Hungary

the Bradt Travel Guide

Adrian Phillips
Jo Scotchmer

With updates from Elizabeth Courage,
Mónika Illés & Márk Kincses

edition

2

www.bradtguides.com

Bradt Travel Gu
The Glob Peo

Sopron
pages 480–7

Szentendre
pages 180–6

S L O V A K I A

Budapest
pages 87–172

AUSTRIA

Hegyeshalom

Moson-Magyaróvár

Danube Komárom

Esztergom

Visegrád

Vác

Duna-Ipoly NP

M2/A

SOPRON

Ferto-Hanság NP

GYŐR

M1

Tata

Szentendre

Kapuvár Csorna

TATABÁNYA

BUDAPEST

M0

KŐSZEG

Pápa

SZÉKESFEHÉRVAR

Danube

Sárvár

Lajosmizse

SZOMBATHELY

Lake Velence

H U N G A R Y

Körmend

Veszprem

Balatonfüred Balatonalmádi

DUNAÚJVÁROS

Balaton Uplands NP
Tapolca

Tihány Siófok

DUNAFÖLDVÁR

Kiskunsá NP

Örség NP

M8

ZALAEGERSZEG

Keszthely

Lake Balaton

M7

SLOVENIA

Kis-Balaton

M6

KALOCSA

NAGYKANIZSA

Tolna

KAPOSVÁR

Szekszárd

M9

Nagyatád

Duna-Drava NP

Bátaszék

Baja

Lake Balaton
pages 493–522

Duna-Drava NP
Szigetvár

PÉCS

M60

Barcs

Mohács

Harkány

Siklós

CROATIA

Pécs
pages 404–17

0 ———— 50km
0 ———— 50 miles

Eger and the Mátra Hills
pages 232–42

Tokaj
pages 261–7

UKRAINE

Aggtelek NP

Aggtelek

Sátoraljaújhely

Záhony

Sárospatak

Kisvárda

Szilvásvárad

Szerencs

Bükk NP

MISKOLC

Tokaj

NYÍREGYHÁZA

Máteszalka

Fehérgyarmat

M30

Pásztó

Mátrafüred

EGER

Tiszaújváros

M3

NYÍRBÁTOR

Gyöngyös

Mezökövesd

Füzesabony

M35

Hajdúböszörmény

M3

Heves

Tiszafüred

Hortobágy

Nyírábrány

ödöllő

Lake Tisza

Hortobágy NP

DEBRECEN

Jászberény

HAJDÚSZOBOSZLÓ

Hortobágy
pages 288–92

Tisza

SZOLNOK

Körös-Maros NP

Szarvas

Lake Tisza
pages 282–8

KECSKEMÉT

Csongrád

BÉKÉSCSABA

ROMANIA

M5

Kiskunfélegyháza

Körös-Maros NP

Szentes

Gyula

Körös-Maros NP

Kiskunhalas

HÓDMEZŐVÁSÁRHELY

SZEGED

N

Bradt

Kecskemét
pages 317–25

Szeged
pages 353–64

SERBIA

KEY
Capital city
Other city
Main town
Other town
Airport
Motorway
Main road
Other road
International boundary

Hungary
Don't
miss...

Vibrant festivals
There are regular festivals across Hungary – from traditional celebrations of folklore to fish-soup-cooking contests (HNTO) pages 67–8

Charming towns
Some of Hungary's towns are lovely places to take a stroll or enjoy a coffee. This is Sopron's quaint central square (HNTO) pages 480–7

Exploring the countryside
The famous Great Plain is a place of grassland and cowboys, but the country has a diverse and wildlife-rich range of landscapes (LN) pages 4–5

Wine tasting
Tour Hungary's vineyards and cellars — there are some top-class wine regions, and Tokaj is renowned worldwide (HNTO)

Wallow in a spa
Hungary sits on a reservoir of thermal water, and Budapest has more thermal spas than any other capital city. This is the Rudas (HNTO) pages 124–5

A snapshot of Budapest

above   The colourful buildings of the Castle District have survived many sieges over the centuries (HNTO) pages 128–32

left   The impressive 36m-high Millennium Monument in Heroes' Square (AP) page 151

below   The interior of the capital's opera house oozes opulence (HNTO) page 116

bottom   On the charge! Memento Park is home to many Communist monuments; this is the Béla Kun memorial (MI) pages 160–1

right	The sculptor Alajos Stróbl took ten years over his meticulously researched statue of St Stephen (AP) page 130
below left	A fun depiction of St Stephen, founder of the Christian state (hence the church he clutches to his chest) (AP) page 167
below right	Our favourite statue — a personification of Buda and Pest reaching across the Danube to each other. It stands on the side of Gellért Hill (AP)
bottom left	Entrance to the Lion Courtyard in the Buda Castle Palace (AP) page 128
bottom right	Mátyás Well, with the much-loved Renaissance king on the hunt (MU) page 128

above   The riverside Parliament building was influenced by that in London, and contains 40 million bricks (MU) pages 170–1

right   The 19th-century Great Synagogue is the second-largest in the world, and is topped with Moorish minarets (HNTO) pages 169–70

below left   The Basilica contains the mummified right hand of St Stephen, the country's holiest relic (AP) page 172

below right   The heavy doors to the Basilica bear the faces of various saintly figures (AP) page 172

Spas and shopping

above   The Neo-Baroque Széchenyi Baths feature thermal outdoor pools in which you can bathe even in the depths of winter (HNTO) page 125

right   Paprika is added to a great many Hungarian dishes. Markets sell the colourful spice in strings or in powdered form (MU) page 336

below left   Buying vegetables is a special experience below the patterned roof tiles and girders of Budapest's Great Market Hall (MU) page 123

below right   Váci utca is the shopping artery running through the heart of Pest (AP) page 145

Intriguing architecture

above Bory Castle, in Székesfehérvár, is an eccentric mongrel of a building that draws on a range of national and international architectural styles (HNTO) page 435

below This 16th-century former mosque in Pécs is one of the few pieces of Turkish architecture that survive in Hungary (WC) page 411

opposite

top left The Votive Church — something of a geometrical jumble — was built by Szeged citizens to honour a vow they made following the great flood of 1879 (HNTO) pages 360–1

top right A view from Templom tér in Szentendre, with the Belgrade Cathedral in the distance (AP) page 185

middle left The Coronation Monument shows the Bishop of Esztergom crowning King Stephen — the anointment is said to have taken place on the site of the Basilica (MI) page 196

bottom The monumental Esztergom Basilica, which took 50 years to build (MI) pages 194–5

The winter freeze

above left Ducks drift as the steam lifts from the surface of the lake in Budapest's City Park (AP) page 153

top right Frost on the branches of trees in the Bükk Hills (LN) page 232

above right The Budapest Christmas market in Vörösmarty tér is the place for hand-crafted gifts and a warming mug of mulled wine (AP) page 146

below The fairytale Vajdahunyad Castle in City Park incorporates 21 different styles in showcasing Hungarian regional architecture (AP) page 153

A spot of wine tasting

top left   A cellar-packed road in the village of Villánykövesd, part of the Villány-Siklós wine route (HNTO) page 399

top right   A Balaton vineyard — the region's white wines have an excellent reputation (WC) page 112

above   Polished oak tables in Tokaj's 15th-century Rákóczi Cellars, where you can take a tour and a tasting (MI) pages 266–7

right   Avert your eyes! A reveller lets it all hang out in shameless celebration of the grape in Tokaj (AP) page 266

A breath of fresh air

above & left   You can enjoy views from land or water in the Balaton region. The flat-topped hill in the distance is Badacsony, which is much loved by walkers and wine tasters alike (both WC) page 507

below   Regions like the Göcsej preserve traditional thatched dwellings of yesteryear. Look out for open-air museums, known as *skanzen* (WC) page 466

above   The pretty village of Máriagyűd in southern Transdanubia is a site of pilgrimage for many thousands of Roman Catholics each year (HNTO) page 400

right   The Magyars were expert horsemen and the Great Plain was once a place of horse-riding outlaws. Today you can watch equestrian feats at a horse show (HNTO)

below   The 13th-century castle at Boldogkőváralja in the Northern Uplands (HNTO) page 261

AUTHORS

Adrian Phillips joined the staff at Bradt Travel Guides in 2001 after completing a PhD in English literature. Two years later, he left his desk for several months to research the first edition of this guidebook with Jo. *Hungary: The Bradt Travel Guide* subsequently won the award for Best Guidebook of the Year. Since then, Adrian has continued to straddle the fence between writing and publishing; a member of the British Guild of Travel Writers, he is author of several guidebooks, and writes regularly for national newspapers and magazines. He is now Publishing Director at Bradt.

Jo Scotchmer is a Public Relations Director who specialises in lifestyle and travel PR. After spending a significant time in Hungary, she fell in love with the place, its culture and its people. Having resolved to take a career break to travel (and to learn something on the way!), she teamed up with Adrian to explore Hungary's highways and byways, and to write the original Bradt guides to Hungary and Budapest.

In addition to this guidebook, the second edition of Adrian and Jo's *Budapest: The Bradt City Guide* is available to buy (*www.bradtguides.com*).

AUTHORS' STORY

Writing a guidebook is like eating an elephant – something best approached one piece at a time. As Jo and I slumped down in our Budapest hotel room on the opening night of our trip, the elephant in the corner seemed to loom uncomfortably large... Where the heck should we start? What had we let ourselves in for? We'd taken sabbaticals from work to do the necessary travel; this was the first guidebook either of us had written from scratch, we didn't know anybody in Hungary, and we spoke no Hungarian. Fortunately, our appetite grew as the first-night flutters settled. There were few corners of Hungary that escaped our scrutiny over the following five months – and few locals who escaped our (frequently mimed) questions. We travelled high and low, from palaces and coronation churches to museums that focused on tarmac and marzipan. Our feet grew tough, our hair grew long and our suitcases groaned under the weight of maps, brochures and handwritten notes. Over the months we became familiar with – and terribly fond of – the ways of Hungary and its people, and we hope this book does them justice. It was no picnic, eating that elephant, but we're awfully glad we did so.

PUBLISHER'S FOREWORD   *Hilary Bradt*

At Frankfurt Book Fair I was showing our just-published Budapest guide to our new representative for eastern Europe. 'But this is amazing!' said Csaba. 'It describes restaurants that I thought only I knew about.' Adrian and Jo have gone one big step further – revealed insider secrets for all of Hungary. Dip into the guidebook at any point and I bet you find something you didn't know: Hungary is home to the furioso horse, for instance, and the 'frizzle' pig (I long to meet the latter). Ice cream is *fagylalt*, which seems to come straight from the pages of the *Hitchhiker's Guide to the Galaxy*, and Hungarians choose a name for their child from an approved list. I even found myself engrossed in a description of a car (that's definitely a first) – although I suppose the Trabant is only just a car. I learned that 52% of storks' nesting sites are on telegraph poles and that there are awards for outstanding service in stork protection. I learned... but why not read it for yourself?

Second edition May 2010
First published September 2005

Bradt Travel Guides Ltd, 23 High Street, Chalfont St Peter, Bucks SL9 9QE, England
www.bradtguides.com
Published in the USA by The Globe Pequot Press Inc, 246 Goose Lane,
PO Box 480, Guilford, Connecticut 06475-0480

Text copyright © 2010 Adrian Phillips and Jo Scotchmer
Maps copyright © 2010 Bradt Travel Guides Ltd
Illustrations copyright © 2010 individual photographers

A catalogue record for this book is available from the British Library
ISBN-13: 978 1 84162 285 9

Photographs Adrian Phillips (AP), FLPA Images (various photographers), Hungarian National Tourist Office (HNTO), Gábor Kovács (GK), László Nehezy (LN), William Courage (WC), Mike Unwin (MU), Mónika Illés (MI)
Front cover Church in Höllökő (Mary Lane/iStockphoto)

Maps Matt Honour, Greg Best, David McCutcheon, Steve Munns. Regional maps based on ITM *Hungary*.

Typeset from the authors' disc by Wakewing, High Wycombe
Printed and bound in India by Aegean Offset (arranged by Jellyfish UK)

MAIN CONTRIBUTORS

ELIZABETH COURAGE was born in 1948 in Western Hungary. She has lived in England for 36 years, but has retained a close contact with Hungary (not least in her capacity working for the Hungarian Tourist Office in London for 13 years). Elizabeth has a keen interest in Central European history, is passionate about the Hungarian countryside and country matters, and is a lover of classical music; her husband, William Courage, contributed photos to this guide.

MÓNIKA ILLÉS helped to update this second edition. She has been living in London for over ten years, but is originally from Budapest and returns to the city regularly.

MÁRK KINCSES graduated from Pannon University in Veszprém, before continuing his tourism studies with a course at the University of Derby, UK. Since then, he has worked for the Hungarian National Tourist Office, both in London and (now) in Budapest. Mark's parents were 'couch surfers' in the 1980s, and instilled in him a love of travel from a young age.

OTHER CONTRIBUTORS In addition, we are grateful to the following for their invaluable assistance: Lucy Mallows (various), Gerard Gorman (wildlife), Carolyn Chapman (various), Kim Lyon (Danube Bend), Marti Andrews (spas, food), József Hunyady, Gábor Orbán, Balázs Szigeti, Shena Maskell, Martin Catt (all wildlife), Stuart Candy (music), Janet Phillips (various) and Bianca Otero (wine).

FEEDBACK REQUEST

We've strived to tramp and nag and eat our way to accuracy. However, a guidebook is a snapshot in time, and we writers feel like painters on the Forth Bridge – once the last page is done the first needs re-checking. Would you lend us your ears and eyes to ensure that subsequent editions keep pace? What was new or different during your visit? What did you like or dislike about the book? We'd love to hear from you, and will be sure to reply personally, as well as crediting your contribution in the next edition. We'll also post useful updates on our updates page at http://updates.bradtguides.com/hungary. You can reach us at e hungarytravelguide@yahoo.co.uk, or write to us c/o Bradt Travel Guides, 23 High St, Chalfont St Peter, Bucks SL9 9QE. And if you've found our book useful, please do let other travellers know by posting a review on the Amazon website (www.amazon.co.uk or www.amazon.com) – drop us a line if you're not sure how to do so.

Happy travels!
Adrian and Jo

Acknowledgements

Never has so much been owed by so few to so many – we salute you all. Thank you to Tsvia Vorley, Ildikó Balogh and Melinda Stein for smoothing the initial path; to Sally Brock, Matt Honour, Dave Priestley, Greg Best, David McCutcheon and all at Bradt for making sense of endless scribbles; to Dr Alex Vida for his information on national parks; to Annalisa Rellie, Tim Burford, Adrian Courage and Neil Taylor for brochures, corrections and notes scrawled on airline sick bags; to Lucy Mallows, Carolyn Chapman, Kim Lyon, Bianca Otero and Marti Andrews for their tireless and expert assistance; to Gerard Gorman for his invaluable 'twitching tips', to Jószef Hunyady, Gábor Orbán, Balázs Szigeti, Shena Maskell and Martin Catt for contributions to the wildlife sections elsewhere, and János Malina for his information on music; to those readers of the last edition who offered feedback and helpful suggestions, including Kate Lach, Martin Evans, Mrs L M Newman, Miss A J Udall, Patricia Smith, John Chan, Henry Long, Anthony Stern, Polly Evans, Sally Brock, Carol Donaldson, Val Reynolds, Mervyn Brown, Ildikó Rékási, László Wagner, Claire and Alan Terrill, Myrna O'Malley, Henry Spratt, Lee Bostock, Mike and Kathy Unwin, Murray Melbin, Daniel Kaali, Scott Brown, David Newton, Tony Brand, Donald McIntyre, David Clarke and Daniel Sollé; to Dóra Helmeczi, András and Zsuzsi Hirschler, Balázs Szűcs, and Adrian and Rita Courage for insider tips and evenings out; to Bánk Gyökhegyi and Ian Traill for restaurant recommendations; and to our families and friends for their support. Thanks to Péter and Zsanett Koltai, who were selfless in their help and guidance during our research for the first edition of this guidebook, and with whom we hope to catch up once more during our next visit. And thank you to Elizabeth and William Courage, Mónika Illés and Márk Kincses for their help in updating this new edition – a book of this length is a labour of love, and they truly devoted heart and soul to the task.

UPDATES WEBSITE

For the latest travel news about Hungary, please visit the new interactive Bradt update website: http://updates.bradtguides.com/hungary.

This update website is a free service for readers and for anybody else who cares to drop by and browse, so if you have any comments, queries, grumbles, insights, news or other feedback, you're invited to post them on the website.

Contents

LIST OF MAPS

NOTE ABOUT MAPS

Several maps in the Budapest chapter use grid lines to allow easy location of sites. Map grid references are listed in square brackets after listings in the text, with page number followed by grid number, eg: [156 C3].

Introduction

It has been said that Hungary 'grows on you and seems to squirt a divine soda water into your blood'. During our first encounter with Budapest we would have gladly swapped the squirt for a healthy splash of brandy. Nerves needed soothing in the back of an airport taxi driven by a man resolute in his commitment to overtaking on blind corners; stomachs needed settling after plates of cockerels' testicles unwittingly ordered from an impenetrable menu; tempers needed calming in the face of an ear-picking manager denying all knowledge of our hotel booking. But romantics know that love can blossom from unpromising first meetings. In the days that followed, the capital offered up its rumbling trams, its faded mansions and its walls pocked with conflict's bullet holes. Yes, we had that brandy – not in trembling glasses but in those raised to a city with bite, elegance and romance.

Budapest's charms are no longer a secret. However, if our hearts were caught there the grip only tightened as we ventured beyond. We discovered a country with the diversity both to indulge established passions and spark new ones. There was wine, plenty of it, in Eger's Valley of the Beautiful Woman. And in the villages of the Tokaj region. And in Szekszárd and Villány. There were lush walking trails in the Northern Uplands, creamy-orange stalactites in Aggtelek and spring-time storms that flashed and crashed above the hilltops. The Great Plain came thick with legends of derring-do, with hairy pigs and 'horny' sheep, and with modern-day cowboys cracking their whips and galloping astride five horses at once. Pécs proudly showed off its Ottoman and Roman legacy, and elsewhere we found Transdanubian forts and thatched dwellings and the prettiest medieval towns you could wish to see. When we fancied a dip, we headed to central Europe's largest lake for windsurfing and wakeboarding, and further bouts of tasting among the vineyards.

Of course, more recently we've returned wearing researchers' hats, and with an unhealthy interest in opening hours and walk-in hotel rates. But, whatever the purpose, we love going back. Travel in Hungary is a varied, rich, exhilarating experience, and one of which we'll never tire.

Part One

GENERAL INFORMATION

Country name The Republic of Hungary (Magyarország)
Language Hungarian
Population 10,006,835
People Hungarian (Magyar) 89.9%, Roma 4%, German 2.6%, Serb 2%, Slovak 0.8%, Romanian 0.7%
Religion Two-thirds of the population are Roman Catholic; other faiths/denominations include Calvinist, Lutheran, Jewish and Greek Orthodox
Neighbouring countries Austria, Croatia, Romania, Serbia and Montenegro, Slovakia, Slovenia and Ukraine
Area 93,000km²
Time Central European Time (GMT +1)
Currency Forint (Ft or HUF)
Flag Three equal horizontal bands: red (top), white (middle) and green (bottom)
Life expectancy Men 68 years, women 77 years
Economy Agriculture 8%, industry and commerce 42%, services 32%, government 7%
Telephone codes Country code 0036, Budapest code 1

KEY TO STANDARD SYMBOLS

Bradt

International boundary	Castle
Chapter content boundary	Church, cathedral
National park boundary	Synagogue
Airport (international)	Archaeological or historic site
Ferry	Old city wall
Railway	Statue, monument
Tram, metro	Zoo
M Metro station	Historical buiding
Bus station	Summit
Motorised train stop	Tourist information
Hotel, panzió	Theatre, cultural centre
Hostel, college with accommodation	Museum, art gallery
Hospital	Bank, ATM
Pharmacy	Internet café
Campsite	Post office
Coffee house, café, café bar	Cave
Wine bar, pub	Beach
Restaurant	Swimming
Nightclub	Golf course

Background Information

GEOGRAPHY

The Republic of Hungary (Magyarország) lies in the Carpathian Basin in central eastern Europe. It occupies 93,030km², is landlocked and bordered by seven others: Austria, Slovakia, Romania, Serbia and Montenegro, Croatia, Slovenia and Ukraine. Budapest – occupying a central-northern position – is the capital and by a distance the largest city (525km²). The Danube runs through the country for 417km, dividing it roughly in half from north to south. The other major river is the Tisza, entering the country from Ukraine, flowing through the plains and exiting into Serbia. As for standing bodies of water, Balaton is comfortably the biggest of the lakes, followed by Tisza (a significant wildlife spot).

A broad-brushed description of the country's landscape can divide it into three main types. Mountain ranges (the Northern Uplands) stretch towards the Ukrainian border to the northeast of the country, with the highest point Mount Kékes (1,008m); the vast area to the east of the Danube (the Great Plain) is characterised by even plains, grasslands and agricultural land; the west (Transdanubia) is the most varied, comprising small mountains, rolling foothills and open plains, punctured by Lake Balaton. Budapest is sliced in two by the Danube; Buda on the western bank is green and hilly, while on the other side Pest is flat and built-up. (See also *Vegetation*, page 4.)

CLIMATE

Three climate systems collide in Hungary, with cold Siberian influences meeting the hot weather cycles from the Mediterranean and mixing with more temperate weather from the Atlantic. With protection from surrounding mountains, the result is a temperate continental climate, with significant, distinct and quickly changing seasonal variations. Winter (Dec–Feb) is icy cold, with temperatures often dropping below freezing and some snowfall possible. Small streams and lakes – even Balaton – can freeze over. Spring arrives and the temperatures begin to perk up properly in April, although showers are also common. You should expect ten daily hours of sunshine during the summer months (Jun–Aug), which are at least warm and can be very hot – the August average is 22°C, but temperatures often break the 30°C barrier. As in other countries in continental Europe, it is also noticeable that temperatures do not peak at midday, but appear to continue rising well into the afternoon, and humidity can be high. Autumn can bring a warm and dry Indian summer, described in Hungarian as 'old women's summer'. The country's moderate rainfall, averaging 600mm per year, falls principally in spring and autumn. March and November are the wettest months, and are neither warm nor bitingly cold. The most extreme weather patterns are found on the Great Plain, where hot, dry summers are followed by bitterly cold and windy winters. Rainfall is highest in the country's southwestern hills. Although average monthly temperatures generally vary in a range of only three or four degrees between such places as Budapest, Miskolc to the north and Szeged to the south, if you're a real heat-seeker you should head for Gyula in the Southern Great Plain; just 4km from the Romanian border, it is Hungary's hottest place and boasts over 2,000 hours of sunshine each year.

The website of the Hungarian Meteorological Service (*www.met.hu*) has detailed **weather reports**; little is in English, but the pictograms and sun/rain symbols are pretty self-explanatory.

NATURAL HISTORY AND CONSERVATION

See also dedicated wildlife colour insert

With a temperate climate and a lack of topographical extremes like high-altitude mountain ranges or scorching deserts, Hungary has – at least since the end of the 18th century – been largely settled, cultivated and grazed. Arable land now covers 50% of its area. Even so, thanks to a relatively low population density and extensive agriculture, the country is surprisingly rich in rare species of plant and animal.

VEGETATION Many of the most important conservation areas in Hungary support **grasslands**, which occupy 12% of the land surface, are predominantly semi-natural in origin and usually comprise swathes of steppe (the so-called Hungarian *puszta*) or wet grassland flood plains. *Puszta* is found mainly in the lowlands, on saline, sandy or peaty soils; prime examples are found in Hortobágy, Kiskunság and Körös-Maros national parks, and are characterised by *Fescues, Festuca rupicola* and *Festuca pseudovina*, the latter being prevalent in degraded or overgrazed grasslands. Steppe grasslands also grow to a lesser degree in the west (in hill ranges such as the Bakony and the Vértes) and northwest (on the Kisalföld, or 'Little Plain', in the Fertő-Hanság National Park). Steppe habitats are often associated with non-intensive methods of arable farming and grazing, and have become fragmented as a consequence of intensified agricultural practices. They are vital for birds like the great bustard (*Otis tarda*), red-footed falcon (*Falco vespertinus*), stone curlew (*Burhinus oedicnemus*), roller (*Coracias garrulous*) and lesser grey shrike (*Lanius minor*).

Wet meadows are found in flood plains throughout the country, but the Ormánság in Baranya county, the Bodrog flood plain in Borsod and the River Ipoly valley in Nográd county are good examples. Upland meadows lie in the hill ranges to the north, while the Kali and Tapolca basins (in the Balaton Uplands National Park) are also notable. Meadows – which depend on regular mowing – contain the most varied plant communities in Hungary. Some meadows have been found to contain over 50 species of grasses, and many orchids are confined to such habitats; globally threatened birds including the corn crake and white stork are often dependent upon them.

Forests cover 19% of the country, a proportion that the government and the EU would like to increase to 25%. Woodlands are mainly composed of oak, hornbeam and beech, with plantations of non-native false acacia, poplar and coniferous species making up half of the total. Hilly areas are usually covered by broad-leaved, deciduous forests, while flood plains feature both soft-wood and hard-wood alluvial forest (willow, alder, ash, etc). Fine pine forests, which were planted at the end of the 19th century, can be found in the Orség National Park in the west, and impressive beech stands are found in the cooler local climates of the Bükk Hills in the northeast. Mixed oak forests are the predominant indigenous vegetation type, with oak-hornbeam and oak-lime in the damper, higher areas; good examples are in the Börzsöny and Zselic hill ranges. Turkey oak and Hungarian oak thrive in the warmer, south-facing slopes of the Bakony, Vértés and the Mecsek hills. The Great Plain is significantly less forested than the north and west; nevertheless, there are areas of flood-plain forest (characterised by willow, poplar and English oak) in the Hortobágy National Park, the Gemenc Forest of the Danube-Dráva National Park and along the upper reaches of the River Tisza. Wet alder forests are typical in parts of the southwest. Scrub habitats usually take the form of scrub encroaching on meadows, but there are also such habitats on the karst rock of the Aggtelek National Park.

Around 14% of the country remains uncultivated, and includes lakes, rivers and wetlands (as well as urban areas and the like). Apart from Lake Balaton, Lake Velence and the major rivers, Hungarian **wetlands** are for the most part man-made. Kis-Balaton (in the Balaton Uplands National Park) was created as a retention reservoir to filter the water of the River Zala before it enters Lake Balaton; eight species of heron now nest among its vast reed beds. The Hortobágy fishponds, one of the best places in Hungary for nesting marsh terns, were created in the 1970s.

FLORA Hungary has a very diverse flora. Its geographic location means it harbours plants that originate from Asia, western Europe and the Adriatic and Mediterranean regions. There are over 3,000 flowering plant species, including many near-endemics which are not found outside the Carpathian Basin. Although much of the countryside is given over to agriculture, farming methods are often less intensive than in western Europe; as a consequence, wild flowers are attractive and plentiful, particularly on roadside verges and along the edges of arable fields. Roadside crop fields take on the glorious hues of plants like the red **poppy**, blue **cornflower**, pink/mauve **corn cockle**, white **mayweed**, yellow **corn marigold** and purple **larkspur**, a canvas of colour found even alongside the major motorways. The greatest variety of wild flowers, however, is found on rocky limestone hillsides such as at Aggtelek in the northeast. Woodlands are home to several species of orchid, among them the very rare **ghost orchid**, as well as **red helleborine**, **violet helleborine** and **greater butterfly orchid**. Grasslands on limestone can have an impressive range of colourful flowers, including some endemic species. Some of the showiest are the blue/purple **knapweeds** and **thistles**, which tower above the lower-growing herbs. Several tall yellow-flowered **mulleins** are widespread within this habitat, and the **purple mullein** is often particularly striking.

The more acidic rock of the Bükk Hills is home to a quite contrasting floral group. Distinctive plants here include the pink/mauve **martagon lily** and several orchid species including **white helleborine**, **butterfly orchid** and **bug orchid**. **Wolfsbane** is a very obvious, buxom daisy occurring at the woodland edges. **Crested cow-wheat** is another summer plant that stands out, with a vivid yellow-and-red spiky flower head. Open areas of uncultivated hillsides, and low hills in general, are usually the richest botanical areas. Many are small and hard to identify but include attractive **clovers, vetches** and **mints**.

The best period for botany is from April to October, with the range of plants changing from month to month. It is possible to see **primroses, Narcissi, snowdrops** and **crocus** on visits in the spring, with most of the **orchids** occurring in early to mid summer, and later the conspicuous grassland plants of **scabious** and **knapweed** appearing. The botany season draws to a close with **autumn crocus** and other **narcissi.**

In lowland and wetland areas there are many interesting plants but few with obvious and colourful flowers. Two notable exceptions are the bright yellow flowers of **yellow iris** and the pink/mauve umbrella-like flowers of **flowering rush**. One distinctive tree of the lowlands is the **black poplar**. Its massive form dominates the landscape and produces millions of fluffy seeds during mid summer.

5

Many species of **fungi** can be found in autumn. Local people collect them for personal consumption and for sale. In season, locals often sell mushrooms at roadsides but – although there are many good edible species – don't be tempted to try any unless you are very sure what you'll be eating. The main markets of large towns have stalls where you can take your mushrooms to be checked by an expert (*gomba vizsgáló*).

FAUNA

Mammals Hungary is not rich in large mammals, although wolf and lynx exist in small numbers. The **European beaver** has been reintroduced into the Gemenc Forest (in the Danube-Drava National Park) and other areas, and is doing well. **Golden jackal** has crept in from the Balkans and **brown bear** occasionally wanders over the border from Slovakia, but these, along with **wolf** and **lynx,** are all very secretive and the chances of seeing them slim (which disappoints naturalists, but rather cheers the average lay hiker!). Hungary's **red deer** are more famous than they probably wish they were among the hunting fraternity, and world-record trophies have been shot in the country. Zala, Somogy, and the area of Tamási and the Gemenc in Tolna – the largest areas of lowland forest – are just some of the places where these deer thrive. **Roe deer** are very common and the introduced **fallow deer** are concentrated in a few hunting areas such as Lábod (in Somogy), Gyulaj and Tamási (in Tolna) and Pusztavacsi (on the border of Pest and Bács-Kiskun).

Mufflon, introduced in relatively recent times, can be found in the rocky wooden terrain of the Zemplén Hills in the northeast and of the Bakony range in the west. The **wild boar** is common throughout the country but especially so in the west and the north where the forest cover is at its densest. As elsewhere in Europe, its numbers have grown in recent years. The **brown hare** is most numerous in the east, on the flat and open terrain of the Great Plain.

Birds – and birdwatching with Gerard Gorman (author of Bradt's Central and Eastern European Wildlife, and leading birdwatching guide in Hungary)
Hungary is a great country for birds and birdwatchers – indeed, for a land-locked European country the avifauna is remarkably rich and varied. Around 400 species have been recorded nationwide and a remarkable 250-plus have been seen in and around Budapest. By way of comparison, Hungary's woodlands are home to eight resident species of woodpecker – of which Budapest has seven – whereas there are just three species in Britain. All this is partly due to Hungary lying at a sort of ornithological crossroads between east and west, with the warm Mediterranean zone to the south and the colder boreal Europe to the north. The fact that the Communist era resulted in large areas of countryside lying untouched (often by accident rather than design), or exploited in a less-than-efficient manner, also means that birds have done well. In addition, Hungarians are not 'trigger-happy' in the way that some other populations are in Mediterranean countries: only gamebirds are shot for food, and people are pleased when white storks nest in their villages. Many towns have birdwatching clubs or branches of the MME (Hungarian Ornithological Society). It's therefore unsurprising that Hungary is now regarded among Europe's best birding destinations by travelling twitchers.

Special birds Many of Hungary's 'specialty' birds reside out on the *puszta* (the flat, lowland grasslands that lie mainly east of the Danube on the Great Plain). Several of the birds of prey found here are very rare or absent altogether in western Europe. These include eastern imperial eagle (*Aquila heliaca*) and saker falcon (*Falco cherrug*), two magnificent species that have their European strongholds in Hungary. The delightful little red-footed falcon (*Falco vespertinus*) is a classic bird of the Great

Plain, and usually breeds in noisy, lively colonies. Lesser grey shrike (*Lanius minor*) and roller (*Coracias garrulous*) are other typical *puszta* birds often seen perched on roadside wires. The wetlands that dot the country also host some decidedly 'eastern' species such as pygmy cormorant (*Phalacrocorax pygmaeus*), ferruginous duck (*Aythya nyroca*), Caspian gull (*Larus cachinnans*), white-winged black tern (*Chlidonias leucopterus*) and aquatic warbler (*Acrocephalus paludicola*). Flocks of bean geese (*Anser fabalis*) and a few parties of the endangered lesser white-fronted goose (*Anser erythropus*), which breed up in Scandinavia, also visit Hungary on autumn and spring migration. All these birds are great draws for birdwatchers from Britain and the rest of western Europe.

Common birds Besides the eastern specialties and rarities that delight the keener birdwatcher, the sheer abundance of more common and widespread species is also an attraction. In spring and summer, the likes of great white egret (*Egretta alba*), white stork (*Ciconia ciconia*), marsh harrier (*Circus aeruginosus*), cuckoo (*Cuculus canorus*), crested lark (*Galerida cristata*), nightingale (*Luscinia megarhynchos*), great reed warbler (*Acrocephalus arundinaceus*) – and many more – are often encountered during a walk or drive in the countryside. Thankfully, birds like lapwing (*Vanellus vanellus*), turtle dove (*Streptopelia turtur*), red-backed shrike (*Lanius collurio*), skylark (*Alauda arvensis*), yellow wagtail (*Motacilla flava*), tree sparrow (*Passer montanus*) and corn bunting (*Milaria calandra*), all of which have declined in Britain, are still doing well and are fairly easy to find in rural Hungary. Urban areas, too, are not without good birdwatching. Syrian woodpecker (*Dendrocopos syriacus*), collared flycatcher (*Ficedula albicollis*), black redstart (*Phoenicurus ochruros*), short-toed treecreeper (*Certhia brachydactyla*), golden oriole (*Oriolus oriolus*), serin (*Serinus serinus*) and hawfinch (*Coccothraustes coccothraustes*) can often be found in gardens, parks and the grounds of hotels. In spring and summer a walk around almost any reed-fringed lake – and even managed fishpond – can take you past herons, egrets, terns, gulls, a range of warblers and penduline tit (*Remiz pendulinus*).

Where to go Arguably the most 'typical' wildlife habitat in Hungary is the *puszta*, and it is often superb for birdwatching. But there are also many wetlands such as floodplain woods along the Danube, Tisza, Drava and other rivers, marshes, salt lakes, reed beds and marshes where birds abound. Straddling the border with Austria in the northwest, **Lake Fertő** is a breeding site for a range of egrets, herons, ducks, birds of prey, crakes and warblers. In winter, large goose flocks roost here after grazing in adjacent farmland.

In the **southwest** (bordering Croatia along the Danube at Gemenc and Béda-Karapancsa) there are riverine woods, ox-bow lakes and pools that are part of the Duna-Dráva National Park. The **Pacsmag fishpond** system is another good Transdanubian wetland for breeding and passage wildfowl. North of here is rolling hilly country dotted with more fish farms and deciduous woodlands; this is a good area to look for white-tailed eagle (*Haliaeetus albicilla*). At the heart of Transdanubia is **Lake Balaton**, which, away from the resorts in summer, is also a decent birdwatching spot. At Balaton's southwest tip is **Kis-Balaton**, a reedy wetland with herons, egrets, wildfowl and white-tailed eagles possible all year round.

Closer to Budapest, lakes Velence and Tata host large numbers of geese in autumn. In the same region the wooded Gerecse and Vértes Hills are home to woodpeckers and birds of prey. **Budapest** itself is a surprisingly good city for birdwatchers, and it's worth exploring Pest's parks, Margaret or Óbuda Islands or Buda's wooded hills. All these places are accessible by public transport. Exciting birds like saker falcon, red-footed falcon, great bustard and a range of woodpeckers can all be seen within an hour's drive of the capital.

A series of forested hill ranges, including the Pilis, Cserhát, Börzsöny, Aggtelek, Bükk and the Zemplén, lie in the **north of the country**. These are mostly blanketed in broadleaved forest where black stork (*Ciconia nigra*), collared flycatcher (*Ficedula albicollis*), black woodpecker (*Dryocopos martius*), honey buzzard (*Pernis apivorus*) and goshawk (*Accipiter gentiles*) are found. In some spots in these forests the huge Ural owl (*Strix uralensis*) is resident. In the **northeast**, near Tokaj, is a vast flood-plain where the Tisza and Bodrog rivers join. In spring this is one of the best places in Hungary to hear corncrake (*Crex crex*), although the downside is that you're at risk of being eaten alive by mosquitoes.

South of the northern hills, to the east of the Danube, is the **Great Plain**. This flat lowland is largely cultivated, but dry and wet *puszta* and the many fish-pond systems that litter the area are often great places to birdwatch. Bács-Kiskun, Heves, Csongrád and Békés all hold flocks of great bustard (*Otis tarda*), Hungary's national bird. Two of Hungary's finest birdwatching areas are also here: the Hortobágy and the Kiskunság, both of which include large national parks. Breeding birds in these regions include most of the species already mentioned, often in good numbers. In spring and autumn, wildfowl and wader passage is often impressive; around 100,000 common cranes (*Grus grus*) stop to refuel in the east in October; and in winter most fishpond systems host groups of white-tailed eagles. The Hortobágy is also home to the country's only breeding population of aquatic warbler – permission is needed from the national-park directorate (see page 290) to visit the reserve in the company of a park ranger.

When to go Key times to visit Hungary to go birdwatching are in **April** (white storks arriving and waders on passage), **May** (all breeding birds present), **June** and **July** (colourful summer visitors like golden oriole, roller and bee-eater all active), **August** and **September** (return migration) and **October** (common cranes and wildfowl). Even **winter**, which usually sees standing wetlands freezing over, has its birdwatching highlights. Any lake with wildfowl sees a few white-tailed eagles in attendance, long-eared owls (*Asio otus*) gather in double-figure roosts, great grey shrikes (*Lanius excubitor*) are not uncommon roadside birds, great bustards flock up

THE ELECTRIC BIRD

A huge, scruffy nest is a familiar sight in many villages, belonging to the fondly loved white stork (*Ciconia ciconia*). Hungary has one of southern Europe's largest nesting populations of this migrating marvel, which has a wingspan of 2.5m and helps to keep pest numbers down in fields and pastures. Before post-war socialist 'reorganisation', the wide chimneys of peasant houses provided natural nesting perches but industrialisation and state-run collectivised farming methods decimated these traditional homes and the stork population in Hungary halved between the late '50s and mid '70s. It was then that some brainy birds discovered they could build their nests on the tops of the telegraph poles and transmission lines that were rapidly appearing over the Hungarian countryside. In 1968, 91 such nests were spotted; by the late 1980s, it had become common practice among stork home-makers and telegraph poles accounted for an astonishing 52% of nesting sites. Aware of the potential danger inherent in combining feathers and high-voltage electricity – and keen to avoid telegraph-top scrambled eggs – a programme of stork protection was implemented. The most precarious nests are carefully relocated, support platforms are added to the poles, special insulation and warning equipment is mounted on lines, and prizes are awarded in recognition of outstanding service in the name of stork protection.

with males, females and young together, and the resident woodpeckers are often easier to see in the leafless woodlands.

Organising a trip Although many birds can be seen in Hungary by simply exploring likely-looking places, local help will be needed to see the specialties, especially the woodpeckers and owls that live in the northern hills, the rarer birds of prey and great bustards which, despite being large, are very localised and tricky to locate in Hungary's vast croplands. All in all, much time and effort can be saved by hiring a **local birdwatching guide**, and a lot can be learnt too. For details of guiding companies (such as Probirder), see pages 39–41.

Joining an **organised birdwatching group** to Hungary from abroad is another option. Such tours are usually escorted by a group leader and met by a local guide and driver upon arrival in Hungary. Group travel is not for everyone but any extra cost will be offset by everything being arranged for you, there being more pairs of eyes to spot things and the fact that most travelling birdwatchers are keen to share what they find with others. Besides being taken to the right places, participants will also benefit from the knowledge passed on by the group leader and local guides. Before signing up for a group-birdwatching holiday try to establish whether the company concerned is experienced in Hungary (or is at least using a good local guide) and whether it operates in a responsible manner and supports local conservation. UK-based birdwatching tour operators who travel to Hungary and fit this bill include Birdfinders, Heatherlea, Naturetrek and WildWings (see pages 39–40). Gerard Gorman himself guides for several of these companies.

What to take You should consider taking binoculars, telescope, tripod, camera, chargers, adaptors, notebook, sun-block, insect repellent and local maps on any birding trip. **Clothing** depends upon the season: in summer think light and wear a cap, in winter warm-wear and decent boots will be needed. Excellent local and national-park **maps** can be bought in bookshops in most towns in Hungary.

As for **reading matter**, Bradt's *Central and Eastern European Wildlife* by Gerard Gorman covers many of the birds and other wildlife that is special to Hungary, while the same author's *Birds of Hungary* (A&C Black) is the only English-language handbook to the status of the country's avifauna. *Birding in Eastern Europe* (Wildsounds) is a guide to the best birdwatching sites in the whole region, including 22 places in Hungary. Any standard European bird field guide will suffice for identification purposes – consider *Birds Of Europe* by Lars Jonsson (Helm) or the *Collins Bird Guide* by Lars Svensson et al (HarperCollins).

Reptiles and amphibians (HERPS) Over 40 species of reptile and amphibian may be encountered within Hungary. Those most likely to make their presence felt are some of the more vocal amphibians, which have loud and distinctive calls and can be heard from some distance. The smallest of these – at less than 4cm long – is the **European tree frog**, which – like some children we've sat next to on planes – produces an incredible volume of sound relative to its size. Its harsh croaking call can be heard for miles, and, besides trees, it often inhabits reed beds. **March frogs** are present in most areas of open water and can be very distinctive with their territorial croaking, disappearing with a loud splash if disturbed. The **fire-bellied toad** is commonly found in the lowlands, while the **yellow-bellied toad** is a rarer upland species. These little toads are dark (olive or black) on the back with a glaring patterned colouration on their undersides. The piping call of the fire-bellied is a familiar sound by wetlands throughout Hungary from May to July. The yellow and black **fire salamander** is widespread in Hungary's hill woodlands, but it is normally secretive and nocturnal, only coming out into the clear during the day after rain when it can be seen crossing roads and tracks. The **European pond terrapin** is scattered around Hungary's standing wetlands, often seen basking on logs or rocks before diving under the water surface when approached. The most common snakes are the **grass snake**, followed by the **dice snake**. Both species are comfortably aquatic, swimming quite happily on the surface as well as hunting for prey in shallow water. They regularly bask to warm their bodies, and this practice means they can often be found in the lowlands at the edges of minor roads. The **meadow viper** (aka Orsini's viper) is at the northern edge of its distribution, and is limited to the Hanság and Kiskunság regions. The **adder**, also a viper, is more common but seldom seen. It inhabits warm, sandy and rocky areas with sparse vegetation.

Hungary has several lizard species, most of which make their presence known when scurrying for cover. The **European green lizard** occurs throughout the country, often climbing into bushes to sunbathe in the morning. Its overall colour of emerald green with a blue throat and yellow underparts makes it a very distinctive and attractive creature. In areas that see high numbers of tourists (like archaeological sites), the lizard can be pretty tame – and in reaching a respectable length of up to 40cm, it is the species that people are most likely to come across. **Sand lizards**, with a broad green stripe down their backs, are fairly common in lowland areas; they can grow up to 25cm. Smaller **wall** and **common lizards** can also be very widespread, but their dull brown colouration means they are generally overlooked. The rare **snake-eyed skink** lives on south-facing hillsides that catch the sun rays, such as the Mecsek, the Börzsöny and the Bakony.

Fish The **European mudminnow**, which lives in small lakes, ponds and swamps, is among the rarest and most protected fish in Europe. It can be found in the Kiskunság National Park and in a few other sites between the Danube and the Tisza. The **pikeperch** (*fogas*)is one of the country's best-known fish – although most people witness it on its journey from plate to mouth aboard fork. **Carp** is bred in fishponds and fish farms all over Hungary, whereas **catfish**, sometime over 3m in length and 50kg in weight, can be found in the waters of the Tisza and the Danube.

Insects The majority of the creepy-crawlies in Hungary are fairly small and dull-coloured, but there are several distinctive and brightly coloured species. Over 40 species of **dragonfly** and **damselfly** occur here. They all breed in water but the flying adults can be seen in many locations between April and October. Although identifying the species can be difficult, the sheer beauty of their colours makes it worthwhile watching for them. They range from the stunningly vivid red of the scarlet darter through the blues of black-tailed skimmers, the yellow-and-black hoops of the golden-ringed dragonfly, to the delicate blues and greens of the emerald and beautiful damselflies.

There are around 180 different **butterfly** species within the diverse habitats of Hungary. On a week-long butterfly tour with an expert guide up to 100 species are regularly seen. Many are difficult to identify and also fairly widespread in the rest of mainland Europe. The more distinctive ones include the bright yellow-and-black swallowtail and the white-and-orange orange-tip. Two of the most striking families of butterflies are the coppers (which are mainly orange/red) and the blues (which are various shades of pastel and metallic blue). Though not endemic to Hungary, the Hungarian glider, which is an elegant black-and-white creature that can be found flying and basking along sheltered woodland edges, is particularly common in the northeast.

Most of the several-thousand **moth** species that occur in Hungary are nocturnal, although in rural parts these will often be attracted to lights. The largest and most spectacular moth is the saucer-sized **peacock moth**, with its distinctive eye patterns on the upper surface of its wings. Its wingspan can reach 10cm across. There are several types of hawk moth, big and pretty creatures with delicate (often pastel-coloured) upper wings that contrast with the striking hues of the hind wings (which they show when disturbed). You might watch seven or more species of these gathering around honey-suckle flowers or outdoor lights during June and July.

During summer evenings visitors cannot fail to notice the magical delights of glow worms and fireflies as they produce their bio-luminescence to attract a partner. Their eerie glow will be seen just after dusk, with the fireflies causing the most spectacular display as they flash their lights on and off while flying around sheltered woodland edges. Despite their names, both of these are **beetles**. Other notable members of this group are the imposing **stag beetle**, the male with antler-like projections on its head. These can be almost 7cm long and are often found near oak woodland in June and July. To see them in flight on a sunny day still captivates us.

Long-horned beetles inhabit old woodlands. These big, narrow beetles, with antennae longer than their bodies, live within dead and dying timber. Their exit holes, often over a centimetre in diameter, can be visible on old tree stumps. The adult beetles feed on the nectar of woodland flowers.

Several species of **preying mantis** occur in Hungary, fascinating creatures that are generally seen sitting on flowers awaiting an unsuspecting insect on which to feast. In late spring and early summer, millions of **long-tailed mayflies** swarm on the River Tisza for a few hours while mating and laying their eggs before falling exhausted (and dead) on the water. This is a quite astonishing spectacle of the natural world.

NATIONAL PARKS AND CONSERVATION AREAS There are ten **national parks** in Hungary, covering over 175,000ha. Hortobágy, on the Northern Great Plain, is the oldest, largest and best-known of these, a UNESCO World Heritage Site and home to the biggest area of *puszta* grassland in central Europe. There are two other parks on the Great Plain (Kiskunság and Körös-Maros), two in the Northern Uplands (Bükk and Aggtelek), one around the Danube Bend (Duna-Ipoly), three in Transdanubia (Duna-Dráva, Őrség, and Fertő-Hanság) and one at Lake Balaton (Balaton Uplands). (See the relevant regional chapter for detailed information on each.) In addition, a total of 26,200ha have been declared **nature conservation areas**, which are smaller (usually under 1,000ha) zones of important natural value; bird sanctuaries generally fall under this category. **Landscape protected areas** (467,000ha in all) fall between the two, providing protection for medium-sized landscapes (over 1,000ha) like Lake Balaton. As such almost 8% of Hungary is nationally protected, and when wetlands, alkaline lakes and areas of local significance are considered we can say that 10% of the territory is under some form of nature protection.

GREEN TOURISM Hungary has a respectable enough history of nature conservation; laws designed to protect its birds and forests were passed well over a century ago, the first landscape-protection area was established in 1952, and the first national parks in the 1970s. Since then, thousands of protected areas have been created at local, county, national and international levels. While there is a danger to wildlife from EU-sponsored 'development', the government is aware of the importance of its habitats for so-called 'green' or 'low-impact' tourism; the Ministry of the Environment, together with national parks, have established information centres, birdwatching hides and nature trails in many areas. The Hungarian tourist board has produced a series of brochures in several languages that focuses on nature. Pollution has declined significantly in recent years, in good part due to the drive to meet EU environmental standards, and 'green' tourism is a relatively new and exciting sector of the tourist market. Hungary is ripe for such tourism: there are around 400 recorded species of bird, around 180 butterflies, over 3,400 species of moth, and thousands of plants. Low-impact tourism can help to protect this abundance of natural riches.

Natural highlights and activities There are several – often spectacular – **seasonal highlights** that those interested in wildlife should pen into their diaries. Some of these are breathtaking for the sheer numbers involved. The flowering of the River Tisza in spring involves the emerging, mating and dying of huge quantities of the ephemeral mayfly; during summer, there are clouds of butterflies in the meadows of the Balaton Uplands, Bükk and Aggtelek; the autumn migration of common cranes in the Hortobágy, when around 100,000 of these birds fly low overhead at sunset, is stunning (see page 289); snowy winters are equally blessed by the massing of geese at the Hortobágy, the Danube Bend and Lake Tata. During the second half of September and the beginning of October, red deer are in rut. Spring, summer and autumn all offer botanical treats too, with the flowering of a great variety of protected plants and wildflowers, including over 50 orchid species. Tours incorporating these can be arranged through nature tour operators (see pages 39–41).

Hungary also holds thousands of limestone **caves**. In Aggtelek National Park alone there are 700, some of which remain to be explored. The Baradla-Domica system (*www.showcaves.com/english/hu/showcaves/Baradla.html*; see pages 256–8) is one of Europe's largest stalactite caves; it is a World Heritage site and ranks among the world's most beautiful and intriguing geographical phenomena. The underworld offers another, rather warmer pleasure – **thermal water**, which bubbles up through rock fissures and forms the raw material for the country's many natural spas. Some of these – such as those at Hévíz and Budapest's City Park – allow you to don your swimming costume in mid winter as snow falls on the water. And where the water is medicinal, you may be tempted to drink an eggy concoction in the hope of relieving respiratory or gastric complaints – or a hangover headache.

For **horse-riding** and **hiking**, see pages 75–6.

Some green tourism projects, centres and events Sustained protection efforts have resulted in stable and growing populations of some globally threatened bird species – notably the **eastern imperial eagle** (*conservation project in the Carpathian Basin, www.imperialeagle.hu/indexa.html*), **saker falcon** (*nest-site-protection project,* ✎ *70 339 5903*) and **great bustard**. One of the most exciting rehabilitation schemes is taking place in the Körös-Maros National Park at Dévaványa, where they are protecting the great bustard. At the visitor centre, you can get close to the birds and enjoy their spectacular springtime display rituals (see page 372).

There are also some curious domestic stock. At Hortobágy, the Puszta Animal Park (see page 292) has an excellent range of **protected breeds** – Hungarian grey cattle, equine species like the Lipizzaner, shagya, nonius, gidran, furioso, kisbér halfbreed, murinsulaner and hucul, sheep including the racka, tsigai and cikta, poultry such as the Hungarian yellow, white, speckled and Transylvanian naked-necked hens, the bronze turkey, and the mangalica pig (sometimes referred to as a 'frizzle' on account of its hairy hide). There are also several intriguing types of **sheep dog** – the long-haired komondor, with a thick fringe covering its eyes, the kuvasz and the puli (see box, page 143). Thatched farms, or *tanya*, dot the *puszta* landscape, and beside them tall wooden structures called 'heron wells' (*gémeskút*) that are reminiscent of Arab *shadoofs*; equestrian shows, riding tours and goulash parties are other highlights.

If you're going to Hungary for the wildlife – on an organised or independent tour – the following are some of the items to be found in the pack of any self-respecting wildlife watcher:

ESSENTIALS
- Small rucksack
- Torch
- Water bottle (and hip flask, for those long hours in the hide!?)
- Notebook and pencil
- Sun hat, sunglasses, towel, lipsalve, handcream, sunscreen and insect repellent
- Field guides: you can purchase the *Collins Bird Guide* (by Mullarney, Svensson et al) from UK bookshops; *Butterflies of Europe* (by Tristan Lafranchis) is available by contacting lafranch@otenet.gr
- Handbooks: Bradt's *Central and Eastern European Wildlife* (by Gerard Gorman) and *The Birds of Hungary* (published by A&C Black)
- Maps of the Hungarian national parks (try the websites www.omnimap.com or www.stanfords.co.uk)

TECHNICAL CLOBBER
- Pair of binoculars (8.5 x 42 a personal favourite)
- Telescope (optional) – carry on the plane as hand luggage, with the tripod in your suitcase
- Camera (with lenses, film or memory cards and spare batteries)
- Hand-lens and specimen inspection pot for examining insects

Some **bird-ringing** stations allow visitors to assist with the work. At Lake Tata, a summer ringing camp welcomes tourists and school parties. For further details contact Peter Csonka (✆ *06 70 339 5903*), nature conservationist at Duna-Ipoly National Park, who also runs the saker falcon nest-site-protection project (see opposite) and the winter bird race (see below). **International bird races** welcome participants too, at the Hortobágy fishponds (Halastó) (usually first weekend in Sep) and Lake Tata (in Nov). The races take place over 24 hours, and have in recent years included entrants from the UK and USA.

Hungarian Moth Nights are run by the Szalkay József Hungarian Lepidopterological Society (*Magyar Lepkészeti Egyesület; Debrecen, Zoványi utca 19/B/9;* e *kadar.mihaly@mail.vpop.hu*), when volunteers join professional lepidopterologists in searching for and identifying moth species in different regions of the country and submitting their data to provide a snapshot of local moth populations. Information about upcoming events can be obtained from the vice-president of the society, Sáfián Szabolcs (✆ *06 20 346 1883;* e *lepkeved@ yahoo.co.uk; www.lepidoptera.freeweb.hu/program/emn/emn1.htm*).

For further details of operators running low-impact nature tours see pages 39–41; the *Charities* section (page 84) lists other worthy conservation projects.

HISTORY

TIME'S MISTS In 1965 the 400,000-year-old bones of a man – nicknamed Samuel by archaeologists – were found at Vértesszőlős (near Tata); he crafted flint tools, bathed in thermal springs and ate (or perhaps was eaten!) in this ancient camp. Several caves show signs of **Stone Age** man, of Neanderthals who picked berries and stalked mammoth, bear and ibex 40,000 years ago. With the thawing of the Ice Age, the Palaeolithic hunter-gatherers moved out and in 5000BC were replaced by migrants from the Near East via the Balkans. These **Neolithic** clans were producers rather than crude predators, and imported knowledge of agriculture, animal husbandry and pot-making, and belief systems based around goddess worship; their 'Körös culture' is named after the southeastern river valley in which their settlements were based, making use of the fertile soil. The advanced Neolithic culture slowly spread through the Danube Basin to the rest of Europe, but the Southern Great Plain is the westernmost region where *tell* can be found – artificial mounds formed by the accumulated remains of long-term habitation, and a feature more typical of the eastern Mediterranean.

From 3000BC fresh tribes arrived from the Balkans, Indo-European herders taking advantage of drier climatic conditions to supplant the agriculturalists. These shepherds stamped their authority with revolutionary technology – notably copper weapons and the four-wheeled cart. (A drinking vessel unearthed at Budakalász, near Budapest, is the earliest known representation of the cart in Europe.) During the early **Bronze Age** there were influxes from the south, and between 1700 and 1300BC a clutch of ethnically different lowland tribes were governed by horsemen living in a system of hillside forts. While the subsequent ebb and flow of migrating peoples was frequently bloody, it also ensured invention's spread; Iranian-speakers from the East introduced iron in 800BC and the Scythians brought with them the potter's wheel in 500BC. By the 4th century BC the **Celts** controlled the Carpathian Basin, their dominance based on the advanced use of iron. However, it was not until the arrival of Roman legions in the 1st century BC that a true, sandal-footed leap was made towards a sophisticated and civilised society.

THE ROMANS AND THE GREAT MIGRATIONS The **Romans** were determined to put proper distance between themselves and the Germanic barbarians to the east, and by 35BC they had extended their imperial boundary as far as the Danube. They protected this border with a line of forts known as the *limes*, and behind it established the province of Pannonia (subsequently divided into lower and upper administrative zones). Between AD106 and 271 they also controlled the province of Dacia further east in today's Transylvania. The strategic importance of Pannonia is evident in the fact that four of the empire's 25 legions were permanently based there. The Latin impact was immense. Remnants of the urban infrastructure – roads, baths, villas, temples and amphitheatres – can still be seen in Óbuda, Szombathely, Sopron, Győr and Pécs; cultural and spiritual influences (in the form of viniculture and Christianity) were no less important. During the 4th century the empire came under mounting pressure from waves of attack, and in the early 5th century they finally abandoned Pannonia.

This triggered the **second age of migrations** as Asiatic peoples from the east moved into the Carpathian Basin. Initially the Huns filled the vacuum under the notorious Attila. After murdering his brother in AD445, Attila commanded unswerving loyalty from his people. Such was the force of his personality that many later claimed blood ties with him, including Magyar rulers. After his death in AD453, however, the Huns' short-lived empire crumbled. Several nomadic tribes rose and fell over the next 400 years, the Avars most successful in grasping the nettle and holding it until the 8th century. By the 9th century, though, no group was in overall control, and the region was ripe for the plucking.

THE MAGYAR CONQUEST The question of true Hungarian ancestry has caused much squabbling and head scratching. The erroneous belief in a blood tie with the Huns continued well into the 18th century, and Attila was a heroic figure in the cultural consciousness during the period of national awakening – indeed Hungarians retain a soft spot for the 'Scourge of God' still. More recently there have been claims of kinship with groups including the Etruscans, Sumers and even the Incas, but scholars usually accept that the Magyars were a Finno-Ugric group hailing from lands between the River Volga and the Urals (in modern-day Russia). In 500BC, a branch of this group splintered off and travelled southwest to Bashkiria in central Asia (north of the Caspian Sea); they called themselves Magyars, a name formed of the Finno-Ugric words *mon* ('to speak') and *er* ('man'). At some point after AD500, some members moved further southwest to the Don River and joined other tribes in a collective known as the Onogur (from which the Western name 'Hungary' stems). Their final journey prior to the conquest took them around the top of the Black Sea to an area called Etelköz, between the Danube and the Dnieper rivers.

The position there was a precarious one, and after an attack by nomads from the Asian steppe the decision was taken to make the short hop west for greater security beyond the Carpathian Mountains. Divided between seven tribes under the overall leadership of a chieftain called Árpád and joined by three smaller groups of Kuns – making a combined invasion force of around 600,000 – the Magyars are said to have crossed the mountains via the Verecke Pass (in Ukraine). The ancestors of today's Hungarians had arrived. Resistance was negligible, and no match for a breed acutely skilled in both horsemanship and archery. In the early years they aspired to even greater things, and their armies travelled light in forging westward with devastating effect (reaching as far as France). However, after a string of losses culminated in a real spanking in Augsburg they elected to cut their losses and consolidate their new homeland.

THE ÁRPÁD KINGS AND THE HUNGARIAN STATE In the following years, **Prince Géza** (great-grandson of Árpád) invited missionaries from the West to introduce the Magyars to Christianity – although he himself never converted, claiming he was 'powerful enough to worship as many gods as he pleased'. Born around AD975, Géza's son Vajk was christened **István** (Stephen), and it was he who pushed on with centralising control – until then, the clans were effectively just a confederation that co-operated in times of war – and establishing a single, powerful state under the banner of Christianity (and, of course, the rule of his own fair hand). Lauded in Hungary as the prince among all their kings, it is forgotten that István was ruthless in his purpose. In snuffing out an alternative challenge to his primogeniture from his older cousin Koppány, István hung pieces of his body from four separate castles as a warning to others.

After his coronation in AD1000 with a crown sent by Pope Sylvester II, István set about bedding in his position, carefully dividing the land into counties governed by royal-appointed officials (not hereditary feudal rulers), fortifying the country borders and founding eight episcopal sees and two archbishoprics (at Esztergom and Kalocsa). Marriage to Gizella (niece of the German King Otto I 'the Great', the victor at Augsburg) and a friendship alliance with the Byzantine empire ensured István could get on with all this undistracted by international struggles. His success was rewarded with the title of 'Apostolic King', bestowed by the pope, and the right to use the double cross (still visible in the country's coat of arms). By the time of his death in 1038, István had transformed the country into a Christian monarchy with legal and administrative structures. When he was canonised 45 years later, his right hand was found still to be preserved and it is now held in Budapest's basilica, Hungary's most holy relic.

As he grew up, István's only son **Imre** had been carefully groomed to continue his father's work. It was therefore a tragic blow when Imre died in a hunting accident in 1031, an event that famously led István to offer the protection of his kingdom to the Virgin Mary. The death of the now-heirless István triggered **four decades of fighting** between a succession of weak kings and the nobility, and a final anti-Christian uprising under the pagan clan-chief Vata (during which Imre's former spiritual tutor, the Venetian Bishop Gellért, was stuffed into a spiked barrel and tossed down a hill into the Danube).

Stability returned with the reign of **László I** (1077–95), a shrewd monarch who governed with an iron fist, made careful alliances, reinforced the authority of the Church and even extended Hungary's influence by adding the crowns of Croatia and Dalmatia to his own (after the death of his brother-in-law and previous ruler of those territories). (The gold bust of László, containing his skull, is on display in Győr Cathedral.) The bookish **'Könyves' Kálmán I** (1095–1116) therefore took over a peaceful place, and was able to indulge and encourage love for the arts. During the 12th century Hungary flourished further, particularly under **King Béla III** (1172–96). Educated in Constantinople, Béla III based himself at Esztergom, quietened threatening rumbles from Byzantium, and went about overhauling the country's administrative framework; one of his enlightened moves was to declare it compulsory that legal and Crown dealings be documented in writing. In the same spirit, this was the era of the unknown scribe **Anonymus**, whose *Gesta Ungarorum* chronicled the events of Hungary's early history and remains a rare source for students today.

András II (1205–35) was feeble by comparison. After attempting to impose a tax to fund his participation in the Crusades, he provoked a rebellion and was forced in 1222 to sign a charter of rights called the **'Golden Bull'**, a sort of Magna Carta that decreed a yearly meeting (Diet) of nobles in Pest and curtailed the powers of the king. His son **Béla IV** (1235–70) was of a very different mould, but his rule was destined to overlap the devastating **Mongol invasion** of 1241–42, when the country was razed and vast swathes of the population massacred. He returned from exile determined to protect Hungary from future hostility – the country's first properly fortified castles, including that on Buda's Castle Hill, dated from the aftermath of the invasion – but the Mongols had wiped out a third of the population and he had to rely on the influx of German immigrants and the assistance of regional magnates. Civil war was almost inevitable in such raw circumstances, and Béla was forced to hand over half the country to his son; the barons capitalised, increasing their power by switching their support from one ruler to the other. The kingdom remained a turbulent one right up until the curtain was finally drawn on the Árpád line with the death of **András III** (1290–1301).

THE GOLDEN AGE A series of foreign dynasties put forward claims to the vacant throne, but the struggle was eventually won by **Károly Robert** (1308–42), an Angevin (or Anjou) king from Naples with the backing of the pope. He settled things down, moving the court to a new palace at Visegrád to negate the threat of disgruntled nobles in Buda and stabilising the economy with proceeds from gold mines in the north. **Lajos the Great** (1342–82) continued the expansion and captured the Polish throne in 1370. When he died without a male heir, **Zsigmond of Luxembourg** (1387–1437) – later King of Bohemia and Holy Roman Emperor – took over; his reign coincided with Turkish expansionist ambitions in Europe which Zsigmond (continually flitting about his territories abroad) did very little to counter. The defeat of his armies at Nicopolis in 1396 signalled the beginning of the Ottoman charge into central Europe.

The Ottoman advance was halted at the **Battle of Nándorfehérvár** (now \belgrade) in 1456 when Hungary's greatest general, the Transylvanian Prince János \unyadi, achieved a famous victory for which he was lauded as the saviour of

Christendom. Pope Callixtus III declared that the noon Angelus should be prayed, and church bells rung across Catholic Europe in grateful remembrance. Hunyadi succumbed to the plague shortly afterwards, but in 1458 his teenage son **Mátyás** (1458–90) took the throne after victory in the baronial struggle that followed the death of Zsigmond's son László V. His reign proved something of a purple patch. The economy prospered, and Mátyás – known as 'Corvinus' after the raven in his coat of arms – and his Italian wife Beatrice made the court at Buda one of the centres of Renaissance art and learning. For men of letters, he put together a stunning library in one wing of the palace; for men of action, he set up the Black Army, one of Europe's first professional units. An able statesman and a famously fair man, he was deeply respected and even liked by his subjects – on his death, it was said truth had died with him. Hungary's political and cultural influence never again blossomed so fulsomely.

There was the familiar feudal infighting following Mátyás's demise, climaxing in the **Peasant Revolt** of 1514. This was provoked by increasing pressures put upon the peasantry by the noble landlords, and was enacted by a peasant army under György Dózsa that had originally been assembled by the Franciscans to embark on a crusade against the Turks. The rebellion made the ruling classes put aside their differences, and they united to crush the peasants ruthlessly – Dózsa was burnt to death on a metal throne – and enforced a Tripartitum law that reduced the peasants to a state of **'serfdom in perpetuity'** whereby they were tied to the estates of their landowning masters. It was a division that remained for several hundred years. Such turbulence, though, was as nothing compared with that to come.

TURKISH OCCUPATION For Hungarians, August 29 1526 is the most tragic date in a past littered with them. On that day the Turks – who were on the march once more and had taken castles in Serbia before crossing the Drava – obliterated the Magyar army under Lajos II at **Mohács** in southern Hungary. Fifteen years later the Ottomans had conquered much of eastern and central Hungary. Lajos II had drowned while fleeing the battlefield, and in the urgent need to prevent the Turks mustering their forces and pressing on to Vienna, **Ferdinand I of Habsburg** (1526–64) – with a claim to the throne through the Habsburg brother-in-law of Zsigmond, who'd briefly ruled Hungary – moved into Transdanubia. Over subsequent years the Turks made further incursions into the north and across into Southern Transdanubia. Instances of bold, last-gasp resistance at the fortresses of Szigetvár and Eger are the stuff of folklore; it is equally true that Habsburg armies often sat back and watched blood spill from a distance, unwilling to risk their troops and ready to sacrifice Magyar fighters as long as the Turks were stalled. This naturally engendered a burning sense of betrayal in the towns that were captured, whose people had accepted Ferdinand's kingship in the expectation he would protect his territories. At the **Treaty of Adrianople** in 1568 the division of land was agreed: the Turks held the Great Plain, areas to the north of it and Transdanubia below Balaton; the west and north of Transdanubia and the remaining parts of the uplands in the north and northeast were subsumed into the Habsburg empire (with Royal Hungary's capital in Pozsony, or Bratislava); and Transylvania – much to the annoyance of the Habsburgs – retained its status as a semi-autonomous principality, permitted its own rulers on the condition of allegiance to the Turks.

Come the dawn of the 17th century, it seemed that Hungary was destined to remain divided in three for ever more. The **Fifteen Years War** (1593–1606) represented the only concerted early effort to boot out the Turks and integrate Transylvania into Royal Hungary. It petered out having wreaked further damage and depopulation and achieved little beyond local successes. For their part, the

Protestant **Transylvanian princes** – István Bocskai (1605–06) and Gábor Bethlen (1614–29) – were keen to shift the Catholic Habsburgs and reunite non-Turkish Hungary with Transylvania once more, often calling on mercenary Hajdúk (Heyduck) peasants soldiers to help in the effort. Imre Thököly led a failed revolt in 1682, but it was Ferenc Rákóczi whose name became synonymous with the anti-Habsburg fight in the early years of the next century. Meanwhile Turkish powers were fading. In 1686 a pan-European army evicted the Turks from Buda after a siege that lasted months, and in 1697 **Eugene of Savoy** secured the conclusive victory at Zenta (now in Serbia).

HABSBURG RULE The Habsburgs were in charge, but they certainly hadn't won over hearts and minds. The blunt policies of **Leopold I** (1657–1705) had made many enemies. Resentment had been heightened by the **Treaty of Vasvár** in 1664, when he handed back to the Turks areas that Hungarian General Miklós Zrínyi had only just recaptured. Like the Romans before, he was using Hungary to put distance between his empire and the threat (now Turkish rather than Germanic) to the east, and the impression he gave was that the bodies in between were dispensable in this cause. In response a **Hungarian plot** had been hatched in 1670; when uncovered, leaders including Péter Zrínyi were executed and the noble privileges dating to the 'Golden Bull' revoked. Counter-Reformatory measures (half the population was Protestant) became violent and land taken back from the Turks was given to favoured courtiers with no concern for legal claims of prior ownership. Against such a backdrop, resistance was gathered around the romantic figure of **Ferenc Rákóczi II**, a member of the Zrínyi plot spared because of his Catholic mother. Nobles and peasants joined the *kuruc* (independence fighters) forces and waged an eight-year rebellion partly financed by Louis XIV of France. The struggle eventually failed, but Rákóczi had been the first to muster Hungarians across the social spectrum in opposition to Habsburg rule.

After the wars, Hungary was but a province of the Habsburg empire, but under the enlightened absolutism of **Maria Theresa** (1740–80) it actually enjoyed a period of sustained growth. **József II** steeped himself in the ideas of the Enlightenment – he even refused to be crowned as he didn't believe in being tied by the Coronation Oath – and his rule divided attitudes. While he ruffled the feathers of feudal nobles by abolishing perpetual serfdom and insisting that German (rather than Latin) was the official language, he garnered support from progressive Hungarians like Ferenc Széchenyi. In part he was let down by tactlessness rather than malevolent intent. **Ferenc I** (1792–1835) was far more conservative; plagued by fear of the revolutionary fire that was raging in France, he came down heavily on a Jacobin plot of 1795 led by the priest Ignác Martinovics (who, ironically, had acted as a Crown informant in the past).

Despite this imperial conservatism, the first decades of the 19th century witnessed the **Age of Reform**, in large part spurred by aristocrats like Count **István Széchenyi** – 'the greatest Hungarian'. His progressive bourgeois vision was influenced by visits to England, and he inspired the founding of the Hungarian Academy of Sciences, the laying of the first railway line and the regulation of the Danube and Tisza rivers. While Széchenyi was radical in a practical sense, politically he was a believer in evolution rather than revolution; however, a group emerged that lacked his patience – its leading beacons Baron Miklós Wesselényi, poet Ferenc Kölcsey, Ferenc Deák and the eloquent lawyer Lajos Kossuth. Their desire to drag Hungary away from its feudal roots was coupled with resentment of absolutist rule by foreign monarchs who neither spoke their language (Ferenc zsef was the first to do so) nor spent much time on Magyar soil. While only 5% adult males had the franchise, and Vienna ensured that the incumbent government had plenty of money to wine and dine come election time, there was nevertheless a groundswell of support for progressive reform both in the chambers of Parliament (or Diet) and beyond. Things were beginning to bubble.

THE 1848–49 WAR OF INDEPENDENCE AND THE 1867 COMPROMISE The catalyst for change came during the revolutions that erupted in Europe in March 1848. The liberals grabbed their chance and the Diet passed a raft of Acts that became known as the **April Laws**. These extended the franchise, made the ministry responsible to Parliament alone, reunited Transylvania with the rest of Hungary and abolished the legal distinctions between citizens (including tax exemptions and the right of nobles to peasant services) – in effect laying the foundations for a constitutional monarchy and the consequent curtailment of royal power. The weak **Ferdinand V** (1835–48) wavered but eventually gave his royal assent and **Count Lajos Batthyány** was appointed as prime minister. However, the poet **Sándor Petőfi** and other young radicals gathered on the streets of Pest to demand that reforms go further, urging Hungarians to rise up in revolution.

In September the Habsburg forces responded by attacking Hungary, and a national defence committee was organised with **Kossuth** – 'the Moses of the Hungarians' – at its head. Initially the independence government – which in April 1849 declared the country free from the rule of Habsburg monarchy – was successful in pushing back the imperial armies. However, the new **Emperor Ferenc József** (1848–1916) enlisted reinforcements from the Russian Tsar Nicholas I, and the revolution was over by August. Petőfi had died in battle and Kossuth went into exile. The notorious Austrian Field Marshall Haynau – the 'Hyena of Brescia' – was tasked with putting on a show of Habsburg might. Batthyány was executed, together with 13 generals in Transylvania (the 'Martyrs of Arad'); thousands were imprisoned and thousands more fled abroad to escape reprisals.

However, renewed hope came more swiftly than expected. The Austrians suffered several defeats to Italian, French and Prussian armies, and – anxious to shore up the Habsburg empire – acceded to an agreement drawn up by the liberal politician **Ferenc Deák**. The **Compromise** (*Ausgleich* or *Kiegyezés*) of 1867 established a dual monarchy, whereby Hungary had its own government, parliament and even small army, but operated jointly with Austria in matters of foreign policy and defence. Hungarians were buoyant, the economy boomed and there was a flurry of cultural and creative activity most evident during the **millennial celebrations** of 1896 commemorating the Magyar conquest. A mighty exhibition showcased Hungarian technology and achievement in Budapest's City Park, and ambitious building programmes were undertaken in the capital and beyond. Not all was rosy though. Minorities in particular felt oppressed by nationalist domestic policies of '**Magyarisation**'; these stemmed from the urge to re-establish a firm sense of national identity, for so long suppressed under the occupation of foreign powers, and demanded full cultural assimilation from non-Magyars. By the early 20th century, there were also discontented stirrings from society's disenfranchised lower echelons.

THE WORLD WARS Hungary was tied to Austria through thick and thin – and in the early years of the Compromise few could see past the current thick to the possible thin, dangerous times ahead. Those came with a bang in 1914. In June a Serbian youth assassinated Archduke Ferenc Ferdinand, the heir to the thrones of Austria and Hungary. Despite the initial objections of Hungarian Prime Minister István Tisza, war was declared on Serbia in July. The Austro-Hungarian empire was decisively defeated in **World War I**, and the Habsburg monarchy collapsed. In the aftermath, a short-lived communist regime known as the **Republic of Councils** was established for 133 days under Béla Kun – using 'Red Terror' to impose nationalisation of land. On June 4 1920 Hungary was forced by the victorious powers to sign the uncompromising **Treaty of Trianon**, which handed two-thirds of its territory to neighbouring countries that even included Austria. Three million Magyars found themselves sudden exiles in foreign states. This division of countryman from countryman had a lasting impact on Hungarian culture and sense of self, and the memory of 'Greater Hungary' – and the treatment of ethnic Hungarians in Romania and elsewhere – remains a hot topic to this day. The exiled Magyars frequently met with little sympathy from those of the Successor States of which they were now members – memories of the punitive measures imposed on minorities who resisted 19th-century 'Magyarisation' remained fresh.

A counter-revolutionary army had begun to form at Szeged; it was headed by **Admiral Miklós Horthy** – the last commander of the Austro-Hungarian fleet that had been bottled up in the Adriatic during the war – who targeted 'Reds' in a regime of 'White Terror' at the other end of the political spectrum and displayed ruthless elements of anti-semitism. When Horthy rode into Budapest with his troops in November 1919, Kun fled abroad (ultimately to be executed by Stalin during 'purges' of the 1930s) and on March 1 1920 Horthy was elected Regent (as the self-declared representative of exiled Habsburg Emperor Karl IV). Horthy led a **right-wing dictatorship** whose policies were conservative, anti-semitic and nationalistic. Its primary aim was to retrieve the lands stripped from Hungary at Trianon, an ambition supported universally by Hungarians. Prime Minister **István Bethlen** (1921–31) was an able administrator well-regarded by the Allied powers, and a few concessions were secured (such as the return of Sopron and Kőszeg after referendums); on the home front, Count Bethlen helped to develop industry and education, stabilise the economy and tone down some of the anti-semitic extremes. However, he leant towards the Catholic Church and the landowners, and the agricultural workers in particular were subject to restrictive controls designed to protect the interests of the gentry. The urge to find a way of reclaiming land confiscated at Trianon, together with the right-wing bent of the governing class, inevitably pushed Hungary towards alliance with fascist Germany.

In 1941 – against the advice of Prime Minister Teleki, who subsequently committed suicide – Horthy supported Germany in the **unprovoked attack** upon Yugoslavia. Hungary was rewarded with the return of some lost lands, but it was now inextricably and actively involved in **World War II**, and its army suffered very heavily on the eastern front. When Horthy secretly entered into negotiation with the Allies, the Germans learned of the betrayal and **occupied** the country in March 1944. They installed the leader of the Hungarian Nazis (the **Arrow-Cross Party**) at the head of the government, ushering in the horrors of the **Holocaust**. Ghettos were established and Adolf Eichmann oversaw a programme of deportation of Jews to death camps that started in the countryside and moved in towards Budapest. Only the intervention of Horthy and the actions of Raoul Wallenberg (the Swedish diplomat), Carl Lutz (the Swiss consul) and the Catholic Church saved those in the capital from the wholesale deportation that was carried out in the rest of the country. The end was nigh for the Germans, however, as the Russians advanced from the east and, after a viciously contested siege at Buda, the Germans finally fled in April 1945.

THE COMMUNIST YEARS The communists came to power in 1947 on the back of a campaign of intimidation and a rigged election. **Mátyás Rákosi** – acting in total subservience to Moscow – imposed a **Stalinist dictatorship** between 1947 and 1953, emulating his mentor in the brutal use of spies, torture and murder. Private

Q 'How do you double the value of a Trabant?'
A 'Fill it with petrol.'

The Berlin Wall fell in 1989, but the blue-smoke-belching Trabant – symbol of the old communist era – is still a visible presence. City governments have tried to run it off the road, but people love their 'soap dishes'. Owners were offered a BKV transport pass worth 30,000Ft in 1995 as an incentive to trade in their Trabis; of 300,000 on the road, just 200 were handed in.

During the 1960s and '70s, the waiting list for a Trabi was 15 years long. It cost a year's wages for an average Hungarian worker, and came in beige, light blue or olive green. On delivery, new owners were advised to tighten visible screws and grease all working parts. In actual fact it was never meant to be a car, but a rainproof motorcycle with a boot, and thus cheap transport for all the family. It was an innovation in the 1950s, the engine so light it could be lifted out by one man – rally-racing Trabants often carried a spare in the boot. In a 'reindeer test' – which simulates the ability of a car to avoid an obstacle (such as an animal) at speed – the Trabant apparently bettered a Mercedes. It was handmade of Duroplast – a mixture of compressed resin and polyester – and is light, rust-proof and cheap. However, it is also totally non-recyclable, has the acceleration of an overweight slug and gets reduced to smithereens in a collision.

In the last days of the Berlin Wall, rickety East German Trabants escaping to the West through Hungarian territory became symbols of freedom. Consumerism, however, and the competing claims of shiny Audis and Fiats, meant it quickly reverted to a sad symbol of socialism: inefficient and dull. There were even small ads in local papers offering to swap cars for packets of cigarettes. The Trabi gained cult status in the West, though; in the early 1990s, U2 took a fleet of them on tour as part of their Achtung Baby set.

The last Trabant was made in 1992, but Zwickau in the former East Germany (where it was manufactured) remains a place of pilgrimage for the annual rally, attended by enthusiasts from all over Europe. The proudly ugly Trabi has outlived the demise of the system and the factory, and remains the most communist car of all – a true car for the people.

Background Information **HISTORY**

businesses were nationalised without compensation, peasants were forced into state farms and the feared ÁVO – the secret police – conducted their dark operations from headquarters at Andrássy út 60 in Budapest. Over 500,000 people were executed or jailed in labour camps at home (there was one at Recsk) or in the Soviet Union. Rákosi's position was undermined by Stalin's death in 1953, and **Imre Nagy** – a reformist in the Communist Party – took over as prime minister. He was expelled for introducing mild reforms, but the spectre of a kindly, humane communism had been raised.

On October 23 1956 a student demonstration in Budapest demanded democracy, neutrality in foreign policy and the reinstatement of Nagy. After gathering for a tentative speech by Nagy outside Parliament, some split off to the radio station on Bródy utca with the intention of voicing their feelings more widely. As they attempted to enter, they were fired upon by members of the ÁVO and peaceful protest flared into **revolution**. The statue of Stalin that stood to the south of City Park was broken to pieces. Nagy set up an administration, declared the country's withdrawal from the Warsaw Pact, and looked hopefully to the West for recognition and assistance. However, Western powers were focused upon the Suez crisis, and – after bloody street fighting – Soviet tanks brutally suppressed the revolution. The Russian military placed **János Kádár** in charge of the 'Revolutionary Worker-Peasant' government; pacification and stabilisation of the country featured the execution of 2,000, the arrest of 20,000, and the shipping off of many more to Soviet labour camps. Around 200,000 people – two per cent of the population – fled to the West, a serious leak of enterprising young talent (the average age was just 20). Nagy was imprisoned and quietly exterminated in 1958; his body, along with many others, was laid in a distant corner of Budapest's Újköztemető (New Public Cemetery), in overgrown 'Plot 301'.

Initially repressive in consolidating his position, and hated for being the Soviets' man, once Kádár was entrenched he managed a delicate balancing act, both appeasing Soviets and introducing liberal policies that gradually thawed the frost between the governing and the governed. Where Rákosi had declared 'Those who are not with us are against us', Kádár's appeasing mantra was 'Those who are not against us are with us'. He instituted a platform of national reconciliation, and from 1968 implemented a programme of radical economic reforms. This 'market socialism' was nicknamed **'Goulash Communism'** abroad, and led to strengthened relations with the West. It also further relieved domestic tensions and gradually improved living standards; Hungary was known as the 'happiest barracks in the Bloc'.

THE FALL OF COMMUNISM By 1988 Kádár was struggling to control a spiralling economic crisis and was finally dismissed after a remarkable 32 years of cautiously responsive rule that had successfully prevented a return to tyranny and revolution. The MSZMP (Hungarian Socialist Workers' Party) recognised the shape of things to come and permitted a series of 'round table' discussions with 'non-official' new 'opposition' parties – the first move positively towards democracy proper. The sign that the worm had turned irrevocably in the modern history of Hungarian politics came during the **reburial of Imre Nagy** in 1989. In a reconciliatory act on the anniversary of the executions, Nagy (and other victims of the revolution) were reburied in a spruced-up Plot 301. During the ceremony a young hippie of a student, Viktor Orbán, gave voice to what many were thinking in demanding that Soviet troops leave his country. The last soldier did so on June 19 1991.

A PECULIAR SORT OF PICNIC

The event that set in chain the final fall of the Iron Curtain didn't involve violence or wrecking balls – rather, it was signalled by a gentle picnic. In August 1989, it was decided to hold a 'Pan-European Picnic' at the Austrian/Hungarian border (near Sopron) – a follow-up to the symbolic cutting of the fence between the two countries by Gyula Horn and Alois Mock (Hungarian and Austrian foreign ministers) a couple of months before. As well as the nibbles you'd expect at a picnic, the border was to be opened for a few hours to allow citizens to pass freely between the two countries. Among the crowd of thousands who turned up for the picnic, though, were some 600 East Germans who'd spotted an opportunity to flee to the West. The Hungarian border guards allowed them through – or pretended they hadn't noticed them! – and a seemingly minor breach kickstarted one of the 20th century's momentous events. Just a few months later the Berlin Wall was brought down. Today the site contains memorials to the picnic, together with a preserved watchtower where soldiers once guarded the wire.

As the Iron Curtain began to draw back, Hungary played a significant role in pulling the cord. Gyula Horn (the foreign minister) allowed East Germans to climb into their Trabants and sputter through the country to reach the West (see box opposite). In 1989, the reform communists declared the advent of **party-political democracy**; the first free elections in March 1990 resulted in a coalition led by the Hungarian Democratic Forum (Magyar Demokrata Forum – MDF), who campaigned on a blend of conservative and nationalist policies. The first president of the new democracy was the enduringly popular Árpád Göncz, a Free Democrat (SZDSZ) translator and author who had been imprisoned after 1956. With a quiet simplicity wholly alien to significant events in Hungary's history, the communists had been voted out. The People's Republic of Hungary became the Republic of Hungary, and the contemporary era of parliamentary democracy had begun. (For details of the landscape since, see *Politics* and *Economy* below.)

POLITICS

DEMOCRATIC HUNGARY In the 20 years since the *rendszerváltás* (change of political system), Hungarian politics has swung backwards and forwards between left and right (or, more accurately, centre-left and centre-right). In 1994, the **Socialist Party** (Magyar Szocialista Párt – MSZP) returned to power on a wave of nostalgia for past stability and dissatisfaction at rising unemployment, rising inflation and rising crime. The government of the MSZP and its coalition partner, the liberal Alliance of Free Democrats (Szabad Demokrata Szövetség – SZDSZ), were led by Gyula Horn, the man who had waved through the soap dishes on their journey to the West five years earlier. The government introduced an 'austerity package' – known as the Bokros package – to set the country back on course towards EU membership.

A policy with 'austerity' as its mantra is rarely a vote winner, and in 1998 (when the four-year tenure came to an end) the country looked rightwards once more in electing a third party, **Fidesz** (Fiatal Demokraták Szövetsége). This Alliance of Young Democrats was originally formed in the late 1980s by Viktor Orbán – who had spoken with such passion and charisma at Nagy's funeral – from a group of law students. In the early days the party was characterised by youthful liberalism, but it became increasingly conservative in the ensuing decade. Orbán began to promote staunchly conservative, Christian family values – 'God, Homeland, Family' (*'Isten, Haza, Család'*). In a move rich with political, religious and social meaning, Orbán shifted the iconic symbol of Hungary – the crown of St István – from the National Museum to the Parliament building.

In 2002, the country elected the socialist **MSZP** once more (again with coalition partners SZDSZ). The elections were savage and the socialists' victory tiny, with a majority of just ten. So narrow was the margin that Fidesz refused to accept the result, and established local action groups to drum up support in the countryside (where conservative values still predominate). However, the slender majority was stable. Hungary had joined NATO in 1999; on May 1 2004, the prime minister, Péter Medgyessy, steered the country into the **EU** before resigning following a failed cabinet reshuffle. Ferenc Gyurcsány was selected to replace him, and in April 2006 he led his socialist-liberal coalition to re-election – the first time this had happened since communism's fall. The 2005 presidential election (characterised by particularly vociferous bickering all round) was, however, won narrowly by the nominee of the centre-right opposition, former chief justice of the Constitution Court László Sólyom. The president (whose official residence is the Sándor Palace) serves for five years, and has relatively little executive power under the constitution, but does provide a check on the constitutionality of government legislation.

Gyurcsány modelled himself on Tony Blair, and made it his mission to revitalise the Socialist Party. However, Gyurcsány's period in office was far from smooth. With a total of 210 seats (out of 386), the coalition government did not have the two-thirds majority required to enact constitutional, legal or procedural changes. In September 2006 recordings emerged of Gyurcsány apparently declaring he'd lied to voters, sparking some of the worst riots in decades – indeed, protesters even seized a Soviet-era tank and drove it at police (until it ran out of fuel!) during clashes on the 50th anniversary of the 1956 revolution the following month. (Since then, riots by thuggish right-wing groups have become a depressingly familiar feature of many of the national holidays.) He fought to tackle a huge budget deficit with tough measures like tax rises, something resented by many Hungarians who remembered the austerity package of a decade ago that was meant to cure such ills. In March 2008, things got worse when several elements of the reform programme – including controversial new fees for higher education and medical visits – were comprehensively rejected by voters during a national referendum. In the aftermath, the SZDSZ (with their 20 seats) withdrew from the coalition (attaching their support to conditions like tax reductions) and Gyurcsány was rendered a toothless tiger at the head of a minority government. Then the global financial crisis blew in. In autumn 2008, Hungary was forced to accept a US$25 billion bailout (see opposite), and in March 2009 Gyurcsány finally resigned. Gordon Bajnai – a relative unknown – took over as prime minister this year (2010). Crises can be the saviours of struggling governments; however, Fidesz are currently 30% ahead in opinion polls, and it would take a resurrection of biblical proportions for the MSZP to win a third straight election. Furthermore, there's been a sinister rise in popularity for the ultra-right party Jobbik (who have three of Hungary's 12 MEPs) – and there's concern that Fidesz's popularity might later drop (when they come to power), leaving them forced to seek Jobbik support.

While smooth and unbloody, the transition from the rule of state to democratic government was nevertheless a significant social, ideological and political change. It's easy to forget this happened just 20 years ago. Parliament is a more exciting place, and a centre of lively argument; it is also a place where debate is often confrontational, and focused upon political points-scoring rather than genuine policy differences. Where consensus comes in the parliamentary chamber is over Euro-Atlantic integration and the development of a free-market economy. Hungary's foreign-policy thrust has been largely consistent since 1990 in prioritising integration into Western economic and security organisations. In addition to joining NATO and the EU, it has signed treaties with neighbours Romania, Slovakia and Ukraine that give up any historical territorial claims and thereby pave the path for smoother relations. Despite that, the thorny subject of the rights of minority ethnic Hungarian populations in Romania and Slovakia does raise its head sporadically and create tensions.

The process and the parties Parliamentary elections are held every four years (the next as we go to press, in spring 2010) on the basis of a complicated, 'mixed' system. The country is broken down into constituencies, in each of which citizens vote for their preferred candidate; in a first-past-the-post system, the one with the majority is elected to parliament. At the same time, however, voters also indicate their choice of party. For this the system is proportionate, and parties receive their mandates according to the percentage of votes they win. At least 5% is required for parliamentary representation. There are 386 MPs in the Hungarian Parliament; 176 MPs are elected from the constituencies, while the rest of the MPs are appointed from the list of parties.

The **main political parties** are the Hungarian Socialist Party (MSZP); Alliance of Free Democrats (SZDSZ); Hungarian Civic Alliance (Fidesz-MPP); Hungarian Democratic Forum (MDF); Hungarian Workers' Party (MMP); Hungarian Justice and Life Party (MIEP) – currently superseded by Jobbik ('the Better'); Christian Democratic People's Party (KDNP; and Hungarian Democratic People's Party (MDNP).

ECONOMY

The economic priority over the last couple of years has been to reduce the nation's worrying budget deficit, and the government pursued a tough programme of tax rises and spending caps. In 2007 the trade deficit was successfully eliminated; however, the strong growth of the previous decade inevitably slowed (to under 2%), inflation rose to nearly 8% and unemployment is over 10%. The government was also defeated in a referendum on parts of its austerity package in 2008 (see opposite), which saw the programme put on hold. The global financial crisis hit Hungary's economy – naturally vulnerable because of its reliance on external financing and high level of foreign-currency borrowing – very hard. At the end of October 2008, Hungary accepted US$25 billion from the IMF, EU and World Bank – a consequence of instability as foreign investors withdrew funds to finance their losses elsewhere as the credit crunch crunched. The bailout was aimed at shoring up Hungary to protect against a domino effect in Central Europe. The loans helped to stabilise things, although the macroeconomic situation remained weak in 2009 as a result of falling demand in Hungary's main export markets and slowing domestic consumption. It is hoped that growth prospects will improve in 2010 as the IMF loan and EU funds (a €22.4 billion subsidy is available until 2013) continue to help, and the country's traditional economic strengths – low wages, high skills, good infrastructure and prime location – bear fruit. However, while there seems to be little concern about repaying the loan – Fidesz are campaigning on lowering taxes and increasing jobs – further austerity measures will be hard to avoid.

Despite current problems, Hungary has demonstrated strong growth since making the transition from a centrally planned to a **market economy** (averaging 4.5% between 1996 and 2006). The high inflation that characterised the early years after its change of political system – 14% as late as 1998 – was brought under control (it fell to 3.9% in 2006), and the reward was EU membership on May 1 2004. A combination of Hungary's relative lack of natural resources and its strategic location in Europe means that it has traditionally relied on foreign trade. Prior to the regime shift in 1989, 65% of the country's trade was with Comecon countries, but afterwards Hungary moved much of its trading relationships towards the West and is now deeply integrated into the European economy. The **private sector** accounts for over 80% of GDP. Since 1989, direct foreign investment has been considerable, attracted by relatively low working costs and wages, and an educated workforce. Foreign firms control 66% of manufacturing, 90% of telecommunications and 60% of the energy sector. Germany is Hungary's most significant economic partner. The Hungarian average wage is £7,200. The aim is eventually to bring the public sector deficit under 3% of GDP, a precondition of Hungary's eligibility to adopt the euro, as outlined in the Maastricht Treaty.

Standing at its crossroads, **Budapest** has emerged as the financial and commercial hub of central Europe. It is inevitably at the forefront of Hungary's economy, and consequently of its economic growth. It is here that the country's important transport arteries are gathered and it is here that 60% of foreign capital investment is funnelled. The GDP per capita is a staggering 90% higher than the average, and the capital generates 35% of the national income.

Hungarians are no grinning Cheshire cats. They are a rare and intriguing breed that looks on the gloomier side of life, that notices the cloud from afar but develops myopia when it comes to its lining. They acknowledge this trait, although typically describing it as 'realism'. They are more Eeyore than Tigger, and hooray for that.

We can look to history to make sense of this tendency towards pessimism. Foreign nations (Ottomans, Habsburgs, Germans and Soviets) have conspired to subject the people and destroy their precious monuments. The Treaty of Trianon stripped the country of two-thirds of its territory. Borders have buckled through the ages, and five million ethnic Hungarians are now 'exiles', dividing families and isolating pockets of the populace. The upshot is a social psyche that expects to be dealt the rough cards in any hand. On an individual level, this melancholy can manifest itself in tragic ways. It is estimated that alcoholism is a problem for ten per cent, and Hungary used to top the 'suicide league table'. It's no coincidence that *Gloomy Sunday* – a song that has been blamed for provoking over 100 suicides and was banned in the UK until 2002 – was written by a Hungarian...

It is therefore surprising that Hungarians are neither lethargic nor submissive; on the contrary, they are fiercely patriotic and take deep pride in their past heroic struggles against oppression. Countless towns and villages are pieces of standing proof of a willingness to rebuild – repeatedly – from conflict's rubble. They have been resourceful, energetic and inventive, claiming a clutch of Nobel prizes and making a bigger splash in the spheres of science, music and medicine than their population size entitles them. As the proverb states, 'only a Hungarian can enter a revolving door behind you and come out in front'. Such nationhood and high achievement stem from a desperate urge to resist forces that might snuff them out.

The issue of where the country stands in relation to its past divides Hungarians. Some – more usually city folk – are westward-facing Europeans. Others are fervent nationalists who believe in a Greater Hungary. They stress the importance of ancient tradition, of their Asiatic roots, and are frequently suspicious of the liberal cosmopolitanism (by which they usually mean 'Jewish-ness') of Budapest. Some right-wing politicians have played upon geographical insecurities, positioning Hungary as an island in a sea of Slav, surrounded by neighbours they cannot trust. This fear of anything that isn't 'pure Magyar' can seem strange when common surnames like Németh (meaning 'German'), Tóth (Slovak), Horváth (Croatian) and Orosz (Russian) are indicative of a more mixed heritage. Nevertheless, such isolationist views make prejudice common; while there is growing public discussion about the shame of the Hungarian Holocaust, anti-Semitism is not unusual and dislike of the Roma minority is often openly expressed. Hungary also lags behind some Western countries in its ready acceptance of feminist views and alternative lifestyles (such as homosexuality).

If it seems paradoxical (even oxymoronic) to talk of people as proud pessimists or suicidal self-improvers, there are other ways in which the Hungarian national character is a coin of two sides. As we've said, Hungarians – even urbanists and the young – are inherently conservative and home loving, preferring the Magyar way of life. Yet they can also be wholly lacking in prudery. Porn-star Michelle Wild is a household name who appears regularly on breakfast television. And while social codes are based on formality and politeness, you may find this difficult to credit in some restaurants, where it is quickly clear that the service industry has yet to recover fully from 40 years of communism.

The Hungarian character evades simple stereotypes. This is a race of people made tough by repeated slaps from history's hand; it is also one with stamina and resourceful answers to difficult questions. Tourists will find that the Budapest

What's in a name? Nothing, it seems, as long as it's not that of Belgian movie star Jean-Claude van Damme or the Olympic cities of Sydney and Atlanta. These were among those submitted to – and rejected by – the Interior Ministry recently. Hungarians are obliged to choose names from an official list, a practice introduced under the communists; while Rózsa would no doubt smell as sweet by any other name, that other name had better be in the approved 'Ládó' book.

Those wishing to deviate from the list must apply for permission at the Hungarian Academy of Sciences, and unusual or foreign-sounding names are often turned down. There are exceptions; 'Jennifer', for instance – very possibly popularised by singer Jennifer Lopez – has made it into the 1,900 permitted first names as 'Dzsenifer'. Historical names are also protected, and applicants would usually have to prove a familial link. Typical requests for name changes come from married women starting in business who want to free themselves of 'né' (see below), or from Roma looking to disguise their roots after marrying non-Roma.

Registered forenames are assigned a calendar 'name day' (*névnap*), which is celebrated with cards and gifts. (The Hungarian section of the website www.behindthename.com has a name-day calendar.) A married woman may either retain her maiden name or adopt her husband's with the appendage 'né' ('belonging to'). As such, if Szabó Anna married Kovács János, she could call herself one of four versions: Kovács Jánosné, Kovácsné Szabó Anna, Kovács Jánosné Szabó Anna or just Szabó Anna. Confused? Well you'll be dismayed to hear that, in addition to all this, in Hungary surnames appear in front of forenames.

boulevard is a purposeful place where people hurry about their business. There are few exchanged smiles on the metro. However, there is never any sense in which this is intimidating or uncomfortable, and it masks a genuine and earnest helpfulness that lurks close beneath the surface. A terse face can be transformed by '*köszönöm*' from a foreign tongue, and more sustained interaction reveals an openness, an engaging and sophisticated humour, and a commitment to friendship that is all the more valuable because not casually offered.

The **ethnic make up** of Hungary is 89.9% Hungarian, 4% Roma, 2.6% German, 2% Serb, 0.8% Slovak, 0.7% Romanian.

RELIGION

Those who regularly attend church are in a minority in Hungary, especially in the cities. **Roman Catholicism** (*Katolikus*) is the main religious denomination (67.5% of Hungarians). István, Hungary's first king, introduced Christianity as the religion of state over a thousand years ago, and it survived in spite of sustained Turkish occupation (when many Hungarians converted temporarily to Islam) and the secularity of communist rule. The largest **Protestant** denomination is the Calvinist or Reformed Church (*Református*; 20% of the population), followed by the Lutherans/Evangelicals (*Evangélikus*; 5%).

Seven per cent are listed as affiliated to other religious orders that include **Serb** and **Greek Orthodox** (*Szerb/Görög ortodox*) and **Judaism** (*zsidó vallás*). Before World War II, Budapest had one of the most significant Jewish communities in the world, estimated at 200,000. However, over half perished during the Holocaust, and after the war only 90,000 Jews remained in the city; populations beyond the capital were all but wiped out during the programme of deportation to Nazi concentration camps. Numbers dwindled further still under communist rule, particularly following the 1956 revolution. The demise of communism saw a revival of sorts, and today 80,000 Jews live in Budapest (the biggest community in central Europe), a number that continues to grow. In addition, as in most post-communist countries, Hungary is seen as fertile ground for the 'new' religions; Mormons, Hari Krishna, Faith Congregation and Scientologists are all commonly found on the streets and subways.

CULTURE

LITERATURE AND ART Hungary has a proud cultural history, but much of its output remains closed to a world that can't speak the tongue. Some of the finest **literature** is set in regions now beyond the country's borders, and represents the constant prick of loss. An early narrative of roaming Magyars fleeing hostile foes in their own land has a strong hold, while there's a tradition of rebellion, isolation and despair among the popular songbooks. The most renowned writers hark from the Romantic age, kings among them being the young revolutionary poet Sándor Petőfi (see page 334) and his friend János Arany. Others you'll come across – often through the names of streets or squares – are the Romanticists Ferenc Kölcsey (author of the national anthem) and Mihály Vörösmarty, the late-19th-century Realists József Eötvös and Mór Jókai, the anguished Endre Ady and the Expressionistic, avant-garde and ultimately suicidal Attila József. In October 2002, Imre Kertész – author of *Sorstalanság* (*Fateless*), a shocking Holocaust novel – won the Nobel Prize for Literature.

Your best bet for getting a flavour of the nation's **art** is to take a spin around the Hungarian National Gallery (see pages 158–9), which encompasses ecclesiastical works – medieval panel paintings and 18th-century masterpieces by F A Maulbertsch (responsible for the wondrous 'Rococo Sistine Chapel' at Sümeg) – as well as late-Renaissance and Baroque courtly portraits. The emergence of recognisably 'Hungarian' art came during the 19th-century creative explosion that went hand in hand with a thriving economy and a new national self-confidence. The Romantic Historicist works of Bertalan Székely (1835–1910) and Gyula Benczúr (1844–1920) were accompanied by pieces of Impressionism by László Paál (1846–79) and Realism by Mihály Munkácsy (1844–1900). The turn of the 20th century saw the establishment of deeply influential artists' colonies at Nagybánya and Gödöllő, each turning away from rigid formalism, the latter by seeking inspiration from folk art. Also of this period were the Post-Impressionist paintings of József Rippl-Rónai (1861–1927) and the vast and visionary canvases of Tivadar Csontváry Kosztka (1853–1919). The Expressionists Gyula Derkovits and József Egry produced inter-war works, while the best-known painter after that, Victor Vasarely (1908–97), created most of his ground-breaking Op-Art in Paris after emigrating in 1930. As for sculptors, 20th-century favourites include Zsigmond Kisfaludi Strobl (1884–1975), notorious for his 'pragmatism' in adapting his output to suit the prevailing political climate, the ceramicist Margit Kovács (1902–77), and Imre Varga, whose polished-metal creations are fabulous (and whom you might bump into during a visit to his collection in Óbuda; see page 160).

While **folk art** is still alive and kicking in areas of Transylvania, within Hungary's borders it's largely the stuff of museums and the odd decorated interior of a Calvinist church. It represents the untutored work of peasant families jazzing up their immediate surroundings with painted domestic items like headboards and chests, patterned or grooved pottery and clothes or bedspreads embroidered with vivid thread. The clearest attempt to preserve (and market) folk heritage can be seen from the Palóc people of Hollókő in the Northern Uplands, but the Mátyó group from Mezőkövesd also has a strong tradition, and the women of Kalocsa are famous for painting the living spaces of their houses. During the search for a Hungarian sense of nationhood in the late 19th and early 20th centuries, these vernacular forms had a significant impact upon 'high art'.

MUSIC If Hungary needs a cultural ambassador, it surely has one in its exotic music. The famous big hitters were of course Ferenc Liszt, Béla Bartók and Zoltán Kodály, each an established name in the canon of European composers. To try to isolate and define Hungarian music would be to overlook the fact that its *diversity* is intrinsic to understanding this corner of the world. The musical landscape in central Europe reflects a tangled web of historical relationships and influences. The base layer is closely related to the folk music of Turkic and Finno-Ugric peoples from the Urals and Siberia (as uncovered by Kodály and his colleagues in the early 20th century). There has also been mutual borrowing from regional traditions – Slavonic, Romany, Jewish and more. It's certainly rich territory for the ethno-musicologist.

That with greatest popular resonance is gypsy music, performed by the dazzling dynasties that have enchanted visitors for centuries. Haydn, who was in the service of the Esterházy family for most of his life, drew extensively upon the gypsy strains around him; Beethoven and Schubert were frequent visitors and Hungarian music informed their work; two of Brahms' major influences were Hungarian concert violinists, and his series of Hungarian dances came as no surprise. The first Hungarian-born composer to achieve fame in Europe was Liszt; although he only lived in Budapest for a few years, he left a lasting legacy by founding the Academy of Music (see page 116). Bartók and Kodály studied and taught at the academy, and it has since produced many other students who have spread Hungarian traditions across the world.

These days, the minimalist textures of modern composer György Ligeti are helping to carry on the Hungarian claim to musical pre-eminence – his compositions featured in *2001 A Space Odyssey*, and his was the eerie piano music in Stanley Kubrick's *Eyes Wide Shut* – while the haunting vocals of folk singer Márta Sebestyén can be heard at the beginning of *The English Patient*. The contemporary Hungarian music scene is one of the most intriguing faces of cultural change underway in the country.

Within Hungary, there is no shortage of music companies or venues. Budapest has five symphony orchestras, two opera houses, the Art-Nouveau Great Hall of the Academy of Music (with its perfect acoustics) and the Palace of Arts (see page 115). All the large cities have their own opera companies and orchestras, and in addition to the standard music arenas you'll be tripping over tickets for concerts hosted in churches and former synagogues around the country. As for annual events, the capital hosts two major arts festivals (the Spring and Autumn festivals), while regional highlights include Miskolc's Bartók Plus opera festival in June, the Sopron Festival (especially the Sopron Early Music Weeks), also in June, the Zemplén Art Days in August (with events in castles, churches and villages halls) and 'Haydn at Esterháza' at Fertőd in August/September.

Folk music Stifled under communism because nationalistic songs were out of keeping with the professed internationalist ethic, folk music now thrives again. The early 1970s saw the emergence of the *táncház* ('dance house') movement, a custom imported from Transylvania in which young villagers would hold a dance in a rented house. The roots of its appearance can be traced to a reaction against sanitised State ensembles, a sense of national pride, a concern for the Magyar minority in Transylvania (where the best music was concentrated), and the influence of research into folk culture by Béla Bartók, Zoltán Kodály, Zoltán Kallós and others. Young urbanites travelled to rural communities to learn and preserve

We can attribute the current abundance of distinguished Hungarian string players to one man: Jenő Hubay. A pupil of Brahms' Hungarian-born friend Ede Reményi, he was the Academy of Music's Professor of Violin between 1886 and 1934 and his chair one of the foremost centres of its kind in Europe. A skilled composer and conductor, he was also a breathtaking virtuoso. However, his greatest achievement was to mould two generations of talented violin and viola players. The individual characteristics of the 'Hubay school' have roots both in the Paris and Brussels traditions and in the virtuoso Hungarian gypsy violinists whom, like Liszt, he much admired. Chamber music was an organic part of his teaching creed. With the Austrian cellist David Popper, he formed the Hubay-Popper quartet – the outstanding Hungarian quartet of the 20th century. Other quartets taught by Hubay and Popper followed throughout the century, and eminent soloists (like today's internationally renowned Barnabás Kelemen) achieved fame after serving apprenticeships under students of those two.

In the 1980s the first chamber orchestra playing period instruments was created in Hungary. Since then orchestras like the Capella Savaria and Concerto Armonico have gained international recognition. Hungary has no fewer than three excellent period-instrument string quartets; the first of them, the Festetics Quartet, is well known outside Hungary, while the violinists István Kertész, László Paulik and Zsolt Kalló and the cellist Balázs Máté travel the globe as soloists, quartet players, leaders of orchestras or teachers.

dying traditional music and dances. They then played and taught these to those in cities. Béla Halmos is an outstanding name in this folk-music renaissance. Such dance houses continue. They are usually held in cultural centres, where traditional dance is accompanied by folk music played on traditional instruments by groups like Muzsikás. Visitors take an active part in the dance, or sit around with glasses of *pálinka* and watch as musicians play and dancers dance. Dance houses take place less often in summer. (For *táncház* venues in Budapest, see pages 117–18.)

For other folk music experiences, try listening to Kaláka, or Muzsikás with Márta Sebestyén. Other notable groups exemplifying distinctive regional music styles include the renowned ambassadors of *klezmer* (a Jewish folk tradition originating in central and eastern Europe) the Budapest Klezmer Band and purveyors of Croatian dance Vujicsics. (There are regular performances by such groups at cultural centres like Fonó in Budapest; see page 118.)

Gypsy music The distinctive and passionate violin-playing of the gypsy bands epitomises the rich and individual identity of Hungarian music. With flamboyance and impromptu innovation, the Roma performers bring an interpretation of the indigenous folk music of Hungary, helping to close the divide between two oft-clashing cultures. It is important to recognise, however, that this is not the traditional music of the Roma – their songs, sung in the Romany language, are for private consumption. Instead gypsy bands perform centuries-old Hungarian popular songs (known as *Magyar nóta*), the themes rooted in sentimentally romanticised versions of the gypsy way of life; the agony of love lost or unrequited and the turbulent history of Hungary's oppression also find outlet in the gypsy tradition. Go to any traditional Hungarian restaurant and you will be serenaded at your table by a violinist of virtuosity (if you are lucky), supported by a strange and characteristically Magyar dulcimer known as the *cimbalom*. (To hear the instrument's capabilities explored in full, look out for Balogh Kálmán and the Gipsy Cimbalom

Band.) Be aware that if the musicians approach your table, and you accept their invitation to play, they will expect to be tipped at the end of the performance. If you are interested in hearing true gypsy music – or modern renditions of it – then Parno Graszt, Romano Drom, Kalyi Jag and Ternipe are all bands that work in the Romany strand. Beyond this true gypsy music and the *Magyar nóta*, there is also the peasant music discovered by the Bartók-Kodály generation that has almost nothing to do with the popular song tradition. The *táncház* movement has mainly resurrected the instrumental part of this; the vocal repertoire has often been arranged in the compositions of Bartók and Kodály (and their successors), and was part of the musical curriculum in schools from the 1930s.

Jazz Jazz fans might try the Dresch Mihály Quartet or the Balázs Elemér Group, while the upcoming group The Next Generation is made up of highly talented young musicians in their teens and 20s. Admirers of instrumental virtuosity should make a note of pianist Béla Szakcsi Lakatos and his son Robi, the latter a rising star in his own right. Dynamic young violinist Lajkó Félix – imagine a kind of Balkan Nigel Kennedy – from northern Serbia now lives and regularly performs in Budapest. The very young and very alternative jazz group Punch boasts a fantastic female player called Luca Kézdy, an artist with a crystal-clear tone and endless musical fantasy.

Popular music In the second half of the last century, while rock and roll boomed in the West, Hungarians only had access to it via Radio Luxembourg and Radio Free Europe (which were illegal). Communism prohibited commercial radio, and the musical diet was officially limited. During this era underground radio played a crucial counter-establishment role, both cultural and political (indeed, some people partly attribute the bloody 1956 Hungarian uprising to its subversive influence). As a consequence, Hungarians are even now 'catching up' with some of the music that passed them by – and it hardly needs stating that Hungarian classic rock is unknown in the West. Although local rock bands required a permit to play for live audiences, there were some very successful home-grown artists in the 1960s and '70s (such as Bikini, LGT, Illés, Metró and Omega).

Popular music underwent a rapid change in the late 1980s. The cultural influx that came with the political shift has continued unabated since. Young Hungarians are generally fashion-conscious and up to date. Nevertheless, seismic cultural change has inevitably resulted in generational differences. Those in their 30s and 40s tend to go out less frequently as family and work commitments take precedence; older Hungarians arguably hold a limited definition of 'culture', partly due to the entrenched Soviet practice of 'cultural houses', which served for the staging of everything from poetry readings to chess games. The established view in Hungary is that pop is a subculture belonging to the commercial – not the cultural – domain, and full acceptance will take time.

DJs Among well-regarded DJs active in Budapest, and at the cutting edge of Hungarian sounds, are turntable veteran Palotai and the talented young Yonderboi. Electronic and dance artists you can pursue in record shops (or perhaps catch live) include Anima Sound System, Korai Öröm, Zagar, Másfél and Yonderboi (again). These acts are notable for fusing global and local elements in a way that is original and eclectic, but avoids seeming contrived. The fusion of new and old is emblematic of the meeting of world and local cultures occurring in this part of Europe. Contemporary Hungarian music is especially interesting for the way many of the artists disregard, and so transcend, boundaries between musical genres and traditions.

Hungary's answer to *Jesus Christ Superstar* is a guitar-strumming tribute to the man who founded the country. The much-loved *István a király* – written by a pair of rock stars from a famous group of the '60s and '70s called Illés – recounts how István overcame his pagan rival Koppány (whom he killed and quartered) to become Hungary's first Christian king. The rock opera was first performed in City Park on 20 August 1983 (and featured a young Márta Sebestyén; see page 29), and encompassed sounds ranging from folk music to hard rock. There's a subtlety to the characterisation that means the opera is not a simple tale of good versus evil; Koppány, for instance, is portrayed as a man motivated by respect for tradition rather than pure lust for power. As such, the rock opera is open to varied interpretations, and the focus upon nationhood and Christianity – and particularly the struggle for control of the state – was a brave one at the time. It isn't hard to find a subversive allegory of the 1956 Revolution in the piece, and János Kádár, who was still in power in 1983, was of course the man who had ridden into town with the Soviet tanks to crush the rebellion. Hungarian minorities in neighbouring countries readily saw a patriotic rallying call in the lyrics of the final song 'Beautiful Hungary, our sweet home'. Alternatively, a pro-communist interpretation might link István and Kádár as men who had to take a tough stance for the greater good. It's perhaps because of this ambiguity that the opera wasn't staged again until after the political changes; since then, however, it's been a perennial favourite, and the film of the original performance is regularly televised on St Stephen's Day.

ARCHITECTURE Where some cultural output can be inspired and concentrated by conflict – just ask Petőfi – architecture is the physical body destined to suffer in the front line. For much of its history, Hungary was forced to pick up the pieces; the country's structural heritage is one of a canvas repeatedly re-painted. The earliest significant remains are those left from the Roman province of Pannonia, evident at Aquincum and in Transdanubian centres like Pécs. Romanesque ecclesiastical architecture of the 11th–13th centuries – including the first reaching cathedrals of István's Christian kingdom – was obliterated by the Mongols in 1240–41, and generally survives as recycled features in later churches or as subterranean crypts. Both the Romanesque and the Gothic buildings that followed them were generally westward-looking (in the cultural sense), frequently showing the hands of immigrant craftsmen from Italy and Germany.

The flowering of the Renaissance occurred during the golden age of Mátyás in the 15th century, and his palaces at Visegrád and Buda were among the very cream of the European crop. Unfortunately a healthy imagination is required to conjure their former splendour from the fragments that remain. While some medieval and Renaissance works still stand in the northwest and northeast, regions that didn't fall to the Turks, the Ottoman occupation wiped out those everywhere else. Nor is there much to show for those 150 years (the odd Turkish bath in Buda, a minaret in Eger, a square mosque in Pécs), which added up to a period of creative stagnation. Instead the towns bear the stamp of the Baroque, Neoclassical and other styles that came during re-building afterwards. Many of the richest 18th-century mansions were those of families who'd profited by cosying up to the Habsburgs when others were fighting alongside Rákóczi in the doomed struggle for independence. Another architectural feature of the 18th century is the divide between the whitewashed Calvinist churches of the Great Plain and Southern Transdanubia, their interiors decorated with the folk art of peasant artisans, versus the grand onion-domed edifices of the Catholic tradition evident in the centre and west of the country.

A growing national self-confidence – manifested architecturally in the monumental Neoclassical designs of men like József Hild and Mihály Pollack – was temporarily dented by the failed revolution of 1848–49, but it bounced back during the reformatory and creative zeal of the century's second half. After the Compromise of 1867, a desire to assert and consolidate Hungarian nationhood took hold. The millennial celebrations in particular spurred an intensive programme of building, and threw up grandiose pieces of Historicist architecture like the Parliament building and Mátyás Church. A separate strand of this impulse expressed itself in a return to rural roots, to the forms of the earthy vernacular, and in striving for a specifically 'Hungarian style' Ödön Lechner employed folkloric and oriental motifs to give Art Nouveau a uniquely Magyar face. The bulk of the 20th century has, of course, been shaped by war and its consequences. The bombardments of World War II had a devastating effect on many cities, Budapest chief among them, and ushered in the functional and drab architecture of communism. You can see the Bauhaus and Socialist-Realist 'aesthetic' – an oxymoron to our ears – at Dunaújváros, but you're probably better looking out for the softer, organic forms of the leading Postmodernist Imre Makovecz, whose wooden creations can take the forms of owls or open books. The definitions below encompass the styles you'll encounter during your travels.

Art Nouveau (Secessionist or Jugendstil) Art Nouveau hit Hungary in the late 1800s and early 1900s, a style characterised by flowing lines and the organic forms of nature. As elsewhere in Europe, it represented a rebellion against imitative forms, but in Hungary it was also something more – an architectural expression of independent national identity. Ödön Lechner was the leader in developing this specifically Hungarian form of Art Nouveau; the Museum of Applied Arts (see page 165) is a prime example. (Reader Alan Terrill wrote to us lauding Budapest's Art-Nouveau highlights, observing that it 'made me feel optimistic about modern architecture in a way other cities don't'.)

Baroque This is the most common historical style you'll find in Hungary, the fashion during the 17th and 18th centuries when there was widespread building – both because of the necessary reconstruction following 150 years of Turkish occupation, and because the Catholic Church erected a wave of new temples as part of the Counter-Reformation. It is characterised by blowzy, barley-sugar twisted columns, sweeping *trompe-l'oeil* deceits, arching domes and complex ornamentation.

Gothic The Gothic style, prevalent in western Europe between the 12th and 16th centuries, came to Hungary after the 13th-century Mongol invasion. The characteristic pointed arches, flying buttresses and soaring, star-vaulted ceilings are beautifully illustrated in the Calvinist church at Nyírbátor. You will more usually come across earlier Gothic fragments incorporated into reconstructed churches and houses.

Eclectic See *Historicism*

Historicism Historicism drew upon the architectural styles of earlier historical epochs during the building boom of the 19th century. It is evident in structures like Steindl's Neo-Gothic parliament, Schulek's Mátyás Church and the mansions lining the avenues of Pest. It is also referred to as Eclectic.

Louis XVI Emerging during the late 1700s, the Louis XVI style was a departure from the Baroque and the precursor to the Neoclassical. It is characterised by straight lines, reflecting the Enlightenment philosophy of order and reason. It is often known by its German label, Zopf – which means 'plait', a reference to the laurel-leaf motifs that adorn the façades and look like pigtails.

Neoclassical This reflects the revival of the Greek classical style of architecture that first arose at the end of the 18th century in a movement away from the extravagance of the Baroque. It is typified by plain, straight (often massive) columns – as seen in the cathedrals at Eger and Esztergom.

Postmodernist The late-20th-century reaction against the functional forms of the Bauhaus and Socialist-Realist schools. Its best exponent is Imre Makovecz, whose designs represent an organic return to nature, and often employ softer materials like wood – he once said 'trees are the most complete representation of life, their branches supernatural aspirations and their roots representative of the mysterious unconscious' – or even turf. Makovecz's buildings were a conscious rebuttal to the anti-aestheticism of the communist regime. Examples of 'organic architecture' can be seen in the community centres at Sárospatak and Kakasd, the forest buildings near the campsite at Visegrád, and the Roman Catholic church at Paks.

Renaissance Italy took the lead in Renaissance architecture – a revival of earlier classical models – but under King Mátyás (and his Italian queen) 15th-century Hungary wasn't far behind, and boasted some breathtaking palaces. Unfortunately most of it was later trampled during history's skirmishes and only fragments remain (such as the Hercules Fountain at the Visegrád Royal Palace and the funerary Bakócz Chapel at Esztergom).

Rococo The Esterházy Palace at Fertőd is one of the few Hungarian examples of this style, a variation of late-Baroque ornamented with swirling, asymmetrical shell and rock (*rocaille*) motifs.

Romanesque The Romanesque style of architecture – typified by rounded arches and vaulting and galleries supported on columns – can be seen in the country's earliest extant ecclesiastical buildings, constructed between the 11th and 13th centuries. The stand-out model is Ják's Benedictine abbey.

Romantic The Neoclassical concern with form and uncluttered line gave way in the 19th century to a style that preferred the grand and picturesque, and featured fantastical medieval ornamentation (with castellations and crenellations galore). It is evident in the highblown Pesti Vigadó of 1865.

Zopf See *Louis XVI*

2

Practical Information

WHEN TO VISIT

Hungary has somewhere offering something all year round, although in winter it is difficult to look beyond the biggest cities or the ski slopes of the Mátra Hills (which are, in fairness, rather feeble by comparison with alpine resorts elsewhere). The cold settles in from the end of October until the middle of March, and bites in December and January when the sun pushes off early at 16.00. However, don't discount the winter period entirely for it's a frosty heart that turns from the romance of Budapest with snow under foot and Christmas markets selling piping mulled wine. Just bring your scarf and gloves. Come in spring or autumn if you want to avoid traipsing in the wake of beetroot-red gaggles of tourists, and to enjoy cultural festivals in Budapest and other towns and cities. These are the seasons to watch nature by, when the climate is warm enough for strolling (although it can be wet between April and mid May and in November) and the play of light beautiful. Autumn is when the grape is harvested and when countless cranes fill the skies at Hortobágy. Furthermore, hotels have not yet hiked their prices for the peak season. That of course comes in summer, which is long and hot (with temperatures hitting up to 32°C). Landlocked they may be, but Magyars adore their water, and you can choose from thousands of outdoor lido-style bathing complexes and swimming areas (strands). Locals traditionally ship out of Budapest and other large cities in the sticky months of July and August, many heading to Lake Balaton (whose southern shore in particular heaves with bodies).

HIGHLIGHTS

Diversity and accessibility come together in Hungary; there's something here for everyone and it's never far away. A highlights list is something of a pick-and-mix, as arbitrary as it is subjective. It also can't allow for that riverside goulash on a canoe trip down the Tisza, that peek into courtyard gardens from a church tower or that winter soak in a thermal bath with the snow falling on the water. Treat the following with caution – and please drop us a line to tell us about the particular places and moments that made your trip special.

Most first steps beyond the capital (for Budapest's best bits, see box, page 98) are to the towns of the **Danube Bend**. The river view here is as good as any in Europe, and the favourable light has traditionally attracted artistic types to Szentendre in particular. Further up is Visegrád and its castle (see page 187), and the one-time royal capital of Esztergom (page 191). For Baroque beauty and fewer crowds, Vác (page 198) should be your target on the outside of the bend. The region has hiking trails in the Pilis, Visegrád and Börzsöny hills, while the orchids at Ócsa (page 176) and the butterflies at Fót (page 180) are wildlife treats known to few.

The **Northern Uplands** to the northeast of the capital have the greatest concentration of high ground. Hungary's tallest peak lies in the Mátra Hills, which

The nature of your holiday will of course be dictated by your particular interests, but the following suggestions offer a decent spread of town culture, outdoor activities and gastronomy. Don't feel pressured into visiting every place we've suggested here – it's a fairly packed programme. We've tried to keep travel to manageable chunks, although there are a couple of longer stretches in the two-week itinerary. We've assumed you'll be driving, although it should be possible to stick broadly to the itineraries using public transport.

ONE WEEK: OPTION A

Days 1 & 2	Budapest.
Day 3	Day trip to Danube Bend (returning to Budapest in evening).
Day 4	Gödöllő (morning), then to Mátra Hills for an afternoon walk (basing yourself at Mátrafüred or Mátraháza or Parád).
Day 5	Eger, with an early evening visit to the Valley of the Beautiful Woman.
Day 6	Either head to Tiszafüred for a day cycling, fishing and kayaking, or spend the morning at Szilvásvárad and then choose between Aggtelek (caves) and Tokaj (wine).
Day 7	Return to Budapest for flight home.

ONE WEEK: OPTION B

Days 1 & 2	Budapest.
Day 3	Day trip to Danube Bend (returning to Budapest in evening).
Day 4	Veszprém (morning), then explore Tihany, and stay in Balatonfüred.
Day 5	Do some sunbathing/cycling at the lake, or take a walk in the Balaton Uplands National Park to the north. Go to Badascony for wine tasting.
Day 6	Explore Keszthely and either head for a dip in the thermal lake at Hévíz or arrange a trip to Kis-Balaton.
Day 7	Return to Budapest for flight home.

TWO WEEKS

Days 1 & 2	Budapest.
Day 3	Szentendre and Esztergom.
Day 4	Győr and Sopron.
Days 5, 6 & 7	Northern shore of Balaton (Balatonfüred, Tihany, Badacsony, Keszthely, Hévíz)
Day 8	Pécs.
Day 9	Mohács (morning) and Szeged.
Day 10	Longish morning drive to Tiszafüred for afternoon at Lake Tisza.
Day 11	Hortobágy (morning) and drive across Great Plain to Tokaj for mid-afternoon wine tasting.
Day 12	Aggtelek (morning) and Szilvásvárad.
Day 13	Eger and its Valley of the Beautiful Woman.
Day 14	Return to Budapest (via Road 24 through Mátra Hills, if time allows).

are dotted with resorts in which to base yourself for local treks. Hollókő (page 213) preserves Palóc peasant houses and traditions, and is a UNESCO World Heritage Site, while there are fossilised trees and animal prints at Ipolytarnóc (page 217). Eger (page 232) is renowned as one of the country's prettiest towns and has its own valley crammed with wine cellars. Take a narrow-gauge railway from Szilvásvárad into the Szalajka Valley (page 246), with its waterfalls and trout ponds, and explore the stalactite caves at the UNESCO World Heritage Site of Aggtelek (page 256). It's in Tokaj (page 261) you'll find what Louis XIV called 'the king of wines, the wine of kings'.

The **Great Plain** covering the bulk of the country's eastern side is the place of the '*puszta*', the grasslands where outlaws and herders roamed in centuries past. Equestrianism is strongest in this region, both in the form of dare-devil horse shows and riding tours and schools. Hortobágy National Park (page 289) is the biggest in Hungary, and is particularly popular with twitchers drawn by over a million migratory waterbirds and raptors. The spectacular autumn arrival of 100,000 cranes is a sight that will impress even the staunchest of urbanites. Lake Tisza (page 282) is another wildlife hotspot, harbouring 150 nesting bird species. Heading right into the northeastern corner you'll reach the most isolated places, many of which retain strong rural traditions; be sure to pop into Szatmárcseke's cemetery (page 315) with its wooden boat-shaped grave markers. Kalocsa (page 335) is the capital of paprika production, while it's salami in Szeged (page 353), a city that also shines a cultural light in the southern part of the plain. Ópusztaszer (page 350) is where the Magyar chieftains are said to have gathered in the aftermath of conquest, and the memorial park contains a quite breathtaking cyclorama.

Transdanubia lies to the west of the Danube, and was the easternmost frontier of the Roman empire. Pécs (page 404) contains early-Christian tombs from that period, as well as rare surviving Ottoman architecture from 150 years of occupation. Villány and Villánykövesd (page 399) are tiny villages lined from top to toe with wine cellars. The Gemenc Forest (see page 391) is Hungary's broadest expanse of flood plain, which you can explore on a narrow-gauge train or in a boat with a guide. Mohács (page 394) occupies a dark place in the nation's heart for the Turkish victory here in 1526 broke the back of Hungarian resistance. Today its citizens don hairy costumes and scary masks to celebrate Shrove Tuesday. Dunaújváros (page 426) is notable for its surviving Socialist-Realist monuments, so many of which were torn down elsewhere after the fall of communism. Veszprém and Székesfehérvár (pages 436 and 431) were early royal centres, the latter the scene for coronations and burials for 500 years. Don't miss the 'Rococo Sistine Chapel' – a masterclass in painting at the Sümeg parish church (page 443). There are further outstanding ecclesiastical trappings to be sniffed out – the painting that shed bloody tears in Győr Cathedral (page 456), the gorgeous 13th-century Romanesque abbey at Ják (page 475), and the Pannonhalma Monastery (yet another UNESCO World Heritage Site; page 460) looming at the edge of the Kisalföld. The medieval squares of Sopron and Kőszeg (pages 480 and 476) are as lovely as they come, while the high-blown Esterházy Palace at Fertőd (page 491) and the restrained Széchenyi Mansion at Nagycenk (page 489) are as different in style as they are close in kilometres.

Lake Balaton, the biggest lake in central Europe, is where Magyars come to play – to sunbathe, paddle and windsurf. Its southern shore is more developed, studded with brash resorts like Siófok (page 495) with its bars and nightclubs. The reeds and deeper water on the other side offer more serene pleasures. Kis-Balaton (page 504) at the western tip is another bird-watching haunt, and also has a bison reserve. Near by, the university town of Keszthely (page 499) has a Neo-Baroque Palace with a fountain that radiates changing coloured lights after dark, and Hévíz (page 505) holds the second-largest thermal lake in the world. Set back a little from the shore, Tapolca (page 509) has an 18th-century watermill and a narrow cave lake that you can boat along. The Tihany peninsula (page 513) is a lovely tongue of land licking into the lake with an abbey church and some interesting geology. You can ride a jeep taxi up to the vineyards above Badacsony (page 507) and enjoy some fabulous views while sipping your wine.

ABROAD

UK 46 Eaton Place, London SW1X 8AL; ☎ +44 (0)20 7823 1032/1055; e info@ gotohungary.co.uk; www.gotohungary.co.uk

Czech Republic Schnirchova 29, 17000 Prague 2; ☎ +42 (0)283 870742; e info@madarsko.cz; www.hungarytourism.cz

France 140 Av Victor Hugo, 75116 Paris; ☎ +33 (0)1 53 70 67 17; e info@hongrietourisme.com; www.hongrietourisme.com

Germany Wilhelmstr 61, D-10117 Berlin; ☎ +49 (0)30 243 1460; e berlin@ungarntourismus.de; www.ungarn-tourismus.de

Italy Via Giotto, 3, 20145 Milano; ☎ +39 (0)2 4819 5434; e info@turismoungherese.it; www.turismoungherese.it

USA 350 Fifth Avenue, Suite 1707, New York, NY 10118; ☎ +1 212 695 1221; e info@ gotohungary.com; www.gotohungary.com

IN HUNGARY Tourist information (*turista információ*) is best sought from a branch of the Hungarian National Tourist Office. These offices are known as **Tourinform**; there are around 140 in the country, manned by (usually) multilingual staff who can offer advice and help on accommodation, restaurants, transport, events and attractions. They also distribute free brochures, leaflets and listings magazines, and sell tourist discount cards, local transport tickets, phonecards and the like. They are open during normal office hours, and often at weekends too in high season. For further details, contact the information centre (*24-hr* ☎ *1 438 8080;* e *hungary@ tourinform.hu; www.tourinform.hu or www.hungary.com*); in addition you can ring a hotline on 06 80 63 0800 (from Hungary) or 0800 36 000000 (free from the UK).

TOUR OPERATORS

Package holidays, city breaks, and tailor-made tours and flights are readily available through UK- and US-based tour operators specialising in eastern Europe. In addition to the companies below, local guides and tour operators are included under the relevant regional sections.

GENERAL
In UK

Dash Travel ☎ 01443 879557; www.dashtravel.co.uk. With the motto 'Go where the wild geese go – everywhere', Dash specialises in tailor-made holidays for those with limited mobility (disabled & senior citizens). See also box, page 41.

Fregata Travel 177 Shaftesbury Ave, London WC2H 8JR; ☎ 020 7420 7305; www.fregatatravel.co.uk. Concise tour of Budapest that includes all the city's main attractions.

Hen Nation ☎ 0800 027 4836; www.hennation.co.uk. Company arranging breaks for hen parties, including some interesting spa options.

Kirker Holidays 4 Waterloo Court, Theed St, London SE1 8ST; ☎ 020 7593 1899; www.kirkerholidays.com. Specialises in short/city breaks.

Our Hungary 17 Sutton Sq, Middx TW5 0JB; ☎ 01173 500857; www.ourhungary.co.uk. Hungary specialists offering a variety of tours & tailored packages (including dental holidays – see pages 41 & 51).

Page & Moy Compass House, Rockingham Rd, Market Harborough, LE16 7QD; ☎ 0800 567 7400; www.page-moy.com. Tours to Budapest & river cruises on the Danube.

Peregrine Adventures 8 Clerewater Pl, Lower Way, Thatcham, Berks RG19 3RF; ☎ 0844 736 0170; www.peregrineadventures.com. Offers 8- or 15-day tours to central Europe that take in Budapest & the Danube Bend.

Regent Holidays Mezzanine Suite, Froomsgate House, Rupert St, Bristol BS1 2QJ; ☎ 0845 277 3317; www.regent-holidays.co.uk. Respected independent operator specialising in eastern European destinations.

Stag Republic ☎ 0800 027 4836; www.stagrepublic.co.uk. Lads' activities & tailor-made stag weekends. Does exactly what it says on the tin: 'no request – from strippers with toys to vegetarian meals – will make us blush'...

Trailfinders 194 Kensington High St, London W8 7RG; ☎ 020 7938 3939; www.trailfinders.com. A one-stop shop for advice, flights & tailor-made packages to Budapest.

Voyages Jules Verne 21 Dorset Sq, London NW1 6QG; ✆ 020 7616 1000; www.vjv.com. Tours include a 4-

night programme taking in all the main city sights, as well as longer tours that feature Budapest, Vienna & Prague.

In USA

Abercrombie & Kent 1411 Opus Place, Executive Tower West II, Suite 300, Downers Grove, Illinois 60515-1182; ✆ +1 630 725 3400; www.abercrombiekent.com. High-end tailor-made private tours for individuals & small groups.

General Tours 53 Summer St, Keene, New Hampshire; ✆ +1 800 221 2216;

e info@generaltours.com; www.generaltours.com. All-inclusive 3–6-day tours of Budapest, or longer ones featuring Budapest, Krakow & Prague.

Grand Circle Travel 347 Congress St, Boston MA 02210; ✆ +1 800 959 0405; e reservations@gct.com; www.gct.com. Offers a variety of all-inclusive tours to Budapest & other eastern European cities.

CULTURAL AND RAIL TOURS

Danube Express See page 46. Railway tours.

Great Rail Journeys Saviour House, 9 St Saviourgate, York YO1 8NL; ✆ 01904 521936; www.greatrail.com. Runs several escorted rail tours departing from Waterloo to European cities including Budapest.

John Whibley Holidays with Music ✆ 01663 746578; www.whibley.co.uk. Cultural breaks in Budapest, including all-inclusive packages during the Autumn & Spring festivals.

Martin Randall Travel Voysey House, Barley Mow Passage, London W4 4GF; ✆ 020 8742 3355; www.martinrandall.com. Culture vultures can join a musical or historical tour of Budapest.

Operas Abroad 80–83 Long Lane, London EC1A 9ET; ✆ 020 7511 9018; www.operasabroad.com. Specialist packages including operas, ballets & concerts.

Travel for the Arts 12–15 Hanger Green, London W5 3EL; ✆ 020 8799 8350; www.travelforthearts.com. Company specialising in arts-related group or tailor-made breaks to cities including Budapest.

ACTIVE, NATURE AND ECO TOURS
In UK

Avian Adventures 49 Sandy Rd, Norton, Stourbridge DY8 3AJ; ✆ 01384 372013; www.avianadventures.co.uk. Fully inclusive escorted birdwatching holidays.

Birdfinders Westbank, Cheselbourne, Dorset DT2 7NW; ✆ 01258 839066; www.birdfinders.co.uk. Organise week-long birdwatching group tours, & can tailor make trips.

Birding Hungary www.birdinghungary.com. Bespoke birdwatching tours & wildlife walks arranged by experts on birding in eastern Europe.

British Trust Conservation Volunteers Sedum House, Mallard Way, Doncaster DN4 8BD; ✆ 01302 388 883; www.btcv.org. BTCV is a charity involved in conservation projects in Hungary. The charity usually organises week-long trips in summer – half hard work, half conservation & nature-related fun – although they don't do so every year. Accommodation is of the simple kind.

Cycle Rides Victoria Works, Lambridge Mews, Bath BA1 6QE; ✆ 01225 428452; www.cyclerides.co.uk. Group tours to Budapest and beyond on 2 wheels.

Earthwatch Institute Mayfield House, 256 Banbury Rd, Oxford OX2 7DE; ✆ 01865 318838; www.earthwatch.org/europe. Non-profit-making

organisation that arranges for volunteers to assist with research & conservation projects around the world. The projects change yearly; Hungary didn't feature in 2009, but in the past Earthwatch volunteers have contributed to research into the decline of songbirds migrating from Europe to sub-Saharan Africa (at a research centre in the Ócsa Wetland; see page 176), so keep an eye on the website. Note that Earthwatch projects are rewarding, but are not guided tours.

Greentours Leigh Cottage, Gauledge Lane, Longnor, Buxton, Derbyshire SK17 0PA; ✆ 01298 83563; www.greentours.co.uk. Small natural-history tour operator running gentle wildlife trips to countries including Hungary. Committed to conservation.

Heatherlea ✆ 01479 821248; www.heatherlea.co.uk. Based in Inverness-shire, Heatherlea is run by birding specialists & offers a spring tour to Hungary that takes in the owls & woodpeckers of the north, & the birds of the Hortobágy.

Limosa Holidays Suffield House, Northrepps, Norfolk NR27 0LZ; ✆ 01263 578143; www.limosaholidays.co.uk. Year-round birdwatching & wildlife tours, including a weekend expedition to witness the spectacular crane migration in autumn.

Naturetrek Cheriton Mill, Alresford, Hants SO24 0NG; ☏ 01962 733051; www.naturetrek.co.uk. Birdwatching & natural-history tours to the hills, plains & wetlands of Hungary led by leading British ornithologists & botanists.

Probirder www.probirder.com. Operating for over 20 years, this is Hungary's most experienced birdwatching guiding outfit. Probirder arranges local English-speaking guides to assist visiting birdwatchers on trips lasting from a few hours around Budapest to week-long tours nationwide. All kinds of birdwatcher are catered for (from the casual to the lister & those with a more ornithological approach), & the company also arranges special trips for bird clubs, societies, families, photographers, sound recordists & disabled birders. A 'meet & greet' service is provided at the airport or any other address in Budapest.

Quest for Nature 29 Straight Mile, Romsey, Hants SO51 9BB; ☏ 01794 523500; www.questfornature.co.uk. Inclusive butterfly-watching trips.

Sherpa Expeditions 131A Heston Rd, Hounslow, Middx TW5 0RF; ☏ 020 8577 2717; www.sherpa-walking-holidays.co.uk. Arranges self-guided cycling tours that take in the Northern Uplands & Danube Bend.

Sunbird PO Box 76, Sandy, Beds SG19 1DF; ☏ 01767 262522; www.sunbirdtours.co.uk. Well-regarded bird-watching tour company that runs programmes in the Hortobágy National Park (where it has its own sponsored observation tower) & bird-watching combined with the Zemplén Festival.

Walking Hungary www.walkinghungary.com. Walks & treks in Hungary's northern hill ranges, ranging from weekend breaks to week-long trips. There are also themed walks focusing on wine & wildlife.

WildWings ☏ 01179 658333; www.wildwings.co.uk. Arrange week-long 'bird festivals', based in the Hortobágy (in spring) & Tata (in winter), where participants can join local guides, do their own thing on foot or bike, or choose a mixture of the two. Suitable for keen beginners or experienced birders; the group size is 20–30.

In USA

Earthwatch Institute 3 Clock Tower Place, Suite 100, PO Box 75, Maynard, MA 01754; ☏ +1 (978) 461 0081 or +1 (800) 776 0188; e info@earthwatch.org. For description, see under *UK*.

In Australia

Earthwatch Institute 126 Bank St, South Melbourne, VIC 3205; ☏ +61 (0) 3 9682 6828; www.earthwatch.org/australia. For description see under *UK*.

In Hungary

Ecotours XI Budapest, Villányi út 62; ☏ 30 606 1651; www.ecotours.hu. Budapest-based specialist company offering tailor-made (birdwatching, butterfly, botanical, canoe, horse-riding, hiking & biking) tours & general nature & culture tours to Hungary's national parks & other eastern European destinations. Claims to be the only officially registered incoming operator in its market.

Hubertus Ltd I Budapest, Ady Endre u. 1; ☏ 1 316 0469; www.hubertus.com. Offers small-game hunting, fishing on Lake Velence & Lake Tisza (& fishing camps for children at Rétimajor & Örspuszta), birdwatching in the Rétszilas fishponds & themed riding holidays in the Kiskunság & Hortobágy national parks.

Jegmadar Viziturak H-9200 Mosonmagyarovar, Vízpart u. 40; ☏ 20 566 8196; www.jegmadarviziturak.hu. Company offering canoe trips on the Moson arm of the Danube in the Szigetköz region, with its beautiful flood forests.

MME ☏ 1 275 6247; www.mme.hu. Budapest-based Hungarian Ornithological & Conservation Association (and Hungarian partner of Birdlife International) that can organise birdwatching tours with an English-speaking guide. Unfortunately the website currently offers no info in English.

Pegazus Tours V Budapest, Ferenciek tere 5; ☏ 1 317 1644; www.pegazus.hu. Arranges all-inclusive riding tours for those of any level, as well as adventure holidays & tours to sports events (including the Hungarian Grand Prix).

Somogy Provincial Association for Nature Conservation (SPANC) H-8714 Kelevíz, Lehner Major; ☏ 85 708142 or 06 30 226 9553; www.hunyady.hu. Friendly & eco-sensitive riding company offering 6-day tours from Lake Balaton to the River Dráva. Can also organise shorter tours on request. Recommended.

STH Special Tours VI Budapest, Paulay Ede u. 5; ☏ 1 267 0125; www.spectours.hu. Includes golfing tours among its offerings.

Vidam Delfin Travel Agency H-4400, Nyíregyháza, Szent Miklós tér 7; ☏ 42 443 519; iroda@vidamdelfin.hu; www.vidamdelfin.hu. Hungarian travel agency through which you can book canoe & cycling trips or arrange equipment hire & boat delivery; the site is in

Facilities for those with limited mobility are improving, but EU laws on wheelchair access have still not been acted upon in many public buildings and access to some public transport can be difficult (particularly beyond the capital). Several vehicles in Budapest do now have low floors or ramps, including buses 4, 15, 16, 26 and 78, trams 4 and 6, and trolley-bus 70. Other routes feature less-regular buses and trolley-buses suitable for disabled passengers (indicated on timetables with a wheelchair symbol). The capital's main railway stations have lifts to assist wheelchair passengers board or leave trains; these should be booked in advance.

The **National Federation of Disabled Persons' Associations** (*MEOSZ; III, San Marco u. 76;* ✆ *1 250 9013; www.meoszinfo.hu/eng/index0x.htm*) is a good source of information; the 'Touristical' page on its website provides lists of Budapest hotels and public-transport routes with facilities for the disabled. The federation also offers a transport service of its own, using minibuses fitted with lifts or ramps. It recommends the **EGALITÁS Foundation** (*contact: Ms Katalin Zákány;* ✆ *1 397 0691;* e *lavorando@mail.datanet.hu*), which can arrange accommodation in a complex of adapted houses in the Buda Hills (17km from the centre), as well as offering sightseeing and other programmes. British tour operator **Dash Travel** (see page 38) specialises in holidays for those with limited mobility.

Hungarian, but the company welcomes English enquiries. They have set annual tour dates into which tourists can slot; a British party of 16 recently went on one, & their feedback was very positive.
Vista Visitor Centre VI Budapest, Andrássy út 1; ✆ 1 429 9999; e incentive@vista.hu; www.vista.hu. Can

organise canoe & kayak trips on the Danube, Rába & Tisza rivers.
Vizitúra IX Budapest, Hurok utca 1; ✆ 1 280 8182; www.vizitura.hu. Organises 'water' tours, including river canoeing & kayaking trips.

MEDICAL AND DENTAL TOURS

Hungarian Dental Travel ✆ 0845 612 1988; international callers: 01522 789157; www.hungariandentaltravel.co.uk (UK), www.hungariandentaltravel.com (US). Deals with several surgeries around Hungary, & provides a guarantee with every treatment (which patients validate with a yearly check-up). Dentists visit the UK every 6 weeks for initial consultations (costing £15) & check-ups on patients who have received treatments.
Operations Abroad Worldwide ✆ 0800 328 1347 or 0161 236 3211; www.operationsabroadworldwide.com. British company specialising in breaks for cosmetic & dental surgery, & running for over 8 years. Can offer a door-to-door service & claims that operations are 50–70% cheaper than in the UK. It works with the Art Medic Clinic in Budapest, which is ISO accredited

& whose cosmetic surgeons are members of the International Society of Plastic & Reconstructive Surgery. See page 49 for further details.
Our Hungary ✆ 01173 500857; m 07515 004752; www.dentalimplantsinhungary.co.uk. UK-based operator working in association with the British Hungarian Medical Service (✆ 1 402 1195; www.bhms.hu). Offers initial London consultations for £40 (free if patients proceed with treatments).
VitalEurope www.vitaleurope.co.uk. Dental travel agency with large clinic in Budapest treating 2,000 patients a year; offers consultations & aftercare at Oxford Circus.
www.ouchmytooth.com A good website providing advice on dentistry abroad & details of dental surgeries in Hungary & elsewhere

See also box, pages 50–1.

RED TAPE

ENTRY REQUIREMENTS European Union (EU) nationals, including those from Britain, may visit Hungary as indefinite tourists providing they have valid passports;

visitors from France, Germany, Italy and Spain require only a national ID card. EU nationals need a European Economic Area resident-citizen permit if staying longer than three months. Apply at the local regional agency of the Hungarian Immigration and Nationality Office before the last two weeks of your stay.

Tourists from all other European countries (excluding Albania, Turkey, Macedonia and Bosnia and Herzegovina), the USA, Canada, Australia and New Zealand can visit without a visa for up to 90 days. Travellers wishing to exceed a 90-day stay should apply for a visa from their country's Hungarian consulate and allow several weeks for it to be processed. More information is available on the website of the Hungarian Immigration and Nationality Office (*www.bm-bah.hu*).

Although in exceptional cases visas can be issued at Hungarian border crossings, the authorities strongly urge you to apply for visas at the embassy. In order to apply for a visa you'll need your passport (valid for at least three months from the time of exit from Hungary), a signed application form, one recent passport-sized photo, return travel tickets and proof of accommodation. All visas (airport-transit visa, transit visa or short-stay visa) now cost US$80 – there are no single-entry or multi-entry visas. Note too that Hungary became a member of the Schengen Agreement in 2007, which means that it accepts visas issued by any other member countries; as such, if you have a visa valid for entry to any of the other 24 Schengen countries then it will be accepted in Hungary. (The UK and Ireland are not members of this agreement, so if you have a visa for UK or Ireland you will still need to apply for a separate visa to enter Hungary.) For additional details about the Schengen Agreement (including a full list of membership) or other visa information, log on to Hungary's foreign ministry website at www.mfa.gov.hu. The Hungarian embassy's websites are www.huemblon.org.uk (UK) and www.huembwas.org (US).

CUSTOMS REGULATIONS Those visitors aged 16 or over from a non-EU country may bring 200 cigarettes, 50 cigars or 250g of tobacco, two litres of wine, one litre of spirits and five litres of beer, 250ml of cologne and 50g of perfume into Hungary. If you are travelling from an EU destination the allowances increase to: 800 cigarettes, 200 cigars or 1,000g of tobacco, 110 litres of beer, 10 litres of spirits and 90 litres of wine. Export of museum pieces or antiques requires an export permit, registered in your name; such permits can usually be obtained from the shop of purchase (see www.muemlekvedelem.hu for more details). If you buy an antique at auction, the organisers will give you an invoice and, for a charge of 2–4% of its selling price, a relevant museum issues the *kiviteli engedély* (export permit). Different museums issue permits for different items; specialist companies can arrange this paperwork for you. The special *bírálati csoport* (appraisal team) evaluates the art work if you do not have an invoice. Importation of any currency worth more than 1,000,000Ft must be declared, and raw meat or milk products and potted or rooted plants cannot be taken in or out of Hungary. Unsurprisingly, it is prohibited to import pornography, drugs and unlicensed weapons. You can only claim back VAT (ÁFA) on goods over a certain value if you are a non-EU citizen. Hand the refund form (available from shops) to customs on leaving the country.

You will find full customs information on the website www.vam.hu.

🄴 HUNGARIAN EMBASSIES AND CONSULATES

ABROAD
Australia 17 Beale Crescent, Deakin, ACT 2600; ☏ +61 (2) 628 23 226; e mission.cbr@kum.hu; www.mfa.gov.hu/emb/canberra

Canada 299 Waverley St, Ottawa, Ontario, K2P 0V9; ☏ +1 (613) 230 2717; e mission.ott@kum.hu; www.mfa.gov.hu/emb/ottawa

Germany Unter den Linden 76, 10117 Berlin; ☏ +49 (30) 203 100; e infober@kum.hu; www.mfa.gov.hu/emb/berlin
Ireland 2 Fitzwilliam Place, Dublin 2; ☏ +353 (1) 661 2902; e mission.dub@kum.hu; www.mfa.gov.hu/emb/dublin
Italy Via dei Villini 12–16, 00161 Roma; ☏ +39 (06) 440 2032; e titkarsag.rom@kum.hu; www.mfa.gov.hu/emb/rome

UK 35 Eaton Place, London SW1X 8BY; ☏ +44 (20) 7201 3440; e office.lon@kum.hu; www.mfa.gov.hu/emb/london
USA 3910 Shoemaker St NW, Washington DC 20008; ☏ +1 (202) 362 6730; e was.missions@kum.hu; www.huembwas.org

IN HUNGARY Note that embassies in Hungary are closed on Hungarian national holidays and those of the country the embassy represents.

Australia XII Budapest, Királyhágó tér 8–9; ☏ 1 457 9777; www.ausembbp.hu. ⊕ Mon–Fri 09.00–12.00.
Canada II Budapest, Ganz u. 12–14; ☏ 1 392 3360; www.kanada.hu. ⊕ Mon–Thu 08.30–16.30, Fri 08.00–13.00.
France VI Budapest, Lendvay u. 27; ☏ 1 374 1100; www.ambafrance-hu.org. Consulate ⊕ Mon–Fri 09.00–12.30.
Germany I Budapest, Úri u. 64; ☏ 1 488 3500; www.budapest.diplo.de. ⊕ Mon–Fri 09.00–12.00.

Ireland V Budapest, Szabadság tér 7; ☏ 1 302 9600. ⊕ Mon–Fri 09.30–12.30, 14.30–16.00.
UK V Budapest, Harmincad u. 6; ☏ 1 266 2888; www.britishembassy.hu. ⊕ Mon–Fri 09.30–12.30, 14.30–16.30.
USA V, Szabadság tér 12; ☏ 1 475 4400; emergency out of hours ☏ 1 475 4703/4924; hungarian.hungary.usembassy.gov ⊕ Mon–Fri 08.00–17.00.

GETTING THERE AND AWAY

Ensure all your documentation is at hand when crossing borders as guards have the right otherwise to refuse entry.

✈ **BY AIR** As with air travel to most European destinations, ticket prices to Hungary are at their highest during the summer period (*Jun–Aug*), and at Christmas and New Year. Costs may also rise during city festivals, and especially during the Hungarian Grand Prix (see page 76). The cheapest season is winter (*Nov–Mar*). Shop around for cut-price flights and last-minute bargains on the internet (try www.expedia.com, www.travelocity.co.uk, www.lastminute.co.uk and www.cheapflights.co.uk). Flight schedules, prices and routes listed below were correct at the time of going to press, but be aware that these are constantly subject to change and you should always check directly with travel agents or airlines. Budapest's Ferihegy International Airport is currently the only entry point for travellers from most countries. For a short time, Ryanair was offering flights from the UK to a small airport – formerly a Soviet airbase – 15km from Keszthely at Lake Balaton. Those flights have now ceased (with no current plans to revive them), although Lufthansa is running services from Germany. Check the Fly Balaton website (*www.fly-balaton.com*).

From the UK and Ireland Several airlines fly to Budapest, including no-frills operators like easyJet and Wizz Air. In addition to London services, easyJet now operates daily flights from Newcastle and Bristol, and Jet2 also flies from Manchester. Aer Lingus offers a service from Dublin, as does Malév.

Aer Lingus ☏ +353 (0)818 365 044; www.aerlingus.com. Daily flights from Dublin starting at around €80 return.

British Airways ☏ 0870 850 9850; www.ba.com. Operates 3 flights a day from London's Heathrow to Budapest (Terminal 2B) from around £100 return. It also has a code-share agreement with Malév, & now offers 2 flights daily from London Gatwick (operated by Malév & arriving at Terminal 2A).

easyJet ⤷ 0871 244 2366; www.easyjet.com. The popular low-cost airline offers direct flights to Budapest twice-daily from London Luton & daily from London Gatwick. Return fares from £65.

Jet2 www.jet2.com. Flights from Manchester 4 days a week, starting at around £70.

Malév Airlines ⤷ 0870 909 0577 (customer reservations); www.malev.com. Fly twice-daily direct from London Gatwick to Budapest (Terminal 2A). Through a code-share agreement with British Airways, customers can also fly 3 times daily from Heathrow (operated by BA & arriving at Terminal 2B). Return fares from £90. There are also indirect flights (via London) from Aberdeen, Edinburgh, Glasgow, Manchester & Newcastle. There are direct flights from Dublin (daily, from €150 return) & Cork (thrice-weekly, from €140 return).

Ryanair www.ryanair.com. Flights from East Midlands (Mon, Fri), Glasgow (Wed, Sun but they don't seem to run beyond Oct) & Bristol (Mon, Fri) & Dublin (Mon, Thu, Fri, Sun) from around £50 return.

Wizz Air ⤷ 0048 22 351 9499; www.wizzair.com. Daily flights between London Luton & Budapest (Terminal 1); return fares from £60.

From the US Malév runs direct flights between New York's JFK Airport and Budapest. There are seven flights a week, taking just over nine hours, and you can expect to pay roughly US$530 return. Delta (*www.delta.com*) also started direct flights from New York in 2006. KLM operates non-direct flights from the US via Amsterdam.

From the rest of the world There are no direct flights from **Australia**; the cheapest way to reach Budapest is to fly to London from Sydney or Melbourne and transfer to a budget airline from there. Qantas offers daily flights direct to London for around US$2,500.

Malév operates five direct flights a week between **Canada** (Toronto) and Budapest costing around CAD800 standard return. You could also try Air Canada and Lufthansa for indirect flights from Vancouver and Montreal. No direct flights are available from **New Zealand**; you'll need to take a flight to London or Paris (with Air New Zealand), and get a connection from there.

In addition to the above, you can catch direct Malév flights to Budapest from **Lyons** (seven flights a week), **Ljubljana** (12 a week), **Vienna** (twice daily) and **Dubrovnik** (three a week). Other international airlines that operate in and out of Ferihegy include Turkish Airlines, Alitalia, Finnair, Czech Airlines and Aeroflot.

Airline/airport contact numbers

Aeroflot +36 1 294 4039
Air France +36 1 294 4201
British Airways +36 1 777 4747
Central airport info +36 1 296 9696
Finnair +36 1 296 5486
Flight information +36 1 296 7000

KLM +36 1 373 7737
Lost luggage Terminal 2A +36 1 296 5449
Lost luggage Terminal 2B +36 1 296 5966
Lufthansa +36 1 296 6192
Malév +36 1 235 3888

Budapest Airport Ferihegy International (⤷ 1 296 9696; *www.bud.hu*) is Hungary's main commercial airport, located 25km southeast of Budapest. There are two adjacent terminals: Terminal 2A services Malév flights, while Terminal 2B looks after most other airlines. The airport is compact and clean, and contains a handful of souvenir and duty-free shops, a bar, coffee shop and restaurant, and currency-exchange bureaux (that in Terminal A charges no commission). A third terminal – Terminal 1 – is located on the same road as Ferihegy 2 but closer to town; it services the budget airlines (as well as private aircraft).

For details on **transfers** from the airport into Budapest itself, see Budapest's *Getting there and away* section, pages 92–3.

⚌ BY TRAIN Unless you're planning to make the train 'a feature' of your trip – perhaps by booking with a specialist tour operator – travelling from the UK to Hungary by train is only worth the time and effort if you're planning a round-Europe trip, would like to stop off along the way, or are afraid of flying. Flights with budget airlines are generally considerably cheaper than return rail tickets; for example, a check on the price of a standard-class return ticket from London St Pancras (via the Eurostar) to Budapest Keleti in October found the cheapest price was over £200. The journey from London takes 22 hours (including the three-hour journey on Eurostar), and you can travel via Cologne and Munich, Frankfurt and Nürenberg or Paris and Vienna. Tickets are usually valid for around three months, allowing you to get off to explore along the way (although you can't depart from your booked route). For information on crossing the Channel from London, contact **Eurostar** (❧ 08705 186186; *www.eurostar.com*). Rail tickets to Budapest can be booked through the **Rail Europe Travel Centre** (❧ 08448 484064; *www.raileurope.co.uk*), who can also help to plan your trip. Alternatively, you can contact **Trains Europe** (❧ 0871 700 7722; *www.trainseurope.co.uk*), a leading supplier of European rail tickets (including, they claim, tickets Rail Europe can't provide) that can also offer advice on itineraries and routes.

As Budapest has direct rail connections with 25 European cities, it can be a great platform from which to delve around in central Europe. All international trains through Budapest are equipped with sleepers in 1st- and 2nd-class carriages, and most (though not all) have dining cars. If you're planning to travel with a bicycle, you'll pay an additional charge of about a quarter of the price of your main ticket. See www.mav.hu or www.mav-start.hu for details of international rail timetables and ticket costs, or call 1 371 9449. Keep your passport and tickets to hand as they are likely to be regularly inspected, and you will usually need to produce them when crossing borders. Snoring soundly in your cabin will not exempt you from this – staff will shake you awake if they need to.

International trains to Budapest arrive at/leave from one of the three main railway stations. The **Eastern Railway Station** (*Keleti pályaudvar; VIII, Baross tér*) handles the bulk of them, including those to/from Belgrade, Bratislava, Bucharest, Kiev, Krakow, Ljubljana, Moscow, Munich, Prague, Sofia, Venice, Vienna and Zagreb. The **Western Railway Station** (*Nyugati pályaudvar; VI, Nyugati tér*) was the city's first main station, built in 1877 by Eiffel, and serves international destinations such as Warsaw, Bratislava, Berlin and Prague. The **Southern Railway Station** (*Déli pályaudvar; I, Krisztina körút*) handles international journeys to and from Cologne, Ljubljana, Munich, Sarajevo, Venice, Vienna and Zagreb. Each of these has a connection to the underground system.

If you're travelling from Budapest, you should aim to buy your ticket (*jegy*) at least a day or two in advance as services can get booked up. Seat reservations (up to 60 days in advance) are essential for those marked with a circled *R* on the timetable. Tickets can be bought from each of the three main Budapest stations, but it might be easier either to deal with a travel agent (page 99) or head for the MÁV central ticket office. Contact details for this office, and other information on train travel, are included under *Getting around* (pages 55–8). There is a 24-hour helpline for international passengers (❧ 1 461 5500). Those aged 65 or over with EU passports can travel anywhere in Hungary on public transport free of charge.

Some international services Rail connections between Hungary, its neighbouring countries and beyond are good. This paragraph provides a brief overview of some of the main routes. It's a three-hour journey from **Vienna** to Budapest Déli passing through the Hegyeshalom border and on via Győr and Tatabánya. It can take as little as 2½ hours to reach Budapest from **Bratislava** either over the Szob

2

border and directly on to Budapest Keleti or via the Rajka border, through Győr to Déli. A full day's travelling is required to reach the Hungarian capital from **Kiev** and usually one change or more is necessary at the border. Trains then continue their journey through the Hungarian entry point at Záhony, to Debrecen, Szolnok and Keleti. From **Bucharest** the train enters Hungarian soil at Lőkösháza before heading to Békéscsaba, Szolnok and Keleti, taking around 13 hours. Trains from **Belgrade** run via Novi Sad and Subotica, with some services crossing the border at Kelebia (travelling via Kiskunhalas to Budapest Keleti) and others at Röszke (going on to Szeged). It's possible to travel from **Zagreb** to Budapest in as little as five hours. The journey cuts the Croatian border at Koprivnica before heading through Nagykanizsa, around the southern side of Balaton and on to Budapest Keleti. Alternatively you can cross the border further east, near Villány, and travel on to Pécs. The quickest route from **Ljubljana** to Budapest is via Zagreb (as above), which takes around 7½ hours. There are also two crossings further north at Hodoš (travelling on to to Zalalövő, Veszprém and terminating at Budapest Déli) and Szentgotthárd at the Austrian border (offering a less direct journey to Budapest via Szombathely). The quickest way from **Prague** is via Bratislava, through the Szob border and on to Keleti, taking from seven hours. The fastest and most direct route from **Warsaw** again goes through Bratislava and Szob before stopping along the way to Keleti at Tata and Tatabánya. It's an epic 35-hour journey from **Moscow** through Poland, with at least one change (and often more), before heading on to Slovakia, the Rajka border, Győr and Tatabánya to reach Keleti. You can also go via Kiev.

Rail passes The **InterRail Global Pass** (*see www.interrailnet.com*) gives European rail travellers the freedom to enjoy unlimited travel across 30 countries on the continent. There are two types of pass – continuous cards (valid for 15 days, 22 days or one month at a time) or flexi cards (allowing travel for five days within a ten day period or ten days within a 22-day period). Cards start from adult €249–599 and under 26s €159–239; they are only available to European residents, and can be bought through the website.

A classic **Eurail Pass** (*see www.eurailnet.com;* e *info@eurailnet.com*) allows limitless travel across 25 European countries, including Hungary. Prices range from US$728 to US$2,040, depending on the duration of the pass's validity (from 15 days to three months). If you're under 26 then you are eligible for a Eurail Youthpass, which dramatically cuts the cost (by around 40%). Holders of both the above passes are entitled to discounts on Eurostar travel.

The Danube Express The **Danube Express** (*Offley Holes Farm, Charlton Rd, Preston, Hitchin, Herts SG4 7TD;* \ *01462 441400; www.danube-express.com*) – billed as a 'hotel on wheels' – is a luxury train (featuring en-suite cabins) based in Budapest and travelling through central and eastern Europe (to destinations like Istanbul, Prague, Krakow, Vienna and Berlin). You can book all-inclusive holidays (of up to 12 days) starting from London (with sightseeing excursions, etc), but the train is also available for use by independent travellers. Meals are included.

BY COACH Travel to Hungary from afar by coach is an exhausting proposition. It used to be the cheapest option, but is now under severe pressure from the budget airlines. As long as you're not overly tall, and can sit still for extended periods, the coaches are comfy enough with reclining seats, TV and video, and washroom facilities. **Eurolines** (\ *0870 5143219; www.eurolines.co.uk or www.nationalexpress.co.uk*) operates in over 30 other countries, and under the National Express banner in the UK and Volánbusz in Hungary. In England, direct and indirect coaches depart from London

Victoria Coach Station and Dover Eastern Docks to Budapest Népliget – the capital's main coach station – via France, Belgium, Germany, Austria and Győr in northwest Hungary. The journey takes a mind-numbing 27½ hours. Coaches depart daily from both coach stations in peak season (*Jun 26–Sep 11*), and every day except Wednesday and Saturday the rest of the year. Standard fares are single £57 and return £85.

If you are planning a European tour, it could be worth investing in a **Eurolines Pass**, which gives holders unlimited deluxe coach travel for between 15 and 30 days to 46 major European cities (including Budapest). Passes start at €175. For more information, visit the Eurolines website, the Eurolines ticket office at Népliget (⊕ *Mon–Fri 06.00–18.00, Sat–Sun 06.00–16.00*), the Volánbusz Travel Office (*V, Erzsébet tér 1;* ✆ *1 382 0888 or the central office at Népliget Bus Station*) or any National Express agent in the UK.

In Budapest, Népliget Bus Station (for contact details, see page 93) deals with all international services, which include Naples via Rome, Toulouse via Vienna and Lyons, Berlin via Prague, Paris via Strasbourg and Amsterdam via Frankfurt. International services also run to and from other towns and cities, including Debrecen, Baja, Szeged, Miskolc, Győr, Szombathely and Siófok.

BY CAR The overland drive from the UK to Budapest would certainly make an epic of a road movie – all 1,684km (1,047 miles) of it – but there's a certain romanticism and some wonderful scenery. Once on mainland Europe the easiest route to Budapest is via Ostend, Belgium, Cologne, Frankfurt and Vienna. On a good day the journey should take around 17 hours but, obviously, this doesn't take into account food (and ablution) stops, sleep breaks, traffic problems, border queues, etc. See www.michelin.com for a detailed route planner. It's important to keep to hand your driving licence, vehicle insurance and registration documents (as well as your passport), and to display your country-identification letter on your vehicle. It is vital to take out adequate breakdown cover in case the unthinkable happens. The AA (✆ *0800 085 7253; www.theaa.com*) operates a European Breakdown Cover policy that will protect you on your trip. Finally, be aware that tolls and high fuel prices in mainland Europe can considerably inflate your anticipated expenses.

To drive in Hungary (on the right-hand side, remember!), you must hold a full driving licence that is valid for at least 12 months upon your return home. Third-party insurance is also a necessity but cars with licence plates and national-identification letter for A, B, CH, D, DK, E, F, FL, GB, HR, I, IRL, IS, L, NL, P, S, SK, SLO countries will already be covered. If your country is not listed above then you'll have to produce a Green Card and may be asked to buy the insurance at the border if you don't already have it. For further details on driving in Hungary, see pages 59–60.

There are 80-odd road border crossings into Hungary, around 40 of which are international stations and open around the clock – you can assume that all those crossings met by major roads are of this type. The remaining smaller border crossings are for locals only (prohibited to foreigners).

BY HYDROFOIL A hydrofoil service operated by **Mahart PassNave** (*V Budapest, Belgrád rakpart;* ✆ *1 484 4000/4010;* e *hydrofoil@mahartpassnave.hu; www.mahartpassnave.hu*) runs between Vienna and Budapest via Bratislava, and takes 5½ hours. Tickets from Vienna to Budapest (*daily Aug 1–29; May–Jul & Aug 31–Oct 3 Wed, Fri & Sun – services the other way Tue, Thu & Sat*) cost adult single/return €89/109, student €66.75/81.75, child €44.50/54.50, and there's a 50% discount if you have a Hungary Card (page 55) on booking. Bicycle carriage costs an additional €20. In Budapest, the ferry departs from Pest (between the Szabadság and Erzsébet bridges), in Vienna from the Reichsbrücke pier.

Generally the standard of public health in Hungary is good, the tap water safe to drink and no vaccinations are legally required. However, it is wise to be up to date with routine vaccinations such as diphtheria, tetanus and polio. Hepatitis A should also be considered.

If you are planning to visit deep-forested areas outside the capital, consult your doctor about getting immunisation against encephalitis, which is carried by forest ticks (*kullancs*). Take precautions by using tick repellents, wearing long-sleeved clothing and a hat, and tucking trousers into boots. After a day in the forest it is important to check yourself for ticks, or get someone else to do it for you. For those travelling with children, concentrate particularly on checking their hair. (See the website www.masta.org/tickalert for more details.) The other primary irritant is the mosquito, which whines around the riverside on summer evenings. Cover exposed skin with a DEET-based insect repellent (*rovarirtó*) and they'll feast on some other suckee.

For those who are going to be working in hospitals or in close contact with children, hepatitis B vaccination is recommended. Pre-exposure rabies vaccine (ideally three doses given over a minimum of 21 days) should also be considered for anyone who is specifically going to be working with animals. For **emergency telephone numbers**, see page 78.

THE EUROPEAN HEALTH INSURANCE CARD

EU nationals who are taken ill or have an accident when visiting Hungary are entitled to healthcare. In 2004, a European Health Insurance Card was introduced to improve access to healthcare in the EU and to speed up the reimbursement of costs (replacing the E111 form). Some countries incorporate this health-insurance card into their national cards while others issue separate ones. UK citizens can apply for this card through the EHIC website (*www.ehic.org.uk*), by calling 0845 606 2030 or by picking up an application form from some post offices.

Only publicly funded health treatment is included in this scheme for the moment. In Hungary, while emergency treatment is free for visiting EU citizens, you have to pay the full cost of drugs and non-emergency treatment and then claim a refund. It is important to keep all your bills, prescriptions and receipts.

TRAVEL CLINICS AND HEALTH INFORMATION

A full list of current travel clinic websites worldwide is available on www.istm.org. For other journey preparation information, consult www.tripprep.com.

IN HUNGARY

Free emergency health care is available to foreigners, but any required medication or follow-up treatment will have to be paid for. It is therefore important to ensure that your travel insurance covers medical costs. Take a copy of your policy certificate with you and keep the policy number to hand in case you are obliged to quote it. Hungarians swear by the curative properties of thermal baths (*gyógyfürdő*), and doctors will frequently prescribe dips for conditions ranging from skin problems to arthritic pains.

For those minor ailments, you'll find Budapest has a rash of pharmacies (*gyógyszertár* or *patika*); all towns and most villages will boast at least one pharmacy. It is nevertheless worth bearing in mind that some medicines available over the counter in the UK and US – like antihistamine – require a prescription in Hungary. If you suffer from allergies, take relevant medication with you. Normal pharmacy opening hours are 09.00–18.00 on weekdays; they often close at lunchtime on Saturday, and don't usually open at all on Sunday. Local listing magazines, Tourinform or signs in pharmacy windows should indicate the nearest all-night pharmacy.

Dentistry Hungary has a first-rate and highly affordable dental service. The *Budapest Sun* and *Budapest Times* often contain advertisements for private dental practices. If you're in need of urgent dental care in Budapest, contact **SOS Dental Service** (*VI, Király u. 14;* ✆ *1 267 9602*), which operates 24 hours a day. There are also English-speaking dentists at Profident (*VII, Károly körút 1;* ✆ *1 268 1097; www.profident.com;* ⊕ *Mon–Sat 08.00–22.00*).

It might well be that, far from an unforeseen inconvenience, a trip to the dentist is the primary motive behind your visit. Brits have started to catch on to the savings available on dental work performed in Hungary, and several tour operators now offer the chance to add a sparkle to your smile during a Budapest break. If you require complicated dental work that goes beyond the standard clean-up or filling, the economic argument is overwhelming, with procedures generally costing at least half – and sometimes as little as a quarter – of the price paid in the UK. Consider the following listed prices for common treatments through the operator Our Hungary: implant from £690 (average UK price £2,200), porcelain crown £200 (average UK price £500), porcelain veneer £250 (average UK price £500). As this suggests, there are potential savings of thousands – and even tens of thousands – of pounds to be made, even allowing for travel costs. Furthermore, it is increasingly common for companies to arrange initial consultations in the UK. See box, pages 50–1, for further details, and page 41 for a list of relevant tour operators.

Cosmetic surgery If you see sunglasses after nightfall, don't assume it's a posing popstar – it might be a visitor recovering from an eyelift. There has been a rise in customers taking advantage of good-value cosmetic surgery in Hungary. One British operator arranging trips for cosmetic (and dental) surgery is Operations Abroad Worldwide (✆ *0800 328 1347 or 0161 236 3211; www.operationsabroadworldwide.com*). The company has been running for over seven years, can offer a door-to-door service and claims that operations are 50–70% cheaper than in the UK. It works with the Art Medic Clinic in Budapest, which is ISO accredited and whose cosmetic surgeons are members of the International Society of Plastic and Reconstructive Surgery. We must stress, however, that we have no direct experience of this (or any other) operator; it is of course of the utmost importance that you thoroughly research the subject, the operator and the surgery – and seek independent, professional medical advice – before considering undergoing cosmetic surgery.

SAFETY

Happily Hungary is a safe country with a low rate of violent crime. However, like many other European countries, incidents of pick-pocketing, mugging, car theft and overcharging with threats are sadly on the increase. The bulging tourist wallet is inevitably at greatest risk, so it is wise to stay vigilant when travelling on public transport, strolling in busy and built-up areas, shopping in markets and malls, and relaxing in restaurants and bars. As a general rule, don't let your belongings out of your sight, try not to flash around valuable items and make use of your hotel safe. Never walk the streets with large sums of cash, or – as we learnt to our cost – leave your cellphone in an unzipped shoulder bag as you peer at the bus timetable.

There have been occasional instances of criminals going to more extreme lengths to extort money from tourists. Examples include conmen posing as policemen and demanding cash (if in any doubt, ask for the 'officer's' credentials and insist on being taken to a police station with access to a translator), and

It's said that there's something in Budapest to interest the crooked set – something to put a smile on the face of the most foul-mouthed of Brits. Yes, dental treatments at a fraction of the bloated prices demanded in the UK. But what of the quality? However tempting the savings, we suspect that even the desperate would shrink from inviting a bearded and bloodstained behemoth to take a drill to their mouths. I therefore bravely volunteered to see how the service compares with that at home, and arranged with two UK-based operators to pay visits to their Budapest surgeries.

HUNGARIAN DENTAL TRAVEL After being whisked by complimentary taxi from my hotel to Villányi Dent, a surgery in Buda that works in tandem with Hungarian Dental Travel (see page 41), I was greeted by the dainty Dr Viktória Portugal, an earnest young dentist with good English and a reassuringly attractive smile. She took me on a tour of the practice, which boasts a state-of-the-art thermograph machine that shows a computerised image of the structure of the patient's mouth and can highlight problem areas in an instant. There's also a cutting-edge, professional system for teeth whitening that avoids using bleach – Dr Viktória strongly recommends avoiding potentially damaging whitening services offered by some hotels. And I then had a scaling and clean-up. I can report, nervous readers, that it was a thoroughly comfortable experience – indeed, more comfortable than many of my trips to the tooth doctor in Britain.

Villányi Dent currently receives around 20 tourists a month, a number that continues to rise year on year. The bulk of visitors require complex dental work such as implants and breaches. It is in such procedures, along with veneers, that the top savings are to be made – you can expect to pay at most half the price of treatments in the UK, and perhaps as little as one-fifth. It's worth noting, however, that routine problems and teeth whitening are only slightly cheaper, and are not worth travelling for in their own right.

thieves posing as motorists in distress, flagging down fellow drivers for assistance before stealing from them and driving away in their cars (be cautious about stopping to help apparent breakdowns). Theft of cars and the possessions inside them is not uncommon, so don't tempt opportunists by leaving things of value on the seats.

Gentlemen, if an attractive young woman approaches and asks you to join her for a drink, consider the possibility that she is drawn by more than your irresistible masculine charms. Unwary, strutting men have lost both their swagger and their swag when, after tripping over their tongues into a seedy joint with a 'consume girl', they have been forced by burly bouncers to pay an extortionate price for the drinks.

On a more mundane level, check your bills in restaurants and bars carefully for 'mistakes' in the maths. Never order from a menu that does not display prices alongside its fare. Always use a recognised taxi firm, and agree a price or check the meter is cleared before climbing in (see pages 96–7). And resist dealing with unlicensed moneychangers in the street.

We must stress again that by Western standards Budapest is extremely safe, and you are unlikely to feel threatened. Please don't have nightmares, do sleep tight. For up-to-date security information, check the Foreign and Commonwealth Office website at www.fco.gov.uk.

WOMEN TRAVELLERS There is a typical central European machismo to Hungarian men, and they can hold attitudes that many in the West would consider sexist. Such thinking tends to manifest itself in high-blown compliments rather than anything

OUR HUNGARY Another free taxi from the hotel, this time heading for a dental surgery in the suburbs of Pest. I arrive at a smart building with pine trees in the garden and a relaxation area in a decked conservatory. I'm greeted by a friendly receptionist, and shown around by an equally affable Dr Balázs Gyovai, one of the dental surgeons here. Dr Gyovai has a beard, it's true, but he's certainly no behemoth and his tunic is spotless. The British Hungarian Medical Service – working with Our Hungary (see page 41) – has been operating for over three years, and 80% of its customers are British. I'm told that most treatments require two visits to the surgery (although occasionally up to four), and generally take place during a city stay of between five and 12 days (offering plenty of time to see the sights). On average, the surgery receives 25 patients a month, with its busiest period coming in spring.

Everywhere is squeaky clean, and the equipment state of the art (even featuring a TV with an oral camera so that you can watch what's going on, if that takes your fancy). I take the chair, and have a thorough clean up; as with my previous experience at a Hungarian dentist, it's all professional and painless, and my teeth feel wonderfully smooth afterwards.

It's as I return to the reception area, however, that the scale of the benefits become fully obvious. There I find a lady from London who has been in Budapest for a few days having some implants fitted. She admitted to being a traditionally nervous patient, but was full of praise for the caring staff and the skill of the dentists. And she still couldn't believe the price. Where she had been quoted £2,000 per implant in the UK, here she was charged just £650; even allowing for accommodation and travel, she reckoned on having saved 60% overall. And savings increase proportionately with the level of work. Where a full arch of implants and crowns might cost £50,000 in the UK, the price here would be under £18,000. Scattering smiles all round, I bid farewell and am whisked back to my hotel.

more sinister. Women will find men unafraid to 'check them out' as they pass in the street and perhaps less inhibited in approaching them in bars than in more reserved cultures such as Britain; however, provided women take sensible precautions they should encounter no harassment.

TERRORISM The threat of terrorist activity is a current danger in Hungary as elsewhere in the world. Obvious targets such as the British and American embassies are presently protected with concrete barriers and armed guards. Tourists are advised to behave as they would at home and be alert to any suspect behaviour, especially in busy public places. The FCO website (see opposite) offers up-to-the-minute advice.

THE LAW It is legal for prostitutes to stand in a 'tolerant zone' (*türelmi zóna*), wait for customers to stop their cars, and then 'conduct their business' in the cars or nearby bushes. You may see scantily clad women beside some of the main roads leading out from Budapest. Other more solid trappings of the trade – pimps and madams, brothels etc – remain illegal (although some strip joints are rather feeble covers for prostitution rackets). Recreational drug use is prohibited. Tourists are most likely to brush with the law as a result of motoring offences. Random road blocks are extremely common – during a four-month period we were pulled over on seven occasions in a Hungarian car. You will be asked to show your passport, driving licence and car registration papers. Minor offences can be punished with on-the-spot fines, while fines for speeding (usually 10,000Ft) must be settled at a post office. It is illegal to drink any alcohol at all prior to driving.

THE POLICE While the police force (*rendőrség*) has enjoyed a better reputation than counterparts in other eastern European nations, it has nevertheless been regarded with suspicion by Hungarians. Accusations of corruption have plagued the constabulary for years. In 2003 the director of police in Budapest went so far as to offer his officers cash rewards in return for their blowing the whistle on instances of bribery in an attempted clean up. On the whole, though, the situation is improving and tourists are unlikely to encounter any problems in their dealings with officers, which will primarily come in being stopped at road blocks (see page 60) or very occasionally during passport inspections. There is a good police presence on the streets of Budapest during high season, when patrols aim at deterring thieves. Officers usually speak little or no English, but in July, August and September such patrols are often accompanied by translators.

Lost passports should be reported immediately to the Office for Immigration and Citizenship (*XI Budapest, Budafoki út 60;* ☎ *1 463 9165*), which is open 24 hours a day. If your passport has been stolen you'll need to report it to the police either by calling one of the emergency numbers or via the tourist police office (*in the Tourinform at V Budapest, Sütő utca 2; 24-hour* ☎ *1 438 8080*).

For emergency telephone numbers, see page 78.

WHAT TO TAKE

There is little that isn't readily available in Budapest and the other main cities. Pack your swimsuit for a spa visit, your driving licence if you are looking to hire a car, and a jacket and tie if you're a gentleman who wants to dine at the Gundel (see page 108). Young women in Budapest like to make an effort when they go nightclubbing, so a set of trendy threads might deserve a place in your suitcase. Some medication that can be bought over the counter in the West requires a prescription in Hungary, so ensure you've got your relevant tablets. Choose your clothes remembering that it can be very cold in winter, wet in early spring and very hot in summer; there are winds and occasional storms in summer, and a jumper is worthwhile for those cave or cellar visits. Take out comprehensive travel insurance before your trip to cover lost baggage, theft and medical emergencies, and bring copies of the documentation with you (or use a computer safe; see box above). A plug adaptor (two-prong, round-pin) will allow you to use your own electrical devices. Beyond that, bring some comfortable shoes, a patient frame of mind and a packet of indigestion tablets. Oh, and *Hungary: The Bradt Travel Guide*!

ELECTRICITY

Hungary's **electrical current** is 220 Volts/50Hz, accessible via the European two-pin plug. Plug adaptors for use with three-pronged plugs are generally available from large supermarkets and chemists in cities.

MONEY The forint (Ft or HUF) is Hungary's official unit of currency and is issued in banknote denominations of 200, 500, 1,000, 2,000, 5,000, 10,000 and 20,000 and coins of 5, 10, 20, 50 and 100. Small shops, cafés or taxis may have difficulty with 20,000Ft notes, so it's worth asking your hotel to break down larger denominations before going out for the day.

While Hungary is a member of the EU, it is not yet ready to switch to the Euro currency. Despite that, some businesses have been accepting the euro for some time, and hotels will often list their prices in euros because of the changing value of the forint. Any goods and services purchased in Hungary require the payment of a value-added tax levy known as ÁFA (between 5 and 20%, but most commonly 15%). Most quoted prices in shops include this tax but it's worth checking in case. Non-EU-country members can claim this tax back if purchasing goods worth over around 45,000Ft (or €175) within six months of purchase. See page 62 for hotel tax rates; see pages 81–2 for a guide to tipping.

The current **exchange rate** (January 2010) is £1 = 300Ft, US$1 = 185Ft, €1 = 270Ft.

Exchanging currency and travellers' cheques

Banks, post offices, hotels, *bureaux de change*, tourist offices and travel agencies usually exchange **currency**. The commission charged by *bureaux de change* (which you'll find in railway stations, shopping centres and on the shopping streets of main cities) can be high (at times extortionate) and their rates of exchange vary considerably so be sure to shop around. Always ask how much it will cost to change £1 or US$1 – some places mislead customers by quoting a rate that only applies if you change over a certain amount of money. The safest place to exchange cash is at a bank, where you should get an acceptable rate and should not be charged commission.

The profusion of ATMs means that **travellers' cheques** are increasingly rare things, and we have found that many *bureaux de change* do not deal with them. You should, in any case, avoid such booths as the rates on offer are likely to be very low. Banks will exchange travellers' cheques (American Express are the most widely used) at decent rates without fuss; travel agencies like Ibusz may be able to exchange them, though usually for a commission. You can also try the post office. Remember to take your passport as a means of identification.

Travelex cash passport

A safe and convenient alternative to carrying cash or travellers' cheques is the Travelex Cash Passport scheme (☎ *020 7837 9580; www.travelex.co.uk*). The system is based on a pre-paid travel card that allows holders 24-hour access to their money in any local currency. You simply load the card up with funds before your trip and draw the cash out as you go along from ATM machines. Once you've exhausted your funds you throw the card away.

Credit cards

Although locals tend to pay for goods and services in cash, major credit cards are accepted in Hungary, particularly in tourist-heavy shops, hotels and restaurants. However, smaller outlets – including some supermarkets, museums and transport ticket offices – may not take them. If your card is lost or stolen, notify your credit-card company immediately to prevent the possibility of fraud.

American Express ☎ 1 235 4349
Visa ☎ 0800 963833 (UK 24-hour hotline)

Mastercard (Hungary) VI Budapest, WestEnd City Center, Tower C, Floor 6, Váci út 1–3; ☎ 1 238 7500

BANKS In general, banks are open 08.00–16.00/17.30 on weekdays and 08.00–12.00 on Saturdays – however, some close as early as 15.00 during the week and don't open at all at the weekend. All are shut on Sundays. Twenty-four-hour automated teller machines (ATMs) are fairly commonplace (you'll find them even in small towns) with most accepting American Express, Visa, MasterCard, as well as debit cards from Cirrus and Maestro. Many are located inside the bank buildings; swipe your card at the door to gain entry out of hours. Check with your bank before you travel whether you'll be charged a commission fee.

DISCOUNT CARDS The International Student Card (ISIC) or International Youth Travel Card (for non-students under 26) will entitle you to reductions on entry to many museums, galleries and other attractions, and on journeys on some public-

---

BUDGETING

Hungary is considerably less of a bargain-bucket destination than it once was, but in general you'll get far more for your money in shops, restaurants, hotels and on public transport than you will in the West. Costs are highest in Budapest and Balaton, and (as you'd expect) things are cheapest in those areas that see fewest tourists (such as the eastern reaches of the Great Plain). For the sake of giving you the 'worst-case' scenario, the budget below is based on staying in Budapest (although costs vary even within the city – a beer in a prime tourist spot will cost over double that of a beer elsewhere). The following rough guide lists daily budgets per person; the calculation is based on two people sharing accommodation (and therefore paying half each of the room cost) – a single traveller may find the accommodation cost slightly higher. Costs beyond Budapest and Balaton should be between one-third and two-fifths lower.

STRAPPED Church mice can scrape by on around 6,000Ft per day by staying in a hostel dorm, eating in a basic büfé and getting around on foot. There might even be change for a decilitre of wine in a backstreet borozó.

MODEST If you can't splash out but can afford a minor ripple, you'll get along with 14,000Ft a day by seeking out a cheapish panzió. This will allow you to have a light snack for lunch, visit the odd museum and gallery, travel around by public transport, and eat a two-course meal with wine at an inexpensive restaurant.

COMFORTABLE A daily allowance of 31,000Ft will permit a stay in a four-star hotel, ample sightseeing, cake stops, a meal in a decent restaurant, some late-night drinks in a bar, and a taxi back to your room.

INDULGENT For 52,000Ft you can kick off your shoes and live the city high life. Stay in a luxury hotel, drink cocktails, eat well and make merry, travel where you want to go and see most of what you want to see. You'll rarely need to check the restaurant prices before taking a table, and you should still have a bit of loose change at the end of the day.

HEY, BIG SPENDER If money is no object, book a plush room at the Four Seasons, dine at the Gundel, drink top Tokaji Aszú until it's coming out of your ears, take in a performance at the State Opera House, bet bravely at the casino and set about the shops of Váci utca. If you want to spend a fortune in Budapest it is quite possible to do so – it will simply take a little longer than in London or Paris.

transport networks. Concessionary rates for pensioners usually only apply to Hungarian nationals, although it is a little-publicised fact that over-65s can travel free on all forms of public transport in Budapest and that elderly EU residents can enter the Parliament building without charge by showing their passports. If you are travelling extensively beyond Budapest, the Hungary Card might be worth investing in. Accepted at participating outlets around the country, it allows discounts on accommodation, restaurants, museums, public transport and certain cultural events – it will even get you 20% off the price of the Budapest Card (see page 100). You'll also receive reductions on highway tolls, the hydrofoil, and car rental. The card is valid for 13 months, is transferable, and can be bought from Tourinform offices for 7,140Ft. For more information, see www.hungarycard.hu or call 1 266 3741.

GETTING AROUND

Public transport within Hungary is efficient, reliable and cheap; most villages and towns are accessible by either train or bus (although certain very remote areas – such as the extreme northeast – are most readily navigated by car). Many settlements can be explored by foot but public transport within larger towns is also excellent. Buses, trolleybuses and trams run throughout the day until around 23.00; tickets can be purchased from newsagents, street stands and some hotels, and should be stamped in the punching machines aboard the vehicles. There are no scheduled internal flights. Note that **EU members over the age of 65** can travel free on public transport anywhere in Hungary – just show your passport. (You'll need to pay a very small reservation fee when buying tickets for express trains, which have to be booked in advance.)

BY TRAIN Trains operated by the Hungarian state railway company MÁV (Magyar Államvasutak) certainly can't be described as modern, but they are comfortable enough. There are first- and second-class carriages, and often a buffet car; you must buy a separate ticket for your bike (costing an additional 25%), and place it in the front or back carriage (if there isn't a specified area set aside for cycles). Budapest is the central hub for all the major rail routes that link the main cities and towns, and in some cases it is quicker to travel via the capital – even if it adds distance to the journey – than taking secondary branch lines where services are slower. InterCity trains (IC) are the quickest services, offering direct routes that stop only at major towns and cities. The InterCity Express (EX) also only halts at main settlements, but doesn't get up the same speed on the way. The 'fast trains' (*sebesvonat* and *gyorsvonat*) cost around 10% less than Express trains, and stop more frequently. Avoid the 'slow trains' (*személyvonat*) unless you only have a short distance to go – they don't miss a station, calling in at even the piddliest little places, and the fares are no cheaper than for the fast trains.

There are three main railway stations in Budapest serving domestic destinations: the Eastern Railway Station (Keleti pályaudvar; see page 45) is the point of arrival and departure for trains from the Northern Uplands and northeast (Gyöngyös, Szécsény, Eger, Miskolc, Tokaj, etc), the Western Railway Station (Nyugati pályaudvar; see page 45) serves the Great Plain (Szeged, Kecskémet, Szolnok, Debrecen, Nyíregyháza, etc) and the Danube Bend (Esztergom, Visegrád, Vác, etc), and the Southern Railway Station (Déli pályaudvar; see page 45) caters for journeys to and from the remainding chunk – Balaton (Keszthely, Siófok, Tapolca, etc) and Transdanubia (Győr, Tata, Pécs, Kaposvár, etc). While these are loosely the rules, there are a few wild cards – Sopron, Szombathely and Herend trains, for example, use Keleti – so be sure to check before travelling. Each of these stations is also on the Budapest underground system.

2

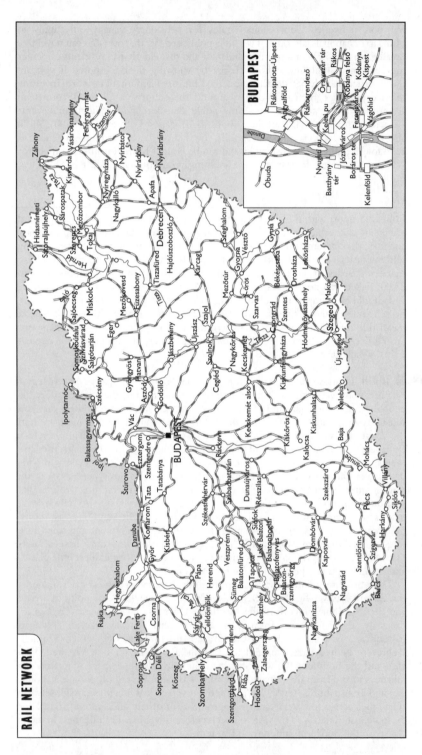

RAIL NETWORK

BUDAPEST

56

Hungarian bus and train timetables seem designed to bewilder even the most rabid Magyar nationalist with their labyrinthine linguistics. *Szabadnap* translates literally as 'free day', usually meaning a Saturday when people beyond the service industry don't work but shops are open. *Munkaszüneti nap* – 'a break-from-work day' – is a Sunday or bank-holiday Monday when everything is closed. Here goes with a few explanations of the abbreviations you'll encounter:

TRAIN

V   *közlekedik: keddtől–szombatig; de nem közlekedik IV.22-én és VI. 10-én*
     train runs Tue–Sat, but not on Apr 22 and Jun 10

m   *munkanap* working day

z   *szombat, vasárnap és ünnepnap*
     Sat, Sun and special hols/bank hols (ie: festival days like Mar 15, Aug 20, Nov 1)

x   *hétköznap* weekday

w   *közlekedik: szombaton és XII. 24-én de nem közlekedik: XII. 28, IV. 26, V.3,*
     X.18, X.25
     train runs on Sat and on Dec 24, but not on Dec 28, Apr 26, May 3, Oct 18
     or Oct 25

u   *közlekedik: vasárnap és IV 21-én, VI. 9-én, de nem közlekedik: IV.20, VI.8*
     train runs on Sun and on Apr 21 and Jun 9, but not Apr 20 and Jun 8

BUS

+   *munkaszüneti napokon* on non-working day (Sun and hols)

D   *naponta, kivéve szabadnapokon* daily except for Sat (literally 'free day')

E   *a hetek első munkanapján*
     on the first working day of these weeks

I   *iskolai előadások napján* on school days

M   *munkanapokon* on working days

O   *szabadnapokon* on free days (usually this means Sat)

U   *a hetek utolsó munkanapján* on last working day of these weeks

V   *a hetek első munkanapját megelőző napon*
     on day prior to first working day of these weeks

X   *naponta, kivéve munkaszüneti napokon*
     daily except non-working days (Sun and hols)

Z   *szabad és munkaszüneti napokon* on free days and non-working days

HF   *hétfői napokon* on Mon

V+   *hetek első munkanapját megelőző napok kivételével munkaszüneti napokon*
     on non-working days except the day prior to the first working day of these
     weeks

W   *hetek első iskolai előadási napját megelőző napon*
     on the day prior to the first school day of the week

VV   *V. hó 25-tol IX. hó 14-ig vasárnapi napokon*
     on Sun May 25–Sep 14

For V, m, z, x, w and u, see entries under *Train* above. And if you are still confused, don't worry – when it comes to the details of Hungarian transport timetables, so's everybody else...

In addition to the standard trains, MÁV Nosztalgia (*www.mavnosztalgia.hu*) operates a number of steam trains in summer months. MÁV also runs four narrow-gauge railways (Budapest Children's Railway, Balaton, Kecskemét and Nyíregyháza), and there are 12 maintained by United Forest Railways (ÁEV), some of them leading through national-park areas. For details of all these, check out the website http://narrowrail.net/hungary.

Tickets and timetables Train timetables can be confusing for the uninitiated (see box, page 56, for help with some of the abbreviations you might encounter). Those indicating arrivals (*érkezés*) are in yellow and those for departures (*indulás*) in white; faster trains are highlighted in red. Where there is automated information, the platform (*vágány*) number/letter will appear when the train is ready for boarding. If you've access to the internet, the MÁV website (see below) is a good way to plan your journey in advance.

Tickets (*jegy*) – single (*egy útra*) or return (*retur* or *oda-vissza*) – can be purchased from the departure station or (in Budapest) from the main **MÁV Ticket Office** (*V, József Attila u. 16;* ✆ *1 512 7918/7919;* ☉ *Mon–Fri 09.00–18.00; there's a second office at Keleti station*), which accepts credit cards. Unfortunately station staff may speak little English; if you want to take the hassle out of booking, deal instead with a travel agent (see page 99) or use the MÁV-Start website. This site – www.mav-start.hu (then click the 'English' button) – allows you to check your train route, timings and prices, as well as buy your ticket; in addition, there's a direct information and booking telephone line called MÁVDIREKT (✆ *1 371 9449 or 06 40 494949*). First-class tickets cost around 20% more than second-class. Where possible reserve your seat in advance, particularly for faster trains and when travelling to popular destinations in the summer period. Reservation is compulsory for intercity express services – look for the letter *R* in a circle or square on the timetable – and can be made up to 60 days in advance at MÁV offices. If you are caught without a ticket you can expect to be fined up to 6,000Ft.

Rail passes The **InterRail One Country Rail pass** allows 'free' travel (for European residents only) on the Hungarian network for between three and eight days within a one-month period. The price (*adult €71–139, under 26 €46–90*) depends upon how many days you want the pass to cover; passes are available from www.interrailnet.com. MÁV sells a **START Klub Card** (*6 months for over 26s/under 26s 14,900/19,900Ft, 1 year 24,900/34,900Ft*) that gives a 50% discount on tickets for second-class travel (excluding pre-booked tickets); on Saturday, it entitles two passengers to the discount. Full details at www.mav-start.hu.

BY BUS Buses reach the nooks and crannies that trains cannot, and can be a quicker alternative to the railway branch lines (although they are a touch pricier than 2nd-class train fares); they are often the only viable option in remoter regions of the Great Plain and Southern Transdanubia. They are generally comfortable, with adequate legroom, and on long journeys the driver will stop every few hours to allow passengers to stretch their legs. In towns and cities, there are usually separate stations for local and inter-city services; for details of those in Budapest, see page 93. The timetables posted in the bus stations are inevitably confusing; for help with the various symbols, see box, page 57. Volánbusz operates most of the domestic buses to and from Budapest as well as the majority of the regional lines (see www.volanbusz.hu for up-to-date timetables).

Tickets You can buy tickets aboard the buses or guarantee a seat by pre-booking from the relevant bus station (the latter is not possible in rural areas with bus stops only). Some routes can be busy, and it's worth turning up at least 30 minutes before departure. Bus fares are based upon the length of road travelled. The following is a guide to Volánbusz charges:

Distance	Cost	Distance	Cost
0–5km	135Ft	30km	480Ft
10km	210Ft	50km	795Ft
20km	320Ft	100km	1,590Ft

BY CAR Hungary is in some ways a walk in the park when you can drive in a car; the country's furthest reaches are within five or six hours of Budapest. The government has recently spent considerably on improving major roads and extending motorways. It's not all dreamy, though. Beyond the main routes, single-lane carriages can prove frustrating when stuck behind a choking Trabant held together with sticking tape and, at the other end of the spectrum, impatient boy racers can be a pain in the rear bumper. Hungarians tend to treat blind bends as overtaking opportunities too, and this can seem hairy at times. If you are involved in an accident, report to the police immediately before contacting Hungária Biztosító (*VII Budapest, kiraly u. 59/b;* ꕔ *1 237 2372*) – part of the Allianz group – a company that helps foreigners with insurance claims. Most petrol stations accept credit cards and sell unleaded fuel, and some are open 24 hours. There are often pump attendants on hand, and it's polite practice to give them a small tip. For information on the required driving licences etc, see page 47.

Roads Hungarian motorways are prefixed with the letter 'M' (see below), international roads with 'E' and smaller roads have two- or three-digit numbers (the first of which reflects the highway it joins). In Hungary there are nine dual carriageways, Roads 1–7 and 10 radiating from Budapest like a wagon wheel and Road 8 beginning at Székesfehérvár (and going westwards). (With typical Magyar perversity, the planners omitted a road numbered 9.) There are eight motorways. The **M0** ringroad half circles Budapest; the **M1** connects Budapest with Vienna via Győr; the **M3** ties the capital with the eastern part of the country, leading into Miskolc and going on to Nyíregyháza; the **M35** branches off the M3 to Debrecen; the **M30** also leads from the M3, going to Miskolc; the **M5** leads in a southerly direction from Budapest to Kecskemét and on to the border town of Röszke (past Szeged), providing access to Serbia and Montenegro and a direct connection to southern Europe; the **M6** goes south from Budapest (parallel with the Danube) and terminates at Dunaújváros (although an extension to Pécs will be completed shortly); the **M7** runs to the southern Balaton shore and on to Croatia.

All motorways require the payment of a **motorway toll permit**. These permits (*vignette* or *matrica*) should be purchased before you set wheel on the motorway and can be bought from petrol stations and post offices. Like the congestion-charge system in London, once you've paid your registration number is recorded – there is no physical permit to display on your car – but you should retain the receipt of purchase. For a car or motorbike whose weight does not exceed 3.5 tonnes, permits cost 1,170Ft for four days (1,530Ft May–Sep), 2,550Ft for seven days, 4,200Ft for a month and 37,200Ft for a year. For more information on the motorways, see www.autopalya.hu.

Emergency telephones (24-hour) are situated every few kilometres along most motorways. The Magyar Autóklub (ꕔ *1 345 1800; www.autoklub.hu*) provides a 24-hour breakdown service.

Driving laws You can't drink a drop of alcohol if you choose to drive as drinking and driving is strictly prohibited and the law fiercely enforced. Outside built-up areas, you should have dipped headlights switched on at all times (even during daylight hours). Seat belts are compulsory for all passengers. Vehicles drive on the right. Overtaking on the right is illegal, as is using a hand-held mobile phone while driving and tooting your horn in urban areas unless in an emergency. Speed limits are 130km/h on motorways, 110km/h on dual carriageways and 90km/h on all other roads (except in built-up areas, where the restriction is 50km/h). The police are hot on traffic violations and will indiscriminately pull over vehicles to check the credentials of both the cars and the drivers. On-the-spot fines of up to 10,000Ft can be issued by the police, with much heavier penalties by the authorities in the event of a more serious infringement. While it recently became compulsory for drivers to give way to pedestrians at pedestrian crossings, some drivers continue to break the rule, so be wary. For information on taxis, see Budapest's *Getting around*, pages 96–7.

Car hire To rent a car in Hungary you must be aged 21 or over, and in possession of a driving licence (valid for at least a year) and passport. You will need to leave a deposit – usually a temporary debit from your credit card. Some companies will deliver the car to your hotel (and pick it up again); the car will have a full petrol tank on delivery and you must ensure it is full when returned.

The following companies have good reputations:

Avis V Budapest, Szabadsag ter 7; ✆ 1 318 4240; international reservations ✆ +36 1 318 4685; e resoffice@avis.hu; www.avis.hu. Reliable company. *Cars from €437/week. Pick up & drop off available at airport.*

Fox Autorent XXII Budapest, Nagytétényi út 48–50; ✆ 1 382 9000; e fox@fox-autorent.com; www.fox-autorent.com. Full range of cars, most with A/C. There is the option of airport/home/hotel

delivery, & 24-hour road assistance. *Cars from €228 week.* ☉ *08.00–20.00 daily.*

Worldwide Rent A Car V Budapest, Sas utca 10–12; ✆ 1 302 0431; www.wwrentacar.com. Situated in front of the Basilica, on the corner of Sas Utca & Zrínyi utca. This is the place to try if you want to pay very little & don't mind an older, unflashy car with a high mileage. *Cars from about €20/day.*

 BY TAXI See pages 96–7.

BY BOAT **Mahart Passnave** (*V Budapest, Belgrád rakpart;* ✆ *1 484 4013/4010; www.mahartpassnave.hu*) operates hydrofoil and riverboat services between Budapest and destinations on the Danube Bend (Szentendre, Vác, Nagymaros, Visegrád and Esztergom) from spring to autumn. Full details are on the website, and we've listed specific information for the relevant towns in the *Getting there and away* sections of *Part Two*. The **Balaton Shipping Company** (*Balatoni Hajózás; Siófok, Krúdy sétány 2;* ✆ *84 310050; www.balatonihajozas.hu*) operates a ferry service (spring to autumn) for foot passengers across 22 ports around Lake Balaton; prices range from 1,040Ft to 1,560Ft depending on the distance you're travelling. In addition, the company offers a service for vehicles between Szántód and Tihany (⚙ *500/250Ft, motorcycle 750Ft, car 1,450Ft; runs all yr, unless the lake is frozen*).

BY BIKE There are 2,000km of cycling paths in Hungary, and this network is being extended all the time – in recent years, the development of the areas around Lake Tisza and Lake Fertő are particularly worthy of note. It's illegal to cycle on motorways or major roads (those marked with a one-digit number) and a white front headlight, and a red tail-light, yellow light reflectors on the spokes of both wheels, a bell (or similar) and working breaks are compulsory. Pedestrians may also use cycle lanes (although cyclists have right of way), so keep your eyes peeled. You may take bikes on trains for an additional 25% of the ticket price. However some intercity trains don't carry bikes – look out for a bicycle symbol on the timetable or check when purchasing your ticket. Before you set off, speak to the **Hungarian**

Bikers Association (*VI Budapest, Bajcsy-Zsilinszky út 31;* ☏ *1 311 2467*); in Budapest, the **Friends of the City Cycling Association** (*VBB; V, Curia u. 3, 2nd floor, Room 1;* ☏ *06 30 922 7064; www.vbb.hu – website in Hungarian only*) is also a good contact point, and arranges tours.

👍 **HITCHHIKING** Hitchhiking is prohibited on motorways, but is legal on all other roads, and is a popular way for students to get about. Hitching is as safe as it can be, but there is always an inherent risk in climbing into the vehicle of a stranger. If you want to hitchhike, travel in daylight and preferably with someone you know (particularly if you are female); if you are alone, keep a mobile phone to hand and notify someone beforehand of your intended destination and anticipated route.

🏠 ACCOMMODATION

There is no shortage of places to stay in Hungary, suiting all budgets and most whims. Once the state monopoly was undone in the 1980s, a wave of visitor accommodation rolled in that shows no signs of breaking (particularly now the country has joined the EU). The gamut of hotels runs from exclusive converted 19th-century mansions, luxury spa centres and upper-end conference hotels based on Western models, through comfortable mid-range affairs that have good facilities without every trimming, and on to basic joints that might be clean and well-kept or downright depressing and tatty. Overlapping them from the mid-range downwards are pensions, an imprecise label that is used equally by private guesthouses (often family-run) and smallish hotels that undercut (or hope the name gives the impression of undercutting) the prices of other hotels in the area. The very cheapest options of all are private rooms, campsites and beds in hostels or university digs. With the exception of campsites, hostels and the very top hotels (generally rooted in big cities or major tourist haunts), you can expect to find examples of each of the above in even little towns.

Deciding whether or not to **book ahead** depends on where you're going and when – and, in all honesty, your character. We've rarely had problems finding somewhere to lay our heads when we've turned up in a town, but we're a fairly happy-go-lucky and unfussy pair; if the day's end is something you'll worry about or you're after something specific, you should certainly make a reservation. Booking during festivals and events is strongly advised; remember too that summer (*Jun–Sep*) is high season, and crowds gather in Budapest, the Danube Bend, Lake Balaton, resorts in the Northern Uplands, and ever-popular pockets like Pécs and Sopron. At this time, spa towns in particular can reach capacity. Large hotels will invariably have English-speaking staff answering their telephones, as well as email and website booking services. It can be more complicated making arrangements with smaller hotels and pensions, who may or may not have English speakers manning the phone – they'll almost always understand some German – and may or may not have websites. In these cases you will usually make yourself understood in the end with a few basic words in Hungarian (see *Appendix 1*, page 523). An alternative is to use a local travel agency, and the Hungarian travel agent Ibusz can usually book private rooms; you'll pay a small fee for the service. Tourinform offices can offer advice on all types of accommodation, but do not themselves arrange bookings.

High-season accommodation **rates** – generally a 15–30% hike – can start as early as April and run as late as mid October; however, some city hotels exclude the hottest months of July and August (when many customers look elsewhere for cool air). The higher rates are also imposed at Christmas and New Year, and during festivals and events. The prices quoted in this book are walk-in high-season rates for a single night's stay; while these are inevitably subject to change, they were all researched during a four-month period and can therefore be used as a comparative guide. You can get reductions for advance and group bookings, and stays of more than one night. A 15% value-added tax (called ÁFA) and a variable local tourist tax (3% in Budapest) are usually included in the quoted price, but it is worth checking before accepting your room.

The following **websites** might prove useful when considering different accommodations types:

www.hah.hu The Hotel Association of Hungary
www.camping.hu Information on campsites & related facilities around the country

www.kastelyszallodak.hu Website listing Hungary's 'castle hotels' (usually converted manor houses & mansions)
www.falusiturizmus.info.hu Details of rural & agro-tourist accommodation

HOTELS While hotels (*szálló* or *szálloda*) are categorised according to a star system, this is a less reliable guide to facilities than in the West; you may find, for instance, that a four-star establishment has a swimming pool where a five-star does not. Nor can a star rating account for character, and some of the historic hotels fall outside the top bands. You can expect as a minimum that rooms in hotels above two-star category will have en-suite bathroom, TV and telephone; where bathrooms are shared, we say so. Top hotels offer satellite TV, fitness suite, sauna, restaurant, bar and sometimes boutiques and a swimming pool; those in the mid range will generally have a restaurant and fitness facilities of some sort, but beyond that are difficult to predict (they can surprise you with luxuries like saunas and swimming pools). 'Wellness' tourism – tapping into Hungary's rich resources of thermal water – is big business, and there are many spa hotels catering both to guests with specific medical complaints and those after a simple pampering.

Breakfast is a buffet spread; a peculiar (irritating!) quirk is that while it is generally included in the price of budget and mid-range accommodation, you may be charged extra in the higher-cost places. Many hotels can arrange bike hire, theatre trips and excursions. Most of the better hotels offer discounted deals on weekend breaks. (Keep an eye on websites like www.lastminute.com and www.expedia.com.) If you are travelling alone, be aware that there are few single rooms; while some hotels will charge a lower rate for a single occupant, others may insist on the full double-room price.

PENSIONS AND INNS At their finest, pensions (*panzió*) or inns (*fogadó*) represent better value than hotels in the same star bracket. Some are simply hotels by another name (and can have facilities including a restaurant, sauna and even, rarely, a small swimming pool). Others are the equivalent of guesthouses or bed and breakfasts – rooms in a family house – and are wholly fashioned by the tastes and energies of the owners. If you find a good 'un, a place run by warm and welcoming people who take pride and care in what they do, the stay can knock spots off that in any luxury hotel.

PRIVATE ROOMS AND APARTMENTS Bagging a bed in someone else's house is usually a far cheaper alternative to hotels and most pensions, and also allows you a peek behind domestic curtains. **Private rooms** can be arranged through an agency like Ibusz. In doing so, you accept a room unseen and clearly take a gamble of sorts; you can cut the odds by specifying a location in the very centre (Belváros), where buildings are likely to be better (and more convenient) than those in the suburbs (which can be tatty high-rise blocks). Alternatively you can knock at houses with *szoba kiadó* or *Zimmer frei* signs. Your hostess is likely to be a retired lady with but a smattering of English, so don't bank on any meaningful chitchat. Rooms usually have TV, bedding and towels. Expect to pay 3,500–6,500Ft for a single room and 4,500–10,000Ft for a double. Rates should include heating and electricity (but not food), and are dependent upon the season and duration (there may be a minimum length of stay to qualify for the quoted rate). Self-contained **apartments** are an alternative for families and small groups. Most come with a fully equipped kitchen, bed linen and towels, TV and radio. Rates include all utility costs.

HOSTELS AND COLLEGE ACCOMMODATION Beyond Budapest, **youth hostels** (*ifjúsági szálló*) can seem thin on the ground and are generally open in summer only. You rarely need a Hostelling International (IYHF) card, although this might get you a small reduction in price. Beds are available from around 2,500Ft. For further information or reservations, contact the Hungarian Youth Hostel Association (*www.miszsz.hu*).

During student vacations (and sometimes all year round), many **colleges** rent out vacant student rooms or dormitories. These can be offered for as little as 1,800Ft per person, and are the cheapest option of any available. Regional Tourinform offices can usually provide a list of colleges and contact numbers.

CAMPSITES It is illegal to camp rough. Camping grounds range from swish sites with restaurants, sports facilities and even swimming pools to lonely fields with little more than pitching space. In addition to a nightly charge for the ground rent for your tent or caravan, and for any other vehicle, you will usually also pay a charge per person per night on top of local tax. The charges vary (and are particularly high around Lake Balaton), but you can expect to pay from 700Ft/person, 700Ft/tent and 1,000Ft/caravan. Most campsites are open between April/May and September/October, although a few open all year. Some have wooden bungalows for those without tents (which may or may not have en-suite facilities), and others pensions and motels within their grounds. Tourinform produces a brochure showing all the country's campsites, or you can check online at www.campings.hu.

 EATING AND DRINKING

> I am not a glutton – I am an explorer of food.
>
> *Erma Bombeck (1927–96)*

FOOD Hungarian cuisine (*Magyar konyha*) has been influenced by the kitchens of Serbia, France and Turkey; the Renaissance court of King Mátyás introduced Italian ingredients like garlic, onion and dried pasta; the Germans and Austrians muscled in during the Austro-Hungarian period with their cream-filled desserts, sauerkraut and dumplings. All these tastes add nuances to a no-nonsense, homely tradition of peasant cookery.

Pork became a staple of the Hungarian diet after the Turkish invasion, when the Muslim occupiers left pigs wholly to the natives. Sour cream is handsomely applied to soups and sauces, as well as dishes of meat, cabbage and sweet pasta. Vegetable accompaniments are pickled or from the freezer, and salads plate-edge afterthoughts. The vegetarian diner may feel put upon in traditional restaurants, where the choice is often restricted to fruit soups and cheese or mushrooms in breadcrumbs. Cumin, caraway, black pepper and marjoram are frequently used for seasoning, but when you think Hungary it's red (*piros*) paprika that sets the tastebuds tingling. Probably introduced from Spain in the 16th century (although not widely used until the 19th), it imparts vivid culinary colour, and ranges in taste from sweet and fruity (*édes*) to fiery (*erős*), the latter proffering a kick like a hussar's horse. And woe betide he who gets between a Magyar and a piece of fresh bread (*kenyér*); it is regarded as the greatest of feasts.

While many busy Hungarians may just grab a roll on the run, if they greet the day properly then it is early and with a **breakfast** (*reggeli*) of open sandwiches. Salami (*szalámi*) or dried, chorizo-like sausage (*száraz kolbász*), ham, cheese, yellow pepper and tomato are eaten with white bread. The weekend may see omelettes on the table, while at Easter there is gammon-like ham with boiled eggs and horseradish. The reviving morning brew is hot (often black) coffee or tea with lemon (not milk).

Lunch is the main event, and comprises two courses. The first is likely to be soup (*leves*). Freshwater lakes like Balaton provide the specimens for fish soup (*halászlé*) – a customary dish on Christmas Eve. Chicken soup (*tyúk húsleves*) is packed with vegetables and light pasta (similar to Italian *vermicelli*), while fruit soup (*hideg gyümölcsleves*) is a refreshing summer slurp, flavoured with cherry or strawberry, topped with cream and served cold. The smoky, meaty kidney-bean soup (*jókai bableves*) can be gorgeous. The international superstar is, of course, goulash (actually *gulyás*, and pronounced 'gooyash'), strictly a soup rather than a stew, and containing beef or pork, pinched dumplings, vegetables and the ubiquitous paprika. Cooked in a cauldron (*bogrács*), its roots can be traced to the country's nomadic ancestors. The meaty Hortobágy pancake (*Hortobágyi húsos palacsinta*) is a speciality of the Great Plain; seasoned minced pork or poultry is folded into thin pancakes and baked in a sauce of paprika and sour cream. Please don't miss this one – it shades the number-one spot on our Hungarian-dish wish list.

The second course is invariably a meat-based rib sticker, usually served with weighty side dishes including egg dumplings (*galuska* or *nokedli*), couscous-type pasta (*tarhonya*), potato croquettes (*krokett*) and rice. A traditional stew (*pörkölt*) might be concocted from any of the main meats, but our vote goes to that with chicken (*csirkepaprikás*) – creamy, golden as toffee, and occasionally with the coxcomb thrown in! Other popular choices are stuffed cabbage (*töltött káposzta*) or pepper (*töltött paprika*) filled with minced meat, a piece of the earthy-tasting pike perch (*fogas*), and a plate-sized slab of Wiener schnitzel (*bécsi szelet*). The latter is often eaten for Sunday lunch.

Pudding (*édességek* or *desszertek*) requires a healthy appetite and a sweet tooth. Any room for a cake, an ice cream, a strudel or a crêpe? At times savoury becomes sweet; *túróscsusza* is a hot pastry with ricotta, sour cream and – believe it or not – pork crackling. Pastas, too, are familiar dessert dishes. *Rétes* is an Austrian strudel filled with either fruit, walnut, peppery cabbage or poppy seeds and ricotta, while walnut cream and chocolate sauce is the heavenly mix in a Gundel pancake (*Gundel palacsinta*). For other sweet options, see box, page 66.

DRINK Thirsty? Big-name fizzy **soft drinks** are available everywhere, as are bottled mineral waters (*ásványvíz*) and fruit juices. Hungarians satisfy regular coffee cravings (see page 67); although they are less enamoured with tea, which is sipped straight or with lemon, teahouses are popping up with growing frequency in Budapest. For something stronger, fruit **brandy** (*pálinka*) is a popular tipple – even at breakfast time for rural diehards. It's distilled from apricots (*barack*), plums (*szilva*), pears (*körte*), cherries (*cseresznye*) or peaches (*őszibarack*), although if you try a home brew – a common hobby of the older generation – you'll get some fire with your fruit. Another *apéritif* is the herbal and distinctive Unicum, said to have been invented by the court physician to József II, and distilled by the Zwack family for 200 years. Many claims have been made for this bitter liquid – that it is an aid to digestion, a restorative and even an aphrodisiac; the only undeniable truth is that it is an acquired taste. Drink it straight, with cola or even as a hot toddy. And give it as many second chances as you feel able. (There is a small museum in the Budapest Zwack plant at Soroksári út 26; contact them on 1 476 2383 to arrange a visit.)

Much **beer** (*sör*) is imported from the Czech Republic or brewed under the licence of foreign companies like Tuborg and HB, but Hungarian beers are deserving of attention. They might be bottled or on tap, and fall into two types – lager (*világos*) and brown (*barna*), the latter similar in colour to English bitter but with a sweet flavour. The leading breweries are Dreher, Soproni and Borsodi, the first marginally our preferred choice, while other regional brands can be found in the supermarkets. The word for 'cheers!' – *egészségedre* – is a mouthful at the best of times, but becomes a particular trial after a drink or two.

It is said that Hungarians can be divided into the few who produce **wine** and the many who would dearly love to. For much of the 20th century, you'd be forgiven for thinking the amateurish majority had been let loose on the vineyards. There was a massive decline in quality behind the Iron Curtain; vineyards were neglected, fine sites abandoned, and state co-operatives devoted themselves to mass production. During the 1980s, Hungary's main export, Bull's Blood, became a byword for vinegar; the Soviets were the sole bulk buyers. However, change has been rapid since the advent of privatisation. Joint ventures with foreign vintners and investment in technology have resulted in some fine wineries, many of them family-owned.

Some facts. There are 22 wine regions and around 20 Hungarian grape varieties. Seventy-five per cent of wines are white (*fehér bor*), although recently it is the reds (*vörös bor*) that have attracted attention. In very rough terms – there are exceptions – white is produced in the north and red in the south. Grapes include Hungarian and imported varieties. Good-to-fine white wines are made from Furmint (the base wine of Tokaji Aszú), Királyleányka, Hárslevelű, Irsai Olivér and Olaszrizling, along with Sauvignon, Chardonnay and Tramini. Quality home-grown reds include Kékfrankos (the most widely planted) and Kadarka, while Cabernet, Merlot and Pinot Noir have all been produced at very respectable levels. Reds are characteristically light because of the country's cold winters, and they are often served at a lower temperature than you might usually expect. There is a Hungarian equivalent of the French *appellation controlée*, so before buying check for *minőségi* (quality) or *különleges minőségi* (special quality) on the bottle. During the day and in bars, wine is sometimes mixed with soda or sparkling water to make a spritzer (*fröccs*).

WHERE TO EAT AND DRINK Light bites of pickles, cold meats and sandwiches are available to take away from delicatessens in towns, while those who want to take the weight off their feet for a short while seek out a *bisztró* or *büfé*, which offer small selections of hot food alongside filled rolls. Burger and sandwich (*szendvics*) stands are burgeoning in cities, together with global fast-food giants that vie with cheaper kebab shops and Chinese buffets. Otherwise seek out a place selling *főzelék*, dishes of puréed vegetables (not unlike baby food) that are cooked in the home but generally overlooked by restaurants. They can be made from whatever vegetables are in season and make great bar food. The pumpkin version is very tasty, if you like gloop. One popular snack on the move is a *perec*, a large and salty piece of pretzel-shaped bread (try to avoid stands where they are uncovered and therefore likely to be stale), and another a *lángos*, something of a bulky hybrid of the Yorkshire pudding and the doughnut. A *lángos* is often topped with ladlefuls of runny garlic sauce, sour cream and cheese, and is enough to give your heart an attack just looking at it. Fresh produce is available in supermarkets, but head instead for outdoor markets or market halls, which have an excellent array of meat, fish, vegetables and fruit.

Restaurants There are several words for different types of restaurant, although in reality some are used interchangeably. *Étterem* or *vendéglő* indicate a restaurant, the latter supposedly a cheaper establishment than the former (although this is by no means always true), while you can usually expect traditional Hungarian specialities

You'll have no problem sating that craving for sweetness. Hungary's restaurants, cafés and (especially) pâtisseries promise things naughty but nice. If you can forget the scales, the doctor's orders and your conscience's wagging finger, below are some of the treats that await you.

CAKE

Dobos torta Dobos József, a master chef, prepared his cake for the Hungarian National Exhibition of 1885, and it worked gourmets and confectioners into a drooling frenzy. Competitors were desperate to learn the recipe, and orders flooded in from home and abroad. It became Hungary's most famous cake. Five layers of white sponge filled with chocolate cream and glazed caramel on top.

Sacher torta Rich chocolate cake with jam running through the middle. Originated in Vienna.

Gyümölcs torta Sponge cake with fruits and whipped cream.

Rigó Jancsi A two-inch-square sponge cake with chocolate cream and chocolate glaze atop.

Somlói galuska Layers of sponge cake, rich chocolate sauce, walnuts, raisins and a whirl of whipped cream served in a bowl.

PANCAKES, PASTRIES AND STRUDELS

Palacsinta Crêpes with a choice of fillings, such as sweet cottage cheese, nuts, fruit, chocolate cream or jam. The classic dish of this family is the Gundel palacsinta, a folded pancake containing walnut and rum filling and drenched in chocolate sauce and more rum. It may be served flaming. Flaming good.

Krémes Square flaky pastries with French pâtisserie and whipped cream.

Rétes Strudels are available with a range of fillings, including cherry (*meggyes*), sweet cottage cheese (*túrós*), and poppy seeds (*mákos*).

ICE CREAMS

Fagylalt There can be no nation more committed in its devotion to ice cream. Roadside vendors, pâtisseries and ice-cream parlours (*fagylaltozó* or *fagyizó*) really are hubs of the community in summer, and they'll do a very respectable trade in winter too. *Fagyi* (the slang term) is served in cones and you pay by the scoop (*gombóc*). The range of flavours can be daunting – anything from vanilla to poppy seed.

in a *csárda* (inn). Lunch is customarily the main meal of the day, but restaurants in cities cater equally for the evening crowd; despite this, you risk bed without supper if you arrive much later than 22.00 (and aim for 20.30 or earlier in the provinces). What, then, can you expect from the dining experience? How long's a piece of string? There are courtyard gardens and river terraces, brick cellar restaurants and dining rooms, modern lounges and rustic spaces strung with dried paprika. Traditional restaurants range from classy and intimate to cavernous coach-party traps. You might be treated to the lively strains of a gypsy violinist, or suffer the tinny torture of a cheap synthesiser. While Hungarians (and especially

Budapesters) no longer double-take on seeing a vegetarian restaurant, in the main those averse to meat are poorly catered for; even the obligatory fried vegetables are sometimes cooked in animal fat. Beyond the top restaurants, the quality of service can vary, and it's not unusual for a waiter to don the proverbial blinkers – although we should stress that we noticed a considerable improvement in service standards when researching this second edition. If you aren't entirely satisfied, don't tip.

What else to bear in mind? You shouldn't have difficulty securing a table in the majority of restaurants, although it is worth booking at the best. Dress codes are generally relaxed; Gundel (see page 108) is the exception rather than the rule in requiring male diners to wear jackets in the evening. Don't order if food or drink menus are missing prices, and always check your bill carefully. Despite the brilliance of the Hungarian mind, errors of calculation are common and curiously tend to fall above the line rather than below it. Ask whether a service charge is included – it usually isn't – and tip ten–15 per cent if you're satisfied. (For tipping etiquette, see pages 81–2.) Major credit cards are usually accepted in cities, but always ask in advance if you haven't got cash in reserve. The individual **price guides** in this book are based on the average price of a main course.

Pâtisseries and coffee houses Hungarians love sugar and caffeine in equal measure. By rights, they should spend their days bouncing off the walls and their nights in wide-eyed insomnia. **Pâtisseries** (*cukrászda*) display a tempting selection of cakes, pastries and ice creams. Some are shops selling sticky things to take away, while others allow you to have your cake and eat it amid chandeliers and marble, and with a coffee at your elbow. You'll find cakes in **coffee houses** (*kávéház*), too. At the turn of the 20th century, there were nearly 1,000 coffee houses in the Hungarian capital, with a staggering 64 places along the Nagy körút alone to drink the 'black soup' (*fekete leves*). As in many continental countries, these places were traditionally kaleidoscopes of social colour where newspapers were read, politics discussed, poems composed and rebellions plotted (see page 109). Penniless poets would famously settle bills with sonnets written on napkins. Coffee still very much matters. The standard cup is a small and strong espresso (*eszpresszó* or *kávé*). You can order it with milk (*tejeskávé*), but beyond that the standard varies. A cappuccino may be little more than a filter coffee with whipped cream, and isn't worth a scribbled couplet.

Bars etc The various categories of watering hole might confuse the raw Western recruit. Far from upmarket, a wine bar (*borozó*) often equates to a den of men drinking rough vintages ladled from metal drums for 30Ft a decilitre. You might find spit and sawdust in a beer hall (*söröző*), too, but you are just as likely to find a well-turned-out pub. The word *pince* indicates a cellar, be that a brick beer tavern with wooden benches or a place for tasting wine (*borospince*) from regional vineyards. Some wineshops (*italbolt*) also offer tastings. Modern bars often bear the name 'café', and are contemporary reinterpretations of an earlier coffee-house culture that declined in the mid-20th century; they may serve food and coffee, and have music and dancing, but they are more bar than traditional café or club. When wetting your whistle, you can order draught beer by the half-litre (*korsó*) or smaller (*pohár*) glass, while wine is served by the bottle (*üveg*), by the glass (*pohár*) or – usually in wine bars – by the decilitre.

PUBLIC HOLIDAYS AND FESTIVALS

Hungary's promotional literature justifiably makes much of its status as a country of festivals. This is a cultured place with a proud musical heritage, a place of wine production and regional variants in cuisine, and one keen to preserve folk

The week leading up to Easter is a busy one for the women of Hungarian households, who perform a thorough spring clean and go into baking overdrive. In addition, they paint hard-boiled eggs with folksy motifs and patterns, and present them to visitors as Easter gifts. The celebrations themselves begin on Good Friday, with mass services held at 15.00 in churches all over the city. On Easter Sunday, following morning services, children are treated with chocolate eggs and small presents from the Easter Bunny. The real fun, though, comes on Easter Monday, when the traditional 'sprinkling' (*locsolkodás*) takes place. Men customarily 'sprinkle' their female relatives and friends with cheap perfume, in return for which they receive a reward – a painted egg, some chocolate coins or a shot of *pálinka* (potent fruit brandy). The latter reward means that by mid-afternoon there can be some rather giddy sprinklers! Originally this ritual was a fertility rite, when men visited the single women of the village and sprinkled their friends and relatives along the way. Even today it is used as a form of courtship. It is less sodden than it was in the past, however – when buckets of water were used in the villages rather than cologne.

traditions (at least for a few days a year). You'll find the staples are performances of music, song, dance and theatre, wine and food galore, processions and floats, and demonstrations of folk art or equestrian pageantry. However, there are some weird and wonderful ones among the line-up – the world's biggest celebration of fish soup in Baja, *gulyás* cooks fighting for the coveted 'golden stirring spoon' in Gyöngyös, celebrants prancing about in hairy suits and sinister masks on Shrove Tuesday in Mohács. And of course on the patron saint's day a 1,000-year-old mummified hand is paraded through the streets. Top that!

Festivals are celebrated throughout the country throughout the year, although the greatest concentration is between June and August, and the real biggies are in Budapest (particularly the Spring and Autumn festivals). Information on regional festivals and events are included under the relevant city, town or village sections. The following public holidays are celebrated annually (note that most businesses and shops close on these days).

January 1	New Year's Day
March 15	Independence Day
March/April	Easter Monday
May 1	Labour Day
May/June	Whit Monday
August 20	St Stephen's Day (founding of the state)
October 23	Republic Day (anniversary of the 1956 revolution and the 1989 proclamation of the republic)
November 1	All Saints' Day
December 25–26	Christmas (*Karácsony*)

Hungarians celebrate Christmas on December 24, so – while it's not an official holiday – companies often grant their employees that day off.

🛒 SHOPPING

Popular gifts or souvenirs include wine, foods and spices (see box opposite), and folk art (embroidered tablecloths and napkins, decorated boxes, hand-made dolls and wooden toys, and painted vases, jugs and mugs) – for the latter you're best to head for the regional sources (like Kalocsa, Hollókő and Mezőkövesd for embroidery, and Hódmezővásárhely, Tiszafüred and Hajdúszoboszló for pottery) rather than tourist-tat shops in Budapest. You won't have difficulty finding a piece of porcelain either, contemporary or antique. There are delicate Hollóháza ceramics and chunky Sárospatak pots. However, Herend and Zsolnay are the premier manufacturers, each established for over 150 years, and producing hand-moulded dishes, bowls, figurines and, in the latter's case, vivid majolica roof tiles. Herend is classy and conservative, while Zsolnay is distinctive for the dark iridescence of some of its pieces, like the feathers of a cormorant. These two are the dinner-service favourites of quality restaurants; discreetly check the maker's mark under your next *gulyás* bowl. Ajkas produces quality leaded crystal.

FOOD GIFTS

If you seek a tasty gift or a flavoursome reminiscence of your trip, there are a variety of specialities available in the shops, market halls and supermarkets. How about:

SAUSAGE/SALAMI (*kolbász/szalámi*) You'll find a wide selection behind the supermarket's meat counter or hanging from market stalls, ranging from mild to spicy (*csípős*). The best-known brand is Pick salami, manufactured in Szeged. Some *kolbász* needs to be cooked, rather like standard English sausages. Be aware that meats brought into the UK must be vacuum packed – you can be fined for packing a bare *kolbász*.

RED PAPRIKA (*piros paprika*) The crimson spice of Hungarian life can be bought as a dried whole or in finely ground form. There are seven strengths: mild (*különleges*), also mild (*csípősségmentes*), mildish (*csemege* – the most commonly used in Hungarian dishes), medium (*édes-nemes*), slightly hot (*félédes*), hot (*rózsa*) and very hot (*erős* or *csípős*). You'll pay more for a fancy presentation bag. One of the main centres of production is Kalocsa.

GOOSE LIVER Available in black-and-gold tins, liver is produced by the Merian Orosháza Rt of Orosháza (in the heart of goose-gagging country), who have a monopoly on the goose-liver market. A 200g tin costs 5,000Ft.

CAVIAR A popular offering among the tins of goose liver and the Tokaji in market halls. It's not Hungarian, but it is cheap by Western standards – ranging from 4,500Ft to 21,000Ft (and small tins of Russian Astrakhan caviar for 4,000Ft). Tins are usually marked '*malosol*' (meaning 'little salt').

WINE (*bor*) 'Wine is sunlight, held together by water', Galileo once observed. He very probably hadn't been to Kecskemét. However, there are some among the country's 22 regional wines that are very worth drinking; those particularly favoured by connoisseurs internationally are the sweet, white Tokaji Aszú (in its distinctive long-necked bottle) and Bull's Blood (Bikavér) from Eger or Szekszárd.

SPIRITS Brandy or grappa (*pálinka*) is a popular digestif. Kecskemét redeems itself with an apricot brandy (*barack pálinka*), and there are other fruity flavours that'll take the skin off your tongue (see page 64). Alternatively, take back some Unicum, a 'healthy' spirit concocted from a secret recipe of herbs. The branding is striking, with its dark orb of a bottle and a disconcerting poster of a man emerging from water that has become an advertising classic, but the taste is of the 'acquired' variety.

The run-away winners in the shopping stakes, both in terms of value for money and all-round atmosphere, are bustling **market halls** (*vásárcsarnok*) and **flea markets** (*bolha piac* or *ócskapiac*). In most cases – and particularly if buying fresh food – it is best to get there early. It's strictly cash only; your flexible friend will be laughed all the way to the nearest bank. You should not try to haggle in market halls, but you can do so in flea markets – although Hungarians are not very enthusiastic barterers, and tend to seem a bit fed up with the process.

Everyday items are widely available in towns and cities. Non-food shops are isually open ☺ 10.00–18.00 on weekdays and 09.00–13.00 on Saturdays, while those selling foodstuffs are open 07.00–19.00 during the week and 07.00–14.00 on Saturdays. Malls will often keep longer hours (that include Sundays), and markets shorter ones that vary from site to site. International stores and malls in cities accept credit cards, but you're best to carry cash to be guaranteed of closing deals elsewhere. See *Money*, page 53, for details of tax that non-Europeans can reclaim on goods.

🎭 ARTS AND ENTERTAINMENT

Since the 19th century, culture has been an important touchstone of Hungarian self-identity – initially as a means of tacit resistance to occupation. It is celebrated in regular festivals, and there are plenty of places in Budapest and other main cities to let dinner settle over performances of folk music, opera, dance or Hungarian takes on jazz, blues and rock. Alternatively you could let good digestion wait on some energetic clubbing.

Hungary has good reason to be proud of its **classical** heritage. Concert performances are two-a-penny, offering home-grown and international talent, although in the hot months these are more likely to be outdoor. **Operas** in Budapest are full-blown affairs, with elaborate sets and luxuriant costume. They are also often performed in Hungarian, which is considerably less romantic than Italian but probably no worse than English. Opera buff or not, you should take advantage of the ridiculously cheap tickets for performances at the stunning State Opera House. Attending performances of Shakespeare in Hungarian probably doesn't sound much fun (and isn't), but you'll find the odd English-language **theatre** and performance (particularly in Budapest – the Madhouse company, for instance, stages English-language performances at the National Theatre, although tickets sell quickly so you'll need to book some time in advance to guarantee a seat).

Most venues have their own box offices, but you can also secure seats for performances at ticket agencies (*jegyiroda*) and cultural centres. Even small towns have **cultural centres**, which are often the first ports of call for information on what's on while you're there. Cultural centres frequently host events and exhibitions themselves, and are also the places for *táncház* evenings (see page 29). Alternatively, pick up a copy of *Programme in Ungarn/in Hungary* (from Tourinform), a bilingual monthly publication listing performances scheduled around the country; *Pesti Est* and its regional equivalents also have such listings, although they are in Hungarian only. Several English-language magazines provide information on forthcoming events in Budapest, including the free magazine *Funzine*.

If you want to watch a Hollywood blockbuster in a mainstream **cinema**, head for an American-style shopping mall, which often holds multiplexes. Many are in the original English with Hungarian subtitles, although comedies are frequently dubbed. If a film is advertised with its English title, you can assume it will be subtitled; alternatively look for *feliratos* (or *fel*) in the listings. Dubbed films are indicated by *magyarul beszélő* (or *mb*). Be wary of the peculiar Hungarian way of displaying times (see *Time*, page 81). It is a source of great shame that some of Budapest's art-house cinemas have been forced to close. Nevertheless, investment by the Budapest Film Company has meant that many others have been renovated, and they showcase art films from Hungary and other countries, often in intimate and ambient screening rooms.

The popularity of **museums** came with the emergence of the middle classes, the growth of an urban population and the 19th-century urge to reassert – and display – Hungarian nationhood and heritage. There was a particular boom between 1867 and 1914, prosperous years, and the period of the Millennial Exhibition. The legacies of these enlightened patrons among the upper-middle or noble classes remain in Budapest, often framed by magnificent works of architecture. There is no shortage of museums and galleries beyond the capital either – Pécs has a specific street devoted to them. Museums are generally closed on Mondays, and open between 10.00 and 18.00 on other days during high season (although ticket offices often shut up to an hour before closing time). Hours are usually shorter in winter. You may be charged an admission fee, and permission to take photos or videos inside costs a significant amount extra. Guided tours may or may not be in English; museum attendants, often elderly ladies, may or may not speak English. We list prices – indicated **with a 'coins' symbol** – for adults and concessions (always children, and often students and EU pensioners over the age of 62). Note that EU citizens of 70 and over should be allowed entry to permanent exhibitions free of charge; show your passport.

Nightlife is best in the capital, which has the choicest clubs (including outdoor beach-style ones in summer), and at the southern shore of Lake Balaton in summer. Beyond that it varies, although you'll be sure to find lively places to dance away the early hours in student cities and towns. As you'd expect, DJs and drum 'n' base are thin on the ground in rural areas.

For further information on arts in Hungary, see the *Culture* section.

THERMAL BATHS

A British novel was once much derided for its all-too-descriptive description of love's 'liquid noises'. Well, there may be no shoreline, but the sounds of Hungarian passion are those of splashing and soaking and dripping and gulping, all liquid noises with bells on. Hungary is afloat on a hot reservoir of water that breaks the surface through natural springs and drilled wells. There are almost 400 registered thermal springs in 85 different locations. The thermal water absorbs minerals from the earth's crust, and the Ministry of Health has recognised the medicinal properties of 50 of the country's baths. Budapest is unique among the world's capitals in offering such a plethora of places to bathe; beyond it, some previously obscure towns now purr under the attention of tourists drawn by the prospect of a warming wallow.

2

HISTORY The **Romans** were the first to take advantage of Hungary's hot springs in any sophisticated sense. There were 14 baths in Budapest alone. Aquincum holds stretches of an aqueduct that channelled spring waters from the hills, and the central military complex at Florian tér is the largest of the country's 21 Roman baths. Many centuries later, Buda became Hungary's courtly centre and a bathing culture bloomed once more. Zsigmond built the Imre Bath (today called Rác fürdő) in the 15th century, and Matyás even added a corridor linking them to the palace. However, it was the Turks who constructed a baths network. They blended Roman bathing traditions with their own, and remains of these bathhouses – with main halls and pools – are the period's noticeable surviving monuments in the capital. Eight were recorded by a 17th-century English traveller, and of these the Rác, Császár, Király and Rudas still stand.

Advances in engineering and the development of '**balneology**' (the science of medicinal waters) provided fresh impetus in the 19th century. Baths were built or renovated by some of the country's greatest architects. In 1937 Budapest received the official title 'Bath Town/Spa City' from the first International Balneological Congress. In the aftermath of World War II, many were subsumed into the social-security system and rendered dull by socialist-style renovation. However, Hungary embarked on a huge programme in the '60s and '70s to develop hotels offering facilities focused around medicinal water. In the past ten years, therapies have come to include gymnastics, massage and electrotherapy, but healing waters remain the mainstay in this natural approach to treatment. In addition, there are numerous (usually seasonal) outdoor pools (*strand*), which are particularly popular on steamy summer days. While some of these have medicinal waters, and are occasionally linked to hotels or day-time hospitals, they are more properly areas for relaxation and recreation.

THERAPY The medicinal spring waters of Hungary are usually over 30°C (although there are a few outdoor medicinal baths that are cooler), and contain a range of minerals. **Spa treatments** are recommended for those suffering from arthritic and rheumatic pain (muscle tension, aches), blood-circulation or breathing difficulties, for those requiring injury rehabilitation, and those with chronic gynaecological problems or certain skin conditions. And some baths have drinking halls where you can swallow as well as wallow.

Visitors can choose how they approach these soups of minerals. Some just enjoy spending a few hours sitting in the regenerative waters and enjoying their warmth. Others take advantage of the packages available at thermal hotels. Treatments beyond general dips in the pools or tubs, or refreshing massages (such as mud or weight baths, healing massages, etc) require a medical referral. Hungarians receive prescriptions from specialised physicians, and they pay a small fee to the cashier (subsidised under the country's social-security system). However, professional bath physicians on site provide consultations for other visitors (for a charge).

Besides the public bathing complexes, there are also **hotels** offering treatment packages. These divide into two types – thermal hotels (*gyógyszálló*) and 'wellness' hotels, which cater for the modern interest in health tourism. Thermal hotels are based at the sites of thermal springs, and have spa therapy centres. They provide traditional Hungarian remedies, and have tended to cater to the older market; however, most offer fitness centres and other 'luxuries', and increasingly attract a younger crowd. While wellness hotels are generally located in spa cities, they have neither on-site medicinal waters nor medical centres. Instead they represent non-medical health retreats, where the focus is upon the promotion of well-being through pampering and exercise.

BATHS AND THE BATHING EXPERIENCE A decade or so ago, **thermal baths** were primarily frequented by the mature lady or gent; however, these days you'll find wrinkled palms among younger Magyars too. Indeed, the pools in some ways fulfil the same function as coffee houses, allowing people to gather, chat and relax.

Thermal baths are very different from recreational swimming pools, and even those with fabulous ornamentation tend to have areas that feel like a sanatorium (with white tiles and staff in starched uniforms). Complexes usually comprise several pools or bathtubs, together with saunas or steam rooms. Bathing is often mixed, although some establishments offer same-sex bathing on different days of the week (and Budapest's Gellért Baths have separate pools). You will be provided with a **changing cabin** or a **locker** (for extra security, the locker number differs from the tag you are issued with – the tag number is chalked on the inside of the locker door by the attendant – so be sure to memorise the locker number itself), and sometimes a bathrobe on getting changed. **Swimming costumes** are usually worn (you can hire a costume or towel if you have come without) – although same-sex pools may allow nude bathing, and men are issued with aprons at baths like the Rudas in Budapest. You will on occasions be required to don a **swimming cap**. The medicinal pools are peaceful places for sitting and soaking. There is usually a **swimming pool** on the same site, however, for those of a more energetic disposition.

It is generally recommended that you spend 20–30 minutes in the **medicinal pools**, depending upon the concentration of the minerals. For the purposes of healing, regular visits are important. Doctors provide patients with prescriptions, and Hungarians receive state-subsidised discounts for up to two courses of 15 visits. Without a doctor's prescription, visitors cannot receive specialised treatments beyond healing massages and bathing; as a tourist, you'll need to join the queue of those with prescriptions to arrange a consultation with the **on-site physicians**. If you receive a treatment, it is good etiquette to **tip** the 'gate keepers'. If you are simply taking a dip in the baths, tip the locker *néni* about 100Ft; masseurs make little in wages, and should be tipped 400Ft or so. Beware, though, that queues to buy tickets can be long because patients with social-security referrals often use the same entrance as 'temporary' visitors. Cashiers rarely speak English.

Where the entrance price to the baths exceeds 1,000Ft, there may be a graded system of **refund** whereby a certain portion of money is returned if the visitor leaves within four hours. Note that children can only use recreational facilities, such as swimming pools, and are prohibited from the medicinal pools. Try too to bring your own towel – while you can hire these at the baths, they tend to be little more than bedsheets and rather lacking in absorbency...

SPORT AND ACTIVITIES

Hungary has no preening, globally recognised sporting icon in the David Beckham mould, but the country has traditionally punched above its weight on the sporting stage. Don't mention the 2008 Olympics (at which Hungary performed poorly), but the 2004 Athens Olympics saw the country finish in a creditable 13th place overall with a haul of 18 medals. Hungarians could actually argue that in a historical context this was a below-par performance; they have won over 160 gold medals in all Olympics, positioning them at eighth in the games' world rankings. They placed third in 1952 and 1968, and were fourth in 1956 (a year that is remembered for other things). The country enjoys an enviable reputation in fencing, the pentathlon and water polo. Among more cerebral celebrated successes was that at chess in 1988, when a quartet of child prodigies – including the three

With 43,252,003,274,489,856,000 possible moves, it isn't surprising that many of us have been driven to breaking open the infamous Rubik's cube with a screwdriver to rearrange the pieces or, more often than not, peeling off the stickers and putting them back one by one (guilty as charged!). What is perhaps more surprising is that the creation of Rubik's *'Bűvös kocka'* ('Magic Cube' in Hungarian) was very much an accident.

Born in a bomb shelter during World War II, Ernő Rubik started out as an architect and teacher, initially interested in investigating the geometry of 3-D forms. His source of inspiration for the cube actually came one summer's day on the banks of the Danube while remarking on the shape of rounded river pebbles. Keen to help his students appreciate the dynamics of three-dimensionality, and fascinated by the possibility of moving the individual blocks of a cube independently without the whole thing falling apart, Rubik began creating the rounded architecture for the interior of the famous cube.

Each coloured face was composed of three rows and three columns; the central cube of each was attached to an internal mechanism that allowed it to rotate through 360°. Rubik began to twist, intrigued to see how 'after only a few turns, the colours become mixed, apparently in random fashion', which brought him face to face with the 'Big Challenge' – how to return the colours to their original positions. He hypothesised that through randomly twisting it could take more than a lifetime. So he began working on a solution, aligning the eight corner 'cubies' and following sequences of moves in an attempt to get back to the start.

Realising what he had hit on, Rubik quickly applied for a patent. The cube became an icon of the 1980s, enchanting people of all ages and nationalities. 'Cubic Rubes' appeared (fans eager to solve the puzzle in the fastest possible time) and formed clubs. Winning the Toy of the Year award in 1980, the Rubik's Cube even got its own entry in the *Oxford English Dictionary*. 'Rubik's wrist' became a medical condition, where cube fanatics developed what we now know as Repetitive Strain Injury. Rubik was perhaps right when he claimed that 'we turn the cube and it, in turn, twists us'.

The mind-bending puzzle can in fact be solved in just 52 moves – an amazing feat when there is only one correct answer and 43 trillion wrong ones! It was at the first World Championships in Budapest in 1982 that a 16-year-old Vietnamese student from the US became champion by unscrambling a cube in less than 23 seconds. This world record has since been beaten by Denmark's Jess Bonde, who solved the puzzle in 16.53 seconds in 2003. Since its appearance 30 years ago, Rubik's brain child has become the best-selling toy in history. As the first self-made millionaire from the communist block, Rubik has also set up a foundation for promising inventors and is still, to this day, creating games and puzzles to continue and develop his theories on geometrics.

Polgár sisters, the youngest just ten years old – won the women's team event at the Chess Olympics in Athens, defeating the seasoned Russian champions.

For Budapest offices selling **tickets** to sporting events, see page 114.

FISHING There are countless places to go fishing, which is a very popular pastime. You'll need to obtain a State Angling Ticket (valid for a year and covering the whole country) and an Area Permission for the particular place you wish to fish (daily, weekly or yearly passes are available). You can usually buy both tickets at the same place – they're sold in angling shops, by angling associations or often at a ticket office at the given body of water. The National Federation of Hungarian Anglers (*MOHOSZ; XII Budapest, Korompai u. 17; www.mohosz.hu*) can provide fuller information on regulations and the best places to cast a line. There is English-language text on the helpful website. Alternatively, you could try the Association of Fishermen in Greater Budapest (*Nagybudapesti Horgászok Egyesülete; V Budapest, Váci u. 46;* ↘ *1 209 5882;* ☉ *Mon–Fri 09.00–17.00*), which can give information, and sells permits. The portal http://horgasz.lap.hu is a starting page with links to many fishing sites.

FOOTBALL Football is the country's favourite game, and Hungary was once a round-ball heavyweight. Between 1950 and 1954, under the leadership of Ferenc Puskás, the national team went unbeaten; its most heralded victory came when pummelling England 6–3 during a friendly at Wembley in 1953. This is now but a distant 1950s memory, a sepia-tinted time of pig-skin balls and long shorts. Poor funding and financial problems have crippled the sport to such an extent that Hungary hasn't qualified for a major tournament since 1986. The most-successful club side is Budapest's Ferencváros, who play at the FTC Stadium (*IX, Üllői út 129; see www.ftc.hu for information on fixtures*).

GOLF Hungary has no tradition in the sport of golf, and courses are inevitably thin on the ground. However, several good-quality courses have been established in recent years, largely because of the influence of foreign investment. Most close during winter, although any hotel/spa facilities remain open. You can find full information on the websites www.golfszovetseg.hu and www.hungolf.hu, but a few of the best 18-hole courses are listed below.

Birdland Golf & Country Club Bükfürdő, Golf út 4; ↘ 94 558700; www.birdland.hu. Built in 1991, Birdland was the country's first international championship course. There's a 5-star hotel & spa facilities too.
European Lakes Golf and Country Club Hencse, Kossuth Lajos u. 1–3; ↘ 30 516 1488; www.europeanlakes.com. Located in the Zselic Nature Reserve in southwest Hungary, the course was influenced in design by Augusta. There's a luxury Country House Hotel (as well as courtyard chalets & modern apartments), a restaurant and Irish pub, & facilities including tennis courts, sauna & spa pool.
Old Lake Golf Club Tata, Remeteségpuszta; ↘ 34 587720; www.oldlakegolf.com. This championship course lies northwest of Budapest, near the border with Slovakia. There's an elegant, 35-room hotel.
Pannonia Golf & Country Club Alcsútdoboz-Máriavölgy; ↘ 22 594200; www.pannonia-golf.hu. Standing 35km west of Budapest (40 mins by car), the course is imaginatively designed. The clubhouse has an

atmospheric terrace restaurant, but there's no onsite accommodation.
Pólus Palace Golf Club Göd, Kádár u. 49; ↘ 27 530500; www.poluspalace.hu. Opened in 2005, the Pólus Palace is the closest course to Budapest (just a 20-min drive from the centre). It is located in a nature reserve, & has a 5-star hotel offering wellness facilities (as well as plastic-surgery & dental treatments).
Royal Balaton Golf & Yacht Club Balatonudvari, Vászolyi u.; ↘ 87 549200; www.balatongolf.hu. The first golf course at Lake Balaton (20 mins from Tihany). A wellness hotel is in the pipeline.
Zala Springs Resort www.zalasprings.com. For several years, a Hungarian-Irish consortium has been building what they hope will be the leading course in eastern Europe. It is part of a broader development containing villas & apartments for sale; there will also be fitness & spa facilities. It isn't clear when it will finally open – keep an eye on the website.

HORSE-RIDING, HIKING AND CYCLING Hungarians arrived in the Carpathian Basin on horseback from Asian steppes in the 9th century AD, and equestrian pursuits remain strong. There are many opportunities for **horse riding** in areas all over the country, and horse-riding holidays are popular. A number of 'horse inns' offer quality rooms and horse-riding at hourly rates. Lipizzaner horses of the famous

Viennese Spanish Riding School are bred at Szilvásvárad (see page 244) and Csipkéskút in the Bükk Hills, and can often be seen in the verdant meadows of the Bükk plateau. Asiatic *hucul* horses graze in Aggtelek National Park. There are horse-riding centres all over the country, although they are particularly prevalent on the Great Plain in places like Lajosmizse. Otherwise, log on to the website of the Hungarian Equestrian Tourism Association (*IX Budapest, Raday u. 8;* ͺ *1 455 6183; www.equi.hu – website in Hungarian only*), which can send out brochures on equestrianism and recommended horse-riding schools. The Hungarian tourist board also produces a couple of weighty booklets covering Hungary on horseback including *Equestrian Centres and Riding Schools*, which lists a selection of reliable riding centres in every region.

If you prefer to stand on your own two feet, the hilly western and northern regions are criss-crossed with excellent and well-marked **hiking** trails, and there are also routes through the Great Plain and other lowland areas. The National Blue Trail is a long, circular hiking path that connects almost all the famous spots. Further information can be found at MTSZ, the Hungarian Ramblers' Association 'Friends of Nature' website (*www.fsz.bme.hu/mtsz/bemutata.htm*). An extensive selection of maps are available from Cartographia, showing educational tracks, cycling, hiking and riding routes; you can buy copies either from their shop in Budapest (see page 123) or through their website (*www.cartographia.hu*). The tourist board also publishes brochures showing regional trails. The country is particularly well suited to **cycling**; the terrain is often gentle, and there are picturesque and well-marked trails. There is an abundance of literature available – start with the tourist board's *Cycling in Hungary* – and bike hire is offered in many resorts and hotels. For further details see pages 60–1, and for tours on two wheels see pages 39–40.

HUNGARIAN GRAND PRIX Undoubtedly the biggest event in the sporting calendar, the annual Hungarian Grand Prix is held at the Hungaroring racetrack 20km northeast of the capital in Mogyoród (see page 179). Late July/early August sees an invasion of F1-lovers and an astronomic hike in hotel and restaurant prices. If the latter doesn't put you off, log on to www.hungaroring.hu for ticket and visiting details.

HUNTING While it's not our bag, hunting is popular in Hungary where game is rich among the hills of the Northern Uplands and the woods of Transdanubia. Contact Hubertus Ltd (see page 40) for information or to arrange tours.

MARATHON The annual Budapest marathon (*early Oct*) starts and finishes in Heroes' Square; if you don't mind the blisters and dehydration, it actually provides an excellent sightseeing circuit of the city. Alternatively you can relax among the spectators lining the streets and enjoy the sight of dehydrated people with blisters. See www.budapestmarathon.com for information.

SWIMMING AND WATERSPORTS Hungary has made quite a splash in the international pool. The country's most-successful individual athlete of all time is swimmer Krisztina Egerszegi, who won gold and silver medals in Seoul, becoming the youngest-ever Olympic champion at just 14 years of age (and a delicate 41kg in weight). She added three further golds to her display case at the 1992 Barcelona Games. The water-polo team has dominated the world, winning Olympic gold on nine occasions (including at the last three games). The most famous victory came in Melbourne in 1956, when Hungary met the Soviet Union. Unsurprisingly in the context of that infamous year, the sporting battle was a brutal one that frothed the water and turned it red; the 5–2 win created global Mexican waves (metaphorically speaking).

If you're looking for a proper **swim** rather than a thermal soak, most towns have open-air and covered pools. Changing facilities include lockers for your clothes; the attendant will shut the door and give you a numbered band or tag. As a security precaution, the locker and tag numbers are different, so be sure to remember your locker number to avoid being caught cold later. In addition to man-made pools, rivers often have grassed sunbathing and swimming areas (*strand*); some are free to use, others charge entrance and might feature *büfé* stands and places to hire boats.

Lake Balaton is the mecca for those seriously committed to **windsurfing** and **sailing**, and Siófok even has **wake-boarding** mechanisms (a popular, cheaper and more practical offshoot of waterskiing); you'll find places to rent equipment around the shoreline. **Canoeing** and **kayaking** holidays are growing in popularity, particularly on the Tisza and Danube rivers. Guided visits to protected wetland habitats like Lake Fertő may also feature canoe trips into the reed channels. For company's arranging canoeing trips or equipment, see *Tour operators*, pages 39–41.

MEDIA

PRINT The Hungarian press is independent (foreign and locally owned), but journalism is not very daring, critical or investigative. Budapest is (relatively speaking) a small town, so that everyone knows everyone and there is a reluctance to give (as well as receive) criticism – however constructive. Items such as restaurant reviews tend to be bought off in advance and lack objectivity. Of the Hungarian-language press, *Pesti Est* and its equivalents produced for other towns around the country are probably the only publications of any practical use to the foreign tourist. This is the weekly pocket-sized listings guide to the best bars, clubs and events in town, and can sometimes help with addresses and opening hours; it's also a good prop for affecting an air of Magyar cool in bars. There are some English translations on the website (*www.est.hu*). Among the mainstream nationals, *Blikk* is now the most widely read daily – full of gossip, naked women, film stars, and no obvious news. It has supplanted the perennial favourite *Népszabadság* (*People's Freedom*), the serious broadsheet and former organ of the one-party ruling MSZP.

English-language press There are a number of English-language publications, several of which are available free of charge from hotels, tourist offices and coffee houses in Budapest. Among the ones to look out for are the weekly *Budapest Business Journal* (*www.bbj.hu*), *Budapest Sun* (local news, reviews and listings; *www.budapestsun.com*) and *Budapest Times* (news, business and culture), the monthly glossy *Where Budapest* (shopping, dining, nightlife and entertainment) and *Funzine* (a fortnightly magazine covering events in Budapest, as well as recommending restaurants, bars, etc; *www.funzine.hu*). Major international newspapers and lifestyle magazines can be picked up from larger newsagents and bookshops, although you should expect to pay considerably above the cover price and foreign newspapers are usually at least a day out of date.

TELEVISION On the whole, the fare on the Hungarian goggle box makes for pretty depressing viewing. The state owns two television channels: MTV1 (Magyar Televízió 1 – not to be confused with the American music channel!) and MTV2 (Magyar Televízió 2). During the communist period, these were used as tools for political propaganda, and even today parliament has a strong influence over their content. Until recently, they aired very conservative programmes featuring serious-looking men with droopy moustaches pontificating on political or literary topics. However, things have improved significantly – even the news programmes are hipper in tone, and there is a variety of foreign films and series. There are three commercial stations, which have traditionally proved colourful – Duna TV (which places emphasis on the 'larger Hungary' of times pre-Trianon Treaty, and now caters almost exclusively for Hungarians living outside the country), RTL Klub and TV2. In addition, there are many local independent stations (among them Bp TV, which is run by a local celebrity who often appears naked during live phone-ins). Almost everyone in Budapest has either cable or satellite, offering dozens of foreign channels and dubbed channels such as National Geographic and Hallmark. At 23.00, the Travel Channel suddenly changes to hardcore porn with local 'stars' performing in tourist spots such as the Gellért Hotel or Fishermen's Bastion – a novel way of showcasing the capital's sights…

RADIO Since the fall of communism, the airwaves have been flooded with commercial stations. Rádió 1 (103.9fm), Danubius (103.3fm), Rádió Café (98.6fm), Roxy Rádió (96.4fm) and Juventus (89.5fm) offer a mix of local and international popular music. Slager Rádió (100.8fm) plays golden oldies. Tilos Rádió (90.3fm) started off as a pirate radio station (*tilos* means 'forbidden') and is liberal in style. Rádió C (88.8fm) is a station for the Roma minority, and popular with younger listeners seeking an alternative to the tired old rotation lists of Juventus and Danubius. There are three state radio channels, including Bartók Rádió (105.3fm), which is devoted to classical music. You can listen to BBC World Service at certain times on BBC-RFI Budapest (92.1fm), a non-profit-making station launched in 2003 in collaboration with Radio France Internationale. For programme schedules, log on to www.bbc.co.uk/worldservice.

COMMUNICATIONS

𝄵 **TELEPHONE AND FAX** Most public telephones in Hungary are operated by **phone cards** (*telefonkártya*), which can be purchased from newsagents, hotels, tourist offices and post offices (800Ft/50 units and 1,800Ft/120 units). The fewer coin-operated public phones take 20Ft, 50Ft and 100Ft pieces. Main post offices offer a **fax** service, as do hotels with business centres and some internet cafés.

Local areas in Hungary each have a two-digit prefix code – except Budapest, whose **area code** is '1'. Budapest telephone numbers are seven digits long (excluding the area prefix), those of other areas six. Local calls can be made by directly dialling the required telephone number. For those beyond Budapest, dial '06' (the inter-area code), wait for a slightly different-sounding dialling tone, and then enter the specific area code and telephone number. (For cellphones, see opposite.) For calls out of the country, dial the international access code '00', listen for the second tone, and proceed with the relevant country code and number. Some country codes are listed below:

Australia	61	Hungary	36	UK	44
France	33	Ireland	353	USA/Canada	1
Germany	49				

Useful/emergency telephone numbers

Ambulance 104
Domestic operator and directory inquiries 198
Fire brigade 105
General emergency (for English, German and French speakers) 112

International operator and international directory inquiries (English spoken) 199
Police 107
Tourinform 24-hour hotline (info and reporting crimes; English speakers) 1 438 8080

Cellphones/mobiles The three cellphone providers are T-Mobile, Pannon and Vodaphone. To call a cellphone from a landline, you must prefix both the standard intercity code (06) and the provider's regional code – 30 or 60 (T-Mobile), 20 (Pannon) or 70 (Vodaphone). Calls between same-network cellphones do not require either of these codes, while a call to a mobile on a different network only requires the regional prefix. If you are taking your cellphone with you, check with your own provider first about call charges.

POST OFFICES Post offices (*posta*) are usually open Monday–Friday 08.00–18.00, Saturday 08.00–12.00. You can post letters and parcels, buy stamps (*bélyeg*) – although you'll save queue time by getting these at newsagents – pay parking and speeding fines, send faxes (main branches only), and exchange Eurocheques, American Express travellers' cheques and postal orders. If you're **sending a letter**, head for the desk marked with an envelope symbol. Letters or postcards to other European destinations will take around five or six days, while those to the US take eight to ten. Letters (up to 30G) or postcards within Hungary cost 75Ft, to Europe letters (up to 20g)/postcards 270/210Ft, to the US 300/230Ft. Be aware that it's far from unusual for 'interesting-looking' packages to go walkabout in the Magyar postal system – a postman somewhere, for instance, is doing his rounds in a fetching pair of pastel M&S knickers. It's safest not to send anything of value by post to/from Hungary, but if you have no choice then do so by registered post. Ask for an *ajánlott levél* form; its instructions are in Hungarian, but it's fairly straightforward to fill out (name, address, weight, value, etc) – the clerk can usually help, especially in larger post offices. You keep the form, which is stamped and numbered, while the letter or parcel is marked with an identification number.

Addresses When sending a letter to a Hungarian address, it's important to list the address details in the following order and on separate lines: recipient name; town name; street and house number; postcode; country name (if writing from abroad). Each digit of the postal code provides a piece of information – the regional area (first digit), the district (second and third) and the precise neighbourhood (fourth). The second and third digits can be particularly useful navigational tools in big cities. In the case of Budapest, for example, you can establish that the address 'Fő utca 4, H-1014' falls in district (*kerület*) 1 (the Castle Hill area of Buda). Floors of buildings (*emelet*) are numbered from the level above ground upwards (as in Britain), written as III emelet (third floor), IV emelet (fourth floor), etc.

INTERNET Internet cafés are commonplace across all main cities and towns; they are less readily found in villages. Most places charge for access by the minute. If you're struggling, head to a hotel as many permit internet use by guests and non-guests, although the charge is generally higher than in the cafés.

MAPS

The Hungarian National Tourist Office is a rich resource for information, and it publishes many maps that might meet your needs – showing campsites, hiking and cycling trails, equestrian centres, etc. These can be picked up (often free of charge) from regional Tourinform offices, which should also be able to provide a tourist map of the town or city you're visiting. Tourist maps are frequently available from hotel receptions too. More detailed or professional maps can be bought from bookshops or, again, from Tourinform offices.

The leading Hungarian map producer is Cartographia, which produces country, city, regional and hiking maps, as well as a couple of road atlases (*Magyarország*

Don't think you've been touched by the brilliance of the Hungarian mind? Consider some of the following contributors to the worlds of science, culture, art and entertainment. And think again.

EDE TELLER (1908–2003) Born in Budapest, Teller was a physicist who co-developed the atomic bomb and invented the hydrogen bomb.

ALBERT SZENT-GYÖRGYI (1893–1986) Awarded a Nobel Prize in 1937 for discovering vitamin C.

OSZKÁR ASBÓTH (1891–1960) A flight-obsessed engineer who invented the propellor helicopter.

ERNŐ RUBIK (1944–) Mathematician and creator of the irritating '80s cubic puzzle the Rubik Cube, which baffled and frustrated millions around the world.

LÁSZLÓ JÓZSEF BÍRÓ (1899–1985) Not content with inventing the ball-point pen (or Biro), he also fashioned the automatic gearbox.

IMRE KERTÉSZ (1929–) Acclaimed Jewish writer, deported from Budapest during World War II (aged 11). His novel *Sorstalanság* (*Fateless*) documented his experiences in Nazi concentration camps, and won him the Nobel Prize for Literature in 2002.

HARRY HOUDINI (1874–1926) Real name Ehrich Weisz. Perhaps the most-accomplished escapologist the world has known.

FERENC LISZT (1811–86) Renowned 19th-century composer and pianist who founded his own music academy in Pest.

BÉLA BARTÓK (1881–1945) Discovered by Liszt, Bartók was one of Hungary's greatest composers of classical and folk music.

ZOLTÁN KODÁLY (1882–1967) A popular composer and teacher who, with Bartók, collected Hungarian folk music. Kodály also devised his own method of music study to encourage the less talented to learn and play.

Hungarians were also responsible for inventing colour television, the hologram, the phosphorus match and the horse-drawn coach. Actors Tony Curtis, Drew Barrymore, Freddie Prinze Junior and Zsa Zsa Gabor have Hungarian ancestry, as do fashion designer Calvin Klein, singer Paul Simon and comedian Jerry Seinfield.

autóatlasza) that show both the country's road network and street plans of individual towns. Cartographia has a shop in Budapest (*VI, Bajcsy-Zsilinszky út 37;* ☏ *1 312 6001; www.cartographia.hu;* ⊕ *Mon–Fri 10.00–18.00*), and you can also order through the website. For travel bookshops in Budapest, see page 123. If you want to buy your maps before you go, Stanfords (*www.stanfords.co.uk*) is an excellent UK specialist in travel books and maps. ITMB (*www.itmb.com*) publishes a full-country *Hungary* map.

BUSINESS

Business etiquette is similar to that in western Europe and the US. The suit is the standard uniform, the handshake is used for greeting (it is customary to wait until the woman offers her hand), business cards (*névjegy kártya*) are exchanged (although Hungarian cards will list the holder's surname before his/her forename), and it is common to give a token gift. The principal language of business is English, although on occasion a translator may be required; it is prudent to ask about this beforehand, and the British embassy can advise on interpretation services. While the usual hours of business are 08.00–16.30 during the week, companies (and especially government offices) often close early in the afternoon on Friday, and spring and autumn are the main business seasons. Budapest's location makes it a popular place for international conferences, and the city has invested heavily over recent years in hotels and other business facilities. The city's flagship is the Budapest Congress and World Trade Center (*www.bcwtc.hu*), which has state-of-the-art audio-visual technology, a large exhibition hall and a conference room that can host 1,800 delegates. The capital's financial district is in Pest. For information on buying property, see box, pages 82–3.

USEFUL CONTACTS

American Chamber of Commerce Budapest V, Szent István tér 11; ✎ 1 266 9880; www.amcham.hu
British Chamber of Commerce Budapest XIII, Szent István körút 24; ✎ 1 302 5200; www.bcch.com
Hungarian Chamber of Commerce and Industry Budapest V, Kossuth tér 6–8; ✎ 1 474 5100; www.mkik.hu

Hungarian Convention Bureau I, Bartók Béla út 105–113; ✎ 1 488 8640; www.hcb.hu. Lists events, industry fairs & relevant industry news.
ITD Hungary Budapest VI, Andrássy út 12; ✎ 1 472 8100; e info@itd.hu; www.itd.hu. Headquarters of the Hungarian government's investment & trade-development agency, which offers consulting, business match-making services, trade directories, conference facilities & a business library. ⊕ *Mon–Thu 08.00–16.30, Fri 08.00–14.00.*

TIME

Hungarian time is one hour ahead of Greenwich Mean Time, six hours ahead of Eastern Standard Time and nine hours ahead of Pacific Standard Time. Bear in mind when checking cinema or theatre listings that when expressing the time Hungarians refer to the full hour *to come* rather than that passed. Thus 6.30 is expressed as 'half to seven' (*fél hét óra*); in shorthand/24-hour forms, it may therefore appear as 'f7', 'f19', '½7' or '½19'. The same applies to ¼- and ¾-hour intervals. In this book, time is given using the 24-hour clock in the usual way.

PUBLIC TOILETS

Hungary isn't dripping with public facilities in which to spend a penny; when you do find somewhere, you'll more frequently spend between 50Ft and 100Ft, and pay it to an elderly attendant. In summer months, cafés and fast-food restaurants (like McDonald's) in tourist-heavy areas occasionally charge even customers a fee for the use of their public conveniences. Doors are marked with *nők* or *női* (women) and *férfiak* or *férfi* (men).

CULTURAL ETIQUETTE

TIPPING It is customary to give a tip (*borravaló*, meaning 'something to buy wine with'...!) to waiters, hotel porters, bath attendants, bar staff, taxi drivers, hairdressers and tour guides. As in most countries, the amount to tip is something of a grey area. Ten–15% is generally acceptable, although with bar and café bills and taxi fares it is common simply to round up to the nearest 'convenient' amount. Give porters 300–500Ft, masseurs 500Ft and locker attendants 100Ft. When paying the bill in a restaurant, do not leave your tip on the table. Instead tell the waiter precisely how much you would like to pay (including the tip); if you say 'thank you' as you pass over payment, the waiter will assume that you don't want any change. Check whether service is included before paying – the staff are unlikely to point out your error if you tip twice – and shelve any embarrassment about refusing to tip if the service is poor. While we've noticed a distinct improvement in the last couple of years, service in Hungary remains variable, and disinterested staff should not expect to get rewarded regardless.

'CHEERS!' The convivial toast when drinking is *'egészségedre'* – a twister for the foreign tongue thickened with wine that often leads to an unwitting toast 'to your arse!' rather than 'to your health!' There are mixed messages as to whether or not the clinking of beer glasses is a social *nem-nem*. After crushing the rebellion against Habsburg rule in 1849, the Austrian military leader Haynau – known as the 'Hyena of Brescia' – toasted the execution of 13 Hungarian generals by clinking his beer glass. Some say that Hungarians swore that for the next 150 years they would refrain from clinking their own glasses out of disgust for what they had seen, and that the custom continues. However, there are others who either haven't heard this story or say it's completely untrue. You decide...

BUYING PROPERTY IN BUDAPEST

If you fancy becoming a property mogul abroad, you could do worse than think about investing in a Budapest flat. There has been significant interest in property in the capital (and at Lake Balaton) in recent years; Irish investors – noting how real estate rose in value after their own country's accession to the EU – led the way in buying up places shortly before Hungary joined in 2004. As a consequence, prices in the most sought-after districts rose by 30–40% in 2003.

Changes in the relative value of the pound against the forint does of course make some periods better to buy than others. Nevertheless, Hungary has enough **key ingredients** to suggest that long-term investment in Budapest property should provide a safe (although perhaps not spectacular) return. The country has proved more successful than other former Eastern-bloc states in attracting direct foreign investment, and the capital sees 60% of it; despite recent spikes, inflation and unemployment are under greater control; Budapest's position offers easy access to other European destinations and makes it a popular centre for business; and, most importantly, the city is a desirable place to be – offering reliable transport, cosmopolitan attractions and good summer weather. Previous trends also suggest that if and when Hungary joins the euro, its interest rates will drop and house prices will see a boost.

The **favoured districts** (for investments rather than for living – property and rental prices are highest in districts II, XII and along the river) are V and VI, and to a lesser extent VII, IX and XIII. Prices in these areas start as low as £25,000 (for a small, one-room flat or something in a poor state of repair). An outlay of £200,000 would get you a spacious three-bedroom flat in excellent condition on Régi posta utca – as central as you could wish; a large, two-bed apartment in an elegant listed building on Andrássy út (in need of a little freshening up) might cost around £130,000. A rather unscientific trawl through estate-agents' offerings suggests an average price of £75,000 or so for a two-bedroom apartment in a decent area of the city.

BARS Most bars in Hungary offer table service. Open a tab and settle the bill with the waiter or waitress before you leave.

SMOKING Smoking is popular in Hungary, and you'll see many a local drawing on a thin, white-tipped cigarette and lingering over a coffee. A law was passed in 1999 stipulating that restaurants must provide a non-smoking section; hunt out the sign reading '*tilos a dohányzás*' (no smoking) – it usually marks the tiny area shoved away at the back. Of course, dividing a single room into smoking and non-smoking areas is about as useful as dividing a swimming pool into peeing and non-peeing areas..

THANKS DOC Hungarian doctors were paid meagre salaries by the state during the communist period, and it became customary for grateful patients to offer physicians a tip (*hálapénz*, or 'gratitude money'), given discreetly in a plain envelope, for their help and advice. Doctors are much better off today, but many Hungarians still adhere to this tradition – a friend recently gave 50,000Ft (around £130), for example, after a small operation.

WHAT'S THE POINT? As a rule of thumb, Hungarians consider it rude to point at other people with the index finger – it is OK, however, to point at an object. When counting on their hands, Hungarians start with the thumb. As such, if a shop assistant wants to check that you really only want one banana, she will give what looks like a thumbs-up sign. Two bananas would be thumb and index finger, and so on.

The opportunity to **rent out** such apartments looks rosy, with tourism being Hungary's primary foreign-currency generator. A one-bedroom flat with views of the Danube costing £70,000 would generate rental income of around £650–700 per month. If you need to borrow, the normal mortgage in Hungary is 50% payable over 20 years, so UK buyers usually raise the additional funds from equity in property at home.

Now a solid member of the EU, the **bureaucratic legacy** of Hungary's communist past is fading rapidly. You would be wise, however, to avoid some of the monstrous buildings that were thrown up in that era, and you will need a good lawyer to protect you against problems that can arise because of outdated land records or dubious evidence of title. Investors should always check the **land registry** (Földhivatali Nyilvántartás) through their lawyer. Agricultural land cannot yet be purchased by foreigners. There are other **potential pitfalls**. Foreign nationals need a permit to purchase property in Hungary. It usually takes a few weeks but a local lawyer will organise this for you. You would have to pay tax at 20% and there may be stamp duty of up to 6%. Other costs to swallow would be the estate agent's commission and transfer tax, together adding about 4% to your outlay. Serious property investors set up as a company in Hungary. This brings advantages of paying a reduced rate of tax, as well as the possibility of multiple purchases in any one district – a right denied to individuals.

Hungarian **estate agents** include Otthon Centrum (*www.oc.hu*), CDC Real Estate Agency (*www.cdci.hu*), Big George (*www.biggeorge.hu*), Central Home (*www.centralhomehungary.com*) and Duna House (*www.dh.hu*); these sites list properties for sale and rent, and you'll also find details of their offices in Budapest. Real Estates (*www.property-hungary.co.uk*) is a Hungarian-based company specialising in property in eastern Europe. You can also check the Hungarian properties advertised under the international section of website www.primelocation.com. For further information, see the trade office website at www.hungarytrade.co.uk/ITD2/realestate.htm.

HOUSE VISITS If invited to a Hungarian's home for a meal, take a bottle of good Hungarian wine with you – a fine Tokaji is always well received – and perhaps some flowers or chocolates. You may be expected to remove your shoes before entering. Few topics of conversation are off limits, but remember that the average Hungarian salary is considerably lower than those of many other Europeans, so be sensitive that discussions of your earnings might cause discomfort.

SHOPPING When entering a chemist or food shop, you must pick up a basket – even if you plan to buy just one item or simply to browse. Large electrical stores often ask customers to leave their bags in secure lockers before they shop to make theft more difficult.

CHARITIES

Hungary ain't Africa, and while it is a poor country by Western standards you are unlikely to find yourself experiencing your pleasures guiltily or having your heartstrings tugged around every corner. You are in any case contributing to an economy that relies heavily on tourism simply by visiting the place, travelling responsibly, spending your dollars and extolling Hungary's charms to others on your return home. However, if you do want to give something more there are plenty of charities and projects that would receive your help very gratefully. Which you choose will depend entirely on your personal interests and cares.

The **Foundation for School Meals** (*Gyermekétkeztetési Alapítvány; XX Budapest, Mária utca 3;* ❧ *1 283 2510; www.gyea.hu*) assists poor and hungry children, many of which are from the Roma community (which remains a deeply hard-pressed and impoverished minority). Children are also the priority for the **Education for Blind Children** (*Vakok Szolgáltató Központja; XIV Budapest, Ajtósi sor 39;* ❧ *1 363 3343; www.vakisk.hu*) and the **Károlyi István Children's Centre** (*Gyermekközpont; web in English: www.gyermekkozpont.hu*). The **Foundation for the Women of Hungary** (*Magyarországi Női Alapítvány; web in English: www.mona-hungary.org*) provides support to women in violent relationships, while the **White Cross** (❧ *in English: 06 20 958 2545; www.feherkeresztliga.hu*) does excellent work rounding up the absurdly high number (two million) of domestic moggies and pooches that go astray annually in Hungary.

If you're a naturalist, you could consider assisting **WWF Hungary** (*XIV Budapest, Álmos Vezér útja 69/a;* ❧ *1 214 5554;* e *panda@wwf.hu*), which has operated here for a decade. Its activities are focused towards the conservation of forests, rivers and endangered fauna, and on helping the country meet the environmental challenges of EU membership. Field projects involve species like the wolf, beaver, lynx and European pond turtle, but equally significant are the attempts to revive the traditional agriculture of floodplains in the Middle Tisza region and the southernmost reaches of the Danube. Volunteer groups are vital to such work, and have so far assisted in constructing nature trails, surveying hiking resorts in the Buda Hills and studying European pond turtles. **Hungary Conservation Volunteers** organises an excellent programme for those who wish to get actively involved in the monitoring of key European butterfly species (including the large copper and anomalus blue) and in the management of their habitat. Contact the Butterfly Conservation Head Office (*Manor Yard, East Lulworth, Wareham, Dorset BH20 5QP;* ❧ *0870 774 4309; www.butterfly-conservation.org*). For further information on wildlife conservation, see pages 11–13.

Part Two

THE GUIDE

Please note that this chapter is aimed at travellers staying in Budapest just for a couple of days prior to visiting other areas of Hungary. As such, we have restricted ourselves to the city highlights. Fuller coverage is available in *Budapest: The Bradt City Guide*.

SYMBOLS are used where appropriate to indicate transport routes:

B̄	bus
M̄1̄/M̄2̄/M̄3̄	metro (number indicates line)
T̄	tram
T̄B̄	trolleybus
H̄ĒV̄	suburban railway

HOTELS are divided by price range (the price for a **double room** in **high season**). The price ranges used are as follows:

€€€€€+	77,500Ft and above
€€€€€	52,000–77,495Ft
€€€€	35,500–51,995Ft
€€€	17,000–34,995Ft
€€	12,000–16,995Ft
€	11,995Ft and below

RESTAURANTS are divided between Buda and Pest, and then further subdivided between districts or convenient areas. Each is given a price code that refers to the cost of an **average main course**. The price ranges used are as follows:

€€€€€	5,000Ft and above
€€€€	3,500–4,995Ft
€€€	2,500–3,495Ft
€€	1,750–2,495Ft
€	1,745Ft and below

MAPS There is a city overview map, as well as several others focusing on particular areas. **Grid references** for these maps are provided next to relevant sites in the text; the grid reference is given after the map page number – so that [144 D4] refers to square D4 of the map on page 144.

The sections *Exploring Buda* and *Exploring Pest and the Islands* guide you to the sights as you walk the streets of Buda and Pest. They include cross-references to the *Museums and More* section, containing full entries for selected museums, galleries and major sights.

3

Budapest

Great cities are forged from moments of tragedy as well as triumph, but Budapest has seen more than its fair share of blood and bullets. Traditionally, when Hungary dropped the toast it landed buttered-side down. The Turks strutted here in the 16th and 17th centuries, Austria ruled during the 18th and 19th, and the 20th century saw the country lurch from one terror regime to another. The citizens did not subject meekly; the capital has witnessed several revolts and some ding-dong street battles, and the nation's revered heroes are those who've fought for freedom.

As we write, however, Hungarians are in charge, and the only gangs of foreigners are coach parties. Tourism is thriving in the capital, and has boomed further since entry to the EU. Budapest is big enough to take it; one of the city's strengths is the elbowroom around its sights. While there are quaint narrow streets on Castle Hill, Budapest is characterised more typically by the broad and the bold. These are features of nature, such as Buda's craggy hills and caves, and the sweeping river; they are also features of architecture, such as Pest's Historicist and Art-Nouveau mansions and Parisian boulevards, which replaced the medieval and Baroque during 19th-century expansion. Another strength is the diversity of attractions. The city is significant both for its museums and its nightclubs, for its opera house and its contemporary music festivals; it suits both the flâneur and the hill walker. For all the exoticism of its Turkish baths and the impact of its communist past, this is a cosmopolitan capital that has always looked longingly westward. However, with the odd smoking Trabant, rumbling tram, and flower-selling *néni* comes destinational bite, and a flavour quite unique.

HISTORY

EARLY Peering through history's early mists, excavations suggest that the site of the capital was inhabited as long ago as the **fourth millennium** BC. There were communities here during the Bronze and Iron ages, including Celts who arrived in the 4th century BC and constructed a citadel on Gellért Hill. In around 35BC the area's strategic advantages were properly exploited for the first time when the **Romans** extended their imperial boundary eastward to the Danube, occupying the Celtic settlement of Ak-Ink (adopting the Latinised form of Aquincum). A legionary camp was established in today's Óbuda and a civilian town to its north; the river formed a natural barrier to attacks from Asiatic tribes, and a couple of advanced fortified positions were constructed on the other bank – including Contra-Aquincum, remains of which still stand in Március 15 tér. Aquincum flourished and became the capital of Pannonia Inferior, one half of the Roman province of Pannonia; as provincial governor, Hadrian built himself a palace on Shipyard Island.

During the 4th century the empire declined, and the Romans finally abandoned Buda at the beginning of the 5th century. When the **Magyars** arrived, Buda and

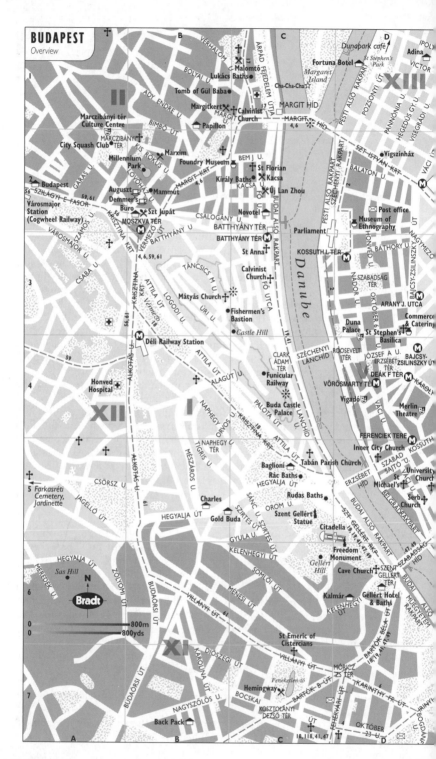

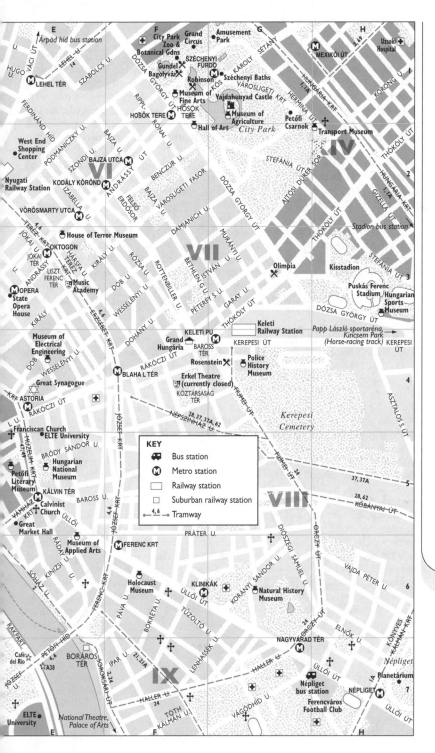

Pest (they weren't joined officially until the 19th century) were still just villages. It wasn't that they lacked for excitement – it was, after all, from Gellért Hill that the spiritual tutor of King István's son was launched in a barrel full of spikes by miffed pagans – but the royal and religious centres were elsewhere. After the Mongol invasion, **Béla IV** fortified Castle Hill, moved the populations of Buda and Pest behind the safety of its walls, and in doing so was lauded as the second state founder. Castle Hill was subsequently ranked a city and named Buda (the area to its north relegated to Óbuda – 'Old Buda'), while Pest developed as a commercial centre and attracted immigrant craftsmen from other corners of Europe.

14TH–17TH CENTURIES The 14th-century **Angevin kings** shifted the royal court from Visegrád to Buda. Subsequent monarchs enlarged upon the regal residence on Castle Hill, in particular Zsigmond of Luxembourg who constructed the beautiful Gothic Friss Palace. King Mátyás extended it further, and the court became a hotspot of European Renaissance art and learning.

In 1541 the **Turks** came, and many of the townspeople cleared out. There were several attempts to re-take Buda before a European army eventually vanquished the Turks in 1686 after a siege that lasted months. Buda was reduced to rubble by the fighting, and Pest was by now a virtual ghost town; their combined population was just 1,000. There was a massive process of rebuilding and re-population ahead (the latter with German, Slovak and Serbian settlers, as well as Hungarians from other parts of the country).

18TH–19TH CENTURIES During the 18th century Pest became an important trading centre and a wealthy town, attracting fresh groups of immigrants including Serbs and Jews. The 19th-century **Age of Reform** saw the construction of the first permanent bridge crossing the Danube here and the founding of the Hungarian Academy of Sciences. It was also during this period that Pest took on its current face. The **Great Flood** of 1838 had an effect as dramatic as London's fire of 1666, flattening the Neoclassical and Baroque dwellings and making way for the broad Parisian boulevards that replaced them. Some surviving churches bear markers recording the height reached by the waters.

On March 15 1848 **revolution** broke out on Pest's streets, its spokesmen the poet Sándor Petőfi and his fellow radicals. Once they'd crushed it, the Habsburgs built a citadel looking down from the Buda bank. The Compromise of 1867 provided new hope, and in 1873 Buda, Óbuda and Pest were **unified** to form Budapest, a union that had been inevitable since the erection of the Chain Bridge linking both banks. The city developed a capitalist infrastructure, the population grew rapidly, Pest became a place of great municipal construction and the hub of the empire's rail system, and cultural output rivalled that of Vienna. This spirit of energy and independence was evident during the **millennial celebrations** of 1896; an exhibition featured 220 halls showcasing Hungarian achievements, while lasting monuments like City Park, Heroes' Square, the first underground railway line, Mátyás Church and the Museum of Applied Arts were also born of this staggeringly ambitious and productive moment.

WORLD WAR II AND THE REVOLUTION OF 1956 World War II hit the city like a hammer blow. A ghetto was established in the area around the Great Synagogue and troopers executed Jews on the Danube banks. Twenty per cent of the capital's inhabitants were Jews, and only the intervention of a precious few souls saved them from the wholesale deportation that occurred in the rest of the country. Allied aerial bombardment took a serious toll on the city, and this was worsened when the Germans made a desperate last stand against the advancing Russians, destroying all the bridges and holing up on Castle Hill. Budapest was surrounded on December 24 1944, and Hitler ordered the 22,000 mainly SS troops to defend it to the last soldier; on February 12 1945, down to just 1,800, they finally succumbed. Three-quarters of Budapest's buildings bore the scars of battle, over a third were destroyed and 38,000 civilians had been killed (through violence, hunger or illness).

Afterwards the daunting process of reconstruction began; historic buildings were restored, and drab, utilitarian residential blocks raised on the outer city limits. However, the buildings bore fresh bullet wounds when blood spilt on the streets once more during the **revolution of 1956**, which started with a student demonstration against the communist government and ended with Soviet tanks in the boulevards.

RECENT TIMES In recent years – with the exception of the riots following political 'indiscretions' (see page 24) – conflicts have largely been restricted to wars of words, at the centre of which has invariably been the combative Mayor Gábor Demszky (now in his fifth term). During the four years that Fidesz ruled (1998–2002), the relationship between the government and the capital scraped rock bottom. Demszky, a former dissident, and Fidesz fought a series of bitter battles over the cost of large projects in the city (such as the National Theatre; see page 115). At the heart of this were contrasting views of the very capital itself, which Demszky promotes as a 'world city' and Fidesz sees as the embodiment of dangerous, non-Magyar forces of cosmopolitanism and liberalism. Given that Fidesz will almost certainly be in power as you read this book (elections are in April 2010), things could get interesting once more.

Practical Information

A PRACTICAL OVERVIEW

The first thing to ask yourself is 'On which side of the river am I?' The 525km^2 city is divided in two by the blue Danube, which runs through here for 28km and is spanned by seven road and two rail bridges. If you're among narrow streets or leafy hills to the west, you are in Buda, which makes up a third of the city; if you're in the more built-up area to the east, with shops, businesses, broad boulevards and squares, you're in Pest. If you're wet and treading water, you've fallen between the two.

Administratively, Budapest is carved into 23 districts (I–III, XI–XII and XXII in Buda, IV–X, XIII–XXI and XXIII in Pest). The tourist is most likely to spend time in districts V (the downtown), I (where you'll find the Castle District), VI (Terézváros, which holds Andrássy út), XIV (home of City Park), VII and VIII (Erzsébetváros and Józsefváros respectively), III (where the Roman ruins of Aquincum lie) and II and XII (the Buda Hills). Districts or areas within them often also bear historic names (such as Erzsébetváros – or Elizabeth Town).

The city's street plan is well laid out. In essence, the centre of Pest is defined by two ring roads – the Kiskörút (Small Boulevard), a semicircular thoroughfare that links the Chain and Liberty bridges and hems in the Belváros (city centre), and the Nagykörút (Great Boulevard), which runs outside it between Petőfi and Margaret bridges. Radiating outward from the Kiskörút are several broad avenues that cut through the Nagykörút and beyond. The result is an easily navigable spider web of tarmac. Buda is characterised more by its features than its roads, with Castle and Gellért hills dominating the immediate riverscape. On a map, Margit körút makes a teasing play of continuing the natural line of the ringroad, before leading off towards Lake Balaton. Attila út, Hegyalja út, Bartók Béla út and Fő utca are Buda's

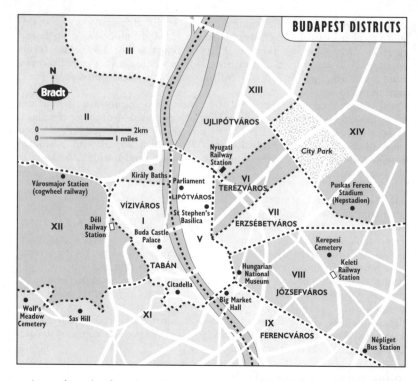

Map labels:
III
N
Bradt
II
0 — 2km
0 — miles
XIII
UJLIPÓTVÁROS
XIV
Nyugati Railway Station
City Park
Király Baths
Városmajor Station (cogwheel railway)
Parliament
VI TERÉZVÁROS
Puskas Ferenc Stadium (Nepstadion)
LIPÓTVÁROS
VÍZIVÁROS
St Stephen's Basilica
VII ERZSÉBETVÁROS
XII
Déli Railway Station
I
Buda Castle Palace
V
Kerepesi Cemetery
Keleti Railway Station
TABÁN
Hungarian National Museum
VIII
Citadella
JÓZSEFVÁROS
Big Market Hall
Wolf's Meadow Cemetery
Sas Hill
XI
IX FERENCVÁROS
Népliget Bus Station

main roads – the first three busy and noisy – while Moszkva tér and Móricz Zsigmond körtér are the transport hubs. In addition to all this, there are three metro lines (all serving Pest, one of which crosses the river to the north of Castle Hill), suburban railways, and three main railway stations (Déli in Buda, and Keleti and Nyugati in Pest) that run trains to national and international destinations.

GETTING THERE AND AWAY

BY AIR For details of international flights to and from Budapest, see pages 43–4. On landing, passengers have the following options for travelling to the city centre:

Airport minibus service Those travelling in ones or twos should consider the minibus shuttle (↘ 1 296 8555; www.airportshuttle.hu). The counter is open round the clock and the bus will drop you off at any address in Budapest. Book at the minibus desk (in the arrivals hall of each terminal); if you need to wait over 30 minutes, the full fare and return ticket may be refunded. A one-way ticket costs 2,990Ft for one and 4,490Ft for two, and a return 4,990/8,490Ft. For your return journey, call the office 24 hours in advance, and quote your flight number and hotel location; it's worth telephoning again on the day to check your booking has been logged.

Airport bus The public bus is the cheapest transfer (270Ft from the airport newsagent, or a little more if you pay the driver). There are two options. Bus 200E is a new airport service running from outside terminals 1 and 2 to Kőbánya-Kispest metro terminal; it operates 04.52–24.15, and has space for luggage. Local bus 93 leaves for Kőbánya Kispest every half-hour from Terminal 1, but is a slower service.

In each case, disembark at the last stop, Kőbánya Kispest metro, and take blue metro line 3 into the heart of Pest (Deák Ferenc tér station) and beyond. Bus 200E back from Kőbánya Kispest runs between 04.30 and 23.45, and the trip takes around 25 minutes.

Taxi For two passengers or more, a taxi should work out better value than the Airport Minibus. Don't simply hail a cab outside the airport – there's a danger of being stung. Either telephone a taxi firm, and agree a price – most offer a flat-rate airport fare (of around 5,000Ft) – or arrange a pick-up at the Zóna desk outside the arrivals hall. Zóna (1 365 5555; www.zonataxi.eu) recently won the airport-transfer contract; it offers fixed prices for various city 'zones', and prices are currently 3,300–4,500Ft (the latter for the city centre). The taxis also run meters, and if the meter price proves lower than the fixed price, then that's what you should pay. Be sure only to pay the lower of the two prices; we've heard word that unscrupulous drivers have charged unwitting tourists the higher fare. If you want to pre-book a cab by email, try http://programs.ohb.hu/; the driver will meet you at the gate with a name board, and the journey costs from €22. It takes around 20 minutes to reach the city centre by car.

Train A new railway line now runs between Nyugati Railway Station and Terminal 1 (not 2 – and the terminals are not within walking distance of each other). The journey takes 30 minutes; a single ticket costs 300Ft. Tickets can be bought from the Tourinform kiosk in the terminal between 09.00 and 22.00, and from the conductor on the train at other times. An express service running from Keleti to both terminals – taking 18 minutes and costing 1,500Ft – should be available shortly.

BY BUS The four primary **bus stations** for domestic services are all on the Pest side of the city. Each station has its own connecting metro station. For details of international services to/from Budapest, see *Chapter 2*, page 46.

Népliget Bus Station IX, Üllői út 131; 1 219 8000. On the blue M3 metro line.
Stadion Bus Station XIV, Népstadion; 1 252 2995 (domestic), 1 252 1896 (international). On the red M2 metro line.

Árpád híd Bus Station XIII, Forgách utca; 1 329 1450. On the blue M3 metro line.
Újpest Városkapu District IV. On the blue M3 metro line. For the Danube Bend and around.

BY TRAIN Budapest has three main railway stations that serve both international and domestic destinations – the Eastern (Keleti), Western (Nyugati) and Southern (Déli) railway stations. Each has a metro station; for full details of getting to/from Budapest by rail, see pages 45–6 and 55–8. In addition, there are four suburban rail lines (known as the HÉV) that run a shortish distance beyond the city to Szentendre, Gödöllő, Csepel and Ráckeve (see page 96).

BY BOAT There is a hydrofoil service operated by Mahart PassNave and running between Budapest, Bratislava and Vienna. For full details, see *Chapter 2*, page 47. The same company runs hydrofoils and ferries connecting Budapest with Esztergom, Visegrád, Szentendre and Vác between spring and autumn. Details are included under the *Getting there and away* sections of each of the Danube Bend towns.

GETTING AROUND

Here are the statistics: 210 buses (*autóbusz*), 16 trolleybuses (*trolibusz*), 32 trams (*villamos*), three underground metro lines (with a fourth on the way), and a

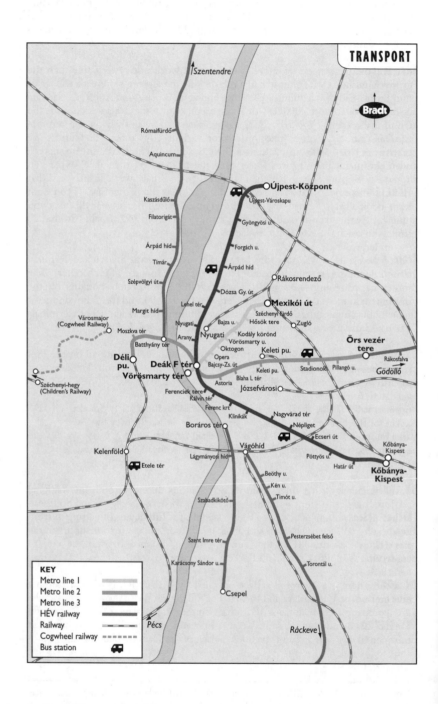

TRANSPORT

Bradt

Szentendre

Rómaifürdő

Aquincum

Újpest-Központ

Kaszásdűlő
Újpest-Városkapu

Filatorigát
Gyöngyösi u.

Árpád híd
Forgách u.

Tímár
Árpád híd

Szépvölgyi út
Rákosrendező

Dózsa Gy. út

Margit híd
Lehel tér
Mexikói út

Városmajor
(Cogwheel Railway)
Moszkva tér
Széchenyi fürdő
Nyugati
Bajza u.
Hősök tere
Zugló

Batthyány tér
Arany
Nyugati
Kodály körönd
Vörösmarty u.
Örs vezér
tere

Déli
pu.
Deák F tér
Oktogon
Opera
Keleti pu.
Rákosfalva

Vörösmarty tér
Bajcsy-Zs. út
Keleti pu.
Stadionok
Pillangó u.
Gödöllő

Széchenyi-hegy
(Children's Railway)
Astoria
Blaha L tér
Józsefvárosi

Ferenciek tere
Kálvin tér

Ferenc krt
Nagyvárad tér
Klinikák
Népliget

Boráros tér
Ecseri út

Kelenföld
Vágóhíd
Pöttyös u.
Kőbánya-
Kispest

Etele tér
Lágymányosi híd
Határ út
Kőbánya-
Kispest

Beöthy u.

Kén u.

Timót u.
Szabadkikötő

Pesterzsébet felső

Szent Imre tér

Karácsony Sándor u.
Torontál u.

KEY
Metro line 1
Metro line 2
Metro line 3
HÉV railway
Railway
Cogwheel railway
Bus station

Csepel

Pécs

Ráckeve

suburban railway (HÉV) – in addition to the Hungarian State Railway (MÁV), which takes passengers to national and international destinations beyond the city. Oh, and there are taxis, and funicular, children's and cogwheel railways. Of course, 89% of statistics mean absolutely nothing, but Budapest is genuinely blessed with an efficient and punctual public transport network, both easy to navigate and cheap to travel on. Getting around is a doddle.

If you wish to **report an incident** that occurs on the transport system, contact the Traffic Security Department of Budapest Transport Ltd (*VIII, Orczy út 34;* ℑ *1 334 1964*). If an **item goes astray**, contact the Budapest Public Transport Company's (BKV) lost-and-found office (*VII, Akácfa u. 18;* ℑ *1 258 4636;* ⊕ *Mon–Tue & Thu–Fri 08.00–17.00, Wed 08.00–18.00*). Up-to-date **public transport information** is available in English from the BKV website at www.bkv.hu/angol – including timetables for all modes (including ferries).

TICKETS Passengers purchase their tickets (*jegy*) before boarding the metro, bus, tram or trolleybus and are trusted to validate them by inserting them into 'punching' machines. (You may be able to buy a ticket from the driver on buses and trolley-buses, but people rarely do, and you'll need the exact money – 400Ft.) On the underground, punching machines are automated and are usually found at the top of the escalators, while buses and trams have them on board (where you have to pull down on the slot to operate the puncher). Inspectors (with red armbands) sometimes patrol to check tickets, and may also wait at the metro station punching machines as you enter; they will issue fines for fare dodgers (6,000Ft if paid on the spot, 12,000Ft if paid within 30 days).

Tickets are available individually or in books, and can be bought at hotels, newsagents and train stations. The same type of ticket can be used on the underground, trams, buses and trolleybuses; one ticket allows one journey on one transport system (without changing). If you're travelling on the underground and intend to change lines then you'll require a transfer ticket that needs to be validated. A Budapest Card allows free use of public transport. The standard single ticket is valid on the HÉV up to the city limits, but you'll need to buy a separate ticket for travel onward. Ferry tickets can be purchased from ticket machines at the docking points. While it's not widely advertised, note that **EU residents aged 65 and over** may travel for **no charge** on public transport in Hungary. Show your passport if confronted by an inspector – although reader Mrs L M Newman found that it was sufficient to point to her grey hair! For information on all tickets for travel on public transport, check www.bkv.hu/angol/jegyek/index.html.

Ticket prices

Single	300Ft (400Ft from the driver)
Book of 10	2,700Ft
One-day ticket	1,550Ft
Tourist ticket	3,850Ft (3 days), 4,600Ft (7 days)
Metro section ticket	250Ft (valid for up to 3 stops only, within 30 mins)
Metro transfer ticket	470Ft (as many stops as you like with 1 line change within 1hr)

BY METRO Budapest's metro was the first underground transport network in continental Europe – the second in the world after London's – and currently consists of three lines: yellow (M1), red (M2) and blue (M3). The yellow line, which travels the entire length of Andrássy út to City Park and beyond, is the oldest and was built to celebrate the country's millennium in 1896. It is affectionately known as the '*kisföldalatti*' (or 'little underground'), and its stations are decorated with patterned tiles.

All three lines are reliable and safe, and the trains arrive at frequent intervals of a few minutes. The metro runs from 04.30 until around 23.00 every day. The three lines intersect at Deák Ferenc tér station in the heart of Pest.

A fourth metro line is under construction, and will run in a northeast direction between Kelenföld in Buda and Bosnyák tér in Pest. The first section (as far as Keleti) was planned to be finished by the end of 2009, but delays mean it's unlikely to open before the second half of 2011. The new line will intersect with M3 line at Kálvin tér and M2 line at Keleti; it is designed to allow for further branch lines in the future – from Kelenföld (via Gazdagrét) to Budaörs, from Bosnyák tér to Rákospalota, and from Bocskai út (via Fehérvári út) towards Budafok.

BY BUS, TRAM AND TROLLEYBUS The blue single-decker **bus** service is frequent and dependable. Busier bus routes have express services – indicated by an 'E' suffix – that only stop at major bus stops. Day buses operate between 05.00 and 23.00, and can get very crowded during the rush hour. They are particularly useful for getting into the Buda Hills; Buda's main terminals are at Moszkva tér and Móricz Zsigmond körtér. **Night buses** (*éjszakai járatok*) run between 23.30 and 04.30, and follow 32 different routes (including those of the red and blue underground lines and the main tram paths); they are always (and exclusively) prefixed with the number '9' (eg: 907). Note that single-journey transport tickets are not valid on night buses – use a daily/tourist ticket, a Budapest Card or pay the driver. Budapest has three bus stations for national and international services (page 93).

There's something slightly special about riding a **tram**, a great unsung yellow rumble of a way to see the city's various aspects; Budapest's hog some of the choice cuts, running over four of the bridges, along both riverbanks and around the Great Boulevard. Trams 4 and 6, covering the Great Boulevard, are the newest in the fleet – bigger and easier to access for those with wheelchairs or buggies. Note that the river-hugging route of tram 2 will be broken at Fővám tér (near the Great Market Hall) until at least the middle of 2010 to allow construction work on the fourth metro line (see above). There are therefore termini either side of Freedom Bridge.

The transport brainchild of the '40s, the **trolleybus** is still surging onward along its overhead cables. It was introduced to commemorate Stalin's 70th birthday in 1949, which is why the first working bus was numbered '70'; each succeeding route was numbered upwards.

Trams, buses and trolleybuses run from around 05.00 to 23.00 daily (excluding night buses). Most stops have a printed **timetable** (*menetrend*).

BY HÉV The suburban railway, known as the HÉV, consists of four lines that run to the outer reaches of the capital and nearby towns of Szentendre, Gödöllő, Csepel and Ráckeve. The green trains are used predominantly by commuters, although the 45-minute journey between Batthyány tér and the picturesque town of Szentendre is very popular with day trippers, and also passes through Óbuda and Aquincum on the way. In daylight hours trains for Szentendre leave every 10–30 minutes.

BY TAXI Taxis are everywhere in Budapest, but tourists are vulnerable to unscrupulous drivers who charge significantly over the odds – and we're sorry to report that such drivers are no rare breed. The best way to avoid this is to order a taxi by telephone from a reputable firm. If you call from a public telephone, you can usually quote the number in the booth and the taxi will know precisely where to collect you. If you must hail a cab in the street, always ensure it is a marked car (with a company name on the side), ask for an approximate cost from the driver, and ensure the meter is visible and re-set. Remember that the driver is unlikely to be able to change large currency bills, and that you should give a tip (either 10% or round the fare up to the nearest convenient amount). Legally, taxis are allowed to charge up to the following rates: (06.00–22.00) 300Ft basic fee, 240Ft/km, 60Ft/minute for waiting; (22.00–06.00) 300Ft basic fee, 336Ft/km, 70Ft/minute for waiting. Firms will usually have a standard charge for the journey to the airport from Pest or Buda. Prices have remained the same for a few years, but a significant increase was being discussed as we went to press.

Reputable taxi firms in the city include Fő (℡ *1 222 2222*), City (℡ *1 211 1111*), Rádió (℡ *1 377 7777*), 6x6 (℡ *1 266 6666*), Tele5 (℡ *1 355 5555*) and Taxi 2000 (℡ *1 200 0000*).

BY CAR There's little joy for the driver in the centre of Budapest, with the congestion and maze of one-way streets that you expect from major capitals. The system of public transport is by far the better option. However, a car can be useful for trips into the hills, and you may anyway have a car for pressing on into the rest of Hungary after your Budapest stay. If you do have a car, good luck finding somewhere to park it – a Herculean task, particularly in downtown Pest. You pay for a space at coin-operated meters or through pay-and-display machines. Time restrictions on parking in the downtown area are enforced by wheel clampers. Multi-storey car parks can be found at V, Szervita tér 8; V, Aranykéz utca 4; VIII, Futó utca 52; and VII, Osvát utca 5. For car rental firms, see *Practical Information*, page 60.

BY BICYCLE While cycling is fraught with danger in the city centre, and bikes are prohibited on most major roads, there are cycle lanes along the Buda bank running to Szentendre and beside Andrássy út up to City Park, and other pleasant rides around Margaret Island or into the Buda Hills. Furthermore, recent changes to the Hungarian highway code have encouraged greater consideration towards cyclists. Grab a copy of the excellent *Biking in Budapest* (1:60,000) map, available free from Tourinform offices. You can carry bicycles on the HÉV, Cogwheel and Children's railways (you will have to pay extra), but not on buses, trolleybuses, trams or the metro. Hotels sometimes offer bikes for rent; alternatively, try:

Budapest Bike VI, Wesselényi u. 18; ℡ 06 30 944 5533; www.budapestbike.hu; ⊕ 09.00–24.00 daily Rent bikes (3,000Ft/day) & mopeds (6,000Ft/day), & run bike tours (10.00 daily, & also at 17.00 in high season). Near Great Synagogue.
Velo Touring XI, Előpatak u. 1; ℡ 1 319 0571; www.velo-touring.hu; ⊕ Mon–Fri 09.00–17.00 [000000] Bike hire for €18/day (for pick up); can also deliver to your hotel for additional charge.

Directions to depot on website. Deposit €100.
Yellow Zebra V, Sütő u. 2 & VI, Lázár u. 16; ℡ 1 266 8777; www.yellowzebrabikes.com; ⊕ Nov–Mar 10.00–18.00, Apr–Oct 8.30–20.00 daily. 2 outlets (one in courtyard just off Deák tér, other behind Opera House). Costs 3,000Ft/1 day & 5,000Ft/2 days, along with a €50–100 deposit. Also offers daily bike tours.

The X-Factor in MOM Park shopping mall (*XIII, Alkotás u. 53*; ℡ *1 487 5606* e *x-factormom@hu.inter.net*) is a bicycle-repair shop.

TOURIST INFORMATION, LOCAL TOURS AND TRAVEL AGENTS

TOURIST INFORMATION All five of the Tourinform (*www.tourinform.hu*) offices in the capital offer excellent (multi-lingual) advice and free tourist literature to help you make the most of your visit. Be sure to pick up the English-language publications *Funzine*, *Where Budapest* and *Budapest Guide* if you can. Tourinform offices can be found at:

IF YOU'RE STAYING A WEEKEND

- Make an early-morning trip to the bustling Great Market Hall, with its salamis and lace and glass and caviar (page 123).
- Ride the funicular railway (page 126) up Castle Hill, trawl a leisurely course around the Castle District (page 125), and scoff a cake at the Ruszwurm (page 109).
- Pick a museum and gallery or two – choose from extensive holdings at the Museum of Fine Arts (page 163), the Hungarian National Museum (page 164) and the Hungarian National Gallery (page 158), or more specialised exhibitions like the polished Imre Varga Collection (page 160) or the sombre, stylised House of Terror (page 162).
- Soak away your aches in a thermal spa – and admire the proud Art-Nouveau architecture and wide-girthed men of the Gellért or Széchenyi baths (pages 124–5).
- Wrap yourself around a pastry in a *fin-de-siècle* coffee house (pages 109–11).
- Take in the sights and shops of the city centre, including the St István Basilica (page 172) and the Parliament building (page 170).
- Join the metro to Heroes' Square and City Park, with its ducks, zoo and eclectic castle (pages 151–3).
- Eat *gulyás* soup, Hortobágy pancakes, and paprika chicken with dumplings.
- Try a shot of fruit brandy, and a glass or three of sweet Tokaji Aszú.
- Watch the day draw to a close in a café-bar on Liszt Ferenc tér (page 113).

AND LONGER...

- Hire a bike and pedal around Margaret Island (page 156).
- Take the cogwheel and children's railways into the Buda Hills (page 139), and return by chairlift from János hegy (page 141).
- Visit the Cave Church (page 166) dug into the side of Gellért hegy, and then push on up to the Freedom Monument (page 133) and Citadella (page 167) on top.
- Take in a performance at the stunning State Opera House (page 116), or an outdoor concert in front of the St István Basilica (page 172).
- Book an evening river trip (see opposite).
- Travel to Memento Park (page 160), the dumping ground for communist statues.
- Eke out the Roman amphitheatres and mosaics of Óbuda (page 136).

ℹ V, Sütő u. 2 (just off Deák tér); ☏ 1 438 8080 (24hr), 1 317 1248; ⊕ 08.00–20.00 daily. The city's main tourist-info office; in addition to the usual services, it now sells tickets to cultural events (inc the Sziget Festival) & concerts in the A38 boat & Palace of Arts (pages 117 & 115). There is internet access (150Ft/15mins) & the police inform office is also housed here.

ℹ V, Városház u. 7; ☏ 1 428 0377
ℹ VI, Liszt Ferenc tér 11; ☏ 1 322 4098; ⊕ daily 09.00–19.00 (Apr–Oct), Mon–Fri 10.00–18.00, Sat 10.00–16.00 (Nov–Mar)
ℹ XVIII, Ferihegy Airport, Terminals 1 & 2A/2B; ☏ 1 438 8080 (24hr)

There are computerised **information touch points** at Blaha Lujza tér, the upper terminus of the funicular railway, Déli Railway Station, both terminals of Ferihegy Airport, the Great Market Hall, Tourinform (*Sütő u. 2*), Moszkva tér and Keleti Railway Station.

LOCAL TOURS There's no shortage of organised tours of the city and beyond, both for those who pre-book and for impulsive types. As well as the buses and boats, there are cycling, nature, walking and horse-riding tours.

General/sightseeing

Best Hotel Service V, Sütő u. 2; ☎ 1 318 5776/4848; www.besthotelservice.hu; ⏱ 08.00–20.00 daily
Budatours VI, Andrássy út 2; ☎ 1 374 7070; www.budatours.hu; ⏱ 08.00–18.00 daily
Cityrama Sightseeing Tours V, Báthory u. 22; ☎ 1 331 0043; www.cityrama.hu; ⏱ Mon–Fri 08.00–18.00, Sat–Sun 09.00–15.00
EUrama Sightseeing Tours V, Apáczai Csere János u. 12–14; ☎ 1 327 6690; www.eurama.hu
Ideal City Tour V, Apáczai Csere János u. I; ☎ 06 20 232 3232/1 212 3131; www.idealtravel.hu; ⏱ office Mon–Sat 09.00–15.00, Sun 09.00–12.00

Koltour Bt XI, Rákó u. 3; ☎ 06 20 935 9511 e peter@koltour.hu; www.koltour.hu
Program Centrum Travel Agency VII, Madách u. 13–14; ☎ 1 317 7767, 1 327 0055; www.programcentrum.hu; ⏱ Mon–Fri 09.00–14.00 (also Sat 09.00–15.00 Apr–Oct)
To-Ma Tour V, Budapest, Október 6 u. 22; ☎ 1 353 0819; e tomatour@tomatour.hu; www.tomatour.hu. Friendly company specialising in tailor-made & group tours of the city, as well as offering a range of private rooms/apts (page 104).

Walking, cycling, cruising

Absolute Walking Tours V, Sütő u. 2; ☎ 06 30 211 8861I; www.absolutetours.com; ⏱ office daily 09.00–20.00 (high season), 10.00–19.30 (other times)
Free Budapest Walking Tours www.triptobudapest.hu. Free 2hr walking tours leave daily at 10.30 from lion fountain outside Gerbeaud (page 110). Tip if happy.
Legenda Travel Agency V, Vigadó tér, Pier No 7; ☎ 1 317 2203; www.legenda.hu. Two (hour-long) boat trips along the Danube.

Mahart Passnave V, Belgrád rakpart; ☎ 1 484 4013; www.mahartpassnave.hu; ⏱ ticket & information office Mon–Fri 08.00–16.00. Sightseeing cruises available.
Yellow Zebra V, Sütő u. 2; ☎ 1 266 8777; www.yellowzebrabikes.com; ⏱ office daily 09.00–20.00 (high season), 10.00–18.00 (other times). Bike tours.

Nature

Caving Under Budapest II, Pálvölgy Stalactite Cave, Szépvölgyi út 162; ☎ 06 20 928 4969. Climbing & crawling through the cave system with qualified guides. Bus 65 from Kolosy tér runs to the cave (5th stop); no experience necessary.

See pages 39–41 for companies like Probirder and Ecotours who can arrange local wildlife tours.

Other

Jewish Heritage in Budapest VII, Dohány u. 2; ☎ 1 317 2754. Tours depart from Great Synagogue (page 169) Mon–Thu 10.30 & 13.30, Fri 10.30, Sun 11.30.
1956 Revolution Tour ☎ 1 269 3843; www.hungary1956revolution.com. Walking tour of the main action sites of the revolution. Tours depart Wed & Sat at 15.00 (Nov–Mar Sat only) from Discover Hungary (VI, Lázár u. 16, just behind Opera House).

LOCAL TRAVEL AGENTS Travel agents can offer assistance with accommodation, programmes and excursions, car rental, and with tickets for shows and international and domestic travel; they can also often provide information, brochures and tourist maps, while some offices exchange travellers' cheques.

Express VIII, Dohány u. 30/a; ☎ 1 266 6188 e info@expresstravel.hu; www.expresstravel.hu; ⏱ Mon–Fri 08.00–18.00, Sat 09.00–13.00
Ibusz Main office: V, Ferenciek tere 10; ☎ 1 485 2700 e info@ibusz.hu; www.ibusz.hu; ⏱ Mon–Fri

09.00–18.00, Sat 09.00–13.00; other offices: II, Margit körút 58 and V, Vörösmarty tér 6. The largest travel-bureau network in Hungary.
Koltour Bt See above

HEALTH In an **emergency**, contact Főnix SOS Ambulance (*XII, Diós árok 1–3;* ℩ *1 200 0100; www.fonixsos.hu*), which provides round-the-clock health care and has its own ambulance service. The private Rózsakert Medical Center (*II, 2nd Floor, Gábor Áron u. 74–78;* ℩ *1 391 5903; www.medical-center.hu*) is housed in the shopping mall of the same name and has helpful, American-trained doctors in residence; it is closed at weekends. A reader has also recommended www.firstmedcenters.com at Hattyú utca, which is just off Széna tér and reached on tram 2 or 4. For **dental services**, see page 49.

Most **pharmacies** close between 18.00 and 20.00, but at least one in every district is open 24 hours a day. If it's very late you may have to ring the bell for admittance (and you may also be charged a small fee). Some pharmacies running non-stop services can be found at the following addresses:

✚ VI, Teréz körút 41; ℩ 1 311 4439
✚ XII, Alkotás u. 1B; ℩ 1 355 4691
✚ II, Frankel Leó út 22; ℩ 1 212 4406/4311

✚ VIII, Baross tér 9. A non-stop pharmacy where a doctor is always on duty & you don't get charged for service outside usual shop hours. Next to Keleti railway station.

BANKS AND MONEY The greatest concentration of banks is in downtown Pest. Twenty-four-hour automated teller machines (ATMs) are fairly commonplace – if in doubt, head to the busy shopping areas of Váci utca or the Great Boulevard. For general information, see pages 53–4.

Exchanging currency Numerous *bureaux de change* booths can be found on Váci utca and the Great Boulevard, as well as in hotels, railway stations and shopping centres. The Interchange counters offer poor rates, and should be avoided. There are also foreign-currency exchange machines at several points around the city (including at II, Margit körút 43–45, V, Károly körút 20, and VI, Andrássy út 49). Dealing with black-market money-changers is illegal, and you run a high risk of being ripped off.

$ **American Express Exchange** V, Deák Ferenc u. 10; ℩ 1 235 4340; ☺ Mon–Fri 07.00–17.30, Sat 09.00–14.00. Exchanges AmEx travellers' cheques commission-free & also dispenses cash to its

cardholders. A smaller branch in the Castle District at the Sisi Restaurant has a currency exchange that operates daily from March to mid-January.

DISCOUNT CARD The **Budapest Card** grants free entry to the permanent exhibitions of the bulk of the museums and galleries, as well as to a few other sights, and discounts on some temporary exhibitions, sightseeing tours (although generally on the big, impersonal coach trips), restaurant meals, shop purchases and thermal baths. It also allows free and unlimited use of public transport, and provides the holder with travel-insurance coverage for the duration of the card's validity. Cards are valid for 48 hours (6,500Ft) or 72 hours (8,000Ft), cover one adult and one child (up to the age of 14), and can be obtained from tourist offices, the airport, travel agencies, hotels and main metro ticket offices. Sign the card and fill in the date from the moment you want to start using it (you can choose when the period begins). You'll find a list of the places where the card is accepted at www.budapestinfo.hu or in a leaflet you can pick up from Tourinform offices.

Whether or not the card is worth getting really depends upon how you intend to spend your time. If you plan to visit three or four of the main (more expensive) museums over a two-day period, and to make good use of public transport, then you'll probably find that it saves you cash. However, if you're eligible for concessions anyway – and remember that senior citizens can travel free on public transport (page 55) – you'll have to do the maths more carefully before buying.

POST OFFICES A few main branches keep later hours; for general info, see page 79:

✉ **Keleti Pályaudvar Posta** VIII, Baross tér 11/c;
🕐 Mon–Fri 07.00–21.00, Sat 08.00–14.00
✉ **Nyugati Pályaudvar Posta** VI, Teréz körút 51;
🕐 Mon–Fri 07.00–20.00, Sat 08.00–18.00

✉ **Posta** V, Petőfi Sándor u. 13–15 (with another entrance at Városház u. 18); 🕐 Mon–Fri 08.00–20.00, Sat 08.00–14.00
✉ **Váci Utca** Posta V, Váci u. 85 (at corner with Fővám tér); 🕐 Mon–Sat 10.00–18.00

INTERNET Most hotels offer internet access, but there are plenty of cheaper internet cafés all over Budapest. You'll find a full list of internet cafés on the excellent website www.caboodle.hu. For other useful website resources, see *Further Information* appendix.

🏠 WHERE TO STAY

HOTELS, PENSIONS & HOSTELS Accommodation fills up in high season, so book ahead where possible. Demand is also fierce during festival periods. Note that for comparative purposes, the price bands refer to walk-in rates (including tax and any breakfast cost) for a standard double room during high season – generally May/June–September/October (although some hotels exclude parts of July and August, when the heat means visitor numbers drop) and the period over New Year. Low-season rates fall by around 30%, and most of the hotels offer heavily discounted deals on weekend breaks. The flipside of the coin is that during days around the Formula 1 Hungarian Grand Prix (end of July or start of August) rates climb extravagantly, often to two or three times the high-season rate.

€€€€€+ (77,500Ft & above)

🏠 **Corinthia Grand Hotel Royal** (414 rooms) VII, Erzsébet körút 43–49; ☎ 1 479 4000; www.corinthiahotels.com [149 D3] M̲2̲ Blaha Lujza tér T̄ 4, 6. There's yesteryear dignity about the marble lobby, sweeping staircase & heritage-protected ballroom, but any stuffiness is tempered by an airy modern layout that pits rooms around atrium courtyards. Rooms are comfortably sized & smartly furnished; all have bath & separate shower. The luxurious adjacent Royal Spa is linked to the hotel via a corridor.

🏠 **Four Seasons** (179 rooms) V, Roosevelt tér 5–6; ☎ 1 268 6000; www.fourseasons.com/budapest [144 A1] A hotel to smack the gobs of the most difficult to please. Fashioned in 1907, the Gresham Palace insurance building was one of the finest examples of Art-Nouveau architecture in the world. Today, the hotel is 5-star-plus, with 12 types of room furnished

in Secessionist style (many with balconies & vaulted ceilings). The immaculate spa is set into the roof. The Páva restaurant is excellent. The hotel was voted the best in Europe in a survey by Condé Nast Traveler. The top-category rooms are well over €5,000. B/fast 5,500–8,300Ft.

🏠 **Hilton Budapest** (322 rooms) I, Budapest, Hess András tér 1–3; ☎ 1 889 6600; www.budapest.hilton.com [127 B2]. Nestles next to the Mátyás Church, its eastern-facing rooms offering unrivalled views over the Danube; the modern meets the historic in a provocative design uniting rows of metallic-tinted windows with the Baroque façade of a 17th-century Jesuits' college, & the ruins of a 13th-century Dominican monastery. The rooms are not enormous, but are elegant & suitably well equipped. You'll pay over €2,000 for the best suites. Excellent buffet b/fast. No swimming pool.

€€€€€ (52,000–77,495Ft)

🏠 **Andrássy Hotel** (70 rooms) VI, Andrássy út 111; ☎ 1 462 2100; www.andrassyhotel.com [149 D1]

M̲1̲ Bajza u. B̲ 105. Once a state-owned hotel hosting foreign communist delegates (including

Gorbachev), the Andrássy is rather different now — classy & contemporary, & holding the well-regarded Baraka restaurant (see page 107). Well situated for City Park & the State Opera House. Guests can use the fitness room & sauna at the Residence Izabella. Entrance on Munkácsy Mihály u.

🏠 **Danubius Grand/Health Spa Resort Margitsziget** (164/267 rooms) XIII, Margit-sziget; ☎ 1 889 4700; www.danubiushotels.com/margitsziget [137 D5] B̲ 26 runs between hotels & Nyugati station every 15 mins;

€€€€ (35,500–51,995Ft)

🏠 **Atrium Fashion Hotel** (57 rooms) VIII, Csokonai u. 14; ☎ 1 299 0777; www.hotelatrium.hu [149 D4] M̲2̲ Blaha Lujza tér. The unassuming façade of this newish hotel belies a stylish interior, where an enormous green clock takes pride of place among the many local artworks.

🏠 **Buda Castle Hotel** (25 rooms) I, Úri u. 39; ☎ 1 224 7900; www.budacastlehotelbudapest.com [127 B2] A new, ship-shape 'boutique' offering in the Castle District that fits nicely into its surroundings. There are no extra facilities such as a gym to go with its 4-star superior status, but rooms are large, contemporary in style & have all the necessary comforts (inc A/C & WiFi). Given this & the pleasant location, the room prices are very reasonable.

🏠 **Hotel Astoria** (131 rooms) V, Kossuth Lajos u. 19–21; ☎ 1 889 6000; www.danubiushotels.com/astoria [144 D3] The Astoria retains much of its fin-de-siècle elegance, & is often used by film-makers producing period pieces. It was here that the first democratic Hungarian government declared independence from Austria in October 1918. Today the rooms vary in size, but are comfortable & classically furnished, & the hotel has a beautiful, recently refurbished café-restaurant.

🏠 **Hotel Gellért** (234 rooms) I, Gellért tér 1; ☎ 1 889 5500; www.danubiushotels.com/gellert [88 D6] T̲ 18, 19, 41, 47, 49. If a dandyish, old-money aristocrat were to meet Medusa's eye, the Hotel Gellért might be the result. It was built in 1918, and became a high-blown Art-Nouveau favourite of the inter-war party set. Michael Palin stayed here during his TV series on 'New Europe' (& we noticed the last edition of this book on his bedside table in one shot — we hope not as an aid to sleep!). Rooms (divided between 3 categories) vary considerably in size & shape. Those facing the river offer wonderful views — although light sleepers should note that trams rumble along the road below. The hotel's café (with terrace) serves great cakes & snacks, & the brasserie offers a Sunday brunch for 5,100Ft/pp

car access via Árpád Bridge. These hotels (linked by underground corridor) sit peacefully together at the northern end of Margaret Island. The mansion-like Grand was designed by Miklós Ybl in 1873. The Health Spa Resort is less noble of aspect but, as its name suggests, it's here that guests (of both hotels) get down to the serious business of health, fitness & beauty. The spa complex makes use of 3 hot springs that feed the island, & there are indoor & outdoor swimming pools. Spa open to non-guests.

(12.00–15.00; 20% off for hotel guests). Free access to adjacent Gellért Baths (page 124).

🏠 **Lánchíd 19** (48 rooms) I, Lánchíd u. 19; ☎ 1 419 1900; www.lanchid19hotel.hu [127 D4] T̲ 19, 41 B̲ 16, 86. A member of the Design Hotels chain. In addition to a cutting-edge façade (featuring moving coloured 'slats'), each room is uniquely & imaginatively designed. Contemporary restaurant. Sits right on the Danube, by the Chain Bridge (Buda side); some rooms face river, others Castle Hill.

🏠 **Promenade Hotel** (45 rooms) V, Váci u. 22; ☎ 1 799 4440; www.promenade-hotel.hu [144 B3] While it lacks facilities like a gym or restaurant, this hotel is shiny-pin new & has a charm that you mightn't expect given its location at the tourist hub. It's narrow in the shoulders, jutting upwards over 6 floors (which you access aboard a glass-walled lift); the simply furnished rooms have space to breathe, & the lofty, top-floor b/fast room is a pleasant spot to ease yourself into the morning. Free WiFi.

🏠 **Radisson SAS Béke Hotel** (247 rooms) VI, Teréz körút 43; ☎ 1 889 3900; www.danubiushotels.com/beke [149 B/C2] M̲3̲ Nyugati T̲ 4, 6. The mid-19th-century façade remains, & the Zsolnay Café is turn-of-the-century elegant, but otherwise this is a modern hotel with swimming pool, sauna, solarium & massage treatments. You're right in the thick of the city here, on the busy Great Boulevard. Comfortable rooms, including large & well-equipped suites.

🏠 **St George Residence** (28 suites) I, Fortuna u. 4; ☎ 1 393 5700; www.stgeorgehotel.hu [127 B2] Occupying the site of the renowned 17th-century Fortuna Inn in the Castle District, this hotel contains imported Italian furniture, rooms decorated with green marble, and a Rococo-style coffeehouse adorned with birds & butterflies floating on the wind. There are 4 categories of suite, each with a kitchen & a few with a Jacuzzi. Small but plush restaurant. No lift or fitness facilities.

🏠 **Zara Boutique Hotel** (74 rooms) V, Só u. 6; ☎ 1 577 0700; www.zarahotels.com [144 C5] The Zara lacks something of the no-expense-spared luxury to its styling that we'd usually expect from a 'boutique' tag. However, there's been no effort spared in making the most of a more limited budget. The décor draws on oriental & European styles; the

standard rooms are small, simple & clean-lined, & all have flat-screen TVs & Wi-Fi. The staff are keen to create a sense of 'community' — there's even a hotel band that sometimes plays in the lobby.

€€€ (17,000–34,995Ft)

🏠 **Burg Hotel** (26 rooms) I, Szentháromság tér 7–8; ☎ I 212 0269; www.burghotelbudapest.com [127 B3] Lacking the river views of its illustrious neighbour the Hilton Budapest (page 101), this 3-star hotel nevertheless has its own piece of courtyard history — a segment of castle wall dating back 300 years — & is very reasonably priced considering its location. Most rooms overlook the square.

🏠 **Gerlóczy** (15 rooms) V, Kamermayer Károly tér; ☎ I 501 4000; www.gerloczy.hu [144 C3] In 2008, the Gerlóczy café (page 111) also started offering accommodation, & we're so pleased it did. You'll struggle to find anywhere with more character. The rooms are wonderfully elegant; the bathrooms have free-standing sinks that might have come straight from the house of a 19th-century nobleman. All rooms cost the same (€85), so request one of the two with balconies overlooking the square. Some rooms have baths & others showers. B/fast €10.

🏠 **Hotel Kalmár** (10 rooms) XI, Kelenhegyi út 7–9; ☎ I 372 7530; e kalmar@ohb.hu [88 D6] B̲ 27. With prices in the lower rather than upper half of this category range, we reckon the superb Kalmár is the city's best-value hotel. It has a faded, aristocratic elegance, & — sitting up a hill behind the Hotel Gellért — its front-facing rooms offer good city views. The current owner's great grandfather built the house for Prime Minister Pál Teleki, who lived

here prior to his suicide (page 129). Each room is different in look, although always large in size; there are several suites (one with a jacuzzi), a massive apt with a dining area, & 2 studios with small kitchenettes. Slightly steep walk to reach it.

🏠 **Hotel Normafa** (62 rooms) XII, Eötvös út 52–54; ☎ I 275 5160; www.normafahotel.com [140 A5] B̲ 90, 90A (from Moszkva tér) Just a few metres from the southern entrance to the wooded Normafa lejtő (page 139) on Sváb hegy, & 2km from János hegy with its biking & walking routes, this handsome alpine-style hotel is a great base for families exploring the Buda Hills. Fitness centre, sauna, swimming pool (with children's pool & play area), bike hire. Reader Mervyn Brown notes that the Normafa Café & Grill (☎ I 395 1771) is one of his favourites, having a diverse world-based menu to suit all tastes.

🏠 **Hotel Pest** (25 rooms) VI, Paulay Ede u. 31; ☎ I 343 1198; www.hotelpest.hu [149 B3] M1 Opera B̲ 105. This lovely hotel really blends in with the neighbours. Occupying half a building wrapped around a quiet inner courtyard, it is part of a typical residential apartment block. Its well-maintained rooms — most of which overlook the courtyard — are very large, with understated décor. There's a small bar & a glass-ceilinged atrium for b/fast. Highly recommended. At the upper end of this price bracket — but still a bargain.

€€ (12,000–16,995Ft) & **€ (11,995Ft & below)** Hotels, hostels and pensions in the budget category will generally have en-suite rooms with a bath and/or shower and telephone (except in hostel dorms); in addition, they may have television, air conditioning, internet access and sauna. Youth hostels (*ifjúsági szálló*) may be open during the summer only, although this is unusual in Budapest. (The Hungarian Youth Hostels Association can provide further information, and make reservations; *VII, Almássy tér 6;* ☎ *1 343 5167; www.miszsz.hu.*) A final cheap-as-chips option is to

COMMIE LOVE

Durex, the condom manufacturer, conducted a survey in 2003 to find the nation that most enjoyed sex. The French? The Italians? Oh, *nem nem*. Hungarians topped the poll as the Buda-best lovers, followed by citizens from Serbia and Montenegro, Croatia, Bulgaria and the Czech Republic. Perhaps a communist past is the Viagra of central Europe…

stay in college accommodation during the summer recess (*Jul & Aug*). A Tourinform should be able to provide a list of these, although local tourist agencies (see *Private apartments/rooms*, page 104) can also make bookings for you. As well as the euro symbol indicating the price of a double (usually the costliest option in this category), we also list individual prices for rooms holding three and above.

🏠 **Hotel Papillon** (30 rooms) II, Rózsahegy u. 3/B; ➷ I 212 4750; www.hotelpapillon.hu [88 BI] B̲ *II from Batthyány tér* T̲ *4, 6*. More family guesthouse than hotel, with homely, modern rooms (standard & superior) & a welcoming owner. There's a garden & tiny pool in which to relax after the sapping climb up Rose Hill. 10 brand-new rooms. The owner also runs a travel agency. Trpl/quad/apt €69/79/90 (excl Tourist Tax). €€

🏠 **Domino Hostel** (26 rooms, 146 beds) V, Váci u. 77; ➷ I 235 0492; www.dominohostel.com [144 C5]. At the Domino, guests can sleep snugly knowing that – in terms of location – they're getting steak at hamburger prices. Rooms are bright & airy; the 4 dbls are en suite, while other rooms share showers on the corridors. There's no kitchen, but a laundry is planned & there's a bar. Entrance on Havas u. Book ahead to guarantee a dbl. 10% discount with student

card. Note payment is accepted in cash only. Quad 5,500Ft/pp, dorms (for 6/8) 4,400/4,950Ft/pp. €€

🏠 **Red Bus Hostel** V, Semmelweis u. 14; ➷ I 266 0136; www.redbusbudapest.hu [144 C3] M̲2̲ *Astoria* M̲3̲ *Ferenciek tere, then few mins' walk*. There's no nonsense here – newly renovated hostel accommodation owned by a friendly South London geezer & his Hungarian wife. On the 1st floor of a residential block; climb the stairs around the inner courtyard after you've passed through the main entrance. Standard dorms, as well as sgl, dbl & trpl rooms, communal kitchen & laundry facilities, internet access, & shared toilets & showers. Centrally located just inside Károly körút, on the corner of Gerlóczy u. & Semmelweis u. The owners run the adjacent shop selling second-hand English-language books (🕐 Mon–Fri 11.00–18.00, Sat 10.00–14.00). Dorms (for 4, 6 & 8) 3,900Ft/pp. Price inc b/fast. €

PRIVATE APARTMENTS/ROOMS Several agencies can organise private apartments and private rooms, including Best Hotel Service (*www.besthotelservice.hu*), Boulevard City (*www.boulevardcity.hu*), Budapest Apartments 4U (*www.budapest4u.co.uk*), Ibusz (*www.ibusz.hu*), Non-Stop Hotel Service (*www.non-stophotelservice.hu*), To-ma Tour (*www.tomatour.hu*) and www.budapestrooms.hu.

CAMPING The best places to pitch up are on the Buda side of the river. Sites are well equipped (without giving Eurocamp undue cause for worry), and can be crowded in high season. The campers' favourite is **Zugligeti 'Niche' Camping** (XII, Zugligeti út 101; ➷ 1 200 8346; *www.campingniche.hu;* 🕐 *all yr [140 B4]*), a characterful site (9km from centre) that occupies a former tram terminus near the lower end of the chairlift (page 141).

✖ WHERE TO EAT

You can't properly enjoy rooting around a city without the anticipation of good food and drink to come. Coffee and cake is the cement between sights in a day spent wandering Budapest, and you'll reflect fondly on that evening passed people-watching on a terrace with a glass of beer and a bowl of bean soup. Hungarian food fuelled shepherds, hunters and fishermen, and it more than fills the legs of today's tourists; it is characteristically hearty, oily and rich, heavy with protein and carbohydrate. Prepare to loosen your belt and lose a few buttons.

RESTAURANTS Greek, Italian, French, Indian, Chinese, Japanese, Mexican, Russian – the whole gamut of global fare is represented in Budapest. You'll even find Hungarian. Prices at the bottom and top ends are higher than elsewhere in the country, considerably so where *haute cuisine* is concerned, and eateries in Váci utca and the Castle District will charge what they know they can get. Nevertheless, the average cost of a meal in any of the brackets remains significantly lower than in Western capitals. Eat-all-you-like brunches and fixed two- or three-course tourist menus offer added value, and an increasing number of restaurants allow those with lighter appetites to avoid waste (of food and cash) by ordering smaller portions at a discounted price. The quality of meals can vary, but tourist expectations are bringing about improvements by the year; good restaurants serving traditional Hungarian – as opposed to international – food remain a little thin on the ground (perhaps because locals rarely eat out).

We've chosen to divide restaurants **by area** (and then **by district order** within each area); euro symbols refer to the **average cost of a main course**. The price ranges are as follows:

€€€€€	5,000Ft and above
€€€€	3,500–4,995Ft
€€€	2,500–3,495Ft
€€	1,750–2,495Ft
€	1,745Ft and below

BUDA
Castle District

✗ **Arany Kaviár** I, Ostrom u. 19; ☎ I 201 6737/225 7370; www.aranykaviar.hu; ⏲ 12.00–24.00 daily [127 A1] This intimate restaurant specialises in Russian, Armenian, Ukrainian & Georgian cuisine; its rich decoration emulates the dining-rooms of the 19th-century Russian bourgeoisie. Have your tastebuds tickled by fine caviar & your head befuddled with frozen glasses of syrupy vodka, thick enough to spread on toast. Just outside Bécsi kapu. €€€€

✗ **Café Pierrot** I, Fortuna u. 14; ☎ I 375 6971; www.pierrot.hu; ⏲ 11.00–24.00 daily [127 B2] The Pierrot is a cellar restaurant that aims for yesteryear class in a 13th-century building – something it largely achieves (in spite of the subversive efforts of its cigarette-toking live pianist & his brimming ashtray during our last visit). Modern European & Hungarian cooking; northern end of Fortuna u. €€€€

✗ **Rivalda** I, Színház u. 5–9; ☎ I 489 0236; www.rivalda.net; ⏲ 11.30–23.30 daily [127 C3] A colourful interior pays homage to those who have trodden the boards, & there is a pretty dining area in the Carmelite courtyard. The menu features inventive Mediterranean & international cuisine. Just off Dísz tér, next to the National Dance Theatre (page 118). 3-course lunch menu for 4,000Ft (11.30–15.30 daily). €€€€

Víziváros

✗ **Le Jardin de Paris** I, Fő u. 20; ☎ I 201 0047; ⏲ 12.00–24.00 daily [127 C2] Ṯ 19, 41 Ḇ 86. Make it an evening meal at Le Jardin de Paris, for the garden is at its most atmospheric after dark. There are fairy lights in the trees, oil lamps on the tables, an al-fresco kitchen & an open-fronted cellar bar. Among the French offerings are snails, frogs' legs, truffles & lobster, as well as crêpes suzette. €€€–€€€€

✗ **Kacsa Vendéglő** II, Fő u. 75; ☎ I 201 9992; www.kacsavendeglo.hu; ⏲ 12.00–24.00 daily [88 C2] M̲2̲ Batthyány tér Ḇ 86. The chef has over 60 duck dishes in his portfolio at 'Duck Restaurant'; on request, he'll put together a plate featuring a 'taste' of several. The menu is interspersed with other international choices, & the goose-liver starter melted on the tongue. The waiters are attentive & knowledgeable. Let them guide you. This is exclusive dining, & very much all it's quacked up to be. Opposite the Király Baths. €€€€

✗ **Margitkert** II, Margit u. 15; ☎ I 326 0860; www.margitkert.com; ⏲ 12.00–24.00 daily [88 B1] Ṯ 4, 6 Ḇ 91. The Margitkert tempts diners with a big cheese. The bald-headed Lajos Boross is the 'Gypsy King' – the chief violin soloist (primás) – of the Budapest Gypsy Symphony Orchestra (www.100violins.com). The orchestra is the largest of its type in the world, & was born at the funeral of the legendary primás Sándor Jároka in 1985, when leading gypsy musicians struck up a spontaneous tune as a mark of respect. The restaurant's food is traditional, wholesome & well priced, the speciality of the rather kitsch house a wooden platter of grilled meats (for 2 or more). Up a steep hill opposite Margaret Bridge. Gypsy music daily from 18.00 (Boross usually from 19.30). €–€€

Moszkva tér

✖ **Marxim** II, Kis Rókus u. 23; ✆ I 316 0231;
⊕ Mon–Thu 12.00–01.00, Fri–Sat 12.00–02.00,
Sun 18.00–01.00 [88 B2] M̲2̲ *Moszkva tér* T̲ *4,
6.* This communist-themed pizzeria revels in a certain
nostalgia for iconography & agitprop murals while
dividing booths with barbed wire. Gorge on pieces of
Gorbi Gorbi or Pizza à la Kremlin. Loud & lively, it's
the only restaurant you'll visit that requests diners
not to scrawl on the walls. Pittas & pastas alongside
good-value pizzas. €
✖ **St Jupát** II, Dékán u. 3; ✆ I 212 2923;
www.stjupat.hu; ⊕ Sun–Thu 12.00–02.00, Fri–Sat

12.00–04.00 (garden 17.00–24.00) [88 B2]
M̲2̲ *Moszkva tér* T̲ *4, 6.* In the morning's early
hours, when the sensible of Budapest are long abed,
the St Jupát is a beacon for those more committed
to an active nightlife. Take a polished booth, cast a
bleary eye over the never-ending story that is the
menu, & prepare to line the stomach with daunting
wooden platters of Hungarian specials. It's busy,
buzzy & the prices please the tightest of wallets. It
also has an adjacent fast-food place. Just behind
Moszkva tér €-€€

Óbuda

✖ **Maligán** III, Lajos u. 38; ✆ I 240 9010;
www.maligan.hu; ⊕ Tue–Sat 12.00–14.00,
18.00–22.00 (wine store 10.00–18.00) [137 B6]
T̲ *17* B̲ *86, 109.* Dedicated to good food & wine
('maligán' refers to a measure of alcohol). There are
over 400 varieties of Hungarian wine on offer, & you
can purchase bottles to take away. €€–€€€
✖ **Symbol** III, Bécsi út 56; ✆ I 333 5656;
www.symbolbudapest.hu [137 B5] H̲E̲V̲ *Szépvölgyi*

út T̲ *17* B̲ *86, 109.* Symbol is like nothing else in
Budapest. At its core is a courtyard cocktail bar
with a glass roof that's open in summer; after a gin
& tonic here, you can choose from several
restaurant/bar areas leading from it, each with its
own style & atmosphere (a sports bar, Italian
restaurant, cellar restaurant & classy café), & there's
a downstairs club. Near Kolosy tér.

The Buda Hills

✖ **Remiz** II, Budakeszi út 5; ✆ I 275 1396;
www.remiz.hu; ⊕ Mon–Fri 11.00–23.00, Sat–Sun
09.00–23.00 [140 B4] B̲ *22* T̲ *18, 56 from
Moszkva tér.* The Remíz ('Tram Depot') blends past
& present; tram paraphernalia & tinkling ivories
evoke an era of silent movies & full moustaches,
while traditional dishes are infused with modern
international influences on the monthly menu. It's
low-lit & graceful without a hint of stuffiness. One
of the city's best; if only it were more central.
€€€
✖ **Jardinette** XI, Németvölgyi út 136; ✆ I 248
1652; www.jardinette.hu; ⊕ 10.00–24.00 daily [140

C6] T̲ *59 (from Moszkva tér)* B̲ *8.* Reader Mervyn
Brown pointed us towards this selection – a garden
restaurant beneath the branches of chestnut trees
where you can enjoy good food & good value.
Mediterranean & Hungarian dishes. Opposite the
Farkasréti Cemetery. €€–€€€
✖ **Arcade** XII, Kiss János Altábornagy u. 38; ✆ I
225 1969; www.arcadebistro.hu; ⊕ Mon–Sat
12.00–23.00 [140 C5] T̲ *59 (from Moszkva tér)*
B̲ *105.* International & Hungarian cuisine; we confess
not yet to having eaten here ourselves, but the
restaurant is a recommendation of co-updater,
Elizabeth Courage – whose taste is faultless! €€€

PEST
Downtown & beyond
✖ **Babel Delicate** V, Váci u. 82; ✆ I 338 2143;
www.babeldelicate.hu; ⊕ 12.00–24.00 daily [144
C5] This sleek newcomer to the city's prime artery
explores food's many flavours (or languages – hence
'Babel'). The evening fare features set, 8-course tapas-
style meals selected from 2 menus
(international/Hungarian 12,900/11,900Ft). If you've
less cash to spend, lunch is much cheaper & takes a
more traditional form, with à-la-carte & set-menu (2-
/3-course 1,490/2,490Ft) options. There's an extensive
list of over 140 wines. Lunch à la carte: €€

✖ **Café Kör** V, Sas u. 17; ✆ I 311 0053;
www.cafekor.com; ⊕ Mon–Sat 10.00–22.00 [144 B1]
A popular restaurant offering good (but not excellent)
food, attentive service, a convivial atmosphere &
reasonable prices. It's a safe bet for a pleasant meal
– it's just not the 88th best restaurant in the world
(as voted in 2007 by *Restaurant Magazine*)…
Choose from Hungarian & international choices.
Payment is accepted in cash only. €€€
✖ **Central Cellar** V, Váci u. 11/A; ✆ I 318 1580;
⊕ 12.00–23.30 daily [144 B3] This restaurant &

wine bar at the northern end of Váci u. has been recommended separately by readers Kate Lach & Martin Evans. Kate calls it a 'treasure of a find slap bang in the centre of Pest'. Martin enjoyed a tender steak with goose liver; he mentions that the service was very good, & that there's live gypsy music. €€€

✘ **Fatál** V, Váci u. 67; ☎ 1 266 2607; www.fatalrestaurant.com; ⏱ 11.30–02.00 daily [144 C5] An atmospheric, cacophonous brick cauldron of chatter & whirring fans. The menu features cheap, super-sized dishes that ooze Hungarian rusticity & manliness, the fare of tough-skinned farmers with big hands: liver sausage, lung, black pudding, dumplings, deep-fried brains, red cabbage. We're fans. Entrance on Pintér u. €€–€€€

✘ **Gerlóczy** See page 111.

✘ **Kyoto** V, Roosevelt tér 7–8; ☎ 1 801 9862; www.kyotoetterem.hu [144 A1] This smart Japanese restaurant has a glass frontage overlooking the square. Among its choices are a Bento Special (4,500Ft), featuring a feast of soup, tempura shrimp & raw delicacies. €€€

✘ **Mokka** V, Sas u. 4; ☎ 1 328 0081; www.mokkarestaurant.hu; ⏱ 12.00–24.00 daily [144 B1] The Mokka has North African styling & a funky elegance. The service is excellent. Its international menu has a Mediterranean flavour, & features tapas selections (for 700Ft) alongside main dishes. €€€€

✘ **Nádor** V, Nádor u. 30; ☎ 1 302 3086; ⏱ 12.00–24.00 daily [149 A3] This atmospheric little cellar restaurant near Parliament was recommended to us by readers Ian Traill and Donald McIntyre, who each observed that the staff were attentive & genuinely helpful, the portions very satisfactory, and the food excellent. Hungarian & international. €€–€€€

✘ **Páva** V, Roosevelt tér 5–6; ☎ 1 268 6000; www.fourseasons.com/budapest/; ⏱ Mon–Sat

Terézváros

✘ **Baraka** VI, Andrássy út 111; ☎ 1 483 1355; www.barakarestaurant.hu; ⏱ 12.00–23.00 daily [149 D1] M1 Bajza u. B 105. In the hands of a former sous chef of the Four Seasons, the Baraka serves good international food with an oriental bent from its home in the Andrássy Hotel (page 101). Set 2-course lunch menu (Mon–Fri 12.00–15.30) for 4,000Ft. Live jazz in the garden on Thu. €€€€

✘ **Chez Daniel** VI, Szív u. 32; ☎ 1 302 4039; www.chezdaniel.hu; ⏱ 12.00–15.00, 19.00–23.00 daily [149 C2] M1 Kodály Körönd TB 70, 78

18.00–22.30 [144 A1] Fabulous north Italian cuisine served in the elegant surroundings you'd expect of the Four Seasons Hotel. Among the offerings is a 6-course degustation menu that changes fortnightly. €€€€€

✘ **Tigris** Mérleg u. 10; ☎ 1 317 3715; www.tigrisrestaurant.hu [144 B1] The Tigris has apparently attracted attention from the reviewers who give out Michelin stars. The elegant restaurant serves haute-cuisiney takes on traditional Hungarian dishes, as well as some international choices; it includes a range of foie-gras specialities.

✘ **Trattoria Toscana** V, Belgrád rakpart 13; ☎ 1 327 0045; www.toscana.hu; ⏱ 12.00–24.00 daily [144 B5] Tuscan cooking by an Italian chef in an open kitchen in a cosy villa facing the Danube. The service is friendly & the restaurant has had a good reputation for several years. Between Erzsébet & Szabadság bridges. The adjacent wine bar & shop (L'Enoteca; www.lenoteca.hu; ⏱ Mon–Sat 11.00–24.00) serves Tuscan food and booze. €€€–€€€€

✘ **Costes** IX, Ráday u. 4; ☎ 1 219 0696; www.costes.hu; ⏱ Mon–Sat 12.00–24.00 [144 D5] M3 Kálvin tér. The arrival of this chic restaurant (in mid 2008) was the clearest evidence that Ráday utca had shed its once-gritty skin. A few years ago, you'd have looked in vain for pot-roasted squab pigeon or prawn tart with aubergine caviar in these parts. Costes serves these dishes among rich furnishings; you'll need some richness in your wallet too, for it ain't cheap. €€€€€

✘ **Kiskakukk** XIII, Pozsonyi út 12; ☎ 1 450 0829; www.kiskakukk.hu; ⏱ 12.00–23.45 daily [149 A1] T 4, 6 TB 75, 76. Reader Martin Evans highly recommends this restaurant, with its lofty ceilings & old-fashioned elegance. He judged his meal here second only to that at Gundel, & he enjoyed some excellent wine. Hungarian & international. Just north of Szent István körút. €€–€€€

B 105. Pay no heed to the tatty homes around it; Daniel's house is very much in order. The staple of the French food is fresh produce from local markets, & there's a sunny courtyard with open-fronted bar. In addition to exclusive à-la-carte options, there are set menus (up to 6 courses) for 3,500–9,000Ft. €€€€

✘ **Donatella's Kitchen** VI, Kiraly u. 30–32; ☎ 1 878 0515; ⏱ 12.00–24.00 [144 D1] M1 Opera TB 70, 78. Despite the gaudy, diamond-effect lighting spelling out its name on the façade, this restaurant has drawn the discerning crowd to its table since opening in 2008. On the menu are Italian dishes of veal, pork & fish, as well as pasta & pizza. Pizzas 1,080–2,700Ft. €€€€

✘ **Fausto's** VI, Székely Mihály u. 2; ✆ 1 877 6210; www.fausto.hu; ☉ Mon–Fri 12.00–15.00, 19.00–23.00, Sat 18.00–23.00 [144 D1] M1 *Opera* B *105*. This remains the city's Italian stallion. It caters for guests wishing to take time to indulge in fine dining. The décor is immaculate & the chef concocts delicate regional dishes. €€€€

✘ **Főzelékfaló Ételbár** VI, Nagymező u. 18; ☉ Mon–Fri 09.00–22.00, Sat 10.00–21.00, Sun 11.00–18.00 [149 C3] M1 *Opera* TB *70, 78* B *105*. A fast-food joint you can visit in all good conscience. This is one in a small chain of food bars specialising in *főzelék* – a quick & convenient Hungarian classic comprising dishes of puréed vegetables thickened with fried flour. 350Ft/dish. €

✘ **Goa** VI, Andrássy út 8; ✆ 1 302 2570; www.goaworld.hu; ☉ 12.00–24.00 daily [144 C1] M1 *Bajcsy-Zsilinszky út* B *105*. Washed walls & hanging lanterns evoke the Indian theme, but the menu reflects influences far more wide ranging – Thai, Japanese, Italian & Argentinian among them. There is also a selection of yuppy sandwiches – on

Heroes' Square & City Park

✘ **Bagolyvár** XIV, Állatkerti út 2; ✆ 1 468 3110; www.bagolyvar.com; ☉ 12.00–23.00 daily [89 F1] M1 *Hősök tere* TB *72* B *105*. 'Owl's Castle' was established by Hungarian-American restaurateur George Lang, who also revived Gundel after communism. While the Baroque & Biedermeier furnishings radiate 19th- rather than 21st-century charm, Bagolyvár is consciously less formal in atmosphere than its neighbour – there's even an outdoor children's play area – as well as less imposing on the pocket. The canopied terrace is a joy in summer months, & the all-female staff are at the heart of the restaurant's lightness of touch. Mild, but traditional, Hungarian flavours dominate. €€€

✘ **Gundel** XIV, Állatkerti út 2; ✆ 1 468 4040; www.gundel.hu; ☉ 12.00–16.00, 18.30–24.00 daily [89 F1] M1 *Hősök tere* TB *72* B *105*. It's fashionable to decry Gundel – indeed, even we were disturbed to hear of a current step towards nouvelle-cuisine-style dishes, which we hope is but a temporary experimental fancy (we find that less is rarely more!). However, the nosh has been top-notch during our visits; Queen Elizabeth II & Pope John Paul II loaded their forks here, and that's good enough for us. The main dining room evokes high *fin-de-siècle* grace. Traditionally the menu has

ciabatta, obviously – & a set lunch menu (Mon–Fri) for 1,800/2,500Ft (2-/3-course). A good choice. €€€–€€€€

✘ **Klassz** VI, Andrássy út 41; ✆ 1 328 0081; www.klassz.eu; ☉ Mon–Sat 11.30–23.00, Sun 11.30–18.00 [149 C3] M1 *Oktogon* T *4, 6* B *105*. Klassz means 'great', & we've twice had greatness thrust upon us at this restaurant. Steaming plates of greatness, featuring a duckleg with crisp, golden skin & goose liver that melted on the tongue. The chef offers twists on Hungarian dishes; a cove lined with wine bottles is a sign of the restaurant's link with the Hungarian Wine Society (Bortársaság), & the booze is good value. So too is the food itself – unlike most top restaurants, the bill won't spoil your night. You can't book ahead. €€

✘ **Marquis de Salade** VI, Hajós u. 43; ✆ 1 302 4086; ☉ 11.00–01.00 daily [149 B2] TB *70, 78*. This characterful restaurant – its cellar section arching & intimate, with woven wall hangings – serves an extensive range of well-prepared & sizeable specialities from Azerbaijan, Russia & Hungary. Alongside the lamb & fish is a fair vegetarian selection. Friendly owner. €€€

✘ **Menza** See box, page 152.

featured refined creations based upon Hungarian classics, as well as dishes from France & elsewhere. The gypsy musical ensemble is as accomplished as any you will find. All this comes at a very high price by Hungarian standards. Enjoy a 5-course set menu with wine for 18,700Ft, 6 courses for 24,200Ft, or a Sunday brunch buffet (*11.30–15.00*) for around 5,900Ft. There are also good-value 3-course lunch menus (*Mon–Sat 12.00–15.00*) for 3,300–4,700Ft. At the other end of the spectrum, the most expensive 5-course set menu will set you back 39,200Ft. Gents require a jacket. €€€€€

✘ **Robinson** XIV, Városligeti tó; ✆ 1 422 0222; www.robinsonrestaurant.hu; ☉ 12.00–16.00, 18.00–24.00 daily [89 F1] M1 *Hősök tere* TB *72* B *105*. On a sun-drenched day, life seems tickety-boo from under a pagoda on Robinson's decked jetty. The lake & its water life are all about, while in front is an expensive menu that makes a good stab at being truly international – Hungarian broth, Thai prawn soup, French onion soup, New Zealand beef. In fact, it's an appealing place during winter too, toasty warm next to the fire in the pavilion's hearth as mist lifts in curls from the lake. The café (☉ *12.00–24.00 daily*) above the restaurant offers a lofty view of the park while you lick your ice-cream. €€€€

Erzsébetváros & Józsefváros

✗ **Carmel** VII, Kazinczy u. 31; ☎ 1 322 1834; www.carmel.hu; ☉ Sun–Thu 12.00–23.00, Fri 12.00–16.00 (evenings for pre-paid bookings only) [144 D2] T̲B̲ 74. Kosher since spring 2008, the Carmel has a cellar dining room studded with pretty windows of stained glass. The menu offers Hungarian & Israeli food, & there are live klezmer concerts by Sabbathsong every Thu from 20.00 (entrance 2,000Ft). €€€–€€€€

✗ **Osteria Fausto's** VII, Dohány u. 5; ☎ 1 269 6806; www.osteria.hu; ☉ Mon–Sat 12.00–15.00, 19.00–23.00 [144 D3] M̲2̲ Astoria B̲ 109. The Osteria offers a deliberately lighter & less expensive dining experience than its big-sister restaurant, Fausto's (see opposite). €€–€€€

✗ **Fülemüle** VIII, Kőfaragó u. 5; ☎ 1 266 7947; www.fulemule.hu; ☉ 12.00–22.00 daily [149 D5] T̲ 4, 6 M̲2̲ Blaha Lujza tér. In the thick of District VIII, Fülemüle specialises in Jewish (non-kosher) dishes typical of central Europe, with goose featuring most prominently. Thanks to András Hirschler for pointing us to it; the Nobel-Prize-winning author Imre Kertész is also a regular diner. Short distance inside József körút. Set 3-/5-course lunches (Sat–Sun 12.00–16.00) for 2,290/3,690Ft. €€€

PÂTISSERIES, COFFEE HOUSES, TEA HOUSES

Coffee houses were traditionally meeting places where views were discussed and grievances grumbled about. The young revolutionaries of 1848 are said to have penned their demands for reform in the Pilvax kávéház, while two decades later Ferenc Deák negotiated the terms of the 1867 Compromise in the coffee house of the Queen of England Hotel. Some establishments even had their own notepaper for artists to use; where they didn't, an impoverished poet would scrawl a sonnet on a napkin in lieu of payment for his drink. At the turn of the 20th century, there were nearly 1,000 coffee houses in Budapest, with a staggering 64 places along the Great Boulevard alone to drink the 'black soup' (fekete leves). (Hungarians were introduced to coffee during the period of Ottoman occupation, and initially it was associated with unpleasant business – after a meal, the Turks would serve coffee while discussing the taxes owed by their Hungarian 'subjects' – hence the unattractive-sounding nickname for coffee.) The importance of the coffee house as a forum for social discussion and expression diminished in the 1940s, and the more staunchly working-class and socialist coffee bar took hold (see page 110), but many of the classics of the era remain. Furthermore, a hundred years on there's been a renaissance, with a crop of new venues. Some fall within the grand Pesti tradition, while others are modern, trendy interpretations that are more properly café-bars. In addition, **tea houses** have become increasingly popular; there is a crop of them, for instance, on Jókai utca (near Liszt Ferenc tér). The following establishments are divided between Buda and Pest, and listed in district order.

Buda

▭ **Ruszwurm** I, Szentháromság u. 7; ☎ 1 375 5284; www.ruszwurm.hu; ☉ 10.00–19.00 daily [127 B3] Ruszwurm is the oldest café in Budapest, operating since 1827, its interior a fine example of the Biedermeier style. Its cakes have graced the tables of palatines & duchesses; Sisi (Empress Erzsébet) came here for hot chocolate.

▭ **Marvelosa** I, Lánchíd u. 13; ☎ 1 201 9221; www.marvelosa.eu [88 C4] Beautiful, Parisian-styled café heartily recommended by reader Daniel Sollé.

▭ **Auguszt** II, Fény u. 8; ☎ 1 316 3817; XI, Sasadi út 190; ☎ 1 249 0134; www.augusztcukraszda.hu; ☉ Tue–Sat 10.00–18.00 [140 D4] The name Auguszt is synonymous with fine pastry in Budapest. Since 1870, 5 generations have strived to maintain the family reputation. The dynasty operates from 3 locations (see also page 110), each managed by a family member. (To get to the Farkasréti tér outlet, take tram 59 from Moszkva tér; it's next to Farkasréti Cemetery.)

▭ **Daubner** II, Szépvölgyi út 50; ☎ 1 335 2253; ☉ 09.00–19.00 [140 D3] It ain't much to look at, but this is the city's sugar daddy. Recollections of banoffee-pie ice-cream make us dribble.

▭ **Szamos** XII, Böszörmenyi út 44–46; ☎ 1 355 1728; www.szamosmarcipan.hu; ☉ 10.00–19.00 daily (10.00–20.00 in summer) [140 C5] One of the city's best pâtisseries – & one of more than 10 run by this company in Budapest. The website lists the locations of all the others.

The *presszó* or *eszpresszó* is less traditionally highbrow than the *cukrászda* or *kávéház*. The author Sándor Márai complained in 1940 that in *eszpresszó* bars 'one can only chat – one cannot write a great work as there is no space on the table'. It's a communal place for the local working class, where groups of ladies enjoy cakes and gangs of workmen play dominoes and eat *somlói galuska* with their beer. The floor is stone or covered with beige linoleum, and there are net curtains, tiled walls and little gnome stools. Surly waitresses wear long, lace-up boots that give support during endless hours of standing. A proper old-style *presszó* has a neon sign proclaiming a socialist name such as 'Terv' (Five-Year Plan), 'Béke' (Peace), 'Haladás' (Progress) or even 'Májas' (Liver Sausage). But the *eszpresszó* is an endangered species. One by one, they have closed as rent soars and the fast-food chains and banks move in.

Budapest was once the city of *eszpresszó* bars, where elderly couples would drink brandy and have sing-songs on Friday nights, where old *bácsis* danced with little girls and *nénis* danced together, where workers spent their wages on beer, and the air was thick with the fog of Munkás (Worker) cigarettes. In 1937, the Quick in Vigadó utca was the first coffee bar to open (it is an office now), and was followed by many more. After 1956, Social-Realist architecture began to wane. Shops destroyed during the uprising were rebuilt in the modern style. There was a craze for neon, and for radical slogans like 'Prosperity' and 'Spartacus'. While some of the 1950s *eszpresszós* still exist, the original style is harder to find. The neon lights are fading, the Traubi (grape-flavoured) and Márka (cherry) soft drinks are hard to find, the Bambi pop has disappeared, the wheels of progress grind on. However, the following are hanging on in there:

Bambi II, Frankel Leó út 2–4; ❯ I 212 3171; ⊕ Mon–Fri 07.00–21.00, Sat–Sun 09.00–20.00 [88 B2] One of the few untouched interiors dating back to the 1960s. Red leatherette seats & old men playing dominoes in the afternoon. A good example of the cheap prices to be found at these places – the most expensive dish is 550Ft, & large beers are around 450Ft.

Ibolya V, Ferenciek tere 5; ⊕ 09.30–24.00 daily [144 C4]

Terv V, Nádor u. 19; ⊕ Mon–Fri 09.00–24.00, Sat 09.00–23.00, Sun 10.00–23.00 [144 A1] Smartened up & with a genuinely characterful atmosphere, the Terv has *cukrászda* pretensions that are nevertheless undermined by the occasional working man drinking beer & spirits in the morning.

Tik-Tak XII, Böszörményi út 17/C; ❯ I 212 3762 [140 C5]

Tulipán V, Nádor u. 32; ⊕ 24hrs daily [149 A3] One of a couple of *presszós* in District V bearing the names of flowers (inc the Ibolya – 'Violet'). Back room of high stools, mushroom tables & walls turned beige by cigarette smoke; the roadside tables are quite popular with locals.

Pest

Auguszt V, Kossuth Lajos u. 14–16; ❯ I 337 6379; www.augusztcukraszda.hu; ⊕ Mon–Fri 10.00–18.00 [144 C3]. Pesti branch of the family chain (see page 109).

Big Ben V, Veres Pálné u. 10; ❯ I 317 8982; www.bigbenteahaz.hu; ⊕ 10.00–22.00 daily [144 C4] Quaint English-themed tea house serving a wide selection of teas & selling teapots & other brewing bits. At corner of Veres Pálné u. & Irányi u.

Centrál V, Károlyi Mihály u. 9; ❯ I 266 2110; www.centralkavehaz.hu; ⊕ 08.00–24.00 daily [144 C4]. In its pomp during the late 1800s & early 1900s, this was a hub of intellectual – &

particularly literary – life. The artist József Rippl-Rónai scrawled 'I drew this in the Centrál Coffee House' on one of his paintings. Today you'll find high ceilings, polite service & snacks for the modest purse (*zóna ételek*) alongside more expensive Hungarian & international dishes. Located on the corner of Ferenciek tere.

Gerbeaud V, Vörösmarty tér 7–8; ❯ I 429 9000; www.gerbeaud.hu; ⊕ 09.00–21.00 daily [144 B2] Hungary's most famous café, Gerbeaud is a refined behemoth in marble, walnut & wicker, a favoured rendezvous spot, an exquisite must in the tourist top 10, & always – always – busy. Service can be slow.

In the café's cellar, accessed via Dorottya u., is a beer hall (⊕ *12.00–23.00 daily*) serving home-brewed drinks, & it has an adjacent restaurant (Onyx).

⚲ **Gerlóczy** V, Kamermayer károly tér; ☏ I 501 4000; www.gerloczy.hu; ⊕ 07.00–23.00 daily [144 C3] Ask café-loving Budapesters in the know, & many will declare the Gerlóczy their current favourite. There's much to recommend it, not least its location overlooking a quiet square; while close to the city's heart, the beat is muffled here. The split-level interior courts an atmosphere of old-fashioned Parisian elegance. In addition to coffee & cake, the menu includes excellent heartier meals (€€€); there are also some lovely guest rooms (page 103).

⚲ **Lukács** VI, Andrássy út 70; ☏ I 373 0407; www.lukacscukraszda.com; ⊕ Mon–Fri 08.30–19.00, Sat–Sun 09.30–19.00 [149 C2] It's changed much since being refurbished during the 1990s & more recently, but this used to be where secret policemen ate pastries in between interrogations at their headquarters (Andrássy út 60; see page 162).

⚲ **Művész** VI, Andrássy út 29; ☏ I 352 1337; ⊕ 09.00–23.45 daily [149 C3] 'The Artist' was a favourite of the upper middle classes during the communist era. It exudes old-world grandeur, & the terrace on a warm evening is great for a pastry before watching the fat lady sing at the State Opera House opposite.

⚲ **New York** VII, Erzsébet körút 9–11; ☏ I 886 6111; www.newyorkpalace.hu; ⊕ 10.00–24.00 daily [149 D4] The New York kávéház could justly claim to be at the birth of modern Hungarian literature. Ferenc Molnár is said to have tossed the café's key into the Danube in protest at its closing at night; he went on to write his great work *Liliom* here. The café re-opened as part of the Boscolo Hotel a couple of years ago; the hotel aimed at absolute authenticity during the renovation, & there are original frescoes on the ceiling; however, you sense it lacks the weighty gravitas of its 19th-century predecessor. Near Blaha Lujza tér.

WHERE TO DRINK

You'll have no trouble finding a place for a proper drink in Budapest; the primary clusters are on the Pest side of the river, and on Liszt Ferenc tér and Ráday utca in particular. During summer, such areas make a very Parisian use of public space as tables spill on to pavements, squares and courtyards. Al-fresco **garden bars** (such as Szimpla kert, page 113) have also become popular in recent years; they make use of decrepit courtyards and, because of their locations in residential areas, tend to be fairly transient. The very latest trendy hangout spots are rooftop **terrace bars** – such as Kópé – perched on commercial buildings like department stores. All of the above are generally open daily from 11.00 or 12.00 until 24.00, although closing times often extend into the early hours on Fridays and Saturdays. It isn't unknown for city-centre bars to raise their prices in the evenings.

The following bars and pubs are divided between Buda and Pest, and listed in district order.

BUDA

♀ **Café Miró** I, Úri u. 30; ☏ I 201 5573; www.cafemiro.hu; ⊕ 09.00–24.00 daily [127 B3] A self-consciously contemporary wine-bar-cum-café. Inspired by the work of Catalan artist Joan Miró, its bold splashes of colour & wiry metal furnishings draw the fashionable & young like moths to its flame. Good view of Mátyás Church – & of old 'golden balls' (page 130).

♀ **Lánchíd söröző** I, Fő u. 4; ☏ I 214 3144; ⊕ 09.00–24.00 daily [127 D3] An authentic pub recommended by ex-resident Lucy Mallows. Great wine, great black-&-white photos on the walls & a great owner who loves to practise his English. On the Buda side of the Chain Bridge.

♀ **Dokk Café** II, Mammut II, 2nd Floor, Lövőház u. 2–6; ☏ I 345 8531; www.dokkcafe.hu; ⊕ Mon–Sat 11.00–24.00, Sun 12.00–24.00 [88 B2] This is an evening's swanky starting point for the élite & beautiful of Budapest. There are club nights between autumn & spring (⊕ *end Sep–May Thu–Sat 20.00–03.00; free entry*), while in summer the clubbers move to Dokk Beach (page 119). Sells the inevitable cocktails, together with surprisingly good international food (€€–€€€).

♀ **Symbol** See page 106.

What should you plump for with dinner? Aged in networks of mould-clad cellars, **Tokaji Aszú** is long-lived and nectar sweet, with a volcanic mineral edge. It was favoured by Europe's royal houses, and Louis XIV declared it 'the king of wines, the wine of kings' – which must have had the marketing people gleefully rubbing their hands. Queen Victoria was presented each birthday with 12 bottles to mark each year of her life, receiving over 900 at the last count. It suffered under the state economy, but is back to its freshest and fruitiest.

Aszú is created from grapes affected by noble rot, and the number of hods (*puttonyos*) of such grapes added to a dry base wine determines the wine's sweetness. Most is produced at levels of between three and six puttonyos, with Aszú Esszencia sweeter still. Top recent vintages were 1996 and 2000, while those of 1993 and 1999 are judged to be classics. Dry Tokaji wines are also available – look out for those of 2000 and 2002 – but more readily acclaimed are the light and young-drinking whites from **Lake Balaton** (especially the Olaszrizling of Badacsony).

If you fancy something bubbly, the country's main sparkling wine (*pezsgő*) is the relatively inexpensive **Törley** champagne. It's produced by Hungary's largest wine company, Hungarovin, and compares favourably with versions from New World countries.

Bull's Blood (Bikavér) derives its name from the period of Turkish occupation; the sober Ottomans thought that their opponents were made brave by consuming flagons of animal blood, when the Hungarians were actually more sensibly seeking Dutch courage in flagons of red wine. Moves are underway to protect Bull's Blood, which became synonymous with a Hungarian product ruined by commercialism, but its definition remains loose – simply encompassing 'quality' blended red wine from Szekszárd or Eger. One problem is that large companies continue to cling to its potential as a brand, looking enviously at the success of Australian Rosemount or Jacob's Creek. A leading firm even attempted to spark success by replacing its bull's head logo with a rather Spanish-looking matador. Stick to bottles from small producers who take time over the product rather than the branding and you'll find some excellent wines. Alternatively, reds from **Villány** are expressive, full-bodied and rightly rated.

PEST

♀ **Becketts** V, Bajcsy-Zsilinsky út 72; ✆ I 311 1035; www.becketts.hu; ☺ Sun–Thu 12.00–01.00, Fri–Sat 12.00–02.00 [149 B2] It's named after Samuel Beckett, there is passable Guinness in the taps & a *Commitments* poster on the wall, which all adds up to about as authentic an Irish pub as Hungary has to offer. Ex-pats love the place, drawn by the promise of 14 draught beers, British sports on TV, & live music from 20.00 on Thursday. The pub grub is also excellent.

♀ **Etno** V, Fehér Hajó u. 5; ✆ I 411 0643; www.etno.hu; ☺ 11.00–23.00 daily [144 B2] Don a pair of shades & a cool expression, & relax in the knowledge that you're among the trendy set. Sip cocktails, coffees, milkshakes or flavoured teas. Statuettes of Hindu elephant gods look on as you tuck into food with an Asian bent. Fits the bill for an afternoon break, an informal meal (€€€) or an evening drink.

♀ **Irish Cat** V, Múzeum körút 41; ✆ I 266 4085; ☺ Mon–Thu 11.00–02.00, Fri–Sat 11.00–04.00, Sun 17.00–02.00 [144 D4] Newly refurbished, this is traditionally one of the city's good-time meat markets. There's flat Guinness & thumping chart music, but also a surprisingly diverse crowd & an unthreatening atmosphere. Opposite the National Museum.

♀ **Negro** V, Szent István tér 11; ✆ I 373 0391; ☺ Mon–Tue 08.00–01.00, Wed–Sun 08.00–02.00 [144 B1] With dark woods & muted orange lighting, this smooth lounge-bar (named after a cough sweet) near the Basilica jostles for the custom of the city's slickers. As you'd expect, there's an interminable list of cocktails, a smaller selection of light meals & a fair share of noses in the air.

♀ **Tom-George** V, Október 6 u. 8; ☏ I 266 3525; 8 www.tomgeorge.hu; ◷ 12.00–24.00 daily [144 B1] One of several trendy restaurant-bars in this pocket near the Basilica. Its menu (€€€€) offers a wide range of international cuisines, & there are 2- & 3-course business lunches for 1,850–2,250Ft. Large selection of cocktails. Popular with local celebrities & porn stars.

♀ **Box utca** VI, Bajcsy-Zsilinszky út 21; ☏ I 354 1444; www.box-utca.hu; ◷ Mon–Fri 08.00–24.00, Sat–Sun 10.00–24.00 [149 B3] The Hungarian boxer István 'Ko-Ko' Kovács was an Olympic gold-medal winner in 1996 & a world champ in 2001, & he's since made a pretty good fist of this upmarket sports bar & restaurant. This is a place of plasma screens & soft lighting, of sports jackets rather than string vests; chunky chips make way for breaded chicken roulade (€€€–€€€€). During his visit, David Coulthard carelessly left behind his racing car in the restaurant. Opposite the Arany János metro.

♀ **Instant** VI, Nagymező u. 38; ◷ Mon–Fri 18.00–02.00 [149 B3] A relative newcomer, Instant has the potential to be a cult classic. It occupies not only a covered courtyard, but also the rooms of the flats surrounding it, each with its own unique styling – including one with furniture stuck to the ceiling, which is sure to confuse those who've had a drink too many.

♀ **Kópé** VI, Nyugati tér 1–2; ◷ mid Jun–mid Sep 18.00–02.00 daily (roof), 12.00–02.00 (downstairs) [149 B2] The latest of the summer roof-terrace bars, & among the best. The Skála was one of the city's main department stores during the communist period; how the reds would have turned in their beds to see its rooftop cradling the city's chic young things. There's an open-fronted beach-style bar, a DJ shack & elevated views over Nyugati station.

♀ **Castro Bisztró** VII, Madách tér 3; ☏ I 215 0184; ◷ Mon–Thu 11.00–24.00, Fri 11.00–01.00, Sat 12.00–01.00, Sun 14.00–24.00 [144 C2] This tatty-chic bar (which serves Serbian food, but is no bistro) is extremely popular, & attracts a mixed crowd – from students to leading city players

(Hungary's hottest film star was at the adjacent table when we visited). Non-smokers beware – there's a perpetual fug. Drinks are well-priced (a mojito costs 950Ft, a pint 450Ft).

♀ **Dupla & Szimpla** VII, Kertész u. 48; ☏ I 321 9119; ◷ 12.00–24.00 daily (Dupla), 10.00–02.00 (Szimpla) [149 C3] These sister establishments – with separate entrances, but linked inside by stairs – have an illicit, speak-easy feel to them that makes them enduringly popular. There's an eclectic mix of furniture, graffiti on the walls & the dingy Szimpla basement is lit with red bulbs. Don't forget the third sister, Szimpla kert (see below), 5 mins away.

♀ **Előre 57** VII, Akácfa u. 57; ◷ Mon–Sat 07.00–02.00 [149 C3] Not for the fainthearted, this modern take on an old-style wine house serves alcohol from metal vats & hosts the odd inebriated regular. Retro, 1960s furniture – & pints from just 300Ft.

♀ **Gozsdu udvar** VII, Király u. 13; www.gozsduudvar.hu [144 D2] A newly renovated string of courtyards in the Jewish district that we tip to develop into a popular evening watering spot.

♀ **Szimpla kert** VII, Kazinczy u. 14; ☏ I 321 5880; www.szimpla.hu; ◷ 12.00–04.00 daily [149 C4] There's a dash of surreality about Szimpla kert, the city's best-known courtyard bar. An elegant archway on this quiet, residential street is a porthole to a flaking other world. The derelict courtyard itself fills with customers drinking at little tables, while there are also quirkily themed rooms inside. In daylight there is a grungy feel to the whole set-up, but the edges are smoothed when night falls & the courtyard lights give it a romantic Mediterranean atmosphere. A kitchen on the first floor provides simple snacks.

♀ **Café Intenzo** IX, Kálvin tér 9; ☏ I 219 5243; www.cafeintenzo.hu; ◷ Mon–Fri 11.00–24.00 [144 D5] This building housed the Two Lions Inn until 1881, but it is now a popular pavement café-bar. Avoid the noise of traffic by sitting in the summer garden courtyard at the back, part of a large square owned by the church.

Liszt Ferenc tér & Jókai tér

Liszt tér is the established scratching post for the city's young and trendy. It is here that they gather in real concentrations around the café-bars that line either side of the square (and on Jókai tér opposite), perched at the tables and chairs that litter it in summer months. Among the most popular bars are Barokko, Buena Vista, Cactus Juice (Western-themed and lively), Café Vian, Fresco, Karma Café and Kiadó, but there's little between them and you're best just to pitch up and park yourself where you fancy.

Ráday utca Linking Kálvin tér and the lower reaches of the Great Boulevard, the regenerated Ráday utca has established itself as the main challenger to the hegemony of Liszt Ferenc tér, sustained by the custom of students from the three universities near by. It's less gritty than it used to be, with charming streetlamps bearing copper shades and outdoor pavement seating in summer. The bulk of the decent bars & restaurants are concentrated in the road's northern portion.

ENTERTAINMENT AND NIGHTLIFE

There's no excuse for calling it a day when the sun sets over Budapest. No city wears night's cloak with more elegance. The castle turns on its illuminations, bridges follow suit, lights ride the river's ripples and romance's stage is set. Choose a bar for that post-dinner digestif, and decide upon where next. There are few people whose darkness hours Budapest can't find a way to fill.

Several publications listing **what's on** are available (often free) from Tourinforms, hotels, pubs and bars. In general, the best bet for English speakers are titles like *Where Budapest*, the *Budapest Sun*, or the *Budapest Times* (with its 11-day calendar detailing upcoming events at bars, cultural houses, etc), and A5-size magazines like *Budapest Funzine, Programme, Key to Budapest, Rhythm of Budapest* and *Budapest Life*. Grab a free copy of *Súgó* for theatre listings that are translated into English in July and August. The comprehensive *Pesti Est* and *Pesti Műsor* give information on arts and entertainment, but are mainly in Hungarian.

TICKET OFFICES Most venues have their own box offices, but the following agencies (*jegyiroda*) sell tickets to sporting events, opera and ballet, concerts (including pop, jazz, classical), theatre performances, and folklore programmes.

Broadway XIII Hollán Ernő u. 10; ℡ 1 340 4883; www.broadwayjegyiroda.hu; ⊕ Mon–Fri 11.00–18.00
Concert & Media IX, Üllői út 11–13; ℡ 1 455 9000; www.jegyelado.hu; ⊕ Mon–Fri 10.00–18.00
Cultur-Comfort VI, Paulay Ede u. 31; ℡ 1 322 0000 w www.cultur-comfort.hu; ⊕ Mon–Fri 09.00–18.00
Jegymester VI, Bajcsy-Zsilinszky út 31; ℡ 1 302 4433; www.jegymester.hu; ⊕ Mon–Fri 10.00–16.00. Has a refreshingly clear website.
Showtime Budapest II, Nyúl u. 24; ℡ 1 354 0224 (office), 06 30 303 0999 (ticket reservations);

www.showtimebudapest.hu (details of upcoming concerts & shows), www.eventim.hu (online tickets); ⊕ Mon–Fri 10.00–18.30
Thália Jegyiroda VI, Nagymező u. 19; ℡ 1 302 3841; ⊕ Mon–Fri 10.00–16.00 daily (in summer). Ticket office for the Thália Theatre, but also sells tickets for performances at other venues.
Ticket Express VI, Andrássy út 18; ℡ 06 30 30 30 999; www.tex.hu; ⊕ Mon–Fri 10.00–18.30, summer only Sat 10.00–15.00

Many of the websites of the above companies offer online ticket sales. Other ticket sites (with information available in English) include www.ticketportal.hu, www.ticketoffice.hu and www.interticket.hu.

THEATRE Budapest has a strong relationship with the theatre, and while it would benefit further from greater financial support, there is a varied selection of plays, musicals and comedies to be found on over 40 stages around the city. The main cluster of these is just off Andrássy út, on Nagymező utca, which is known as the Pest Broadway. Alongside productions by domestic playwrights such as Mihály Babits and Ferenc Molnár, there is international drama including Shakespeare. However, the Anglo-Saxon visitor yearning to see *The Tempest* in Hungarian is a breed we've yet to meet, and only the Merlin is a safe bet for English-language drama. Curtains usually rise at 19.00; remember that most theatres – including the Merlin – close during the hottest summer months (from mid June to late August).

Merlin Theatre V, Gerlóczy u. 4; ☏ 1 317 9338; www.merlinszinhaz.hu; ⊕ box office Mon–Fri 14.00–19.00 [144 C2] There's contemporary dance at the Merlin, but it's also known for its classical, modern & alternative English-language productions. You can purchase tickets via the website (in English), & there's a 15% discount with a Budapest Card. Popular with ex-pats & foreigners. Has a restaurant. Tickets 1,500–3,500Ft.

National Theatre (Nemzeti Színház) XI, Bajor Gizi Park 1; ☏ 1 476 6800; www.nemzetiszinhaz.hu; ⊕ ticket office Mon–Fri 10.00–18.00, Sat–Sun 14.00–18.00 T̄ 1, 2, 24. The National Theatre was for some time a subject of drama. Thirty years after the communists demolished the splendid original in Blaha Lujza tér, an almighty slanging match erupted over its replacement. As the Fidesz government bickered with the Budapest mayor over costs (page 91), the enormous foundation hole at Erzsébet tér was tagged the 'National Pit' by city wags. Eventually a new site was chosen near Lágymányosi híd to the south of the centre, & the theatre – a bold, self-consciously modern building, resembling a ship's prow – opened in 2002. It is a showcase for

Hungarian drama – & very Magyar – but Sándor Román's ExperiDance (a famous local company) also performs dance here & there are a few English-language productions (by the Madhouse company, for instance).

Palace of Arts (Művészetek Palotája) XI, Bajor Gizi Park, Komor Marcell u. 1; ☏ 1 555 3001; www.mupa.hu; ⊕ ticket office Mon–Fri 13.00–18.00, Sat–Sun 10.00–18.00 T̄ 1, 2, 24. The Palace of Arts – between Lágymányosi híd & the National Theatre – has been criticised as a concrete cube, but reader David Clarke rightly points out it's far less architecturally brutal than London's National Theatre. Home of the Ludwig Museum (page 165) & the National Philharmonic Orchestra.

Thália Theatre VI, Nagymező u. 22–24; ☏ 1 312 1280; 8 www.thalia.hu; ⊕ ticket office Mon–Fri 10.00–18.00, Sat–Sun 14.00–18.00 [149 C3] **M1** Opera **TB** 70, 78. Well-respected theatre. Links up with the Operetta Theatre for musicals & operettas (page 116), & – now that the Erkel Theatre is closed for extensive refurbishment – is also a secondary venue for companies linked to the Opera House (including the leading ballet company).

MUSIC

Opera and classical Whether or not you're a regular **opera** goer, it would be a shame not to take advantage of some of the cheapest ticket prices in the world (from as low as 600Ft, but around 4,000–6,000Ft for a good view), and a sumptuous setting at the State Opera House. You don't need to wear top hat and tails, but jeans distress the usherettes. The 'father of Hungarian opera' was Ferenc Erkel, who conducted his own *Hunyadi László* and *Bánk Bán* at the opening of the State Opera House. Both operas remain popular today; there are also performances throughout the year of work by foreign masters like Mozart and Wagner.

Hungary has good reason to be proud of its **classical** heritage. Concert performances are two-a-penny, offering home-grown and international talent, although in the hot months these are more likely to be outdoor. The Budapest Philharmonic Orchestra was founded by Erkel in the mid-19th century; when it is not touring, its home is at the State Opera House. Buda Castle Summer Nights – opera, classical and jazz concerts in the Hilton Budapest's Dominican Courtyard (page 101) – run every other evening for much of July (book tickets through the hotel or on the website below), while there are concerts every five days or so in July in Szent István tér, the Basilica providing a stunning backdrop. In addition, regular organ recitals, choral performances and classical concerts are hosted in the city's churches – including the Lutheran Church (*V, Deák tér*), Mátyás Church (*I, Szentháromság tér*), St Michael's Church (*V, Váci u. 47/B*) and St Anna Church (*I, Batthyány tér 7*) – as well as at the Vajdahunyad Castle in City Park and the Dome Hall of the Parliament building. Information is available from Tourinforms, ticket offices or listings magazines (pages 97–8 and 77); alternatively, details are given at www.viparts.hu, where you can also reserve tickets online, and in the *Koncert Kalendárium* (*www.koncertkalendarium.hu; in Hungarian*).

Budapest Operetta Theatre (Budapesti Operettszínház) VI, Nagymező u. 17; ☏ 1 472 2030; www.operettszinhaz.hu; ⊕ ticket office (next door) Mon–Fri 10.00–19.00 (closed 14.30–15.00), Sat–Sun 13.00–19.00 [149 C3] M̲1̲ Opera T̲B̲ 70, 78 B̲ 105. Along with Vienna, Budapest is a capital of operetta (light musicals); this is the best place to watch one, in glamorous Art-Nouveau surroundings & beneath a magnificent century-old chandelier. Classic Magyar operettas (usually subtitled in German) & modern musicals (usually subtitled in English). (See also Thália, page 115.) Tours available at weekends – call in advance.

Danube Palace (Duna Palota) V, Zrínyi u. 5; ☏ 1 235 5500; www.bm.hu/dunapalota [144 A1] Neo-Baroque palace & base for the distinguished Danube Symphony Orchestra. Classical performances are held every Sat at 20.00 May–Oct & once/twice monthly the rest of the year (with the option of a cruise with candlelit dinner afterwards). There is folk dancing by the Danube Folk Ensemble or Rajkó Folk Ensemble at 20.00 on other evenings of the week. The building has a restaurant & hosts temporary exhibitions. Concert tickets ✍ 6,400–8,100Ft/ 5,600–7,200Ft; cruise with dinner 7,900Ft.

Hungarian State Opera House VI, Andrássy út 22; ☏ 1 331 2550 (ticket office), 1 353 0170; www.opera.hu; ⊕ Mon–Sat 11.00–17.00 or start of performance, Sun 16.00–19.00 [149 B3] M̲1̲ Opera B̲ 105. The Austrians apparently only agreed to the construction of Budapest's opera house on the condition that it was smaller than that in Vienna. When completed in 1884, it was certainly relatively small in size; however, Ferenc József lamented that he hadn't stipulated it be less pretty too. Designed by Miklós Ybl, it's a breathtaking neo-Renaissance

building. The entrance hall has a winding staircase, swirling blue pillars & an opulent ceiling that undulates like a choppy ocean, while the horseshoe-shaped auditorium glows golden-red. The Historicist artists Károly Lotz, Bertalan Székely & Mór Than painted the frescoes, influenced by those of Paris & Vienna in illustrating music's power, while Alajos Stróbl created the sculptures of Erkel & Liszt in alcoves at the entrance. As well as looking great, it sounds pretty good too, the acoustics reputedly second only to La Scala. And it's cheap. Box office inside main entrance (also selling tickets to the Thália Theatre); guided tours at 15.00 & 16.00 daily (✍ 2,600/1,400Ft).

Liszt Music Academy (Liszt Zeneakadémia) VI, Liszt Ferenc tér 8; ☏ 1 462 4600; www.zeneakademia.hu [149 C3] M̲1̲ Oktogon T̲ 4, 6 T̲B̲ 70, 78. Situated on the lively Liszt Ferenc tér, this turn-of-the-20th-century Art-Nouveau music academy has 2 auditoria – the huge Nagyterem (closed Jul–Aug), seating 1,200 people, & the smaller Kisterem. The acoustics are fabulous, like the décor; pop your head into the entrance hall, with its greens & golds, mosaics & marble columns. A seated bronze of Ferenc Liszt is positioned above the entrance, & gargoyles leer at passers-by. The academy's central library contains the country's most extensive music-related collection.

Nádor Concert Hall XIV, Ajtósi-Dürer sor 39; ☏ 1 363 3343; www.vakisk.hu [89 H2] T̲B̲ 72, 74 T̲ 1. A recommendation of reader Mervyn Brown, this concert hall inside the Institute of the Blind – a beautiful Art-Nouveau building (on the corner of Hungaria körút) – offers excellent musical performances of various types at bargain prices. Near City Park.

Jazz and easy listening

♪ **Cotton Club** VI, Jókai u. 26; ☏ 1 354 0886; www.cottonclub.hu; ⊕ 12.00–24.00 daily [149 B2] M̲1̲ Oktogon T̲ 4, 6. Old-fashioned speak-easy club, bar & café with a determined whiff of 1920s America. There are varied live performances of music & dance at the weekend & on some week nights, featuring jazz, blues & revue-style shows.

♪ **Fat Mo's** V, Nyáry Pál u. 11; ☏ 1 267 3199; www.fatmo.hu; ⊕ Mon–Tue 12.00–02.00, Wed 12.00–03.00, Thu–Fri 12.00–04.00, Sat 18.00–04.00, Sun 18.00–02.00 [144 C4] Early 20th-century-themed club whose disco on Saturday is popular with prowling meat marketeers. However, there are live jazz, blues & country performances on other evenings (Sun–Tue & Thu).

♪ **Jazz Garden** V, Veres Pálné u. 44/A; ☏ 1 266 7364; www.jazzgarden.hu; ⊕ 18.00–02.00 daily [144 D5] The outside's in at this romantic little club, decorated to feel like a pavement café under a starry sky. A firm favourite among lovers of jazz & blues, it attracts top Hungarian & international musicians who perform live in the evenings between 21.30 & 24.30. You can also eat here.

♪ **New Orleans Jazz Club** VI, Lovag u. 5; ☏ 1 451 7525; www.neworleans.hu; ⊕ 18.00–02.00 daily [149 B2] T̲B̲ 70, 78. A classy modern club that features big international jazz names, who perform at 21.00 every evening except Sunday & Monday. The website (in Hungarian) lists the monthly programme.

Contemporary The electronic music scene is strong. As in western Europe, some musical events are managed by the same company at different locations, while other venues run consistently interesting programmes.

For electronica and dance-music fans, Cinetrip, a regular party whose venue varies, is just as remarkable for its large screens and VJs (improvisational video-based DJs) as its music. It has been staged at the Railway Museum and at Turkish baths, where fans take along a towel and a swimsuit to change into. You might also try Trafó (page 118) or A38 (below). The municipal government-owned Petőfi csarnok is a large 'youth leisure centre' in City Park, which aims for more mainstream appeal. Large international acts appear at the Puskás Stadion or at the smaller arenas in the vicinity (such as the Kisstadion).

In warmer weather, the Sziget Festival is an August staple of the partying calendar (page 120), while the day-long Budapest Parade is a huge rave similar to the Berlin Love Parade (page 120). In addition, outdoor clubs like Zöld Pardon, Rio and the roof of the A38 boat take advantage of the summer months.

The music scene is inevitably in a perpetual state of flux. Check English-language listings magazines for up-to-date information (useful websites like www.port.hu and www.est.hu are unfortunately only in Hungarian). Tickets for performances are available from the city-centre ticket offices (page 114).

♪ **A38 Club** XI, Állóhajó, near Petőfi híd; ☎ 1 464 3940; www.a38.hu; ⊕ Mon–Sat 11.00–24.00 (until 04.00 on performance dates) [89 E7] Ṯ 4,6. The A38 is a renovated Ukrainian stone-carrier ship (originally the *Artemovsk 38*) moored near Petőfi Bridge, & serves as an innovative live-music venue, restaurant & nightclub. The website lists a monthly programme including jazz, rock, drum 'n' bass, hip hop & classical. The ship also hosts parties, festivals & other events.

♪ **Gödör Klub** V, Erzsébet tér; ☎ 06 20 201 3868; vwww.godorklub.hu [144 B2] With a glass-bottomed artificial lake & a sunken terrace on to which a stage opens in summer, this is a popular spot to enjoy both music events & a casual drink. Inside is another stage (with the lake above it) & a bar & café.

♪ **Millennium Park** (Millenáris Park) II, Fény u. 20–22; ☎ 1 336 4000; www.millenaris.hu [88 B2] M2 Moszkva tér Ṯ 4, 6. Two concert halls — one a vast brick hangar (the Teátrum) & the other a more informal space — that host world music & folk. Always a diverse programme of music, dance & entertainment. See also pages 159–60.

♪ **Old Man's Music Pub** VII, Akácfa u. 13; ☎ 1 322 7645; www.oldmans.hu; ⊕ Sun–Thu 15.00–04.00, Fri–Sat 15.00–04.30 [149 D4] M2 Blaha Lujza tér Ṯ 4, 6. Lively basement bar in the Jewish quarter,

with friendly staff & live jazz, blues, Latino, swing or rock acts (21.00–23.00 most nights).

♪ **Papp László Sportaréna** XIV, Stefánia út 2; ☎ 1 422 2600; www.budapestarena.hu M2 Stadionok B̲ 178. Known affectionately as 'the pebble', this arena is the venue for sporting & live music events.

♪ **Petőfi Csarnok** XIV, Zichy Mihály út 14; ☎ 1 363 3730; www.petoficsarnok.hu [89 G1] Ṯ 1 T̲B̲ 70, 72, 74. Concert venue in City Park. Also has an open-air stage & arena, with folk-music performances in summer & bands like Massive Attack, Placebo, & Earth, Wind & Fire.

♪ **Puskás Ferenc Stadion** XIV, Istvánmezei út 3–5; ☎ 1 471 4100; [89 H3] M2 Stadionok Ṯ 1 B̲ 178. The national sports stadium — named after the country's star footballer of the 1950s — can hold almost 70,000 people, & hosts concerts, as well as matches.

♪ **Tűzraktér** VI, Hegedű u. 3; ☎ 70 321 3536; www.tuzrakter.hu [149 C3] Newly moved from its original slot in a factory, this trendy indie arts centre was established with the aim of bringing artists & art lovers together. It's all encompassing in its cultural embrace — serving as a gallery, theatre, studio, music venue, café & nightclub. Website lists events (although when we checked the listing was in Hungarian).

DANCE

Folk The dance-house (*táncház*) movement began over 30 years ago (see pages 29–30). Dance houses take place less often in the summer. Entertainment listings magazines will show what's on, or log on to www.tanchaz.hu. If you want a polished performance rather than a workshop, it's worth checking the programmes at the National Dance Theatre or the Danube Palace.

🎭 **Aranytiz Cultural Centre** (Művelődési Központ) V, Arany János u. 10; ☎ 1 354 3400; www.aranytiz.hu [149 A3] Every Saturday (21.00–24.00) the Kalamajka táncház is found here, with Béla Halmos (the founder of the dance-house movement) & his band playing. Listen while enjoying *pálinka* from the makeshift bar. There's also a *táncház* for the children in the afternoon.

🎭 **City Cultural House** (Fővárosi Művelődési Ház) XI, Fehérvári út 47 ⊤ 18, 41, 47. A concrete block with regular dance houses, featuring Balkan & Moldavian troupes.

🎭 **Fonó Buda Music House** (Zeneház) XI, Sztregova u. 3; ☎ 1 206 5300; www.fono.hu ⊤ 41, 47, 18

🅱 103, 114 stop near by. Slightly out of the centre, Fonó is a cultural centre & live-music venue. There are regular performances by Hungarian & eastern European folk bands & dance troupes – including Muzsikás – as well as modern concerts. Dance-house events take place on Wednesday, & there's an excellent CD shop. Closed in high summer (Jul–Aug).

🎭 **Marcibányi tér Cultural Centre** (Művelődési Központ) II, Marcibányi tér 5/A; ☎ 1 212 2820; www.arczi.hu [88 A2] 🅱 11, 149 run near by. Performances of Csángó music (the ethnic Hungarians from Moldavia), as well as informal sessions by Muzsikás on some Thursdays from 20.00 & a weekly dance house every Wednesday (from 20.00).

OTHER Ballet has been popular in Hungary for 200 years; the most prestigious of today's companies is the National Ballet Company, the country's first ensemble, which is based at the State Opera House. The National Dance Theatre also includes ballet among its repertoire. There are several venues offering **contemporary dance**.

🎭 **Central Europe Dance Theatre** (Közép Európa) VII, Bethlen Gábor tér 3; ☎ 1 342 7163; www.cedt.hu [89 F3] Ⓜ2 Keleti, then short walk along Bethlen Gábor u. ⊤🅱 73, 74, 78. Quality contemporary dance, with frequent workshops. Alongside the modern dance, there is a strong folkloric heritage with traditional dances deriving from the Carpathian Basin.

🎭 **National Dance Theatre** (Nemzeti Táncszínház) I, Színház u. 1–3; ☎ 1 356 4085 (theatre), 1 201 4407 (ticket office), 1 375 8649 (box office); www.dancetheatre.hu [127 C3] The country's only 18th-century theatre still functioning as such. Previously a Carmelite monastery, it became a place of drama when József II dissolved the religious order in 1784. Although the theatre primarily catered to the German population, the first professional Hungarian-language theatrical production (of *Igazházi* by Kristóf Simai) was staged here in 1790. Haydn attended a performance of his own 'Creation' oratory in 1800, & Beethoven played a concert in

the same year. Since 2001, the theatre has specialised in dance & related performing arts – ranging from folklore to classical ballet & contemporary dance. There are 2 auditoria, & during August performances (usually folkloric) are held outside in the Carmelite courtyard. Next to the Sándor Palace. Ticket office at front (🕐 11.00–18.00/ 19.00 daily), box office behind theatre (🕐 Mon–Thu 10.00–18.00, Fri 10.00–17.00).

🎭 **Trafó House of Contemporary Arts** (Trafó Kortárs Művészetek Háza) IX, Liliom u. 41; ☎ 1 456 2040; www.trafo.hu; 🕐 ticket office Mon–Fri 14.00–20.00, Sat–Sun 17.00–20.00 (gallery 16.00–19.00) [89 F6] Ⓜ3 Ferenc körút ⊤ 4, 6. Housed in a former electrical transformer station, Trafó is now a contemporary cultural centre & nightclub with a diverse programme. It hosts international-standard contemporary dance, theatre & music, as well as temporary exhibitions of graphic art. Tickets also available from Ticket Express (page 114).

NIGHTCLUBS While Budapest isn't a clubbing mecca in world terms, and you'll come across the odd trashy Euro-pop track, there are some excellent nightclubs to be sought out – both indoor and out – and some talented Hungarian DJs (page 31). A good starting point is **Shipyard Island** (Hajógyári-sziget), which now functions primarily as a night spot and which holds no fewer than seven clubs (from the slick to the enjoyably cheesy where you can get your disco digits out). Clubbing is popular and nightclubs crowded, particularly after midnight. There is sometimes (although not always) an **admission charge**, which varies between about 500Ft and 5,000Ft depending on the event and venue. It is unjust, but not uncommon, for clubs to make only the men dip into their pockets at the entrance. Jeans and smart trainers are usually acceptable. When it comes to the clubbing uniform,

Hungarian women seem to believe that 'less is more' when dressing and 'more is more' when applying make-up! Many clubs are connected to a bar, and so open for most of the day; the remainder open between 18.00 and 21.00, and usually continue until 03.00 or 04.00. If you like a club to have warmed up by the time you arrive, don't bother getting there until at least 22.30. Clubs can appear and disappear very quickly – criminal gangs have their fingers in the pie of nightclub ownership, and as a consequence the scene can be unstable.

Buda

☆ **Bed & Bed Beach** III, Reményi Ede u. 3 (just off Szentendrei út); www.bed.hu; ⊕ Sat 21.00–05.00 (end of Dec–May 2 only); Hajógyári-sziget; ☏ 06 30 436 4400; www.bedbeach.hu; ⊕ Fri–Sat 21.00–05.00 (May 3–Sep/Oct only) [137 D1] Bed is something of a blend of warehouse & basketball court, with bleachers stacked around the main dance floor. The atmosphere is heady but friendly, the music a contemporary fusion of funky house & dance played by DJs who know how to work a crowd & attract more serious clubbers than those at the Dokk. During the summer, the club moves outside to a man-made beach on Shipyard Island. ☞ Free entry (1,500Ft for men after 24.00).

☆ **Dokk Beach** III, Hajógyári-sziget 122; ☏ 30 436 3666; www.dokkbeach.hu; ⊕ Fri–Sat 22.00–05.00 [137 D1] An uber-cool summer club (linked to the Dokk Café; page 111) that drags Budapest's young élite to its breast from June to August. The action is al fresco, with a bridge leading to a timber platform on the water, & a venue that rivals the Ibiza beach clubs.

☆ **Romkert** XI, Budapest, Döbrentei tér 9; ⊕ May–Sep Sun–Mon 12.00–02.00, Tue–Sat 12.00–04.00 [88 C5] Burnt down by arsonists in 2007, the Romkert – one of the original garden-style clubs – has risen from the ashes. Popular for coffee &

snacks during the day; come evening, partygoers flood the al-fresco bar & dance floor as the DJ takes over (from 22.00 daily). There's a lively buzz & a notable lack of elbowroom on Friday & Saturday nights.

☆ **Sláger Terasz** III, Hajógyári-sziget; ☏ 06 30 408 8030; www.slagerparty.hu; ⊕ Sat–Sun 20.00–04.00 (summer only) [137 D1] 'Sláger' is the name for pop classics, & they're exactly what you get at this raised terrace club on Shipyard Island. You won't know any of the Hungarian boppers' favourites of the last couple of decades, but you might recognise the odd poached Abba strain & it's all good fun.

☆ **Studio Lounge** III, Hajógyári-sziget; ☏ 06 30 436 3600; www.studio-eh.hu; ⊕ Sat 22.00–05.00 (lounge area), 23.00–05.00 (main room) [137 D1] Quickly established as one of the city's premier clubs, the massive, upmarket Studio stands next to Dokk on Shipyard Island. Opens every second Saturday, & has theme nights & shows (*Pesti Est* lists details of upcoming shows). ☞ Entry 1,000Ft (women), 2,000Ft (men).

☆ **Zöld Pardon** XI, Goldmann György tér 6; www.zp.hu; ⊕ 09.00–06.00 daily (mid Apr–mid Sep) [89 E7] Sprawling al-fresco club on the south side of Petőfi Bridge, next to Café del Rio; frequented by younger revellers who come for live rock acts & music at the harder jungle & drum 'n' base end of the spectrum.

Pest

☆ **Buddha Beach** IX, Közraktár u. 9–11; ☏ 1 210 4872; www.buddha-beach.hu; ⊕ 18.00–05.00 daily (summer only) [144 C6] Sitting on the riverbank behind the Great Market Hall, the big Buddha Beach (summer sister club of a winter venue, Inside) features 3 cocktail bars, Thai 'sungalows' to chill out on & a giant golden statue of Buddha.

☆ **Cha-Cha-Cha Terasz** XIII, Margitszigeti Atlétikai Centrum; www.chachacha.hu; ⊕ 16.00–dawn daily (summer only) [88 C1] Newish al-fresco nightspot on

Margaret Island that attracts a good mix; its sister bar (VI, Bajcsy-Zsilinszky út 63) is near Nyugati tér.

☆ **Holdudvar** XIII, Margit-sziget; ☏ 1 236 0655; www.holdudvar.net; ⊕ 11.00–05.00 daily (May–Sep) [88 C1] Long-time popular 'Moon Courtyard' has moved to Margaret Island – and is 4 times bigger, with an indoor area (including restaurant & bar), a gallery & outdoor cinema. Stands next to Sarkkert, another summer favourite.

GAY BUDAPEST After a slow start the gay scene has perked up somewhat in the capital, and there seem to be more openly gay couples on the streets than there were. It's worth balancing this evidence of a thawing in old-fashioned prejudices by adding that there have been some ugly scenes during the last two Gay Pride parades, when right-wing groups organised violent demonstrations at Liszt Ferenc tér and Heroes' Square (and later beat up a gay politician). There seems to be a failure of political will to quell these demonstrations (perhaps because the ruling party makes capital by claiming such incidents represent an unsavoury underbelly of the Fidesz-led opposition); until that will hardens and laws are changed, there's likely to be a nervous edge to the annual celebrations.

There are several bars, clubs and cafés in Pest (districts V, VI, VII and IX). Most clubs either charge an entrance fee or require a minimum drinks spend (running a tab that you settle on leaving). Some of the thermal baths are established gay meeting points (Király the current favourite, according to reader Scott Brown). For information on bars, clubs and gay-friendly accommodation, log on to www.gay.hu or www.gayguide.net. Be sure to pick up a copy of *Na Végre* (or check the website www.navegre.hu); this free monthly magazine (available in Tourinform and elsewhere) is mainly in Hungarian, but has a section for tourists (including a map marking the city's gay bars and clubs) and an easily followed calendar of upcoming events.

MAIN FESTIVALS AND EVENTS

Budapest celebrates a range of festivals devoted to sport and the arts. The country's two biggest cultural events are the Spring (Tavaszi) and Autumn (Őszi) festivals. Tickets are available from the Budapest Spring-Autumn Festival Office (*V, Szervita tér 5;* ↘ 1 486 3300; *www.festivalcity.hu*). Tourinforms and listings magazines will offer precise details of the attractions on offer and their venues; you might also try www.budapestinfo.hu/en/calendar_of_events/. There are also events on all national holidays (see page 68).

Budapest Spring Festival (mid Mar–early Apr) 17-day national arts festival. The capital hosts 200 events, including orchestral recitals, & opera, ballet & folk-dancing performances. See www.festivalcity.hu.

Danube Carnival International Cultural Festival (mid Jun) The capital jigs to a 10-day festival of music & dance, held at various locations. See www.dunaart.hu/carnival.

Budapest Equestrian Summer Festival (late Jun) Thousands of spectators flock to Shipyard Island for thrilling displays of equestrian martial arts, show-jumping, dressage, stunt shows & carriage driving. See www.karneval.hu.

National Gallop (end May/start Jun) First hosted in 2008, this weekend equestrian celebration sees competitors from different regions of Hungary racing horses around Heroes' Square. There are also parades & folklore displays along Andrássy út. See www.vagta.hu.

Summer on the Chain Bridge (Jul–mid Aug) Budapest's most famous bridge is closed to traffic every w/end during Jul & the first half of Aug. Stalls sell food & items of folk art, & there are performances of traditional music & dance. Popular with tourists, less so with motorists.

Sziget Festival (end Jul/start Aug) Budapest's very own Glastonbury is held on Shipyard Island, & is

gaining in international importance. There's a broad spectrum of music from some of Europe's best bands, & those who fancy it can camp. Lots of other entertainments too. See www.sziget.hu.

St Stephen's Day (Aug 20) Public holiday in honour of Hungary's patron saint & first king, St István (1000–1038). His mummified right hand is paraded through the streets, & church services are held across the capital, along with plays, shows, dances & a craft fair in the Castle District (see www.nesz.hu). Climaxes with a spectacular river procession & fireworks on Gellért Hill.

Budapest Parade (late Aug) Thumping carnival & street party modelled on Berlin's Love Parade, with colourful floats & parades, & a massive disco afterwards in the Stadionok complex. See www.sziget.hu/budapestparade & www.sziget.hu/afterparty.

Jewish Summer Festival (late Aug–early Sep) Celebration of Jewish culture, music, dance, cuisine & film. Good opportunity to watch a concert inside the breathtaking Great Synagogue. See www.jewishfestival.hu.

Budapest International Wine Festival (early–mid Sep) Merry festival concentrated on the Castle District (with smaller events in Budafok & Szentendre). Wine auction, harvest procession & plenty of tasting. See www.winefestival.hu.

Budapest Autumn Festival (mid–late Oct)
Contemporary arts festival that has been running for over 20 years.

Budapest Antiques Fair (last w/end of Nov) Held in the Hall of Arts (Műcsarnok) on Heroes' Square. See www.antik-enterior.hu for details on Antik Enteriőr.

New Year's Eve Gala Ball (Dec 31) The capital's glitterati dig out their penguin suits & ball gowns, & step out to the State Opera House for a wonderful gala concert performed by some of the country's leading musicians & dancers. There's a banquet & dancing until dawn. Tickets are sought after & very expensive. See www.viparts.hu.

SHOPPING

Budapest is no Rome or Paris, and the shops don't have the expensively labelled flocking from afar. Nevertheless, elegant boutiques are now as much a part of the scene as the noisy market halls. The city is a fun-time place to browse and buy. Pest is where the retail action's at. The touristy Váci utca, Vörösmarty tér, Petőfi Sándor utca and the streets branching from them are lined with glamorous international designer outlets, and stores selling antiques, paintings, folksy items and cosmetics. Products here are pricier than elsewhere (and beyond the means of many Hungarians), but what stroll isn't enhanced by a spot of leisurely window shopping? Get your nose up to the windows, work yourself into the narrow aisles, and cast a curious eye over coloured glass, quirky antiques and hanging lace.

Budapesters target the **Great Boulevard** and streets stemming from or out towards it, such as Rákóczi út and Kossuth Lajos utca. Shops here are lower key, generally a touch shabbier, and more affordable. In addition, American-style **shopping malls** have sprung up like mushrooms; they are not particularly cheap, but they open late, have everything under one roof – including restaurants, bars and cinemas – and have inevitably placed pressure on small independent retailers. For information on opening hours and popular gifts, see pages 68–70.

ANTIQUES, ART, FURNITURE & JEWELLERY Just off Szent István körút, **Falk Miksa utca** is the first stop for those in quest of antiques. The street is lined with commanding six-storey residences, and a rash of shops – over 40 – selling collectibles. Elsewhere there are a number of shops selling antiques in both the Castle District and on Váci utca, but these tend to be significantly overpriced. Instead look out for **BÁV stores and auction houses**, outlets of a well-respected Hungarian chain that are dotted all around the city. These usually have a range of period furniture, porcelain, fine art and glassware, and also stage auctions throughout the year. For more information (and upcoming auction dates), log on to their website (*www.bav.hu*). Some BÁV stores and others are listed below. Superior modern furniture and furnishings can be found on **Király utca** in District VI. Remember when making purchases that antiques require a **permit for export** (*kiviteli engedély*), so be sure to pick up the necessary paperwork at the shop. The form requires a special stamp of permission if antiques are over 70 years old. (See page 42 for further details.)

🏛 **Antik Bazár** VII, Klauzál u. 1; ☎ 1 322 8848; ⊕ Mon–Fri 10.00–18.00, Sat 10.00–14.00 [149 D4] The hoarding owner offers a sprawling collection of anything & everything dating to the period 1900–1960, from walking sticks to broken opera glasses.

🏛 **BÁV** Outlets around the city include: V, Falk Miksa u. 21 (☎ 1 353 1975; ⊕ Tue–Fri 09.30–18.00, Sat

10.00–14.00; specialises in jewellery); V, Ferenciek tere 10 (☎ 1 318 3733; ⊕ Mon–Fri 08.00–16.00); V, Szent István körút 3 (☎ 1 473 0666; ⊕ Mon–Fri 10.00–18.00, Sat 09.00–13.00; good for antique jewellery); V, Bécsi u. 1–3 (☎ 1 429 3020; ⊕ Mon–Fri 10.00–18.00, Sat 10.00–14.00).

🏛 **Dunaparti Aukciósház** V, Váci u. 36; www.dunapartiaukcioshaz.hu; ⊕ Mon–Fri

10.00–18.00, Sat 10.00–16.00 [144 B4] Large auction house & gallery near the bridgehead of Erzsébet híd. It sells glass, paintings, china, silverware & furniture; the website lists upcoming auctions, which are usually on Monday at 17.00 (lots can be viewed 10 days in advance).

☗ **Ernst Galéria** V, Irányi u. 27; ☎ 1 266 4016; www.ernstgaleria.hu; ☉ Mon–Sat 11.00–19.00 [144 C4] Impressionist & modern Hungarian art works & furniture from the 19th & 20th centuries, as well as a collection of vintage film posters.

☗ **Nagyházi Galéria** V, Balaton u. 8; ☎ 1 475 6000; www.nagyhazi.hu; ☉ Mon–Fri 10.00–18.00, Sat 10.00–14.00 [149 A1] Large gallery & auction house selling collectible works of art. Just off Falk Miksa u.

☗ **Polgár Galéria és Aukciósház** V, Kossuth Lajos u. 3; ☎ 1 318 6954; www.polgar-galeria.hu; ☉ Mon–Fri 10.00–18.00, Sat 10.00–13.00 [144 C3] Gallery & auction house offering paintings, antique furniture & jewellery; there's also a larger sister establishment (V, Váci u. 11B; ☎ 1 267 4077; ☉ Mon–Fri 10.00–18.00).

☗ **Varga Design** V, Haris köz 6; ☎ 1 318 4089; www.vargadesign.hu; ☉ Mon–Fri 10.00–18.00, Sat 10.00–14.00 [144 C3] Sells the striking creations of master silversmith Miklós Varga, who has been working for 30 years & employs a 'cobweb' technique in his recent jewellery – criss-crossing threads of gold or silver.

FOLK-ART CENTRES
The centres of folk art lean very heavily towards the kitsch, and they are marketed firmly at the tourist; nevertheless, the craftsmanship is often good, and folk items make super souvenirs.

☗ **Folkart Centrum** V, Váci u. 56–58; ☎ 1 318 5840; www.folkartcentrum.hu; ☉ 10.00–19.00 daily [144 C5] Broad selection of lace, china & craftworks from all regions of Hungary.

☗ **Folkart Kézmüvesház** V, Régi posta u. 12; ☎ 1 318 5143; www.folkartkezmuveshaz.hu; ☉ 10.00–19.00 daily [144 B3] A busy craft house, with quality evident in the hand-painted plates, carved chess sets & traditional textiles.

☗ **Folkart Nepmüvészeti** VIII, Rákóczi út 34; ☉ Mon–Fri 10.00–18.00, Sat 10.00–13.00 [149 C4] Folksy craftworks, lace & Hollóháza pottery.

☗ **Holló Mühely** V, Vitkovics Mihály u. 12; ☉ Mon–Fri 10.00–13.00, 13.30–18.00, Sat 10.00–14.00 [144 C3] Quaint craft shop selling pottery, furniture & other painted knick-knacks.

FOOD & DRINK (See also *Markets*, opposite).

☗ **Bortársaság** I, Batthyány u. 59; ☎ 1 212 2569; www.bortarsasag.hu; ☉ Mon–Fri 12.00–20.00, Sat 10.00–18.00 [127 C1] Knowledgeable staff & free tastings on Saturday (14.00–17.00) make this Wine Society shop a favourite. There are now 5 outlets: V, Bazilika, Szent István tér 3; IX, Ráday u. 7; II, Budagyöngye shopping centre, Szilágyi Erzsébet fasor; II, Rózsakert shopping centre, Gábor Áron u. 74–78.

☗ **House of Royal Wines & Cellar Museum** (Királyi Borház és Pincemúzeum) I, Nyugati sétány, Szent György tér; ☎ 1 267 1100; ☉ Tue–Sun 10.00–18.00 [127 C4] Opened in August 2008, this place occupies a 15th-century cellar of the royal palace, & is reached via steps at the far side of Szent György tér. Wine tastings are available for individuals or groups: 1,350–2,100Ft (3 wines), 1,800–2,800Ft (4 wines), 2,700–4,200Ft (6 wines). Entrance ☞ 900/500Ft.

☗ **ÍzLelő** V, Arany János u. 12; ☎ 1 269 0494; www.izlelo.hu [149 A3] 'Taster' – owned by Károly Gundel, who presumably shares blood with Hungary's most-famous culinary family – offers speciality chocolates, pralines & Hungarian wines.

☗ **La Boutique des Vins** V, József Attila u. 12; ☎ 1 317 5919; www.malatinszky.hu; ☉ Mon–Fri 10.00–18.00, Sat 10.00–15.00 [144 B1] Decent selection of wines from the southern region of Villány (home of the winemaker-owner). On Hild tér, just off József Attila u.

☗ **Magyar Pálinka Háza** VIII, Rákóczi út 17; ☎ 1 338 4219; ☉ Mon–Sat 09.00–19.00 [149 C4] Throat-rasping drops of traditional brandy & other spirits.

☗ **Szeged Pick Salami Shop** V, Kossuth Lajos tér 9; ☎ 1 331 7783; ☉ Mon–Thu 06.00–19.00, Fri 06.00–18.00 [149 A2] Salami show-house for the famous Pick company; also has a restaurant. There are other Pick outlets in the city, including one on Pilvax köz.

☗ **Unicum Museum & Store** IX, Soroksári út 26; ☎ 1 456 5247; ☉ Mon–Fri 9.00–18.00 [89 F7] Buy bottles of the bitter spirit (page 64) or tour the museum (book ahead).

☗ **Vinum Primatis** I, Úri u. 18; ☎ 1 356 5828; www.vinumprimatis.hu; ☉ Tue–Sun 10.00–18.00

[127 B3] This wine shop represents the Primatical Wine Guild, which was established in 2007 with the aim of increasing the profile of Hungarian wines worldwide. The owner hopes shortly also to take over the former premises of the House of Hungarian Wines, opposite the Hilton Hotel.

MARKETS For general details on markets, see page 70. During December, festive markets pop up in many of the city's squares. The biggest is in Vörösmarty tér, where wooden booths are draped with fairy lights, and you can choose from handicrafts and wooden Christmas toys while clasping a plastic cup of piping mulled wine.

When the Nagycsarnok opened in 1897, four smaller roofed markets were also opened on the same day. Each was given a number (the Nagycsarnok was No I); look up for the numeral carved in stone or forged in metalwork above the csarnok sign and the entrance/exit. The other four markets can be found at: Rákóczi tér (No II), Klauzál tér/Akácfa utca 42–48 (No III, and now operating under the Kaiser's supermarket chain), Hunyadi tér (No IV) and Hold utca (No V). There is also one on Batthyány tér.

🏛 **Great Market Hall** (Nagycsarnok) IX, Vámház körút 1–3; www.piaconline.hu; ⊕ Mon 06.00–17.00, Tue–Fri 06.00–18.00, Sat 06.00–15.00 [144 C5] The Great Market Hall's Art-Nouveau styling, with patterned bricks & coloured ceramic roof tiles, was the work of architect Samu Pecz in 1897. It was designed as a sheltered area for traders, who previously sold their wares from beneath umbrellas on the Danube bank. When first constructed, the hall had an indoor canal running through it along which goods were delivered to the stalls. It's a privilege to shop beneath its girders.

On the ground & lower-ground floors are fresh produce (vegetables, meats of all shapes & sizes, chickens' feet, river fish mouthing furiously in cramped tanks), pickles, wines & spices, while upstairs are stalls selling Hungarian handicrafts. Prices are good by Hungarian standards & cheap by those of western Europe, & there is usually a little room for negotiation (a 10% reduction the limit). There are also some cheap & hearty büfés. One of the ground-floor stalls proudly displays a photo of Margaret Thatcher haggling over some paprika in 1984; the Iron Lady was the first foreign dignitary to visit the hall. Southern end of Váci u.

NEWSPAPERS, BOOKS & MAPS The following is a list of the main bookstores in the city. We've indicated English-language specialist shops, although all big stores will have an English-language section.

📚 **Alexandra** V, Nyugati tér 7; ℡ 1 428 7070; ⊕ 10.00–22.00 daily [149 B2] Largest bookshop in Hungary. Among others in Budapest: VII, Károly körút 3c/Dob u. 1 & Andrássy út 35.

📚 **Bestsellers** V, Október 6 u. 11; ℡ 1 312 1295; www.bestsellers.hu ⊕ Mon–Fri 09.00–18.30, Sat 10.00–17.00, Sun 10.00–16.00 [144 B1] English-language bookshop.

📚 **Cartographia Map & Globe Shop** VI, Bajcsy-Zsilinszky út 37; ℡ 1 312 6001; www.cartographia.hu; ⊕ Mon–Fri 10.00–18.00 [149 B2] National & international maps & globes by Hungary's leading cartographic company.

📚 **Freytag & Berndt** V, Kálvin tér 5; ℡ 1 318 5844; www.freytagberndt.hu; ⊕ Mon–Fri 10.00–18.30, Sat 10.00–13.00 [144 D5]

📚 **Libri** V, Váci u. 22; ℡ 1 318 5680; www.libri.hu; ⊕ Mon–Fri 10.00–19.00, Sat–Sun 10.00–15.00

[144 B3] Foreign-language bookshop (mainly English). Other outlets: in Mammut (page 124) & at Rákóczi út 12.

📚 **Pendragon** XIII, Pozsonyi út 21–23; ℡ 1 349 3049; www.pendragon.hu (under construction); ⊕ Mon–Fri 10.00–18.00, Sat 10.00–14.00 [149 A1] English-language books, at good prices. Second outlet: Zrínyi u. 12; ℡ 1 327 3096.

📚 **Térképkirály** VI, Bajcsy- Zsilinszky út 23; ℡ 1 472 0505; www.mapking.hu; ⊕ Mon–Fri 09.00–18.00, Sat 09.00–13.00 [149 B3] 'Map King' is a chain selling maps & a few guidebooks.

📚 **Treehugger Dan's Bookstore Café** VI, Csengery u. 48; ℡ 1 322 0774; www.treehugger.hu; ⊕ Mon–Fri 10.00–19.00, Sat 10.00–17.00 [149 C2] Second-hand English-language books. Second outlet: VI, Lázár u. 16.

PORCELAIN, POTTERY & GLASS

⚜ **Ajka Kristály** XIII, Szent István körút 18; ☎ |
340 5083; V, József Attila u.; ☎ | 317 8133;
www.ajka-crystal.hu; ⏰ Mon–Fri 10.00–18.00, Sat
10.00–13.00 [149 B1]

⚜ **Herend Porcelain** V, József nádor tér 11; ☎ | 317
2622; www.herend.com; ⏰ Mon–Fri 10.00–18.00,
Sat 10.00–14.00 [144 B2] Beautiful examples of
Herend porcelain. Another outlet: VI, Andrássy út 16.

⚜ **Herend Village Pottery** II, Bem rakpart 37; ☎ |
356 7899; ⏰ Tue–Fri 09.00–17.00, Sat
09.00–12.00 [88 C2] Specialises in the more 'rustic'
– rather than refined – pieces.

⚜ **Zsolnay** V, Kecskeméti u. 14; ☎ 318 2643;
www.zsolnay.hu; ⏰ Mon–Fri 10.00–18.00, Sat
10.00–13.00 [144 D5] An array of hand-made
Zsolnay pieces, including vases, plates, cups &
saucers. Many other outlets in the city (see website).

SHOPPING MALLS IN THE CENTRE

⚜ **Duna Plaza** XIII, Váci út 178; ☎ | 465 1666;
www.dunaplaza.hu; ⏰ Mon–Sat 09.00–21.00, Sun
10.00–19.00

⚜ **Mammut** II, Lövőház u. 2–6; ☎ | 345 8020;
www.mammut.hu; ⏰ Mon–Sat 10.00–21.00, Sun
10.00–18.00 [88 B2]

⚜ **Westend City Center** VI, Váci út 1–3; ☎ | 238
7777; www.westend.hu; ⏰ Mon–Sat 10.00–21.00,
Sun 10.00–18.00 [149 B1]

THERMAL BATHS

Budapest stands on a fault line dividing the Buda Hills from the Great Plain; three
million litres emerge daily, feeding around 40 baths and seasonal pools, 15 with
medicinal ranking. For the sake of this guide, we've listed only the main ones. For
information on the history and etiquette of bathing, see pages 70–3; see
www.spasbudapest.com for up-to-date info.

Gellért Baths XI, Kelenhegyi út 4–6; ☎ | 466 6166;
⏰ high season (May–Sep) thermal baths &
indoor/outdoor swimming pools 06.00–20.00 daily;
low season (Oct–Apr) thermal baths & indoor
swimming pool 06.00–19.00 daily; steam bath all yr
Mon–Fri 06.30–20.00, Sat 06.30–13.00;
💲 2,900Ft (locker), 3,200Ft (cubicle); note there are
reduced afternoon rates (2,700/3,000Ft after 17.00);
discount with Bpest Card [88 D6] 🚇 18, 19, 41, 47,
49 🚊 7. Here, one feels, a decadent of ancient Rome
could draw contented breath, cast off toga & sandals,
& plunge in with a hearty 'Carpe diem!' The domed
hall, frescoed ceilings, neo-Romanesque columns &
spouting gargoyles ooze opulence; a visit is as much
about gawping as soaking. There is a pool for mixed
bathing, as well as separate areas for men & women
– where you can choose between your moon & your
costume. Outside is a summer terrace & pool with
vigorous wave machine. It's worth saying that the
staff here are notoriously unhelpful, & many tourists
prefer to visit the Széchenyi (see opposite) than
suffer their rudeness. Guests of the Gellért Hotel may
use the baths gratis. A sliding refund is available for
shorter stays (400/200Ft if you leave within 2/3hrs,
except on already-discounted afternoon tickets) –
retain the coupon issued as you enter & collect your

refund from the cash desk on leaving (ensure you
ask for this).

Király Baths II, Fő u. 82–86; ☎ | 201 4392;
⏰ 09.00–20.00 Mon & Wed (women), Tue, Thu–Sat
(men), Sun (men & women); 💲 1,200Ft [88 C2]
🚇 4, 6 🚊 86. The Király (King) Baths date to the 16th
century. Some swear that bathing here is a mystical
experience. The baths are certainly the most
atmospheric of any in the country, with lowly shafts of
daylight from the original Turkish dome casting a
murky, steamy haze. Open to men or women only on
alternate days (the baths are popular with the gay
community), visitors are issued with an apron to wear.
There are just 2 warm indoor pools, with a dry & wet
steam room & saunas (under the smaller dome). The
main pool is on the cosy side, so it is best visited on
weekdays to avoid the crowds. On purchasing your
ticket, go upstairs & take a bath towel from a
uniformed staff member. Choose a cabin along one of
the long corridors; ensure that you return within 90
minutes or you'll be charged extra. The shower facilities
are next to the pool, under the second dome, & so it
is probably worth taking your shampoo & soap with
you on heading down to the baths. Children prohibited.

Rudas Baths XI, Döbrentei tér 9; ☎ | 356 1322;
⏰ steam baths: Mon, Wed–Fri 06.00–20.00 (men),

Tue 06.00–20.00 (women), Fri 22.00–04.00, Sat 06.00–17.00 & 22.00–04.00, Sun 06.00–17.00 (both); swimming pool: Mon–Fri 06.00–18.00, Sat–Sun 06.00–14.00; ♨ thermal baths 2,200Ft (refund of 400/200Ft if leave within 2/3 hrs; no concessions), swimming pool 1,200/1,000Ft [88 C5] T̲ 18, 19, 41 B̲ 5, 8. Constructed by the Turks in the mid-16th century, the Rudas has an octagonal steam pool & turquoise cupola & is the favourite of many of the city's male bathers (who are issued with aprons to spare blushes) — indeed, it has traditionally been a popular meeting place for gay bathers. There is now a women-only day, as well as mixed late-night bathing at weekends. The indoor swimming pool is open to both sexes. Immediately to the south of Elizabeth Bridge. Massages from 2,500Ft.

Széchenyi Baths XIV, Állatkerti körút 11; ✆ 1 363 3210; www.szechenyifurdo.hu; ⏱ 06.00–22.00 daily; ♨ adult 2,600/2,400Ft (before/after 16.00) [89 G1] M̲1̲ Széchenyi fürdő T̲B̲ 72. Opposite the circus in City Park is the mustard-yellow, neo-Baroque edifice housing Europe's largest spa. It's cheaper than the Gellért Baths, & is generally regarded as being friendlier in atmosphere. Built in 1913, the 16 indoor sitting-pools are set in enormous halls, suggestive of the Roman bathing culture, while a steam room, 4 saunas & cold-water tubs draw on Turkish & Nordic traditions. Outside is a lukewarm swimming pool, a jacuzzi pool (with underwater jets) & the main hot bathing pool (37–38°C — the spring actually emerges at 76°C & has to be mixed with cooler water); all pools (including those outside) are open all year. Prepare for hot, hot water, & bathers playing chess on stone boards jutting from the pool sides.

Let's help you get your bearings. Head for one of the cash desks inside the entrance facing the circus, & buy a cabin ticket (if you're with a friend & aren't bashful, just buy one ticket — cabins are big enough for two). Take your ticket through the revolving barriers into the changing area, which has something of the feel of a sanatorium. Show your ticket to the attendant, & you'll be led to a cabin; once you've changed, the attendant will chalk a letter on the inside of the door to indicate the time of your arrival, lock the cabin & and give you a disk with a number on it that matches a disk left inside. Be sure to remember your locker number, which differs from the disk; if you leave within 2 hours, some money will be returned to you as you swipe your card on departure.

Exploring Buda

CASTLE HILL

QUICK CROSS-REFERENCES

Map page 127
Museums & galleries
  pages 157–9
Restaurants page 105
Cafés page 109
Bars page 111

Castle Hill (Várhegy; in District I) rises 60m above the Danube, bears aloft the former royal palace, and is the master of the western bank. It is often overcrowded and some of its services are overpriced; however, visit at the right time of day (earlyish morning or lateish afternoon) and in a patient frame of mind, and cobbled streets and Baroque dwellings provide a backdrop for some of the city's most pleasant strolls and river views. The museums and galleries of Buda Castle Palace, the wonderfully extravagant Mátyás Church, and the natural caves running beneath also make this a short-break must-see.

Inhabited since the early stages of pre-history, it was not until after the **Mongol invasion** of 1241–42 (page 16) that Castle Hill was considered as a potential stronghold. **King Béla IV** (1235–70) resolved to protect his homeland; he moved the country's capital from Esztergom to Buda, and constructed a fort to the south of Castle Hill and a royal residence to the north, near Vienna Gate (Bécsi kapu). Citizens from the Víziváros and other vulnerable areas were moved to residences in a new burghers' town (the Castle District or Várnegyed) that occupied the remaining two-thirds of the hilltop, and which was surrounded by fortified walls.

A diverse community grew up around the hill's castle and churches. **Germans and other European traders** contributed to a community that flourished until the arrival of the **Turks**. Castle Hill's fortifications did not deter conflict. There were over 30 sieges during subsequent centuries, and the district had to be rebuilt on numerous occasions. Following the **1686 siege** that drove the Turks from Buda, most of the houses were reconstructed over two (rather than the original three) storeys in Baroque and Louis-XVI styles by successive Habsburg rulers. Similarly, few buildings escaped unscathed after the last gasp of the German army here in 1945.

GETTING UP THERE The **funicular railway** or cable car (*Budavári sikló;* ✆ *07.30–22.00 daily, closed 1st & 3rd Mon of month for maintenance;* ✆ *sgl/rtn adult 800/1,400Ft, concessions 500/900Ft*) offers the most direct and sedate journey up Castle Hill, while also providing goodly views of Budapest. It is accessed at the western side of Clark Ádám tér. There is also a **lift** running from Dózsa tér up to the palace complex, next to the Lions' Courtyard (same hours as Széchényi Library; page 159).

The '**Várbusz**' – a dinky little chap that bears a castle symbol rather than a number – runs from Moszkva tér to Dísz tér every six or seven minutes, while 16A and 116 also follow this route. Alternatively, bus 16 travels between Déak Ferenc tér on the Pest side and Dísz tér throughout the bulk of the day.

Much of the Castle District is pedestrianised, and most **cars** can only drive as far as Dísz tér – via Palota út or the one-way Hunyadi János út – where you must park and disembark. Only authorised vehicles and hotel residents may enter via Bécsi kapu. Another option is to drive up below the Fishermen's Bastion and park on the street there. Drivers collect a ticket on entering the district and pay on leaving (currently 500Ft/hr, but this changes regularly). If you are staying in one of the hotels, the receptionist will stamp your card to allow you to exit through the barrier. Parking is free for guests at the Hilton, while the Kulturinnov charges a daily fee for the use of its car park.

There are approaches from most sides for those with the energy to puff and pant up Castle Hill **on foot**. Several roads lead up to Bécsi kapu. Steeper flights of stone steps (*lépcső*) snake up the hill's eastern side and provide more taxing but ultimately rewarding routes to the top. One set finishes next to the upper station of the funicular railway, another at the Fishermen's Bastion; these can be picked up at various points on and around Hunyadi János út, including from Clark Ádám tér. Alternatively you can take a route up from Szarvas tér to the southern end of the hill, and there are further flights leading up the western slope.

THE CASTLE COMPLEX *(For details of the palace itself, see pages 165–6; for its museums and galleries, see pages 157–9.)* There are two points of access to the **Buda Castle Palace** complex (✆ *06.00–24.00 daily*) in Szent György tér, near the upper terminal of the funicular railway. That immediately to the left – a black ornamental gate with an intricate stone-carved arch – is most striking for its fierce neighbour, a huge bronze *turul* (see box, page 128) (Gyula Donáth, 1905). As it glares grumpily over the city from its prime perch, you'd be forgiven for thinking that it finds the view a little irksome. If so, it's feathered of brain; on passing through the gate and down to the cobbled terrace, you can look unhindered over the river as it cuts forcefully between Buda and Pest, and sweeps away around the bend.

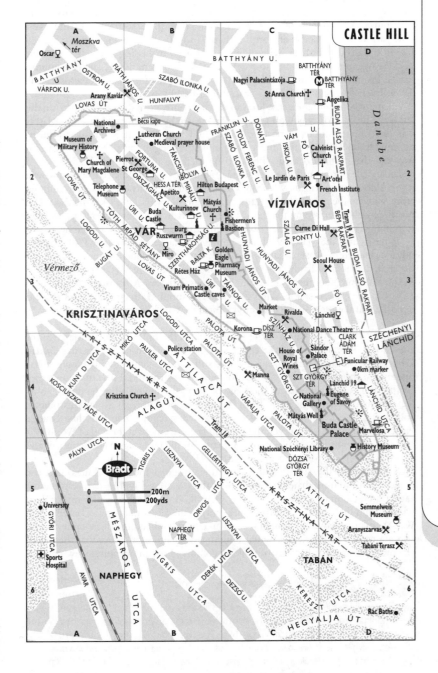

CASTLE HILL

A **B** **C** **D**

Moszkva tér

Oscar

BATTHYÁNY U.

BATTHYÁNY U.

BATTHYÁNY TÉR

BATTHYÁNY U. OSTROM U. FIÁTH JÁNOS U. SZABÓ ILONKA U. Nagyi Palacsintázója BATTHYÁNY TÉR

VÁRFOK U.

Arany Kaviár

St Anna Church

Angelika

LOVAS ÚT HUNFALVY U.

BUDA ALSÓ RAKPART

Bécsi kapu

National Archives

FRANKLIN U. DONÁTI U.

VÁM U.

Danube

Museum of Military History

Lutheran Church

Medieval prayer house

SZABÓ ILONKA U. TOLDY FERENC U.

ISKOLA U. FŐ U.

Calvinist Church

Church of Mary Magdalene Pierrot St George

FORTUNA U. TÁNCSICS MIHÁLY U. ORSZÁGHÁZ U.

Le Jardin de Paris

Art'otel

Telephone Museum

HESS A TÉR

Apetito Kulturinnov Hilton Budapest

French Institute

2 Buda Castle Mátyás Church **VÍZIVÁROS** **2**

ÚRI U. Burg Ruszwurm

Fishermen's Bastion

LOVAS ÚT TÓTH ÁRPÁD SÉTÁNY

VÁR

SZENTHÁROMSÁG U. Carne Di Hall

Vérmező

LOGODI U. BUGÁT U.

Miro

BALTA K. HUNYADI JÁNOS U.

SZALAG U.

PONTY U.

BEM RAKPART BUDAI ALSÓ RAKPART

Golden Eagle Pharmacy Museum

Rétes Ház

Seoul House

3 Vinum Primatis Castle caves HUNYADI JÁNOS ÚT FŐ U. **3**

ÚRI U. TÁRNOK U.

KRISZTINAVÁROS

LOGODI UTCA PALOTA ÚT

Market

Rivalda

Lánchíd

SZÉCHENYI LÁNCHÍD

Korona DÍSZ TÉR National Dance Theatre

MIKÓ UTCA PAULER UTCA ATTILA UTCA Police station

House of Royal Wines Sándor Palace

CLARK ÁDÁM TÉR

4 KOSCIUSZKO TÁDÉ UTCA KUNY D UTCA Manna SZT GYÖRGY TÉR Funicular Railway 0km marker **4**

Krisztina Church ALAGÚT UTCA

National Gallery

Eugene of Savoy

Lánchíd 19

LÁNCHÍD U.

Tram 18 VÁRALJA UTCA PALOTA ÚT

Mátyás Well

Buda Castle Palace

Marvelosa

PÁLYA UTCA TIGRIS U. LISZNYAI UTCA GELLÉRTHEGY UTCA National Széchényi Library

History Museum

N DÓZSA GYÖRGY TÉR

Bradt

0 200m

0 200yds

ATTILA ÚT

5 University ORVOS UTCA LISZNYAI UTCA KRISZTINA KRT **5**

GYŐRI UTCA MÉSZÁROS UTCA NAPHEGY TÉR

Semmelweis Museum

Aranyszarvas

Sports Hospital

TIGRIS UTCA DERÉK UTCA DEZSŐ U.

TABÁN

Tabáni Terasz

6 AVAR UTCA **NAPHEGY** KERESZT UTCA **6**

HEGYALJA ÚT

Rác Baths

A **B** **C** **D**

Budapest **CASTLE HILL**

3

The vast neo-Baroque equestrian statue is that of **Prince Eugene of Savoy** (1663–1736), who led the armies that liberated Hungary from Ottoman rule, forcing the Turks to sign the Treaty of Karlowitz in 1699 that ceded Hungary to the Habsburgs. The citizens of the town of Zenta (133 miles southeast of Buda, and now part of Serbia), scene of a seminal battle in 1697, commissioned this statue by József Róna 200 years later. When they made the embarrassing discovery that their pockets weren't deep enough to pay for the work, Ferenc József stepped in with funds. Prince Eugene had attacked Sultan Mustafa II's forces as they crossed the Tisza River, overcoming an army twice the size of his own.

An archway behind the statue leads to another courtyard at the palace's rear. On the left is the bronze **Mátyás Well** (*Mátyás-kút*) created by Alajos Stróbl in 1904. Mátyás was one of the country's most renowned and respected kings. He was fond of donning the clothes of commoners and mingling among his people; when he died, it was said that truth had died with him. As such, he made the ideal subject for a legendary tale of romantic love, recorded originally by his chronicler and then woven into a 19th-century ballad by Mihály Vörösmarty. Here Mátyás is shown in hunting attire, while to the right is the beautiful peasant girl, Ilonka Szép (Helen the Fair). The poem describes her seeing this handsome huntsman and falling deeply in love; on learning his identity, and the impossibility of a match, she dies of a broken heart.

To the right of the Mátyás Well is the entrance to the **Lion Courtyard** (Oroszlános udvar), guarded by a pair of kingly beasts looking faintly aloof. On the other side of the arch, they roar violently at the temerity of those who have crossed between them. At the courtyard's southern end is the **Budapest History Museum** (Wing E; page 157). On the eastern side is Wing D of the **National Gallery** (pages 158–9), and opposite that the **National Széchényi Library** (Wing F; page 159).

THE OLD TOWN If the palace is the noble head of the hill, and the prime target of any knockout punch during the epic fights that have taken place here, the **Castle District** or burghers' town has inevitably suffered the sapping body blows. It has undergone the same cycle of destruction and reconstruction. Little of its medieval Gothic apparel remained after the siege of 1686; the town had to be pulled to its feet, brushed down and given a fresh Baroque set of clothes. It gained in strength, and during the late 19th century even boasted splendid mansions like Sándor Palace (see opposite). However, the Russian bombardment at the end of World War II brought it to its knees once more. A quarter of the buildings were flattened, and a measly group of just four escaped unscathed.

Nevertheless, the streets still follow their original medieval routes, and the recycling of building materials means that the eagle-eyed will recognise pieces of earlier architectural features – sections of wall, Gothic arches, stone niches, and window and door frames. Furthermore, during the clear-up operation after World War II, many medieval remnants were uncovered, shedding fresh light on the appearance of the district's original buildings – including the fact that they were elaborately painted in a range of striking colours. This architectural stew endows

THE TURUL

This mythical bird, resembling an eagle, is said to have sired Árpád's father, Álmos, and thus brought forth the Árpád dynasty. It became a symbol of national identity during the millenary celebrations of 1896. The weapon in its talons is the sword of Attila. While elsewhere in the world he was about as popular as a garlic mouthwash, Attila became a heroic figure in Hungarian cultural consciousness during the 18th century because of theories of an ancestral link between the Huns and the Magyars.

Ludwig Koch, the Viennese painter, much admired the great horsemanship of the Hungarians. Upon returning to Austria in 1923 he pushed artistic licence to the full in painting an imaginary scene in which a single horseman rode five steeds at the same time. Intent on further proving their skills of horsemanship, Hungarians successfully imitated the painting; the stunt became known as the 'Koch (or puszta) five'. Riders have raised the bar ever since – the current world record is for one man on 12 horses!

the district with its charm and interest. For all the pretty restoration, it is in such historical flotsam that the area's violent past is revealed, together with the resilience of the people who kept on piecing it back together.

Szent György tér The stony rubble of some of the noble mansions that once stood in Szent György tér can be seen towards the back of the square. The squat, neo-Classical **Sándor Palace** (nos 1–2) still stands, to the right of the funicular railway. Built in 1806 for Vince Sándor, it even had marble mangers in the stables. Later used as the prime minister's official residence, it was the scene of Pál Teleki's suicide in 1941. Just months after signing a friendship treaty with Yugoslavia, Admiral Horthy committed Hungary to the Nazi attack on its new 'ally'; his prime minister felt unable to live with the dishonour. The building was gutted by fire during World War II; renovations costing two billion forints were completed in 2002, and it is now the president's official residence. The yellow **National Dance Theatre** (page 118) – graced by performers including Haydn and Beethoven – is next to the Sándor Palace.

Dísz tér Walking up one of either Szent György utca or Színház utca you will reach Dísz tér and the southern extent of the burghers' town proper. Here it was that market sellers plied their trades during the Middle Ages, and where parades by the palace guards took place in the years after the expulsion of the Turks. Today it is the main point of traffic access to the Castle District. At the centre of the square is the **Honvéd statue** by György Zala, cast from cannon metal and erected in 1893 as a memorial to those 'defenders of the homeland' who fought in the 1848–49 War of Independence. On the eastern side is a quaint **Folk Art Market** (⊕ 09.00–19.00 daily) selling lace, wooden toys, football shirts and etchings at prices reflecting its prime pitch. In a corner just off the square's southeastern end sits a slouching statue of the neat-bearded Zoltán Kodály (page 29).

Two roads forge away from the top of the square – Úri utca (page 132), which hugs the remaining length of the district's western side as far as Kapisztrán tér, and **Tárnok utca**. Take the latter for the moment, with its collection of little shops to interest you on the way towards Mátyás Church. Keep an eye out for the **Tárnok Café** – with its swirling red and orange sgraffitoed walls – and **Arany Hordó Vendéglő** at nos 14 and 16 respectively. Their Renaissance exteriors were exposed following damage during World War II.

The **Golden Eagle Pharmacy Museum** (Tárnok u. 18; ☏ 1 375 9772; ⊛ 500/250Ft; ⊕ Oct–Mar Tue–Sun 10.30–15.30, Apr–Sep Tue–Sun 10.30–17.30) originally housed the district's first apothecary. In an upper-storey niche of the neo-Classical façade stands a curious **painted statuette** – almost a sculpted cartoon – of the Madonna and child by Margit Kovács (pages 184–5). Moving just beyond the museum, you pass the tiny side street of **Balta köz**. Claustrophobic and darkly romantic, 'Axe Alley' is said to be where the brothers Hunyadi (László and Mátyás) were captured by László V, and where they defended themselves with axes during the violent struggle.

Szentháromság tér We have now reached the highest point of Castle Hill and one of the pouting cover girls of Budapest's picture postcards – the bustling and asymmetrical Szentháromság tér (Holy Trinity Square).

The Council of Buda erected the Baroque **Trinity Column** (1711–14) on behalf of plague survivors. It was funded in part through a system of fines imposed on naughty citizens found guilty of offences like adultery. Around the column are carved saints who stand as guardians of the city.

The two-storey building with the diminutive green clock tower across from the Burg Hotel is the **former town hall** (no 2), constructed by the Italian architect Venerio Ceresola in the late 1600s. A chapel was later added specifically to hold a holy relic – one of the feet of St János the Charitable. Originally a gift to King Mátyás from the Turks ('Hmmm, just what I've always wanted...'), the foot now 'stands' in the church of his name (pages 167–9). Artúr Görgey – young commander of the Hungarian forces – stayed in the town hall after capturing the area from the Austrians during the 1848–49 War of Independence. The statue in a niche at the building's corner is Pallas Athene, the 'Protector of Buda'.

A few metres to the west along Szentháromság utca is a horsey **statue by György Vastagh** (1936). The noble animal's green-and-black colouring is broken by its golden 'crown jewels' (ahem!), polished by generations of students who give them a rub for luck. The figure atop is the popular András Hadik (1710–90), a man who rose through the ranks to become a hussar general – and later chairman of the Vienna Military Council, the only Hungarian to reach such dizzy heights under the Habsburgs – and was a favourite of Maria Theresa. The original of the sabre at his side can be seen in the Museum of Military History (page 157). A document bearing the name of every soldier to fall during the life of the Third Royal and Imperial Hussars (1702–1918) lies in a glass case entombed in the statue's pediment.

The square's show stealer, of course, is **Mátyás Church** (pages 167–9). Next to this is the **Fishermen's Bastion** (*Halászbástya*); you might think that its stones are too brightly white and its medieval silhouette too sharp and unworn to have weathered the storms of several centuries – and you'd be correct. It was erected by Frigyes Schulek in 1902 as a purely decorative companion for his church, and stands at the section of the hill supposedly defended in the past by the guild of fishermen. The coned turrets symbolise the tents of the nomadic Magyar tribes (page 15). The largest of the seven represents the leader Árpád.

In front of the bastion is an equestrian **statue of St István**, the country's first king, founder of the Hungarian state and convert to Christianity. It was commissioned of Alajos Stróbl at the time of the millenary celebrations, although the great Historicist sculptor took ten years over his masterpiece – he even researched the history of the 11th-century stirrup. The altar-like pedestal was designed by Schulek, a man whose fingers were in so many of the square's pies; it is inset with carved reliefs depicting defining moments in the king's reign, including his coronation and his founding of Székesfehérvár Church.

Hess András tér The funnel-shaped square immediately to the north of Szentharomság tér is named after the first printer of Buda who lived here in the 15th century. The Hess press printed the earliest Hungarian book in 1473, the only remaining complete copy of which is in the Széchényi Library (page 159). At the square's centre is a **statue of Pope Innocent XI**, who is known as the 'saviour of Hungary' because of his endeavours in funding the European forces that freed Hungary from Turkish rule.

The **Budapest Hilton** at no 1 is a heady mix of Baroque, Gothic and 20th-century tinted chic. Opened in 1977, it was built on the site of a Dominican church and monastery of 1252 and incorporates the remains of its walls, together with a 15th-century tower and the reconstructed Baroque façade of a 1688 Jesuit college.

Táncsics Mihály utca & Fortuna utca From Hess András tér, streets strike out northwards in a two-pronged attack on Bécsi kapu tér. In taking that on the right, **Táncsics Mihály utca**, you follow a curving road of two-storey houses painted from a pretty pallet of fading pastel shades. From the 15th century, this street was the hill's **Jewish quarter**. The Castle District had traditionally been a haven for religious groups. Béla IV granted legal privileges to Hungarian Jews in the 13th century, attracting those suffering from persecution in western European countries. They eventually settled along Táncsics Mihály utca, remaining here throughout the period of Ottoman occupation – indeed, at that time the road was called Zsidó (Jew) utca. You can visit a **16th-century prayer house** (*Táncsics Mihály u. 26;* ✆ *1 225 7816;* ✆ *500/250Ft;* ⊕ *May–Oct Tue–Sun 10.00–17.00*).

No 9 is believed to have been the site of the original royal residence, before the monarch's quarters were relocated to the hill's southern end. Much later it was transformed into a barracks whose armoury was used as a **prison** from the early 19th century. Behind the huge gates, still visible today, several prominent anti-Habsburg 'subversives' were confined, including Lajos Kossuth (1837–40) and Mihály Táncsics (1847–48 and 1860). The prison was stormed during the uprising of March 15 1848, and Táncsics was freed and carried through the streets by the revolutionaries.

The parallel left-hand road from Hess András tér is **Fortuna utca**, named after the goddess of Fortune, and featuring a sprinkling of shops and galleries.

Bécsi kapu tér Vienna Gate (Bécsi kapu) is the northern entrance to the old town. It has stood in its present incarnation since 1936; its medieval ancestor was reduced to gravel during the 1686 siege. The **glazed relief** outside bears the distinctive style of Margit Kovács (pages 184–5), who here depicts a violent assault upon Buda's walls. It is a fitting companion for Ostrom utca – or 'Siege Street' – and for the square it introduces, once site of the medieval Saturday market but later marked as a place of remembrance for those who fell for freedom in 1686.

Next to the gate is a drab academic in harlequin's headgear – the **National Archives** (Országos Levéltár; nos 2–4) building, its sombre stone blocks capped with a majolica-tiled celebration of colour. Raised between 1913 and 1920, its roof betrays its designer – Samu Pecz – who was also responsible for the Great Market Hall (page 123).

Don't leave without taking in the sights from the **outer walls**. The fortifications were primarily the work of the Turks, who incorporated medieval walls wherever possible. One way of joining these is from Bécsi kapu tér, with access next to the archives building on to a promenade leading around the northern tip of the district. After 100m you will pass the **memorial to Abdurrahman** on the Anjou bástya, a symbolic grave dedicated to the last Turkish governor (pasha) of Buda. He was 70 years old when he was killed in battle, and with this monument the Hungarians honour a heroic adversary. Further round, the path is lined with chestnut trees and the Buda Hills are presented in all their splendour. The entrance to the **Museum of Military History** (page 157) can be found on Tóth Arpád sétány. Also along this western stretch is the **monument of the Second Transylvanian Hussars**, an inter-war interpretation of Leonardo da Vinci's Renaissance horse and rider (as seen in the Museum of Fine Arts; page 163). The promenade leads eventually into Dísz tér.

Kapisztrán tér Petermann bíró utca carries you westwards from Vienna Gate into the cobbled Kapisztrán tér. The square is striking for the lonely Gothic tower of the **Church of Mary Magdalene** (page 167). Next to the **town hall** (no 1) at the northern side of the square stands a neo-Classical palace, built as a barracks in 1847. At its entrance are two formidable cannon; the **Institute and Museum of Military History** (page 157) are now housed inside. Cannon balls are embedded in the façade, reminders of the Hungarian army's liberation of the Castle District in 1849. Also here is a **statue of János Kapisztrán** (1386–1456), stepping over the body of a slain Turk. The Italian Franciscan monk fought with his private peasant army alongside János Hunyadi in the famous victory at Nándorfehérvár in 1456, succumbing to the plague shortly afterwards. A fresco in the Mátyás Church (opposite the Loréto Chapel) also commemorates this battle; Kapisztrán actually used the church for a troop-recruitment speech in 1455.

Országház utca Országház (Parliament) utca runs between Kapisztrán tér and Szentháromság tér, and is so named because parliamentary sessions were held in no 28 at the turn of the 19th century. There are several Gothic features to be seen on buildings along the street, most obviously extant alcoves or '*sedilia*' set within the openings of gates. Such intriguing architectural characteristics – unique to Hungary – came to light all over the district during post-war excavations and have perplexed boffins ever since. The educated assumption is that they were covered niches for nightwatchmen or for citizens and servants to duck into for rest or shelter. Whatever their purpose, they became canvases for carved decoration and display, as neighbourly peacocks strove to out-strut each other.

Úri utca Úri utca is the final piece in the district's jigsaw, the only street to last the course through the whole length of the town, and connecting Kapisztrán tér and Dísz tér. Its location next to the promenade overlooking the hills to the west was enough to make medieval estate agents drool, and noble residences were hot property.

Religious devotees once shut themselves away from earthly pleasures in the Franciscan monastery at **no 53**, while the followers of Martinovics were more reluctant detainees here in the 1790s (see box above).

The 15th-century house at **no 31**, looking down upon its neighbours, is something of a historical 'storey teller' – providing us with the only standing evidence that there were once three-floor houses on the hill. There are medieval *sedilia* sunk into the gateway walls at **no 32**. The massive lucky charm that is the Hadik statue (page 130) is at the junction with Szentháromság utca. Finish off with a visit to the dank cave system – the **Buda Castle Labyrinth** (*Budavári Labirintus; Úri u. 9;* ✆ *1 212 0207; www.labirintus.com;* 🎫 *1,500/600–1,100Ft, small discount with Bpest Card or Hungary Card;* ⊕ *09.30–19.30 daily [127 C3]*) – and then on to the creamy offerings at **Ruszwurm** (page 109) – the café that's served buns to burghers since 1827.

QUICK CROSS-REFERENCES

Maps pages 149 & 127
Museums & galleries
  page 159
Cafés page 109
Bars page 111

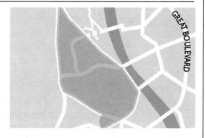

GELLÉRT HILL Gellért Hill (Gellért hegy; District XI) raised its granite head over 200 million years ago, a craggy henchman to the south of Castle Hill. From deep in its bowels spews water that feeds the three thermal baths (pages 124–5), while at the top the fortress and monument to freedom represent rather unlikely bedfellows. Inhabited since Neolithic times, transcripts of witch trials during the 17th and 18th centuries reveal that the rock was a favoured gathering place for exponents of the dark arts, and this is also supposedly where the Venetian monk Gellért (page 16) – after whom the hill was named in the 18th century – was martyred.

You are less likely these days to encounter witches' spells or falling bishops, but it still takes a certain commitment to brave the 140m on foot. The panoramic views, however, reward any effort. A series of stone steps and sloping paths lead up the southeastern side of the hill (from opposite the Gellért Baths), while there are walkways from the north too. If you'd prefer to have some breath left for the views to take, there is a **car park** on Citadella sétány, while **bus 27** (from Móricz Zsigmond körtér) stops 300m below the Citadella (outside the Búsuló Juhász restaurant).

At the Buda foot of Freedom Bridge (Szabadság híd), **Gellért tér** is a beacon for those hankering after some stylish soaking or a turn-of-the-20th-century flourish to their hotel stay (pages 124 and 102). **Freedom Bridge**, topped with *turul* birds (see box, page 128), was built for the millennial celebrations and initially bore the name of Ferenc József. While it would be an exaggeration to say that the latter was a key construction worker, he did push a button that activated a hammer that drove the final rivet into the bridge. The rivet was silver and bore his initials; unsurprisingly it was later stolen.

Across the road from the Gellért Baths is the romantic **Cave Church** (pages 166–7), beyond which you can begin the ascent to the summit. With its 14m poker-straight woman thrusting high above the hill's peak, the **Freedom Monument** is visible from miles around. Finally erected in 1947, it was commissioned originally by Admiral Horthy as a memorial to his son, who had died during a wartime test flight. In an ironic twist, the Russians arrived before the sculpture was complete, and Zsigmond Kisfaludy Stróbl adapted the design to suit his new patrons. A palm

Budapest **GELLÉRT HILL AND THE TABÁN**

3

HALLO EVERYONE!

The name Tivadar Puskás may not ring any bells, but this ex-student of the University of Technology invented the telephone exchange in 1877 and was a colleague of the rather better-remembered Thomas Edison. He is said also to have brought us the world's most familiar greeting. On testing his invention, and hearing a voice at the other end of the telephone line for the first time, he cried out 'Hallom!' meaning 'I hear you!' in Hungarian. A slight mishearing and a dropped consonant later, and the word 'hallo' was born.

frond (instead of the intended propellor) was placed in the hands of the woman, transforming the piece from a personal – if very public – tribute into a political symbol of Russia's role in liberating the city. After the demise of communism, the bronze soldier was moved to Memento Park (pages 160–1), leaving the muscle-bound beast slayer and striding torchbearer to convey an allegorical message shorn of specific historical associations. The plinth's inscription now reads 'In memory of all of those who sacrificed their lives for Hungary's independence, freedom and prosperity'. Next to the monument is the imposing **Citadella** (page 167).

A little further down the hill's northern end, Gellért (or 'Gerard') flourishes a cross above the traffic passing back and forth over Elizabeth Bridge. A waterfall flows beneath **Gyula Jankovics's statue** of 1904, and a walkway – guarded by a pair of *turul* birds – begins directly below it. It is said that at this point in 1046 the bishop took a more direct and less leisurely trip down the hill in a barrel full of spikes. The Italian missionary had been appointed Bishop of Csanád by King István, before becoming the country's first Christian martyr during the power struggle and pagan backlash that followed the monarch's death (page 16).

THE TABÁN Plugging the gap between the two hills on the river's bank is the Tabán (in District I), an area of grass, a large traffic junction and two of the city's thermal spas. In summer it is the site of al-fresco concerts, while sledding and snowballs are popular during the snowy season. In Turkish times, foreign artisans set up shop here, and in the 18th century a village was built by Serbian settlers. It became a lively place, with many restaurants and bars, but in 1933 the bulk of the single-storey houses were demolished for hygiene reasons (open sewers and diseased grape vines). Just outside it, on the lower southeastern slope of Castle Hill, is the zigzagging ceremonial pathway of the **Várkert bazár**. In its heyday this was a splendid pleasure garden designed by Miklós Ybl in 1872 (and there are plans to renovate it). A **statue of Ybl** (1814–91), laden with dividers and architectural plans, stands near by, as does the **birthplace of Ignác Semmelweis** (page 159).

Immediately to the north of Elizabeth Bridge is the pedestrianised Döbrentei tér, its paths leading away underneath the busy flyover that circles overhead. Here sits a **youthful Erzsébet** (1837–98), fondly sculpted in a flowing gown with roses lying beside her. She was a popular queen, who made determined efforts to engage with the Hungarian people, and her assassination by an Italian anarchist was met with genuine sadness. Underneath the bridge is a **drinking hall**, while on the southern side are the **Rudas Baths** (pages 124–5).

Nine statues – grim-faced toughs with axes in hand and violence in mind – stand with Dózsa György tér at their backs and the rear of the Buda Castle Palace looming above. They represent participants in the peasant uprising of 1514 (page17), and were sculpted in 1961 by István Kiss.

THE VÍZIVÁROS

QUICK CROSS-REFERENCES

Maps page 127 & 88
Restaurants page 105
Café pages 109
Bars page 111

The Víziváros (Water Town; in Districts I–II) squeezes between Castle Hill and the Danube, before breathing out and filling the space northward to Margit híd and westward to Moszkva tér. The main street (Fő utca) follows the route of a Roman road that linked the hill and Aquincum, and retains a healthy dash of old-world romance. In the years prior to the Turkish occupation, fishermen and artisans dwelt here; today it offers a straight-lined, uncomplicated **walk** between the Chain and Margaret bridges. If you do it one way, choose Fő utca; if you have the stamina for a return journey, walk back along the parallel Bem rakpart next to the river.

Start at **Clark Ádám tér**, named after the 19th-century Scottish engineer who constructed both Széchenyi Lánchíd (the Chain Bridge) and the tunnel through the hill that connects the city centre with the western parts of Buda. The **tunnel** is 350m long. The original **Chain Bridge** itself was designed by Englishman William Tierney Clark (responsible for the first Hammersmith Bridge in London) in 1824, replacing a pontoon that had to be dismantled with the arrival of winter's ice. In December 1820, István Széchenyi was called to Buda on learning of the death of his father; however, the bridge was down, he could find no ferryman willing to navigate the drifting chunks of ice, and he very nearly missed the funeral. He campaigned thereafter for a permanent structure; it was finally opened in 1849, although Széchenyi himself was by then incarcerated in a mental asylum, and unable to cross the bridge he had inspired.

Fő utca straddles districts I and II, carrying you north of Clark Ádám tér as far as Bem József tér. Some buildings appear sunken into the surface – this is because at the end of the 19th century the street level was raised by over a metre to reduce its vulnerability to flooding.

The **church** at the south side of **Corvin tér** (Fő u. 30–32) was originally constructed in the medieval period, used as a mosque during the Ottoman occupation (note the Turkish ogee-arched door in the southern wall) and then as a Capuchin monastery in the 18th century. A statue of St Elizabeth gazes down from high above the entrance.

You'll emerge for a few paces before disappearing into **Szilágyi Dezső tér**. The red-brick neo-Gothic **Calvinist church** has a slender steeple – the tallest in Buda – and a roof adorned with ceramic Zsolnay tiles. A pint-sized statue of Samu Pecz, who clearly enjoyed playing with geometry in constructing the church in 1893–96, stands outside dressed in the garb of a medieval master builder. On the river bank is a memorial to the March 15 1848 revolution, bearing the message 'Steadfastly for your homeland'. It was at this place that the Arrow Cross murdered hundreds of Jews in 1945, dumping their bodies in the water.

Batthyány tér (named after the prime minister of the 1848 government) contains the Baroque **St Anna Parish Church** (1740–62). The church wasn't actually consecrated until 1805 because the finishing touches were hampered by an earthquake. Organ concerts are held inside (ticket info; ↘ 1 317 2754), with a sightseeing dinner cruise afterwards if you choose. On the northern side of the square is a **former hospital** run by Elizabethan nuns; a statue in front depicts Ferenc Kölcsey (1790–1838), the bald-headed Romantic poet who composed the Hungarian national anthem 'Hymn' ('Himnusz'). Batthyány tér is served by both the metro (M2) and the HÉV, while tram 19 terminates here.

Cross Csalogány utca and join **Nagy Imre tér**. Nagy was leader of the government during the 1956 revolution (see pages 21–2); it was in the midst of the intimidating symmetry of the **military court and prison** building (Fő u. 70–78) to the square's north and northwest that he was sentenced to death two years later. Luckier was Attila Ambrus, the 'Whisky Robber', who in 1999 escaped from an upper storey with a rope he'd fashioned from bed sheets.

Just beyond the junction with Kacsa utca are the **Király Baths** (page 124), while on the other side of Ganz utca is the **Chapel of St Flórián** (*Görögkatolikus templom; Fő u. 88*). This tiny church – as yellow as egg yolk, and with just eight pews either side of a golden altar – was built in 1759–60 and later given to the Greek Catholics. After the raising of Fő utca, the church's portico slipped over a metre below street level; in the 1930s the church was itself lifted by 1.4m to minimise future flood damage.

Fő utca culminates at **Bem József tér**. The Polish General József Bem, known as 'Papa Bem' (Bem Apó), fought with the Hungarians in the 1848 revolution, scoring victories over Austrian and Russian armies in Transylvania. Bem fled to Turkey after the collapse of the uprising, and died in 1854 bearing the name Amarut Pasha after converting to Islam. The statue in the centre commemorates the 1849 Battle of Piski – 'I will take this bridge or I will die. Go Hungarians!' – and was a rallying point for students during the 1956 revolution. It was here that the Russian hammer and sickle was cut from the Hungarian flag, creating an instant gaping touchstone of the revolutionary cause.

From here, the Rózsadomb and **tomb of Gül Baba** (page 169) are a short but steep walk away. Alternatively make your way back along the river on **Bem rakpart**, running the gauntlet of speeding cyclists and enjoying the views of Parliament on the opposite bank.

ÓBUDA AND AQUINCUM

QUICK CROSS-REFERENCES

Map page 137
Museums & galleries
    page 160
Restaurants page 106
Cafés page 109
Bars page 111

The primary concentration of ancient history is to be found in Óbuda (Old Buda; District III), which became 'old' in the 13th century when Béla IV shifted the centre of the region's power behind new walls on Castle Hill. Occupying a northern portion of the city, the early provenance is difficult to credit at a passing glance, for parts of District III sprouted high-rise flats during the '60s and a large carriageway was driven through the centre. However, two millennia ago the area was occupied by Celts and then Romans. The Danube represented the eastern boundary of the Roman empire; Flórián tér was the site of a camp supporting 6,000 legionaries, while to its north was a civilian settlement called Aquincum. The sites

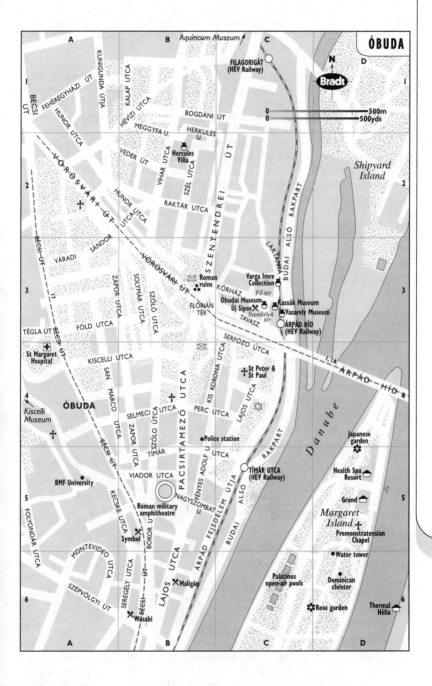

ÓBUDA

137

of interest are scattered between – and even sheltered beneath – highways and residential blocks, and as such it is best to move about by **public transport** if you want to avoid long treks through concrete jungle. You can travel here on bus 86 or tram 1 (over Árpád híd), but the HÉV suburban railway provides the simplest route; pick it up from Batthyány tér or Margit híd.

Alight at Timár utca and walk southwest to the corner of Nagyszombat utca and Pacsirtamező utca where you'll find a 2nd-century **military amphitheatre**. Holding 15,000 spectators, this was the largest of its type outside Italy (indeed some claim it was larger than the Colosseum – although it seems unlikely to us that the Romans would trump their capital card in this way); here gladiators fought with beasts or took part in naval battles in the flooded arena.

Head further north up Pacsirtamező utca past Flórián tér, duck under the Szentendrei út flyover and you'll enter a subway like no other – an unexpected trove of Roman ruins. These were the **legionary baths**, excavated in 1778, and the tiled heating courses are still evident. A few hundred metres east along Kórház utca is the former market place and present-day haven of **Fő tér** (behind Árpád híd station in Szentlélek tér). This pretty, cobbled square contains a daffodil-yellow **town hall** (*Fő tér 3*) at its northern side, with a little balcony and acorn finials, while on the eastern edge is the 18th-century **Zichy Palace**. Inside its Baroque wings, and those of an adjacent Trinitarian monastery, are the **Óbuda History Museum**, and collections of works by avant-garde artist **Lajos Kassák** (*Fő tér 1;* ＼ *1 368 7021; www.pim.hu;* ₰ *300/150Ft;* ✆ *Wed–Sun 10.00–17.00 [137 C3]*) and leading Op-artist **Victor Vasarely** (*Szentlélek tér 6*; page 160) – the latter including kaleidoscopic pieces that will make your head swim. Pass out of the square's northeastern corner (*Laktanya u.*) and take a photo with the four ladies strolling towards you beneath their umbrellas. Imre Varga's intriguing sculpture is a taster for the fabulous exhibition of his layered and polished metal works near by (page 160).

For a real orgy of Roman ruins, take the HÉV to the **Aquincum** stop; this area was the heart of what became the principal town of the province of Pannonia Inferior until the soldiers (and consequently the civilians too) pulled out in AD404. It was established as the base for those civilians associated with the military camp 3km to the south, but quickly became a major administrative and commercial centre in its own right, with an amphitheatre, law courts, baths and temples. Walk across the road and south to the neo-Classical **museum** (page 160), which makes sense of the stone lines and piles, and displays other archaeological finds.

BUDA HILLS

QUICK CROSS-REFERENCES

Maps pages 140 & 88
Museums & galleries
 pages 160–1
Restaurants page 106
Cafés page 109

There are few large cities where natural greenery is so readily accessible. The Buda Hills are known as the 'lungs' of the capital, and – clichéd as it sounds – the woodlands and clearings really do promise kisses of life on stifling days. In winter, they are places to sledge, or even ski. The Buda Landscape Protection Area (Budai Tájvédelmi Körzet) covers 10,000ha in total, and is characterised by outcrops of white dolomite and limestone rock, by forested areas and grasslands, and by over 150 caves.

Some of the most fragile habitats are barred to the casual tourist boot, but Hármashatár, Kis- and Nagy-Hárs, Remete, János and Széchenyi hills are all within easy reach and feature trails for ramblers, families and cyclists. Over 100 species of bird breed up here, wild boar and deer (fallow and red) inhabit the forests, scarce reptiles like the Armenian whipsnake (*Coluber jugularis*) bask in the sun, and edible funghi are to be found such as the brown-capped common mushroom (*Agaricus sp*) – although check before guzzling a handful as there are also poisonous varieties. Botanical gardens and other sites of natural interest wait beyond the designated protection area too, and those who wish to go further can explore the footpaths of the Pilis, Visegrád and Börzöny hills in the Danube-Ipoly National Park (*park directorate: II, Hűvösvölgy út 52;* ☎ *1 391 4610; www.dinpi.hu*) to the north of Budapest. We've merely scratched a muddy surface with the following, and green fingers will find value in probing deeper. For operators running **nature-related tours**, see pages 39–41 and 99.

THE RAIL TRAIL Several buses run to points along the edge of the Buda Landscape Protection Area, but the train is an enjoyable way to ignore these limits and plunge straight on in. It also affords an easy introduction to a decent chunk of nature.

The **Cogwheel Railway** (*Fogaskerekű vasút; XII, Szilágyi Erzsébet fasor 14–16*) is the first stage of your two-track journey. Its lower end station (*vá*) is Városmajor, opposite the Budapest Hotel, and best reached by tram (59 or 61 – the latter going on all the way to Hűvösvölgy) from Moszkva tér. Trains run every 15–20 minutes to Széchenyi hegy (*between 05.00 & 22.20 daily; last train back leaves around 23.30*) and you can travel using an ordinary bus/train ticket. Don't expect a quaint or relaxing ride; toothed cogs pull the carriages uphill, and it's something of a brain-sloshing 20 minutes.

On disembarking, signposts offer several options. You can walk a short distance along Rege út to the **Széchenyi kilátó** (a TV tower at the top of the hill), you can follow Golfpálya út on the considerably longer route on foot to János hegy (page 141), or you can take a few steps to the second stage of the railway trail 200m away.

The **Children's Railway** (*Gyermekvasút; Hegyhát út;* ☎ *1 397 5392; www.gyermekvasut.com;* ☏ *sgl/rtn: adult 700/1,400Ft, child 350/700Ft; Nov–mid Mar, Tue–Sun 09.05–17.05 every hr, mid Mar–end Oct, Mon–Fri 09.05–17.05 every hr, Sat–Sun 08.00–17.45 roughly every 30 mins*) is a narrow-gauge line that preserves the tradition – established by the communist youth movement and the Hungarian State Railway in 1948 – of giving work experience to children aspiring to a career on the railways. The kids collect and sell tickets conscientiously, but are not yet trusted with driving the engine. The carriages are wooden-benched and open-sided; they snake their way into the landscape protection area, and proceed northwards for 11km as far as Hűvösvölgy. The whole journey takes 45 minutes, but you may wish to alight at one of the eight stations along the way. The track passes Normafa lejtő, János hegy and Hárs hegy, while the Budakeszi Game Park (*Vadaspark; XII, Budakeszi;* ☎ *1 2345 1783; www.vadaspark-budakeszi.hu;* ☏ *400/200–250Ft;* ⊕ *(Mar–Oct) Mon–Fri 09.00–16.00, Sat–Sun 09.00–17.00; (Nov–Feb) Mon–Fri 09.00–15.00, Sat–Sun 09.00–16.00*) is accessible from Szépjuhászné (*alight and take bus 22 from Budakeszi út to Szanatórium u.*). You can return to town from the Children's Railway aboard tram 61.

NORMAFA LEJTŐ & JÁNOS HEGY Normafa – Róza Klein once sang an aria from Bellini's *Norma* under a tree (*fa*) here – is a very popular walking, biking, jogging and picnicking spot, particularly at weekends. At 479m above sea level it is one of the highest points in town, and offers some snow sports in winter; in truth,

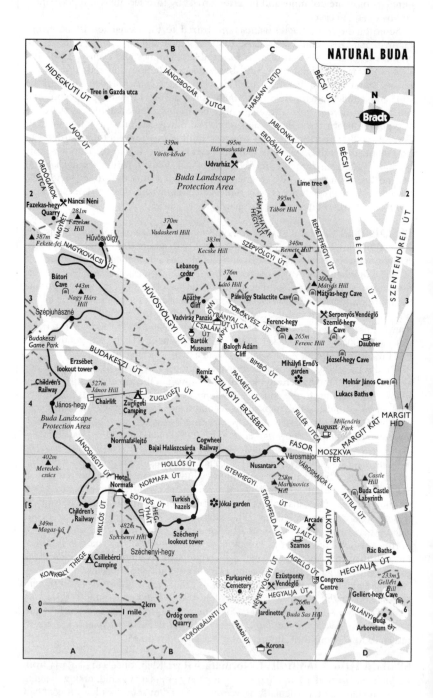

Bradt

HIDEGKÚTI ÚT

Tree in Gazda utca

JÁNOSBOGÁR UTCA

HARSÁNY LEJTŐ

BÉCSI ÚT

LAJOS ÚT

ORDOGÁROK UTCA

339m
Vörös-kővár

495m
Hármashatár Hill

Udvarház

JABLONKA ÚT

ERDŐALJA ÚT

Lime tree

*Buda Landscape
Protection Area*

Náncsi Néni

Fazekas-hegy
Quarry

281m

NAGYRÉT U. ÚT

*Fazekas
Hill*

▲ 387m
Fekete-fej

NAGYKOVÁCSI ÚT

Hűvösvölgy

370m
Vadaskerti Hill

395m
Tábor Hill

HÁRMASHATÁR HEGY ÚT

BÉCSI ÚT

SZENTENDREI ÚT

REMETEHEGYI ÚT

383m
Kecske Hill

SZÉPVÖLGYI ÚT

348m
Remete Hill

Bátori
Cave

443m
*Nagy Hárs
Hill*

Lebanon
cedar

376m
Látó Hill

300m
Mátyás Hill

Szépjuhászné

HŰVÖSVÖLGYI ÚT

Pálvölgy Stalactite Cave

Mátyás-hegy Cave

Serpenyős Vendéglő
Szemlő-hegy
Cave

Budakeszi
Game Park

Apáthy
Cliff

NAGYBÁNYAI ÚT

TÖRÖKVÉSZ ÚT

Ferenc-hegy
Cave

Vadvirág Panzió

CSALÁN ÚT

KAPY UTCA

▲ 265m
Ferenc Hill

Daubner

BUDAKESZI ÚT

Bartók
Museum

Balogh Ádám
Cliff

BIMBÓ ÚT

Mihályfi Ernő's
garden

József-hegy Cave

Erzsébet
lookout tower

Remiz

PASARÉTI ÚT

Molnár János Cave

Children's
Railway

527m
János Hill

Chairlift

ZUGLIGETI ÚT

SZILÁGYI ERZSÉBET

FILLER UTCA

Lukács Baths

Millenáris
Park

Auguszt

MARGIT KRT

MARGIT
HÍD

János-hegy

Zugligeti
Camping

*Buda Landscape
Protection Area*

JÁNOSHEGYI ÚT

Normafa-lejtő

Cogwheel
Railway

FASOR

MOSZKVA
TÉR

402m
*Meredek-
csúcs*

Hotel
Normafa

Bajai Halászcsárda

Railway

Városmajor

VÁROSMAJOR U.

MIKLÓS ÚT

NORMAFA ÚT

HOLLÓS ÚT

ISTENHEGYI

Nusantara

258m
*Martinovics
Hill*

*Castle
Hill*

Buda Castle
Labyrinth

ATTILA ÚT

Children's
Railway

EÖTVÖS ÚT

EÖTVÖS HEGY

XI HÁT

Turkish
hazels

Jókai garden

STROMFELD A. ÚT

349m
Magas-kő

482m
Széchenyi Hill

Széchenyi
lookout tower

Arcade

KISS J. ALT. U.

Szamos

ALKOTÁS UTCA

Rác Baths

KONKOLY THEGE

Csillebérci
Camping

Széchenyi-hegy

Farkasréti
Cemetery

Ezüstponty
Vendéglő

NÉMETVÖLGYI ÚT

HEGYALJA ÚT

JAGELLÓ ÚT

Congress
Centre

HEGYALJA ÚT

233m
Gellért
Hill

Gellért-hegy Cave

0
0
2km
1 mile

Ördög orom
Quarry

TÖRÖKBÁLINTI ÚT

SASADI ÚT

266m
Buda Sas Hill

Jardinette

VILLÁNYI ÚT

Buda
Arboretum

Korona

though, the views are more thrilling than the skiing. Bus 21 runs here from Moszkva tér at regular intervals; alternatively, you can take the Children's Railway to Normafa station (and follow Eötvös út north). If you want to escape the crowds, and enjoy a gentle downward lope, follow the route marked with a green cross next to the final bus stop (on the other side from the Danube view). Cross the Children's Railway line, and head down the valley, through Budakeszi forest towards Makkosmária Church in its lovely clearing. After the church, continue down Makkosmária út towards the centre of Budakeszi. From here you can take bus 22 back to Moszkva tér, passing the wildlife park on the way.

A more strenuous walk from Normafa is northwards to **János hegy**, the capital's highest peak (527m), along the blue-circle route. Up here you'll find the **Erzsébet-kilátó** (⊕ *08.00–20.00 daily*), a white-stone viewing tower that is a view in itself. You can see the hand of Frigyes Schulek in an elegant design with a strong flavour of the Fishermen's Bastion; its namesake 'Sisi' (page 134) – Empress Erzsébet to you and me – visited the spot in 1882. You can climb its steps for a tower-top vantage point and superb views over the hills. There are also further sign-posted walking routes (including a nature trail). Best of all, however, is the **chairlift** (*libegő*; ⊕ *Mon–Fri 10.00–17.00, Sat–Sun 09.00–18.00, closed every other Mon; 🚠 adult 500Ft, student/pensioner 400Ft, child 200Ft*), which offers peaceful carriage down the hill to Zugligeti út (from where you can take bus 158 to Moszkva tér – after grabbing a *lángos* from the shack at the Zugligeti campsite near by; page 104). It can get chilly up there, so take a sweater. There's a walking/cycling route running beneath the lift, but it's very steep.

CAVES Budapest is unique as a world capital in being riddled with caves (*barlang*). There are over 60 thermal springs in Buda, welling up in groups at Gellért hegy, Hármashatár hegy and in the Csillaghegy-Rómaifürdő area; over thousands of years, the corrosive, toasty water broadened rock faults into chambers. The Bátori Cave on top of Hárs hegy was mined for iron ore during the Middle Ages, and the caves under the Castle District were used variously as cellars, burial vaults and air-raid shelters. Lime material deposited by the water as spring travertines at the surface was used in building the city, while the very name 'Pest' probably derives from the slavic word for cave.

The five largest cave systems – Pál-völgy, Mátyás-hegy (a popular cavers' training site), Ferenc-hegy (a maze of narrow passages), Szemlő-hegy and József-hegy (only discovered in 1984) – are all located within an area of a couple of square kilometres, and are strictly protected. Despite this, there is limited access to a few of them for non-specialists. In addition to those below, some companies offer more active tours with qualified cavers, usually of the Mátyás-hegy system. For **further information** on caves, contact the Danube-Ipoly National Park (*park directorate: II, Hűvösvölgy út 52;* ✆ *1 391 4610; www.dinpi.hu*).

Pálvölgy Stalactite Cave II, Szépvölgyi út 162; ✆ 1 325 9505; 1,000/750Ft, free with Bpest Card, combined ticket 1,250/850Ft; ⊕ Tue–Sun 10.00–16.00 [140 C3] Ⓑ 65 (*from Kolosy tér – alight at 5th stop*). You'll need to scale a ladder & 417 steps in your tour of the stalactite cave (*cseppkőbarlang*), with formations that as crocodiles to the imaginative eye, & fossils of 40-million-year-old sea urchins in the limestone. At over 19km, this is the second-longest cave in Hungary; the public may see 500m of it. Guided tours (50 minutes)

leave 15 minutes past every hour; children under 5 may not enter. (If you purchase a combined ticket for both Pálvölgy & Szemlő-hegy caves, the tour times suit a visit to the latter first.)

Szemlő-hegy Cave II, Pusztaszeri út 35; ✆ 1 325 6001; 800/600Ft, free with Bpest Card, combined ticket (see above); ⊕ Wed–Mon 10.00–16.00 [140 D3] Ⓑ 29 (*from Kolosy tér – alight at 5th stop, on Felsőzöldmáli út*). The 2.2km-long cave is nicknamed 'the underground garden of Budapest' because of its popcorn-coralloid & other speleothems

– in English, pretty mineral & crystal formations. The cave's glories were revealed in 1930, when a slim lady was passed through a narrow slit (later named the 'Needle's Eye'). Fat ladies (opera singers) now visit the 'Giant Corridor' to benefit from the curative effects of the cave's humid air. A 300m stretch is open to the public; tours (35 mins) start on the hour.

Exploring Pest and the Islands

THE DOWNTOWN

QUICK CROSS-REFERENCES

Maps page 144 & 149
Museums & galleries
    page 161
Restaurants pages 106–7
Cafés page 110
Bars pages 112–13

The downtown (District V) is Pest's beating heart, a gathering point for the city's shopping, commercial, banking and tourist centres. The bulk of the Belváros (inner city) portion is hemmed in by the Kiskörút (Small Boulevard), a near semi-circle of road running from Freedom Bridge along the original lines of the medieval walls (dismantled during 19th-century expansion) before becoming a little ragged on its way to the Chain Bridge. It is lanced by Kossuth Lajos utca, running from Erzsébet híd out to Keleti station. The Lipótváros (Leopold Town) north of József Attila utca holds two of the country's most significant buildings in the Parliament and St Stephen's Basilica. The tracks of tram 2 run alongside the Danube and circle the Parliament, offering views to rival those from public transport anywhere in Europe. Moving in from the tracks, though, the downtown is a compact area of one-way or pedestrianised roads that's best explored on foot.

BELVÁROS There's no simple way of tackling the inner city – the chances are that you will start somewhere in the vicinity of Váci utca and dive off into those squares and side streets that take your fancy. No single linear walk properly covers the sights of interest; for the purposes of this guide, therefore, we've divided it into two chunks, south and north of Erzsébet híd. Pick and mix your way around.

The southern half At the southern end of the inner city is **Szabadság híd** (page 133), spanning the river to Gellért Hill (page 133). Near it is the magnificent **Great Market Hall** (page 123).

Kálvin tér Vámház körút leads in an easterly direction around to Kálvin tér, a busy square rather dominated by the glass building of the Erste Bank. The white neo-Classical **Calvinist Church** (Református templom) was built by József Hofrichter and József Hild (1813–51). The sandy building (*Kálvin tér 9*) next to it – now holding a café and flower shop – was once the **Two Lions Inn** (see the weather-worn beasts above the doorway); Hector Berlioz first heard the 'Rákóczi March' while staying here – a stirring tune originally used to recruit freedom fighters to the anti-Habsburg cause in the early 1700s. Berlioz drew from the song in composing his own version over a century later. One of the **medieval gates** through the city walls stood at Kálvin tér. Branching southeast from the square (further into Ferencváros) is **Ráday utca** (page 114), one of the stars on the city's drinking circuit.

When we first saw a *puli* running down the street in Budapest, we looked around with some chagrin for the joker who was throwing mop heads around. It is one of the oddest dogs you'll see, a compact canine whose shaggy coat forms a series of natural cords – often mistaken for dreadlocks – that reach to the ground, covering its whole body. If the dog is standing still, it can be difficult to tell whether it is wagging a tail or shaking a head. When lying flat, you'd be forgiven for thinking it was a bath mat – although it would be a poor performer in this respect, for the *puli* can take three days to air dry, and will walk carefully around a small puddle.

Despite appearances, the *puli* is highly agile. It looks more sheep than shepherd, but was brought to Hungary by Magyar tribesmen over 1,000 years ago as a herder of livestock on the plains. The dogs gathered the stock from the villages, and drove them between grazing areas or to market. *Pulis* differed from other working dogs, such as border collies, in having to move huge numbers of sheep – often upwards of 400, many with foot rot – in tall grass. As a result, theirs was a vigorous and less-refined method than other breeds – bouncing to see over the grass and yelping to spur the flock into motion. They are usually black in colour (originally to distinguish them from the sheep), highly intelligent, extremely active, and expressive watchdogs. Bred to be the sole companion of the shepherd during months of isolation, they are also affectionate and loyal. Indeed the bond was so strong between man and dog, that shepherds would only ever sell *pulis* between themselves, believing that others could never properly understand the dog's unique temperament.

Múzeum körút If you follow the Small Boulevard northwards you'll join Múzeum körút, with a cluster of shops hawking antique books, maps and coins. Addresses on the opposite side of the road actually have a District VIII postcode (page 155), and these include the **Hungarian National Museum** (page 164). The museum is difficult to miss – it's the largest in the country – and you certainly shouldn't, because it holds the Hungarian coronation mantle and some breathtaking ceiling frescos. It was from the museum steps that Petőfi's 'National Song' was recited at the outset of the 1848 revolution, and from the **radio station** on the adjacent Bródy Sándor utca that secret police fired the opening salvos at student demonstrators during the revolution of 1956 (pages 21–2).

Cross the road and head back towards the depths of the inner city along Ferenczy István utca to **Károlyi kert**, an enclosed and peaceful park. This was a private garden belonging to the palace behind it, once home of Mihály Károlyi, the president of the 1918–19 Hungarian Republic. During the mid-19th century, the notorious Baron Haynau ('the Hyena of Brescia'; page 19) took the place as his headquarters after crushing the 1848 revolution, and from here dictated those vengeful measures designed to dampen future thoughts of rebellion. It is now the headquarters of the **Petőfi Literary Museum** (*V, Károlyi Mihály u. 16;* ☎ *1 317 3611; www.pim.hu;* 💰 *480/240Ft;* ⊕ *Tue–Sun 10.00–18.00 [144 C]4*).

Ferenciek tere To the right along Károlyi Mihály utca is Ferenciek tere, named after its Franciscan church (*Ferences templom; Ferenciek tere 9*). The current church was completed in 1743, the Turks having trashed its 13th-century Gothic predecessor in 1526. Look out for the pew where Ferenc Liszt used to park himself while staying in the adjacent monastery. A relief on the wall outside shows the nobleman **Miklós Wesselényi** in action during the murderous flood of 1838 (page 90). His valiant efforts in a rowing boat saved many lives – and unlike others who milked

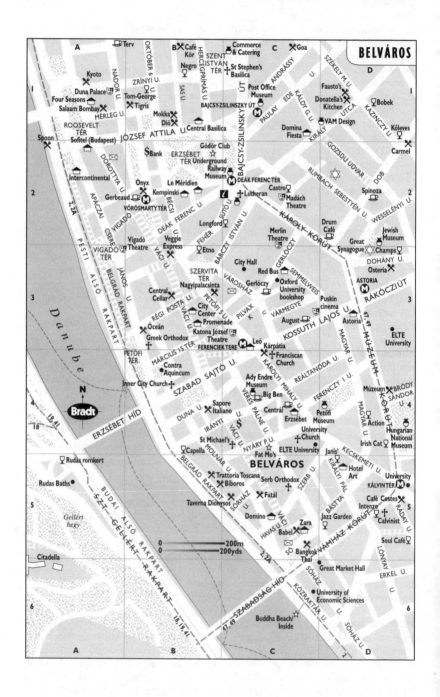

BELVÁROS

desperate people by demanding payment for access to their boats, Wesselényi's bravery came free of charge.

Egyetem tér Taking Károlyi Mihály utca in the other direction from the Károlyi Palace brings up Egyetem tér. The **University Church** (*Egyetemi templom; Papnövelde u. 9*) needs a good bath, but beneath the grime of time and car fumes is a beautiful Baroque surface of terracotta and white. It was constructed by the Paulines – the country's only indigenous monastic order – in 1748. They were booted out not long afterwards when József II dissolved the orders in 1782, and the church was taken over by the university. Parliament met for a short time here after the 1848–49 War of Independence. High above the altar, angels bear a copy of Poland's 'Madonna of Czestochowa'.

Moving southwest from the square along Szerb utca, the **Serb Orthodox church** (*Szent György Nagyvértanú Szerb Orthodox templom; Szerb u. 6*) was constructed in 1698 by Serbs arriving after the Turkish occupation. The tower and façade were added in 1750, probably to the plans of the renowned architect András Mayerhoffer, and the nave divides male and female worshippers over two levels. The iconostasis is a replacement for an original that fell victim to the 1838 flood; a marker by the southern entrance shows the level the waters reached – fully two metres high.

Váci utca The Serb church is an incense whiff from Váci utca, which runs through the whole of the Belváros, linking our northern and southern halves and marking the length of medieval Pest. It is the primary tourist street, pedestrianised most of the way, and characterised by cafés, restaurants, and shops selling goods from designer clothes to folk art and antiques (see *Shopping*, pages 121–4). Prices are as high as you'll find anywhere in the city, but it's busy and colourful. On meeting a sculptural tree of life – which actually looks more like a stick of celery – you'll have arrived at **Szabad Sajtó út** at the top of the inner city's southern segment.

The northern half Look to the left along Szabad Sajtó út and you'll see **Erzsébet híd**, crossing the river at its narrowest point. When originally opened in 1903, this was the longest single-span chain bridge in the world (at 380m). Destroyed by the retreating Germans in 1945, it was the last of Budapest's bridges to be replaced and – with its new cable design – the only one not restored to its former shape. A significant slice of medieval architecture was sacrificed to make way for the bridge, and the **Inner City Parish Church** (page 170) had to close its eyes and pray as the wrecking ball whistled past its left cheek. In front of the church in **Március 15 tér** are remains of **Contra-Aquincum**, a 3rd-century fort built by the Romans to protect their settlement on the other side of the river.

Duck under the subway (containing some 19th-century photographs of the city) to continue on Váci utca, which leads uninterrupted to Vörösmarty tér. If you take the direct route, keep your eyes peeled for the the jagged line of marble cobblestones (a little further on from the 'Fisher Girl' statue), which traces the position of the northern medieval **Vác Gate** before it was removed in 1789.

Petőfi tér, Vigadó tér and Vörösmarty tér Alternatively, take a slight detour left into Régi posta utca, looking up to the painted relief of a stagecoach by ceramicist Margit Kovács (pages 184–5) on the building at **no 13**. At the end of the street you'll emerge into **Petőfi tér**, a square with strong symbolic significance and a favoured rallying point for both protest and celebration. The cloaked and goateed statue at the centre is Sándor Petőfi (see box, page 147), around which students gathered to denounce the Rákosi regime on October 23 1956. The **Greek**

Orthodox church was built by 18th-century Greek and Macedonian merchants; one of its two towers was destroyed in World War II and never replaced.

Move northwards along the Duna-korzó to **Vigadó tér**. Some impish boys play by the fountain at the grassy centre, while on the railings next to the tram track sits the harlequinesque statue of the '**Little Princess**' ('Kiskirálylány', Marton László, 1989). The square takes its name, however, from the ornamental and high-blown 19th-century **concert hall** at the eastern side. The promenade continues on to the Chain Bridge and Roosevelt tér, but we'll take a right down Vigadó utca – which has recently been reconstructed – to the side of the concert hall and on to **Vörösmarty tér**. It is broad and elegant, filled with portraitists and plane trees, with seasonal markets (the Christmas market in December is one of Europe's best) and performances of folk music. At its centre the poet **Mihály Vörösmarty** rests his pins; the opening line of 'Szózat' ('Admonition'), an appeal in 1836 for Hungarian unity, is inscribed on the statue's plinth – 'Be steadfastly faithful to your homeland, oh Magyars'. At the square's northern side is the celebrated **Gerbeaud** (page 110).

Szervita tér, József nádor tér and Erzsébet tér Southeast of Vörösmarty tér is **Szervita tér**, which used to belong to the Order of Servites whose Baroque church (Szervita templom) was consecrated in 1748. The relief above the portal's pediment depicts the order's founding saints – Julianna on the right and Peregrin (the patron saint of leg-pain sufferers) on the left. The square's three **Art-Nouveau façades** are wonderful, particularly Miksa Róth's 1906 allegorical mosaic of Hungary on the Turkish Bank House (Török Bankház) at no 3.

North of Vörösmarty tér, **József nádor tér** is bordered by heavy neo-Classical residences and the magnificent **Postabank Headquarters** (1860–61), which fills the entire western side. At the square's centre is a statue of Archduke József, the Habsburg palatine for 50 years from 1797. As palatines went, he was relatively popular in Pest; he loved the city, and made determined efforts to improve it – he was, for instance, the instigator for the planting of its greatest parks (at Margaret Island and City Park). The nearby **Erzsébet tér** contains a modern park, with a glass-bottomed pool covering a cultural and conference centre (the Gödör Klub; page 117). The **Danubius Fountain** is a replacement for a 19th-century original (Miklós Ybl and Leó Feszler, 1880–83) destroyed in World War II; its broad bowls are topped by an allegory of the Danube, with its half-naked tributaries seated around the base.

Deák Ferenc tér Deák Ferenc tér meets at the east. The simple **Lutheran Church** (*Deák téri evangélikus templom*) was designed at the turn of the 19th century by Mihály Pollock; the sons of Lajos Kossuth were baptised inside, and Sándor Petőfi was schooled here. The **Lutheran Museum** (*V, Deák tér 4;* ☏ *1 317 4173;* ☞ *400/200Ft, free with Bpest Card;* ⊕ *Tue–Sun 10.00–18.00 (10.00–17.00 in winter) [144 C2])* is next door, while the **Underground Railway Museum** (*Deák tér underpass;* ☏ *1 461 6500; www.bkv.hu;* ☞ *270/220Ft, free with Bpest Card;* ⊕ *Tue–Sun 10.00–17.00 [144 C2])* in the station underpass tells the story of the continent's oldest metro line, one of several ambitious constructions built as part of the millennial celebrations. The beige and fading **Anker Palace** (*Deák Ferenc tér 6*), with its helmet turrets, was an insurance building that many felt a blight on the cityscape when it first appeared. It now contains a series of shops.

LIPÓTVÁROS & BEYOND The area north of József Attila utca is known as Leopold Town, which developed following the construction of the Chain Bridge (page 135). It is still part of District V but a world away from the Belváros; colourful side streets make way for straight roads and broad squares, and shops and cafés for

To this day, the nation's favourite versifier – the man who has made the deepest dent on the national and literary consciousness – is the 19th-century poet Sándor Petőfi (1823–49). He was a writer who brought the vernacular into Hungarian poetry, and a fervent patriot. Most of all, he was a newlywed who provided the voice and impulse for the revolution that broke out on March 15 1848. In his 'National Song' – recited from the steps of the National Museum – he pleaded 'Rise, Hungarians!' ('Talpra, magyar!'). And they did. A year later – at just 26 – he was dead, killed in Transylvania during one of the last battles of the War of Independence. His cult status was sealed as the young, passionate, revolutionary romantic – the eloquent James Dean of his age.

offices and 19th-century residential blocks. It feels a more serious place, one of industrious commerce and government, and holds pockets that resonate strongly with some of the city's tragic moments.

Roosevelt tér Start with the elliptical Roosevelt tér at the foot of the Chain Bridge. The grassed island in the centre was the site of **Coronation Hill**, a mound of soil gathered from points all over Hungary. Following the 1867 Compromise (page 19), and the crowning of Ferenc József in Mátyás Church, Hungary's new king clambered the hillock, pointed to the four compass points with St István's sword, and pledged to be the country's defender – a symbolic act that harked back to pagan clan ceremonies. The **Four Seasons Hotel** occupies the renovated Gresham Palace, an Art-Nouveau jewellery box originally built for an English insurance company. There are statues to Ferenc Deák, the architect of the Compromise, and István Széchenyi, who made possible the **Hungarian Academy of Sciences** (*Magyar Tudományos Akadémia; Roosevelt tér 9*) at the square's northern side. The count donated a year's income to the founding of the society in this neo-Renaissance palace, with its chunks of creamy-orange stone. A relief at one side of the building records the moment on November 3 1825; when asked how he'd live for a year with no money, Széchenyi replied 'My friends will help me'.

Szent István tér and Kossuth Lajos tér Zrínyi utca leads eastwards as far as **Szent István tér**, a pedestrianised space that seems rather undersized in the presence of the looming **Basilica** (page 172). Behind it is Bajcsy-Zsilinszky út – named after a politician who stood up to the Nazis and was executed for it in 1944 – which links Deák tér to Nyugati tér; the latter holds the iron-and-glass **Western Railway Station** (Nyugati pályaudvar), built by Gustave Eiffel's firm (1874–77). Adjacent is 'the world's most beautiful McDonald's', and to the rear the Westend City Center shopping mall (page 124).

If, instead of going east, you follow Széchenyi rakpart north from Roosevelt tér, you'll arrive at **Kossuth Lajos tér**. (While in the vicinity, it's worth pointing out a sculpture – 'Cipők a Duna-parton' or '**Shoes on the Danube Bank**' by Gyula Pauer – that was placed on the stretch of the riverside Pesti also rakpart running between the two squares in 2005. Comprising 60 pairs of empty shoes, it commemorates the 60th anniversary of the Holocaust, and is sited at one of the spots at which Jews were murdered by Arrow-Cross troopers and their bodies cast into the river.) Imre Steindl was victorious in the competition to build **Parliament**, and his vision stands overlooking the river on the western side (pages 170–2). Remarkably, however, the second- and third-placed entries were also constructed, becoming the Palace of Justice (no 12, now the **Museum of Ethnography**; page 161) and **Ministry of Agriculture** (no 11) respectively. At the northern end of the square is a **statue of Kossuth** (1802–94), leader of the ultimately failed 1848–49 War of Independence, while the Transylvanian Prince **Ferenc Rákóczi II** (1676–1735) – another anti-Habsburg freedom fighter of the previous century – is opposite. Also on the lawn are memorials – a **symbolic grave** and an **eternal flame** – to victims of October 25 1956 when ÁVO shooters fired on a peaceful crowd. Each metal 'bullet' set into the walls of the Ministry of Agriculture represents one of the dead. Two days before, revolutionaries had torn the Soviet emblem from the Hungarian flag during the uprising, and the gravestone bears a relief of this symbol of freedom.

Szabadság tér Leaving via the southeast corner, however, you'll pass through the tiny **Vértanúk (Martyrs')** tere; standing on a bronze bridge and looking westward for American support is a **statue of Imre Nagy** (1896–1958), the communist reformer and prime minister during the '56 revolution who the Soviets executed two years later (page 22). Beyond it, at the end of Vécsey utca, is the lengthy **Szabadság (Liberty) tér**. Until the late 1800s, this was the site of a barracks, where significant participants in the 1848–49 War of Independence were incarcerated and then executed by Baron Haynau (page 19). Among them was Lajos Batthyány, prime minister of the 1848 independent government, and close by on Aulich utca an **Eternal Light** in a greening casket glows perpetually in remembrance. The **Soviet monument** was placed in the square in 1945; after the fall of communism, the Russian government was allowed to nominate one public piece to remain in situ (rather than being carted off to Memento Park), and this was the choice. The **Hungarian National Bank** (*Szabadság tér 8*) bears reliefs showing personifications of art, industry and commerce (among them the building's architect, Ignác Alpár, in the clothes of a medieval master builder).

TERÉZVÁROS

QUICK CROSS-REFERENCES

Map page 149
Museums & galleries
  pages 161–2
Restaurants pages 107–8
Cafés pages 110–11
Bars page 113

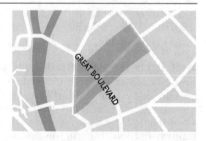

Falling on the eastern side of Bajcsy-Zsilinszky út, and locked between Király utca, Dózsa György út and the tracks of Nyugati Railway Station, much of Theresa Town (District VI) is a touch shabby. **Király utca** (named after the king of England in 1860) was a major thoroughfare at the end of the 19th century, and has a thriving collection of shops selling second-hand clothes and electrical goods, some swanky interior-design showrooms at its western end, the Liszt Ferenc Academy of Music at nos 64–66, and the district's 19th-century parish church (where it meets Nagymező utca), with chapels by Mihály Pollock and spire by Miklós Ybl. Liszt Ferenc tér and Jókai tér are popular drinking and meeting spots, and Nagymező utca contains the city's main clutch of theatres. However, the splendid big boy of the district is Andrássy út, the main avenue flying arrow straight from the Small Boulevard to Heroes' Square, and rated by many as the city's prettiest.

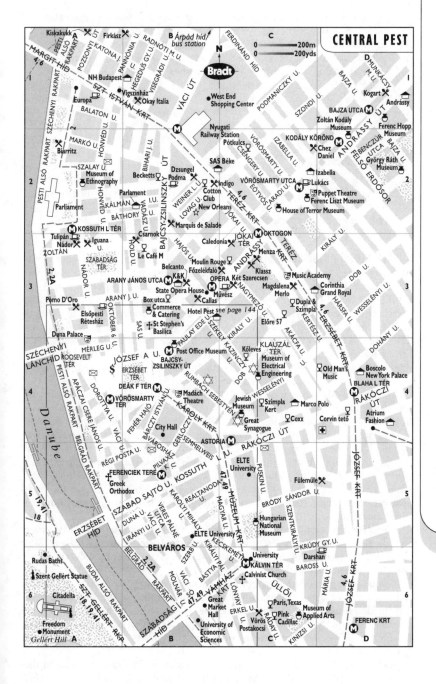

CENTRAL PEST

0 ——— 200m
0 ——— 200yds

N

Bradt

Kiskakukk · Firkász · B Árpád híd/ bus station · C · D MUNKÁCSY M.U.

PESTI ALSO RAKPART · POZSONYI · KATONA J. U. · PANNÓNIA · HEGEDÚS GY.U. · VISEGRÁDI U. · RADNÓTI M.U. · VÁCI ÚT · FERDINÁND HÍD · PODMANICZKY U. · SZONDI U. · BAJZA U. · Kogart · Andrássy

MARGIT HÍD · 4, 6

NH Budapest · West End Shopping Center · BAJZA UTCA M

Európa · Vigszínház · Okay Italia · SZT ISTVÁN KRT · BALATON U. · Zoltán Kodály Museum · Ferenc Hopp Museum

MARKÓ U. · HONVÉD U. · Nyugati Railway Station · Pótkulcs · KODÁLY KÖRÖND · ANDRÁSSY ÚT

Biarritz · BIHARI J. U. · VÖRÖSMARTY U. · IZABELLA U. · FELSÓ ERDÓSOR · BAJZA U.

SZALAY U. · Museum of Ethnography · Becketts · Dzsungel Podma · SAS Béke · CSENGERY U. · György Ráth Museum

Parlament · Parliament · KÁLMÁN I.U. · VADÁSZ U. · WEINER U. · Indigo · Cotton Club New Orleans · VÖRÖSMARTY UTCA M · Izabella · Lukács · Puppet Theatre

BÁTHORY · HOLD U. · BAJCSY-ZSILINSZKY ÚT · LOVAG U. · TERÉZ KRT · EÖTVÖS U. · VÁRADI U. · JÓKAI U. · Ferenc Liszt Museum

KOSSUTH L TÉR M · Csarnok · Marquis de Salade · House of Terror Museum

Tulipán · Nádor · Iguana · HAJÓS U. · Caledonia · JÓKAI TÉR · OKTOGON M · KIRÁLY U.

ZOLTÁN · NÁDOR U. · SZABADSÁG TÉR · Le Café M · Belcanto · Moulin Rouge · Menza · ANDRÁSSY ÚT · TERÉZ KRT

Pomo D'Oro · ARANY JÁNOS UTCA M · K&K · Belcanto · Főzelékfaló · Klassz · Music Academy · DOB U.

State Opera House · OPERA M · Két Szerecsen · Magdalena Merlo · Corinthia Grand Royal · WESSELÉNYI U.

ARANY J.U. · Box utca · Művész · NAGYMEZÓ U. · Dupla & Szimpla · HARSFA U. · ERZSÉBET KRT

Elsőpesti Rétesház · Commerce & Catering · Hotel Pest see page 144 · Előre 57 · DOHÁNY U.

Duna Palace · St Stephen's Basilica · SZÉKELY · KIRÁLY U. · AKÁCFA U.

SZÉCHENYI LÁNCHÍD · ROOSEVELT TÉR · MÉRLEG U. · JÓZSEF A. U. · Post Office Museum · Kőleves · KLAUZÁL TÉR · Old Man's Music · Boscolo New York Palace

PESTI ALSO RAKPART · BAJCSY-ZSILINSZKY ÚT · RUMBACH SEBESTYÉN · KAZINCZY U. · Museum of Electrical Engineering · BLAHA L TÉR M

ERZSÉBET TÉR · DEÁK F TÉR M · Madách Theatre · DOB U. · WESSELÉNYI · RÁKÓCZI ÚT

DOROTTYA U. · VÖRÖSMARTY TÉR · Jewish Museum · Szimpla Kert · Marco Polo · Corvin tető · Atrium Fashion

APÁCZAI CSERE JÁNOS U. · FEHÉR HAJÓ · KÁROLY KRT · GERLÓCZY U. · Great Synagogue · Coxx · JÓZSEF KRT

Danube · City Hall · SEMMELWEIS U. · ASTORIA M · RÁKÓCZI ÚT

RÉGI POSTA U. · VÁROSHÁZ · ELTE University · PUSKIN U.

FERENCIEK TERE · PILVAX · BRÓDY SÁNDOR U. · Fülemüle

Greek Orthodox · SZABAD SAJTÓ U. · KOSSUTH · REÁLTANODA U. · MAGYAR U. · MÚZEUM KRT · SZENTKIRÁLYI U.

ERZSÉBET HÍD · DUNA U. · VÁCI UTCA · VERES PÁLNÉ · KÁROLYI MIHÁLY · Hungarian National Museum

18 · 19, 41 · IRÁNYI U. · ELTE University · SZERB U. · KECSKEMÉTI U. · KRÚDY GY. U.

BELVÁROS · BELGRÁD · 2, 2A · VÁCI · KIRÁLY PÁL · University · Darshan · BAROSS U.

Rudas Baths · BUDAI ALSÓ RAKPART · BÁSTYA U. · KÁLVIN TÉR M · Calvinist Church · MARIA U. · 4, 6

Szent Gellért Statue · SZT GELLÉRT RKP · MOLNÁR U. · VÁMHÁZ KRT · LÓNYAY U. · ÜLLÓI ÚT · JÓZSEF KRT

Citadella · SZABADSÁG HÍD · 47, 49 · Great Market Hall · ERKEL U. · Paris, Texas · Pink Cadillac · Museum of Applied Arts · FERENC KRT M

Freedom Monument · University of Economic Sciences · Vörös Postakocsi · RÁDAY U. · KINIZSI U.

Gellért Hill **A** · **B** · **C** · **D**

You know you've made it when streets in more than one continent are named after you and your face smiles out from your nation's banknotes. Hungary's great bourgeois nationalist Lajos Kossuth, born in 1802 and dying in exile in Turin almost a century later, claims such fame. A man of fine intellect, and trained as a lawyer, his early career was temporarily halted by a spell in prison, accused of sedition. On his release he established the *Pesti Hirlap*, and became one of the chief advocates of the revolutionary drive towards liberty. By 1847 he was the most prominent opposition leader, and when the revolution came he took up the post of Chairman of the National Defence Commission in the Independence government. When that government declared the country a republic, Kossuth was the putative Head of State. The press of the day hailed him as the 'Moses of the Hungarians'. But the Promised Land failed to materialise – crushed by the Habsburgs, Kossuth fled to Turkey, and from there to England, America and Turin. While his political clout fell after the Compromise of 1867, over the 50 years following his departure from Hungary his radical ideas excited and influenced thinkers in diverse political movements from hard-line republicans to communists (although Karl Marx condemned him as bourgeois).

A WALK ALONG ANDRÁSSY ÚT In the 1860s, politician and nobleman Count Gyula Andrássy returned to Hungary after a period in France determined that Budapest should have its very own Champs Elysées. The elegant avenue – declared a UNESCO World Heritage Site in 2002 – went some way towards fulfilling the dream; when the underground railway was constructed underneath in 1896 (three years before the Parisian metro), it could justifiably claim to have gone one better. The street is a showcase for turn-of-the-century star talent (including Alajos Strobl, Károly Lotz and Miklós Ybl). The avenue stretches for over two kilometres; if you don't fancy strolling the whole length, break your walk by joining the **metro** for a stop or two, or hopping on bus **no 105**.

The **Postal Museum** (no 3; page 162) is your first stop, if only to see the frescoed stairwell. The breathtaking **State Opera House** (no 22; page 116) is a little further on. Strobl was just 26 when he carved the marble sphinxes outside; poet Endre Ady, who was fond of a drink, slipped off the back of one and cracked his head on the pavement. The literary world of the coffee house is well represented by the **Művész** (no 29; page 111) and the **Lukács** (no 70; page 111). The eclectic **Dreschler Palace** (no 25) was designed by Ödön Lechner (who famously explained that he decorated the roofs of his buildings to give the birds pleasure), and used to house the Ballet Institute. Just north of the opera house is **Nagymező utca**, the 'Hungarian Broadway'.

Take a break at a café-bar on **Jókai tér** or **Liszt Ferenc tér** (page 113), which straddle the avenue shortly afterwards. The **Liszt Music Academy** (page 116) is at the southeastern end of the latter; László Márton's statue near by shows the great composer in mid, manic flow.

Beyond the eight-sided **Oktogon** – today dominated by fast-food restaurants – stands a building at no 60 that chilled hearts during much of the 20th century; it now holds a **museum to the terror regimes** (pages 162). Ferenc Liszt lived in an apartment of the Music Academy at no 67 (the academy moved to its current location in 1907), and a **memorial museum** there allows you to have a snoop (pages 161–2).

Kodály Körönd is the most atmospheric circus in Pest, and the one in the worst state of repair. Its flaking buildings have dark turrets, rounded towers and Transylvanian-style boxed roofs. The statues gracing its four corners are fighters for freedom – the lyrical poet Bálint Balassi (who died in battle against the Turks), Miklós Zrínyi and György Szondi (16th-century heroes), and Vak Bottyán (a leader of the 18th-century anti-Habsburg independence war) – while the composer Zoltán Kodály lived at no 89, where there's now a **museum** (*Kodály körönd 1;* ☎ *1 352 7106;* ✆ *230/120Ft, free on Sun & with Bpest Card;* ✆ *Wed 10.00–16.00, Thu–Sat 10.00–18.00, Sun 10.00–14.00; closed Mon–Tue, Aug 18–31 & Dec 4–21 [149 D2]).* From here onward the spacious villas have fenced gardens, originally the homes of 19th-century industrial magnates but now belonging to embassies and law firms. Two collections of Asian art can be found at the **Ferenc Hopp** (*Andrássy út 103;* ☎ *1 322 8476; www.hoppmuzeum.hu;* ✆ *1,000/500Ft, discount with Bpest Card;* ✆ *Tue–Sun 10.00–18.00 [149 D1])* and **György Ráth** (*Városligeti fasor 12;* ☎ *1 342 3916;* ✆ *600/300Ft;* ✆ *Tue–Sun 10.00–18.00 [149 D2)* museums, before the avenue reaches its dramatic climax in the vastness of Heroes' Square.

HEROES' SQUARE AND CITY PARK

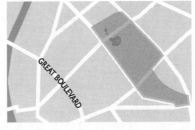

QUICK CROSS-REFERENCES

Map page 89
Museums & galleries
    pages 162–4
Restaurants page 108

HEROES' SQUARE Heroes' Square (Hősök tere; in District XIV) was one of the millennial projects, constructed to celebrate the anniversary of the supposed date of the Magyar arrival in the Carpathian Basin. It is a monumental, triumphalist expression of Hungarian patriotism and confidence at a time when the Compromise had restored a nation's self-respect and the economy was buoyant; aside from the odd glaring omission (read on below), its statues represent a chronological catalogue of the nation's first 1,000 years. In 1896, it also formed the gateway to the celebratory exhibition, whose 200 pavilions attracted visitors from all over the world.

At the square's centre is the 36m-high fluted column of the **Millennium Monument** (which wasn't completed until 1929), with the Archangel Gabriel atop bearing the Holy Crown that he is said to have offered to István in a dream. Around the base are the menacing Magyar tribal chieftains. A marble tablet in front covers an **empty coffin**, laid in 1989 to honour those killed during the 1956 revolution, and inscribed with 'In memory of our heroes'. All this is framed by a **pair of colonnades** bearing statues of the country's major leaders, starting with István and culminating in Lajos Kossuth, who headed the 1848 revolution before going into exile in America. One dynasty is noticeable by its absence; originally the last five statues in the sequence depicted the Habsburgs (Leopold II, Charles VI, Maria Theresa, Joseph II and Francis Joseph). The latter was an unpopular figure whose statue was quickly torn down when the monarchy fell at the end of World War I, and the others were later removed by the communists. The replacements are all heroes of the independence struggle against Turks, Habsburgs or both, with Ferenc Rákóczi II (page 18) among the Transylvanian princes alongside Kossuth. The chariots charging above are allegories of work and welfare, war, peace, and art and science.

Splendid examples of neo-Classical architecture, the **Museum of Fine Arts** (pages 163–4) and the **Hall of Arts** (page 162) stand to the north and south. **Dózsa György út** – which runs across the square – was a Soviet parade ground, and site of a massive statue of Stalin that insurgents subsequently bashed to bits during the '56 revolution; a reconstruction of the huge base is shown in Memento Park (page 160). In 2006, a **huge memorial** marking the 50th anniversary of the '56 revolution was erected a short distance southeast of Heroes' Square on Városligeti fasor. The abstract monument comprises tall, polished and tight-packed silver posts giving way to shorter, rusting and more scattered ones. Less abstract is **'The Timewheel'**, which you'll pass on your way there from Heroes' Square and which is the world's largest hour glass. Weighing 60 tonnes, it was commissioned to mark Hungary's accession to the EU in 2004 and represents continuity and eternal movement.

THE COMMIE TOUR

The last Soviet soldier left in 1991, but there are communist reminders to be found in places other than Memento Park (page 160). Pest contains the odd shop with swirling neon sign, typical of the communist era. The former state-owned bookshops are still marked by a blue neon owl. A *közért* (literally 'for the public') is a local corner shop stocking traditional items. Try District VIII, which hasn't changed much, and you'll find unusual products in tins and jars – Traubisoda and Márka (fizzy drinks), Túró Rudi (a tube of cottage cheese with a hint of vanilla and covered in plain chocolate, found in the chiller cabinet), and Munkás (Worker) cigarettes.

In the garden at Puskás Ferenc Stadion (the country's main stadium, in District XIV) are **16 Socialist-Realist statues**, depictions of health and sport that lined the avenue leading to the stadium (built in 1953). On the corner of Dózsa György út and Városligeti fasor, near City Park, is a massive **mural** showing labourers on the wall of a former trade-union office. The **Workers' Pantheon** of Kerepesi Cemetery (page 170) is inscribed with 'They lived for communism and the people'; despite the law banning 'images of oppression', a nearby plot for fallen Soviet soldiers displays a hammer and sickle. This also features on the World War II monument in Szabadság tér (page 148). The island of Csepel in southern Budapest was always a stronghold of the workers' movement, and a statue called 'Olvasó Munkás' (**'Reading Worker'**) by András Beck adorns Béke tér. The Young Pioneers built what is now the Children's Railway (page 139) in 1950. A **museum at Hűvösvölgy station** has a charming collection of memorabilia, while Virágvölgy displays a plaque with three pioneers pointing towards a brighter socialist future.

Several restaurants preserve flavours of the socialist era. For details of **Marxim**, see page 106.

Menza (VI, Liszt Ferenc tér 2; ☎ 1 413 1482; ⏰ 10.00–24.00 daily; €€€) – or 'Canteen' – opened in 2003, and is an upmarket, stylish take on the Socialist-Realist dining-hall aesthetic of the 'Goulash Communism' period, with brown colours, polyester tablecloths and boarding to protect the walls from splashes of soup. The 'best-of' menu even includes socialist favourites like *lángos* (page 65); the restaurant has always been highly rated, although a trusted colleague told us that he'd been less impressed during his last two visits – let's hope success hasn't gone to the restaurant's head.

Paprika gyorsétterem (V, Pilvax köz 3) was once the Hungarian version of a fast-food restaurant chain, with goulash in plastic dishes and red wine sold in little paper cups. The restaurants gradually disappeared during the 1990s, but this last hanger-on is enjoying a renaissance.

CITY PARK City Park (Városliget) is grassed and wooded, accessed from the back of Heroes' Square via a bridge (designed by Gustave Eiffel) over an artificial lake. The water is ideal for a summery splash around in a pedalo, or for a spot of ice-skating during winter when the southern portion is transformed into a massive rink. Standing on an island is the fantastical **Vajdahunyad Castle**. Ignác Alpár used 21 buildings as the models for a design that incorporated all the styles of Hungary's architectural heritage. Its most striking sections were based upon the former castle of the Hunyadi clan in Transylvania, after which the creative mishmash is named. Originally fashioned from wood, the fairytale castle so enchanted those who saw it that it was rebuilt in stone as a permanent fixture. Just outside is a **statue of Alpár** surveying his masterpiece, and in the courtyard of the Baroque wing (which holds the **Agricultural Museum**; page 163) sits the hooded '**Anonymus**' (Miklós Ligeti, 1903). While his true identity is lost to us, the 12th- or 13th-century 'Anonymus' chronicled the country's early history in his *Gesta Hungarorum*, which is now held by the Széchényi Library (page 159). Touch his pen – it's considered good luck.

In summer, there are outdoor concerts at the castle, while at the park's eastern edge is the **Transport Museum** (page 164). To the north of Kós Károly sétány are the country's biggest **zoo** (page 163), most famous **restaurant** (page 108) and largest **spa** (page 125), together with a **circus** and an **amusement park** (page 164). It is difficult to find nothing to do.

Public transport Hősök tere and Széchenyi fürdő stations are on the M1 underground line, while buses 105 and 30 and trolleybus 72 also serve City Park et al.

ERZSÉBETVÁROS

QUICK CROSS-REFERENCES

Maps pages 144, 149 & 89
Museums & galleries
   page 164
Restaurants page 109
Cafés page 111
Bars page 113

District VII – Elizabeth Town – runs from the Small Boulevard's outer rim as far as Dózsa György út, and is bordered by Király utca to the north and **Rákóczi út** to the south. The latter is one of the city's main shopping streets, the route linking the Eastern (Keleti) Railway Station to the city centre a natural magnet for traders. It used to be a seedy area frequented by prostitutes, but it's cleaner now and the popular choice for well-priced clothes.

At the corner with Gyulai Pál utca, the Baroque **St Rókus Chapel** (no 31) was built in 1711 in the hope that it would secure saintly protection for the citizens of Pest during a period when the plague was hitting hard. Next to the chapel, is the **capital's oldest hospital** (*Gyulai Pál u. 2*), constructed in 1796 – at that time well outside the city walls – to treat infectious diseases. It is named after the 19th-century head doctor **Ignác Semmelweis**, who was christened the 'saviour of mothers' after discovering that soaped and scrubbed staff reduced incidents of child-birth fever (see page 159). Further on, **Blaha Lujza tér** on the Great Boulevard is named after a 19th-century actress (nicknamed 'the nation's nightingale') and used to be the site of the National Theatre; a memorial stone marks where it stood before making way in the 1970s for the metro station. The nearby **New York Coffee House** (page 111) is one of the city's classics.

THE JEWISH QUARTER The Jewish quarter falls in the area between the Small and Great boulevards. The first major influx of Jews to Budapest came during the tolerant reign of Béla IV in the 13th century, and they assisted with the process of rebuilding following the Mongol invasion (page 16). There were periods of repression in centuries to come, but Hungary more usually represented a haven from harsher persecution elsewhere. The community's contribution has been valuable; during the 20th century, seven of Hungary's 12 Nobel Prize winners were of Jewish descent. By 1939 there were 200,000 Jews living in Budapest. Then came Adolf Eichmann and the **Holocaust** in 1944; 600,000 were murdered or deported nationwide, the population in the countryside obliterated. In Budapest, the Nazis established a ghetto between Dohány utca, Király utca and Erzsébet körút; 70,000 were crammed in here under brutal conditions, the majority around Klauzál tér. Bodies of the dead were kept in fridges at Klauzál tér market before burial in the square. Fortunately, however, annihilation was averted by the arrival of the Soviets. Today there are 80,000 Jews, less than half the pre-war number but still the largest community in central Europe. You can buy tickets for a guided **walking tour** of the Jewish quarter from the Great Synagogue (page 169).

A walk along Dob utca The district's prime sight is the **Great Synagogue** (*Dohány u. 2*; page 169), one of the city's foremost architectural works; the silver willow in its memorial park is both a striking sculpture and a touching tribute. If you fancy a walk through the district, however, your best bet is **Dob (Drum) utca**, which traverses the very heart. Along its length a dying breed of craftsmen ply their trades – goldsmiths, engravers, tailors and stocking repairers.

Keep an eye out early on for the **memorial to Swiss consul Carl Lutz** who, like Wallenberg after him (see box, page 171), saved many Jews from deportation. Placed at the one-time entrance to the ghetto, it depicts a gold angel offering a cloth lifeline to a figure lying prone below. An inscription from the Talmud reads 'He who saves one single person could also save the world.'

A modest sign at Dob utca 22 heralds one of the street's treasures; the **Fröhlich cukrászda** offers delicious cakes, and claims to be the only genuine kosher café in Hungary. At the corner of Kazinczy utca, look right to see Pest's **Orthodox Synagogue** (*Kazinczy u. 29–31*), designed by the Löffler brothers (Béla and Sándor) in 1913, and serving the city's small community of just over 3,000 Orthodox Jews. It looks dark and forlorn, but the Hebrew lettering at the top of the façade – 'This is the House of God and the Gate of Heaven' – remains in good condition. It isn't open to visitors. Further down Kazinczy utca is the **Museum of Electrical Engineering** (*Kazinczy u. 21; ✆ 1 342 5750; www.emuzeum.hu; 💰 400/200Ft; ⊕ Tue–Fri 10.00–17.00, Sat 09.00–16.00; closed Sun–Mon [149 C4]*), while further up Dob utca is **Klauzál tér**, which was at the centre of the ghetto. Today, gypsies make up a high proportion of the residents in the single-room flats with outdoor toilets that are common in the area. Before leaving the district, be sure to run the gauntlet of a *néni*'s wrath by peering through the odd doorway to the leafy courtyards within; in these nooks you'll find children playing football, housewives beating carpets and grandmothers watching from balconies above. We're especially fond of that at Dob utca 82.

QUICK CROSS-REFERENCES

Map page 144, 149 & 89
Museums & galleries
  pages 164–5
Restaurants page 109
Bars page 113

The segment south of Rákóczi út to Üllői út is **Józsefváros** (Joseph Town, District VIII). East of the Great Boulevard has traditionally been the haunt of scoundrels and ne'er-do-wells, but as long as you keep your purse safe from wayward fingers, there are some real gems here. The **Eastern (Keleti) Railway Station** is surely one of the most beautiful and romantic in the world, a monumental eclectic structure in iron and glass. It was constructed in 1882 by Gyula Rochlitz, and outside are statues of the great English rail pioneers George Stephenson and James Watt. A short distance away is **Kerepesi Cemetery** (page 170), its paths the city's most peaceful.

Several university buildings are located inside the sweep of the Great Boulevard, and this was a hot spot during the '56 uprising. **Bródy Sándor utca** was where it all erupted on October 23 after students were fired on outside the **Hungarian Radio headquarters** (no 7); there is a famous black-and-white photograph showing a Hungarian flag fluttering from an upper window of the building, the Soviet crest ripped from its centre. Opposite, a marble tablet commemorates 18-year-old János Vizi, who was the first to die that day. Múzeum körút, with its **National Museum** (pages 164–5) and **antiquarian bookshops** (page 143), is dealt with under the Belváros.

Ferencváros (Francis Town, District IX), framed by Üllői út and the river, was flattened by the Great Flood in 1838; it is now an area dominated by blue collars and green-and-white flags, the latter the colours of the local football team Ferencvárosi Torna Club (FTC; page 75). The **Great Market Hall** (page 123) near Szabadság híd is an absolute must; we've dealt with this and **Kálvin tér** (page 142) during our walk around the downtown. **Ráday utca**, forging southeast from Kálvin tér, is a trendy night spot (page 114). At the junction with Ferenc körút is the **Museum of Applied Arts** (page 165), a veritable Art-Nouveau free-for-all. A **Holocaust Memorial Centre** (*Páva u. 39;* ＼ *1 455 3333; www.hdke.hu;* ＠ *1,000Ft, guided tours 7,500Ft/group;* ⊕ *Tue–Sun 10.00–18.00 [89 F6]*) stands a short distance east in a former synagogue (and former internment camp).

THE ISLANDS

QUICK CROSS-REFERENCES

Map page 137
Bars/nightclubs
  page 119

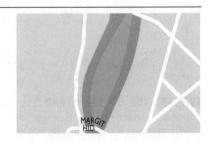

MARGIT
HÍD

MARGARET ISLAND Shady chestnut trees, quiet walkways and open pieces of grass make it the playground of sunbathers, joggers and strollers without time to head for the hills. Formed from three islets that were artificially fused in the late 19th and early 20th centuries, the island now measures 2.5km long by 500m wide, and settles between Margit and Árpád bridges. Before World War II, 'undesirables' were deterred from the gardens and medicinal baths by an entrance fee, but you may now visit freely, however undesirable you are.

Motorists can access the island via Árpád híd, and must pay to leave their vehicles in a car park at the northern tip. Bus 26 traverses the island on its journey between Nyugati station and Árpád híd; alternatively, alight from tram 4 or 6 on Margit híd. If you fancy sparing some shoe leather once there, you can hire a variety of bicycles, pedal cars or electronic buggies from near the southern end.

Approaching from **Margit híd**, you'll be using the city's second permanent river crossing, built 1872–76. It was designed in Parisian style by a colleague of Eiffel, and predictably became nicknamed the 'French Bridge'. Scores of pedestrians were killed when the retreating Germans blew up the structure during World War II. Follow the pedestrian bridge that runs from here down to the island, and ahead will be the **Centenary Monument**, erected on the 100th anniversary of the union of Buda, Pest and Óbuda. A short distance beyond that is the country's largest **fountain**; it is illuminated at night, and if you're lucky you'll catch its water spurts dancing to snatches of music.

Walk on past the **Hajós Alfréd Swimming Pool**. Before reaching the Palatinus – an enormous strand a few hundred metres further up from the swimming pool – to the right of the path lie the remains of a 13th- to 14th-century **Franciscan church**, with a Gothic tracery window.

Leave the track and aim towards the centre ground, walk between the blooms of an **elliptical garden**, and then bear northeast a short while to the island's main archaeological site – the **cloister and church of the Dominican nuns**. When the Mongols sacked the country in 1241, Béla IV swore an oath that his future daughter would devote her life to God if his people were delivered from the hordes. Margit was born the following year, and the king had the complex built in honour of the Blessed Virgin. Margit lived a life of utmost piety here, and was famed for performing curing miracles; she was also known never to wash above the feet, so perhaps her greatest achievement was in persuading people to let her near enough to heal them. The cult of Margit began soon after her death at 28, although she wasn't finally canonised until 1943. The foundations – and the marble coffin of Margit's brother, István V, complete with golden funeral crown (now in the Budapest History Museum) – were discovered during the clear up after the Great Flood of 1838.

Look westward above the treeline to the 57m-tall **water tower** (*víztorony*), constructed in 1911 and a protected industrial monument. Beneath it is an open-air theatre that hosts performances in summer. Directly northward is the reconstructed medieval **Premonstratensian chapel**, originally erected in the 12th century. In its tower hangs the oldest bell in Hungary, dating back to the 15th century; the bell lay hidden – probably from the Turks – until 1914, when a storm brought down a tree and revealed it among the roots. Near here too is the **Artists' Promenade**, a series of busts depicting greats of Hungarian literature, music and art.

The northern portion of the island contains two hotels (page 102), which make use of the thermal medicinal waters that have been tapped here since the 1860s. The excellent spa is open to non-residents.

SHIPYARD (OR ÓBUDA) ISLAND The island to the north of Margit-sziget was where the **palaces of the Roman proconsuls** stood when Aquincum was at its height, and much later where an industrial **shipyard** was sited. Today tourists will be less interested by the warehouses than by the tennis courts, assault course, horse-riding opportunities and several achingly trendy or cheesy nightclubs (page 119). The island is invaded by music lovers during the **Sziget Festival** (page 120) and by horsey types for the **Budapest Equestrian Summer Festival** in June (page 120). While cars can drive on to the island, buses 34, 42 and 106 only run as far as Szentendrei út, from where you'll need to walk on along Mozaik utca.

Museums and more

Budapest has some fabulous museums and galleries – the Hungarian National Museum, the Hungarian National Gallery and the Museum of Fine Arts could float happily among the cream of European cultural houses, while individual attractions like the Imre Varga Collection are real treats. For details of exhibitions during your stay, grab a copy of *Pesti Műsor PM Tárlat*, an A5-sized guide that is published quarterly, has English translations and is available free from tourist and ticket offices, coffee houses, museums and exhibition centres. **Note** that we only have the space in this guide for a small selection of the best and most central attractions; for a fuller list, see *Budapest: The Bradt City Guide*.

MUSEUMS, GALLERIES ETC

BUDA
Castle Hill
Budapest History Museum *(Budapesti Történeti Múzeum) (I, Budavári Palota, Épület E, Szent György tér 2; ↘ 1 487 8800; www.btm.hu; ℰ 1,100/550Ft, free with Bpest Card; ⊕ May 16–Sep 15 daily 10.00–18.00, Nov–Feb Wed–Mon 10.00–16.00, Mar 1–May 15 & Sep 16–Oct 31 Wed–Mon 10.00–18.00)* [127 D5] The popularly known 'Castle Museum' can be found at the southern side of Lion Court. Reached from the basement below the museum itself are **remains of the medieval palace** at various stages and under various rulers. The greater share belongs to the Gothic **palace of Zsigmond of Luxembourg** (1387–1437), including the elaborately restored **Knights' Hall**, which now contains a series of Gothic statues (of contemporary courtiers and biblical apostles) that were unearthed from a ditch in 1974. Evidence of Mátyás's pad is largely restricted to stove tiles and fragments of red-marble balustrades, which can be viewed in the **Renaissance Hall**. The lower portion of the **Royal Chapel**, constructed by Nagy Lajos (Louis the Great) in the 1360s, also survives. Among the museum's other permanent displays are finds dating from prehistory to the end of the Avar period (second floor), and exhibits charting those moments that have caressed or buffeted the capital over the years since 1686, from transient domestic fashions to the devastating flood of 1838 and the tragic consequences of 20th-century war (first floor).

Institute & Museum of Military History *(Hadtörténeti Intézet és Múzeum) (I, Tóth Árpád sétány 40; ↘ 1 325 1600; www.hm-him.hu; ℰ 700/350Ft, foreign-lang tours from 4,000Ft for a group of up to 10; ⊕ Oct–Mar Tue–Sun 10.00–16.00, Apr–Sep Tue–Sun 10.00–18.00)* [127 A2] There are enough boys' toys in here to satisfy the most macho of holidaying males. You'll find weapons dating from the Turkish period & before, as well as more modern machinery, medals and uniforms worn by the Hungarian Hussar regiment. The royal army of Regent Horthy is represented, together with an excellent exhibition devoted to the national army (Honvéd) of the 1848–49 War of Independence. The display related to the 1956 uprising will move even the stoniest of hearts. Admission to the museum is just behind the square's western side, on Tóth Árpád sétány, with its spanking views of the Buda Hills (page 13).

Hungarian National Gallery (*Magyar Nemzeti Galéria*) (*I, Budavári Palota, Épület B, C, D, Szent György tér 2;* ✆ *06 20 439 7325; www.mng.hu;* ✐ *permanent exhibitions 800/400Ft, special shows 1,600/800Ft, guided tours in Eng from 3,200Ft, crypt (phone in advance to arrange a visit) 500Ft; on 3rd Sat each month, admission free for visitors under 26 & 2 adults accompanying someone under 18;* ⊕ *Tue–Sun 10.00–18.00*) [127 D4] The National Gallery is daunting in size, sprawling across 3 wings of the Buda Castle Palace. Of course, size isn't everything – it's what you do with it. Well, they've done well; this is one of the country's most significant museums.

The foundations of a public collection of Hungarian art can be traced to the middle-class reform drives of the early 1800s. There are now around 100,000 works in the gallery. On the ground floor of Wing D is a **lapidarium** containing medieval and Renaissance stone carvings, including fragments of 11th- to 15th-century architecture and marble carvings from King Mátyás's palace. The twin reliefs of the king and his wife by an Italian master are first-class examples of the craft. In vaulted rooms facing the Danube are **medieval panel paintings and wooden sculptures**, such as the *Madonna and Child from Toporc* of around 1420, with its milky-faced Mary and curly-haired Christ. In the first-floor throne room is an array of dazzling late-Gothic winged altars that adorned churches in northern Hungary.

Next door is the collection of **late-Renaissance** and **Baroque art**. Among the works are effigies of Eszterházy family members, a 1712 portrait of the Transylvanian Prince Ferenc Rákóczi II by the court painter Ádám Mányoki, and 18th-century religious paintings by F A Maulbertsch. Towards the end of the period more secular genres emerged that embraced allegory and scenes of country life, thus anticipating the full flowering of Romanticism.

The same floor of Wings C and B holds the **19th-century collections**, which display the main parallel strains of Romanticism – the portraiture typical of the neo-Classical form and the landscapes of Biedermeier (or middle-class Romanticism). Head for the works of János Donát and Károly Kisfaludy respectively for these genres at their early stages. Historical painting, another related branch of the Romantic tradition, is represented by Bálint Kiss and Mihály Kovács; the infusion of Realism in the latter half of the century is embodied in works such as the *Condemned Cell I* (1870) by Mihály Munkácsy, itself strongly reminiscent of social commentary by other Europeans like Victor Hugo and Charles Dickens. Among the sculptors, Miklós Izsó was a true exponent of National Romanticism in tackling both rural working life and portrait sculpture. National self-confidence after 1867 manifested itself in competitions to shape the city's buildings and public spaces. Many of the models on display by sculptors like Izsó, Alajos Stróbl, János Fadrusz and György Zala are entries to such competitions.

Art of the first half of the 20th century occupies the second floor of Wing C. Here you'll find works by Károly Ferenczy, the leading artist of the supremely influential Nagybánya artists' colony (an area now part of Romania); some vast canvases (such as *Ruins of the Greek Theatre at Taormina*, 1904–05) by Tivadar Csontváry Kosztka, visionary and drenched in colour; a range of Post-Impressionist paintings by József Rippl-Rónai, including the beautiful *Woman with Bird Cage* (1892), with her ivory-hued features (painted during the artist's 'black period'); and inter-war Expressionist pieces by Gyula Derkovits and József Egry. Picasso was a fan of Csontváry, apparently requesting that he be left alone to admire the paintings during an exhibition of 1949. He was lucky to be able to see them at all; on Csontváry's death, his family had arranged to sell some of the pieces as tarpaulin before someone fortunately intervened to buy the canvases – to hang on walls rather than tent poles. On the third floor is a collection of **post-1945 art**. The **Habsburg Crypt** (Nádor kripta), the remaining part of the Chapel of St Sigismund, can also be accessed from the museum. It is here that Archduke József – the son of Leopold II and the Habsburg representative in Hungary (the Palatine, or *nádor*) between 1796 and 1847 – was buried.

The museum's main entrance is near the statue of Eugene of Savoy (page 128) on the eastern side of the palace, although there is also access from the western side.

National Széchényi Library *(Országos Széchényi Könyvtár)* *(Budavári Palota, Épület F;* ❧ *1 224 3700; www.oszk.hu; foreign-lang tours of the library (by appointment only;* ❧ *1 487 8637)* ✆ *200Ft, day reader pass 1,000/300Ft;* ☉ *reading rooms Tue–Sat 10.00–20.00, closed Aug)* [127 D5] Some people collect stamps or beer mats; during the 18th century, Count Ferenc Széchényi, father of István (page 18), set himself the modest task of collecting every available example of 'Hungarica' – literature by Hungarians or about Hungary. His obsession stemmed from a desire to reinforce Hungarian nationhood and establish the country's place as an 'intellectual' centre of Europe. Based on his hoardings, the national library opened in 1803 in Pest.

The library now occupies 8 floors of the palace (the entrance in the Lion Courtyard is on the library's 5th floor). There are currently 10,000,000 items. Among the holdings are the only complete copy of the first book published in Hungary (the *Chronica Hungarorum* of 1473) and the *Gesta Hungarorum*, the early-13th-century work of an unknown chronicler (labelled Anonymus by the history books) charting the early centuries of Hungarian history. There are also 33 surviving 'corvina' codices from the acclaimed 15th-century library of King Mátyás (see page 17). A museum on the 8th floor includes a filing cabinet damaged by gunfire in 1956.

Gellért Hill, the Tabán & surrounds
Semmelweis Museum of Medical History *(Orvostörténeti Múzeum)* *(I, Apród u. 1–3;* ❧ *1 375 3533; www.semmelweis.museum.hu;* ✆ *700/350Ft, guided tour in English 1,000Ft;* ☉ *Nov 1–Mar 14 Tue–Sun 10.30–16.00, rest of yr 10.30–18.00)* [127 D5] ⊤ 18, 19, 41 Ⓑ 5, 86, 178. Ignác Semmelweis (1818–65) solved one of medicine's tragic mysteries by discovering that grime was the primary cause of puerperal (childbirth) fever. In pioneering hospital cleanliness and antiseptics, the surgical scrubber slashed mortality rates in his Viennese maternity hospital by 80%, and was labelled the 'saviour of mothers'. Fate and irony colluded to ensure that Semmelweis died of septicaemia in a mental asylum. The house in which he was both born and buried (the urn containing his ashes was placed in a wall of the building) stands to the south of Castle Hill, and charts the history of medicine from the Stone Age through to the 19th century. Along with medical instruments, a reconstructed 19th-century pharmacy and a medieval chastity belt, a memorial room preserves some of the man's furnishings.

Around Moszkva tér
House of the Future *(Jövő Háza)* *(II, Millenáris Park, Kis Rókus u. 16–20;* ❧ *1 336 4000; www.jovohaza.hu;* ✆ *1,200/890Ft, family 2,990Ft, combined tickets (for Palace of Wonders too) 1,790/1,190Ft, family 4,590Ft;* ☉ *Tue–Sun 10.00–18.00)* [88 B2] Ⓜ2 Moszkva tér or ⊤ 4, 6, then follow Lövőház u. An interactive, science-based exhibition devoted to subjects like space travel, gene research and astronomy. Visitors are greeted by robot 'hosts'. In the Millennium Park, which also holds the Palace of Wonders (see below).

Palace of Wonders *(Csodák Palotája)* *(II, Millenáris Park, Kis Rókus u. 16–20; www.csodapalota.hu;* ✆ *1,090/890Ft, family 2,990Ft, combined tickets see House of the Future above;* ☉ *10.00–18.00 daily)* [88 B2] Ⓜ2 Moszkva tér or ⊤ 4, 6, then follow Lövőház u. An interactive educational centre where children can bang, press buttons, take things apart, climb walls, ride a high-wire tricycle, and generally have a jolly good mess around while weary parents reassure themselves it's all in the name of learning. Young children revel in the energy and din; adults should take a cool flannel and a headache pill. Just to the north of Moszkva tér.

Óbuda & Aquincum

Aquincum Museum (*III, Szentendrei út 139;* ☏ *1 250 1650; www.aquincum.hu;* ✆ *900/450Ft, free with Bpest Card;* ⊕ *Apr 15–30 & Oct Tue–Sun ruins garden 09.00–17.00, exhibition 10.00–17.00; May–Sep ruins garden 09.00–18.00, exhibition 10.00–18.00; closed rest of yr)* HEV *to Aquincum stop; turn right & the museum is 200m away, on the opposite side of the road* B *34, 106.* The civilian Roman town of Aquincum was an important place, situated as it was at the eastern frontier of the empire (page 14). The artisans, tradesmen and vintners left over a million artefacts for archaeologists to unearth, including early-Christian religious items, an altar dedicated to Mithras, and even a portable organ. The grounds surrounding the museum encompass one-third of the town, and there are remains of the courthouse, the great shrine, the public baths and the market, as well as evidence of a sophisticated sewage system – featuring flush toilets. The lapidarium has stone finds, while the civilian amphitheatre, which could hold 6,000 spectators, is near Aquincum station. A new exhibition space has opened showing mosaics that adorned the floor of the Governor's Palace on Shipyard Island.

Imre Varga Collection *(Varga Imre Kiállítása) (III, Laktanya u. 7;* ☏ *1 250 0274; www.budapestgaleria.hu;* ✆ *500/250Ft;* ⊕ *Tue–Sun 10.00–18.00)* [137 C3] HEV *Árpád híd* T *1* B *86.* All that glisters is not gold; polished sheet metal glisters too, and in the hands of Varga is moulded, bent and folded into layered and textured works of art that delight those with eyes for shiny things. Varga came to major prominence in the 1960s and – despite being a favoured sculptor under János Kádár, crafting statues that were subsequently banished to Memento Park (see below) – sustained his popularity after the political changes. This concentrated collection shows why: a rich feast of statues, busts and sculptures that includes the gaunt figure of St István (the original of which is in St Peter's Basilica in Rome), the behatted Béla Bartók, and, leaning against a wooden gate, the tormented Jewish poet Miklós Radnóti, who was killed on a forced march from a labour camp in 1944. You can sit in the museum café while admiring the collection. Varga often holds court here on Saturday from 10.00, and speaks English. Greatly admiring his works, we try to forget that he is supposedly a rather unlikeable chap…

Vasarely Museum *(III, Szentlélek tér 6;* ☏ *1 388 7551; www.vasarely.tvn.hu; ✆ 800/400Ft (adult 600Ft with Bpest Card);* ⊕ *Tue–Sun 10.00–17.30)* [137 C3] HEV *Árpád híd* T *1* B *86.* Yet another museum in a pocket of the Zichy Mansion, this one devoted to 20th-century Hungarian artist Victor Vasarely, famous for his optical, 3-D-illusion art. The extensive collection includes early Matisse-like sketches and distorted Picasso-like still-life paintings. Of most interest, however, are the stylised later pieces of the 1960s and '70s that make kaleidoscopic use of coloured geometrical shapes, playing with expectations of dimension and space. The effect can be giddying, almost psychedelic, as squares and dots swim before your eyes; take an anti-nausea pill before you visit.

Buda Hills & beyond

Memento Park *(Szoborpark) (XXII, corner of Balatoni út & Szabadkai u.;* ☏ *1 424 7500; www.mementopark.hu;* ✆ *1,500/1,000Ft, free entry with Bpest Card; return bus ticket (from Deák Ferenc tér, inc entrance to park) 3,950Ft (discount with Bpest Card or student* *card*); ⊕ *10.00–sunset daily*) **B̲** *Special bus from Deák Ferenc tér (near the Volánbusz terminus; the timetable faces away from the square), leaving at 11.00 daily (Jul–Aug 11.00 & 15.00); standard bus 150 from Kosztolányi Dezső tér (every 20 mins weekdays, every 30 mins w/ends); or red 7 bus or bus 173 (from Ferenciek tere or Astoria to Etele tér), then yellow Volán bus (every 15 mins from stall 7–8 to Diósd-Érd).* 'Heroic' monuments to communism were not only symbols of ideology, but vast instruments of repression that bullied public spaces. The undersized Memento Park – until recently (and more appropriately) called Statue Park – divests them of such registers, and makes them seem faintly pathetic. Of course, the setting is as much a product of its historical moment as the statues are products of theirs. When communism fell, this wasn't intended as a memorial; by contrast it was a dumping ground for beacons of the socialist period, an insignificant place 15km from the centre, a country's act of closure. And it feels like it. But don't be unimpressed; try to imagine the statues in their original political and historical context, as they stood on hills, on squares, on boulevards. Remember the backdrop to the 1956 publication of Gyula Illyé's poem 'One Sentence of Tyranny', which greets visitors at the gates. And remember that, because so many other nations destroyed such monuments as the Iron Curtain fell, these 42 bulky relics are rare extant markers of one of the significant periods of 20th-century European history.

To the right as you enter is the figure of the **Soviet soldier** by Zsigmond Kisfaludy Strobl that used to stand beneath the Freedom Monument (page 133). You'll find statues of **communist martyrs**, memorials to Lenin, Marx, Engels, and **Hungarian communist leaders** like Béla Kun and Árpád Münnich. What you won't find is an image of Stalin; the city's only statue was cut off at the boots during the 1956 revolution, and many Budapesters still own fragments of the metal torso. You can see the boots at actual size in the **Barrack Exhibition**; in here too is a theatre showing film archive of the methods used by the Ministry of Interior Affairs to train its secret police in the dark arts of bugging and shadowing… The souvenir shop sells model Trabants (see box, page 21), Soviet medals, CDs containing songs of the Movement, and T-shirts.

PEST
Downtown & beyond
Museum of Ethnography (*Néprajzi Múzeum*) (*V, Kossuth Lajos tér 12;* ❏ *1 473 2400; www.neprajz.hu;* 🎫 *800/400Ft;* ⊕ *Tue–Sun 10.00–18.00*) [149 A2] Like the Ministry of Agriculture next door, this building (by Alajos Hauszmann) was a losing entry in the fierce 19th-century contest to design Parliament. It was constructed nevertheless, destined to look greenly upon Steindl's victorious vision across the square, and until 1949 served as the Supreme Court. Its interior includes a gorgeous fresco by Károly Lotz depicting 'The Triumph of Justice'. The present museum collection is founded on the late-19th- and early-20th-century interest in national folklore. The exhibition displays costumes, craftwork and photos of the peoples of historical Hungary, as well as artefacts gathered during expeditions further afield. There are frequent temporary displays too.

Terézváros
Ferenc Liszt Memorial Museum (*Liszt Ferenc Emlékmúzeum*) (*VI, Vörösmarty u. 35;* ❏ *1 322 9804; www.lisztmuseum.hu;* 🎫 *600/300Ft, foreign-lang tour 9,000Ft;* ⊕ *Mon–Fri 10.00–18.00, Sat 09.00–17.00, closed Aug 1–20*) [149 C2] **M̲1̲** *Vörösmarty u.* **B̲** *105.* One of music's masters, the silver-haired Liszt (1811–1886) was a symbol of Hungarian nationhood, his very concerts bold statements of opposition to the absolutism that followed the 1848–49 Independence War. He was elected president of the Academy of Music on its inauguration in 1875, and lived out his final years

on the first floor of the academy's neo-Renaissance building. There's a bovine-legged Chickering grand piano, a gift to Liszt from the manufacturers, and a tailored writing desk with a pull-out keyboard. The man behind the music played whist (there's a card table and a card box); he smoked cigars (there's a case and a few coronas); he took snuff from a silver box. He needed a cognac snifter before a composing session. And his fingers! A bronze replica of his elderly hand – cast by Alajos Kisfaludy Stróbl – shows a thumb that reached to the upper knuckle of the forefinger! These lengthy digits cascaded over the keyboard; as one observer remarked, 'We had never been confronted by such passionate, demonic genius.' The building also holds a research library, and a small concert hall. On the corner where Andrássy út meets Vörösmarty u.

House of Terror *(Terrorháza) (VI, Andrássy út 60;* ❧ *1 374 2600; www.terrorhaza.hu;* ❧ *1,500/750Ft (students free on Sun);* ☉ *Tue–Fri 10.00–18.00 (last admission 16.30), Sat–Sun 10.00–19.30 (last admission 18.00))* [149 C2] **M̄1** *Vörösmarty u.* **B̄** *105.* Among the stately apartments of Andrássy út is one painted in powder blue that bore witness to some of the blackest acts of the blackest years of the 20th century. During the short and bloody reign of the Arrow Cross regime in 1944, the Hungarian Nazis set up their party headquarters here, torturing and murdering Jews in the former coal cellars. The address was subsequently used for interrogations and executions by the communist political police (the PRO, ÁVO and ÁVH) until 1956. Prisoners were beaten with rubber truncheons, given electric shocks and burnt with cigarettes; among the cells was one in which the occupant was forced to sit for days in water. Citizens as young as 15 were arrested for resistance to communist rule. Closer to a piece of installation art than a traditional museum, this represents a sensual assault more about atmosphere than artefacts; a stylised use of light, space and music aims to educate through emotional engagement. The displays include video footage of communist propaganda, photographs of political leaders and prisoners, screen prints and props, and there are useful sheets in each room explaining the history of the terror regimes.

Postal Museum *(Postamúzeum) (VI, Andrássy út 3;* ❧ *1 269 6838; www.postamuzeum.hu;* ❧ *500/250Ft, free for under 7s, over 65s, & with Bpest Card;* ☉ *Tue–Sun 10.00–18.00)* [144 C1] **M̄1** *Bajcsy-Zsilinszky út* **B̄** *9, 105.* Wooden doors flanked by winged figures open on to an eclectic mansion, built 1884–86 and owned formerly by the merchant Andreas Saxlehner (whose family fled to America in 1938). You'll have to buzz for entry; as you climb the stairwell to the 1st floor be sure to admire the ceiling frescos by Károly Lotz, which give an insight into the splendour of a wealthy 19th-century townhouse. The museum holds the trappings of postal history, and items relating to telecommunications and broadcasting. King Mátyás established the very first mail coach in 1458, which delivered missives between Buda and Vienna.

Heroes' Square, City Park & around

Hall of Arts *(Műcsarnok) (XIV, Dózsa György út 37;* ❧ *1 460 7000/7014; 3-D film info: 1 460 7033; www.mucsarnok.hu;* ❧ *1,200/600Ft, combined ticket (with Erst Museum) 1,400/700Ft, free with Bpest Card;* ☉ *Tue–Wed, Fri–Sun 10.00–18.00, Thu 12.00–20.00)* [89 F1] **M̄1** *Hősök tere* **B̄** *105.* One half of the exquisite neo-Classical brace of buildings on Hősök tere, the Hall of Arts represents the country's largest gallery space and hosts temporary lashings of contemporary art, as well as exhibitions of antiques and furniture. Regular screenings of a 3-dimensional film about Hungary's highlights take place in the exhibition hall.

Hungarian Agricultural Museum *(Magyar Mezőgazdasági Múzeum)* *(XIV,*
Vajdahunyadvár, Városliget; ❯ *1 422 0765; www.mezogazdasagimuzeum.hu;*
🎫 *500/250Ft, guide 8,000Ft;* ☉ *Mar–Oct Tue–Sun 10.00–17.00, Nov–Feb Tue–Fri*
10.00–16.00, Sat–Sun 10.00–17.00) [89 G1] **M1** *Széchenyi fürdő.* Europe's largest
agricultural museum is held in the intriguing Vajdahunyad Castle (see page 153).
The museum's collection is planted in the Baroque and Gothic wings, and is
devoted to animal husbandry (István Széchenyi imported English methods of
horse-breeding during the 19th century), hunting and wine production.

Hungarian Railway History Park *(Magyar Vasúttörténeti Park)* *(XIII, Tatai út 95;*
❯ *1 450 1497/238 0558; www.vasuttortenetipark.hu & www.mavnosztalgia.hu;*
🎫 *950/500Ft, family 1,900Ft, interactive rides 100–1,000Ft;* ☉ *Tue–Sun (Mar 15–31*
& Oct 31–Dec 17) 10.00–15.00, (Apr 1–Oct 29) 10.00–18.00) **B̄** *30 (from Keleti*
Station to Rokolya u.) **T̄** *14 (from Lehel tér to Dolmány u.). Vintage diesel shuttle runs*
between Nyugati Station & museum (Apr–Oct, departing 09.40, 10.40, 13.40 & 15.40).
Central Europe's largest outdoor railway museum is a real heavyweight. The
bays of the former North Depot's 1911 roundhouse are crammed with carriages
and engines dating back to the late 19th century. Among them are the Árpád rail
car, which ran between Budapest and Vienna from 1937, and an *Orient Express*
dining carriage. Many are used for tourist trips by MÁV Nosztalgia. You can
drive a steam engine or a horse tram, and there's a model railway. The interactive
rides are only ☉ Apr–Oct 10.00–16.00.

Municipal Zoo and Botanical Garden *(Fővárosi Állat-és Növénykert)* *(XIV, Állatkerti*
körút 6–12; ❯ *1 273 4901; www.zoobudapest.com;* 🎫 *1,690/1,190Ft;*
☉ *(Nov–Feb) 09.00–16.00 daily, (Mar & Oct) Mon–Thu 09.00–17.00, Fri–Sun*
09.00–17.30, (Apr & Sep) Mon–Thu 09.00–17.30, Fri–Sun 09.00–18.00,
(May–Aug) Mon–Thu 09.00–18.30, Fri–Sun 09.00–19.00; cash desk closes 1hr earlier)
[89 F1] **M1** *Széchenyi fürdő* **TB** *72.* Few elephants around the world trumpet away
beneath a turquoise domed roof. The Moorish enclosure – whose tower you can
climb – was inspired by the remains of a Turkish mosque, but there is early-20th-
century architectural adventure elsewhere, not least in the garish Secessionist
entrance gate. At the western side of City Park (next to the circus), the zoo is also
home to Hungary's only gorillas, and holds a good children's playground and a
botanical garden.

Museum of Fine Arts *(Szépművészeti Múzeum)* *(XIV, Dózsa György út 41;* ❯ *1 469*
7100; www.szepmuveszeti.hu; 🎫 *permanent exhibitions 1,200/600Ft; guided tours*
8,000Ft, free (in English) on Tue–Fri at 11.00 & 14.00, Sat 11.00; ☉ *Tue–Sun*
10.00–17.30, Thu 10.00–22.00) [89 F1] **M1** *Hősök tere* **TB** *72* **B̄** *105.* Indisputably
Hungary's premier collection of international art, and very arguably one of
central Europe's. The building has the look of a classical temple and the interior
is a shrine to past masters. The place to head in a hurry is the renowned **Old**
Picture Gallery, occupying the first and second floors; there are paintings by
Raphael (including *Madonna and Child with the Infant St John,* a small work flooded
with light, and known as the 'Esterházy Madonna') and Titian in the Italian
collection, works by Breughel and Rubens in the Dutch one, and – in an 11-
room extravaganza featuring El Greco, Murillo and Goya – the richest group of
Spanish pieces outside Spain itself. Room 7 (on the first floor – walk through
the display of 'Romanticism to Post-Impressionism' to reach it) flies a fairly
diminutive British flag, with works by Reynolds, Gainsborough and Constable.
You'll find Monet, Manet, Renoir, Delacroix, Gauguin, Cézanne and Hungary's
very own Op-Artist Vasarely (page 160) popping their heads up in the modern

department, while Pisano's marble *Madonna and Child* is one of the darlings among the sculpture. If that isn't enough, the small **Egyptian section** in the basement has mummies and painted sarcophagi, and there are statues and pottery in the display of **Greek and Roman finds** on the ground floor. The cream of the exhibition was gathered between the 17th and 19th centuries by the aristocratic Eszterházy family; keep these princes fondly in your thoughts, for they left a wonderful, inspiring, sense-stirring hoard of art. Note there's late opening on Thursday, when there are sometimes special programmes.

Transport Museum *(Közlekedési Múzeum) (XIV, Városligeti körút 11;* ℡ *1 273 3840; www.km.iif.hu;* ✆ *800/400Ft, foreign-lang guide 5,000Ft;* ☺ *(Oct–Apr) Tue–Fri 10.00–16.00, Sat–Sun 10.00–17.00, (May–Sep) Tue–Fri 10.00–17.00, Sat–Sun 10.00–18.00)* [89 H2] T̄ *1* T̄B̄ *70, 72, 74.* This is no 'tram, bam, thank-you ma'am' museum; the collection of trains, boats, motorcycles and vintage cars – both replicas and the real things – is vast. The model train engines, intricate and precise copies, are magnificent. In front of the museum are pieces of the Chain Bridge that was destroyed by the Germans during World War II. On the edge of City Park.

Vidámpark *(XIV, Városligeti körút 14–16;* ℡ *1 363 8310; www.vidampark.hu;* ✆ *(depending on season) 3,700–3,900/2,300–2,500Ft, children free if under 100cm!;* ☺ *10.00/11.00–19.00/20.00 daily (Apr–Oct), 10.00–19.00 Sat–Sun (Nov–Mar))* [89 G1] M̄1̄ *Széchenyi fürdő* T̄B̄ *72.* The 1906 merry-go-round (immortalised in the Rogers and Hammerstein musical *Carousel*) is a protected national monument encased in a glass building, and the roller-coaster terrifies not because of the dips and lurches, but because it is made of wood and feels a bit overly rickety... Generally quite deserted, this is a fun place on a dreary Sunday afternoon.

Erzsébetváros

Jewish Museum *(Zsidó Múzeum) (VII, Dohány u. 2;* ℡ *1 342 8949;* ✆ *1,400/750Ft, free with Bpest Card;* ☺ *Sun–Thu 10.00–17.00, Fri 10.00–14.00, closed Sat)* [144 D2] M̄2̄ *Astoria* T̄ *47, 49* B̄ *7.* Little more than a decade after opening in 1932, the exhibits were destined for dark corners and dank cellars away from the keen eyes of German occupiers. The first of the two exhibitions focuses upon religious objects associated with Jewish holidays. As well as silver menorahs and chalices, borrow someone's reading glasses and take a careful look at the tapestry on the left as you enter. The words of the Torah are embroidered in tiny script; it was made in 1828, and used for covert worship during World War II. Contemporary photographs in the Holocaust exhibition bring up close the chilling plight of Hungarian Jews in 1944, many of whom perished in labour camps. There is also a more uplifting tribute to those who strove to help them, among them Raoul Wallenberg (see box, page 171). Next to the Great Synagogue (page 169).

Józsefváros, Ferencváros & beyond

Hungarian National Museum *(Magyar Nemzeti Múzeum) (VIII, Múzeum körút 14–16;* ℡ *1 338 2122; www.mnm.hu;* ✆ *permanent exhibitions 1,000/500Ft;* ☺ *Tue–Sun 10.00–18.00* [144 D4] M̄3̄ *Kálvin tér* T̄ *47, 49* B̄ *109.* The largest museum in Hungary, and regal with it. Among its garden statues is that of Ferenc Széchényi (1754–1820), the enlightened rock on whose collection the museum was founded. The neo-Classical palace, with its busty embodiment of Pannonia on the tympanum, was built in 1847 by Mihály Pollack and became a symbol of the Independence War a short time later. On March 15 1848, radical intellectuals gathered outside and demanded reform, and copies of Petőfi's 'National Song' were distributed.

Your entrance fee is justified immediately by the **rich frescos** that adorn the main stairwell. The work of Mór Than (1828–99) and Károly Lotz (1833–1904), those on the ceiling show allegories of virtue and learning, while the wall friezes depict a broad sweep of Hungarian history, from the Huns leaving Asia up to the birth of the museum. The collection at the top of the stairs charts the **period between 1000 and 1990**, from the Árpád dynasty (including goods buried with Béla III, the era's only royal grave to survive intact) to the collapse of communism. Descend from the foyer to a **lapidarium** and a 3rd-century mosaic excavated from a villa in Balácpuszta. To the right of the entrance hall is an exhibition with artefacts dating from the prehistoric **Palaeolithic Age to the Age of the Avars** (AD567–804), prior to the Hungarian conquest. To the left, though, is the museum's star attraction. You can take your Holy Crown and sceptre – the more lauded items of the coronation regalia that in 2000 were moved from here to the Parliament building; for us, the **cloak** is the true crowning glory. This semi-circular stretch of purple silk, shimmering with gold embroidery, is a textile masterpiece, and the sole item among the regalia that actually belonged to St István. He gave it to the church in Székesfehérvár in 1031, and he is included with his wife Giselle among the angels at the bottom of the cloth.

Ludwig Museum – Museum of Contemporary Art (*Kortárs Művészeti Múzeum*) (*IX, Palace of Arts, Komor Marcell u. 1;* ☎ *1 555 3444; www.ludwigmuseum.hu;* 🎫 *1,200/600Ft;* ☺ *Tue–Sun 10.00–20.00 (until 22.00 every last Sat of month))* Ⓣ *1, 2, 24.* This museum was the first of international contemporary art in Hungary, and represents a bite-sized romp through works by some of the 20th century's most flamboyant artists. It is based on donations and long-term loans by the German collectors Peter and Irene Ludwig. There are three late Picassos here (including *Matador and Nude*, 1970), examples of American pop art by Andy Warhol and Roy Lichtenstein, and European trans-avantgarde works. The Ludwigs were also among the first to collect from former socialist countries, and so there is material by artists from the Soviet Union, Bulgaria, East Germany and Hungary. In addition, an exhibition charts Hungarian art in the 1990s, and there are regular temporary displays that are generally significant, interesting and worth a snoop.

Museum of Applied Arts (*Iparművészeti Múzeum*) (*IX, Üllői út 33–37;* ☎ *1 456 5100; www.imm.hu;* 🎫 *600–1,000Ft/300–500Ft;* ☺ *Tue–Sun 10.00–18.00)* [149 C6] M3 *Ferenc körút* Ⓣ *4, 6* Ⓑ *15.* Thoroughly, blissfully over the top, the Art-Nouveau building was designed for the millennial celebrations of 1896 by Ödön Lechner and Gyula Pártos. The pair clearly had some fun. Lechner – whose hunched statue sits outside – determined to create a uniquely Hungarian style, and there are folksy and oriental elements, as well as Indian influences deriving from the contemporary belief that the Magyar tribes arrived from the subcontinent. The portal looks like a piece of Moorcroft pottery, while the crown-like dome of the roof is coated with coloured ceramic scales. Indeed, the extravagance of the design was initially controversial, many angered by the eastern styling – which they accused of representing a celebration of 'gypsies'. The white interior hosts primarily temporary exhibitions devoted to arts and crafts, textiles and other artworks, although there is a single permanent one displaying items relating to the history of the museum.

MAJOR SIGHTS

BUDA

Buda Castle Palace (*Budavári Palota*) (*I, Vár hegy*) [127 D4] The vast pile that commands the southern end of Castle Hill is the last in a line of palaces built on the hill since the early-medieval period. **Béla IV** first chose to construct a town here in

3

the 13th century, surrounded by a defensive wall and with a fort to the south. After the demise of the Árpád dynasty, the **Angevin kings** also established strongholds, with Prince István 'the Angry' ('Haragos') building a keep whose foundations still exist, and Lajos Nagy (Louis the Great) erecting his palace on the same site.

However, the golden age of the royal complex came during the **15th century**. First Zsigmond of Luxembourg (1387–1437), King of Hungary and Holy Roman Emperor, established a considerably larger Gothic palace (featuring the renowned Knights' Hall; see page 157). After that the cultured and progressive Mátyás Hunyadi (also known as 'Corvinus'; 1443–90) expanded upon it with a Renaissance flourish. His second wife, Beatrice, was from Naples, and she brought with her a gaggle of Italian artists and a legendarily hospitable nature. Scholars and gentlemen from all over Europe flocked to the majestic palace, with its fine art and marble details. The king's library – the Bibliotheca Corviniana – was among the world's richest, holding 2,000 books and manuscripts. Scattered by the Turks, today only 200 remain worldwide (33 of them in the current National Széchényi Library; page 159).

The palace fell into decline under **Ottoman occupation**. It was finally put out of its misery in 1686, when Buda was liberated but its greatest building reduced to rubble. The country's **Habsburg rulers** began anew. Maria Theresa (1740–80) enlarged upon her father's Baroque palace; it became the residence of the palatines, and from 1776 also held the Holy Right Hand of St István – the country's most prized and revered relic.

The palace's feathers were ruffled once more during the 1848–49 War of Independence, when it was occupied by Hungarian forces struggling against imperial rule. Restoration came on a grand scale following the Austro-Hungarian Compromise of 1867, first to the designs of Miklós Ybl and then, after his death, to those of Alajos Hauszmann. The expansion was an expression of a fresh sense of independence, and it was hoped that the splendacious palace would shift the dual monarchy's beating heart from Vienna to Budapest. Hauszmann doubled the length of the palace's façade (to over 300m) and added its outstanding feature, the central dome. Ferenc József, who had been crowned in Buda, laid one of the foundation stones during the millenary celebrations of 1896. Once completed, it formed the impressive backdrop to the coronation procession in 1916 of Károly IV, the last, short-lived Habsburg king.

In the **aftermath of World War I**, the newly elected governor, Admiral Miklós Horthy, moved into the palace and lived the right royal high life. Shortly after his removal in a German coup of 1944, the Buda Castle Palace was brought down for the 31st and final time. The German army's centre of operations was based here, and as the soldiers holed up in a doomed final stand, the palace was battered by Russian bombardment. The **post-war reconstruction** incorporated those walls that were still standing, and included Gothic and Baroque elements, but paid little regard to many aspects of the original design. However, archaeological excavations went hand in hand with the reconstruction and revealed previously hidden medieval sections that can be viewed on the lower levels of the **Budapest History Museum** (page 157). A series of Gothic statues of saints, knights and bishops found in 1974 probably date to Zsigmond of Luxembourg's time. In 1959 the decision was made to devote the building to Hungarian culture, and, as well as the history museum, it now houses the **Hungarian National Gallery** (pages 158–9) and the **National Széchényi Library** (page 159).

Cave Church *(Sziklatemplom) (I, Gellért tér; ⊕ 09.00–21.00 daily)* [88 D6] T̲ *18, 19, 41, 47, 49* B̲ *7, 86.* A jagged-walled cavern and rugged place of worship. Its hill was originally called Mount 'Pest', the Slavic word for 'cavity', while the cave itself was named St Iván after a medieval healing hermit who lived inside. In 1926 the grotto church was built, inspired by a pilgrimage to Lourdes. During World War II, Pauline monks disguised Jews in their robes and hid them in the adjacent turreted cloister. In 1950, however, the saviours turned victims when communists seized monasteries all over Hungary. In total, over 10,000 of the country's monks and nuns were forced out, and many executed or imprisoned. The cave entrance was blocked with concrete, the cloister became a dormitory for students of the state ballet school and the Paulines had to wait almost 40 years for the political climate to permit their return. To the right of the cave entrance, a piece of the concrete wall remains as reminder of the enforced period of exile. A **statue of St István**, his toes curling over the plinth, is positioned outside. Masses are held daily at 11.00, 17.00 and 20.00, and on Sunday and holidays at 08.30. Non-observants may not visit at these times.

Church of Mary Magdalene (*Mária Magdolna templom*) (*I, Kapisztrán tér*) [127 A2] The first church was erected in Romanesque style in the 13th century, and traditionally served the Hungarian population of the burghers' town. During the Turkish occupation, for some time it was the only church in the Castle District where Christian services were permitted; making the best in difficult times, Protestants used the nave and Catholics the chancel. The Habsburg Ferenc I was crowned here in 1792, adorned in ceremonial Hungarian garb, and the neo-Classical porch facing on to Úri utca was commissioned at the same time. Shortly afterwards Martinovics was stripped of his priesthood in the church, a further humiliation prior to his execution (see box, page 132). Massive World-War-II damage led to the demolition of most of the walls in 1952 and only the tower was preserved. The pathetic ruins of what was the church's main body lie behind it, culminating in an unsupported and fragile arched window, assembled from gathered fragments. It is said that if you look through the window your wishes will come true. This sounds laced with irony; in the face of this phantom of a church we're reminded of a dog with one ear and one eye called 'Lucky'.

Citadella (*I, Gellért hegy; www.citadella.hu; ☞ citadella 400Ft, bunker exhibition 1,200Ft, children (under 14) free; ☉ open-air exhibition & panoramic views 12.00–24.00 daily, bunker Mon–Fri 09.00–21.00, Sat–Sun 08.00–22.00*) [144 A6] **B** 27 to Busuló Juhász restaurant, then few mins' walk. Like the Freedom Monument (page 133), the stronghold next to it had significant symbolic overtones when constructed by the Habsburgs following the 1848–49 War of Independence. Built with Hungarian forced labour, its forbidding presence against the skyline was designed to quash further rebellious impulses. However, tempers had cooled by the time the Austrian garrison took up residence, and the grey fortress began to look something of a white elephant. In 1894 it was handed over to the city, and parts of it demolished as a token of the country's unshackled self. It subsequently served, among other things, as a prison and a hostel for the homeless, but its walls now contain an **open-air exhibition** devoted to Gellért Hill, covering its history from ancient times up until the 20th century. There is a section on the martyrdom and cult of Gellért himself that challenges the traditional legend of the bishop's death (pages 16 and 134), arguing instead that the pagan insurgents of Vata tied him to a chariot, stoned him to death and pierced his heart with a lance. Infinitely preferable! There's also a **World War II Bunker Exhibition**, a waxwork display devoted to the air-defence stronghold established here by the Hungarian army in 1943. Sellers of items irresistible to coach parties cluster outside the walls of the fort.

Mátyás Church (*Mátyás templom*) (*I, Szentháromság tér 2;* ☏ *1 488 7716; www.matyas-templom.hu;* ☞ *700/480Ft, family 1,200Ft, audio guide 400Ft, free entry with Bpest Card;*

⊕ *Mon–Fri 09.00–17.00, Sat 09.00–12.15 & 13.45–16.30, Sun 13.00–17.00*) [127 B2]
Different brushstrokes for different folks. Some deplore the old town's centrepiece
as a tattooed millionaire of a church, all chunky jewellery and no class; others see a
triumphant marriage of 13th-century Gothic design and late-19th-century national
pride. It is something of a miracle that there is anything left to argue about. During
World War II, tanks rammed through its main gates, the roof was burned out, and
it was used alternately as a German field kitchen and a stable for Soviet horses.
Mátyás was twice married here, and the walls – or parts of them – witnessed the
coronations of Károly Róbert (the first Angevin king, in 1309), Ferenc József (for
which Liszt's 'Coronation Mass' was composed, in 1867) and Károly IV (the
country's last, in 1916).

The church was first raised on this site by Buda's **German population** in the
reign of Béla IV. It was reconstructed by **King Lajos** in the 14th century (when the
Maria portal was added) and **Mátyás** in the 15th (who oversaw the construction of
the bell tower), and subsequently appropriated by the **Turks** as their main mosque
during the 150 years of occupation. As part of the 1896 millenary celebrations, the
architect **Frigyes Schulek** stripped away many of the later architectural layers in
his quest to remain faithful to the spirit of the Gothic original. The result is a hall
church characterised by its elegant Mátyás Tower, complete with lace-like
stonework and bobbly spire, a fabulous Zsolnay-majolica-tiled roof, and interior
decoration that thumps the eyeballs.

The **14th-century relief** above the southern Maria portal depicts the death and
Assumption of the Virgin Mary (after whom the church is properly named); the
raven perched on the easternmost turret recognises the mighty impact of Mátyás
Hunyadi's patronage (the raven his symbol). Inside, candy-sweet paints adorn every
pillar of the nave and vaulted undulation of the ceiling. The geometric and floral
designs were supposedly based upon Middle Age fragments, although the influence
of Hungarian Secessionism (Art Nouveau) is also clear. Other frescoes and stained-
glass windows depict events of Hungarian history, and make the church as much a
shrine to national consciousness as religious worship. These are the work of the
renowned Romantic historicist artists Károly Lotz and Bertalan Székely, who were
responsible for other paintings in the opera house and Parliament.

There are subtler details to be winkled out inside. Our favourites can be found
near the Mátyás coat of arms, within the arch of the organ loft to the left after you
pass through the Maria portal. Look carefully, and among the leafy motifs adorning
two 15th-century capitals you will spot **four carved heads** – the wispy-bearded face
of János Hunyadi, the curtain-haired Mátyás, the lopped-off noggin of László and,
gazing towards the chancel, what is presumed to be a representation of the tower's
builder. Next to the Hunyadi capital is the **Loréto Chapel**, the first of several side
chapels. There's a legend attached to its statue. When the Turks converted the church
into a mosque, they walled up a Madonna statue rather than taking the trouble to
remove it. During the siege of Buda 145 years later, an explosion caused the wall to
fall away, revealing the long-forgotten figure to startled Muslim worshippers. This
was regarded as a sign, and a contributing factor in accelerating the Christian victory
– although the current statue was sculpted later than 1686, and could not itself be the
Madonna of the legend.

The **St Imre Chapel** is dedicated to the son of István (the first king of the
Árpád dynasty), who died in a hunting accident in 1031. Without an heir, the
monarch symbolically offered the crown to Mary. Next to it is the **Béla Chapel**,
containing the remains of Béla III (1173–96) and his wife, moved here in the 19th
century. The sarcophagus was paid for by Ferenc József, an act more political than
benevolent: Béla's daughter had married a Habsburg, thus establishing a historic
link between the dynasties, and justification for Habsburg claims to the throne.

The **St László Chapel**, to the left of the altar, contains a replica of the reliquary – a stunning gold bust of László (reigned 1077–95) – held in Győr Cathedral. One fresco shows the famously tall king saving a Hungarian maiden from a pagan Cuman chief, while in another he summons water from a stone to quench the thirst of his soldiers. The **crypt and royal oratory** hold stonework remains, a collection of ecclesiastical art (none medieval, as József II auctioned most of this in 1785) and copies of the Hungarian crown and coronation regalia. In **St István Chapel** is the right foot of St János (page 130). Holy Mass Mon–Fri 07.00, 08.00 and 18.00, Sun and public holidays 07.00, 08.30, 10.00 (choral, and in Latin), 12.00 and 18.00. Regular organ recitals and concerts; tickets can be purchased at the entrance.

Tomb of Gül Baba *(Gül Baba türbéje)* *(II, Mecset u. 14;* ☏ *1 326 0062;* 🎫 *500/250Ft;* ⊕ *(Jan–Apr) 10.00–18.00 daily, (May–Sep) Tue–Sun 10.00–18.00, (Oct) Tue–Sun 10.00–17.00, (Nov–Dec) 10.00–16.00 daily)* [88 B1] **B̄** *91, 191.* The cobbled stairway of Gül Baba utca leads you up the peaceful Rózsadomb (Rose Hill). In an octagonal mausoleum at the top lies the Turkish dervish Gül Baba, who took part in the capture of Buda but dropped dead during the thanksgiving service afterwards in Mátyás Church; Süleyman the Magnificent attended his funeral prayer and may even have helped carry his coffin. The dervish later became known as the 'Father of Roses', reputedly because he grew flowers on the hillside but more probably either a reference to tributes left at his tomb or to a case of metaphorical Chinese whispers – his mysticism meant he was referred to as the most 'fragrant' of his order, which may have been misinterpreted. The shrine was erected in 1548, the tablet pointing towards Mecca, and is a place of Muslim pilgrimage. Remove your shoes before entering. There's a small adjacent café.

PEST

Great Synagogue *(Nagy Zsinagóga)* *(VII, Dohány u.;* 🎫 *1,600/750Ft, tours 1,900–2,600Ft/1,450–2,150Ft (discount with Bpest Card);* ⊕ *Sun–Thu 10.00–18.00, Fri 10.00–15.00)* [144 D2] **M2** *Astoria* **T̄** *47, 49* **T̄B̄** *74* **B̄** *7.* The 'Tobacco Street Synagogue' (named after a factory here) was raised in 1859, its Moorish minarets the work of Austrian architect Ludwig Förster. It is the world's second largest (after that in New York), and seats 3,000. The magnificent interior – which caters for the Neolog community (a Hungarian denomination) – is unusual in several ways. As well as containing an organ, and 25 copies of the Torah (rather than the usual 12), it also has two pulpits from which the words of the rabbi are repeated so that all can hear (there are no microphones). Neglected under communism, renovation came in the 1990s, funded partly by the Emanuel foundation (established by actor Tony Curtis and named after his father, who emigrated in the 1920s). Today, festivals attract worshippers from all over Europe, and at other times there are concerts.

There was a ghetto here at the end of World War II, and a portion of the wall can be found in the **central courtyard**. The wall was demolished by the Soviets on January 18 1945, but a mass grave contains those who perished in the months before. Towards the back is **Heroes' Temple**, built in 1931 to commemorate Jews who died fighting at the front in World War I, often so poorly equipped that they didn't even have uniforms. The **Raoul Wallenberg Memorial Park**, behind the complex on the site of a mass grave, is dedicated to the Swedish saviour (see box, page 171); its silver willow tree (by Imre Varga) remembers the 600,000 Jews who died and the heroes of all faiths who risked their lives to save others. Relatives pay to have the names of victims inscribed upon the leaves. Next to the synagogue's main entrance is the **Jewish Museum** (page 164); Tivadar (Theodor) Herzl

(1860–1904) was born on this site, the journalist who founded the modern Zionist movement after witnessing anti-Semitism in Paris.

Inner City Parish Church *(Belvárosi plébániatemplom)* (*V, Március 15 tér 2*) [144 B4] Nestling tight against Erzsébet híd, the Inner City Parish Church is Pest's oldest building. It was first constructed in the 12th century over the southern wall of the Roman fort at Contra-Aquincum, and actually recycled some of the stones; the south tower contains remnants of this original. (There had been an even earlier church on the site, where the martyred Bishop Gellért was buried in 1046.) The current Gothic sanctuary was raised in the 15th century, although there was a Baroque overhaul in 1739 and 19th-century renovation by Imre Steindl (at which time little shops operated from the spaces between the exterior buttresses). Work in the 1930s and 1940s uncovered *sedilia* in the sanctuary, together with a prayer niche (*mihrab*) that proves Turkish worship here during the occupation. The fragments of a medieval tabernacle were also found in the clear up after World War II; pieced together, it sits to the left of the high altar.

Kerepesi Cemetery (*VIII, Fiumei út 16;* ⊕ *daily Jan–Feb, Nov–Dec 07.30–17.00, Mar & Oct 07.00–17.00, Apr & Aug 07.00–19.00, May–Jul 07.00–20.00, Sep 07.00–19.00*) [89 G4] **M2** *Keleti* **T** *24* **B** *5, 7*. In our view, this is the city's prime haven – 56ha of parkland criss-crossed with paths and chestnut avenues, and history's movers all around. It's peaceful and fascinating. It's also one of the few places you'll see the red star and the hammer and sickle (officially outlawed as symbols of oppression). In one corner is the 1958 **Workers' Pantheon**, a white-stone piazza with Socialist-Realist statues and the words 'They lived for communism and the people'. The red-marble gravestone of **János Kádár** (page 22) stands near by. Fallen revolutionary heroes of 1956 are buried in a plot behind the pantheon; secret policemen (ÁVO) who died 'upholding the system' lie on the opposite side of the cemetery to prevent fights during memorial services. There are **magnificent mausoleums** for Ferenc Deák (page 19), Lajos Kossuth (page 19) and Lajos Batthyány (page 19) – the latter raided by robbers in 1993, who stole a sword but overlooked the earrings of Batthyány's wife (now safe in the National Museum). József Antall – the first post-communist leader – is also here. Teenager Mária Csizmarovits is buried close to the Russian memorial; she died during the 1848 revolution, having disguised herself as a man to gain admission to the army. In the **artists' plot**, look out for sculptor János Pásztor, whose round-buttocked wife was the model for the statue on his grave; a widow was later so affronted to hear her husband was to be buried in the face of this peachy backside that she ordered the newly deceased be interred in another cemetery altogether!

Parliament *(Országház)* (*V, Kossuth Lajos tér 1–3;* ↘ *1 441 4904; www.mkogy.hu;* ✆ *2,000/1,000Ft (tickets available at Gate X from 08.00 – ask guard for permission to pass);* **note** *EU residents may visit Parliament for no charge (show your passport at the ticket desk);* ⊕ *tours (in Eng) start at 10.00, 12.00 & 14.00 daily (tourists may only visit on a tour)*) [149 A2] The symmetrical Parliament is a grandiose counterweight to the palace across the river, the symbol of democratic rather than aristocratic governance. (With this in mind, it is a typical irony of Hungarian history that for much of the 20th century, this 'democratic' institution simply rubber-stamped authoritarian decisions taken elsewhere.) It was the winning entry in a competition of 1882, its neo-Gothic aspect influenced by London's Parliament. However, Imre Steindl brought eclectic elements such as the central dome to the medieval-style buttresses, spires and archways. The statistics are staggering. The building took 17 years to construct, with 1,000 (often convict) labourers working at any one time; it

Raoul Wallenberg is cherished as foremost among the 'righteous gentiles'. In 1944, SS officer Adolf Eichmann was arranging the annihilation of Hungary's Jewish population, & mass deportations were taking place daily. By summer, 400,000 had been carried away to concentration camps, the majority to Auschwitz. Wallenberg – a 32-year-old Swedish businessman – was sent to Budapest as secretary of the Swedish legation in the hope that he could stem the tide. He had no diplomatic experience, but was a tough man, ready to use bribery and extortion as necessary. He distributed protective passes to Jews that granted them protection as Swedish (neutral) citizens, and set up 30 safe houses in Pest under the Swedish flag. As deportations intensified, he even ran alongside the wagons, handing out passes & offering aid; German soldiers were so impressed with his bravery that they aimed high when ordered to shoot. It is estimated that Wallenberg saved the lives of 100,000. When the Russians arrived, however, he was taken to their military headquarters – and never seen again. It seems that he was arrested on suspicion of spying for the Americans, but his fate thereafter is unknown. The Russians claimed he had died of a heart attack, while many others claimed he was still alive in a Soviet prison. The likelihood, however, is that he was executed.

A less-celebrated figure is the British agent in Switzerland, **Elizabeth Wiskemann.** In May 1944 – just as deportations from Hungary were beginning – the location of the 'unknown destination' to which European Jews were being taken was revealed by two escapees to be Auschwitz. A request was sent for the allies to bomb the railway lines. However, resources were stretched and the request was denied. As a cunning ploy, Wiskemann therefore sent a deliberately uncyphered message providing the addresses of individuals and government offices involved in the deportation plans and asking for target bombing of these should deportations continue. As expected, it was intercepted and passed to Regent Horthy. Six days later, entirely coincidentally, American raids on Budapest's marshalling yards accidentally hit some of the government buildings listed in the telegram. This caused panic in Budapest, and Horthy demanded an immediate end to deportations; without the assistance of Hungarian police and rail workers, the last major removal of Jews to Auschwitz had come to an end on July 6.

is 268m long, its dome 96m high (a measured reference to the Magyar arrival in AD896), and contains 40 million bricks and 40kg of gold gilding. It is said that the cost of the project was equal to that of building a town for 60,000 people.

The true splendour of the place is evident as soon as you enter (via the south side, facing Kossuth tér). A **vaulted hall** is supported by eight columns carved from a single block of Swedish marble, a gift from the Swedish king (there are four of these in the English Parliament too); the imposing staircase carries you up to the **Dome Hall**, beneath frescos by Károly Lotz and an allegorical portrait of Hungary with István Széchenyi and Sándor Petőfi at her feet. The Dome Hall itself is surrounded by Zsolnay ceramic statues of the country's rulers (Árpád, the original Magyar, casting dagger eyes towards the Habsburgs to his right). The glass-cased centrepiece is the **coronation insignia**, with the Sacred Crown (Hungary's national symbol), sceptre, orb and sword, which were placed here in 2000 (the mantle remains in the National Museum; see page 165). While the legend goes that the crown was presented to István in 1000 as a sign of papal support for his rule, it was actually bashed together from two different pieces in the 12th century. Its skew-whiff cross is evidence of a turbulent history that saw it lost, dropped, buried in a bog and transported to various safehouses over the centuries, eventually ending up in America's Fort Knox before being returned in 1978. Since 1944, the legislature has been monocameral, and members sit in the **Chamber of Representatives** in the southern wing; the Upper House to the north is now used for international conferences. The **Hunter Hall** opposite the main staircase is the official dining area.

St Stephen's Basilica *(Szent István Bazilika)* *(V, Szent István tér; ☏ 1 403 5370; www.basilica.hu; ☒ church free entry, treasury 400/300Ft, Panorama Tower 500/400Ft, guided tours in English (Mon–Fri 11.00, 14.00, 15.30, Sat 11.00, other times by appointment; ☏ 20 257 5329) 2,000Ft; ⊕ Panorama Tower (Apr–May) 10.00–16.30, (Jun–Aug) 09.30–18.00, (Sep–Oct) 10.00–17.30; Treasury (Apr–Sep) 09.00–17.00, (Oct 10–Mar 31) 10.00–16.00)* [144 B1] The Basilica got off to something of an inauspicious start. The first version of the capital's largest church, designed in 1845 by József Hild and constructed with inferior materials, had to be demolished after the dome collapsed. Miklós Ybl began anew, basing his Renaissance-inspired plan around a dome of 96m (like Parliament; see page 171) flanked by stocky towers. During World War II, the dome was hit by a bomb that mercifully failed to detonate, but a fire in 1946 brought it down once more. After restoration, Pope John Paul II took Mass here in 1991.

As you move up the steps and through the entrance's triumphal arch, you'll pass beneath a tympanum of carved Hungarian saints worshipping Mary and Christ, a statue of St István (the founder of the Christian state) in Italian marble, and a gilded mosaic of Christ by Mór Than. The **interior** – laid out in the shape of a Greek cross – strikes you with contrasts, of light and dark, black and white, sturdy architecture and delicate art. Like the Mátyás Church (page 168), the artists present the Christian story very much in the context of Hungary's history, using Szent István as the focus. His statue (by Alajos Stróbl) graces the high altar, while major events in his significant life are played out in bronze reliefs on the walls behind. It is interesting to note that, for all the iconography portraying István's saintliness, he was actually a brutal and brooding king, merciless in suppressing perceived challenges to his authority. Look up to the dome, and mosaics by Károly Lotz, and to the Altar of the Virgin Mary at the southern end of the transept where Gyula Benczúr records the moment that István offered his crown to Mary on the death of his only son. There is a tiny **treasury** to the right of the entrance, and you can climb 300 steps (or take the lift most of the way) up to a **gallery** running around the outside of the Basilica's drum. However, the primary draw is the gnarled **right hand of István** himself, mounted in a casket in the Chapel of the Sacred Right. It is paraded through the streets during celebrations of the saint's day on August 20. Check listings magazines for details of **concerts** in the church or on the square outside. Note the church is free to enter (it has been known for conmen to try to charge tourists at the entrance).

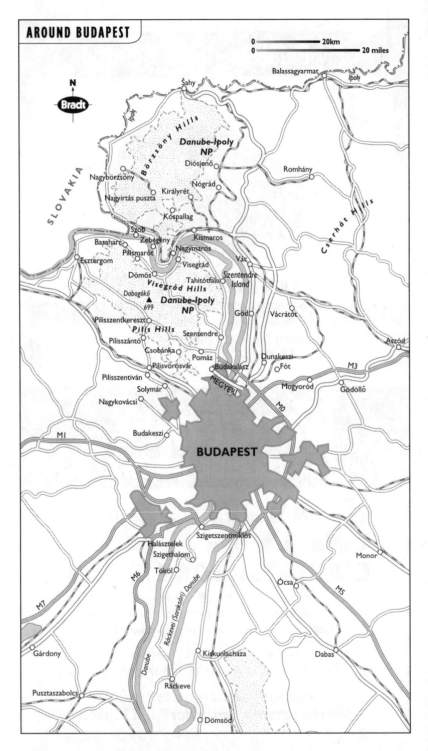

AROUND BUDAPEST

0 ——— 20km
0 ——— 20 miles

N
Bradt

Balassagyarmat

Ipoly

Šahy

SLOVAKIA

Ipoly

Börzsöny Hills

Danube-Ipoly NP

Diósjenő

Nagybörzsöny

Nógrád

Romhány

Királyrét

Nagyirtás puszta

Kóspallag

Cserhát Hills

Szob

Kismaros

Zebegény

Basaharc

Nagymaros

Pilismarót

Vác

Esztergom

Visegrád

Dömös

Szentendre Island

Tahitótfalu

Visegrád Hills

Dobogókő

Danube-Ipoly NP

699

Göd

Vácrátót

Pilisszentkereszt

Pilis Hills

Szentendre

Pilisszántó

Aszód

Csobánka

Pomáz

Dunakeszi

Pilisvörösvár

Fót

M3

Pilisszentiván

Budakalász

Solymár

MEGYERI

Nagykovácsi

Mogyoród

Gödöllő

M0

Budakeszi

M1

BUDAPEST

Szigetszentmiklós

Halásztelek

Szigethalom

Monor

Tököl

M6

Ócsa

M5

M7

Ráckevei (Soroksári) Duna

Gárdony

Kiskunlacháza

Dabas

Danube

Ráckeve

Pusztaszabolcs

Dömsöd

174

4

Around Budapest and the Danube Bend

While we've included a few places of interest running around Budapest's nether regions, the main concentration of sights hover above. The Danube Bend (Dunakanyar) is just what it says it is – the point at which Europe's second-longest river (after the Volga) alters its west–east course to slice Budapest and surge southwards through the rest of the country. There's beauty here – the river views match those you'll find anywhere in Europe; there's nature, with rich birdlife and striking rock formations among the peaks and valleys of the Pilis, Visegrád and Börzsöny hill ranges; and there's history, with the remains of Roman forts and watchtowers – this area represented the northern boundary of the Roman empire – and the palatial and ecclesiastical trappings that signal its importance as a medieval royal and episcopal centre. Szentendre in particular is close enough to the capital to allow a day trip, but that is to do the Danube Bend an injustice by attempting to bolt down a rich meal in a few high-piled spoonfuls; instead linger awhile, allow yourself time to taste and digest, for the bend both deserves and rewards a few days of your time.

A rail line from Budapest passes through Vác and follows the outside of the Danube Bend, but the inside is less well served by train; there are services to Szentendre and Esztergom, but not to Visegrád (which requires a ferry crossing from Nagymaros on the opposite bank). Fortunately there are frequent buses both direct from Budapest and running between the towns, while the ferry from Vigadó tér is a more leisurely option and particularly pleasant in summer.

AROUND BUDAPEST

RÁCKEVE A little under 50km south of Budapest, towards the lower end of Csepel Island, Ráckeve reveals a Serb (Rác) heritage in its name. Refugees arrived in the 15th century, fleeing Turkish advances in the south, and in 1487 hoisted what is now the country's oldest **Serb Orthodox church** (*Viola u. 1*). The 16th-century freestanding tower had a Baroque extension plonked on top in the 18th century, but otherwise the exterior of the Gothic church is largely unaltered. Inside the walls are thick with Byzantine frescoes that were added in 1771 but are thought to have traced and revived the fading 15th-century ones already there; the iconostasis was painted at the same time. There are still services on Orthodox festival days, but the villagers themselves can no longer fill the pews and the congregation has to be reinforced with people from other local communities.

During the 17th century, Ráckeve was bought by Prince Eugene of Savoy, hailed victor over the Turks at the Battle of Zenta in 1697 and subject of the equestrian statue outside Buda Castle Palace (see page 128). Basking in the glory, he had a young Johann Lucas Hildebrandt – later responsible for Vienna's Belvedere Palace – design him a **mansion**; built between 1702 and 1720, this is the second of the town's country 'firsts', being the oldest Baroque palace in Hungary. As a campaigning soldier, the prince actually never stayed here; however, you can for it is now the **Savoyai Kastély Hotel** (*Kossuth Lajos u. 95;* ↘ *24 485253; www.savoyai.hu; 30 rooms; sgl 8,800Ft, dbl 14,000Ft, trpl 17,500Ft; b/fast 1,500Ft*), and has a decent restaurant.

Also on Kossuth Lajos utca, which runs level with the Danube, is the **Árpád Museum** (*Kossuth Lajos u. 34;* ↘ *24 385364;* 🎫 *200/100Ft;* ⊕ *Tue–Sun Mar 16–Oct 31 10.00–18.00, Nov 1–Mar 15 10.00–16.00*), with a collection of local history and folk art. A statue of the leader of the Magyar tribes stands in Árpád tér, sculpted for the millennial celebrations and showing the festivities held on Csepel Island at the birth of Árpád's son.

Ráckeve is within easy reach of the capital. By **car**, take Road 51 south from Budapest and turn right after passing Kiskunlacháza; by **train**, board the HÉV at Budapest's Vágóhíd (regular services), and buses carry you the final stretch to town from the station; there are **buses** (taking about an hour) from Budapest's Népliget (five direct on weekdays, one on Sunday with a change at Kiskunlacháza), while at weekends you can take direct buses from Koltói Anna utca (up to eight) in District XXII (southwestern part of the city).

ÓCSA Thirty kilometres to the southeast of Budapest, Ócsa's 13th-century Romanesque **Calvinist church** (*Bercsényi u. 2*) was originally built by Premonstratensians, and has medieval wall paintings and a Turkish prayer niche (*mihrab*) from the period of occupation. Moving outside, the **Ócsa Landscape Protection Reserve** covers 3,576ha, the most valuable habitat being wet meadow. The depressions hold bogs and alder trees, while there are broad buckler ferns beneath ash trees and European mud minnows, pond tortoises and moor frogs (with their blueish breeding colours) in the marshes. The reserve also has a cemetery with wooden grave markers, which vary in size according to the sex and age of the deceased; opinion is divided as to whether these are shaped like boats or human profiles. The reserve's **visitor centre** (*Bercsényi u. 4–6;* ↘ *06 30 948 9150;* ⊕ *Feb–Nov Tue–Fri 09.00–16.00, Sat–Sun 09.00–18.00*) next to the church has an ethnographical exhibition (as well as a collection devoted to the flora and fauna of the conservation area), while twitchers make a beeline for the bird hide (↘ *28 454443*). If you contact the hide in advance, you may also be able to participate in bird ringing. Ócsa's real treasures, however, are its spectacular orchids in the peat bog meadows. Enjoy them on two walking trails, one of which (Selyemrét) is freely accessible. You'll need a guide for the second; contact Ágnes Pap (↘ *06 30 948 9150;* e *tarnics@vipmail.hu*), who can arrange one for 2,500Ft/hour (as well as offering bikes for hire). Wildlife-dedicated tour operators (see pages 39–41) should be able to arrange tours to the area.

There are branches to Ócsa off both Road 5 and the M5 from Budapest, as well as a **railway station** reached from Budapest's Nyugati (you can also join at Kőbánya-Kispest, at the end of metro line 3). Otherwise catch one of the regular **buses** from Népliget bus station.

GÖDÖLLŐ Gödöllő town is the centre of the Gödöllő hill region 30km east of Budapest. It was but a prettily situated village until the 18th-century noble Antal Grassalkovich I got his hands on it. He built up his estate near the then town of Pest and went about constructing the largest Baroque palace in Hungary (and supposedly the second-largest in Europe, after Versailles). The village grew into market town, attracting craftsmen and shopkeepers; baths and pleasure grounds were added, and it became a favourite summer resort of the Habsburgs. In 1901 the little town's significance was cemented further by the establishment of the hugely influential Gödöllő Artists' Colony. In the town's coat of arms, a pelican feeds her chicks with her own blood, a symbol of a town proud of its repeated investment in its own.

Getting there and away Gödöllő can be reached from Budapest on both the MÁV network (regular services from Keleti) and the bone-rattling HÉV (frequent departures from Örs vézer tere, with the last return at 22.51; alight at Szabadság tér). If you're going by **car**, take either the M3 or Road 3 towards Miskolc, which can be picked up from the top of Rákóczi út; the motorway is quicker, but there's no toll to use Road 3. There are numerous daily **buses** from Stadion, taking between 35 minutes and an hour.

Information and other practicalities
🏛 **Cultural centre** Szabadság út 6; ☎ 28 514130. Concerts, plays & exhibitions, together with information on what's on. *Ticket office* ⊕ *Mon–Tue 08.30–13.00, 08.30–12.00, Fri 08.30–13.00.*

🏛 **Tourinform** Gödöllő Royal Palace; ☎ 28 415402; e godollo@tourinform.hu. Located inside the palace, & offering information on the town & broader region. ⊕ *Tue–Sun Apr–Oct 10.00–18.00, Nov–Mar 10.00–17.00.*

🏠 **Where to stay and eat** You're unlikely to need to stay overnight in Gödöllő when the capital is within spitting distance.

🏠 **Galéria** (7 rooms) Szabadság tér 8; ☎ 28 418691; www.galeriamotel.hu. Gets the thumbs up for colourful, light & comfortable rooms in the main square. Its restaurant (⊕ *11.00–23.00 daily*) is superb, with an intriguing & extensive menu that features choice dishes such as wild boar, shark & fried brains. *Sgl 10,300/6,900Ft, 8,900/12,900Ft en-suite/not en-suite.*
✗ **Kastélykert** Szabadság út 4; ☎ 28 527020; www.kastelykertterem.hu. On the opposite side of the road from the Town Museum, this restaurant is fair value; its extensive menu focuses on traditional Hungarian dishes. The outdoor area is a good place

for a drink. *Mains avg 1,600Ft;* ⊕ *daily 12.00–22.00.*
✗ **Pizza Max** Dózsa György u. 36; ☎ 28 416207. A modern, fashionably turned-out restaurant. In addition to a long list of pizzas, there are pastas, sandwiches & other international fare. *Mains avg 1,800Ft;* ⊕ *12.00–late daily.*
🏠 **Sunshine Hotel** (20 rooms) Szabadság út 199; ☎ 28 420602; e sunshinehotel@vnet.hu. The Sunshine is 1.5km east along the road towards Aszód; its restaurant (⊕ *07.00–22.00 daily*) serves Chinese, Hungarian & international food. *Rooms €45–75 (depending on size).*

What to see and do The 136-room **Gödöllő Royal Palace** (*Gödöllői Királyi Kastély;* ☎ 28 415402; *www.kiralyikastely.hu;* 🎫 1,800/900Ft, *guided tours 3,300–5,300Ft;* ⊕ *Tue–Sun Apr–Oct 10.00–18.00, Nov–Mar 10.00–17.00*) was commissioned by Grassalkovich in 1741, designed by Antal Mayerhoffer in a style that became tagged 'Gödöllő Baroque'. It very quickly became a Habsburg playground and has more than a few tales of mystery and eccentricity (as all self-respecting palaces should have). In the summer of 1751, the notoriously spoilt Empress Maria Theresa is said to have insisted on going sledging; a year's yield of salt from the Felvidék mine was laid down to humour her, while lackeys sweated in winter coats. Rumours abounded about secret tunnels leading from the palace to the town, and in recent years they were found, big enough to accommodate a coach and horses; they were possibly dug by the Habsburgs, who used the palace as a headquarters during the Napoleonic Wars, but nobody knows for sure. There is a deep irony in the fact that in 1849 Lajos Kossuth drafted the motion demanding the overthrow of the Habsburg monarchy from within the palace, for after the Compromise in 1867 it was bought by the State and converted by Miklós Ybl into a residence for Ferenc József; Queen Erzsébet (the popular 'Sissi') loved it here – particularly when hubby wasn't, for she apparently loathed him and preferred the company of the dashing Count Andrássy.

When the Romanians invaded to remove the short-lived communist regime in 1919, they allegedly stripped the palace of many of its artworks. Between the wars

Admiral Horthy used it as a summer residence, while after World War II the edifice entered its worst period of neglect. The Soviet army stored petrol in the stables, painting everything a dull grey and stencilling the red marble arches and watering troughs with 'no-smoking' signs; some of the magnificent rooms were used as an old people's home, and the park was chopped up into smaller plots. Conservation and restoration couldn't begin in earnest until the final troops had left their 'barracks' in 1990.

Inside there are banqueting rooms to be seen, as well as an exhibition covering the first century of the palace's existence on the first floor. You can visit the suites of Ferenc József and his queen, including Erzsébet's dressing room, decorated in violet (her favourite colour) and with portraits of her on horseback (she was a mad-keen rider). From there you move through into her bedroom, which before that had been a room set aside by Grassalkovich for Maria Theresa and adorned with marble and gilding. Next are memorial rooms to Erzsébet, one of which was formerly used by her during quiet moments; among the Biedermeier furnishings are the settee on which she read, and paintings of her ladies in waiting. The final room in the set records the outpouring of grief following the queen's assassination, and her subsequent immortalisation – the newspaper article announcing her death, the tribute coins issued afterwards, and 20th-century postcards of sites that came to bear her name. In 2003, the renovation of the Baroque theatre in the southern wing – which hadn't been used for over two centuries – was finally completed at a cost of over US$5 million, and was unveiled with a performance by the Hungarian State Opera House. (There are also open-air concerts in the courtyard in summer.) The palace chapel, to the far right of the main entrance, was built in 1749 in place of an earlier Calvinist church on the spot. There's a mosaic of Grassalkovich on the back wall.

In the main square northwest of the palace, the **Town Museum** (*Gödöllői Városi Múzeum; Szabadság tér 5;* ✎ *28 422002;* ✆ *600/300Ft;* ☉ *Tue–Sun Mar–Oct 10.00–18.00, Nov–Feb 10.00–16.00*) shows works by the massively influential Gödöllő School, a collection of artists brought together by Sándor Nagy and Aladár Kőrösfői Kriesch whose colony operated in town between 1901 and 1920. Inspired by the Pre-Raphaelites, Tolstoy and the idealistic Englishmen artist William Morris and essayist John Ruskin, the group developed an Arts-and-Crafts movement that was anti-capitalist in thrust and that aimed to nurture a uniquely Hungarian brand of earthy, folkloristic Art Nouveau. As well as paintings, they produced book illustrations, stained glass and textiles (employing local girls to operate looms brought from a bankrupt weaver's factory), and were among the pathfinders of Hungarian Secessionism. In addition, the museum has an exhibition of local history documenting the golden years first under Grassalkovich and then under the royals, a natural-history display, a collection devoted to the Hungarian scout movement (including a letter of 1933 from Baden-Powell to the town governor), and items gathered by the 20th-century priest Mihály Zoltán that includes Ferenc Deák's pipe, Prime Minister Gyula Andrássy's inkwell and a dress worn by Erzsébet's sister to the 1867 coronation. An **applied arts workshop** (*Iparművészeti Műhely Alkotóháza; Körösflői u. 15–17*) and a walking tour taking in the various artists' houses are open at weekends only.

Other The village of Máriabesnyő, 3km to the east of Gödöllő on the way to Aszód (Road 30), was part of the Grassalkovich estate. The great landowner arranged for a church to be built here by Antal Mayerhoffer (designer of the palace) in the 1760s. Nothing unusual about that, of course, except that during the laying of the foundations a 13th-century *Madonna and Child* statuette came to light. Word of the find got around, as did tales of miracles in connection with it, and the so-called **Pilgrimage Church** (*Kapucinusok tere 1;* ✎ *28 510025;* ☉ *Mon–Fri 09.00–12.00,*

15.00–17.00) became a site of … well, pilgrimage. Grassalkovich had a precious container made for the relic, and the family vault was sunk into the crypt. In the 20th century, Pál Teleki (see pages 20 & 129) was also buried at the church, which is at the top of a 200m dust track off the main road, lined with stations of the cross. The interior is breathtaking in its opulence; behind it is a former Capuchin monastery, with a statue of Pope Pius XI in the courtyard. If you're in the area, it would be criminal not to make a brief visit; you can catch the bus from Gödöllő, alighting at the Máriabesnyő templom stop outside.

In August, thousands of petrol heads make a pilgrimage of a different sort to Mogyoród, 8km northwest of Gödöllő on Road E71. Just outside the village is the **Hungaroring**, the Formula 1 racetrack built in 1986 and central European stage for the Hungarian Grand Prix (see page 76).

ASZÓD Situated in the Galga valley 12km east of Gödöllő, Aszód – from *aszó*, meaning 'dry valley' – was once a Stone-Age 'metropolis', its hill settled by Neolithic man 5,000 years ago. Kurszán, one of the 9th-century conquering Magyar chieftains rooted his clan here, making use of the fertile land. However, the arrival of the Turks emptied the town; the revival came after the occupation, when János Podmaniczky – a Protestant noble who acquired the territory through a marriage tie – repopulated it with Slovaks, Germans and Jewish traders. Thanks to Podmaniczky's enlightened farming methods, the town (and its vegetables) grew quickly. In 1914, it was home to the country's largest munitions factory, producing biplanes and automobiles.

The 18th-century former **Podmaniczky Palace and residence** (*Szabadság tér 7–8*), a sandy-yellow Baroque structure whose neglect during the communist period is very evident, provides the backdrop to the main square. Despite its broken windows and flaky plaster, you can get a sense of past grandeur as you walk the grounds and courtyard. In the square outside is a white war memorial bearing both a Christian cross and a menorah, the latter a tribute to the Aszód Jewish victims of the Holocaust.

Follow Petőfi utca for 100m and turn left into an uneven cobbled street holding the **Petőfi Museum** (*Szontágh lépcslő 2;* ☏ *28 500650;* ✆ *400/200Ft;* ☉ *Tue–Sun Apr–Oct 09.00–17.00, Nov–Mar 09.00–16.00*), housed in a Neoclassical former Lutheran grammar school completed in 1771. The Hungarian poet Sándor Petőfi – whose name then was Alexander Petrovics – was dispatched here in 1835 at the age of 13 after his parents became concerned by his slack attitude to scholarship (he was more interested in loitering around theatres, apparently). He spent three years under the direction of István Koren, who kindled in him a love for verse. A room displays items relating to those days, including Petőfi's school reports written by his tutor, while other collections showcase Neolithic finds from the hill above (look out for the pottery bird walking on human legs, reckoned to represent early beliefs about life and the afterlife), agricultural and industrial life in the Galga valley between the 18th and 20th centuries, and various village folk costumes (which conveyed subtle messages about the wearers, from marital status to wealth).

In the garden outside are three gravestones representing the religions of the town's settlers (Roman Catholic, Lutheran and Jewish). The adjacent **Lutheran church**, originally built in the 15th century and re-vamped in the 18th, witnessed both the marriage of Petőfi's parents and later their young son's first poetic effort (*Búcsúzás*, or 'Farewell').

There are very regular **buses** from Budapest's Stadion, as well as from Gödöllő. The **railway station** is to the east of the centre (follow the road in front of the station and turn left at the top), and lies on the line to Budapest Keleti (that passes through Gödöllő). You can also travel northeast on the route towards Miskolc (some direct, others with a change at Hatvan) and northwest to Balassagyarmat.

Other The **Lázár Equestrian Park** (*Lázár Lovaspark; Domonyvölgy, Fenyő u. 47;* ↘ *28 576510; www.lazarlovaspark.hu*) lies a short distance northwest of Aszód in the Domony Valley. Established by the Lázár brothers – a pair of world-champion carriage riders – the 9ha park hosts horse shows, coach trips into the forest, team-building events (Trabant rallies, quad-biking races, etc), and traditional feasts and wine tasting for groups. Its farmyard contains ancient Hungarian livestock breeds. There's accommodation on offer in several wooden lodges, in addition to a new four-star wellness hotel adjacent to the park. Horse shows are held daily at 11.30 and 17.00 (if there are a minimum of 20 spectators), but you'll need to phone in advance to book.

FÓT To the northwest of Gödöllő (and 25km northeast of Budapest), the village of Fót on the edge of the Gödöllő hills has a **palace** (*Vörösmarty tér*) in its main square commissioned by the Károlyi landowners – the family of politician Mihály Károlyi, president of the first republic in 1919 – and rebuilt by Miklós Ybl in 1847; today a children's care home (with a memorial plaque to Mihály on its wall) fills part of the mansion, together with other buildings in the surrounding park. Ybl was also behind the four-towered **Roman Catholic church** (*Vörösmarty u. 2;* ☉ *08.00–12.00, 14.00–18.00 daily*), completed in 1855 and comprising eastern, Arabic and Moorish features. The crypt holds the Károlyi family vault, and a side chapel contains the relics of St Lucentius donated to the church by Pope Pius IX. However, naturalists rate Fót's Somlyó Hill as the place to see **butterflies**. The path starts at the **Fáy Présház**, the 19th-century winery built by the writer András Fáy, which is signposted in the village. You can get here via turn-offs from both the **M3** motorway and Road 2/A; alternatively, there are very regular **buses** from the Újpest Városkapu terminus. Up to 25 **trains** run daily to Fót from Budapest Nyugati (taking 30 minutes) on the line that loops eastward before heading back towards Vác and the Danube Bend.

NAGY-SZÉNÁS Standing 25km northwest of Budapest, in the outer parts of the Buda Hills between Nagykovácsi and Pilisszentiván, the 550m Nagy-szénás is a beautiful place, and one with a botanical rarity – the *Pilis flax*. Contact Pál Kézdy (↘ *06 70 330 3812*) for an English-speaking guide. Note that it is a strictly protected area, and if you come by bus or car you will have to alight and walk from the village. Follow the path marked with a yellow stripe heading south from the edge of the village for about 2km. To get to the village from Budapest, drive north towards Szentendre, fork left on Road 10 towards Pilisvörösvár, and turn left after 10km to Pilisszentiván. Alternatively, you can follow the marked (green line) path from Solymár, which has a railway station on the line passing through Aquincum and Óbuda and is near the British Military Cemetery where RAF pilots downed over Hungary are buried. From Nagy-szénás, you can pick up red trails to Pilisszentkereszt (see page 187) around 15km to the north.

SZENTENDRE

Szentendre (St Andrew), bustling and touristy, is the first town of the Danube Bend, 19km north of Budapest. There was an influx of Serb refugees fleeing the Turks in the 14th century and, after depopulation during the occupation, another surge during the 17th century when Hungary was freed of Ottoman shackles but fighting still raged in the Balkans. Wooden buildings were replaced with stone ones, and Szentendre became the ecclesiastical centre for the diaspora Serb Orthodox Church; four remain of the several temples they built during their time here, each named after the region from which their congregation originated. The citizens were farmers and vintners, but many left after phylloxera and floods hit the area in the 19th century, and those who stayed replaced the vines with fruit orchards. Only a dozen or so Serbian families remain now, but the cosmopolitan legacy is reinforced by the modern flood of visitors from the capital.

The sun smiles on Szentendre, and artists are attracted like moths to its favourable light. In the 1920s an artists' colony was established, and many continue to paint the town red. You can admire their handiwork in the seeming myriad of galleries, many ensconced in beautiful old town houses. Szentendre's virtues give rise to its faults: you'll barely scratch the rich surface of the art on a day trip, you'll need to jostle with many others in the museums during summer months, and the cheerfully coloured buildings are too often occupied by fleecers, whose tat laminates rather than celebrates Hungarian culture. However, such qualms aside, there are few livelier places beyond the capital to enjoy the national artistic output, go shopping or stroll along winding alleys and the Danube banks.

GETTING THERE AND AWAY The HÉV commuter train takes about 40 minutes from Budapest's Batthyány tér. **Trains** run every 30 minutes on weekdays and every 20 minutes at weekends; remember that the outer limit of the Budapest local transport tickets is Békásmegyer, and you need to pay extra to travel on to Szentendre. Many trains also terminate at Békásmegyer, necessitating a platform change for the connecting service. **Buses** run at least once every hour from Budapest's Újpest Városkapu. Both railway and bus stations are 800m south of the centre. By **car**, take Road 11 (cross Árpád híd to join it) all the way. If you're north of the centre, you can take the new, 2km-long Megyeri híd from Újpest, which crosses the Danube just below Szentendre Island to Budakalász (where you join Road 11).

The romantic way to get there is by **river boat** (☎ 1 484 4013; www.mahartpassnave.hu), taking 1½ hours and departing from Pest's Vigadó tér and Batthyány tér (10 mins later). Mahart runs services daily (*except Mon*) in high season (*May 1–Sep 26*) and at weekends (*Sat & Sun*) in low season (*Apr 3–25 & Oct 2–31*); boats depart at 10.30 (with the return leaving Szentendre at 17.00). Adult tickets cost 1,490/2,235Ft (*sgl/rtn*); children get a 50% discount, and students/pensioners 25%. The Mahart ferry pier is 600m or so north of the centre along the Dunakorzó; a closer, second pier serves hourly ferries across to Szentendre Island (see page 186).

INFORMATION AND OTHER PRACTICALITIES

Z Ibusz Bogdányi u. 11; ☎ 26 500178. Arranges private rooms & tours. ☉ May–Sep Mon–Fri 09.00–17.00, Sat–Sun 10.00–14.00, rest of yr Mon–Fri 08.00–16.00.

Z Tourinform Dumtsa Jenő u. 22; ☎ 26 317965; e szentendre@tourinform.hu; www.szentendreprogram.hu. To the south of the main square; very helpful. ☉ approx Mar 15–Oct 15 Mon–Fri 09.30–16.30, Sat–Sun 10.00–14.00, rest of yr Mon–Fri 09.30–16.30.

WHERE TO STAY

Centrum Panzió (6 rooms) Bogdányi u. 15; ☎ 26 302500; e hotelcentrum@t-online.hu. As central as its name suggests, with well-cared-for (slightly twee) rooms & good views of the Danube. The friendly owner grew up in Canada after his father left in 1956, but he later returned to his homeland to set up this place. Entrance on Dunakorzó. *Sgl €50, dbl €55.*

Corner Panzió (6 rooms) Dunakorzó 4; ☎ 26 301524. Spacious panzió on the river, sharing a building with the Corner restaurant. *Dbl 12,000Ft.*

Hotel Waterfront (20 rooms) Dunakorzó 5; ☎ 26 500478; e info@waterfront.hu. This riverside former workers' hotel was being refurbished during our visit, but promises to be spick & span by the time you read this. The renovated rooms we saw were nicely decorated in neutral tones, those on the first floor with balconies. There's a jacuzzi & sauna, & they're building a pier & outdoor eating area. 5-min walk north of centre. *Sgl €60, dbl €70, trpl €80, quad €95.*

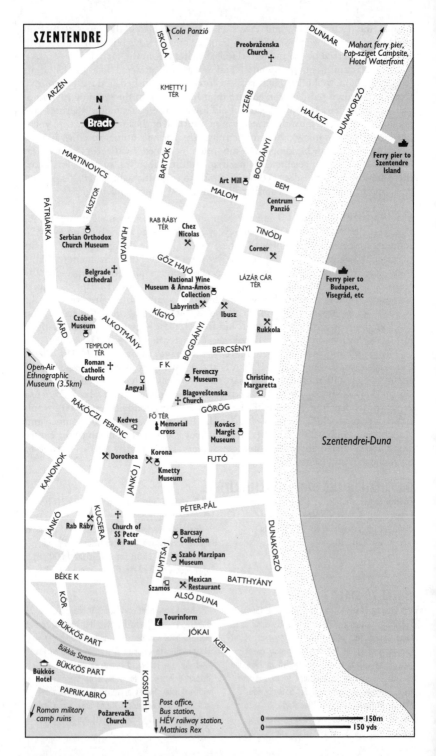

SZENTENDRE

Cola Panzió

ISKOLA

Preobraženska Church

DUNAÁR

Mahart ferry pier, Pap-sziget Campsite, Hotel Waterfront

KMETTY J TÉR

ARZÉN

N

Bradt

SZERB

HALÁSZ

DUNAKORZÓ

BARTOK B

BOGDÁNYI

MARTINOVICS

Art Mill

BEM

MALOM

Centrum Panzió

Ferry pier to Szentendre Island

PÁTRIÁRKA

PÁSZTOR

RAB RÁBY TÉR

Chez Nicolas

TINÓDI

Serbian Orthodox Church Museum

HUNYADI

GÖZ HAJÓ

Corner

Belgrade Cathedral

National Wine Museum & Anna-Ámos Collection

LÁZÁR CÁR TÉR

Ferry pier to Budapest, Visegrád, etc

Czóbel Museum

ALKOTMÁNY

KÍGYÓ

Labyrinth

Ibusz

BOGDÁNYI

Rukkola

VÁR

TEMPLOM TÉR

BERCSÉNYI

Open-Air Ethnographic Museum (3.5km)

Roman Catholic church

F K

Ferenczy Museum

Christine, Margaretta

Angyal

Blagoveštenska Church

RÁKÓCZI FERENC

GÖRÖG

Kedves

FŐ TÉR

Memorial cross

Kovács Margit Museum

Szentendrei-Duna

KANONOK

JANKÓ J

Dorothea

Korona

FUTÓ

Kmetty Museum

PÉTER-PÁL

JANKÓ

KUCSERA

Rab Ráby

Church of SS Peter & Paul

DUMTSA J

Barcsay Collection

DUNAKORZÓ

Szabó Marzipan Museum

BÉKE K

KÖR

Mexican Restaurant

BATTHYÁNY

Szamos

ALSÓ DUNA

Tourinform

JÓKAI

KERT

BÜKKÖS PART

Bükkös Stream

BÜKKÖS PART

Bükkös Hotel

KOSSUTH L

PAPRIKABIRÓ

Roman military camp ruins

Požarevačka Church

Post office, Bus station, HÉV railway station, Matthias Rex

0   150m
0   150 yds

Mathias Rex (12 rooms) Kossuth Lajos u. 16; 26 505570; www.mathiasrexhotel.hu. A nicely thought-out hotel whose décor is sympathetically in keeping with the adjacent Roman ruins. There's something of a lodge/villa feel; the cellar restaurant (mains avg 2,000Ft; ⏱ daily 12.00–22.00) hosts medieval-style feasts for groups, when diners are issued with bibs & eat with their hands. Friendly staff. Sgl 9,500Ft, dbl 13,500Ft, apt 18,000Ft.

Pap-sziget Campsite Pap-sziget; 26 310697. Found on the recreational island 2km north of the centre (accessed via a wooden bridge), this lovely site is popular with families & the riverside location makes it an excellent choice. The bungalows have kitchens, showers & toilets, & there's a pension. Take any bus running up Road 11 on the way to Visegrád & Esztergom. Camping 1,200Ft/pp, tent 700Ft, c/van €17; bungalows €40 (for 2), €45 (for 3), €48 (for 4); panzió dbl €25; ⏱ May–Oct.

✗ WHERE TO EAT AND DRINK
There are plenty of pleasant cafés and restaurants (including a clutch along the Dunakorzó) in which to take refreshment, although – as with everything – they can be crowded in high season.

Angyal Alkotmány u. 4. Traditional, below-street wine/beer cellar. ⏱ Mon–Fri 06.00–22.00, Sat–Sun 07.00–22.00.

✗ Café Christine Görög u. 6; 26 950407. Tastefully styled waterfront café-cum-restaurant serving international & Hungarian food. Mains avg 2,300Ft; ⏱ daily 08.00–23.30.

✗ Chez Nicolas Kígyó u. 10. This characterful restaurant, with its quirky layout over several levels, is located up an uneven cobbled alleyway. Specialities include goose liver, gulyás, soups & fish, & it also offers some French cuisine. Mains avg 2,200Ft; ⏱ Tue–Sun 12.00–22.00.

✗ Corner Dunakorzó 4; 26 300027; e milenko@vipmail.hu. The choice of Serbian, in addition to Hungarian, dishes makes this an interesting choice. There's a montage of old money above the bar, but with the efficiency of service here you might not have much time to look at it. Mains avg 1,900Ft; ⏱ daily 10.00–23.00.

Dorothea Jankó János utca; 06 20 579 3800. A dream of a café. Homely & cosy, with comfy cushioned seating, games to play & plenty of magazines to read. Popular with locals & tourists. There are many home-made cakes, dips, & fancy coffees available; you'll probably stay longer than you intended. ⏱ Mon–Fri 08.00–22.00, Sat–Sun 11.00–22.00.

Kedves Fő tér 13; 20 474 6554. Welcoming coffeehouse popular for its free access to WiFi for those with laptops. ⏱ daily 09.00–24.00.

✗ Korona Fő tér 18–19; 26 313651; www.korona-etterem.hu. While touristy in thrust, the Korona is more intimate than many such establishments. Its folksy décor includes wagon-wheel lighting & wooden benches, while each table has an individual wine dispenser. Hungarian food sits alongside some international dishes (including frogs'

legs & snails). Mains avg 1,500Ft; ⏱ daily 09.00–23.00.

✗ Labirintus Bogdányi u. 10; 26 317054; www.bor-kor.hu. The restaurant is divided into various rooms, each uniquely styled & given names like 'Hunting Hall', 'Cup Hall' & 'Cellar'. The 'big fish dish of Szentendre' is exactly that – they aren't shy with portions here. As part of the National Wine Museum (see page 185), there is the perfect glass for every dish. Good range for vegetarians. Dishy waiters too. Mains avg 2,700Ft; ⏱ daily 10.00–23.00.

Margaretta Cukrászda Görög u. 4; 26 319345. Cool, faux-marble-floored courtyard parade offering fancy ice-creams & cakes; a separate part sells baked potatoes. ⏱ Mon–Fri 10.00–18.00, Sat–Sun 10.00–19.00.

✗ Mexican Restaurant Dumtsa Jenő 14/A; 26 302418; www.palapa.hu. You can base an evening around this lively, colourful garden eatery. The quirky menu (featuring a dessert called 'Very Hot Love') can make a welcome change from typically lardy Hungarian norms. Great cocktails. Enchiladas 1,480Ft; ⏱ Mon–Fri 17.00–24.00, Sat–Sun 12.00–24.00.

✗ Rab Ráby Kucsera Ferenc u. 1/A; 26 310819; www.dunakanyar.net/~rabraby. As over-the-top as any restaurant you'll ever see, the Rab Ráby is crammed to the gills with tankards, musical instruments, suits of armour & old Hungarian tools. Serves traditional Hungarian food. Mains avg 1,750Ft; ⏱ daily 12.00–23.00.

✗ Rukkola Dunakorzó 7; 26 500048. It looks nothing special, but Rukkola serves excellent pizzas, along with pastas, salads & soups. Pizzas 1,290–1,750Ft, mains avg 1,400Ft; ⏱ daily 11.00–22.00.

Szamos Marzipan Cukrászda Dumtsa Jenő u. 12; 06 30 330 6044; e info@elender.hu. When you

4

visit a café whose tables are reserved on a sleepy Sunday morning, you can be sure the cakes taste as good as they look. There's also a museum display across the road (see below). ⊕ *daily 10.00–19.00.*

WHAT TO SEE AND DO It's nice just ambling around the cobbled streets of Szentendre, but there are lots of museums, galleries and churches to structure a day, most of which are close to Fő tér. Before digging in to these, though, you might want to have a peek at the lapidarium containing the stone remains of a **Roman military camp** (*Dunakanyar körút*), on the southern side of the Bükkös Stream; Ulcisia Castra was built in the 2nd century, and was an important station on the Danube. To get there, follow Római sánc köz away from Kossuth Lajos utca. On the same side of the stream is the **Požarevačka Church** (*Kossuth Lajos u. 1*), one of the permanent stone Serb Orthodox churches built in 1759 (the tower added in 1794), and holding a Byzantine-style iconostasis.

Crossing the water and taking the right-hand fork, the first exhibition you'll reach is the **Szamos Marzipan Museum** (*Dumtsa Jenő u. 12, entrance from Batthyány u., across the road from the cukrászda;* ☏ *26 311931;* ⊜ *adult 400Ft;* ⊕ *daily May–Sep 09.00–19.00, Oct–Apr 10.00–18.00*). It's a feast for the eyes, with marzipan 'sculptures' of Hungarian historical figures, Princess Diana, cartoon figures and many more. You can watch one of the sculptors at work too. Further along, the **Barcsay Collection** (*Dumtsa Jenő u. 10;* ⊜ *600/300Ft;* ⊕ *Wed–Sun 10.00–18.00, rest of yr 10.00–16.00*) shows the art of Jenő Barcsay (1900–88), an influential 20th-century artist and one of the founders of Szentendre's colony. His early pieces were dark – *The Madman of the Village*, painted when he was 23, a good example – while his later works fall into the abstract genre of Constructivism. His anatomical drawings were used for training medical students.

On the other side of the Péter-Pál Gallery (*Péter-Pál u. 1*), which sells lace and pottery, is the **Church of SS Peter and Paul** (*Péter-Pál u. 6*). Completed in 1791 (and refurbished in 1991 to mark both its 200th anniversary and the pope's visit to Hungary), this was formerly owned by the Dalmatians, who arrived from the shores of the Adriatic, and is one of the town's two Roman Catholic churches. From there it's a short hop north into **Fő tér**, lined with 18th- and 19th-century trade houses; those on the eastern side (*Fő tér 2–5*) were built in the 1720s after a fire, and share a common gabled roof. They now contain the Szentendre Gallery, which hosts temporary exhibitions. The Merchant Cross in the middle of the square was erected in the aftermath of a plague outbreak in 1763; it is said that there are bodies buried upside down beneath it. On the square's southern side is the **Kmetty János Memorial Museum** (*Fő tér 21;* ☏ *26 310244;* ⊜ *600/300Ft;* ⊕ *Wed–Sun 10.00–18.00*), devoted to an artist who belonged to the Szentendre colony in the 1940s, and who brought the influence of French Cubism into the sphere of Hungarian fine art.

The little Baroque **Blagoveštenska Church** (⊜ *250Ft;* ⊕ *Apr–Oct Tue–Sun 10.00–17.00, Mar & Nov Fri–Sun 10.00–17.00*) across the way was built in 1752 on the site of a previous 17th-century wooden version, and is thought to be the work of Antal Mayerhoffer. It is known as the 'Greek Church' – a headstone near the gate suggesting that the church was actually founded by Greek merchants – and has a Rococo iconostasis (whose subjects' eyes follow you all about).

The **Margit Kovács Museum** (*Vastagh György u. 1;* ☏ *26 310244;* ⊜ *700/350Ft;* ⊕ *09.00–18.00 daily*): you'll either love it or hate it, but you have to see it. The ceramics of Margit Kovács (1902–1977) are often poo-pooed in elevated art circles but they are widely adored by down-to-earth bods. We're in the love camp. Her statuettes and reliefs appear all over the world – from the walls of Budapest's Castle District to those of the Vatican. Kovács had many artist friends in Szentendre, and she decided to donate these works to the city (and personally arranged the exhibits in the basement area). Her early art featured religious themes, but she was ordered to change tack by the Communists, and so moved to folk-inspired pieces. The top floor contains the only bust she ever sculpted of her mother, and there's also a piece of her favourite tree (which blew over during a storm on Margaret Island). The final exhibit on display is the last she made – a relief of 1975 called *The Dance*.

Heading north from the square, a tasty way to end a cultured day is in the **National Wine Museum** (*Nemzeti Bormúzeum*; *Bogdányi u. 10*; ☏ *26 317054*; *www.bor-kor.hu*; ☞ *1,500Ft/pp for a tasting tour that includes 5 wine samples and snacks*), which is linked to the Labirintus Restaurant. An exhibition area in the 220-year-old cellar showcases the 22 wine regions; there are tastings of wine and palinka, and 250 different wines for sale. Be sure not to dull the senses before a visit to the captivating **Imre Ámos & Margit Anna Memorial Museum** (*Bogdányi u. 10/B*; ☞ *600/300Ft*; ☉ *Wed–Sun 10.00–18.00*), where quality prevails over quantity in the collection of husband and wife Margit Anna and Imre Ámos. Anna's post-war self-portraits reveal her profound despair in the aftermath of the Holocaust, when her Jewish husband died in a labour camp.

A short distance further, a square opens to the right with a **memorial cross** at its far corner. The cross marks the spot of a former wooden church where 17th-century Serbian refugees kept the bones of Tsar Lázár – the Serbian king executed by the Turks after the 1389 Battle of Kosovo – before the Treaty of Karlowitz allowed the coffin's return to their homeland in 1699. Continue to the **Art Mill** (*Művészet Malom*; *Bogdányi u. 32*; ☏ *26 319128*; e *malom@mail.matav.hu*; ☞ *free admission*; ☉ *daily 10.00–18.00*), a former 19th-century sawmill converted with government funding into an exhibition hall for 'serious' contemporary local artists. A sound collection has been established here already, but it continues to expand. Beyond that is the **Preobraženska Church** (*Bogdányi u. 40*), built in 1746 by the tanners' guild and containing a gilded iconostasis. The church is the focal point for the traditional Serbian festival on August 19.

A small hill rises above Fő tér, reached via steps leading up either from the northern end of the square or from Rákóczi Ferenc utca, and provides an ideal vantage point from which to peek into the town's gardens and courtyards below. It originally held a medieval castle, but that's gone; the **Roman Catholic church** (*Templom tér*) dates to the same period, and retains some Romanesque and Gothic features, although 18th-century reconstruction means that it is primarily Baroque in style. The Gothic sanctuary is decorated with inter-war frescoes by members of the Artists' Colony. Near the church is the **Czóbel Museum** (*Templom tér 1*; ☏ *26 310244*; ☞ *600/300Ft*; ☉ *Wed–Sun 14.00–18.00*), occupying the building of a former school. Béla Czóbel (1883–1976) – who studied under Matisse – lived and worked in Szentendre between 1940 and 1966, and his landscapes and portraits from this period are on display, together with nudes painted during the last decade of his life in Budapest.

To the north of Templom tér, the **Belgrade Cathedral** (*Belgrád Székesegyház*; *Pátriárka u., with small gate on Alkotmány u.*) is the Hungarian Serbian Orthodox episcopal seat, completed in 1764. In addition to its dark red tower it has an altar of red marble; the Baroque iconostasis was painted by an artist from Novi Sad, and a Rococo doorway fashioned by a local craftsman. Its chancel has a fresco showing a rich man revelling in his wealth, ignorant that behind him stalks Death with his scythe. Near the courtyard at the back of the cathedral is the **Serbian Orthodox Church Museum** (*Pátriárka u. 5*; ☏ *26 312399*; ☞ *500/250Ft*; ☉ *May–Sep Tue–Sun 10.00–18.00, Mar–Apr & Oct–Dec Tue–Sun 10.00–16.00, Jan–Feb Fri–Sun 10.00–16.00*), an Aladdin's cave of ecclesiastical art and vestments from churches all over the country that gradually declined as Serb settlers returned to the Balkans.

Other A couple of kilometres north of the centre, **Pap Island** (*Pap-sziget*) is a recreational area where you can swim, play tennis, catch some rays or rent a boat; there's a strand and a swimming pool. You can get there by boarding any bus running northward along Dunakanyar körút (Road 11).

Szentendre's prize museum is 3km to the northwest of town on Sztaravodai út, reached by a direct bus service from the town's central bus station; there are seven or eight a day in high season (buy a ticket from the driver). The **Open-Air Ethnographic Museum** (*Szabadtéri Néprajzi Múzeum; Sztaravodai út;* ⟍ *26 312304/502500; www.skanzen.hu;* ✆ *1,000/500Ft;* ⊕ *Mar 22–Oct 31 Tue–Sun 09.00–17.00, Nov 2–Dec 14 Sat–Sun 10.00–15.00*) – or *skanzen* – is a massive, 50ha showcase of Hungarian regional architecture that gives urbanites a rich sense of what rural Hungary was and is about. The original structures from villages and small towns range in date from the 18th to the early 20th centuries, and represent the Upper Tisza, Western Transdanubia, the Kisalföld in Northwest Transdanubia, the Bakony and Balaton Uplands, and a market town from the Great Plain (with an animal farm). It has been a work in progress since its initiation in the 1960s, and ten areas are planned in total. There are regular interactive folk displays – usually, but not always, on Sundays – and the site also hosts events during festivals. Tourinform (see page 181) can furnish you with a current programme of events.

SZENTENDRE ISLAND Curving scimitar-like from below Szentendre up around Visegrád, the 31km-long Szentendre Island is the source for much of Budapest's drinking water. Standing at the divide between lowlands and hills, its wildlife includes hill-loving flora, rare floodplain snails on the riverbanks, foraging upland raptors and bee eaters nesting in the hollows of sand dunes at the northern end. **Kisoroszi** was named after the members of a Russian Basilite Order who settled here at the turn of the 11th and 12th centuries; there is a **campsite** (⊕ *May–Sep*) among the willow trees to the west of the village, from where you can enjoy watching Visegrád across the water. (Hourly ferries cross between Kisoroszi and the bank to the southwest of it.) Moving down the island, you will pass a golf course and several riding schools on your way to the resort at Surány and Szigetmonostor, once owned by the Zichy family.

While the new Megyeri híd crosses the Danube at Szentendre Island's southern tip, there is no access from it to the island itself. There is just one usable bridge spanning the Danube at Tahitótfalu (burial place of architect Mihály Pollack), further up Road 11 from Szentendre, and a single **vehicle ferry** running from Tahitótfalu to Vác (*regular services between 05.40 & 20.15;* ✆ *400/330Ft*). Szentendre has a **ferry** taking foot passengers to the island (*one an hour 07.00–19.30 daily;* ✆ *adult 250Ft*), as do a couple of villages to the north of it. The alternative is to **row across** (boat hire is available at Pap Island; see above).

THE PILIS AND VISEGRÁD HILLS

The Pilis and Visegrád hill ranges, spanning more than 400km^2 and reaching 756m at Pilis-tető, are part of the Duna-Ipoly National Park (see box, page 203). The **Pilis Hills** – their once treeless peaks inspiring their name, which means 'tonsure' in old Hungarian – are formed of limestone and dolomite, their forests the hunting grounds for medieval aristocrats; as well as ravines and hot springs, the landscape is characterised by karstic features common when limestone and water come together. There are hundreds of caves, many of them showing evidence of ancient occupation; Stone-Age tools were found in Kőfülke in Pilisszántó and a 4,000-year-old drinking vessel in the shape of a clay wagon unearthed near Budakalász.

This is a region of beautiful hikes, and mountain bikers, climbers, horse-riders and skiers will find an ample playground around Oszoly Rock, the River Dera Canyon, the Vaskapu Pass and the Holdvilág Ditch. The Vaskapu Pass represents a pair of natural portholes – formed after the collapse of a cave roof – jutting from the side of Vaskapu Hill.

Pomáz – 17km from Budapest, and once site of a medieval royal hunting lodge – is the gateway for walks into the Pilis, easily reached from Budapest by train (on the HÉV line running to Szentendre), and with several walking trails leading away from it. To the west, Csobánka is an ethnically mixed bag, founded by Serbs fleeing the Turks at the end of the 17th century, swelled by Germans and Slovaks during the 18th, and Romanians in the 20th. If you follow the red trail northwards, you will come to the Holdvilág Ditch (Holdvilág-árok); the limestone ravines can be tough walking terrain, and you'll need to climb an iron ladder to reach the Lajos Spring (Lajosforrás). A blue trail leads northwest along the Dera Valley to Pilisszentkereszt, which has the scant remains of a 12th-century Cistercian monastery. This was occupied by monks brought to Hungary by the French wife of Béla III, and the tomb of Gertrude of Andechs-Meran, András II's wife, was found here (now in the Hungarian National Gallery; see pages 158–9); Gertrude was murdered in 1213, and the monastery was the scene for József Katona's drama *Bánk Bán*. From here you can take a trek through the Kovács Stream Canyon, in the shadow of Pilis-tető; the trail begins at the lime kiln. The Esztergom Education Centre (*Esztergom-Kertváros;* ✆ *33 435015*) is in the Pilis Hills southwest of Esztergom, and has a nature trail.

The bridge between the Pilis Hills and the **Visegrád Hills**, which follow the line of the Danube, is the resort of Dobogókő; it can be reached by bus from Pomáz, Esztergom, Budapest (Árpád híd), Visegrád or Dömös, or by walking north from Pilisszentkereszt. At 699m, it is the highest spot of the range and has a lookout tower with views towards the river that include the romantically named Sorrow Valley (Búbánat völgy), opening up from the end of Pilismarót, and the Shivering Cross (Hideglelős Kereszt) jutting above the Danube at Basaharc. The area is clearly blessed with some mystical force. A report on Magyar television named Dobogókő as the site of the natural heart chakra of all Europe, a powerful source of healing, while the Shivering Cross was erected in the 18th century to inspire religious feelings in those using the river and is said to cure those who walk around it of the shakes (very useful for those hangover mornings). The resort was popular with the communist élite in the 1950s. From here you can hike for 8km (aided by fixed chains) along the narrow gorge called the Rám Precipice (Rám-szakadék) down to Dömös (taking approximately 4hrs), which is on the river bank and has a beach. You can also pick up routes into the hills from Dömös; follow Duna utca (south of the village along the Malom Spring) for 2–3km to marked trails leading right to the Rám Precipice or left to the saw-edged formations of the Vadálló Rocks (Vadálló-kövek) and the lookout tower of Pulpit Seat (Prédikáló-szék) above, the latter a steep and potentially dangerous rock of 640m that should be attempted only by experienced climbers. Kő-hegy has mushroom-shaped stones and a crater lake on top, home to the protected spade-foot toad. If you're going to hike in the hills, buy a copy of Cartographia's *A Pilis és a Visegrádi-helység* (1:40,000), which shows the routes in full.

VISEGRÁD

Above Szentendre, the eastward-flowing Danube changes its mind and decides to make a swan dive south. Just before it does, though, there's a moment of indecision as it makes a last-ditch attempt to chart a course through the Pilis and

Börzsöny hills. This wiggle of uncertainty formed a commanding strategic position utilised first by the Romans and then by Slav immigrants, who built a fort called '*Vyšehrad*' ('high fortress'). A Hungarised version of the name stuck, and became synonymous with the settlement at one of the country's prettiest points.

In the 11th century András I built a monastery here, but construction began in earnest under the Angevin king Károly Róbert. The king was intent on quashing challenges to his authority by Buda's German population, and moved the royal seat to Visegrád in 1326; he based his palace in the lower castle erected the century before (along with the hilltop citadel) by Béla IV after the Mongol invasion. Subsequent kings enlarged and improved, and after King Mátyás's Italian architects had provided a monumental Renaissance flourish in the 15th century, a papal legate declared it 'a paradise on earth'.

Things were less heavenly after a siege by the Turks in 1543, which destroyed much of the palace and overran the seemingly invincible upper fortress; the town was utterly unloved during occupation. Afterwards, the Habsburgs detonated the citadel to deny independence fighters a stronghold and German settlers raided the town's rubble for material to build their houses; Visegrád's status as a royal seat was downgraded to that of market town and what remained of the palace gradually disappeared beneath earth sliding from the hillside. The fall from grace was so complete that until excavations began in the early 20th century, many dismissed talk of a former riverside edifice as so much pie in the sky. However, restoration of the castle began in the 1870s, and doubting Thomases were put straight in 1935 when archaeologists located the site of the 600m-long palace.

GETTING THERE AND AWAY Trains from Budapest's Nyugati station take 45 minutes on their way to Visegrád-Nagymaros (✆ *ticket sgl 955Ft*), on the line to Szob; from there you can board one of the hourly ferries (✆ *26 398344; last ferry 20.45*) across to Visegrád itself. There are **buses** at least every hour from Budapest's Újpest Városkapu station (on the M3 line), as well as from Esztergom and Szentendre. The pier for the Visegrád–Nagymaros ferry is 500m south of the palace, and there's one bus stop here and another by the Mahart pier.

Mahart (✆ *1 318 1223; www.mahartpassnave.hu*) operates a **river-boat** service (*May 1–Aug 29 daily except Mon; Apr 3–24 Sat only; Sep 3–26 Fri, Sat & Sun; ✆ sgl/rtn 1,790/2,685Ft, child 50% discount, student/pensioner 25% discount*) to Esztergom that stops at Visegrád on the way. Ferries depart from Pest's Vigadó tér at 09.00 (return departure 17.45), stopping to pick up passengers five minutes later from Buda's Batthyány tér, and take around three hours. There's also a **hydrofoil** service (*May 1–Oct 3 Fri, Sat, Sun 09.30; return departure at 17.30; ✆ adult sgl/rtn 2,690/3,990Ft, child 50% discount*); the journey takes an hour and departs from the same landing stage. A special service is offered during the Visegrád Palace Games (see page 190; check the Mahart website for details).

INFORMATION AND OTHER PRACTICALITIES

🖥 **Video Café** Rév u. 13. Offers internet access, as well as coffee. ⊕ *daily 09.00–22.00.*

📸 **Visegrád Tours** Rév u. 15; ✆ 26 398160; www.visegradtours.hu. Organises tours & programmes in & around the Danube Bend, & owns the Hotel Visegrád (it's next to the entrance to the Sirály Restaurant). They should be able to provide information if you need it. ⊕ *daily May–Sep 08.00–19.00, Oct–Apr 09.00–16.00.*

 WHERE TO STAY It's unlikely you'll be stuck for accommodation in Visegrád, as '*Zimmer frei*' signs abound.

🏠 **Hilton Visegrád** (213 rooms) Road 11; ☎ 33 482107 (pre-opening office); www.hilton.com. This new 5-star hotel was under construction as we went to press, but will be open by the time you read this. It is Hungary's third Hilton, & sits on the river to the south of the centre. There are good views over the Danube, & a large wellness centre located over 2 floors.

🏠 **Hotel Honti** (7 panzió rooms, 23 hotel rooms) Fő. u. 66; ☎ 26 398120; www.hotelhonti.hu. Set on the bank of the Apátkuti Stream on the main road towards Esztergom, the Honti is a hotel & panzió suiting those seeking a quiet & romantic stay. *Hotel sgl 12,000Ft, dbl 15,000Ft, trpl 19,500Ft; panzió sgl 10,000Ft, dbl 14,000Ft (excl Tourist Tax).*

🏠 **Hotel Visegrád** (40 rooms) Rév u. 15; ☎ 26 397034; www.visegradtours.hu. This centrally located hotel houses the pricey Sirály Restaurant & the Visegrád Tours travel agency. Its classy rooms have balconies, with splendid views of Visegrád Castle or the Danube. Guests have free use of a sauna & jacuzzi, but if it's a pampering you want, the Thermal Hotel down the road is better. Guests can eat at a discount in the Sirály or the Renaissance restaurant (see below). *Sgl 15,700Ft, dbl 19,400Ft (excl Tourist Tax).*

🏠 **Mátyás Tanya** (9 rooms) Fő. u. 47; ☎ 26 398309 or 1 313 1420 (reservations). A characterful & cosy (if slightly tatty) inn with old-fashioned, faintly austere-looking rooms, & a friendly owner.

Opposite car park for the palace. *Dbl 11,900Ft (excl Tourist Tax).*

🏠 **Silvanus Hotel** (138 rooms) Fekete-hegy; www.hotelsilvanus.hu. Sitting right on top of Fekete-hegy (further up the road beyond the castle), this is a pleasant hotel with great views (Danube-facing rooms higher in price). It has a wellness centre with a pair of pools, Jacuzzi, tepidarium & massage rooms, as well as a pub with bowling lane & an airy buffet restaurant. All rooms have balconies. Note that there is no bus service up here, so you'll need either to drive yourself or request a hotel pick-up. *Sgl €85–118, dbl €118–144 (excl Tourist Tax).*

🏠 **Thermal Hotel Visegrád** (174 rooms) Lepence-völgy; ☎ 26 801900; www.thv.hu. Located 2km beyond Visegrád on the main road to Esztergom, this family-friendly spa hotel has good-sized, understated rooms with balconies overlooking the river bend (ask for one on the 3rd floor). The spa facilities – fed by a natural mineral spring – are excellent, & include thermal pools, swimming pool, Finnish sauna, steam bath & aroma cabin. The medically-registered water (39°C) is used in the treatment of muscular & allergic conditions, & there are drinking cures for digestive problems. A number of spa packages are available (a weekend ½-board package is €350, a 4-day option during the week is €258). Excellent restaurant service. *Sgl €119–139, dbl €169–195, suite €209–319; €6/pp supplement for Danube-facing room.*

✖ **WHERE TO EAT AND DRINK** There are few restaurants or cafés in Visegrád, and it's worth considering the restaurants of the hotels featured above to supplement those that follow. Nagymaros, across the river, has a wider and more inspired choice. With walls plastered in jazz memorabilia, a working juke box and piano in the corner, **Don Vito Pizzeria** (*Fő u. 83;* ☎ *26 397230; www.donvitovisegrad.hu; pizzas from 990Ft;* ⊕ *daily 12.00–22.00*) feels more like a music bar than a restaurant. There's a cosy leather-seated *salsa di cosa nostra* and a bright, sun-lit room if you prefer a quieter eating environment. Some pasta and meat dishes are offered, but the focus is definitely pizza, with interesting sweet pizzas to boot. It stands next to the church; look out for jazz and karaoke nights at the weekends. Near the Mahart pier, the massive **Renaissance** (*Fő u. 11;* ☎ *26 398081; mains avg 2,500Ft;* ⊕ *daily 08.00–22.00*) – attached to Hotel Visegrád by a corridor – is targeted at tourist groups and is as tacky as hell with its medieval theme, men in tights and wenchy waitresses. It's also not cheap, but in for a penny (or many pennies)... **Gulyás Csárda** (*Nagy Lajos király u. 4;* ☎ *26 398329; mains avg 1,800Ft;* ⊕ *daily 12.00–22.00*) stands on the right on the main road towards Fellegvár. Cluttered with strings of garlic and paprika, it also has charming thatch-covered tables outside, and specialises in traditional cuisine.

WHAT TO SEE AND DO The main sights are all ranged along or above the river to the north of the central pocket. The **Royal Palace** (*Királyi palota; Fő u. 23; 26 398026;* 🎫 *1,000/500Ft; www.visegradmuzeum.hu;* ⊕ *Tue–Sun 09.00–17.00*) is the first of them, reached after a 500m stroll up Fő utca. This was a palace of European significance; in 1335, for instance, a two-month summit was hosted here by Károly Róbert at which Polish, Czech, Saxon and Lower Bavarian heads met to resolve territorial disputes and forge a trade agreement that bypassed the increasingly powerful Habsburgs. The terraced complex – its Gothic styling complemented by the Renaissance additions made by King Mátyás – was reconstructed after 20th-century excavations, and was a hefty project given that the Court of Honour was buried beneath a layer of stones 15m deep.

Behind the ticket office is a field that hosts displays of medieval crafts, jousting and archery during the annual Visegrád Palace Games (*www.palotajatekok.hu*) on the second weekend in July. In front is a collection of stone finds dating from Roman times up to the medieval period, and beyond that the palace itself. Much of what you see dates to Mátyás's reign, when there were apparently 350 rooms, and a plethora of courtyards, fountains and hanging gardens. At its heart is the ornamental Court of Honour on the second tier, flanked by a Gothic arcade and holding a copy of the Hercules Fountain bearing Mátyás's crest. The third level holds the chapel and queen's apartments (where Beatrix held court); on the uppermost terrace at the palace's rear is a bathing area, and a courtyard holding a replica of the Lion Fountain with its beasts and basins (the original is in Solomon's Tower). The Mátyás Museum tells the palace's tale, and has red marble columns among its display.

Continue along Fő utca and keep right at the fork in the road on to Salamon-torony utca, where you'll find **Solomon's Tower** (*Salamon Torony u.;* ↘ *26 398026;* ✆ *600/300Ft;* ☉ *May–Sep Tue–Sun 09.00–17.00*), the lower of the castle fortifications built by Béla IV in the 13th century. The tower is one of the best-preserved Romanesque keeps in central Europe, and formed part of a connected defensive system with walls running up to the citadel and down to a water bastion from where guards kept watch on the Danube. You can get a bird's eye view of these from the top of the tower; the structures were in part funded by the sale of jewellery brought from Byzantium by Béla's wife, Queen Maria Lascaris. Inside the keep – which is oddly named after the son of András I, whom King László imprisoned in Visegrád during a power struggle fully 200 years before the thing was built – are fragments from the Renaissance palace, including the original Hercules and Lion fountains, and altar pieces (the best being the so-called Madonna of Visegrád). The top floor contains a collection devoted to the history of the town.

Atop the rock directly above is the citadel or **Upper Castle** (*Fellegvár;* ✆ *1,100/550Ft (or 1,400/700Ft for access to the waxworks exhibition);* ☉ *Mar 15–Oct 15 10.00–17.00 daily, Oct 16–Mar 14 09.30–16.00 Sat–Sun only*). It was constructed between 1245 and 1255 as a bolt hole for Dominican nuns from Hare (now Margaret) Island in case of further Mongol raids; among the nuns there was Princess Margit, whom Béla had pledged to God and who was famous for never washing above the ankle (see page 156). The precious Holy Crown was housed here for 200 years up until the Turkish invasion, save for a period during the 15th century when it went walkabout. During a vacuum in which several factions were claiming the right to succession of the throne, a lady-in-waiting to the widowed Elizabeth of Luxembourg (daughter of Zsigmond) stole it away in an attempt to settle things in favour of her mistress's unborn child. The baby was actually crowned with it when born, but it all came to nothing when the Hunyadis won through and the crown was returned to the fortress in 1464.

On entering, you'll pass an inconspicuous collection charting the history of the castle and its restoration, using drawings and archive photographs; there are keystones carved with the coats of arms of Mátyás and his queen, window and door frames from the Angevin and Zsigmond years, and part of a 13th-century fireplace from Solomon's Tower. Moving on, the southern wing of the citadel's lower courtyard has a waxwork display of a medieval feast, while the wings of the innermost courtyard contain rooms devoted to aristocratic hunting, early coats of arms and weaponry. The exhibitions themselves are unimpressive, and aren't worth the visit in themselves (or paying the extra to do so). Instead it's the views that offer the value. The ramparts were built in several rings, and you can clamber over them and admire views that include ruins of the 4th-century Roman military camp on Sibrik Hill.

There are two routes up the 350m hill to the citadel. The steeper of these runs from Solomon's Tower, but if you fancy taking it slightly easier follow Kálvária sétány from the centre, leading off Nagy Lajos Király utca from the back of the Roman Catholic church.

Other As you move away from the river you start to hit the Visegrád Hills, which form a belt running behind Visegrád around to Esztergom and are themselves buttressed by the Pilis Hills at their back. From Visegrád, the best starting point for proper bracing hikes into these ranges is Dömös (see page 187), around the lower western side of the river wiggle; buses run there along Road 11 *en route* to Esztergom. On the way, after 2km you'll pass a road leading left to Pilisszentlászló and Szentendre; at the junction lies Lepence and the **Visegrád-Lepence Baths** (*Visegrád-Lepence; www.castrum-visegrad.hu; closed until 2011*). It was closed for renovation as we went to press (due to re-open in 2011 with new sunbathing terraces, a club restaurant and spa hotel), but if it retains its previous character you'll search in vain for a more picturesque wallowing hole. Circular thermal pools on terraces cling to the wooded hillside, decorated with an unusual concrete structure that is somewhat '60s *szocreál* in style. The pools, in concentric rings and nicknamed 'onion skins', are supplied by thermal waters gushing from springs below at 39°C. Jets of water burst from the walls and provide an excellent underwater massage. Spectacular.

There are some gentle hikes in the immediate area of the citadel. The paths from Solomon's Tower and the centre become one to the north of the citadel, and this meanders up towards the **Nagy-Villám lookout tower**. (You can marginally shorten the trip by following the main road from the citadel car park for the first half, picking up the last section of the path at the second, higher car park.) Beyond a campsite to the north of the tower (take the left branch of the path as you ascend) are some **forest buildings** constructed by the nationalist architect Imre Makovecz, whose organic designs spoke loud in defiance of communist homogeneity during the Kádár years. The turf-roofed cultural centre has a woodland display. To the south of the tower (opposite the road leading to the Silvanus Hotel) is a **'bobsleigh' run** (*Nagy-Villám bob-pálya;* ✆ *26 398169; www.bobozas.hu;* ✉ *350/280Ft;* ⏰ *daily Nov–Feb 11.00–16.00, Mar 11.00–17.00, Apr–Aug 09.00–18.00 (19.00 w/end), Sep–Oct 10.00–17.00 (17.30 w/end)*), a 700m winding metal track down which riders can whizz in sled carts.

ESZTERGOM

If Budapest is central Europe's definitive city of superlatives, Esztergom is the town. Facing Slovakia across the water, it boasts the first and largest church in Hungary, and the oldest synagogue; as a settlement with a heritage spanning over 1,000 years, Esztergom has plenty to offer history buffs. The site was originally a Roman outpost, part of the fortifications lining the Danube that represented the empire's eastern border, and one where the future emperor Marcus Aurelius wrote his *Meditations* while waging a campaign against Germanic tribes. A fortress was constructed on Castle Hill in AD972, and the town – the 'Cradle of Hungary' – was the place of birth and coronation for King István, founder of the State and Church. Esztergom remained the royal capital until Béla IV shifted to Buda after the Mongol invasion in the mid 13th century. The Treaty of Trianon reduced the town's secular importance by stripping away two-thirds of Esztergom County, and it wasn't until after the fall of communism that attempts were made to re-instate some political power by relocating the constitutional court here. However, as the seat of Roman Catholicism in Hungary its religious role has remained enormously significant for much of a millennium, interrupted only by the Turkish occupation when the clerics fled to safer havens. The Archbishop of Esztergom, who lives in the Primate's Palace, traditionally wielded great authority, and during medieval flashpoints over legitimate royal succession it was the archbishop who assumed control until the squabbles were resolved. Such privileges were enjoyed until World War II, when Cardinal Mindszenty – a reactionary who couldn't stomach even democratic socialism, and faced the considerable consequences of saying so – was relieved of them. Today Esztergom is a favourite tourist town, conveniently laid out, readily walked around and signalled from afar by the dominant form of the 'enormous snail'.

GETTING THERE AND AWAY Trains from Budapest's Nyugati station take 90 minutes, departing up to 25 times a day (✆ ticket 955Ft). Esztergom's station (*Bem József tér*) is 2km south of the centre; you can pick up local buses 1 and 5 the rest of the way.

Yellow **buses** run twice an hour (*the last at 23.00*) from Budapest's Árpád híd bus station to Esztergom, via Visegrád or Dorog (the latter 45 mins quicker); there are services every hour from Újpest Városkapu and a few from Széna tér. There are regular services to Visegrád (taking 40 mins) and Szentendre (90 mins). The bus station is on Simor János utca, which leads south from Rákóczi tér.

Mahart (✆ 1 318 1223; *www.mahartpassnave.hu*) operates a **river-boat** service to Esztergom (*May 1–Aug 29 daily except Mon; Apr 3–24 Sat only; Sep 3–26 Fri, Sat & Sun; ✆ sgl/rtn 1,990/2,985Ft, child 50% discount, student/pensioner 25% discount*). Ferries depart from Pest's Vigadó tér at 09.00 (return departure 16.30), stopping to pick up passengers five minutes later from Buda's Batthyány tér, and take 4½ hours. There's a **hydrofoil** service (*May 1–Oct 3 Fri, Sat, Sun 09.30; return departure at 17.00; ✆ adult sgl/rtn 3,290/4,990Ft, child 50% discount*); the journey takes 1½ hours and departs from the same landing stage. The ferry pier is on Nagy-Duna sétány, to the south of Mária Valéria Bridge.

INFORMATION AND OTHER PRACTICALITIES

🏛 **Cathedral Tours** Bajcsy-Zsilinszky u. 26; ✆ 33 520260; ⏰ Mon–Fri 09.00–16.00
🏛 **Gran Tours** Széchenyi tér 25; ✆ 33 413756. Travel information & currency exchange bureau that can organise private accommodation. ⏰ Sep–May

Mon–Fri 08.00–16.00, Jun–Aug Mon–Fri 08.00–17.00, Sat 09.00–12.00.
🖥 **Internet** There's an internet terminal at the Hotel Esztergom.
Listings magazine Komárom-Esztergomi Est

🏠 WHERE TO STAY

🏠 **Alabárdos Panzió** (22 rooms) Bajcsy-Zsilinszky u. 49; ✆ 33 312640. You'll probably see the large but harmless dog called 'Gigalo' as you enter the gates! Although the rooms are small, this is a comfortable pension hung with historical paintings of the town & with great views of Castle Hill. You couldn't ask for

friendlier or more welcoming staff. *Sgl 9,500Ft, dbl 12,500Ft.*
🏠 **El Greco Kávéház** (4 rooms) Pázmány Péter u. 15; ✆ 33 631064; www.elgrecocafe.hu. A decent coffeehouse & bar that also has some stylish, modern & well-equipped rooms. It's a pity that there was a

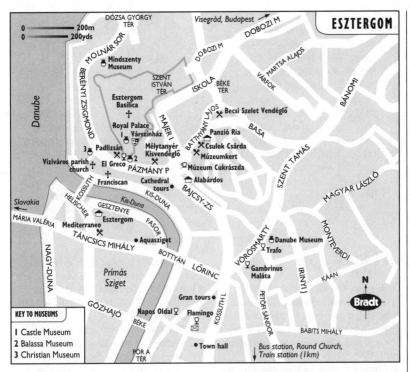

KEY TO MUSEUMS

1 Castle Museum
2 Balassa Museum
3 Christian Museum

rather surly waitress on duty during our visit because this place otherwise has a lot to recommend it. *Dbl 12,000Ft, apt 14,400Ft (excl Tourist Tax).*

🏠 **Hotel Esztergom** (36 rooms) Prímás sziget, Nagy-Duna sétány; ☎ 33 412555; www.hotel-esztergom.hu. We're unsure what the interior designers were thinking when decking the reception hall in dull beige, yellow & pink but the effect is outmoded & drab. The rooms themselves – all with balconies – are better, although ours could have done with a hoovering. The hotel restaurant (⊕ *daily 18.00–21.00*) serves Hungarian classics. *Sgl 16,000Ft, dbl 18,000Ft, apt 22,000–25,000Ft.*

🏠 **Mediterraneo** (3 rooms) Prímás sziget, Helischer út 2; ☎ 33 311411; www.mediterraneo.hu. Opened in 2008, the Mediterraneo has simple but serviceable rooms above the restaurant (see below). *Dbl 13,900Ft, quad 20,000Ft.*

🏠 **Panzió Ria** (15 rooms) Batthyány u. 11–13; ☎ 33 401429; www.riapanzio.com. This is a pension with that little bit extra – spacious rooms facing a pleasant courtyard, an internet room, sauna, fitness room & bike hire. If exploring the basilica – standing virtually on the doorstep – isn't enough, the staff will help you arrange excursions beyond. *Rooms 13,000Ft.*

Contact Gran Tours (see opposite) if you wish to book **college** or **private accommodation**. **Gran Camping** (*Prímás sziget, Nagy-Duna sétány 3;* ☎ *33 402513; www.hotels.hu/gran_camping;* ⊕ *May 1–Oct 15*) is the best & most central of the campsites, & has bungalows.

✕ WHERE TO EAT AND DRINK

✕ **Bécsi Szelet Vendéglő** Téglaház u. 4; ☎ 33 404090. Specialises in *wiener schnitzels*, including a giant one of 30dkg for 1,940Ft. *Mains avg 1,400Ft;* ⊕ *daily 11.00–22.00.*

✕ **Csülök Csárda** Batthyány Lajos u. 9; ☎ 33 412420; www.csulokcsarda.hu. Brick-cellar restaurant serving

traditional dishes like knuckle of ham, belly of pork & veal stew. *Mains avg 2,400Ft;* ⊕ *daily 12.00–22.00.*

✕ **Mediterraneo** See above. One of the few non-smoking restaurants you'll come across, this restaurant is based in a brick-and-glass pavilion & has a multi-level terrace. International & Hungarian

The conservative cleric Cardinal József Mindszenty famously became a figure of resistance first to the Germans and subsequently to the communists, who subjected him to a show trial in 1949 before imprisoning him. There are transcripts recording his suffering at the hands of secret-police torturers on display in the House of Terror (see page 162). During the revolution of 1956 he was freed, and took haven in the US Embassy in Budapest – where he stayed for a full 15 years, becoming a focal point for communist opposition and rejecting State proposals such as the secularisation of Roman Catholic schools. It was only in 1971 that he was persuaded by the Vatican to leave the embassy and move to Austria, where he died four years later at the age of 83. In 1990, shortly after the change of political system, the cardinal's body was returned to Hungary and buried in Esztergom Basilica; Pope John Paul II knelt before his grave during his papal visit to Hungary the year after, and since then the crypt has become a place of pilgrimage for Roman Catholics. It is hoped – nay, expected – that Mindszenty will one day be canonised.

food, & friendly service. *Mains avg 1,700Ft;* ⏲ *daily 12.00–22.00.*

✘ **Mélytányér Kisvendéglő** Pázmány Péter u. 1; ☎ 33 412534; www.melytanyer.hu. This cheerful restaurant is a good choice for families, with gingham furnishings & a wall of football scarves. Service is quick & the atmosphere relaxed. *Mains avg 1,900Ft;* ⏲ *daily 12.00–21.30.*

🍴 **Múzeum Cukrászda** Batthyány Lajos u. 1. Cakes, pancakes & other sins. The colour-clashing walls are lively & the sweetmeats are sumptuous. ⏲ *daily 09.00–22.00.*

✘ **Múzeumkert** Batthyány Lajos u. 1; ☎ 33 404440. Múzeumkert offers a wide choice of traditional dishes, including a good spread of fish options, & its cobbled courtyard is a pleasant place to eat. *Mains avg 2,000Ft (½ portions at 30% discount);* ⏲ *daily 11.00–24.00 (disco Tue, Fri–Sat until 03.00).*

🍴 **Napos Oldal** Széchenyi tér 24. Serving sandwiches & popcorn, the 'Sunny Side' is a cheerful little café-bar on the western side of the square. ⏲ *Mon–Thu 07.00–23.00, Fri 07.00–24.00, Sat 08.00–24.00, Sun 10.00–22.00.*

✘ **Padlizsán** Pázmány Péter u. 21; ☎ 33 311212. 'The Aubergine' is an upmarket, drape-curtained restaurant that teeters on the ostentatious. It has an international menu, & a courtyard seating area. *Mains avg 1,800Ft;* ⏲ *12.00–22.00 daily.*

✘ **Pizzéria di Stefarta** Lőrinc u. 5; ☎ 33 312952. Recommended by locals, this lively spot is the most popular eatery in town. The staff may not speak English, but they do know how to make a fantastic pizza & there's a magnificent list of toppings from which to select. *Avg pizza 1,200Ft;* ⏲ *daily 11.00–22.00.*

ENTERTAINMENT AND NIGHTLIFE Esztergom has various drinking holes. The **Gambrinus Maláta Bár** (*Vörösmarty u. 5;* ☎ *33 402844; www.gastroport.hu;* ⏲ *Mon–Thu 13.00–01.00, Fri 13.00–02.00, Sat 15.00–02.00, Sun 15.00–24.00*) is one of them, with loud and funky beats, wood panelling and a collection of Hungarian ornaments. **Múzeumkert** (see above) holds a disco on some evenings. You can drink and squander your spare coins in the **Flamingo**, a very dark bar on Széchenyi tér which is open 24 hours and has a small casino at the rear. **Trafo Café** on Vörösmarty utca is a café-bar in a pavilion on an island in the road. There are **organ concerts** held in the basilica in summer months and drama and dance in the Rondella. Buy tickets or get details from Grantours (see page 192) or from the ticket office (*Széchenyi tér 7;* ⏲ *Mon–Fri 09.00–16.00*).

WHAT TO SEE AND DO

Castle Hill Esztergom Basilica (*Szent István tér 1;* ☎ *33 411895;* e *bazilika.esztergom@ museum.hu;* 🎫 *admission free;* ⏲ *Apr–Oct daily 07.00–18.00, rest of yr Mon–Fri 07.00–16.00, Sat–Sun 07.00–17.00*) crowns the town; it is the country's biggest, erected on the spot where Prince Géza's 30-year-old son was anointed King István in AD1000 with a crown sent by Pope Sylvester. In replacing the 12th-century Gothic St Adalbert Cathedral that was maimed by the Turks, the 19th-century planners worked with the grandiose aim of producing a Magyar version of the Vatican's St Peter's Square. The behemoth is 100m high and 107m long, and took almost 50 years to build; it was completed by József Hild, who added the last piece of the monumental jigsaw – the dome – in 1869. Liszt had composed and conducted its consecration mass 13 years before. Regarded as a masterpiece of Neoclassical architecture, the basilica is actually formally rigid and rather stark; it doesn't float everybody's boat.

The main altar in the cavernous interior has an appropriately over-sized copy of Titian's *Assumption*, the largest single-canvas oil painting in the world. The highlight though is the **Bakócz Chapel** on the southern side of the nave, built by Archbishop Tamás Bakócz in 1507 as his future sepulchre. Carved of red marble from nearby Süttő, this wonderful piece of Renaissance work stood in St Adalbert's before its demolition; at that time, the chapel was carefully dismantled and later re-assembled to adorn the new basilica. It is unsurprising that Bakócz should have commissioned Italian craftsman of the highest order in constructing this tribute to himself in death; in life he was notorious as a brilliant but deeply conniving and greedy prelate, who used all means possible (including conning Queen Beatrice after the death of Mátyás) to accrue a massive personal fortune. He is also remembered as the man tasked with raising a peasant army to tackle the Turks in 1514 – an army whose appointed commander, György Dózsa, ended up leading his peasants in revolt (see page 17).

Through a door to the right of the main altar painting is the nation's most precious liturgical collection, a trove that looks to have been manhandled by Midas himself. The **cathedral treasury** (*☞ 600Ft/300Ft; ☉ Mar–Oct 09.00–16.30 daily, Nov Sat–Sun 10.00–15.30, Dec Mon–Fri 11.00–15.30, Sat–Sun 10.00–15.30, closed Jan–Feb*) has been raided on several occasions over the centuries, but it still contains 400 items of ecclesiastical jewellery and textiles dating back as far as the Árpáds. Chief among the attractions are a 13th-century coronation cross on which Hungarian kings swore the oath of accession, the beautiful 16th-century Suki Chalice, and the Calvary of King Mátyás. The latter comprises two parts, the Gothic upper portion presented to Zsigmond by the French Queen Isabelle in 1424, and the lower Renaissance part made for Mátyás by Italian goldsmiths working in Buda. Beside the entrance to the basilica are two sets of stairs, one leading down to the **crypt** (*☞ adult 150Ft; ☉ daily 09.00–17.00*) – the resting place for archbishops and other clergy (including Cardinal Mindszenty; see box opposite), and straight out of a Gothic novel – and the other up to the **cupola** (*☞ adult 250Ft; ☉ May–Oct daily 09.30–17.00*), equally chilling for those lacking heads for heights.

GOD'S YOUNG GUN

There was more than a whiff of nepotism involved in the appointment of Ippolito d'Este as archbishop in 1477. At just eight years old, it could have been argued that he lacked for something in experience; however, he was the nephew of Mátyás's wife and this put him at something of an advantage over the other candidates. He took over after the death of János Vitéz, and held the post for a decade. Queen Beatrice certainly lacked such sway after the death of Mátyás; instead it was the scheming Archbishop Bakócz who was able to manipulate things, and Beatrice lived unhappy in a tower of the palace before eventually returning to her native Italy.

If you prefer your vantage points less dizzying, walk behind the basilica for a lovely view of the Danube's curve. Here too is the **Coronation Monument**, erected to mark the millennium, and depicting the crowning of King István by the Bishop of Esztergom. The **Mindszenty Memorial Museum** (*Mindszenty Emlékhely; Bazilika templom tér;* ↘ *06 3340 3162;* ✎ *adult 400Ft;* ☉ *Tue–Sun 09.00–17.00*) displays items belonging to the cardinal (see box, page 194), as well as featuring a film showing his reburial and the papal visit of 1991.

A short step south of the basilica is the former **Royal Palace**, whose partly reconstructed remains represent the earliest structure extant in Hungary. They were excavated during the 1930s, the palace having sunk beneath the earth after being destroyed during the Turkish occupation. At the southern end are walls dating to Prince Géza's 10th-century palace, including the St István Hall where his son (called Vajk before he received the baptismal name by which he was revered for ever more) was supposedly born. The bulk of the building though was added in the 12th century by Béla III, with subsequent decorative alterations by the archbishops who occupied the palace from the 13th century (after the royal capital was moved to Buda). The first-floor Hall of Virtues, which once hosted royal receptions, was used as a study by Archbishop János Vitéz in the 1470s; it gets its name from the painted allegories of Intellect, Temperance, Fortitude and Justice that were added shortly afterwards, perhaps by Ippolito d'Este (see box, page 195). Just to the north is the 12th-century late-Romanesque/early-Gothic royal chapel with a splendid rose window; among the frescoes are a tree of life and a lion whose style reflect the Byzantine background of Béla III, and eight later half-length apostles from the 14th century. All these remains are part of the **Castle Museum** (*Szent István tér 1;* ↘ *33 311821;* ✎ *adult/child 400/200Ft;* ☉ *Tue–Sun mid Mar–Oct 31 10.00–18.00, Nov 1–mid Mar 11.00–15.30*), which also contains finds from the local area (including stonework from St Adalbert Cathedral), 18th- and 19th-century weaponry, a history of Hungarian minting and a panopticon of wax statues bedecked in regal dress. There are summer arts performances hosted in the **Rondella**, one of the bastions that made up the fortifications surrounding Castle Hill.

The rest of town If you descend the steps leading down the hill's southeastern side, and then pick up Pázmány utca bearing westwards around the bottom, you'll enter the Baroque **Víziváros** (Watertown) district. At the eastern end of Pázmány utca is the **Archdiocesan Library** (*Bibliotéka*), which is among the country's oldest collections of books, while further on you'll find temporary exhibitions of archaeology and local history at the **Balassa Museum** (*Pázmány Péter u. 13;* ↘ *33 412185;* ✎ *200/100Ft;* ☉ *Nov–Apr Wed–Sun 09.00–17.00, May–Oct Tue–Sun*

A LOVER AND A FIGHTER

Bálint Balassi (1554–94) was one of the great Renaissance poets, innovative in experimenting with form, writing in the vernacular and producing a significant body of love poetry. But he was a maverick who broke moulds beyond the sphere of art, and was a man of his 'sword' (metaphorically and literally) as much as his pen. He embroiled himself in a series of notorious sexual relationships that resulted – among other things – in a prosecution for incest (after he married his first cousin, the daughter of István Dobó; see page 232). His fondness for battling the Turks brought about his final downfall at the age of just 40; during the attempt to recapture Esztergom in 1594 he was injured in the legs, dying of blood poisoning a short while later. There is a statue of him in Szent István tér.

09.00–17.00). Opposite is the two-steepled Baroque **Franciscan church** and adjoining monastery (*Pázmány u. 18*).

A short distance further west is the early-18th-century **Víziváros Parish Church**, and the **Christian Museum** (*Keresztény Múzeum; Mindszenty hercegprímás tere 2;* ℻ *33 413880;* ✆ *700/350Ft;* ⊕ *Wed–Sun mid-Mar–Apr & Nov–Dec 11.00–15.00, May–Oct 10.00–18.00*) in the Neo-Renaissance former Primate's Palace. Founded in 1875 by Archbishop János Simor, it represents Hungary's stand-out display of medieval and Renaissance religious art. As well as native works (from 15th-century painted panels to a 17th-century portrait of the poet Balassi, who turned to religion at the end of a far from virtuous life; see box opposite), there is a particularly rich collection of Trecento and Quattrocento paintings (Italian art of the 14th and 15th centuries), as well as Austrian, German, Flemish and French pieces. Be sure not to miss the two works most commonly mentioned in association with this museum – Tamás of Kolozsvár's *Calvary* altarpiece (1427), where Christ's suffering is emphasised in his hollow face and distorted toe joints, and the wooden *Coffin of Our Lord* (c. 1480), a symbolic sepulchre on wheels that was used in liturgies at Easter and whose carved figures were modelled on actors in passion plays of the time. Both came from the Benedictine monastery of Garamszentbenedek in Slovakia.

A bridge at the southern side of Mindszenty hercegprímás tere crosses over to **Prímás sziget** (Primate's Island), and Nagy Duna sétány leads around the island's outer edge. After 100m you'll reach a second bridge, this time spanning the water to the Slovakian town of Átúrovo ('Párkány' in Hungarian). For nearly 60 years the **Mária Valéria Bridge** meant a forlorn pair of twisted stubs protruding from the water after the retreating Germans detonated it during World War II. During those years the opposite bank could only be reached by ferry. However, after protracted discussions the 500m-long 19th-century structure was finally resurrected, and opened at a ceremony attended by the Hungarian and Slovakian prime ministers in 2002. The island holds the **Aquasziget Adventure Baths and Spa** (*Táncsics Mihály u. 5;* ℻ *33 511100; www.aquasziget.hu;* ✆ *day ticket 2,950Ft;* ⊕ *Sun–Fri 09.00–20.00, Sat 09.00–21.00; outdoor pools May–Aug, rest all yr*), which opened in 2005. The complex includes indoor and outdoor pools, a wellness centre (with saunas, massages, a hammam, fitness facilities, etc) and a medical/beauty treatment centre.

Moving back off the island, the river-hugging Kis-Duna sétány is a pretty promenade and a pleasant way of moving towards the heart of town to the south of Castle Hill. On the way, it passes the invigorating **Szent István Thermal Baths** (*Bajcsy-Zsilinszky u. 14;* ℻ *33 312249;* ✆ *1,100/800Ft;* ⊕ *May–Sep daily 06.00–19.00, Oct–Apr Mon–Fri 06.00–19.00, Sat 06.00–18.00, Sun 08.00–16.00*), which has indoor and outdoor pools, as well as massage facilities and sauna. The second road on the left takes you to the recently renovated (and pedestrianised) Széchenyi tér and its Baroque, Rococo and Neoclassical architecture. The **town hall** (*Széchenyi tér 1*) – conspicuous for lacking a fresh lick of paint when the other buildings sparkle around it – was originally built in the 17th century, and was home to János Bottyán, the one-eyed general known as 'Bottyán the Blind' who served under Rákóczi II; there used to be a sword suspended outside reminding those with crime on their minds that murderers could be sentenced to death. Kossuth Lajos utca passes to the square's eastern side and continues south to Hősök tere where stands the **Round Church**, inspired by Rome's Pantheon, intended as a practice run for the basilica, and completed in 1835.

To the northeast of Rákóczi tér, at the top of Vörösmarty utca, the **Danube Museum** (*Kölcsey Ferenc u. 2;* ℻ *33 500250; www.dunamuzeum.hu;* ✆ *500/250Ft;* ⊕ *Wed–Mon Nov–Dec & Feb–Apr 10.00–16.00, May–Oct 09.00–17.00*) is devoted to water administration and environmental protection, and has exhibitions showing the solutions and equipment used in regulating Hungary's main river during the 19th century.

FESTIVALS AND EVENTS The town is at its liveliest in summer, with an annual drama festival in the open-air Castle Theatre (*Vörösmarty u. 2;* ↘ *33 501175;* e *varszinhaz1@invitel.hu; www.esztergomkultura.hu*), which runs from the middle of June until the end of August (*performances Fri, Sat & Sun 20.30*). There is an International Guitar Festival in August (contact Gran Tours above for more information) and a Gizella Festival in May.

VÁC

On the eastern bank 35km north of Pest, Vác is a walkable town less tourist-infested than elsewhere on the Danube Bend and seems laid back by comparison. This atmosphere belies a very active and frequently influential past, however; the town basked in the immortal glow of Ptolemy's *Geographia* (in which it was recorded as an ancient river crossing called Uvcencum), and in the 11th century it was one of the ten episcopal sees founded by King István. One theory regarding its current name posits that before their battle to decide the Hungarian succession in 1074, the princes Géza and László met a hermit called Vác while riding in a nearby forest. After the Mongols had ripped out its early-medieval heart – including Géza's Romanesque cathedral, where he was buried in 1077 – Béla IV gathered his noblemen here to decide the way forward in protecting the country from future attack. During the 14th century, it benefitted from close proximity to the royal capital at Visegrád and for a time Vác's silver coinage served as the national currency. However, a position of strategic importance meant it featured heavily in the struggles when the Turks came on the scene, and changed hands 40 times before finally succumbing to Ottoman occupation – and a second episode of heart ripping.

Fate conspired against the town's revival when a fire in 1731 razed 90% of the buildings. The Baroque town you see now is the result of successive bishops' efforts during the rest of the 18th century to haul it back up by its bootstraps, a period that also saw repopulation with Germans, Czechs, Slovaks, Croatians and Serbs. Confirmation that things were back on track came literally in 1846 with the construction of the rail link with Budapest, the first in the country. A memorial at the town's southern gate commemorates two battles during the 1849 War of Independence, but during the 20th century the town was linked inexorably with its fearsome prison, a place used first by Miklós Horthy and then by Rákosi to incarcerate their political opponents.

GETTING THERE AND AWAY Vác can be reached via roads 2 or E77/2A, which run parallel to the river from Budapest. The **bus station** (*Szent István tér*) is 300m northeast of the centre; there are loads of daily buses from Budapest's Újpest Városkapu and Árpád híd stations, as well as services between Vác and Vácrátót (21), Balassagyarmat (14 direct), Salgótarján (three direct), Gödöllő (ten direct) and many other towns. The **railway station** is 500m from the centre, at the northeastern end of Széchenyi utca. There are very regular train services from Budapest Nyugati to Vác, most of which continue around the Danube Bend to Szob. Vácrátót is on the same line (a 12-minute trip southeast of Vác); there are also trains northwards terminating at Balassagyarmat (up to 11).

A **ferry** going across to Szentendre Island (see page 186) leaves fairly regularly from the pier at the junction of Ady Endre sétány and Eszterházy utca, and can take both foot passengers and cars. Further north along the bank is the Mahart ferry pier (*Liszt Ferenc sétány*). Mahart (↘ *1 318 1223; www.mahartpassnave.hu*) operates a **river-**

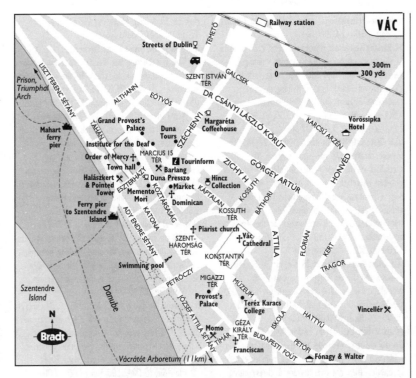

VÁC

- Railway station
- Streets of Dublin
- SZENT ISTVÁN TÉR
- LISZT FERENC SÉTÁNY
- Prison, Triumphal Arch
- Mahart ferry pier
- Grand Provost's Palace
- Duna Tours
- Institute for the Deaf
- Order of Mercy
- Town hall
- Halászkert & Pointed Tower
- Memento Mori
- Ferry pier to Szentendre Island
- MÁRCIUS 15 TÉR
- Tourinform
- Barlang
- Duna Pressszo
- Market
- Hincz Collection
- Dominican
- KÖZTÁRSASÁG
- KATONA
- ADY ENDRE SÉTÁNY
- Margaréta Coffeehouse
- Vörössipka Hotel
- DR CSÁNYI LÁSZLÓ KÖRÚT
- KARCSÚ ARZÉN
- GÖRGEY ARTÚR
- ZICHY H
- KOSSUTH
- BÁTHORI
- KOSSUTH TÉR
- Piarist church
- Vác Cathedral
- SZENT-HÁROMSÁG TÉR
- KONSTANTIN TÉR
- ATTILA
- FLÓRIÁN
- KERT
- TRAGOR
- Swimming pool
- PETRÓCZY
- MIGAZZI TÉR
- Provost's Palace
- MÚZEUM
- Teréz Karacs College
- Szentendre Island
- Danube
- JÓZSEF ATTILA SÉTÁNY
- Momo
- TIMÁR
- GÉZA KIRÁLY TÉR
- Franciscan
- ISKOLA
- HATTYÚ
- BUDAPESTI FŐÚT
- PETŐFI
- Vincellér
- Fónagy & Walter
- Vácrátót Arboretum (11km)
- Bradt
- N
- 0 — 300m
- 0 — 300 yds
- ALTHANN
- EÖTVÖS
- GALCSEK
- TEMETŐ
- SZÉCHENYI
- ESZTERHÁZY
- KÁPTALAN
- HONVÉD

boat service to Esztergom that stops at Vác along the way (*May 1–Aug 29 daily except Mon; Apr 3–24 Sat only; Sep 3–26 Fri, Sat & Sun; ♨ sgl/rtn 1,490/2,235Ft, child 50% discount, student/pensioner 25% discount*). Ferries depart from Pest's Vigadó tér at 09.00 (return departure 18.30), stopping to pick up passengers five minutes later from Buda's Batthyány tér, and take two hours.

INFORMATION AND OTHER PRACTICALITIES

Dunatours Széchenyi u. 14; ⁜ 27 310950. This office can arrange local, domestic & international tours, & private rooms; it stands on the road running from the eastern side of the main square. ⏰ *Mon–Fri 08.00–16.00, Sat 08.00–12.00.*

Tourinform Március 15 tér 16–18; ⁜ 27 316160; www.tourinformvac.hu. At the eastern side of the square. ⏰ *Jun–Sep Mon–Fri 09.00–18.00, Sat–Sun 09.00–17.00, rest of yr Mon–Fri 09.00–17.00.*

WHERE TO STAY

Fónagy & Walter (3 rooms) Budapesti fő út 36; ⁜ 27 310682; www.fonagy.hu. The 'antique' furnishings of this pension 400m southeast of the cathedral could have been pinched from your grandmother's, but the rooms are large & have sofas. It also has a wine cellar. *All rooms 9,500Ft.*

Teréz Karacs College Budapesti fő út 8; ⁜ 27 315480. Just beyond the southern corner of

Konstantin tér, the college has dorm rooms available during vacation periods. *Beds from 2,500Ft/pp.*

Vörössipka Hotel (16 rooms) Honvéd u. 14; ⁜ 27 501055; www.vorossipkahotel.hu. To the east of the centre, this fire-engine-red hotel has spotless rooms with gleaming floors, although the service was poor during our stay & the rooms lack telephones. *Sgl 8,600–13,500Ft, dbl 10,800–16,600Ft.*

WHERE TO EAT AND DRINK

Aredo Március 15 tér 22; ⁜ 27 308309; www.aredo.hu. In the main square, the Aredo is a

bar & restaurant with contemporary furnishings & a summer terrace. The menu offers Hungarian fare, with a few international options. *Mains avg 1,800Ft;* ⊕ *daily 10.00–24.00.*

✘ **Barlang Restaurant** Március 15 tér; ✆ 27 315584. At the heart of the square – indeed running beneath it – this cool cellar bar brims with Gothic character, with torch light & a hanging iron candelabra. Pizza is the order of the day. *Mains avg 1,500Ft;* ⊕ *Mon–Thu 11.00–23.00, Fri–Sat 12.00–01.00, Sun 12.00–22.00.*

☕ **Choco Café** Március 15 tér 20; ✆ 27 305839; www.chococafe.hu. As the name suggests, this café specialises in chocolate – hot & cold. How about a chili hot chocolate, one with strawberry & pepper or even a Japanese wasabi concoction? There are alcoholic takes on the chocolate theme, as well as standard teas/coffees & sandwiches for the less adventurous. ⊕ *Sun–Thu 10.00–20.00, Fri–Sat 10.00–21.00.*

☕ **Duna Presszo** Március 15 tér 13; ✆ 27 310569; www.dunapresszo.hu. Enjoy the square in this 25-year-old coffee house & bar next to the town hall. ⊕ *Mon–Thu 08.00–23.00, Fri 08.00–13.00, Sat 08.00–24.00, Sun 08.00–22.00.*

✘ **Halászkert** Liszt Ferenc sétány 9; ✆ 27 315985. On the old-fashioned side, the Halászkert serves up traditional fare – featuring a good number of fish specialities. There's a river terrace & cheesy music

(live on Fri & Sat). *Mains avg 2,200Ft;* ⊕ *12.00–22.00 daily.*

☕ **Margaréta Coffee House** Széchenyi u. 19; ✆ 27 311524. This buzzing bar & café is a good people-watching spot, & sells ice cream by the bucket load in summer. ⊕ *Mon 06.00–16.00, Tue–Fri 05.00–16.00, Sat 05.00–13.00, Sun 06.00–12.00.*

✘ **Momo** Timár u. 9; ✆ 27 306777. Overlooked by the spire of the Franciscan church & fronting on to the Danube, this is a decent place for a beer/cocktail or meal. Outside it spreads over a three-tiered terrace, while the modern interior has wicker chairs & lots of space. The menu includes Hungarian & international dishes. *Mains avg 2,500Ft;* ⊕ *daily 11.00–23.00.*

♀ **Street of Dublin Irish Pub** Zrínyi u. 3; ✆ 27 306785. Up some steps opposite the bus station, the Street of Dublin is the favourite drinking hole for the locals. It has Kilkenny beer in the pipes, & decent enough steaks. Live music some evenings. ⊕ *Mon–Sun 12.00–24.00.*

✘ **Vincellér** Dr Csányi Lászlo körút 85; ✆ 27 301521. Hungarian specialities, along with a few international dishes, in a cosy enough restaurant with a small terrace. As the name suggests, they pride themselves on their selection of wines. *Mains avg 1,700Ft;* ⊕ *Mon–Sat 12.00–22.00, Sun 12.00–17.00.*

WHAT TO SEE AND DO

Március 15 tér and around Március 15 tér looks like a Neapolitan ice cream, lined with civic buildings and town houses in shades of pink, yellow and brown. It gained its triangular shape in 1761 when a church at the southeastern end was demolished, bringing into view the newly completed **Dominican church** (*Március 15 tér 22*). Known as the Church of the Whites (after the habit worn by the monks), the Baroque exterior hides rich Rococo furnishings inside, while next door is the monastery. In 1994, a forgotten, sealed crypt was found in the church that had served as a burial chamber during the 18th century. The conditions had led to mummification of the corpses, many of which were interred in formal costume – the women in bonnets, the men in jackets or cloaks – and the children in coffins of blue or green. In the cellars to the right of the church, the **Memento Mori** (*Március 15 tér 19*; ✆ *27 305988;* ✆ *1,000/500Ft;* ⊕ *Tue–Sun 10.00–18.00*) displays some of the discoveries – jewellery, rosaries and children's shoes – as well as three of the mummies themselves, lying with their arms folded. It's fascinating stuff, and sombre rather than creepy.

On the other side of Eszterházy utca is the custard-yellow Baroque **town hall** (*Március 15 tér 11*), built in 1764 in time for the visit of Maria Theresa to the town. On the gable is an allegory of Justice, with reclining figures either side bearing the coats of arms of Hungary and Bishop Kristóf Migazzi. Migazzi was incumbent during Vác's golden age, and presided over the building of the cathedral, the Triumphal Arch and the town hall itself; he went on to become Archbishop of Vienna and a cardinal. Next to the town hall is the 18th-century former **monastery of the Order of Mercy** (*Március 15 tér 7–9*), while the **Institute for the Deaf and Dumb** (*Március 15 tér 6*) has functioned in the building opposite

Probably the most varied of Hungary's national parks – with hill ranges, river valleys and flood plains – the Danube-Ipoly National Park was founded in 1997. Over 63,000ha, it covers the Pilis and Börzsöny hills, Szentendre Island, the valley of the River Ipoly (which runs along the Slovakian border), and the Danube valley between Vác and Pest. Its renowned feature is the Danube Bend close to Esztergom, with stunning views of the terraced valleys and the majestic river below. The hill ranges vary in composition, the Pilis Hills formed from marine sediment and the Börzsöny and Visegrád hills from volcanic stone. On the steep slopes of the Börzsöny Hills are karst bush forests, and rare dolomite grasslands and slope steppes; in the flatter parts are *puszta* oak forests. Over half of the country's bird species twitter in these peaks, and there are several glacial plant relicts among the 70 protected types. The River Ipoly on the border with Slovakia, which used to meander profusely, has undergone a process of artificial straightening; as well as the resulting dead channels and ox-bows, 12km have been left unaltered, resulting in one of the last relatively undamaged river-catchment basins in the Carpathian Basin. The river here is allowed to flood, and the valley holds wet meadows, alder wood, marshes, more birds and representatives of virtually every one of Hungary's amphibian species. The park harbours the endemic butterfly *Dioszeghyana schmidtii*, and vulnerable species including the European mudminnow and striped ruffe, the lesser white-fronted goose, the lesser horseshoe bat and the otter. Among the species you might spot springing about in the Pilis and Visegrád hills is the saw-legged grasshopper, one of the country's longest insects. It's a blinder of an area for nature walks, and there are also narrow-gauge railways into the Börzsöny Hills from Kismaros to Királyrét and Nagyirtás to Nagybörzsöny (see page 204). For more information, contact the Danube-Ipoly National Park Directorate (*Main office: Budapest XII, Költő u. 21;* ℐ *1 391 4610;* e *dinpi@dinpi.hu; www.dinpi.hu*).

since 1802, although in the aftermath of Turkish occupation it served for a while as the Bishop's Palace and was where Maria Theresa stayed. The former **Grand Provost's Palace** (*Március 15 tér 4*) stands adjacent to it.

There is a lovely promenade running along the river bank, and you might wish to enjoy a short stretch of it before rejoining Köztársaság utca and its notorious **prison** (*Köztársaság u. 64–66*) 600m north of Március tér. (You'll pass the **Pointed Tower** at Liszt Ferenc sétány 12 on the way, which was a corner turret of the medieval town walls and is now incorporated into the structure of a residential building.) The jail was originally a school, one of Maria Theresa's institutes for the education of noble children (known as Theresianums), but since 1855 its watchtowers and gridded windows have restrained prisoners rather than pupils. Its hulking form stands at a particularly pretty point, and inmates no doubt request a river-facing room. Just beyond it is the Neoclassical **Triumphal Arch** (commonly called Kőkapu, or Stone Gate), another of Bishop Migazzi's monuments erected specifically for Maria Theresa's visit in 1764. It is said that the bishop actually placed theatrical scenery props along her route through the town to screen any unappealing architecture.

Konstantin tér and around Moving out through the southeast corner of Március 15 tér, behind the Dominican church is an **outdoor market** (⊕ *Mon 06.00–16.00, Tue–Fri 05.00–16.00, Sat 05.00–13.00, Sun 06.00–10.00*) selling clothes, flowers and vegetables, and further down on the other side of the road is the **Hincz Collection** (*Káptalan u. 16;* ℐ *27 313463;* & *600/300Ft; contact in advance for access –*

Around Budapest and the Danube Bend VÁC

4

min of 5 visitors). The museum has two permanent exhibitions showcasing the history of Vác and the work of avant-garde painter and graphic artist Gyula Hincz (1904–86).

Konstantin tér was the ecclesiastical engine room of the town, and is bullied by the vast and boxy **Vác Cathedral**. It was built between 1763 and 1767, originally to the plans of the Austrian architect Franz Anton Pilgram before Bishop Migazzi brought in the Frenchman Isidore Canevale to finish the job. Many regard the cathedral as a supreme example of Hungarian Neoclassical architecture, but to us the proportions feel uncomfortable, both in the building itself and its surroundings, like the first pupil in class to hit his growth spurt. Enormous Corinthian columns dominate the façade, with six enormous statues by József Bechert peering down from above them; the green cupola is hardly visible. The interior is considerably lighter in touch, with cream walls and a fresco of the triumphant Holy Trinity by Franz Anton Maulbertsch giving a splash of colour to the dome; the main altar painting (*The Meeting of Mary and Elizabeth*) by the same artist was only discovered during restoration in the 1940s – it was not to Migazzi's taste, and had been covered over. Pieces of the sanctuary rail are taken from the earlier Renaissance cathedral built by Bishop Miklós Báthori – a bishop whom King Mátyás threatened to chuck in the Danube if he continued to torture his tenants – and there are other stone fragments in the crypt.

On the western side of the square, paved with stones of grey, blue and terracotta, and dotted with ornate lamp posts, is one side of the late-Baroque **Provost's Palace** (*Migazzi Kristóf tér*), which faces on to Migazzi tér and was built between 1782 and 1784 by Viennese architect József Meissl. Múzeum utca runs northwards to Szentháromság tér and the flaking **Piarist Church**, finished in 1741; inside is as spartan as outside, with the notable exception of its carved and gilded Venetian mirror altar. Keep a look out too for the graceful statue of a timid Mary in a red dress. The sandstone **Trinity Column** was erected by Bishop Althann in 1755.

To the south of Konstantin tér is a **Franciscan church** (*Géza Király tér 18*), built in the 18th century with stone from the old fortress destroyed by the Turks; the pulpit bears exuberant allegories of the Virtues, while the church's centrepiece is the elaborate, two-storey Rococo altar. Continue further southwards on Budapesti főút and you'll reach a **stone bridge** that has spanned the Gombás Stream since 1757, and is adorned with seven statues of saints by József Bechert. It is the country's only surviving Baroque bridge of its type. Beyond that is a monument to those who died in the battles at Vác during the 1849 War of Independence, topped with a cannonball, and the early-18th-century **Chapel of the Seven** (*Hétkápolna; Derecske dűlő 2*) named after the seven sorrows of the Virgin Mary.

Other Vácrátót, 11km to the southeast of town, has a super **arboretum** (*Alkotmány u. 2–4;* ✆ *28 360122; www.botkert.hu;* ✉ *740/350Ft;* ☉ *daily Apr–Oct 08.00–18.00, Nov–Mar 08.00–16.00; greenhouses closed Mon*), complete with waterfalls, a water mill and exotic plant species. A visitor centre within the garden showcases the flora of the local protected area, and explains how man is affecting the planet's ecology. There are trains and buses there from Vác (see page 198; a bus takes you the final 3km from the railway station to the garden); if you're driving, follow Road 2 or 2/A south for a short distance, turn left towards Aszód and then right towards Gödöllő. There is also a 500m-long **nature trail** managed by the Göncöl Foundation (*Ilona u. 3;* ✆ *26 304484*) on the flood plains near Vác. It can be reached from the stone bridge over the Gombás Stream; the wooden path takes you through forest containing aquatic flora including the rare broad-leaved helleborine orchid, and there are two bird-observation towers.

During the 1950s, negotiations began between the Czechoslovakian and Hungarian governments to construct a dam at Gabčikovo (now in Slovakia). Originally envisaged as a way of altering the shallow Danube to allow navigable access for transport ships, in the 1970s the focus changed to hydroelectric energy production with two dams and plants planned at Gabčikovo and Nagymaros. In Hungary there was widespread concern at the prospect of the Czechs having control of the river upstream, but the Soviets pushed the idea forward. Increasingly the project became a target for anti-communist demonstration; those supporting it were labelled Stalinist traitors, and in the 1980s there were protest marches in Budapest. In 1990, the newly elected right-wing coalition unilaterally cancelled the agreement.

However, the dam at Gabčikovo was almost completed, and the project became a symbol of strength for the newly independent Slovakians. They pushed forward and diverted water through the turbines of the Slovakian plant; but the second plant had been intrinsic to the design, and little energy was squeezed at the cost of significant environmental damage to the river at Győr. Both sides turned to the International Court of Justice in 1993. A year later the socialists were back in power in Hungary, and when the court decreed the governments should negotiate a way out, they returned to the table. With eyes on European Union membership, the neighbours were anxious to show they could resolve their squabbles and it was agreed that the project should proceed and that ecological concerns would be addressed. But the swings and roundabouts of Hungarian politics intervened; the right-wing opposition joined forces with the Greens, anti-dam rallies were held and the issue helped lever the socialists out in the elections of 1998. The new right-wing government had promised to put an end to the idea once and for all, and spent millions of dollars dismantling the half-built Nagymaros dam. The matter is no longer in the political limelight, and ecologists on both sides agree that the environmental damage has already been done. The Slovaks remain quite proud of their dam – which is fully operational (extra water is allowed into other arms of the Danube at Szigetköz to limit the eco impact) – and you can take a boat trip to see it from Bratislava. On the Hungarian side, there remain some apartments in Nagymaros built to house the dam workers, but there are no dam workers to live in them.

NAGYMAROS, ZEBEGÉNY AND SZOB

Road 12 follows the line of the upper bank of the Danube and there are a few riverside towns and villages that serve as starting points for an exploration of the Börzsöny Hills behind them. **Nagymaros** stands directly opposite Visegrád (see page 187), and provides the rail link (and then the ferry across the river) for visiting the former royal capital. You'll need an active imagination to envisage the town that prospered here during the Middle Ages, bolstered by the significant status of its neighbour across the water and lined with the mansions of nobles. The Turkish occupation resulted in destruction and depopulation, and plague swept through in 1709; German immigrants started again in 1715, and many among today's raspberry-growing population of 5,000 are their descendants. The main point of historical interest is the Gothic-Baroque Roman Catholic church (*Szent Imre tér*), standing on the upper side of the rail track from the ferry pier. Its 14th-century nave was reconstructed after the Turks left, but the tower of 1509 is as originally constructed. You can follow a path leading to the Julianus Lookout Tower on Hegyestető (Pointed Peak), which gets the better of 480m and offers a spectacular view of the river's curve. Standard Mahart ferry services to Esztergom (see page 191) also stop at Nagymaros (*docking ten mins later than the stop at Visegrád; return departure 17.40; ⚓ sgl/rtn 1,790/2,685Ft*).

There are several hiking trails running around and through **Zebegény**, which sits at the point where the Danube makes its first charge south. This is another fruit-growing town, the good times of wine production brought to a halt by the phylloxera epidemic. If you're interested in architecture, its Roman Catholic church (*Petőfi tér*) is an absolute unmissable, an invigorating piece of late-Secessionist design by the Transylvanian Károly Kós and Béla Jánszky in 1908. A ten-minute walk or so behind the church along Szőnyi utca brings up the István Szőnyi Memorial Museum (*Bartóky u. 7;* ℡ *27 370104;* ⚓ *600/300Ft;* ⊕ *Jan–Oct Tue–Sun 10.00–16.00*); this was the house of Szőnyi himself, a leading 20th-century Hungarian artist who spent his life in Zebegény making use of the beautiful location to create warm and gentle canvases. A school for fine arts is hosted in its gardens during the summer.

Five kilometres further west, **Szob** lies where the Danube and the Ipoly meet, and is the railway crossing point into Slovakia – indeed, Zoltán Kodály's father was once the station master. (You cannot cross here by car, though – for that you must head 25km north to Parassapuszta.) The Börzsöny Museum (*Szent László u. 14;* ℡ *27 372037;* ⚓ *600/300Ft;* ⊕ *Tue–Sun 09.00–17.00*) has carved tombstones, ethnographic costumes and a wildlife display, while (like Zebegény) the town offers a variety of summer programmes during the Danube Bend Art Days.

BÖRZSÖNY HILLS

The Börzsöny Hills lie on the northern side of the Danube, and are part of the Danube-Ipoly National Park. There were once over 20 fortresses in the range, including the formidable Nógrád Castle. Lightning hit this castle in 1685, igniting the gunpowder store, and leading to the surrender of the Turkish occupiers. The best known, however, is that on top of the **Drégelypalánk peak** close to the northern border with Slovakia; here in 1552 a force of 150 under the command of György Szondi held out valiantly for three days before being overrun and killed by a far superior Turkish force. (You can get there along Road 2, or by train from Budapest, Vác or Balassagyarmat.) Numerous springs feed the local habitat, creating a damp and mild microclimate in the valleys. Among the fauna, the spotted salamander is found only in the Börzsöny, while a significant population of the strictly protected white-backed woodpecker can be found in the beech woods at the centre. The hills are characterised by volcanic cones with sharp ridges and steep sides; some of the lava trails are still visible and there are areas of boulders deposited during the Ice Age. The highest peak (and most testing to climb) is that of Csóványos at over 900m, while the most beautiful meadows are the Királyrét, around the Foltánkereszt, and the Ispán Meadow. Buy a copy of Cartographia's *Börzsöny-hegység* (1:40,000) before setting out, which shows the trails and accommodation options.

Királyrét, named after Mátyás who used to hunt in the region, is a popular weekend destination because it is served by a 55-year-old narrow-gauge railway (*www.kisvasut-kiralyret.hu;* ⚓ *adult sgl/rtn 600/1,000Ft, concessions 350/600Ft; Apr–Oct up to 7 daily, rest of yr up to 5 at w/ends only*) running 10km through the Valley of the Morgó from **Kismaros**; the Kismaros main station (across the road) is on the line running through Vác from Budapest Nyugati. Királyrét has an education centre (*Szokolya, Királyrét;* ℡ *27 585625*) that organises programmes for schools or nature enthusiasts. In addition, there are several hiking trails; you can strike east to **Nógrád**, southwest to **Kóspallag** or northwest to the peaks of **Magas-Tax**, **Nagy**

Hideg and finally **Csóványos**. The latter route continues around to the village of **Diósjenő** (to the north of Nógrád). Diósjenő is the alternative departure point for hikes, particularly for those climbing Csóványos; its railway station is on a branch that breaks north shortly before Kismaros, and can be reached from Vác and Budapest. Kóspallag is worth mentioning because 6km northwest of it is the second of the hills' narrow-gauge railways, running from Nagyirtás to Nagybörzsöny (*www.kisvasut-kiralyret.hu; ✍ adult sgl/rtn 650/1,200Ft, concessions 350/600Ft; 3 trains a day Jun–Aug Fri–Sun, Apr–May & Oct Sat–Sun*). (Alternatively, start from Nagybörzsöny – take the train from Budapest Nyugati to Szob, take bus 355 from stop number 2 to Nagybörzsöny, and from there it's a 15-min walk to the narrow-gauge.) The Szent Orbán Erdei Hotel (*Kóspallag-Nagyírtáspuszta;* ✆ *27 378047; www.szentorban.hu; 31 rooms; dbl 30,800–43,800Ft, suite 79,700Ft, apt (for 4) 61,100Ft*) is an atmospheric, wood-cabin-like hotel set deep in the forest near Kóspallag (follow signs from the village). There's a swimming pool, saunas and wellness facilities. Not cheap, but worth the money if you have it.

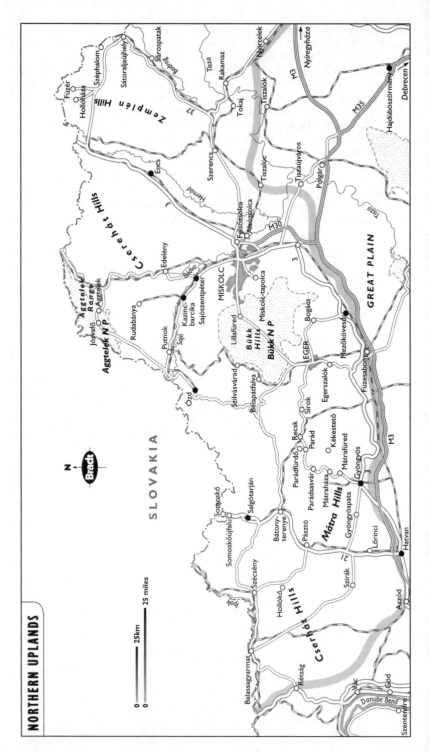

NORTHERN UPLANDS

5

Northern Uplands

Castles and caves, wildlife, wine and a valley of beautiful women – what more could you wish for? The Northern Uplands fill an area between the Great Plain and the border with Slovakia, extending in a west–east direction from the Danube Bend to Sátoraljaújhely. This is hill country, the Bükk and Mátra holding the highest peaks, and a place of forests and valleys, clear springs, startling rock formations and caves dripping with creamy stones. Some areas were once the hub of the iron industry, thriving on ore mined from the hills, while others – notably Eger and the Tokaj-Hegyalja region – represent vinicultural strongholds. A fierce national pride burns among the towns and villages of the region; it was a centre of resistance to Turks and Habsburgs, and the grasp on folk tradition is firmer here than elsewhere in Hungary. For all the passion, though, this is a spot to relax – to quaff a glass of wine after a day spent cycling, hiking or riding a narrow-gauge railway.

The Cserhát Hills Region

While the Cserhát Hills were formed at the same time as the Mátra (see page 220), fashioned from the same material (andesite) and by the same violent volcanic forces, they are a poor relation when it comes to hiking opportunities. They are stunted in height by comparison, and much of their original forest cover has been cleared for ploughing or housing. As they look over the 2,500km² of Nógrád County, they instead promise cultural highlights – notably the colourful peasant traditions of the Palóc people from the Cserhátalja, most famously preserved in the UNESCO-protected village of Hollókő.

BALASSAGYARMAT

At the border with Slovakia, 80km from Budapest, Balassagyarmat's unwieldy eponym is the result of the coming together of the names 'Gyarmat' (one of the seven tribes that conquered the Carpathian Basin in the 9th century) and 'Balassa', the family who later owned the area. There are scanty remains on Bástya utca of the fortress they built following the devastating Mongol rampage of 1241. The castle was eventually destroyed by the Turks in 1663; in the aftermath of the Turkish occupation, an ethnically diverse population of merchants and manufacturers filled the vacuum, and in 1790 the town was made the capital of Nógrád County. Harder times were to come. The Treaty of Trianon divided the place, with the portion north of the River Ipoly absorbed into Czechoslovakia, while in 1950 the town's status as main county seat was lost to Salgótarján.

Nevertheless, Balassagyarmat retains its claim to being the capital of the Palóc region in the Cserhát Hills. The Palóc people are noted for their strong folk traditions and for their dialect – the latter unusual (and essentially unexplained) in Hungary, where speech and accents are remarkably consistent from region to

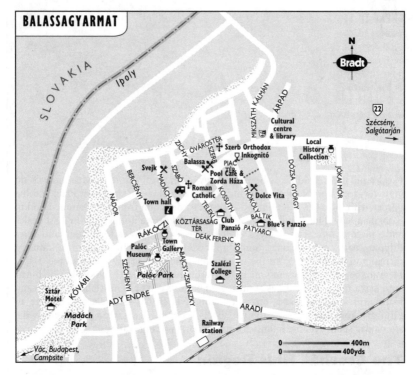

BALASSAGYARMAT

region. The origins of the Palóc Hungarians remain something of a mystery; some believe that they are of ancient Hungarian ancestry, while others argue a Mongol link. Whichever is true, cultural expression burned strong in generations past, who produced decorative furniture and donned distinctive colourful costume. It is rare now to see such dress worn in everyday life – the inhabitants of Hollókő (see page 213) are the exceptions that prove the rule in doing so, and attract the tourist pound as a consequence – but you can see examples of it in Balassagyarmat's Palóc Museum.

GETTING THERE AND AWAY The **railway station** is located 500m from Köztársaság tér, at the southern end of Bajcsy-Zsilinszky utca, while the **bus station** is centrally located behind the town hall. Trains run to Balassagyarmat from Vác (14 daily) and Aszód (nine daily), the former journey taking a little over two hours with the latter around half an hour quicker. (From the capital, trains to Aszód depart from Budapest Keleti, while to Vác they run from Budapest Nyugati.) From Balassagyarmat, you can catch trains further northeast to Szécsény and Ipolytarnóc. There are up to 15 buses a day from Budapest's Árpád híd, travelling via Vác; the total journey takes about two hours, which makes it a quicker proposition than the train (once changes are factored in). Frequent services run to/from Szécsény and Salgótarján.

INFORMATION AND OTHER PRACTICALITIES

Tourinform Köztársaság tér 6; ☎ 35 500640;
e balassagyarmat@tourinform.hu;

www.balassagyarmat.hu. Housed in the former County Hall.

Rákóczi fejedelem útja contains the main **shops**, a couple of **banks** and a **post office**.

WHERE TO STAY, EAT AND DRINK

✗ **Balassa** Rákóczi fejedelem útja 34–36; ↘ 35 500321. Fairly spartan restaurant serving low-priced East European dishes. ⊕ *Mon–Thu 10.00–2.00, Fri–Sat 10.00–24.00.*

🏠 **Blue's Panzió** (10 rooms) Baltik Frigyes u. 3; ↘ 35 300189; e blues@enternet.hu. Cosy, family-run place with restaurant, bar & terrace over the summer. *Dbls 12,000–19,200Ft.*

🛖 **Campsite** Kővári út 13; ↘ 35 300404. As well as pitching space, there are 3 cabins for 12 guests, & tennis courts & a lido next door. ⊕ *Jun 15–Aug 31.*

🏠 **Club Panzió** (18 rooms) Teleki út 14; ↘ 35 301824. Central & simple, with nicely appointed rooms, & a bar & moderately priced restaurant to wet whistles & silence stomach rumbles. *Dbl 8,000Ft, apt 20,000Ft.*

✗ **Dolce Vita** Thököly u. 20; ↘ 35 300810. Has a family feel, & cooks pizzas to eat in or take away. *Pizza 320–650Ft;* ⊕ *Mon–Thu 11.00–22.00, Fri–Sat 11.00–23.00, Sun 17.00–22.00.*

♀ **Inkognitó** Tihanyi u. 1. A suitably understated & dark little bar near the market on Thököly utca. ⊕ *Mon–Thu 08.00–22.00, Fri–Sat 08.00–24.00.*

▱ **Pool Café** Rákóczi fejedelem útja 28; ↘ 35 302898. Café with games machines & pool tables; in a courtyard at the end of an alleyway leading from the main high street. ⊕ *Mon–Thu 09.00–23.00, Fri–Sat 09.00–02.00, Sun 14.00–22.00.*

✗ **Svejk** Szabó Lőrinc u. 16; ↘ 35 300999. Specialises in food Magyar & Czech from its position behind the bus station. ⊕ *daily 11.00–22.30.*

🏠 **Sztár Motel** (8 rooms) Kővári út 12; ↘ 35 301152; e sztarmotel@is.hu. En-suite dbl rooms & a cheap restaurant ⊕ 24hrs; to the west of the centre. *Dbl 5,500Ft.*

✗ **Zorda Háza** Rákóczi fejedelem útja 28. Pizza joint in the same courtyard as Pool Café. ⊕ *Mon–Thu 11.00–22.00, Fri–Sat 17.00–23.00, Sun 17.00–22.00.*

WHAT TO SEE AND DO Located in an early-20th-century building in a green park to the southwest of Köztársaság tér, the **Palóc Museum** (*Palóc liget 1;* ↘ *35 300168;* 🏛 *600/300Ft;* ⊕ *Tue–Sat 10.00–16.00*) is the town's prime attraction. Devoted to the lives lived by the Palóc peasants of Nógrád County – from the chores of the house to festival feasts – it features folk art, traditional costumes and everyday utensils. Among the early crafted furniture is a *szuszék* – an etched chest used for storing grain – together with corner benches bearing paintings of noble hussars. Next to it is an **outdoor exhibition** (*closed Oct–Apr*) of outhouses and white thatched buildings typical of the Palóc architectural style, and including a reconstruction of the church at Szanda and a 200-year-old home dismantled and transported here from Karancslapujtő.

Köztársaság tér runs across the northern end of Bajcsy-Zsilinszky utca. The **Town Gallery** (*Városi Képtár; Köztársaság tér 5;* ↘ *35 300186;* 🏛 *100/50Ft;* ⊕ *Tue–Sun 10.00–12.00, 13.00–17.00*) is painted in gaudy turquoise and displays the works of Vladimir Szabó (the painter and graphic artist born in Balassagyarmat in 1905) and other modern artists of Nógrád County. Opposite stands the Neoclassical former **County Hall** (*Köztársaság tér 6*), completed in 1835, and now housing the Tourinform. Either side of its entrance are plaques devoted to two of Hungary's great 19th-century writers. A carving of a man wreathed in a serpent's coils reminds us that Imre Madách (1823–64) – responsible for the universal drama *The Tragedy of Man* – once worked here as a notary, judge and county chief assessor. This was also the workplace of the outstanding novelist Kálmán Mikszáth (1847–1910), who garnered material for his humorous satires on the Hungarian nobility. There are more substantial statues of each near by, and the names of the lettered men are linked once more in the **Imre Madách Town Library** and **Kálmán Mikszáth Cultural Centre**, both behind the arching brick façade at Rákóczi fejedelem útja 50 (↘ *35 300622;* ⊕ *Mon–Fri 08.00–20.00, Sat 13.00–20.00*). The latter contains a gallery named after the graphic artist Endre Horváth, whose work included coins and stamps depicting the scenery of the Palóc region and who lived in the town. On the other side of Madách utca is the immaculately painted **Town Hall**, Eclectic in style and constructed in 1914, while facing that is a monument of a smiling, bare-

5

breasted female warrior spearing a snarling mythical beast – honouring Balassagyarmat's title as the bravest town ('**Civitas Fortissima**'), earned after citizens helped to drive Slovak forces from the region in 1919.

The **Roman Catholic church** (*Rákóczi fejedelem útja*) was built between 1741 and 1746; it holds a barrel-like oak pulpit, along with the relics of Szent Felícián in a glass sarcophagus, donated by Pope Clement XIII in the 18th century. The **Serb Orthodox church** (*Szerb u. 5;* ☎ *35 300622;* ☞ *free admission;* ⏰ *Tue–Sun 14.00–18.00*) on Óváros tér culminates in an onion spire and now serves as a small gallery space. For the **Collection of Local History** (*Helytörténeti Gyűjtemény; Csillag-ház, Rákóczi fejedelem útja 107;* ☎ *35 300663;* ☞ *300/150Ft;* ⏰ *Tue–Sun 08.00–12.00, 13.00–16.30*), head further eastward along the town's main road to an L-shaped 18th-century mansion, set back on the right-hand side and once home of Horváth (see page 209).

SZÉCSÉNY

Move a little under 20km eastwards along the Ipoly Valley and you'll reach Szécsény, a town whose diminutive size belies its historical importance. The town is first mentioned in written records of the 13th century, when a villager sued his neighbours to the value of ten oxen. A touch more significant, however, is the fact that in 1705 a Diet was held here in Borjúpást Meadow (just north of the centre) at which the Transylvanian Ferenc Rákóczi II was declared the country's ruling prince (and leader of the independence struggle against the Habsburgs). It's a peaceful spot with several sights deserving of attention – notably a Baroque mansion, a Gothic monastery and a leaning fire tower.

GETTING THERE AND AWAY The **train station** lies on Vasút utca, 1,500m north of the centre along Rákóczi út, and is on the line connecting Balassagyarmat and Ipolytarnóc (up to seven trains a day); you will need to change at Balassagyarmat for trains to/from Vác or Aszód. The **bus station** is on Király utca, immediately to the east of Fő tér. There are nine direct buses on weekdays from Budapest's Árpád híd (taking a little under 2½ hours), as well as indirect services (with a change at Balassagyarmat); buses from Budapest Stadion require a change at Salgótarján. There are regular buses to Balassagyarmat and Salgótarján, and a handful to Hollókő (taking half an hour).

INFORMATION AND OTHER PRACTICALITIES

🖼 **Tourinform** Ady Endre u. 4; ☎ 32 370777; ⓔ szecseny@tourinform.hu; www.szecseny.hu. Opposite the bastion (see page 212), in the

Kézművesház (Craftsman's House – there is a small exhibition of local craftworks, with items for sale). ⏰ Mon–Fri 08.00–18.00, Sat–Sun 10.00–18.00.

A **bank** and a **post office** sit either side of the town hall, just to the south of Fő tér.

 WHERE TO STAY, EAT AND DRINK Szécsény certainly does not spoil you for accommodation choices.

✗ **Al Capone** Gábor Áron út 1; ☎ 32 372606. Around 60 types of pizza to choose from (420–780Ft). ⏰ Sun–Thu 11.00–23.00, Fri–Sat 11.00–24.00.

🏠 **Bástya Panzió** (18 rooms) Ady Endre u. 14; ☎ 32 372427; www.bastyapanzio.hu. The Bástya's

building dates to 1664, & was where the servants of Forgách Mansion curled up for the night. It became a pension in 1991, & is comfortable enough without being anything to shout about. The restaurant (⏰ daily 12.00–22.00) serves fair regional fare, & there's a disco, pizzeria & bar (see

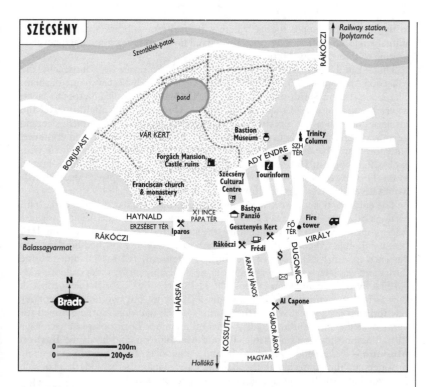

SZÉCSÉNY

Railway station, Ipolytarnóc

Szentlélek-patak

RÁKÓCZI

pond

VÁR KERT

BORJUPAST

Bastion Museum

Trinity Column

Forgách Mansion, Castle ruins

ADY ENDRE

SZH TÉR

Szécsény Cultural Centre

Tourinform

Franciscan church & monastery

XI INCE PÁPA TÉR

Bástya Panzió

HAYNALD

ERZSÉBET TÉR

Iparos

Gesztenyés Kert

FŐ TÉR

Fire tower

RÁKÓCZI

Rákóczi

Frédi

KIRÁLY

Balassagyarmat

ARANY JÁNOS

DUGONICS

N

Bradt

HÁRSFA

KOSSUTH

GÁBOR ÁRON

Al Capone

0 ——— 200m
0 ——— 200yds

Hollókő

MAGYAR

---

opposite). *Sgl 5,500Ft, dbl 8,500Ft, trpl 11,500Ft, quad 15,000Ft. Varying discounts for children, according to age.*

🍴 **Frédi Cukrászda** Rákóczi út 85; ☎ 32 370372. Cakes & ice creams, & a few pavement tables. ⊕ *Mon–Sun 09.00–18.00.*

✖ **Gesztenyés Kert** Rákóczi út 87; ☎ 32 372600. The interior is pink & vibrant, but head instead for its large chestnut-shaded garden. There's a barbecue & live music out here in summer months. Mainly Hungarian food, with some international dishes. *Mains avg 900Ft;* ⊕ *Sun–Thu 08.00–21.00, Fri–Sat 08.00–22.00.*

✖ **Iparos** Erzsébet tér 3; ☎ 32 370091. Like the rest of the town's restaurants, there's nothing decadent or luxurious here. The Iparos stands near the Franciscan church, & serves Palóc specialities in

understated surroundings. *Mains avg 900Ft;* ⊕ *Tue–Sat 11.30–22.00.*

✖ **Paradiso Disco Bar & Pizzeria** Ady Endre u. 14; ☎ 06 20 912 6422; http://paradiso.gyaloglo.hu. The disco (affiliated to the Bástya Panzió) offers Sat-night cheesiness & seediness aplenty, with theme nights & dance shows that feature much female skin. *Disco* ⊕ *Sat 21.00–05.00.*

✖ **Rákóczi** Rákóczi út 95; ☎ 32 370277. No-frills bar & canteen restaurant selling cheap Hungarian cuisine (*mains all under 1,000Ft*). There's something of a youth-centre atmosphere, & if you're intolerant of listening to kids playing table football while you eat, it's probably best avoided. On corner of Rákóczi út & Ady Entre u. *Restaurant* ⊕ *Mon–Thu 11.00–20.00, Fri–Sat 11.00–16.00; bar* ⊕ *11.00–22.00 daily.*

WHAT TO SEE AND DO The bright-yellow, Baroque **Forgách Mansion** (*Forgách-kastély; Ady Endre u. 7;* ☎ *32 370 143; www.museum.hu/szecseny/kubinyi*) was erected in 1770 from the stones of the medieval castle that previously filled the site (see page 212). Inside now is the **Kubinyi Ferenc Museum** (🎟 *600/300Ft;* ⊕ *Tue–Sun 10.00–16.00*), named after a palaeontologist of the Reform era from Ipolytarnóc. Among the exhibits are items detailing the archaeology of Nógrád County, including a reconstruction of a Neolithic house, Bronze Age tools and jewellery, and Turkish swords and stirrups dating to the Ottoman occupation. Taxidermy is to the fore in the upper rooms, where – from ducks to bears – you'll find the animal kingdom stuffed. There are also carved horns and long guns, paraphernalia relating to three famous Hungarian hunters.

There can be few Europeans whom Buddhists revere as saints, but the collection (🎫 *adult 140Ft*) contained in the gatehouse is dedicated to one of them. The Transylvanian **Sándor Csoma Kőrösi** (1784–1842) travelled on foot to Tibet, where he was convinced there were monastic chronicles that might unravel the mysteries of Hungarian ancestry. He spent nearly a decade in the country, sleeping in unheated monks' cells in temperatures as low as minus 16°C, and compiled both the first Tibetan–English dictionary and a book of Tibetan grammar with explanatory notes in 16 languages. He eventually died of malaria, and was buried in the Himalayas. Some of his original artefacts are here, displayed in a cell that would have been typical of his humble and chilly quarters.

The entrance ticket to the Kőrösi exhibition also allows access to the two extant bastions of the medieval **Szécsény Castle**. Foundations for the original fortress were probably sunk in the 14th century; the structures that remain date to the 16th century, though, when the castle was an important link in a fortified border chain designed to resist expansion of the Turkish empire. It fell several times to the Turks, and was later a place of struggle during the 17th-century independence wars led first by Bocskai and then (against the Habsburgs) by Gábor Bethlen. Most of the castle was eventually destroyed by the Habsburgs, but two northern **corner bastions** survived. That within the grounds of the mansion can be climbed for views over the surrounding fields – where the famous Diet took place (see page 210). The northeastern one stands 100m down the road, and holds the **Bastion Museum** – comprising a set of stocks and some other chains used to incarcerate prisoners in the dungeon at the bastion base. The park behind the Forgách Mansion has a small pond, and is a pleasant spot for a stroll.

A short distance to the southwest of Forgách Mansion is a **Franciscan church and monastery** (*Ferences templom és kolostor; Haynald Lajos út 9;* ✆ *32 370076; requested donation* 🎫 *500/250Ft;* 🕐 *Tue–Sat 10.00–16.00*), constructed in 1332 to house 12 mendicant monks. The current Baroque façade is the result of early-modern face-lifts, but inside there are significant original Gothic features, including carved animals, rosettes and an octagonal pillar in the sacristy. Ferenc Rákóczi is said to have prayed in the oratory above the sacristy. Looking around, you will see that some of the statues are faceless, their visages cut away by the Turks when they used the church for worship; there is a further reminder of Ottoman occupation in the *mihrab* (prayer niche), set into the south wall and the

PALÓC COSTUME

The Palóc people form an ethnic group that – in pockets such as Bugac, Rimóc and Hollókő – serves as one of the last examples of living folk tradition. The most visible aspect of such tradition is in costume; while it is rare now to see folk dress worn in everyday life, it is brought out during festivals. The rich Palóc garments probably originate from the mid-19th century (in contrast to the medieval-style garb of the Matyó people of Mezőkövesd). Women don several layers of embroidered short underskirts – young girls as many as 20 – over which are added decorated aprons. Unmarried girls wear ribbons and braid their hair, while wives cover their heads with scarves. Strings of pearls are hung around their necks, and the ensemble is completed with a pair of high-heeled boots. The costume of the menfolk is a touch less extravagant (though impressive still), with black trousers, embroidered shirts, colourful belts, felt jackets, black boots and upturned hats.

northernmost remnant of Turkish architecture in the country. During the communist era, the Franciscan order was disbanded and a single parish priest was charged with caring for the buildings; since 1990, novice Franciscan monks have come here to undertake a year's quiet contemplation. A smartly dressed guide will lead you around the complex, but he speaks no English. (You may be lucky enough – as we were – to pass a monk prepared to break his silent vow, and answer a few whispered questions in English before he hurries guiltily on his way.)

During the 19th century, a lookout would keep watch from the town's two-storey **fire tower** (*Rákóczi út 86;* ❧ *32 370199*); a further storey was later added after the new town hall blocked the view. However, it would take a dedicated sentry to take up position now in this tilting tower, whose foundations have subsided in the clay beneath. To the north is an 18th-century **Trinity Column**, placed in grateful thanks for the passing of plague, while behind that is the oldest serving **pharmacy** (*gyógyszertár; Rákóczi út 67*) in Nógrád County, snuffing out sniffles since 1741.

HOLLÓKŐ

Hungarians are proud of Hollókő; as they watch the fading ways of bygone days – and sense a cultural heritage being lost – this little village 15km southeast of Szécsény serves as a defiant last hurrah in the face of historical pressures and the march of modern progress. Here the 400 villagers – who average over 50 years old – speak with the Palóc dialect, they celebrate the Palóc Easter Festival, they live in traditional vernacular houses, and some still wear Palóc costumes that they've made themselves. It is undoubtedly a beautiful place, snug in a valley and protected by the forested Cserhát Hills. When it was added to the UNESCO World Heritage List in 1987, it was the first village in the world to receive such an accolade.

And yet from the moment you pay 500Ft to leave your vehicle in the large car park at the village entrance, something doesn't quite ring true. The peasant rusticity feels contrived, as though the village is forever competing in a 'Hungary in Bloom' contest, and there is an inevitable tension in adhering to a sleepy, past-century existence while basking under the attention of coach loads of 21st-century tourists. Of course, the collective attempt to guard folk traditions is laudable, deeply valuable and inherently fascinating; however, the village is equally a testament to a shrewd understanding of modern wants, and the truth of a life lived apart from that world is as illusory as the truth purveyed by the makers of reality television programmes.

Settlement of the village dates back to the 13th century, when the castle was built on Szár-hegy (Stalk Hill) in the aftermath of the Mongol invasion. As with all castles worth the name, there is a legend that goes with it. A maiden was supposedly abducted by András Kacsics, the main landowner of the area; her nurse – who happened to be a witch – arranged for the devil to secure the maiden's release. The devil sent ravens to rescue her and demolish the warlord's fort; with the stones, the birds constructed the castle here – hence Hollókő, or 'Raven Stone'. The ravens subsequently kept watch over the damsel as she ruled from her new castle. It is said that the women of the village are her descendants, and that the ravens continue to protect them from the unwanted advances of men. Gents, you have been warned!

Until the 20th century, the houses of the village were thatched, and fire ravaged them on several occasions. After the last of these infernos in 1909, the buildings were restored with tiled roofs. Beyond that, however, the 58 protected structures in the Old Village (Ófalu) remain faithful to the layout of 17th-century Palóc peasant homes, with wooden verandas, protruding roofs and three distinct rooms. The Old Village consists of two streets running either side of the church, and

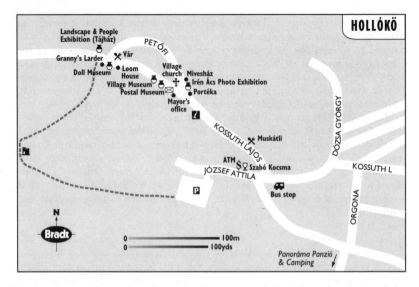

makes a romantic ramble; there are also easy marked trails snaking around the village and leading up to the castle. Be mindful that the day closes early here, and it is generally as dead as a doornail after 20.00.

GETTING THERE AND AWAY The **bus** stop is at the southeastern end of Kossuth Lajos utca. There is a solitary 15.15 service direct from Budapest Stadion via Pásztó (taking just over 2 hours), which is an option only if you wish to stay overnight; alternatively, an earlier one at 09.00 involves a change at Pásztó (be aware you'll wait an hour for the connection). There are four buses from Árpád híd via Szécsény (with a 20-minute connection delay) at 07.10, 12.35, 16.30 and 17.35. Buses run regularly between Hollókő and Szécsény (note the last bus back leaves at about 20.00), although there are just five on Sunday; there are up to four a day to Pásztó, and two direct between Hollókő and Salgótarján in the early morning and late evening (although otherwise you'll need to change at Szécsény or Pásztó).

If you are **driving**, take the M3 motorway from Budapest as far as Hatvan, where you pick up Road 21; the route branches off towards Hollókő just before Pásztó.

INFORMATION

Tourinform Kossuth Lajos u. 68; ☎ 32 579 011;
e holloko@tourinform.hu; www.holloko.hu;
⏰ Mon–Fri 08.00–18.00, Sat–Sun 10.00–16.00.

There is an **ATM** next to the Szabó Kocsma.

WHERE TO STAY, EAT AND DRINK Most people staying overnight do so to sleep in one of ten **traditional Palóc houses** lining Petőfi utca that can be booked through the Foundation for Hollókő (*Hollókőért Közalapítvány;* ☎ *32 579011; e kozalapitvany@holloko.hu; rooms from 7,500Ft, houses from 14,000Ft*), which shares the Tourinform office. The Tourinform can provide a list of private houses offering rooms. There are only two restaurants in Hollókő, and we wouldn't hurry back to either. Considering the village is so popular with tourists, however, the prices are as cheap as chips (which, judging by our meals here, would be greasy). Note their early closing times.

Hungary wildlife

below The crow-sized black woodpecker is Europe's largest woodpecker species (Duncan Usher/Minden Pictures/FLPA)

right Ural owls are secretive inhabitants of Hungary's northern hills and will attack any intruder near their nest site (Imagebroker/FLPA)

bottom The pygmy cormorant, smallest and rarest of Europe's cormorant species, breeds in small numbers throughout the Danube basin (Martin Woike/Minden Pictures/FLPA)

left   The great white egret (foreground) can be distinguished from the little egret (background) by its larger size and yellow base to the bill (LN)

below   Lesser grey shrikes arrive each spring from their African wintering quarters to spend summer on the *puszta* (LN)

above   European bee-eaters (*left*) and European rollers (*right*) are dazzling summer visitors to Hungary from Africa. Both species are hole-nesters, the bee-eater forming large colonies in sandbanks while the roller prefers an old tree hole (both LN)

right   In Hungary, the endangered aquatic warbler breeds only in the Hortobágy National Park (GK)

below   An intimate moment between two red-footed falcons reveals the great contrast in plumage between male (on top) and female (LN)

above   Great bustards gather at a courtship arena, or 'lek'. Around 1,200 of these enormous birds inhabit Hungary's lowlands (GK)

left   The outsized bill of a hawfinch is powerful enough to crack cherry kernels (LN)

below   Around 100,000 common cranes stop over in eastern Hungary every autumn en route to their wintering quarters in Turkey and the Middle East (GK)

right   Hungary is arguably the best country in Europe to look for the powerful saker falcon (GK)

bottom Hungary hosts key European populations of the eastern imperial eagle (*left;* GK) and white-tailed eagle (*right;* Ingo Arndt/Minden Pictures/FLPA). The latter is larger, with a shorter tail and broader wings, and generally found close to water

✘ **Muskátli** Kossuth Lajos u. 61; ✆ 32 379262. As you'd expect, the waitresses are wrapped in folk dress, & there's traditional Palóc food on the menu. The colourful terrace – rather than any great wizardry in the kitchen – gives it the edge over Vár. Mains avg 1,250Ft; 2-course set meals (inc wine, beer or coffee) 2,400Ft; ⊕ Wed–Fri 11.00–17.00, Sat 11.00–18.00, Sun 11.00–17.00.

⌂ **Panorama Panzió & Campsite** Orgona út 31; ✆ 32 379 048. Perched on a hill just to the south of the village. As well as pitches for caravans or tents, Panorama offers 9 rooms (sleeping 2–4) & 5 bungalows (for 4), all with bathrooms. There's an on-site restaurant. Panzió dbl 5,000Ft, quad 7,000Ft; bungalow 6,000Ft; camping 500Ft/pp, tent/caravan 450/600Ft.

⌷ **Teaház** Petőfi u. 4. Booth-like tea house adjacent to the church. ⊕ Tue–Sun 11.00–17.00.

✘ **Vár** Kossuth Lajos u. 93–95; ✆ 32 379029. Choose the brick-floored restaurant or its shady garden to sample fatty & rather uninspiring plates of traditional Palóc cuisine. Mains avg 1,300Ft; ⊕ 11.00–19.00 daily.

⚲ **Szabó Kocsma** The spartan, unloved 'Tailor Inn' is the only pub in the village. ⊕ daily 07.00–13.00, 14.00–20.00.

WHAT TO SEE AND DO

The church, shops and museums There are several small museums and craftshops in the Palóc houses ranged along Kossuth Lajos utca and Petőfi utca. We list them in the order they appear on a stroll starting from the lower (eastern) end of the village. Opposite the Tourinform, **Portéka** (*Kossuth Lajos u. 75*) sells examples of folk arts and crafts. Two houses further on is the **Irén Ács Photo Exhibition** (*Ács Irén Fotóművész; Kossuth Lajos u. 79;* ⊕ *Apr–Oct 10.00–17.00 daily;* ✆ *120/60Ft*); as well as showcasing the superb photos of Palóc villages by Ács, the exhibition also displays wood carvings by local master Ferenc Kelemen (who lives next door). For further information, contact the village hall (*Kossuth Lajos u. 74;* ✆ *32 379255*).

Just north of here Kossuth Lajos utca passes to the left of the **village church**. A medieval predecessor was razed by the Turks, and the current building dates to 1889. It is elegant in its plainness, a lime-washed lower portion capped with a brown wooden spire. Inside are a flag and a crucifix from the 18th century, donated by the Museum of Christianity in Esztergom.

The **Postal Museum** (*Kossuth Lajos u. 80;* ✆ *32 379288; www.postamuzeum.hu;* ✆ *400/200Ft;* ⊕ *Apr–Oct Tue–Sun 10.00–17.00*) is devoted to the postmen of Nógrád County, who had more to contend with than dogs barking at letter boxes – among the exhibits are weapons they had to carry to deter attacks from highwaymen. Next door is the **Village Museum** (*Falumúzeum; Kossuth Lajos u. 82;* ✆ *32 379258;* ✆ *250/100Ft;* ⊕ *Mar 15–Nov 15 daily 10.00–18.00*), which allows you to look around the typical layout of a peasant house: three rooms, including a 'Sunday room' at the front (where beds were stored and guests entertained), a living area (where the family slept and spent the majority of their time), and a kitchen. There is a 19th-century oak winepress in the yard.

Kosaras (*Kossuth Lajos u. 86;* ⊕ *10.00–17.00 daily*) sells charming handmade goods, including children's prams, rocking chairs and baskets; next to it is **Csuhé Csodák** (⊕ *Tue–Sun 10.00–18.00*), where you can shop for crafted lamp shades, wine-bottle holders and bags. The **Loom House** (*Szövőház; Kossuth Lajos u. 94;* ✆ *150/100Ft;* ⊕ *daily 10.00–17.00*) is a workshop containing two weaving machines – one of which harks back to old methods of textile production, while the other has a flying shuttle. There is a small shop.

Maybe we've watched too many horror movies, but **doll museums** give us the heeby-jeebies; hopefully the multi-layered Palóc dresses worn by the china-faced specimens here (*Babamúzeum; Kossuth Lajos u. 96;* ✆ *32 379088;* ✆ *150/100Ft;* ⊕ *Apr–Sep daily 10.00–17.00*) would slow them down if they sprang to life and gave us chase. Drop in at **Granny's Larder** (*Nagymama Kamrája; Kossuth Lajos u. 98; Mon 12.00–18.00 Tue–Sun 10.00–18.00*) for homemade pickles and honey; the entrance is from the back. The Tájház contains a **Landscape and People**

If you're after a little aristocratic, old-world luxury during your stay in Hungary, you could do worse than check yourself into the Baroque **Hotel Kastély** (*Szirák, Petőfi u. 26;* ✆ *32 485300;* e *kastelyszirak@globonet.hu; 25 rooms; dbls from 9,950Ft/pp, suite from 14,450Ft/pp*) for a night or two. Sitting on the southern slopes of the Cserhát Hills, it's 90km from Budapest and 26km from Pásztó, and was originally built in 1748 by Tamás Királyfalvi Róth. His daughter married the cultured Count József Teleki – a man no stranger to the Parisian court of Louis XV, and one who numbered Voltaire and Rousseau among his acquaintances – and the pile became the Róth-Teleki Castle. The village itself offers little for those after excitement; this is a place to come to be peaceful. The surrounding parkland is well tended and there are 18th-century paintings on the walls of the opulent banqueting hall; the rooms themselves are immaculate, and the suites have period features. In addition, there's a library, sauna, solarium, pub, international restaurant (*mains avg 1,800Ft*), and opportunities for tennis (*free for hotel guests, 1,500Ft/hr for non-guests*) and horse-riding (*3,000Ft/hr*). They can even arrange hot-air ballooning. The park and the restaurant of the castle are open for visitors too.

To get there, take the bus from Budapest Stadion; there are up to 15 daily, five of these direct, and the journey takes up to two hours. Indirect services require changes at Aszód or Hatvan, among others. Buses at weekends are less frequent. There are also buses from Pásztó. The bus stops outside the village church (300m away).

Exhibition (*Táj és a Nép; Kossuth Lajos u. 99–100;* ✆ *160/120Ft;* ⊕ *Apr–Oct Tue, Thu–Sun 09.00–17.00, Nov–Mar Tue, Thu–Sun 10.00–15.00*) featuring the natural history of the 141ha Eastern Cserhát Landscape Protection Reserve – the country's smallest – that surrounds the village.

A little shop at Kossuth Lajos utca 105 (⊕ *Wed–Sun 10.00–17.00*) peddles local crafts (pottery, candles and dolls), while **Mívesház** (*Petőfi u. 4;* ✆ *32 379257;* ⊕ *Tue–Sun 11.00–17.00*) offers a broader selection including tablecloths, wine, peasant costumes and pop-up puppets.

Hollókő Castle and some walking trails

The **fortress** (*www.hollokoivar.hu;* ✆ *600/300Ft, family 1,800Ft;* ⊕ *Apr–Oct 10.00–17.30 daily, Nov Sat–Sun 10.00–15.30*) on the volcanic-rock hilltop above the village was constructed in the 13th century by the local landowner, András Kacsics. During the period of Turkish occupation, it fell alternately into the hands of Turks and Hungarians before the Polish King Jan Sobieski finally banished the Ottomans in 1683. When the Habsburg Leopold I decreed that Hungarian fortifications should be demolished two decades later, Hollókő Castle had already fallen into disrepair and was consequently left alone. After a programme of reconstruction in 1996, it is the best surviving example of 13th-century defences in Nógrád County; there is now an exhibition showing some of the finds made during excavation.

The hill is also worth visiting for its views – over narrow agricultural plots and forested areas that are steadily reclaiming land formerly cleared for pasture. You can follow **trails** leading up there either from the car park or from opposite the Tájház on the western section of Kossuth Lajos utca. The walks take around 15 minutes, but are fairly steep in places. If you'd like a closer view of the local habitat of the Cserhát region, a longer green 'study trail' – with information boards – follows a loop into the nature conservation area and around the northern side of Stalk Hill. It can be picked up a few hundred metres along the castle trail (from either starting point), and is around 5km in length. For more information, contact the **Bükk National Park Directorate** in Eger (✆ *36 411581*).

FESTIVALS AND EVENTS The best time to visit is during one of the festivals, when the villagers are dressed to the nines in traditional costumes. During the Easter Festival (*late Mar/Apr*), there is song, dance, folk crafts and food aplenty. In addition, the Raspberry Festival and Nógrád Folklore Festival take place in July, the Castle Tournament – with medieval jousting – in August, and the Grape Harvest Parade in September.

LUDÁNYHALÁSZI AND IPOLYTARNÓC

If you fancy your history more natural than human, there are a couple of convenient excursions within a relatively short distance north of Szécsény. The nearer of these is **Ludányhalászi**, which stakes a claim to being central Europe's longest village; on its western side lies a series of lakes fed by the River Ipoly. The wildcat prowls the area, while in the waters anglers can try for pike, catfish and pike perch (*contact the Öreg Potyka Fishing Association for further information;* \ *32 556011*). Or you can simply enjoy the sight of sand-martins careering above the surface at dusk. You won't have to wait long for a bus to take you the 4km from Szécsény; alternatively, it will take under ten minutes by train.

Follow the Ipoly for another 18km as it wriggles north, and you'll reach the village of **Ipolytarnóc**. There are up to 11 trains daily, running from Balassagyarmat via Szécsény; there are buses from Szécsény, most of them requiring a connection change, and regular direct services from Salgótarján (taking about an hour). You'll need to walk 2km up to the visitor centre on alighting at the village. Twenty million years ago, a massive volcanic eruption buried the area in hot, fine ash, and – like Pompeii – in doing so entombed a prehistoric time capsule. In the Csapás Valley, 2km from the village, are petrified the delicate marks of that prehistoric period, including leaf impressions and the footprints of birds and rhinoceros, as well as the trunks of massive pine trees and the teeth of sharks that had patrolled the waters of an earlier tropical sea. There are trails on which to explore this protected geological site (*Ipolytarnóc, Ősmaradványok TT;* \ *32 454113;* e *itarnoc@gmail.com; www.web.kvvm.hu/ipolytarnoc*). The **biological study paths** (*Tue–Sun 09.00–14.30*) – of either 2km or 4km in length – can be followed unaccompanied, and take in some of the native species that are returning after deforestation during the 18th century. However, it's on the 800m-long geological study trail that you'll see the fossilised imprints; this can only be visited with a guide, and takes just under an hour. The visitor centre hosts a new 4D cinema (in which your seat shakes, etc); following some EU funding, several other attractions are on the way – including a playground and treetop walkway – and the plan is to apply for UNESCO World Heritage status. Tours are available in English, and depart Tue–Sun 09.30, 10.30, 11.30, 12.30, 13.30, 14.30, 15.30, 16.00 (*Apr–Oct*) and 09.30, 10.30, 11.30, 12.30, 13.30, 14.30 (*Nov–Mar*); *&* 800/450Ft, 10-min 4D movie 950Ft.

If you want to stay in the area, the **Christina Park Hotel** (*16 rooms; Kossuth Lajos u. 56;* \ *32 454066;* e *christinaparkhotel@gmail.com; www.cphotel.hu; dbl 18,900–24,500Ft, apt 30,900–43,900Ft*) in Ipolytarnóc village is a new wellness hotel based in a former 19th-century brick factory. The modern furnishings – trying achingly hard to be fashionable – offer a contrast with the style of the original building. The sauna and jacuzzi will open shortly; there's a good-value restaurant.

SALGÓTARJÁN

J B Priestley once described a certain town as having been planned by an enemy of the human race; the phrase sprung to mind when we first saw the capital of

5

Nógrád County. It seems astonishing today that Salgótarján's 1960s facelift – when the existing houses and streets were levelled to make room for a modern city centre – won a prominent architectural award. It's a place of industrial constructions and sterile residential blocks 2km from the Slovakian border. The limited colour brought by Fő tér is drained by stark buildings and the unforgiving Rákóczi út that runs it through; there's little to see for a town of its size. Thank goodness for the forest and hills either side, which – while making the man-made scar glare angrier still by contrast – nevertheless offer respite and peaceful walks. This was where the Tarján tribe settled after the Magyar conquest, and the Salgó fortress protected the area from the 13th century. However, it was with the discovery of coal that expansion came; mining began in 1845, and related industries – iron, glass and power – soon followed. The miners have gone, but the town preserves its past with the country's first underground mining museum. A reminder of a grimmer period in the town's history is found in December 8 tér, to the south of Nógrád History Museum, where a monument of an agonised, modern-day martyr pays respect to demonstrators killed by secret police in 1956. There are 53 names in the black marble, although these probably reflect fewer than half the actual death toll.

GETTING THERE, AWAY AND AROUND The **bus** station is just to the west of Erzsébet tér; take the subway beneath the railway track to reach the square. The **train** station is even more central. There are no direct trains from Budapest; there are up to14 services with a change at Hatvan to join the line branching northwards to Somoskőújfalu (and over the border to Luāenec in Slovakia). The train also passes through Pásztó. There are buses every 30–40 minutes from Budapest's Árpád híd and Stadion bus stations, the majority of them direct. Among the many other destinations are frequent services to Szécsény and Balassagyarmat, and to Ipolytarnóc (up to ten direct), Eger (nine), Gyöngyös (five), Hatvan (four), Hollókő (three), Miskolc (two), Parádfürdő (one). If you need a **taxi**, try 6x6 Taxis (✆ *32 666666*).

INFORMATION AND OTHER PRACTICALITIES

Ⓣ Ibusz Fő tér 6; ✆ 32 511634; e salgotarjan@ibusz.hu. Located at the back of the Karancs Hotel, on the eastern side of the square; can exchange money, book private accommodation & arrange tours to the castles (see page 220). ⊕ Mon–Fri 08.30–16.30.

Ⓒ József Attila Cultural Centre Fő tér 5; ✆ 32 310503. In the same building as the Tourinform, the cultural centre hosts performances of theatre & music, as well as exhibitions of art & photography. The poet Attila József is honoured in a Pál Kő relief in the foyer; look out too for Imre Varga's statue of another poet, Miklós Radnóti, in Fő tér outside. This

stringy Jewish figure, shown swamped in a long coat & leaning against a gate, died during a march from a labour camp in 1944. ⊕ Mon–Fri 10.00–18.00 (ticket office 14.00–18.00 daily).

Listings magazine Nógrádi Est

Ⓣ Nógrád Tourist Erzsébet tér 5; ✆ 32 310660. Can offer information & exchange money. Situated on 1st-floor walkway of the shopping arcade. ⊕ Mon–Fri 08.30–16.00, Sat 09.00–12.00.

Ⓣ Tourinform Fő tér 5; ✆ 32 512 315; e salgotarjan@tourinform.hu. ⊕ Mon–Fri 09.00–17.00, Sat 10.00–13.30.

WHERE TO STAY

🏠 Galcsik Fogadó (34 rooms) Alkotmány út 2; ✆ 32 422660; e www.galcsikhotel.hu Located 200m from the city centre, on the corner of Alkotmány út & Karancs út, the pension rooms are clean without being special. The lively restaurant (⊕ Mon–Sat 07.00–22.30, Sun 07.00–21.00; mains avg 1,000Ft) is probably the best in town, with an elevated terrace, welcoming staff & a Hungarian & international menu. Sgl 3,980–7,900Ft, dbl

5,980–10,900Ft, trpl 10,480–12,900Ft, quad 12,980–13,980Ft (higher prices for air-con).

🏠 Halász Fogadó (Tó Strand) Füleki út; ✆ 32 432400. The open-air lido — itself something of an oasis from the industrial heart — has a pension (25 rooms), motel & campsite. 3km north of the centre. Pension dbls 8,980Ft, trpl 11,480Ft; motel 1,200Ft/pp.

🏠 Karancs Hotel (48 rooms) Fő tér 6; ✆ 32 410088. The exterior is 1960s bleak, & the rooms depressingly drab. The view over the town from its roof garden is apparently beautiful. *Sgl 7,500Ft, dbl 9,300Ft, apt (for 2) 11,600Ft.*

⌂ **Kulacs Szálloda** Bartók Béla út 14; ☎ 32 310993; e pentasystem@freemail.hu. A good class of hotel, with a restaurant serving Palóc & international dishes (☺ *daily 11.00–23.00; mains avg 1,500Ft*). *Sgl 9,500Ft, dbl 12,500Ft.*

⌂ **Vörösfenyö Apartman** Salgóbánya, Szapolyai út 3; ☎ 30 2196675; www.vorosfenyo-apartman.hu. Comfortable, new apartments with a great garden & a terrace. The complex is away from the centre (7km from Salgótarján, at the end of Vár út, 50m from Salgó Castle's main car park; see page 220), but you might feel that's not such a bad thing...

✗ **WHERE TO EAT AND DRINK** Galcsik and Kulacs have their own restaurants (see above).

✗ **CZZ Kisvendéglő** Fő tér 1; ☎ 32 311384. Opposite the Karancs Hotel, this is no-frills dining – the most expensive main course a trifling 1,000Ft. ☺ *Mon–Sat 07.30–21.00.*

✗ **Godó Cukrászda** Rákóczi út 12; ☎ 32 416068. An elegant terrace, good cakes, ice creams, cocktails & frothy cappuccinos with whipped cream & cinnamon. ☺ *Mon–Fri 10.00–19.00, Sat–Sun 09.00–17.00.*

✗ **La Fiesta** Pécskő út 15; ☎ 32 512622. Based over 2 floors, La Fiesta has both a restaurant & a vendéglő, & is trying hard to be the town's best place to eat. The elegant restaurant even features seafood. Located off Rákóczi út. *Mains avg 1,500Ft;* ☺ *Sun–Thu 11.30–22.00, Fri–Sat 11.30–23.00.*

✗ **Old Timers Pub** Rákóczi út 13; ☎ 32 422509. A fat chef bears a gargantuan tankard of beer at the entrance & invites you into a comfortable, informal interior. A place to eat as well as drink, the menu includes pastas, salads & Hungarian cuisine. *Mains 750–1,800Ft;* ☺ *Sun–Thu 10.00–22.00, Fri–Sat 10.00–23.00.*

♀ **Svejk Söröző** Erzsébet tér 6; ☎ 32 423191. Low-priced brews & snacks beside the railway track. ☺ *Mon–Wed 09.00–23.00, Thu–Sat 09.00–24.00, Sun 10.00–23.00.*

WHAT TO SEE AND DO Constructed in the aftermath of World War II, the building housing the **Nógrád History Museum** (*Nógrádi Történeti Múzeum; Múzeum tér 2;* ☎ *32 314169;* ☙ *600/300Ft;* ☺ *Tue–Fri 09.00–16.00, Sat 09.00–13.00*) has soft corners and a space-age feel. Inside is an exhibition devoted to the history of Nógrád County, and including the mining heritage of the area. A sculpture of Count István Széchenyi – whose progressive reforms earned him the tag 'the greatest Hungarian' – stands in front, a sleepy-eyed pelican perched above his head.

A few minutes' walk away to the west of the railway track (behind the Spar supermarket), the **Underground Mining Museum** (*Földalatti Bányamúzeum; Zemlinszky Rezső u. 1;* ☎ *32 420258;* ☙ *600/300Ft;* ☺ *Tue–Sun Oct–Mar 10.00–14.00, Apr–Sep 09.00–15.00*) preserves the memory of the town's mining past. Outdoors are the little grey coal trains and carriages, while there is further paraphernalia in the shaft itself and in a former official's flat.

The 18th-century Baroque **Roman Catholic church** (*Rákóczi út 24*) elevated above Rákóczi út has something of the fantastical castle about it, with turreted towers either side of the main gun-blue spire. It is believed that a church has stood at this site since the Árpád era. Further north on Acélgyári út, **Szent József Church** is also Roman Catholic, but forbidding and jail like. Outside it is the **Millennium Monument**, a pole bearing a Holy Crown and carved representations of significant events over Hungary's 1,000-year history.

You can take a tour of the **Glass Factory** (*Huta u. 1;* ☎ *32 410433*), a working, industrial complex to the south of December 8th tér; contact Tourinform for details. Keep an eye out for Viktor Kálló's sculpture of glass blowers outside one of the gates – a surreal depiction of faceless figures puffing coloured balloons of glass. There is a small **Jewish cemetery and Auschwitz Memorial** (*Füleki út 57*) opposite the hospital.

FESTIVALS AND EVENTS The annual celebration of jazz – the International Dixieland Festival – takes place at the beginning of May, concentrating on the cultural centre and the square outside.

SALGÓ AND SOMOSKŐ CASTLES

The crow would need to fly 7km northeast from the centre of Salgótarján to the ruins of **Salgó Castle**; *you* can take the 11B bus on its slightly longer route to the nearby village of Salgóbánya, alighting at the end stop, and following Vár út and the path it leads in to. If you fancy a longer walk, pick up a wriggling path from near the Strandfürdő campsite. The castle – on which Sándor Petőfi based his poem 'Salgó' in the mid 19th century – looks down precariously from a 625m basalt cone and affords good views of the surrounds. The castle was originally constructed by a member of the Kacsics clan in the 13th century. In 1554 it fell to the Turks, the defenders fleeing after seeing their attackers carrying wooden logs up the hill and mistaking them for cannon. You can visit at any time for no charge. There is a nature trail among the rock flora of Boszorkány-kő, a few hundred metres to the south of the castle. You can stay in some new apartments in the village (Vörösfenyő Apartman – see page 219).

Three kilometres further north is the village of **Somoskő**, which boasts a second, better-preserved castle *(& adult 150Ft/20 Slovak crowns, concessions 75Ft/10 Slovak crowns; ⊕ daily autumn/winter 08.00–16.00, spring/summer 08.00–20.00).* This one stands on top of a 526m hill, on the cusp of the Medves Plateau – the largest basalt plateau in central Europe (and presenting fascinating 'organ-pipe' geological formations). The hill is actually bisected by the Hungarian-Slovakian border, and the 14th-century fortress lies on the wrong side. The border crossing can be made at Somoskőújfalu (you'll need your passport or ID card), a couple of kilometres to the west – bus 11 runs here. Alternatively you can hop on bus 11A to Somoskő village, from where the castle is visible if not visitable.

The Mátra Hills Region

The Mátra Hills stretch for around 50km and are divided between five regions – the western Mátra, central Mátra (containing the country's highest peak – that of Kékes, at 1,015m), eastern Mátra, Mátralába and Mátraalja. The villages of the area have little in the way of varied attractions, but then the thousands who come here each year are after life's simple pleasures – to hike among the forested hills and enjoy some of the country's most beautiful scenery. There is also some rather tame skiing in the winter, and opportunities for hunting if that's your bag. A network of trails connects the major villages, with lookout points along the way. To make the best use of them, pick up a copy of the *Mátra és a Mátraalja* map (1:30,000) by Imre Faragó, which is available from Tourinform and some local hotels. The snaking Road 24 also provides a gorgeous drive through the oak and beech trees for those making their way between Gyöngyös and Eger.

PÁSZTÓ

Tucked next to the River Zagyva as it runs between the Cserhát and the Mátra hills, Pásztó is a good starting point for those trekking into the western Mátra. However, the town itself has some historical buildings to look at before you don your hiking boots. An 11th-century Benedictine monastery stood on the site of the current Cistercian one, and Pásztó represented an important religious centre in the Middle Ages. The citizens packed up and shipped out during the period of Turkish occupation, and for a century this was a virtual ghost town; things didn't pick up again until the mid 1600s. The air is fresh and the hills scenic, and this has helped the town develop into a centre for rehabilitation; its hospital (recently renovated) is key to local employment.

GETTING THERE AND AWAY Pásztó is near Route 21, 30km from Hatvan. The **railway station** is a short distance west of the centre; it is on the line running north between Hatvan and Somoskőújfalu. There are three direct trains from Budapest Keleti; all others require a change at Hatvan (regular trains from there). There are regular **buses** from Budapest Stadionok, as well as services from Salgótarján, Balassagyarmat (two daily), Gyöngyös (eight), Hatvan (nine), Mátrafüred (two).

WHERE TO STAY AND EAT The sleeping and scoffing options are limited here, although there's a stretch of cafés, bars and restaurants on the main street (Fő utca).

✗ **Bence** Fő út 92; ☏ 32 460687. Decent enough pizzas. *Mains 550–900Ft;* ⊕ *Mon–Sat 11.00–22.00.*

⌂ **Hotel Zsigmond** (26 rooms) Nagymező út 4; ☏ 32 460442. An uninspiring little place to crash for the night, although desperately cheap. The rooms are big but barren, & have fridges; the café-style restaurant serves Hungarian food & snacks (*mains 600–1,150Ft*). Twin 2,500Ft.

✗ **Ózon** Deák Ferenc u. 3; ☏ 32 461 713. Near the post office, this is a decent place to fill the stomach. Pizzas, soups, salads, pastas, burgers, cakes & ice creams. *Mains 880–2,300Ft;* ⊕ *daily 10.00–21.00.*

⌂ **Verzsó Guesthouse** (3 rooms) Pásztó-Hasznos, Alkotmány u. 99; ☏ 32 462111; e mischi2@aktivi.hu; www.verzso.hu. This lovely self-catering apartment in the Hasznos district (a few miles from Pásztó, towards Galyatető) gives you a chance to enjoy rural Hungary at its best. You can stock up on the owners' homemade wine & *pálinka*, & they can arrange bike rental, carriage rides, fishing in the nearby lake & tours. *Apt 3,000Ft/pp.*

WHAT TO SEE AND DO St **Lawrence Parish Church** (*Szent Lőrinc plébániatemplom; Múzeum tér 1*) is something of an architectural mishmash, its Baroque and Gothic elements the result of reconstructions to the original church, which was built in the 15th century over 13th-century Romanesque foundations. We particularly like a pair of chubby angels inside that spread their arms towards a painting on a side altar, and rather cheekily display an oversized rump. The eastern windows were only discovered in 1959; one of these bears a rose-like detail that is unique in Hungary. The Baroque **parsonage** (*Múzeum tér 2*) was constructed in the 18th century. Outside the church railings is Sándor Kiss's **statue of King Zsigmond** – who bestowed town status on Pásztó in 1407 – standing on top of a resting lion.

The garden of medieval ruins is at the ancient centre of the town. At its heart is the whitewashed **schoolmaster's house**, first mentioned in a will of 1428, and the country's last 15th-century market town house. During excavations in 1978, a hoard of 16th-century domestic items was found buried in containers beneath the floor – doubtless hidden by the occupant before he fled from the advancing Turks. These are now exhibited inside, together with instruments used for medieval wine production in the cellar. At its southern side the **remains of a workshop** were uncovered, used by the monks to make glass during the 11th and 12th centuries before burning down in 1230.

At the western side of the square is the Baroque **former Cistercian monastery**, completed in 1720. There was a monastery here much earlier, though – mentioned in town charters of 1138, and belonging initially to the Benedictine order before passing to the Cistercians in 1190. It lay dilapidated following the Turkish invasion (the stones of its base walls still litter the ground about), before the Cistercians returned and rebuilt. Today it houses the **Local History Museum** (*Helytörténeti Múzeum; Múzeum tér 1;* ☏ *32 460194;* ⊕ *Apr–Sep Mon–Sat 09.00–15.00, Oct–Mar 31 Mon–Fri 08.00–16.00, Sat 10.00–14.00*), with an exhibition of prehistoric finds, a memorial room to Benjámin Rajeczky, the musicologist and last prior of the town, and details of the history of the Cistercian order. The nearby bronze **statue of Szent István** was sculpted by Sándor Kiss as part of the 2000 millennium celebrations.

The **Csohány Kálmán Gallery** (*Múzeum tér 4;* ➲ *32 460194; Mon–Fri 08.00–16.00, Sat 10.00–14.00 in winter, 09.00–15.00 in summer*) shows 150 of the works of 20th-century graphic artist Csohány, who was born and buried in Pásztó. There is an open-air **strand** (*Kossuth Lajos út 116;* ➲ *32 460750;* ⊕ *Jun–Aug daily 06.00–19.00*) at the northern end of the town; its water is 33°C and registered as medicinal. For some final ruins, visit **Hasznos** a short distance to the northeast. In the past, a series of castles defended the route through the Mátra Hills, and this settlement (belonging to Pásztó) bears the remnants of one of them. The hill on which the tower foundations lie also offers splendid views of not only the Mátra Hills, but the Cserhát and Karancs hills to the west and north respectively.

EXCURSION The village of **Mátraverebély-Szentkút** lies a few kilometres to the northeast of Pásztó, on the road to Salgótarján. Its **Holy Well** (Szentkút) is ranked among Hungary's most important shrines dedicated to the Blessed Virgin Mary. The Well of St László has been a site of Catholic pilgrimage since as early as the 13th century. It is said that St László and his soldiers were surrounded here by the Cumans; having run out of water, some of the Hungarians told the Cumans they'd switch religion in return for their release. St László was so angered by this that he threw his spear into the rocks – and when he pulled it free, water flowed from the place. The Baroque **Church of Szentkút** – near the well – was built in 1763, and in 1970 was granted the title of basilica minor by Pope Paul IV. In the middle of Mátraverebély village, there's a lovely Gothic church. On the hill above it are some **hermit caves** (*remetebarlang*); these were dug by hand by Adam Antal Bellagh, the priest of Feldebrő (20km southeast of Eger), in around 1757. There is even a kitchen and latrine dug into the limestone.

GYÖNGYÖS

The 'gateway to the Mátra' stands 80km from the capital, at the meeting point of the forested hills and the northern cusp of the Great Plain. The second-largest town in Heves County, Gyöngyös has traditionally been noted for its textiles and handicrafts, and as the centre of wine production in the northern hill ranges (see box, page 224). It was declared a market town by the Anjou king Károly Róbert in 1334, and continued to flourish throughout the period of Turkish occupation when it was granted protected status by the sultan. It didn't have all its own way, however. In the 1880s its vineyards were blighted by the phylloxera plague, and in 1917 a fire sparked in the hospital and wiped out 549 houses, leaving 8,000 homeless. As the inferno raged, the citizens even used their stores of wine in their desperate attempts to douse the flames. The long process of construction began in the years following World War I.

GETTING THERE, AWAY AND AROUND The main **railway station** stands to the east of the centre, on Vasút utca – follow Kossuth Lajos utca into the centre. The **bus station** is 600m closer in on Koháry út. Gyöngyös is at the end of a short spur off the main Budapest–Miskolc line. The spur comes at Vámosgyörk, and you'll have to change there for the final push. There are up to 13 trains daily from Budapest Keleti and Kelenföld stations to Vámosgyörk. There is also a **narrow-gauge railway** departing from Előre station (*Mátravasút;* ➲ *37 312447*) close to the Mátra Museum. It started a century ago as a forest railway, but today transports tourists

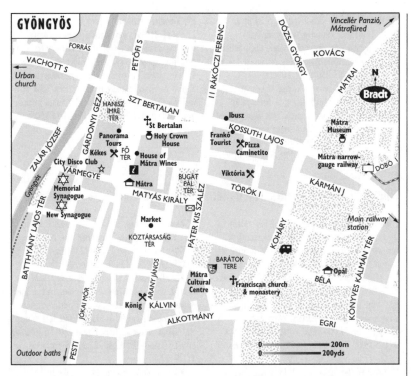

rather than dead wood; there are services to Mátrafüred (*Mar–Sep daily every hour between 08.00 & 18.00, Oct–Feb Sat–Sun & 4 trains each way only; ⊜ sgl/rtn adult 200/380Ft, concessions 100/200Ft*) and Lajosháza (*May–Sep Sat–Sun between 08.00 & 16.00, with additional trains in high season on Wed & Fri; ⊜ adult 240/450Ft, concessions 120/240Ft*). In addition, a 3½km extension to Szalajkaház has just opened. There are two buses an hour from Budapest Stadion, and regular runs between Mátrafüred, Mátraháza, Hatvan and Eger; you can also reach Salgótarján (five), Miskolc (two) and Debrecen (two). If you need a **taxi**, call Mátra Taxi (☎ 37 313033).

INFORMATION AND OTHER PRACTICALITIES

🔲 **Franko Tourist** Kossuth Lajos u. 13; ☎ 37 311339; e franko@mail.datanet.hu. Offers various sightseeing programmes around the Mátra region, including trips by coach & narrow-gauge railway to Eger & Mátrafüred (where it has its own guesthouse). A 6-day tour costs around €340/pp.
🔲 **Ibusz** Kossuth Lajos u. 6; ☎ 37 311861; e gyongyos@ibusz.hu. ⊕ Mon–Fri 8.00–17.00.
🔲 **Panorama Tours** Fő tér 5; ☎ 37 500885. ⊕ Mon–Fri 08.00–17.00, Sat 08.00–12.00.

✉ **Post office** Mátyás Király u. (in Bugát Pál tér). ⊕ Mon–Fri 08.00–20.00, Sat 08.00–12.00.
🔲 **Tourinform** Fő tér 10; ☎ 37 311155; e gyongyos@tourinform.hu. Housed in the 3-storey avocado-coloured Baroque Grassalkovich Mansion, which also holds the town's library & an exhibition of 20th-century paintings by Herman Lipót. ⊕ Jun 15–Sep 15 daily 09.00–18.00, rest of yr Mon–Thu 07.30–16.00, Fri 07.30–13.30.

There is an **open-air market** (*Termelői piac*) on Köztársaság tér (⊕ *Fri 05.00–13.00, Sat 06.00–13.00, Sun 06.00–12.00*).

🔺 **WHERE TO STAY** Ask at Tourinform for their *Gyöngyös Mátra Accommodation* booklet, which gives a list of **private rooms**; these can also be booked through Ibusz.

🏠 **Hotel Mátra** (40 rooms) Mátyás király út 2; ☎ 37 313063; e inn-side@mail.matav.hu. Uninspiring hotel on the main square, albeit better since its recent refurbishment. The restaurant has a small terrace. *Sgl 6,250Ft, dbl 9,000Ft.*

🏠 **Hotel Opál** (16 rooms) Könyves Kálmán tér 13; ☎ 37 300455; www.opalhotel.hu; e hotelopal@karolyrobert.hu. An unostentatious little hotel, located 600m east of the centre in between the bus & train stations. Convenient for the Mátra Museum & its gardens. *Sgl 9,500Ft, dbl 14,500Ft, suite (for 4) 21,500Ft.*

🏠 **Vincellér Panzió** (15 rooms) Erzsébet királyné u. 22; ☎ 37 311691; www.vincellerpanzio.hu. Apart from the dawn squawks of an inconsiderate cockerel outside our window, we were satisfied with compact & clean rooms. The pension's popular restaurant has a good ambience, friendly staff, a garden patio lit with candles, & a varied selection of dishes (*mains avg 1,400Ft*). *Dbl 9,200Ft, apt (for 4) 14,500Ft; b/fast 1,500Ft.*

✖ **WHERE TO EAT AND DRINK** The Vincellér has a decent restaurant (see above).

♀ **House of Mátra Wines** (*Mátraaljai Borok Háza*) Fő tér 10; ☎ 30 9787151; e matraiborokhaza@tvnetwork.hu. The most convenient place to have a glug of the region's bottles. The house showcases 100 of the wines produced in the 22 villages of the Mátraalja – the region at the 'foot of the Mátra Hills'. With advance notice, the cellar can accommodate up to 50 tasters. *Wine shop* ⊕ *Mon–Thu 11.00–18.00, Fri 10.00–18.00, Sat 09.00–15.00, Sun 10.00–14.00; wine tasting Fri 18.00–22.00, Sat 19.00–22.00.*

✖ **Kékes** Fő tér 7; ☎ 37 311915. Specialising in Hungarian food, this is the town's most expensive restaurant. It boasts an elegant interior, with a wooden upper seating section & low-hanging lights, & an outdoor area sheltered by a canopy. *Mains avg 2,400Ft;* ⊕ *12.00–23.00 daily.*

✖ **König** Arany János u. 13; ☎ 37 315809. Spartan restaurant serving good Hungarian fare. *Mains avg 1,000Ft;* ⊕ *Mon–Thu 12.00–22.00, Fri–Sat 12.00–23.00, Sun 12.00–22.00.*

✖ **Pizza Il Caminetto** Kossuth Lajos u. 19; ☎ 37 312652. Watch pizzas being freshly prepared in the restaurant's open kitchen; eat them while enjoying the atmosphere on the al-fresco terrace. There are also pastas to choose from. *Pizzas 710–1,120Ft, avg 800Ft;* ⊕ *Sun–Thu 11.30–22.00, Fri–Sat 11.30–23.00.*

✖ **Viktória** Török Ignác u. 24/2; ☎ 06 30 504 3626. Hungarian & international dishes, & courtyard seating. Situated in the narrow side-street linking Török Ignác u. & Kossuth Lajos utca. *Mains 800–1,600Ft;* ⊕ *daily 12.00–22.00.*

ENTERTAINMENT AND NIGHTLIFE The ticket and information centre of the **Mátra Cultural Centre** (*Barátok tere 3;* ☎ *37 312281/2/3*) is open Monday–Friday

WINES OF THE MÁTRAALJA WINE REGION

Formerly known as Gyöngyös-Visonta – the name was altered in the 1960s – the region at the foot of the Mátra Hills is the second-largest of the country's 22 regions. It occupies a 20km strip of land on the southern slopes of the Mátra Hills, bordered by the Tarna River to the east and the Zagyva River to the west. There is an ancient tradition of viniculture here, its climate and soil types most suited to flowery, fruity whites – today including Italian riesling and Ottonel muskotály, Szürkebarát or Leányka, as well as global varieties of Chardonnay. There was wine-making here even prior to Hungarian settlement, but the golden age came during the period of the Napoleonic Wars, sustained during Habsburg rule. The phylloxera plague of 1880 was devastating, and the region relied on significant government assistance in its rejuvenation. Today the region's big-boy wineries are Szőlőskert and Danubiana, but there are also many small, family-run ones. An increasing number of these offer tastings for visitors – particularly since the founding of the Wine Route Association in 1998 – but the simplest way of sampling what is on offer is at the Mátraalja House of Wine (see above).

14.00–18.00. Just off the main square, **City Disco Club** (*Fő tér 9;* \ *37 312281*) – with a pizzeria and three dancefloors – was being refurbished during our last visit, but should have re-opened by the time you read this. There are several bars to the south of Fő tér.

WHAT TO SEE AND DO Fő tér is the pedestrianised main square containing **St Bertalan Parish Church** (*Szent Bertalan út 1*) at its northern end. The twin-towered 'Big Church' is appropriately nicknamed – it is the country's largest Gothic temple, although its face became more properly Baroque during rebuilding in the 18th century. Original features of the 15th-century hall church (built on the site of a church that had stood here since 1301) remain in the form of Gothic twin windows on either side of the apse, and in a bronze Gothic baptism font at the southern side of the shrine. Look out too for the frescoes of Hungarian freedom fighters (*kuruc*). Near the church is a skinny **statue of Károly Róbert**, commissioned to mark the 650th anniversary of the settlement's accession to town status. The **town hall** (*Fő tér 13*) bears the town's coat of arms – depicting a howling wolf beneath a golden sun and moon – and these images are replicated in three of the square's corner fountains. The fourth shows the vine, a nod towards the strong tradition of wine production in the region.

The **Holy Crown House** (*Szent Korona Ház; Szent Bertalan út 3;* \ *37 311143;* ⊕ *Tue–Sun 10.00–12.00 & 14.00–17.00*) is to the south of the church, so-named because the Hungarian crown was three times hidden in an upper room during the Napoleonic Wars. This is commemorated in the painted ceiling of the ceremonial hall. The building now holds the **treasury** (*kincstár*) of the St Bertalan Church, said to be the third-richest ecclesiastical collection in the country. Here are works by medieval and Renaissance goldsmiths, as well as vestments and statues. To the east of the church is a music school that was once a **secondary school** for Jesuits and then Franciscans. Its niches hold Baroque wooden statues of St Ignatius and St Francis; the original stone versions are in the Mátra Museum.

Two former synagogues stand southwest of the main square, testament to the strength of the town's Jewish population prior to the horrors of World War II. Opposite the County Hall is the classicist **Memorial Synagogue** (*Vármegye u.*), built between 1816 and 1820 by Károly Rábl, a local of the town. Next to it is the domed **New Synagogue** (*Kőrösi Csoma Sándor u.*), a Moorish edifice designed by Lipót Baumhorn in 1930.

Franciscan monks arrived during the 14th century, and their **church and monastery** (*Ferences templom és rendház; Barátok tere 1–2*) were founded in 1370 (although the 18th century saw a Baroque overhaul). Gyöngyös was in the thick of the struggle for independence led by Ferenc Rákóczi II between 1703 and 1711, and the prince held negotiations with the Habsburg ambassador here. One of the insurrection's best-known generals – János Vak (Blind) Bottyán – is buried in the crypt. The monastery houses the **Memorial Library of the Hungarian Franciscan Friars** (*Magyar Ferencesek Műemlék Könyvtára;* \ *37 311361;* ⊕ *Tue–Fri & Sun 14.00–18.00, Sat 10.00–18.00*), a collection of 16,000 volumes (including antique decorative works by various European printing houses, five codices and 210 incunabula) preserved by the religious order since the Middle Ages and uniquely surviving the Turkish period unharmed. There is a permanent exhibition covering the history of the Franciscan order in the entrance hall.

The **Mátra Museum and Mikroárium** (*Kossuth Lajos u. 40;* \ *37 505530; www.matramuzeum.hu;* 🎫 *1,000/500Ft;* ⊕ *Tue–Sun Mar–Oct 09.00–17.00, Nov–Feb 09.00–14.00*) can be found in the Neoclassical and tatty 18th-century Orczy Mansion. There are carved lions guarding the entrance, while another (sculpted by István Ferenczy in 1840) sleeps in the lovely gardens. The iron fence is said to have

5

been fashioned from gun barrels of the Napoleonic Wars. In the museum is the second-largest natural-scientific collection in Hungary. The ground floor holds an exhibition about the history of the town and surrounding region, from 13th-century Kisnána tombstones discovered at Benevár, Mátrafüred, through Turkish weapons to items melted by the devastating fire of 1917. Upstairs is a selection of the geology of the Mátra Hills, as well as a mammoth skeleton and hunting items.

There are indoor pools and open-air **thermal baths** (*Pesti út;* ✆ *37 311561;* 🎟 *400/190Ft;* ☉ *Jan 1–May 15 Tue–Fri 06.00–18.00, Sat–Sun 08.00–17.00, May 16–Sep 14 Mon–Fri 09.00–19.00, Sep 15–Dec 31 Tue–Fri 06.00–18.00, Sat–Sun 08.00–17.00*) a kilometre or two to the south of the centre. Follow Jókai Mór utca to Pesti út.

GYÖNGYÖSPATA

Twelve kilometres west of Gyöngyös (and accessible by bus), Gyöngyöspata is worth a trip for its **15th-century Gothic church** (✆ *37 364250; telephone in advance*). Inside is an 8m-tall high altar – probably the work of Polish artists of the 17th century – bearing the carved and painted **family tree of Jesus Christ**. This 'Tree of Jesse' is a Baroque masterpiece, although late-Gothic in look.

VILLAGES OF THE MÁTRA HILLS

MÁTRAFÜRED Although Mátrafüred is a small and pretty resort, it is nevertheless a lively place – particularly at weekends, when several of the restaurants and pensions put on music (inevitably of the cheesy, synthesiser brand). A dainty **Baroque church** opposite the narrow-gauge railway station was built in 1767, and is now almost swallowed by horsechestnut trees. At the **Palóc Private Ethnographic and Doll Exhibition** (*Palóc Néprajzi Magángyűjtemény, Palóc Babák; Pálosvörösmarti út 2;* ✆ *37 320137;* ☉ *Mon–Fri 09.30–17.00*) there are dolls dressed in the traditional costumes of Nógrád and Heves counties, from feasting outfits to casual clothes. The former primary school also contains woven textiles and other works of folkloric art. However, most people come here to **walk**. To get started, head for Tornyos Panzió (see opposite), from where eight marked trails (of varying lengths) depart to other villages to the north and northeast, including Mátraháza (5km), Sástó (3km) and Kékestető (8km). There are **cycling** routes too; pick them up from near the ethnographic museum.

Getting there and away Mátrafüred – like the other villages of this region – can be accessed by **car** on Route 24, which runs through here on its way between Gyöngyös and Eger. There are up to eight **buses** daily from Budapest Stadion; of these, all also go to Mátraháza and Sástó, three of them to Kékestető and two to Parád, Parádfürdő, Recsk and Sirok. There are regular buses from Gyöngyös, and less-frequent services from Eger and Miskolc. Far more enjoyable, though, is the **narrow-gauge railway** to Mátrafüred from Gyöngyös; the trip takes around 20 minutes, and there are as many as ten departures a day (although four only outside peak season). Tickets cost 200/380Ft sgl/rtn; there is a discount with the Hungary Card.

 Where to stay and eat You'll be tripping over **private rooms** here – try along Béke út – and there are **stalls** aplenty on Parádi út selling pancakes, pizzas and alcohol, and opening late.

🏠 **Anna Hotel** (18 rooms) Üdülősor 55; ✆ 37 520058; www.anna-hotel.hu. Situated on a quiet street

a few minutes' walk from the main strip (with its snack stands), this 3-star hotel is clean & pleasant enough. It has wellness facilities (inc sauna, gym & massage) & a pool. Sgl 17,000Ft, dbl 22,000Ft.

✗ **Benevár** Parádi u. 10. The most popular place to eat Hungarian food; the restaurant is divided inside between 3 simple rooms & has hanging baskets in the garden. Mains avg 750Ft; ⊕ daily 11.00–23.00.

🏠 **Diana Hotel** Turista út 1; ✆ 37 320136. Basic accommodation. Dbl 7,000Ft, trpl 9,000Ft, apt 15,000Ft.

✗ **Feketerigó** Avar út 2; ✆ 37 320052. Serves cheap if unexceptional food like deer goulash & turkey breast stuffed with goose liver. Its accommodation lacks the modern touch – & rooms don't have bathrooms – but they are comfy enough, & similarly lowly in price. Sgl 2,000Ft, dbl 3,200Ft, trpl 4,200Ft, suites 7,400–8,600Ft; ⊕ Tue–Sun 12.00–21.00.

✗ **Füredi Terasz** Parádi u. 3; ✆ 37 320240. A wide selection of well-priced pizzas & pastas. Pizza/pasta avg 680Ft, Hungarian dishes 780–1,680Ft; ⊕ daily 12.00–23.00.

🏠 **Hegyalja-Fenyveskert** (13 rooms) Béke út 7; ✆ 37 320027; e foglalas@matraigidak.hu; www.matraigidak.hu. A handsome guesthouse & restaurant (serving Hungarian grills & stews; ⊕ daily 12.00–22.00) with a well-maintained interior & log

furniture shaded by pine trees outside. You can buy local produce, & even try milking a goat. Sgl 7,000Ft, dbl 12,500Ft, trpl 16,500Ft, quad 21,500Ft.

🏠 **Hotel Avar** (94 rooms) Parádi út 24; ✆ 37 320400; e avarhotel@mail.datanet.hu; www.avarhotel.hu. Standard 3-star hotel. Its rooms are light & airy, & have balconies, while there is also an indoor pool. It's due a renovation. Sgl 11,200Ft, dbl 15,400Ft, apt (for 2) 20,400Ft.

🏠 **Hotel Füred** (10 rooms) Kékesi u. 1–3; ✆ 37 520030. Around 500m from the village centre, this hotel is tucked among blue-green fir trees. Its rooms are clean, & its facilities include a sun terrace, a football field & an area for clay-pigeon shooting. Sgl 6,500Ft, dbl 7,500Ft.

🏠 **Hotel Gyöngyvirág** (25 rooms) Béke út 8; ✆ 37 520001; e info@gyongyvirag.hu; www.gyongyvirag.hu. Has a beer garden & grill buffet during the summer months, & an outdoor swimming pool. Sgl 7,500–10,000Ft, dbl 8,800–13,000Ft, apt 13,000–16,000Ft.

🏠 **Tornyos** (8 rooms) Parádi u. 25; ✆ 37 320236; Restaurant with good fish & friendly staff; it also has a small attached pension. Dbl 8,000Ft, apt (for 4) 15,000Ft; mains avg 900Ft; restaurant ⊕ Sun–Fri 08.00–22.00, Sat 08.00–23.00.

SÁSTÓ Located bang in between Mátrafüred and Mátraháza on the winding Road 24 that leads from Gyöngyös, Sástó is one of the highest lakes in the country (500m above sea level) and is a popular spot for fishing or messing about in boats. There are numerous stalls selling refreshments around the water's edge, and you can cross wooden bridges that straddle the lake to access a 50m-high **lookout tower** (Sástói Kilátó; & adult 45Ft). If you fancy further thrills, you can follow signs on Road 24 for **adrenalin park** (✆ 37 600 074; www.adrenalin-park.hu), which offers the chance to try some 'extreme' activities including climbing, quad biking and bobsleighing.

Sástó is a pleasant 30-minute walk uphill from Mátrafüred (follow the yellow-circle trail from Tornyos Panzió), although there are also buses running here from Budapest, Eger, Gyöngyös and Miskolc. The bus stops directly outside **Mátra Camping** (Farkas u. 4; ✆ 37 374 025; e info@matrakemping.hu; www.matrakemping.hu), a large and pretty site that offers accommodation of some sort all year round, and has a snackbar, pub, restaurant and supermarket. There's space for 200 tents (available Apr–Oct), while there are also welcoming bungalows (with TV & refrigerator; trpl 9,900Ft), less-comfortable huts (dbl 4,300Ft, trpl 5,900Ft) and a motel (shared bathrooms; dbl 5,900Ft, trpl 6,900Ft). The **Tourinform** in Gyöngyös can provide any further information you might need.

MÁTRAHÁZA A little further north of Sástó, Mátraháza is like an understudy for Mátrafüred – slightly less pleasing on the eye and with fewer amenities, but with a good spread of choice walks. Join the marked trails from close to the bus stop – to Sirok (blue horizontal line; 24km), Kékestető (red plus sign; 3km), Sástó (yellow plus sign; 3km), Lajosháza (yellow plus sign; 4km), Galyatető (the country's second-highest peak at 965m; blue horizontal line; 10km) or Párádsasvár (red horizontal line; 6km). The village stands in the shadow of Mount Kékes, and is consequently also a base for skiers in winter.

Where to stay and eat

Bérc Hotel Mátra (128 rooms) ⟍ 37 374102; e berchotel@t-online.hu. One of a brace of big hotels on the Panorama Road (No 24) that you'll pass on your way from Sástó to Mátraháza. It was closed for refurbishment as we went to press, but will re-open as a 4-star wellness hotel. *For rates, contact hotel.*

Borostyán ⟍ 37 374090. Next to the Pagoda Hotel (and belonging to the same owner), Borostyán serves fair traditional cuisine with game specialities. It is elevated from the road, with animal skins on the walls & seating outside in individual wooden pavilions. *Mains avg 1,100Ft;* ⊕ *daily 09.00–22.00.*

Hotel Edzőtábor ⟍ 37 374016. An ex-trade-union hostel, with a canteen-style restaurant & a preponderance of school parties among its guests. *Rooms 2,500Ft/pp; b/fast 700Ft.*

Ózon Hotel (59 rooms) ⟍ 37 374004; e info@hotelozon.hu; www.hotelozon.hu. On the same road as the Bérc (and a slightly more upmarket proposition), the Ózon is divided between 2 buildings. Some of its rooms are a touch old fashioned, but pleasant nonetheless, with balconies attached to those on the 1st & 2nd floors. (Request a room at the back for hill views.) The hotel can organise horse-riding trips, wine tasting & forest walks, bikes can be hired for 400Ft/hr, & there are tennis courts, a fitness room & sauna. *Sgl 8,260–11,860Ft, dbl 11,220–16,120Ft.*

Pagoda Hotel (26 rooms) ⟍ 37 374023; e ingrid.kocsis@gastrotourist-egyesules.hu. The name refers to the multi-tiered roof of its main building. Indeed, this 19th-century structure in the middle of the village was once the only house in the area, & gave its name to Mátraháza itself – 'the house of Mátra'. There are several wings spread over the hotel's grounds; among the facilities are tennis courts & free bike hire. *Sgl 5,900Ft, dbl 10,000Ft, trpl 14,500Ft, quad 19,000Ft; b/fast 800Ft.*

KÉKESTETŐ At 1,015m, 'Blue Peak' is Hungary's highest point; it also enjoys more autumn and winter sunshine than anywhere else, and is thus regarded as a therapeutic spot. It is a short distance up a steep, winding road from Mátraháza; you can take one of the marked walking trails or a bus. In snowy months, there are two **ski slopes** available, one of them running down to Mátraháza (⊕ *Sun–Thu 09.00–16.00, Fri–Sat 09.00–20.00*). The upper section has a ski lift (ℰ *1 ride 500Ft, day pass 4,000/3,000Ft, Night pass (Wed, Fri, Sat) 2,500 Ft*), but those continuing further down need to jump on a bus for the re-ascent. You can rent skis here during the season, and there is a ski school for children. Alternatively you can climb 38m to the lookout gallery of the 187m **TV tower** (ℰ *400/250Ft;* ⊕ *daily May–Sep 09.00–18.00, Oct–Apr 09.00–16.00*).

Next to the tower is the forbidding-looking **Hotel Hegycsúcs** (14 rooms; ⟍ *37 567004; http://kekesteto-hotel.internettudakozo.hu; dbl 8,300Ft, trpl 10,800Ft, suite 14,900Ft*), on whose upper floors you can rest satisfied that you are above every other tourist in any other hotel in the country. More fusty and basic – verging on the time-warped – is the **Kányai Uram Fogadó** (*Üdülőtelep 1;* ⟍ *37 367064; 15 rooms; 2,000Ft/pp*). Its rooms have shared bathrooms, and there's a Hungarian restaurant (*mains avg 1,000Ft;* ⊕ *07.00–21.00 daily*).

PARÁDSASVÁR Just to the east of Galyatető (at 965m, the country's runner-up in the highest-hill stakes), in a valley at the northern foot of the Mátra, Parádsasvár *is*

THE BIRTH OF THE COACH

The word *kocsi* derives from the Hungarian village of Kocs in Komárom County, a stage on the road from Buda to Vienna during the reign of King Mátyás when nimbler, light-weight carriages replaced clumsier wagons in use up until then. They were quickly adopted elsewhere around the world; the Hungarian *kocsi* is evident in the word *coach* – one of the few to leap the linguistic divide from Hungarian to English – and the German *Kutsche*.

significant for glassworks – established by the Orczy family in 1767, and still going strong – and sulphurous medicinal water from the Csevice Spring. The latter is reputedly effective in treating not only respiratory and stomach complaints, but hangovers. The **Parád Crystal Factory** (*Kristály Manufaktúra; Rákóczi u. 46–48;* ⟍ *36 364353;* ⊕ *Tue–Sat 10.00–15.00*) produces crystal and glass as fine as you'll find anywhere. You can buy pieces from its shop (⊕ *Mon–Fri 09.00–15.00, Sat–Sun 09.00–13.00*), and there are further examples in the **Sasvár Galéria** (⊕ *Mon–Fri 09.45–12.30, 13.45–14.30, Sat 08.00–09.00, 09.50–11.30*) opposite. Several residential houses also have small glass workshops that can be visited, and which offer decanters, drinking vessels and novelty bits and bobs – try **László Ólomkristály Üzlet és Műhely** (*Arany János u. 13;* ⟍ *36 373574; laszlokristaly@ gmail.com*). You can have a go at decorating your own glass too.

If you fancy a **walk**, there are a couple of trails signposted as you enter the village. Alternatively you can head for the **Fényes Major Equestrian Farmstead** (*Fényes Major Lovastanya;* ⟍ *36 444444;* e *info@khs.hu; www.khs.hu;* ⌂ *entrance adult 500Ft, child under 12 free; riding lesson 3,000Ft/hr, cross-country riding with guide 4,000Ft/hr, carriage ride 8,000Ft/hr;* ⊕ *Wed–Sun 08.00–18.00*), 30 minutes' walk east of the centre or a short bus ride (alight at the Fényespusztai Elágazás stop). Follow the track adjacent to Túra Camping for 1km. The 32ha ranch holds Lipizzaners and Hungarian half-breds, as well as donkeys, buffalo, goats and sheep. Lessons and excursions are available for riders of all levels, as well as carriage trips, paintball for groups, jeep tours and quad-bike rental.

One hundred kilometres from Budapest, take the Gyöngyös exit off the M3 motorway, and follow Road 24 for 24km. **Buses** run to and from Eger, Párad, Páradfürdő, Recsk and Sirok; alight just outside the St Hubertus Panzió.

Where to stay and eat The former mansion of Mihály Károlyi (1875–1955) – Hungarian prime minister of the republic in 1918 – was designed in the late 19th century by Miklós Ybl and was refurbished in the 1990s to become the **Kastély Hotel Sasvár** (*Kossuth Lajos u. 1;* ⟍ *36 444444;* e *info@khs.hu; www.khs.hu; 57 rooms; sgl 30,000–50,000Ft, dbl 40,000–60,000Ft, suites 70,000–270,000Ft*). 'Eagle Castle Hotel' is an impressive, turreted affair, with super facilities – bowling alley, squash courts, pools indoor and out. Each of its suites has its own sauna and Jacuzzi, and there are separate wings for honeymooners and families. For all its splendour, however, we felt there was something slightly soulless about the place, as though the restoration had been done by a team from Disney World. Non guests can pay 10,000Ft for a day ticket, which gives them access to the facilities and restaurant (*for an extra 5,000Ft*).

More rustic and less pressing on the pocket is the nearby **St Hubertus Panzió** (*Rákóczi út 2;* ⟍ *36 544060; 10 rooms; dbl 8,800–11,800Ft, trpl 12,500–17,600Ft, quad 16,000–23,000Ft, b/fast 600Ft*), a renovated 19th-century 'Bailiff House'. Its restaurant specialises in game dishes (*mains 580–1,700Ft, avg 1,100Ft;* ⊕ *Sun–Fri 12.00–21.00, Sat 12.00–22.00*).

Túra Camping (⟍ *36 364079; camping* ⌂ *700/300Ft, tent 700Ft, c/van 1,100Ft, dbl 5,000Ft*) is located just off Road 24 on the way out of Parádsasvár towards Eger, next to a small go-kart track. The facilities are basic, and include an on-site restaurant more reminiscent of a school canteen and some plain rooms.

PARÁD AND PARÁDFÜRDŐ Parád and Parádfürdő stand shoulder to shoulder, and – like Parádsasvár – have traditionally drawn those seeking therapy from the area's odoriferous medicinal water. Behind Parád's church, in the northwest of the village on the bank of the Tarna Brook, is a traditional, thatched **Palóc Cottage** (*Palócház; Sziget u. 10*). Built at the end of the 18th century, it serves as a museum of folk art

5

and peasant architecture, with hand-woven embroidery and painted wooden furniture – although at the time of research it was closed for renovation. Another exhibition displays the masterful **wood carvings** of Joachim Asztalos (*Fafaragó kiállitás; Hársfa u. 6;* ☉ *daily 09.00–18.00*).

The State Hospital of Parádfürdő holds a collection of bottles of mineral water from countries around the world in its **Medicinal Water Museum** (*Gyógyvíz Múzeum; Kossuth Lajos út 221;* ☏ *36 364233;* ☏ *100/50Ft*). You'll need to ask at the hospital reception for access, and it isn't really worth the effort. Far better is the **Coach Museum** (*Kocsi Múzeum; Kossuth Lajos út 217;* ☏ *36 364384;* ☏ *350/220Ft;* ☉ *Apr–Oct daily 09.00–16.50, Nov–Mar Tue–Sun 10.00–16.00*), housed on the site of the Cifra Istálló (Decorated Stable) that Count György Károlyi commissioned in 1880. He was determined to own a splendid stable that would shade all others, and put the job into the hands of Miklós Ybl, who made use of red marble in his design. Today you'll find an array of coaches and horsey paraphernalia dating to the 19th and early 20th centuries. Lipizzaners are still bred in two wings.

BÜKK NATIONAL PARK

Established in 1976, no less than 90% of the 43,200ha that make up Bükk National Park – encompassing Eger, Lillafüred, Bükkszentkereszt, Bélapátfalva, Felsőtárkány, Szarvaskő, Szilvásvárad, Répáshuta and their surroundings – is covered by forest (predominantly beech, *Fagus sylvatica*). But in addition to towering trees, there are open limestone meadows displaying various karst forms produced by erosion – fissures, sinkholes, underground streams and caverns. Indeed the surface is riddled with caves – around 850 at the last count, with a total length of 35km – and many have yielded rich collections of Stone Age tools. The region's communities tap into the huge quantities of pure karst water, which doesn't need filtering or chlorinating. Crags and cliffs afford excellent vantage points, while water has fashioned weird and wonderful rock formations, the best-known of which are Három-kő, Tar-kő, Vörös-kő, Őr-kő and Bél-kő in the 'rock parade' (Kövek Vonulata); this can be reached on hiking trails to the north of Répáshuta village and east of Szilvásvárad.

Among the highlights of the park is the stepped waterfall on the Szalajka Stream (see page 247); another notable place is the Őserdő (Ancient Forest; head for the Olaszkapu car park from Szilvásvárad, and hike the rest of the way) where there has been no felling for over a century. Lillafüred is home to the Szent István and Anna caves (see page 249), with their stalactites, stalagmites and fossilised trees. The central part of the hills comprises the Bükk Plateau, 20km in length, surrounded by ridges, pocked with sink holes, and very popular with hikers. Nagymező contains some of the Bükk's rarest plants.

There are over 22,000 species of animal living in the Bükk. With its many cliffs, the park offers ideal nesting conditions for rare raptors, and most valued among the 90 types of bird are the imperial eagle, the lesser-spotted eagle, the short-toed eagle and the saker, while Ural and eagle owls are the largest of the nocturnal hunters. Dense deciduous forest harbours numerous warblers and woodpeckers; warm limestone rocks and flowering meadows are ideal for butterfly spotting. The long-eared bat breeds and hibernates in some of the caves, and the wolf and lynx – up until 30 years ago declared extinct in Hungary – have recently made a comeback.

The Orbán House Exhibition (see page 247) examines the natural features of the Bükk. For further information, contact the Bükk National Park Central Office (*Eger, Sánc u. 6;* ☏ *36 411581;* e *bnptitkatsag@bnp.kvm.hu; www.bnpi.hu;* ☉ *Mon–Thu 07:30–16.00, Fri 07.30–13.30*).

Where to stay and eat On the main street running through Parád, **Parádi Kisvendéglő** (*Kossuth Lajos u. 234;* ❧ *36 364831*) serves traditional Hungarian dishes and Palóc specialities (*mains avg 1,500Ft;* ⊕ *Apr–Sep Wed–Mon 12.00–21.00, Oct–Mar Wed–Sun 12.00–21.00*) and has a few rooms (*dbl 5,200Ft*).

Parádfürdő has a greater choice of accommodation. A few minutes east, the **Erzsébet Királyné Park Hotel** (*Kossuth Lajos u. 372;* ❧ *36 444044;* ℮ *info@ erzsebetparkhotel.hu; www.erzsebetparkhotel.hu; 99 rooms; sgl 15,500–17,500Ft, dbl 19,500–22,500Ft, suites 32,500Ft*) is another of Ybl's creations, a beautiful building and a sprawling, comfortable hotel. Among the amenities are swimming pools, sauna, massage and fitness room, tennis, bowling and pool.

Hotel Freskó (*Kossuth Lajos u. 221;* ❧ *36 544083; 38 rooms; sgl without bathroom 4,400Ft, dbl with/without bathroom 5,800/7,000Ft, apt with kitchenette 12,000Ft; b/fast 1,400Ft*) stands next to the medicinal hospital and has a vast dining hall decorated with painted panels of battle and hunting scenes, and a limited Hungarian menu (*mains 800–1,500Ft, avg 1,000Ft;* ⊕ *daily 08.00–22.00*). Its rooms are basic but cheap.

There are several pensions on Peres út (just off the main thoroughfare); **Muflon Panzió** (*Peres út 8;* ❧ *36 544086;* ℮ *muflon.panzio@netquick.hu; rooms from 3,800Ft/pp*) is slightly tatty but has neat rooms sleeping two–eight guests; not all of these are en suite, and most don't have TV. Other recommended guesthouses are **Valentin Panzió** (*Peres út 16;* ❧ *36 364295*) and **Boróka Mini Hotel** (*Peres út 18;* ❧ *36 364527*).

RECSK Many Hungarians make the trip a couple of kilometres further east along Road 24 to pay their respects to the memory of countrymen who toiled here in the early 1950s. Mátyás Rákosi established a secret labour camp in Recsk in 1950, where opponents of the communist regime were transported after being sentenced (without trial) to forced labour. They mined the quarries close by, and hundreds died under appalling conditions. Imre Nagy shut the place down in 1953, but it was the recollections of the only prisoner to successfully flee the camp that revealed its existence to the West. Gyula Michnay was one of eight prisoners who escaped after disguising himself as a guard (even fashioning a wooden gun) and escorting the other seven out of the camp. He was the only escapee not to be recaptured. In the book *My Jolly Days in Hell* (*Pokolbeli Víg Napjaim*), György Faludy describes how Michnay had memorised the names of 600 fellow prisoners, and eventually got these names broadcast by Szabad Európa Rádió. It was the first that the relatives knew of the plight of their 'disappeared' loved ones, and it kick-started the process that led to the dismantling of the gulag camps. It was later revealed that 1,300 prisoners had passed through the camp, with the last delivered here in January 1951. A memorial to the **labour camp** (*Recski Kényszermunka Haláltábor;* ✍ *300/150Ft;* ⊕ *May–Sep daily 09.00–17.00, Oct–Apr Sat–Sun 09.00–15.00*) is 6km south of the village. After Nagy closed the camp, it was entirely dismantled, and today you can only see the outlines of the buildings and a reconstruction of a wooden barracks. There's little information in English. (Note that the camp is reached via a sharp turn-off after a bend on Road 24, and it's easy to shoot past it.)

SIROK Continuing yet still eastward along Road 24, the ruins of the **Castle of Sirok** provide great views over the eastern and western sides of the Mátra and Bükk hills respectively, as well as ranges on the Slovakian side of the border. The 13th-century castle was constructed of rocks chiselled from the 296m-high hill on which it sits; it was blown up by the Habsburgs in 1713 in the aftermath of the War of Independence.

The Bükk Hills Region

The Bükk Hills protect Eger from the bullyingly industrial Miskolc, and derive their name from the beech (*bükk*) trees that carpet them. King of the hills in this range is the Istállóskő, which is 958m tall and can be accessed from Szilvásvárad; the average height of the hills tops that of any in the uplands. The hills were formed of calciferous sediment left by an ocean that covered the region for 70 million years. The area is awash with springs and streams, and there are caves aplenty in the limestone surface. Although from the 19th century the region was plundered for the iron ore and timber that fed the iron-working towns in the Sajó Valley (running around the hills' eastern side), much of it remains strikingly beautiful. A large portion has been declared a national park (see box, page 230), and the combination of interesting geology and rich wildlife makes it excellent territory for hiking. Be sure to purchase a decent map – look for those produced by Cartographia.

EGER

Resting in the valley of the River Eger, between the Mátra and Bükk ranges, Eger – from the Latin word *ager* (earth) – is one of the country's charmers, an enchanting town of cobbled streets, Baroque buildings and Bull's Blood (*Egri Bikavér*). It is easy to see why visitors flock here and coo. But Eger is not just a pretty face; its defiance of Turkish force in 1552 was immortalised in the 1901 novel *Egri Csillagok* (*Eclipse of the Crescent Moon*) by Géza Gárdonyi (1863–1922), and its citizens became linked in the Hungarian mind with the most spirited of patriots.

Settled by the Magyar tribes, Eger was made a bishopric by King István in the 11th century. Its rise as a significant centre of Renaissance culture was curtailed by the Turks. The womenfolk of the town famously fought shoulder to shoulder with István Dobó's 2,000 soldiers in repelling the first siege in 1552. The victory over a far superior force was acclaimed around Europe, and effectively stalled (temporarily) the spread of the Ottoman empire. It was also during this struggle that Dobó's troops are said to have been issued with wine – which the attackers mistook for bull's blood – to assist them in screwing their courage to the sticking place. There was considerably less backbone on display when the Turks returned in 1596, however, and a defending garrison of mercenaries surrendered with barely a whimper (excepting, it is hoped, the trumpeter, who was apparently a deep-chested Englishman). Despite a promise of safe passage, the Walloons (who had re-populated the town after the Mongol invasion in 1241) among the many foreign fighters were slaughtered mercilessly in revenge for their part in an earlier massacre of Ottomans living in nearby villages. Today a solitary minaret and a few bath stones are the only reminders of the occupation that lasted until 1687.

Eger was heavily involved in the War of Independence led by Rákóczi, and the Habsburg Emperor Leopold crippled some of the castle fortifications to ensure it couldn't be used by freedom fighters. There was swift development of the town during the rest of the 18th century, with the construction of private houses and ecclesiastical buildings. Look down from the fortress at the many church steeples spiking the skyline and you'll understand why it earned the nickname 'the Hungarian Rome'.

GETTING THERE AND AWAY The **bus** station is in Pyrker János tér, around 500m southwest of Dobó István tér. There are 28 direct buses from Budapest Stadion, taking three hours; Eger is well served by buses to/from many other destinations, including Miskolc (18), Mezőkövesd (up to 35), Aggtelek (one direct, leaving Eger

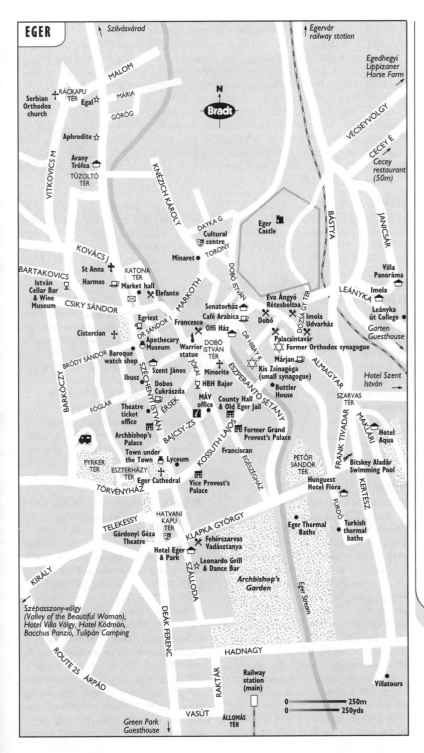

at 08.45), Gyöngyös (49), Mátrafüred (three), Tiszafüred (up to 11), Szilvásvárad (32) and Salgótarján (ten). There is an information bureau at the bus station.

The main **railway station** is to the south, on Vasút utca; follow Deák Ferenc utca northwards for a kilometre to reach the centre. There are nine direct trains a day to Eger from Budapest Keleti, the journey taking about two hours; the indirect route requires a change at Füzesabony on to the line running northwards to Putnok. There is a single daily direct train from Debrecen (two on Sun), but all others require a connection at Füzesabony, as do all trains to and from Miskolc. The Füzesabony–Putnok line includes Szilvásvárad (seven daily). Egervár – a very small station near the castle on Vécseyvölgy utca – is on the same line. You can book train tickets at the **MÁV Office** (*Jókai u. 5;* ☎ *36 314264;* ☺ *Mon–Thu 09.00–17.00, Fri 09.00–13.30*).

GETTING AROUND Bus numbers 10, 11 and 12 run along Deák Ferenc utca (close to the main train station) into the middle of town. Two motorised **sightseeing trains** trundle around the town, and one goes out to Szépasszony-völgy; they leave from Dobó István tér on the hour from 09.00, and tickets (*300Ft*) are purchased on board. **Taxi** firms include City Taxi (☎ *36 555555*) and Panta Taxi (☎ *36 333333*).

INFORMATION AND OTHER PRACTICALITIES

ℹ️ **Bükk National Park Directorate** Sánc u. 6; ☎ 36 411581. Information on the region's nature.

🎫 **Express** Széchenyi u. 28; ☎ 36 427757. Bookings for tours & private accommodation. ☺ Mon–Thu 08.00–16.30, Fri 08.00–16.00.

🎫 **Ibusz** Széchenyi u. 9; ☎ 36 312652; e eger@ iroda.ibusz.hu. Can exchange currency, as well as arranging tours & private rooms.

📧 **Internet** There are terminals at Broadway Studio & Egriest Café (see pages 236–7)

ℹ️ **Listings magazine** Egri Est

ℹ️ **Tourinform** Bajcsy-Zsilinszky u. 9; ☎ 36 517715; e eger@tourinform.hu. The usual first port of call for local information, including recommendations for English-speaking tour guides. There's an internet terminal. ☺ Jun–Aug Mon–Fri 09.00–19.00, Sat–Sun 10.00–18.00, Sep–May Mon–Fri 09.00–17.00, Sat 09.00–13.00.

🎫 **Villa Tours** Kertész u. 84; ☎ 36 518072; e villatours@villatours.hu. Can arrange accommodation, guided walking tours, themed sightseeing, wine tours, full-day birdwatching, truffle hunting & other gastro tours. Rents out bikes too. ☺ Mon–Fri 08.00–16.00.

🏠 WHERE TO STAY

🏠 **Bacchus Panzió** (24 rooms) Szépasszony-völgy u. 29; ☎ 36 428950; www.bacchuspanzio.hu. With a name like Bacchus, it could only be in the valley of wine cellars – & the old soak would enjoy sleeping off his excesses in one of the spacious, comfortable & modern rooms at this welcoming guesthouse. He may not be the type to appreciate them, but the grounds are lovely too, & there's a patio area from which to enjoy them. Rooms with balconies are slightly more expensive. *Standard sgl/dbl €45/53, superior sgl/dbl €52/60, dbl with jacuzzi €70, apt with jacuzzi €75, excl Tourist Tax.*

🏠 **Garten Guesthouse** (11 rooms)Legányi Ferenc u. 6; ☎ 36 320371. If you prefer to be ensconced away from the thick of things, the Garten is a 15-min walk east of the centre – & it's pretty, with a shady garden & a light conservatory in which to breakfast. The lady owner is a dear. *Dbl 9,000Ft, apt 18,000Ft.*

🏠 **Hotel Arany Trófea** (14 rooms) Széchenyi u. 41/b; ☎ 36 510 840; e hotel@aranytrofea.hu; www.aranytrofea.hu. It looks rather like a doll's house from the outside, & some of the rooms are also on the diminutive side, but the Arany Trófea is central, bright & furnished with mod cons. *Sgl 8,200–10,900, dbl 12,500–18,500Ft, apt (for 4) 13,500–37,900Ft.*

🏠 **Hotel Eger & Park** (177 & 34 rooms) Szálloda u. 1–3; ☎ 36 522221; www.hotelegerpark.hu. Located in the northwestern corner of the Archbishop's Garden, the Eger & Park are two hotels in one. The former is a blocky '70s affair, the latter a 4-star hotel with an elegant early-20th-century atmosphere. Both parts were recently renovated, the location is pleasant, & there's a wellness centre with adventure pool, sauna, ice-, steam-, aroma-, light-, infra- & salt cabins, body treatments, aqua programmes, massages, tennis courts, squash & fitness room. *Sgl €68–114, dbl €80–130, deluxe €170.*

🏠 **Hotel Flora** (184 rooms) Fürdő u. 5; ✆ 36 513300; www.hungesthotels.hu/flora. A blocky hotel with direct access to the thermal baths. The rooms are a touch tired, but are soon to be freshened up with a refurb. Its location makes it a favourite with families, & there's a wide choice of programmes, as well as in-house medical treatments. *Sgl €42, dbl €64–77.*

🏠 **Hotel Ködmön** (20 rooms) Szépasszony-völgy; ✆ 36 516174; www.szepasszonyvolgy.eu. New 4-star property in the Valley of the Beautiful Woman (opposite the Ködmön Csárda & Café Habana, & sharing the same owner). Rooms are good-sized & comfortable, there's a small wellness area & a nice rooftop terrace. *Dbl 24,500–28,500Ft, suite 36,500Ft.*

🏠 **Hotel Senator Ház** (11 rooms) Dobó István tér 11; ✆ 36 320466; www.senatorhaz.hu. Right in the historical heartland, the Senator Ház is a charming 250-year-old town house with a café & restaurant at the front, & green-shuttered windows peeping from among the roof tiles. Half its rooms overlook the square. *Sgl 10,700–13,000Ft, dbl 15,000–17,200Ft, apt from 19,000Ft.*

🏠 **Hotel Villa Völgy** (62 rooms) Tulipánkert u. 5; ✆ 36 321664; www.hotelvillavolgy.hu. A well-located hotel near the Valley of the Beautiful Woman with a mixture of 3- and 4-star rooms. There's a restaurant & cellar, & the 4-star building contains a pool & fitness area. The surrounding garden is beautiful, & hides a romantic little chapel. Ask for a room with a balcony. *Sgl 11,900–21,500Ft, dbl 15,500–27,500Ft, suite 35,000Ft.*

🏠 **Imola Hostel** Leányka u. 2; ✆ 36 520430; www.imolanet.hu/hostel. This hostel is very well located near the castle, & was renovated fairly recently. It has doubles, triples & apartments for 6; rooms have microwave, fridge & are ensuite. *Rooms 3,000Ft/pp.*

🏠 **Imola Udvarház** (6 apts) Dózsa György tér 4; ✆ 36 516180; www.imolanet.hu. Adjacent to the castle entrance, the Imola has well-equipped apartments (choose rooms 1 or 2 for the best views) & an excellent restaurant (see page 236). *Dbl 22,000Ft.*

🏠 **Hotel Szent István** Legányi u. 12; ✆ 36 511300; www.hotelszentistvan.hu. Spread between 5 buildings, this hotel has doubles, apartments & luxury suites. There's a characterful garden (complete with chapel for weddings), a wellness area & restaurant; it's only a 3-star, but really merits a higher ranking. Follow Diófakút utca eastwards from Szarvas tér until it leads into Legányi utca. *Dbl (for 1) 14,000Ft, dbl (for 2) 19,000Ft, apts 20,000–65,000Ft.*

🏠 **Tulipán Camping & Hotel Rubinia** Szépasszony-völgy 71; ✆ 36 410580; www.hotelrubinia.hu; www.eurocampings.net. The ideal site for campers who've sampled the cellars until they're several sticks short of a teepee. While the site itself is simple, there's free access to the facilities (inc swimming pool with view over the valley) at the Hotel Rubinia (same owner). There's a laundry, shop & restaurant, & you can rent old, fixed caravans. (It should be noted that the location makes access for caravans & motorhomes tricky.) *Tent/caravan 600/1,000Ft, plus 1,050Ft/pp; panzió dbl 12,000Ft, apt (for 4) 16,000Ft; bungalow 6,000Ft.* ☺ May–Sep.

🏠 **Villa Citadella** Bálint pap u. 3; ✆ 36 410121; www.villacitadella.hu. It's a bit of a schlep from the centre, but there are superb views over the town from this contemporary villa. It is also very well equipped, with a sauna, solarium & swimming pool. *Sgl 7,000Ft, dbl 14,000Ft.*

Tourinform can provide details of further budget options. There are, for example, several pensions and houses on Joo János utca or Cecey Éva utca offering **private rooms**. There are good views of the city from here, but it's a steep walk up to these roads from the castle's eastern side; if you catch a bus along Bástya utca for a short distance, it will bring you closer and take much of the strain for you. Ibusz and Express (see opposite) can also arrange private lodgings.

✗ **WHERE TO EAT AND DRINK** While there is no shortage of cafés, restaurants are perhaps Eger's blindspot – great places to eat are thin on the ground in the centre.

✗ **Arany Oroszlán** Dobó István tér 5; ✆ 36 311005. The restaurant of the Offi Ház Hotel stands next to the little bridge leading into the larger portion of the square, & serves international cuisine. There are pew-like benches inside & further seating outdoors.

Mains 550–1,200Ft; ☺ *daily 11.00–24.00.*

✗ **Arany Trófea** See opposite. This intimate & chintzy hotel restaurant specialises in game. If you'd prefer, there's less frilly clutter on the grill & beer terrace. *Mains avg 1,600Ft;* ☺ *10.00–22.00 daily.*

☕ **Café Arabica** Dr Hibay Károly u. 22. Quaint café on a corner just outside Dobó István tér; you can choose from vast arrays of teas & coffees – the friendly staff will let you sniff the leaves or beans before making your selection – & either drink your brew among the doilies & bean barrels or buy a packet to take away. ☀ *daily 10.00–19.00.*

☕ **Dobos Cukrászda** Széchenyi u. 6; ☎ 36 413335. The best cakes are probably to be had here, near the Archbishop's Palace, among the wood panelling, chandeliers & stained glass. Such upmarket ambience is reflected in the price. There are also ice creams, coffees & cocktails. ☀ *daily 09.30–21.00.*

☕ **Egriest Café & Internet** Széchenyi u. 16; ☎ 36 411105. A relaxed place for a coffee that also offers internet access. Opposite St Bernard's Church. ☀ *Mon–Sat 11.00–24.00.*

✕ **Elefanto** Katona István tér 2; ☎ 36 412452; www.elefanto.hu. A wooden terrace wraps itself around the elevated restaurant; we love it here at night, when its lanterns & fairy lights in the surrounding trees are at their best. Game is the speciality, but there is also a wide range of pizzas. There is a determined anti-smoking policy inside. *Mains avg 2,000Ft;* ☀ *daily 12.00–23.30 (earlier closing in winter).*

☕ **Éva Ángyo Rétes Boltja** Dobó u. 10. Tasty 'granny-made' strudels. *340Ft/piece;* ☀ *daily 10.00–17.00.*

✕ **Fehérszarvas Vadásztanya** Klapka út 8; ☎ 36 411129; www.feherszarvasetterem.hu. The 'Farm of the White Stag Hunter' looks like a theme restaurant gone mad, with hunting paraphernalia stuffed (literally!) in every cranny. Naturally game is the order of the day, & the quality is as good as anywhere in town. The spicy stews are recommended. Next to the Park Hotel. *Mains avg 2,000Ft;* ☀ *daily 12.00–24.00.*

✕ **Francesco Kávéház és Étterem** Dobó István tér; ☎ 36 515422; www.francesco.hu. Small restaurant on the northern side of the square, opposite the Minorite church. It specialises in Mediterranean food – pizzas & pastas – although there are Hungarian dishes too. *Mains avg 2,100Ft, pizzas 790–1,200Ft, ½ portions at 70% of full price;* ☀ *Sun–Thu 11.30–21.30, Fri–Sat 11.30–22.00.*

☕ **Harmos Cukrászda** Széchenyi u. 25; ☎ 36 517608. Dreamy & creamy ices are popular with the locals, who often queue at the street-level hatch. ☀ *daily 09.00–19.30.*

♀ **HBH Bajor Sörház** Bajcsy-Zsilinsky u. 19; ☎ 36 515516; www.hbh-eger.hu. Beer house with Hungarian & Bavarian brews – including home-made tipples – & food specialities. *Mains avg 1,800Ft;* ☀ *daily 10.00–22.00.*

✕ **Imola Udvarház** Dózsa György tér 4; ☎ 36 414825; e udvarhaz@imolanet.hu; www.imolanet.hu. Situated near the entrance to the castle, this is one of Eger's best. It has a plant-festooned courtyard with waterwheel, & serves well-presented nouvelle-Hungarian cuisine. Overseen by the 'celebrity chef' Viktor Segal. *Mains avg 2,500Ft.*

✕ **Ködmön Csárda** Szépasszony-völgy; ☎ 36 413172; www.kodmoncsarda.hu. The valley's restaurants almost inevitably cater for tourist parties attracted by the wine-sampling opportunities. The Ködmön nevertheless serves tasty Hungarian fare. *Mains avg 1,800Ft;* ☀ *daily 10.00–24.00.*

✕ **Kulacs Csárda** Szépasszony-völgy; ☎ 36 311375; www.kulacscsarda.hu. Kulacs is cut from Ködmön's cloth, trapping tourists with local dishes, gypsy music, vines & lanterns. The dish of cockerel testicles wrapped in onion & egg was something to crow about. They've got a few guestrooms upstairs too. *Mains avg 1,800Ft;* ☀ *daily 12.00–23.00.*

☕ **Marján Cukrászda** Kossuth Lajos u. 28; ☎ 36 312784. An elegant interior with high-backed seating & a daunting selection of cakes piled with cream, cherries, chocolate, walnuts... There's a terrace outside. ☀ *daily May–Sep 09.00–22.00, Oct–Apr 09.00–19.00.*

✕ **Palacsintavár** Dobó u. 9; ☎ 36 413980. There's a bustling atmosphere at Palacsintavár, set deep below street level near the castle, & a serious commitment to calorie counting – think of a number & multiply it many, many times! Among a staggering choice of pancakes is 'Lucifer's palacsinta' – featuring pork, turkey, chicken, potato & cream. Fabulous. *Pancakes 850–1,500Ft;* ☀ *daily 12.00–23.00.*

The main **market hall** (*Katona tér;* ☀ *Mon–Fri 06.00–18.00, Sat 06.00–13.00, Sun 06.00–10.00*) sells fresh fruit, vegetables and cakes.

ENTERTAINMENT AND NIGHTLIFE The Tourinform or main **ticket office** (*Széchenyi u. 5;* ☎ *36 518347*) have details of drama and concerts. The **Gárdonyi Géza Theatre** (*Hatvani kapu tér 4;* ☎ *36 310026; www.gardonyiszinhaz.hu; ticket office* ☀ *Tue–Sat 14.00–19.00*) stands near the basilica, and is named after the literary son the town clutches tight to its bosom (see page 241); unfortunately the drama, musicals and children's productions are in Hungarian.

Perhaps more likely to leap the linguistic gap is the **Harlekin Puppet Theatre** (*Harlekin Bábszínház; Bartók Béla tér 6;* \ *36 413073*), its auditorium hosting shows for adults and children. Alternatively, in summer there are **organ recitals** in the basilica (*May 15–Oct 15 Mon–Sat 11.30, Sun 12.45*), and plays at the **Lyceum** (see below). The **cultural centre** (*Knérich Károly u. 5*) also hosts concerts and local productions.

Broadway Studio (*Pyrker tér 1–3;* \ *36 517220;* ☉ *café daily 09.00–23.00, club Thu–Sat 22.00–06.00*) is sequestered beneath the basilica steps, operating as a bar and internet café by day and a club by night. **Aphrodite Nightclub** (*Széchenyi u. 53*) is a rather cheesy, Euro-pop-tune club at the end of Széchenyi utca. The **Egal Cult Club** (*Széchenyi u. 57;* \ *36 436295;* e *info@egal.hu*) is one of the great underground places in town, with live concerts and DJs every Wednesday, Friday and Saturday evening. They have exhibitions too. The **Hippolit Club** (*Katona István tér 2;* \ *36 412452;* e *hippolit@agria.hu;* ☉ *Tue–Sat 21.00–04.00*) is a disco and karaoke bar at the Elefanto (see opposite), while **Champ's Pub** (*Maklári út 9;* \ *36 512512*) in the Hotel Aqua has draught beer and a summer grill terrace.The **Leonardo Grill & Dance Bar** (*Klapka út 8;* \ *36 312058;* ☉ *Tue–Sat 22.00–03.00; Wed–Thu 19.00–22.00 for speed dating*) offers the chance for a disco dance; if you arrive early on Wednesday or Thursday you can try to find someone to dance with during a speed-dating session. And don't forget the 200 wine cellars to move between in the **Valley of the Beautiful Woman** – more than enough to fill an evening…

WHAT TO SEE AND DO

Eszterházy tér, Széchenyi István utca and around There were no horses spared in building the Neoclassical **Eger Cathedral** (*Eszterházy tér*); József Hild's design – the country's second-largest church (after Esztergom) – was finished in 1836 after just six years' work. The cupola is 40m in height, while two broad flights of steps lead up to the colonnade's eight monumental Corinthian pillars at the basilica's entrance. Statues of kings Laszló and István and apostles Peter and Paul either side of the steps are the work of Venetian sculptor Marco Casagrande, who had a hand in many of the church's artistic adornments. Inside are clusters of chocolate- and caramel-coloured marble columns, an altar painting (*The Martyrdom of St John*) of 1835 by Viennese artist Joseph Danhauser, and the biggest organ in Hungary. (For details of recital times, see above.) The cathedral was raised to 'basilica' rank by the pope in 1970.

Just to the north of the basilica is the **Archbishop's Palace** (*Érseki Palota; Széchenyi István u. 5*), the Baroque residence of the town's bishops for over 250 years. Its **Ecclesiastical Collection** (*Egyházi Gyűjtemény;* \ *36 421332;* ◈ *500/300Ft;* ☉ *Apr–Oct Tue–Sat 09.00–17.00, Nov–Mar Mon–Fri 08.00–16.00*) charts the history of Eger's top ministers between 1699 and 1943, featuring canonical treasures of the 18th and 19th centuries. Some of the items were gifts to Bishop Gábor Erdődy from Empress Maria Theresa, including the cloak she wore at her coronation.

To the right of the base of the steps leading to the basilica is the **Town Under the Town** (*Város a Város Alatt; Malomárok u. 10;* \ *20 961 4019; www.varosavarosalatt.hu;* ◈ *950/500Ft; 45-min tours every hr;* ☉ *daily 10.00–20.00 Apr–Sep, 10.00–17.00 Oct–Mar*). This is the entrance of the former archiepiscopal wine cellars. Visitors can walk a few hundred metres of a system that measured kilometres in length; historical tours are led in English, Hungarian and German.

The rectangular **Lyceum** (*Eszterházy tér 1;* \ *36 520400;* e *kincsmarti@ektf.hu;* ◈ *700/500Ft;* ☉ *by prior arrangement Apr–Sep Tue–Sun 09.30–15.30, Oct–Mar Sat–Sun 09.30–13.30*) faces the basilica across Széchenyi István utca. It was built in late-Baroque style during the mid-18th century as a school. Bishop Károly Eszterházy (1725–99) subsequently expanded the building with the intention of developing it into a Hungarian-language university, establishing an extensive library and an astronomical tower. However, Maria Theresa scuppered these plans by decreeing that there should be no further higher-education institutions under church control, and denying Eger the right to university rank.

While it now operates as a teacher-training college, the Lyceum also houses the splendid **Archdiocesan Library** on its first floor, the Hungarian Church's only public holdings. Presiding over Louis-XVI-style oak furnishings and creaking floorboards, the ceiling is decorated with a 1778 fresco by János Kracker and József Zach depicting the Council of Trent (held between 1543 and 1563). Among the important decisions taken during the synod debates was the censorship and destruction of heretical writings, symbolised in the painting by a flash of lightning. Comprising 20,000 volumes when opened in 1793, the library now has 130,000, among them medieval codices, the first book printed in Hungarian (the *Buda Chronicle* of 1473) and a letter in Mozart's hand (the only one in Hungary).

A big trek up to a small collection, the **Astronomical Museum** (🎫 600/400Ft) is on the sixth floor of the east wing, and displays refracting and reflecting telescopes and quadrants from the 18th century, together with a horizontal sundial found in the small village of Mezőnyárád. Climb higher for a reconstruction of an astronomer's room, and a viewing gallery running around the outside of the tower. A final push brings you to the **camera obscura**, the 'eye of Eger'; a twiddle of the periscope's mirrors and lenses projects an image of the town outside on to a table inside the pitch-black Dark Chamber. Constructed in 1776 by the Viennese astronomer Miksa Hell – purely to amuse himself and his pals – the device is the second-oldest of its type in the world (pipped by Edinburgh).

Széchenyi utca is the strollers' street of choice, with its atmospheric restaurants, bars and terraced patisseries. There's plenty to keep you interested as you move northwards from the Lyceum. Look out for the Baroque **clock shop** (*no 13*) at the corner with Bródy Sándor utca, designed by Italian architect Giovanni Carlone in 1725; there's a statue of a lady ruffling a cherub's hair in a niche above the entrance. Next door is the **Cistercian Church** (*Széchenyi u. 15*), constructed on the site of an earlier Turkish mosque. Originally a Jesuit church, the foundation stone was laid by Bishop István Telekessy in 1700, but the Rákóczi Uprising put a halt to work and the church wasn't completed until 1743. It was taken over by the Cistercians at the end of the 18th century. While the frescoed ceilings and walls are not as sharply colourful as they once were, they remain impressive; the statue on the Rococo high altar depicts the kneeling Jesuit St Francis Borgia, and dates to 1770.

Opposite is an **Apothecary Museum** (*Apothekemúzeum Telekessy Patikamúzeum; Széchenyi u. 14;* ☏ *36 312744; free;* ☉ *May–Aug Tue–Sun 09.00–17.00*), its Baroque and florid Rococo furnishings crafted in the Jesuit monastery during the mid 1700s. The pharmacy was established in the monastery on the back of a donation from Bishop Telekessy, and moved to its current location in 1900. Further up, the stones of a mosque were recycled in the construction of **St Anna Church** (*Széchenyi u. 29*) in 1731; a plaque records the height reached by a flood that wrought havoc in 1878. You can access the **Serbian Orthodox Church** (*Szent Miklós Görögkeleti; Széchenyi u. 55;* ⊗ *adult 200Ft;* ☉ *Tue–Sun 10.00–16.00*), with its magnificently gilded Louis-XVI-style iconostasis (1789–91), via some covered steps at no 55. Alternatively you can go around the corner to a door at Vitkovics utca 30. It was established in 1789 by Serbs and Greeks who settled here after fleeing the Turks; in a deliberate snub to the intolerant archbishop, who had previously forbidden any non-Roman-Catholic churches in Eger, József II personally granted permission for its construction. In the former parsonage – the **Vitkovics Ház** (☏ *36 412023;* ⊗ *300/150Ft;* ☉ *May–Sep Tue–Sun 10.00–16.00, Oct–Apr Mon–Sat 10.00–16.00*) – is the memorial room of the Serbian poet Mihály Vitkovics and an exhibition of the work of 20th-century Hungarian artist György Kepes.

Kossuth Lajos utca Kossuth utca is studded with fine 18th-century Baroque buildings, many adorned with intricate wrought-iron work. The heavy-metal master was Henrik Fazola, hailing originally from Germany, whose hand was in the balcony and billowing window covers of the peach-coloured **Vice-Provost's Palace** (*Kispréposti Palota; Kossuth Lajos u. 4*). Your eyes will need some time to adjust on entering the dimly lit **Franciscan church** (*Kossuth Lajos u. 14*), famed for its altar by painter Pál Kronewetter and sculptor Antal Steinhauser, with branching vines like tinsel on a tree. The church's foundation stone was laid in 1736, and many of the monastery's doors and fittings are original.

The genius of the ironwright Fazola is evident again in the gates and door of **County Hall** (*Kossuth u. 9*), where metal twists and turns and blooms into flowerbuds, where branches form a bower of justice, and the golden figures of Faith, Hope and Justice sit among dark stems. We also love the cuddly lions that hold the door knockers. The building itself was finished in 1756, based on the designs of Mátyás Gerl. Moving through to the courtyard, you'll reach the former Eger prison; today it houses the **Local History Museum** (covering Heves County and Eger between the 18th century and now) and the **Sports Museum** (showing over 1,800 trophies won by the county's star swimmers and waterpolo players; *both museums* ⊗ *120/80Ft;* ☉ *May–Sep Tue–Sun 09.00–17.00*).

The former **Grand Provost's Palace** (*Kossuth Lajos u. 16*) now contains the county library; doubtless among its books is Kálmán Mikszáth's *A Strange Marriage*, which featured **Buttler House** (*Kossuth Lajos u. 26*) – now a decrepit building just beyond the bridge over the Eger Stream. A smidgen further, set back on the left, is a former 19th-century **Orthodox synagogue** (*Kossuth Lajos u. 17*), which – after decades of neglect – now hosts temporary exhibitions. Near by too is the former **Small Synagogue** (*Kis Zsinagóga; dr Hibay Károly u. 7*), which was built in the 1840s and served as a centre for the Jewish community until World War II. It has been renovated by a local NGO and opened as a gallery for local artists, with regular exhibitions and workshops.

Dobó István tér and the minaret Bisected by a stream, the pleasingly asymmetrical Dobó István tér was the town's market square from the Middle Ages; in summer, bursting window boxes adorn the houses, and there's an unbroken murmur from customers seated at the cafés. The eponymous commander and defiant Eger hero (see page 232) is remembered in **Alajos Stróbl's statue**, flanked by one of the local women who pitched in to assist in repulsing the attack. A second monument – *Soldiers of the Border Fortress* – is all movement and wild-eyed, gaping-mouthed stallions in its depiction of a fearless Hungarian assault on a pair of Turks.

The prime sight, though, is the twin-towered **Minorite church** (*Dobó István tér 4*), rated among the most handsome pieces of Baroque ecclesiastical architecture in Europe. It was designed by the Prague master Kilián Ignaz Dientzenhofer, and finished in 1767; the altarpiece showing St Anthony and the Virgin Mary is a cracker of a painting by the painter János Kracker. Look up also to the piggy-faced gargoyles running around the outside, with their double chins and sausagey lips. If you're there on the hour, you'll enjoy as charming a musical chiming as you're likely to hear from a church – a lurching, lilting melody that stumbles its way through to the tune's conclusion. Near by is the **Palóc Folk Art Exhibition** (*Dobó István u. 12:* ❧ *36 312744;* ✆ *200/100Ft;* ☉ *Apr–Oct Tue–Sun 09.00–17.00*), an ethnographic collection of Palóc ceramics and costumes.

A shortish distance to the north of Dobó tér is one of the lonely reminders of Turkish occupation in Eger – and Europe's northernmost remnant – a spindly sandstone finger in the middle of Knézich Károly utca. You can take a vertiginous and cramped climb up the 40m **minaret**'s 97 steps to a narrow viewing ledge (✆ *adult 100Ft;* ☉ *Apr 1–Oct 31 Tue–Sun 10.00–18.00*) – pity the 17th-century Muslim crier who had to do this five times a day in calling the faithful to prayer.

The castle and around From Dobó István tér, a steep cobbled lane brings you to **Eger Castle** (*Egri Vár; Vár 1;* ❧ *36 312744; www.div.iif.hu;* ✆ *grounds only 700/350Ft, grounds & Castle Museum 1,200/600Ft (concessions inc under 26s); grounds* ☉ *daily Apr–Aug 08.00–20.00, Sep 08.00–19.00, Oct 08.00–18.00, Nov–Feb 08.00–17.00, Mar 08.00–18.00*), which is virtually synonymous in national consciousness with the heroic stand made against the Turks in 1552. It means István Dobó, it means 2,000 men seeing off a force of 80,000, it means women hurling boiling pitch from the ramparts, it means red wine or bull's blood to fortify wilting spirits (see page 232). The 13th-century castle – built in the aftermath of the Mongol invasion – had actually fallen into disrepair in the years leading up to this first siege, and it wasn't until after 1552 that Dobó properly set about strengthening and updating its fortifications. However, the Turks were unwilling to give up on a castle that they saw as strategically vital to the northern portion of the country, and successfully captured it 44 years later. In 1702, 15 years after the departure of the Ottomans, the castle was blown up by the Habsburgs.

The majority of the buildings now inside the walls are the result of modern reconstruction – the exception being the ruined foundations of the 11th-century **Romanesque cathedral** in the eastern section. The restored **Bishop's Palace** was originally built in Gothic style during the 1470s. The occupying Turks later used the ground floor as a prison, but the palace is now home to the **Dobó István Castle Museum** (☉ *Tue–Sun Nov–Feb 09.00–15.00, Mar–Oct 09.00–17.00*), whose exhibitions include a history of the complex (complete with Turkish items), artefacts from villages of the region, the 'Heroes' Hall' (resting place of Dobó himself) and a collection of instruments of torture and execution. An **art gallery** near by in the courtyard displays works by Italian, Dutch and Austrian artists, as well as pieces by Mihály Munkácsy, while other attractions for which you'll need to pay extra are a **coinage** and a **waxworks** (featuring characters from Gárdonyi's *Eclipse of the Crescent Moon;* ✆ *250/175Ft;* ☉ *08.00–18.00*) in the northwestern Föld Bastion.

The soft stone beneath Eger allowed the digging of a series of **underground passages** (*kazamaták*) that connected various parts of the castle and were used as storage rooms. Subterranean battles were intrinsic to the struggle for the castle. In 1552, Hungarian defenders watched peas on drums to detect the vibrations of Turkish picks as they attempted to tunnel beneath the walls. The Hungarians would then dig towards the sounds and detonate explosives to snuff out the invaders. You can visit a section of the system on a guided tour (*leaving from information desk beside arched gateway;* ⊕ *until 17.00*), although it's in Hungarian. The last, collapsed piece of the tunnel contains a memorial plaque to 50 soldiers who died during the second siege in 1592; they were killed after foreign mercenaries turned traitors – the Turks detonated this portion after being informed that the Hungarian soldiers were in the process of launching a counterattack here.

On top of the southeastern Várkoch Bastion is the **grave of Géza Gárdonyi**, marked as he wished with the simple words 'Only his body lies here'. The writer lived in the town for his last 25 years; his house lies 50m to the north of the castle and now contains a **memorial museum** (*Gárdonyi u. 28;* ☏ *36 312744;* 🎟 *400/200Ft;* ⊕ *Tue–Sun Mar–Oct 09.00–17.00*). The 'hermit of Eger', as he became known, took two years to compose *Eclipse of the Crescent Moon* and did so with his windows boarded up and his doors stuffed with pillows to guarantee privacy and focus. His library, desk and a few writings (some in code) are on display. To the south of the castle complex in Dózsa György tér are the ruins of a **Turkish bath** (*Válide Szultána fürdő*), currently under a corrugated covering; it is hoped that this will eventually be reconstructed.

Valley of the Beautiful Woman At the end of an afternoon's sightseeing, take a 20-minute walk west along Király utca to Szépasszony-völgy – where there are 200 numbered wine cellars carved into the valley sides, looking like a series of dungeon cells. The name is intriguing. Some say it harks back to a goddess of love named Szépasszony to whom sacrifices were made in the valley; some say it refers to a particularly lovely lady who once ran a cellar here. We're not sure, but it could be because everybody looks beautiful after a few glasses of wine!

The mould-clad cellars were dug from the tufa centuries ago, and they remain at a constant temperature of 10–15°C. Cellars have variable hours, but generally there are some open at 10.00 and some still going at 21.00 or 22.00. Wine by the glass costs as little as 50Ft; it is also common to purchase by the refillable plastic bottle. Tamás Sike's cellar (no 43 in the row) has excellent Cabernet Franc, and the staff speak a bit of English – if you ask, they might show you the wooden barrels deep within the cellar's belly. Beyond that, dip into those caverns that take your fancy – but remember to dedicate your last drink to St John, protector of the vines. There's an area for picnics or barbecues, and a couple of restaurants (see page 236).

If you don't want to walk to the valley, one of the motorised tourist trains runs there (see page 234); alternatively, a taxi should cost approximately 800–1,000Ft.

Other There is a cluster of places to take a dip. The pleasant **Eger Thermal Baths** (*Petőfi tér 2;* ☏ *36 412202;* 🎟 *1,250/1,080Ft;* ⊕ *May–Sep Mon–Fri 07.00–19.00, Sat–Sun 08.00–19.00, Oct–Apr daily 09.00–18.30*) is an area of open-air and adventure pools in the Archbishop's Garden; the mildly radioactive thermal water is said to ease rheumatic and locomotor disorders. Our favourite spot is the Roman-style hydromassage near the paddling pools. There's also a wellness centre with saunas and massage (for an extra charge). (Note that guests of the Hunguest Hotel Flora can enter the baths free.) Adjacent is a **Turkish Bath** (*Fürdő u. 1–3*), which was originally completed in 1617. (While few Turkish traces remain now, the bathing culture remained popular after their departure. In 1791, the mayor decreed that 'any persons found in the bath after ten o'clock by the city guards shall be given 24 lashes with a stick in the market place.' We're assured the current authorities are more lenient...) The baths were closed for refurbishment during our last visit, but will re-open as a Turkish hamam and with a therapy centre, making use of its curative waters.

The **Bitskey Aladár Indoor Swimming Pool** (*Frank Tivadar u.;* ❧ *36 511810; ❧ 850/550Ft;* ☉ *Mon–Fri 06.00–21.30, Sat–Sun 07.30–18.00*) is an impressive modern structure containing an Olympic-sized pool. It's worth remembering that Eger is a stronghold for waterpolo and swimming, and so the pool is sometimes closed to the public while athletes train. If you're lucky, you might get the chance to catch a live waterpolo match.

The **Egedhegyi Lippizaner Horse Farm** (*Lipicai Lovastanya; Noszvaji út mellett;* ❧ *36 517937; www.matyusudvarhaz.hu; ❧ riding from 3,500Ft/hr, carriage rides from 3,500Ft/pp/hr*) is 2km from Eger on the way towards Noszvaj (the bus from the centre stops outside). Its stables can cater for riders of all levels, and the farm also offers hunting, wine and cross-country programmes, as well as carriage driving. Board is available in the Mátyus Udvarház (*6,000 Ft/pp*), which also has a restaurant.

FESTIVALS AND EVENTS Among the town's annual events are the Eger Spring Festival (featuring performances of contemporary art, folklore, theatre and ballet; *last two weeks of Mar*), Army Bands' Festival (brass and woodwind bands; *Jun*), Agria Summer Games (theatrical events; *Jun–Jul*), the Eger Wine Festival (a celebration of Bull's Blood, with food to accompany it, in Dobó István tér; *Jul*), the Castle Festival (medieval tournaments, battle re-enactments and processions, together with puppetry and other street performances; *mid Jul*), the Baroque Festival (three weeks of dance music and street activities; *late Jul/early Aug*), the Musical August Festival (concerts of jazz, popular and classical music; *Aug*), the Szépasszony-völgy Festival Mátra (wine, wine-songs competition and food; *Aug 20–22*), the Agria International Folk Festival (a convention of international folk-dance groups, who put on shows in the streets and squares; *late Aug*) and the lively Eger Harvest Days (folkdancing, parades of floats and various wine-related events; *Sep*).

EGERSZALÓK, DEMJÉN AND BOGÁCS

When we first came here a few years ago, we came close to double-taking on seeing **Egerszalók's hot spring** (*Forrás u. 2;* ❧ *30 4765736; ❧ adult 1,000Ft;* ☉ *Tue–Thu 15.00–22.00, Fri–Sat 13.00–01.00, Sun 13.00–22.00*), and people lounging around what looked like icebergs in their bathing suits in the dead of a winter's night. The water emerges at 70°C (and is 20,000 years old), and contains calcium, sulphur, sulphide – and the salt whose deposits form the 'icebergs'. This was by far the most

---

LIPIZZANERS

Contrary to popular belief, you can find the world-famous Lipizzaner horses (which were originally trained as nimble battle steeds) outside Vienna – indeed, they are bred at the Slovenian karst village of Lipica (meaning 'small linden tree' in Slovenian, and from where the horse's name derives), as well as in Hungary. The dazzling white coat comes with time; Lipizzaners are actually grey or black at birth, and gradually whiten with age – if you see a pure white, it is at least six years old. Aside from the beautiful colour, Lipizzaners are distinctive for their broad and muscular frame, reaching a height of over 2m, and for their graceful movement and thick manes.

romantic spa we'd seen. However, we returned more recently and discovered they'd spoiled the whole thing. Dirty lucre has clearly played its part: the quiet spot has been converted into a spa complex, the 'icebergs' part of a giant, artificial pool area. Next to the older lido, the new **Salt Hill Thermal Spa** (*Forrás út 4;* ℡ *36 688500; www.egerszalokfurdo.hu;* ✆ *2,400/1,200Ft;* ⊕ *daily 10.00–20.00*) covers 11,000m² (with a water surface area of 1,900m²), and has 17 outdoor and indoor pools, as well as a variety of saunas, massages and medical treatments. A luxury hotel is being built adjacent to the spa – the rotten cherry on top of a spoiled cake – and the surroundings are currently a giant construction site.

It's just a 13-minute bus ride southeast from Eger to Egerszalók; buses leave regularly, passing through Egerszalók on their way to Kerecsend via Demjén. The spring itself is on the main road between Egerszalók and Demjén – follow the wooden signposts for the short walk from the road.

If you'd rather something a little more peaceful, you might consider moving a few kilometres to **Demjén** (*Demjén Thermal Völgy;* ✆ *990/790Ft;* ⊕ *09.00–02.00*). This thermal spa has something of the isolated feel of the Egerszalók of yesteryear; it uses the same spring and is favoured now by many locals (although the pools themselves are standard). Southeast of Eger (and 10km north of Mezőkövesd), the village of **Bogács** is also popular for its thermal baths (*Dózsa György u. 16;* ℡ *49 534410;* e *bogacs-strand@t-online.hu;* ✆ *950/700Ft;* ⊕ *daily Jun–Aug 09.00–20.00, May & Sep 09.00–19.00, Oct– 09.00–17.00, closed Mon in winter*). There are seven outdoor thermal pools. Regular buses run from Mezőkövesd station on the Budapest–Miskolc railway line.

MEZŐKÖVESD

South of Bogács, Mezőkövesd is the capital of the 'Matyóföld' – where the Matyó people are responsible for Hungary's brightest and most vivid folk art. The settlement is defined by the floral-patterned needlework that its people have developed over the last 150 years, and which is renowned even beyond the national borders, while the protruding roofs of its houses – reminiscent of the Palóc style (see page 212) – also mark it out. It is thought that the ethnic group derived its name from that of Mátyás, the Renaissance monarch who conferred market status on the town. There's no point in staying here overnight when Eger is under 20km away. The best time to visit is Easter, when the Matyó Easter Festival comes to town – featuring folk dance, handicraft exhibitions, egg painting and the traditional 'sprinkling' (see box, page 68).

GETTING THERE AND AWAY Mezőkövesd is on the line from Miskolc to Budapest, and there are up to nine direct **trains** a day from Budapest Keleti or Kelenföld. Hatvan is also on this line; you'll need to change at Füzesabony if you're travelling from Debrecen or Eger. There are three direct **buses** a day from Budapest Stadion, the rest requiring a change at Eger. There are regular buses to Eger and Miskolc, and services to Debrecen (two), Gyöngyös (four) and Tiszafüred (five).

INFORMATION
🛈 **Tourinform** Szent László tér 23; ℡ 49 500285;
e mezokovesd@tourinform.hu; www.mezokovesd.hu;
⊕ Mon–Fri 10.00–16.00.

WHAT TO SEE AND DO The **Matyó Museum** (*Szent László tér 20;* ℡ *49 311824;* ✆ *400/200Ft;* ⊕ *Tue–Sun 09.00–17.00; prior notice through Tourinform is advised in winter*) reveals the life, times and culture of the Matyó people. There are displays of coloured furniture, crockery, rich head gear and bell-shaped skirts. At the entrance is a bust of Bori Kis Jankó, the 'woman of a hundred roses' who founded a Matyó folkart school. The **Bori Kis Jankó Memorial House** (*Kis Jankó Bori Emlékház; Kis Jankó Bori u. 22;* ✆ *49 411873;* 🎫 *200/100Ft;* ◷ *May–Oct Tue–Sun 09.00–16.00*) shows some of her rosy embroidery in the 19th-century cottage in which she lived, and also provides an insight into the lifestyle of the area's peasant workers.

The **Agricultural Machine Museum** (*Eötvös u. 32;* ✆ *49 312820*) is an exhibition (indoor and out) of threshing equipment, tractors and other tools used by the farmers here, and focuses too on the work of local blacksmiths. St László Church (*Szent László tér 28;* ◷ *daily Mar 21–Sep 21 08.00–16.30, Sep 22–Mar 20 08.00–15.30*), near the Matyó Museum, has a 15th-century Gothic sanctuary inside its primarily Baroque body. The frescoes were by István Takács, whose art adorns many churches around the country. In 1806, the Holy Crown spent a night in the parsonage, one among the numerous places it was hidden during its fugitive history.

Zsóry Thermal Baths (*Napfürdő u. 2;* ✆ *49 412844; www.zsory-furdo.hu;* 🎫 *1,200/900Ft;* ◷ *Sep–May 07.00–18.00, Jun 07.00–19.00, Jul–Aug 07.00–20.00*) – 3km away from central Mezőkövesd – is the main tourist attraction nowadays. The baths complex has indoor and outdoor pools, and its waters are curative.

BÉLAPÁTFALVA

Moving north from Eger – three-quarters of the way to Szilvásvárad – Bélapátfalva was named after the Bél clan. Its cement factory would usually make it a place to scurry past, but the **abbey church** was part of a monastery constructed by Cistercian monks in 1232 and, as such, is a rare surviving Romanesque building (with later Gothic additions). Most buses and trains running between Eger and Szilvásvárad stop at Bélapátfalva. The church is 2km east of the centre along Apátság utca; you may need to ask for the key (*kulcs*) at Rózsa Ferenc utca 42.

SZILVÁSVÁRAD

At the northwestern edge of the Bükk Hills, 30km from Eger, the area around Szilvásvárad has been inhabited since the Palaeolithic Age – evidence of ancient occupation was found in the cave at the foot of Istállóskő (itself the highest Bükk peak, at 958m). The village is now a focal point for the breeding of Lipizzaners, those snowy equine aristocrats. There are excellent indoor and outdoor equestrian arenas – where Prince Philip once competed in the '80s – and September sees the Lipizzaner Horse Festival, while each summer the national coach-riding championships are held here. The primary attraction, however, is the Szalajka Valley, one of the country's most captivating corners. Waterfalls and trout ponds dot its length, and you can visit them on foot, by bike or by boarding a wooden carriage of the narrow-gauge railway.

GETTING THERE AND AWAY There are **bus** stops in the middle of the village, with between two and four daily buses going to Budapest and regular services to Eger (up until around 18.30 at weekends and 20.30 on weekdays). Among other destinations on the bus route are Gyöngyös (five a day), Parádfürdő and Mátraháza (one), and the pretty village of Szarvaskő (regular). The village has two **train** stations (on the Füzesabony–Putnok line, which includes Eger and Egervár); the main one is 3km to the north but you are better to alight at Szilvásvárad-Szalkavölgy just under a kilometre to the southeast along Egri út. If coming from Budapest, you'll need to change at Füzesabony.

WHERE TO STAY AND EAT There's oodles of accommodation in Szilvásvárad – the only times you might struggle are during the horse festival or carriage championships.

✕ **Csobogó Étterem** Szalajka-völgy út; www.csobogoetterem.hu. Standing almost opposite the Lovas (see below), this decked bar & restaurant has a staggered waterfall as its central feature, & is a good spot for a beer or bite.

✕ **Fenyő Vendéglő** Szalajka-völgy út; ✆ 36 564015; www.fenyovendeglo.hu. Like Lovas, this is a good 'un with very friendly staff & local specialities. You can rent a private apartment here too (from 2,700Ft/pp), & book a variety of programmes. Mains avg 1,900Ft; ⊕ daily Apr–Oct 08.00–22.00, Nov–Mar 10.00–20.00.

⌂ **Gasthaus Szilvásvárad** (9 rooms) Egri út; ✆ 36 355185. A modern guesthouse just outside the barrier marking the entrance to Szalajka Valley. The owner is a surly chap, but the rooms are tidy enough & the restaurant (mains avg 1,400Ft; ⊕ Tue–Sun 07.00–22.00) specialises in local game & trout. Dbl 9,600Ft.

⌂ **Hegyi Camping** Egri u. 36A; ✆ 36 355207; www.hegyicamping.com. This large site at the base of Kalapot Hill has log cabins, dorm rooms & tent-pitching space. You can also hire horses (3,000Ft/hr). Cabin dbl 5,500Ft, trpl 6,500Ft, quad 7,500Ft; tent/caravan/motorhome 1,300/3,500/3,000Ft; ⊕ Apr 15–Oct 15.

⌂ **La Contessa Kastély Hotel** (44 rooms) Park u. 6; ✆ 36 564064; www.lacontessa.hu. Housed in the former Neo-Baroque Pallavicini Castle (designed by the prolific Miklós Ybl), this recently overhauled hotel drips comfort & style, & is set in 40ha of beautiful grounds. It has wellness facilities, & half of the rooms even have their own saunas. Impressively luxurious. Note that prices are lower on weekdays & when booking online. Dbl 18,700–49,000Ft.

⌂ **Lipicai Tourist House** (29 rooms) Egri út 12–14; ✆ 36 564036; www.szilvasvarad-lipicaihotel.hu. A hostel popular with student groups & consequently both lively & lacking in luxury. The rooms (sleeping 2–5), however, do have showers & TVs. There's a small restaurant attached, & the hotel can arrange excursions on foot, by horse or by jeep. Rooms 4,400Ft/pp; b/fast 500Ft.

✕ **Lovas** Szalajka-völgy út; ✆ 36 564056; www.lovasetterem.hu. We really enjoyed eating at Lovas, next to the open equestrian arena. It's rustic & atmospheric, & the service is excellent. We love the way the menus are printed like newspapers. The cuisine is Hungarian & international, many dishes served with truffles sourced from the local forest

(indeed, they run a truffle-hunting expedition for guests in October). We found the food top drawer, & the portions large. Highly recommended. Mains avg 2,100Ft.

⌂ **Szalajka Fogadó** Egri út 2; ✆ 36 564020; www.szalajkafogado.hu. Shaded by trees at the bank of a little stream (300m north of the Lipicai), the recently renovated inn has a fountain bubbling at its entrance, contemporary rooms & a small wellness area. Its restaurant is rather good, with a decent-sized alfresco eating area; game & trout again feature prominently on the menu (mains avg 1,600Ft). The hotel can organise programmes including horse-riding, paragliding & cycling. Sgl 9,700Ft, dbl 13,500Ft, trpl 17,800Ft, apt (for four) 20,800Ft, excl Tourist Tax.

⌂ **Szalajka Liget Hotel & Villas** Park u. 25/A; ✆ 36 564020; www.szalajkaliget.hu. This new 4-star wellness hotel is in a scenic spot; its rooms are comfortable, & the villas have open kitchens & fireplaces in the sitting room. Dbl 18,500–26,000Ft, suite 34,500–37,000Ft, apt (for 4/6) 34,500–39,900Ft/39,500–45,000Ft.

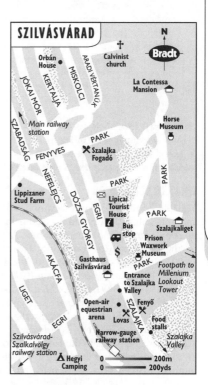

The **common alder** (*Alnetum glutinosae-incanae*), which thrives in the alluvial deposits at the edges of streams, is the valley's dominant tree species; its cones grow in bunched groups, while in spring catkins appear. The shallower valley sides also harbour willows, particularly the **white willow** (*Salix alba*). Spring sees the valley's damper areas blanketed with the **common marsh marigold** (*Caltha palustris*), also known as the 'kingcup', its five petals flowering between March and August. There are many species of **fern** among the alder groves, along with the **butterbur** (*Petasites hybridus*), which flowers between March and May and whose roots were once used to treat the plague.

The fauna is typified by wet-loving species. The **common brown trout** (*Salmo trutta fario*) is as wet as you can get in the streams, and is also reared in artificial ponds. The creeks – fed by karstic springs – shelter species that are sensitive to environmental change. Here are **snails** (like the endemic *Sadleriana pannonica*), **sand-hoppers** (which are found under pebbles and leap about when disturbed), **bloodworms** (larvae of the midge family *Chironomidae*, which degrade organic material in the water), **may flies** (*Ephemeroptera*, fans of fresh flowing water during their notoriously short lives), **beetles** (like rhynchites, plant beetles), **dragon flies**, **caddis flies**, **caperers** and **lace wings**. Amphibians such as **salamander**, **common brown frog** (*Rana temporaria*) and **brown toad** (*Bufo bufo*) enjoy the ponds and creek overflows in spring. **Water rats** hunt the waterside butterbur meadows.

The **wood warbler** (*Phylloscopus sibilatrix*) is common to deciduous forests; it has a yellow throat and eye stripe, but is small and difficult to see – listen out for its hissing song. The **robin** (*Erithacus rubecula*), a red-breasted and sparrow-sized bird found all over Europe, nests in scrubby forest. The **grey wagtail** (*Motacilla cinerea*) is found near water, and favours brooks and mountain streams. It is unfortunately decreasing in number. The distinctive **dipper** (*Cinclus cinclus*) – dark, dark brown, with a bright-white belly – is common in much of Europe. In Hungary, however, its population fell to under ten pairs, and a couple of these nest in the Szalajka Valley. Dippers have an unusual feeding method – they run along the bed of the brook, catching snails, crayfish and insect larvae. The **blue tit** (*Parus caeruleus*) nests in hollow trees.

🏠 **Villanegra** (9 rooms) 📞 36 355240 ℮ villanegravendeghaz@t-online.hu. Real romance in the heart of the Szalajka Valley. The panzió is tastefully furnished & squeakily clean, & its rooms are of a reasonable size. It also has its own little restaurant (*mains avg 1,800Ft*). You'll find it well signposted along the walking trail once you've alighted from the narrow-gauge railway. *Dbl 14,500Ft.*

WHAT TO SEE AND DO

Szalajka Valley The 5km valley itself is presaged by a road buzzing with places to eat and huts selling pottery and faux animal skins. The main walking trail can be picked up 300m south of the entrance barrier. A path branching immediately to the left leads to the **Millennium Lookout Tower** (🎫 *300/200Ft;* ⊕ *Nov–Feb Wed–Sun 10.00–16.00, Mar–Apr Wed–Sun 10.00–17.00, May & Sep–Oct Tue–Sun 10.00–17.00, Jun–Aug Mon 12.00–19.00 Tue–Sun 10.00–19.00*). There is also an **Adventure Forest** (*kalanderdő;* 🎫 *1,500/1,300Ft;* ⊕ *Jun 15–Aug 31 11.00–19.00 daily, Apr 15–Jun 15 & Sep 1–Oct 15 11.00–17.00 weekends only*), a playground for younger and older alike in the trees with rope bridges and high walkways, and a place to hire **bicycles** (*kerékpár;* 📞 *30 335 2695;* 🎫 *800Ft/hr, 2,000Ft/day*). (We hired bikes and followed a route map on a 2½-hour, 18km ride to the Fátyol Waterfall, past some soldiers' graves in the forest, on to Bélapátfalva and then back to Szilvásvárad. It was very enjoyable – albeit tough in places – largely because we managed to lose the marked path on occasions…)

Opposite that, however, is the Szalajka-völgy 6 station for the **narrow-gauge railway**, which operates between April 1 and October 31 and during the summer runs seven daily trains on weekdays (*first at 09.25, last at 16.10; final return train 16.40*) and ten at weekends and holidays (*first at 08.20, last at 18.00; final return train 18.30*). A one-way ticket on the regular train costs 700/400Ft, while the nostalgia steam train is pricier at 1,000/800Ft. The journey in the open carriages is a real treat, weaving through leafy glades pierced by beams of sunlight and past trickling streams and still ponds. Alight at Szalajka Fátyolvízesés, from where it is a few minutes' walk further south to **Mount Istállóskő** and the **cave** at its base.

If you can, make the return trip under your own steam; the main trail back to Szilvásvárad takes you to a treasure of the Bükk – the **Fátyol Waterfall**, where the Szalajka stream cascades over 17m of staggered limestone shelves, throwing a veil (*fátyol*) of fine droplets into the air. The steps grow by a couple of millimetres a year as further lime is deposited. Further along (at the juncture with the start of the Horotna Valley) is the **Open-Air Forestry Museum** (*Szabadtéri Erdei Múzeum;* ⊕ *all year*), erected in the 1970s as a monument to the men who have lived and worked in the forests, and featuring wood carts, the slatted huts of lumbermen and shinglers, and lime and charcoal kilns. A wonderful cameo is a warning sign of 1834 that reads 'Do not fish, you villain!' Continue following the stream, with its eddying pools and quaint wooden bridges – past the Rock Spring (*Szikla-forrás*), a waterfall that emerges from underground caves (but can dry up in summer) – and after 20 minutes you will reach the indoor **Forestry Museum** (*Erdészeti Múzeum; for info, contact Egri út 16;* ℡ *36 355197;* ✆ *300/150Ft;* ⊕ *Tue–Sun Nov 1–Apr 15 08.30–14.00, Apr 16–Apr 30 08.30–16.00, May–Oct Mon–Fri 08.30–16.30, Sat–Sun 10.00–18.00*). Held in a 19th-century manor house that was once the headquarters of the mining authorities, the museum includes hunting knives and horns, a massive wild-boar pelt, forestry tools and documents (some dating back to the 18th century), and flora and fauna of the Mátra and the Bükk.

Other sights Staying with the nature theme for a while, in the village itself the **Orbán House** (*Miskolci út 58–60;* ℡ *36 355133;* ✆ *200/150Ft;* ⊕ *Apr–Oct Tue–Sun 09.00–17.00*) covers the creation and natural history of the Bükk. You can learn about Lipizzaners at the **Horse Museum** (*Lovas Múzeum; Park u. 8;* ⊕ *Apr–Oct Tue–Sun 09.00–12.00, 13.00–17.00, Nov–Dec weekends only*) – which also has coaches and a blacksmith's workshop – and ride them at the **Lippizaner Stud Farm** (*Lipicai Ménesgazdaság; Fenyves u.;* ℡ *36 355155;* ✆ *riding from 2,500Ft/hr*).

The **Prison Waxwork Museum** (*Panoptikum Börtön Múzeum;* ℡ *20 969 3017*), near the barrier entrance to the valley, is rather lightweight but entertaining nevertheless. Among its exhibits are shame masks (used to ridicule prisoners) and stocks. There is also a record of the fees earned by 17th-century executioners – 1Ft for torture, 18Ft for the burial of hanging victims and 24Ft for impalement or quartering. Criminals paid a high price, it seems.

The **Calvinist Church** (*Aradi u. 30*), dominating the northern end of the village, was built in 1840 by József Hild; it is Neoclassical, with a domed roof and Doric columns. One of the bells in the 17th-century belfry dates to 1488.

Pack your Toblerones and fondue forks, for Sándor Petőfi wrote in his *Travel Letters* of 1847 that Lillafüred was as 'nice a place as Switzerland'. When Count András Bethlen, the agriculture minister, stumbled across it while hunting in 1892, he was so enchanted that he dedicated it to his wife, Lilla Vay. It's certainly romantic; mist hangs in the early morning, and flashing thunderstorms illuminate the hills on May evenings. The diminutive resort lies on the eastern edge of the Bükk Hills (and is an excellent base for hiking), at the meeting point of the Szinva and Garadna valleys on the shore of Hámori-tó. It is said that when they were forbidden from marrying, a mill-owner's daughter and her mill-hand lover threw themselves from the white limestone Molnár-szikla – a couple of kilometres east of the lake – into the Szinva ravine. Miskolc is 10km – and a world – away.

GETTING THERE AND AWAY You can take the **bus** (nos 5 or 15) to Lillafüred from Diósgyőr Villamos in the western portion of Miskolc; get to Diósgyőr by taking bus or tram 1 from Tiszai railway station. More enjoyable though is the **narrow-gauge railway**, which stops at Lillafüred on its journey between Kilián-Észak (in western Miskolc) and Garadna stations; on the way you'll cross the country's highest narrow-gauge viaduct. There are at least four a day between May and September (fewer during other months; *≋ 200/170Ft*). Be wary not to board one of the infrequent weekend services that branch north at Papírgyár to Taksalápa.

INFORMATION

🗗 **Lillafüred Foundation** Erzsébet sétány 69; ✎ 46 403 387; e foldshe@gold.uni-miskolc.hu. A small organisation that helps to promote tourism in the area, & can provide information. Alternatively head for the Tourinform in Miskolc.

There's also a useful **area map** on a large board in the Palota Hotel car-park.

🏠 WHERE TO STAY AND EAT

⋏ **Lillafüred Camping** Erzsébet sétány 39; ✎ 46 333146; www.eurocampings.hu. Further south from the Ózon along the same road to Eger. The amenities are not top class, but the setting is perfect. Tents & caravans only. *Adult/concessions 800/500Ft, tent/caravan/motorhome 500/700/1,200Ft; ⊕ May–Sep.*

🏠 **Ózon Panzió** (19 rooms) Erzsébet sétány 19; ✎ 46 532594; www.ozon-panzio.hu. Large pension a short distance further up the hill from the railway station. Set in pleasant grounds, it is comfortable but unexciting. *Dbl from 7,500Ft, trpl from 12,900Ft (rooms with balcony are more).*

🏠 **Palota Hotel** (129 rooms) Erzsébet sétány 1; ✎ 46 331411; e hotelpalota@hunguesthotels.hu; www.hunguesthotels.hu. This former Neo-Renaissance castle of the 1920s is the resort's focal point, & undoubtedly rules the roost. Surrounded by a hanging garden & a large park, the best of the rooms offer views of the Szinva Stream & Hámori-tó. Among the facilities are a fitness centre, swimming pool, sauna, salt chamber & bowling lanes. Of the three restaurants, the Mátyás (⊕ *daily 12.00–22.00*) is the swankiest, with its stained lead-glass windows; however, we felt it was over-priced & its international fare no better-tasting than the cheaper Tókert. *Sgl 20,500–27,600Ft, dbl 27,200–36,700Ft, suites 33,800–51,900Ft.*

🏠 **Tókert Panzió** (11 rooms) Erzsébet sétány 3; ✎ 46 533560; www.tokertpanzio.hu. Next to the Palota, & with good-sized rooms. The restaurant's elevated eating area outside is bedecked with fairy lights, & provides a pretty space from which to watch the resort below; inside it is too brightly lit (*mains avg 2,500Ft, with daily set menus for 1,500–2,000Ft; ⊕ daily 07.00–23.00). Sgl 9,000–10,800Ft, dbl 12,600–14,500Ft.*

Stalls near the narrow-gauge station sell fast and fatty **snacks** like *lángos*, pancakes and doughnuts.

WHAT TO SEE AND DO The area's prime attraction is the limestone stalactite cave system. A large number of Ice-Age flint tools and laurel-shaped spearheads were discovered in **Szeleta Cave**, but this isn't open to the public. Head instead for **Anna Cave** (✆ *46 370239; 25-min tours leave every hr if there are 10+ visitors, with guaranteed departures at 12.00 & 15.00;* ✆ *900/600Ft;* ⊕ *Apr–Oct 10.00–16.00*), whose entrance can be found near the **Szinva Stream waterfall** in the park surrounding the same hotel. Follow the rumbling sound of the water as it tumbles from a height of 20m. The travertine formations show the imprints of mosses, pine needles, roots and grasses that became covered with deposits of freshwater limestone 40,000 years ago.

Around 400m south of the station, **Szent István Dripstone Cave** (✆ *46 334130; guided tours on the hr;* ✆ *900/600Ft;* ⊕ *daily Apr–Oct 09.00–17.00, rest of yr 09.00–15.00*) is one of the biggest and deepest in the region – its passages reach for 700m, of which 170m are accessible. The cave came to light when an unfortunate dog fell through an opening. The chambers hold a variety of stalactite formations. Both caves are managed by the Bükk National Park Directorate; for the more adventurous, it also organises full-day caving tours.

The **Herman Ottó Memorial House** (*Peleház; Erzsébet sétány 33;* ✆ *46 370703;* ✆ *600/300Ft;* ⊕ *Apr–Oct Tue–Sun 10.00–16.00*) was the villa of the naturalist who revealed in the late 19th century that the caves around Miskolc had been inhabited by prehistoric man. His collections of Bükk flora and fauna are on display.

The 1.5km-long **Hámori-tó** (Foundry Lake) came to be when Henrik Fazola built a sluice dam at the juncture of the Garadna and Szinva streams in the early 19th century to power the ironworks of Hámor. In summer you can hire rowing boats (✆ *350Ft/30 mins*) or pedalos (✆ *300Ft/30 mins*).

There are several marked **hiking trails**, a couple following the Szinva and Garadna valleys, others snaking through the surrounding hills; plan any walk carefully (and take a good map), however, because the forest can be dense and there are few alternative settlements in which to seek refuge should the weather turn or the night fall. One possible excursion is to the **ancient foundry** (*őskohó*), 4km west at Újmassa. Henrik Fazola originally established a furnace in the 1770s to produce crude iron for processing at the Hámor ironworks; his son Frigyes later expanded it, and there's now an adjacent museum (✆ *46 379375; www.fazolanapok.hu;* ⊕ *Apr 15–Oct 15 Tue–Sun 09.00–16.00*). Follow the blue-cross trail from the Palota Hotel around Hámori-to and then along the Garadna Valley.

Further west, Bánkút holds Hungary's largest **ski centre** (✆ *46 390135;* e *www.bankut.hu;* ✆ *1-day ski pass 4,000Ft; depending on conditions,* ⊕ *daily 09.00–16.00, as well as Wed, Fri–Sat 17.00–20.00 under lights*) with eight pistes running down the Borovnyák and Bálvány peaks, the longest of which is 1,500m. There is accommodation and ski hire; for further information, contact the Bánkút Ski Centre on 46 390135. If you don't have a car, follow the S+ (yellow cross) trail markings for 4.6km from Ómassa (bus 15 runs from Miskolc to the latter).

MISKOLC

Miskolc has nearly 200,000 residents, and is Hungary's third-largest city. There are 14,000 students at the country's biggest university, and the city also claims the nation's earliest stone-built theatre (of 1823) and the first public tramline (of 1897). However vigorously it wags such statistics, though, this is a practical rather than a pretty city. Rising, green tower blocks and defunct factory buildings – hulking relics of the heavy industry that thrived here until its collapse in the 1990s – offer a drab welcome. While still having the highest unemployment in the country, the town has reinvented itself and is surrounded by state of the art green-

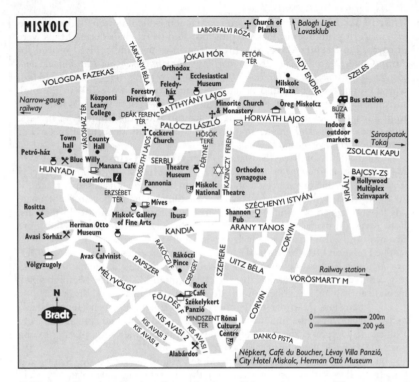

MISKOLC

field manufacturing that is reflected in the well-kept city centre, There are some good restaurants, coffee shops and bars, together with a sprinkling of Eclectic, Neo-Renaissance and Baroque architecture, but generally it will struggle to capture your heart. Rather it is a functional gateway to Lillafüred and the hills of the Bükk National Park, and the caves at Aggtelek.

The Miskóc tribe settled here in the 11th century, but the industrialisation began in 1770 with the arrival of Henrik Fazola from Germany and the iron furnace he constructed in Ómassa (see page 249). Flame and then flood devastated the city in the 19th century, after which it all had to be put back together again.

GETTING THERE, AWAY AND AROUND The main, renovated **railway station** (Miskolc Tiszai) is to the southeast on Kandó Kálmán tér; outside is the terminus for trams 1 and 2, which run into the centre and on as far as Diósgyőr. There is a second, smaller station (named Gömöri) – board a bus to the centre from nearby Zsolcai kapu. There are up to 39 daily trains direct from Budapest Keleti to Miskolc Tiszai. Miskolc is also on a line running to Nyíregyháza (28) that passes through Tokaj and Szerencs on its way, and less frequently continues to Debrecen (eight; if there's no direct train, pick up a connection at Nyíregyháza). Change at Nyíregyháza for services to Nyírbátor. A fork at Mezőzombor leads up to Sárospatak and Sátoraljaújhely (12). There are up to eight trains a day to Aggtelek on a line branching northeast. As for international services, some trains on the line to Hidasnémeti continue over the border to Kosice (three direct) in Slovakia. Change at Nyíregyháza for Kiev and Moscow. There are three trains a day to Oradea in Romania, with a change at Püspökladány.

The intercity **bus station** is on Búza tér, within walking distance to the east of the centre. There is just one direct bus to/from Budapest early in the morning, and you must otherwise travel via Eger or Ózd. There are up to 18 a day to Eger (taking about 1½ hours), Debrecen (29), Mezőkövesd (half-hourly), Nyíregyháza (two on weekdays, one on Sat), Szerencs (up to 11) and Sátoraljaújhely (one daily, except Sun).

You can catch a **narrow-gauge railway** (*Dorottya u. 1;* ↘ *46 379086*) to Lillafüred and further to the Trout Farm about halfway to Szilvásvárad from Kilián-Észak to the west of the city, near Diósgyőr (accessible by bus or tram 1); for further information, see page 248. For **taxis**, try Hellotaxi (↘ *46 333444*) or Nonstop Taxi (↘ *46 333333*).

INFORMATION AND OTHER PRACTICALITIES

i **Forestry Directorate Building** Deák tér 1; ↘ 46 501526; www.eszakerdo.hu. Information on the nature of the surrounding area, based in a lovely Neo-Renaissance building that is worth a look in its own right. Accommodation in hunting lodges in the Bükk forests is also available outside the shooting season.
Ibusz Széchenyi út 15; ↘ 46 508211. Accessed via a courtyard; help with private accommodation & tours, & can exchange travellers' cheques. ⊕ *Mon–Thu 08.00–16.30, Fri 08.00–14.00.*

i **Listings magazine** *Miskolci Est*
i **Tourinform** Városház tér 13; ↘ 46 350425; e miskolc@tourinform.hu. A friendly & helpful office; there's a touch-screen information machine inside offering details of transport timetables etc. ⊕ *Jun 15–Sep 15 Mon–Fri 09.00–18.00, Sat–Sun 09.00–13.00, rest of yr Mon–Fri 09.00–17.00, Sat 09.00–13.00.* There is also a Borsod County Tourinform office; Mindszent tér 1; ↘ 46 508773.

Beyond the smaller **shops** on Széchenyi út, the swanky **Miskolc Plaza** (*Szentpáli u. 2–6;* ↘ *46 504002;* ⊕ *Mon–Sat 09.00–21.00, Sun 09.00–19.00*) is a modern precinct within easy reach. Alternatively there is an indoor and outdoor **market** behind Búza tér, selling snacks, fruit and veg among the diesel fumes from the bus station.

WHERE TO STAY There is but a limited choice of accommodation, much of it at the budget end of the spectrum. It is worth throwing the pensions at Miskolc-Tapolca (see pages 255–6) into the mix before making your decision.

City Hotel Miskolc (23 rooms) Csabai kapu 6; ↘ 46 555100; www.cityhotelmiskolc.hu. An ugly outer shell masks spacious & pleasant rooms, together with a bubbling, glass-roofed jacuzzi. *Sgl 18,900Ft, dbl 24,800Ft, suite 29,500Ft.*
Hotel Pannonia (34 rooms) Kossuth Lajos u. 2; ↘ 46 504980. Slap in the city centre, the Pannonia has compact rooms (with bath or shower) painted in burgundy, 2 restaurants & a set of 7 apts (each with kitchen) in a separate building 100m away. *Sgl 16,900Ft, dbl 18,900Ft; b/fast 1,600Ft.*
Központi Leány College Palóczy László u. 1; ↘ 46 508356. College dormitories, holding 6 to a room; limited capacity outside summer. *Beds 1,000–1,600Ft (discounts with student card).*
Lévay Villa Hotel (21 rooms) Lévay József u. 13; ↘ 46 500890; www.levayvilla.hu. In a greenish suburb just south of the Népkert public garden (bus 31 stops outside), the Lévay combines the looks of an early-20th-century villa with freshly furnished rooms. Among the facilities are a sauna, fitness room & cold plunge pool & 2 Finnish saunas. Recommended. *Sgl 14,900Ft, dbl 19,900Ft, trpl 26,900Ft.*

Öreg Miskolcz (26 rooms) Horváth Lajos u. 11; ↘ 46 550550; www.oregmiskolcz.hu. Completely blending into the streetscape, this brand-new hotel in a quiet & central road has spacious, tastefully furnished rooms, saunas, a plunge-pool & hydromassage shower. Secure parking. *Sgl 17,300Ft, dbl 22,900Ft, apt 29,900Ft.*
Székelykert Panzió (7 rooms) Földes Ferenc út 4; ↘ 46 411222. This guesthouse is a short walk from the main area, & as such the prices are reasonable; expect the rooms to be on the old-fashioned & fusty side. Perhaps more notable for its restaurant (see page 252) than its accommodation. *Dbl 12,000Ft, trpl 14,000Ft.*
Szeleta Hotel (21 rooms, 15 apts) Miskolc-Alsóhámor, Szeleta u. 12–14; ↘ 46 531130; www.harmorholiday.hu. The village of Alsóhámor is 15km from the centre, overlooking the Szinva Stream a short distance north of Lillafüred, & as such is a convenient & picturesque base both for the city & for Bükk walks. The site is superb, with a hotel & apartments; among the facilities are a restaurant, sauna, gym, open-air swimming pool, solarium, snooker

room & bar. Rooms are comfortable, if kitsch. *Hotel sgl/dbl 14,000/17,000Ft, apt (for 3) 25,000Ft.*

🏠 **Völgyzugoly Vendégház** (5 rooms) Toronyalja u. 61; ☎ 46 353676; www.volgyzugolyvendeghaz.hu.

Friendly little place close to Avas Church in a village-like atmosphere. They are proud of the murals by a local artist, Tamás Kettős, in the corridor & rooms. *Sgl 6,000Ft, dbl 8,000Ft, apt 10,000Ft.*

✕ WHERE TO EAT AND DRINK

✕ **Alabárdos** Kisavas, Első sor 15; ☎ 46 412215; www.alabardos-miskolc.hu. On the road leading up to Avas Hill, Alabárdos has both a brick-floored beer hall & a wine cellar. The décor in the medieval-theme restaurant is pleasingly understated, & there's an open fireplace in the centre of the room. One of the city's oldest restaurants, it is also one of the better places to chow down; good-quality traditional food is served on Herend crockery, & the final preparatory flourishes to the dishes are made at the table. Commendable wine list. *Mains avg 2,800Ft; restaurant ⊕ 18.00–24.00 daily, beer hall 16.00–24.00 daily.*

✕ **Avasi Sörház** Meggyesalja u. 1; ☎ 46 340071. This restaurant would not be out of place in an alpine village but here the backdrop is the Avas Hill. Extensive Hungarian menu & friendly atmosphere. *Mains avg 2,100Ft; ⊕ 11.00–23.00 daily.*

✕ **Blue Willy Étterem** Hunyadi János u. 4; ☎ 46 323844. The latest kitchen in town, the owner/chef will cook for you up to midnight! The location is central, the interior simply panelled, the terrace spacious, the wine list of good quality, & some of the prices on the hefty side. *Mains avg 2,800Ft; ⊕ Sun–Thu 08.30–23.00, Fri–Sat 8.30–24.00.*

♀ **Café du Boucher** Görgey Artúr u. 42; ☎ 46 432320; www.belgianbeercafe.hu. The first in the international 'Belgian Beer Café' chain to open in Hungary has Belgian beer & Flemish, Walloon & Hungarian delicacies. The food is pricey, but high quality. *Mains avg 2,690Ft; ⊕ Mon–Thu 11.00–24.00, Fri–Sat 11.00–01.00.*

💻 **Műves Kávézó** Rákoczi u. 2; ☎ 70 4311758; ⊕ 09.00–17.00. Located in the vaulted Rákóczi House, this a cosy little place where you can enjoy a cup of Fairtrade coffee & a piece of cake surrounded by books & friendly chatter.

✕ **Rákóczi Pince** Rákóczi u. 23; ☎ 46 343916. Like a familiar pair of slippers, this cellar-style restaurant is comfy & reliable without courting excitement. Specialities on a menu of Hungarian & Bavarian dishes include catfish & carp. There's a bar at its top end. *Mains avg 2,200Ft; ⊕ 11.00–22.00 daily.*

✕ **Rossita** Meggyesalja u. 18, ☎ 46 344300. Fantastic smells waft from behind an unpromising entrance. This small, unpretentious Italian restaurant offers pasta & pizzas, but also has an extensive Hungarian menu. 2-course set lunch 790Ft. *Mains avg 1,800Ft; ⊕ Mon–Fri 11.00–22.00, Sat–Sun 12.00–22.00*

✕ **Székelykert** See page 251. A classy little restaurant – attached to the panzió – that successfully blends relaxed, peasant styling with a hint of luxury. The varied menu features very good Székely & Borsod dishes; the management are justly proud of their jaunty gypsy players. *Mains avg 2,000Ft; ⊕ 11.00–23.00 daily.*

ENTERTAINMENT AND NIGHTLIFE Miskolc National Theatre (*Miskolci Nemzeti Színház; Déryné u. 1;* ☎ *46 344711; www.miskolcinemzetiszinhaz.hu*) was Hungary's first permanent playhouse – erected in 1823 – and the first to perform drama in the Hungarian language. Unfortunately it was destroyed by fire in 1843 (learn more in the Theatre Museum; see opposite); parts of the theatre that replaced it in 1857 are incorporated into the current Neoclassical structure that was resurrected in the 1990s. Today there are plays, musicals and concerts by ensembles such as the Miskolc Symphonic Orchestra and the National Philharmonic. The ticket office is next door (*Széchenyi u. 23;* ☎ *46 344864; ⊕ Mon–Fri 10.00–19.00, Sat–Sun 15.00–19.00*).

The **Rónai Cultural Centre** (*Mindszent tér 3;* ☎ *46 342408*) hosts concerts and other productions, while you can catch a blockbuster at the **Hollywood Multiplex Szinvapark** (*Bajcsy-Zsilinszky út 2–4;* ☎ *46 502700; www.hmpix.hu*).

Shannon Pub (*Széchenyi István út 54;* ☎ *46 413904; ⊕ Mon–Sat 11.00–23.00*) has flat Guinness, fiddle music and a 'fresco' of the emerald isle. There are hearty plates of stew, fish and sandwiches for the peckish (*mains avg 2,000Ft*).

Manana Café (*Városház tér 3;* ☎ *46 323429; mains avg 1,500Ft; ⊕ Mon–Thu 08.00–00.00, Fri–Sat 10.00–02.00*) is a relaxed and intimate bar; funk, jazz and blues fill the air, and a younger crowd lounge under the low lighting. During the day you can enjoy their home–made strudels (*rétes*); at lunchtime, there's a set menu costing 890Ft, while at other times sandwiches, tapas and simple meals are available. Choose from a limited but excellent selection of Hungarian wines or cocktails.

WHAT TO SEE AND DO Széchenyi út is the city's main thoroughfare, running horizontally through its belly and hoarding several pretty residences in Baroque and Neoclassical styles. The National Theatre (see opposite) stands at the junction with Déryné utca, while beside it is the **Museum of Theatre and Acting** (*Színháztörténeti és Színészmúzeum; Déryné u. 3;* ✆ *46 327900;* 💲 *400/200Ft;* ⊕ *Tue–Sat 09.00–17.00*). As well as an exhibition of costumes and playbills, there are drawings of the original theatre and photographs of Róza Déryné, the popular actress who performed many times in Miskolc during the early 19th century. There's also a stage lighting machine from England, used between 1959 and 1990. The explanatory notes are in Hungarian.

Further west along Széchenyi út is an 18th-century passage known as the **Dark Gate** (*Sötét kapu*) that leads to Rákóczi utca. Since 1996, Rákóczi-ház has held the **Miskolc Gallery of Fine Arts** (*Városi Művészeti Múzeum; Rákóczi u. 2;* ✆ *46 500680; www.miskolcigaleria.hu;* 💲 *400/200Ft;* ⊕ *Tue–Sun Jun–Sep 10.00–18.00, Oct–May 09.00–17.00*) – with its permanent and temporary collections of modern fine, applied and photographic art – but much earlier the 17th-century Baroque mansion was home to Prince Rákóczi. There are further art exhibitions in the **Feledy-ház** (*Deák Ferenc tér 3;* ✆ *46 355472;* 💲 *400/200Ft;* ⊕ *Tue–Sat 09.00–16.30*), presenting the life work of Hungarian graphic artist Gyula Feledy, and the **Petró-ház** (*Hunyadi u. 12;* ✆ *46 355472;* 💲 *400/200Ft;* ⊕ *Tue–Sat 09.00–17.00*), former abode of the doctor Sándor Petró where you'll find photos, reliefs and other pieces by painter Lajos Szalay (1909–95).

A short distance to the west of the Dark Gate is **Erzsébet tér**, with its bathhouse and assured statue of Lajos Kossuth. It opens into **Városház tér**; the 18th-century County Hall (*no 1*) is dressed in yellow, while the peach-coloured town hall (*no 8*) is a favourite venue for musical concerts.

The **Herman Ottó Museum** (*Papszer u. 1;* ✆ *46 346875; www.hermuz.hu;* 💲 *600/300Ft;* ⊕ *Tue–Sun 10.00–16.00*) occupies a former school building dating to the 15th century. There's a statue of Herman Ottó the scientist outside, with his short calves and slight paunchiness, while inside there are temporary exhibitions. A main museum building (*Görgey Artúr u. 28;* ✆ *46 560170*) houses permanent exhibitions of rocks and minerals, archaeological finds dating as far back as the Magyar arrival, and a display of some masterpieces from the Petró collection (see above), but perhaps the most unique is a huge collection of ethnographic material of the Palóc and Matyó people.

From Papszer utca, some steps lead up to the late-Gothic **Avas Calvinist Church** (*Papszer u. 14;* ✆ *46 358677 to arrange visit;* ⊕ *Jun–Aug Mon–Sun 14.00–17.00*), built after the Turks levelled a 13th-century church on the site in 1544. There is a beautiful painted and coffered ceiling that was added in the 1700s, and outside is an elegant 16th-century **belfry**, constructed from wood and stone and topped with a steep-tiled 'wizard's hat' of a roof. Gravestones crowd in upon the church and add to a sense of Gothic mystery. Push on up Avas Hill along a zig-zagging cobbled path to a **TV tower** and glass-enclosed viewing gallery; its coffee shop (⊕ *10.00–22.00 daily*) can slake parched throats. The hill is also notable for the many **wine cellars** lining its narrow streets.

In the area north of Széchenyi út are several houses of worship that testify to the Jewish and Greek communities that once thrived here. The **Orthodox synagogue** (*Kazinczy u. 7*) is a sparrow-brown lump of a building that has seen better days; its Neo-Romanesque and Moorish design was the work of Ludwig Förster, but the

Jewish population can no longer fill its three-aisled interior after being decimated during the deportations of World War II. Overlooking it is the Baroque **Minorite church and monastery** (*Hősök tere 5*) of 1740, with two towers, vast frescoed ceilings, a Rococo pulpit and attractive iron doors added in 2000.

To the west in Deák Ferenc tér is the Calvinist '**Cockerel Church**' (*Kakas templom*), so-named after the bird perched on its steeple. The 18th-century **Hungarian Orthodox church** (*Deák Ferenc tér 7*) behind the Minorite church was built by the offspring of Greek merchants who set up home here after fleeing the Turks. They traded in wine and grain as far as St Petersburg. The gem-studded Mount Athos Cross was brought by the original settlers. Also inside is one of central Europe's biggest iconostases; its 88 painted panels were crafted in 1793, and make up a whole that measures 16m in height. The icon known as the 'Black Mary of Kazan' was a gift from the Russian Tsarina Catherine II ('the Great'). The congregation is still 59 strong, augmented by Russians and Ukrainians resident in Miskolc. Services sung by five cantors are wonderful to hear. During the opera festival, concerts are held here and the acoustics are fantastic. In front of the church, in the old Greek School built in 1805, is the **Hungarian Orthodox Ecclesiastical Museum** (*Magyar Orthodox Egyházi Múzeum;* ✆ *46 415441;* 🎟 *400/200Ft;* ☉ *Tue–Sun Nov–Mar 10.00–16.00, Apr–Oct 10.00–18.00*), whose books and manuscripts chart both the assimilation of the Greeks into Miskolc society and the Byzantine traditions they brought from the Balkans. The highlight is the 'Good-Friday grave pall', embroidered in Vienna in 1760. Ask for Zsuzsa Néni in the museum, and she will open the church for you (🎟 *entrance 150Ft*).

The **Church of Planks** (*Deszka templom; Tetemvár;* ✆ *46 506613 to visit*) looks over Petőfi tér, an asymmetrical and angular wooden Calvinist church that dates to 1938 but had to be reconstructed following a fire in 1997. It emulates the Transylvanian style, and has floral, swirling patterns cut and painted into its wood.

FURTHER OUT

Diósgyőr Castle Eight kilometres west of the centre, Diósgyőr Castle (*Miskolc-Diósgyőr, Vár u. 24;* ✆ *46 533355; www.diosgyorivar.com;* 🎟 *600/250Ft;* ☉ *daily May–Sep 09.00–18.00, Oct–Apr 10.00–16.00*) stands on a hill by the Szinva Stream. The scribe Anonymus – writing during the reign of Béla III in the late 12th and early 13th centuries – documented a structure here, but the current castle came into being between 1342 and 1382 under Lajos I. It was used as a residence by several kings and queens before stagnating after damage in the early 18th century. Restoration during the 20th century lacked finesse. Today there are several permanent exhibitions here, including a selection of medieval weaponry, a minting press and some waxworks. The northeast tower offers grand views, while in summer there are a series of open-air concerts, theatre productions and games (programme of events on the website). The nearby **lido** (*Vár u. 1;* ✆ *46 379146;* ☉ *May–Sep 09.00–18.00 daily*) has a hot sauna and a cold rock plunge-pool. Buses 1, 101 and 101B and tram 1 run out here from Miskolc. If you need a bite, Déryné Ház is a pleasant café within the castle (and once the post-retirement residence of the famous actress and singer, Róza Déryné). It also offers accommodation.

Miskolc-Tapolca Bus 2 from Miskolc journeys 7km southward to the quaint resort of Miskolc-Tapolca, whose waters have been used in cures since the 16th century. The **Cave Bath** (*Barlangfürdő; Miskolc-Tapolca, Pazár István sétány;* ✆ *46 304128; www.barlangfurdo.hu; day pass* 🎟 *2,400/1,600Ft;* ☉ *daily summer 09.00–19.00, winter 09.00–18.00*) consists of a series of pools in a natural cave system. The water temperature ranges between 27°C and 31°C, there's a waterfall or 'thrashing shower', and the humid air is reputedly good for bronchial complaints. Massages and other treatments are available, and there are cooler pools and sun terraces outside. In addition, the town's park holds a lively **lido** (*Miskolctapolcai u. 1;* ☏ *46 368127;* ☉ *May–Sep daily 09.00–18.00*), complete with separate pools for the kiddies, and a lake on which you can go **boating** (*boat hire May–Sep daily 10.00–16.00;* ✆ *800Ft/30 mins*). If you fancy a decent stretch, there is a walking trail (marked by a yellow square with a blue diagonal line) from the Cave Bath entrance to Diósgyőr Castle; it will take a little over two hours.

There is no shortage of accommodation in Miskolc-Tapolca. **Hotel Kolibri** (*Fecske út 15–17;* ☏ *46 555010; www.hotelkolibri.hu; 9 rooms*) is well kept, and has a swimming pool and pleasing views. There's wood galore at the quirky-looking **Tapolca** (*Csabai út 36;* ☏ *46 562215; www.tapolca-fogado.hu; sgl 8,000Ft, dbl 15,000Ft*). **Bástya** (*16 rooms; Miskolctapolcai út 2;* ☏ *46 369154;* e *bastyahotel@ axelero.hu; www.bokik.hu/bastya*) is a decent pension 100m from the lido, while **Hotel Kitty** (*25 rooms; Pazár István sétany 1;* ☏ *46 508042; www.hotelkitty.hu; dbl 24,500Ft, excl tourist tax*), with its 'Classical-style' turrets, is clean, spacious and even closer.

Balogh Liget Riding Club (☏ *46 712899*) is beautifully situated among the vineyards 3km north of Miskolc on Road 26. Open all year, it has a large indoor arena and specialises in show jumping and carriage riding. Lessons are available (✆ *3,600Ft/hr for riding, 3,000Ft/hr for carriage riding*). Two cottages offer pleasant accommodation (*3,000Ft/pp*).

FESTIVALS AND EVENTS A string of festivals starts with the weird Jelly Festival in February. However, the main programme of events takes place during Miskolc Summer (Miskolci Nyár). Among these are the Bartók + International Opera Festival (*mid Jun; www.operafesztival.hu*; top European performers, including soloists from the Scala and Bolshoi); the Borsodi Fonó International Folk Festival (*end Jun*); Kaláka International Festival of Folk Music (*start Jul*; folk performances at the Diósgyőr Castle); and the Diósgyőr Revels (*mid Aug*; a range of events culminating in a feast for 5,000 in the castle moat). In addition, there are concerts and fireworks on May 11 to commemorate the day in 1909 that Ferenc József made the town an independent municipality, while at the end of the same month there is medieval jousting and archery during the Castle Games.

THE AGGTELEK RANGE

Established in 1985, Aggtelek National Park lies on the border with Slovakia, its limestone bed formed almost 250 million years ago by a shallow sea. Divided in two by the Bódva River valley, its densely forested 20,000ha present oodles of opportunity for hiking and cycling, enhanced by diverse species of flora and fauna (see box, page 256; Cartographia's *Az Aggtelekeki Karszt* map, 1:40,000, shows walking and cycling trails in the region). Its real prizes, though, are the karst cave systems – most notably that of Baradla-Domica, whose chambers spread over 25km (a quarter of the length on Slovak territory) and are filled with gorgeous dripstones of orange and cream. These caves rank as high as any in Europe; they have enjoyed international protection since 1979 and were added to the Unesco World Heritage List in 1995. The Baradla is flanked by the villages of Aggtelek and Jósvafő; there are entrances at each of these, and a third at Vörös-tó (Red Lake), close to Jósvafő. You can cross overground into Slovakia to the western Domica entrance, but you cannot pass between the two sections via the caves themselves.

GETTING THERE, AWAY AND AROUND There are two daily direct **buses** from Budapest Stadion (taking four hours), stopping at both Aggtelek and Jósvafő; there

This relatively small area is home to species of flora and fauna whose ecological demands are often very different. Typically northern Carpathian montane species grow in the beech forests on the northern slopes and in the cool ravines. Dog's tooth violet (*Erythronium dens-canis*) is a beautiful early-spring bloomer in the linden-ash woods of steep escarpments. The grasslands and oak parklands harbour steppe-woodland species, while in the rocky karst of drier slopes you'll find even sub-Mediterranean and Balkan elements. Juniper-heath tracts and plants similar to those that thrive on western European heaths inhabit covered karst areas, and enrich the natural scene further; the most renowned native plant of the Aggtelek karst is the Tornaian yellowdrop, with its drooping, bell-like flower.

The diverse geological, relief, climatic and phytogeographical conditions of the Aggtelek National Park (as well as its geographical situation) ensure that the area's fauna is also wide ranging. The insect world is very rich. Hungary's largest species, the sparsely distributed matriarchal katydid (*Saga pedo*) is here, as well as several unusual butterflies – the clouded Apollo (*Parnassius mnemosyne*), the purple-edged copper (*Palaeochrysophanus hippothoe*) and the poplar admiral (*Limenitis populi*). The longest watered caves – such as the Baradla Cave – are inhabited by some intriguing arthropods like blind carabid beetles, blind crayfish and micro-whip scorpions (*Palpigradi*). Indeed there are around 500 animal species in the cave system, most of them microscopic, with 40 species of plants (mainly white algae and moss).

The springs and brooks represent another special habitat. In addition to certain invertebrates, some protected fish species – like the bait minnow (*Phoxinus phoxinus*), the Mediterranean barbel (*Barbus meridionalis*) and the Danubian lamprey (*Petromyzonidae*), a brook-trout parasite – also occur in the waters. The most valuable reptile species of the Aggtelek karst is a little lizard called the snake-eyed skink (*Ablepharus kitaibelii*).

The imperial eagle (*Aquila heliaca*), lesser-spotted eagle (*A pomarina*), short-toed eagle (*Circaetus gallicus*) and honey buzzard (*Pernis apivorus*) are among the feathered fliers that nest here, as are the hazel grouse and the dipper. The dipper nests at mountain streams (sometimes in Jósvafő village), while the hazel grouse frequents denser woodland and is very rare, very shy and very hard to spot. Other highlights are the Ural and eagle owls, and – during spring – the rock bunting and rock thrush. As for furry fliers, the park numbers 21 of the 28 European bat types, including the Mediterranean horseshoe (*Rhinolophus uryale*) variety. And the region is notable for its big game; the wolf and the lynx, for example – animals that had died out in Hungary – have reappeared over the last two decades, and there are also deer, boar and wild cat.

are also buses from Miskolc (one) and Eger (one). Up to ten **local buses** link Jósvafő and Aggtelek.

Jósvafő-Aggtelek **railway station** is around 15km from Jósvafő and 20km from Aggtelek – a coach will take you from the station the rest of the way. There are no direct trains from Budapest (change at Miskolc); six services run to/from Miskolc.

INFORMATION AND OTHER PRACTICALITIES

Aggtelek National Park Directorate Aggtelek, Tengerszem oldal 1; ☎ 48 506000; e info.anp@ t-online.hu; www.anp.hu. In the middle of Jósvafő. An educational centre, offering study tours for schoolchildren (and on-site dorm rooms), as well as grown-up information on the region's nature.

✉ **Post office** Aggtelek, Kossuth Lajos u. 39
Tourinform Aggtelek, Baradla oldal 1; ☎ 48 503003; e aggtelek@tourinform.hu. Opposite the Baradla Restaurant. Contains useful information on the caves & trails in the area, & walking & cycling maps. ⊕ *Apr–Sep daily 08.00–19.00, Oct–Mar 08.00–16.00.*

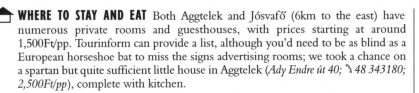

WHERE TO STAY AND EAT Both Aggtelek and Jósvafő (6km to the east) have numerous private rooms and guesthouses, with prices starting at around 1,500Ft/pp. Tourinform can provide a list, although you'd need to be as blind as a European horseshoe bat to miss the signs advertising rooms; we took a chance on a spartan but quite sufficient little house in Aggtelek (*Ady Endre út 40;* ↘ *48 343180; 2,500Ft/pp*), complete with kitchen.

🏠 **Baradla Hostel and Campsite** Aggtelek, Baradla oldal 1; ↘ 48 503005; e szallas@anp.hu. Near the cave entrance. There are 9 hostel rooms with shared bathrooms; 25 huts (a few with kitchens & bathrooms) & camping pitches (*available Apr 15–Oct 15*). Prepare for squealing school parties. *Hostel room 1,900Ft/pp, huts (for 4–6) 5,200–18,000Ft, tent 1,000Ft plus 1,200Ft/pp.*

✗ **Baradla Restaurant** Aggtelek, Baradla oldal 1. Next to the cave entrance, & offers Hungarian dishes.

🏠 **Cseppkő Hotel** (70 rooms) Aggtelek, Baradla oldal; ↘ 48 343075; e hcseppko@freemail.hu. This hotel has a good vantage point 200m from the cave entrance, but its rooms are drab. The hotel also serves grub. *Sgl 8,900Ft, dbl 14,000Ft, trpl 20,000Ft.*

🏠 **Kővirózsa Apartman** Aggtelek, Deák Ferenc u. 18. Book rooms at this nice guesthouse through Baradla Hostel & Campsite or Tourinform (see opposite).

🏠 **Tengerszem Hotel** (18 rooms) Jósvafő, Tengerszem oldal 2; ↘ 48 506005. A pretty outside – in a scenic & peaceful spot – & a basic centre. Few animals are safe from its restaurant (*mains avg 1,600Ft*), whose meat-heavy menu includes venison, boar & veal. It's a relaxed, student-tuck-shop of a place, & the staff aren't precious about muddy boots; the food is unexceptional but filling. *Sgl 7,800–9,000Ft, dbl 13,100–15,500Ft.*

🏠 **The Cottage (Kisház)** Berecz-szőke Jósvafő, Dózsa György u. 5; ↘ 48 350053; e josvafo_kishaz@freemail.hu. A better choice than the Tengerszem for accommodation in Jósvafő, this is an atmospheric cottage for 4 by the village's babbling brook. It nestles a few yards up a track, between the museum & the bell tower (see page 258). *2,500Ft/pp.*

WHAT TO SEE AND DO

Caves Baradla Cave (⊕ *daily Apr–Sep 08.00–18.00, Oct–Mar 08.00–16.00*) was first mentioned in literature of 1549, although prehistoric finds (including pottery and bears' bones) show it was inhabited much earlier, and ancient torches have left their sooty marks in places. This is the country's longest and richest, packed full of nobbly stalactites and stalagmites in which you're invited to see the shape of a dragon's head, a Chinese pagoda or a mother-in-law's tongue. The main branch runs between Aggtelek and Jósvafő. You can listen to classical music in the domed 'Concert Hall' chamber as lights play over its otherworldly dripstones, and – if the water is high enough – float in a boat on the subterranean Styx Stream. It's damp and cold, so wear an extra layer.

There are three entrances to the cave on the Hungarian side – at Aggtelek, Jósvafő and Vörös-tó – and tours of varying lengths (*one, two, five & seven hrs*) to choose from. The Aggtelek end of the cave has more wonder in a concentrated space, and is a better option for the shortest tours; the very longest generally leave from the artificial entrance at Vörös-tó, and should be booked in advance. The regular one-hour tours are not strenuous, but be sure you are up to it before booking the more extended options. There are reductions for those who wish to do more than one of the tours on consecutive days – retain your ticket from the first tour, and receive a discount on a subsequent purchase at the other ticket office.

Aggtelek entrance Baradla oldal 1; ↘ 48 503000; www.aggtelek.hu. The 1-hr tour is 1km long, & includes music in the 'Concert Hall'. Tours depart at 10.00, 11.30, 13.00 & 15.00 (with additional tours in high season). ✍ 2,200/1,100Ft.

Jósvafő entrance Tengerszem oldal 3; ↘ 48 506009. The entrance is just to the west of the village, next to the Tengerszem Hotel. The 1-hour tour is 1.5km long, & includes the 'Giants' Hall' (the largest chamber in the system). Tours depart at 09.00 &

17.00 (high season) & 10.00 & 15.00 (low season). ☜ 1,400/900Ft.

Vörös-tó entrance In between Aggtelek & Jósvafő. The Red Lake — now largely overrun with rushes — was so-named after a herd of wallowing pigs stirred up ferric oxide in its bed & turned the water crimson. A 2-hour, 2.3km tour leaves from here; it follows the course of the Styx Stream, & takes in the 'Astronomical Telescope' (Hungary's tallest stalagmite) & 'Giants' Hall' on the way to its finish at the Jósvafő end. Tickets should be bought from the Jósvafő ticket office. Tours depart at 10.00, 12.00, 13.30 & 15.00 (high season) & at 10.00 & 12.00 only in low season. ☜ 2,800/1,400Ft.

If you're still hankering for things speleological, there are several other caves that can be visited. Tickets for the **Vass Imre Cave**, to the north of Jósvafő and with its 'Orange Cascade' formation, can be purchased from Jósvafő (*tours depart at 15.00 in high season, and by advance booking only in low season;* ☜ *adult 3,200Ft*); the price includes a 2km guided nature walk from the ticket office to the cave itself. There are longer visits to a 1,200m stretch of **Béke (Peace) Cave**, and its gravel terraces and rimstone dams. The tour lasts three hours and comes on top of a two-hour hike to get there; while torches are provided, waterproofs and sturdy footwear are essential as you'll need to negotiate an underground stream. (Overalls can be hired for 800Ft.) Book at least two weeks in advance from Aggtelek (☜ *adult 7,000Ft, no children under 14*). The humid air in both the Vass Imre and Beké caves is thought to be beneficial to those with respiratory disorders. Trips into **Rákóczi Cave**, near the village of Bódvarákó, can be arranged (*with 2 weeks' notice; maximum group size of 10;* ☜ *adult 3,500Ft*) at either Jósvafő or Aggtelek. All tickets also grant access to the **Kessler Hubert Memorial House** (next to the Jósvafő entrance), which highlights the work (and potholing conquests) of the respected director and researcher of the Aggtelek Caves in what was his home.

Nature tours Those who prefer to feel soil underfoot and sky overhead can take one of several eco tours or nature trails available. Guided tours eke out the region's wildlife and geology; there are advanced as well as more general tours. Prices start at 600Ft, and should be booked ahead at Jósvafő and Aggtelek. Alternatively, you can contact Litkei Krisztina (*Gömörszőlős, Kassai u. 37;* ✆ *48 434181*) who organises three-hour tours in the company of a local qualified biologist (☜ *5,000Ft/pp*), as well as 'herbal' walks that feature stops for herbal tea (☜ *3,000Ft/pp*). If you're happy to go it alone, follow one of the park's educational trails. Among these are the **Baradla Trail** (a 7km route running between the Aggtelek and Jósvafő caves, over open and covered karst areas; yellow waymarking) and the **Tohonya-Kuriszlán Trail** (a 9km geological path in Jósvafő; yellow waymarking). Tourinform can provide fuller details of these and others.

Other sights A **Village Museum** (*Tájház; Dózsa György u. 3;* ✆ *48 350072;* ☜ *150/75Ft;* ☉ *daily Apr–Sep 10.00–16.00; for visits during rest of yr,* ✆ *48 350084*) in Jósvafő is held in a traditional group of buildings from the late 19th century, and has exhibitions on local industry, agriculture, domestic life and cave exploration. The ticket office can provide an English-language leaflet, but it wants for much in detail. Behind the museum is the 13th-century **Calvinist church** (*Faluséta 11*) a white-washed villa-like building with a coffered ceiling and a detached belfry.

The **Hucul Stud** (*Táncsics Mihály út 1;* ✆ *48 350052 for info;* ☉ *daily 08.00–15.00, by advance booking only*) is the only one of its kind in the country; the *hucul* is a small-bodied horse that is indigenous to the Carpathian region, and the purpose here is to preserve the breed. Horse and carriage riding is available (☜ *from 2,500Ft/hr*). To the north of Petőfi Sándor út (up Ady Endre utca), you can reach the stud via the National Blue Trail from Jósvafő or the yellow-marked Tohonya-Kuriszlán Trail.

FESTIVALS AND EVENTS The **Gömör-Torna Festival** in the latter part of July features pop, classical and percussion concerts in Baradla Cave and the local churches, as well as 'village days' of folk events, fireworks and sport. Other performances of chamber music in the cave take place during the summer and at the end of December; contact Tourinform for details. Cycling, climbing and nature events are held between March and October.

EXCURSIONS There are many pretty villages in the surrounding area that are worth a visit if you have a bicycle or car. In the southern portion of the national park (3km from Martonyi) are the ruins of the medieval **Háromhegyi Pálos church and monastery**, built by the only monastic order founded in Hungary. The monastery was erected in 1341 and the church in 1411, and functioned up until the Turkish occupation; today the nave, gable and side-walls remain, and there is talk of reconstruction. Close by is **Szalonna**, notable for its 11th-century frescoed church with an odd-shaped 13th-century nave. Southwest of that (and 20km from Aggtelek) is **Rudabánya**, where iron ore was once mined; in 1967, an ancient monkey jaw – ten million years old – was found in one of the shafts, and is now on display.

The Zemplén Hills and around

The region of the Zemplén Hills is something of a split personality; divided by the River Bodrog, the territory falling to the north and reaching to the Slovakian border is proper tough highland stuff of significant natural beauty, while that below is more plain-like in character. The tallest peak in the volcanic range is Nagy-Milic, a touch short of 900m. The bulk of visitors make the pilgrimage here in the name of wine – specifically the Tokaj-Hegyalja wines that are produced from vines on the warm slopes at the south and southeastern edges. The communities of historical significance are Sárospatak, Sátoraljaújhely, Szerencs and Tokaj; the region was a hotbed of Rákóczi-fuelled anti-Habsburg sentiment and action, but there was brain here as well as brawn, and some of its sons were prominent in the 19th-century literary and linguistic reform movements. In recent years, the area has become known as a centre of art; its peaceful and scenic villages have attracted artists to settle here (as, perhaps, has its good-quality wine!). Year by year, the Zemplén Festival in August attracts the best performers.

SZERENCS

Standing at the meeting point of the Great Plain and the Zemplén Hills, Szerencs is the gateway to the Hegyalja. It is frequently overlooked by tourists, but the whiff of history hangs strong and one of its churches hides a fascinating relic that adds real bones to tales of the past.

Szerencs has been inhabited since the Neolithic age, and developed into an important trade route – the Transylvanian salt road, for example, ran through here on its way from Tokaj to Buda and Pest. Devastated by the Mongol invasion in 1241, Szerencs's purple patch was to come between the 16th and 18th centuries. A castle was built in the 1550s, incorporating an earlier Benedictine monastery; the area and its fort quickly came into the possession of the Rákóczi family, leading participants in the independence struggles against the Habsburgs. In 1605, a parliament here elected the Transylvanian István Bocskai reigning prince, and he subsequently bestowed royal rank upon the town. On his death, Zsigmond Rákóczi was voted to succeed him, and the town remained at the forefront of resistance up until the suppression of the War of Independence led by Zsigmond's famous great-grandson, Ferenc Rákóczi II. In the aftermath, the fort declined in significance, and was gifted to more loyal nobles by the victorious Habsburgs. Economic revival came with the building of a sugar plant in 1889 and a chocolate factory in 1923 – sweet success once more.

GETTING THERE AND AWAY The **bus** and **train** stations are situated next to each other. On alighting, turn right to the end of the road, turn left on to Rákóczi út at the top, past the Nestlé factory on the left, move over the crossroads and continue straight to the centre – it's around a 15-minute walk. The train station is on the line running between Miskolc and Nyíregyháza (that also includes Tokaj), and there are frequent services to each of these. There are 11 direct daily trains from Budapest Keleti, as well as several indirect (change at Miskolc). Buses run to Tokaj (up to nine), Miskolc (12) and Monok (12).

INFORMATION AND OTHER PRACTICALITIES

🎭 **Cultural centre** ❱ 47 362290. In summer months, the centre organises folklore events, wine exhibitions, art days & outdoor concerts. Opposite the library in the castle.

📋 **Zemplén Tourist** Rákóczi út 67; ❱ 47 362952; e zemplen.tourist@t-online.hu. Tourist information, accommodation & Tokaj wine tours. Currency exchange available. ⊕ Mon–Fri 07.30–16.00.

There's a **bank** at Kossuth Lajos tér 3A, & a **post office** at Rákóczi út 74–80.

🏠 **WHERE TO STAY AND EAT** You're unlikely to stay in town with Miskolc and Tokaj so relatively close, but if you do the **Hotel Huszárvár** (*Huszárvár út 11;* ❱ *47 563050;* e *info@huszarvarszallo.hu; 20 rooms; dbl 6,200–8,000Ft, b/fast 900Ft*) occupies an outer wing of the castle. It's lacking in mod-cons, and rooms on the second floor have shared toilets, but both the location and price defy whining. Its restaurant (*mains avg 1,500Ft;* ⊕ *daily 10.00–22.00*) is kitted out medieval-banquet style. Snacks are available at **Sörház Za-nor** (*Petőfi út 5;* ❱ *47 364029;* ⊕ *Mon–Fri 08.00–21.00, Sat 08.00–14.00 & 18.00–22.00*), pizzas and other fast food at **Postakocsi Pizzeria & Pub** (*Rákóczi út 60;* ⊕ *Mon–Thu 09.00–21.00, Fri–Sat 11.00–23.00*), and sweet things at **Kovács Cukrászda** (*Rákóczi út 25;* ❱ *47 362693;* ⊕ *daily 08.00–20.00*).

WHAT TO SEE AND DO Rákóczi Castle (❱ *47 362121;* ⊕ *Tue–Fri 09.00–17.00, Sat 08.00–14.00*) is the hub of town. Zsigmond Rákóczi – whose barrel-chested statue stands in the castle grounds – acquired the estate in 1586, and after reinforcing the fortress and adding outer bastions, the family lived within its thick walls until 1616. It is said that Ferenc Rákóczi II spent time here on his 18th birthday. The castle witnessed several battles against the Turks during the 1600s; after the War of Independence, the new occupiers restructured things to make it more palatial than military.

Today the **Zemplén Museum** (❱ *47 362842;* 🎫 *600/300Ft;* ⊕ *Mon–Fri 10.00–16.00*) fills the eastern wing. Its exhibitions include the world's third-largest collection of postcards (some dating back to 1860), period furniture and costumes from the Rákóczi era, and the work of Fery Antal (a local graphic artist). The castle also holds a library and cultural centre, and hosts several events during the year (see page 262).

The **Sugar Museum** (*Cukor Múzeum; Gyár u. 1;* ❱ *47 565100;* 🎫 *300/200Ft;* ⊕ *Tue, Thu, Sat 10.00–17.00, Wed, Fri, Sun by pior appointment only*) stands to the east of the castle, at the junction of Rákóczi út and Road 37; it was unwrapped on the centenary of the town's sugar plant, and tells its history.

For us, though, the town's jewel is its 13th-century Gothic **Calvinist church** (*Kossuth tér 3;* ❱ *47 362090*), a short distance northwest of the castle up a sloping track where Kossuth Lajos utca and Rákóczi út touch. You may need to get the key from the vicarage at the bottom of the pathway up to the church itself. Thick metal doors protected the church from Turkish attack. In 1605 parliament was held inside, and István Bocskai declared Prince of Hungary. His successor was Zsigmond Rákóczi II. A red marble sarcophagus stands to the right, while a trapdoor beneath the carpet leads into a dank chamber and to a casket bearing the bones of Zsigmond and his second wife. The prince died peacefully, but two slashes across his skull testify to a life spent battling Turks and Habsburgs. The bones had to be re-gathered after they were scattered by the Habsburgs during the Revolution of 1849.

Szerencs celebrated the 2002 inclusion of the region and its Tokaj vineyards on the UNESCO World Heritage List by erecting two towers – each 30 metres tall – on Road 37 at the entrance to the town to mark the **gateway to the Tokaj Wine Region**. There's an information booth and temporary exhibitions in one of the towers.

FESTIVALS AND EVENTS A wine exhibition and folklore events are held in June, while August sees both the Zemplén Art Days (open-air concerts and drama at the castle) and the International Folk Dance Festival.

EXCURSIONS FROM SZERENCS The western side of the Zemplén Hills is relatively free of the tourist boot, and is consequently light on accommodation and other facilities, but there is some beautiful landscape and some villages with merit. It's most easily accessed by car, although there are buses from Szerencs, as well as stops on the railway as it travels up the Hernád Valley from Szerencs to Hidasnémeti at the border with Slovakia.

The nearby village of **Mád** has a Louis-XVI-style synagogue from 1795, which was restored in 2004 after a long period of neglect. Around 15km north of Szerencs, **Monok** was the birthplace of Lajos Kossuth, and there is a memorial museum (*Kossuth Lajos u. 18*) in his residence. **Boldogkőváralja** has a 13th-century castle (🏰 *500/300Ft;* ⊕ *mid-Apr–mid-Oct Tue–Sun 09.00–17.00*), which declined after the suppression of Imre Thököly's revolt in the late 1600s. There's a themed restaurant at the foot of the castle (*Castrum Boldua; mains avg 2,400Ft;* ⊕ *daily 09.00–22.00*). At the peak of a commanding hill, the vistas are lovely; the castle is a couple of kilometres east of the railway station.

At the end of the 16th century, the first Hungarian translation of the Bible was printed in **Vizsoly**, the work of Gáspár Károlyi who was a priest at Gönc. The Calvinist church has a copy of the original, together with some beautiful medieval frescoes. Twelve kilometres further on, **Gönc** gives its name to the Tokaji wine barrels that were produced here in the past. **Telkibánya**, to the east, was once a centre of gold mining, while **Abaújvár**, to the north, has some faded frescoes in its 14th-century Gothic church.

TOKAJ

The statue of a naked Bacchanalian reveller in the centre is a prominent clue; a registered 'International Town of Vine and Wine', Tokaj is all about grapes and glasses. It is 'capital' of the Tokaj-Hegyalja (Tokaj Foothills) region, where the country's most-lauded wine is produced. The quality nose-dived with the mass production typical of the socialist market economy, but since 1991 private estates have re-emerged in place of the massive state-owned factories. Tokaj is just one of almost 30 wine towns in the area; it's pretty enough, but wine is the religion here, and teetotallers will find little else to occupy their time.

GETTING THERE AND AWAY The main **bus stop** is south of the town's synagogue on Serház utca. There are no direct buses from Budapest – the single daily indirect service involves a change at Nyíregyháza. There are two a day to Debrecen, two to Nyíregyháza, nine to Szerencs (four at weekends) and two to Sárospatak. The **railway station** is a kilometre to the south of the town (buses run from outside to the centre approximately hourly until early evening). Tokaj is on the line running between Miskolc and Nyíregyháza, and there are regular services to Budapest and

THE WINE OF KINGS, THE KING OF WINES

Tokaji is an amber-hued white wine from the Zemplén Hills or the Tokaj-Hegyalja, a location considered a sacred part of Hungary; its rich colour, texture and taste are unique, and earn it a distinct place in the world of plonk. During the 16th century, Italian writers documented that it contained gold. In 1703, Ferenc Rákóczi II – who used it to secure political favours – presented Louis XIV of France with bottles from his own vineyards. Louis pronounced it the 'wine of kings, king of wines', and since then it has been considered one of the world's noblest. It is claimed that Peter the Great of Russia insisted on Tokaji for special occasions (and that he regarded it as a tonic for the troops), and that it was the favoured tipple of Catherine the Great, Frederic II of Prussia, Voltaire, Goethe and Schubert. And many thought it had medicinal properties; George V of England was one of those who drank it to speed recovery from illness, and early-18th-century European physicians swore by the healing power of the soil itself. One bevvie legend was that if a man drank Tokaji on his wedding night, his wife would give birth to a son. (Interestingly, it is thought that Tokaji may have been a dry wine until the 17th century. The significance of *aszú* – botrytis-affected berries – was only discovered when the threat of Turkish invasion pushed harvests back in the region, and 'noble rot' set in; the consequent deeper and sweeter flavour was revealed when the wine was later tasted.)

The paradox is that, despite dripping with pride in its past, Tokaji is in some ways just 15 years old. For over 40 years the wines lost their lustre as state farms and wineries (imposed under the state monopoly) modified them with sugar and alcohol to serve the masses back in the Soviet Union. It is only since communism's fall that the age-old traditions have been resurrected (often after foreign investment), and that the wine has made its mark once more.

Only four white-grape types are allowed to be grown in the region: Furmint, Hárslevelű (both original Hungarian varieties), Muscat Lunel and Oremus. Seven wines can be made from them. Furmint is the most famous, a light, dry white, produced by a reductive procedure. Szamorodni can be sweet or dry, its Polish name translating as 'as it was born'. Aszú – produced only in Tokaj according to traditional methods – is divided into wines of three, four, five and six *puttyonyos* (tub or butt), referring to the number of 30-litre tubs of Aszú paste added to the fermenting must. Aszúesszencia is prepared in the same way, but a greater amount of paste is used – equivalent to a seven- or eight-*puttonyos* Aszú wine. The other wines are Hárslevelű (as in Linden leaf), Muscat Lunel (different from the Italian Muscat, and with a wonderful bouquet and tart flavour) and Oremus (both the name of a grape and a major vineyard in the Tokaj region). Tokaji wines are usually very sweet, and drunk as an aperitif or with dessert. However, you can also now get good dry whites like the Degenfeld 2003 Tokaji Muscat Lunel from the vineyards belonging to the German-Hungarian Count Degenfeld in Tarcal (see box, page 264). A good year for Aszú wine is one that is hot but moist; top recent years include 1993, 1996, 2001 and 2003.

these destinations (as well as Szerencs), and most of them continue to Debrecen. Change at Mezőzombor for Sárospatak and Sátoraljaújhely.

INFORMATION AND OTHER PRACTICALITIES

☑ Tourinform Serház u. 1; ☏ 47 352259; e tokaj@tourinform.hu. ☉ Jun–Sep daily 09.00–18.00, Oct–May Mon–Fri 09.00–16.00.

There's a **post office** (*Rákóczi út 24*) opposite Makk Marci Pizzeria, and a **bank** opposite the town hall on Rákóczi út.

WHERE TO STAY

⌂ Degenfeld Panzió (4 rooms) Kossuth tér 1; ☏ 47 552173; e palota@degenfeld.hu; www.degenfeldpalota.hu. Linked to the central Degenfeld Restaurant, the rooms here are excellent – spacious, contemporary & with small kitchens. Highly recommended. Sgl 9,000Ft, dbl 13,000Ft.

⌂ Lux Panzió Serház u. 14; ☏ 47 352145. You'll search in vain for a cheaper pension, but rooms are rather archaic. The staff fall over themselves to be helpful; they also play origami with the bath towels. Dbl 6,000Ft, trpl 8,000, b/fast 700Ft/pp.

⌂ Makk Marci Panzió (7 rooms) Liget köz 1; ☏ 47 352336; www.makkmarci.hu. Spotless rooms in a

pension attached to the pizza parlour. Sgl 5,000Ft, dbl 9,000Ft, trpl 12,000Ft, quad 15,000Ft, apt 18,000Ft.

⌂ Millennium Hotel (18 rooms) Bajcsy-Zsilinszky út 34; ☏ 47 352247; www.tokajmillennium.hu. Built in – you guessed it – the year 2000, the Millennium has something of a Travel-Inn feel, but the rooms are roomy & the staff friendly. Dbl 16,900Ft, trpl 19,900Ft, apt (for 4) 25,000–29,900Ft.

Å Tisza Camping 4465 Rakamaz, Szent István út 116; ☏ 47 352012; e info@tokajtiszakemping.hu. At the foot of the Tokaj Bridge, this campsite (1 of 3 in close proximity) has its own hostel with 24 simple but clean rooms (only 6 have en-suite facilities). You can make use of the riverside location by renting kayaks or canoes (500Ft/day), or splash out on a motorboat for a fishing excursion (5,000Ft/day). There's also bike hire (1,000Ft/day). (Note that in mid July, this is the site of the Hegyalja music festival, & the place is alive with thousands of young hippies & other music lovers.) Hostel room/bungalow 1,600Ft/pp; tent/caravan 900Ft/pp; ☉ mid-Apr–mid-Oct.

⌂ Toldi Fogadó (20 rooms) Hajdú köz 2; ☏ 47 353403; www.toldifogado.hu. This is a lovely place with large rooms, a small pool & wellness centre, & an excellent restaurant (see page 266). Sgl 14,000Ft, dbl 17,000Ft, trpl 21,000Ft, apt (for 5) 27,000Ft.

⌂ Vaskó Panzió Rákóczi u. 12; ☏ 47 352107. Comfortable boarding house with a cellar bar next door – not far to stagger after a night on the local vino. Dbl 7,000Ft, b/fast 700Ft/pp.

WHERE TO EAT AND DRINK Also see *Wine cellars and shops*, pages 266–7.

✗ Bacchus Kossuth tér 17; ☏ 20 494 8850; www.borostyanbacchus.extra.hu. This newly renovated restaurant & pizzeria beside the Rákóczi Cellars offers cheap eats. Mains avg 1,100Ft, pizzas from 850Ft; ☉ 08.00–21.00 daily.

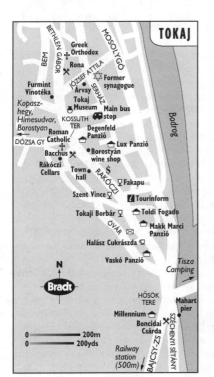

TOKAJ

Greek Orthodox
Rona
Former synagogue
Furmint Vinotéka
Kopasz-hegy, Himesudvar, Borostyan
Tokaj Museum
Main bus stop
KOSSUTH TÉR
Degenfeld Panzió
DÓZSA GY
Roman Catholic
Lux Panzió
Bacchus
Borostyán wine shop
Rákóczi Cellars
Town hall
Fakapu
Szent Vince
Tourinform
Tokaji Borbár
Toldi Fogadó
Makk Marci Panzió
Halász Cukrászda
Vaskó Panzió
Tisza Camping
N
Bradt
HŐSÖK TERE
Mahart pier
Millennium
Boncidai Csárda
0 ___ 200m
0 ___ 200yds
Railway station (500m)

BETHLEN GÁBOR
BEM
MOSOLYGÓ
JÓZSEF ATTILA
SERHÁZ
Árvay
Bodrog
RÁKÓCZI
ÓVÁR
BAJCSY-ZS
SZÉCHENYI SÉTÁNY

The Tokaj-Hegyalja (Tokaj Foothills) make up the southernmost part of the volcanic mountains that branch from the Carpathian chain, the region filling a triangle between the slopes of Sátorhegy-Sátoraljaújhely, the Sátorhegy-Abaújszántó and the Kopasz mountains. Fifty-five kilometres long and 15km wide, the mountains fill the horizon; tucked away here are 28 diverse villages. German, Slovakian and Jewish communities settled in the past, and linguistic variations persist. Spring and autumn are the seasons to visit, particularly during the Tokaj Spring Festival (last weekend of May) and the Harvest Festival (last week of October).

GETTING AROUND Tokaj-Hegyalja is simple. Road 37 from Szerencs runs through the centre to its end at Sátoraljaújhely. Every village is within 8km of turn-offs from the highway. There are buses from Szerencs and Tokaj to most villages, but it's easiest with a car.

Starting at the southwestern end of Tokaj-Hegyalja and passing eastward through Szerencs, the last town before entering the region, you'll reach a sign indicating **Mád** to the left. Hills full of the distinctive cellar doors embedded in their rocky sides surround this little village and its single main road, Rákóczi út. Mád is currently the home of the premier wine maker in the whole area. István Szepsy (*Szepsy Mád-Királyi Szőlészet; Batthyány u. 59; \ 47 348349; www.szepsy.hu*) has been producing wines since communist times; although Szepsy does host tastings in his cellar, his workload means that such opportunities are rare, and it is better instead to head for the Királyudvar winery in Tarcal (see below), where he joins forces with another celebrated winemaker, Zoltán Demeter. The other big name is Tokaj Classic (*Rákóczi út 45, opposite the town hall*), owned by a Hungarian-American couple, András and Phyllis Bruhács. There are also many smaller winemakers scattered in Mád, offering full cellars and visitor tastings. Alternatively, consider the cellars at Oroszlános Borvendéglő in **Tállya** (*Rákóczi u. 23, \ 47 598 888; www.oroszlanos.hu; sgl 6,000–8,000Ft, dbl 12,000–14,000Ft*), in the 17th-century stately home Szirmay-kúria.

Joining Road 37 once more, and going due southeast towards Tokaj, the renowned **Disznókő (Rock Boar) winery** (*Mezőzombor, Disznókő dűlő; \ 47 569410; www.disznoko.hu*), a dome-shaped building perched on a hill, stands just before the turn off for Tarcal. What makes Disznókő particularly unusual is its white pavilion atop a jetting boulder; the boulder is said to look like a wild boar, and the structure was designed by the organic architect Imre Makovecz. **Tarcal** is a town located on the western side of Bald Mountain (see page 266), and has several wineries worth seeing: the Dorogi Vineyard (*Klapka u. 7; \ 20 9576470; e dorogibor@freemail.hu*), Tokaj Nobilis, Királyudvar (*Fő u. 92; \ 47 380111; www.kiralyudvar.com*), Kikelet and Degenfeld (*Terézia kert 9; \ 47 380173; www.grofdegenfeld.com*). The last of these has the Gróf Degenfeld Castle Hotel (\ 47 580400; www.hotelgrofdegenfeld.hu; *21 rooms; sgl 27,600–30,000Ft, dbl 30,000–32,400Ft, suite 36,000–38,400Ft*) in its grounds, an elegant place with 19th-century ambience but modern facilities. The nearby Andrássy Kúria Wine & Spa (*Fő u. 94; \ 47 580015; www.andrassy.hu; 40 rooms; dbl from 28,000Ft, suite from 41,000Ft*) opened in 2008 and has everything promised in its name. Spa treatments play on the anti-ageing properties of grapes and grape seeds.

Continue southwards and around the bottom of Bald Mountain, you'll reach **Tokaj** itself. One of the gurus of this area is János Árvay, the top vintner after Mád's Szepsy.

The Bodrog River courses through **Bodrogkeresztúr**, which stands beside Route 38 on the way back to Road 37. The Dereszla Estate (*Felső u. 2; \ 47 396004; www.dereszla.com*) here is half-owned by French Wine Makers, the D'Aulan family from Champagne. In the immediate aftermath of the political changes of 1989, several French investors and wine makers arrived to work with the locals in harnessing traditional regional techniques with contemporary machinery. The result is spectacular. The Dereszla wines are full-flavoured and wonderful; the Dereszla cellars are a favourite of the region, winding deep underground. Supping direct from the barrels is a frequent pleasure during tours of this winery, but there is also a recently refurbished tasting room. Choosing the best of their wines is a tough task, but special mention should go to the Muskotály 2000; free of the acidic taste that usually characterises Tokaji Muscat, this one yields a soft, slightly sweet wine with a swift and sharp finish. Füleky (*Iskola köz 15;* \ *47 396478; www.fuleky-tokaj.com*), one of the leading smaller wineries, is also in Bodgrogkeresztúr. Judit Bott is the wine maker and in recent years she has received rave reviews. The Furmint 'Pallas' is the most popular of the wines. Judit speaks excellent English and is a super wine guide.

Back on Road 37, vineyards envelope the landscape. The majority are owned by Hétszőlő, Dereszla and private landowners. The turn for **Erdőbénye** is further northeast along the highway. Tiny in size but beautiful in look, it is known for its makers of traditional Tokaji barrels (*gönci*), which hold 136 litres. Attila Homonna came to Tokaj ten years ago, and has been making his name during the past few of them with his fantastic Szamorodni and Furmint wines.

Olaszliszka is the next stop, 5km further along our route, where just one maker plies his trade. Samuel Tinon is a Frenchman who moved to Tokaj 14 years ago to revamp many of the larger wineries, introducing up-to-date processes and techniques. Eight kilometres on is **Tolcsva**, home of the Spanish/Hungarian Tokaj Oremus winery (*Bajcsy-Zsilinszky u. 45;* \ *47 384505; www.tokajoremus.com*). Oremus is internationally known, and boasts one of the most advanced wine-making systems (with a 'gravity-flow' process, considered to provide the 'clearest' extract from the grapes). The estate is huge. Of all the cellars of the wineries, this is the one to go to. Mouldy, low-ceilinged corridors are lined with backlit bottles that project shafts of amber-coloured light all around. Oremus also holds the 'Wine of the Century' – voted the best dessert wine in the world – from the 1972 vintage. Keep an eye out for the 1999 Hárslevel late harvest and Szamorodni dry and sweet wines.

At the heart of the town is the Ős Kaján (*Kossuth u. 14–16;* \ *47 384195; www.oskajan.hu;* ⊕ *Tue–Sat 12.00–22.00, Sun 12.00–17.00*), a restaurant owned by a French couple, Anne and Pascal, who have contributed greatly to the process of resurrecting Tokaji's place in the tradition of Hungarian cuisine. They have studied old Hungarian recipes, and reinvented the art of the true Hungarian kitchen; their restaurant is rustic, antiquated and intimate. A garden holds plum, apple and peach trees, and is the venue for summer concerts on Fridays and Saturdays, while inside are regular exhibitions of Hungarian and foreign artists. As for food, ingredients are home grown and dishes carefully matched with the right Tokaji wine.

Sárospatak (see page 267) is 20km on, while another 10km of tarmac brings up **Sátoraljaújhely**, right on the Slovakian border. This town is home to the Tokaj Pendits (MWB) winery (*Abaújszántó, Béke út 111, Pf 27;* \ *47 330567; www.pendits.de*), owned by the Wille-Baumkauff family, who have just renovated and restored their estate; the views from the hill here are top-notch, and make this winery the perfect place to take a final draught, draw a deep sigh and complete your tour of Hungary's prime wine region.

Wine tasting on the estates usually **costs** between 500Ft and 1,500Ft, although occasionally it is free. For **further information**, contact Tokaj Renaissance (*Tokaji Nagy Borok Egyesülete; Tokaj, Pf 17;* \ *47 353612; www.tokaji.hu*). The headquarters of the state-run wine company **Tokaj Kereskedő Ház** – whose wines are considered good but not the best – are in Sátoraljaújhely (*Mártírok u. 17;* \ *47 384164;* e *marketing@tkrt.hu*).

✗ Bonchidai Csárda Bajcsy-Zsilinszky út 21; ✆ 47 352632; www.hollandrt.hu. Large, traditional-style restaurant opposite the Millennium Hotel. It specialises in classics like fish soup, & has a lovely riverside terrace. ⊕ 10.00–22.00 daily.

✗ Degenfeld Restaurant & Wine Pub Kossuth tér 1; ✆ 47 552202; e palotaetterem@degenfeld.hu. Fresh international & Hungarian fare in highly polished surroundings. They take pride here – this is one of the region's best. There's occasionally wine-tasting available in the wine pub – although most tastings are held at the vineyard itself (see page 264), which is 10km away. There's a wine shop next door. Mains avg 2,000Ft; restaurant ⊕ 12.00–21.00 daily.

✗ Fakapu Pinceborozó Falatozó Rákóczi út 27; ✆ 20 519 0390; e fakapu@citromail.hu. Newish cellar bar offering wines from all the local cellars & traditional Hungarian dishes (always fish soup & goulash, with other daily choices depending on what's being cooked in the courtyard cauldron). ⊕ daily 11.00–23.00.

✗ Makk Marci Pizzéria Liget köz 1; ✆ 47 352336. Cheap & cheerful pizza & pasta joint – the ravenous can tuck in to a 40cm pizza for 1,800Ft. ⊕ daily 10.00–20.00.

♀ Szent Vince Rákóczi út 42. Around since early 2009, this bar opens later than anywhere else in the centre. ⊕ Mon–Thu 12.00–22.00, Fri 12.00–late, Sun 10.00–22.00.

♀ Tokaji Borbár Rákóczi út 34; ✆ 47 352320. An elevated bar with minimal furnishings; wine available by the glass or bottle. ⊕ daily 12.00–22.00.

✗ Toldi Fogadó See page 263. Inviting interior with high wooden benches & stained glass, as well as an outdoor area at the back. The menu features fish & game dishes. Mains avg 1,600Ft; ⊕ daily 11.00–23.00.

WHAT TO SEE AND DO The **Tokaj Museum** (*Bethlen Gábor u. 7;* ✆ *47 352636;* 🎟 *600/300Ft;* ⊕ *Tue–Sun 10.00–16.00, Tue–Sat in winter*) stands at the northern end of the main square, its building constructed by a Greek merchant in 1790. It holds a collection of religious art representative of northern Hungary's churches, including icons, Baroque statues and Russian and Ukrainian woodcuts, as well as Jewish artefacts from the former synagogue. Here too is an exhibition devoted to life along the Tisza and Bodrog rivers, and another displaying the tools of winemaking (from transportation carts to bottle labels). The cellars – that 'world under the ground where the world above is forgotten', as Kálmán Mikszáth once wrote – contain casks and bottles from the best of the region's producers. Further up the same street, the late-Baroque **Greek Orthodox Church** (*Bethlen Gábor u. 17;* ✆ *47 352003; free entry;* ⊕ *May–Oct daily 10.00–16.00*) was built in the 1780s, and now has a gallery showcasing local artists.

The **former synagogue** (*Serház u. 55*) is east of the gallery, a sad and broken reminder of the significant Jewish presence in the town (and in the town's wine trade) prior to World War II. It has been earmarked for conversion into a conference hall, and there's a Jewish cemetery (with Classicist tombstones) a few kilometres north in Bodrogkeresztúr. By contrast, the **Roman Catholic church** on Kossuth tér is spick and span, its interior a beautiful example of understated decoration. We particularly like the juxtaposition of the church and the half-naked figure of the Bacchanalian reveller outside – which inevitably highlights wine's contrasting roles as symbol of sacrifice and practical means to excess.

To the west, **Kopasz-hegy** (Bald Mountain) has a TV tower and splendid views. There are several **hiking trails** in the hills, whose flora includes the woolly Michaelmas daisy, footgrass, fringe flower, desert bloodgrass and red lednek. Alternatively you can stroll the Széchenyi Trail, which starts at the confluence of the Bodrog and Tisza. On the opposite bank there is a **beach** and camping, from where you can hire canoes (see page 263). Between spring and autumn, **ferry tours** leave from the Mahart pier (✆ *47 352937*) at Hősök tere, running between Tokaj and Sárospatak.

Wine cellars and shops Wine is Tokaj's *raison d'être*. The **Rákóczi Cellars** (*Kossuth tér 15;* ✆ *47 352408;* e *info@rakoczipince.hu;* ⊕ *May–mid Oct Tue–Sun 10.00–18.00 or*

20.00 in summer) are the town's most renowned. the history of the cellars is impressive. The 24 tunnels, branching from a central hall, were built in the 15th century, and in 1526 formed the backdrop to the Hungarian Diet that elected János Szapolyai king. Oak barrels line the chambers as Tokaji Aszú and Szamorodni mature inside. One of the main cellar passages collapsed during bombing in World War II; originally kilometres long, it's now cut short to 600m. Today the cellars are owned by the Hétszőlő company, which has vineyards on a hill in southern Tokaj. English-language tours and tastings (*☞ from 2,700Ft/pp*) begin on the hour. The rare Esszencia – a wine made from far more of (or even exclusively from) the botrytis-affected grapes – is low in alcohol but highly prized as an elixir. In 1993 (a good year), the company here made only 30 bottles and a single one now will set you back 233,000Ft!

The **Hímesudvar Pince** (*Bem út 2;* ☎ *47 352416; www.himesudvar.hu;* ⊕ *Mar 15–Oct 31 Sun–Thu 10.00–18.00, Fri–Sat 10.00–21.00, Nov 1–Mar 14 Fri–Sat 10.00–18.00, Sun–Thu by prior appointment*) is a short walk northwest of Kossuth tér; the building was constructed by Szapolyai in the 16th century as a hunting lodge and cellar. The Várhelyi family restored it in the 1980s, and now offers its own wines and others from the region (*☞ tastings from 1,200Ft/5 wines*). **Tokaji Hétszőlő** (*Bajcsy-Zsilinszky út 19–21;* ☎ *47 352009;* e *hetszolo@t-online.hu*) – the company that owns the Rákóczi Cellars – has an impressive cellar burrowing through the ground with corridor after corridor of rooms with barrels and traditional tasting areas.

Borostyán Wine Cellar (*Dozsa György u.6/B;* ☎ *47 352054; www.borostyanbacchus.extra.hu;* ⊕ *10.00–20.00 daily*) offers tastings (*☞ 500Ft/decilitre, ½-litre bottle from 3,000Ft*) of wines from the Borostyán family winery. (The cellar is almost opposite Hímesudvar Pince, around 100m along the road running away behind the church.) You can also buy wines by this producer from **Borostyán Pince** (*Kossuth tér;* ⊕ *10.00–18.00 daily*), a specialist wine shop in the centre where you can choose from an extensive list of wines by the glass or bottle. **Furmint Vinotéka** (*Bethlen Gábor u. 12/A;* ☎ *47 353340;* e *vinoteka@enternet.hu;* ⊕ *daily 09.00–17.00*) has a wide range of wines from over 30 of the region's wineries. You can also book tours or tastings, and purchase gifts such as personalised bottles.

János Árvay makes just about every kind of Tokaji and is one of the region's top vintners. His winery is in the former town hall (*József Attila u. 2;* ☎ *47 552155; www.arvaybor.hu; ☞ tastings from 1,900Ft*), its renovation completed in 2004. Inside are a coffee shop, a wine-tasting room, cellars below and a pressing room on the top floor.

FESTIVALS AND EVENTS Inevitably the main events are wine soaked – there are festivals in May; The five-day Hegyalja Music Festival (*www.hegyaljafestival.hu*) takes place in Mid July at Tisza campsite (see page 263); August sees the Zemplén Festival; and In October it's all about harvesting and celebrating the wine.

SÁROSPATAK

The 'Hungarian Cambridge' or 'Athens on the Bodrog' – so named because of the formidable reputation of its Calvinist college – lies 20km north of Tokaj; the actual meaning of Sárospatak is rather less salubrious – 'muddy stream'. The college was founded in 1531, and numbers some greats among its alumni: the Czech humanist and teacher J A Comenius studied here in the 1650s, and other past pupils include the Enlightenment poet Mihály Csokonai Vitéz, the language reformer Ferenc Kazinczy, the statesman and 'Hungarian Moses' Kossuth Lajos, and the 20th-century author Géza Gárdonyi. The town is also inextricably linked with the Rákóczis, who acquired it in 1616 and ensured that it was at the forefront of the revolutionary struggles. In 1708 it hosted the last Diet during the War of Independence, and Sárospatak was also the town from which Rákóczi II was exiled

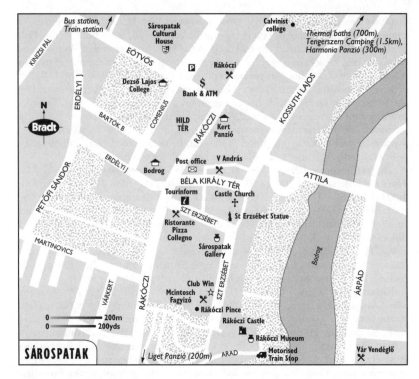

after the dream had died. There's plenty in its compact centre to fill an enjoyable day, and a couple of spanking pensions for overnight stays.

GETTING THERE AND AWAY The **bus** and **train** stations are next to each other, a short distance to the north. On alighting from either station, follow Táncsics Mihály utca for a short distance to the Calvinist college; turn right to reach the centre. Sárospatak railway station lies on an offshoot northeast from the main line running between Miskolc and Nyíregyháza. There are eight daily direct trains from Budapest Keleti. Alternatively there are nine from Miskolc; from Debrecen or other towns to the east, change at Szerencs or Mezőzombor. There are no direct buses from Budapest; there are two daily services to Debrecen (one early morning and one afternoon service) which stop at Tokaj and Nyíregyháza. For Miskolc, the train is a better option as there's only one service on weekdays. There are frequent connections to Sátoraljaújhely.

INFORMATION AND OTHER PRACTICALITIES

$ Bank Eötvös út 2
⚡ **Listings magazine** *Miskolci Est*
⚡ **Tourinform** Szent Erzsébet u. 3; *☏* 47 313150;
e sarospatak@tourinform.hu; www.sarospatak.hu. In

the same building as the ÚjBástya Café, which has good coffee & an internet corner. ☉ *Jun 15–Aug 31 Mon–Fri 09.00–19.00, Sat–Sun 10.00–20.00, rest of yr Mon–Fri 09.00–16.00, Sat 10.00–14.00.*

🏠 WHERE TO STAY

🏠 **Dezső Lajos College** Eötvös u. 7; *☏* 47 513000/2847; e mihalkoerika@citf.hu. Cheap dorm beds during student vacation periods. *Beds from 2,000Ft/pp.*

🏠 **Hotel Bodrog** (50 rooms) Rákóczi út 58; *☏* 47 311744; www.hotelbodrog.hu The building is stale & dated (& its 4-star rating ambitious), but the rooms themselves are spacious & light, & there's a sauna &

fitness room. More costly rooms on the 1st & 2nd floors are bigger & have balconies. *Sgl 14,400–17,700Ft, dbl 17,300–20,900Ft (excl local tax of 250Ft/pp).*

🏠 **Harmónia Panzió** (5 rooms) Dobó Ferenc u. 39; ☎ 47 889111; www.harmoniapanzio.hu. The brand-new Harmónia is further to the south & has comfortable rooms & apartments with cooking facilities & a café. The apartments (for up to 6) are large & the garden is good. *Dbl 5,000Ft/pp, apt (for 4) 17,000–27,000Ft, b/fast 1,000Ft.*

🏠 **Kert Panzó** Rákóczi út 31; ☎ 47 311559; www.kertpanzio.hu. Sparkling, wood-floored rooms with everything you need – inc use of a communal kitchen & pretty garden. It's centrally positioned, but quiet. And crumbs it's cheap. They have their own wine cellar, & bike rental is available (1,200Ft/day). *Sgl 4,700Ft, dbl 7,000Ft, trpl 9,000Ft.*

🏕 **Tengerszem Camping** Herczeg Ferenc u. 2; ☎ 47 312744; ℮ info@tengerszem-camping.hu. Just 2km northeast of the centre (close to the thermal baths), this manicured campsite has an outdoor pool, restaurant, tennis courts, cute bungalows (all with bathrooms & most with small kitchens & TVs) & new superior apartments. Hedges provide privacy between camping pitches. *Bungalow from 6,500Ft (for 2), from 7,500Ft (for 4); apt from 14,900Ft (for 4); tent/caravan 1,100/1,600Ft, plus 1,100Ft/pp; b/fast 1,500Ft.* ⊕ *Apr–Oct.*

🏠 **Vár Vendéglő** Árpád Út 35; ☎ 47 311370; www.varvendeglo.hu. Spacious, clean rooms above a good restaurant (see below). Those with a view are slightly more expensive, but strongly recommended. *Sgl 7,400–9,800Ft, dbl 11,200–13,600Ft.*

✗ WHERE TO EAT AND DRINK

🍨 **McIntosch Fagyizó** Szent Erzsébet u. 22; ☎ 47 312929. Ice-cream parlour that also serves burgers, pizzas & pancakes. ⊕ *Mon–Thu 10.00–22.00, Fri–Sat 10.00–22.00, Sun 10.00–20.00.*

🍷 **Rákóczi Cellar** Szent Erzsébet u. 26; ☎ 47 311902; ℮ info@pajzos-megyer.com. Dug deep beneath the castle grounds & snaking to around 1km in length, the cellar has changed little in the centuries since it was constructed in 1530 – dim corridors, mould-clad walls & oak barrels. The humidity is 96% & the temperature a constant 12°C. The Szamorodni, Tokaji Aszú & Esszencia of Chateau Megyer (the current owners) mature inside. The entrance is just to the right of the castle complex. *Wine tastings (starting on the hour) from 700Ft;* ⊕ *daily 10.00–18.00 (but best to call ahead).*

✗ **Rákóczi Restaurant** Rákóczi út 30; ☎ 47 511423. Specialises in game, as well as a dish of pork & chicken for the carnivorous to share. They have a few rooms upstairs too (*sgl 6,500Ft, dbl 12,000Ft, trpl 18,000Ft*). The English-speaking manager was very welcoming during our visit. *Mains avg 1,800Ft;* ⊕ *daily 07.00–22.00.*

✗ **Ristorante Pizza Collegno** Szent Erzsébet u. 10; ☎ 47 314494. Atmospheric cellar & a good selection of pizzas. *Pizzas 700–1,500Ft;* ⊕ *Mon–Sat 11.00–24.00, Sun 16.00–23.00.*

✗ **V András Restaurant and Coffee House** Béla Király tér 3; ☎ 47 312415; www.otodikandras.hu. Standard Hungarian cuisine; there are set menus (read 'bland-but-cheap') for around 1,800Ft. It's nice to sit outside, if the weather allows. *Mains avg 1,400Ft;* ⊕ *daily 10.00–22.00.*

✗ **Vár Vendéglő** See above. Top of the food tree – a rustic restaurant with upbeat staff across the water from the castle. Fish is the dish of the house, & there's a good wine selection. If you choose to sit outside of an evening, bring some insect repellent – mosquitoes enjoy dining by the Bodrog River too. *Mains avg 1,800Ft;* ⊕ *Mon–Sat 12.00–22.00, Sun 12.00–20.00.*

ENTERTAINMENT AND NIGHTLIFE Club Win (*Szent Erzsébet u. 22;* ⊕ *Mon–Tue 19.00–23.00, Wed 19.00–24.00, Thu 19.00–23.00, Fri–Sat 19.00–02.00*), on the road leading to the castle, is a student favourite and is packed to the rafters at the weekends. Next to the Tourinform, the **Sárospatak Cultural House** (*Eötvös u. 6;* ☎ *47 311811; www.sarospatak.hu/muvhaz;* ⊕ *Mon–Fri 08.00–20.00, Sat–Sun 10.00–18.00*) hosts theatrical productions, concerts, dance classes and discos; its adventurous, exhilarating building was designed in the 1970s by Imre Makovecz, and is intended to resemble a human face or an open book. Makovecz was something of an outcast of the establishment during the communist period, when his organic, natural designs ran visibly counter to the rigidity of the prevalent architectural style and its associations with the party.

WHAT TO SEE AND DO Slightly south of the town centre, **Rákóczi Castle** (*Szent Erzsébet u. 19–21; www.spatak.hu;* 🎫 *500/250Ft, Eng-lang tours from 1,000Ft/pp;* ☉ *Tue–Sun 10.00–18.00*) stands in an area that was a royal estate from the 11th century, positioned at the crossing point of the River Bodrog. It is an eclectic patchwork in stone, the product of several centuries of architectural tinkering – but tinkering of the very finest. The oldest portion is the late-15th-century Red Tower – 'red' because of coloured plaster that originally covered its walls – while Renaissance wings were constructed in the next century. The complex came into the possession of the Rákóczis on the marriage in 1616 of its owner, Zsuzsanna Lorántffy, to György I (later elected Prince of Transylvania). It stayed in the family until the failure of Ferenc Rákóczi II and his *kuruc* armies, after which the Habsburgs demolished its fortifications and handed it over to foreign aristos.

The **Rákóczi Museum**, which is housed in the Renaissance building, holds permanent exhibitions devoted to the castle, the Rákóczi family, the history of the Independence War, and period furniture and weaponry. Carved door and window frames in the Perényi wing and a beautiful open-sided arcade of 1646 that leads from the courtyard to the Red Tower are first-class examples of Renaissance artistry. In the corner of the northeast bastion, the Knights' Hall was the site of a Diet during the War of Independence; there had been anti-Habsburg plans afoot in 1670 too when plotters met in the adjacent balcony room, congregating beneath the stone rose in its ceiling. The leaders subsequently got the chop, but the conspiratorial connotations of the Latin term '*sub rosa*' lived on in the room. (The rose as a symbol of silence dates back to antiquity; it came to be a popular decoration in banqueting halls, reminding diners to guard against wine's power to loosen their tongues!)

If you're feeling lazy, you can hop on a motorised **tourist train** that departs each hour from the car park behind the castle on Arad utca. It takes you as far as the thermal baths (📞 *20 3886241;* 🎫 *adult 400Ft*)

Moving away from the castle, north along Szent Erzsébet utca, the **Sárospatak Gallery** (*Szent Erzsébet u. 14;* 📞 *47 511012;* 🎫 *400/200Ft;* ☉ *Tue–Sun 10.00–16.00*) sits in an 18th-century Baroque building just inside the outer fortified wall. It hosts temporary exhibitions, and is presaged by a statue of a boy riding a distinctly giraffe-like horse outside. Close by is the 14th-century **Castle Church** (*Szent Erzsébet u. 7;* 🎫 *150/80Ft;* ☉ *Tue–Sat 09.00–16.00, Sun 11.30–16.00*), every part of which shouts 'big'. This is one of the largest Gothic hall churches in the country, its enormous interior supported by enormous columns and punched with enormous arched windows. The wooden altar – inevitably Hungary's biggest – originally stood in Buda Castle's Carmelite church until the monastic order was outlawed in the late 1700s. Regular concerts are played on the Baroque organ, which is rather small… Only joking!

The main building of the **Calvinist college** (*Sárospataki Református Kollégium; Rákóczi út 1;* 📞 *47 315256;* 🎫 *400/200Ft;* ☉ *Mon–Sat 09.00–17.00, Sun 09.00–13.00*) – imposing, Neoclassical and based around a central courtyard – was completed in 1834, although there had been a college on the site since 1531. Between 1650 and 1654, the Czech humanist Johannes Amos Comenius taught here, and wrote the pioneering educational work *Orbis Sensualium Pictus* (*The Visible World*). Other significant alumni are commemorated by statues in the college garden. The stock of the library – in a stunning oval hall designed by Mihály Pollack – includes 2,000 volumes remaining from the original 16th-century holdings. (Another 15,000 were taken by Russian troops in 1945, and have not yet been returned.) There are hourly tours. An 18th-century Baroque side wing has scientific collections, an exhibition of religious art and details of the college's history.

The town's outdoor **thermal baths** (*Végardó;* ☎ *47 311639;* 🎫 *900/600Ft;* ⏰ *daily 08.00–18.00 in summer*) are around a kilometre north of the centre, just beyond the Tengerzem campsite.

FESTIVALS AND EVENTS The primary festival takes place in mid August, when a series of classical-music concerts are staged in conjunction with other towns and villages as part of the region's Zemplén Arts Days. There's a two-day festival in commemoration of Szent Erzsébet (who was born here in 1207) at the start of June, while the Dixieland and Blues Festival comes to town at the latter end of July.

SÁTORALJAÚJHELY

What's in a name? Well, in Sátoraljaújhely's case, many syllables – *Sha-tor-a-ya-ooi-hay*. There's little else of significant interest in a one-street town bereft of decent restaurants, dead as a doornail by mid evening, and blighted by surrounding residential blocks. From the 18th century, this was actually a prosperous wine-trading town and capital of Zemplén County until the Treaty of Trianon broke the country and shifted power to Sárospatak, 12km to the south. Like Sárospatak, the town stands on its history. In 1697 a peasant rebellion broke out here that spread throughout the Hegyalja region, and it was at the heart of the 17th-century struggles led by the Rákóczis, the landowners of the period. It was later to witness the first flowerings of Lajos Kossuth's political career. Today, though, it functions primarily as a board for springing elsewhere – be it into the hills, to nearby villages or over the border at the crossing into Slovakia.

GETTING THERE AND AWAY The **bus** and **railway** stations both stand to the south. On exiting the stations, walk straight ahead up Fasor utca (past the Temple of Wine), and at the top of the road turn right on to Kossuth Lajos utca to the centre. It is about a 15-minute walk. The railway station is on the same line as Sárospatak (the next stop northwards). There are five trains direct from Budapest Keleti; otherwise you can access the town from Miskolc (up to 11) or Szerencs (14). Destinations further east require a change at Mezőzombor. You can also take occasional daily services across the border into Slovakia.

There are frequent buses to Sárospatak (5km away). You can pick up services to other places in the northern Zemplén too, including Hollóháza (up to ten), Füzér (four) and Hidasnémeti (one); the latter offers trains over the border.

INFORMATION AND OTHER PRACTICALITIES

$ **Bank** Széchenyi tér 13. ⏰ Mon–Fri 08.00–16.00.

📧 **Internet Café** Rákóczi u. 30a; ☎ 47 325150. A shop rather than café, with 4 computer terminals (350Ft/hr). ⏰ Mon–Fri 08.00–17.00, Sat 09.00–12.00.

📺 **Kossuth Cultural Centre** Táncsics Mihály tér 3; ☎ 47 321727. Regular theatre productions & other events.

ℹ️ **Listings magazine** Miskolci Est

ℹ️ **Tiszi BT** Kossuth tér 22; ☎ 47 322563. Super-helpful office that can arrange tours &

accommodation, & provide information on Zemplén County. ⏰ Mon–Thu 09.00–17.00, Fri 09.00–15.00.

🎫 **Tiszi és Újhelyi Írisz** Kossuth Lajos tér 26; ☎ 47 321757. Private accommodation, transport & money exchange. ⏰ Mon–Fri 08.00–16.00, Sat 08.00–14.00.

ℹ️ **Tourinform** Hősök tere 3; ☎ 47 321458. Have information on guides, tours & accommodation; in the very centre of town. ⏰ mid Jun–mid Sep Mon–Fri 09.00–18.00, Sat–Sun 09.00–17.00, rest of yr Mon–Thu 07.30–16.00, Fri 07.30–13.30.

🏠 WHERE TO STAY

🏠 **Csillagfény Panzió** (10 rooms) Mártírok u. 29; ☎ 47 322619; e csillagfenypanzio@t-online.hu.

Comfortable & characterful guesthouse close to the Greek Orthodox church; ski-hire available. *Dbl*

5

10,000Ft, trpl 12,000Ft, quad 14,000Ft, apt (for 2) 15,000Ft.

🏠 **Hotel Henriette** (9 rooms) Vasvári Pál u. 16; ☏ 47 323118. If you've packed one, there's plenty of room to swing a cat in the rooms of the Henriette, a short distance east of the Ferenc Kazinczy Museum. The furnishings are more than adequate too. Dbl 9,000Ft, trpl 10,500Ft; b/fast 1,000Ft.

🏠 **Hotel Hunor** (30 rooms) Torzsás u. 25; ☏ 47 521521; www.hotelhunor.hu. Situated at the foot of Magas-hegy, next to the lower station of the chairlift (see opposite), the Hunor has well-appointed rooms & excellent facilities (including a fitness centre, bowling alley, tennis court & small swimming pool). A little out of the centre, it is on the bus route towards the village of Rudabányácska. Bike & ski hire available. Dbl 19,900Ft, apt 25,000Ft.

🏠 **Hotel König** (27 rooms) Széchenyi tér 5; ☏ 47 523400; e konighotel@t-online.hu. A gleaming-floored, Holiday-Inn-type hotel right in the centre, with a fitness room & sauna. The standard rooms are compact, while the 3 larger suites have the luxury of baths. Sgl 11,200–12,700Ft, dbl 12,800–14,600Ft, suite 17,300Ft.

✘ WHERE TO EAT AND DRINK

✘ **Black Coffee** Széchenyi tér 2; ☏ 30 981 3817. Standing next to the Roman Catholic church (accessed via an archway), Black Coffee has an elegant but cheerful restaurant, serving international food, & a coffee house with some outside seating. Mains avg 1,200Ft; café ⏱ 10.00–22.00 daily, restaurant 12.00–22.00 daily.

🍷 **Bodnár Wine House** Pincék-völgye 16; Balassi Bálint u. 31 (mail address); ☏ 30 9951115; e bodnarpinceszet@freemail.hu. To the north of the centre up a steep track running off Kazsincy Ferenc utca. The friendly owner – whose family runs 6ha of vineyards – will show you around the computer-regulated pressing room, mouldy cellar & collection of 5,000 ex libris wines, before plying you with glasses in a rustic tasting room. Telephone in advance of a visit. Tasting 2,500Ft/7 wines.

✘ **Csillagfény Restaurant** See page 271. The panzió restaurant offers Hungarian fare in a dated dining area decorated with kitsch mountain scenes & faux-candle chandeliers. Mains avg 1,400Ft; ⏱ daily 11.00–22.00.

☕ **Henriette Café House** Dózsa György utca. The pavement corner outside the café is a popular place for the 20- & 30-somethings to pass time. ⏱ daily 10.00–22.00.

✘ **Spaten** Kossuth Lajos u. 10; ☏ 47 321527. Rather dingy pub serving pasta, pancakes & other Hungarian dishes. Mains avg 1,000Ft; ⏱ Mon–Sat 09.00–22.00, Sun 10.00–22.00.

✘ **Zempléni Casinó** Kazinczy u. 1–3; ☏ 47 321470. Airy pizzeria. Pizzas 570–2,160Ft; ⏱ daily 11.00–21.00.

WHAT TO SEE AND DO The **Kazinczy Ferenc Museum** (Dózsa György út 11; ☏ 47 322351; ☞ 600/300Ft; ⏱ Tue–Fri 09.00–16.00, Sat 09.00–16.00, Sun by prior arrangement only) is housed in a Neoclassical building that between 1835 and 1850 was the site of the Zemplén Casino, where the progressive movers and shakers met to chew the cud. Between 1894 and 1954 it served as the town hall. An exhibition charting the town's history between 1261 and 1848 includes a reconstruction of the casino and a room devoted to Kazinczy, the leader of the language-reform movement (which established Hungarian as the literary lingo rather than German) during the Enlightenment period. Kazinczy had a colourful life during which he was imprisoned for six years – narrowly avoiding the death penalty – after implication in Martinovics's Jacobin conspiracy (see box, page 132). He was superintendent of the Sátoraljaújhely Calvinist Church (to the west of the museum) and the county archivist from 1820 in the current town hall. (He lived and was buried in nearby Széphalom, where there is an Ybl-designed literary memorial and a new Museum of Hungarian Language; see opposite.) There is also a natural-history display, heavy on stuffed and pinned fauna from around Zemplén County.

Towards the northern end of Kossuth Lajos tér, the Baroque **town hall** (Kossuth Lajos tér 5) was erected in 1768, and is special for its rather unspectacular balcony; it was from here that Lajos Kossuth, the soul of the 1848–49 Revolution and War of Independence, delivered his first public speech in 1830. There is a **statue** of the man in the centre of the square, with a sword at his hip (as well as a musical fountain opposite Tourinform on Hősök tere).

To the south of the statue is the broad and understated **Roman Catholic church** (*Széchenyi tér 10*), completed in 1792. More elaborate is the former **Piarist church** (*Deák u. 14*) to the northeast of the centre, with its extravagant altarpiece. A succession of churches rose and fell on this site – succumbing to the Turks, *kuruc* insurrections and fire – and the current late-17th-century incarnation only narrowly survived after Ferenc Rákóczi's instruction to level it was overlooked. Several earlier portions remain, such as the Gothic tower and northern wall of the Anjou-funded 14th-century church. The adjoining Pauline monastery became defunct after József II disbanded the order in 1786. A **Greek Orthodox church** (*Benczur Gyula utca*), slightly northwest of here on the other side of Kazinczy Ferenc utca, is also worth a peek for its peacock-iridescent iconostasis of 1759.

Before World War II, a significant proportion of the population was Jewish, and the town has two cemeteries. Among the stunted, sorry-looking gravestones of that to the south, in the fork between Kossuth Lajos utca and Esze Tamás utca (*to gain access,* ⚲ *47 312029*), is a restored memorial to rabbi Mózes Teitelbaum – who expounded an 18th-century form of Jewish mysticism, and purportedly performed miracles. A short distance further south, opposite the train and bus stations, is the early-20th-century turreted **Temple of Wine** (*Bortemplom; Fasor utca*), with colourful reliefs depicting towns of the region; the cellars of its decaying interior can store up to 12,000 hectolitres of wine.

The **Town Swimming Pool** (*Városi uszoda; Balassi Bálint u. 6;* ⚲ *47 321116;* 🎫 *400/300Ft;* ☼ *daily 06.00–19.00*) is just beyond the eastern end of Dózsa György utca, but those after exercise would do better to head for **Magas-hegy** (Tall Hill). There are walking trails and ski and sledge runs in winter. The **chairlift** (*libegő; Torzsás út 5;* ⚲ *47 322346;* 🎫 *750/500Ft one way;* ☼ *daily 10.00–16.30, later opening in summer*) is a real treat, the country's longest and cutting a 1,333m-long gash through the trees. In addition, a new adventure park features Central Europe's longest bob-sleigh track (☼ *Mon–Fri 09.00–17.00, Sat–Sun 10.00–17.00; also Fri–Sat 18.00–20.00 in winter;* 🎫 *500–750Ft*) – 2km in length – which is open all year, and a summer dry-ski slope. Buses to Rudabányácska can drop you here; specify your destination to the driver. There are great views from the narrow-stepped (be careful if you're larger of foot) lookout tower (*kilátó*) at the top.

EXCURSIONS FROM SÁTORALJAÚJHELY There are a couple of villages worth sniffing out beyond the Zemplén hills, tucked into the very northernmost tip of the country. **Széphalom** – with the Kazinczy Mausoleum (see opposite) – falls on the way there, 6km north of Sátoraljaújhely. The Museum of Hungarian Language (*Sátoraljaújhely-Széphalom, Kazinczy u. 275;* ⚲ *47 521236; www.nyelvmuz.hu;* 🎫 *400/200Ft;* ☼ *Tue–Sun 08.00–16.00*) was opened in 2008, and has an extensive exhibition covering the past, present and future of the baffling Magyar lingo (info leaflets in English; Eng-lang tours by prior arrangement). **Füzér** is 10km from Pálháza (with its narrow-gauge railway running to Rostalló), and has some wonderful and romantic peasant houses. On a hill above it (and giving spectacular views) are the remains of a 13th-century fortress razed by the Habsburgs in the aftermath of the Rákóczi-led War of Independence; its claim to fame is that the holy crown was kept within its walls following the devastating defeat by the Turks at Mohács. East of that, **Hollóháza** is renowned for its porcelain factory, producing pieces characterised by bright floral decoration. The modern church contains religious works by the renowned Margit Kovács. Buses run to these villages from Sátoraljaújhely, but you'll be less restricted if you visit by car.

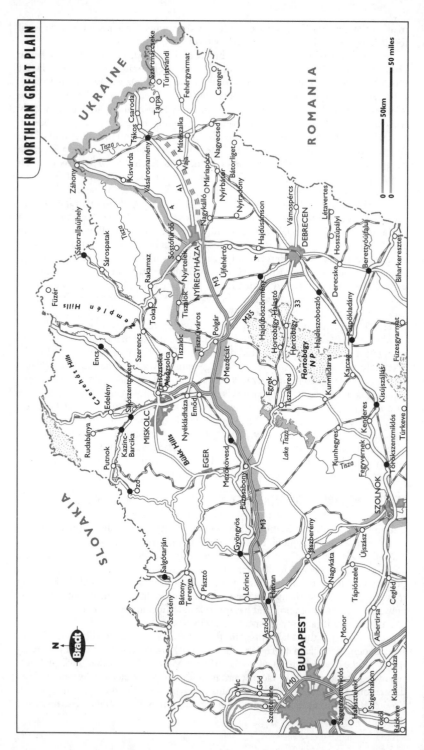

6

Northern Great Plain

The Great Plain (Nagyalföld) is the heartland of Hungarian romanticism. It is a profoundly enigmatic place, a landscape occupied by the minds of poets and storytellers, by legends and folklore, a territory where the imagined and the actual blend like ink in water. Mirages deceive the weary traveller through the summer heat, and Petőfi observed that 'the earth and sky flow together'; it has been said that if your eyesight is good, gaze across the flat expanse and a week later you will see the back of your own head. Here the real can be unreal.

The Great Plain covers half of Hungary, filling a tract of lowland framed by the Danube in the west, the upland foothills in the north and the borders with Ukraine, Romania and Serbia. Perhaps appropriately, it has proved to be of shifting appearance. Originally it was forested and fertile, watered by regular floods from the Danube and Tisza. However, the Turks raped the land, stripping it of vegetation in their hunt for rebels and need for timber, and laying the topsoil bare to the wind. With no roots to bind the earth or suck up moisture, some portions turned to sandy wasteland and others to saturated marsh barely navigable in flat-bottomed boats. Fear of harsh Ottoman rulers drove country folk to the towns, particularly those towns under the direct protection of the sultan. A few brave toughs tilled in summer, living on isolated farmsteads (*tanyák*) – you'll come across them occasionally as you journey between settlements – but in essence this was inhospitable, bleak land. It became known as '*puszta*' – or 'abandoned'.

With the land uncultivated for such an extended period, and travel tricky, when life picked up again it was livestock and lawlessness that held sway. Domestic animals included racka sheep, hairy pigs and ill-tempered white cattle; the hardy shepherd, with his fleece coat and odd-looking herding dogs (see box, page 143), is a perennial figure in the colourful folklore of the plains. However, it was the horse and its uniformed herdsmen (*csikós*) that fully fired the imagination. This was – at least retrospectively – the age of romance, the Hungarian variation on the American 'Wild West', a time of hard riding and hard drinking, of horsemen and highwaymen, and the flamboyant, unbending, whip-cracking human spirit unbowed by the bully-boy force of authority.

Of course, the *csikós* of today are simply strutting showmen for tourists, and the *puszta* a shadow of its former barren self. In the 19th century a massive programme of river regulation tamed the Danube and the Tisza, and reclaimed much of the marshland for planting. It didn't achieve its purpose everywhere, though; the soil in some parts became increasingly alkaline, and came to harbour swathes of grassland rather than vegetables. The livestock and herders frolicked, but the days of the cowboys were numbered. With advances in industrial agriculture and irrigation, landowners were able to cultivate crops and needed fewer hands to do so. Agrarian movements did their best to fight – often bloodily – for the evicted peasant small holders and herders, but the intensive agricultural economy had arrived; romance was no match for mechanisation.

All is not lost. Sand dunes, alkaline lakes, grasslands and bogs remain preserved in national parks like Hortobágy, as do some of the ancient livestock breeds, curious creatures of corkscrew horns and matted fur. Horse shows replay the tricks that were once the trade of the manly herdsmen. One can clutch at the will o' the wisp of past isolation while journeying between towns and villages, lonely farmsteads forming islands in a considerable landscape. With the exception of a few pockets, the region remains Hungary's least touched by tourism and least readily travelled.

The colour and richness to be found elsewhere can at first sight seem thinly spread in the Great Plain. This is a place of dogged Calvinism rather than ebullient Catholicism, a place with a scarcity of historic buildings, a place where big towns are few and far between. However, there are several globally significant national parks, strong folk traditions, some important ecclesiastical, cultural and academic centres, the River Tisza (increasingly popular for kayak trips) and a few lively and pretty towns.

★   ★   ★

The Northern Plain (Észak Alföld) is the wilder section, the northeastern pocket Hungary's remotest region. In the past, this was somewhere to fear, its marshes difficult to navigate and prowled by wolves in winter. After the Turkish occupation the pastures between the swamps were leased to herders and shepherds who would drive their livestock to markets in Turkey, Poland, Austria and Italy. Debrecen, second-biggest city in the country, is its main staging post, reached from Budapest on the M3 motorway in just two hours. Alternatively, you can leave the motorway at Füzesabony and travel on Road 33 via Tiszafüred and Hortobágy – this is a longer route but gives a better introduction to the *puszta* landscape. Nyíregyháza can also be reached on the M3 followed by the M35; an extension is underway heading northeast to the Ukrainian border. To the west of Debrecen is the famous Hortobágy National Park, which is a Unesco World Heritage Site and maintains the grassy steppe that thrived after the regulation of the Tisza in the 1840s, and Lake Tisza, an excellent spot for birdwatching and watersports. Other highlights include painted churches, wooden water mills and boat-shaped grave markers.

SZOLNOK

Lying at the confluence of the Tisza and Zagyva 100km east of Budapest, Szolnok has been an important river-crossing point for centuries. As such, its 11th-century fortress had a particular significance, which was why the Habsburgs decided to do away with it after the town supported Rákóczi's War of Independence. The great reformer István Széchenyi also saw the potential of the place for the control of steamboating on the Tisza and in the development of rail; the Pest–Szolnok line – the country's second – opened in 1847, just in time to help in moving troops of the Hungarian army during the 1848–49 Independence War. By the turn of the 20th century, industry was thriving on the excellent transport links and the good times rolled. Not for long, though. World War I brought growth to a juddering halt, particularly towards the latter stages when the town found itself at the front and taking some serious pummelling. More was to come in 1944, when many, many buildings were destroyed during air raids in the summer and in the final autumnal fights before capture by the Soviet army. This was known as the Battle of Hortobágy, the second-largest tank battle of the war (after that at Kursk in Russia). Historic buildings are thin on the ground – unsurprising given that the city suffered no fewer than 68 sieges during its history – but who needs them when there are spas, riverbank promenades and watersports?

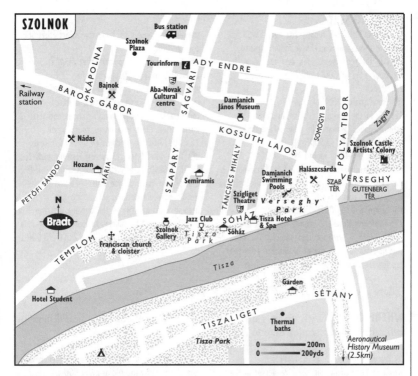

GETTING THERE AND AWAY Route 4 links Szolnok with Budapest and Debrecen. The **bus station** (*Ady Endre u.*) is northwest of the Tourinform, on a road parallel with the main Baross Gábor út. There are direct services to and from many towns, including Budapest (Népliget and Stadion, but those from the former take half the time), Cegléd (up to four), Hatvan (one on weekdays), Kecskemét (up to ten), Szeged (six), Szentes (up to six), Kalocsa (one on weekdays) and Jászberény (19). Buses to Debrecen require a change, usually at Tiszafüred.

The modern **train station** (*Jubileum tér 1–3*) lies on 1,100 pillars sunk down to a depth of 11m, and is 2km west of the centre along Baross Gábor út; local bus numbers 6, 7, 8 and 15 run from there into the middle. Szolnok is the hub of a railway-line wagon wheel, with no changes required for Budapest (Nyugati and Keleti), Debrecen, Békéscsaba, Cegléd, Jászberény and Nyíregyháza. There are six trains direct to Kecskemét but none to Szeged (you'll need to change at Cegléd); change at Hatvan for Miskolc. You can take international trains to destinations over the Romanian border like Arad, Baia Mare and Bucharest.

INFORMATION AND OTHER PRACTICALITIES

📛 **Aba-Novák Cultural centre** Hild János tér 1;
📞 56 514569. Close to the Tourinform, the cultural centre can give details of what's happening entertainment-wise.

🔃 **Listings magazine** Szolnoki Est

🏬 **Szolnok Plaza** Ady Endre u. 28; 📞 56 506502. Large American-style shopping mall. As well as shops, there is a multi-screen cinema & casino.
🕐 Mon–Sat 09.00–21.00, Sun 10.00–19.00.

🔃 **Tourinform** Ságvári Endre körút 4; 📞 56 420704; e szolnok-m@tourinform.hu. Hidden in one corner of a block of offices, behind Baross Gábor út. It has a useful eco-tourist map of Jász-Nagykun-Szolnok county, & also sells tickets to performances at the Szigligeti Theatre. 🕐 Jun 15–Aug 31 Mon–Fri 08.00–17.00, Sat– 09.00–13.00, rest of yr Mon–Thu 08.00–16.00, Fri 08.00–15.00.

⌂ WHERE TO STAY

⌂ **Garden Hotel** (46 rooms) Tiszaliget; ☎ 56 520530; www.gardenhotel.hu. A rather expensive, hotel in the recreational area over the bridge from the centre. *Sgl 18,600Ft, dbl 24,200Ft, apt 29,700Ft.*

⌂ **Hotel Student** Mártírok útja 12–14; ☎ 56 421688. In the low-price bracket, but with accommodation available Jul–Aug only. Right on the river. *Rooms 3,000–3,500Ft/pp.*

⌂ **Hozam Hotel** (11 rooms) Mária u. 25; ☎ 56 510530; www.hozamhotel.hu. The first 4-star hotel & the best in town, with a fine swimming pool, saunas & fitness facilities. Located in a quiet area close to the centre. *Sgl 16,000Ft, dbl 22,000Ft.*

⌂ **Semiramis Hotel** (12 rooms) Magyar út 23; ☎ 70 3966910; www.semiramishotel.hu. The latest 4-star hotel in town. It sits on a peaceful road near the theatre, & is aimed more at the business traveller. Well-appointed, large rooms. *Sgl 16,900Ft, dbl 22,900Ft.*

⌂ **Sóház Hotel** (12 rooms) Sóház út 4; ☎ 56 516560; e reserve@sohazhotel.hu; www.sohazhotel.hu. The Sóház perches near the river; its rooms come in 3 sizes, & have comfortable (if slightly flimsy) fixtures, including kitchenettes. There is a tennis court. *Small 12,000–13,000Ft, medium 14,000–15,000Ft.*

⌂ **Tisza Hotel & Spa** (33 rooms) Verseghy park 2; ☎ 56 210850; www.hoteltisza.hu. Near by – indeed, a step even closer to the water – is the town's Neo-Baroque old duchess, with rooms that are in keeping with the style of the building. Attached is a Turkish-style spa & rounded, vaulted swimming halls (entrance inc in room price). *Sgl 12,000–13,000Ft, dbl 15,500–17,500Ft.*

There is **camping** at the western end of Tiszaligeti sétány.

✗ WHERE TO EAT
With up to a quarter of the population students, you'll have no difficulty finding somewhere to pick up a pizza.

✗ **Bajnok** Baross u. 3; ☎ 56 421089; www.bajnoketterem.hu. Big cellar restaurant in the centre, & popular with the locals. Extensive Hungarian menu with some unusual twists, & a good selection of wines. *Mains avg 2,300Ft;* ⊕ *11.30–24.00 daily.*

✗ **Galéria** Szapány út 1; ☎ 56 513053. Has a park terrace by the Tisza promenade, good food & a good atmosphere. There's an international & Hungarian menu, & a lengthy wine list. *Mains avg 2,400Ft;* ⊕ *12.00–23.00 daily.*

✗ **Halászcsárda** Damjanich u. 1; ☎ 56 429519; www.halaszcsarda-szolnok.hu. Within a maggot's throw of the bridge, this traditional fish restaurant offers a variety of fish soups & other fish dishes, as well as non-fishy Hungarian fare. Little has changed here in 30 years. *Mains avg 2,000Ft;* ⊕ *11.00–23.00 daily.*

✗ **Hozam** Mária u. 25; ☎ 56 510530. High ceilings & a classy ambience. *Mains avg 1,800Ft;* ⊕ *12.00–23.00 daily.*

✗ **Nádas Étterem** Petőfi Sándor u. 6; ☎ 56 421242. The name means 'thatched', but refers to the owner's surname rather than the look of the place. To the northwest of the centre, serving mainly Hungarian dishes. The courtyard garden is lined with conifers & trellised creepers, & an outdoor grill quietens growling tums in summer months. Rightly popular. *Mains avg 1,900Ft;* ⊕ *Mon–Thu 11.00–22.00, Fri–Sat 11.00–24, Sun 11.00–16.00.*

✗ **Tisza Hotel Restaurant** See above. Like the Hozam, this is an elegant place to eat. *Mains avg 2,200Ft;* ⊕ *12.00–23.00 daily.*

ENTERTAINMENT AND NIGHTLIFE The **Irish Pub** (*Szapáry u. 24*) is a fairly lively spot for a pint. **Jazz Club** (*Sóház u.8;* ☎ *56 341071; www.jazzclubszolnok.hu; mains avg 2,000Ft; set menu 900Ft, Mon–Fri 11.00–14.00;* ⊕ *Sun–Thu 18.00–24.00, Fri–Sat 18.00–02.00*) is a good place to enjoy a bite to eat and some live jazz (*Thu–Sat*). The **Szigligeti Theatre** (*Szigligeti színház; Tisza park 1*), opposite the Tisza Hotel, blends elements of the modern and the Art Nouveau in its handsome look, a reflection of amendments made in 1991 to its original 1912 form. Beside the theatre is a statue of the theatre's eponym, the Hungarian dramatist Ede Szigligeti. Buy tickets at the **box office** (*Kossuth tér 17–23;* ☎ *56 422902;* ⊕ *Mon–Fri 09.00–13.00, 14.00–17.00*) or Tourinform.

WHAT TO SEE AND DO Across the River Zagyva just east of Szabadság tér, you could very easily miss the lone standing piece of wall that is the sum remaining total of the once-formidable **Szolnok Castle** (*Gutenberg tér*). It was built in the 11th century, renovated and reinforced in 1550 (with the help of the renowned warden and hero of Eger Castle, István Dobó; in an attempt to stave off the Turks, before finally being obliterated by the Habsburgs in 1710.

On the site of the former castle, the **Artists' Colony** (*Gutenberg tér 4;* ✆ *56 425549;* ⊕ *Tue–Sun 10.00–16.00 – prior notice required*) was established in 1902 and is one of the leading of its kind in the country. It has been the hive for great 20th-century artists like Béla Iványi Grünwald, Vilmos Aba-Novák, János Vaszary and Adolf Fényes. Temporary exhibitions are hosted at the **Szolnok Gallery** (*Templom u. 2;* ✆ *56 378023;* ⊕ *Tue–Sun 09.00–17.00*), housed in the Moorish former synagogue designed by Lipót Baumhorn in 1899; concerts are also held here. There are summer organ concerts in the nearby 18th-century Baroque **Franciscan church and cloister** (*Templom u. 8*) too; the church is one of the town's oldest extant buildings.

Just to the north of Kossuth Lajos út is Kossuth tér, home to the town hall of 1884 and the **Damjanich János Museum** (*Kossuth tér 4;* ✆ *56 421602; www.djm.hu;* 🎟 *1,000/500Ft;* ⊕ *Mon–Tue May–Oct 10.00–17.00, Nov–Apr 10.00–16.00*). The late-Classical museum is named after the celebrated general who led the victorious fight against the Habsburgs at the 1849 Battle of Szolnok; he was later among the 13 generals martyred in Arad (now Romania) at the conclusion of the war (see page 19), and there is a marble memorial to him in Gutenberg tér. Exhibitions of archaeology, folk art (primarily pottery and fur) and ethnography chart the history of the Jász-Nagykun-Szolnok County, and there are works by the artists of the local colony and caricatures by Tibor Pólya.

The **Tabáni Tájház** (*Tabán u. 24;* ✆ *46 421602; adult 100Ft;* ⊕ *May–Sep Thu–Sun 13.00–17.00 – prior notice required*) – a peasant house next to the River Zagyva, 15 minutes from the centre – preserves the domestic set up in the Tabán district during the 1930s. This was a neighbourhood of water people; the fishing equipment in the yard was used for fixing nets, the main trade for anglers in winter.

If you follow Road 442 south out of the city for a few kilometres to Szandaszőlős, you'll come to an **Aeronautical History Museum** (*Hadtörténeti Aero Múzeum; Kilián u. 1;* ✆ *56 505100; www.museum.hu/szolnok/aero.hu;* 🎟 *200/150Ft;* ⊕ *Apr–Oct Tue–Fri 10.00–15.00, Sat–Sun 10.00–14.00*), with MIGs and other aircraft on the grass outside. Buses 34B and 37A run here.

Other Other attractions inevitably feature water. **Tisza Park Thermal Baths** (*Tiszaligeti sétány; www.szolnokfurdok.hu;* 🎟 *970/720Ft;* ⊕ *daily May–Aug 08.00–18.00*) are outdoors in Tiszaliget, while the **Damjanich Swimming Pools** (*Damjanich u. 3;* 🎟 *750/300Ft;* ⊕ *daily May–Sep 07.00–21.00, rest of yr 06.00–18.00*) are situated near the bridge on the other side of the Tisza, and have been something of a bastion for champion waterpolo players. The 'Dami' has thermal water too. There's a Turkish-style spa attached to the Hotel Tisza (see opposite), and an international rowing course on a dead channel of the Tisza.

FESTIVALS AND EVENTS Szolnok certainly isn't short of celebrations. Among the excuses for a party are the Music Festival in March and April, the Etelköz Festival in August, the Tisza Water Parade (along the promenade by the Hotel Tisza) on August 20, and the Goulash Festival in September. During the Tisza Summer Festival, there's a re-enactment of the Battle of Szolnok.

Fifty kilometres east of Budapest, near the northern edge of the Great Plain, Jászberény is the cultural centre and largest town of the area known as the Jászság region, which was originally settled by an ethnic group of Iranian origin. The Jász (Jazygians) are said to have arrived here in the 13th century, Orthodox Christians who had split from the Alan clan. The dozen or so surrounding towns whose names begin with 'Jász-' bear testimony to the extent to which this ethnic group once controlled the region; the prefix is equally, however, one of the few remaining traces of the Persian-speaking people, whose mark is invisible even in the folk art. The citizens nevertheless still proudly refer to themselves as 'Jász's'. Their pride is justified; when in 1702 Leopold I pawned the whole region to the mighty Teutonic Knights (who fought in the wars against the Turks), the locals mounted a huge fundraising campaign and by 1745 had bought back their freedom. This is the Act of Redemption that formed the basis for the region's prosperity.

Jászberény is relatively spread out, but everything of interest lies in the compact town centre. The majority of the structures worth seeing can be found on Lehel vezér tér – the leafy central square – or within a block or two of it. Lehel vezér tér is lined with Baroque buildings, churches, and monuments and plaques to the town's heroes of war and revolution. A narrow portion of the River Zagyva flows through the middle of town (parallel to Lehel Vezér tér, and one block north of it), and there are walking paths along the river bank.

GETTING THERE AND AWAY The railway station is on Vaspálya utca, almost 2km from the centre, and a 30-minute walk down Rákóczi út. The bus station is a 20-minute walk, on Petőfi tér. Buses and trains run regularly between Jászberény and Budapest. There is one daily **bus** to Debrecen, nine to Kecskemét, two to Miskolc and four to Szeged. Direct **train** connections are limited – you need to transfer at Szolnok for most destinations – but there are regular trains to Szolnok and Hatvan. There is a train to Budapest nearly every hour.

INFORMATION AND OTHER PRACTICALITIES

Ibusz Szövetkezet u. 7/A; ↘ 57/412 143; e i056@ibusz.hu. Can arrange stays in private rooms, which cost around 2,500Ft/pp. ⊕ Jun–Aug Mon–Fri 08.00–16.00, Sat 08.00–12.00, weekdays only rest of yr.

J-Bike Centre Palotási János út 7; ↘ 57 503075. Bike rental from near the bus station.

Tourinform Lehel vezér tér 33; ↘ 57 406439; email jaszberenyi@tourinform.hu. Offers good town maps for 400Ft & small booklets describing the town's sights for 30Ft, & can provide contact numbers for private rooms. It also sells tickets to local events & festivals. ⊕ Mon–Fri 08.00–17.00.

 WHERE TO STAY AND EAT Private rooms can be arranged through Ibusz (see above); however, if you'd like to book in advance, the house of the Sárközi family (Mályva u. 8; ↘ 57 410 301 or 06 30 258 8736; e sarkozi@citrommail.hu) comes highly recommended. There are two small panziós in town.

Arizona Steakhouse Serház u. 1; ↘ 57 412 042. Offers a decent range of steaks & ribs with a Hungarian accent, as well as typical national specialities. Its terrace in the street gets crowded in good weather. Mains avg 1,900Ft; ⊕ daily 11.00–24.00.

Jóbarát Panzió Dózsa György u. 22; ↘ 57 412646. This is the cheaper of the town's pensions,

although the drop in price is matched by a drop in quality. Rooms 3,000Ft/pp.

Krémes Mézes Dózsa György út 1; ↘ 57 412207. Has the largest selection of pastries & cakes, if you fancy something sugary to finish. ⊕ daily 08.00–18.00.

Lehel Gyöngye (25 rooms) Neszür 10 Dülő; ↘ 57 415025; www.lgyongyhotel.jaszbere.hu. This thatched hotel is set in idyllic surroundings in the middle of nowhere (take Road 31 to Nagykáta for 10km until you turn off on a sandy road running through faded vineyards). The rooms have balconies, & are good. There is also a restaurant. *Sgl 12,900Ft, dbl 14,400Ft.*

✗ River Restaurant & Bowling Club Lehel Vezér tér 15; ✆ 57 407500; www.egyunkigyunk.hu. Tucked at the back of the former prison, this place is popular with locals. The extensive menu offers some interesting Hungarian twists on international food. *Mains avg 2,000Ft;* ⊕ *Mon–Thu 12.00–24.00, Fri 12.00–02.00, Sat 11.00–02.00, Sun 11.00–24.00.*

⌂ Sólyom Panzió Sólyom u. 8; ✆ 57 401267. Simple, clean & comfortable. *Rooms 7,000Ft/pp.*

⌂ Touring Hotel (26 rooms) Serház u. 3; ✆ 57 412051; email hoteltouringjb@vnet.hu. Refurbishment is close to completion on what was an outdated hotel. Touring is quite friendly (and is, in any case, the only real hotel in town). It is located between the bus station & Lehel Vezér tér, & does much of its business with the huge manufacturing company across the street. *Sgl 8,400–12,000Ft, dbl 9,700–13,500Ft.*

WHAT TO SEE AND DO If your time is limited, you won't miss much by skipping the town's two museums. The main attraction of the **Jász Múzeum** (*Táncsics Mihály u. 5;* ✆ *57 502610; www.djm.hu;* ✆ *260/130Ft;* ⊕ *Apr–Oct Tue–Sun 09.00–17.00, Nov–Mar Tue–Fri 09.00–16.00, Sat–Sun 09.00–13.00*) is the Lehel horn, which is the symbol of the town and the entire region. Legend states that the intricately carved ivory horn belonged to a Magyar general named Lehel, who helped to conquer the area. It was said that after defeat by the German emperor in AD955 Lehel requested that he be allowed to blow his horn for a final time; when permission was granted, he killed the emperor with it. Academics have spoilt the story, though, by proving that the Byzantine horn actually dates back only to the 11th century, and was probably originally used as a circus prop (it depicts circus acts). The rest of the museum has sections on the Jazygian region, but (like many small town museums) is slightly amateurish and has few explanations in English.

The **Hamza Collection and Jász Gallery** (*Gyöngyösi u. 7;* ✆ *57 503260; www.hazamuzeum.hu;* ✆ *200/100Ft;* ⊕ *Apr–Oct Tue–Sun 10.00–18.00, Nov–Mar Tue–Sun 10.00–16.00*) is held in the former home of local artist Ákos Hamza. The museum presents his paintings and sculptures, his library, and hundreds of intriguing sketches by his fashion designer wife, Mária, who began her career in Paris.

Jászberény's **thermal spa** (*Hatvani u. 5;* ✆ *57 412108;* ✆ *800/550Ft; thermal baths* ⊕ *all year Tue–Sun 09.00–18.00, outdoor pool May–Aug only*) has five pools, a sauna, a fitness room and offers various massages.

The **Jászberény Equestrian Circus** (*Jászberény Lovasbaráti Kör; 10km out of town on Route 31; entrance opposite Lehel Gyöngye;* ✆ *30 2913392*) is a beautifully kept establishment in the middle of the forest. They have around ten horses, and the sandy soil is ideal for riding; the company specialises in showjumping and riding tours (✆ *2,500Ft/hr*), and also offers carriage drives.

FESTIVALS AND EVENTS Jászberény has one of the best folk-dance ensembles in the country; their annual festival is the Csángó Festival (*end Jul/early Aug; www.csangofestival.hu*). The Csángó comprise a splinter group of Hungarians in Moldavia (on the eastern side of the Carpathians, and featuring 13 villages in all) who maintained their distinct ethnicity for centuries but are quite threatened now. The festival's origins lie in the *táncház* movement (see pages 29–30), which grew up in the 1980s as a form of civic resistance against the officially sanctioned culture of the Communist period. The festival celebrates village musicians and dances (mainly from Transylvania), and the action is not unlike a barn dance or Scottish *ceilidh* in Britain. Other small European ethnic minorities are invited to participate. Immediately afterwards is the Honey Fair of Jászberény.

Lake Tisza is the place for those interested in fish, birds and nature photography. It was created in the 1960s and '70s, when the River Tisza was dammed as part of the development of an irrigation system on the Great Plain. A happy by-product, it was hoped, would be a lake to rival Balaton. Lake Tisza spans 127km², and is treasured for its pristine natural environment, water-chestnut fields, mass of lily pads, winding channels surrounded by lush flora, and thriving birdlife. Two-thirds of it comprises significant wetland areas best visited in small boats capable of navigating the dozens of narrow courses. Scores of small islands, dead river arms and marshes make the lake popular with anglers, the experienced among whom know the deep or shallow points, the portions where catfish lurk and where carp are abundant. Indeed, it's claimed that there are more than 50 types of fish in the Tisza river and lake, which are stocked to keep supplies plentiful. Because the river runs through the lake, there are also sections of choppy water that are ideal for water sports.

The lake can be divided into three parts. That north of Highway 33 is a bird reserve and part of Hortobágy National Park, as is the middle portion with its giant white water lilies and colonies of heron and cormorant that can be visited by following established trails (many of which are barred to motorboats). Other parts of the lake (the Sarud and Tiszafüred basins and the southern Abádszalók section) are where the splashing and sporting takes place.

Those who want to avoid the crowds of Balaton come here instead. Bird lovers delight in nearly 150 species of bird nesting around the lake, and generally visit during the months between April and October. Note that it is forbidden to approach nests during the hatching period in April and May. Besides bird watching, the lake's shores are popular with cyclists, horse riders, boaters, fishers and sunbathers. Since the last edition of this guidebook, the tourist infrastructure has developed significantly around the lake, and it's somewhere that will genuinely reward 'outdoorsy' types.

TISZAFÜRED AND AROUND Archaeological artefacts have been found in Tiszafüred dating back to 4500BC, and the settlement was first mentioned in 13th-century documents. From the Middle Ages, it was on the salt route running between

Transylvania and western Hungary, and large herds of cattle were also driven through here en route to western Europe. However, beyond being an army headquarters during the 1849 War of Independence, when Lajos Kossuth spent quite a bit of time in town, very little of note happened here until the lake came into being. Now Tiszafüred is the central town, and with 15,000 residents it's the largest. This is where you are likely to base yourself, for it has the lion's share of the accommodation and facilities; there's a big, grassy strand, with lots of eateries, rental companies, open-air showers and stores. While Lake Tisza generally attracts bird spotters rather than night owls, Tiszafüred is one of the few towns that doesn't shut down after dinner and where sunbathers are prevalent during the day. Nevertheless, Tisza isn't like Balaton, and even in the height of the tourist season it's more about wildlife than wild nights.

Getting there and away Tiszafüred is on the Füzesabony–Debrecen rail line, and is 1½ hours by **train** from Debrecen (ten daily trains). There are eight trains to Karcag, two trains to Eger (changing at Füzesabony), and 12 daily trains to Egyek. The railway station (*Vasút u. 29;* ✆ *59 352648*) is a few blocks north of the Tourinform.

The **bus** station (*Bartók Béla út 37;* ✆ *59 351044*) is just south of the train station. There are nine daily direct buses to Debrecen (taking about 1½ hours). There are four daily buses to Budapest, but it's also possible to reach the capital by

---

THE BIRDS OF LAKE TISZA

The bird sanctuary at Lake Tisza, to the north of the Debrecen–Füzesabony railway line (and close to Tiszafüred), is technically part of the Hortobágy National Park and is one of the best places in the country for bird watching and observing the rest of the lake's largely unspoiled flora and fauna. The western half of the reserve is covered in water during summer (the floodgates open in spring, filling the reservoir, which reaches its peak level by June), while to the east the oxbow lakes, ponds, marshes and scrubland form a varied landscape. You should employ a guide to take you to the most protected areas. A good way to see birdlife is with a walk on the dyke at Poroszló as far as Négyes, a stretch that offers decent views over the reserve. Lake Tisza's combination of two very different habitats – the river bed (with its currents attracting fish like the sturgeon) and the atmospheric dead channels and basins (most of which were cut off during the river regulation, and now home to bream, pike and carp) – is unique, and pulls in animals aplenty. Over 147 species of bird nest at the lake, and expert bird guides are easy to find (see page 284). In addition, there is a bird rescue centre at the Górés Tanya (✆ 30 515 3463), where you can mingle with recuperating storks; the Egyek-pusztakócs marshland bicycle track (at the Egyek exit of Highway 33) takes in the farm.

Hortobágy is said to be the largest bird migration congregation point in central Europe, and after Lake Tisza was created the same types of birds began to migrate there. It's estimated that 80,000–100,000 birds inhabit Lake Tisza during the spring migration, with over 250,000 passing through. Wild geese are visible in the open areas; shore birds like ruffs, black-tailed godwits, and lapwings are abundant; heron and cormorant colonies are plentiful; ducks, particularly mallards, are everywhere towards the end of the summer; and white-tailed eagles are regular winter visitors. Among the others you might encounter are the osprey, common gull, great reed warbler, kingfisher, common tern, whiskered tern, white-fronted goose, grey duck, golden-eye, tufted duck, little egret, great white egret, greylag goose, black stork, night heron and tufted heron. Don't forget your binoculars!

transferring at Eger or Szolnok. There are at least seven daily buses to Eger, eight to Szolnok and eight to Hortobágy village. There's one direct bus to Hajduszoboszló, but it's easy to transfer there from Debrecen.

Information and other practicalities

ℹ️ Lake Tisza Regional Marketing Directorate Kossuth tér 1; 📞 59 351753; www.tiszatoinfo.hu. This organisation will mail details about the Tisza region to those who want it in advance of their trip – they publish lots of information, especially on angling, cycling & water tours (those serious about touring the area will find their cycle & water tour guide, with detailed maps, particularly useful).

ℹ️ Tourinform Fürdő u. 29; 📞 59 511123; e tiszafured@tourinform.hu. On entering Tiszafüred from the direction of Hortobágy (to the southeast), the office stands at the point where Highway 33 meets Fürdő utca. ⊕ Jun–Aug Mon–Wed 08.00–18.00, Thu–Fri 08.00–20.00, Sat–Sun 10.00–19.00, Sep–May Mon–Fri 08.00–16.00.

For **fishing information** (including regulations, varieties and seasonal differences), contact MOHOSZ (Örvénzi út 46; 📞 59 352113; www.mohosz.hu; ⊕ 08.00–16.00); they can also provide the state angling ticket for foreign residents and a local permit. Water quality is measured regularly; details about current **water conditions** can be found on the website of the Ministry of Environment and Water (www.ktm.hu).

Tours and rentals For further companies offering nature tours in Hungary, most including Lake Tisza, see *Tour operators*, pages 39–41. The national park directorate can also arrange guides; most of these don't themselves speak English, but there is apparently an English teacher who can accompany them and translate as necessary. You can book these guides through hotels such as the Tisza Balneum (see page 286).

Bird Watching Hungary 📞 06 30 490 9303; www.birdwatching.hu. Organise nature tours & sightseeing trips by 4x4 at Lake Tisza. These range from a few hours to several days in length, & cost from 15,000Ft/day.
EuroRiver Cruises 📞 800 5434504; www.eurorivercruises.com. Offers 2 trips in early summer on the Danube & Tisza (starting from Budapest or Tokaj) that are described as focusing on 'nature, authenticity & tradition'.
Gábor Füstös Tiszafüred-Örvény, Kossuth u. 7; 📞 59 350963. A fishing guide who rents motor boats & provides private accommodation.
Gulyás Tanya Tiszafüred-Örvény, Esze Tamás u. 2/B; 📞 59 351814. A farm run by Kálmán Gulyás that has a riding school (riding 3,000Ft/hr), carriage rides & equestrian shows from Easter to the end of October. It can also arrange riding tours (except during the winter) of up to a week & 'goulash parties' to accompany the equestrian shows. There are boats for hire & boat trips can be mapped out. The farm, 1½km from the lake, operates a small pension (dbl 9,000Ft).

Horgász Centrum (Fishing Centre) Kasfonó út 12; 📞 59 353443 or 06 30 965 9824; www.horgaszcentrum.hu. The proprietor, Sándor Szövetes, has been fishing on the Tisza for decades, & has made this store near the lake shore an indispensable stop for all things fishing related. You'll find fishing supplies (for sale & hire), & boat rentals & instruction; you can also book fishing trips (of up to a week). ⊕ Apr 15–Oct 15, 24 hrs a day.
Imre Fatér 📞 06 30 445 6856; e fater.imre@mme.hu. Imre works for the Hungarian Ornithological Society, & offers bird-watching tours at Lake Tisza for groups of no more than 8 (Apr–Oct). Guests are transported by Land Rovers, & binoculars, telescopes & field guidebooks are provided.
Imre Szabics 📞 06 30 954 8620. Offers boats for rent & organises other activities.
Kormorán Kft Ady Endre u. 16; 📞 59 350350. Fishing guides, canoe & motor-boat rentals, & 2-hour boat tours (max 4 people/boat; Apr–Nov). See also Kormorán Kikötő, opposite.

 Where to stay Tiszafüred has developed into a thriving tourist centre offering a broad selection of accommodation. However, the other villages around the lake are also worth considering if you want a little more quiet. There are dozens of private

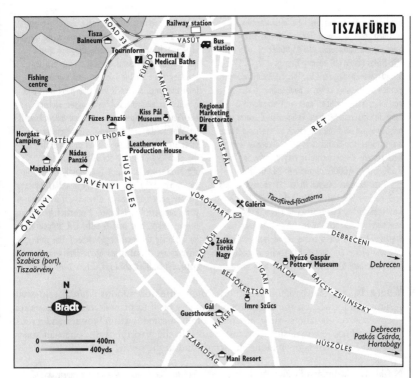

pensions, and you could also consider renting an apartment (which can work out very cheap if you're travelling with others). There are several campsites – most of the ports, for instance, have one alongside (see page 288); bungalows generally cost 2,000–3,000Ft/night, and tent space 500Ft (plus 500Ft/pp).

🏠 **Füzes Panzió** (10 rooms) Húszöles út 31/B;
☎ 59 351854. Near the lake, rooms here are comfortable & clean, although the décor is nothing to shout about. Breakfast isn't included, but there's a restaurant next door. *Sgl 2,900Ft, dbl 5,900Ft.*

🏠 **Gál Guest House** (5 rooms) Hársfa út 2; ☎ 59 352359. A family-run pension with a yard, terraces & a kitchen that guests are free to use. *Rooms €10/pp; b/fast €2.*

🏠 **Horgász & Családi Camping & Panzió** (29 apts, 39 bungalows) Kastély út; ☎ 59 351220; www.campings.hu. The owners reel in the anglers by offering special fishing packages, organising fishing trips, helping with fishing licences & serving as tour guides. The complex also has plenty of dry-land entertainment — including volleyball & tennis courts. *Accommodation 7,000Ft/pp, camping 500–600Ft/pp;* ⏰ *Apr–Nov.*

🏠 **Kormorán Kikötő** (6 houses) Tiszafüred-Örvény, Kormorán Kikötő; ☎ 59 350350; www.kormorankikoto.hu. Inside the flood defences on the shore, the small boat harbour is surrounded by spacious self-catering wooden cottages. The calm is wonderful, & you really feel as though settled in nature's lap. Each cottage has a pair of twin rooms, bathroom & kitchen, & a terrace overlooking the water (don't forget your mosquito spray!). There's a pub offering wine & beer. The cottages are available all year, but the best times to visit for fishing or birdwatching are May/Jun & Sep/Oct. You can hire outboard motors (3,750Ft/hr), kayaks, canoes (500Ft/hr), bikes (2,000Ft/day) & fishing boats (7,000Ft/day); angling & birdwatching guides are also available (2,500Ft/hour), but book in advance for an English speaker. *Cottage (for 4) 28,000Ft/night; discount for 5 nights or more.*

🏠 **Magdalena Guest House** (3 rooms) Gesztenyés u. 22; ☎ 06 30 349 8299. Pleasantly decorated pension with a yard, standing just 300m from the lake. *Rooms 3,000Ft/pp;* ⏰ *Mar–Oct.*

🏠 **Mani Resort** (10 apts) Szabadság u. 20–22; ☎ 59 350484. A small apartment-complex of a hotel about 1km from the lake, with traditional thatched roofs & a pool. The apartments (for 4) have private bathrooms. *Apt 15,000Ft; ☺ Mar–Oct.*

⌂ **Nádas Panzió** (18 rooms) Kismuhi u. 2; ☎ 59 551401; www.nadaspanzio.hu. This fabulously appointed pension has a wine cellar, a pool, sauna, jacuzzi, a host of sporting facilities, open grill, breadoven & camp fire. Its cottages have well-furnished rooms with fully equipped kitchens; the rooms in the main house are spacious, the breakfast room is decorated with local pottery, & the service is very friendly. *Sgl 7,500Ft, dbl 14,000Ft, apts (for 4) 24,000Ft.*

⌂ **Tisza Balneum Thermal Hotel** (51 rooms, 18 apts in 9 houses) Húszöles út 27; ☎ 59 886200; www.balneum.hu. The understated elegance of this new hotel is enhanced by its fabulous location on the lake. Most of the spacious rooms look onto the lake; the wicker furniture & basketware is made by local craftsmen, & the walls are hung with bird photos. Its wellness facilities make use of thermal water, & you can swim outdoors even in the depths of winter. It's pricey, but there are good special offers. It also represents a great launch pad for kayaking tours on the lake. You can hire kayaks from the hotel, & launch from the hotel pier. Bike hire is also available, but we'd suggest looking elsewhere for cheaper deals – if you follow Road 33 for 5km to the bridge, there's a campsite on the other side that rents good bikes at less than half the price. *Sgl 27,000Ft, dbl 30,000Ft.*

⌂ **Tisza Lodge** (6 rooms) Tiszaderzs; Ady Endre út 16; ☎ 59 355507; www.tiszalodge.com. This converted granary on a side road of a small, traditional village is an unexpected find. Owned & operated by a young Belgian couple, it is neat & tasteful, & a good base for exploring the local neighbourhood. The only disadvantage is that it lies about 3km from the water. *Sgl 8,500Ft, dbl 13,000Ft.*

✗ **Where to eat** This region is famous for its inns or saloons (*csárda*), old-style restaurants located on the highways. Originally built to provide resting places for shepherds or travellers, they are most often located outside towns and cities. Tiszafüred has few real, sit-down restaurants. In the warm months, open-air snack bars and food stands open along the strand and in the town.

✗ **Fehér Amur Halászcsárda** Tiszacsege, by the river; ☎ 52 373 832. The locals wax lyrical about the fish soup served here, & in gourmet circles it is famed nationally for its traditional fish dishes. Other ingredients (including brain) also feature on the menu. It has the feel of an old-fashioned fish restaurant, decorated with reeds & nets, & has a mosquito-proof outdoor eating area. *Mains avg 1,800Ft, with ½ portions at 70% of the full price; ☺ 12.00–21.00.*

✗ **Galéria Café Restaurant** Fő u. 15; ☎ 59 350512; wwwgaleria-etterem.hu. This is a good meeting place in the centre of town with a roof terrace in summer. Our helping of breaded catfish with chips was enormous, & the service speedy. *Mains avg 1,500Ft; ☺ daily 11.30–22.00 (mid Jun–Sep).*

✗ **Hableány Hotel-Restaurant** Tiszafüred-Örvény, Hunyadi út 2; ☎ 59 353333; e hableanyhotel@ dunaweb.hu. The traditional & international food is good at this riverside restaurant in the village of Tiszafüred-Örvény (south of Tiszafüred itself); it also has a decent outdoor terrace. The hotel has 20 simple rooms.

✗ **Molnár Vendéglő** Húszöles út 31/B; ☎ 59 352705. A popular tourist restaurant in Tiszafüred, serving typical Hungarian specialities, & a huge variety of fish (particularly pike perch & trout). It has fancier stuff too (like caviar), & a decent vegetarian selection. *Mains avg 2,000Ft; ☺ daily 11.00–20.00.*

✗ **Öreg Pákász** Poroszló, Fő u. 15; 36 535983; www.oregpakasz.hu. On the northern side of the Tisza Bridge, in the centre of the village, the 'Old Marshdweller' has been here for 100 years & is well known for its Hungarian travellers' fare (this was the Budapest–Debrecen road for centuries before the motorway was constructed). The food is simple but tasty, featuring five fish soups & traditional peasant dishes. A walkway on stilts stands 200m away, leading to a bird hide; keep your ticket as it will secure you a 10% discount at the restaurant. *Mains avg 2,400Ft; ☺ Easter–Nov daily 10.00–22.00, winter Mon–Fri 12.00–20,00, Sat 10.00–22.00, Sun 10.00–20,00.*

✗ **Park** Kossuth tér 15; ☎ 59 350649. This large restaurant in the centre of town is a relic of Socialist times, but the prices are reasonable. Expect the usual Hungarian fare. *Mains avg 1,200Ft; ☺ daily 12.00–22.00 (closed Mon in winter).*

✗ **Patkós Csárda** ☎ 52 378605. A traditional-looking place between Tiszafüred & Hortobágy that cooks up regional specialities, & is one of the best inns. There is frequently live gypsy strumming, & if you're really lucky you'll pitch up during an ox roast. The Patkós also operates a pension & campsite. On Highway 33, by the turn off to Egyek. *Mains avg 1,200Ft;* ⊕ *daily 09.00–20.00.*

✗ **Tisza Balneum** See opposite. The hotel offers a short menu containing mainly Hungarian dishes with a contemporary twist. Choice wine list including Tokaj wines from the owner's cellar. Beautiful terrace overlooking the lake. *Mains avg 2,200Ft.*

What to see and do The Lake Tisza region is rated highly for its **folk art**, particularly basket weaving, pottery and leather work, and the bulk of the non-wet attractions revolve around such cultural output. Many local artists throw open their workshops and homes to visitors, to show and sell their colourful creations; there are no fixed opening hours for these places.

Imre Szűcs (*Belső kertsor u. 4/A;* ☎ *59 351483; ✆ free admission*) is one of the best-known potters in the area, and holds the title 'Master of Folk Art'. In the 1970s when folk-style pottery was steadily going out of fashion, Szűcs endeavoured to revive the old traditions. His most popular creations revolve around animals – pigs, hens, roosters and other birds – but he uses a range of motifs and shades. Some of his pieces have found their way into museums. Imre often gives demonstrations at his workshop, and his wife and daughters are also potters; there is a 'house museum' in the basement where all of the items on view are for sale. **Zsóka Török Nagy** (*Szőlősi út 27;* ☎ *59 353538*) once worked at Imre Szűcs's studio, but her style is quite different since she also studied under other potters. At Zsóka's studio, you can get your hands dirty and have a bash at making a pot yourself.

The **Nyúzó Gáspár Pottery Museum** (*Malom u. 12;* ☎ *59 352106;* ⊕ *May–Sep Tue–Sat 14.00–17.00 – you might need to ask at the Kiss Pál Museum for entry*) is located inside the former home of two of Tisza's most-famous potters (father and son). Nyúzó junior died in 1922. The house is still furnished as it was when inhabited by the Nyúzó family, and the museum shows how the old potters from the region lived and worked. This whole area is representative of the 'old' Tiszafüred, before the tourist development of the 1970s.

The **Kiss Pál Museum** (*Tariczky sétány 6;* ☎ *59 352106; ✆ 260/130Ft;* ⊕ *Thu–Sat 09.00–12.00, 13.00–17.00*) displays further craftwork in the Neoclassical Lipcsey Hall, particularly the leather saddles produced by highly skilled artisans. You can learn how to create such masterpieces yourself at the **Leatherwork Production House** (*Ady Endre út 45;* ☎ *59 353501; ✆ 500Ft/hr, plus materials*); there is also a collection of leatherwork by a regional craftswoman.

As we've indicated, the Northern Great Plain is a heartland of Hungarian pottery. If you want to see more, Karcag has both a museum (*Kántor Sándor Fazekasház*) and a working potter (*Mihály Szabó, Bethlen u. 31*). Nádudvar (*www.nadudvarifazekas.hu*) is a centre for active potters, who are the main producers of black pottery (Baja and Transylvania are the other prime production areas).

Other activities The main attractions at Lake Tisza are **swimming**, **rowing** or **kayaking** among water lilies in secluded channels, but there's also fishing, hiking, cycling and horseback riding. The southern part of the lake is the place to head for **motor boating** and other **watersports**, and boats can be hired from most of the 'ports' around the lake; motor boats (*✆ 3,500–4,800Ft/day, plus petrol, for 5 people*) or canoes (*✆ 1,500–2,000Ft/day*) can be rented on the spot with no training necessary. A **canoe** is the ideal way to explore the lake; motor boats are banned beyond the southern section, and can't in any case reach the smaller, narrower channels and canals or many of the islands that are most worth experiencing. For **birdwatching**, see box page 283.

If you are unsure of how to get started, or want a more thorough tour of the lake, you should enlist the services of a guide. There are six specified tour routes on the lake; of these, one requires a guide and Tourinform recommends the use of

Northern Great Plain **LAKE TISZA**

6

a guide for four of the others. **Tour guides** can be booked at the ports, along with **boat trips** (*8,000Ft/2 hours*) and **fishing trips** (*3,000–5,700Ft/day, plus petrol; rowing boat 2,500Ft/day*). Details of the ports in the vicinity of Tiszafüred are as follows; alternatively see page 284 for details of local tour and rental companies.

Albatrosz Port Tiszafüred, Bán Zsigmond u. 67; 06 30 967 6037
Kormorán Port Tiszafüred-Örvény; 06 20 939 1979
Szabics Port Tiszafüred-Örvény; 59 353250; www.szabicskikoto.hu
Katamarán Port Tiszafüred-Örvény; 06 30 952 7039

From Szabics, a boat takes you over the water to an island where walking trails lead to **birdwatching towers**. When the lake is frozen – which is quite often in winter because of the shallow depth – popular **ice-walking tours** are held at weekends; the photo opportunities are outstanding. In June, when the **mayflies swarm**, special tours are laid on (*700/400Ft*); this is one of nature's real spectacles (see page 12). Fishing expeditions with an English-speaking guide are available all year (prior booking required). Look out for a catfish head as big as a shark's on the wall of the Szabics reception – 100kg catfish lurk in these waters.

There are **hiking** and **biking** trails around the lake, with no steep hills to spoil the fun; Tourinform can provide detailed maps. We spent a happy, peaceful day cycling the entire circumference of the lake and would highly recommend it (if your thighs can bear the strain). One of the most popular tours is a cycling route along the dykes. It's thirsty work, so consider making pitstops at Szőlőszem Okofarm (*30 485 1025*) in Tiszaszőlős, Lila Akác (*30 903 1330*) in Abádszalók, Ezüst Horgony (*36 358130*) in Kisköre, Eurostrand (*36 462030*) in Sarud or Öreg Pákász (*36 353983*) in Poroszló. Try if you can to pay a visit to **Sarud** village, which has quite a number of protected old peasant houses; given the building boom of the last 40 years, these are an increasing rarity in Hungary. Another **one-day cycle trip** not to miss starts at the Nyugati entrance (*8km along Road 33 to Debrecen, next to Patkós Csárda*) to Hortobágy National Park (*entry 900/600Ft*) and takes in Meggyes Csárda (*70 231 5073*), a small museum dedicated to the way of life of past travellers and highwaymen, and the plains, swamps and forests of the park. Bicycles can be rented at the entrance (*1,800Ft/day*). It is worth taking a guide (*2,000–3,500Ft/hr*) to properly explore the natural world of the *puszta* – a book that's closed to those who don't know where to look. There are also opportunities for **riding** (*3,000Ft/hr*) and two-, three- and five-hour carriage trips (*3,000Ft/hour*). You'll find simple **accommodation** (*30 278 7378; e nyugatifogado@t-email.hu; dbl 6,000Ft, dormitory 2,000Ft/pp; Apr–Oct*) at the entrance too. Further information on all this is available from the Meggyes Csárda or at the Nyugati entrance.

HORTOBÁGY

Hortobágy, 25 miles west of Debrecen, is a tiny village in the thick of the vast Hortobágy National Park. This area looms very large in Hungarian folklore and poetry, and the image of horsemen in traditional garb galloping across the wide plain is as much a part of the country's identity as goulash and Bull's Blood. The place drips with romance, the legends alive from the days when cattle herders, shepherds and cowboys were abundant on the *puszta*. There are homesteads, barns and long-handled *shadoof*-like wells (*gémeskút*); ancient burial mounds (*sírdomb*) are also conspicuous when they break the pancake-flat landscape. A recurrent phenomenon recorded in literature is the appearance of ghostly forms here, from broad cities to solitary human figures. These mirages (known as *délibáb*) are said to form during muggy summer days, when layers of humid air with different temperatures come

Hortobágy is Hungary's biggest and oldest national park, founded in 1973 and now spreading over 81,000ha. Up until the drainage project undertaken in the middle of the 19th century, the area was regularly flooded by the Tisza; at that time, boats (not wagons) were the chosen means of transport. The engineering resulted in a landscape dominated by alkaline floodplains covered with grasslands – known as *puszta*. The park's flat expanse of *puszta* grassland is not only the largest in Hungary, but in the whole of central Europe. And on it graze traditional national livestock breeds – Hungarian grey cattle and racka sheep – just as they have done for hundreds of years. This is shepherd country.

Apart from the *puszta*, the national park is characterised by two other main habitats. The first is floodplain forest and oxbow lakes, lush left-overs from the days when the Tisza oozed free on the plain. The second is similarly sodden, comprising marshes and lakes. The park holds over 5,000ha of fishponds, together with 7,000ha of Lake Tisza; these bodies of water in part compensate for the surface water lost during the drainage programme. Such diverse habitats spawn unique species, including salt-tolerant types in the seasonal salt marshes, aquatic sedge and rush communities, loess deserts, grasslands and special woods. The entire wetland complex forms a very significant breeding, feeding, staging and wintering site for many species of migratory waterbirds and wetland-related raptors – indeed, the total number exceeds a million. Among these, Hortobágy regularly supports 60–80,000 European cranes, lesser white-fronted and red-breasted geese, dotterel and black-tailed godwit during migration periods; with a permit (from the Visitor Centre or Hortobágy National Park Directorate; see page 290) you can observe these from birdwatching towers at the fishpond system.

together. The tourist industry has very much hitched its wagon to the Hortobágy's mystique; be prepared for the ubiquitous overblown horse shows and busloads of tourists ushered in for packaged versions of old-style Hungarian living.

Although Hortobágy includes the largest area of grassland in central Europe, it also has its marshy swampland. Hortobágy village is the place to start your exploration, and is where the majority of the restaurants, hotels and facilities are located (although most visitors come on day trips). Animal breeding and keeping is one of the prime occupations at Hortobágy, and it is famous for its animal park. The animals presumably keep a wary eye on the Hortobágy Csárda across the river, which dishes up some of the Hungarian special breeds for eating. Another classic Hortobágy site is the Nine-Arch Bridge, where the Bridge Festival is held each year.

This is horse country, and riding schools abound; for the less active, there are carriage tours too. Otherwise the national park is full of walking paths and bird-watching areas, and is best visited in the warmer months. Few come in winter, but if you do, be prepared for biting winds blowing across the flat landscape. An admission ticket is required to visit a few protected areas of the park (*900Ft/day from the visitor centre*), including some cycling routes, and some others are only accessible with a guide (contact a specialist tour company; see pages 239–41 and 284).

GETTING THERE, AWAY AND AROUND Hortobágy is best explored by **car**, since trains and buses won't take you to the lesser-visited pockets. Highway 33 cuts through the park, and you can take in a traditional *csárda* along the way. There are, however, decent train and bus connections to the village itself. From Debrecen, **trains** in the direction of Tiszafüred and Füzesabony call at Hortobágy (over a dozen daily trains in the summer from Debrecen, and around ten the rest of the year). From

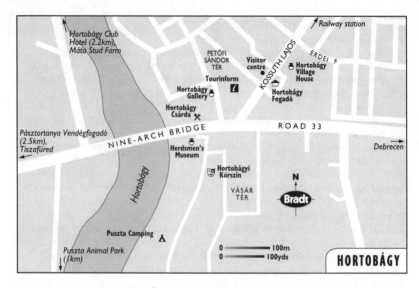

HORTOBÁGY

Nyíregyháza, trains stop at Óhat-Pusztakócs (a few kilometres west of Hortobágy village), and you can pick up a connecting train from there. There are no direct trains to Budapest and Eger; instead you'll need to change at Füzesabony. The train station (Dékány köz) is a few blocks from the Hortobágy Csárda, via Kossuth utca.

Buses leave from the Hortobágy Csárda. The bus service is less frequent into the park, but there are buses from Debrecen, Hajdúszoboszló, Eger and Tiszafüred. There are no direct buses between Budapest and Hortobágy; the most convenient route is to make a transfer at Eger. There are eight daily buses from Hortobágy to both Debrecen and Eger. Once there, Tourinform can advise of places to hire **bikes**.

INFORMATION AND OTHER PRACTICALITIES

☑ Hortobágy National Park Directorate Debrecen, Súmen u. 2; ☎ 52 529920; e hnp@hnp.hu; www.hnp.hu. If you're coming from Debrecen, you might pop into the national-park office first for information.

☑ Hortobágy National Park Visitor Centre Petőfi tér 13, ☎ 52 589321; www.hnp.hu. The visitor centre is the main stopping place for tourist information, including detailed maps, programmes, admission tickets for the protected areas, guided tours & even

help with accommodation. The centre contains a wildlife exhibition, & there are folk-art workshops where you can watch craftsmen making herdsmen's clothing & whittling wood. ⊕ Oct–Apr Mon–Fri 08.00–16.00, May–Sep Mon–Fri 08.00–16.00, Sat–Sun 10.00–16.00 (Jul–Aug until 17.00).

☑ Tourinform Petőfi tér. There is a small, high-season Tourinform office in the shops at the centre of Petőfi tér. ⊕ mid-Jun–Aug daily 09.00–17.00.

Tour guides

Bird Watching Hungary ☎ 06 20 955 6758; e info@birdwatching.hu; www.birdwatching.hu. Organises nature tours & sightseeing trips by 4x4 in the Hortobágy. These range from a few hours to several days in length, & cost 14,490–18,900Ft/day. **Imre Fatér** ☎ 06 30 4456856, e fater.imre@mme.hu. Imre works for the Hungarian

Ornithological Society, & offers bird-watching tours at Hortobágy for groups of no more than 8 (Apr–Oct). Guests are transported by Land Rovers, & binoculars, telescopes & field guidebooks are provided. He leads tours to other destinations in the country too; check with him in advance.

For further details of companies arranging nature tours, see pages 239–41.

WHERE TO STAY AND EAT Accommodation options are limited in Hortobágy, but the Tourinform does have a list of more than 40 families offering **private rooms**. Many people prefer to stay in Debrecen and take day trips to Hortobágy.

☖ **Hortobágy Club Hotel** (54 rooms) Hortobágy-Máta Pf 11; ✆ 52 369020; www.hortobagyhotel.hu. Just north of Hortobágy village, this is one of the best-equipped (and most expensive) hotels in the area, with 2 pools, a sauna, a tennis court, spa facilities & 2 restaurants. There are great views of the plain from the grounds, & rooms are spacious & comfortable. It also operates an equestrian centre (see page 292). The hotel sells visitor permits. *Rooms 18,900–33,600Ft.*

✗ **Hortobágy Csárda** Petőfi tér 2; ✆ 52 589339. The area's most-renowned restaurant by a country mile. The 300-year-old building sits at the head of the Nine-Arch Bridge, & specialises in traditional, organic dishes, some concocted from animals bred in the national park (including Hungarian grey cattle, buffalo, mangalica pig, racka lamb & guinea fowl). The grey-cattle sirloin slices are among the tenderest you'll taste. *Mains avg 2,300Ft;* ⊕ *daily 08.00–22.00.*

☖ **Hortobágy Fogadó** (11 rooms) Kossuth u. 1; ✆ 52 369137. Simple rooms with no fancy extras. The whole place is slightly run down, but it's one of the few places to stay in the centre of Hortobágy

village. The restaurant downstairs (*mains avg 1,000Ft;* ⊕ *Mon–Sat 06.00–20.00*) has cheap tucker, but has little else to tempt you away from the superior Hortobágy Csárda. *Sgl 3,500Ft, dbl 6,000Ft, trpl 8,000Ft, quad 10,000Ft.*

✗ **Kadarcsi Csárda** ✆ 52 370101. The first restaurant on this site was built in 1761, although the current incarnation has stood since 1843 & is considered a historical monument. The whitewashed walls, period furnishings & old-style atmosphere is typical of the region's *csárda*; as you'd expect, there's traditional Hungarian food with occasional live gypsy music. The regional specialities are excellent. On Highway 33, at the 86km mark. *Mains avg 2,100Ft;* ⊕ *daily 10.00–22.00.*

✗ **Pásztortanya Vendégfogadó** (3 rooms) Hortobágy Halastó; ✆ 52 369127; e pasztortanya@ freemail.hu. Sparse rooms & a small restaurant with a limited Hungarian menu & a pleasant terrace. On Highway 33, near milepost 67. *Dbl 6,000Ft.*

⚐ **Puszta Camping** ✆ 52 369300. Stands on the river bank, 200m south of the Nine-Arch Bridge. ⊕ *May–Oct.*

WHAT TO SEE AND DO The **Nine-Arch Bridge** is the longest stone road bridge (167m) in Hungary, and is the symbol of Hortobágy village. Constructed in 1826, it replaced earlier wooden bridges at the same point that gave way during floods; considering it's the park's leading architectural monument, it is surprising that cars are still allowed to cross (it forms part of Highway 33).

The **Herdsmen's Museum** (*Pásztormúzeum; Petőfi tér 2;* ✆ *52 369119;* 🎫 *500/300Ft;* ⊕ *daily Mar 15–Mar 30 10.00–14.00, Apr 10.00–16.00, May–Sep 09.00–18.00, Oct 10.00–16.00, Nov 10.00–14.00, Dec–Mar 14 by prior arrangement*) commemorates the shepherds and herders of the Great Plain, showcasing the trappings of their everyday lives – embroidered leather cloaks, cooking utensils and equestrian clobber. The building, raised in 1785, was once the coach house for patrons of the Hortobágy Csárda across the street. Opposite the museum is the **Körszín** (*Round Theatre;* ✆ *52 589000; free admission; opening hrs same as museum*), a roundhouse containing full-scale dummies of herders on the plain and local artisans (a cartwright, a blacksmith, etc) at work.

There are several other little collections to visit. The **Hortobágy Gallery** (*Petőfi tér;* ✆ *52 369401;* 🎫 *free admission;* ⊕ *daily 10.00–17.00 May–Nov*) shows temporary exhibitions of art taking the *puszta* for their muse. The **Meggyes Csárda** (*Highway 33, 60km mark – a few kms from Hortobágy towards Tiszafüred;* ✆ *06 70 231 4073;* ⊕ *by appointment only*) is a tavern museum with ethnographical pieces celebrating life in the Hortobágy and the *puszta* around the turn of the 19th century, when there were over 40 *csárdas* touting for business. The three-room building was constructed in 1760, and contains tables, benches and shepherds' cloaks (*szűr*) hanging from the coat peg. The **Hortobágy Village House** (*Kossuth Lajos u. 8;* ✆ *52 369570*) hosts temporary art exhibitions and cultural events.

The **Puszta Animal (or Rare Breed) Park** (📞 *52 701037;* ⊕ *daily Mar 1–Nov 15 09.00–18.00, Nov 16–Dec 31 09.00–16.00, closed Jan–Feb; adult 500Ft*) rears traditional Hungarian species, several of which are native to the Great Plain. Among the animals snuffling, trampling or fluttering around are curly haired mangalica pigs, Hungarian grey cattle, racka sheep (with horns like twists of ribbon), domestic water buffalo, Transylvanian bald-neck hens, several types of turkey, and Hungarian pigeons. The striking dreadlocked dogs that you'll see springing around here (and throughout the region) are sheep herders called *puli* (see box, page 143). An exhibition gives some background to the animals. This place makes meaty forkfuls at Hortobágy Csárda guilty ones. To get to the park, turn left after the Nine-Arch Bridge, and it's around 2km away.

Hortobágy-Halastó Six kilometres west of Hortobágy village (and one stop on the train), the Hortobágy-Halastó (fishpond) is ideal for bird watching. The area covers approximately 2,000ha, and has a bundle of watch towers offering fantastic views of the storks, mallards and cranes. The fishponds also harbour the strictly protected spoonbills and great white egrets; even the retiring grey heron is found among its old reedbeds. Spring and autumn are ideal twitching times, with flocks of thousands of birds filling the sky in preparation for their migration. It is said that 342 bird species have been spotted in Hortobágy, and 152 of those nest in the park. An educational track embarks from between kilometre markers 64 and 65 on Highway 33. An admission pass is required to visit Halastó. For details of guides, see page 290.

Horseriding Two kilometres from the village, the **Hortobágy Máta Stud Farm** (*Hortobágy-Máta, Czinege János u. 1;* 📞 *52 589369*) is one of the country's major breeding centres, much of its effort directed towards the preservation of the *noniusz* – considered an ideal horse. There are over 250 horses at this 300-year-old farm, and some of these are available for hire. Cross-country and short-distance riding options are available, together with lessons, carriage tours, competitions and equestrian shows.

The **Hortobágy Club Hotel** (*Hortobágy-Máta;* 📞 *52 369020*; see also page 291) operates what is claimed to be Hungary's largest riding centre, in the Hortobágy equestrian village (1½km from the bridge). You can watch a touristy horse show, take riding lessons or carriage trips, or hire your own horse for gallops across the *puszta*.

FESTIVALS AND EVENTS The annual Bridge Fair is one of Hortobágy's big events, and takes place at the foot of the Nine-Arch Bridge on August 20 (and a weekend either before or afterwards). Originally a livestock market, you no longer need to work out how to fit a cow in your suitcase; the fair sells a range of goods, from local foods and wines to arts, crafts and folk items from all over Hungary. The highlight for many is the traditional ox roast, and the preparation of other specialities like *slambuc* (a *puszta* potato-and-pasta dish). The music and dancing isn't bad either!

On Village Day (*May*), there are folklore programs, traditional games and food, equestrian events, and folk song and dance. International Hortobágy Equestrian Days (*first weekend in Jul*) has show jumping, carriage-driving competitions, a folk-art fair and horse-herding shows, while at the Herdsmen's Goulash Contest (*Jun*) you can learn how to cook goulash and other *puszta* shepherds' favourites. If cooking isn't your thing, sit back and taste all the expert efforts of the locals.

DEBRECEN

Debrecen is the second-largest city in Hungary, a lively university town, and a significant centre for Hungarian Calvinism. Less than 50km from the Romanian border and 100km from Ukraine, it is off the beaten tourist track; nevertheless it is a good base for exploring eastern Hungary. In the 14th and 15th centuries, Debrecen was an important and wealthy market town – indeed, it still hosts several annual markets – and during the 15th century its citizens were granted rights and privileges only equalled by those of Buda. Trouble came in the 16th century when the country was split (see page 17), and Debrecen ended up on the border; residents were obliged to pay taxes both to Austria and Turkey, a financial burden that hit hard. Things improved with the introduction of Calvinism, which rapidly spread in the mid 16th century and proved a durable faith – today 20–30% of Hungarians are Calvinists.

The Calvinist Reformed College was founded in 1538, and students from all corners of the country gathered to participate in its rigorous programme. After the departure of the Turks, Debrecen was granted the title of 'free royal town' by the Habsburgs. It continued to grow, and when the Great Reformed Church was erected in 1821 (becoming the symbol of the city), Debrecen began to take its modern face. During the 1848 revolution, the nation's capital was transferred from the embattled Budapest and parliament met in the Great Reformed Church. Kossuth gave a famous speech there before the revolution was quashed. The suppression of the revolution didn't prevent Debrecen from expanding rapidly over subsequent decades; its population steadily increased and several universities were established. The city was severely hurt during World War II, and much of it was bombed and burned. Now, however, Debrecen is one of Hungary's great university cities and an important cultural centre of eastern Hungary. It attracts many international students, especially for its renowned, intensive Hungarian-language course (*www.nyariegyetem.hu*); it is said that after a month of lessons students leave speaking fluent Hungarian – an impressive (and questionable) boast when many English ex-pats still struggle after a decade's exposure to the lingo.

GETTING THERE, AWAY AND AROUND The **railway station** (*Petőfi tér 12;* ↘ *52 346777*) is a few blocks south of the end of Piac utca, which leads to the city centre. There are good train connections in and out of Debrecen, including almost a dozen daily services to Budapest, trains to Nyíregyháza every half an hour, and regular services to Hortobágy. The **bus station** is conveniently located too, near the meeting point of Széchenyi utca and Nyugati utca. To reach the centre, walk east on Széchenyi utca until you hit the pedestrian Piac utca. Hajdú Volán (*Külső Vásár tér 12;* ↘ *52 413999*) offers frequent connections to all the small towns of the region (including Hajdúböszörmény and Hajdúszoboszló), and tickets can be bought on board the buses. To get to Hortobágy National Park, however, the train is preferable since there are few daily buses. Getting to other regions of the country is more difficult from Debrecen via bus, although there are daily buses to Békéscsaba, Eger, Gyula, Jászberény, Nyíregyháza, Szeged and Tiszafüred.

Debrecen has reliable **tram** and **bus** networks, but unless you are heading out to the university area, the thermal baths or the Nagyerdei Park you will have little need to use them. For a good and cheap sightseeing tour of the city, take the number 1 tram (the only tram line) out to the leafy university area and Nagyerdei Park. You can pick up the tram from its terminus at the train station, or along Kossuth tér. It runs in a circle, and riding its length will allow you to get your bearings. For **taxis**, try Főnix Taxi (↘ *52 444444*), Főtaxi (↘ *52 444555*), City Taxi (↘ *52 422222*) or FanTaxi (↘ *52 888444*).

INFORMATION AND OTHER PRACTICALITIES

i **Hajdú-Bihar County & Debrecen Hiking Association** Simonffy u. 1/C; ↘ 52 342951. Information on walking, hiking & nature in the region. ⊕ Wed 15.00–17.00.

i **Hortobágy National Park Directorate** Sumen u. 2; ↘ 52 529 920. The national park office, which can offer advice on where to go, what to see & which areas can only be accessed with a guide or pass.

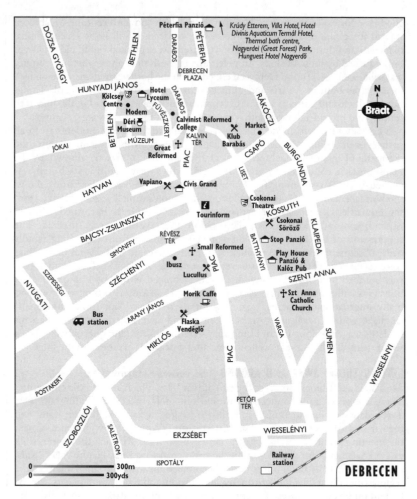

Map labels (Debrecen):

Péterfia Panzió — Krúdy Étterem, Villa Hotel, Hotel Divinis Aquaticum Termál Hotel, Thermal bath centre, Nagyerdei (Great Forest) Park, Hunguest Hotel Nagyerdő

DÓZSA GYÖRGY
BETHLEN
DARABOS
PÉTERFIA
DEBRECEN PLAZA
HUNYADI JÁNOS
Hotel Lyceum
Kölcsey Centre
Modem
Déri Museum
Calvinist Reformed College
Market
KALVIN TÉR
Klub Barabás
RÁKÓCZI
BURGUNDIA
Bradt
N
FÜVÉSZKERT
DARABOS
BETHLEN
MÚZEUM
JÓKAI
Great Reformed
PIAC
CSAPÓ
LISZT
Vapiano
Cívis Grand
HATVAN
Csokonai Theatre
KOSSUTH
Tourinform
Csokonai Söröző
Stop Panzió
BAJCSY-ZSILINSZKY
RÉVÉSZ TÉR
SIMONFFY
Small Reformed
BATTHYÁNYI
Play House Panzió & Kalóz Pub
KLAIPEDA
SZÉCHENYI
Ibusz
Lucullus
PIAC
SZENT ANNA
NYUGATI
SZEPESSÉGI
Morik Caffe
Szt Anna Catholic Church
ARANY JÁNOS
Bus station
Flaska Vendéglő
MIKLÓS
VARGA
SUMEN
PIAC
WESSELÉNYI
POSTAKERT
SZOBOSZLÓI
SALÉTROM
PETŐFI TÉR
ERZSÉBET
WESSELÉNYI
ISPOTÁLY
Railway station
0   300m
0   300yds
DEBRECEN

t Ibusz Révész tér 2; ☏ 52 415555; e debrecen@ ibusz.hu. ⏰ Mon–Fri 08.00–17.00, Sat 08.00–12.00.
i Tourinform Piac u. 20; ☏ 52 412250; e debrecen@tourinform.hu. Centrally located next

to Kossuth tér & the Great Reformed Church. ⏰ Jun–Aug daily 08.00–20.00, Sep–May Mon–Thu 09.00–17.00, Fri 09.00–16.00.

WHERE TO STAY It's prudent to book in advance during main festivals, but at other times there's enough room space – from expensive spa hotels to budget options. Tourinform holds a list of families offering **private accommodation**; prices are 3,000–8,000Ft/pp.

Aquaticum Termál & Wellness Hotel (96 rooms) Nagyerdei Park 1; ☏ 52 514111; www.aquaticum.hu. With thermal water & a wellness centre attached, this is worth a splash if your budget allows. Sgl 19,900–22,900Ft, dbl 23,900–26,900Ft, apt 30,900–42,900Ft.

Cívis Grand Hotel Aranybika (205 rooms) Piac u. 11–15; ☏ 52 508600; www.civishotels.hu. The Art-Nouveau 'Golden Bull' is Debrecen's oldest & most-famous hotel, & is centrally located. Designed by Alfréd Hajós – Hungary's first Olympic champion before turning to architecture – the hotel was built in 1915 & is chock-full of amenities (including a wellness centre), although it could perhaps do with a spruce-up. *Sgl 14,500–21,600Ft, dbl 17,400–25,700, apt 25,700–48,000Ft.*

⌂ **Divinus Hotel** (150 rooms) Nagyerdei körút 1; ☎ 52 510900; www.hoteldivinus.hu. A brand-new luxury hotel with roof-top apartments. There are restaurants, a bar, pools, sauna, steam room, massage options & a great terrace to enjoy a coffee & cake from the patisserie. The staff are welcoming & enthusiastic. During summer, grilled dishes are prepared under the sunshades. *Sgl 24,000–33,500Ft, dbl 25,500–35,500Ft, suite 46,500–96,000Ft (excl b/fast).*

⌂ **Lycium Hotel** (92 rooms) Hunyadi u. 1–3; ☎ 52 506600; www.hotellycium.hu. Sitting next to the Kölcsey Központ (convention centre), this is a popular choice with businessmen. It has a central location, & is just a step away from MODEM (if you've a thirst for contemporary art). *Sgl 23,000Ft, dbl 28,000Ft, apt (for 4.) 43,900Ft.*

⌂ **Péterfia Panzió** (19 rooms) Péterfia u. 37/B; ☎ 52 418246; e peterfiapanzio@peterfiapanzio.hu.

There are simple & clean rooms, & a nicely manicured little backyard. *Sgl 8,200Ft, dbl 9,600Ft; trpl 11,000Ft; b/fast 1,200Ft.*

⌂ **Play Pub House Panzió** (12 rooms) Batthány u. 24–26; ☎ 52 411252; e playpubhouse@ t-online.hu. Despite being above an Irish bar, this pension has quiet, pleasant rooms with TVs & private bathrooms. *Rooms 5,000Ft/pp.*

⌂ **Stop Panzió** (14 rooms) Batthány u. 18; ☎ 52 420301; e stoppanzio@vnet.hu. A few doors down from Play House, Stop has a more retro, 1960s feel to it, with chunky brown furniture & red fittings. It has laundry facilities, & all rooms have bathrooms, TVs & fridges. *Sgl 6,900Ft, dbl 8,900Ft, trpl 11,900Ft; b/fast 900Ft.*

⌂ **Villa Hotel** (15 rooms) Medgyessy sétány 4; ☎ 52 442244; www.villahotel.hu. An elegant 19th-century villa in the green heart of Debrecen. Rooms are well furnished & comfortable; there's a sauna & jacuzzi in the garden cottage, & a good restaurant (see Krúdy below). *Sgl 13,200Ft, dbl 17,500–19,700Ft, apt 26,400Ft.*

✗ **WHERE TO EAT AND DRINK** There are numerous eating options, from fine dining to simple, local cooking. This is also a prime place to sample some regional specialities, like the Hungarian grey cattle and Mangalica pigs that are raised on the Great Plain. Hotel Aranybika and the Aquaticum Wellness Hotel (see above) both have nice but pricey restaurants. You'll get better value elsewhere; Piac utca has many scoffing spots and watering holes.

✗ **Csokonai** Kossuth u. 21; ☎ 52 410802; www.etterem.hu/6191. Debrecen's most celebrated restaurant, based in a cellar with heavy wooden seats & tables. The food is mainly Hungarian, although their 'ironed steak' – finished at your table with a sizzling iron – is something to try too. ⊕ *Mon–Sat 11.30–23.00, Sun 12.00–23.00.*

✗ **Flaska Vendéglő** Miklós u. 4; ☎ 52 414582. A local favourite ensconced in a vaulted cellar; the décor is peasant-style, & the place has a super selection of local & regional specialities. Try the Debrecen stuffed cabbage or the Hortobágy stuffed pancakes. *Mains avg 1,500Ft;* ⊕ *Mon–Sat 11.30–23.00, Sun 11.30–22.00.*

♀ **Kalóz Pub** Batthyány u. 24; ☎ 06 30 588 7575. Next door to the Play Pub House, the Kalóz has occasional live music. ⊕ *Tue–Sat 20.00–04.00.*

✗ **Klub Barabás** Vár u. 11; ☎ 52 502231. Purportedly 'English' in style, the Klub Barabás serves excellent food. It's more Hungarian than English, though. *Mains avg 1,800Ft;* ⊕ *Mon–Thu 11.00–23.00, Fri–Sat 11.00–24.00, Sun 12.00–17.00.*

✗ **Krúdy Étterem** Medgyessy sétány 4; ☎ 54 442244; www.villahotel.hu. Famous restaurant of the Villa Hotel (see above), & favoured by the locals for special occasions. The Hungarian dishes are excellent, & have a real traditional flavour. If you've a sweet tooth, try the 'lover misses' favourite soup'. *Mains avg 2,000Ft;* ⊕ *daily 07.00–24.00.*

✗ **Lucullus** Piac u. 41; ☎ 52 418513. Housed in an early-19th-century building, Lucullus is a folksy restaurant with good, traditional food. *Mains avg 1,800Ft;* ⊕ *daily 11.30–23.00.*

☕ **Morik Caffe** Miklós u. 1; ☎ 52 310550. The Debrecen branch of this café empire. There are delicious coffee & sweets, & the café even has its own special coffee blend on sale. ⊕ *Sun–Fri 07.00–23.00, Sat 09.00–24.00.*

♀ **Play Pub House** Batthyány u. 24–26; ☎ 52 451987. Below the Play Pub House Panzió, this popular Irish-themed pub has a cosy bar, comfy leather couches & occasional live music. It also serves full meals & lighter pub food. *Mains avg 1,200Ft;* ⊕ *Sun–Thu 07.00–24.00, Fri–Sat 07.00–02.00.*

✖ **Trendo** Piac u. 11–13; ☎ 20 286 2860. This is a busy, trendy place in the Civis Grand (see page 294) that serves pasta & Hungarian choices. There are daily 3-course menus for 990Ft. Mains avg 1,800Ft; ⊕ Mon–Fri 10.00–23.00, Sat–Sun 11.00–24.00.

✖ **Vapiano** Piac u. 1; ☎ 52 531101. International chain serving freshly made salads, pasta & pizza. Mains avg 1,490Ft; ⊕ daily 11.00–23.00.

WHAT TO SEE AND DO One block east of Piac utca, **Batthyány utca** represents a pleasing stroll; it has a couple of lively pubs, and vendors selling fruit, vegetables, clothing and other items.

Most of Debrecen's sights are concentrated around the central pedestrianised area leading from Piac utca through Kossuth tér to Kálvin tér. Your first port of call is likely to be the Neoclassical **Great Reformed Church** (*Nagy templom; Kossuth tér;* ☎ 52 412694; ✚ 300/150Ft; ⊕ Mon–Sat 09.00–16.00, Sun 12.00–13.00), which has been the city's symbol since it was constructed 1819–23 to the design of Mihály Péchy (who attended the adjacent school); it occupies the site of a medieval church destroyed by fire in 1802. The interior is stark white, with little embellishment. While the organ is among the largest in Hungary, the bricks and mortar go one better – this is the country's biggest Protestant church. The chair that Lajos Kossuth sat in when he read the Declaration of Independence (from the Habsburg empire) during the Diet of 1849 has been proudly preserved inside. Climb the tower for a panoramic view of the city.

North of the church, the **Calvinist Reformed College** (*Református Kollégium; Kálvin tér 16;* ☎ 52 414744; ⊕ Tue–Sat 09.00–17.00, Sun 09.00–13.00) was founded in 1538, although much of the current building was the 19th-century work of Péchy. Its library contains an important collection of more than 600,000 volumes. There's a small **museum** (✚ adult 100Ft) telling the history of the college, and a courtyard in the middle.

The main attraction of the Neo-Baroque **Déri Múzeum** (*Déri tér 1;* ☎ 52 322207; www.derimuz.hu; ✚ 1,000/500Ft; ⊕ Tue–Sun Apr–Oct 10.00–18.00, Nov–Mar 10.00–16.00) is its collection of enormous Mihály Munkácsy paintings – and particularly the so-called 'Jesus trilogy'. Munkácsy, who lived during the second half of the 19th century, spent half his life in Paris but is nevertheless one of Hungary's best-known artists, renowned particularly for religious and historical works. There is also an exhibition on the history of Debrecen, a selection of works by other well-known and minor Hungarian artists, and ethnographic exhibits including some beautifully embroidered leather clothing worn by shepherds. The recently renovated Déri tér is a good spot for a picnic.

MODEM (*Baltazár Dezső tér 1;* ☎ 52 525018; www.modemart.hu; ⊕ Tue–Wed & Fri–Sun 10.00–18.00, Thu 16.00–24.00) is Debrecen's modern exhibition hall and museum, displaying contemporary art over three floors. The gigantic space in front of the building hosts outdoor exhibitions. Next to it is the **Kölcsey Központ** (*Hunyadi u. 1–3;* ☎ 52 518400; www.kolcseykozpont.hu), which is eastern Hungary's biggest convention centre; it hosts exhibitions and concerts, and offers a wide choice of programmes all year round.

Szent Anna Catholic Church (*Szent Anna u.*) was an important addition to the city in the 18th century for it wasn't until the predominantly Calvinist community also had a Catholic church and parish that it could be granted the title of 'royal free town'. The **Nagyerdei (Great Forest) Park** is a ten-minute tram ride (number 1) northwards, and spreads over 1,000ha. The forest contains university buildings, streets lined with splendid villas, a zoo and botanical garden, and the **Thermal Bath Centre** (*Gyógy & Fürdőközpont; Nagyerdei Park 1;* ☎ 52 514100; www.aquaticum.hu; ⊕ daily 07.00–21.00 (✚ from 1,050Ft), strand & outdoor pools May–Sep daily 06.00–19.00 (✚ from 1,000Ft), indoor pool Sep–May 06.00–19.00

(☞ 620Ft), water park all yr Mon–Thu 11.00–21.00, Fri–Sun 10.00–22.00 (☞ 2,300–4,400Ft). The latter has both indoor and outdoor pools (complete with tropical plants), steam baths, saunas, an assortment of therapeutic treatments, and an expansive children's section with slides, cave pools and waterfalls. The medicinal waters are similar in mineral content to those of Hajdúszoboszló.

The **Great Forest Cultivated Park Zoological and Botanical Gardens** claim to hold 170 animal species and 700–800 varieties of plants. The spiky stars of the botanical garden *(Egyetem tér 1;* ☏ *52 316666; free admission;* ☉ *08.00–18.00 daily)* are its cacti – there are thousands of them. Although fully open to the public, the garden is also used by the university for research. The zoo *(Ady Endre u. 1;* ☏ *52 310065;* ☞ *900/600Ft;* ☉ *daily summer 09.00–18.00, rest of yr 09.00–16.00)* has 1,400 animals.

FESTIVALS AND EVENTS Debrecen's Spring Festival *(Mar or Apr;* national and international performers at over 50 concerts and exhibitions), Flower Carnival *(Aug 20;* flower-festooned floats, folklore programmes and a firework display in celebration of St Stephen's Day) and Jazz Days *(Sep;* the country's oldest jazz festival, attracting musicians from as far afield as America) are all worth checking out.

THE HAJDÚ REGION

The Hajdúk people (Heyducks) were herders who also fought as mercenary soldiers, and had a ferocious reputation. They formed guerilla armies, and took up arms initially during the Peasant's Revolt of 1514 led by György Dózsa and in 1604–6 during war against the Habsburgs under István Bocskai. Bocskai, who owned vast estates in the region, had originally joined the Habsburgs in opposition to the Turks, but he found himself disgruntled with Habsburg policy towards his homeland. He masterminded a successful insurrection against his former allies (ironically with Turkish assistance), and secured concessions at the Treaty of Vienna – including the right of nobility to govern themselves and freedom of worship for Protestants. The Bocskai Uprising was the first Hungarian revolt against the Habsburgs, and an important chapter in Europe's Fifteen Years' War involving France, the Holy Roman Empire and the Turks. The Hajdúk were rewarded for their military support with land and privileges, and seven Hajdú towns were established. At the end of the 17th century they joined forces into a specific Hajdú district, with Hajdúböszörmény at the centre.

HAJDÚBÖSZÖRMÉNY Hajdúböszörmény is 19km northwest of Debrecen, and represents an easy day trip from the city. With its 15th-century circular layout, this is one of the most interesting towns in the Hajdúság. Originally there was a fortress at the centre, and houses have been built in concentric circles around it ever since. In addition to the struggles against the Habsburgs under Bocskai (see above), the citizens played another important part in the Hungarian Revolution of 1848. Even prior to that, however, Hajdúböszörmény was the centre of the Nyírség Muslims; in old Hungarian, 'Böszörmény' meant Muslim, but little is known of this group of people and no traces of them remain.

Getting there and away The **train** station *(Baross Gábor tér 2;* ☏ *52 227960)* is a ten-minute walk from the centre, and is on the Debrecen–Tiszalök line, with trains to Debrecen roughly hourly. The **bus** station is on Kálvin tér, and is little more than a few covered bus stops where regional buses pick up and drop off. There are three daily buses to Hajdúszoboszló; you'll need to change at Debrecen for services to Békéscsaba and Gyula. Several local buses run each hour to Debrecen, up until 23.00. Unfortunately, the regional transportation system makes it difficult to travel

6

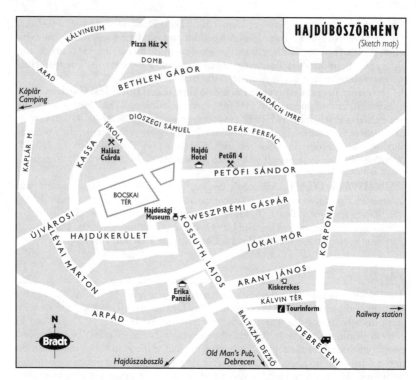

HAJDÚBÖSZÖRMÉNY
(Sketch map)

direct to many other towns, and it is often necessary to return to Debrecen, and then catch another bus or train from there.

Information

🛈 **Tourinform** Kálvin tér 6; ✆ 52 561851; e hajduboszormeny@tourinform.hu. Next to the bus station, & a 10-min walk from the train station (via

Rákóczi Ferenc u.). ⊕ daily Mar–Oct 09.00–17.00, Nov–Feb 09.00–15.00.

Where to stay and eat Tourinform can assist with arranging private accommodation, and there is one hotel, a campsite and three pensions.

🏠 **Hajdú Hotel** (10 rooms) Petőfi Sándor u. 2; ✆ 52 228307. The town's only hotel – a pleasant 3-star located just off Bocskai tér. Most of the rooms have sofas & desks, & are tastefully decorated with watercolour paintings of the region. *Sgl 8,000Ft, dbl 9,000Ft, apt 12,000Ft; b/fast 1,200Ft.*
🏠 **Erika Panzió** (3 rooms) Mester u. 3; ✆ 52 280684. No-frills accommodation in a local family's home; guests share a common bathroom. *Rooms 4,500Ft/pp.*
✕ **Halász Csárda** Iskola utca; ✆ 52 229227. It is a curious fact that there's not much fish on the menu (beyond a fish soup) at the Fisherman's Inn; choose instead from simple dishes of fried or stuffed meat, breaded vegetables or gulyás. *Mains avg 500Ft;* ⊕ *daily 08.00–22.00.*

🏠 **Káplár Kemping** Polgári u. 92–100; ✆ 52 227408; www.vendegvaro.hu/kaplar-kemping. Although there's tent-pitching space, this is considerably more than a campsite; instead it is an ethnographic museum & skanzen (preserved folk village) of adobe & thatched-roof houses, replete with folk-style furnishings, which can be rented. If you don't object to the 1km walk to the centre, a night at the skanzen is preferable to the town's pensions. *Dbls 4,000Ft; trpl 5,000Ft; tent space 400Ft (May–Sep).*
🍺 **Old Man's Pub** Baltazár Dezső u. 83; ✆ 06 70 281 0718. The place to get a strong drink. ⊕ *Sun–Thu 14.00–24.00, Fri–Sat 14.00–02.00.*
✕ **Petőfi 4** Petőfi Sándor u. 4; ✆ 52 228490. Offers a simple selection of Hungarian food (with 650Ft

daily specials), & is one of the few late-night hangouts. *Mains avg 800Ft;* ⊕ *Sun–Thu 11.30–24.00, Fri–Sat 11.30–04.00.*

✕ **Pizza Ház** Domb u. 11; ↘ 52 280498. Average pizzas. *Pizzas 600–2,000Ft;* ⊕ *Mon–Thu 11.00–22.00, Fri 11.00–02.00, Sat 16.00–02.00.*

What to see and do Bocskai tér (where the town's four main avenues intersect), named after the town's hero, is at the centre of the settlement's circle; it is where you'll find City Hall, a big Protestant church, a monument to Bocskai, and the Bocskai Grammar School. Just off the square, the **Hajdúsági Múzeum** (*Kossuth u. 1;* ↘ *52 229038;* ᵺ *300/150Ft;* ⊕ *Tue–Sat 10.00–16.00*) is located inside the town's oldest public building. The museum spreads over more than a dozen rooms, and gives a thorough ethnographic, archaeological and local history of the town. In the museum's courtyard is a statue park filled with busts of famous artists and scientists connected to the town.

Even if you're not staying there (see opposite), the *skanzen* on Polgári utca is worth seeing for its open-air presentation of folk-village life. The town hosts a community event of some sort almost every week; in August it celebrates **Hajdú Week**, with exhibitions about the region, fireworks, traditional music and dance, and other cultural programmes.

HAJDÚSZOBOSZLÓ Hajdúszoboszló is famous for its thermal bath complex, which – occupying an area of 30ha – it claims is the biggest in Europe. It attracts over 1½ million visitors annually, mainly from Poland, Austria, and Germany, and the town is the self-proclaimed 'mecca of the rheumatics'. If you're not a mecca-seeking rheumatic or a lover of a warm soak, you'll miss little by skipping this town. Everything is geared to the business of bathing, and there are hotels everywhere.

Getting there and away The **train** service to Hajdúszoboszló is excellent, since it lies on the Budapest–Debrecen–Nyíregyháza–Záhony line; the station (↘ *52 362391*), however, is 4km from the town centre. Taxi rides (*Főnix Taxi;* ↘ *52 434343*) are a fixed 700Ft; alternatively local buses leave from the bus station. All fast trains and 14 daily inter-city trains call at Hajdúszoboszló, and there are services nearly every hour to Budapest, Debrecen, Nyíregyháza, Záhony and stops in between. During the summer there is also a direct connection to Lake Balaton. The **bus** station (↘ *52 361408*) is opposite the entrance to the baths, near the intersection of Fürdő utca and Sport utca. Local buses to Debrecen leave several times hourly. Like Hajdúböszörmény, regional bus services often require a trip back to Debrecen for the necessary connection.

Information
🛈 **Tourinform** Szilfákalja út 2; ↘ 52 558928; e hajduszoboszlo@tourinform.hu. A 10-min walk

southwest of the bath complex & bus station. ⊕ *Mon–Fri 09.00–17.00, Sat 09.00–14.00.*

Where to stay and eat The town has dozens of hotels and pensions to suit all tastes and budgets, and until the day Hajdúszoboszló hosts a global convention of rheumatics, you'll have no problem finding a room. Many of the hotels are concentrated along Mátyás Király sétány. **Tourinform** has a list of over 1,300 families providing private accommodation; you can also keep your eyes open for the '*Zimmer frei*' signs, which are everywhere. There are, however, few independent restaurants – although most of the hotels have their own restaurants and cafés. During the summer, fast-food-type places open along Mátyás Király sétány.

🏠 **Civis Hotel Délibáb** (240 rooms) József Attila u. 4; ↘ 52 360366; www.civishotels.hu. Among the

biggest hotels, & has spacious rooms to boot. The service is reliable, the restaurant has live gypsy music on most evenings & rooms are well priced. *Sgl 10,000–14,000Ft, dbl 14,000–17,400Ft.*

⌂ **Hajdúszoboszló Thermal Baths, Hotel & Thermal Camping** (117 rooms) Böszörményi u. 35/A; ☏ 52 558552; www.hungarospa.hu. There is a 3-star hotel & camping ground adjacent to the spa, for which campers receive discounted day passes. The site also has a restaurant & a small supermarket. *Rooms 15,400–28,800Ft, tent 890Ft.*

⌂ **Hotel Aqua-Sol** (142 rooms) Gábor Áron u. 7–9; ☏ 52 273310; www.hunguesthotels.hu. This is one of the fanciest – indeed it even has an air-conditioned bridge linking it to the bath complex next door. *Sgl 19,500Ft, dbl 27,100Ft.*

⌂ **Hotel Aurum** (74 rooms) Mátyás király sétány 3; ☏ 52 271431; www.hotelaurum.hu. Brand-new hotel with spacious, modern & comfortable rooms, all equipped with kitchens. *Dbl 21,000–32,500Ft, suite 40,000–75,000Ft.*

⌂ **Hotel Mátyás Király** (106 rooms) Mátyás Király sétány 17; ☏ 52 360200; www.matyashotel.hu. A nice one close to the spa; all rooms have balconies, & there are fitness & spa facilities, & a large restaurant. *Sgl 16,500–27,900Ft, dbl 19,800–33,200Ft.*

✗ **Kemencés Csárda** Szilfákalja u. 40/1; ☏ 52 362221. One of the better restaurants, serving traditional Hungarian food to the sound of Hungarian folk music. It has an attached pension with 20 rooms (sgl 6,600Ft, dbl 9,200Ft). *Mains avg 1,500Ft;* ⊕ *08.00–24.00.*

✗ **Nelson** Hősök tere 4; ☏ 52 270226. Has a nautical theme, & serves good food in hearty portions. *Mains 1,300–2,400Ft;* ⊕ *daily 09.00–24.00.*

✗ **Szilfa** József Attila u. 2–4; ☏ 52 363087. Szilfa is splayed out & touristy, & the food is fair rather than fantastic. On the plus side, it is central, it offers regional specialities, & a plate for 2 is piled high enough to feed 4. *Mains avg 1,400Ft;* ⊕ *11.00–24.00.*

What to see and do The baths are considered to be the town's point of focus. Mátyás Király sétány – where most of the hotels are concentrated – is a good place to start. Besides a few scattered churches and monuments, there's little else to see in town, and the several large roads don't make for the most enjoyable walking routes.

The **Hajdúszoboszló Thermal Baths** (*Szent István park 1–3;* ☏ *52 558558; www.hungarospa.hu;* ⊕ *thermal bath 07.00–19.00 daily; outdoor bath May–May 08.00–18.00, Jun 1–Aug 22 08.00–20.00, Aug 23–Sep 30 08.00–18.00; aquapark May & Sep Sat–Sun 12.00–16.00, Jun–Aug 10.00–18.30; indoor swimming pool Jun 16–Aug 31 09.00–19.00, Sep 1–Jun 15 Mon–Fri 15.00–19.00, Sat–Sun 09.00–19.00*) is a sprawling complex. The thermal water – nicknamed 'hot gold' by residents – was discovered during a search for oil in 1925. The spa opened two years later, and in 2000 was expanded into what you see today. There are 13 thermal pools, an indoor lap pool, an outdoor aquapark with nine water slides, a wave pool, a sandy strand (complete with palm trees), and several enormous swimming pools. There's even a naturist island in one of the outdoor pools, and an open-air stage for summer performances; over 40 different kinds of medicinal and relaxation treatments are available. It's a humungous theme park of a place, and can feel overwhelming. Admission starts at 700Ft and varies depending on what type of ticket and services you want. Construction of the indoor aquapark was underway when we visited, and should be open shortly; it aims to be the largest and best of its kind in Central Europe.

The holdings of the **István Bocskai Museum** (*Bocskai u. 12;* ☏ *52 362165;* 🎫 *adult 400Ft;* ⊕ *Tue–Sun Apr–Sep 10.00–18.00, Oct–Mar 10.00–16.00*) are divided between three different buildings. The permanent exhibitions represent an eclectic mix of folk art, town history, relics of the area's military past and the work of local artists.

SZABOLCS-SZATMÁR-BEREG COUNTY

The northeastern chunk of Hungary – bordered by Slovakia, Ukraine and Romania – falls under the administrative blanket of the huge Szabolcs-Szatmár-Bereg County. Beneath this blanket live the poorest of the country's people – many of them Roma – a population that suffers from a paucity of employment opportunities and whose

The largest ethnic minority in the country, the Hungarian Roma number an estimated 500,000–700,000 people (5–6% of the current population). The Roma arrived in Europe in waves starting in the 9th century, and were recorded in Hungary from the end of the 14th century. Their name derives from the Romany word for 'men', but European confusion surrounding the origins of the Roma peoples is evident in the alternative names used to describe them. The English 'gypsy' (and Spanish equivalent 'gitano') stems from 'Egypt', reflecting a wide belief that the Roma were descendants of an Islamic sect. The Hungarian 'cigány' has its roots in a corruption of the Greek term 'atsingani', a heretical sect of Asia Minor. It wasn't until 1753 that a Hungarian student spotted linguistic ties between Romany vocabulary and a central group of Hindi tongues, tying the Roma to a homeland in northern India. In 1976, at the first Roma festival in Chandigarh, Mrs Indira Gandhi pledged her support for recognising the Roma as a national minority of India.

Only 25% of Hungarian Roma are now Romany speakers, these are divided into two clearly distinct groups, one speaking the lovári language, the other beás. Historically the lovári speakers were horse traders and metalworkers, while the beás Roma worked with their hands, making baskets and traditional wooden tubs used for washing clothes or storing meat. However, the itinerant Roma lifestyle militated against steady education and reduced employment prospects, and they gradually lost not only their traditional professions and language, but their social structure as they moved into cities. Although now largely settled, unemployment among Hungarian Roma currently runs at 60–70%; they live in greatest concentrations in the country's poorer areas, such as the northeastern corner.

It is in gypsy music (cigányzene) that one might see a solitary surviving strain of cultural identity. In its purest form, this has deep historical roots; Roma musicians were reported on Csepel Island in Hungary in 1489, and Romany bands played in the Austro-Hungarian court of Esterháza (at Fertőd) in 1714. However, the variant played by 'musical gypsy families' in today's restaurants is as far removed from original gypsy folk songs as it is from the tunes of Hungarian peasants (with which it is often confused abroad). Instead the ensembles play mainly Magyar songs, and are dressed in Magyar-type costumes.

Historically and across Europe, the Roma have been persecuted; floggings, the shaving of heads, beatings, deportations and hangings were once commonplace. Such prejudice culminated in the extermination of 1½ million Roma during the Holocaust. Interestingly, in 19th-century Hungarian literature the gypsy was treated with a certain affection, as a comic figure or symbol of romantic freedom. However, this was supplanted by images of crime and poverty, and hostility to the Roma people is still very evident. While in politically correct circles the word cigány is becoming taboo, this is counterbalanced by expressions like 'cigányútra ment' ('gone the gypsies' way') – to describe the moment when food goes down the wrong channel – that is still heard beyond these circles. Roma feature little in Hungarian cultural, commercial or political life (although Hungary has a Roma MEP), and despite the country's progress since the fall of communism continue to feel an isolated and persecuted minority.

most easterly communities are decreasing as sons and daughters are drawn by brighter city lights elsewhere. With the exception of the county capital of Nyíregyháza, whose success was founded on an industry that has itself suffered significantly since the political changes of the 1990s, the way of life here is agricultural, the sandy, undulating landscape – formed by soil blown from the Tisza flood basin by northerly winds – peppered with orchards and crop fields. This is a corner with a history of isolation and sadness, imposed upon it by forces geographical and political. Prior to the 19th-century drainage project that regulated the River Tisza, boggy land made travel in or out difficult, while the 1920 Treaty of Trianon slashed away Transylvania and Ruthenia (in the far east of Slovakia) at a stroke and the deportations during World War II decimated the strong Jewish community. It is no surprise that fresh licks of paint are unusual in this pocket, that there is more than a hint of dilapidation and little in the way of sophisticated tourist infrastructure.

Yet these very pressures have created a rough diamond that will reward those who've the energy and spirit to seek it out. Isolation breeds preservation; here is rural life laid out, and tradition, culture and architecture less damaged or altered by hostile invasions of the past or progressive moves of the present. Painted medieval churches, wooden belfries, water mills and boat-shaped grave markers are among the region's human highlights, while fishing and canoeing is good on the Tisza (you can book canoe trips or arrange equipment hire and boat delivery through the website www.vidamdelfin.hu; it is in Hungarian, but the company welcomes English enquiries), and naturalists will not be disappointed by the varied habitats of the marshes, wooded pasture and grassland.

THE NYÍRSÉG REGION The towns and villages of the Nyírség region – many of whose names are helpfully prefixed with 'Nyír' (meaning 'birch', after the forests that grew in the depressions) – lie north and northeast of Debrecen on Hungary's second-largest sand bed. Nyíregyháza is the focal point and the main town not just of the Nyírség but of the northeast as a whole; this is the place to stock up on tourist information before taking a deep breath and plunging into the remoter spots out towards the borders.

Nyíregyháza A town of squares and statues, Nyíregyháza lacks thrills but its eclectic architecture, mixed bag of churches and wide-ranging museum provide enough to fill a pleasant day. Owned by the Transylvanian Prince István Bocskai in the early 17th century, a series of violent squabbles between town and county factions caused many to up sticks and move out – the dawn of the 18th century was greeted by just 50 families still resident in Nyíregyháza. However, it was re-settled by Slovaks, and went on to become the easternmost market town of the Eastern Bloc during the communist period. (The Slovak descendants continue to speak an archaic form of Slovakian.) While its industry has died with the times in which it thrived, the town remains nevertheless the county seat of Szabolcs-Szatmár-Bereg and the main centre of the Nyírség. The resort of Sóstófürdő a few kilometres to the north, with its open-air village museum and baths, is a major bonus.

Getting there, away and around Both the bus and train stations are 1.5km from the action, at the ends of Széchenyi utca and Arany János utca respectively (as they run westwards out of the city). You can catch local buses 7 or 8 from here to the centre. The **train station** is a modern affair, and stands at the junction of two main lines running west–east and south–north. Twenty-nine trains run daily from Budapest (either Keleti or Nyugati), taking between three and four hours; there are a good number to Miskolc (passing through Tokaj and Szerencs on the way) and Debrecen, and services to Nyírbátor (ten, with some also stopping at Máriapócs and Nagykálló) and Záhony (20). The latter also passes through Kisvárda, and up to two continue over the Ukrainian border to Csop. A smaller third line also links the town with Vásárosnamény.

The **bus station** is 150m north of the train station on Petőfi tér. One daily bus runs direct between Nyíregyháza and Budapest Stadion, except on Saturday when

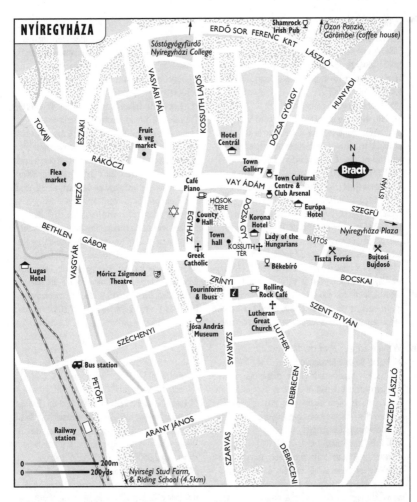

you have to change at Eger or Gyöngyös. There are services to Debrecen (five, taking between one and two hours), Eger (two), Sárospatak (two), Tokaj (two), Miskolc (up to two), Gyöngyös (up to two) and Kisvárda (five on weekdays, two at weekends). In addition, there are regular services to Nagykálló, Máriapócs and Nyírbátor, and daily international buses to Košice, Satu Mare and Uzhgorod.

Taxis can be arranged through **Fő Taxi** (↘ *42 444444*) or **Radio Gold FM Taxi** (↘ *42 414414*).

Information and other practicalities

$ **Bank** Kossuth Lajos tér 2. Worth a peek for its Neo-Baroque styling, neat balconies & decorative supporting pillars. ⊕ *Mon 07.45–18.00, Tue–Thu 07.45–17.00, Fri 07.45–16.00.*

🖾 **Europa Net Café** Hunyadi u. 2; ↘ *42 508670.* A two-floor café next to the Europa Hotel with comfy sofas & 10 internet terminals.

🖾 **Ibusz** Országzászló tér 6; ↘ *42 312695.* Can

arrange private accommodation & local tours, & change travellers' cheques. ⊕ *Mon–Thu 08.00–16.00.*

🖾 **Listings magazine** *Nyíregyházi Est*

🖾 **Tourinform** Országzászló tér 6; ↘ *42 505697.* All the usual information; the theatre ticket office is also here. ⊕ *Jun 15–Oct 15 Mon–Fri 09.00–19.00, Sat–Sun 09.00–18.00, rest of yr Mon–Fri 09.00–17.00.*

⌂ Where to stay

⌂ **Európa Hotel** (60 rooms) Hunyadi u. 2; ☎ 42 508670; www.europahotel.hu. Standing on Szabadságág tér, the Európa looks like a hotel from Legoland, but its rooms are more ordinary. *Sgl 9,000Ft, dbl 11,000Ft.*

⌂ **Hotel Centrál** (33 rooms) Nyár u. 2–4; ☎ 42 411330; www.centralhotel.hu. Modern hotel with comfortable charm in a quiet spot just to the north of Hősök tér. Among the facilities are a pleasant little indoor pool & a jacuzzi. *Sgl 13,000Ft, dbl 15,000Ft, apt 17,000Ft.*

⌂ **Korona Hotel** (35 rooms) Dózsa György u. 1; ☎ 42 409300; http://members.chello.hu/korona. Grand, characterful, stunning inside & out, the century-old Korona is an excellent choice. It also has its own pub, pizzeria, café, casino, solarium & sauna. *Sgl 12,800Ft, dbl 13,900Ft, apt 17,000Ft; b/fast 1,500Ft.*

⌂ **Lugas** (26 rooms) Prága u. 3; ☎ 42 342777; www.lugashotel.hu. On the outskirts of town, the Lugas is worth the effort. As well as a landscaped garden area, it has a pool, bowling alley & a top-notch restaurant (see below). From the centre, travel westwards along Bethlen Gabor utca, cross the rail tracks, take the first left into Derkovits Gyula u. followed by the first right into Prága utca. *Dbl 17,000Ft, trpl 19,500Ft, apt (for 2) 24,000; b/fast 1,500Ft.*

⌂ **Nyiregyházi College** Sostoi u. 31/B; ☎ 42 599419. The college is located around 2km north of the centre, & has rooms available in Jul & Aug. To reserve one, you must call ahead or make arrangements through Tourinform. If you're walking it, follow Kossuth Lajos utca, cross Ferenc körút & the college is 800m or so up on the left; alternatively, buses 13, 20, 19, 8 & 8A stop near by. *Rooms 1,500Ft/pp.*

⌂ **Ózon Panzió** (19 rooms) Csaló köz 2; ☎ 42 402001; www.ozonpanzio.hu. The Ózon has a chalet feel to it, in a leafy (or pine-needly) suburb on the way out towards Sóstófürdő. The hotel operates as a training school for local catering students, who enjoy firing up barbecues in the summer. The dbl rooms are smallish, but comfortable; the apts are rather fusty. Bus 9 stops 200m away. *Dbl 9,200Ft, apt 12,200Ft; b/fast 1,100Ft.*

✗ Where to eat and drink

✗ **Bujtosi Bujdosó Restaurant** Bujtos u. 34, ☎ 42 411433. Five minutes east of the centre, this café-style restaurant has staff as eager as puppies & a menu that's as cheap as the chips that accompany a number of its dishes. *Mains avg 1,000Ft;* ☺ *Mon–Sat 10.00–22.00.*

☕ **Café Piano** Hősök tere 8; ☎ 42 400377. There's a trombone & other brass instruments, together with an obligatory piano. Selling cocktails & cakes at the northern end of the square, this is a popular coffee house, although its high ceiling & tiled area at the front dilute the atmosphere somewhat. ☺ *Mon–Thu 09.00–22.00, Fri 09.00–23.00, Sun 15.00–20.00.*

✗ **Centrál Restaurant** Nyár u. 2–4; ☎ 42 411330. We haven't tested the chef's expressed willingness to prepare any dish you desire, but we can vouch for the foie gras starter. The restaurant of the Hotel Centrál (see above) isn't bad at all, although we'd prefer the lighting a little less glaring. *Mains avg 2,000Ft;* ☺ *07.00–23.00 daily.*

☕ **Görömbei Cukrászda** Korányi Frigyes u. 23/A; ☎ 42 500795. As nice as they are naughty, the cakes, biscuits & ice creams at Görömbei are the town's best. Burn off the guilt with the 2km walk there (northeast along Dózsa György u. & beyond the ring road) – or squeeze into buses 5, 7 or 12. ☺ *daily 10.00–20.00.*

✗ **Lugas Restaurant** Prága u. 3; ☎ 42 342777. Hotel restaurant serving high-class international nosh in an airy, cheerful conservatory-style dining room. The line-up includes veal, crêpes, pastas & fish dishes. *Mains avg 2,000Ft;* ☺ *10.00–23.00 daily.*

✗ **Rolling Rock Café** Geduly ház, Luther u. 5, ☎ 42 401915. One in the chain of America-theme bars, the Rolling Rock is a busy haunt serving American-sized portions of fajitas, steaks & burgers (alongside traditional Hungarian specialities). *Mains avg 1,700Ft;* ☺ *Mon–Fri 10.00–24.00, Fri–Sat 10.00–02.00, Sun 11.00–23.00.*

✗ **Tiszta Forrás Bioétterem** Bujtos u. 27, ☎ 42 402 306. Healthy food – all ingredients are free of preservatives, & only organic vegetables are used. While the family is keen to promote the wonders of the vegetable kingdom, & there are dishes for meat eaters too – including Hungarian specialities like gulyás & pörkölt. *Mains avg 1,990Ft;* ☺ *Mon–Sat 11.00–23.00.*

There is a **fruit, meat and veg market** on Búza tér (☺ *Mon 06.00–13.00, Tue–Fri 06.00–17.00, Sat 06.00–14.00, Sun 07.00–11.00*), where you can also pick up a cheap snack.

Entertainment and nightlife Ferenc Bán's **Town Cultural Centre** (*Szabadság tér 9;* \ *42 411822*) was acclaimed when finished in 1981, but the concrete block with its cylindrical protrusions won't be to everybody's taste; this is, however, the place to head for details of listings and events. The palatial **Móricz Zsigmond Theatre** (*Bessenyei tér 13; ticket office* \ *42 507007; www.moriczszinhaz.hu*) is considerably easier on the eye, and can also offer help; the theatre hosts some acclaimed international orchestras and choirs, including the American Cantemus Chorus. The ticket office is in the Tourinform. Outside is a statue of the Hungarian socialist poet Mihály Váci, dressed in a shabby polo neck; the book in his hand had been graffitied with 'porno mag' when we last visited, but we suspect it's more likely to represent a collection of his verse. The **Palace Cinema** (*Nyíregyháza Plaza, Szegfű u. 75;* \ *42 499412; www.palacecinemas.hu*) has big-screen blockbusters.

If you need to wet your whistle, you can try the seedy-looking **Békebiró Söröző** (*Bocskai u. 1;* \ *06 20 414 0411;* ⊕ *Mon–Thu 09.00–24.00, Fri 09.00–02.00, Sat 17.00–02.00, Sun 17.00–22.00*), the **Shamrock Irish Pub** (*Korányi Frigyes utca;* \ *42 403717*) just to the north of Ferenc körút, or the **John Bull** (*Dózsa György u. 1*), a cellar-like piece of Blighty at the Korona Hotel. Below that, the **X Café** doubles as a dance club; alternatively, you can cut some shapes to thumping base lines at the dark and smoky **Club Arsenal** (*Szabadság tér 9;* \ *42 411 825;* ⊕ *Tue–Sat 21.00–05.00*), underneath the cultural centre.

What to see and do The town centre consists of a series of interlinked squares, prime among which is Kossuth tér, built in 1910 and paved with coloured stones. At its heart is a huge statue of a barrel-chested Kossuth (by Gyula Bethlen, 1912), while on the western side is the **town hall** (*Kossuth Lajos tér 1*) – Neoclassical when built in 1841, but later restyled – with its long balcony and iron fretwork. Facing it across the square is the Neo-Romanesque **Lady of the Hungarians Church** (*Kossuth Lajos tér 15*), a magnificent twin-steepled Roman Catholic temple built in 1904 by József Kommer and Virgil Nagy. A pastel rainbow of colours covers the grey stone inside, as though a class of innocents was given free rein to make the church its own, and the effect is completed by vivid stained glass adorning the nave and chancel.

If you're feeling particularly ecclesiological, there are other churches to see. Behind the town hall, the Art-Nouveau **Greek Catholic Church** (*Görög Katolikus Egyház; Bethlen Gábor u. 5*) has cheerful orange patterning; there's a collection of ecclesiastical art in the nearby episcopal palace and college. The **Lutheran Great Church** (*Evangélikus nagytemplom; Luther tér 14;* \ *42 508770*) was built in 1786 by Italian master Giuseppe Aprilis, and is sited at the town's highest point. (Keep an eye out for organ and choral concerts held here.) Changing religious tack, the pink **synagogue** (*Mártírok tere 6*) was designed by Lipót Baumhorn (1924–32), is adorned inside with animal motifs, and has a small Holocaust exhibition next door (where you also ring for access; ⊕ *Mon–Thu 09.00–12.00*).

Hősök tere is home to the Eclectic **County Hall**, an elegant brute of a building designed by Ignác Alpár in 1892. To the northeast, opposite the cultural centre, the **Town Gallery** (*Selyem u. 12;* \ *42 408720; free admission;* ⊕ *Tue–Sat 09.00–17.00*) displays the 20th-century work of Pál Gyula, which has something of the J S Lowry about it. There are also temporary exhibitions by contemporary artists.

To the south is Országzászló tér, with its late-20th-century **Hungarian Hussars Monument** (Sándor Győrfi, 1997) commemorating the role of the cavalry in the bloody battles of the Napoleonic Wars. Southwest of that (linked by Széchenyi utca), the narrow Benczúr Gyula tér holds the **Jósa András Museum** (*Benczúr Gyula tér 21;* \ *42 315722;* 🎟 *400/200Ft;* ⊕ *Tue–Sun 10.00–17.00*), guarded by a brace of pint-sized lions. Benczúr Gyula (1844–1920) – whose statue also stands outside – was born in the town and numbered among his works the altar painting and mosaic in Budapest's St István Basilica. András Jósa (1834–1918) was a famous archaeologist and doctor (turning to medicine after medical men failed to diagnose his own illness). He lived in the Neoclassical building, and founded the museum in 1868. The exhibitions include paraphernalia from the local regiment of the 4th Hussars and other fearsome weaponry, coins dating back to the Roman Age and a display of local history. Most valuable are the pieces relating to Nyíregyháza's two renowned Gyulas – the painter Benczúr and the writer Krúdy (1878–1933).

For some colourful bustle, head for the outdoor **flea market** (*Tokaji út;* ☺ *Mon–Sat 06.00–16.00*), just beyond the train track at the meeting point of Rákóczi utca and Tokaji út, where you'll find traders hawking anything and everything. Buses 1 and 1A run there.

Horse-riding The **Szil-Ko Stud Farm and Riding School** (*Bem József u. 22–23;* ☏ *42 728826; www.kovacslovarda.hu*) offers an extensive range of programmes, including a week-long Tokaj riding tour and three-day hunting tour. It also has an indoor arena for riding lessons (☞ *from 1,750Ft/hr*). The on-site panzió has five cosy rooms (*dbl 6,000Ft*). Ask for Kovács István. Turn on to Simai utca (near the bus and train stations) and then left into Bem József utca.

Festivals and events Nyíregyháza Arts Week takes place in April, when there's also a regional ballet festival. The main annual event is the Autumn Festival (*Aug–Sep*), but there is also an International Bird Exhibition (*Oct*) and even a Father Christmas Beauty Contest (*Dec*). The mind boggles.

Sóstófürdő 'Salt Lake Baths' is 6km north of Nyíregyháza, and derives its name from a 10ha saline lake upon which the resort has grown since the 1920s. The mineral-rich water is said to aid recovery from a range of ills, but the lake is also popular for boating. An even more worthy attraction is the excellent Village Museum, and the surrounding oak forest promises cooling walks.

Bus 8 (not 8A) runs here from Nyíregyháza, and there are regular trains to Sóstó station (on the southeastern side of the zoo). Alternatively, you can take the narrow-gauge train from Nyíregyháza NyK through the Sóstó Forest (*Sóstó-erdő*) on the Balsa/Dombrád line; trains leave every three hours or so. Buses and the narrow-gauge train stop near the Krúdy Hotel, a short distance southeast of the Village Museum and west of the lake.

Information and other practicalities

🖪 **Szabolcs-Szatmár-Bereg County Nature Lovers' Association** Mártírok tere 9; ☏ 42 311577. Information on walks & other nature highlights of the region. ☺ Thu 15.00–20.00.

🖪 **Tourinform** Water Tower (Víztorony); ☏ 42 411193; e sostofurdo@tourinform.hu. The town's distinctive octagonal monument was built in 1911 & originally functioned as a well, but is now home to the helpful seasonal tourist office. ☺ May 21–Jun 14 Mon–Fri 08.30–16.30, Jun 15–Sep 15 Mon–Fri 08.30–17.30, Sat–Sun 08.30–15.30.

 Where to stay There are several campsites near both the Village Museum and the outdoor baths. Alternatively there are several decent guesthouses.

🏠 **Hotel Sóstó Turistaszálló & Camping** Sóstói út 76; ☏ 42 402011. A fairly new campsite in between the Village Museum & outdoor baths; it is well kept & well equipped (with swimming pool, tennis courts, a restaurant & horse-riding opportunities). It also has a no-frills hotel. *Hotel sgl 7,000Ft, dbl 8,900Ft, trpl 11,900Ft, apt 12,800Ft; tent/caravan 800/3,000Ft, plus adult/child 800/500Ft.*

🏠 **Blaha Panzió** (12 rooms) Blaha Lujza sétány 7; ☏ 42 403342. Blends contemporary furnishings with a hint of simple rusticity, & is superbly located. It's also pretty cheap.*Sgl 7,300Ft Dbl 9,800Ft; b/fast 850Ft.*

🏠 **Hotel Svájci-Lak** (10 rooms) Sóstói út; ➘ 42 411191; www.furdohaz.hu. Once frequented by Gyula Krúdy & Lujza Blaha, this is a tidy hotel linked to the adjacent Fürdőház Panzió & Bath House (see below). *Sgl 9,200Ft, dbl 13,800Ft, trpl 19,800Ft, apts 18,900–15,200Ft.*

🏠 **Hotel Tara** (21 rooms) Fürdő u. 51; ➘ 42 475903; e bchu@t-online.hu. Offers plain accommodation 2 mins from the outdoor baths, & is

run by an Irishman (whose son, Brian Carney, used to play for the Great Britain rugby league team).

🏠 **Krúdy Hotel** (20 rooms) Sóstói út 75; ➘ 42 596 187; e info@krudyvigado.hu; www.krudyvigado.hu. An Eclectic, achingly romantic hotel overlooking the lake & next to the Irish Pub.

🏠 **Sóstói Szinbád Hotel** (21 rooms) Sóstói út 66, ➘ 42 506 500, e hotel@sostoiszinbadhotel.hu. This was once a railway station, before being converted into the current hotel. A standard 3-star inside; the staff are unhelpful. *Sgl 17,500Ft, dbl 20,500Ft.*

✖ *Where to eat and drink*

♀ **Beatles Nosztalgia Club** Szódaház u. 14; ➘ 42 475731. This is a real gem, an outlandish bar filled with plush red seating & varnished tree trunks a short distance east of the northern section of the lake. It's a curious blend of indoor forest, cavern & beach bar, & like nothing else we've ever seen.

✖ **Krúdy Hotel Restaurant** See above. A fabulous place to dine, with its canopied terrace illuminated with fairy lights. *Mains avg 1,800Ft;* ⏲ *12.00–24.00 daily.*

✖ **424 Irish Restaurant & Pub** Blaha Lujza sétány 1; ➘ 42 424000. The Irish Pub has a rounded outdoor terrace set among the trees. Beyond the Murphy's & Guinness, & the green furnishings, there's little obviously Irish here but it bursts at the seams in summer. We found the food – Hungarian, with fish the speciality – fairly average. *Mains avg 2,000Ft;* ⏲ *10.00–23.00 daily.*

What to see and do The **Open-Air Village Museum** (*Sóstói Múzeumfalu; Tölgyes u. 1;* ➘ *42 479704;* ✆ *600/300Ft; Eng-speaking guide 4,000Ft;* ⏲ *Tue–Sun Apr 1–Jun 14 09.00–17.00, Jun 15–Aug 31 09.00–18.00, Sep–Oct 09.00–17.00*) is devoted to the architecture and lifestyles of people from five ethnographic regions in the county (Szatmár, Rétköz, Nyírség, Nyíri Mezőség and Bereg). Among its buildings are a school, church and belfry, grocery store, pub and fire station, together with a farmhouse typical of the Slovakian settlers (Tirpák) who repopulated Nyíregyháza in the 18th century. A cemetery contains distinctive Szatmár grave markers, while Roma huts nestle tellingly at the edge of the village – indicative of the social segregation that remains evident even today. Craft shows and demonstrations are often held here devoted to traditional trades, and on Wednesdays regional dishes are cooked up for visitors to sample. The 7½ha site has much to see; join Tölgyes utca from near the Krúdy Hotel.

The **Sóstó Lake Baths** (*Tófürdő; Blaha Lujza sétány 1;* ➘ *42 475736;* ⏲ *May 27–Aug 31 daily 09.00–19.30;* ✆ *600/400Ft*) is on the other side of Sóstói út from the museum, its upper section given over to boating and its lower to a cold-pool beach. There are snackbars, a volley-ball court and waterslide, and ladies can go topless if so inclined. The **Park Baths** (*Berenát u. 3;* ➘ *42 475736; www.aquariusfurdo.hu;* ✆/*family from 800/600/2,500Ft;* ⏲ *May 27–Sep 10 daily 09.00–19.00, indoor pools are all yr*) were opened to the north when the lake began to suffer from overcrowding in the 1950s, and the water is equally mineral-rich. Alongside the various pools, there are go-karts, tennis courts, an inflatable trampoline and an area for nude sunbathing. In addition, there's a new indoor baths complex here called **Aquarius Fürdő**, which is very popular with families, and features slides and a variety of pools. If you're here out of season, the **Bath House** (*Fürdőház; Sóstói út;* ➘ *42 411191;* ✆ *adult 1,500Ft;* ⏲ *daily 10.00–20.00*) is open all year round too (having been resurrected in 2000 after stagnating for 25 years), and has bathing tubs and opportunities for massages.

Sóstó Zoo (✆ *42 479 702; www.sostozoo.hu;* 🎫 *family 1,600/1,100/4,700Ft;* ☉ *daily Apr–Sep 09.00–19.00, Oct–Mar 09.00–16.00*) is southwest of the lake; it is Hungary's second-largest, and has nearly 300 species including rare snow leopards and Mexican macaws. Our feeling is that some of the cages holding the bigger beasts are on the small side, and some of the pacing cats looked pretty miserable. You can watch them being fed every second hour on Sat and Sun.

Other excursions from Nyíregyháza Twelve kilometres to the southeast Nagykálló was the county capital until 1876 and former site of a Heyduck fort (levelled in 1769); today, however, the town is more popularly associated with the mental hospital in the old County Hall than for its past history. There are some handsome Neoclassical buildings and two 15th-century churches, but most visitors are either Hasidic Jews making a pilgrimage to the tomb of the mystical Rabbi Isaac Taub (in the Jewish cemetery) or those drawn by a folk-art festival at the end of June. Details can be obtained from the Tourinform in Nyíregyháza. The railway station is on the line between Nyíregyháza and Nyírbátor; change at Nyíregyháza or Nyíradony for Debrecen. There are very regular buses from Nyíregyháza, and on to Máriapócs.

Just off the road running between Nagykálló and Nyírbátor (another 8km on), **Máriapócs** is a settlement of just 2,000 that was first mentioned as 'Pócs' in records of 1280. 'Mária' was added when the village was declared a holy place; Pope John Paul II visited in 1991, and each year a million pilgrims make the trip. Why? Because of a special icon of the Virgin Mary at the northern end of the village's 18th-century Greek Catholic Basilica (*Görög katolikus bazilika; Kossuth tér 25*). In 1696, this votive picture – painted in 1676 by a travelling artist who had escaped the Turks – was seen to shed tears. When Lipót I heard of this, he moved it to Vienna (it is still there, in St Stephen's Cathedral), but a copy was made in Kosice and proved to be equally weepy – crying in 1715 and again for 18 days in 1905. The current twin-towered Baroque church was completed in 1756 after the number of worshippers outgrew the original wooden version; it was raised to 'basilica' status in 1946. The days that see the most traffic – thousands upon thousands of Greek Catholics – are August 15 (Feast of the Assumption) and the nearest Sunday to September 8 (Feast of the Blessed Virgin Mary). The **train station** is a couple of kilometres from the church, and there are daily services between Nyíregyháza (nine), Mátészalka (seven) and Fehérgyarmat (one). **Buses** stop near enough outside the church; there are regular buses to Nyírbátor, as well as to Nyíregyháza (26) and Nagykálló (26).

If you follow Route 41 northeast from Nyíregyháza for just under 40km, and turn right on to Road 49, you'll come to **Vaja**, notable for the 16th-century Vay

THE BÁTHORI FAMILY

The Báthori dynasty was one of the most important in Transylvania between the 15th and 17th centuries. Born in Somlyó, István Báthori lived 1533–86 and was a *fejedelem* or Transylvanian prince (1571–86). He married a Jagello princess and became King of Poland (1575–86) after fighting off an attack in 1578 from Gáspár Bekes, a pretender to the throne supported by the Habsburgs. Báthori ascended to the Polish throne and moved to Krakow for a while, leaving the rule of Transylvania to his elder brother Kristóf. In 1579 he set off with a conscripted army to fight the Russian Tsar Ivan the Terrible, and in 1582 struck a ten-year ceasefire deal with Ivan. Towards the end of his life he created an alliance against the Turks, with the help of Pope Gregory III and comprising Transylvania, Hungary and Poland. He died in Grodno.

family mansion and grounds. Ádám Vay was a supporter of the Rákóczi-led independence struggle against Habsburg rule; the building now houses a museum of local history (⊕ *Apr–Oct Tue–Sun 10.00–18.00, Nov–Mar Mon–Fri 08.00–16.00; ☞ adult 200Ft*). There's also a Gothic Calvinist church nearby, originally built in the 15th century but reconstructed in the 19th. Buses run here from Nyíregyháza, Mátészalka and Vásárosnamény. **Mátészalka**, from where the parents of Hollywood star Tony Curtis herald, is a few kilometres further along Road 49. Its railway station is on the same line as Nyíregyháza, and also on that running north to Záhony (and on over the Ukrainian border) and south to Ágerdőmajor (and on over the Romanian border).

Nyírbátor Nyírbátor is undoubtedly the town of the Báthori family – hence the 'bátor' in the town's name – a significant aristocratic clan whose most famous member was István, Prince of Transylvania and King of Poland. The Báthoris owned it for four medieval centuries and left their powerful stamp on its main monuments: the Calvinist church, which ranks among the country's best late-Gothic religious architecture, and the former Minorite church, containing some magnificent Baroque wood carvings.

Getting there and away Nyírbátor is on Road 471 leading northeast from Debrecen. The **railway** and **bus** stations (*Ady Endre u.*) are a few hundred metres north of the centre along Kossuth Lajos utca. Trains run west through Nagykálló on their way to Nyíregyháza (change there for Miskolc), and are also on the Apafa–Zajta line (including Mátészalka and Fehérgyarmat). There are 11 daily direct to Debrecen (or change at Apafa). Buses run very regularly to nearby Máriapócs, and to Nyíregyháza and Nagykálló; there are four daily services to Debrecen.

Where to stay, eat and drink

♀ **Bowling Club & Bar** Pócsi út; ☎ 42 284488. Has a lively reputation, & is where the young head to let off steam & knock over some pins. It is 2km outside the centre on the road to Máriapócs (just beyond the railtrack). ⊕ *Mon–Tue 16.00–22.00, Fri–Sun 16.00–24.00.*

♀ **Café Code** Szabadság tér 7. One of the few places that opens late. The Ibiza Klub is next door. ⊕ *Mon–Thu 08.00–22.00, Fri 08.00–02.00, Sat 08.00–14.00, 19.00–03.00, Sun 17.00–22.00.*

🏠 **Éltes Mátyás Általános Iskola és Diákotthon** Debreceni u. 67, ☎ 42 281244. A cheap option in college accommodation. There are dorm beds & 2 single rooms. *Sgl 1,230Ft/pp, dorm 2,460Ft/pp.*

🏠 **Hotel Bástya** (26 rooms) Hunyadi u. 10; ☎ 42 281657. You won't lose the Bástya in a crowd; its vivid colour & central bastion make it something of an attention seeker. A step inside is a step back to the '70s – the bathrooms in particular could do with an overhaul – but it's kitschly comfortable & there are moderately modern conveniences such as

air conditioning. *Sgl 6,960Ft, dbl 9,360Ft, trpl 12,000Ft (excl tourist tax); b/fast 1,010Ft.*

🏠 **Hotel Hódi** (17 rooms) Bátori u. 11; ☎ 42 281012. The top hotel by a long chalk is based in a former Báthori residence & has played host to some big guns. The Hungarian president stayed here in 2001, & if you want a right royal night's kip choose room 16 where the King of Spain laid his head in 2002. As you'd expect, the accommodation is of a high standard & full of character; there's also a wonderfully opulent indoor swimming pool, a friendly owner, & a reasonable price tag. Unless there's no room at the inn, there's no need to look elsewhere. *Sgl 11,900Ft, dbl 12,900Ft; b/fast 1,300Ft.*

✗ **Kakukk** Szabadság tér 21; ☎ 42 281050. The main eatery in the town's main square, serving Hungarian & international cuisine. It has an enormous terrace, & there are 5 guest rooms available above the restaurant (*from dbl 9,000Ft*). *Mains 780–2,000Ft, avg 1,500Ft;* ⊕ *daily 11.30–21.00 (until 22.00 in summer).*

What to see and do The 15th-century **Calvinist church** (*Báthori u. 24*) is a Gothic masterpiece; its vast ceiling is adorned with geometric vaulting, and there are 12m lancet windows and Renaissance *sedilia*. This was originally a Roman Catholic church, before falling into Calvinist hands in the 16th century. A red-marble sarcophagus was fashioned in 1493 to cover the bones of the church founder, the Transylvanian Prince István Báthori, while an adjacent tomb holds a second István of the family, one who served as lord chief justice and sponsored German and Hungarian translations of the Bible before leaving this earthly sphere in 1605. (For details of the third István, see box, page 308.) There is a pair of organs; the Neo-Gothic one has stood in the centre for over a century, while the other is just a decade old, a pipsqueak in years but well endowed with pipes (over 2,000 of them). During the Nyírbátor Music Days in August, audiences enjoy the magnificent acoustics. Outside, the free-standing and oriental-looking wooden **belfry** has a shingled roof and reaches 35m skywards; it was built in 1640, and the bigger of its brace of bronze bells weighs 600kg and is engraved with images of the four evangelists. The tower is a beautiful example of craftsmanship, but is only made of wood because non-Roman-Catholic denominations were forbidden from erecting attached stone belfries during the Counter-Reformation. Be careful on the uneven stairs if you choose to climb it.

The **Báthori kastély** (*Vár u. 1;* \ *42 410216; www.bathorivarkastely.hu; 800/400Ft;* ⊕ *daily Oct–Mar 10.00–17.00, Apr–Sep daily 10.00–18.00*) is a newly renovated 15th-century castle containing an information centre and a good exhibition about the Báthori family. The basement holds a restaurant where waiters in medieval costume serve excellent food based on traditional 15th-century recipes.

The **Minorite church** (*Károlyi Mihály u. 19;* ⊕ *Apr–Sep daily 09.00–17.00, Oct–Mar Tue–Sun 08.00–16.00*) was also built by Báthori as a Roman Catholic church in 1480, in the aftermath of his victory at the Battle of Kenyérmező in 1479. In 1587, however, the marauding Turks claimed vengeance and went to work on the place, and it was members of the Franciscan Minorite order who resurrected it in its current Baroque form during the 18th century, adding the adjacent monastery. Among several splendid altars, that known as the Krucsay Altar of the Passion (first on the left) is most worthy of attention. János Krucsay suspected his first wife, Borbála Tolvay, of playing away from the marital home; she was found guilty of adultery at the county court and subsequently executed. Just three months later Krucsay was married again, and – perhaps in an effort to appease a troubled soul and dull conscience's prick – he commissioned this carved and painted altar in the 1730s. He is buried in the crypt. Ring at the side door to the left (with the tiny painted statuette above its porch) for admission if the church is locked.

The **Báthori István Museum** (\ *42 281760;* *200/100Ft, free on Sun;* ⊕ *Apr–Sep Tue–Sun 10.00–18.00, Oct–Mar Mon–Fri 08.00–16.00*) is housed in the former monastery next door, and contains a rich collection of local artefacts dating from the Middle Ages to the middle of the 20th century. Among them are stones and glazed tiles from the fortified castle that once stood near the Calvinist church, as well as a row of 15th-century choir stalls from the same church, produced in Florence in 1511 and the largest extant example of such Renaissance carving in Europe.

Excursion from Nyírbátor Let's get primeval. About 15km to the southeast, tucked beside a tributary of the River Kraszna, is a 53ha relict bog conservation area at **Bátorliget**. The special characteristics of this area, and the consequent importance of its wildlife, were recognised in 1913; the microclimate of the spot, in a depression sheltered from warm air currents by hills and oak groves, has helped to preserve glacial flora that has died out elsewhere. The sunnier southern slopes of the surrounding dunes harbour earlier-still heat-loving species that were able to cling on here during the Ice Age. In all, there are over 1,000 types of plant (such as the globe flower, Siberian iris, turban lily, flesh-coloured orchid and a plethora of fungi) and 7,000 of fauna (including the viviparous lizard, roller, black stork, 18 snail species and many of the insect kingdom). The Museum of the Primordial Marsh (*Bátorligeti Ősláp Múzeum; corner of Bajcsy-Zsilinsky u. and Botanikus u.;* ✆ *42 269708;* ✆ *admission free;* ☉ *May–Sep Tue–Sun 10.00–16.00*) can fill you in further; the marsh itself can only be visited on a guided tour (telephone the museum in advance). There are **buses** from Nyírbátor, Nyírvasvári, Terem and Vállay.

THE RÉTKÖZ REGION Settled in a dip to the northeast of Nyíregyháza, with the Tisza above and its tributaries wrapping round below, the Rétköz (Meadow Land) used to be a particularly swampy and tough place to be. Things have eased considerably, but it doesn't clammer for your attention; you're more likely to pass through on the way to Záhony, the crossing point for the Ukrainian border. If you need to stop for any reason on the way, choose Kisvárda, 24km from the border, which is preferable to Záhony itself.

Kisvárda Kisvárda reached its zenith during the Ottoman occupation, when its castle cast an important defensive glow, but after that its status faded. These days it is best known for its distillery (Várda Drink), which produces enough low-priced alcohol to keep the country afloat… The **fortress** (northwest of Flórián tér) was originally constructed in the 15th century, before corner towers were added in the 16th. Very nearly demolished in the 19th century, the ruins survived to serve as a venue for al-fresco summer-time **theatre** productions, while the grounds contain some **baths** (*Városmajor utca*). At the town centre, Flórián tér has a **Roman Catholic church** (*Flórián tér 11*) bearing a few Gothic features (such as traceried windows) of its original 15th-century self prior to a late-Baroque overhaul.

Just to the east of the square, the **Rétköz Museum** (*Csillag u. 5;* ✆ *45 405154;* ✆ *200/100Ft;* ☉ *Apr 1–Oct 15 Tue–Sun 08.30–16.30, Oct 15–Dec 1 Mon–Fri 08.30–16.30*) is within a former synagogue built in the early 1900s. A Jewish community grew in the town from the 18th century. The descendants were to suffer desperately during World War II; those that hadn't already been sent to perish at forced labour camps in Ukraine were placed in a regional ghetto in April 1944 before being deported to Auschwitz. A stone at the entrance commemorates the 1,000 who died there. The museum itself contains several exhibitions of folk art and craft, as well as a local-history display.

If you're staying, your best bet is the central **Bástya Hotel** (*18 rooms; Krucsay Márton u. 2;* ✆ *45 421100; dbl 5,000–5,500Ft, sgl 4,000Ft, excl b/fast*). For food, the **Opál Vendéglő** (*Csillag u. 33;* ✆ *45 406007; mains avg 1,200Ft;* ☉ *daily 10.00–22.00*) is 200m from the museum and has palatable enough fare. The **bus** and **train** stations are around 2km southwest of the centre (with local bus connections). There are between five and 11 daily trains to Budapest's Nyugati and Keleti (the latter the quicker journey), and very regular services from Nyíregyháza on the line running up to the Ukrainian border. There are direct buses from Nyíregyháza (up to four), Vásárosnamény (up to 12) and Sárospatak (one on weekdays).

THE TISZAHÁT AND ERDŐHÁT REGIONS The remotest areas of Szabolcs-Szatmár-Bereg County (and of Hungary as a whole) lie in the bump at the country's most easterly point, sandwiched between the border and the Tisza's banks – the Tiszahát on the northeastern side and the Erdőhát to the south. Navigating the swamps and water channels was traditionally tricky, and while things are drier now, transport remains far from a breeze; roads are rarely in tip-top nick, and, while there are local buses, they are not always regular or convenient. The main – in the loosest sense of the word – towns are Fehérgyarmat and Vásárosnamény. This region retains an unbroken link with its past, largely untouched by invaders that had such an impact

THE RIVER TISZA

The Tisza is Hungary's second river, originating in the eastern Carpathian mountains where the 'White' and 'Black' branches come together. Running north to south through Hungary, via Tokaj in the Northern Uplands and on through the Great Plain past Szolnok and Szeged, its extravagant bends and curves slowed its flow and made it prone to regular flooding. As such, it was an ever-present force for both good and bad on the Great Plain, providing many with their livelihoods but equally – particularly after the deforestation of the Turkish period – transforming significant areas into unmanageable marshland. In the 1840s, on the initiative of Count István Széchenyi, a river regulation programme was begun, the architect Pál Vásárhelyi overseeing a straightening of the channel to allow the water to run more quickly. The result was that much boggy land became cultivable once more.

Things haven't been wholly rosy since then, however. The citizens of Szeged were victims of a fit of the river's pique in 1879 when it flooded and obliterated their city overnight (see page 353), and more recently the levels have risen dangerously again on several occasions in the late 1990s and early 2000s, possibly as a result of global warming. A disaster of a different sort hit the river in January 2000, when a cyanide leak had a devastating impact on its wildlife, poisoning the poissons and hitting tourist numbers hard. The eco disaster made itself felt even on the sporting stage. The leak allegedly emanated from a mine in Romania part-owned by Australians, and during a football match between the two countries a month later, Hungarian fans jeered their way through *Advance Australia Fair*, held up banners accusing the Socceroos of being 'fish murderers' and threw dead fish on to the pitch.

The river has largely recovered. It is increasingly popular for canoeing and kayaking tours (see pages 39–41), while many of its dead channels – those bends cut off from the main course during straightening – have become wildlife reserves, or haunts for anglers, sunbathers and watersports enthusiasts.

elsewhere; even the Turks steered clear, judging that anyone willing to live in such inhospitable terrain was welcome to it.

Vásárosnamény The gateway to the Bereg stands at the meeting point of three rivers – the Tisza, Szamos and Kraszna – and was once a trading post on the 'Salt Route' between Transylvania and Debrecen. The inhabitants make their living the agricultural way – their main produce the red Namény apple – but this is nevertheless one of the significant town centres of the region (with seven churches, six schools and a cinema). Among some decent hotels are the **Marianna Center** (*Szabadság tér 19;* ☎ *30 976 3347; sgl 5,000Ft, dbl 7,000Ft, excl b/fast*) and the **Kovács Hotel and Restaurant** (*Bereg köz 1–4;* ☎ *45 470854;* e *hotelfeher@t-online.hu; 16 rooms; sgl 8,000Ft, dbl 9,500Ft*), the latter a clean and modern place in front of the sport centre, with a recently refurbished restaurant. The main square also holds a **Tourinform** (*Szabadság tér 33;* ☎ *45 570206;* e *vasarosnameny@tourinform.hu*). In 1969 the town was connected with the villages of Vitka and Gergelyiugornya, the latter having wooden huts on piles and a willow-strewn beach beside the bridge over the Tisza, making it a popular summer resort. There are two campsites – **Diófa Camping** (*Gulácsi út 71;* ☎ *45 712298*) and **Tiszavirág Camping** (*Tisza-part;* ☎ *45 570062*).

The **Bereg Museum** (*Rákóczi u. 13;* ☎ *45 470638;* 🎫 *400/200Ft;* ⊕ *Apr–Oct Tue–Sun 08.30–16.30, Nov–Mar Mon–Fri 08.00–16.00*) has permanent exhibitions of archaeological finds, cast-iron stoves and local folk art, including traditional Bereg embroidery. The varied patterns of the rich textiles were personalised to the wearer, indicating age and marital status. There are no direct **buses** to Vásárosnamény from

Budapest (you'll need to change at Nyíregyháza); you can catch direct services from Nyíregyháza (ten), Kisvárda (up to 12), Fehérgyarmat (five most days, but just three on Sunday) and Mátészalka (up to five, but none on Saturday). The **railway station** is the terminus for the line running from Nyíregyháza (eight daily), and on the line between Záhony and Ágerdőmajor that includes Mátészalka (nine).

Tákos Ten kilometres further along Route 41 (between four and 11 buses from Vásárosnamény), Tákos has a wattle-and-daub **Calvinist church** (*Bajczy-Zsilinszky u. 25;* ⊕ *daily 08.00–19.00;* ☙ *150/100Ft*), known variously as the 'peasants' cathedral' or the 'barefoot Notre Dame'. Built in the 1760s, the white-washed exterior contrasts powerfully with folksy paintings inside, the ceiling adorned with 58 panels of floral patterns, the work of Ferenc Lándor in 1766. A wooden belfry stands in front. The village is a centre for the production of hand-made crossed embroidery, the women employing two colours in stitching images of deer, tulips and roses.

Csaroda Csaroda lies on a stream a short distance eastward on Route 41, just to the south of the Báb Lake bog-moss moor (with its trees of birch, willow and poplar). During renovation of its tiny 700-year-old Romanesque **Calvinist church** (*Kossuth u. 2*), some 14th-century frescoes were uncovered from beneath whitewash and floral patterns added during the Reformation. Among the apostles in the Byzantine frescos are the so-called 'smiling saints' of Peter and Paul, an unusual detail in church paintings. The stylised red tulips and leafy decorations (many of which remain on the northern and southern walls) were evidently done by a Calvinist village craftsman; his inscription records that they were completed in 1642 – and suggests that his talents were rather unrefined, judging by the piling together of the final letters as the available space ran out. Nevertheless, the rich – if raw – artistic effort in such a diminutive church offers a glimpse of a heritage that was all but eradicated through war and occupation. The 14m-high turreted wooden belfry was built in the 18th century. Characteristic peasant houses can be found on Kossuth utca (*nos 13 & 21*), while you'll have to travel to the Village Museum at Sóstó (see page 307) to see the Calvinist vicarage that originally stood here from the 1870s. The same buses to Tákos from Vásárosnamény run on to Csaroda.

Tarpa Storks, grey herons and waterfowl live in the pastures and marshes along the riverside at Tarpa; the villagers themselves grow fruit (used in jams and brandies) and produce wine. Tarpa is known, though, for its 19th-century **dry mill** (*Árpád utca;* ⊕ *daily Apr–Oct 10.00–18.00, Nov–Mar 10.00–15.00*), the only one of its kind in the northeast. The mill has a conical roof covered with Tokaj wooden shingles, and was once powered by horses; you can only gain access if a worker is there. The **Calvinist church** (*Kossuth Lajos u. 13*) has a 15th-century oak door with original hinges, and Gothic frescoes on the northern wall. Near by, in the former granary, is a **Museum of Local History** (*Kossuth u. 25/A*), among its exhibitions a display dedicated to Endre Bajcsy-Zsilinszky. Bajcsy-Zsilinszky was a politician during the 1930s and 1940s, and took up arms against the Germans in spring 1944; he is buried in the village. There are **buses** from Vásárosnamény (up to 11) and Fehérgyarmat (up to nine, but just two on Sunday).

Fehérgyarmat Fehérgyarmat is the main centre in the section south of the Tisza, located on Road 491 as it crosses the River Szamos. The reference to 'Gyarmat' in its name suggests that it was occupied by one of the conquering Hungarian tribes during the 10th century. It is said that Lajos Kossuth gave a recruiting speech here in 1848, and there is a memorial to this in the park. By the 19th century the town was making its money from the production of tobacco, but it smoked itself in 1872,

1895 and 1900, a series of fires that proved very bad for its health. In 1970 it was water that caused the damage during the Tisza-Szamos flood that destroyed many of the traditional peasant houses.

The 15th-century Gothic **Calvinist church** (*Kossuth u. 29*) has four pinnacles on its steeple and a bell presented by István Báthori (see page 308). The late-Baroque **Roman Catholic church** (*Kossuth u. 1*) originally dates to 1816, but was reconstructed in 1900. Telephone in advance if you'd like to visit the exhibition of **Szatmár-Bereg Nature Reserve** (*Vörösmarty u. 1;* ◖ *44 364060;* ⊜ *adult 200Ft;* ⊕ *Tue–Sun 09.00–14.00*), which teaches about the region's wildlife and includes some mammoth bones that were unearthed near by. (See also box below.)

There's precious little accommodation in town, and you're best looking elsewhere. The **railway station** is a couple of kilometres south of the centre, and is on the Mátészalka–Zajta line. There are up to ten trains to Mátészalka, where you can change for Vásárosnamény; you can also change for Nyíregyháza or Debrecen, although there are also a few daily direct services. The **bus station** is central; there are regular services to Mátészalka and Nyíregyháza, as well as to the villages of the region (including Tarpa, Túristvándi, Szatmárcseke and Tivadar). For Debrecen, you'll need to change at Mátészalka.

Túristvándi On the bank of the River Túr at the heart of Szatmári plain, Túristvándi's wooden **water mill** (*vízimalom;* ⊜ *200/100Ft;* ⊕ *daily Apr–Oct 09.00–18.00*) was originally built in 1800 (and reconstructed in the 1960s). Inside is a complex set of cogwheels and pulleys that clatter and ring and work the millstones when the sluice is opened. A small display explains how the mechanism works, and gives a bit of history. If there's nobody there, contact Madics Illés (*Zrínyi út 8;* ◖ *44 721073*). A memorial tablet on the corner house in the village, with its belltower, records that the writer Zsigmond Móricz spent childhood days here with his blacksmith uncle in 1885–87.

Vízimalom Camping (*Malom u. 3;* ◖ *42 437053; tent/caravan 1,000/2,000Ft, plus 1,000Ft/pp; panzió room 10,000Ft;* ⊕ *all yr*) is a small grassy site in a charming spot

WILDLIFE OF THE SZATMÁR-BEREG NATURE RESERVE

The Szatmár-Bereg Nature Reserve covers 22,246ha in the region of the Tisza, Szamos and Túr rivers, and features the volcanic peaks of Kaszonyi-hegy near Barabás and Tarpa Nagy-hegy, as well as former streams, oxbows and sediment-filled river beds. Fish species of the rivers include Danube trout, grayling, Tisza lamprey, gudgeon and loach, while several strictly protected peat bogs (such as those at the Nyíres, Báb, Zsig and Bence lakes) provide the habitat for marsh cinquefoil, cranberry, common sundew, cottongrass and eared willow. Half of the reserve has tree cover, comprising willow-poplar and ash-elm-oak gallery forests on the floodplain and hornbeam-oak forests further from the water.

Among the mammals of the region are the wild cat, otter, numerous bat species and a stable population of red deer. Reptiles are represented by the common viper and viviparous lizard, while birds of prey include the goshawk, buzzard, sparrow hawk and harrier (and more unusually the honey buzzard, black kite and saker falcon). The black stork lives in the mature forest, the kingfisher and bee eater dart among the river and sand banks, and there are around 100 species of passerines (most interestingly the thrush nightingale). Other rare birds are the corn bunting and the country's largest number of corncrake (over 100 pairs), breeding in freshly mown grasslands and wet meadows. For further information, visit the exhibition centre in Fehérgyarmat (see above).

Most people associate *szatmári szilva* (the 'Szatmár plum') with the fiery fruit brandy (*pálinka*) that is unique to Hungary. However, the fruit itself (and the jam that's made from it in this region) also enjoys a considerable reputation. The Szatmár plum is a wild and savoury fruit. Plum jam is produced here using a process of gentle reduction (the plums are heated for 12 hours in copper cauldrons until thick enough to stick to a spoon), so the jam is naturally conserved without the need for artificial preservatives.

The region boasts four main centres of 'plumming'. Every summer, one of the key events of the Szatmár Festival is held in **Szatmárcseke**: the 24-hour plum-jam cooking competition! The nearby settlement of **Penyige** has its own variety of plum – the so-called '*penyigei*' or '*dunno*' plum; the village is also home to Hungary's first Plum and Jam Museum (*Lekvárium; Penyige, Kossuth út 31;* ☎ *44 709004;* ⊕ *Jun–Aug Tue–Sun 09.00–17.00*), which contains displays of traditional fruit-processing tools. The plum also looms large in the life of **Tarpa**, on the other bank of the River Tisza, while your fourth stop on any plummy tour should be **Panyola** and its fruit distillery (*Szilvórium, Mezővég út 31;* ☎ *30 645 3319;* e *info@panyolai.hu;* ⊕ *by prior arrangement*). This *pálinka* plant is open to the public, so you can learn about the brandy-making process.

If you follow the 'Plum Route', you'll get a good flavour of the values and traditions of Szatmár-Bereg County – and the fruity goings-on in this part of Hungary. For more information, visit www.szilvaut.hu.

on the river bank near the mill. There's a no-frills panzió and a restaurant (*mains 750–2,200Ft, avg 1,500Ft;* ⊕ *daily 09.00–21.00 in summer*), and little else to do beyond swim, canoe (*1,000Ft*), float on an inflatable ring and enjoy the surroundings. There are regular **buses** from Fehérgyarmat and Turistvándi; the bus stop is 100m from the mill.

Szatmárcseke Szatmárcseke is a plummy place (see box above), growing the fruit that is used for the fiery national brandy (*pálinka*); it is said that the drink can raise the dead. This claim is rather undermined by the village's **cemetery** (*Tancsics Mihály u.*), its pride and joy. Its wooden gravemarkers are quite unique, shaped like vertical rowing boats; they have earned the site protected status since 1973. Various theories have been mooted as to the significance of the shape. Some say it harks back to a Finno-Ugric belief in death as a journey, others that it refers more simply to the time centuries ago when the cemetery was on a peninsula and bodies had to be rowed across the water. You may notice letters carved on the wood; 'ABFRA' stands for 'under the hope of happy resurrection' and 'BP' for 'peace to his ashes'. Breaking the trend in the centre of the plot is a tomb in white stone, that of Ferenc Kölcsey – poet, language reformer and the man who penned the Hungarian national anthem in 1823. Kölcsey lived in the village for over 20 years; the **cultural centre** (*Kölcsey u. 31*) stands on the site that once held his house, and has a room dedicated to him. The **Kölcsey Ferenc Memorial House** (*Kölcsey u. 46;* ☎ *70 3778570;* & *200/100Ft; usually* ⊕ *daily 09.00–16.00, but telephone ahead*) has another exhibition about the poet, containing books, pictures and photos. Opposite the entrance to the cemetery is a **world map** with a plaque showing the number of Hungarians living abroad.

Szatmár Fogadó (*Petőfi u. 7;* ☎ *20 468 7882; 12 rooms; dbl 2,500Ft*), opposite the Calvinist Church, offers simple rooms with bathrooms and a restaurant serving regional specialities.

The **bus** stop is opposite the post office, just off the main street. There are services to Féhérgyarmat (up to nine), Kömörő (nine), Turistvándi (nine) and Mateszalka (with a change at Fehérgyarmat).

Csenger On the border with Romania, Csenger has a Gothic 14th-century **Calvinist church** (*Hősök tere*) whose polygonal tower is topped with a parapet and shingled spire. The coffered ceiling was painted in the mid 18th century. Calvinist Protestantism was adopted at a synod convened in the church in 1576. A second, modern church – together with several other buildings in the village – are the work of renowned architect Imre Makovecz. The **Local History Museum** (*Hősök tere 3; & entry free; ⊕ Tue–Sat 09.00–17.00, Sun 10.00–17.00*) has archaeological artefacts and pieces of folk art, as well as a reconstruction of a room in a peasant home.

The **Hotel Schuster** (*Ady Endre u. 12;* ✆ *44 520146; 14 rooms; sgl 10,900Ft, dbl 14,400Ft, apt 18,400Ft*) is a charming hotel, housed in a 200-year-old building set in pretty grounds and with well-furnished rooms. There are **buses** between Csenger and Fehérgyarmat (up to six) and Mátészalka (16); the **railway station** is on the line from Mátészalka (eight daily). There is a road border crossing into Romania at Csengersima, a short distance to the north.

7

Southern Great Plain

(For background to the whole Great Plain, see pages 275–6.)

The Southern Plain (Dél-Alföld), covering the counties of Bács-Kiskun, Békés and Csongrád, is more cultivated than the north, with large areas of farmland and a greater number of towns. In the 19th century, acacias, poplars, fruit trees and vines were planted to bind the barren earth; the river courses were straightened in an effort to reclaim land saturated by floodwater, and the resulting dead channels – those bends cut off during the process – now form fishing lakes, reserves and bathing spots. There is still *puszta* to be found – notably at Bugac – and wildlife must-sees include the great bustard reserve at Dévaványa and Lake Fehér, a significant stop-over site for migrating birds.

The south was hit hard during the Ottoman occupation; a lucky few like Kecskemét and Szeged came under the direct administration and protection of the sultan, but the regional architecture generally dates from the period afterwards. There is also a multi-ethnic feel, a result of Slovak, Serbian, Romanian and German immigrants who repopulated (and rebuilt) certain towns and villages in the 18th century. Both Kecskemét and Szeged are sophisticated and attractive towns, and others like Hódmezővásárhely and Gyula are equally deserving of attention. Horse-riding is widely offered in centres like Lajosmizse, and there are spas galore to the east of the Tisza, fed by thermal water discovered during surveys for oil in the mid 20th century. The memorial park at Ópusztaszer, the supposed meeting place for the Magyar chieftains after the 9th-century land taking, has become one of the most-visited attractions in the country; Árpád Feszty's breathtaking cyclorama alone makes the admission fee money worth spending. In addition, the region is the country's warmest, enjoying over 2,000 hours of sunshine a year.

KECSKEMÉT

Equidistant from the Danube and the Tisza, Kecskemét is the principal town of Bács-Kiskun County. *Kecske* means 'goat' in Hungarian, and it is said this derives from the peculiar practice of the 13th-century bishop in presenting an animal to each convert to Christianity. History does not record how successful he was in appealing to them with the Father, the Son and a holy goat … Youthful in feel, architecturally adventurous in look, it isn't hard to see what people like about Kecskemét. Once you've accustomed yourself to what at first feels a confusing centre – a merging cluster of squares – it's worth putting aside a couple of days rather than hours to gape at some beautiful buildings, peruse a good selection of museums, shop from a decent range of boutiques and eat in some above-average restaurants. Kecskemét will keep you busy.

Kecskemét was a prosperous market town by the 15th century, and its layout – surrounded by a belt of farmsteads that give way to gardens and orchards – is typical of such settlements on the Great Plain. It suffered less than most during the Ottoman occupation, governed as it was directly by the sultan and enjoying his

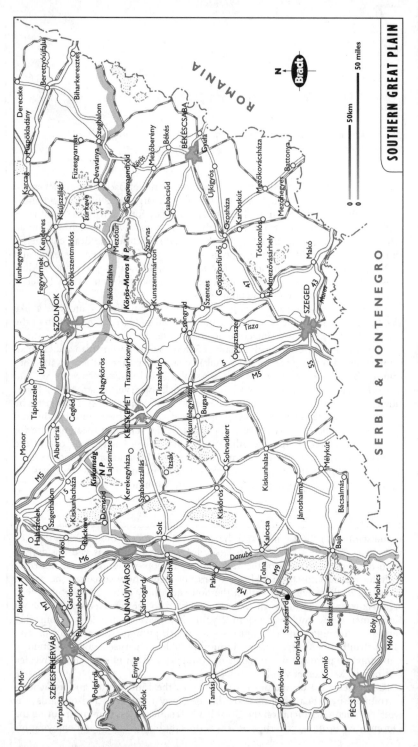

SOUTHERN GREAT PLAIN

0   50km
0   50 miles

protection from the Turkish officers that intimidated and exploited the unfortunate towns that fell under their administration. Turning in earnest to viniculture in the 19th century, the citizens were fortunate once more when the rampant phylloxera louse decided it disliked the area's sandy soil. The luck ran out in 1911 when an earthquake caused severe damage. 'Twas but a temporary set back; today the town rivals Szeged and Debrecen as the region's major educational and cultural player, and its apricot orchards yield renowned, throaty bottles of brandy (*barackpálinka*).

GETTING THERE, AWAY AND AROUND The composer Zoltán Kodály was born in the building now housing the **railway station** (*Kodály Zoltán tér 7*), just behind József Katona Park to the northwest. From the station it is a 500m walk through the park (where you should keep an eye out for the busts of some of the town's famous citizens) and along Nagykőrösi utca to the centre. Kecskemét is on the Szeged line; there are trains from Budapest Nyugati (regular) and Szeged (up to 13), as well as Kikunfélegyháza and Nagykőrös. There are direct trains to Szolnok (seven), although it's better to take the indirect route with a change at Cegléd – the direct train stops at all stations and takes two hours (as opposed to the one-hour indirect journey). Change at Cegléd for services to Debrecen too. In addition to the main station, the narrow-gauge Kecskemét KK station has two branches, one going to Kiskőrös and the other Kiskunmajsa. The latter passes through Bugac felső, and can thus be taken to get to Bugac and the Kiskunság National Park (see page 327); there are three a day, but it is a two-hour journey and there remains a 3km walk from Bugac felső to Bugac itself. (As such, you are probably better to take the bus.) Kecskemét KK is 1km southwest of the centre on Halasi út (which joins Batthyány utca); you can catch bus 2 there from the local bus station.

The **bus station** is near the train station, at the northern end of József Katona Park. There are services to a good number of towns around the country, including Budapest Népliget (regular), Szolnok (eight), Szeged (ten), Debrecen (seven, although not direct) and Pécs (two). The station for **local buses** is on Széchenyi tér, opposite the Otthon Cinema. If you need a **taxi**, try Hírös (↘ *76 484848*) or Zebra (↘ *76 444444*).

INFORMATION AND OTHER PRACTICALITIES

🅱 Bugac Tours See page 327.

🅴 EuroNet Internet Café Beniczky u. 1; ↘ 76 516221. There's no coffee at this café, but you can surf the net for 400Ft/hr. ☺ *Mon–Sat 10.00–22.00, Sun 16.00–22.00.*

🅱 Ibusz Korona u. 2; ↘ 76 486955; e kecskemet@ibusz.hu. Located next to the bus station, in the Malom shopping centre behind Hotel Aranyhomok. Book private accommodation, tours & exchange travellers' cheques & currency. ☺ *Mon–Sat 10.00–19.00, Sun 10.00–14.00.*

🅸 Listings magazine *Kecskeméti Est*

🏛 Market Piac tér. North of the centre at the point where Budai utca & Erdosi Imre u. meet. Sells fresh produce, flowers & household goods.

☺ *Sep–Apr Tue–Fri 06.00–14.00, Sat 06.00–13.00, Sun 06.00–11.00, May–Aug Tue–Fri 05.30–14.00, Sat 05.30–13.00, Sun 05.30–11.00.*

🅴 Piramis Internet Café Csányi u. 1–3; ↘ 76 418134. Next to the Hotel Udvarház, this cybercafé offers internet access for 480Ft/hr. ☺ *Mon–Fri 10.00–20.00, Sat–Sun 13.00–20.00.*

🅸 Tourinform Kossuth tér 1; ↘ 76 481065; e kecskemet@tourinform.hu. This office, in the northern corner of the town hall, can give details of cheap student digs & private accommodation. It also arranges bike hire. ☺ *Jun–Aug Mon–Fri 08.00–17.00, Sat 08.00–18.00 (rest of yr 09.00–13.00).*

WHERE TO STAY

⛺ Autós Camping Csabay Géza körút 5; ↘ 76 329398. This campsite is adjacent to the water park, & therefore no stranger to excited squeals & splashes. As well as tent & caravan space, there are

25 bungalows (for 4) with showers. Bungalow 5,800Ft, tent/caravan 550/1,600Ft (15% discount with student card); ☺ Apr 15–Oct 15.

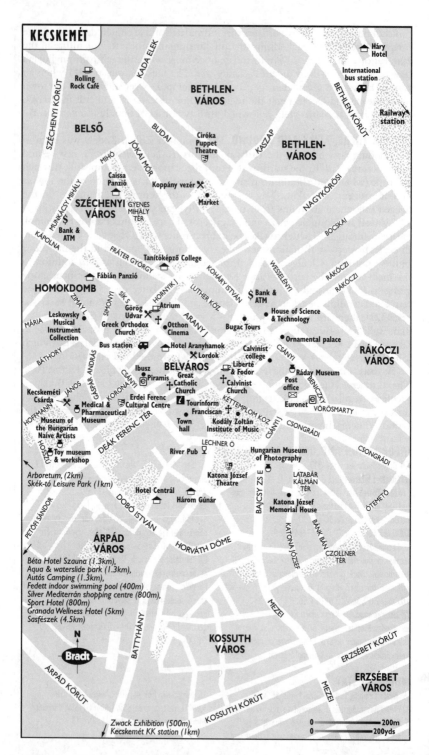

KECSKEMÉT

Háry Hotel

International bus station

Railway station

Rolling Rock Café

KADA ELEK

SZÉCHENYI KÖRÚT

BETHLEN-VÁROS

BELSŐ

BUDAI

Ciróka Puppet Theatre

BETHLEN-VÁROS

BETHLEN KÖRÚT

JÓKAI MÓR

MIHÓ

Caissa Panzió

Koppány vezér

NAGYKÖRÖSI

SZÉCHENYI VÁROS

GYENES MIHÁLY TÉR

Market

KASZAP

MUNKÁCSY MIHÁLY

Bank & ATM

BOCSKAI

KÁPOLNA

FRÁTER GYÖRGY

Tanítóképző College

WESSELÉNYI

RÁKÓCZI

Fábián Panzió

KOHÁRY ISTVÁN

Bank & ATM

RÁKÓCZI

HOMOKDOMB

ZIMAY L.

SIMONYI

SÍK S.

HORNYIK I.

LUTHER KÖZ

ARANY J.

House of Science & Technology

MÁRIA

Leskowsky Musical Instrument Collection

Görög Udvar

Atrium

Bugac Tours

Ornamental palace

RÁKÓCZI VÁROS

Greek Orthodox Church

Otthon Cinema

BÁTHORY

GÁSPÁR ANDRÁS

JÁNOS

Bus station

Hotel Aranyhamok

Lordok

CSÁNYI

Calvinist college

HOFFMANN

KORONA

CSÁNYI

Ibusz

Piramis

BELVÁROS

Great Catholic Church

Liberté & Fodor

Calvinist Church

Ráday Museum

BENICZKY

Kecskeméti Csárda

Medical & Pharmaceutical Museum

Erdei Ferenc Cultural Centre

Tourinform

Franciscan

Post office

Euronet

VÖRÖSMARTY

NÉGSŐ

Museum of the Hungarian Naïve Artists

DEÁK FERENC TÉR

KÉTTEMPLOM KÖZ

Town hall

Kodály Zoltán Institute of Music

CSÁNYI

CSONGRÁDI

Toy museum & workshop

River Pub

LECHNER Ö

Hungarian Museum of Photography

CSONGRÁDI

Arboretum, (2km)
Skék-tó Leisure Park (1km)

Katona József Theatre

LATABÁR KÁLMÁN TÉR

ÖTEMETŐ

PETŐFI SÁNDOR

Hotel Centrál

Három Gúnár

DOBÓ ISTVÁN

BAJCSY ZS E

Katona József Memorial House

ÁRPÁD VÁROS

HORVÁTH DÖME

Béta Hotel Szauna (1.3km),
Aqua & waterslide park (1.3km),
Autós Camping (1.3km),
Fedett indoor swimming pool (400m),
Silver Mediterrán shopping centre (800m),
Sport Hotel (800m)
Granada Wellness Hotel (5km)
Sasfészek (4.5km)

KATONA JÓZSEF

BÁN BÁN

CZOLLNER TÉR

BATTHYÁNY

MEZEI

N

Bradt

KOSSUTH VÁROS

ERZSÉBET KÖRÚT

ERZSÉBET VÁROS

ÁRPÁD KÖRÚT

MEZEI

Zwack Exhibition (500m),
Kecskemét KK station (1km)

KOSSUTH KÖRÚT

0 ————— 200m
0 ————— 200yds

🛏 **Caissa Panzió** (10 rooms) Gyenes Mihály tér 18;
📞 76 481685; www.caissachessbooks.com. Standing
among flats on a quiet square shrouded by trees,
Caissa has rooms that vary in size & facilities (with
or without bathroom & TV), some of which are very
cheap & therefore popular with students (who
choose them rather than dorms). There are regular
chess tournaments held here. *Sgl 4,800–7,900Ft, dbl
5,900–9,800Ft.*

🛏 **Fábián Panzió** (10 rooms) Kápolna u. 14; 📞 76
477677; www.panziofabian.hu. A short walk from
Széchenyi tér, this family-run guesthouse is blessed
with good looks, a central garden & an owner as
keen as mustard. It's been here for 15 years, but
has clearly been loved & cared for. WiFi available.
Well recommended. *Sgl 9,800 Ft, dbl 11,800 Ft.*

🛏 **Granada Konferencia Wellness & Sport Hotel**
(70 rooms) Harmónia u. 12; 📞 76 503130;
www.granada-konferencia.eu. This newish 3-star hotel
is located slightly outside the centre, but offers some
fitness & wellness facilities in compensation. *Sgl
14,900Ft, dbl 17,500Ft, apt 21,900–24,900Ft (for
1), 25,900–28,900Ft (for 2).*

🛏 **Hotel Aranyhomok** (108 rooms) Kossuth tér 3:
📞 76 503730; www.hotelaranyhomok.hu. It's unpretty
from the outside, but it's what's inside that counts;
the rooms are modern, & there's a fitness centre. It's
worth paying the extra to bag a room with a
balcony overlooking the square. *Sgl 9,500–26,200Ft,
dbl 14,200–30,500Ft, suite 28,200–35,700Ft
(wellness facilities included).*

🛏 **Hotel Udvarház** (17 rooms) Csányi u. 1–3; 📞 76
413912; www.hoteluh.hu. In the Piramis Udvarház,
next to the Great Catholic Church. Simple but well
located. *Sgl €47, dbl €55.*

🛏 **Háry Hotel** (21 rooms) Kodály Zoltán tér 9;
📞 76 480400; e hotel@hary.hu; www.hary.hu.
Recently refurbished, the Háry — named after a
Falstaffian soldier of the Napoleonic Wars
immortalised in a musical piece by Kodály in 1927
— has rooms that are on the 'cosy' side for 2, but
are airy nevertheless. The location is handy for the
bus station, but the surroundings are correspondingly
drab. Sauna & fitness room. *Sgl €50, dbl €60, trpl
€70 (excl tourist tax).*

🛏 **Hotel Talizmán** (19 rooms) Kápolna u. 2; 📞 76
504856; e talhot@t-online.hu;
www.hotels.hu/talizmanhotel. On the same road as
the Fábián, the Talizmán lacks for character by
comparison, but its whitewashed rooms are
contemporary & have air-con. *Dbl 13,600Ft, trpl
16,500 Ft, family 20,400Ft.*

🛏 **Sport Hotel** (55 rooms) Izsáki út 15; 📞 76
496822; www.shk.hu. Around 1km southwest of the
centre (on Road 52), the Sport has a swimming pool
& fitness room, & adequate rooms lacking in homely
touches (those with a double bed slightly better).
Well situated for the leisure park & arboretum. *Sgl
9,500Ft, dbl 12,990–13,990Ft.*

🛏 **Tanítóképző Főiskola Kollégiuma** (100 rooms)
Piaristák tere 4; 📞 76 486977. Central college
offering accommodation in summer (Jul–Aug). *Rooms
1,600Ft/pp.*

✕ WHERE TO EAT AND DRINK

🍽 **Atrium Coffee House** Hornyik János körút 2;
📞 76 486793. Busy & intimate backstreet bar with
outdoor terrace. ⊕ Mon–Thu 08.00–22.00, Fri–Sat
08.00–23.00.

🍽 **Fodor** Szabadság tér 2; 📞 76 496545. Sit in
the pink parlour or on the outdoor terrace, & enjoy
excellent ice cream & cake. There is a second branch
at Nagykőrösi u. 15, although the views of the main
road make it less enticing. ⊕ 09.00–18.30 daily.

✕ **Görög Udvar** Széchenyi tér 9; 📞 76 492513;
www.gorogudvar.hu. The name & music might suggest
otherwise, but there are as many Hungarian as
Greek dishes on the menu here. The outdoor
courtyard, with its hanging baskets, is the place to
dine; it's atmospheric, & the food is good. *Mains avg
2,000Ft;* ⊕ 11.00–23.00 daily.

✕ **Három Gúnár Fogadó** Batthyány u. 1–7;
📞 76 483611; www.hotelharomgunar.hu. A
restaurant, hotel & conference complex. It's far from

beautiful, but serviceable enough for a night or two.
Sgl 10,500Ft, dbl 13,800–14,500Ft, trpl 21,100Ft.

✕ **Kecskeméti Csárda** Kölcsey u. 7; 📞 76 488686.
Around the corner from the Pharmacy Museum, the
Kecskeméti Csárda is the town's top restaurant. The
menu features generously ladled Hungarian food with
Mediterranean specials, & dishes like venison steak
with roasted apple & walnut sauce are worth the
extra few forints. The peasant-style décor is
nevertheless sophisticated — rustic chic — & the al-
fresco area is beautiful on a balmy night. The
language on the English menu could do with some
polishing — we avoided the 'fish food' option, &
wished the 'obsessed goose liver' would lighten up.
Mains avg 2,000Ft; ⊕ daily 12.00–23.00.

✕ **Kisbugaci Csárda** Munkácsy u. 10. Unfussy &
understated restaurant serving Hungarian grub. *Set
menus 1,900–2,300Ft; mains avg 1,500Ft;*
⊕ Mon–Sat 12.00–22.00, Sun 12.00–15.00.

✕ **Koppány Vezér** Erdősi Imre u. 6; ✆ 76 480779. Medieval-theme restaurant serving 'feasts' for up to 10. The menu is inevitably meat-heavy. Located next to the market. *Feasts 3,200–24,600Ft; mains avg 2,400Ft;* ⊕ *12.00–23.00 daily.*

✕ **Liberté** Szabadság tér 2; ✆ 76 509 175 or 30 820 3362. A tasteful jewel of a place for a coffee, a beer or a meal, with a lengthy terrace overlooking Szabadság tér. Hungarian cuisine with a few beef steaks thrown into the line-up. Connected to California Coffee Company chain. *Mains avg 2,500Ft;* ⊕ *daily 11.00–22.00.*

⌷ **Lordok Café** Szabadság tér. Trendy bar & fast-food restaurant on the main square. Perfect place for an early breakfast or a beer at the end of the day. ⊕ *Mon–Sun 06.00–22.00.*

♀ **River Pub** Lestár tér 1; ✆ 76 415405. A pubby pub serving Kilkenny & Guinness & with a mural of a paddle steamer dominating the back wall. International food is served in hearty platefuls, & there's also a wide winelist. *Mains avg 1,900Ft;* ⊕ *Mon–Sat 11.00–23.00.*

✕ **Sasfészek Étterem** Alsócsalános u. 3; ✆ 76 507 563; www.sasfeszek.hu. Its been open since 1982, & is a local favourite (despite being a little out along Izsáki út, near the M5 motorway). There's a decent summer terrace; the cuisine is primarily Hungarian, although they've added some good steaks to menu too. *Mains avg 1,700Ft;* ⊕ *daily 11.00–24.00.*

⌷ **Teátrum** Kéttemplom köz. A cosy café with foreign-language magazines & country-style cookies. Opposite the Kodály Institute. ⊕ *Mon–Sun 09.00–22.00.*

ENTERTAINMENT AND NIGHTLIFE A mischievous smile plays about the lips of the 19th-century Eclectic **Katona József Theatre** (*Katona József tér 5;* ✆ *76 483283; www.katonaj.hu*), with cherubs cavorting above its entrance and tooting on horns. Good humour was in short supply when the contract to design the theatre – part of the millennial celebrations – was awarded to foreign (Viennese) architects Fellner and Helmer (also responsible for Budapest's Vígszínház, and the resemblance is clear). The **ticket office** (✆ *76 501174;* e *jegyiroda@ katonaj.hu;* ⊕ *Tue–Fri 10.00–13.00, 15.00–19.00, Sat 10.00–14.00*) can tell you what's on. The Holy Trinity Monument outside was erected in 1742 by survivors of the plague, which had claimed 5,000 lives two years before.

Ciróka Puppet Theatre (*Bábszínház; Budai u. 15;* ✆ *76 482217; www.ciroka.hu*) stages performances for kids of kindergarten age and upwards; shows run most days and usually start at 10.00–10.30 and 14.00 – although this can vary, so check beforehand at the ticket office (⊕ *Mon–Fri 09.30–15.00 & 1hr before performance at weekends*). **Otthon Cinema** (*Kossuth tér 4;* ✆ *76 490640; www.otthon-mozi.hu*) is the only traditional film house in town, open for 60 years and decorated with folk motifs. It screens children's, European and Hungarian classic movies, as well as Hollywood blockbusters. The **Erdei Ferenc Cultural Centre** (*Deák Ferenc tér 1;* ✆ *76 503880;* e *efmk@t-online.hu;* ⊕ *Mon–Sat 11.00–13.30, 16.00–19.00*) hosts temporary exhibitions and a variety of cultural programmes, and is the best place to go for information on other events in town.

A couple of kilometres southwest of the centre, the buzzing **Silver Mediterrán Club** (*Izsáki út 2;* ✆ *06 20 919 0392; www.clubsilver.hu;* ☒ *admission 700/1,000Ft before/after 24.00, but may vary;* ⊕ *Sat 22.00–05.00 & occasional Fri*) is in a shopping mall. Based over two levels, you can dance on the first and chill out on the second. Down an alley, **Xtreme Music Club** (*Kisfaludy u. 4;* ✆ *76 500926;* ⊕ *Wed, Fri–Sat 10.00–04.00*) plays rock, dance or disco, depending on the day of the week. Wednesday is student night, and Saturday usually rock night (when there may be an admission charge).

WHAT TO SEE AND DO

Kossuth tér and around If you can unravel the tangle of squares, then Kossuth tér is just about the centremost of them; bustling and spacious, its monuments include a statue of Kossuth and a cone-shaped distance marker, a popular slippery playground with the town's kiddies.

In 1891, a competition was opened to design the **town hall** (*Kossuth tér 1*), with entrants asked to follow the theme of the town's motto – 'Neither height nor depth deter me'. Ödön Lechner and Gyula Pártos were the victors, and put together the salmon-pink building with its stained glass and majolica roof of yellow diamonds; the result was one of Lechner's early attempts at a distinctive national style, an influential masterpiece of Hungarian Art Nouveau (Secessionism). It is adorned with fire-glazed tiles of floral motifs, and contains a ceremonial hall bearing frescoes by Bertalan Székely (1897) in the pseudo-historical romantic style of the period and a bronze chandelier weighing in at a mammoth 1,200kg. (*To visit the hall,* ✆ 76 483683 *in advance, & between 10.00 & 11.30;* 🎫 *300/150Ft, guide 700Ft.*) The glockenspiel above the entrance plays snatches of music on the hour – including Kodály and Erkel (*12.00*), Handel, Beethoven and Mozart (*18.00*) and Hungarian folk songs (*20.00*). A broken block of stone in one of the flower beds out front marks the spot where playwright József Katona (see page 324) collapsed and died of a heart attack in 1830 at the age of just 39.

Adjacent to the town hall, the Piarist Gáspár Oszwald's late-Baroque **Great Catholic Church** (*Nagytemplom; Kossuth tér 2;* ⊕ *May–Sep Tue–Fri 09.00–12.00, 15.00–18.00, Oct–Apr Tue–Fri 09.00–12.00*) nudges 75m – the largest on the Great Plain – and was built 1774–1806. Somehow the very vastness of its interior presses the fragility of the human condition upon you, a feeling reinforced when looking down from the frightening height of the gallery running around the clock tower. Niches above the entrance hold statues of saints István and László; the dongs of the church's bell used to call the workers in from the fields at lunchtime.

At the square's eastern side, the **Franciscan church** (*Szent Miklós ferences templom; Kossuth tér 3*) is the town's oldest building, originally constructed in the 14th century before later Gothic and Baroque reconstruction. The modern frescoes inside – with a hieroglyphic feel to them – are striking, although they may not appeal to traditionalists. The **Kodály Zoltán Pedagogical Institute of Music** (*Zenepedagógiai Intézet;* ✆ *76 481518;* 🎫 *120/60Ft;* ⊕ *daily 10.00–18.00*) occupies the former early-18th-century monastery next door. The institute – whose staff follow Kodály's revolutionary teaching method – has a small museum devoted to the man himself. Kodály was born in Kecskemét in 1882; he was a composer, but is best remembered for his theory that music skills should be acquired through singing and the programme he devised based upon Hungarian folk songs.

Szabadság tér To the northeastern side of its bigger brother, Szabadság tér has trees and benches to enjoy their shade. The **Calvinist church** (*Szabadság tér 7*) was completed in 1684, the only stone church to be built during the era of Turkish rule. While religious tolerance – as evidenced by the churches of various denominations in close proximity – was a feature of the town, this church actually replaced a wooden version burnt by Catholics in 1678 during a spell of Counter-Reformatory pique. The Art-Nouveau **Calvinist college** (*Szabadság tér 7*), with its terracotta roof and Transylvanian motifs, was built in 1912 and holds the parish library and the **Ráday Museum** (✆ *76 486226;* 🎫 *400/200Ft;* ⊕ *Tue–Sun 10.00–18.00*). The latter has displays of Calvinist religious art from the region, as well as a translation of the New Testament by János Erdősi Sylvester in 1541 – the first work printed wholly in Hungarian. The promulgation of vernacular Christianity was a prime reason for the rise in Calvinism's popularity (in contrast to the Latin used by the Catholic clergy), and it became entrenched in many areas of the Great Plain during the 16th century.

The **Ornamental Palace** (*Cifrapalota; Rákóczi út 1*), to the college's right, houses the town gallery (✆ *76 480776;* 🎫 *500/250Ft;* ⊕ *Tue–Sun 10.00–17.00*), with works by László Mednyánszky (1852–1919), Auschwitz-victim István Farkas (1887–1944) and Menyhért Tóth (1904–80). The building itself, though, is the outstanding work of art; constructed in 1902 by Géza Márkus – originally as a town house with ground-floor shops – its façade has floral decoration and its roof of green, orange and blue supports seven glazed chimneys. The Peacock Hall boasts several of the favoured motifs of the Hungarian Art Nouveau inspired by Lechner – flowers, lianas and peacocks.

Across Rákóczi út, the **House of Science and Technology** (*Tudomány & Technika-háza; Rákóczi út 2;* \ *76 487611; & free admission;* ⊕ *Mon–Fri 08.00–16.00*) occupies the Moorish-Romantic former synagogue (built 1864–71), and is used as a conference centre. Winding stairs lead to a gallery of plaster-cast copies of Michelangelo sculptures; some of these look forlorn and faintly ridiculous in such a limited space, but the resplendent stained-glass windows are beautiful.

Museums and galleries The **Hungarian Museum of Photography** (*Magyar Fotográfiai Múzeum; Katona József tér 12;* \ *76 483221; www.fotomuzeum.hu; & 400/200Ft;* ⊕ *Wed–Sun 10.00–17.00*) has temporary exhibitions of work by Hungarian photographers old and new, as well as a library, shop and collection of technological bits and bobs. The 18th-century building has had a varied existence, serving over the years as a horse-changing station, restaurant, dance club and Orthodox synagogue.

The **Katona József Memorial House** (*Katona József u. 5;* \ *76 328420; & 150/100Ft;* ⊕ *Jan 20–Dec 20 Tue–Sat 10.00–14.00*) pays tribute to one of the town's past leading lights. Katona wrote the classic drama *Bánk Bán* (on which Ferenc Erkel based his opera), which features the murder of a German-born queen by a servant, and addresses the inherent tension between an individual's duty to his own conscience and that due to a foreign-controlled government. Katona's talent was not properly recognised prior to his premature death in 1830 (see page 323), and the drama was not published until after it.

To the west of Deák Ferenc tér, the **Museum of the Hungarian Naive Artists** (*Gáspár András u. 11;* \ *76 324 767;* e *naivmuzeum.kecskemet@museum.hu; & 210/160Ft;* ⊕ *Mar–Oct Tue–Sun 10.00–17.00*) is inside an 18th-century nobleman's mansion. The 'naive' style originated in the early 20th century, practised by artisans with no formal artistic training who anchored their work in the themes of rural peasant life – the world of markets, harvest festivals and local celebrations. Among the leading early artists were Rezső Mokry-Mészáros and the 'peasant painter' Péter Benedek, and the pieces are raw, instinctive and refreshingly clumsy.

The adjacent **Toy Museum and Workshop** (*Szórakaténusz Játékmúzeum & Műhely; Gáspár András u. 11;* \ *76 481469; www.szorakatenusz.hu; & 450/220Ft;* ⊕ *museum Mar–Oct Tue–Sun 10.00–12.30, 13.00–17.00, Nov–Feb Tue–Sun 10.00–12.30, 13.00–16.00, workshop Wed & Sat 10.00–12.00, 14.00–17.00, Sun 10.00–12.00*) is a child's paradise, with dolls, puppets, carved wooden wagons and a jigsaw puzzle made in the 1760s. The workshop organises programmes where children can have a go at making wooden toys.

Just 100m away, the **Medical and Pharmaceutical History Museum** (*Orvos & Gyógyszerészettörténeti Múzeum; Kölcsey u. 3;* \ *76 329964; & 200/100Ft;* ⊕ *May 15–Oct 31 Tue–Sun 10.00–14.00*) has medical objects used in Bács-Kiskun county over the past 200 years. Follow Petőfi Sándor utca a block beyond the ring road and turn right to reach the **Museum of Hungarian Popular Arts and Crafts** (*A Magyar Népi Iparművészeti Múzeum; Serfőző u. 19;* \ *76 327203; & 400/200Ft;* ⊕ *Jan 6–Dec 19 Tue–Sat 10.00–17.00*), which has a daunting collection of wood carvings, embroidery, pottery, basketwork and more in a 200-year-old former brewhouse.

The **Leskowsky Musical Instrument Collection** (*Zimay László u. 6/A;* ✆ 76 486616; 🎫 *500/300Ft; visits by prior registration only*) has a private collection of 1,500 instruments from all over the globe, which the owner will play for you.

The **Zwack Fruit Brandy Distillery and Exhibition** (*Gyümölcspálinka-főzde & Kiállítás; Matkói út 2;* ✆ 76 487711; 🎫 *adult 1,500Ft; visit on Fri at 13.00 or groups on weekdays by prior registration*) is a temple for lovers of fruit brandy, for which Kecskemét is renowned. The English King Edward VIII remarked that 'when mixed with sparkling water, this brandy is better than whisky; with tea, it is better than rum'. Zwack Unicum is the market leader, and you can look around the plant, learn a little about the Zwack family, and have a taste. You'll find it just over 1km to the south of the centre; follow Batthyány utca into Halasa út, and turn left immediately after the rail track.

Other activities There are several places to take a dip to the west of the centre. The **Szék-tó Leisure Park** (*Szabadisopark;* 🎫 *entrance to lake 50Ft, fishing 990/590Ft;* ⊕ *in summer Mon–Fri 06.00–21.00, Sat–Sun 05.00-21.00, variable hours other seasons*), just beyond Csabay Géza körút, comprises a large artificial lake and swimming pools. The relatively new **Aqua and Waterslide Park** (*Élményfürdő & Csúszdapark; Csabay Géza körút 2;* ✆ 76 417 407, 76 481724; *www.csuszdapark.hu;* 🎫 *1,700/1,400Ft, reduced cost after 15.00 mon–fri, waterslide tickets 600–850Ft;* ⊕ *May–Aug/Sep 09.00–19.00 daily*) has pools, slides, whirlpools and wave machines. (Local buses 1, 11 and 22 run out here from Széchenyi tér.) The **Fedett Indoor Swimming Pool** (*Izsáki út 1;* ✆ 76 482152; 🎫 *620/440Ft;* ⊕ *Mon–Fri main pool 06.00–21.00 Sat–Sun 06.00–23.00, thermal pool 06.00–19.00*) has regular and thermal pools, as well as sauna, solarium and massage options.

A few kilometres northwest of the centre, the 62ha **arboretum** (*Nyíri út 48;* ✆ 76 492455; 🎫 *free admission*) operates not only as a nature haven but also as a natural wind shield for the town. There are species common to the Great Plain, as well as more exotic types. The wood-chipped paths, wooded picnic area and wooden viewing tower make this an excellent spot for walks or picnics. The main entrance and car park are at the southern end. The path here leads past a series of statues of Hungarian saints beyond which is the Mary Chapel (*Mária-kápolna;* ⊕ *daily summer 08.00–20.00, winter 08.00–16.00, spring–autumn 09.00–17.00, closed in Dec*). It is said that a man was chased by a bull here in 1718, and built the chapel to thank the Virgin Mary for his escape.

Equestrian tourism is strong in these parts, and Tourinform can provide details of farms in the vicinity offering horse-riding, horse shows and private accommodation.

FESTIVALS AND EVENTS There are concerts and exhibitions during the Kecskemét Spring Festival in March, while Summer in the Main Square (*end Jun–start Jul*) sees folk performances and an open-air folk-art fair. The Kodály Seminar and Festival takes place every other July, with educational programmes and concerts. The Hírös Week Festival (*end Aug*) showcases traditional crafts and food. The aerobatics during the International Airshow and Military Display (*Aug*) are astounding, and well worth seeing.

KISKUNFÉLEGYHÁZA

The 'Kiskun-' ('Little Kun') prefix to this and other towns in the region refers to a nomadic Turkic people called the Cumans (or Kun), skilled horsemen who settled here during the 13th century and were gradually assimilated into Hungarian society. They arrived in Kiskunfélegyháza in 1239, but the town was deserted during the Turkish invasion and had to be repopulated all over again (this time by Jazygians) in the mid 18th century. It developed as a market town and rose to be administrative centre of the Kiskun district between 1753 and 1876. Its main claim to fame, though, is that it was the birthplace of Ferenc Móra, one of the country's most significant writers of the early 20th century.

GETTING THERE AND AWAY The **bus station** is to the south of the parish church on Bajcsy-Zsilinszky Endre utca; there are services to Budapest Népliget (17), as well as to closer destinations like Kecskemét (regular), Szeged (11), Csongrád (20) and Bugac (11). The **railway station** is at the western end of Kossuth Lajos utca; there is a taxi rank outside, but it is a relatively easy walk to the centre (straight ahead from the station and up Kossuth Lajos utca). Kecskemét is at the meeting point of several lines, including those to Szeged and Kiskunhalas. There are regular services to Budapest Nyugati and Szeged (every hour), Cegléd (ten), Kecskemét (17), Kiskunhalas (eight) and Szolnok (three); for trains to Kelebia (and onward journeys to Belgrade), change at Kiskunhalas.

INFORMATION

🆔 **Kiskun Nova** Martirok utja 1; ☎ 76 4333243; e kiskunnova@kiskunnova.hu. Travel agency organising foreign & domestic travel, & able to

provide limited information about the town. 🕘 Mon–Fri 09.00–17.00.

WHERE TO STAY

🏠 **Borostyán Panzió** Szőlő u. 1; ☎ 76 466785; e pepu@netquick.hu. Staying here is rather like staying in the spare room of someone's house; there's little luxury, but it's low in price. To get there, follow Szentesi út off the main high street, turn right into Nefelejcs u. and, after 500m, turn left into Szőlő utca. *Sgl/dbl €2–7, trpl €32.*

🏠 **Hotel Oázis** (16 rooms) Szegedi út 13; ☎ 76 461427. To the south of the main square, this hotel is more central than the other options & marginally more appealing. *Sgl 5,500Ft, dbl 11,000Ft.*

🏠 **Malom Hotel** (18 rooms) Szentesi út 23/A, ☎ 76 560668; www.malomhotel.hu. This newish 3-star hotel is clean & well located. More like a panzió. *Sgl 6,000–9,700Ft, dbl 11,700–14,000Ft.*

🏠 **Mónika Panzió** (10 rooms) Szőlő u. 1; ☎ 76 466022. Next to Borostyán Panzió, Mónika could hardly be called modern & could certainly be called basic. Rooms are en suite, though. *Dbl 7,000Ft, quad 11,000Ft.*

WHERE TO EAT AND DRINK
There are several pizza and pasta places on Kossuth Lajos utca, and in terms of location and atmosphere they are probably the best eating bet.

✖ **Csillag Vendéglő** Szegedi út 41; ☎ 76 462640. A minimalist affair serving goodly portions of average but cheap Hungarian food. *Mains avg 1,000Ft;* 🕘 *Mon–Sat 11.00–22.00, Sun 11.00–15.00.*

✖ **Gyorsétkezde** Kossuth Lajos u. 76; ☎ 76 462273. The most popular of the pizzerias. It is also a pub

& coffee house. *Pizzas 600–1,800Ft, avg 740Ft;* 🕘 *Mon–Thu, Sun 09.00–24.00, Fri–Sat 09.00–02.00.*

✖ **Hotel Oázis** See above. This hotel restaurant is plasticky, overly bright & distinctly forgettable. *Mains avg 1,400Ft;* 🕘 *daily 06.00–10.00, 18.00–22.00.*

WHAT TO SEE AND DO The town consists of three main streets – Szegedi út, running through its centre, and Kossuth Lajos utca and Bajcsy-Zsilinsky Endre utca perpendicular to it – with the primary square, Petőfi tér, merging with Béke tér and Szent János tér. The citizens' pride and joy is their **town hall** (*Petőfi tér*), a beautiful monument to the vernacular Hungarian Art-Nouveau style of the early 20th century, and looking like a Zsolnay-majolica-studded princess's castle.

Opposite is the white **Swan House** (*Hattyúház; Szent János tér 9;* ☎ 76 461429; 🕘 *Mon–Tue 08.00–17.30, Wed–Thu 12.00–17.30, Fri 08.00–17.30, Sat 08.00–12.00*), built in 1819 in Neoclassical style; today it houses a library, but between 1824 and 1830 there were sausages – Sándor Petőfi's father ran a butcher's shop from here. A short distance to the east, behind the Roman Catholic church, the **Petőfi Memorial Museum** (*Petőfi Sándor u. 7;* ↘ *76 461468;* ✆ *220/110Ft;* ☉ *Mar 5–Oct 31 Wed–Fri 09.00–12.00*) has various bits and pieces connected with the future poet in the house where he spent much of his childhood. Although he wasn't born in Kiskunfélegyháza, Petőfi was to say that 'This is the town where I first saw the light'.

The terracotta-coloured mid-18th-century **Roman Catholic church** dominates Béke tér, a Baroque building with colourful Rococo pulpit and side altars. Among the monuments to the right of the church is one to Károly Kertbeny, a Hungarian-German writer who devoted his life to popularising Hungarian literature abroad – and gave the world the terms 'homosexual' and 'heterosexual'.

Continue east along Bajcsy-Zsilinszky utca and turn right into Móra Ferenc utca for the **Móra Ferenc Memorial House** (*Móra Ferenc u. 19;* ↘ *76 461468;* ✆ *220/110Ft;* ☉ *Wed–Fri 09.00–12.00*); this thatched cottage set back from the road was the birthplace and childhood home of the writer. The top collection in town, however, is at the **Kiskun Museum** (*Dr Holló Lajos út 9;* ↘ *76 461468;* ✆ *320/160Ft;* ☉ *Mar 15–Oct 31 Wed–Sun 09.00–17.00*) in the former county prison house. There are paintings by László Holló, a local and prominent Expressionist artist who depicted the misery of peasants, and died in 1976; there are archaeological and ethnographic items relating to the region, including a reconstruction of a peasant living room; there is the butcher's block and cleaver used by István Petrovits (Petőfi senior) and Ferenc Móra's school desk; and there are torture tools used at the jail, as well as toys made by prisoners – chief among which is a fabulous wooden clock of 1918. In the courtyard is a windmill that operated on a nearby farm between 1860 and 1942; windmills were once plentiful in Kiskunság, with 62 in and around Kiskunfélegyháza alone in the 1850s. It is a shame that few remain.

The **swimming pool and lido** (*Blaha Lujza tér 1;* ↘ *76 463201;* ✆ *950/700Ft;* ☉ *Mon–Fri 06.00–20.00, Sat–Sun 09.00–20.00; Fri–Sat 20.00–23.00 also*) has indoor and outdoor pools, sauna and steamroom; it lies towards the western end of Kossuth Lajos utca, near the train station.

KISKUNSÁG NATIONAL PARK

BUGAC Bugac – the 'pearl of the Kiskunság', a few kilometres southwest of Kiskunfélegyháza – is the second-largest *puszta* in Hungary and a good introduction to the national park. **Bugac Tours** (*Kecskemét, Szabadság tér 5A;* ↘ *76 482500;* e *bugacpuszta@invitel.hu;* ☉ *Mon–Fri 08.00–16.30*), with a small office (*Nagybugac 135;* ↘ *76 575112*) at the gateway to the national park, have something of a monopoly here. As well as organising a variety of programmes featuring horse shows and horse-riding, they can arrange accommodation in thatched farmhouses (*from 8,000Ft/night*). Next to the office is the **Bugaci Karikás Csárda** (*Nagybugac 135;* ↘ *30 416 6439;* e *bugacpuszta@invitel.hu; www.bugacpuszta.info.hu; mains avg 1,400Ft;* ☉ *09.00–22.00 daily*), a traditional 'folksy' restaurant that makes the bulk of its cash from serving clients on programmes organised by Bugac Tours. There is also a basic **campsite** (*arrange through Bugac Tours; 700Ft/pp*) in a field behind the restaurant.

A track running into the *puszta* leads 1.5km to a farm and stables of 100 halfbreds. During **horse shows** (*daily at 13.15, with a second at 15.15 if there is sufficient demand*), the brightly waistcoated herders (*csikós*) perform the famous 'Puszta Five' (see page 332), as well as making their steeds go through a range of equestrian tricks; you can walk, drive or take a carriage ride from the entrance (✆ *1,000Ft/pp*). In addition, there is **horse-riding** on offer (✆ *riding from €8/hr, instruction from €32/hr, full-day tour with picnic from €56/pp*). Near by is the **Pastoral**

Museum (*Pásztormúzeum;* 🎫 *800/400Ft;* ⊕ *Apr–Oct daily 10.00–16.00*), housed in a circular hut and displaying shepherding memorabilia – musical instruments, sheep identification tags, tools, bells and the shepherd's ubiquitous sheepskin coat. Bugac Tours arrange a programme that includes the museum, a show and lunch at the csárda (🎫 *from 4,500Ft/pp, with optional carriage ride extra; May–Sep, departing from the entrance at around 12.00 daily*).

There are several marked **walking trails**; it might help to purchase a map of the national park from the House of Nature (see box below) or Bugac Tours (*Kiskunsági Nemzeti Park*, 1: 90,000).

If you have a car, you can park at the park entrance; otherwise the journey is a slightly awkward one, and you may not arrive to coincide with a programme.

KISKUNSÁG NATIONAL PARK

The second-biggest national park in Hungary (covering 76,000ha), the Kiskunság was founded in 1975 and is, like the Hortobágy, a UNESCO World Heritage Site. Comparisons with the Hortobágy don't stop there, for the landscapes and the species to be found in them are similar, and there are opportunities in both for enjoying horse shows and *puszta* parties. Located between the Danube and the Tisza, the Kiskunság is composed of nine separate areas covered with loess or sand, and dotted with reeds, wet marshes, bogs, pastures, forests and steppe; much of this is barred to the casual tourist boot.

Lake Kolon in Izsák is a typical example of a freshwater marshy area in a former river branch, and is characteristic of the Danube floodplain; the site hosts a strong population of the globally threatened European mudminnow, and all of Hungary's eight heron species breed here. During the Turkish occupation, locals often hid from the Ottoman armies among the lake's reeds. Head with your binoculars to the Bikatorok Hill, just west of the lake, to watch the birds without disturbing them.

The **Fülöpháza** area is known for its mobile sand dunes, which are blown in the direction of the prevailing wind (from northwest to southeast); there is a 1.5km study trail, departing from near kilometre marker 20 on Road 52. The **Bócsa-Bugac** is the most extensive and diverse area of the park; as well as dunes, you'll find alkaline grasslands, oak forests, ancient juniper stands, wet meadows, bogs, marshes, cultivated fields and exposed sandy soil.

The most frequently visited part of the park – the River Tisza oxbow at Szikra and the surrounding Tőserdő, 27km east of Kecskemét – is also the smallest. Many head for Szikra (the riverside part of Felső-Alpár *puszta*) to fish or bathe, but others follow the trails through the bog woods that flank the oxbow. The southernmost section holds the Alpár meadow, where it is said a great battle took place between the invading Hungarian tribes and the Bulgars, who inhabited the site in the 9th century; here the water violet blooms in spring and whiskered terns nest in the fens.

The **Upper Kiskunság** in particular is notable for being a stronghold of the great bustard, as well as of the saker falcon, stone curlew, collared pratincole, roller and bee-eater. In addition, the national park actively preserves the natural and human features fashioned by the traditional rural way of life on the Great Plain, including isolated farmsteads (*tanya*), wells and wooded pastures. In keeping with this, significant herds of old Hungarian domestic animal breeds are reared here.

The national park's official HQ and visitor centre is the **House of Nature** (*Liszt Ferenc u. 19;* ☏ *76 482611;* 🎫 *200/150Ft;* ⊕ *Tue–Fri 09.00–16.00, Sat 10.00–14.00*), standing a few kilometres to the north of Kecskemét's centre. It features a display of the park's various habitats, together with photos and the obligatory stuffed fauna.

Bugac itself is 6km from the entrance, so if you take a **bus** from Kecskemét you'll need to ask the driver to drop you at the most convenient stop along the way – and you'll still have 1½km to walk. At the weekend, you can take the **narrow-gauge railway** from Kecskemét KK (south of the centre); alight at Bugac-felső (not Bugac Puszta or Bugac), which is 2km south of the entrance. Trains depart Kecskemét KK at 08.00, 14.00 and 19.50 for the 1½ hour journey; the last train back leaves Bugac-felső at 18.09.

NAGYKŐRÖS

Like Cegléd 15km to its north (see below), Nagykőrös goes all gooey over Lajos Kossuth, who gave a speech from its **town hall** (*Szabadság tér*) balcony on September 25 1848 (the day after he addressed the citizens of Cegléd). However, another favourite also stamped his name on the town. The poet János Arany lived here in the 1860s (at what is now Arany János utca 28, south of the main square), teaching grammar and literature at the **high school** (now called the Arany János Gimnazium; *Szabadság tér 8*) for nine years. In the grounds of the **Calvinist church** (*Szabadság tér 6*) is Alajos Stróbl's statue of him, slumped in a chair with his dog by his side.

To the north of the centre, the **Arany János Museum** (*Ceglédi út 19;* ☏ *53 350770;* 🎟 *400/200Ft;* ⊕ *Tue–Sun summer 10.00–18.00, winter 09.00–16.00*) – once a hussars' barracks – tells the story of Nagykőrös, and displays the detritus of its history from 5000BC up to the period of socialist construction. Of particular interest are the years following the failed War of Independence, when the market town was nevertheless able to fall back on its relative wealth and retain a degree of autonomy. In an extraordinary act of patronage, seven distinguished scholars from the Hungarian Academy of Sciences were invited to teach at the secondary high school. One of these was the patriotic Arany, who had lost his job because of his support for the rebellion; he went on to write many of his poems here – inspired by English classical ballads and Hungarian folk songs – and to attract a steady stream of cultural lions to his door (such as Mór Jókai and Mihály Tompa). Among the extensive holdings (accompanied by notes in English – oh, were all museums so helpful!) are some of his personal belongings, while outside is a satisfyingly tactile statue of the *Great Teachers* by Imre Varga.

The hungry can head for the Wild-West-themed **Pizzeria Saloon** (*Szechényi tér 2; pizzas 500–800Ft;* ⊕ *Mon–Thu 10.00–22.00, Fri–Sat 10.00–24.00, Sun 10.00–23.00*) or the peasant-style **Cifra Csárda** (*Nagykőrös út 21;* ☏ *53 351212; www.cifracsarda.hu; mains avg 1,400Ft;* ⊕ *Mon–Sat 09.00–23.00, Sun 09.00–22.00*), a few hundred metres north of the museum.

The **railway station** is 1km from the centre, along Kossuth utca; there are regular services to Kecskemét, as well as trains to Cegléd (up to 14 daily), Szeged and Budapest Nyugati (every hour); for Szolnok and Debrecen you'll need to change at Cegléd. Buses depart for Kecskemét every 30 minutes from the **bus station** (*Derkovits utca*), across the road from Szabadság tér; they also go to Szolnok and Jászberény (six), Eger (three) and Miskolc (one). For Budapest, Szeged and Gyula you'll need to travel via Kecskemét.

CEGLÉD

Thirty kilometres north of Kecskemét, Cegléd's marketplace was where Lajos Kossuth first urged the people of the Great Plain to cast off the Habsburg shackles. On September 24 1848, he declared 'I have come to you, good Hungarians, hope, bastion and pillar of my betrayed homeland'. Agitated speechifiers were clearly fond of the spot for in 1514 György Dózsa, leader of the peasant revolt (see page 17), also spoke here (his second-in-command, Lőrinc Mészáros, heralded from Cegléd). The town makes much of its Kossuth connection, but it has also recently directed attention to its thermal baths in the hope of building a reputation for health tourism.

GETTING THERE AND AROUND The **bus station** is at the northern end of Kossuth Ferenc utca (follow it into the centre); it serves destinations including Szolnok and Gyöngyös (four daily), Eger and Lajosmizse (three), Baja and Kalocsa (two), and offers regular services to Kecskemét and Nagykőrös. The **railway station** is 100m away, with trains to Kecskemét (12), Debrecen and Szeged (seven), and Nyíregyháza (six). It also has regular (every 30 mins) connections to Budapest Nyugati and Szolnok.

INFORMATION AND OTHER PRACTICALITIES

⊞ Tourinform Kossuth tér 1; ✆ 53 500285; e cegled@tourinform.hu. In the town hall building. ☺ Mon–Tue & Thu 08.00–16.00, Wed 08.00–18.00, Fri 08.00–14.00.

⊞ Ibusz Kossuth tér 8; ✆ 53 314717; e cegled@ibusz.hu. Private accommodation & currency exchange. ☺ Mon–Fri 08.00–17.00.

☷ Kossuth Cultural Centre Kossuth tér 5/A; ✆ 53 311004; e cegledi.muv.kozpont@axelero.hu. The town's main arts centre, site of concerts & plays & a gallery of temporary exhibitions. ☺ Mon–Fri 10.00–18.00, Sat–Sun 08.00–20.00; gallery Mon–Fri 09.00–16.00, Sat–Sun variable times.

WHERE TO STAY, EAT AND DRINK

☖ Best Western Hotel Aquarell (92 rooms) Fürdő út 24; ✆ 53 510900; www.aquarellhotel.hu The town's first 4-star hotel opened in 2007, & is another of the country's new wellness hotels. Rooms are comfortable without being anything special; the suites have sauna or jacuzzi. Located next to the baths, a little out of the centre. Sgl/dbl 15,850–16,200/20,900–34,400Ft.

✗ Arizona Pizzeria & Burger Bar Kossuth tér 8; ✆ 53 321480. An understated 'Wild-West' theme inside, with shady outdoor seating overlooking the square. Good fast food. Mains avg 900Ft; ☺ Mon–Tue, Sun 09.00–24.00, Fri–Sat 08.00–01.00.

Å Castrum Thermal Camping Fürdő u. 27; ✆ 53 505009; e info@castrum-group.hu; www.castrum-group.hu. Campsite in the grounds of the super-duper aqua park & thermal baths. ☺ Apr 15–Oct 15.

☖ Kossuth Hotel (11 rooms) Rákóczi út 1; ✆ 53 310990. An estate agent would describe the rooms as 'compact', but they are clean & welcoming nonetheless. Some are not en suite. The restaurant (mains 750–2,500Ft, avg 1,400Ft; ☺ Mon–Sat 07.00–15.00) is open for lunch only, & has a patchy choice of Hungarian food & token pasta dishes. Sgl/dbl (without bathroom) 6,000/6,500Ft, dbl/trpl (with bathroom) 8,200/11,000Ft.

WHAT TO SEE AND DO Kossuth tér is dotted with flowerbeds and trees; at its very heart is the Neoclassical **Church of the Holy Cross**, completed in 1825 on the site of a Gothic predecessor demolished in 1821. The Calvary scene on the main altar was painted by Pest artist József Schöfft in 1830, while the Trinity Column outside was sculpted by György Kiss – and marks the place of Kossuth's ne'er-forgotten recruitment speech. At the square's northern end is the imposing late-19th-century **town hall**, also Neoclassical in style.

Kossuth's son Ferenc assisted János Horvay with getting the likeness of his father just right in the statue standing in **Szabadság tér**; so fine was it that it became the template for the version erected in New York in 1928. The Neo-Gothic **Lutheran church** (Bercsenyi u. 2) of 1896 represents an allusion in brick to the greeting 'A mighty fortress is our God'. However, it is the **Calvinist Great Church** (Szabadság tér) across from it that really holds court, designed by József Hild, finished in 1857 and successfully fusing sturdiness with elegance. It is the biggest Calvinist church in central Europe, seating over 2000; concerts are held beneath its turquoise dome. In the garden behind is a sculpture of a figure trapped in a tree trunk; the *Freedom Tree* was erected in 1989 to commemorate the 1956 revolution, the first such monument in Hungary. The millennium belfry above it was added in 2000, its bells etched with significant dates in the country's history. Remarkably, the garden also holds the balcony once belonging to the Zöldfa (Green Tree) Inn in Bratislava, from where Kossuth declared the March Decrees (later ratified by Ferenc József) and introduced the country's first prime minister, Lajos Batthyány (see page 19).

North of Szabadság tér, the **Kossuth Museum** (*Múzeum u. 5;* ❨ *53 310637;* e *kossuth.cegled@museum.hu;* ❨ *350/150Ft;* ❨ *Tue–Sun Nov–Feb 09.00–17.00, Mar–Oct 10.00–18.00*) displays works by 'peasant painter' Péter Benedek, a leading exponent of the Naive School. The main draws, though, are items relating to Kossuth – including his curved pipe, a locket containing his hair and his death mask. There is a reconstruction of his study in Turin, where he went into exile after the failure of the War of Independence, and a letter to the *Manchester Guardian* in 1860 accusing the newspaper of infringing his copyright by printing a lecture he gave while visiting England. A fascinating collection, it is a crying shame that there are no explanations in English.

Follow Rákóczi út away from Szabadság tér, and turn right for the **thermal baths** (*Fürdő út 27;* ❨ *53 505000;* ❨ *1,000/500Ft;* ❨ *Mon–Sun 09.00–19.00, Thu–Sat also 20.00–24.00*), the centrepiece of the town's drive towards health and leisure tourism. It's a large complex, featuring ten pools altogether – pools indoor and outdoor, pools medicinal and swimming, pools for children and pools set with splashing fountains – and a range of 'wellness' treatments. There's also a park with boating lake, sports fields and al-fresco theatre; the intention is to expand it further in the coming years and establish a resort-style village.

LAJOSMIZSE

If you thought that one-street and one-horse towns were one and the same, Lajosmizse (to the northwest of Kecskemét) will change your mind. There are few in the way of permanent sights here beyond **Szent Lajos Church** (*Cégledi út*), built in 1896 and with a carillon above its entrance, and the **Hungarian Farm Museum** (*Magyar Mezőgazdasági Múzeum Tanyamúzeum;* ❨ *1 341 2011;* ❨ *150/70Ft;* ❨ *Mar 15–Oct 14 Tue–Sat 10.00–17.00, Sun 10.00–18.00*), an outdoor ethnographic collection in 19th-century thatched cottages beside the Öreg Tanyacsárda (see page 332). No, this is an area of farmsteads and the venue for galloping horse shows, monthly horse markets and horse-riding tours. For **further information** on equestrian tourism here and elsewhere in the county, contact the Tourinform in Kecskemét (see page 319).

GETTING THERE AND AROUND The **railway station** is 1km west of the centre at the far end of Rákóczi utca (follow dirt track on to Rákóczi utca, continue to the end, and turn right to the centre); there are up to 15 trains a day to Budapest, as well regular trains to Ócsa and Dabas and up to 4 a day to Kecskemét. The main **bus stop** (*Cégledi út*) in town is by St Lajos Church; there are two buses an hour to Kecskemét, up to 19 daily to Budapest Népliget, three to Cegléd and two to Szeged. There is a cycle track between Lajosmizse and Felsőlajos.

WHERE TO STAY, EAT, DRINK (AND HORSE AROUND) The places offering accommodation and victuals are also often the places offering riding and horse shows. Some can be tough to get to, scattered not only outside the town centre but at times set well back from the roads.

There is an inextricable link between Hungary and horses. The Magyar warrior horsemen brought with them equestrian skills which, preserved for more than 1,000 years, can be seen today on the *puszta*. In days gone by, *csikós* (herdsmen) of the Great Plain – a wild breed that harboured an innate antipathy to authority, particularly when agricultural developments hit their herding rights – would collude with and protect wandering highwaymen. They learnt to stand on bare-back galloping horses, deterring bounty-hunting pursuers with whips (*karikásostor*) they cracked like pistols. They taught their horses to lie down on command, disappearing among the grasses in an instant. An obedient steed would sit on its haunches so its weary master could rest safe against its stomach, protected from the elements in his '*puszta* armchair'. Come evening, herdsmen vied for the attention of the village beauty, chasing each other in an attempt to capture the prized scarf she gave to her favourite – the winner's reward the privilege of dancing with her for the rest of the night.

By the 19th century this distant relative of the cowboy was no more, but his romantic memory burned on. In shows to rival the American Wild West, modern-day herdsmen parade their skills for wide-eyed tourists. Their repertoire includes all the age-old tricks – scarves are stolen, horses sit and lie down, whip-cracking riders stand atop their speeding steeds. Art imitates life for the body of the display – at least a romanticised perception of it – but the climax turns this usual truth upon its head. Greatly impressed by Hungarian horsemanship, Viennese artist Adam Koch used a healthy dollop of artistic licence in painting an imagined scene where a single rider stood atop two horses' rumps and used reins to guide a further three horses ahead of them. Macho Magyars were determined to bring the canvas to life and in 1953 Béla Lénárt succeeded in this feat of horse-surfing; the 'Koch (or Puszta) Five' was born, and has become a staple of horse shows ever since. Bravado always dictated that others would strive to do better still – the current world record is for one man on 12 horses!

🏠 **Gerébi Kúria** Alsólajos 224; 📞 76 356555; www.gerebi.hu. Set in extensive grounds surrounding a 19th-century mansion, the Gerébi Kúria can cater for those who want rustic without the rough. There is little the site can't provide for – it boasts a whirlpool bath, Finnish sauna, solarium, gym, swimming pool, wine cellar, folklore shop, restaurant (*avg 1,500Ft*; ⏱ *daily 07.00–22.00*) & sports courts. The riding school runs lessons, cross-country gallops, carriage rides & much more, & there are horse shows every couple of days in high season. Accommodation is available in the main 17–room hotel & a 41-room 'Arcade' annexe. Guests can be collected from the bus or train stations in Lajosmizse; the site sits 2km back from Cégledi út, 5km east of the town centre. *Main hotel sgl 20,900Ft, dbl 22,900Ft, suite 29,900–31,900Ft; 'Arcade' sgl 15,900Ft, dbl 17,900Ft, suite (for 4) 43,900Ft; f/bd & h/bd options.*

🏠 **Kobza Tanya Panzió** (15 rooms) Közös 168; 📞 76 555173; e kobza@mail.datanet.hu. A kilometre northwest of the centre (along Route 5), &

opposite the Új Tanyacsárda (see opposite), this pretty guesthouse has a swimming pool & wine cellar. The owners organise horse-riding for all levels – from lessons for beginners through 5-day cross-country treks to equestrian paintballing. Turn off the M5 between the 64km & 65km markers. *Sgl 5,000Ft, dbl 7,500Ft; f/bd & h/bd options.*

✗ **Öreg Tanyacsárda** Bene 65 (Route 5); 📞 76 356166; www.tanyacsarda.hu. The 'Old Inn' is a thatched peasant-style restaurant with a muscular statue by Imre Varga sewing seed at the front. Its menu, served by costumed staff, features classic Hungarian dishes. However, together with the Új Tanyacsárda (same company), it is as much a programme organiser as a restaurant. There are myriad folk events – the advertised line-up includes a horse show after dark, a camp fire with 'witches' dance', goulash parties, peasant wedding feast, *puszta* Olympics, ox roasts & assorted excursions. If you choose the trip aboard a nostalgia train from Budapest to Felsőlajos (and then on to the inn), the ladies in the party should be prepared to be 'abducted' from the train by a gang of horsemen. All good fun. Each of the taverns can accommodate up to 1,000 guests; if you're interested in participating in a programme, you'll need to gather a group of 30 or more & book at least a week ahead (contact the sales manager; ✆ 76 356166/356010; m 06 30 958 9460; e tanyacsarda@tanyacsarda.hu). Horse shows start at 2,500Ft/pp & themed events go as high as 350,000Ft/group; riding lessons are 3,000Ft/hr. Located 3km southeast of the centre (on Route 5 in the direction of Szeged). Mains avg 1,600Ft; ⊕ 11.00–22.00 daily.

🏠 **Ricsováry Major** (30 rooms) Mizse hrsz 0505, off Ceglédi út; ✆ 76 716000, 20 915 6225; www.ricsovary.hu. Set fully 3km back from the main road, this is a treat of a retreat, a family-run estate as secluded, idyllic & downright peaceful as you could wish. There are few distractions in the rustic chalets – no TV, telephone or minibar; rather you must relax in the gazebo outside the main house, lounge by the swimming pool or wine taste in the cellar. An unfancy 3-course meal is served each evening (2,000Ft/pp; daily 19.00–22.00), & the

owner can arrange horse-show programmes for guests (to which you are taken by carriage – horse-drawn, naturally). The estate is at the top of a dirt track leading from Ceglédi út, 10km east of Lajosmizse centre (turn off the M5 near the 66km marker, in the direction of Nagykőrös-Cegléd); there is a local bus stop at the entrance to the track, & the owner can pick you up from there. Apt 13,000–20,000Ft, dbl 9,200–16,000Ft; ⊕ Apr–Oct (other periods on request).

✗ **Új Tanyacsárda** See Öreg Tanyacsárda, opposite. The counterpart of the 'Old Inn', the 'New Inn' has more of the same, & is targeted heavily at the tourist market. The horse shows offered in the programmes are held here – during high season there are performances daily at 12.30 & in the evening too if demand dictates. (See Öreg Tanyacsárda for booking details.) There is also a campsite & stalls for those bringing horses. The inn is 5km the other side of town from its sister, set back 1km from Route 5 (in the direction of Budapest). Menu prices as above; ⊕ 08.00–22.00 daily.

Other places with a horsey bent include **Dechy Lovaspanzió** (Mizse 339; ✆ 76 715248) and **Bujdosó Tanya** (Alsólajos 92; ✆ 76 356551).

KISKŐRÖS

There's nature all about Kiskőrös, including the oak, ash and elm trees of Szűcsi Forest (a nature reserve to the north), and acacia and pine woods filling the westward space up to the Danube Valley Canal (Duna-völgyi-főcsatorna). Such landscape is crowded with croaking frogs, flitting butterflies and singing songbirds; there are 300 species of plant. The name of the town derives from the indigenous ash tree, and it features in the coat of arms. However, pilgrims to Kiskőrös do so in the name of art rather than nature. After the Turkish occupation, the area was settled by Lutheran Slovaks, and in the 19th century the son of István Petrovics and Mária Hrúz was born. The inhabitants supported the 1848 uprising and War of Independence but that son went further – he impacted upon national and literary consciousness, instilled revolutionary fervour and became the very voice of the struggle. He was Sándor Petőfi. Such is the reflected glory cast upon Kiskőrös by the poet that in 1973, on the 150th anniverary of his death, it was declared a town – a status it had lost two centuries before.

GETTING THERE AND AROUND The **train station** is 1km west of the town centre – turn right from the station and left into Kossuth Lajos út. There are trains to Kiskunhalas (nine daily), Budapest Keleti or Kőbánya-Kispest station (nine), Kalocsa (four) and Baja (one). The **bus stop** is next to the town hall; there are regular services to Kiskunhalas and Kecskemét, as well as buses to Szeged (14), Baja (eight), Kalocsa (six) and one daily to Budapest Népliget. Romantics can board a narrow-gauge train running between here and Kecskemét. The train leaves three times a day (04.07, 11.24 & 17.48) from Kiskőrös KK station, arriving 2½ hours later at Kecskemét KK.

To this day, the nation's favourite versifier – the man who has made the deepest dent on the national and literary consciousness – is the 19th-century Sándor Petőfi (1823–49). Branded vulgar by some, he wrote copiously and empathetically in the vivid vernacular of 'the common man', travelling the countryside on foot and rooting his language and imagery in that of the Great Plain. He wrote earthy cycles of love poetry, but he is best remembered for his fervent, patriotic and radical narratives. Though personally fractious, socially awkward and discontented, his brilliant writings were inspirational. As a newlywed, he provided the voice and impulse for the revolution that broke out on March 15 1848. In his 'National Song' ('Nemzeti Dal') – recited from the steps of the National Museum – he pleaded 'Rise, Hungarians!' ('Talpra, magyar!'). And they did.

However, he was more than a man of words and his greatest fear was to fade away rather than fighting for the sacred ideal of liberty. In 1846 'One Thought Worries Me' he wrote:

One thought worries me:
To die in bed, amongst the pillows,
To slowly wither away like a flower.

Three years later (aged just 26) he was dead. Dispute surrounds his final flourish on a field in Transylvania during one of the last battles of the War of Independence. Some reports speak of him wearing a conspicuous white shirt (having scorned to wear military dress) and falling to a Russian lance. Others claim he was thrown alive into a mass burial pit and crushed by corpses. His body was never found, and there was a spate of Elvis-like sightings in the following years. Whatever the truth, his cult status was sealed as the passionate, revolutionary romantic of his age – an eloquent rebel with a cause.

INFORMATION

Petőfi Sándor Cultural House Petőfi tér 4/A; 45 312315. Next to the Petőfi Museum, the cultural house is the only place to head for information on what's on. Mon–Fri 08.00–20.00, Sat–Sun 16.00–19.00 (variations if a programme is on).

WHERE TO STAY AND EAT

Thermal Camping & Baths Erdőtelki út, 78 311524. Next to the thermal baths. Tent/caravan 600/1,000Ft, plus 1,600/800Ft/pp; Apr–Oct.

Hotel Imperial (53 rooms) Erdőtelki út 21; 78 514400; www.hotelimperial.hu. The newest on the block is an ugly looking lump of a hotel opened in 2002 to the west of the centre; however, the Imperial compensates with its own thermal baths (free for guests), swimming pool, fitness room, sauna & massage options. The rooms are sterile in every sense – spotlessly clean but characterless. The restaurant (mains avg 1,300Ft; 08.00–24.00 daily) specialises in goose liver & other Hungarian delicacies. Sgl 7,000Ft, dbl 8,500Ft, trpl 11,000Ft, apt 12,000Ft (excl tax); b/fast 800Ft.

Kurta Kocsma Restaurant Csokonai u. 51; 78 311821; www.kurtakocsma.hu. A little southwest of the centre (just off József Attila út), it's difficult to miss the Kurta Kocsma, with the bright mural of horses & carriage on its façade. This is the most popular restaurant in town. There's nothing fancy about the menu; the portions are substantial, & you can have breakfast. Live entertainment is often staged here. Mains avg 1,700Ft; 08.00–22.00 daily.

Szarvas Fogadó (20 rooms) Petőfi tér 17; 78 511500; e szarvash@hu.inter.net. Built in 1914, Szarvas remains the best place to stay, with elegant looks & a prime spot on the main square. There is a fitness room & sauna, & the stylish, wood-panelled restaurant (mains avg 1,500Ft; 07.00–23.00

daily) serves international cuisine. *Sgl 9,400Ft, dbl 9,800Ft, apt 11,800Ft.*

🏠 **Vinum Hotel** (23 rooms) Petőfi Sándor u. 106; ✆ 78 511050; www.vinumhotel.hu. Looking like a Dallas ranch, the sprawling Vinum settles around a grassed courtyard. Rooms vary, but are generally pleasant, & feel as though given a woman's finishing touch. The owner produces his own wine, which you can sample in the cellar, & there is a restaurant (for groups only). *Sgl 9,500Ft, dbl 13,900Ft, trpl 18,300Ft, apt (for 4) 22,500Ft (excl tax).*

WHAT TO SEE AND DO The predictably named main square eggs the pudding further with a statue of the town's cultural behemoth, erected in 1927 (the country's first). The peach-coloured **town hall** (*Petőfi tér 1*) bears Kiskőrös's crest (showing hunting, bee-keeping, agriculture and forest).

The **Petőfi Memorial House and Literary Museum** (*Szülőház Emlékmúzeum; Petőfi tér 5;* ✆ *78 312566; www.petofimuzeum.hu;* 🎫 *200/100Ft;* ☺ *Tue–Sun 09.00–17.00*) is first stop for most visitors. On January 1 1823 Petőfi gasped his first breaths within the mud-walled 18th-century house. This was restored to its original state – with family furniture and documents collected from various later residences, and the only existing picture of the whole Petrovics family (the poet later changed his name to one more 'Hungarian') – and opened to the public by Mór Jókai in 1880.

Outside are busts of 11 of the translators who've tackled the closed book of Hungarian language and opened up Petőfi's work to those in other countries; inside the museum proper (beyond the statue park) is a map showing just how far the Petőfi cult has reached. There are also archaeological, ethnographical and wildlife displays, and documents that relate to the Wattay family – who were gifted the region at the end of the 17th century as reward for their resistance to the Turks, and who brought 700 Slovak peasants from northern Hungary to re-establish the settlement. A gallery upstairs shows art connected with Petőfi.

Your ticket to the museum also allows admission to the **Slovakian Folk House** (*Szlovák Tájház; Szent István u. 23;* ✆ *78 312566;* ☺ *Tue–Sun 09.00–12.00, 13.00–16.00*), which was the initiative of pupils at the local school. The kids spent a decade collecting dishes and furniture in order to resurrect a typical dwelling of the 18th-century Slovak settlers. Follow Kossuth Lajos utca northeast a short distance and turn left on to Szent István utca. If you enjoy watching tarmac dry, push on to the **Public Road Construction Collection** (*Útügyi Kiállítás; Dózsa György út 38;* ✆ *78 311935; www.museum.kozut.hu;* ☺ *Mar–Nov 09.00–16.00 daily*) near the campsite and baths. The museum details the history of Hungarian road laying and bridge building, and showcases maintenance tools and heavy machinery like steamrollers. Pun aside, you really can learn about the invention of the tar 'macadam' by Scottish engineer John McAdam, which replaced cobbles as the road surface of choice at the start of the 19th century.

Other activities The **thermal baths** (*Dózsa György 43;* 🎫 *300/260Ft;* ☺ *daily Jun–Aug 09.00–19.00, Apr–May & Sep–Oct 09.00–17.00*), on the western side of town, can be used freely by those staying at the Imperial Hotel or the campsite.

Around 4km southwest of Kiskőrös (near Road 54, on its way to Kecel), the **Henry Lovasfarm** (*Soltvadkert, Felsőcsábor 39;* ✆ *78 311898;* e *henrylovasfarm@ hotelimperial.hu*) offers horse-riding lessons and tours, and has a panzió. You can also rent bicycles here, or take a carriage ride.

KALOCSA

Wake up and smell the paprika – Kalocsa is liberally peppered with the stuff! There are paprika factories and museums, a Paprika Street, pottery decorated with

Although originally a native American plant – and probably introduced to the Balkans by the Turks, and to Hungary by Bulgarian refugees fleeing the Turks – the milder Hungarian pepper, ripened to vibrant red and dried into the paprika (*Capsicum annuum*) spice, has become associated worldwide with Hungarian cuisine. It is the mainstay of renowned national dishes like *gulyás* and *paprikás*, and is invariably the 'natural colour' mentioned in ingredient lists of red-coloured foods.

The rich source of vitamin C in fresh peppers are largely destroyed by the high temperatures used in the paprika drying process, though if it's betacarotene you're after, to convert into vitamin A, then this spice has few rivals. (Incidentally, the story goes that the wife of the scientist Albert Szent-Györgyi used to swear by the healthy properties of paprika and included it without fail in his lunch. Szent-Györgyi was himself no great fan of the pepper, and conducted tests in his lab trying to disprove his wife's claims. It was while doing so that he discovered vitamin C – and unwittingly proved the old adage that behind every successful man is a paprika-pushing woman.) Szeged and Kalocsa are the centres of paprika production. Over 40 types are grown in the area around Kalocsa (the variety grown each year is determined by the predicted weather conditions) and the crop is graded into six classes, from the pungent and hot *erős* to the exquisitely delicate *különleges*. Like fine wine, the quality of the crop is critically affected by the amount of sunshine in the weeks immediately preceding harvest.

paprika, and shops filled with paprika souvenirs and low-hanging strings of paprika. You might even find paprika imagery incorporated into embroidery, the other string to Kalocsa's bow. In autumn, the fields flame red with the fruit of the pepper plant that is dried and ground into 'red gold'. The town has been the centre of such spice production since the start of the 20th century.

Kalocsa used to stand right on the Danube, but after a manipulation of the river course it came to lie 6km away. It was one of the two original archbishoprics established by King István in the 11th century as he Christianised the country, and as such has always been an ecclesiastical big hitter (second only to Esztergom). Its first prelate was Asztrik, who was sent by Pope Sylvester II as a sign of papal support for the establishment of the Hungarian Church and is said to have presented István with the Holy Crown. Some believe Asztrik is buried in the cathedral crypt, and others trace the word *érsek* (archbishop) to his name. This was a burgeoning medieval settlement, but the population seeped away during Turkish rule and then fire swept through and brought the whole place to earth, including the basilica. The Baroque town and ecclesiastical buildings of today are the 18th-century versions that were raised from those ashes. It's an intimate place where neighbours know each other; the majority of the action goes on around Szent István Király út, which holds the shops, bars and cafés.

GETTING THERE AND AROUND At the southernmost end of Szent István Király út is the town's **bus station**, from where buses travel frequently to Baja. There are also services to Kiskunhalas, Kecskemét and Szeged (seven), Kiskőrös (five) and Székesfehérvár. The **railway station** (*Mártírok tere*), decorated with folk motifs, is 2km northeast of the station and only serves Kiskőrös, and then only four times daily; you can get connections to Budapest from Kiskőrös. Turn right from the station on to Kossuth Lajos utca and follow the road straight into Szentháromság tér.

INFORMATION AND OTHER PRACTICALITIES

Cultural and Youth Centre Szent István Király út 2–4; ☎ 78 462200. The Baroque building was completed in 1787, serving as a religious training college. Today it hosts concerts & plays, as well as having exercise & dance classes. Call in here for details of productions at the Archbishop's Palace across the way. ⏰ *Mon–Sat 08.00–20.00, Sun 09.00–12.00, 15.00–20.00.*

Ibusz Szent István Király út 37; ☎ 78 462012; e kalocsa@ibusz.hu. In the same building as the Hotel Piros Arany; the office can change currency (but not travellers' cheques), provide information on tours & book private accommodation. ⏰ *Mon–Fri 08.00–16.00.*

Kalocsa Gold Tours Szent István Király út 35; ☎ 78 465347; www.kalocsagoldtours.hu. Next to Ibusz. Organise a good variety of local tours, including 'tastes of Kalocsa'. Can also book accommodation.

Korona Tours RT Szent István Király út 68; ☎ 78 461819; www.koronatours.hu. Opposite the Paprika Museum. You can choose from an array of local tours – including trips to Bakodpuszta (see page 339), & paprika harvesting in late Sep/early Oct – or arrange local private accommodation. ⏰ *Mon–Fri 08.00–16.00.*

WHERE TO STAY, EAT AND DRINK

Barokk Coffee House Kossuth Lajos u. 46. Bubbly little joint serving pizzas, cakes, ice cream & ice-cold beer. The outdoor seats are shaded by trees & face the cathedral. There are pool tables inside. *Pizzas 540–700Ft;* ⏰ *Mon–Thu 08.00–22.00, Fri–Sat 08.00–24.00, Sun 09.00–22.00.*

Casablanca Szent István Király út 36. Sells burgers, sandwiches, tortillas & ice cream, & has a pub attached that opens into the wee weekend hours. ⏰ *Mon–Thu 08.00–22.00, Fri–Sat 08.00–04.00, Sun 09.00–22.00.*

Club 502 Hotel & Pizzeria (7 rooms) Szent István Király 64; ☎ 78 562804; www.club502.hu. Cheaper than the Hotel Kalocsa & considerably less shabby than the Piros Arany, this guesthouse has a few big & clean rooms. It also has a large bar with a wide drinks menu, & rustles up a decent pizza *(pizzas 840–1200Ft;* ⏰ *daily 08.00–24.00, kitchen from 12.00). Rooms from 3,500Ft/pp.*

Hotel Piros Arany (20 rooms) Szent István Király út 37; ☎ 78 462220. Not much more than a hostel; some rooms are en suite, others have shared

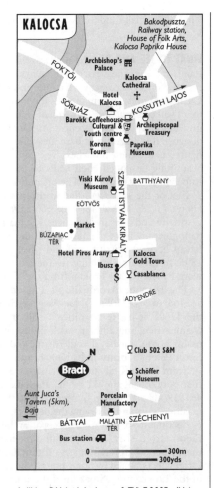

facilities. *Dbl (with bathroom & TV) 7,200Ft, dbl (no frills) 5,400Ft.*

Wellness Hotel Kalocsa (29 rooms) Szentháromság tér 4; ☎ 78 561200; www.hotelkalocsa.hu. Kalocsa's top place to lay a hat is this 200-year-old Baroque former mansion directly opposite the cathedral in the main square. Rooms are spacious & plush; on some mornings a free alarm call comes at 06.30, care of the cathedral bells. The hotel recently received a facelift, & now also has a small wellness centre. The restaurant *(mains avg 1,400Ft)* is very good, with fish, veal & – unusually for Hungary – a vegetarian selection. The garden dining area is pleasantly quiet & the cellar offers a good range of quality Hungarian wines. *Sgl 13,500–15,500Ft, dbl 20,000–22,000Ft, trpl 28,000Ft (excl Tourist Tax).*

There is a small outdoor covered **market** on Búzapiac tér, at the western end of Városház utca.

WHAT TO SEE AND DO The pretty Szentháromság tér, with its cobbles and lanterns, stands at the northeastern end of town, dominated by the cathedral in its face and the Archbishop's Palace, set back a little and coated in a loud mustard yellow. **Kalocsa Cathedral** in its current guise is the fourth to have stood here; the first was built in the 11th century, and subsequent versions were burned down during Mongol invasion and Ottoman occupation. Once the Turks had left, András Mayerhoffer designed this magnificent Baroque edifice (1735–54), its ceiling bearing white carved figures like cameo brooches. The intricate detail – from subtle gilding through beautifully fashioned choir stalls to the altar painting by Austrian artist Leopold Kupelvieser – is stunning. The organ first piped to the tune of Ferenc Liszt himself.

East of the cathedral, the **Archiepiscopal Treasury** (*Főszékesegyházi kincstár; Hunyadi u. 2;* ✆ *78 461860;* 💰 *500/250Ft;* ⊕ *May–Oct Tue–Sun 09.00–17.00*) has vestments and treasures (chalices, reliquaries, pontifical rings set with topaz stones) dating mainly from the 18th and 19th centuries; the star of the show is the Szent István herm, a bust of gold and silver crafted for the millennial celebrations of 1896. In the same building (to the left at the top of the stairs) is an exhibition of work by artist Péter Prokop from the 1970s.

The Baroque **Archbishop's Palace** (*Érseki palota; Szentháromság tér 1;* ✆ *78 362166;* 💰 *500/250Ft;* ⊕ *Apr–Nov Tue–Sun 09.00–12.00, 14.00–17.00*) was built in the 1760s; it has a magnificent hall and chapel adorned with frescoes by F A Maulbertsch, and a library with illuminated manuscripts (notably a 15th-century psalm book), medieval codices (the oldest dating to 1040), a letter by the great Jesuit Péter Pázmány and a bible bearing Martin Luther's scrawl.

Szent István Király út runs arrow-straight southeast from the main square. Your first port of call should be the **Paprika Museum** (*Szent István király út 6;* ✆ *78 461819;* 💰 *500/300Ft;* ⊕ *Mar–Nov 10.00–17.00 daily*), replete with the tools for mashing, cutting and drying the peppers, and puppets showing the process at work. A document in the archiepiscopal archives records the growing of paprika in Kalocsa from 1729 – the hot stuff came to the fore when the Habsburgs prohibited the import of foreign spices, stimulating the popularity of domestic versions. Originally operated by horse power, the grinding mills ran on fuel from the middle of the 19th century. Stock up at the small souvenir shop.

Further along, the **Viski Károly Museum** (*Szent István Király út 25;* ✆ *78 462351;* 💰 *250/120Ft;* ⊕ *Tue–Sun 09.00–17.00*) has ten collections featuring minerals, coins and an ethnographic exhibition of regional textiles and folk art dating from the 19th century. The vivid furniture bears testimony to the colour cravings indulged by the town's 'painting women', skilled groups of female artisans who decorated the main rooms of peasant houses.

On crossing Városház utca, you'll enter a pedestrianised section lined with shady trees and benches; along the centre is an **open-air pantheon** to some Kalocsan colossi of a millennium, ranged chronologically and kicking off with the statue of Asztrik at the southern end. Keep walking until you reach the fascinating **Schöffer Museum** (*Szent István Király út 76;* ✆ *78 462253;* 💰 *200/100Ft;* ⊕ *Tue–Sun 10.00–12.00, 14.00–17.00*), devoted to the Parisian artist Nikolas Schöffer, who was born in this house in 1912. In exploring themes of space, time and light, his pieces incorporate computer automation, mirrors, clockwork mechanisms and cinematography to illusory and energetic effect. Gaze into his mirrored prism and believe you're glimpsing eternity. The French-speaking director is imbued with wonder, and it's easy to see why. Look out for one of Schöffer's bigger works at the bus station.

The **Kalocsa Paprika House** (*Kossuth Lajos u. 15;* ↘ *78 465049;* ☉ *May–Oct daily 10.00–16.00, Nov–Apr by prior arrangement*) claims to hold Europe's biggest paprika museum, although it's really for dining tour groups and has little to get excited about – some processing tools and photos of the 50 members of the Order of the Knights of Kalocsa Paprika in their regal robes (we kid you not!). The museum is run by the Kalocsa Spice Paprika Company, established in 2002 and enjoying 3% of the world market. From Szentháromság tér, head northeast along Kossuth Lajos utca for around ½km.

A short distance further along Kossuth Lajos utca, turn right to the **House of Folk Arts** (*Népművészeti tájház; Tompa Mihály u. 5–7;* ↘ *78 461560;* ✍ *500/300Ft;* ☉ *Apr–Oct 10.00–17.00 daily, Nov–Mar by prior arrangement*), a reed-thatched peasant dwelling with the signature painted walls and items of folk art. It is surprising to learn that Kalocsa's embroidery was traditionally rather plain; the explosion of floral motifs (an extension of those added to the walls) came in the 20th century as coloured cotton became more prevalent and folk dancers were used as the canvases for jazzier designs. For all its folkloric authenticity, the house is something of a tourist trap. The same can be said of **Aunt Juca's Tavern** (*Juca Néni Csárdája; Meszesi út*), an old ferry inn converted into a peasant-style barn where costumed women showcase (and sell!) their handicrafts. Programmes here featuring food, gypsy music and *pálinka* can be arranged through Korona Tours (see page 337).

You'll find the **Kalocsa Porcelain Manufactory** (*Porcelán Manufaktúra; Malatin tér 5; 78 462017; www.porcelanfesto.hu; admission 300Ft*) on the way to Aunt Juca's from the town; here you can see the painting of china and the whole process of making porcelain kitchenware. The visit takes about an hour.

Bakodpuszta Ten kilometres from town – on the way towards Dunapataj (turn left on to Route 51 from Kossuth Lajos utca) – Bakodpuszta has horses and traditional Hungarian livestock on 400ha of land. It hosts five or six horse shows a week and its inn has a huge dining area. You can book through Korona Tours (see page 337).

HAJÓS AND HAJÓS-PINCÉK

Southeast of Kalocsa (just above Route 54), the pretty village of **Hajós** is notable for an airy Baroque Roman Catholic church on Köztársaság tér, its stained-glass windows casting shafts of piercing coloured light. Inside is a Gothic statue of Madonna brought by German (Swabian) Catholics settlers; outside is a grassed avenue with intricately painted stations of the cross made from Zsolnay china. Keep an eye out too for the pleasing pharmacy building in a corner of the square, with its angular rooftop.

Once you've wandered the square, head 1km or so further for **Hajós-Pincék**, whose sole reason to be is wine. Tidy rows of cellars – over 1,000 in total – line the road like hotel pieces on a Monopoly board. Tastings are on offer at some, although opening hours are hit-and-miss affairs. A safe bet, however, is the family-run Judit Panzió, whose charming cellar is divided between several chambers and which can offer food and accommodation once you've had your boozy fill. The village is at its most lively in May, during the celebration of St Orbán (the guardian saint of vintners).

At the top end of Hajósi utca (just before Route 54), **Judit Panzió** (*Borbíró sor 1–3;* ↘ *78 404832; 10 rooms; dbl 6,000Ft*) is friendly, clean and ideal for an evening of wine tasting. The restaurant (*mains avg 2,000Ft;* ☉ *daily 07.00–22.00*) serves traditional Hungarian cuisine. You can also pick up a walking trail from outside. Alternatively, the **Kellermotel Hajós** (*Hajós Kút tér 1;* ↘ *78 504010; www.kellermotel.com; 21 rooms; dbl 47–55*) stands on the road between Hajos and Hajós-Pincék. If ever pride went into a hotel then here it is; the Dutch owners have put whirlpools in some of the rooms, and there's a sauna and well-equipped fitness room. They can arrange wine tastings in their cellar, and also keep seven horses for tailor-made riding tours. Superlatives were made for surprising gems like this.

Buses running between Kalocsa and Baja stop at Hajós (with some going on to Hajós-Pincék), and there are services from Hájos-Pincék to Kiskőrös (about ten daily) and Kecskemét (15).

BAJA

If there's something fishy going on and you sense you're in the soup, the chances are you're in Baja, a town lodged between the Danube and one of its branches (the Sugovica), and bisected horizontally by Route 55 and vertically by Route 51. On the second Saturday every July, 2,000 cauldrons bubble over open fires in Szentháromság tér; the big event of the Baja Folk Festival has earned the town a place in the Guinness Book of Records, under the category of fish soup (greatest quantity of, cooked at one time). Carp is the soup's main ingredient, although catfish, pike and other fish may play their parts. Thousands of people gather to get thoroughly piscivorous. The citizens of Baja are fond of fish during the rest of the year too – indeed, it is said that they consume an average of 66kg a year, more than anywhere else in Europe.

In medieval times, this was a commercial centre, and under the Turks a town fortified by a stockade castle. A massive fire in 1840 cleared many of its buildings and in doing so ensured that its architectural landscape changed from the Baroque to the Neoclassical. Today Baja prides itself on being a cosmopolitan community – with German, Serbian and Croatian influences stemming from 18th-century immigrant settlers – and is a popular resort, tourists attracted by several little river islands, woodland and a beach or two. Its bridge is also key, representing one of only two main river-crossing points on the Danube stretch between Budapest and the southern country border.

GETTING THERE AND AWAY From the **bus station** (*Állomás tér*) it's about a 15-minute walk to the centre (turn right and along Szegedi út, which leads into Arany János utca), or you can catch a local bus from the stop at the end of Állomás tér. Baja is well served by bus and there are frequent connections with Mohács, Szeged, Kalocsa and Pécs, as well as to Szekszárd (11), Budapest Népliget (ten), Kecskemét (eight) and Hevíz (one). It's a ten-minute walk southwest from the **railway station** (*Vonat kert*) to the centre. Only a handful of towns are accessible by train, including Kiskunhalas (12 daily), Kiskunfélegyháza, Kiskőrös and Szekszárd (one); there are regular services to Budapest (with a change at either Sárbogárd or Kiskunhalas).

INFORMATION AND OTHER PRACTICALITIES

$ **Bank** Szentháromság tér 10

🎫 **Info Tourist Travel Agency** Halász-part 4/C; ☏ 79 427533. Can arrange private accommodation & tours by boat, canoe or hiking boot. ☉ *Mon–Fri 09.00–16.30, Sat 09.00–12.00.*

🎫 **IBUSZ** Kossuth Lajos u. 11/A; ☏ 79 524534; e baja@ibusz.hu. Money exchange, tours & accommodation. ☉ *Mon–Fri 09.00–17.00.*

🖳 **Internet Café** Tóth Kálmán tér 7. Internet access in this café near Vörösmarty tér costs 10Ft/min, 500Ft/hr. ☉ *Mon–Fri 09.00–13.00, 17.00–21.00, Sat 09.00–13.00.*

📖 **Listings magazine** Bajai Est

📖 **Tourinform** Szentháromság tér 5; ☏ 79 420793; e baja@tourinform.hu. Can provide details of recommended cycling routes along the Danube, as well as other information. Near the Hotel Duna. ☉ *Mon–Fri 09.00–17.00 (w/end too May–Jul).*

🏠 WHERE TO STAY

🏠 **Az Eötvös József College** Szegedi út 2; ☏ 79 321655. The office here organises rooms in 3 hostels in the city (at Széchenyi u. 18/B, Bajcsy-Zsilinszky út 16 & Deszkás u. 2). *Rooms from 1,500Ft/pp.*

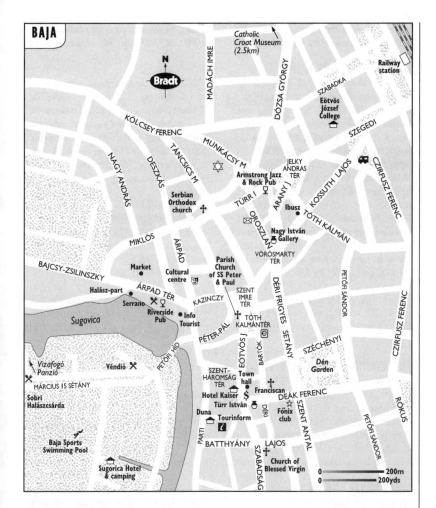

BAJA

Catholic
Croat Museum
(2.5km)

Railway
station

N

Bradt

SZABADKA

Eötvös
József
College

KÖLCSEY FERENC

MADÁCH IMRE

DÓZSA GYÖRGY

SZEGEDI

MUNKÁCSY M

TÁNCSICS M

JELKY
ANDRÁS
TÉR

KOSSUTH LAJOS

CZIRFUSZ FERENC

NAGY ANDRÁS

DÉZSKÁS

Armstrong Jazz
& Rock Pub

Serbian
Orthodox
church

TÜRR I

ARANY J

Ibusz

TÓTH KÁLMÁN

MIKLÓS

ÁRPÁD

OROSZLÁN

Nagy István
Gallery

VÖRÖSMARTY
TÉR

BAJCSY-ZSILINSZKY

Market

Cultural
centre

Parish
Church
of SS Peter
& Paul

SZENT
IMRE
TÉR

DÉRI FRIGYES SÉTÁNY

PETŐFI SÁNDOR

CZIRFUSZ FERENC

Halász-part

Serrano

ÁRPÁD TÉR

KAZINCZY

Riverside
Pub

Info
Tourist

PÉTER-PÁL

TÓTH
KALMÁNTÉR

SZÉCHÉNYI

Sugovica

Vizafogó
Panzió

Véndió

MÁRCIUS 15 SÉTÁNY

PETŐFI HÍD

EÖTVÖS J

BARTÓK

Dén
Garden

Sobri
Halászcsárda

SZENT-
HÁROMSÁG
TÉR

Town
hall

Hotel Kaiser

Türr István

Duna

Tourinform

Franciscan

DÉRI

Fönix
club

DEÁK FERENC

SZENT ANTAL

RÓKUS

PETŐFI SÁNDOR

Baja Sports
Swimming Pool

PARTI

BATTHYÁNY

LAJOS

SZABADSÁG

Sugorica Hotel
& camping

Church of
Blessed Virgin

0 —————— 200m
0 —————— 200yds

🏠 **Country House Panzió** Petőfi-sziget, Március 15
sétány 20; 📞 79 326585. Family-run guesthouse
on Petőfi-sziget whose rooms could do with a
little updating but are nevertheless clean & tidy.
*Sgl 6,500Ft, dbl 8,500Ft, trpl 11,000Ft, quad
14,000Ft.*

🏠 **Hotel Duna** (50 rooms) Szentháromság tér 6;
📞 79 323224; e hotel-duna@baja.hu;
www.hotelduna.hu Staring greenly from the
southern side of the main square, the Hotel Duna
is far from luxurious but is reasonably priced &
centrally located. *Sgl 7,600Ft, dbl 9,600Ft (excl
taxes & b/fast).*

🏠 **Hotel Kaiser Panzió** (15 rooms) Szentháromság
tér 8–10; 📞 79 520950, 30 223 6633;
www.hotelkaiser.hu. New hotel opposite Hotel Duna.
Good location & good rooms with luxurious showers

at a good price. The pension also offers a few other
rooms around town (at Hattyú u. 2 & Tóth Kálmán
u. 12). *Sgl 8,500 Ft, dbl 11,500 Ft; b/fast 1,000
Ft/pp.*

🏠 **Sugovica Hotel & Camping** Petőfi-sziget; 📞 79
321755; www.hotelsugovica.hu. A little further down
the same road as the sports centre, this is a large
32-room hotel & campsite set in 5ha of lush
surroundings (and inc outdoor swimming pool,
children's playground & small bowling alley). It
was closed for refurbishment during our last
visit, & it isn't clear when it will re-open. *Sgl
8,700Ft, dbl 15,400Ft, apt (for 2) 21,400Ft;
bungalows from 6,500Ft, caravan/tent 1,400/590Ft,
plus 440Ft/pp.*

🏠 **Vizafogó Panzió** Petőfi-sziget, Március 15 sétány
27; 📞 79 326585, e vizafogo@citromail.hu. At the

341

northern end of the island, Vizafogó has dbls with decent-sized bathrooms; like a couple of other places in town, one senses its prices are inflated. *Sgl 6,500Ft, dbl 8,500Ft, trpl 11,000Ft, quad 14,000Ft.*

✗ WHERE TO EAT AND DRINK

♀ **Riverside Pub** Halászpart; ↘ 30 3996655. One of a number of bars offering snacks at Halász-part (in the shadow of Petőfi Bridge), the unimaginatively named Riverside has Guinness & Kilkenny on the drinks menu & pizzas, pastas & grilled dishes by way of food. It's the favoured party spot on Fri & Sat nights. *Mains avg 1,200 Ft;* ⊕ *daily 09.00–02.00.*
✗ **Serrano Saloon** Halászpart; ↘ 79 421909. Chow on tortillas, burritos & fajitas in a saloon hung with cattle skulls. *Mains avg 1,200Ft;* ⊕ *daily 10.00–24.00.*
✗ **Sobri Halászcsárda** Petőfi-sziget; ↘ 79 420654; www.sobrihalaszcsarda.hu. Named after a famous fish-soup specialist chef, this fish restaurant takes some beating (or battering?!). There are also 4 guest rooms (*sgl 4000Ft, dbl 6,000Ft, trpl 9,000Ft, quad*

10,000Ft) above the restaurant, facing towards the Sugovica. *Mains avg 1,500Ft;* ⊕ *daily 11.30–22.00.*
✗ **Véndió** Petőfi-sziget; ↘ 79 424544. Rising to the Sobri's challenge, Véndió is a very smart restaurant in a lovely setting on Petőfi-sziget, & serves quality tucker. The dishes are Hungarian, with fish & game the house specialities. It's more expensive than other restaurants in town, but it's worth it. Live music on Sat. *Mains avg 2,200Ft;* ⊕ *Mon–Fri 12.00–22.00, Sat–Sun 11.00–23.00.*
✗ **Vizafogó** See page 341. Another riverside offering with a healthy stock of fish on the menu, & a tasty soup. Take a table on the terrace, but bring some mozzie spray or you'll be the one getting eaten. *Mains avg 1,600Ft;* ⊕ *daily 12.00–23.00.*

The bustling **market** (⊕ *Wed & Sat 08.00–12.00*) is on Szenes utca, just north of the Halász-part. If you're brave enough to try making your own fish soup, you can buy yourself a **cauldron** from the Swobodas (*Arató u. 11;* ↘ *79 422448;* ↘ *06 30 928 5215*).

ENTERTAINMENT AND NIGHTLIFE **Baja marketing ltd** (*Árpád tér 1;* ↘ *79 324229;* ⊕ *Mon–Thu 09.00–12.00, 13.00–16.00, Fri 09.00–12.00, 13.00–15.00*) can provide information on concerts, plays and other entertainment events; you can also purchase theatre tickets here.

There are several bars on the river bank near Petőfi Bridge at the Halász-part. Alternatively, the **Armstrong Jazz and Rock Pub** (*Türr István u. 1;* ↘ *79 428015;* ⊕ *Mon–Thu 13.00–24.00, Fri 13.00–03.00, Sat 18.00–03.00*) is a dark cellar bar with live bands on Sat night (usually from 23.30)..

WHAT TO SEE AND DO The cobbled, recently restored and beautiful Szentháromság tér is at the town's centre, surrounded on three sides with Renaissance, Eclectic and Neoclassical buildings. The square is further enhanced when cleared of parked cars, but that generally only happens when it's being used as the backdrop for a period film. The open fourth side is framed by the Sugovica branch of the Danube and Petőfi-sziget over the water. The **Trinity Column** is Baroque in design and foisted in 1881; on it are the four evangelists with Mary above them, while the seated figures hugging the cross at the top represent the Holy Trinity. The **town hall** (*Szentháromság tér 1*), once home to the Grassalkovich family, was originally Baroque but received a Neo-Renaissance-style overhaul in 1896 as part of the millennial celebrations.

Just to the square's east, the **Türr István Museum** (*Deák Ferenc u. 1;* ↘ *79 324173;* ⊘ *entrance adult 300Ft, explanatory talk 800Ft;* ⊕ *Mar 15–Dec 15 Wed–Sat 10.00–16.00*) has exhibitions spreading over two floors that deal with three centuries of Baja's history. There are archaeological and artistic items, displays devoted to life on the Danube – shipping and fishing – and to the town's ethnic minorities. Many towns of the plain were heavily influenced by such minority groups, formed either of refugees fleeing the Turks and seeking haven or settlers repopulating towns after the Turks had left. István Türr was born in Baja and went on to join the revolution in Italy, fighting alongside Garibaldi; on his return to Hungary after the Compromise, he worked in water management and was involved in the Panama and Corinthian canals. However, perhaps the most quirky of the town's citizens commemorated in the museum was András Jelky – the 'Hungarian Robinson Crusoe'. During the 18th century, this apprentice embarked on a journey to Paris to improve his tailoring skills; he somehow succeeded not only in getting lost but in running out of money, enlisting with the Dutch army and wandering around Asia. On eventually returning to Hungary, he wrote his memoirs – and doubtless prayed for the invention of satnav; there's a statue of him by Ferenc Medgyessy on Jelky András tér. The main entrance is on the other side of the museum, in Roosevelt tér.

Behind the town hall, the Baroque **Franciscan Church of St Anthony of Padua** (*Bartók Béla u. 1*) was completed in 1756 (and remodelled in 1780). The standing, blue-robed Mater Dolorosa is the oldest of the town's Baroque statues – dating to 1740 – but looks rather lonely in its niche at the southern side. The right-hand church spire was once used as a firewatch and lookout tower.

Among other places of worship to look out for are the **Parish Church of SS Peter and Paul** (*Tóth Kálmán tér*), built in 1765 with funding from the contemporary landowners (the Grassalkovich family) and with 1930s frescoes by local art teacher Sándor Éber; the late-Baroque **Serbian Orthodox Church of St Nicholas** (*Miklós u.;* ☏ *79 423199;* ⊕ *Wed 09.00–12.00, call in advance at other times*), like a piece of confectionery in raspberry and custard colours, and with a stunning iconostasis; the 18th-century **Serbian Orthodox Church of the Blessed Virgin** (*Batthyány Lajos u.*), rougher around the edges, jammed cheek by jowl with residential houses and serving as a concert hall; and the proud, Neoclassical former synagogue of 1845, a wing of which used to serve as a home for elderly Jewish folk but which now holds the **Ady Endre Town Library** (*Munkacsy Mihály u. 9;* ⊕ *Mon–Thu 13.00–18.00, Fri 10.00–18.00, Sat 08.00–12.00*). The library stock is graced by fabulous surroundings, with layered chandeliers and high galleries; the most precious incunabula is the first full edition of the great 18th-century encyclopaedia of Denis Diderot and Jean le Rond D'Alembert (the product of their Enlightenment quest to summarise all knowledge), and there is also a bible once owned by the poet Endre Ady.

At the northern side of Vörösmarty tér, the **Nagy István Gallery** (*Arany János u. 1;* ☏ *79 325649;* ⊛ *300/150Ft;* ⊕ *Mar 15–Dec 15 Wed–Sat 10.00–16.00*) has the work of 20th-century national artists in a Neoclassical mansion once home to an artists' colony. Among the pieces are those by Nagy István (1873–1937), a Transylvanian artist who lived in Baja and was the leading member of the so-called Alföld School; there's also a bronze bust of the man outside by the brilliant Imre Varga.

Around 2.5km north of the centre – follow Dózsa György út, turn left into Templom utca and Pandor utca is the first on your right – stands a thatched village house painted with ducks and roses and containing the **Catholic Croat Museum** (*Bunyevác Tájház; Pandor u. 51;* ☏ *79 324173;* ⊛ *150/75Ft;* ⊕ *Mar 15–Dec 15 Wed–Sat 10.00–14.00*). It represents the typical home of a family of Catholic Croats at the turn of the 19th century, an ethnic group who settled in this region after the end of Ottoman rule.

The stretch known as the **Halász-part** (Fishermen's Beach) is a good spot to drink a beer and enjoy the sight of the river bending away. The sandy section for sunbathing is a further 200m along (moving away from Petőfi Bridge). Another place for strolls and quiet contemplation is the **Déri Garden** (*Déri-kert*), a block east of the Franciscan church. At the western entrance is a bust of Frigyes Déri (1852–1924), the Baja-born silk maker and art collector, as well as a 23m-tall World War I memorial and a rock monument commemorating the 1956 revolution.

Other activities Scheduled **boat trips** (☏ *79 426525; Jun 1–Sep 28 Sat from 16.00*) depart from the Halász-part area on summer Saturdays. The one-hour tour circles Petőfi-sziget before travelling along the Gemenc Forest (see page 391). **Admirál** (☏ *06 30 938 2149*) also arranges one- and two-hour tours with a boat leaving from the Sugovica Yacht Basin – including water-skiing if you wish; prices start at around 16,000Ft. As well as the **beaches** on Petőfi-sziget, there are others near the Halász-part and on Nagy Pandúr sziget.

The **Baja Sports Swimming Pool** (*Petőfi-sziget;* ☏ *79 326773;* 🏊 *500/330Ft;* ☉ *Mon–Tue 06.00–19.30, Thu–Fri 06.00–19.30, Sat–Sun 08.00–19.30*), a short distance from the bridge, is a leisure centre with exercise classes, solarium and sauna alongside the main and children's pools.

There are plenty of places to cast a line at Baja, but you'll need an angling permit; **Baja Anglers Association** (*Petőfi-sziget 1;* ☏ *79 321343*) can sell daily, weekly or annual ones. **Baja Rowing Club** (*Garibaldi u. 25;* ☏ *06 30 243 8656*) rents kayaks, canoes and sailboats between March 1 and November 1.

Tourinform can suggest a series of **cycling** routes of between 5km and 60km. Rent bicycles from Rausch Bicycle Shop (*Czirfusz Ferenc u. 4;* ☏ *79 325336;* ☉ *Mon–Fri 09.00–17.00, Sat 09.00–12.00*). The **Gemenc Forest** (☏ *74 491483; www.gemenczrt.hu;* see page 391) – part of the Duna-Dráva National Park – is just across the bridge from Baja; you can pick up walking trails from the bridgehead, but between May and October it is better to take the train to Pörböly from where you can pick up the narrow-gauge railway northward into the region. One daily service runs the 30km to Bárányfok (with its excursion centre), from where it's a short hop to Szekszárd. Two other trains only go as far as Gemenc Dunapart, from where you have to wait for a connection. However, be sure to check the times beforehand as you don't want to get stranded. Pörböly itself has a museum dedicated to the forest's wildlife, and is the starting point for several new marked trails (one to an arboretum and others to birdwatching towers).

FESTIVALS AND EVENTS Fish soup inevitably features heavily in the town's events, not only as the star attraction of the Baja Folk Festival in July but also during the Autumn Festival in September, alongside drama and music. At 174km, the Budapest–Baja International Boat Race is the longest in Europe, and takes place on the second weekend of August.

CSONGRÁD

Directly east of Kiskunfélegyháza, Csongrád falls close to the confluence of the Tisza and Körös rivers. Árpád granted the Tisza region to the ruler Ond, and Ond made this the chief settlement in his territory; its name – a Hungarian corruption of the Slav for 'black castle' – stems from the earthwork built by Ond's son Ete, which stood here up until the Mongols came in the 13th century, laying it waste and thereby stripping the town of the status it had maintained during István's rule. Its layout is linear, with everything spread along Fő utca before it leads out to the Belváros, a winding street with protected 200-year-old fishermen's cottages that was once the settlement's core. Less historic is the resort-style 'beach' on the river bank 50m away.

GETTING THERE AND AWAY There are no shortage of **buses** to Szentes and Kiskunfélegyháza, while a regular service also runs to Szeged; other destinations are Kecskemét (12), Budapest (nine), Orosháza (seven), Szolnok (five), Eger and Gyula (two). The **bus station** (*Hunyadi tér*) is in the centre. Csongrád lies on the same **railway** line as Szentes and Kiskunfélegyháza and there are up to eight trains a day to both destinations. To reach either Budapest, Szeged or Kecskemét you'll need to

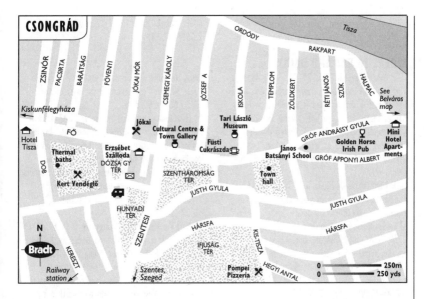

change at Kiskunfélegyháza, and for Orosháza or Hódmezővásárhely at Szentes. The station (*Vasút u.*) is southwest of the main strip; walk across the grassed area in front to the main road 100m ahead, turn left and continue until you join Fő utca.

INFORMATION AND OTHER PRACTICALITIES

🎭 **Cultural Centre & Town Gallery** Szentháromság tér 8; ☏ 63 483414/481034; e muvkozpont@ freemail.hu. There is no independent theatre in Csongrád, but the hall of the cultural centre stages productions by the amateur local group Csongrád Színtársulat, as well as other programmes. The gallery (*Kossuth tér 9–11; admission free*) hosts temporary exhibitions. *Cultural centre opening hours dependent*

on events; gallery ⊕ Mon–Fri 10.00–12.00, 14.00–17.00, Sat–Sun variable.
📕 **Listings magazine** Szegedi Est
📕 **Tourinform** Szentháromság tér 8; ☏ 63 570325. In the cultural centre building. ⊕ Jun 15–Sep 15 Mon–Sun 08.00–16.00, rest of yr Mon–Fri 08.00–16.00.

WHERE TO STAY

⌂ **Erzsébet Szálloda** (13 rooms) Fő u. 3; ☏ 63 483960. Don't be deterred by a forbidding exterior for this is a perfectly comfortable, if old-fashioned, 2-star hotel, centrally located & reasonably priced. There is a coffee house underneath. *Sgl 6,500Ft, dbl 8,000Ft, trpl 10,000Ft.*
⌂ **Fishermen's cottages** Fő u. 16 (contact address); ☏ 63 483631/06 30 239 4701. The charming place to spend a night is in one of the thatched fishermen's cottages, each with kitchen & courtyard. They are mainly situated along Öregvár utca & can accommodate 2–6 people. Contact László Erdős (details above). *Cottages 6,000–14,000Ft.*
⌂ **Hotel Tisza** (15 rooms) Fő u. 23; ☏ 63 483594; ☏ 30 383 0913; e hoteltisza@vnet.hu. Close to the thermal baths, this is a so-so hotel that did not have a restaurant during our visit (and, as such, to

our minds struggles to justify its 3 stars). *Sgl 9,500Ft, dbl 11,000Ft, trpl 12,500Ft.*
⌂ **Köröstoroki Campsite** Köröstorok, Nyárfa utca; Fő u. 14 (contact address); ☏ 63 481185; e idegenforgalom@vnet.hu. Set back from the beach at the Tisza bend, to the east of the centre, this shady campsite has wooden bungalows on stilts (with kitchens & bathrooms) as well as tent space. It is a very popular sunbathing spot in summer, & can be correspondingly 'lively'. Hire fishing equipment from 1,200Ft/day. *Bungalow 6,500Ft (for 2), 8,500Ft (for 3); tent/caravan 3,000/3,500Ft; ⊕ May–Sep.*
⌂ **Mini Hotel Apartments** (4 apts) Gróf Andrássy Gyula utca; ☏ 63 473322; m 06 20 922 9319; e apartments@netposta.net. On the way out towards the Belváros, these well-appointed & cared-for apartments (with small kitchens & bathrooms)

345

for 3–4 are excellent value. The owners will leave a b/fast in the fridge for you for an additional

600Ft. Apts 6,000Ft *(for 1)*, 7,000Ft *(for 2)*, 8,000Ft *(for 3)*.

✗ WHERE TO EAT AND DRINK

🍽 **Bohém Kávéház** Fő u. 20–24; ✆ 63 483651. This first-floor café & ice-cream parlour also serves light meals & snacks; there is a chilled, cavernous bar to the right as you enter, which features some good bands (particularly jazz). There's usually something happening at weekends. *Mains avg 1,100Ft;* ⊕ *Mon–Thu, Sun 09.00–24.00, Fri–Sat 09.00–01.00.*

🍽 **Füsti Cukrászda** Iskola u. 1; ✆ 63 483367. Popular cake & ice-cream place next to the Tari Museum. ⊕ *09.00–19.00 daily.*

🍺 **Golden Horse Irish Pub** Gróf Andrássy Gyula u. 17/A; ✆ 63 483834. A pleasant pub with a large wooden terrace, & Guinness & Kilkenny. The menu has an extensive choice of steaks, fish, chicken & pasta dishes. *Mains avg 1,000Ft;* ⊕ *Mon–Thu, Sun 12.00–22.00, Fri–Sat 12.00–24.00.*

🍺 **House of Csongrád Wines** (Csongrádi Borok Háza) Szentháromság tér 8; ✆ 63 482557. The showcase for the area's vintners since 2002, the House of Csongrád Wines (beneath the cultural centre) hosts pre-arranged tastings, organises tailored programmes & offers information about wine tours & the wines themselves. Wine-making is taken seriously in the region, which has a decent share of sunshine, &

there are some good reds. If you wish to sample direct, head for the cellars to the west of town. ⊕ *09.00–16.00 daily.*

✗ **Jókai Restaurant** Jókai Mór u. 1; ✆ 63 475010. Accessed through an archway opposite the Erzsébet Szálloda, this restaurant serves Hungarian food in goodly portions & has a delightful garden with fountain at the back. Its plush cocktail bar upstairs is closed in the heat of summer. *Mains avg 1,100Ft;* ⊕ *Mon–Sat 10.00–23.00, Sun 10.00–22.00.*

✗ **Kert Vendéglő** Dózsa György tér 6; ✆ 63 483199. Reach the Kert via an arch on Dózsa tér, behind the thermal baths. Outdoor dining is beneath a bamboo-thatch roof; there's a wide selection of fish & grilled dishes, as well as standard Hungarian fare. The pancake desserts are definitely worth a try; settle your food by locking horns on the giant chess set or with a game of mini golf. *Mains avg 1,000Ft;* ⊕ *11.30–22.00 daily.*

✗ **Pompei Pizzeria** Kis Tisza 6; ✆ 63 470160. Pizzas in 4 sizes to suit bellies great & small. The garden at the rear, as well as pool & football tables, makes this a hangout spot for youngsters too. *Mains avg 1,000Ft;* ⊕ *daily 16.00–22.00.*

WHAT TO SEE AND DO Szentháromság tér is a characterful, unkempt square offering cool shade in the heat of the day. Its Trinity Monument was erected in 1869. Just north of Kossuth tér, the **Tari László Museum** (*Iskola u. 2;* ✆ *63 483103; www.tarilaszlomuzeum.hu;* 🎫 *250/150Ft;* ⊕ *Mon–Fri 13.00–17.00, Sat 08.00–12.00, Sun 08.00–17.00*) – named after a local dentist and amateur historian – has a range of ethnographic and archaeological artefacts. Its Bronze-Age display includes excavated skeletons, and there are ancient swords, stirrups, coins, fishing nets and boating equipment, as well as more recent items like military uniforms from the Independence War of 1848–49. The museum also remembers the mid-19th-century peasant labourers who broke their backs with the spade work required in regulating the Tisza, draining the swampland and making habitable a massive area of the Great Plain.

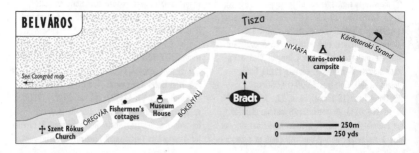

Across the road, the Baroque **Parish Church of the Virgin Mary** (*Nagyboldogasszony templom; Kossuth tér*) was built on an earlier cemetery in 1762, part of the construction of a new town centre with more space to breathe to the west of the traditional Belváros. There are statues of the kings István and László either side of the altar, while the altarpiece itself was painted in 1917 by Lajos Tari, a copy of *Assunta* by Tiziano from the Frári Church in Venice. The wonderful frescoes on the ceiling depict the Annunciation, the Nativity and the moment when István offered the Holy Crown to the Virgin Mary. When the church is lit for a service, its magnificent gilding – and particularly that of the pulpit, looking like an extravagant, wall-mounted bathtub – leaps from the darker nooks and crannies behind, and is a real spectacle. The Art-Nouveau **János Batsányi School** (*Kossuth tér*) at the eastern end of the square was designed by Miklós Ybl in 1914, and has majolica floral motifs above its windows and a steep black roof.

Moving eastwards, Gróf Andrássy Gyula utca leads to Öregvár ('Old Castle') utca and the Belváros, a pleasant 1km walk from the modern centre. You'll pass the shabby white **Szent Rókus Church** (*Szent Rókus tér*) before reaching the cobbled streets and fishermen's cottages. Some of these 200-year-old dwellings – unique in the Great Plain, and 17 were placed under heritage protection in the 1960s – can be rented (see page 345); alternatively you can take a peek inside one at the **Museum House** (*Gyökér u. 1;* \ *63 481052;* ✆ *admission free;* ⊕ *May–Oct Tue–Sun 13.00–17.00*). (Another, that wasn't accorded protected status, was moved for display at the Ópusztaszer National Memorial Park; see page 351.) Until the 1950s, fishermen maintained their traditional lifestyles here by the river bank. Families would take their water from the Tisza, filling jugs and leaving them until the sediment had settled to the bottom. Climb the bank running next to the road for views of the river bend, particularly pleasing during early evening. At the tip of the bend (facing the mouth of the Hármas Körös) is the 700m-long **Köröstoroki Strand**, crowded with sunbathers on the sand and those messing about in boats. This resort-style beach has a couple of places to eat (as well as accommodation; see page 345).

Heading towards the river northwest of the contemporary centre, a pontoon bridge crosses the Tisza to Nagyrét; from there it is a 3km walk to some Roman remains and those of the **Ellés Monastery**, a very significant site dating to the 11th and 12th centuries and excavated during the 1990s.

Other activities As well as the strand (see above), the **thermal baths and swimming pool** (*Dob u. 3–5;* \ *63 481915;* ✆ *360/250Ft;* ⊕ *Mon 07.00–19.00, Tue–Wed 07.00–22.00, Thu 07.00–19.00, Fri 07.00–22.00, Sat 08.00–22.00, Sun 08.00–20.00*) to the west of Dózsa György tér are set among sycamore trees. There are a number of indoor and outdoor pools whose medicinal water is said to help rheumatic and gynaecological disorders.

The **Pejkó Riding Club** (*Szántó Major Tanya 95;* \ *63 483460*) is a few kilometres south of the centre – follow Vasút utca (Road 451) towards Szentes. The horse farm offers riding lessons and cross-country tours, and has an eight-room guesthouse, swimming pool and tennis courts.

FESTIVALS AND EVENTS There are wine festivals in early April and mid August, while those preferring beer are catered for in May. The main event is Csongrád Days, over two weeks in August.

SZENTES

It is surprising that Szentes, on the banks of the River Kurca southeast of Csongrád, is not more popular with tourists for it has much to recommend it. Its main museum is well worth seeing, there are a couple of decent places to stay and eat, a sports complex offers activity a few minutes' walk from the centre and there are pleasant riverside strolls to be had. True, it's regrettable that some of the significant buildings have been allowed to stagnate; in the centuries following the Turkish occupation, the town rebuilt with an architectural flourish seldom found elsewhere on the Great Plain, and one senses that if some of these monuments were to enjoy a lick or two of paint, Szentes could become one of the must-sees of the region. As it stands it is noted for its vegetables (the greenhouses powered by 32 wells, which produce thermal water at temperatures close to boiling point) and athleticism – in the 1990s, Szentes was named National Sporting Town.

GETTING THERE AND AWAY The **bus station** (*Szabadság tér*) is just south of Kossuth tér, offering up to six direct buses a day to Budapest Népliget and a very regular service to Csongrád, Hódmezővásárhely, Szeged and Kiskunfélegyháza; there are also buses to Orosháza (up to 42), Szolnok (ten), Tiszaföldvár (four), Tiszafüred (two), Gyula (eight), Lajosmizse (eleven), Miskolc (four) and once-daily to Mátraháza, Mátrafüred, Parádfürdő and Pécs. The **railway station** – on the lines east–west between Kiskunfélegyháza and Orosháza and north–south between Hódmezővásárhely Népkert and Tiszatenyő – is a 20-minute walk northeast of the centre. There are frequent trains to Budapest Nyugati, nine to Hódmezővásárhely, six to Orosháza, six to Csongrád and six to Kiskunfélegyháza; change at Hódmezővásárhely for Szeged. There's a local bus stop outside the station; on foot turn left from the station on to the main road (*Atilla út*), then right to Kossuth Lajos utca which leads into town. For taxis, try ÁSZ (🕿 *63 444444*).

INFORMATION AND OTHER PRACTICALITIES

🖳 **Arabella Internet Café** Nagy Ferenc u. 1. Internet café next to the cinema. ⊕ *Mon–Thu 10.00–22.00, Fri–Sat 10.00–24.00.*

🎫 **Gold Sun Travel Agency** Kossuth tér 5; 🕿 63 560160. Tour company offering information about what's on, as well as assistance with private accommodation. At the eastern side of the square.

⊕ *Mon–Fri 09.00–13.00, 13.30–17.00, Sat 09.30–12.00.*

📖 **Listings magazine** Szegedi Est

🎭 **Móricz Zsigmond Cultural Centre** Ady Endre u. 36; tel; 63 312623. Entertainment programmes, dance & fitness classes & folk exhibitions. *Opening hrs vary.*

WHERE TO STAY, EAT AND DRINK

🏕 **Camping** Széchenyi liget. There is a campsite near the sports complex in the town's recreational park (see page 350).

🍺 **Chicago Pub, Billiard & Bowling** Nagy Ferenc u.; 🕿 63 562002; www.chicagobowlingpub.hu. A relatively new venue on the pedestrianised street, offering food, drink, bowling alleys & pool tables over 3 floors. *Mains avg 1,800Ft;* ⊕ *Sun–Thu 11.00–22.00, Fri–Sat 11.00–24.00.*

✗ **Főnix** Mátyás király u. 2; 🕿 63 316282. This 1st-floor restaurant is bedecked in purple & has a good range of Hungarian dishes. Follow Kossuth Lajos u. east, & turn right on to Mátyás király utca. *Mains avg 1,200Ft;* ⊕ *11.00–23.00 daily.*

🏨 **Holdfény Panzió** (9 rooms) Arany János u. 8; 🕿 63 444076; e hpanzio@szentes.hu. Just off Ady Endre u., north of Kossuth tér, Holdfény Panzió is comfortable & family run. It has a communal kitchen available to guests; the 2 sgl rooms are not

en suite. Air-con, internet, parking. Rooms *Sgl 5,500Ft, dbl 9,500Ft, quad 12,000Ft.*

🏨 **Hotel Szentes** www.petofiszallo.hu. This new hotel on the corner of Kossuth u. & Petőfi u. was still under construction when we visited. It will be 4-star, & the area's top accommodation.

✗ **Liget** Széchenyi liget, Csallány Gábor part 4; 🕿 63 400397. Provided you can put up with the noise from the baths behind it, the Liget has a covered terrace, an elegant interior & an excellent range of creative, gourmet choices – among them whole roast suckling pig & stuffed pigeon. You shouldn't go wrong here. *Mains avg 1,200Ft;* ⊕ *Mon–Thu 11.00–21.00, Fri–Sat 11.00–22.00, Sun 11.00–21.00.*

✗ **Nádas Csárda** Nádas sétány 1/C; 🕿 63 315941. With its gorgeous thatch & bubbly atmosphere, this is the leading contender in the ambience stakes. There is national & international cuisine, including a Transylvanian mixed grill & the house special of

'Nádas' dish for 2 (a selection of fried meats & cheese). It's next to the river, so try to secure a table outside in the shade. Located 2km north of the centre, but worth the effort; follow Tóth István u. & then Sima Ferenc u., before turning left on to Szalai u. & then first left again. Mains avg 1,200Ft; ⏰ Mon–Fri 11.30–22.00, Sat–Sun 11.30–23.00.

🏠 **Páterház Panzió** (8 rooms) Kossuth u. 1; ➘ 63 444112. While its façade faithfully preserves the early-20th-century style of bourgeois architecture, the interior is modern. The rooms won't disappoint – spick & span, & with large bathrooms. The restaurant (mains 900–1,880Ft, avg 1,500Ft; ⏰ 11.00–22.00 daily) serves quality Hungarian cuisine in an airy dining room with attentive staff. Centrally located, in front of the bus station. Sgl 7,200Ft, dbl 15,000Ft.

✘ **Taverna Pizzeria** Horváth Mihály u. 7; ➘ 63 401051. Pizzas & snacks for those hankering after non-Hungarian food. There's a patio garden at the back. Mains avg 880Ft; ⏰ 11.00–23.00 daily.

WHAT TO SEE AND DO The main square is **Kossuth tér**, with black iron lamps, criss-crossing paths and a fountain whose nozzles spurt water to varying heights. There are statues of Lajos Kossuth (István Tóth) and Mihály Horváth, the latter – a great 19th-century theologian, historian and later MP – with quill in hand and skull cap on head, while around the edges are some of the town's architectural heavy hitters. At the western side, the stateliness of the Neoclassical **former County Hall** (*Megyeháza; Kossuth tér 1*) is sadly compromised by crumbling stonework and pigeon poo. It was completed in 1883, and has carved allegories of agriculture, industry, sailing, hunting, trade and fishing around its windows.

The early-20th-century **town hall** (*Kossuth tér 6*) is an altogether different affair, with a pristine façade and two mansards flanked by cylindrical corner turrets. The Art-Nouveau **Hotel Petőfi** (*Petőfi Sándor u. 2*) also bears ornamental turrets, but one now tilts tiredly. In its prime this was a significant piece of architectural art, the work of Ödön Lechner's disciples Marcell Komor and Dezső Jakab; it now houses a shabby taxi office and an ice-cream parlour, together with the **Tóth József Theatre** (*ticket office* ➘ 63 311166; ⏰ 10.00–13.00, 15.00–18.00 daily). The only ray of hope is that there are restoration plans.

To the east of Kossuth tér, the dinky **Greek Orthodox church** (*Görögkeleti Egyházközösség; Kossuth Lajos u. 4*) is painted strawberry red. This is the oldest building in Szentes, built in Baroque style in 1786, and has a beautiful iconostasis decorated with roses and gilded leaves by István Tenecki (an outstanding 18th-century artist working in Arad, now part of Romania). The church's diminutive stature is reduced further by being set three feet below street level. The fresco in an outer niche depicts Szent Miklós.

Further along Kossuth Lajos utca, the brick Neo-Gothic **Lutheran church** (*Kossuth Lajos u. 9*) was built in 1905, boasting buttresses plated with glazed tiles and floral ironwork on its gate. The stained-glass windows around the altar portray events in Jesus's life; at the southern side of the nave is a marble tablet commemorating Lutherans who died in World War I, framed with Art-Nouveau carvings by Antal Koncz. Continue to the eastern end of Kossuth Lajos utca and the Romantic-style former **synagogue** (*Kossuth Lajos u. 33–35;* ➘ 63 400271) of 1870, now housing the town's library and a wonderful place to read a book.

The **Péter-Pál Town House Museum** (*Polgárház Múzeum; Petőfi Sándor u. 9;* ➘ 63 316678; e *polgarhaz.szentes@museum.hu;* ➹ *admission free;* ⏰ *Tue & Thu 10.00–12.00, 14.00–16.00, Sat 13.00–17.00*) is south of Kossuth tér; the 19th-century doctor (Pál Péter) and his family who lived here clearly did so in some luxury. As well as medical objects, there are musical instruments (the good doctor was a keen collector of such paraphernalia) and textiles. The house was originally built for a wine merchant in 1830, and the fine cellar is the venue for temporary exhibitions.

We have a soft spot for **Erzsébet tér**, with its gravelled pathways and grey-blue conifers. The Art-Nouveau **Roman Catholic school** at the southern side was constructed in 1912, and looks like an overblown doll's house. In the middle of the square stands a poignant **World War I monument** (János Pásztor, 1926) showing a mother and child cowering behind a dying soldier, while at the back is the Neoclassical **Roman Catholic church** (*Szent Anna templom; Szent Imre Herceg u.*) of 1847. Its Baroque tower survives from an earlier 18th-century church; inside, the triumphal arch is adorned with a wonderful secco of Hungarian saints paying homage to the holy sacrament, while the Secessionist ceiling was painted by Béla Endre and Gyula Rudnay in 1910.

Tucked into the crook of a bend in the River Kurca, **Széchenyi liget** is the town's recreational area, a tree-filled park a short walk west of Kossuth tér. Towards the back you'll find a sports complex featuring **outdoor swimming pools** (*Széchenyi liget, Csallány Gábor part 4;* ✆ *63 314167;* 💲 *650/450Ft;* ☉ *05.00–21.00 daily*), water slides and tennis courts (*1,320Ft/hr*), as well as a campsite. At the park's heart is the excellent **Koszta József Museum** (*Széchenyi liget 1;* ✆ *63 313352;* 💲 *200/100Ft;* ☉ *Tue–Sun 13.00–17.00*). The diverse local-history and ethnographic collection includes agricultural and military items, Turkish finds of the 16th and 17th centuries, bottles and coins, and the famed black ceramics crafted by Szentes potters. Keep a look out too for an intriguing novelty musical instrument of 1780, a multi-tasker of a thing with a drum, cymbal and strings operated by a revolving pin cylinder. Most significant, however, are the 35 paintings of József Koszta, whose oeuvre was the Great Plain and its peasant people. Koszta lived and worked on a farmstead near Szentes for over 25 years up until his death in 1948. Outside, Zoltán Kovács's statue of a labourer – all spade and meaty forearms – recalls the town's agricultural lifeblood, so easily overshadowed by the extravagant bourgeois architecture that sprung up in the centre during the prosperous 18th and 19th centuries.

Other activities As well as the swimming pools (see above), there are **thermal baths** (*Ady Endre u. 44;* ✆ *63 401573;* 💲 *530/300Ft;* ☉ *Mon 08.00–16.00, Tue–Fri 08.00–20.00, Sat–Sun 09.00–20.00*) at the northern end of Ady Endre utca. These have an oriental look to them, and make use of the fact that Szentes is perched upon Europe's largest geothermal field.

ÓPUSZTASZER

The village of Ópusztaszer 11km east of Kistelek is itself unremarkable, but the unsnappily named Ópusztaszer National Historical Memorial Park drags it very close to the top of Hungary's tourist tree. Occupying a patch that was once the town of Szer, it was here that Árpád and the other Magyar tribal leaders are said to have assembled in the immediate aftermath of their successful campaign to conquer the Carpathian Basin in the 9th century (see page 15). According to the *Gesta Hungarorum* (see page 16), the warriors camped on the land for 34 days while thrashing out mundane details like rules of governance and justice in their freshly acquired territory. Of course, Anonymus was recording this history fully 300 years after the event, and would probably struggle under cross examination to prove beyond doubt that this was the site of the first Hungarian 'parliament'; however, with no-one sticking their hand up with alternative suggestions, the country has taken the scribe's account to its bosom and celebrates this as the hallowed ground where Hungary was born.

GETTING THERE AND AWAY To reach the park take the **train** to Kistelek from Budapest Nyugati (just over two hours) or Szeged (40 mins); from here up to 13 buses daily stop at the park entrance (15-min journey). MÁV offers a 50% discount on return train tickets for park visitors arriving at either Kistelek or Szeged stations – get your ticket stamped the park entrance. Alternatively, up to 25 **buses** daily run from Szeged to Ópusztaszer Park.

INFORMATION
📋 **Tourinform** Szoborkert 68; ☎ 62 275257;
✉ opusztaszer@tourinform.hu. Can provide
information on the horse shows & other programmes
that regularly take place here. Housed in the
rotunda. ⊕ *same hrs as park.*

🏠 WHERE TO STAY, EAT AND DRINK
🏠 **Erdei Vendégház** Erdei Ferenc u. 58–60; ☎ 06
30 303 4195. We can't recommend this guesthouse
highly enough, set in beautiful grounds hung with
flower baskets 2km from the park entrance (on
Road 5411, running from Kistelek to Ópusztaszer).
There are self-contained apts in the main house
(for 4 or 8) & smaller ones (without kitchens)
encircling the garden. The owners are friendliness
personified, & can organise shooting & riding tours,
& there's a sauna, swimming pool & outdoor
cooking facilities. Relax with a gin & tonic & watch
the sun go down. The same family runs Szeri
Csárda, so ask there if necessary. *Main house*

6,500–7,000Ft/pp, apt from 5,000Ft/pp;
⊕ *spring–autumn.*
✘ **Szeri Csárda** Pusztaszeri major 111; ☎ 62
275165; ✉ szericsarda@invitel.hu. If you time it
right, & avoid the coach parties crashing around,
this is a pleasant peasant-style restaurant serving
Hungarian dishes of game, fish, pork & poultry. It
stands a ½km from the entrance to the memorial
park, & has a campsite (☎ 62 275123; dbl 3,600Ft,
apt for 4 12,000Ft; ⊕ Apr–Oct) next door with
chalets (for 2 or 4); the larger ones have
kitchenettes. *Mains avg 1,300Ft;* ⊕ *daily*
11.30–22.00.

ÓPUSZTASZER NATIONAL HISTORICAL MEMORIAL PARK The 55ha park (*Ópusztaszeri Nemzeti Történeti Emlékpark; Szoborkert 68;* ☎ *62 275133; www.opusztaszer.hu;* 🎟 *park entrance ticket 800Ft, Feszty Panorama 4,000Ft; show tickets 400/300Ft; combined ticket for Panorama & Rotunda 2,000Ft in winter & 2,500Ft in Summer; free for EU residents over 70;* ⊕ *Apr–Oct daily 09.00–18.00, Nov–Mar Tue–Sun 10.00–16.00, open-air museum buildings closed in winter*) stands 1km from the road running between the village and Szeged, and is made up of several parts. (Note the value of a combined ticket, which gives access to the Feszty Panorama and Rotunda (excluding the missable Panopticon) at a price lower than that for the Panorama alone.)

An avenue of lime trees leads from the entrance to the **Árpád Memorial**, a massive Neoclassical monument designed by Gyula Berczik and Ede Kallós and raised in 1896 as part of the millennial celebrations. Árpád sits atop, while around the front is a pantheon of former rulers of Hungary, set here in 2001 on the 1,000th anniversary of István's founding of the Hungarian state. István wears the golden crown. Beyond the memorial are the remains of the medieval **Monastery of Szer**, which was the largest on the Great Plain until its destruction by the Mongols and some of whose parts date to the 11th century; it was first excavated in the 1970s, when skeletons of the original settlers were also unearthed from an earlier pagan cemetery on the site.

In front of the memorial (to the left of the path) is the park's prime attraction, the gigantic **rotunda**; designed by architect István Novák (a follower of Imre

LATE ARRIVALS
As every Hungarian knows, the millennial celebrations of 1896 commemorated the
1,000th anniversary of the greatest hour – the 'land taking' (*honfoglalás*) by their
tribal ancestors, the Magyars. Only the celebrants actually missed the boat by a year
or two. A group of academics commissioned in the 1890s found that the tribes had
probably arrived between AD893 and AD895. Unfortunately this came just too soon
for the government, who couldn't ready themselves in time for the anniversary; not
ones to let inconvenient points of historical accuracy poop their party, however,
they declared that the official date had been AD896 – and the festivities began.

Makovecz), it nods towards the shape of a Magyar chieftain's tent. Inside is the spectacular **Feszty Cyclorama** (*Feszty-Körkép; groups admitted every 30 mins*), which imagines the journey made by the Magyar tribes as they entered the Carpathian Basin, and was created by Árpád Feszty and his colleagues for the millennial celebrations. What a piece of work; this is surely the cream of Hungarian National Romanticism. The canvas is 120m long and 15m tall, and took 24 painters two years (1893–94) to complete; it includes 2,000 figures and 1,500 horses. There are some fascinating details to winkle out. Feszty had a sense of humour, and included personal portraits in the piece; playing on his own name, he painted the chieftain Árpád in his own image, while a black-clad enemy chieftain bears a striking (and cheeky!) resemblance to his father-in-law (the writer Mór Jókai). His wife – the red-headed lady in the painting – is said to have fainted on hearing that Feszty had taken on such a daunting commission; she pleaded to be involved, and her husband finally relented in letting her paint some of the corpses (which required less detail). If you look very carefully, you may spot camels (there are 32 in total) among the horses, assisting in carrying provisions from the east; such is the level of detail that a guide we spoke to worked here for a full year before noticing them. The cyclorama was badly damaged during World War II – indeed, over half was destroyed – and the restoration by Polish experts (using 2,500l of solvent, 7,000kg of sawdust and a hell of a lot of sweat) is very nearly as remarkable as the original work. It was returned to public view in 1995.

Elsewhere in the rotunda are a 'Panopticon' featuring some rather crummy dummies of historical Hungarian greats (& *adult 1,000Ft*), a reconstruction of a street in 1896 (complete with more dummies, in period costume), a gallery showing temporary art displays, an exhibition devoted to the 33 other panorama paintings around the world (a form invented by British artist Robert Barker), and an archaeological collection of finds made during excavation of the market town of Szer and its monastery.

Moving outside again, a cluster of **ten yurt houses** holds the Men and Forest Exhibition (*Erdő & Ember*), devoted to forestry, nature and the history of wood production in the Tisza region, the House of the Hungarians (paying tribute to Hungarian communities abroad) and the Crown House (containing a section from a giant redwood tree felled during a storm in California, and brought here by an ex-pat). Beyond is the sprawling **Open-Air Ethnographic Museum**, comprising a dozen typical buildings from the turn of the 19th and 20th centuries, transported from villages in the Great Plain; among them are a paprika and grape farmstead from Szeged, the house of an onion producer from Makó, a fisherman's cottage from Csongrád, a windmill from Szentes and a forester's lodge from Imrehegy with a wildlife exhibition of the Pusztaszer Nature Protection Area (including Fehér-tó; see opposite).

There are regular **craft shows** held among the buildings of the open-air museum. In addition, twice-daily performances (*11.30 & 14.30*) of the **Nomadic Ancestors Show** take place in the field beside the forester's house, with mounted warriors recreating the Magyar skills of horsemanship by firing off arrows while at full gallop. Test your own skills at riding (*from 300Ft*) and archery (*from 150Ft*), or take a more sedate turn around the park in a motorised buggy, which can be picked up from outside the rotunda (& *300/200Ft*).

FESTIVALS AND EVENTS A wine show takes place on St Vincent's Day in January, while there are folklore programmes (with cauldrons of goulash) on August 20 (St Stephen's Day), Easter and Whitsun. On the last Saturday in June, the 'Hunniális' celebrates the arrival of the Magyar tribes with a handicraft show and an equestrian programme that runs from dawn until dusk.

FEHÉR-TÓ

Fehér-tó (White Lake), just to the east of the road running between Kistelek and Szeged (and not to be confused with the lake of the same name further northeast at Kardoskút), is a very important conservation area. Part of the wetland habitats of the Pusztaszer Landscape Protection Area – the biggest such area in the country – the lake was once little more than a shallow, sodium-rich pond that dried up in summer. However, in the 1930s it was transformed into a fish hatchery and steadily enlarged. It is now home to a plethora of rare aquatic birds, including stilts, avocets, Kentish plover, great white egret, spoonbill, squacco heron and purple heron. Falling as it does near the Tisza, in spring and autumn it attracts flocks of migrating ducks and geese that follow the river route and stop here to rest, while Korom Island holds colonies of nesting black-headed gulls. While you need special permission to visit the 350ha conservation area, you can get a bird's eye view from a lookout tower on the island; to get there leave Road E75 at the Bronze Age cemetery hill at Szatymaz. There are exhibitions covering the lake at Ópusztaszer and Szeged.

SZEGED

Szeged rivals any city in Hungary, and is a thriving rebuttal to those who view the Great Plain as an architectural and cultural wasteland. On the map, its layout – cut through by the Tisza and ringed by inner and outer semi-circular boulevards – bears a passing resemblance to the eastern side of Budapest, and in some ways it can hold its own in such exalted company. In the aftermath of destruction (see below), the city aimed to reinvent itself as the most harmonious provincial settlement in the country. It carefully crafted its public spaces, and each of the squares has a character all its own: the green Széchenyi tér honours greats of the past; Klauzál tér cultivates an atmosphere of theatre and performance, studded with statues of harlequins and street artists (and is, appropriately, the place where Kossuth gave his last public 'performance'); Dóm tér is more austere, institutional and 'Victorian', reflecting its academic and religious heritage (although revellers invade during the Szeged Festival); Aradi vértanúk tere commemorates the 13 Martyrs of Arad, executed after defeat in the 1848–49 War of Independence. The result is a dynamic blend of significant past and carnivalesque present, a city whose spaces value both the contemplation of broad historical perspective and the escapist, bustling act of the here and now. There are decent restaurants, theatres and nightclubs, a nationally renowned opera, several universities, and one of the country's best cathedrals. If one were to be ultra picky, it could be said that the city is light on heavyweight museums, but in every other way Szeged shines bright.

Around 15km from the Serbian border, Szeged sits just below the confluence of the Tisza and Maros rivers and during the early medieval period was a distribution centre for salt shipments brought on the Maros from Transylvania. Szeged was traditionally favoured by Hungarian monarchs, and flourished as a result. Its growth was inevitably stunted between 1543 and 1686 under Turkish occupation, although it represented the centre of the sultan's lands and came under his protection. The real setback came a couple of centuries later. During the night of March 12 1879 the city was engulfed by floodwater from the Tisza. Morning revealed the horrible extent of the damage: 95% of the buildings – 5,700 of the 6,000 – had been wiped away. A massive programme of reconstruction followed, bold Eclectic and Art-Nouveau architecture and avenues emerging from the muddy slush; sections of the Great Boulevard bear the names of European cities (such as Vienna, Paris and London) that aided the recovery. Szeged went from

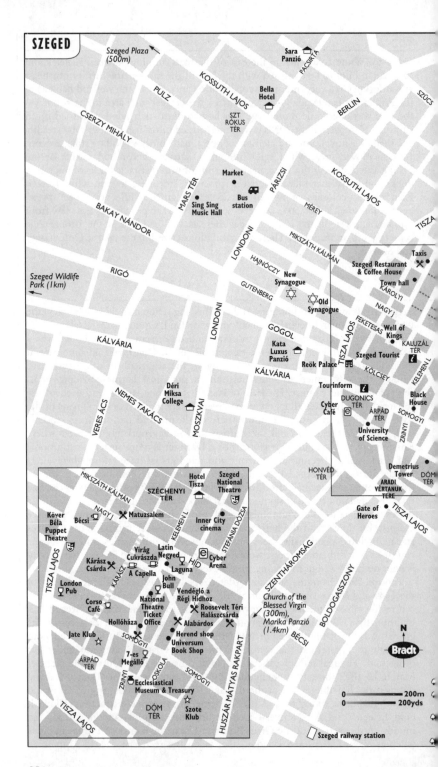

SZEGED

Szeged Plaza (500m)

Sara Panzió
PACSIRTA

KOSSUTH LAJOS

PULZ

Bella Hotel

BERLIN

SZŰCS

SZT RÓKUS TÉR

CSERZY MIHÁLY

KOSSUTH LAJOS

Market

PARIZSI

MÉREY

TISZA

MARS TÉR

Sing Sing Music Hall

Bus station

MIKSZÁTH KÁLMÁN

BAKAY NÁNDOR

LONDONI

HAJNÓCZY

Taxis

Szeged Restaurant & Coffee House

Town hall

KÁROLYI

Szeged Wildlife Park (1km)

RIGÓ

New Synagogue

GUTENBERG

Old Synagogue

NAGY J

FEKETESAS

Well of Kings

KALUZÁL TÉR

KÁLVÁRIA

LONDONI

GOGOL

Kata Luxus Panzió

Szeged Tourist

TISZA LAJOS

Reök Palace

KÓLCSEY

KELEMEN L

KÁLVÁRIA

NEMES TAKÁCS

Déri Miksa College

MOSZKVAI

Tourinform

DUGONICS TÉR

Cyber Café

ÁRPÁD TÉR

SOMOGYI

Black House

ZRÍNYI

VERES ÁCS

University of Science

HONVÉD TÉR

Demetrius Tower

DÓM TÉR

ARADI VÉRTANUK TERE

Gate of Heroes

TISZA LAJOS

Hotel Tisza

Szeged National Theatre

MIKSZÁTH KÁLMÁN

SZÉCHENYI TÉR

NAGY J

Köver Béla Puppet Theatre

Bécsi

Matuzsalem

KELEMEN L

Inner City cinema

STEFÁNIA DÓZSA

TISZA LAJOS

Virág Cukrászda

Latin Negyed

Cyber Arena

HÍD

Kárász Csárda

KÁRÁSZ

Á Capella

Laguna

John Bull

London Pub

Vendéglő a Régi Hidhoz

Roosevelt Téri Halászcsárda

SZENTHÁROMSÁG

Church of the Blessed Virgin (300m), Marika Panzió (1.4km)

BOLDOGASSZONY

Corso Café

National Theatre Ticket Office

Hollóháza

Alabárdos

Herend shop

BÉCSI

Jate Klub

SOMOGYI

Universum Book Shop

ÁRPÁD TÉR

7-es Megálló

ZRÍNYI

ISKOLA

SOMOGYI

HUSZÁR MÁTYÁS RAKPART

Ecclesiastical Museum & Treasury

DÓM TÉR

Szote Klub

TISZA LAJOS

N

Bradt

0 ————— 200m
0 ————— 200yds

Szeged railway station

354

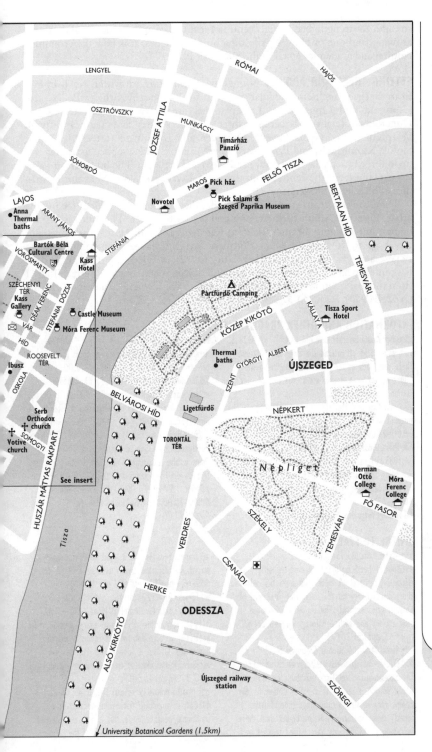

LENGYEL

RÓMAI

HAJÓS

OSZTRÓVSZKY

JÓZSEF ATTILA

MUNKÁCSY

SÓHORDÓ

Timárház
Panzió

FELSŐ TISZA

MAROS Pick ház

Pick Salami &
Szeged Paprika Museum

BERTALAN HÍD

LAJOS

Anna
Thermal
baths

ARANY JÁNOS

Novotel

STEFÁNIA

TEMESVÁRI

Bartók Béla
Cultural Centre

VÖRÖSMARTY

Kass
Hotel

SZÉCHENYI
TÉR

Kass
Gallery

DEÁK FERENC

STEFÁNIA DÓZSA

Castle Museum

Móra Ferenc Museum

Partfürdő Camping

KÖZÉP KIKÖTŐ

KÁLLAY

Tisza Sport
Hotel

ÚJSZEGED

VÁR

HÍD

ROOSEVELT
TÉR

Thermal
baths

SZENT GYÖRGYI ALBERT

Ibusz

OSKOLA

BELVÁROSI HÍD

Ligetfürdő

NÉPKERT

Serb
Orthodox
church

SOMOGYI

Votive
church

TORONTÁL
TÉR

See insert

HUSZÁR MÁTYÁS RAKPART

Tisza

N é p l i g e t

Herman
Ottó
College

Móra
Ferenc
College

FŐ FASOR

VERDRES

SZÉKELY

TEMESVÁRI

CSANÁDI

HERKE

ODESSZA

ALSÓ KIKÖTŐ

SZŐREGI

Újszeged railway
station

University Botanical Gardens (1.5km)

strength to strength, becoming a centre of textiles, salami production and paprika growing, and one of Hungary's leading university cities. It is now the economic, cultural and academic capital of the Southern Plain.

GETTING THERE AND AROUND Numerous destinations are within reach by bus from Szeged, including regular services to Hódmezővásárhely, Békéscsaba, Csongrád and Ópusztaszer. Other towns are Szentes, Kecskemét (nine), Dunaföldvár (eight), Jászberény (three), Mohács (six) and Szekszárd (two), Veszprém (four), Gyula (seven), Debrecen and Lajosmisze (three), Tatabánya, Siofók, Szombathely and Eger (two). There is also a Friday service to Vienna and up to three buses a day to Subotica and Novi Sad in Serbia. The **bus station** (*Mars tér*) is 600m from the centre; from the station, walk east along Mikszáth Kálmán utca, which leads to Széchenyi tér.

There are two **train stations** in Szeged – the main one on Indóház tér and the other, Újszeged, south of the centre and across the river. The latter is a small branch line running through Makó to Kétegyháza. From the main station trains travel up to 16 times daily to Budapest Nyugati via Kecskemét, and also to Békéscsaba via Hódmezővásárhely (up to 12), Cegléd (up to 17), and to Kiskunfélegyháza (regularly). Two trains a day go to Subotica in Serbia. Tram 1 from the main station is the quickest way into town. If you need a **taxi**, try Tempo (♦ *62 490490*), Radió (♦ *62 480480*) or Gabriel (♦ *62 555555*).

INFORMATION AND OTHER PRACTICALITIES

◉ **Cyber Arena Internet Café** Híd u. 1; ♦ 62 422815. Surf your socks off around the clock for 10Ft/min. There are loads of terminals, & a chance to win 500Ft by rolling a double six at the end of your session. ⊕ 24hrs daily.

◉ **Cyber Café** Dugonics tér 11; ♦ 62 425816. Internet access for 10Ft/min. ⊕ Mon–Fri 08.00–24.00, Sat–Sun 09.00–24.00.

◪ **Ibusz** Oroszlán u. 3; ♦ 62 471177; e 1085@ibusz.hu. Small but helpful office arranging tour programmes & private accommodation. ⊕ Mon–Fri 09.00–18.00, Sat 10.00–13.00.

◪ **Listings magazine** Szegedi Est

◪ **Szeged Tourist** Klauzál tér 7; ♦ 62 420428. Arranges cultural & entertainment tours (but not private rooms). ⊕ Mon–Fri 09.00–17.00.

◪ **Tourinform** Dugonics tér 2; ♦ 62 488699; e szeged@tourinform.hu. The best place to start for maps & information on what's on. A second office (Tábor u. 7/B; ♦ 62 548092; e csongradm@tourinform.hu; ⊕ Mon–Fri 09.00–17.00) has information on Csongrád county as a whole, while there is also a summer Tourinform booth (Széchenyi tér; ⊕ Jun 15–Sep 15 daily 09.00–20.30). ⊕ Jun 15–Sep 15 Mon–Fri 09.00–20.00, Sat–Sun 09.00–18.00, Sep 16–Jun 14 Mon–Fri 09.00–17.00.

⌂ WHERE TO STAY

⌂ **Hotel Bella** (25 rooms) Pacsirta u. 31; ♦ 62 498208; e hotels.hu/ujbella. A modern, fairly characterless hotel 15 mins' walk from the centre (a short distance beyond the outer ring road, just off Kossuth Lajos sugarút). The rooms are generous in size; ask for one with a balcony. Sgl €45, dbl €55, trpl €65, apt (for 2) €75.

⌂ **Hotel Tisza** (80 rooms) Széchenyi tér 3; ♦ 62 478278; e info@tiszahotel.hu; www.tiszahotel.hu. The Secessionist Hotel Tisza was built in 1886; after World War II, it served as a police station & cells. Rooms vary in size & furnishings (not all have toilets): those in category II are bigger than those in category I, while apts have period touches such

as draped beds. This is a good hotel, reasonably priced. Rooms without/with toilet sgl €39/52, dbl €57/65, trpl €70; apts €91 (for 1), €104 (for 2), €113 (for 3), €122 (for 4).

⌂ **Kata Luxus Panzió** Bolyai János u. 15; ♦ 62 311258. This is the city's most central pension, more accurately a large apt (with 4 rooms & shared bathrooms, kitchen & lounge). The facilities are excellent, & the place is clean & buxom. Good value. Sgl 7,300Ft, dbl 10,600Ft.

⌂ **Marika Panzió** (9 rooms) Nyíl u. 45; ♦ 62 443861; e marika@tiszanet.hu. Located in a traditional peasant house, this is a lovely, peaceful guesthouse around 1km southwest of the centre (follow Szentháromság u. from Aradi vértanúk tere past Mátyás király tér, & look out for a right turn into Nyíl utca). The rooms are a little old-fashioned, the owners are welcoming, & there's a pleasant garden with a pool. You'll enjoy staying here. *Sgl 8,000Ft, dbl 9,500Ft, trpl 11,500, room for 4 15,500Ft.*

⌂ **Novotel** (136 rooms) Maros u. 1; ☎ 62 562200; www.novotel-szeged.hu. Although this is a chain, & you'll probably have an inkling of what to expect, this modern hotel on the river bank is nevertheless one of the better ones in the city. The older rooms on the first 2 floors don't have AC, but are 10% cheaper. All rooms have balconies. *Dbl €82, dbl €93, trpl €113.*

⋏ **Partfürdő Camping** Közép-kikötő sor; ☎ 62 430483. On the river bank in Újszeged, just north of Belvárosi híd, next to a couple of pools & a small beach. The site also has some chalets. *Camping:* ⛺ *1,000/700Ft, tent/caravan 700/800Ft (excl tax); chalets 6,000–13,500Ft;* ⊕ *May–Sep.*

⌂ **Royal Hotel** (80 rooms) Kölcsey u. 1–3; ☎ 62 475275; www.royalhotel.hu. The Royal certainly isn't regal – in fact, it's bloated & slightly tatty, with narrow rooms – although it was being refurbished

when we visited so might be ship-shape now. The bathrooms are a good size, & it is central. *Sgl 14,100Ft, dbl 16,500Ft.*

⌂ **Sára Panzió** Pacsirta u. 17/A; ☎ 62 498206; e sarapanzio@freemail.hu. Further along the same road as the Hotel Bella, the Sára's rooms are on the small side but comfortable nevertheless. *Sgl 6,500Ft, dbl 8,500, trpl 11,000Ft.*

⌂ **Tímárház Panzió** (14 rooms) Maros u. 26 utca; ☎ 62 425485; www.timarhazpanzio.fw.hu. Comfortable pension with a garden, a friendly owner, a friendly dog & even a parrot (not sure how friendly it is). On a peaceful street just behind the Pick salami factory. *Sgl 9,500Ft, dbl 12,000Ft, trpl 18,000Ft, family room 21,000Ft.*

⌂ **Tisza Sport Hotel** (106 rooms) Kállay u. 6–10; ☎ 62 431429; www.tiszahotel.hu. This hotel, on the other side of the river in Újszeged (near Bertalan híd), has a variety of accommodation options from dorm-style rooms (for 3–4) to superior & modern dbls. Caters for pockets deep or shallow. *Superior/classic sgl €53/40, dbl €68/59; rooms not en suite sgl €27, dbl €42, trpl €52, quad €62; suite (for 4) €101.*

In a city with such a healthy student population (speaking numerically rather than medically), there are many cheap college rooms available during holiday periods. Those closest to the centre include the **Déri Miksa College** (*Moszkai körút 11–13;* ☎ *62 547058; rooms available Jun 15–Aug 31*), the **Herman Ottó College** (*Temesvári körút 50–52;* ☎ *62 544311;* e *iroda@novell.ohsu.u-szeged.hu*) and the **Móra Ferenc College** (*Közép fasor 31–33;* ☎ *62 544101;* e *info@mora.u-szeged.hu*). All offer dorm beds for around 2,000Ft/pp and rooms from 3,000Ft.

⋏ WHERE TO EAT AND DRINK

⛾ **A Capella Kávéház** Kárász u. 6, 62 559966. You can't go wrong with any of the fabulous array of cakes on offer, but the hot *krémes* available on Sat (until 15.00) are a must! Otherwise, try a special Szeged bun or a 'pig' (*röfi*) sandwich, & enjoy the view of the busy square. ⊕ *Mon–Sun 07.00–21.00.*

⋏ **Alabárdos Étterem & Borozó** Oskola u. 13; ☎ 62 420914. Housed in a Louis-XVI-style building of 1810, the former Zodiákus reopened as a fine dining restaurant & wine bar that plays on the 'knightly' theme & offers international & Hungarian dishes. The décor is subtler than you might expect & the atmosphere relaxed. *Mains avg 1,500Ft;* ⊕ *Mon–Sat 12.00–24.00, Sun 12.00–17.00.*

⛾ **Bécsi** Feketesas u. 19–21; ☎ 62 550725. The large Vienna coffee house has a pub-like feel to it, & is highly recommended by younger locals; to the north of Klauzál tér. ⊕ *Mon–Sat 07.00–23.00, Sun 09.00–23.00.*

♀ **John Bull Pub** Oroszlán u. 6; ☎ 62 484217. This is probably the best 'English' pub in the country; at night the courtyard garden flickers with candles & torches, & there's an al-fresco bar as well as a plush interior. The snack menu has steak & chips, chilli con carne & Hungarian food. *Mains avg 2,500Ft;* ⊕ *Mon–Sun 12.00–24.00.*

⋏ **Kárász Csárda** Klauzál tér 5; ☎ 62 550627. The former Arany Oroszlán serves Hungarian & international dishes (including fish soup); it is located in a courtyard behind the square (accessed via an archway). There is pizza & other snacks available at pavement seating on the square itself. *Mains avg 2,000Ft;* ⊕ *Sun–Thu 10.00–22.00, Fri–Sat 10.00–23.00.*

⋏ **Matusalem** Széchenyi tér 13; ☎ 62 420435. The former Boland has very good food & attentive service, with a position that overlooks both the leafy square (nice) & a car park (not so nice). Hungarian cuisine dominates, although there are some German & Serbian choices too. We really enjoyed our meals here, & found the potato doughnuts delicious. *Mains avg 1,700Ft;* ⊕ *10.00–24.00 daily.*

♀ **No 1 Sports Pub** Kölcsey u. 11; ↖ 62 470111. New sports pub & karaoke bar, with a good selection of wines & *palinkas.* ⊕ *Mon–Thu 07.30–24.00, Fri 07.30–02.00, Sat 09.00–02.00.*

✕ **Roosevelt Téri Halászcsárda** Roosevelt tér 14; ↖ 62 555980; www.sotarto-halaszcsarda.hu. Among other things, Szeged is noted for its fish dishes; this fish restaurant looks less upmarket than you might expect for the price, but it is highly regarded & the fish soup as good as you'll find. Next to the Belvárosi híd. *Mains avg 2,300Ft;* ⊕ *11.00–23.00 daily.*

✕ **Szeged Restaurant & Coffee House** Széchenyi tér 9; ↖ 62 555400. This restaurant, bar & coffee house has a terrace that fills a considerable chunk of the square. Its limited menu features international dishes, but you're probably best just coming here for a slurp of beer or a cocktail. There is live (synthesiser) music or other entertainment in the evenings. *Mains avg 1,600Ft;* ⊕ *Mon–Thu 09.00–22.30, Fri 09.00–01.00, Sat 11.00–01.00, Sun 11.00–18.00.*

✕ **Taj Mahal** Gutenberg u. 12; ↖ 62 452131. The Taj Mahal isn't shy, proclaiming that 'Just like the 7th wonder of the world, it will leave an everlasting

impression on you'. Well, that's perhaps a touch ambitious, but this is a good traditional curry house in a country where Indian cuisine is thin on the ground. It's located in the Jewish quarter; each table has an electronic buzzer with which to summon the waiters. *Mains avg 1,600Ft;* ⊕ *Mon 17.00–23.00, Thu–Sat 11.00–23.00, Sun 12.00–22.00.*

✕ **Vendéglő a Régi Hídhoz** Oskola u. 4; ↖ 62 420910. This folksy restaurant (which looks better from inside than out) deals in traditional Hungarian food & puts together a mean fish soup. *Mains avg 1,400Ft;* ⊕ *Sun–Thu 11.30–23.00, Fri–Sat 11.30–24.00.*

⊑ **Virág Cukrászda** Klauzál tér 1; ↖ 62 541360. The biggest & the best of the city's patisseries dominates the square's eastern side, with a takeaway outlet (Kis Virág) opposite & tables filling the area between them. ⊕ *08.00–21.00 daily.*

⊑ **Zacc Café** Kölcsey u. 11; ↖ 30 376 2113. A newly opened café that serves as a meeting place for uni students. Pitchers of cocktails & beers available for about 1,500–2,000Ft. ⊕ *Mon–Thu 08.00–22.00, Fri–Sat 08.00–02.00.*

♀ **7-es Megálló (Tram Bar)** Somogyi Béla u. 20, 70 931 2190. An old tram on the corner of Somogyi u. & Toldy u., converted into a fun bar with pavement seating & cheap drinks. ⊕ *Mon–Fri 10.00–24.00, Sat–Sun 12.00–24.00.*

ENTERTAINMENT AND NIGHTLIFE

The Eclectic and Neo-Baroque **Szeged National Theatre** (*Nemzeti Színház; Deák Ferenc u. 12;* ↖ *62 479279; www.szabadterijatekok.szeged.hu*) was built in 1883, designed by the Hellmer and Fellner company responsible for Budapest's Vígszínház; it had to be reconstructed after burning down just two years after opening. In niches either side of the entrance are statues of Ferenc Erkel and József Katona. It hosts performances of drama, opera and ballet, with music performed by the Szeged Symphony Orchestra. Its main event is the **Szeged Open-Air Games** (*Szegedi Szabadtéri játékok*), an arts festival on a stage erected in Dóm tér. For information on the festival or theatre programme, as well as to buy tickets, contact the **ticket office** (*Kelemen u. 7;* ↖ *62 554713;* e *ticket@szinhaz.szeged.hu;* ⊕ *Mon 13.00–17.00, Tue–Fri 10.00–17.00, Sat 10.00–12.00*).

Performances at the 150-seat **Kövér Béla Puppet Theatre** (*Bábszínház; Tisza Lajos körút 50;* ↖ *62 420912*) usually start at 10.00, 11.00 and 14.30, but check the programme listings outside beforehand. The **Inner City Cinema** (*Belvárosi Mozi; Deák Ferenc u. 14;* ↖ *62 543185; ticket office* ⊕ *14.00–20.45 daily*) has Hollywood blockbusters and Hungarian films. **Bartók Béla Cultural Centre** (*Vörösmarty u. 3;* ↖ *62 542825*) has information on cultural events.

Night owls are well catered for in a city with a high number of students, but be aware that – as with many university towns – mid-week evenings (particularly Thursdays) are often bigger than weekends. The **JATE Klub** (*Toldy u. 2;* ↖ *62 321245; www.jateklub.hu;* ⊕ *Mon, Wed & Thu 09.30–04.00, Tue & Fri 09.30–24.00, Sat 21.30–05.00*) is a basement venue at the back of the science university that hosts regular parties, discos on Mondays and Wednesdays, and cultural events such as traditional dance (*táncház*; see page 29), concerts, poetry readings and drama. The **Sing Sing Music Hall** (*C Pavilon, Mars tér; www.sing.hu;* ⊕ *Wed, Fri & Sat 23.00–05.00*) is a trendy warehouse club (all lasers and balconies), featuring dance music, classic nostalgia tunes, hip-hop and Ibiza-style parties. Just beyond the Great Boulevard, northwest of the centre; the main nights are Wednesdays and Saturdays. The **SZOTE Klub** (*Dóm tér 13*) is frequented by the medical students.

Corso Café (*Kárász u. 16;* ✆ *62 557457*) is a funky café-bar playing jazzy music; it stands on a pedestrianised street between Dugonics and Klauzál squares. The **Gin Tonic Club** (*Széchenyi tér 1;* ✆ *62 559559;* ⊕ *Mon–Fri 12.00–02.00, Sat–Sun 20.00–03.00*) has house and dance classics, as well as the odd live gig and karaoke nights. **Laguna Cocktail Bar** (*Híd u. 6;* ✆ *06 70 201 9818;* ⊕ *Wed–Sat 22.00–05.00*) has a choice of over 80 cocktails, and has DJs as well as funk, hip-hop, R'n'B and Latino theme nights. It's on the corner of Deák Ferenc u. and Híd utca.

WHAT TO SEE AND DO

Széchenyi tér, Klauzál tér and around The Belváros is enclosed by the inner boulevard, **Széchenyi tér** its initial focal point. It is an enormous square, the 50,000m² filled with plane trees, flowerbeds and statues. As well as István Széchenyi himself, Ferenc Deák, Szent István and Queen Gizella are here, as is the vast white head of Count Kuno Klebelsberg (1875–1932). Klebelsberg was a professor at Szeged University and a politician after 1920 who established universal primary-school provision, moved the universities that fell beyond the post-Trianon borders back into Hungary, and founded the Szeged Summer Festival; his red-marble tomb can be seen in the Votive Church (see page 360). Two monuments commemorate the 1879 flood that levelled the city, including a fountain of townsfolk riding on the back of fish. Elsewhere a plinth bears the behatted Pál Vásárhelyi, the engineer who worked with Széchenyi in regulating the Danube and Tisza rivers in the 1840s.

The **town hall** of 1799 was a flood casualty and was afterwards given an Eclectic-Baroque facelift by Ödön Lechner and Gyula Pártos, who aimed towards a uniquely Hungarian national style. Mihály Babits – employing a healthy dollop of that licence available to the poetic – described the tower as 'a young woman with a lace bonnet dancing in the moonlight'. It is certainly a captivating building; in summer, concerts are held in its courtyard. The 'Bridge of Sighs' linking the hall to an adjacent building was erected during the stay of Ferenc József in 1883 to allow him easy access to his entourage ensconced next door. Just northwest of Széchenyi tér, across Vörösmarty utca, are the 19th-century **Anna thermal baths** (*Tisza Lajos körút 24;* ✆ *62 487711;* ✆ *1,500/1,200Ft;* ⊕ *Mon–Fri 06.00–20.00 & 21.00–24.00, Sat–Sun 08.00–20.00*). The indoor pools are fed by naturally hot medicinal water, and can be enjoyed all year round. The complex includes pools, steamrooms, saunas, whirlpools; after a recent renovation, it might claim to be the smaller twin brother of the famous Széchenyi Baths in Budapest.

The pedestrianised Kárász utca is the inner-city spine, a promenade running southwest from Széchenyi tér. Along its way is the atmospheric and romantic **Klauzál tér**, a place for meeting and cake-eating, and lined with grand Neoclassical abodes. Towards its eastern end is a life-size statue of Lajos Kossuth; it commemorates Kossuth's last speech in Hungary, which he delivered from the pink marble balcony of **Kárász House** (*Klauzál tér 5*) on July 14 1849 before fleeing to Turkey (see page 19). Ferenc József stayed in the building in 1857, but it now holds banking clerks. At the opposite side of the square is the **Well of Kings** (*Királyok kútja*) by Tóbiás Klára, featuring four regal lions dribbling into a marble basin.

Continuing along Kárász utca, a brief diversion right along Kölcsey utca leads to the **Reök Palace** (*Tisza Lajos körút 56*), called the 'Horse's Rump' by locals because it stands behind an equestrian statue. The palace is perfect enough to eat, a dazzling example of Hungarian Art Nouveau; it was built in 1907 by Ede Magyar-Oszadszki, a designer who spent most of his short career in Szeged before dying in 1912 at the age of just 35. The wrought-iron flowers blossoming on the façade were made by Pál Fekete, based on drawings by Magyar-Oszadszki.

Dugonics tér, Dóm tér and Aradi vértanuk tere A pair of charming bronze statues entitled *Street Music* (*Utcai Zene*) – a fiddle-playing street performer and a watching child with her *puli* dog – stand at the southern end of Kárász utca, the companions to harlequins at the street's northern end; these pieces are symbolic of the city festivals in summer. They bring up **Dugonics tér**, once the site of a wheat market. On the northern side is the caramel-coloured, Romantic-style **Vajda House** (*Dugonics tér 2*), holding the main Tourinform office; in front is the pensive figure of András Dugonics, clasping his novel *Etelka*, the first printed in Hungarian. Another Szeged resident was Attila József, who was expelled from the Eclectic **University of Science** (*Szegedi Tudományegyetem; Dugonics tér 13*) in 1924 after penning the revolutionary poem 'With a Pure Heart' during the rule of Admiral Horthy. Imre Varga's statue of the poet is outside, as is a modern multi-spouted and music-playing fountain surrounded by concrete seating; stalls purvey various wares around the fountain in summer.

Walk east along Somogyi utca to the brown **Black House** (*Fekete ház; Somogyi u. 13;* ✆ *62 425872;* ✉ *300/150Ft;* ◷ *Oct–Jun Tue–Sun 10.00–17.00, Jul–Sep 10.00–18.00*), named after its earlier blackened walls. Built in 1857 in Romantic style for a wealthy merchant, its most striking feature is the gorgeous corner balcony. Unusually, the merchant also asked the architect Károly Gerster to design the furniture inside; the house is now used by the Móra Ferenc Museum, with a permanent social-history display and other temporary exhibitions.

The brooding **Dóm tér** (Cathedral Square) has an air of the Dickensian Victorian about it, more enclosed than other squares in the city and surrounded by institutional buildings of forbidding brick. During July and August it is the scene for Szeged's great open-air festival, something that can seem difficult to imagine at other times, like picturing a stern headmaster in a Hawaiian shirt. The **Votive Church** (✉ *400/250Ft, free on Sun;* ◷ *Mon–Wed & Fri 09.00–17.30, Thu 12.00–17.30, Sat 08.00–15.00, Sun 13.00–17.30*) was the product of a vow made by city fathers after the 1879 flood, and – whether to your taste or not – is undoubtedly among the outstanding pieces of ecclesiastical architecture in the country. Built between 1913 and 1930, the exterior is a Neo-Romanesque clutter of triangles and rectangles, spires and spanning arches. The two main clock towers are each 93m; at certain times you can climb the 300 steps of one of them (✉ *600Ft; climbs depart Mon–Fri 16.00, Sat 13.00*). The façade bears mosaics of the apostles either side of a marble Mary and child above the portal, while the interior is crawling with frescoes and paisley patterning reminiscent of Budapest's Mátyás Church – unsurprising, as both churches were designed by Frigyes Schulek. A mosaic on the sanctuary ceiling shows Mary in shepherd's cloak and slippers; the dome fresco was added to celebrate the millennium, and beneath it are allegorical paintings of Justice, Fortitude, Prudence and Temperance. Look out for a statue of the crucifixion in wood and marble by János Fadrusz, and hope to hear a snatch from the 10,000 pipes of Europe's third-largest organ.

The **Demetrius Tower** (*Dömötör torony*) is the city's earliest structure, with foundations dating to the 11th century and upper Romanesque and Gothic portions from the 13th century; it was discovered in 1925 during the demolition of a nearby Baroque church (which had been in danger of cramping the style of the square's new darling). The doorway arches contain carved stones salvaged from the former castle. At the northeastern corner of the square, the **Serb Orthodox church** was Baroque when built in 1778 before being remodelled in Louis-XVI style in the 1830s. It contains a beauty of an iconostasis by János Popovics; enquire at the priest's house opposite if the church is locked.

There are several research buildings in Dóm tér, including the biochemistry institute where Albert Szent-Györgyi conducted his 1937 Nobel-Prize-winning work (see box, page 336). An arcade running around the square's southern end holds a **pantheon** of Hungarian stars, from royals to revolutionary poets and egg-headed scientists. On the hour, the **musical clock** chimes above, and carved figures emerge representing graduating students passing before the university council; the woodcarver took Sándor Petőfi and András Dugonics as his models, among others. There is a small collection of items from the churches of Csongrád and Békés counties in the **Ecclesiastical Museum and Treasury** (*Egyházmegyei Múzeum & Kincstár; Dóm tér 5;* \ *62 420932;* æ *100/50Ft;* ⊕ *Mon–Sun Apr–Oct 10.00–18.00, rest of yr 10.00–16.00*), the oldest from 15th-century Franciscan friaries. The friars were particularly important during the Turkish occupation as they were the sole priestly community widely tolerated by the Turks, and were consequently the only ones carrying out pastoral services in southern Hungary.

Behind Dóm tér is **Aradi vértanúk tere**, with a monument to the Martyrs of Arad (see page 19) and an equestrian statue of Rákoczi II. Most striking, however, is the arch leading out on to Boldogasszony sugárút. The **Gate of Heroes** (*Hősök kapuja*) was erected in 1937 ostensibly to honour the soldiers of World War I but more specifically the commandos of Admiral Horthy. In 1919 the counter-revolutionary government (including Horthy) sat in Szeged, and it was from here that the 'White Guard' left to scour the Great Plain for 'Reds' after the defeat of the Republic of Councils. It was the spark for the neo-fascist terror that followed the communist terror under Béla Kun. Vilmos Aba-Novák's cartoon-like frescoes on the underside of the arch were painted over during the communist period; it took 23 artists and 60 million forints to restore them between 1995 and 2001. If you look left from the arch along Lajos körút, you'll see the steel **Flood Memorial**, erected on the river bank to mark the centenary of the great flood.

Roosevelt tér and beyond Moving northwards, Roosevelt tér stands at the western bridgehead of the Belvárosi híd. The **Móra Ferenc Museum** (*Roosevelt tér 1–3;* \ *62 549040;* e *info@mfm.u-szeged.hu;* æ *600/300Ft;* ⊕ *Tue–Sun Jul–Sep 10.00–18.00, rest of yr 10.00–17.00*) stands in the 1896 Neoclassical former Palace of Education and Culture. It is a weighty museum, with late-19th- and early-20th-century art (by painters like József Rippl Ronai and Vilmos Aba-Novák, the latter of Heroes' Gate fame) – keep an eye out for Pál Vágó's depiction of the devastation wrought by the 1879 flood – a display of natural history and geology, the furnishings of an 18th-century pharmacy moved here from Klauzál tér, and a memorial room devoted to Ferenc Móra. Móra was a writer and amateur archaeologist, one-time director of the museum and responsible for unearthing many of the finds on show. The richest collection documents the arrival of early tribes, including the Huns (whose 5th-century campaigns in Europe triggered the age of migrations by Asiatic peoples into the Carpathian Basin), the Avars who came in 567ad and finally the Magyars in the 9th century; it was a time of warriors, and there are fearsome bows and swords among the grave goods, as well as a double burial of an 8th-century Avar couple excavated by Móra at Fehér-tó.

In the riverside garden behind the museum are the remains of Szeged Castle, which was originally built in the 13th century and survived several battles over its walls, both prior to Turkish occupation and during the War of Independence. During the 19th century it operated as a prison, before finally being brought down by the 1879 flood, when the eastern wall and northeastern tower collapsed into the river. The **Castle Museum** (*Stefánia sétány;* ❧ *62 470370;* e *varmuseum.szeged@ museum.hu;* ✆ *300/150Ft;* ◷ *Tue–Sun Jul–Sep 10.00–18.00, rest of yr 10.00–17.00*) has some stonework, a local-history display and temporary art exhibitions. (The Castle Garden itself has a great little space-age playground!)

A short distance west is the **Kass Gallery** (*Vár u. 7;* ❧ *62 420303;* ✆ *300/150Ft;* ◷ *Tue–Sun Jul–Sep 10.00–18.00, rest of yr 10.00–17.00*), with a permanent exhibition of works by graphic artist János Kass. In 1897 his grandfather designed the **Kass Hotel**, huddled at the split between Stefánia utca and Dózsa utca, just outside the Castle Garden. It was a place of luxury in its heyday, but was closed in 1977 and now stands gutted and empty, a forlorn Medusa's head looking down from the tympanum.

Continue northwards parallel with the river, and beyond Tisza Lajos körút is the **Pick Salami and Szeged Paprika Museum** (*Felső-Tisza-part 10;* ❧ *62 421814, 20 4689185 (info in Eng);* e *pick.szeged@museum.hu;* ✆ *640/480Ft;* ◷ *Tue–Sat 15.00–16.00 or by prior appointment*) at the Pick factory. Szeged is one of the country's leading manufacturers of salami, which was introduced to Hungary from Italy in the 19th century. Márk Pick produced salami from 1869 and had a paprika mill too. The museum charts the history of the factory and the salami-making process. Winter salami is the best-selling sausage, making up 47% of sales; when buying some, try to forget that horses' guts are apparently the special ingredient. In 1998 the Szeged Paprika Stock Company became part of the Pick Group, and there is now also a paprika museum on the first floor.

The Jewish quarter and beyond Moving northwest from Klauzál tér along Kígyó utca, and crossing the boulevard, you'll reach the old Jewish quarter. The Neoclassical **Old Synagogue** (*Régi Zsinagóga; Hajnóczy u.*) was constructed in 1843, a plain whitewashed building that is now used for concerts and drama during the summer festival. It was here that Rabbi Lipót Löw first preached in Hungarian and incorporated organ music into the Jewish liturgy; beside the entrance is a plaque marking the height to which the water rose in 1879.

Protected by yew trees behind it, the brick **New Synagogue** (*Új Zsinagóga; Gutenberg u. 13;* ✆ *600/300Ft;* ◷ *Sun–Fri 09.00–14.00*) is considerably more impressive – indeed, is probably the most splendid synagogue outside the capital. It is one of 22 in Hungary designed by Lipót Baumhorn, completed in 1903 with Moorish-Art-Nouveau styling, and capped by a main cupola that reaches 48m. The interior is chock full of golds and blues and pink marble columns. Chief Rabbi Immanuel Löw (son of the rabbi mentioned above) was a botanist who had compiled lists of the flora and fauna mentioned in ancient Jewish literature, and the architect incorporated these species into the motifs of the walls, ceilings and windows. The drum of the cupola is held by 24 columns – symbolic of the hours of the day – and the glass dome is studded with stars against a darkening blue, conveying a sense of infinite space. On the supporting arch are painted the Hebrew words for work, culture and good deeds, the tenets by which the moral Jew should live. The altar stone was fashioned of marble from Jerusalem, and there are six bronze menorah set with semi-precious stones. Two black coffins in the entrance hall commemorate the innocents old and young who died during the Holocaust; a poem on the memorial plaque asks 'Do you see the baby choking with gas, /Carefully hidden in mother's embrace?/ Do you see the child standing next to the mother,/ Gazing upon its death with trembling heart and terror?'.

Out to the west, the **Szeged Wildlife Park** (*Szegedi Vadaspark; Kálvária sugárút;* \ *62 542530; www.zoo.szeged.hu;* 💲 *900/650–750Ft;* ☼ *daily Jan–Mar 09.00–16.00, Apr 09.00–17.00, May & Sep 09.00–18.00, Jun–Aug 09.00–19.00, Oct, Nov & Dec 09.00–16.00*) can be reached on trams 3 or 3F or bus 35. Just beyond the outer boulevard to the south (follow Szentháromság utca from Aradi vértanuk tere) is the Alsóváros (Lower Town), which preserves a rural, peasant feel and is the Roman Catholic heart. The Gothic **Church of the Blessed Virgin** (*Mátyás tér*) is a former Franciscan church built at the end of the 15th century, with a tower and Baroque furnishings added in the 18th century. Pilgrims come to see its *Black Madonna* of 1740, the focal point of an annual patronal festival on the first weekend in August. It was here and in the friary that the Franciscan monks carried out their pastoral work during the Turkish occupation (see page 361).

Újszeged New Szeged lies on the other side of the river from the centre, across Belvárosi híd. Industrial buildings and modern housing blocks are over here, but the area on and near the bank is where the people come to rest and play. The **Partfürdő** (*Közép-kikötő sor;* \ *62 430483;* 💲 *1200/900Ft; tickets valid also for Thermal Baths & Ligetfürdő;* ☼ *May–Sep daily 08.00–19.00*) is a strand right on the water, with a couple of pools, a small beach and a campsite. Behind it are the **thermal baths** (*Fürdő u. 1;* \ *62 431133;* ☼ *Oct–Apr Mon–Fri 06.00–20.00*), containing two mineral-enriched pools to soak your bones in winter, and next to them the **Ligetfürdő** (*Torontál tér 1;* \ *63 431672;* 💲 *1200/900Ft;* ☼ *May–Sep 06.00–20.00 daily*), with a large outdoor swimming pool and some smaller ones for children.

Further back from the shore is the Népliget, the city's largest park; it has tennis courts and an outdoor theatre. Even better, though, are the **University Botanical Gardens** (*Egyetemi Füvészkert; Lövölde út 42;* \ *62 454 236;* 💲 *250/170Ft;* ☼ *Mon–Fri Apr–Oct 10.00–18.00, green house 10.30–16.00, Nov–Mar 09.00–16.00, greenhouse 10.30–15.00*), where you can enjoy evergreens, rose and rock gardens, dawn redwoods and pink sacred lotuses on a lake. The greenhouse has species ranging from harvested crops like pepper, coffee and cocoa to orchids and tropical plants. The gardens are south along the river-bank road; buses 70 and 84F run there.

SHOPPING

🏬 **Herendi Porcelán** Oskola u. 21. The place to come for pieces of Herend china. ☼ *Tue–Fri 09.00–17.00, Sat 09.00–13.00.*

🏬 **Hollóháza** Kárász u. 13. Porcelain outlet specialising in Hungary's second-most-famous breakables. ☼ *Mon–Fri 09.30–18.00, Sat 09.00–13.00.*

🏬 **Latin Negyed** Kelemen u. 11. Next to the Virág Cukrászda, the 'Latin Quarter' is a large, elegant shop selling a massive variety of chocolate from all over

the world: fresh bonbons, truffles & marzipan from Szamos. There's also a selection of teas, fine wines & pálinkas. ☼ *10.00–20.00 daily.*

🏬 **Mars tér Market** Standing next to the bus station, this outdoor market has rows upon rows of stalls selling clothes, flowers, fruit & veg. ☼ *Mon–Fri 05.00–18.00, Sat 04.00–15.00, Sun 04.00–12.00.*

🏬 **Pick ház** Szabadkai út 18. This small supermarket is one of the outlets selling the famous Szeged sausage, together with an assortment of accompaniments. ⊕ Mon 15.00–18.00,Tue–Fri 07.00–18.00, Sat 06.00–12.00.

🏬 **Szeged Plaza** Kossuth Lajos sugárút 119. Large shopping mall containing bars & multi-screen cinema in the northwest of the centre. ⊕ 08.00–02.00

daily; shop hours Mon–Sat 09.00–21.00, Sun 10.00–19.00.

📚 **Universum** Oskola u. 23; ✎ 62 486984; www.bnb.hu. Foreign-language bookshop that serves universities & has a fair range of books in English. ⊕ Mon–Fri 09.00–18.00, Sat 09.30–13.00.

FESTIVALS AND EVENTS The Szeged Open-Air Games (see page 358) in July and August are the city's main event; there are also beer festivals in June and July.

MAKÓ

If Szeged's the local big cheese then it is appropriate that Makó provides the onion. Twenty kilometres to the east, Makó is the undisputed champion of the onion, with an **Onion Festival** in September and an **Onion House** (*Posta u.*), designed by Imre Makovecz to look as though 'growing out of the soil'. A Calvinist priest began cultivating the vegetable during the 18th century; he leased plots to tenant farmers and by the 19th century it had taken root to such an extent that it was being exported all over Europe.

This is also where Attila József (see box, page 360) went to school and published his first poetry. He stayed for a time at the **Espersit House** (*Kazinczy u. 6; 🎫 200/100Ft; ⊕ Tue–Sun 09.00–17.00*), home of a periodical editor and literary patron; today there is a collection devoted not only to Attila, but also to Gyula Juhász (who wrote here) and Ferenc Móra (a frequent visitor). The **Attila József Museum** (*Megyeház u. 4; ✎ 62 213540; 🎫 200/100Ft; ⊕ Tue–Sun 09.00–17.00*) has an exhibition covering the story of paprika production in Szeged, as well as 700 years of Makó history – including, inevitably, a section on onions in the gardening building of its *skanzen*.

The **town hall** (*Széchenyi tér 22*) was originally built in 1780 before taking its current Neoclassical aspect in 1836, while the **summer residence and adjacent chapel** (*Kossuth utca*) of the Bishop of Csanád date to 1826. The **thermal baths** (*Marcibányi tér 6; ✎ 62 212590; 🎫 850/520Ft; ⊕ Mon–Fri 08.00–19.00, Sat–Sun 09.00–19.00*) are in the centre of town, and offer treatments using radioactive mud from the River Maros that'll leave you glowing.

There are numerous **buses** running to Hódmezővásárhely, one every 15 minutes to Szeged and up to five buses a day to Budapest Népliget. Makó **railway station** is on a small branch line which runs between Újszeged and Kétegyháza, and also on that north to Hódmezővásárhely.

HÓDMEZŐVÁSÁRHELY

Its folk-art heritage has earned Hódmezővásárhely (25km northeast of Szeged) the nickname 'Peasants' Paris'; surviving pottery from the 19th century can be attributed to the hands of over 400 potters. The artistic seam continues to run strong, playing a prominent role in festivals and museum exhibitions, and there are two artists' colonies. Interestingly, rivalry led to traditional variations in style that you wouldn't usually expect to find within such a relatively small area; the output from Újváros (southeast of the centre) was a murky green in colour, while potters in the Tabán (northwest) used a bright yellow background, and those in Csúcs (northeast) preferred blue and white. The town is also renowned for its embroidery – table cloths and bed linen adorned with stylised motifs of plants and birds.

Hódmezővásárhely has been inhabited for 6,000 years, and in the medieval years between the Mongol invasion and the Turkish occupation (when the inhabitants

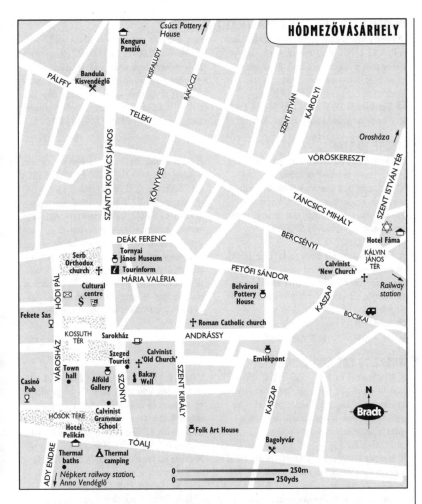

fled and the structures were destroyed) it was made up of around 20 individual villages. When the peasants returned, they brought a radical fire with them – János Kovács Szántó led a revolt in 1894 over the failure to redistribute land after the abolition of serfdom, and the town continued to feature in agrarian proletarian movements up until World War II. Today the town is a pretty one, its streets lined with fragrant flowers; cycling is a popular way to get about, so keep your wits about you if you're walking near the pavement cycle paths.

GETTING THERE AND AWAY The **bus station** (*Bocskai u.*) is 500m east of the centre – walk along Andrássy utca. Regular buses run to Békéscsaba, Csongrád and Szentes, and there are less frequent services to Budapest Népliget (five), Kecskemét (six), Szolnok and Debrecen (three). As well as the main **train station** (*Mérleg u.*), there's a second station, Hódmezővásárhely Népkert, in the southern part of the town. All trains stop at both stations. There are up to 14 departures a day to Szeged, 11 to Békécsaba, eight to Szentes and seven to Makó. To get from the main station to the centre, turn left and walk into Kistópart utca before turning right into Bajcsy-Zsilinszky Endre utca, which leads into Kálvin tér.

INFORMATION AND OTHER PRACTICALITIES

🎭 **Petőfi Sándor Cultural Centre** Szántó Kovács János u. 7; ☎ 62 214750. Hosts cultural events (such as touring plays & folk-dance troops), & can get you up to speed on current entertainment in town. *Ticket office ☺ Mon–Fri 15.30–17.30.*

Szeged Tourist Szőnyi u. 1; ☎ 62 534916. Can book rooms in private houses, arrange domestic

tours & provide information – all the usual. ☺ *Mon–Fri 09.00–12.00, 13.00–17.00.*

Tourinform Szegfű u. 3; ☎ 62 249350; e hodmezovasarhely@tourinform.hu. A short distance northeast of the main square, the tourist office can give you a list of private rooms, as well as answer queries. ☺ *Mon–Fri 08.00–12.00, 13.00–16.00.*

🏠 WHERE TO STAY

🏠 **Hotel Pelikán** (19 rooms) Ady Endre út 1; ☎ 62 245072. There's something of Butlins about the Pelikán, caught in a time warp where lurid sofas & bedspreads are *de rigueur*. Nevertheless, it is centrally located on the main road adjacent to the thermal baths. *Sgl 9,950–13,500Ft, dbl 11,500–13,500Ft.*

Thermal Camping Ady Endre út 1; ☎ 62 245033. Adequately equipped site next to the thermal baths (and behind the Hotel Pelikán). The bungalows are not en suite. *Camping ⛺ 990/640Ft, tent 1,200Ft, bungalow (for 2) 6,900Ft.*

🏠 **Hotel Fáma** (15 rooms) Szeremlei u. 7; ☎ 62 222231. A good 2-star hotel with a small garden &

rooms of varying size & price. Located just northeast of Kálvin tér. *Sgl 6,500–7,500Ft, dbl 7,900–8,900Ft; apt 9,500Ft (for 1), 11,500Ft (for 2).*

🏠 **Kenguru Panzió** (18 rooms) Szántó Kovács János u. 78; ☎ 62 534842; www.kenguru.vasarhely.hu. This first-rate guesthouse is the town's best, its AC rooms fresh & contemporary with wooden flooring & whitewashed walls. There's a little outdoor pool, a solarium & sauna. The young staff are on the sullen side, but otherwise all's hunky-dory. To the north of town, on Road 45 (that runs towards Szentes). *Dbl 12,000Ft, apt 14,500Ft (excl tourist tax); b/fast 950Ft.*

🍴 WHERE TO EAT AND DRINK

🍴 **Anno Vendéglő** Road 47; ☎ 62 713145. It's 4km from the centre (just before the 204km marker) in the direction of Szeged, but worth the journey for excellent Hungarian & international cuisine, & a romantic ambience. *Mains avg 1,600Ft; ☺ 11.00–23.00 daily.*

🍴 **Bagolyvár** Kaszap u. 31; ☎ 62 245726. On a road branching from the eastern end of Andrássy út, 'Owl Castle' has delicious food, attentive staff & a top-notch atmosphere. There's an extensive choice – including spaghetti, steaks, vegetarian paella & shark fillet – & a charming dining area akin to an open-fronted pince. *Mains avg 1,400Ft; ☺ 11.00–24.00 daily.*

🍴 **Bandula Kisvendéglő** Pálffy u. 2; ☎ 62 244234. Good international food & a menu that offers almost too many options, among them paella, chicken with Greek salad, pizza, spaghetti, chilli & steak. Also does takeaways. Stands just off Szántó Kovács János utca, 500m north of Kossuth tér. *Mains avg 1,300Ft; ☺ 11.00–23.00 daily.*

🍷 **Casinó Pub** Hősök tere 2; ☎ 62 246964. Sit out on the elevated terrace & shoot the breeze with an ice cream or an ice-cold beer. There's a selection of chicken & pork dishes. *Mains avg 1,100Ft; ☺ Mon–Thu 12.00–24.00, Fri 12.00–02.00, Sat 12.00–04.00, Sun 12.00–24.00.*

🍴 **Fekete Sas** Kossuth tér 3–5; ☎ 62 249363. At the western side of the main square, the custard-yellow Neo-Baroque 'Black Eagle' was built in 1905 by Gyula Pártos, & was once a hotel favoured by foreign merchants. The interior of the café-cum-brassiere is shabbily chic, & it spills outside with wicker chairs & parasols. Outside is János Pásztor's *Girl with a Jug.* ☺ *Mon–Thu 08.00–22.00, Fri–Sat 08.00–24.00, Sun 09.00–22.00.*

☕ **Sarokház** Kossuth tér 7; ☎ 62 243384. Set back from the road among Kossuth tér's greenery, this café is the perfect place to catch up with people or watch them go by. While stuffing down cake. ☺ *Sun–Thu 09.00–21.00, Fri–Sat 09.00–22.00.*

WHAT TO SEE AND DO Kossuth tér is popular with smoochers and cyclists, but it's also a shady square in which to enjoy a rest and survey some of the town's statues and architecture. A representation of Kossuth by Kallós Ede stands in the northern segment in front of a pink-faced **bank** (*Kossuth tér 5*) with a black dome and winged Mercury (next to the Fekete Sas; see above). The heavyweight sights of interest fall at the southern end, however. The Eclectic **town hall** (*Kossuth tér 1; ☺ Mon–Fri*

08.00–15.30) was built 1892–93 by Lajos Ybl, and has a 56m central tower with a viewing balcony. When there aren't functions going on, you can also visit its luxurious ceremonial hall. Outside is a rearing equestrian statue by János Pásztor, erected to commemorate World War I.

The **Alföldi Gallery** (*Kossuth tér 8;* ✆ *62 242277;* e *alfoldi.hodmezovasarhely@ museum.hu;* 🎫 *400/200Ft;* ⏲ *Thu–Sun 10.00–17.00, Tue–Wed 10.00–16.00*) occupies a Neoclassical former grammar school of the 1820s, and is dedicated to art of the Great Plain between the mid 19th and mid 20th centuries. Among the sculptors represented are János Pásztor, Miklós Izsó and Ferenc Medgyessy, while the paintings include some of the forgotten 718 canvases by local artist János Tornyai (1869–1936) that were found below the floor of his former Budapest studio in 1984. Across the road is the **Calvinist 'Old Church'** (*Református Ótemplom; Kossuth tér*), Romanesque in style and constructed in 1713–14. A rampart with loopholes was added in 1941, part of which still remains behind the church. The **Bakay Well** next to Szeged Tourist, with water pouring from the mouths of lions, was the town's first artesian well. Zsigmond Béla actually sunk it at another spot in 1880, but it was moved hither later.

South of the gallery is a **Calvinist grammar school** (*Szőnyi u. 2*) that has operated here since 1896, while behind that runs a 3km-long **defensive wall** representing a lesson learnt after floodwater devastated Szeged in 1879. Move northward from Kossuth tér to a crumbling late-18th-century Baroque Greek Orthodox church (*Görögkeleti-templom; Szántó Kovács János u. 7*) in dire need of work, and the **Tornyai János Museum** (*Szántó Kovács János u. 16–18;* ✆ *62 242224;* 🎫 *400/200Ft;* ⏲ *Thu–Sun 10.00–17.00, Tue–Wed 10.00–16.00*) opposite. The museum exhibitions (which have explanatory notes in English) include local archaeological finds (a corn jar from 2,600BC, a 'God with a Sickle' from 2,700BC, and a fertility statuette of the New Stone Age dubbed the 'Kőkénydomb Venus'), a memorial room devoted to the ethnographer Lajos Kiss (who was born here in 1881, and who provided many of the exhibits), a display of the popular art in which the town is steeped, and paintings by János Tornyai.

If you want to see some more vernacular art, the **Folk Art House** (*Népművészeti tájház; Árpád u. 21;* ✆ *06 20 444 0560;* 🎫 *200/100Ft;* ⏲ *09.00–12.00, 15.00–18.00*) is situated in the middle of a grassed area surrounded by residential blocks southeast of the Old Church. It is actually made up of two 18th-century houses, and has collections of local pottery and embroidery. Around 1,500m north of the centre, the **Csúcs Pottery House** (*Fazekasház; Rákóczi út 101;* ✆ *62 242224;* ⏲ *Apr 16–Oct 14 Tue–Sun 13.00–17.00*) shows the workshop and living space of Sándor Vékony, a past master potter, together with pieces by other renowned craftsmen. You can watch the workers in action – and buy samples – at the **Embroidery Workshop** (*Bajcsy-Zsilinszky u. 18–22;* ✆ *62 241284;* ⏲ *Mon–Thu 07.30–16.00, Fri 07.30–13.00*) and the **Belvárosi Fazekasház** (*Lánc u. 3;* ✆ *62 533024;* e *keramix@ freemail.hu;* ⏲ *Mon–Fri 10.00–18.00, Sat 10.00–14.00*), where Sándor Ambrus turns his wheel. Tourinform can provide a list of other craft workshops, with artisans involved in wood carving, basket weaving and lace making.

Hódmezővásárhely has its share of houses of worship, representing various creeds; if you head east from Kossuth tér along Andrássy út you'll pass an 18th-century **Roman Catholic church** (*Andrássy út 11*), with Baroque and Neoclassical styling, and 19th-century additions that include aisles designed by Miklós Ybl. On the same road is the **László Németh Town Library** (*Városi Könyvtár; Andrássy út 44;* ✆ *62 245378;* e *nemeth.hodmezovasarhely@museum.hu;* ⏲ *Mon 13.00–18.00, Tue–Fri 09.00–18.00, Sat 09.00–16.00*), whose adjacent memorial exhibition contains some of the personal effects of László Németh; the great writer and thinker taught at the girls' grammar school in the late 1940s.

Andrássy út culminates in Kálvin János tér, with the white **Calvinist 'New Church'** (*Újtemplom; Kálvin János tér* 7), younger counterpart to that in Kossuth tér; built in 1799, it's one of the largest of its denomination in the Great Plain. The square's **artesian well** was designed by András János Nagy in 1884; the mayor had requested that it be placed in the grounds of a school, but Nagy insisted that it be enjoyed by the whole community. To the north of it is the mid-19th-century cream-coloured **synagogue** (*Szent István tér*), with a Secessionist façade added in 1908 by Miksa Müller; the stained-glass panels in its doors remind us of Moorcroft pottery. The **Roman Catholic church** (*Szent István tér 4*) was erected in the style of an old Christian basilica in 1936. István Maté's young Szent István – to whom the church is dedicated – patrols atop his steed outside.

The **Centre of Remembrance** (*Emlékpont; Andrássy út 34;* ✆ *62 530940; www.emlekpont.hu;* ✆ *800/400Ft;* ☉ *Tue–Fri 10.00–18.00, Sat–Sun 10.00–19.00*) is a fascinating and unique exhibition that charts the period between 1945 and 1990, and arguably rivals Budapest's Memento Park (see page 160) for interest and importance. In 2005, an appeal was made to the people of the town to send photos, documents, memories and other items relating to the time of Soviet occupation and the single-party state; thousands of pieces were submitted, and it makes for a stimulating collection.

Other activities South of Kossuth tér, the **thermal baths** (*Ady Endre út 1;* ✆ *62 244238;* ✆ *990/600Ft;* ☉ *08.00–21.00 daily*) sit in an 8ha park; there are eight pools, with medicinal water, as well as sauna and massage facilities.

Aranyági Stud Farm (*Serháztér u. 2;* ✆ *06 30 218 3354;* e *hodmgrt@ hodmgrt.hu*) is a century-old breeding and training farm for Furioso-North Star half-breds from Mezőhegyes. It has an inn, and you can take riding lessons, have a turn in a carriage or watch a horse show. You'll find it 4½km northeast on Road 47 (follow Szent István utca out of town towards Orosháza). Alternatively, the **Dél-Alföldi Lovasudvar** (*Tanya 4010;* ✆ *06 30 514 8860*) is an equestrian yard 2½km west of the centre that can organise riding tours and shows, and has a small guesthouse.

FESTIVALS AND EVENTS During the St George's Day Agricultural Festival at the end of April, farmers gather to celebrate spring with an animal show and competition. There are cultural events during the Autumn Weeks in October, and – as elsewhere in the country – the town goes big on celebrating Szent István on August 20 (and the days around it).

MÁRTÉLY

Ten kilometres to the northwest, Mártély is a resort village by a backwater of the Tisza. There's a sandy bank for sunbathing, trees under which to picnic and water craft to paddle around in (✆ *pedalo 900Ft/hr, rowing boat 600Ft/hr*). Beyond the Tisza embankment is a landscape protection area, a region of floodland that holds frogs, great white egrets and herons. For those who want to stay, a number of private holiday homes (*üdülős*) are set back from the bank – the Tourinforms in Szeged and Hódmezővásárhely have a list, and can also provide information on fishing here. **Hunnia Panzió** (*Árnyas u. 5–7;* ✆ *06 30 507 6692; www.hunia.de; Jul–Aug €285/week, May, Jun & Sep €200/week*) is one such, with two self-contained sections holding five guests each. Otherwise **Tiszapart Camping** (✆ *62 228057; camping 800/600Ft, tents 800Ft, cabins 1,800Ft*) is a lovely site 300m from the water with wooden cabins. Regular **buses** run here from Hódmezővásárhely.

There is little of note to send you charging to Orosháza itself – the odd museum and church won't detain you for long. However, people *are* drawn by the resort of Gyopárosfürdő 3km to the west, with its lake and thermal baths, and this is also a good base for exploring one pocket of the Körös-Maros National Park. Fehér-tó at Kardoskút is of genuine value to birdwatchers, and is but 12km away as the short-toed lark flies.

The proud spirit of resistance blazed strong in Orosháza. Some of its people fought with the Rákóczi battalion founded by Pál Vasvári (which was obliterated in 1849 during a struggle against Romanian insurgents fighting for the Habsburgs), and in the aftermath of the War of Independence the wife of Lajos Kossuth was one among many refugees who sheltered here. That single night of safety cost Ferenc Mikolay dear; the son of the pastor was given a ten-year prison sentence for harbouring the lady fugitive.

Ask Hungarians about Orosháza and 'goose liver' will spring to their lips. Orosháza goose liver (*Orosházi libamájpástétom*) is the country's most famous. The *foie gras* is packed into its stylish black tins before being sent for export. Hungary is a prime exporter of *foie gras*, and sells over 90% of its produce abroad (mainly in France). The farming process is, of course, one that attracts controversy, with animal-welfare groups strongly critical of the way in which the geese are machine-fed. The producers themselves argue that this method is actually far kinder to the animals than feeding them by hand. Whatever your opinion on this, it's certainly the case that goose-liver production provides a living for many of the region's farmers.

GETTING THERE AND AWAY The main Orosháza **railway station** (*Állomás tér*) is at the junction of three lines; trains through this station also serve the town's other three smaller stations. There are trains to Szarvas (five), Békéscsaba (14), Szeged and Hódmezővásárhely (12) and Szentes (five). It's 600m from the station to the centre; walk straight ahead, turn right into Október 6 utca and first left on to Kossuth Lajos utca, which leads to the centre.

The **bus station** (*Március 15 tér*) is 150m south of the railway station; there are very regular services to Békéscsaba, and regular to Szeged, Szentes and Hódmezővásárhely. You can also access towns including Debrecen (seven), Szarvas (12) and Csongrád. Buses to Budapest require a change at Szentes.

For Gyopárosfürdő, you can follow Szentesi út west from Orosháza's Kossuth tér, or take local buses 2 or 4.

INFORMATION

ℤ **Tourinform** Fasor u. 2/A; ↘ 68 414422; e oroszaza@tourinform.hu. The staff of this office were tripping over themselves to be helpful during our visit. Found behind the train station at the top of Fasor u. in Gyopárosfürdő. ⊕ Mon–Fri 08.00–16.00.

WHERE TO STAY, EAT AND DRINK There are very few places to stay in Orosháza; unless otherwise indicated, those below are in Gyopárosfürdő.

⌑ **Amadeus Coffee House** Orosháza, Győri Vilmos tér 2; ↘ 68 472573. Centrally located café, serving coffee, alcohol & ice cream.
🏠 **Fehér Hattyú Panzió** (7 rooms) Fasor u. 13; ↘ 68 510330; www.feherhattyu.hu. The swish 'White Swan' is best for eats & sleeps. Its delightful rooms are tastefully decorated & have a real holiday feel to them. The restaurant (*mains avg 1,300Ft; ⊕ 06.00–24.00 daily*) serves tasty food, its menu featuring Hungarian classics with an international twist in places. *Dbl 12,000Ft, apt (for 4) 27,000Ft.*

 Hotel Corvus Aqua (36 rooms) Hűvös u. l;
20 923 5650; www.hotelcorvus.hu. This new 4-star has comfortable rooms & its great location provides direct access for hotel guests to the thermal baths. *Sgl 12,500–17,500Ft, dbl 16,500–24,900Ft, suite 24,900–34,900Ft.*

 Hotel Flóra (15 rooms) Hűvös u. 8; 68 680753; www.hotelflora.hu. Small but friendly 2-star hotel on the bank of the boating lake, north of the thermal baths. Its grounds are green, there's a tennis court, sauna & solarium, & the simple (but sizeable) rooms have balconies. *Sgl 9,800Ft, dbl 11,800Ft, apt (for 4) 17,500Ft.*

 Napfény Recreation Centre Orosháza, Táncsics Mihály u. 26; rekreal@rekreal.hu. The 'Sunshine' centre (follow Táncsics Mihály u. north from the top of Győri Vilmos tér) is a jack of all trades, a meeting point offering services to townsfolk & tourists alike – there are fitness classes, tennis

courts, wine-tasting sessions, a gym, a beauty parlour, a restaurant & a bar. Some guestrooms are squeezed in among the other facilities. *Dbl 9,000Ft.*

 Thermal Camping Fasor u. 3; 68 512260; www.gyoparosfurdo.hu. There are various accommodation options here, right on top of the baths complex. Wooden bungalows on the lake shore sleep 3–5 (only the largest have bathrooms & cooking facilities), there's a basic hotel & space on the site for 30 tents & 8 caravans. Guests can enter the thermal baths free. *Camping 900/700Ft, tent 200Ft/m2, c/van 300Ft/m2; bungalows: 6,800Ft (for 3), 8,400Ft (for 4), 10,000Ft (for 5).*

 Tópart Panzió Tópart u. 11; 68 413202. On the opposite side of the lake from the Flóra, the 'Lakeshore' is an adorable panzió in a restful setting. The rooms are furnished with pine & flooded with light. You'll try in vain not to love it. *Dbl 11,500Ft, apt 16,500Ft; b/fast 1,000Ft/pp.*

WHAT TO SEE AND DO

The town The **Szántó-Kovács Museum** (*Dózsa György u. 5;* 68 412853; 300/150Ft; Tue–Fri 08.00–16.00, Sat–Sun 10.00–15.00), to the west of Szabadság tér, is an ethnographic and historical collection relating to Orosháza and surrounding villages, and displaying items ranging from the military to the agricultural (including those of the Lutheran peasant families from Zomba near Szekszárd, who repopulated the town after the Turkish occupation). Further along the same street, the **Darvas József Literary Memorial House** (*Irodalmi Emlékház; Dózsa György 74;* 68 311693; admission free; Tue–Fri 08.00–12.00, Sat–Sun with prior notice) occupies the childhood home of early-20th-century writer and socialist cultural politician József Darvas. The front room has the family furniture, together with photos and documents, while a memorial room is devoted to the work of the man himself. A wheelwright workshop at the back was used by the writer's brother, and a building in the garden now holds the Békés County Literary Collection, whose purpose is to gather the manuscripts and other objects belonging to local artists.

The oldest building in town is the late-Baroque **Lutheran Church** (*Győri Vilmos tér*), its clocktower constructed in 1777 and the southern transept added in 1830. This was the house of worship for the original Lutherans who set up shop after being hounded from Zomba because of their religion; in front of the altar is the bell they brought with them. To the east of it is the **Táncsics Mihály Grammar School** (*Mikszáth u.*), a broad Neoclassical building named after the politician who represented the town between 1869 and 1872. The memorial park in front – with scattered chunks of stone and a central bell bearing the date 1744 – was erected on the 250th anniversary of the settlers' arrival.

Head northwards up Táncsics Mihály utca for the **Calvinist church** (*Könd u.*), a palatial white church with three towers that was built in 1917. Opposite it is the **Well Museum** (*Kút Múzeum; Könd u. 1;* 68 417707; admission free; Apr–Sep Mon, Wed & Fri 12.00–16.00, other times by prior notice), a tiny former water tower displaying disused pumps and photos of shadoofs. It's Hungary's only museum devoted to wells, and a visit here will show you why; it puts the 'well' in to well dull. Better is the **Town Gallery** (*Thék u. 1;* 68 412523; Tue–Fri 10.00–12.00, 14.00–17.00, Sat 10.00–16.00), near the bus and train stations, which has works by artists including István Boldizsár, Ferenc Bolmányi, Gyula Pap and Orosháza-born photographer

Miklós Müller. The **arboretum** (*Gárdonyi Géza u. 12;* ⊕ *08.00–17.00 daily*) is off Rákóczi Ferenc utca, just beyond the railway track, and contains over 2,000 plant species.

Gyopárosfürdő Go west for 3km to Gyopárosfürdő, a spa resort (since 1869) concentrated around a natural saline lake. Reed beds and carpets of grass make this a verdant spot for a stroll, and you can swim in, fish in or boat on the water. (There is even an international model-boat competition on the lake at the start of May.) The adjacent complex of **thermal baths** (*Fasor u. 3;* ❧ *68 512260; www.gyoparosfurdo.hu;* ✆ *1,000/700Ft;* ⊕ *outdoor baths May–Sep, indoor baths all yr, Sun–Fri 10.00–20.00, Sat 10.00–24.00; health centre Mon–Fri 07.00–15.00*) is a big thing, fed by two deep wells and including indoor and outdoor pools, saunas, a health centre offering therapies, an assortment of sports facilities and a campsite. The mineral-rich water is thought to be good for treating rheumatic and skin complaints. You can climb the former water tower for views of the lake system.

FESTIVALS AND EVENTS The Summer Cultural Days feature a week of concerts and cabarets at the end of June, while the Bread Festival in August reminds that the town had an international reputation for baking at the start of the 20th century. The inaugural, two-day Foie Gras Festival took place in 2009, and is set to be an annual gourmet event each June.

KARDOSKÚT (AND FEHÉR-TÓ)

Twelve kilometres south of Orosháza is Kardoskút, a diminutive village surrounded by agricultural land. To the west of that (next to the road running between the village and Hódmezővásárhely) is the strictly protected Fehér-tó (White Lake), so-named because of the colour of the sodium carbonate deposited on the lake bed during periods of drought. Part of the Körös-Maros National Park (see box, page 372), this is regarded as one of the country's most valuable conservation areas. It represents a vital stop-over site for aquatic and grassland birds, which rest here and feed on the surrounding *puszta* and farmland. Among the nesting birds are the avocet, Kentish plover, godwit, short-toed lark and lapwing, while migrating species alight in vast numbers – in spring and autumn there might be as many as 50,000 geese, 100,000 ducks and flocks of up to 20,000 common cranes (1% of the entire central European crane population) spending a night. Other occasional visitors are the critically endangered slender-billed curlew, the demoiselle crane, the red-breasted goose, the lesser-white-fronted goose and the white-tailed eagle (drooling at the beak as it eyes up this preening smorgasbord). Around 142 bird species have been recorded at the lake, and this is ornithologist heaven. In addition, long-horned grey cattle graze on the saline pasture near by.

On entering Kardoskút from the Orosháza direction, follow the Hódmezővásárhely-bound road to the right for 3km and you'll arrive at the **Kardoskút Museum** (*Kardoskút;* ❧ *68 429262;* ✆ *160/110Ft;* ⊕ *only with prior notice*), which has a small exhibition of the wildlife of the national park. Continue for a further 1km to the **White Lake Lookout Tower** (*free admission;* ⊕ *all yr*), a wooden viewing point where you can survey the birds and other wildlife of the surrounding flatlands. The lake itself lies to the west, and can only be visited with special permission; however, the watchtower provides an excellent platform, particularly during migratory periods. For further information, contact the Körös-Maros National Park Directorate (*Szarvas, Anna liget;* ❧ *66 313855*).

There are up to 15 buses a day to Orosháza. The **bus stop** is on the main road, just before the turn off for the watch tower and museum. The odd bus also runs

7

The Körös-Maros National Park, divided into 13 different pockets between the Tisza-Körös and Maros rivers, was established in 1997 and covers 51,000ha in total. It includes flood-plain forests, fishing lakes and the dead channels of the two rivers, as well as the remains of habitats left after the Sárrét regulation project (of the 1850s) such as marshes and saline meadows. The park plays host to some exceptionally rare plants, among them the pheasant's eye and nodding sage; the *Adonis transylvanica* and *Salvia nutans* are found only here. There are unusual species of fauna too, like the great owl moth, the steppe moth and the Mediterranean blind mole-rat.

In the northern part of Békés County (northwest of Békéscsaba), the Dévaványa-Ecseg Plain is a place of scattered farmsteads. Much of the landscape is barren steppe, but the area is particularly significant for holding a third of the country's population of the great bustard (and the largest population of the beefy bird in Europe). In 1941, 8,500 of them were counted here, but this had declined to 2,500 by 1985. The **Great Bustard Reserve** on the road running between Dévaványa and Ecsegfalva was established to protect and boost its numbers. While parts of the park can only be visited with special permission, the Réhely Visitor Centre (*Dévaványa-Réhely;* \ *66 483083;* e *rehelyi.devavanya@ museum.hu;* & *350/250Ft;* ⊕ *Apr 15–Oct 31 Tue–Sun 09.00–17.00*) in a former granary is open to all. You can get close to the chicks, and adjoining fields and compounds hold traditional livestock – rare breeds such as the majestic Hungarian grey cattle, the curly-haired mangalica pig and spiral-horned racka sheep. These protected national herds provide an important gene pool. There are observation towers, nature trails, a permanent wildlife exhibition and video displays documenting the great-bustard programme; rooms are available to rent above the visitor centre. You can also follow several nature and cycling trails (*bikes for rent 300Ft/hr, 1,000Ft/day*).

Further south near Orosháza, **Fehér-tó** at Kardoskút (see page 371) is one of the top bird-conservation sites in the country. The Körös-Maros National Park Directorate (see page 379) can provide further information about the park's highlights, and arrange guides to the protected areas (*2,200Ft/hr*) and specialist guides for birdwatching or visiting some strictly protected areas (*5,500Ft/hr*). The *Körös-Maros Nemzeti Park* (1:90,000) map, produced by the national park, shows all the 13 areas and includes brief descriptions of each.

to the museum. Kardoskút **train station** is on a small branch line that links Mezőhegyes to Mezőtúr, passing Szarvas and Orosháza along the way. There are up to seven trains a day along this route.

BÉKÉSCSABA

Settled by Magyars during the 10th century, at the conclusion of the Turkish occupation the population of Békéscsaba amounted to a grand total of just 22 families. After victory in the War of Independence, the emperor gave Békés County to János György Harrucken, supplier of army provisions to the Viennese court; from 1715 Harrucken went about repopulating the village (which by the 19th century was apparently listed as Europe's largest) with Protestant Slovak immigrants drawn by the promise of religious tolerance. In 1841 it was raised to the rank of market town, and the subsequent construction of railway lines from Pest to Arad and Nagyvárad (Oradea) to Fiume (Rijeka) led to economic development so significant that in the mid 20th century the town claimed the title of county seat from Gyula. Today, along with remnants of its Slovak and Lutheran heritage, Békéscsaba is associated with its prized *csabai* sausage (the three-day Sausage Festival takes place in autumn) and its rebellious political past. The region was at the eye of the 'Stormy Corner' (*Viharsarok*), where 19th-century agrarian movements struggled for the rights of workers on feudal estates and initiated a series of violent rebellions.

GETTING THERE AND AROUND The **bus station** (*Andrássy út 58*) is 1½km south west of the town centre – follow Andrássy út northeast to the centre. There are regular buses to Békés, Gyula, Orosháza and Szarvas. There are also up to 15 buses a day to Szeged, 11 to Debrecen, six to Kecskemét, three to Budapest and Szolnok and one to Pécs and Miskolc. Békéscsaba **railway station** – just behind the bus station – is well-connected train-wise. There are up to 16 a day to Szolnok and Gyula, ten to Szeged and Hódmezővásárhely, up to 12 to Budapest and a handful to the Romanian capital of Bucharest.

INFORMATION AND OTHER PRACTICALITIES

Békés Tourist Andrássy út 10; ℡ 66 323448; e bekestourist@t-online.hu. Travel agency that specialises in tours of the Békés region, & can also answer questions. ⊕ Mon 14.00–18.00, Tue–Fri 10.00–18.00, Sat 10.00–14.00.

Csaba Centre Andrássy út 37–43; ℡ 66 524530. Large American-style shopping centre at the western end of Andrássy út with all the usual retail suspects & a multi-screen cinema complex. ⊕ Mon–Sat 09.00–20.00, Sun 10.00–18.00 (although the cafés & cinema keep later hours).

Ibusz Szent István tér 9; ℡ 66 325554. Exchange currency, & book private accommodation & tours. ⊕ Mon–Fri 08.00–16.00.

Listings magazine Békési Est

Tourinform Szent István tér 9; ℡ 66 441261; e bekescsaba@tourinform.hu. Next door but one to Ibusz & opposite the Hotel Fiume. ⊕ Mon–Fri 09.00–17.00.

Weol Internet Café Gyóni Géza u. 14–16.00; ℡ 66 452175. Internet access – 16 terminals costing 10Ft/min (students get a discount) – & coffee bar. ⊕ 10.00–24.00 daily.

BIG FAT BUSTARD

In steppic habitats – most notably the Körös-Maros, Hortobágy and Kiskunság national parks – you might spot one of the world's threatened species, the great bustard or sand grouse. This impressive 20kg giant of a turkey, with a wingspan of 2.3m, stands as tall as a mature roe deer. Threatened by hunting, habitat destruction and its unfortunate deliciousness to the human palate, Hungary treasures up to 1,300 (about 4%) of the heaviest flying bird on Earth.

Dedicated ornithologists may be lucky enough to see this bird's extraordinary mating display, which starts in March. Male birds appear virtually to turn themselves inside out, twisting their feathers by inflating special pouches to transform their normal brown colouring to a brilliant white. The great bustard's succulent meat was a favourite of banquets from Neanderthal times up to the Victorian era when, in one of the most elaborate dishes ever concocted (taking a whole day to cook), the bustard was stuffed, Russian-doll-like, with 15 other birds.

The Great Bustard Reserve at Dévaványa aims to conserve and consolidate. The bustard prefers large areas of cultivated land, and lays its eggs in fields of corn or alfalfa in early May. However, the harvesting of alfalfa often overlaps with the brooding period and the female can be scared away from her nest. The reserve incubates abandoned eggs in the hope of hatching the chicks and raising them until they are capable of fending for themselves.

WHERE TO STAY Békéscsaba is sparing in its variety of accommodation options, and it might be worth considering staying at nearby Gyula.

Arany János College Lencsési út 136; ↘ 66 459366. Dorms rooms at rock-bottom prices in summer months; stands across the water south of Parkerdő in the Ifjúsági-tábor. *From 1,200Ft/pp.*

Hotel Fiume (39 rooms) Szent István tér 2; ↘ 66 443243; www.hotelfiume.hu. The Neoclassical building housing the hotel was constructed in 1868 on the site of a former medieval inn, & is named after the Nagyvárad–Fiume railway line. The rooms try hard to live up to the elegant promise of the restaurant (see below) – half of them containing Secessionist-style furnishings – but the accommodation is over-priced in spite of its central position. *Sgl 10,150Ft, dbl 13,650Ft, trpl 15,750Ft.*

House of Slovak Culture (*Szlovák Kultúra Háza*; 11 rooms) Kossuth tér 10; ↘ 66 441750; www.slovak.hu. This culture house was established in 1996 with the aim of promoting Slovak traditions & maintaining relations with Slovaks in neighbouring countries. As well as hosting temporary exhibitions & other programmes, it has a restaurant (see below) & good rooms with pine floors. *Sgl 7,000Ft, dbl 10,000Ft, apt 9,240–16,800Ft.*

✖ WHERE TO EAT AND DRINK

✖ **Hargita Kisvendéglő** Tavasz u. 7; ↘ 66 435419; ℮ hargitavendeglo@t-online.hu. True to its name – a region of Transylvania – this restaurant serves the best of traditional Transylvanian & Hungarian cuisine. It's something of a hidden gem, lying to the west of town (beyond the railway station) in the Jamina district. Groups of up to 8 people can sample the oven-baked specialities of the house (although preparation time means advanced warning is necessary). Definitely worth searching out – take local buses 2 or 14 to the Tavasz u. stop. *Mains avg 1,500Ft;* ⊕ *daily 11.30–22.00.*

✖ **Hotel Fiume Restaurant** See above. The classy hotel restaurant has an excellent reputation, & is the pick of the town's eateries. Eat outside among the flowerboxes on a warm evening. *Mains avg 1,700Ft;* ⊕ *Mon–Sat 07.00–22.00, Sun 07.00–18.00.*

⎘ **Jankay** Csaba Centre, Andrássy út 37. A permanently busy café where quiet moments are rare & the iced tea is beautifully refreshing. ⊕ *Sun–Thu 08.00–22.00, Fri–Sat 08.00–24.00.*

⎘ **Márvány Cukrászda** Andrássy út 21; ↘ 06 30 409 6962. The best spot for cake & ice cream. ⊕ *08.00–22.00 daily.*

✖ **Pipacs Restaurant** Gyóni Géza u. 19. Nearly 100 years old, the restaurant has re-opened after a recent refurbishment. In winter, the fireplace gives a warm atmosphere; the food is Hungarian & international, the portions are big & the prices are reasonable. *Mains avg 1,500Ft;* ⊕ *Mon–Thu 11.00–21.30, Fri–Sat 11.00–22.30, Sun 11.00–15.00.*

✖ **Rolling Rock Café** Mednyánszky u. 1–3; ↘ 66 430265. Set back from the main street & overlooking a large fountain, the Rolling Rock has a canteen-style buffet selling dishes of pasta & traditional Hungarian food. This is the place for a good budget lunch – a soup starter & pasta main course will set you back less than 1,000Ft. Expect to queue.

✖ **House of Slovak Culture** See above. The house has a low-priced restaurant serving Slovak specialities & beer. *Mains avg 1,100Ft;* ⊕ *11.00–23.00 daily.*

✖ **Uj Trencsén Restaurant** Luther u. 17; ↘ 66 326830. Slovak & Hungarian cuisine in comely surroundings with fishing nets strung from the ceiling & tables divided by trellises. The atmosphere is lovely & the food very decent. *Mains avg 1,500Ft;* ⊕ *Mon–Thu 11.00–21.30, Fri–Sat 11.00–24.00, Sun 11.00–21.30.*

ENTERTAINMENT AND NIGHTLIFE The town's cultural events take place in the town hall, the Lutheran Great Church (see opposite) and the **Jókai Theatre** (*Színház; Andrássy út 1;* ↘ *66 441527*). The latter was the first stone-built theatre in the area, erected in the 1870s and Eclectic in style, with white reliefs of musical muses on its exterior. You can find out what's on at the **County Cultural Centre** (*Luther u. 6;* ↘ *66 442122;* ⊕ *Mon–Fri 10.00–16.00, variable at w/ends*), including dates and times when the Philharmonic is performing in the Great Lutheran Church.

The wine bar **Gazsó** (*Andrássy út 10;* ↘ *66 323597;* ⊕ *07.00–22.00 daily*) generally bursts at the seams with pavement drinkers chatting beneath the tables' parasols, while **Narancs Klub** (*Szent István tér 3;* ⊕ *Thu–Sat 17.00–04.00*) is a sweaty underground basement bar and club – all low ceilings and brick arches –

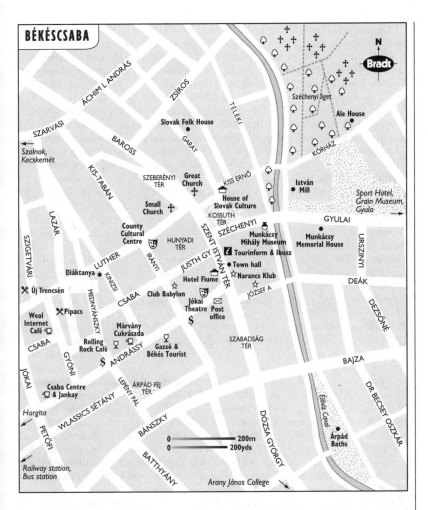

BÉKÉSCSABA

ÁCHIM L ANDRÁS
ZSÍROS
TELEKI
Széchenyi liget
Ale House
SZARVASI
BAROSS
GARAY
Slovak Folk House
Szolnok,
Kecskemét
KÓRHÁZ
KÍS-TABÁN
SZEBERÉNYI TÉR
Great Church
KISS ERNŐ
István Mill
LÁZÁR
Small Church
House of Slovak Culture
Sport Hotel, Grain Museum, Gyula
SZIGETVÁRI
KOSSUTH TÉR
SZÉCHENYI
County Cultural Centre
HUNYADI TÉR
GYULAI
URSZÍNYI
IRÁNYI
Munkácsy Mihály Museum
Munkácsy Memorial House
LUTHER
Diáktanya
KINIZSI
JUSTH GY ISTVÁN TÉR
SZENT ISTVÁN TÉR
Tourinform & Ibusz
Town hall
DEÁK
Új Trencsén
CSABA
Club Babylon
Hotel Fiume
Narancs Klub
DEZSŐNÉ
MEDNYÁNSZKY
Pipacs
Jókai Theatre
JÓZSEF A
Weol Internet Café
Márvány Cukrászda
Post office
SZABADSÁG TÉR
BAJZA
CSABA
GYÓNI
Rolling Rock Café
ANDRÁSSY
Gazsó & Békés Tourist
JÓKAI
Csaba Centre & Jankay
LÉPÉNY PÁL
ÁRPÁD FEJ TÉR
Hargita
WLASSICS SÉTÁNY
BÁNSZKY
0   200m
0   200yds
DÓZSA GYÖRGY
Élővíz Canal
Árpád Baths
DR BECSEY OSZKÁR
PETŐFI
Railway station, Bus station
BATTHYÁNY
Arany János College

haunted by the young. There are places to sit and chill, but they're fewer and further between on club nights (*Thu–Sat*), when booming base lines prevail. The hi-tech **Club Babylon** (*Irányi u. 12; www.babylonclub.hu;* Ⓜ *800–3,000Ft*) features some of the country's best DJs, and attracts young clubbers from far and wide. The main events are on Saturdays, although there are some mid-week parties.

WHAT TO SEE AND DO The speed of the town's 19th-century growth means that architecture pre-dating that period is in short supply. There's a 'David meets Goliath' face-off between the two Lutheran churches straddling Szeberényi tér. The '**Small Church**' (*Szeberényi tér 2*) of 1745 is one of the county's oldest. Until the end of the 1800s, services here were conducted in Slovakian before they became bilingual. The '**Great Church**' (*Szeberényi tér 1*) is a huge, Zopf-style affair completed in 1824 – at the time, the largest Lutheran place of worship in central Europe (and still the largest in Hungary); its tower reaches 70m, and the hall church can hold 6,000 people. Of course, the bigger they are the harder they fall, and in 1978 the building was badly damaged by an earthquake; renovation wasn't finished until 1983. The acoustics are first-rate, and there are regular concerts inside.

7

The cobbled **Kossuth tér** holds János Horvay's statue of the statesman; locals used to queue to drink yellowish water from the square's artesian well, but this was blocked up after World War II and now only the loin-clothed fisherwoman remains. Garay utca runs from the square's northeastern corner and leads to the **Slovak Folk House** (*Tájház; Garay János u. 21;* ✆ *66 321771;* ✆ *100/50Ft;* ☉ *Tue–Sun Apr–Oct 10.00–12.00, 14.00–18.00, Nov–Mar 10.00–12.00*), owned by a wealthy Slovak family in the 19th century. The ornate wooden verandah is typical of Slovak peasant architecture and would have been a meeting place for friends and neighbours, while inside is an open chimney that was used for smoking sausages. The **Diáktanya** youth centre (*Kinizsi u. 12;* ☉ *Mon–Fri 10.00–17.00*) is housed in a beautifully preserved traditional peasant dwelling; it hosts exhibitions, handicraft workshops and the occasional concerts.

Széchenyi liget is a small and peaceful park east of the folk house, on the other side of the Elővíz-csatorna (the canal that splits the town, and around which you'll hear the stuttered groaning of frogs on summer evenings). An **obelisk monument** is dedicated to the 2,000 victims of a cholera outbreak in 1831, which killed 2,000 locals. At the southern end of the park is the Neoclassical former **Ale House** (*Sörház; Kórház u. 4*), built in 1840, while across Kórház utca stands the hulking, six-storey **István Mill** (*Malom; Gőzmalom tér*), built in the early 20th century and still going strong. If you want to know more about the settlement's agricultural past, the **Grain Museum** (*Gabonamúzeum; Gyulai út 65;* ✆ *66 441026;* ✆ *200/100Ft;* ☉ *Apr–Oct Tue–Sun 10.00–17.00*) lies 2km east of here in the Parkerdő, along Road 44 (heading towards Gyula). The thatched dwelling dates to 1824, and there is a romantic brick windmill, a statue park commemorating the 'personalities' in the history of grain improvement and a garden displaying the various grains grown in the county.

On the opposite side of Gyulai út from the mill is the **Munkácsy Memorial House** (*Gyulai út 5;* ✆ *66 442080;* ✆ *500/200Ft;* ☉ *Jan 7–Apr 30 Tue–Fri 08.00–16.00, Sat 10.00–16.00, May–Oct Tue–Fri 08.00–17.00, Sat 10.00–16.00*), a mansion built by the Steiner family in the 1840s. The Steiners and Munkácsy were relatives, and the famous artist lived here for some time as a boy after the death of his parents. Some of Munkácsy's paintings are on display, as well as late-Biedermeier furniture belonging to the noble Omaszta family who inhabited the place after the Steiners. Look out too for one of the doors, which was fashioned by Munkácsy and betrays his initial training as a carpenter (see below).

Back on the western side of the canal, the **Mihály Munkácsy Museum** (*Széchenyi u. 9;* ✆ *66 328040; www.munkacsy.hu;* ✆ *800/400Ft;* ☉ *Tue–Sun Apr–Sep 10.00–18.00, Oct–Mar 10.00–16.00*) has more of the 19th-century artist's work. Munkácsy was a 'boy done good', an orphan and former joiner's apprentice born in 1844 who went on to become one of the country's premier painters. He settled in Paris in 1872, married the widow of a French baron, and devoted himself to painting religious scenes and portraits of society's cream (and their servants). The museum has the world's largest permanent collection of Munkácsy's paintings, as well as exhibitions of ethnography (charting the 18th-century influx of ethnic groups that included Serbs, Romanians and Germans alongside the Slovaks), natural history and modern fine art.

The imposing **town hall** (*Szent István tér 7*) was completed in 1873, its Eclectic façade orchestrated by Miklós Ybl. Its lovely central courtyard is the venue for Békéscaba's main cultural event, the Town Hall Nights (Városházi Esték), which feature concerts and plays over three weeks in June. The pedestrianised **Andrássy út** launches itself westwards from the bottom of Szent István tér; the lively, tree-lined promenade is the main shopping street. The **Árpád Baths** (*Árpád sor;* ✆ *66 549800;* ✆ *1200Ft/800Ft;* ☉ *08.00–20.00 daily*), south of the centre on the other side of Bánszky utca, have thermal baths as well as a large swimming pool and fun slide.

SZARVAS

Szarvas – 'Stag' – is at the western gateway to Békés County, lying on a backwater of the River Körös formed during 19th-century river regulation. After the Turks had run amuck, Count Harruckern (see page 372) settled Slovak peasants here. Real improvement came at the end of the 18th century, however, when a Lutheran priest, Sámuel Tessedik, introduced a building programme and agricultural reforms. After him, the aristocratic Bolza family continued the development, constructing several mansions and founding the arboretum. A sleepy place – when the college students aren't breaking the silence –it is nevertheless not immune to big events; it has twice hosted the four-day Equestrian World Festival (most recently in July 2005), when the town is overrun with people watching performances by 1,000 horsemen from 30 different countries.

GETTING THERE AND AROUND The **bus station** is at the corner of Szabadság út and Bocskai István utca, and runs regular services to Békéscsaba. There are also buses to Szeged (eight), Gyula (seven), Budapest Népliget and Kecskemét (six), Miskolc and Debrecen (two). The **train station** (*Állomás tér*) is 1km east of the centre. From here turn left along Állomás utca and right into Szabadság út. Szarvas is on a small rail line running between Mezőhegyes and Mezőtúr via Orosháza, and there are up to seven trains a day along the route.

INFORMATION AND OTHER PRACTICALITIES

🖳 **Internet** The Panoráma Caffé (see page 378) has an internet terminal.
📔 **Listings magazine** Békési Est
📺 **Sugár Travel** Kossuth u. 23; ☎ 66 215690; e sugartravelzso@globenet.hu. Accommodation, tours, etc. Stands next to the Irish pub & opposite the Jazz Café. ⊙ Mon–Fri 10.00–17.00.

📌 **Tourinform** Kossuth tér 3; ☎ 66 311140; e szarvas@tourinform.hu. Maps, information & lists of cheap accommodation options. ⊙ May Mon–Fri 09.00–17.00, Jun 1–Jun 14 Mon–Fri 09.00–17.00, Sat 09.00–13.00, Jun 15–Sep 15 Mon–Fri 09.00–18.00, Sat–Sun 10.00–18.00, Sep 16–Oct 31 Mon–Fri 09.00–17.00, Sat 09.00–14.00, Nov–Apr Mon–Fri 09.00–16.00.

WHERE TO STAY

🏠 **Aranyménes Panzió** (10 rooms) Arborétum út; ☎ 66 313046; e menes-szarvas@freemail.hu; www.hotels.hu/menes_szarvas. This thatched, peasant-style guesthouse successfully blends the traditional with the modern, & is a superb choice. The rooms are clean & well equipped, & the staff can arrange carriage rides or horse-riding lessons. It stands on the other side of Road 44 from Erzsébet liget, just beyond the road running off to the arboretum. *Rooms €30–40.*

🏠 **Aranyszarvas** Arborétum út 36; ☎ 66 216480; www.aranyszarvas-apartmanhaz.hu. Smart new self-contained apts further along the road leading to the arboretum. The complex has its own outdoor pool & direct access to the Körös riverside.

🏠 **Cséke Tanya** Szarvas-Ezüstszőlő, III. Ker 415; ☎ 66 313601 or 20 456 7801. This lovely peasant house is like a living museum – you can stay among original 19th-century furnishings that you'd usually expect to see bearing signs warning you not to touch. The

house has 2 rooms & can accommodate 4 or 5 people. The owners live near by; they can help with anything you require (including the preparation of dinner on an open fire in the garden if you wish). Located on the second small lane in the Ezüstszőlő district of Szarvas, a few miles from the centre along Road 44 towards Békéscsaba. If you're arriving in winter, give a few days' notice so the owners can get the house heated up. *2,500Ft pp.*

🏠 **Halászcsárda Panzió** I Ker 6; ☎ 66 311164; e halaszcsarda@szarvasnet.hu; www.szarvaslux.hu. Tight up against the bridge over the Holt-Körös, the setting is as romantic as they come. The rooms are on the small side, but comfortable. *Dbl 9,000Ft.*

🏠 **Liget Wellness & Conference Hotel** (39 rooms) Erzsébet liget; ☎ 66 311954; www.ligetszarvas.hu. A former campsite & pension has been transformed into family-friendly 4-star hotel perched on the river bank in the town's park. Its main building has

7

bright, good-sized rooms, Indonesian furnishings & a wellness centre with pools, saunas, steam room & aroma cabin on the ground floor. The separate Magnolia building offers 5 rooms of 3-star status for a slightly lower price. The surroundings are lovely, there's an outdoor pool (as well as the river) to swim in, & you can hire both bikes & boats. *Dbl 18,400–29,200Ft, apt (for 4) 46,800–52,300Ft, deluxe suite (for 2) 43,500Ft.*

⌂ **Lux Panzió** (11 rooms) Szabadság út 35; ☎ 66 313417; e lux@szarvas.hu. Located in the centre, this elegant pension has large rooms & is highly recommended. You'll wake to a good brekkie too. Fitness room, sauna & solarium. The owner also rents out summer cottages in the arboretum. *Sgl 9,500Ft, dbl 11,000–12,000Ft, apts from 14,000Ft.*

✖ WHERE TO EAT AND DRINK

✖ **Ciprus** Arborétum út 1/A; ☎ 66 311700. On the opposite side of the road from the Erzsébet liget, the Ciprus has an undulating roof that reaches to the ground, a tiered outdoor dining area overlooking the Bolza Mansion, & a Hungarian menu. *Mains avg 1,600Ft;* ⊕ *Sun–Thu 09.00–22.00, Fri–Sat 09.00–23.00.*

✖ **Club 44 Pizzeria** Szabadság út 40; ☎ 66 313183. Opposite the Lux Panzió, Club 44 is popular after dark. You can eat pizza on the pavement terrace or play a game of pool inside. ⊕ *Mon–Fri, Sun 08.00–24.00, Sat 08.00–02.00.*

🍺 **Kiszely Cukrászda** Kossuth tér 3; ☎ 66 311551. The pretty pink roundhouse next to the cultural centre serves cakes & ice-cream cones. ⊕ *09.00–21.00 daily.*

✖ **Halászcsárda Vendéglő** See page 377. The restaurant of the Halászcsárda Panzió is lit with lanterns, & is the best of Szarvas's places to eat. The specialities are platters of fish. *Mains avg 1,600Ft;* ⊕ *Mon–Thu, Sun 09.00–23.00, Fri–Sat 09.00–24.00.*

✖ **Panoráma Caffé & Pizzeria** Kossuth tér 3. Next to the Tourinform, the Panoráma is offers shade if you get hot under the collar. The pizzas are fine. *Pizzas 500–1,400Ft;* ⊕ *daily 09.00–22.00.*

ENTERTAINMENT AND NIGHTLIFE The **Vajda Péter Cultural Centre** (*Kossuth tér 3;* ☎ *66 311464;* ⊕ *Mon–Sat 08.00–17.00*) next to the Tourinform has concerts, plays and aerobic classes, and can offer information on arts events in town. In addition, there's a small cinema (Turul Mozi) inside.

There are several lively night spots in Szarvas. **Club Azték** (*Erzsébet liget/Szabadság út 12/C;* ☎ *06 20 9288098;* ⊕ *Fri–Sat 10.00–05.00*) hosts outdoor parties in Erzsébet liget in summer months on every Saturday and most Fridays; to get there, take the first left at the Halászcsárda and then the first right. In winter, the action moves to Szabadság út. **Club Marsall** (*Szabadság út 20;* ☎ *66 210218;* ⊕ *Wed 20.00–04.00, Sat 20.00–05.00*) is another winter disco venue.

The **Jazz Café** (*Kossuth u. 34;* ☎ *66 311652;* ⊕ *daily 10.00–02.00*) has a pleasant garden and mellow jazzy sounds, and is a better option than the very large Green House Irish Pub opposite.

WHAT TO SEE AND DO There are only a few sights of interest in town, and most will head for activities on or along the the **Körös River** (like canoeing, hiking, cycling or horse riding). During the summer season, you can take a cruise on the river aboard the *Katalin II*; Tourinform can provide details of current departure times and bookings.

The **Tessedik Sámuel Museum** (*Vajda Péter u. 1;* ☎ *66 216608;* e *museum@ szarvas.hu;* 🎟 *200/100Ft;* ⊕ *Tue–Sun Apr–Sep 10.00–18.00, Oct–Mar 10.00–15.00*) is housed in the former agricultural school, which was the first of its kind in eastern Europe. Today the museum has ethnographic and archaeological exhibits, together with a display about the 19th-century scientist and Lutheran priest who contributed so significantly to the town in ways agricultural and otherwise. There's a statue of Tessedik near by on Szabadság út, and a plaque to him outside the 18th-century Baroque **Old Lutheran Church** (*Vajda Péter u.*) – which he built – just north of the museum.

The Neoclassical **Bolza Mansion** (*Szabadság tér*) of 1780 stands on the bank of the Holt-Körös, and testifies to another family that put some plums in the town's pudding. The Bolzas came originally from Rome, and in front of the mansion is a statue of the babies Romulus and Remus being suckled by a wolf. You can't go inside, but you can walk in the grounds. There is a strand beyond the mansion where people swim and boat from the bank, while further up still is a historical park with a monument marking the geographical centre of historical Hungary (pre-Trianon; see page 20).

On the other side of the bridge from the mansion is **Erzsébet liget**, a charming little wood with walking trails and the Szarvas Watersport Camp (*Erzsébet u. 4;* ✆ *66 216369*), where you can hire kayaks and play tennis. In the southeastern section is the **Ruzicskay-ház** (*Erzsébet liget;* ✆ *66 312042;* ₰ *200/100Ft;* ☉ *Tue–Sun 10.00–16.00*), containing the private collection of Szarvas-born painter György Ruzicskay in his former residence, and including folk items gathered during his life.

In a crook of the river to the south is Anna liget, where you'll find the **Körös-Maros National Park Visitor Centre** (*Anna liget 1;* ✆ *66 313855;* e *kmnp@kmnp.hu; www.kmnp.hu;* ₰ *250/150Ft;* ☉ *May 10–Jun 15 Tue–Sat 09.00–17.00, Jun 16–Oct 31 Tue–Sun 09.00–17.00*). The centre is one of two in the national park (the other at Réhely; see box, page 372); it charts the history of the landscape between the Körös and Maros rivers, shows finds (including a skeleton dating back 6,000 years) and stuffed animals, and has a room detailing moves to prevent the smuggling of endangered species. There is a butterfly house too. A nature trail winds for 2km, with information boards in English and Hungarian; the walk takes two–three hours (depending how quickly you walk – and read). You can also organise tour guides here for visiting protected areas of the park (see box, page 372).

Anna liget was originally the site chosen by József Bolza to plant some botanical rarities at the end of the 18th century. This seed was nurtured by subsequent generations of the family and now blooms as one of the country's premier arboretums 2km to the north (where it was moved by Pál Boza). The **Szarvas Arborétum** (✆ *66 312344;* e *kert@szarvas.arbor.hu;* ₰ *400/300Ft;* ☉ *daily Mar 15–Nov 15 08.00–18.00, Nov 16–Mar 14 08.00–15.00, closed Dec 15–Jan 5*) covers 82ha and has 1,600 species of plant from all over the globe, among them swamp cypresses and a mammoth pine; to get there, pick up Arborétum út from opposite the entrance to Erzsébet liget.

Back on the other side of the river, the Gothic **New Lutheran Church** (*Szabadság út 70*) – with its slim, 67m tower – was constructed in 1896 as the congregation outgrew the Old Church; it catered for the Hungarian-speaking minority who requested that some services be held in their tongue. The interior is surprisingly rich for a Protestant church. A short distance northeast of Kossuth tér, the thatched **Slovak Folk House** (*Szlovák Tájház; Hoffmann u. 1;* ✆ *66 312492;* ₰ *120/60Ft;* ☉ *Apr–Oct Tue–Sun 13.00–17.00*) represents a typical 19th-century dwelling belonging to Slovak descendants of the immigrants who repopulated the town from 1722. At the end of Hoffmann utca, there's an intact **horse-driven dry mill** (*Szárazmalom; Ady Endre u. 1;* ✆ *66 313850;* ₰ *300/175Ft;* ☉ *Apr–Oct Tue–Sun 13.00–17.00*) that worked from the early 19th century up until the 1960s.

Szarvas sits on natural thermal water that has been used by locals since the Turkish occupation; the first permanent public baths were built in 1884. The current **Szarvasi Gyógyfürdő** (*Kossuth u. 23;* ₰ *870/550Ft;* ☉ *Tue–Fri 08.00–20.00, Sat–Sun 10.00–20.00*) were originally constructed in 1902 (and fully refurbished in 2004), and include hot tubs, steamrooms and a swimming pool.

Four kilometres from the border with Romania, Gyula is a compact settlement with a spa and the Great Plain's only surviving medieval brick fort. Sources disagree on whether the town was named after a Magyar chieftain of the conquest, a grandson of a chieftain, or the title by which the chieftains were known, but what is beyond doubt is that Gyula and its castle represented a regional stronghold – until the mid 20th century this was the county capital – and that the Turks were in possession of it from 1566 up until 1694. Like Békéscsaba, in the aftermath of the War of Independence the town fell under the ownership of Harruckern (see page 372), and was repopulated with Hungarian, Romanians and Germans – indeed, between 1734 and 1857 the town was divided into Hungarian Gyula (Magyargyula) and German Gula (Németgyula) – but unlike Békéscsaba its economic development was gradual, and the citizens retain something of a chip on their shoulders about the shift in power and county status.

GETTING THERE AND AROUND The **bus station** is in the centre of town on Vásárhelyi Pál utca and the only frequent service is to Békéscsaba. There are less-regular buses to other destinations including Szeged (eight), Debrecen (five), Kecskemét (four), Budapest Népliget (two), Miskolc, Szolnok and Siofók (one). Gyula **railway station** is on an offshoot of the line from Békéscsaba and there are 11 trains a day running between the two towns. There are also trains to Budapest Keleti and Kecskemét (two), Szolnok and Eger (one). Up to three trains a day cross the Romanian border to Salonta. The station is at the northern end of Béké sugárút.

INFORMATION AND OTHER PRACTICALITIES

Gyula Tourist Eszperantó tér 1; ↘ 66 463026. Can organise private rooms & local tours. ⊕ Mon–Fri 08.00–17.00, Sat 09.00–12.00.
Listings magazine Békési Est

Tourinform Kossuth Lajos u. 7; ↘ 66 561680; e gyula@tourinform.hu; www.gyula.hu. ⊕ Jun 15–Sep 15 Mon–Fri 09.00–20.00, Sat–Sun 09.00–18.00, rest of yr Mon–Fri 09.00–17.00.

WHERE TO STAY

Corvin Hotel (26 rooms) Jókai u. 9–11; ↘ 66 362044; e corvinhotel@t-online.hu. One of the friendliest hotels in town – in a town where friendly hotels are unusually well represented – has bright, modern rooms, a good restaurant (see page 382) & its own jazz garden. It's worth the slightly higher price. Sgl 12,900Ft, dbl 15,900Ft.
Csigaház Panzió (11 rooms) Csiga u. 12; ↘ 66 362417. You won't be blown away by the rooms – which are sufficient rather than special – but this is a very welcoming family-run guesthouse a short 50m from the baths. Bag one of the rooms with a balcony. Room 4,000Ft/pp.
Elizabeth Hotel (49 rooms) Vár u. 1; ↘ 66 560240; www.elizabeth-hotel.hu. The city's new 4-star property is located next door to the castle in a fully refurbished classicist building; it offers comfortable rooms & a small wellness centre with pool, steamroom & sauna (although it's in any case only a few mins from the Várkert Baths. Have a drink on the hotel's sun terrace overlooking the

castle. Sgl 16,400–18,300Ft, dbl 24,500–36,100Ft, suite 49,100–54,100Ft.
Family Appartements (4 apts) Kossuth Lajos u. 13; ↘ 66 463725. Housed in the same building as the theatre box office, these exclusive apartments – with bathrooms & shared kitchens – are well recommended. To book one, ask at the ice-cream booth outside. Sgl 6,000Ft, dbl 10,000Ft, trpl 12,000Ft, quad 15,000Ft, room for 5 19,000Ft.
Gyula Panzió (13 rooms) Megyeház u. 10; ↘ 66 464644; www.gyulapanzio.hu. Very nice, family-friendly pension in the heart of the city with bright airy rooms & apartments equipped with kitchenettes. Near the Tourinform & Maestro Restaurant. Sgl 7,500Ft, dbl 10,000Ft, apt (for 4) 20,000Ft.
Hotel Park (56 rooms) Part u. 15; ↘ 66 463711; e parkgyula@civishotels.hu; www.civishotels.hu. Standing across the Élővíz Canal from the Castle Bath, the Hotel Park's rooms are nicely kitted out, if a little on the cramped side.

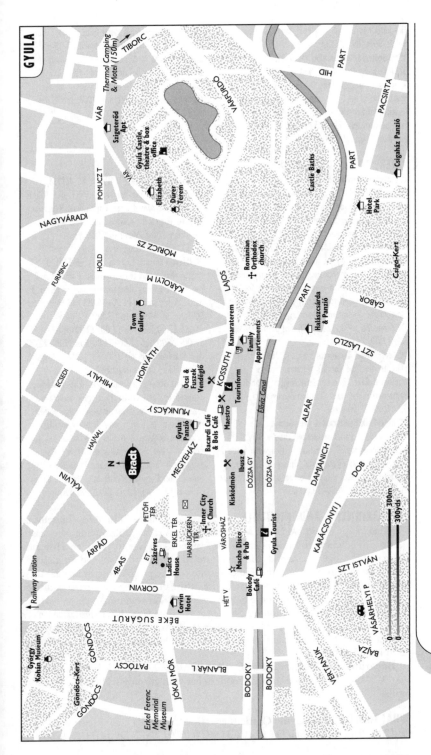

The hotel has a swimming pool, sauna & solarium. *Sgl 9,500Ft, dbl 12,900Ft.*

⌂ **Szigeterőd Apartmanház** Vár u. 29; ☏ 70 457 5781 (ask for Éva or her husband); www.apartman-sziget.com. One of several great apartments around the castle. New, clean, great location, kitchenette & a big terrace. If they are fully booked, they will recommend a suitable alternative. *Apt 5,000–12,000Ft.*

⌂ **Thermal Camping & Motel** Szélső u. 16; ☏ 66 463551; e thermalcamping@bhn.hu. A 15-min walk from the baths – & consequently less rowdy than 2 other campsites located closer – there's a 27-room motel as well as oodles of space for tents. *Camping: ⌂ 800/600Ft, tent 800Ft; mo ☏ dbl 10,500Ft; ⊕ all yr.*

✗ WHERE TO EAT AND DRINK

▭ **Bodoky Kávémühely Café** Városház u. 1; ☏ 20 961 8584. This cosy place at the end of the pedestrian street (on the bridge above Élővíz Canal) is perfect for a terrace coffee. ⊕ *Mon–Fri 07.00–20.00 Sat–Sun 07.00–22.00.*

♀ **Bols** Kossuth Lajos u. 18; ☏ 30 9787407. If ours were anything to go by, this coffee-and-cocktail bar serves the worst cappuccinos in the country. Stick to the cocktails. There's a menu of snack-type food (grills, salads, spaghettis, pizzas) in large portions. Close to the Tourinform. *Mains avg 900Ft;* ⊕ *Mon–Thu 09.00–24.00, Fri–Sat 09.00–02.00, Sun 11.00–24.00.*

✗ **Corvin Hotel Restaurant** See page 380. A great place to dine, the Corvin's restaurant offers traditional Békés & continental choices, & holds barbecues in the warm months. *Mains avg 1,950Ft;* ⊕ *10.00–23.00 daily.*

✗ **Hotel Park Restaurant & Beer Garden** See page 380. The Hotel Park's restaurant offers a very pleasant backdrop, & specialises in Hungarian kettle dishes as well as international cuisine. In summer, the food is cooked outside over an open fire. *Mains avg 1,700Ft;* ⊕ *08.00–23.00 daily.*

✗ **Kisködmön** Városház u. 15; ☏ 66 463934. Standing next to the Romantic former town hall, the Kisködmön is named after a traditional Hungarian costume & aims to provide some traditional Hungarian eating. *Mains avg 1,500Ft;* ⊕ *12.00–24.00 daily.*

✗ **Maestro** Kossuth Lajos u. 3; ☏ 66 560120. Maestro has a well-tended garden, a small bar & two menus offering Hungarian cuisine or pizzas & pastas. A set lunch (11.00–15.00) can be had for 500Ft or so. *Mains avg 1,300Ft;* ⊕ *Mon 11.00–22.00, Tue–Thu 11.00–23.00, Fri 11.00–24.00, Sat 12.00–24.00, Sun 12.00–22.00.*

▭ **Százéves** Erkel tér 1; ☏ 66 362045. Hungary's second-oldest patisserie (after Ruszwurm in Budapest), Százéves opened in 1840 in a building designed by Antal Czigler. Its elegant Biedermeier interior, with white carrara-marble tables, presents a ready excuse to scoff a cake. It offers top-class handmade bonbons & truffles – &, never fret, you can buy a box to take away too. There's a sister patisserie – Kézmőves Cukrászda – on the pedestrianised street (as well as a third in Budapest on Veres Pálné u.). ⊕ *10.00–22.00 daily.*

ENTERTAINMENT AND NIGHTLIFE The **Gyula Castle Theatre** (*Várszínház; Várfürdő utca;* ☏ *66 463148; www.gyulaivarszinhaz.hu*), occupying the castle courtyard, is where the town's main arts events take place in summer. Historical drama, opera, ballet, jazz and folk dance are all performed here, and on a second stage jutting into the lake. Check the website for the programme timetable; there is a summer ticket office in the gatehouse at the entrance to the park (although tickets are also available from the box office at the Kamaraterem).

The **Kamaraterem** (*Kossuth Lajos u. 13;* ☏ *66 463148; ticket office* ⊕ *Mon–Fri 09.00–16.00*) is a 200-seat playhouse where the Castle Theatre company performs during winter (although there is talk of adapting the castle courtyard so it can be used in all seasons).

Bacardi Café (*Kossuth Lajos u. 3;* ⊕ *Mon–Thu 09.00–22.00, Fri 09.00–24.00, Sat 10.00–24.00, Sun 11.00–22.00*) is a modern bar with chrome seating and terracotta walls.

WHAT TO SEE AND DO **Gyula Castle** (*Várfürdő utca; 66 460417; www.corvinmuzeum.hu;* ⌂ *1200/500Ft;* ⊕ *Tue–Sun Jun 15–Aug 31 09.00–19.00, Sep 1–Jun 14 09.00–17.00*) was built in 1445. Alterations were made in subsequent years, and by the 16th century its walls were 3m deep. They repelled Dózsa's rebellious peasants in 1514, but were finally overrun by the Turks in 1566 (and held by them for 129 years). You can walk around the rectangular walls and climb its tower (*várkilátó*); the view is somewhat marred by the hulking presence of a nearby hotel. In the past there was an exhibition of cannon balls and other artefacts in the former chapel, and this might be resurrected at some point. The castle courtyard hosts theatre performances (see page 384), and the 16th-century round tower – added by János Corvin (the son of King Mátyás), and once holding gunpowder – has a café and bar. Beyond the walls is a **lake** surrounded by weeping willows trees, and you can hire little boats (or pedal cars from outside the Hotel Erkel). Near by too is the 18th-century **Almásy Mansion**, rebuilt in 1803 after a fire; it was here that 1,300 Hungarian officers surrendered to the Russian tsarist army on August 23 1849, among them nine of the Martyrs of Arad.

Lying to the south of the park are the **Castle Baths** (*Várfürdő; Várkert u. 2;* ✆ *66 561350; www.varfurdo.hu;* 💰 *1,450/1,200Ft, night baths 1,500Ft;* 🕐 *daily indoor pools 08.00–20.00, outdoor pools May–Sep 08.00–20.00, Fri–Sat also 20.00–24.00*), which rank high among the country's spas. The water is medicinal, and the high mineral count gives it a brownish hue. The huge complex includes a new medical centre, open and covered pools (some of them curative and others recreational), saunas, wave machines, water slides, a children's playground and more. Snatch a moment's peace at the **Romanian Orthodox church** (*Gróza tér*), a slightly fusty-smelling church built in 1825, and with a floor-to-ceiling iconostasis depicting the 12 disciples and scenes from Christ's life.

Dürer Terem (*Kossuth Lajos u. 17;* 💰 *500/250Ft;* 🕐 *Tue 13.00–17.00, Wed–Sat 09.00–17.00, Sun 09.00–13.00*) – named after Albrecht Dürer, the German Renaissance artist whose father originally heralded from Gyula – has temporary exhibitions. The nearby **Town Gallery** (*Városi Képtár; Károlyi Mihály u. 13;* 💰 *300/150Ft;* 🕐 *Wed–Sun 9.00–13.00*) contains the private art collection of Dr Lajos Bene, featuring 19th- and 20th-century works, while to the west the **György Kohán Museum** (*Béke sugárút 35;* ✆ *66 361795;* 💰 *500/250Ft;* 🕐 *Tue 13.00–17.00, Wed–Sat 09.00–17.00, Sun 09.00–13.00*) displays the distinctive art of the Cubist painter. Kohán was born in the town and bequeathed his paintings to the museum; they blend symbolic perception with the influences of folk art.

The **Inner City Church** (*Belvárosi templom; Harruckern tér*) was built in the 1770s, but its most spectacular feature is more modern. The ceiling frescoes show poignant historical moments – among them periods of famine in Africa and man's successful launch into space. A mother and child release doves, indicative of the artist's plea for peace and unity. Northwest of it is the **Ladics House** (*Jókai u. 4;* ✆ *66 463940;* 💰 *500/250Ft;* 🕐 *Tue 13.00–17.00, Wed–Sat 09.00–17.00, Sun 09.00–13.00*), which – like the adjacent Százéves Cukrászda (see page 382) – was designed by Antal Cziegler. The house has been preserved to showcase the inside of a typical 19th-century town house owned by a wealthy family. There's a library, Venetian mirrors and Chinese porcelain; it must have been a pig of a place to dust.

If you follow Jókai utca westward, you'll come to Apor Vilmos tér, with its late-Baroque **Roman Catholic church** of the 1860s. Next to it is the **Erkel Ferenc Memorial Museum** (*Apor Vilmos tér 7;* ✆ *66 463552;* 💰 *500/250Ft;* 🕐 *Tue 13.00–17.00, Wed–Sat 09.00–17.00, Sun 09.00–13.00*), where the 19th-century 'father of Hungarian opera' and composer of the music to the national anthem was born. Among the objects relating to his life are a gold wreath that was presented to him and model stage sets of some of his operas. It is said that he wrote some of his pieces from beneath a maple tree in the castle park. The **Virgin Mary Collection** (*Apor tér 11;* ✆ *66 362169;* 💰 *300/150Ft;* 🕐 *Tue–Sun Mar–Nov 09.00–15.00, Dec–Feb 09.00–12.00*) displays devotional objects and souvenirs.

FESTIVAL AND EVENTS The Festival of Arts at the Castle Theatre runs from late June until early August, and includes days of folk dance and folk music, and performances of ballet, operetta, jazz and drama. In addition, other main events include the Renaissance Carnival (*end of Feb*), the Pálinka Festival (*Apr*), the Flower Festival (*May*), Castle Evenings (*Jul*), Castle Garden Festivities (*end of Aug*) and Advent in the Castle (*Dec*).

8

Southern
Transdanubia

Transdanubia (Dunántúl) covers the whole of Hungary's left-hand side, filling the area between the Danube and the borders with Croatia, Slovenia and Austria to the west and south of it, abutting the Danube at the Slovakian border to the north, and diagonally slashed across the middle by Lake Balaton. The region's landscape picks and chooses a little of everything, featuring hills, plains, brooks and lakes. It is economically richer than the eastern half, its industry drawing on supplies of minerals and fossil fuels; the workers can also enjoy a good spot of plonk, with the wines of Villány and Szekszárd among the best. With money comes architectural flourish, and there are beautifully kept centres. Western Transdanubia remained part of Royal Hungary during the Ottoman occupation and it both benefited from Habsburg building and preserved the monuments of earlier centuries that were ravaged by the Turks elsewhere. The Danube represented the eastern extent of the Roman empire in the first centuries of the first millennium, and Transdanubia – then the province of Pannonia – is where the residue of their stay lies in the pockets of Pécs, Szombathely, Sopron, Győr and Szekszárd. As you explore the region you'll also see regular evidence of much later struggles to consolidate territory, with fortified castles dotting the region's peaks.

* * *

Southern Transdanubia falls below Lake Balaton, running down to the Croatian border. The star of the show is Pécs, a cultured, pretty and welcoming city that offers a host of museums, some significant Ottomon and early-Christian architecture, and several vibrant festivals. There are hills to the north and south of it, the Mecsek the place for hiking and the Villány Hills for wine tasting, the district noted for its Cabernet-Sauvignon, Merlot and Kékoportó (Portugizier). The region also signals historical moments of tragedy and courage. Mohács is associated with one of the lowest points in Hungary's history, when the Turks massacred the Magyar forces in 1526 and effectively broke the country's back; by contrast, Szigetvár represents the ultimate display of bravery under fire, if still in a losing cause. For naturalists, the Duna-Dráva National Park plays host to the Gemenc Forest, an area of woodland and marshy lakes that is one of the country's richest nature reserves.

SZEKSZÁRD

Around 50km northeast of Pécs, Szekszárd lies among hills above the River Sió. A Roman settlement called Alisca once stood here, on the Aquincum military route, and Béla I established a Benedictine monastery in 1061. The town thrived during the 15th century, although its castle was demolished by King Mátyás when he learnt of the landowner's involvement in a conspiracy against him. After the

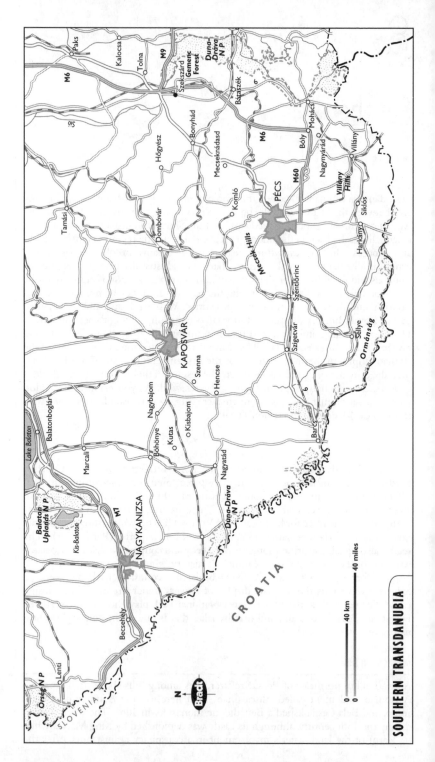

SOUTHERN TRANSDANUBIA

Turks had ravaged the place, it was repopulated with Germans, one legacy of which is the German-language theatre (the only one of its kind beyond Budapest). It was made the seat of Tolna County during the 18th century, but the important architecture dates from the 19th century after a fire blazed through in 1794. Today it is renowned as the birthplace of the poet Mihály Babits and as a centre for some excellent red wine, notably Szekszárdi Kadarka and Bull's Blood. It is also close to the Gemenc Forest, numbered among the country's prime nature and game reserves.

GETTING THERE, AWAY AND AROUND Regular **bus** services run to Pécs, Dombóvár and Baja, and there are up to 19 buses a day that make the three-hour journey to Budapest Népliget. There are direct routes to Szeged (three daily), Kecskemét (three), Győr (two), Veszprém (four), Mohács (seven) and Keszthely (one). To reach Villány, Siklós or Harkány you will need to change at Pécs, while access to destinations in the Southern Great Plain including Szolnok and Debrecen require a change at Szeged or Kecskemét. There are six direct **trains** a day to Budapest Déli, and a further three to Budapest Keleti. Seven direct trains a day go to Baja.

The bus and train stations (*Pollack Mihály u.*) are both located to the east of the town centre, which can be reached on foot in 15 minutes. Turn left from the train station (right from the bus station) and head westwards along Bajcsy-Zsilinsky utca. Turn left again into Mészáros Lázár utca and right into Mártírok tere which leads into the centre. **Taxis** usually gather outside Amaretto Cukrászda; one company is Rádió (❂ 74 555555).

INFORMATION AND OTHER PRACTICALITIES

🖳 **Csetlak** Garay tér 12; ❂ 30 9467309. Internet access (1st hour free). ⊕ *Mon–Sat 14.00–18.00.*

🔲 **Ibusz** Szent István tér 3; ❂ 74 319822. Can arrange private accommodation, local tours & currency exchange (there is also a Western Union office inside). ⊕ *Mon–Fri 08.00–17.00.*

🔲 **Listings magazine** Szekszárdi Est
Tolna Tours Tinódi u. 8; ❂ 74418365;
🔲w.toltours.hu. Specialises in regional excursions, including wine tours. ⊕ *Mon–Thu 09.00–16.30, Fri 08.00–16.00, Sat 08.30–12.00.*

🔳 **Tourinform** Béla Király tér 7; ❂ 74 315198; e szekszard@tourinform.hu. The helpful staff can provide timetables for the trains (inc the narrow-gauge railway at the nearby Gemenc Forest) & buses, as well as assist with lists of college & private accommodation & wine houses. ⊕ *Jun 15–Aug 31 09.00–17.00 daily, Sep 1–Oct 15 & May 1–Jun 14 Mon–Sat 09.00–17.00, Sun 10.00–16.00, Oct 15–Apr 30 Mon–Fri 09.00–17.00, Sat 09.00–14.00.*

WHERE TO STAY

🏠 **Hotel Gemenc** (92 rooms) Mészáros Lázár u. 1; ❂ 74 311722; www.hotels.hu/gemenc_hotel. This ugly '70s block next to the synagogue is better inside than out. Among the facilities are a bar & nightclub, & all rooms have balconies (although not all have TV & minibar). *Sgl 8,500Ft, dbl 11,500Ft.*

🏠 **Gróf Apponyi** (30 in country house, 30 in modern block) Ady Endre u. 2, Hőgyész; ❂ 74 588800; www.apponyi.hu. Standing 30km from Szekszárd on route 65 towards Siófok, this 18th-century building stands in a mature park. While the family that lived here doesn't leap out of the history books, there is a collection of Herend china named after it. While there's no grand lobby or

drawing room (& it's slightly 'institutional' in feel), the building is pretty, the swimming pool is huge, there are 2 thermal pools, & a comprehensive wellness area. Standard rooms are in the modern block. The restaurant (*mains avg 2,500Ft;* ⊕ *07.00–22.00)* looks better than its food tastes. *Standard sgl 15,000Ft, dbl 20,000Ft, main house sgl 22,425Ft, dbl 30,000Ft.*

🏠 **Hotel Zodiaco** (21 rooms) Szent László u. 19; ❂ 74 511150. Each room is allocated a sign of the zodiac, & each is clean, modern, tastefully decorated & furnished with complimentary chocolate bars. Through sweet teeth, we recommend this hotel highly. *Sgl 9,700Ft, dbl 13,100Ft, trpl 16,500Ft.*

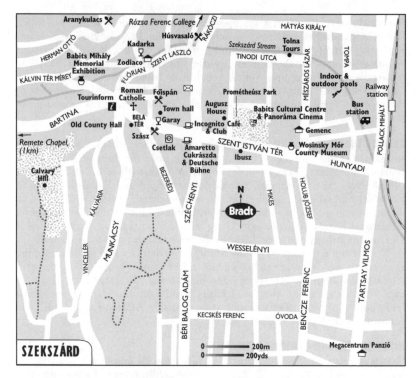

SZEKSZÁRD

0 ‖‖‖‖‖‖ 200m
0 ‖‖‖‖‖‖ 200yds

Megacentrum Panzió

⌂ **Megacentrum Panzió** Tartsay u. 8; ☎ 74 511060. Housed above a motorcycle showroom 1km southeast of the centre, this guesthouse has spacious rooms cheaply priced. It also owns an adjacent pizzeria. *Sgl 6,000Ft, dbl 8,000Ft, trpl 9,600Ft, quad 10,800Ft.*

⌂ **Rózsa Ferenc College** Kadarka u. 29; ☎ 74 315833; e rozsa@webmail.hu. One of several dorm-room options available in summer. Tourinform can provide a full list; this college is to the north of the centre. *Dorm beds €4–5/pp.*

⌂ **Villa Weber** (11 rooms, 3 apts) Bonyhád, István major; ☎ 74 550244; www.villaweber.eu. For a deluxe touch, travel 16km south of Szekszárd. This immaculate complex is based in a country house typical of the 19th-century lesser nobility; its converted outbuildings contain swimming pool, jacuzzi, tennis courts, horses & bikes. The restaurant (*mains avg 2,200Ft;* ⊕ *07.00–23.00*) serves cuisine using organic ingredients. *Sgl 19,200Ft, dbl 20,800Ft*

✗ WHERE TO EAT AND DRINK

⌑ **Amaretto Cukrászda** Garay tér 6. 'Show me the way to Amaretto', the locals cry when in need of cake, ice cream & coffee. ⊕ *09.00–20.00 daily.*

✗ **Aranykulacs** Nefelejcs köz 3; ☎ 74 413369; www.aranykulacs.hu. A small, family-run restaurant offering rustic food in rustic surroundings but still close to the town centre. *Mains avg 1,900Ft;* ⊕ *12.00–24.00 daily.*

✗ **Főispán** Béla tér 1; ☎ 74 312139; www.foispanetterem.hu. A smart & atmospheric restaurant in a 17th-century cellar. Hungarian dishes prevail, including delicious goose liver in local red wine & platters of poultry & fish. There are a few cases holding wine memorabilia at the back,

although they stretch the definition in calling it a 'wine museum'. *Mains avg 1,650Ft;* ⊕ *Mon–Sat 11.30–24.00, Sun 11.30–22.00.*

✗ **Húsvasaló** Rákóczi u. 10; ☎ 06 30 225 7119. This intimate cellar restaurant & bar has a courtyard area. Good Hungarian food. *Mains avg 1,900Ft; restaurant* ⊕ *Mon–Sat 12.00–23.00; pub Sun–Thu 18.00–02.00, Fri–Sat 18.00–04.00.*

♀ **Kadarka** Fürdooház u. 1; ☎ 20 4407445. This wine bar has an extensive selection of Szekszárd wines – & the pleasant staff know their wines too. Cheese & cold meat platters are also available. ⊕ *Mon–Fri 13.00–23.00, Sat 13.00–24.00*

✂ **Szász** Garay tér 18; ☎ 74 312463. Medieval-theme restaurant & bar with typically meat-heavy choices, including venison meatballs & the biggest pork chops we've ever seen. A set lunch menu is available. There's also a new adjacent café. *Mains 1,100–2,700Ft, avg 1,500Ft;* ⏲ *Mon–Sat 10.00–24.00, Sun 10.00–16.00.*

ENTERTAINMENT AND NIGHTLIFE The **Deutsche Bühne** (*Garay tér 4;* ☎ *74 510257*) is the country's only German-language theatre outside the capital. The **Babits Cultural Centre** (*Szent István tér 10;* ☎ *74 311119; www.babitsmuvhaz.hu;* ⏲ *Mon–Fri 08.00–18.00*) can get you up to speed on current performances and exhibitions in the former synagogue and elsewhere in town, while the Youth House at the back can help with cultural events for the 'younger' crowd. The **Panoráma Cinema** occupies the same building.

Incognito Café and Club (*Garay tér 7;* ☎ *74 511010;* ⏲ *Fri–Sat 21.00–05.00*) is a dark cellar bar awash with photos of old films stars; there's funky house and dance music into the wee hours. You can also have a drink at Szász and Húsvasaló (see above). The best of the region's wine cellars are the **Vesztergombi Cellar** (☎ *74 511846*) and **Takler Cellar** (☎ *74 725004*); visits and tastings available with prior arrangement. **Garay Cellar** (*Garay tér 19;* ☎ *74 412828;* ⏲ *Mon–Fri 10.00–16.00, Sat 09–12.00*) is a wine shop where, as well as bottles, you can buy a glass of wine to enjoy on the spot.

WHAT TO SEE AND DO The heart of Szekszárd is sliced vertically by the main Széchenyi utca and horizontally by Szent István tér (which runs west into Garay tér and Béla tér). Béla tér holds a **Trinity Column**, with cherub faces hanging from it like baubles on a Christmas tree; the monument was erected in 1763 in memory of the plague that swept through in 1738–40. The early 19th-century Louis-XVI-style **Roman Catholic church** at the northern side is the largest single-nave church in central Europe, and has some fabulous interior columns painted in pink, purple and mint green.

The Neoclassical **Old County Hall** (*Vármegyeháza; Béla tér 1;* ☎ *74 316222;* *500/300Ft;* ⏲ *Apr 1–Sep 30 Tue–Sun 09.00–17.00, Oct 1–Mar 31 Tue–Sat 09.00–15.00*) was built between 1823 and 1833 by Mihály Polláck on the site of Béla I's Benedictine abbey, the ruins of which are in its central courtyard. There are several exhibitions in the building. The richly preserved suites of the 19th-century lord lieutenant who occupied them include the empire-style armchair in which he was inaugurated. In the **Liszt Ferenc Memorial Room** you'll see a cast of the great man's hand, together with the piano he played (and signed) when

MIHÁLY BABITS

The poet Mihály Babits (1883–1941) was among the élite of 20th-century literati, influential not only in his avant-garde verse but through the journal Nyugat (West), which he edited from 1919 until his death. He used this to open Hungary to trends in Western art and offer an outlet for new talent; he (together with his contemporaries Endre Ady and Dezső Kosztolányi) can be said to have guided the development of Hungarian literary modernism. As well as poetry, Babits was a master of translation. Among the classics that he tackled were Shakespeare's Tempest and the entire body of Dante's *Divine Comedy*. His poetry was deep, inward-looking and characterised by elaborate artifice – indeed, literary historians have labelled him 'the Hungarian T S Eliot'. During his final years he suffered from throat cancer, dying in 1941 shortly after completing his masterpiece *The Book of Jonah* (*Jónás Könyve*), a creative warning against the evil of fascism. He did not live to see just how evil it could be.

visiting the house of landowner Antal Augusz (see below). Across the hall is the **Mattioni Eszter Room**, devoted to the 20th-century Szekszárd-born artist who took traditional peasant life and festivals for her subjects, and committed them to vivid paintings and mosaics.

During festivals, actual wine flows from the playful **Wine Well** (*Borkút*) in the garden to the County Hall's left. Liszt attended the official opening of the **town hall** opposite, with its unfortunate tangerine colouring. Next to that is the **Abbot's Residence**, constructed in 1765 and the earliest of the town's buildings. The nearby **Babits Mihály Memorial Exhibition** (*Babits Mihály u. 13;* ↘ *74 312154;* ✆ *500/300Ft; www.wmmm.hu*) occupies the house in which the poet was born. While he lived here only up to the age of six, he would return to visit as a student and stayed in the third of the rooms. There you'll see a chest of drawers that served as his writing table and the armchair in which he liked to sit and ponder. Pál Farkas's bronze statue in the garden shows him doing just that.

Moving east, Garay tér bears a statue of its namesake, the poet János Garay (1812–53), who conjured the Falstaffian character of Háry János on whom Zoltán Kodály based his opera. Garay was also effusive in his written praise for Szekszárd wine. Nip up Széchenyi utca to see the **Augusz House** (*Széchenyi u. 36–40*), rather a crude piece of pink turretted architecture built for Baron Antal Augusz. Liszt was a visitor here on four occasions, and Augusz apparently had considerable influence in securing for him the commission to write the *Coronation Mass* of 1867 (see page 168). Appropriately, the building now holds a music school.

The **Wosinsky Mór County Museum** (*Szent István tér 26;* ↘ *74 316222;* ✆ *500/300Ft;* ☉ *Apr 1–Sep 30 Tue–Sun 10.00–18.00, rest of yr Tue–Sat 10.00–16.00*) has an extensive and excellent collection – the only shame is that there are no explanations in English. The museum was founded by the priest and amateur archaeologist Mór Wosinsky, who made a Europe-wide name for himself on excavating the Neolithic site of Töröksánc near Lengyel. One exhibition digs deep into time's mists, showcasing skeletons and grave goods from as far back as 20000BC, and moving forward through carved animals from 5000BC up to ornate jewellery and weapons from 2400BC. Another room has stone remains from Roman Christian temples unearthed in the region, and elsewhere there are finds relating to the various nomadic groups that passed through the Carpathian Basin during the first millennium ad. The display of local town history upstairs includes reconstructions of 19th-century shops and houses, and a healthy gathering of German, Serbian and Sárköz ethnographic items.

Set back from the road behind the museum is the **Arts House** (*Művészetek Háza; Szent István tér 28;* ↘ *74 511247;* ✆ *entry 200Ft;* ☉ *Tue–Sun 10.00–18.00*), a Moorish former synagogue in sand- and rust-coloured brick that served the Jewish community from 1897 until World War II. It was later converted into an arts centre; as well as temporary exhibitions, concerts are held here (some on the synagogue's organ). A gnarled *Tree of Life* stands near by, cast in bronze and dedicated to the war victims. Some of Imre Varga's sheet-metal creations can be seen beside the cultural centre to the west, in the grassed **Prométheúsz Park**; Zeus's eagle swoops to strip at the flesh of the unfortunate Prometheus, who had stolen fire and given it to the mortals, thereby unleashing their appetite for culture and art.

Climb **Calvary Hill** (*Kalvaria-hegy*), a short distance to the west of the centre, for views of the town below, the Great Plain beyond, and the vineyards on the surrounding slopes. There's a massive shining sculpture of a vine on top, as well as the crucifixes bearing Christ and the robbers – erected in 1832 by parents mourning the loss of a child – after which the hill is named. Around a kilometre further out is the flaking **Remete (or 'Hermit') Chapel** (*Kápolna tér 10*), a diminutive Baroque church built 1775–78 and a site of pilgrimage. Crowded by trees in a steep field, and reached via a long set of shallow steps, the church seems made for a scene from an Austen novel – perfect equally for a charming midsummer wedding or a moment of foul intrigue on a moonless night. To get there, follow Bartina utca out from Béla tér.

Other There are **indoor and outdoor pools** (*Toldi u. 6/B;* \ *74 412035; ☎ 600/450Ft; ⊕ Mon 1.00–20.30, Tue–Sun 06.00–20.30*) a short distance from the railway and bus stations, beside the Szekszárd Stream. In addition to the wine houses and cellars of the town, Tourinform can provide a map of the **Szekszárd Wine Route** – which includes the 340 cellars at Sióagárd-Leányvár (the 'cellar village') 6km to the northwest. Alternatively, you could head for the **Szent Gaál Winery** (*Zomba-Szentgál-szőlőhegy, 7173 Szentgál-szőlőhegy 83;* \ *74 431256; www.szentgaal.hu*), 12km northwest of Szekszárd. The winery has accommodation in a restored 19th-century mansion (*7 rooms; sauna, swimming pool; dbl 19,800Ft*) set in parkland, and offers wine and cheese tastings (wine tastings 300–600Ft/glass), as well as other programmes. From Road 6, turn off onto Road 65 (towards Siófok) and follow it until you turn left at a sign to Szentgál-szőlőhegy; passing through the village, you'll take a sharp right for the road to the winery.

This area is famous for its **embroidery**, and a few enthusiastic locals make heroic efforts to keep it alive. A remarkable collection of local village embroidery can be found in **Sióagárd-Leányvár** (follow the sign to Margit Pince before the bridge over the Sió). The area south of Szekszárd was isolated by frequent floods in the past and thus preserved its peasant culture well into the 20th century. A collection of costumed dolls celebrating local life and traditional occupations is displayed by their creator at **Decs** (*to the southeast of Szekszárd; Kossuth u. 8;* \ *74 495734, turn right at the war memorial and first left*). Further down the same street is a preserved village house (Tájház; ⊕ *Apr–Oct Mon 13.00–15.00, Fri 10.00–13.00*).

FESTIVALS AND EVENTS The biggest folk festival in the area is the annual **Szekszárd Vintage Festival** on the last weekend in September, which attracts around 50,000 people.

THE GEMENC FOREST

Starting 12km to the east of Szekszárd and following the Danube south for 30km, the Gemenc Forest is the country's largest flood plain. The Danube used to be particularly wriggly at this point and subjected the Sárköz – the 'Muddy Area' home to five villages south of Szekszárd (Őcsény the first of them and Báta the last) – to regular flooding. Mid-19th-century river regulation cut off many of the curves (on a detailed map you'll see that the area is littered with crescent-shaped river-channel fragments), and put a stop to the worst of the deluge. Nevertheless, features of the primal, pre-regulation habitat remained – boggy land, ponds and meadows, woodland of willow, poplar and oak – and the area is rich in wildlife. Herons and other waterbirds, black storks, brown kites and white-tailed eagles nest here, while among the mammals are wild boar, red deer (which have traditionally made the area a favourite with hunters) and even the beaver, which was reintroduced in the year 2000 after dying out in the 20th century. Much of the park is protected, and can only be visited by boat, on the narrow-gauge railway or with a guide, but the national blue and red hiking paths run through the park, and there is a cycle route too.

THE GEMENC EXCURSION CENTRE You can pick up the hiking and cycling routes towards the park's southern end at the bridge across the Danube to Baja (see page 340), but the real gateway is at the Gemenc Excursion Centre (*Gemenci kiránduló* *központ; Bárányfok;* ☏ *74 312552/410151;* ⊕ *May–Oct 09.30–18.00 daily*). Buses to the centre in Bárányfok run from Szekszárd (up to five a day). Bárányfok is on the road running between Szekszárd and Keselyűs (further around the park's western edge).

A couple of hundred metres from the entrance is the **National Park Museum** (☞ *500/300Ft;* ⊕ *Mar 15–Oct 31 Tue–Sun 09.00–17.00*), whose pine lodge was originally constructed in Budapest as part of the millennial celebrations to display the hunting trophies of Archduke Frederick. The latter was a member of the Hungarian branch of the Habsburgs, descendants of Archduke Joseph (who was pivotal in the development of Budapest in the early 19th century; see József nádor tér in Budapest, page 146). It was positioned here as the Trophy Museum in the 1980s, but re-opened in 2003 with a more eco-friendly face, showcasing the region's flora and fauna, and the tools of former forest vocations – fishing, animal husbandry and bee keeping.

If you want to stay, there are 20 Finnish-style **wooden bungalows** that can hold up to three people (☏ *74 312552; 9,800–10,300Ft*); each has a shower, toilet, fridge and TV. There is also a small patch where you can pitch a tent. The **Trófea Restaurant** (☏ *20 226 0904; mains avg 1,300Ft;* ⊕ *May–Oct 09.00–22.00 daily*) is a large and touristy restaurant that caters mainly for tour groups, and specialises in game dishes.

INTO THE PARK One way into the park is via the forest **narrow-gauge railway**, which runs 30km between Keselyűs (the Bárányfok terminus is currently closed) and Pörböly in the southern section. It operates May–Oct, and tickets are available from the centre. Trains travelling the whole way depart at 15.35 daily, while a further two leave at 13.35 (daily) and 10.40 (weekends only) going the first 11km to Gemenc Dunapart (on the Danube bank). (You'll have to wait 2–3 hours for a connection if you wish to continue on to Pörböly from Gemenc Dunapart.) You can't return the same day by narrow-gauge from Pörböly as the last train back is at 13.30 on weekdays and 13.15 at weekends (both of which require changes); instead catch a bus to Szekszárd (the journey takes 40 minutes and there are up to 11 buses a day), or perhaps consider taking a normal train to Baja. A nostalgia steam train (*350Ft supplement*) runs at the weekends only between Gemenc Dunapart and Pörböly.

The railway passes the **birdwatching tower** overlooking the strictly protected Malomtelelő-tó (Lake Winter Mill) around 5km from Pörböly; to visit, alight at the Lassi stop and follow the blue-cross path north for a few hundred metres. The odd name derives from the 19th century, when two boats were moored either side of the river near here, with a wheel between them that the water turned to work some milling machinery. The lake was used as a winter shelter for the boats to prevent damage from floating river ice. As well as the tower, there is a study trail.

If you wish to **hike** into the park, you can join the national blue-horizontal-line trail from the excursion centre; the 40km stretch hugs the forest's western side, takes in the birdwatching tower and then heads east to the bridge across to Baja. If that sounds like rather too much hard work, there's a circular 2.5km **nature trail** leading from the centre that will take around 45 minutes; unfortunately the information boards about the wildlife and the lives of the foresters are in Hungarian. A **cycle path** also leaves from the excursion centre, and there is bike hire available (☞ *1,500Ft/day*). Alternatively you can go **horse-riding** (☞ *around 700Ft/hr*) or take a carriage ride into the woods (☞ *1,200/800Ft/hr*).

If you'd prefer to take to the water, a **motorboat** leaves from Árvízkapu (6km east of the excursion centre) along the River Sió and then up the Danube; the hour-long journey only runs if there is sufficient demand. Gemenc is at its prime when the river level rises above 3m and fills its water courses, which can be explored in **rowing boats** or kayaks (motorboats are only permitted on the River Sió). There are signs to assist those travelling by boat, and permits to tie up on the Grébeci Danube, the Rézeti Danube and the left bank of the Koppányi Old

The Danube-Dráva National Park is not what it was originally planned to be. It had been hoped to establish a park straddling the River Dráva and thereby falling on both the Hungarian and Yugoslav sides of the border. However, the break-up of Yugoslavia and the ensuing bloody conflict put paid to such a vision, and in 1996 the park was formed in Hungary alone. It comprises two riverside sections – the lower Hungarian course of the Danube flowing from north to south, including parts of its floodplain, oxbow lakes and dead channels from the confluence of the Sió in Bogyiszló to the Serbian border, and the entire Hungarian course of the Dráva, running west to east from Őrtilos in Somogy to Matty in Baranya. In total it covers 49,500ha, of which 13,400ha are strictly protected.

The bulk of the protected Danube section of the park is made up of two areas. The first is the **Gemenc** (see page 391), holding the largest riverine forest in Hungary; in it are ash, elm, alder and oak forests, as well as oxbow lakes, marshlands, meadows, reed-beds and willow stands. The second, in the floodplain of the lower course of the Danube, is the **Béda-Karapancsa** (see page 398). This hosts a wide variety of floodplain habitats, including rivers, oxbow lakes and ponds. The areas of open water are flanked by marshlands, reed-beds, meadows and gallery forests of ash, elm, alder and oak. Between them, this pair supports a high density and diversity of endangered species. The globally threatened ferruginous duck quacks happily here, and the region is also home to over 20 pairs of white-tailed eagles and a good number of black storks. The lesser-spotted eagle is present, and many great white egrets, along with probably the greatest concentration of the endemic hawthorn species, *Crataegus nigra*, which is only found in the lower floodplains of the Danube.

The Dráva is the last untamed river in central Europe, its course forever changing under the bullying of the fast-moving waters. The protected stretch is 170km in length, with around 30 oxbows, the same number again of lakes and ponds, and flood plains and marshes supporting thousands of birds. The bee-eater and sand martin nest on its sandy banks, while the little tern prefers the gravelled parts for its dwelling. Fifty species of fish live in the waters, 24 types of dragonfly hover around its streams and the meadows are rich in butterflies and moths. Probably the king of the Dráva valley is the **juniper grove at Barcs**, special in the hearts of horticulturalists for the exceptionally rare royal fern (Osmunda regalis) and the shepherd's cress (*Teesdalia nudicaulis*) that grow there.

In addition, the national park has authority over three protected areas of southern Transdanubia: the Eastern Mecsek, the Boronka and the Zselic natural preserves. All are for the most part forested. The **Eastern-Mecsek** is a mountainous reserve known primarily for its grasslands; the **Boronka** hosts healthy populations of otters, white-tailed sea eagles and black storks; the **Zselic** is a range of hills holding various traditional villages. For further information, contact the **Duna-Dráva National Park Directorate** (Pécs, Tettye tér 9; ℄ 72 517227; www.ddnp.hu).

Danube are available from the Duna-Dráva National Park office in Pécs (see page 405). The excursion centre can provide details both of the motorboat trip and rowing-boat outings. **Fishing** is allowed in designated areas; the excursion centre sells permits (℗ 200Ft/day), but you'll need your own rod.

If you are taking to the park on foot, buy a copy of the *Gemenci tájegység* map, which shows the hiking routes and protected areas; surprise surprise, the map is available from the excursion centre. If you'd prefer to visit the park on an **organised tour**, contact Tolna Tours in Szekszárd (see page 387) or Attila Papp (℄ 06 30 377 3406).

MOHÁCS

To look at Mohács, with its charming main square and attractive riverside promenade, it is difficult to believe that it occupies a place as dark as the local pottery in the hearts of Hungarians. Its name is associated with the grand-daddy of all nadirs, a point so low that it has become the stuff of proverbs. Reminded that 'more was lost at Mohács', a man will stop crying over his spilt milk, nod in agreement and put a braver face on things.

Weakened by inner anarchy and social conflict, in 1521 Hungary lost Nándorfehérvár (today's Belgrade) and Szabács to Sultan Suleiman the Great, two of the key fortresses in its southern defences. In April 1526, the sultan continued his advance. The teenage King Lajos II hastily mustered an army of 25,000, and on August 29 1526 met a Turkish force three times its size in a field 9km to the southwest of Mohács. After a stand-off of several hours under the hot sun, the Hungarians charged and the Turks countered. Evening fell and the smoke cleared to reveal the corpses of 15,000 Hungarian soldiers, among them the commander-in-chief (and Archbishop of Kalocsa) Pál Tomori. Legend has it that King Lajos II drowned trying to flee across the Csele Stream. The Turks went on to capture Buda, and while they had to withdraw temporarily through lack of sufficient reserves, they returned 15 years later to occupy the country. The Battle of Mohács is regarded as the fight that broke Hungary's back.

GETTING THERE AND AWAY Lying on the bank of the Danube, at the junction of Road 56 leading north to Szekszárd and Road 6 east to Pécs, Mohács is a gateway to Croatia (the border crossing is at Udvar, 10km or so to the south). The **bus** is the best way to get to and from Mohács. There are Three services to Budapest Népliget and Baja as well as direct buses to Villány (eight daily), Harkány (nine), Kaposvár (two), Dombóvár (one), Kecskemét (two), Székesfehérvár (one) and Szeged (eight). It's a short walk from the bus station (*Rákóczi út*) to the centre – head north along Rákóczi utca, before turning right into Szabadság utca. You can also catch a number of local buses to the memorial park (see page 396) from outside the station and from bus stops in the town centre. Look for those travelling to Nagynyárád or Lippó.

The only direct **train** services are to Villány (seven daily) and Pécs (seven); for Harkány and Siklós, change at Villány. The station is north of the centre, just beyond the swimming pool. In addition, there's a car **ferry** (*Mohácsi Révhajózási; \ 69 311129*) at the end of Szabadság utca (turn left on to Ságvári Endre utca and it's on the right) across the Danube to the Southern Plain. During summer the ferry (*⊕ 160Ft/pp, bike 150Ft, car 580Ft*) departs every half-hour with the last leaving at 20.00; the ticket office is in front of the Révkapu Motel.

INFORMATION AND OTHER PRACTICALITIES

🗷 **Listings magazine** *Pécsi Est*

🗷 **Tourinform** Széchenyi tér 1; \ 69 505515; e mohacs@tourinform.hu. Located in the town hall & helps with private accommodation. ⊕ Jun 15–Sep 15 Mon–Fri 08.00–18.00, Sat–Sun 10.00–17.00, rest of yr Mon–Thu 08.00–16.00, Fri 08.00–13.00.

WHERE TO STAY

🏠 **Duna Panzió** (7 rooms) Felső Dunasor 14; \ 69 302450. If you're anti-hunting you'll have to stomach the animal-skin rugs in some of the rooms, but otherwise the accommodation is spacious & very good value. The owner is also a jolly & welcoming chap. The guesthouse is to the north of the Kanizsai Dorottya Museum. Sgl 6,000Ft, dbl 7,000Ft.

🏠 **Gerber Birtok** (3 rooms) Kölked, Külterület; \ 20 9914270; www.gerberbirtok.hu. The 3 simple but spacious rooms share a bathroom. The estate has 32 horses & works closely with the nearby national park. Both the riding & the carriage trips go into the national park, while canoeing is also available for min 5 persons. 5,000Ft/room; riding from 1,500Ft/hr.

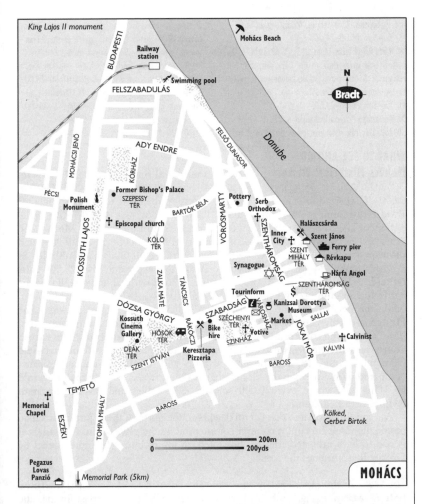

King Lajos II monument

Mohács Beach

BUDAPESTI

Railway
station

Swimming pool

FELSZABADULÁS

N

Bradt

FELSŐ DUNASOR

ADY ENDRE

Danube

MOHÁCSI JENŐ

KÓRHÁZ

PÉCSI

Polish
Monument

Former Bishop's Palace
SZEPESSY
TÉR

Pottery
Serb
Orthodox

Halászcsárda

BARTÓK BÉLA

VÖRÖSMARTY

Szent János

Ferry pier

Épiscopal church

Inner
City

Révkapu

SZENT
MIHÁLY
TÉR

KOSSUTH LAJOS

KÓLÓ
TÉR

SZENTHÁROMSÁG

Synagogue

Hárfa Angol

ZALKA MÁTÉ

TÁNCSICS

RÁKÓCZI

SZENTHÁROMSÁG
TÉR

Tourinform

$

DÓZSA GYÖRGY

SZABADSÁG

Kanizsai Dorottya
Museum

Kossuth
Cinema
Gallery

SZÉCHENYI
TÉR

Bike
hire

Market

SALLAI

JÓKAI MÓR

HŐSÖK
TÉR

Votive

SZÍNHÁZ

Calvinist

DEÁK
TÉR

Keresztapa
Pizzeria

KÁLVIN

SZENT ISTVÁN

BAROSS

TEMETŐ

Memorial
Chapel

TOMPA MIHÁLY

BAROSS

Kölked,
Gerber Birtok

ESZÉKI

0   200m
0   200yds

Pegazus
Lovas
Panzió

Memorial Park (5km)

MOHÁCS

🏠 **Hotel Szent János** (49 rooms) Szent Mihály tér 6–7; 🔌 69 511010; www.hotel-szentjanos.hu. The biggest hotel in town re-opened in 2008 after total refurbishment; owned partly by the church & partly by the town, it's a good choice. Ask for a room overlooking the river. There's a lovely grill terrace on the roof during fair weather. Air-con, internet, wellness, sauna, massage, fitness room. Sgl 14,750Ft; dbl 17,250Ft; restaurant mains avg 2,000Ft; ⏰ 10.00–22.00 daily.

🏠 **Pegazus Lovas Panzió** (9 rooms) Eszéki út; 🔌 69 301244/305500. This wonderful guesthouse & riding

school stands in scenic surrounds 1km to the south of the centre. The rooms are large & comfortable, with good-sized bathrooms. Even if you don't fancy horse-riding, this is a relaxing spot to stay. We recommend it highly. Riding costs from 2,000Ft/hr (they cater for all levels). Dbl 11,000Ft.

🏠 **Révkapu Motel** (5 rooms) Szent János u. 1; 🔌 69 322228. The Révkapu Restaurant has a small motel above it, although we found it difficult to find anyone to show us around. It does overlook the river & is cheap, but if the staff remain the same you'll waste less time looking elsewhere. Dbl 9,000Ft.

✗ WHERE TO EAT AND DRINK

✗ **Halászcsárda** Szent Mihály tér 5; 🔌 69 322542. The fish could leap straight from the water on to your plate in this first-floor river-facing restaurant.

Despite the dickie-bowed waiters, the school-dinner-hall décor rather undercuts any grand aspirations. Fisherman's carp soup & pike goulash are among the specialities. Rude service. *Mains avg 2,000Ft;* ⊕ *Tue–Sun 11.00–24.00.*

✘ **Hárfa Angol** Szent János u. 3; ☎ 69 302477. On a leafy side street close to the ferry pier, this restaurant & café serves steak, Indonesian curry, turkey dishes & the like. *Mains avg 1,600Ft;* ⊕ *Tue–Sun 16.00–24.00.*

✘ **Keresztapa Pizzeria** Szabadság u. 22; ☎ 69 303259. This café-style joint offers pizzas in 2 sizes & many varieties, & there's also a selection of salads, burgers & spaghettis for those averse to the Italian tomato bread. If you want to eat in, there's some seating overlooking Széchenyi tér, but you can also take away. *Mains avg 900Ft;* ⊕ *daily 10.00–23.00.*

✘ **Révkapu Vendéglő** See page 395. Terraced eating area with great views over the Danube, & live music most nights. *Mains avg 2,000Ft;* ⊕ *09.00–23.00 daily.*

WHAT TO SEE AND DO

Mohács Historical Memorial Park The **memorial park** (*Történelmi Emlékpark;* ☎ 69 382130; ☞ 550/350Ft; ⊕ *Apr Wed–Sun 10.00–16.00, May–Sep Tue–Sun 09.00–16.00, Oct Wed–Sun 10.00–16.00*) stands on the route to Sátorhely, just off Road 56 running south from Mohács. There is a bus stop directly outside the entrance. The park was established in 1976 at the site of the Battle of Mohács 450 years earlier, on what Károly Kisfaludy referred to in his poem as the 'blooded mourning field'. The massive reticulated entrance arch by goldsmith József Pölöskei looks oddly triumphal until you learn that every one of its 28,000 bolts represents a fallen soldier. A sunken atrium is lined with tableaux depicting the battle and an unimpressive fountain by Gyula Illés symbolising a broken flower, while the grassed circular park beyond is believed to be the place where the Hungarian army camped prior to the fight. Five mass graves were uncovered here containing the remains of 400 soldiers, and rose beds and carved Transylvanian-style posts mark the spots. A 10m-high cross overlooks the field from the far end. It won't detain you long, and is sobering and understated compared with a memorial park like that at Ópusztaszer, but that is as it should be. This was where over 20,000 soldiers, 500 nobles and seven Hungarian bishops breathed their last.

A second memorial to that fateful day lies to the north of town, just off Road 56 beside the Csele Stream. A column commemorates the place where King Lajos II is said to have drowned after his horse fell on top of him. The bronze relief by György Kiss imagines the scene.

The town At the eastern side of the wide and cobbled Széchenyi tér is the **town hall** (*Széchenyi tér 1*), built in 1926 with Moorish dome turrets. Inside, the assembly room at the top of the stairs (⊕ *Mon–Fri 08.00–16.00*) contains a large tapestry of the Busó Carnival (see opposite) woven in 1922 by István Bán. Like the town hall, the **Votive Church** (*Fogadalmi templom; Széchenyi tér;* ☎ 69 303279; ☞ *admission 150Ft;* ⊕ *09.00–12.00, 13.00–16.00 daily*) was designed by Aladár Arkay, and it is similarly Moorish in look. The foundations were filled with earth from over 3,000 towns and villages as a symbol of national unity. Stained-glass windows around the 30m dome swirl with colour; mosaics in the side chapels were crafted by Mihály Kolbe (see opposite) to the designs of Lili Sztehlo in 1956, while the mosaic floor alludes to the battle of 1526.

Walk west along Szabadság utca to **Hősök tere**, which holds a 24m monument to the 439 soldiers from Mohács who died during World War I. At the centre there is a stone cube added on the 40th anniversary of the 1956 revolution. The square also has a sombre statue by Imre Varga of Miklós Radnóti leaning against a fence post. One of Hungary's outstanding 20th-century poets, the Jewish Radnóti passed through Mohács in 1945 on a forced labour march destined for Vienna. He would never get there; when he became too tired to continue, an Arrow Cross trooper executed him by the road side. His last poems were discovered on his body in a mass grave.

The ground floor of the **Kossuth Cinema Gallery** (*Filmszínház; Deák tér 1;* ☏ *69 510177;* ✆ *250/150Ft;* ☺ *Tue–Sun 10.00–18.00*) has a cinema screening Hollywood blockbusters, but more interesting is the exhibition space upstairs. There is a display of the distinctive **ceramics** of the town, charcoal black and cut with grooves and notches. The style developed in the 18th and 19th centuries, and was shipped to the Balkans where it became very popular. During the 20th century, János Horváth (1905–75) was the acknowledged master of the craft, and you can see his work together with that of other local potters. There are also pieces to buy. Another room contains **paintings by Mihály Kolbe** (1907–90), who lived in Mohács from 1931 after studying in Budapest, and was responsible for mosaics in the Votive Church. His work shows the clear influence of Cubism, and artists like Matisse and Picasso. In a third room is a selection of fearsome **Busó masks** and sheepskin coats. These are worn during the Busó Carnival (*Busójárás*), a Shrove Tuesday celebration derived from the Sokác people, a Croatian minority who (along with Serbs and Germans) repopulated Mohács after the Turkish occupation. During the carnival, a noisy procession wearing the horned and hairy masks symbolically drives out winter and welcomes in spring. It is said by some that the Sokác people donned frightening masks and drove the Turks from Mohács, but they actually arrived a decade after the occupation had ended and so if there's any truth to such an event it must have taken place in their native land. The Busó celebrations were added to UNESCO's 'Intangible Cultural Heritage' list in 2009, aimed at the preservation of ancient traditions. An **ethnographic exhibition** shows the costumes of the various groups that settled and rebuilt the town in the 17th century.

In the immediate aftermath of the Battle of Mohács, the widow of Imre Perényi from Siklós approached the Turkish camp and asked permission to bury the slain. The commander was so moved by her courage that he ordered some of his men to help her. They worked all night and for the following week laying the corpses in shallow graves (some of which were discovered in the 1970s at the site of today's memorial park. To the east of Széchenyi tér, the **Kanizsai Dorottya Museum** (*Városház u. 1;* ☏ *69 311536;* ✆ *300/150Ft;* ☺ *Apr–Oct Tue–Sat 10.00–17.00, Sun 10.00–12.00, 14.00–16.00, Nov–Mar Tue–Sat 10.00–16.00*) is named after her. The permanent exhibition contains ethnographic items belonging to the Croatian, German, Slovenian and Serbian immigrants to Mohács, including costumes, painted furniture, icons of the Orthodox Church and grave markers. There are pieces of local pottery and Busó masks too. The entrance ticket also allows access to a second exhibition space (*Szerb u. 2*) near the Serbian Orthodox church, which details the history of the Battle of Mohács.

Near the ferry dock, the Roman Catholic **Inner City Church** (*Szent Mihály tér;* ☺ *08.00–12.00 daily*) was built in Baroque style in 1766, while across Szentháromság utca in the garden of the former **synagogue** (*Báró Eötvös u. 1*) is a memorial to World War II Jewish victims of the fascist extermination programme. The key to the gates is held in the town library (☏ *69 311347*). Continue north to the **Serb Orthodox church** (*Szerb u. 2*) of 1732, with a 48m tower and spectacular iconostasis by Mór Csóka. You'll need permission from the priest to get in; ring the bell to the right as you enter the church grounds through the low arch on Korsós utca. By the river to the south of the centre is the pretty, late-Baroque **Calvinist church** (*Kálvin u.;* ☏ *69 311336*), built in 1790 and capped with a grey onion spire. Telephone beforehand for admittance.

The **Episcopal Church** (*Gólya u.*), to the northwest of the centre, was commissioned by Bishop Zsigmond Berényi of Pécs in 1742 and his coat of arms sit above the entrance. Across the road is the **Firemen Statue** of St Flórián, which was erected in 1896 after a spate of fires had hit the town, while a touch further north is the **former Bishop's Palace** (*Szepessy tér 6*) where the clerics would come to recuperate in summer. It now houses the Kisfaludy Károly School. The park in the middle of the square contains a monument to the 1,600 Polish soldiers killed at the Battle of Mohács, who were serving in the Hungarian army.

The **Memorial Chapel** (*Emlékkápolna; Eszéki út*) 700m south from here along Kossuth Lajos út is set in a peaceful and beautifully maintained graveyard filled with horse-chestnut trees. The chapel itself was built in 1816, and has a stained-glass portrait of Dorottya Kanizsai (see above). There are also two paintings by István Dorfmeister, showing the 1526 defeat and the second less-remembered Habsburg victory over the Turks at Mohács in 1687. In effect this simply resulted in one occupier replacing another, and isn't a battle greatly celebrated by Hungarians.

Other activities There is a large outdoor **swimming pool** (*Indoház u. 1;* \ *69 303246;* ✆ *1,500/1,000Ft; Mon–Thu 06.00–21.00, Fri 06.00–22.00, Sat/Sun 08.00–22.00*) near the railway station. A **sandy beach** is a popular sunbathing spot on the opposite bank of the river from the ferry pier. During the summer season **bike** and **canoe hire** and **pleasure boating** can be arranged with Beda Tours (\ *30 695 4797*), while if you prefer your rides with four hooves then the **Pegazus Lovas Panzió** or **Gerber Birtok** (see page 395) can help. Wine fanciers can follow the **Mohács-Bóly Wine Route**; pick up a map from Tourinform, or contact the Mohács-Bóly Wine Route Association (*Bóly, Erzsébet tér 1;* \ *69 368100;* e *tourinform@boly.hu*).

Nature lovers should follow the Danube 8km south to the **Béda-Karapancsa flood plains** (to the east of the memorial park), which are part of the Duna-Dráva National Park (see page 393) and feature several dead branches of the river and 10,000ha of woodland lying on either side. The oak trees harbour a significant population of the black stork, while the Kölkedi Nagyrét (meadow) is a stop-off point for migrating birds. Much of the area is protected and can only be visited with permission (*to organise a tour,* \ *72 213236*), but there are cycle and walking routes. **Kölked** also has a White Stork Museum (\ *30 4632295;* ☉ *Nov–Mar Sat–Sun 10.00–17.00, Apr–Oct Wed–Sun 08.00–17.00*), which showcases the habitats, migration routes and family life of storks. Tourinform should be able to furnish you with a map (*Béda-Karapancsai tájegység*) produced by the national park. It is also a good **fishing** haunt; for information on the prime spots and on the necessary angling permits, contact the Mohács Anglers' Association (*Kisfaludy Károly u. 6;* \ *69 322123*). You can buy daily passes for the Kadia Duna and Ferenc Canal, on the eastern side of the river, from the shop at the adjacent village of Budzsák.

The distinctive black colour of the **pottery** for which Mohács is renowned is produced by smothering the fire in the kiln towards the end of firing and thereby filling it with dark smoke. You can look in at the workshop of László Lakatos (*Bárány u. 1, off Vörösmarty u.;* \ *69 301934*), and also buy his pieces.

In the nearby village of **Nagynyárád**, you'll find one of the few remaining indigo (blue) dyers. Andor Auth (*Dózsa György u. 5é;* \ *69 374142*) works on machinery over a century old. Blue dyed material was once the everyday wear of the Danube German (Swabian) population, but these days the old printing blocks are used to make tablecloths, aprons and curtain material. Turn left at the lovely church of **Nagyharsány** into Dózsa György utca. This is still a majority German village, and the difference in the style of the buildings – more town- than village-like, with broad façades and a carriage entrance to the yard – is immediately obvious.

FESTIVALS AND EVENTS The annual Busó Carnival (see page 397) is celebrated before Lent in February or March. The parade kicks off from Kóló tér (with its bronze Busó Statue), and there is a bonfire in the main square.

Around 30km southwest of Mohács, Villány is the best-known village of the Villány-Siklós wine region (see box, page 400). Wine's long been the winner here, Bishop Mihály Haas writing in 1845 that of Hungarian vintages 'the Villány red towers as a hundred-year-old oak above the shrubs'. At the eastern end of the hill range, the vineyards of Villány occupy the slopes of Mount Szársomlyó, which is a nature conservation area and habitat for the Hungarian crocus. The sunny clime has been enjoyed and utilised since prehistory, and wine production is reputed to date back to Celtic times. The area has recently introduced its own '*appellation contrôlée*'.

The Turks destroyed the village in the 16th century, but it was pay-back time at the Battle of Nagyharsány a short distance to the southwest in 1687; the Ottomans were pushed down into the marshes around the River Dráva and mercilessly put to the sword. Afterwards Serbs and Germans made Villány their home, the latter bringing with them a greater wine-making expertise and the Oportó (today Kékoportó – or more accurately Portugiezer, since an EU ruling prohibited the use of Portó or Oportó on the label) vine variety. However, the phylloxera epidemic reached the region in 1875 and blighted everything. The recovery – which took 20 years – was largely thanks to Zsigmond Teleki, who established an experimental vineyard in the village with the aim of breeding a hardy grape that could replenish the vineyards. He sunk all his money into the project, and by the time of his death in 1910 had laid the foundations for what became the biggest root stock and graft producer in central Europe. Things worsened again at the conclusion of World War II, when most among the German population – judged 'guilty by association' – were deported. The Hungarian farmers who replaced them often knew little about vine growing and many went bankrupt, while the nationalisation of estates – which started as soon as 1945 – also drove the quality down. Only since the 1990s has it picked up with a rise in private enterprises and modern techniques; the red wines are generally full-bodied, and characterised by a high alcohol and tannin content.

Villány essentially means the single, cellar-lined street of Baross Gábor utca. In theory the cellars open between 10.00 and 18.00, but in practice they keep their own hours and you'll take your chance on the day. Among those to try are Fritsch Pince (*no 97*), Havas Borház (*no 81*), Boncz Pince (*no 75*) and Maul Pince (*no 39*); alternatively the guesthouses often have connections with local wineries and can organise tastings. The big names to look out for are Attila Gere (widely regarded as the country's top maker of red wine; see Gere Panzió below), Ede Tiffán, Jószef Bock and Csaba Malatinszky. A **Wine Museum** (*Bem József u. 8;* \ *72 492130; & free entry;* ⊕ *Tue–Sun 09.00–17.00*) stands in a 200-year-old cellar that once belonged to the Teleki family. The **Red Wine Festival** takes place on the first weekend in October, and November 10 is St Martin's Day (when there is a feast of wine and goose); you're advised to book accommodation in advance for either period.

A couple of kilometres northwest on the road towards Pécs, **Villánykövesd** is similarly rooted in the grape. The cellars are crammed along two roads (Petőfi utca below and Pincesor above); those especially valued are Polgár Pince (*Pincesor 51–52*), Blum János Borozó (*Pincesor 4–5*), Tiffán Imre Pincéje (*Pincesor 14–15*) and Schwarzwalter Ferenc Pincéje (*Pincesor 16*). There is only one hotel and a couple of guesthouses; during the second half of October the village hosts the opening ceremony of the **Pécs Drinking Song Festival**. Wine culture has gained momentum in Hungary and Villány is at the forefront.

GETTING THERE AND AWAY The main **bus** stop in Villány is outside the town hall on Baross Gábor utca – just to the left of the OTP Bank. From here you can travel to

The 30km-long Villány-Siklós Wine Route was the first to be established by any of Hungary's main wine-making regions, and wends its way around the limestone Villány Hills and through the 11 settlements nestling on the slopes – Palkonya, Villánykövesd (see page 399), Villány, Nagyharsány (with an artists' camp, sculpture park and 13th-century Calvinist church), Kisharsány, Nagytótfalu, Kistótfalu, Vokány, Siklós (see opposite), Máriagyűd (with its Roman Catholic church, which became a pilgrimage site and centre of the Maria cult during the Counter-Reformation in the 18th century) and Harkány (see page 403). The region is well suited to wine production, enjoying 2,000 hours of sunshine a year, and ten million vines grow on the hills over an area of 1,000ha. The eastern slopes yield red wines (notably from the Kékfrankos, Kékoportó or Portugiezer, Cabernet Franc, Cabernet Sauvignon and Merlot grapes), while the central and western slopes produce white wines (Italian Riesling, Hárslevelű, Chardonnay, Tramini and Rhine Riesling). If you require further information on the route and its wines, contact the office of the Villány-Siklós Wine Route Association (see below).

Budapest Népliget (one daily), Harkány (ten), Szigetvár (two), Szekszárd (four) and Pécs (two daily). There are also fairly regular services to Siklós and Mohács. Up to six buses a day make the seven-minute journey to Villánykövesd. The **train station** (*Ady Endre fasor*) is 1km north of the centre (on the way to Villánykövesd). There are direct trains to Pécs (11 daily), Mohács (seven), Siklós and Harkány (up to six), as well as a service across the Serbian border to Sarajevo (taking 8½ hours). From the station turn left and follow the road in front of you, which leads to the village centre.

INFORMATION AND OTHER PRACTICALITIES

$ **Bank** Baross Gábor u. 36 (opposite the town hall)

✉ **Post office** Baross Gábor u. 35 (next to Oportó Panzió)

Villány-Siklós Wine Route Association Deák Ferenc u. 22; ☏ 72 492181; e iroda@borut.hu;

www.borut.hu. Standing just off Baross Gábor u., the office of the region's wine association can provide information on wine festivals & cellars in the area, & organise tours.

 WHERE TO STAY AND EAT Other than the Hotel Cabernet, the places to stay or grab a bite below are in Villány; you'll also find that there are many houses offering private rooms.

🏠 **Bock Pince** (21 rooms) Batthyány u. 15; ☏ 72 492919; www.bock.hu. This beautiful guesthouse is away from the main thoroughfare, the rooms are quiet & the ambience is 'unhurried'. You can enjoy excellent cuisine to accompany award-winning wines on the large terrace in the yard (or the cosy dining room in winter). Sgl 13,250Ft, dbl 16,500Ft; mains avg 2,600Ft; ⏲ all yr except Christmas.

🏠 **Crocus Gere Bor Hotel** (23 rooms) Diófás u. 4; ☏ 72 492195; www.gere.hu. Owned by the revered vintner Attila Gere, the cellar here is probably the best in the village (the winery itself is 5 mins away); taste 5 wines for 1,800Ft or 7 wines for 2,200Ft, & enjoy a plate of cold meats with them if the fancy takes. The new wing of the hotel opened in 2008;

crash afterwards in excellent, modern, apartment-like rooms. Sgl 18,500Ft, dbl 22,000Ft; cellar & restaurant ⏲ Mon–Sat 09.00–18.00, Sun 09.00–12.00.

🍰 **Flamingo Cukrászda** Dózsa György 4; ☏ 72 492207. Where the locals head for their ice cream & cake. ⏲ daily 09.00–20.00.

🏠 **Hotel Cabernet** (25 rooms) Villánykövesd, Petőfi u. 29; ☏ 72 493200; e info@hotelcabernet.hu; www.hotelcabernet.hu. This 3-star doll's house of a hotel is next to the stop for buses from Villány & 100m from the railway station. The hotel's Görbe Pince ('Curvy Cellar'; mains avg 1,800Ft; ⏲ 11.00–22.00 daily) serves regional specialities & holds wines from all the area's producers. Sgl 12,000Ft, dbl 15,000Ft, trpl 19,500Ft.

Oportó Panzió (11 rooms) Baross Gábor u. 33; ℡ 72 592032; e www.oporto.hu. In front of the town hall, this pension & restaurant is Villány's best. The elegant restaurant (*mains avg 1,800Ft;* ⊕ *daily 10.00–22.00*) serves well-presented Hungarian food with an international influence; its intimate terrace is festooned with creepers & feels like a leafy tent. The rooms are large & smartly furnished – in 2003, they played host to the Hungarian president &

prime minister. You can hire a bike & take a sauna, & the family owns a cellar 50m away. *Sgl 11,000Ft, dbl 15,000Ft.*

Polgár Inn (16 rooms) Hunyadi u. 19; ℡ 74 492053; www.polgarpince.hu. This Mediterranean-feeling guesthouse is situated around an inner courtyard. It is run by the Polgár family, another famous wine-making dynasty. *Sgl 10,200Ft, dbl 13,400Ft.*

SIKLÓS

Siklós is Hungary's most southerly town, 15km to the west of Villány. In contrast to the rated reds of its neighbour, Siklós flies the flag for white wines like Italian Riesling, Rhine Riesling, Chardonnay and Traminer. However, it is best known for its castle, which – unlike so many medieval forts – managed to escape Turkish cannon and Habsburg explosives. **Note** that as we went to press the castle was closed for refurbishment, with planned re-opening in 2011.

GETTING THERE AND AWAY The **bus station** (*Szent István tér*) is northwest of the centre. Upon arrival here turn left (and keep left) until the road meets Felszabadulás utca, which leads to the right into Kossuth tér. There are one or two buses an hour to Pécs and Harkány, and a regular service to Villány. Direct routes run to Mohács (up to ten), Szigetvár (up to three), Szekszárd (two) and one daily to Budapest and Székesfehérvár.

Siklós is on the Villány line. There is a **train station** (*Gyűdi út*) to the northwest of the centre, on the road towards Máriagyűd, but the main one (*Vasút út*) is northeast of the centre, at the top of Táncsics Mihály utca (which leads into Kossuth tér). Direct trains run to Harkány (seven), Villány (six), Sellye (four) and Barcs (one), while a change is required at Villány for access to Pécs and Mohács.

INFORMATION

Tourinform Felszabadulás u. 3; ℡ 72 579090; e siklos@tourinform.hu. ⊕ *Jun 15–Aug 31*

Mon–Fri 09.00–17.00, Sat–Sun 10.00–19.00, Sep–Jun 14 Mon–Fri 08.00–16.00.

WHERE TO STAY, EAT AND DRINK

Központi Hotel and Restaurant (25 rooms) Kossuth tér 5; ℡ 72 352513; www.kozponti.hu. The hotel rooms are modern & tastefully done, & there's the opportunity to use a sauna & fitness room. The restaurant (⊕ *08.00–22.00 daily; mains avg 1,800Ft*) is popular in a town with few eateries to spare, but it is basic in its furnishings & lacking in atmosphere.

Its fare is Hungarian with some international choices. *Sgl 8,200Ft, dbl 10,600Ft, trpl 14,400Ft.*

Vasúti Vendéglő Vasút út 9; ℡ 72 579053. Situated directly opposite the main train station, this spartan – somewhat out of the way – restaurant deals in Hungarian food. *Mains avg 1,200Ft;* ⊕: *Mon–Sat 07.00–21.00, Sun 11.00–21.00.*

WHAT TO SEE AND DO

Siklós Castle Kids will be disappointed by some of Hungary's castles – either because they are more mansion than fortress or more broken parts than ramparts – but Siklós Castle (*Vajda János tér;* ℡ 72 351433; ✆ *760/540Ft;* ⊕ *daily Apr 15–Oct 14 09.00–18.00, rest of yr 09.00–16.00, exhibitions closed Mon; note that the castle is closed for refurbishment during 2010, due to re-open in 2011*) is the real old-fashioned deal, with a drawbridge and dungeons and crenellations. A Romanesque castle was constructed on the hill in the 13th century by the Siklós family, but there was rebuilding in the 15th and 16th centuries, and it took its current form in the 18th century after remodelling by Count Caprara and then Count Batthyány (who served under his cousin, Prime Minister Lajos Kossuth – subsequently executed – as foreign minister in 1848–49). Gothic, Renaissance and Baroque features are indicative of the castle's evolution. Although it remains in good shape, its history is not uneventful. In 1401 King Zsigmond was kept here for five months 'under arrest' by an oligarchy unwilling to accept his primogeniture after the death of his first wife, daughter of King Lajos); in 1543 it fell to the Turks, who held it for 143 years; and in 1705 it was captured by the insurrectionist troops of General János Bottyán, who defended it for a year against the imperial army.

You can reach the drawbridge leading into the castle complex from Kossuth tér via Batthyány utca. Running around it is a belt of Renaissance bastions, and above the museum a crenellated terrace (complete with coffee bar) affords spectacular hill views. The 14th–15th-century narrow **Gothic chapel** has vaulted ceilings, long stained-glass windows in pastel shades and niches decorated with faded frescoes of saints and kings, while the nearby bleak **dungeon** cells and torture chambers hold stocks and ankle clamps. To the left of the dungeon is the entrance to the main **Castle Museum**, in the southern wing of the Baroque courtyard palace. Inside is a collection devoted to the history of the glove trade, with prominence given to the Hunor garment company of Pécs that was known all over Europe. Alongside gloves from the late 19th and early 20th centuries, the display includes the tools with which they were made and prints of various styles of the day. A local history exhibition has models of the castle and details of the families who lived in it – uniquely in the country, it was continuously inhabited from the time of its construction up until the 20th century – while the cellar below contains stone pieces from the various earlier incarnations. The rest of the museum includes a memorial room to Ferenc Őrsi (author of the novel *Captain of Tenkes*, about a Robin-Hood-like character who protected people from Habsburg villainy), the 20th-century ceramics of István Gádor and a small gallery of modern art. Leading off from the courtyard, the Wine House (*Borok Háza*) is a limited museum devoted to the history of wine production in the area, and sells locally made bottles of white.

Other the **Franciscan church** to the south of Vajda János tér has Gothic windows and fragments of frescoes dating to the early 15th century. It was here that Miklós Garai was buried, one of the most powerful nobles of his age and palatine of Hungary for 30 years; King Zsigmond confiscated the castle from the Siklós family and gave it to Garai – the oligarch who subsequently imprisoned him until he agreed to hand over control of Hungary's internal affairs – in 1387, and it was he who oversaw the Gothic phase of its rebuilding. The adjacent former Franciscan monastery now holds the **Ceramics Gallery** (*Kerámia Alkotóház; Vajda János tér 4; admission free; when attendant is there*), which exhibits the work of local and international ceramicists. The cloister is home to the Baranya County Art Colony, whose kilns and benches fill the cells; each year around eight potters are invited to a month-long artists' camp, and the rooms, corridors and courtyard of the gallery include their pieces.

Moving away from the castle on Batthyány Kázmér utca, on the right beyond Kossuth tér is the **Malkocs Bej Mosque** (*Dzsámi; Vörösmarty u. 14; 300/200Ft; May–Sep daily 10.00–12.00 & 13.30–18.00*), a chunky little relic of the Turkish era. The restored Muslim prayer house – one of the few to survive in Hungary – was built between 1543 and 1565, and has a square stone base and an octagonal brick upper portion topped by a crescent moon. A short distance to the north is **Serb Orthodox church** (*Táncsics Mihály u. 2; 200/Ft; look for attendant to open it*) in Louis-XVI style, which reopened a decade ago after lying closed for half a century. Built in 1700, it has a fabulous iconostasis crafted in 1800.

Northeast of the square (follow Táncsics Mihály utca, and turn left on to Dózsa György utca) is a lively **market** that sell clothes, fast food, shoes, souvenirs and much more besides.

FESTIVALS AND EVENTS At the beginning of August, the Tenkesalja Festival takes place with concerts and theatre performances in the castle, while the last saturday of the month is devoted to a chicken paprikás event. The harvest parade features folk events during Siklós Autumn at the start of October.

HARKÁNY

At the western end of the Villány Hills, on Road 58 heading north up to Pécs, Harkány is the place to take some water with your wine. The spa resort was established by the Batthyány family in the early 19th century after a peasant, János Pogány, found that the shooting pains in his feet were relieved as he spent days digging canals in the marshlands near Harkány. The sulphurous spring that worked this magic now attracts thousands upon thousands in summer months (indeed, over a million annually), and certainly isn't the place for those averse to crowds – indeed, it's probably best treated purely as an outing from Villány rather than a place to stay.

The **Harkány Spa and Outdoor Pools** (*Harkányi Gyógyfürdő; Kossuth Lajos u. 7*) have thermal baths ($\textcircled{s}$ *2,2500/1,590Ft;* $\oplus$ *daily 09.00–18.00*) and open-air baths ($\textcircled{s}$ *1,090/790Ft;* $\oplus$ *Sun–Thu 09.00–18.00, Fri–Sat 09.00–20.00*), and are set in a 14ha park. The complex boasts two medicinal thermal pools (35–37°C), five swimming pools (25–35°C), a giant water slide, jacuzzi and whirlpool baths, a playground and a scattering of food huts. There are mud treatments as well as water ones, and you can take part in two daily sessions of water gymnastics (*11.00 & 15.20*). The spa's rheumatism hospital stands on the other side of Zsigmond sétány, and administers traditional and modern thermal therapies. The entrance to the thermal baths is also on Zsigmond sétány, while you can access the outdoor pools from Bajcsy-Zsilinszky utca or Kossuth Lajos utca.

The **Tourinform** (*Kossuth Lajos u. 2;* \ *72 479624;* e *harkany@tourinform.hu;* $\oplus$ *Jun 15–Aug 31 Mon–Sat 08.00–17.00, Sep–Jun 14 Mon–Fri 09.00–16.00*) shares a building with the cultural centre and public library.

GETTING THERE AND AWAY Buses (*Bajcsy-Zsilinszky u.*) run every 30 minutes or so to Siklós and Pécs. Direct routes also operate to Villány (six), Mohács (nine) and Sellye (two); there is a twice-daily service to Budapest Népliget and Szekszárd and once-daily buses to Veszprém, Kecskemét and Kalocsa. A summer service provides once a week access to Stuttgart and Frankfurt.

Reach the centre of town from the **railway station** (*Táncsics Mihály u.*) by turning left and walking along Táncsics Mihály utca, turn right on to Petőfi utca and follow this road along until it becomes Kossuth Lajos utca. Harkány is on the line between Barcs (one) and Villány (six), with direct trains also going to Sellye (four) and Siklós (six). For trains to Pécs and Mohács change at Villány.

THE ORMÁNSÁG

The region stretching west from Harkány to Sellye, bordered to the south by the River Dráva, is known as the Ormánság. Flooding in past centuries meant that villages were established on raised platforms, hence its name (*orom* means 'summit' in Hungarian). The area sees few tourists; the wooded landscape is ideal cycling country, while the dead channels of the Dráva will suit those interested in nature.

The villages are perhaps most valued, though, for their **painted Calvinist churches**. These were constructed after József II introduced a greater degree of religious tolerance in 1781; while puritan asceticism generally led to spartan, whitewashed churches, those here are adorned with bright peasant art and coffered ceilings bearing folk motifs. The best examples are in Kóros, Drávaiványi, Adorjás and Kovácshida. You can learn more about the local folk traditions at the **Kiss Géza Ormánsági Museum** (*Sellye, Köztársaság tér 6;* \ *73 480245;* & *300/150Ft;* ⊕ *Tue–Sun Apr–Oct 10.00–16.00, rest of yr 10.00–14.00*), which also has a stilted house that once stood in Csányoszró. It is easiest to travel into the Ormánság from Harkány; the **train** is the quicker mode and there are services to Sellye and Vajszló (which are served by **buses** too). Buses also run from Szigetvár, and trains from there require a change at Szentlőrinc.

PÉCS

It would be a cantankerous soul who didn't like Pécs, a shifty sort who'd tell you that right was left and red was green before wriggling out of paying his bar tab. A man not to be trusted, you understand. Once you pass through the featureless modern suburbs, you're greeted by a wonderful city that combines old-world charm with contemporary vibrancy, one that contains a premier cathedral, a host of conveniently placed museums and some worthy restaurants, and that is atmospheric by night and friendly by day. You'll see in a shot why it is second only to Budapest on the tourist itinerary.

Summer lingers long in Pécs, which is shielded from northern winds by the Mecsek Hills and wallows in a sub-Mediterranean microclimate. It's no surprise that the Romans felt at home here, establishing a town called Sopianae that was by the 3rd century one of the administrative centres of the province of Pannonia. They cultivated vineyards and fruit trees on the southern slopes, a sweet and lasting legacy that in the 15th century inspired the humanist poet Janus Pannonius to trill (in Latin) about the wonders of the late-blossoming almond trees. As the city grows and houses creep up the hillsides, viniculture is less of an enveloping presence than it once was, but vines are still harvested to the east and west of the centre, and older residents refer to themselves as *tüke* (a word deriving from the Hungarian for 'vinestock').

In 1009 King István made the town an episcopal see, and Lajos the Great opened the country's first university in 1367, when it became a stronghold of Hungarian Renaissance culture. Ottoman occupation had a significant impact; while other settlements during this period were often left to rot, Pécs developed into a thriving oriental centre of commerce and academia. The city held 17 mosques. The residue of this Turkish influence is clearer in Pécs and its architecture than anywhere else in Hungary. Damage was heavy during the fight to remove the Turks, but the city rose again on the shoulders of vintners, coal miners digging in the Mecsek, and leather workers continuing an industry imported by Balkan immigrants. Factories producing luxury goods sprouted, among them Hamerli Gloves, Angster Organ

JANUS PANNONIUS

Pannonius was a colourful character, who had enjoyed a humanist education in Italy and was unafraid to attack the greed of the papacy. He was made Bishop of Pécs in 1458 and even served as Chancellor to King Mátyás; however, he had to flee after becoming involved in the doomed Vitéz conspiracy against the king, and died on the run of tuberculosis at the age of just 38.

and Zsolnay Ceramics. After the reshaping of borders through the Treaty of Trianon, Pécs's traditional place as a hive of learning was restored when the Hungarian University of Arts and Sciences was moved here from Pozsony (Bratislava) in 1921; in the 1970s, the city's 'Museum Street' was established. The fresh intellectual and cultural energy is palpable, particularly when festivals are in full swing.

It's therefore appropriate that Pécs is the **2010 European Capital of Culture** (together with Essen in Germany and Istanbul). As we go to press (at the start of 2010), refurbishment of the central public squares is complete; parts of the old Zsolnay Factory are being converted to house a new exhibition hall, arts and crafts centre, and theatre (the largest such project to revive an industrial historical building in Central and Eastern Europe); and the museums in Káptalan utca are being cleaned up, and work on the Museum of Hungarian Modern Art is ongoing. For fully updated details, see www.pecs2010.hu.

GETTING THERE, AWAY AND AROUND The recent completion of the M6 motorway has improved road links to the city. The intercity **bus station** (*Zólyom u.*) is 700m southeast of the town centre, next to a large market. Turn right into Bajcsy-Zsilinszky utca, before following Irgalmasok utcaja into Széchenyi tér. There are no shortage of buses to Siklós, Harkány and Mohács, while Szekszárd, Kaposvár and Szigetvár are also well served. Up to five buses a day make the four-hour journey to Budapest Népliget and there are direct routes to Baja (12), Szeged (eight), Zalaegerszeg (five), Székesfehérvár (five), Keszthely (five), Szombathely (three) and Veszprém (two). There are daily buses to Frankfurt/Main. The local bus station is also here, from where services leave for villages of the Mecsek Hills.

The elegant twin-turreted **railway station** (*Indóház tér*) is around 1km south of the Belváros – follow Jókai utca (directly in front of you). Up to nine trains a day take the three-hour journey to Budapest Déli, and there are also direct connections to Dombóvár (16), Villány (nine), Szigetvár (eight), Barcs (eight), Mohács (five), Kaposvár (five), Nagykanizsa (three) and Keszthely (two). For Siklós and Harkány change at Villány, and for Szekszárd and Veszprém at Sárbogárd. One train a day links Pécs with Sarajevo – a journey that takes nine hours – while Osijek in Croatia can be reached via a two-hour express train. For Zagreb catch the train to Gyékényes and pick up the connection.

A **sightseeing tourist train** (*Janus Pannonius u.;* ✆ *06 704 5451;* ✇ *950/500Ft; opposite Csontváry Museum*) runs through the city, departing from opposite the Csontváry Museum. The commentary is in Hungarian so don't expect to learn a great deal. The ride takes 40 minutes and leaves roughly on the hour. **Taxis** line up in front of the Trinity Column in Széchenyi tér; try Volán (✆ *72 555555*).

INFORMATION AND OTHER PRACTICALITIES

$ **Banks** There are plenty of banks & ATMs, but note that in Pécs banks don't open at all at the weekend.

✇ **Corvina Bookshop** Széchenyi tér 8; ✆ 72 310427. A good selection of English-language books about Hungary by the country's main publisher.
⊕ *Mon–Fri 09.00–18.00, Sat 09.00–13.00.*

⌕ **Duna-Dráva National Park Directorate** Tettye tér 9; ✆ 72 517200; www.ddnp.hu. Information on the nearby national park (see page 393).

⌕ **Ibusz** Király u. 7; ✆ 72 212176. Sightseeing tours, currency exchange & private rooms.

⊕ *Mon–Thu 09.00–18.00, Fri 09.00–16.30, Sat 09.00–12.00.*

⌕ **Listings magazine** Pécsi Est

⌗ **Markets** The biggest market is on Vásártér (⊕ *Sun 06.00–14.00*) – just off Megyeri út 3km to the southwest – where everything is for sale (from antiques to cars!). It's open every Sunday, although at its best on the first Sunday of the month; you can catch bus 50 there from the railway station.

⌕ **Mecsek Tours** Kórház tér 1; ✆ 72 513370; www.mecsektours.hu. This office somewhat away from the centre provides information on tours in &

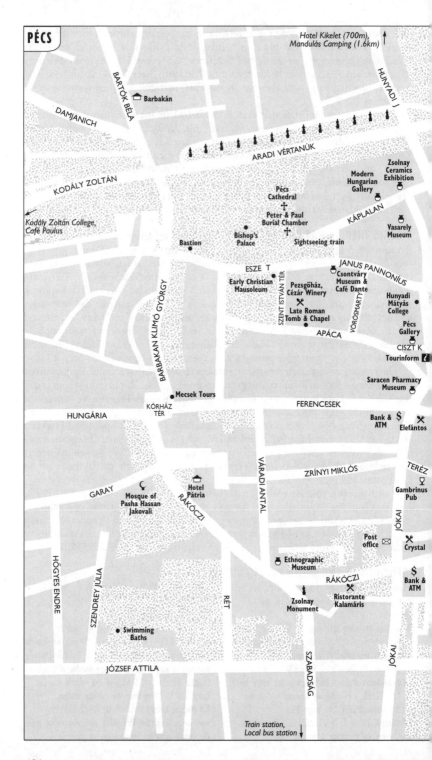

PÉCS

Hotel Kikelet (700m),
Mandulás Camping (1.6km)

Barbakán

BARTÓK BÉLA

DAMJANICH

HUNYADI J

ARADI VÉRTANÚK

KODÁLY ZOLTÁN

Kodály Zoltán College,
Café Paulus

Zsolnay
Ceramics
Exhibition

Modern
Hungarian
Gallery

KÁPLALAN

Pécs
Cathedral

Vasarely
Museum

Peter & Paul
Burial Chamber

Bishop's
Palace

Bastion

Sightseeing train

JANUS PANNONÍUS

ESZE T

SZENT ISTVÁN TÉR

Csontváry
Museum &
Café Dante

Early Christian
Mausoleum

Pezsgőház,
Cézár Winery

Hunyadi
Mátyás
College

BARBAKÁN KLIMÓ GYÖRGY

VÖRÖSMARTY

Late Roman
Tomb & Chapel

Pécs
Gallery

APÁCA

CISZT K

Tourinform

Saracen Pharmacy
Museum

Mecsek Tours

KÓRHÁZ
TÉR

FERENCESEK

HUNGÁRIA

Bank &
ATM

Elefántos

VÁRADI ANTAL

ZRÍNYI MIKLÓS

TERÉZ

GARAY

Mosque of
Pasha Hassan
Jakovali

Hotel
Pátria

RÁKÓCZI

Gambrinus
Pub

JÓKAI

HŐGYES ENDRE

SZENDREY JÚLIA

Post
office

Crystal

Ethnographic
Museum

Bank &
ATM

RÁKÓCZI

Zsolnay
Monument

Ristorante
Kalamáris

RÉT

Swimming
Baths

JÓZSEF ATTILA

SZABADSÁG

JÓKAI

Train station,
Local bus station

Villa Panzió (700m), Pintér Park (800m),
Valcsics Villa Panzió, Pécs Zoo (1.2km),
TV Lookout tower (2km), Duna-Drava
National Park Directorate (700m),
Renaissance Bishop's Summer Palace

Havihegy Chapel (200m),
Amusement park (2km)

✝ All Saints Church

ISTVÁN

Hotel Millennium 🏠

KÁLVÉRIA

ÁGOTA

DR MAJOROSSY IMRE

ALSÓ HAVI

PAPNÖVELDE

ARANYOSKÚT T R

HUNYADI J

Croatian Theatre 🎭

Főnix Hotel & Celláriun 🏠

🏺 Archaeological Museum

Bóbita Puppet Theatre 🎭

KIRÁLY

✝ Inner City Church

Mecsek 🍰 Cukrászda

Hotel Palatinus 🏠 ◫ IBUSZ

SZÉCHENYI TÉR

Webforrás ⓔ

KIRÁLY

🍴 Enoteka & Bistro Zona ●

National Philharmonic ticket office

✝ Lyceum Church

LICEUM

FELSŐMALOM

Market ●

Virág Cukrászda ●

● County Hall, Mecsek Tours, Cultural Centre, Murphy's Pub

National Theatre

PERCZEL

Ábrahám Kishotel 🏠

🏺 Town History museun

Corvina bookshop ●

Akvárium Terrárium ●

KOLLER

IRGALMASOK

✝ Church of the Order of Mercy

MUNKÁCSY MIHÁLY

Lenau Haus (cultural centre)

RÁKÓCZI

→ Zsolnay Factory

🍴 Aranykacsa

Synagogue ✡

TIMÁR

CITROM

◫ Lemon Café

RÁKÓCZI

BAJCSY ZS

Centrál 🏠

N
Bradt

ALSÓMALOM

BACSÓ BÉLA

NAGY LAJOS KIRÁLY

SOMOGYI BÉLA

BAJCSY ZS

Fruit & veg market ●

Inner city bus station 🚌

0 ▬▬▬▬ 150m
0 ▬▬▬▬ 150yds

Southern Transdanubia PÉCS

8

around Pécs, & can aid with booking private accommodation. ⏰ *Mon–Fri 08.30–16.30.*
✉ **Post office** Jókai Mór u. 10. This grand post office deserves a mention for its coloured majolica roof tiles.
📖 **Tourinform** Széchenyi tér 9; ✆ 72 213315; e baranya-m@tourinform.hu. Housed in the County Hall building. ⏰ *Jun 15–Aug 31 Mon–Fri*
08.00–18.00, Sat–Sun 10.00–20.00, Sep–Oct Mon–Fri 08.00–17.30, Sat–09.00–14.00, Nov–Apr Mon–Fri 08.00–16.00, May 1–Jun 14 Mon–Fri 08.00–17.30, Sat–Sun 09.00–14.00.
🖥 **Webforrás** Boltívköz 2. Small internet place tucked off Király u. *6Ft/min (min spend of 100Ft);* ⏰ *Mon–Fri 10.00–22.00, Sat 11.00–18.00, Sun 12.00–18.00.*

🏠 **WHERE TO STAY** There isn't a great deal of cheap accommodation in the centre – which is primarily limited to three- and four-star hotels. The majority of the pensions are located in the surrounding hills. Tourinform or Ibusz can help with college rooms in this university city, which are generally available in summer and cost from 1,500Ft per person. Two among many student residences are **Hunyadi Mátyás College** (*Széchenyi István tér 11*) and **Kodály Zoltán College** (*Kodály Zoltán u. 20;* ✆ *72 326968*).

🏠 **Ábrahám Kishotel** (5 rooms) Munkácsy Mihály u. 41; ✆ 72 510422. An excellent little find a short distance east of the hustle & bustle of the centre, this tastefully furnished boutique hotel has rooms superior to most others in its price bracket. *Sgl 8,100Ft, dbl 11,000Ft.*

🏠 **Bagolyvár Panzió** (19 rooms) Felsőhavi dűlő 6; ✆ 72 211333, www.bagolyvarpecs.hu. This spanking guesthouse is perched on Havi-hegy to the northeast of the centre, 100m up a steep track near Tettye tér. Its dbl rooms vary in price according to whether you choose one at the back – stupid – or at the front, with superb views down the hill. Bus 33 runs to the bottom of the track before doubling back to Tettye tér & down to the centre. *Dbl 8,000–16,000Ft, apt 18,000Ft.*

🏠 **Barbakán** (16 rooms) Bartók Béla u. 10; ✆ 72 517692; www.barbakanhotel.hu. Just north of the cathedral, this hotel has comfy rooms (although the décor is a little over the top). There's underground parking. *Sgl 9,600Ft, dbl 12,500Ft, trpl 15,300Ft.*

🏠 **Diána Hotel** (20 rooms) Tímár u. 4/A; ✆ 72 328594, www.hoteldiana.hu. This bright & fresh hotel stands just beyond the southeastern corner of Kossuth tér, next to the synagogue. If you can stretch to it, the plush apartment is worth the extra & has its own little kitchen. Excellent value. *Sgl 9,500Ft, dbl 13,000Ft, apt 20,000Ft.*

🏠 **Fönix Hotel** (14 rooms) Hunyadi út 2; ✆ 72 311682; www.fonixhotel.hu. Considering its location just north of Széchenyi tér, the prices are more than affordable – although it's basic. *Sgl 7,790Ft, dbl 13,00Ft, trpl 14,990Ft, apt (for 4–6) 19,900Ft.*

🏠 **Hotel Centrál** (17 rooms) Bajcsy-Zsilinszky u. 7; ✆ 72 525602; www.centralpanzio.hu. Unpromising entrance hides spacious, quiet rooms close to the

city centre. *Sgl 12,500Ft, dbl 16,500Ft, trpl 19,000Ft.*

🏠 **Hotel Kikelet** (33 rooms) Károlyi Mihály út 1; ✆ 72 512900; www.hotelkikelet.hu. Set in the hills to the north, the 3-floor Kikelet offers stunning vistas from some of its rooms & has 2 restaurants & wellness facilities. The rooms themselves (standard or superior) are on the sterile side. Stands up a very steep road south of the zoo (see page 416); buses 34, 35A & 35 stop close to hotel. *Sgl 20,500Ft, dbl 21,400Ft.*

🏠 **Hotel Millennium** (25 rooms) Kálvária u. 58; ✆ 72 512222; www.hotelmillennium.hu. Designed by an award-winning architect, this smart hotel is as clean as they come – positively rosy-cheeked with scrubbing. Ask for one of the 3 ground-floor rooms (nos 17, 18 or 19), which have their own patio doors leading on to similarly well-groomed grounds. A 10-min walk north from the centre, just outside the city walls. *Sgl 17,900Ft, dbl 19,900Ft.*

🏠 **Hotel Palatinus** (100 rooms) Király u. 5; ✆ 72 889-400; www.danubiusgroup.com/palatinus. The grandest hotel in town, with a sumptuous lobby & a position at the very heart of things. It's turn-of-the-century elegant, & Béla Bartók once played here, but it's on the pricey side. Standard & superior rooms are available. *Sgl 15,600–24,300Ft, dbl 17,600–27,000Ft.*

🏠 **Hotel Pátria** (116 rooms) Rákóczi út 3; ✆ 72 889500; www.danubiusgroup.com/patria. Unfortunate-looking from the outside, it's much better inside with comfortable & well-equipped rooms. Those on the 3rd floor are superior to (and more expensive than) than those below. *Sgl €45–76, dbl €53–86.*

🏠 **Lenau Haus** (5 rooms) Munkácsy Mihály u. 8; ✆ 72 332515. The German cultural house (see page 410) has some super rooms for a very reasonable price. All have refrigerators & good-sized bathrooms; Otto von Habsburg (the eldest son of Hungary's last king, now approaching 100 years old, & a vocal, Austrian-accented champion of the country) [???ELIZABETH] stayed in room 3. *Sgl 8,700Ft, dbl 12,000Ft.*

⌂ **Mandulás Camping** Ángyán János u. 2; ✆ 72 315981; e mandulas@mecsektours.hu. Situated up in the hills, near the zoo, the campsite has bungalows & hotel accommodation in addition to the tent pitches. Contact Mecsek Tours for information (see page 405). ⊕ *Apr 15–Oct 15.*

⌂ **Valcsics Villa Panzió** Tettye tér 2; ✆ 72 515506. Positioned near the ruins of the Renaissance bishop's summer palace (see page 415), with the rocky hills behind, the Villa's rooms are fabulous, & guests have the use of a shared kitchen. *Sgl 7,500Ft, dbl 9,700Ft, room for 4 13,500Ft.*

✖ WHERE TO EAT AND DRINK

✖ **Aranykacsa Restaurant** Teréz u. 4; ✆ 72 518860; www.aranykacsa.hu. South of Széchenyi tér, the 'Golden Duck' serves very good, stylish Hungarian & international cuisine & is often recommended by locals. *Mains avg 1,500Ft;* ⊕ *Tue–Thu 11.30–22.00, Fri–Sat 11.30–24.00, Sun 11.30–15.30 .*

✖ **Bistro Zona** Király u. 14; 72 525198; www.JTrestaurants.hu. Sitting beneath Enoteka Corso, the ground-floor Bistro Zona serves breakfast, set lunch menus, & fresh bistro courses. Fine terrace overlooking National Theatre. The food is fantastic – indeed, the best food we ate outside Budapest during a recent trip to Hungary. *Mains avg 2,000Ft;* ⊕ *08.00–24.00.*

✖ **Cellárium** Hunyadi út 2; ✆ 72 314453. Based in what was once apparently part of a Turkish catacomb complex, the Cellárium has an extensive choice of primarily Hungarian food (with a good game selection) & a pleasant ambience. It's a cut above, & that's reflected in the prices. *Mains avg 1,900Ft;* ⊕ *11.00–23.00 daily.*

♀ **Cézár Winery** Szent István tér 12; ✆ 72 224839. If you can handle your bubbles, the Cézár Winery (opposite the Pezsgőház) is Hungary's first 'champagne' factory. Its cellars date to the Turkish era, & extend over 2.5km. The company was founded in 1859, & it uses wine from Siklós to create 13 different types of sparkling wine. You can buy bottles from its shop & tours of the cellars (together with tastings) are available for groups by prior arrangement.

✖ **Crystal Restaurant & Coffee Shop** Citrom u. 18; ✆ 72 516720. This contemporary & sleek restaurant has a small courtyard nestling under the city walls & serves Italian food with some Hungarian dishes. Duck breast with morello cherry sauce & polenta was excellent, & nicely complemented by a fine rosé from Villány. *Mains avg 1,700Ft;* ⊕ *Mon–Sat 11.00–23.00, Sun 11.00–16.00.*

✖ **Elefántos** Jókai tér 6; ✆ 72 216055. Busy pizzeria serving grills, pastas, salads & some seafood dishes. *Mains avg 1,600Ft;* ⊕ *11.30–24.00 daily.*

✖ **Enoteka Corso** Király u. 14; 72 525198; www.JTrestaurants.hu. Elegant restaurant in trendy Király u., and recently voted best restaurant outside Budapest. Wonderful selection of wines; fine dining, with prices to match. 5-course degustation menu with matching wines 11,900Ft. *Mains avg 4,500Ft;* ⊕ *Mon–Fri 12.00–14.30 & 18.30–22.30, Sat 18,30–22.30.*

▯ **Lemon Café** Citrom u. 7; ✆ 72 532848. This swanky, youthful hangout hidden behind the fountain off Citrom u. has a range of light meals including crêpes, omelettes, pastas, sandwiches & salads. Otherwise it's cocktails & alcoholic milkshakes. *Mains avg 1,000Ft;* ⊕ *08.00–24.00 daily.*

▯ **Mecsek Cukrászda** Széchenyi tér 16; ✆ 72 315444. Squeezed between Maria u. & Király u., Mecsek vies with Virág for the gong for best *cukrászda* in Pécs. For us, the outdoor seating just swings it the Virág's way, but we've sampled many a pastry at each in reaching the decision. ⊕ *09.00–22.00 daily.*

✖ **Pezsgőház** Szent István tér 12; ✆ 72 522598; www.pezsgohazhu. Choose between the super-elegant cellar or the more relaxed, al-fresco terrace overlooking the square. The menu is international & upmarket – you can enjoy a glass of champagne with your caviar entrée, before tucking into a menu that bandies about options like foie gras, homemade pasta, pink duck breast & the like. There is also a range of healthy dishes – grilled meat with salad & yoghurt dressings. If you feel that food is a distraction from concentrated wine-tasting time, the Cézár Winery can help. *Mains avg 3,000Ft;* ⊕ *Mon–Sat 11.30–23.00.*

✖ **Ristorante Kalamáris** Rákóczi út 30; ✆ 72 312573. Plush country-style restaurant that aims at old-fashioned hospitality. Service is admirably unrushed compared with many restaurants in Hungary; the menu includes specialities of the Baranya region alongside some international flavours. Draws diners away from the very centre. *Mains avg 1,900Ft;* ⊕ *11.00–22.00 daily.*

✗ **Tettye Vendégő** Tettye tér 4; ☎ 72 532788; www.tettye.hu. Large restaurant with a gravelled outdoor eating area at the edge of the hills. Hungarian & German cuisine, along with a few pasta dishes. Live music most evenings from 19.00. *Mains avg 2,000Ft;* ⊕ *11.00–23.00 daily.*

⌑ **Virág Cukrászda** Széchenyi tér 7; ☎ 72 222223. Excellent cakes & ices, as well as cocktails, milkshakes & coffees. Opposite the town hall. ⊕ *Sun–Thu 10.00–23.00, Fri–Sat 10.00–24.00.*

NIGHTLIFE The high number of students means a proportionately healthy number of clubs and bars. Those that follow don't even tickle the iceberg's tip; check *Pécsi Est* for the full run-down.

♀ **Café Dante** Janus Pannonius u. 8–10; ☎ 72 210361. Relaxed, studenty café/bar/club on the ground floor of the Csontváry Museum. It also has internet access (*from 10Ft/min*). ⊕ *10.00–01.00 daily.*

♀ **Café Paulus** Ifjúság út 6; ☎ 72 503636. This bar with two-tiered decked terrace is another popular hangout, although it's 1.5km west of the centre on the main road running past the northern city walls. Buses 30 & M55 stop near by. *Mon–Fri 09.00–24.00, Sat–Sun 16.00–24.00.*

♀ **Gambrinus Pub** Teréz u. 17; ☎ 72 327350. Cheap booze & snacks; festooned with bamboo (the place,

not the snacks). ⊕ *Mon–Thu 08.30–23.00, Fri–Sat 08.30–24.00, Sun 10.00–23.00.*

☆ **Hard Rák Café** Ipari út 7. There's hard rock, obviously, but also other music from hip-hop to Hungarian 'classics'. Don't bother getting there earlier than 23.00. ⊕ *Thu–Sat 22.00–05.00.*

♀ **Murphy's Pub** Király u. 2; ☎ 72 325439. Attracts the English speakers & serves the worst Guinness we've ever tasted (we've seen a bigger head on a cup of tea). The interior makes a fair stab at a British pub; housed at the rear of the town hall building. ⊕ *10.00–24.00 daily.*

ENTERTAINMENT As a city of culture, Pécs holds its own with any city in Hungary, and has traditionally been one of the prime provincial centres of national drama. Its ballet and opera companies are well respected, as is its 92-member orchestra. The **National Theatre** (*Nemzeti Színház; Színház tér 1;* ☎ 72 811965; *www.pecsinemzetiszinhaz.hu*), set back from Király utca, is the place to head. Its box office (*Perczel u. 17;* ☎ 72 512675; e *szervezes@pnsz.hu;* ⊕ *Tue–Fri 10.00–19.00, Sat–Sun 1hr prior to performance*) also sells tickets for the smaller adjacent **Chamber Theatre** (*Kamaraszínház*). The website provides a programme listing for both – and it's in English. The **Pannon Philharmonic Orchestra** holds concerts at the university (*Szigeti u. 12*) and in the cathedral, as well as at the National Theatre; tickets and information are available from the **Philharmonic Ticket Office** (*Filharmónia; Király u. 18;* ☎ 72 437975; e *filharmonia@freemail.hu;* ⊕ *Mon–Thu 09.00–16.00, Fri 09.00–15.00*). The **cultural centre** (*Széchenyi tér 1;* ☎ 72 336622; e *pkk@mail.pserve.hu; www.pecsikult.hu;* ⊕ *Mon 08.00–16.00, Tue–Fri 09.00–17.00, Sat 10.00–14.00*), sandwiched between Mecsek Tours and McDonald's in the town hall building, should be able to assist with queries about other arts events. There is a **ticket kiosk** (*Sétatér;* ⊕ *Tue–Sun 15.00–20.00*) near Janus Pannonius utca that operates during festival periods.

The **Bóbita Puppet Theatre** (*Bábszínház; Mária u. 18;* ☎ 72 211791; e *bobita@bobita.hu; www.bobita.hu; box office* ⊕ *Tue–Fri 09.00–11.00, 13.00–15.00*) puts on plays of classic children's tales, as well as holding outdoor shows for adults. Performance times vary, although there is usually one at 10.00. The ruins of the **Renaissance bishop's summer palace** (*Tettye tér;* see page 415) form a wonderful backdrop for outdoor concerts, mainly held during festivals; you can get tickets from the kiosk listed above or from the **Croatian Theatre** (*Horvát Színház; Anna u. 17;* ☎ 72 210197; *www.horvatszinhaz.hu; ticket office* ⊕ *Mon–Fri 08.30–16.00*). Another venue for concerts and cultural events is the **Lenau Haus** (*Munkácsy Mihály u. 8;* ☎ 72 322515; *www.lenauhaus.hu;* ⊕ *08.00–15.00 in summer & 08.00–16.00 during other months*), an institute for German minorities. It hosts temporary art exhibitions by

German and Austrian artists in Hungary and ethnographic displays. Its garden contains the remains of a 13th-century Dominican monastery that was destroyed during the Turkish occupation. Also here is a statue of a German youth with staff and bag, a monument to the 230,000 ethnic German Hungarians who were felt to be 'guilty by association' and driven from the country after World War II. Otto von Habsburg (see page 409) used to be a regular visitor.

WHAT TO SEE AND DO

Széchenyi tér The city's nucleus is Széchenyi tér, divided between upper and lower sections and giving way to streets feeding from it in all directions. During the Middle Ages it was the market place and in the Turkish period was filled with Ottoman vendors manning bustling bazaars. The 18th century saw the oriental atmosphere seep away as the buildings were torn down and replaced with Baroque ones. The square became the public face of political life; here the 12 points were read during the revolution of 1848, and here the local revolutionaries were flogged when the uprising was quashed. The Eclectic and oversized **former town hall** (*Széchenyi tér 1*) stands at the southeastern corner, built in 1907 and now housing Murphy's Pub among other things.

To the west of it is **County Hall** (*Széchenyi tér 9*), constructed in 1898 with colourful roof tiles and reliefs from the Zsolnay factory (see box, page 413). The Zsolnay family lived at no 17, and the factory was also responsible for the glazed ox-headed gargoyles in front of the 18th-century **Church of the Order of Mercy** (*Széchenyi tér 5*); the fountain was modelled on an ancient drinking vessel unearthed at Nagyszentmiklós (now in the Schatzkammer in Vienna) and positioned on the spot of an earlier Turkish well.

As well as the **Trinity Column** of 1908 by György Kiss, the centre of the square holds the **statue of János Hunyadi** by Pál Pátzay; Pátzay was the 1956 winner of the competition to design a monument on the 500th anniversary of victory over the Turks at Nándorfehérvár. But the main sight of the square – indeed, one of the symbols of the town – is the **Inner City Church** (*⌨ adult 60Ft; ⊕ Apr 15–Oct 15 Mon–Sat 10.00–16.00, Sun 11.30–16.00, Oct 16–Apr 14 Mon–Sat 10.00–12.00, Sun 11.30–14.00*) rising at the northern end. We forgive you for a quick double take for it's an unlikely place of Roman Catholic worship. When originally built in 1579 by Pasha Gazi Kassim, the *djami* was the biggest mosque in Hungary. The pasha used money from the ransom of a prisoner to fund the project, tearing down the Gothic St Bertalan Church that occupied the spot and recycling its stones in the structure of the mosque. After the Turks had gone, Jesuits made changes, but 20th-century renovations stripped some of these back and uncovered a prayer niche facing Mecca, painted Turkish epigraphs from the Koran (to the left as you enter) and the base of a minaret that had been replaced with a tower. The organ was crafted by the famous Angster firm of Pécs. The mosque is one of the most significant pieces of remaining Turkish architecture in Hungary.

Király utca, Kossuth tér and around Király utca runs east from the bottom of Széchenyi tér, and is a tourist hub with its pizzerias, bars and cafés. The Baroque **Lyceum Church** (*Líceum templom; Király u. 44*) was built by the Pauline order in the mid 18th century, while its adjacent monastery now holds a school. The **Akvárium Terrárium** (*Munkácsy Mihály u. 31; ☎ 75 532151; ⌨ 890/690Ft; ⊕ Oct–Feb 09.00–17.00 daily*) sits on the second parallel road to the south; it has a varied collection of fish and reptiles (some of the larger of which look rather cramped), and a small aviary.

To the south of Széchenyi tér, the oblong Kossuth tér has a Romantic-style **synagogue** (*Kossuth tér 1–3; ☎ 72 315881; ⌨ adult 500Ft; ⊕ May–Sep Sun–Fri*

10.00–17.00) at its eastern side, raised in 1865 and containing the first organ ever made by the Angster factory. A book of remembrance commemorates the 4,000 Jews that were deported from Pécs to death camps in 1944. The bright, Eclectic building on the northern edge now houses offices of the town hall. Kids will love the risqué detail on a corner of the shopping parade at the square's western end, which includes some suggestively arranged pieces of sculpted fruit. Melons feature.

Apáca utca and Szent István tér The area to the west of Széchenyi tér held an early-Christian cemetery of the Roman town of Sopianae, and over 100 graves have been excavated; these were awarded UNESCO World Heritage Site status in 2000. The first lie on Apáca utca, and comprise a **late Roman tomb and chapel** (*Ókeresztény Sirkapolna; Apáca u. 8 and 14;* ☎ *72 312719*) from the 4th century AD. There are the graves of three adults and a child, complete with sepulchral statues, and the remains of a chapel used by Christians (who arrived during the 3rd and 4th centuries). Viewing is only possible on a guided tour; book in advance.

Szent István tér is divided from Dóm tér above it by Janus Pannonius utca. During festival times, this area of the city is a focal point, and Janus Pannonius utca is filled with stalls peddling food, drink and souvenirs. In 1975, during the demolition of an artificial waterfall, an **early Christian mausoleum** came to light. The outline of the walls of the single-naved 4th-century chapel are open to the elements in a sunken section of the square, while below them is a burial chamber containing a 3rd-century white marble sarcophagus. On the walls are some well-preserved painted biblical scenes, including Daniel in the lion's den and the original guilty pair in the Garden of Eden holding fig leaves over their bits. After the site was awarded World Heritage status, the **Cella Septichora Visitor Centre** (*joint ticket* ☞ *1,900/1,000Ft;* ☉ *Apr–Oct Tue–Sun 10.00–18.00, Nov–Mar Tue–Sun 10.00–16.00*) was created in Szent István tér; it connects several burial chambers underground (some of which were first opened to the public in 2007), and guided tours in English are available.

Dóm tér and around Dóm tér was originally surrounded by fortified castle walls, and the area of Szent István tér was kept clear to ensure that the guns had a free line of fire. The battlements were considerably stronger than the outer city walls, and they repelled attack by Miklós Zrínyi in 1664 and could have held out during the 1696 siege had the Turkish water supply not dried up. The four-towered Neo-Romanesque **Pécs Cathedral** (*Székésegyház;* ☎ *72 513030;* ☞ *800/500Ft for church, 1,100/600Ft for crypt, treasury, burial vaults & wine cellar;* ☉ *Apr–Oct 15 Mon–Fri 09.00–17.00, Sat 09.00–14.00, Sun 09.00–17.00, Oct 16–Mar Mon–Fri 10.00–16.00, Sat 10.00–14.00, Sun 13.00–17.00*) is of course the square's dominant force. Its earliest parts date to the 11th century, but it has endured several reconstructions, most recently in the 19th century when both Mihály Pollack and Friedrich von Schmidt had a stab (the latter tasked with restoring its appearance to that of the original church from the Árpád period). The late Pope John Paul II visited in 1991 and raised it to the rank of 'basilica minor'.

The interior is decorated with paintings by premier historicist artists Bertalan Székely and Károly Lotz, while the Corpus Christi Chapel – one of the side chapels that stand beneath each of the towers – holds a fine work of the Hungarian Renaissance, the red marble altar commissioned by Bishop Szatmáry in 1521. (Note too the wonderful bronze handle on the chapel doors, held tightly in the teeth of a mythical beast.) During the Turkish period, this chapel was used for Muslim worship, while all the others served as stables. Staircases either side of the apse lead to the vaulted crypt, which is the oldest part of the cathedral; evidence suggests that it probably incorporated an early-Christian burial chamber. The combined entrance ticket (see opposite) gets you a complimentary glass of wine in the nearby Püspöki Pince, as well as access to the nearby tomb sites and to the Bishop's Palace (⊕ *Wed only*).

Looking like a slab of Dairy Milk, the **Bishop's Palace** (*Püspöki Palota;* ✆ *72 513030;* ✆ *1,500/700Ft;* ⊕ *Jun 22–Sep 15 Thu only 14.00–17.30*) has stood at the western side of the square since King István first established Pécs's cathedral, although it has been rebuilt on several occasions. Bishop György Klimó instigated one such reconstruction in the 18th century, and unselfishly opened up his library in the western wing to the public. The benevolent Klimó was a favourite of Maria Theresa, and she presented him with the Gobelin tapestries on the staircase. The sculpture of the long-haired Liszt leaning on the southern balcony was added in 1983. Beside it is a gate leading around the 15th-century castle wall and bastion (supposedly built under the supervision of Pál Kinizsi), which links up with the extant northern section of the main city walls.

In front of the cathedral at the eastern side of the square is the **Peter and Paul Burial Chamber** (*Péter Pál Sírkamra*), which was discovered in 1782 and excavated by the historian József Koller. The surface chapel hasn't survived, but the crypt is decorated with Christian paintings including Jonah and the whale, the Fall, a rare early depiction of Christ and Mary, and the saints after whom the site is named. The richness of the decoration suggests that this was the resting place of an influential member of Sopianae. A small aperture in the northern wall probably originally held a martyr's bones. The **Wine Jug Burial Chamber** (*Korsós Sírkamra*) stands 20m away, where two sarcophagi were found during 20th-century explorations; a niche bears a painting of an amphora – probably symbolic of the Eucharist – while the side walls are adorned with floral motifs. Recent studies date the crypt to around ad395. (These chambers are part of the visitor centre, and can be accessed with the joint ticket; see opposite.)

Around 500m southwest of Dóm tér, the **Mosque of Pasha Hassan Jakovali** (*Rákóczi út 2;* ✆ *72 227166;* ✆ *500/250Ft;* ⊕ *Apr–Oct Thu–Tue 10.00–13.00, 14.00–18.00*) was built in the latter half of the 16th century, and is remarkable for being the only place in Hungary where both the minaret and the Muslim prayerhouse remain intact. It's easily missed, jammed up against larger modern buildings; inside is a display of Ottoman artefacts. A little further out are some **swimming baths** (*Pécsi Hullámfürdő; Szendrey Júlia u. 7;* ✆ *72 512955;*

ZSOLNAY CERAMICS

The Zsolnay ceramics dynasty began in 1853 when the merchant Imre Zsolnay established a stoneware factory, but it really took off under his brother Vilmos in 1865. An innovator and a perfectionist, Vilmos worked with a Budapest chemist to create 'eosin', an iridescent metallic glaze named after the Greek goddess of dawn that became a unique and instantly recognisable hallmark of some Zsolnay pieces – you can see it in the ox-head fountain in Széchenyi tér (see page 411). Perceptive and experimental, Vilmos put Zsolnay at the forefront of the Hungarian Art Nouveau movement; its vases and jugs decorated with folk motifs, together with tiles used to adorn the roofs and facades of turn-of-the-century buildings, meant that the name rapidly became renowned all over Europe. For a time, a third of the ceramics produced in the Austro-Hungarian empire came from the Pécs factory. Unfortunately, when his son Miklós inherited the business the quality started to fall away, and the company reached a new low under nationalisation when it was forced to make ceramic electrical insulators. While it resumed the production of luxury pieces in 1957, it never again scaled those Vilmos-inspired heights.

Southern Transdanubia PÉCS

8

≋ 800/700/450Ft; ☉ daily indoor pool 06.00–22.00, outdoor pool 09.00–19.00); the open-air pool has a wave machine.

Museums and galleries
Pécs is saturated with museums and collections, each a mark of the city's conscious effort to remain at the country's cultural and intellectual top table. There is even a dedicated street – Káptalan utca – along which the bulk are ranged. Most are run by the Baranya County Museum Authority, and you can buy a daily ticket (*≋ 2,000/1,000Ft*) that allows access to any of the museums under its umbrella. This ticket is on sale at all the participating museums; it excludes entry to sights like the cathedral, burial vaults, synagogue and mosque.

⛏ Archaeological Museum (*Régészeti Múzeum*) Széchenyi tér 12; ✆ 72 312719. Behind the Inner City Church, this museum displays finds from Baranya County dating from the Neolithic period up to the age of the Great Migration (when the Carpathian Basin was occupied by a series of nomadic tribes, including the 5th-century Huns, the 6th-century Avars & finally the Magyars, who pitched up in the 9th century). There are also artefacts from the Roman settlement of Sopianae, among them tombs & votive altars in the courtyard dating from the 2nd to the 4th centuries AD. *≋ 350/180Ft; ☉ Nov–Mar Tue–Sun 10.00–16.00; Apr–Oct Tue–Sat 10.00–18.00, Sun 10.00–16.00.*

⛏ Csontváry Museum Janus Pannonius u. 11; ✆ 72 310544. Originally a pharmacist, Tivadar Csontváry Kosztka (1853–1919; see also *Hungarian National Gallery*, page 158) developed into a quite extraordinary artist. Like all true geniuses – & Picasso declared him to be his only 20th-century equal, so who are we to argue? – there was a healthy dollop of madness in the man. He died insane, penniless & largely unrecognised, but not before producing a body of work that is as visionary as it is at times disturbing. Among masterpieces that took Hungarian landscapes for their theme is *The Storm on the Great Hortobágy* (1903), but he also tackled biblical & historical subjects in attempting to reconcile the various strands of his philosophical & spiritual make up. Perhaps the most ambitious example of this comes in *Baalbeck*, a massive canvas measuring 30m. Unmissable. *≋ 700/350Ft; ☉ Tue–Sun Apr–Oct 10.00–18.00, Nov–Mar 10.00–16.00.*

⛏ Ethnographic Museum (*Néprajzi Múzeum*) Rákóczi út 15; ✆ 72 315629. Here you'll find 18th- & 19th-century folk art, embroidery & costume of some of the ten ethnographic groups to be found in Baranya County. Follow Jókai u. south from Széchenyi tér, & turn right on to Rákóczi út. The museum stands near the Zsolnay Monument. *≋ 350/180Ft; ☉ Tue–Sun 11.00–15.00.*

⛏ Mining Museum (*Mecseki Bányászati Múzeum*) Káptalan u. 3; ✆ 72 324822. Underneath the Vasarely Museum (see opposite), this museum tells the tale of mining in the Mecsek Hills – an industry significant in Pécs's growth after coal was discovered in the mid 18th century. The 400m-long cellars are set up like a real mine shaft, & the drop in temperature at the bottom is startling (fortunately the friendly curator is on hand to loan a sweater to T-shirt-wearing tourists). Alongside the miners' tools, there's a mineral display. *≋ 400/200Ft; ☉ May–Oct Tue–Sat 10.00–18.00, Sun 10.00–16.00, Nov–Apr Tue–Sun 10.00–16.00.*

⛏ Modern Hungarian Gallery Káptalan u. 4 & Papnövelde u. 5; ✆ 72 324822. This is the largest collection of 20th-century Hungarian art outside Budapest's Hungarian National Gallery. Currently the museum is undergoing complete refurbishment & the collection will be re-hung (slated to open again in late summer 2010). It is divided in two. Gallery I (on Káptalan u.) will house the Martyn Ferenc Collection, & also works by Amerigo Tot, Slatko Prica & Endre Nemes. Ferenc Martyn (1899–1986) was a painter, sculptor, graphic artist & disciple of József Rippl Rónai. Martyn led the way in Hungarian non-figurative art after spending 15 years in Paris; among the exhibited pieces are illustrations he painted for a Hungarian translation of James Joyce's *Ulysses*. The main museum in Papnövelde utca will cover the years between 1890 & the present, including the leading lights of the Nagybánya (Hollósy & Ferenczy) & Szentendre (Vajda, Barcsay, Kmetty & Álmos) artists' colonies, & greats like Rippl-Rónai in between. This epoch spanned the emergence of modernist tendencies up to the radical political changes of the late 1940s, the emergence of Socialist-Realism & the development of art in the aftermath of Socialist-Realism. *Opening hours & prices still to be announced.*

⛏ Natural Sciences Exhibition Szabadság u. 2; ✆ 72 213419. To the south of the centre, in between the

Zsolnay Monument & the Zsolnay House, the Natural Science Department has displays of insects & other regional wildlife, & an exhibition of the natural heritage of 'Mediterranean Baranya'. *300/150Ft; Tue–Sat 10.00–15.00.

Pécs Gallery Széchenyi tér 11; 72 210436; www.pecsgallery.hu. Temporary exhibitions of modern art; the entrance is on Ciszterci köz, near the County Hall. *200/100Ft, free entry on Sun; Mon–Sat 10.00–18.00, Sun 12.00–18.00.

Saracen Pharmacy Museum (*Szerecsen Patika Múzeum*) Apáca u. 1; 72 315702. This working pharmacy has stood here since 1764, & bears a sculpture of a Moor by Gyula Zsolnay above the entrance. Behind County Hall. *Admission free; Mon–Fri 09.00–18.00, Sat 09.00–12.00.

Town History Museum (*Várostörténeti Múzeum*) Felsőmalom u. 9; 72 310165. Covers the period from the end of Turkish occupation up to the post-war political changes of 1948. The museum is inside an 18th-century tanner house (*tímárház*) just to the south of Király utca, leather-working being one of the prime occupations during the city's industrial boom. *300/150Ft; Tue–Sat 10.00–15.00.

Vasarely Museum Káptalan u. 3; 72 514045. Victor Vasarely (1908–97), the original 'Op Artist', was born in this house & since his death it's become something of a place of pilgrimage. Like the museum in Budapest (see page 160), here you'll find paintings that incorporate geometrical, kaleidoscopic designs to play with notions of space & depth – & not infrequently to make the viewer feel mildly queasy. In addition to 700 of his own works, you'll also see pieces by Victor's wife & son. *700/350Ft; Tue–Sun Nov–Mar 10.00–17.00, rest of yr 10.00–18.00.

Zsolnay Ceramics Exhibition (*Zsolnay kerámia kiállítás*) Káptalan u. 2; 72 512045. On the first floor of the city's oldest residential building – dating to the 14th century – is an exhibition devoted to the ceramics produced by the famous Zsolnay company (see box, page 413). The Pécs factory produced ornamental & everyday pieces, & the collection shows the evolution from handicraft to industrial technology through the 19th & 20th centuries. The work reached its zenith at the turn of the 20th century when architects developing a specifically Hungarian Art Nouveau style – known as Secessionist – employed Zsolnay reliefs & tiles in their designs. A memorial room contains personal items of the Zsolnay family, including some early paintings by Vilmos. You can press a button in each of the rooms to hear a commentary in English. A small room on the ground floor displays some of the works donated to the city by Amerigo Tot (1909–84), the Hungarian-born sculptor who lived in Italy from 1937. There's something deeply satisfying about his big-bottomed & thick-wristed figures. *1,000/500Ft; Apr–Oct Tue–Sun 10.00–18.00, Nov–Mar Tue–Sun 10.00–17.00.

Beyond the centre Unusually in Hungary, the medieval walls to the north of the city remain in good condition; in part this is because they were so ineffectual – too long to be successfully defended and too low to shield shots from attackers on the hillside – that invaders didn't inflict too much damage in breaching them. The suburb of Budaiváros lies to the northeast, where the Hungarians settled after being banished from the centre by the Turkish occupiers. They congregated around the 13th-century **All Saints' Church** (*Mindenszentek temploma; Tettye u. 14*), which was the only Christian church of the period and had to be shared – deeply reluctantly – by three different denominations. Ironically, after the Turks had gone the Hungarians returned to the centre and Bosnians (Christian converts from Islam who remained in Pécs) were displaced to Budaiváros.

Continue up Tettye utca (which runs north from Kálvária utca) to Tettye tér, a park that holds the ruins of the **Renaissance bishop's summer palace** (*Szathmány püspök reneszánsz nyaralójának romjai*); built as a relaxing bolt-hole by Bishop György Szathmáry in the early 16th century, it was used as a dervish monastery by the Turks. Today it forms the venue for outdoor concerts . **Pintér Park** (*Tettye tér 9*; 72 517223; *entrance 200Ft; May–Sep Mon–Thu 08.00–16.00, Fri 08.00–14.00, Sat–Sun & hols 10.00–18.00, other times Mon–Thu 08.00–16.00, Fri 08.00–14.00*), at the western side of the square, is a small arboretum managed by the Duna-Dráva National Park. The strictly protected Banat peony thrives here. Up the

road on Tettye téris the **Lime Tuff Cave** (₰ *600/400Ft;*
⊕ *May–Sep 10.00–19.00, Oct–Apr 10.00–18.00*). If you follow the rising road east
from Tettye tér, you'll come to **Havihegy Chapel** (*Havihegyi út*), a Baroque votive
church built in 1697 after a bout of plague. The stones to build it were carried up
the hill by hand. Phew! It's an hour's walk from the centre up to Tettye tér;
alternatively bus 33 runs up there every 20 minutes or so from the centre.

Heading further north, the foothills get steeper as they approach the Mecsek
Hills proper. To the northwest of Tettye tér, Fenyves sor leads to **Pécs Zoo** (*Fenyves
sor; office at Munkácsy Mihály u. 31;* ☏ *72 317005; www.zoo.hu/pecs;* ₰ *890/690Ft;*
⊕ *daily summer 09.00–18.00, winter 09.00–16.00*). It's had a troubled past – there
were shockwaves when it was alleged that rogue keepers had been allowing hunters
in after dark to shoot rare animals – but there's been extensive recent improvement
of the enclosures. Buses 34, 35 and 35A stop outside.

A narrow-gauge railway runs northeast from the zoo up to a fairly tame
amusement park (*Vidámpark; Dömörkapu;* ☏ *72 315985;* ₰ *400/150Ft, plus 450Ft
per amusement;* ⊕ *Mar 15–Aug 31 Tue–Sun 10.00–17.00*), while the left-hand road
from the lower station takes you up to the Misina peak and its **TV Lookout
Tower** (*Misina tető;* ☏ *72 336900;* ₰ *650/550Ft;* ⊕ *09.00–17.30 daily*). The tower
stands 200m above the 550m peak, and provides stunning views over the Mecsek
Hills and beyond the River Dráva; you can board a lift to the top. Bus 35A chugs
to a car park near the amusement park, while bus 35 goes to the tower. Several
walking trails kick off from here into the Mecsek (see below).

FESTIVALS AND EVENTS There is no shortage of festivals in Pécs. Among the main
ones are the three-week Promenade Festival in June and the Heritage Festival in
September (programme details on www.pecsikult.hu), the latter including
traditional music and dance by minority ethnic groups and featuring the Drinking
Song Festival. There is a festival information bureau in the town hall building
(*Széchenyi tér 1;* ☏ *72 336622;* ⊕ *Mon–Fri 09.00–17.00, Sat 10.00–14.00*), and don't
forget that a ticket kiosk (⊕ *Tue–Sun 15.00–20.00*) near Janus Pannonius utca
operates during festival periods.

For 2010, of course, there is a plethora of events to celebrate the city's status as
European Capital of Culture. The programme heats up from the summer onwards,
with an International Adult Puppet Festival in August, and the 'Mediterranean' at
the beginning of September (focusing on the architectural heritage of the city centre
as a backdrop to music, dance and theatre). A Balkan World Music Festival is
planned for November, while the Bauhaus Exhibition will be open until October
15 (when it transfers to Berlin). (A host of Bauhaus members hailed from Pécs, the
most prominent being Marcell Breuer, designer of the iconic armchair.) The
Zsolnay Factory will be home to an ongoing contemporary design exhibition and
young art and design workshop. For the latest updates, see www.pecs2010.hu.

EXCURSIONS Pécs is the ideal starting point for trips into the **Mecsek Hills**, which
border it to the north. Favourite destinations in the nearby foothills include Misina
Peak and Dömörkapu, each of which can be reached by local bus. Hiking trails
forging out into the hills can be picked up from there – for example from the base
of the TV Lookout Tower – but if you are planning to hike be sure to buy a map
(such as *A Mecsek,* 1: 40,000, by Cartographia). The highest peak is at Zengő
(682m) at the eastern end of the range. Another hill over 600m lies to the
northwest of Pécs; the plateau at the top of Jakab-hegy (602m) holds the remains
of a medieval Pauline monastery, and is surrounded by a 7th-century earthwork.
To the south, the Zsongor Rock (Zsongor-kő) is a great lookout point, and near it
are the so-called 'baby-shaped' rock formations (Babás szerkövek). The West-

Two Zrínyis have made their significant marks on Hungarian history; both were called Miklós and both were military generals, but one was also a poet and penned an epic tribute to the last days of his great-grandfather. 'The Peril of Sziget' ('Zrínyiász') is a must-read in the Hungarian literary canon, written in 1651 about the Battle of Szigetvár nearly a century before.

Since 1556, the rather insignificant-looking castle at Szigetvár had been cocking a snook at the Turks. In that year, Márk Horváth successfully defended the fort against attack and killed 10,000 of his foes in the process. A decade later, Suleiman the Magnificent determined to exact revenge and then march on to Vienna. He arrived in 1566 with an army of 90,000, and was unimpressed by what he referred to as 'a molehill'; arraigned within the molehill were just 2,500 Hungarian and Croatian soldiers under the command of Count Miklós Zrínyi, the Viceroy (Ban) of Croatia.

Rarely have odds been stacked so unfairly. Not only was Zrínyi vastly outnumbered, but the marshes around the castle had dried up during a particularly warm summer. Not far to the north, Habsburg Emperor Maximilian II waited with 80,000 troops to cut off the anticipated Turkish advance to Vienna; he refused to come to Zrínyi's aid, calculating that a few thousand Hungarian lives were worth sacrificing if they could delay the Turks awhile. The cause was a hopeless one, but for 33 days the fort held firm; Zrínyi rebutted Turkish attempts at bribery, and his men ignored messages attached to arrows entreating them to open the gates. Deeply frustrated, Suleiman mounted an all-out assault on August 29 – 40th anniversary of the Battle of Mohács – but wave after wave were cut down, the bodies piling up around the castle walls. As the survivors retreated, the furious sultan suffered a massive stroke.

To preserve what little morale remained, the Turkish leadership concocted an elaborate act to conceal the sultan's death from their soldiers. They propped his body up inside his tent so that from a distance it appeared that he was watching the battlefield. (The pretence continued even after victory in an attempt to stave off any potential power struggle before the arrival of Suleiman's son and heir, Selim II.) By now there were just 300 defenders still standing, and these made a pact to go down in one final glorious blaze. Zrínyi removed his armour, filled his pockets with gold coins to provide for his funeral, and charged with his men through the gates. All were slaughtered, and Zrínyi's severed head rushed to the sitting sultan as proof of victory. In a last bloody twist, a single surviving Hungarian detonated the fort's gunpowder store as the Turkish janissaries poured through the walls. In total, the battle claimed the lives of 25,000 Turks, as well as the 2,500 Hungarian and Croatian soldiers.

Mecsek Rural Tourism Association (*Cserkút, Alkotmány u. 10;* ☎ *72 731988*) can give information on accommodation and programmes in the locality.

Directly to the north of Jakab-hegy are two popular resorts. Orfű is 16km from Pécs and based around four artificial lakes, which offer watersports possibilities. There is a Mill Museum near the smallest of the lakes, Lake Orfű, and the Tekeresi Lovaspanzió (*Petőfi Sándor u. 3;* ☎ *72 498032; www.tekeresilovaspanzio.hu; 14 rooms; dbl 6,300Ft;* ☞ *riding 2,000Ft/hr*) arranges horse-riding (from yard riding to a six-day mounted tour into the surrounding hills). In Orfű village, next to the charming St Martin Church (part of the European Cultural Road of St Martin; see box, page 462), is the award-winning restaurant Muskátli (*Orfű, Széchenyi tér 13;* ☎ *72 498283; www.orfumuskatli; mains avg 2,000;* ☉ *Mar 21–Dec 31 daily 11.30–22.00*). It is festooned with geraniums in the summer; among its drinks is Magyarhertelendi draught, a beer from a small local brewery. The real draw, however, is the Kemencés Udvar behind the restaurant; this is an outdoor area with several bread ovens in which food is cooked on summer weekends (*16.00–22.00*). (The most famous example of bread-oven cookery is the Jewish Sholet – a dried-bean dish with smoked goose meat that was placed in ovens on Friday to be ready for Sabbath the next day.) A couple of kilometres to the west is Abaliget, where you can visit a 1,500m-long stalactite cave set into the side of Bodó-hegy, and where there is also a bat cave and museum (*Denevér Múzeum;* ↘ *72 498684;* ✆ *combined ticket 950/700Ft;* ⊕ *Tue–Sun Mar 15–Oct 15 09.00–18.00, Oct 16–Mar 14 10.00–15.00*). Both Abaliget and Orfű can be reached by bus from Pécs, and have pensions and campsites. For further details on hiking in the Mecsek, contact the Baranya County Naturalist Association in Pécs (*www.baranyatermeszetbarat.hu*). On route 66, 2km out of town, the Mecsextrem Park (*Árpádtető 1;* ↘ *72 244440; www.mecsextrem.hu;* ✆ *prices from 700Ft;* ⊕ *Sep–Nov Fri–Sun 10.00–18.00 – although next yr's opening hrs may change, so check website*) is an outdoor activity park featuring rope walkways through the trees, etc.

Head 25km north of Pécs on Road 6 and you'll reach the small village of **Mecseknádasd**, familiar to admirers of St Margaret of Scotland. She was born here in the 11th century and educated at the court of St Stephen in Esztergom. At the edge of the village is the simple Romanesque church associated with her life. The St Margaret pilgrimage tour in the surrounding hills starts here. Close by is Hetényi János' Cellar and Guesthouse (*Rékavölgyi út 17;* ↘ *20 2228481; www.indivinum.hu; 4,000Ft/pp, 4,700Ft with b/fast*); self catering is also possible. The apartments are well equipped and the surroundings restful.

Head west from Pécs for 33km on Road 6 and you'll reach **Szigetvár**, whose castle is a monument to a supreme historical moment of brave patriotism that was immortalised by the poet Miklós Zrínyi and that – though still in a lost cause – acted in small measure as a counterweight to Mohács. For 33 days of 1566, the great-grandfather of the poet resisted a Turkish force over 30 times the size of his own, before leading his men on a final charge to their deaths when it was clear the game was up (see box, page 416).

Originally constructed in the 14th century on an island among the marshes of the Almás Stream – hence the name 'Island Castle' – the four-towered fort was rebuilt by the Turks in the aftermath of the battle. The Zrínyi Miklós Castle Museum (*Vár u. 9;* ↘ *73 311442;* ✆ *600/500Ft;* ⊕ *Apr–Oct Tue–Sun 09.00–17.00*) has artefacts and documents relating to the battle, and there is also a mosque (*Szulejmán pasa dzsámija*), built by the Turks in the aftermath of victory, and a Baroque tower within the castle walls. On the way south along Vár utca you'll pass a café and Museum of Local History (*Vár u. 1*) before reaching Zrínyi tér, with its lion monument to the fallen heroes. Believe it or not, the St Rókus Roman Catholic church (*Zrínyi tér 9*) is another vestige of the Turkish era, built as the Pasha Ali Mosque in 1589; it was converted into a Baroque church in the 18th century. Near the bus station to the southeast is the country's only extant Turkish House (*Bástya u. 3*), which served as an inn during the Ottoman occupation.

A few kilometres to the north, on the way to Kaposvár, the Park of Turkish-Hungarian Friendship (*Török Magyar barátság parkja*) was funded in 1996 by the Turkish government as a token of wounds healed between the nations. A symbolic tomb marks the spot where Suleiman the Great's tent stood – from which his corpse surveyed the battlefield (see box, page 416) – while next to each other in front are massive busts of the Turkish ruler and Zrínyi. The one-time türbe at Turbékpuszta, to the east of here, is where Suleiman's remains were held before being returned later to his homeland; it is now a Roman Catholic church, but also a place of pilgrimage for Muslim Turks.

There is no Tourinform, but Tájolo Tourist (*Zrínyi tér 3;* ↘ *73 312654;* ⊕ *Mon–Fri 09.00–13.00, 13.30–16.00; Sat 09.00–12.00*) should be able to help. The bus and railway stations are 500m south of the centre; follow Rákóczi utca north to Zrínyi tér. A regular bus service operates to Pécs while there are also direct links to Kaposvár (four daily), Barcs (four) and Nagykanizsa (three), and one-daily buses to Hévíz, Mohács and Veszprém. Direct trains go to Barcs (nine), Pécs (seven) and Nagykanizsa (one); for Budapest, catch a connecting train at Szentlőrinc.

KAPOSVÁR

The capital of Somogy County has few hairs out of place. Nestled in the Kapos Valley, 50km to the south of Lake Balaton, Kaposvár is squeaky clean, due in part to the fact that it hasn't yet had time to get grubby. It prides itself on its flowers, which is no bad thing to be proud about. The majority of its buildings were constructed during the 20th century, and few medieval monuments survived the protracted skirmishes that took place here during the Turkish period. The castle that gave the settlement its name was one such victim of the violence, and there are but scant remains at the end of Vár utca. Kaposvár's modern contribution has been in the spheres of radical politics and art. In the aftermath of the 1867 Compromise, the citizens campaigned to elect the exiled Lajos Kossuth as their parliamentary representative, and there was strong support here for the shortlived communist Republic of Councils set up under Béla Kun in 1919. The painters József Rippl-Rónai (1861–1927), János Vaszary (1867–1939) and Aurél Bernáth (1895–1982) all had connections with the town. Beyond being left-leaning and art-loving, Kaposvár has several good museums and offers easy access both to hiking trails in the Zselic region to the south and the lovely Lake Deseda to the north.

GETTING THERE, AWAY AND AROUND The intercity bus station and adjacent local bus terminus (*Budai Nagy Antal u.*) are both a short walk away from the city centre. There are very regular connections with Pécs (hourly), Nagykanizsa and Siófok. Other buses to Lake Balaton include Fonyód (two), Tapolca (two), Balatonlelle (eight) and Balatonboglár (six), there are twice-daily services to Győr, Székesfehérvár and Veszprém, and thrice-daily buses to Szombathely and Szekszárd. A weekly Sunday service also operates to Frankfurt.

It's a quick five-minute trot to the centre from the **train station** (*Baross Gábor u.*) where connections can be make to Budapest Déli (two), Siófok (three), Balatonfenyves (two), Keszthely (two), Pécs (five) and Nagykanizsa (seven). There are regular services to Dombóvár and Fonyód, where trains to Székesfehérvár and Veszprém can be picked up. If you need a **taxi**, try Tele (✆ *82 555555*).

INFORMATION AND OTHER PRACTICALITIES

🛈 **Listings magazine** Kaposi Est

🛈 **Tourinform** Fő u. 8; ✆ 82 512921; e kaposvar@ tourinform.hu. Can help with private accommodation too. ⊕ Jun 15–Sep 15 Mon–Fri 09.00–18.00, Sat–Sun 09.00–17.00, Sun 09.00–14.00, Sep 16–Jun 14 Mon–Fri 09.00–17.00, Sat 09.00–14.00.

🔢 **Ibusz** Széchenyi tér 8; ✆ 82 512665; www.ibusz.hu. In the same building as the Dorottya Hotel; private accommodation & money exchange. ⊕ Mon–Fri 08.00–17.00, Sat 08.00–12.00.

⌂ WHERE TO STAY

⌂ **Borostyán Vendégház** (13 rooms) Rákóczi tér 3; ✆ 82 320735; www.hotelborostyan.hu. This Art-Nouveau hotel is less impressive inside than you might expect it to be, & the over-the-top rooms won't be to all tastes. Room prices depend on whether you are on the ground floor or levels above. Sgl 6,900–11,900Ft, dbl 10,900–14,900Ft, suite 18,900Ft.

⌂ **Csalogány Panzió** (12 rooms) Csalogány u. 70; ✆ 82 314773; www.csaloganypanzio.hu. Set in a wild garden, this pension has good-sized rooms that are basically furnished. It's 2km or so southeast of the centre (up Róma-hegy, in the vicinity of the Rippl-Rónai Memorial House), but the price is right; bus 15 from the local bus station runs to the southern

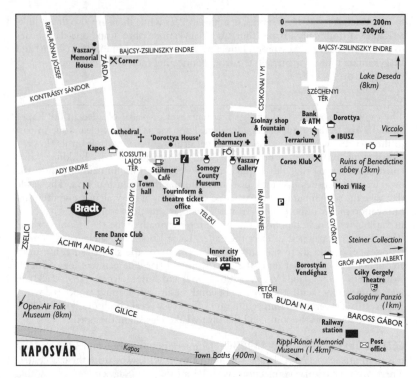

KAPOSVÁR

Map labels:
RIPPL-RÓNAI JÓZSEF · ZÁRDA · Vaszary Memorial House · Corner · BAJCSY-ZSILINSZKY ENDRE · CSOKONAI V M · BAJCSY-ZSILINSZKY ENDRE · Lake Deseda (8km) · KONTRÁSSY SÁNDOR · SZÉCHENYI TÉR · Cathedral · 'Dorottya House' · Zsolnay shop & fountain · Bank & ATM · Dorottya · Viccolo · Golden Lion pharmacy · Terrarium · IBUSZ · FŐ · Kapos · KOSSUTH LAJOS TÉR · ADY ENDRE · Stühmer Café · Somogy County Museum · FŐ · Vaszary Gallery · Corso Klub · Ruins of Benedictine abbey (3km) · N · Town hall · Tourinform & theatre ticket office · IRÁNYI DÁNIEL · DÓZSA GYÖRGY · Mozi Világ · Bradt · NOSZLOPY G · TELEKI · P · Steiner Collection · ZSELICI · Fene Dance Club · ÁCHIM ANDRÁS · Inner city bus station · Borostyán Vendéghaz · GRÓF APPONYI ALBERT · Csiky Gergely Theatre · Open-Air Folk Museum (8km) · GILICE · PETŐFI TÉR · BUDAI N A · Csalogány Panzió (1km) · Railway station · BAROSS GÁBOR · Kapos · Town Baths (400m) · Rippl-Rónai Memorial Museum (1.4km) · Post office

end of Csalogány u. Dbl 10,000Ft, apt (for 2) 14,000Ft.

🏠 **Hotel Dorottya** (26 rooms) Széchenyi tér 8; ☏ 82 315055; www.hoteldorottya.hu. There are 3 categories of room; the most expensive have the better views & furnishings, but the cheaper ones — some with wooden beams in the centre — are full of

character. Right at the heart of town; the prices are fair value. Sgl 5,600–9,800Ft, dbl 6,600–13,600Ft.

🏠 **Hotel Kapos** (80 rooms) Kossuth tér; ☏ 82 316022; www.kaposhotel.hu. The plain-looking rooms come in 4 sizes. There's a coffee house, & a restaurant (see below). Sgl 7,500–12,000Ft, dbl 10,200–16,200Ft, apt (for 4) 26,000Ft.

✗ WHERE TO EAT AND DRINK

✗ **Corner** Bajcsy-Zsilinszky u. 2; ☏ 82 526326; www.corneretterem.hu. Despite its location on a busy street corner, this restaurant has a good terrace & a spacious interior. The menu contains hungarian & international food made with local ingredients. Mains avg 2,000; ☉ Mon–Thu 10.00–23.00, Fri 10.00–24.00, Sat 11.00–24.00, Sun 11.00–23.00.

✗ **Corso Klub** Dózsa György u. 2; ☏ 82 416614. Don't be misled by the name for there's no nightclub here. Rather this is an excellent restaurant & bar, with an inventive menu of international & Hungarian food. The house speciality is 'Vecsési libalakoma', comprising most of a goose on a sauerkraut bed. Mains avg 2,000Ft; ☉ Mon–Thu 10.00–23.00, Fri 10.00–24.00, Sat 11.00–24.00, Sun 11.00–23.00.

✗ **Hotel Kapos Restaurant** See above. We've heard good things about the restaurant at the Hotel Kapos, & the terrace was full on a lovely summer Sunday. Mains avg 1,800Ft; ☉ 07.00–24.00 daily.

✗ **Mozi Világ** Dózsa György u. 3; ☏ 82 512863. This fun restaurant & 'Wild West saloon' in a former cinema serves hearty steak 'n' ribs & the like. The bar stays open late on Fri & Sat, & is a popular spot for letting hair down. Darts, table football, pool. Mains avg 1,600Ft; ☉ Mon–Thu 12.00–01.00, Fri–Sat 12.00–03.00, Sun 12.00–22.00.

☕ **Stühmer Café** Fő u. 4. On the site of the former chocolate factory, this elegant coffee house with original furnishings serves a good selection of coffees & teas, as well as lovely cakes & Italian ice-cream. It also has a whisky & cigar club. ☉ Mon–Sat 07.00–22.00, Sun 08.00–22.00.

ENTERTAINMENT AND NIGHTLIFE The **Csiky Gergely Theatre** (*Rákóczi tér 2;* ☎ *82 528458; www.csikygergelyszinhaz.hu*) is a striking Secessionist building opened in 1911, and had a reputation for provocative and anti-establishment plays during the communist period. Its ticket office is in the same building as the Tourinform. **Somogy County Cultural Centre** (*Somssich Pál u. 18;* ☎ *82 310282;* ⊕ *Mon–Thu 08.00–16.00, Fri 08.00–15.00*) can provide information on arts events, and puts on temporary exhibitions.

WHAT TO SEE AND DO Running east from Kossuth Lajos tér, Fő utca is the prime meeting, eating and drinking street, and few of the sights are far from it. Starting on Kossuth tér itself, the Neo-Romanesque **cathedral** (*Székesegyház; Kossuth tér*) – which attained cathedral status in 1993 when the town became an episcopal centre – was built in 1886 and contains 20th-century frescoes of the stations of the cross by György Leszkovsky. The renowned craftsman Miksa Róth made the stained glass windows of the Neo-Renaissance **town hall** (*Kossuth tér 1*), constructed in the early 1900s. A set of bells play music on the hour.

To the northwest of Kossuth tér on Zárda utca is the **Vaszary Memorial House** (*Zárda u. 9;* ☎ *82 414999;* ⊕ *Tue–Sun 10.00–16.00*), where you can see 30 works by artist János Vaszary in the place he was born in 1867. Passing the Dorottya House on Fő utca, the **Somogy County Museum/Rippl-Rónai Museum** (*Fő u. 10;* ☎ *82 314011; www.smmi.hu; individual exhibitions:* 🎟 *400/150Ft, combined ticket: 1,200/600Ft;* ⊕ *Apr–Oct Tue–Sun 10.00–16.00, Nov–Mar 10.00–16.00*) is in the Neoclassical former County Hall, and has five permanent exhibitions. Among these is an ethnographic display with items relating to the county's shepherds, peasants and even outlaws (*betyár*), a natural-history section, and the private collection of 20th-century art donated by Ödön Rippl-Rónai, the younger brother of the famous József. The latter was born above the nearby **Golden Lion Pharmacy** (*Arany Oroszlán patika; Fő u. 19*), which is itself next to the **Zsolnay Shop** (*Fő u. 21*), where you can admire the ram-head fountain outside and buy pieces of the porcelain inside.

The **Vaszary Gallery** (*Fő u. 12;* ☎ *82 314915;* 🎟 *free admission;* ⊕ *Mon–Fri 09.00–17.00, Sat 09.00–12.00*) showcases contemporary art, but also has a permanent collection of photographs by Juan Gyenes (1912–1995), who was born in Kaposvár but made his name in Spain as the court photographer; among the images are portraits of famous figures from the spheres of art and science. The same building contains a small reconstruction of **a turn-of-the-20th-century shop** (*Fő u. 12;* ☎ *82 311587;* 🎟 *free admission;* ⊕ *Mon–Sat 09.00–12.00 or by prior arrangement*). The **Terrarium** (*Fő u. 31;* ☎ *82 424460;* ⊕ *Mon–Fri 09.00–17.00, Sat 09.00–12.00, Sun 14.00–17.00*) is the country's only private collection of rare reptiles.

Take a right down Anna utca and second left on to Gróf Apponyi Albert utca for the **Steiner Collection** (*Albert u. 29;* ☎ *82 311327;* 🎟 *free admission;* ⊕ *Mon–Sun 10.00–18.00*), whose owner's obsession with cast iron began in 1989 when he installed an iron (rather than tile) stove in his workshop. He went on to gather a huge range of 19th-century objects crafted from the metal, including things you'd expect (wells, cookers, etc) and things you wouldn't (table clocks, chandeliers and pictures).

There are seven hills around Kaposvár, and you'll find the **Rippl-Rónai Memorial Museum** (*Róma-hegy;* ☎ *82 422144;* 🎟 *500/250Ft;* ⊕ *Apr–Oct Tue–Sun 10.00–18.00; Nov–Mar Tue–Sun 10.00–16.00*) up Róma-hegy, 2.5km southeast of the centre. The villa was bought by József Rippl-Rónai (1861–1927) in 1908 when he returned to his native town to spend his remaining years after living in Paris. Surrounded by his cattle, peacocks and bees, the painter was content here and abandoned his 'black period' for pieces full of sunlight whose vivid colours were initially lambasted by the art establishment. Rippl-Rónai had studied under Mihály

Munkácsy before breaking away to experiment with Art Nouveau and Post-Impressionism. He was Hungary's first and arguably best 'modern' artist, although he was a middle-aged man before his talents were properly acknowledged. As well as some of the artist's Biedermeier furnishings (which feature prominently in his paintings), the villa also contains 80 of his works. Good English commentary. Bus 15 stops 400m west of the entrance on Lonkahegyi utca; it's not easy to find by car – from route 67 follow the sign to Szenna after the railway overpass, go under the bridge and follow Zrínyi utca.

Other activities The **town baths** (*Csík Ferenc sétány;* ☎ *82 321044;* 💲 *680/3100Ft,* ☉ *Tue–Sun 09.00–18.00; aqua pools 2,100–1,450Ft,* ☉ *May–Sep*) sit behind the train station, and are the pride of Kaposvár. They include medicinal thermal baths, covered and outdoor swimming pools and other sports facilities.

There are horse-riding lessons and competitions at the **Pannon Horse School** of Kaposvár University (*Lovasakadémia; Guba Sándor u. 40;* ☎ *82 528313; www.lovasakamedia.hu;* 💲 *from 1,700Ft/hr*) to the northeast of the centre; Mező utca runs from the eastern end of Fő utca into Guba utca.

EXCURSIONS There are several points of interest within a few kilometres of Kaposvár. Following Pécsi út from the eastern end of Fő utca, after 4km you'll reach Várdomb and the **ruins of a Benedictine abbey** (*Várdomb 1;* ☉ *Tue–Sun Apr–Sep 10.00–18.00, Oct–Mar 10.00–14.00*) originally founded in 1061. As well as the 11th-century sections, there are the remains of later additions, including an octagonal chapel from the 14th century that is now used for open-air concerts (see Tourinform for programme). It's a steep climb up from the car park on Monostor utca; bus 7 runs along Pecsi út.

There are some lovely walks in the hills and villages of the **Zselic region** to the south of Kaposvár; buy a map (such as Cartographia's *Á Zselic,* 1:60,000) for the routes. In the peaceful village of Szenna, 8km southwest of Kaposvár, there is an Open-Air Folk Museum (*Szennai Szabadtéri Néprajzi Gyűtemény; Rákóczi u. 2;* ☎ *82 712223;* 💲 *500/250Ft;* ☉ *Tue–Sun Apr–Oct 10.00–18.00, Nov–Mar 10.00–16.00*) comprising five 19th-century peasant houses moved here from other villages of Somogy County and settled around Szenna's Calvinist church. The church itself has a coffered ceiling of 117 painted panels completed in 1787; this was within a decade of József II's edict permitting freedom of worship to non-Catholics, and you'll find that many Calvinist churches date from this period. Buses run from Kaposvár to a stop just outside the museum.

Lake Deseda, 8km to the north of the centre in the suburb of Toponár, was formed by the damming of a stream; lined with bullrushes and reed beds, it is a relaxing spot to fish, sunbathe or boat. Much of it is protected, but there is a strand at the southern end, a couple of places to hire kayaks further up the eastern bank, and hiking and cycling routes around it. Ask at the Tourinform in Kaposvár for the *Deseda-tó* booklet, which includes a simple but adequate map of the lake. You can take the train or buses 8 or 18 from Kaposvár to Toponár, just under a kilometre to the southeast; alternatively a bus runs all the way to the campite in summer (*Jun–Sep 1*). At the northern end, the Gombás and Deseda forests are on either side, and there is an arboretum on the lick of land dividing the two prongs of the lake's fork (accessed via a 100m-long footbridge). The hiking and cycling routes run up and in to these. By car, take Road 67 north from Kaposvár; after you've passed Kaposfüred, keep left towards Magyaregres for Gombás Forest and right towards Somogyaszaló for Deseda Forest. Bus 11 stops at Gombás Forest on its way to Magyaregres.

On the first Saturday in every month, the **Kassai Lovasíjászat** ('Riding Archers'; ☎ *82 477061; www.kassai-lovasijaszat.hu;* 💲 *adult 500Ft; begins 11.00*) re-

To the west of Kaposvár, on Road 61 towards Nagykanizsa, keep your head up as you pass through Nagybajom. Signs as you enter proudly declare this the 'European Village for White Storks', and you'll quickly see why. While many villages are fond of their solitary pair of resident storks, Nagybajom harbours around a dozen of the twiggy nests, built on circular platforms atop the telegraph poles (see box, page 8). As elsewhere in Hungary, the birds turn up in spring and leave as summer draws to a close, a reliable sign that winter is on its way.

enact aspects in the lives of the nomadic people of the great migrations (Huns, Avars, Magyars). Mr Kassai's speciality is archery from horseback, for which these people were famed. (The Avars are credited with introducing the stirrup that made this particular type of attack possible.) The display takes place on route 61 (by the Kaposmérő turn-off on a dirt road to Kaposdada).

South of Kaposvár (towards Szigetvár) is the 18-hole championship golf course of the **European Lakes Golf & Country Club** at Hencse (*50 rooms; Kossuth u. 3; ꔫ 82 481245; www.europeanlakes.com; dbl 17,500Ft, apt 32,500Ft*). The estate covers 120 hectares of mature park, and you can stay in the former hunting lodge or in bungalows. Golf is played here from April to November (*⚑ 11,000–18,000Ft/day*). It is recommended that you book in advance.

If you want to escape the madding crowds, you could do worse than visit the **Hertelendy Kastély** (*14 rooms, 5 apts; Kutas-Kozmapuszta; ꔫ 82 568400; www.hotel-hertelendy.hu; dbl €150–300*). This small country house, built in 1922 at the heart of Somogy's rolling countryside, has comfort to complement its peaceful location. Among the excellent facilities are a wellness centre, thermal lake, tennis, riding (9 horses) and an Olympic skeet shooting range. The chef also conjures top nosh using ingredients from their organic farm (*mains avg 6,000Ft; prior booking necessary*). While you're in this neighbourhood, the village of **Kisbajom** is worth searching out; there are some lovely thatched cottages to see beyond the Calvinist church.

FESTIVALS AND EVENTS Dorottya Day culminates in a ball on the first Saturday in February, and opens a series of cultural programmes known as Carnival Days. The Spring Festival includes theatre, music and art exhibitions for a fortnight in March.

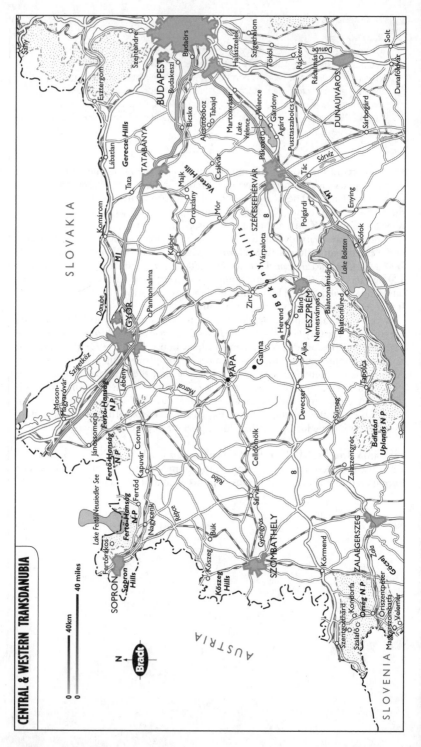

CENTRAL & WESTERN TRANSDANUBIA

N

Bradt

0 ——— 40km
0 ——— 40 miles

9

Central and Western Transdanubia

(For an introduction to Transdanubia as a whole, see page 385.)

Central Transdanubia

Central Transdanubia wraps around Lake Balaton (which is given a separate chapter) and fills the area east to the Danube and northeast to the border with Slovakia. It lacks the density of sights to be found in the southern and western portions of Transdanubia, but nevertheless has some diverse Hungarian highlights. Dunaújváros is the place to see the trappings of the 20th-century Socialist-Realist movement that have been done away with elsewhere, while by contrast Székesfehérvár (the 'first Magyar town') and Veszprém (the 'City of Queens') were important early royal centres. Veszprém is in the foothills of the Bakony, the traditional playground for romantic outlaws in bygone days. Lake Velence plays piggy in the middle with Lake Balaton and Budapest, and is a favoured bird-watching and angling spot. The factory at Herend is the source for the country's best-known porcelain, while F A Maulbertsch went to town in Sümeg's parish church, producing some gob-smacking frescoes that have been compared to those in the Sistine Chapel.

DUNAFÖLDVÁR

Dunaföldvár lies on the Danube between Paks and Dunaújváros. The 9,000 residents are proud of the bridge just outside the town; built in 1930, it used to be the only connection between Transdanubia and the Great Plain and earned the settlement the title of 'gateway to the *puszta*'. Dunaföldvár ('Danube earthen fortress') is more properly named after a 7–8th-century Avar fortification, although it also has a 16th-century stone castle that was erected to protect the town from the approaching Turks.

GETTING THERE AND AWAY Dunaföldvár is a 20-minute **drive** from Dunaújváros on the M6, following the seemingly endless oil pipe that runs beside the road. There are frequent **buses** (almost hourly) from Budapest Népliget and Dunaújváros – all those from the former also stop at the latter. The bus station (*Mészáros u. 2;* ℡ 75 343926) is close to the town centre, by the main junction leading to the Danube bridge. The **train** offers a less-regular service, with four daily trains to Dunaújváros, two to Pusztaszabolcs and three to Paks; the station (*Batthyány Lajos sor;* ℡ 75 343031) is about 2km south of the centre.

INFORMATION
🔲 **Tourinform** Várudvar; ℡ 75 341176. ⊕ *Tue–Sat 09.00–17.00*

WHERE TO STAY AND EAT Despite its size, Dunaföldvár offers a wide selection of places to stay; food, however, is harder to come by (the centre has only two proper restaurants).

✗ **Halászcsárda** Hősök tere 25; ☎ 75 541080. The best bites choice, a rustic restaurant serving good traditional food while barges float by on the Danube. It specialises in fish dishes of carp, catfish & pike perch. *Mains avg 1,750Ft;* ⊕ *daily 11.00–22.00.*

⌂ **Jurik Motel** (7 rooms) Váci u. 2; ☎ 06 30 997 7605. Although it's 1.6km from the town centre, this is one of the better places to stay, with a restaurant, tennis, & horse-riding possibilities. *Dbl 3,500Ft.*

⌂ **Kék Duna Camping** Hősök tere. Riverside camping, with some chalet accommodation. *Adult/child 650/350Ft, chalet rooms (for 1–6) 2,100–8,000Ft, tent 550Ft.*

▱ **Marcipán Cukrászda** Béke tér 3; ☎ 75 541055. Centrally located, & has the usual selection of Hungarian cakes, pastries, & sweets. ⊕ *daily 09.00–18.00.*

⌂ **Panoráma Üdülőfalu** (7 apts) Templom u. 78; ☎ 75 342748. Apartment houses (for up to 5) with kitchens, living rooms & a swimming pool. The main draw is the location, with its village atmosphere & panoramic views of the rooftops & church towers. *Apt 4,000Ft/pp.*

⌂ **Prajda Panzió** (3 rooms) Kossuth Lajos u. 22; ☎ 75 342182. One panzió in a cluster on Kossuth u. & Ilona u.. It has a pretty courtyard, & the rooms have kitchens & sleep up to 5 people. *Rooms from 2,500Ft/pp.*

✗ **Vár** Rátkai köz; ☎ 75 342405. Stands across from the Vár Museum, & is geared towards tourists. Its dishes – fried or stuffed with cheese – are as uninspiring as they are cheap. *Mains avg 1,100Ft;* ⊕ *daily Sun–Thu 11.00–21.00, Fri–Sat 11.00–22.00.*

WHAT TO SEE AND DO Dunaföldvár has five cemeteries and seven churches and chapels, but most of the sights of interest are found within the compact town centre and on Vár domb. Just west of Béke tér is the **town hall** (*Kossuth Lajos u. 2*), with its Art-Nouveau clock tower. A walk up Rákóczi utca will take you past the lovely late-Baroque **Franciscan church** (*Rákóczi u. 3*), built in 1786 and with ornately frescoed ceilings. Continue up Rákóczi utca and turn left on to Templom utca, which leads to another church and a statue of the Holy Trinity.

The **Vár Múzeum** (*Rátkai köz 2;* ☎ *75 541000;* 🎟 *300/160Ft;* ⊕ *Apr 15–Oct 15 Tue–Sun 10.00–17.00*) can be found through the wooden carved *várkapu* (fortress gateway), and offers pleasing views over the Danube; it has a small exhibition about the history of the area. The **Fafaragó Galéria** (☎ *75 541000; Tue–Sun 10.00–18.00*), opposite the museum, hosts temporary art exhibitions. Next to the gallery is **Fazekasműhely** (☎ *06 30 234 6596;* ⊕ *summer daily 09.00–18.00, closed Jan–Mar*), the pottery workshop of artist Zsuzsa Alberczki, where she makes and sells all of her creations. From Vár domb, there is a view of the Danube and the bridge to the northeast and Kálvária Hill to the southeast. The entire area of Fortress Hill, including the museum and an abandoned building, has been impressively renovated in the last few years from EU funds. Stroll Petőfi Sándor utca, Templom utca and the winding cobblestone streets that cross them (such as Ilona utca and Flórián utca) to look at the **traditional houses** and **old wine cellars** built into the ground.

DUNAÚJVÁROS

Dunaújváros, 70km south of Budapest, makes hay of Socialist-Realist monuments that residents of most other towns would consider eyesores. In fairness, they have scant choice since the entire town consists of big, blocky houses, mazes of tall apartments, busy streets – and massive Socialist-Realist-style statues. Originally called Sztálinváros (Stalin Town), it was raised in 1951 next to a snorting beast of an iron factory that was seen by the communist party as an integral component in its industrialisation plan of the 1950s. The Intercisa Museum celebrates the communist past – apparently without irony – and provides an interesting local history. Excavations have unearthed artefacts from the Roman age and the time of the original Magyar settlement. But Dunaújváros likes to advertise itself as Hungary's newest town, and the fall of communism has done little to alter the face of the place. The 60,000 residents also like to see themselves as athletic, and proclaim their town the 'sports capital of the nation'; the football club, Dunaferr SE, is one of the country's best.

It is easy to become disorientated in Dunaújváros since one row of building blocks looks much the same as another. Furthermore, there is no real town centre in the traditional sense; the area that comes closest to it is Városháza tér. You can be forgiven for feeling you've wandered on to a Soviet-era film set, and a couple of hours should suffice for all but those with a diehard fascination for Socialist-Realist architecture.

There is, though, a well-kept, wooded park that might persuade you to linger a while longer. It has several walking paths; a 2km trail 50m above the shoreline affords a wonderful view of the Danube as it flows around the lush Szalki sziget in its navel. Here too reside over 60 statues in a curious open-air Steel Statue Park on the upper bank of the river, most in the Socialist-Realist style.

GETTING THERE AND AWAY There are frequent local **buses** running between Dunaújváros and Dunaföldvár, and buses from Budapest leave from Népliget hourly. The bus station is a few blocks south of Városháza tér, and buses often also stop at the square. The **train** station is 2km west of the centre, down Dózsa György út; there are two daily trains to Budapest Déli, three to Dunaföldvár, nine to Pusztaszabolcs and three to Paks.

INFORMATION
🛈 **Tourinform** Vasmű út 10/A; ☎ 25 500148; e dunaujvaros@tourinform.hu. A 5-min walk from the bus station. ⊕ *Mon–Thu 08.00–16.00, Fri 8.00–15.00.*

WHERE TO STAY AND EAT New and sporty it might be, but its relative unpopularity with tourists is evident in the fact that Dunaújváros is distinctly short on hotels. Tourinform can provide numbers for private accommodation, but many of these rooms can be difficult to find and are quite a distance from the centre. The dearth of accommodation is matched by a dearth of quality restaurants, and an abundance of fast-food joints; for a large town, the eating scene is drab.

🍽 **Corner Café** Dózsa György tér 2; ☎ 25 413322. Serves mostly cold light meals & drinks. *Mains avg 600Ft;* ⊕ *daily 07.30–24.00.*
✗ **Diablo** Bartók Béla tér 5; ☎ 25 420450. Has pizza, pasta, average Hungarian food & a disco on Saturdays. *Mains avg 1,200Ft;* ⊕ *daily 10.00–24.00; disco Sat 21.00–03.00.*
🏠 **Dunaferr Hotel** (52 rooms) Építők útja 2; ☎ 25 500476. Pretty good, with a sauna, gym, games rooms & pleasant accommodation. Hungarian & Chinese are the unlikely partners on the restaurant menu, & there's a wine tavern. *Dbl 17,500Ft, apt 23,500Ft.*
🏠 **Dunaújvárosi Főiskola Kerpely Antal Kollégium** Dózsa György u. 33; ☎ 25 551123;

www.kac.duf.hu/kollegium. The local college also serves as a youth hostel, offering a variety of types of room – some of which even have internet access, televisions & kitchens – at several locations. *Rooms 2,000–3,000Ft/pp (Jul–Aug), 1,500–2,500Ft/pp (rest of yr), apt 10,000–15,000Ft.*
🍽 **Gourmand Kávéház** Korányi Sándor út 1; ☎ 25 410113. Close to the Tourinform, this is 1950s America as imagined in Dunaújváros. It is retro – but more fancy in feel than the usual Socialist-Realist take. Good selection of light meals & pancakes. *Mains avg 1,150Ft;* ⊕ *Mon–Thu 07.30–23.00, Fri 07.30–02.00, Sat 09.00–02.00, Sun 11.00–21.00.*

WHAT TO SEE AND DO Tourinform has a brochure listing 33 of the most important Socialist-Realist monuments and buildings, and outlining a sightseeing path to see them. The walk is hardly worth the effort since the buildings look largely the same, and the brochure doesn't explain their importance.

One block north of Tourinform, the **Intercisa Museum** (*Városháza tér 4;* ☎ *25 411315; www.dunaujvaros.hu/intercisa;* 🎟 *600/300Ft;* ⊕ *Tue–Sun 14.00–18.00*) has a giant left-over statue of Lenin leaning against a wall in the courtyard. The museum contains items dating from the Roman era (when this was an important border fortification) up to the Stalinist period, and is popular with student groups. Standing next to the Tourinform, the **Institute of Contemporary Art** (*Vasmű út 12;* ❧ *25 412220; www.ica-d.hu;* ☞ *admission free;* ☉ *Tue–Sun 12.00–18.00*) holds interesting occasional exhibitions of Hungarian and foreign artists. There's also a café with internet access.

Other The village of **Rácalmás**, 12km north of Dunaújváros, is a perfect illustration of what EU entry can achieve in a short period. A Korean tyre factory was established near by, and the village was thereby able to apply successfully for EU regional development funding to restore its Jankovich manor house as a conference facility. Its outbuildings host local exhibitions and the surrounding garden is well stocked. The brand-new **Jankovich Kúria & Étterem** (*25 rooms; Jankovics Miklós köz 1;* ❧ *25 507817; www.jankovichhotel.hu; sgl 20,000Ft, dbl 27,500Ft; mains 2,000–3,000Ft*) is high quality and – surprise, surprise – features Korean delicacies on its restaurant menu.

LAKE VELENCE

Lying halfway between Budapest and Lake Balaton, the 26km² Lake Velence is a pint-sized version of the latter, and the summer brings sunbathers, swimmers, anglers and stalls hawking *lángos, palacsinta*, cheap beer and wine. During winter, however, the area is empty of visitors beyond the odd ice skater and ice surfer. The shallow lake is both one of the warmest in Europe and one of the best for angling in Hungary; it is surrounded by small fishing villages, and the moored boats are indicative of the local fondness for casting a line or two. The western shore is a nature reserve where 28 protected bird species hatch, drawing twitchers during the migrating seasons in spring and autumn. On the northern shore rise the Velence Hills, with their thick forests, unique rock formations and hiking trails offering respite from the tourist masses at the strand. The northern shore is also less touristy and more residential than the southern. Lake Velence (meaning 'Venice' in Hungarian, and as big a misnomer as you'll come across) and its villages are probably best treated as an excursion point from Székesfehérvár/Budapest rather than a place to stay overnight.

GETTING THERE AND AWAY Lake Velence is readily reached from Budapest, especially by **train**, and is a popular day trip. The villages of Agárd, Gárdony and Velence are on the same railway line, about three or four minutes from each other; there are a couple of dozen daily trains from Budapest Déli, continuing on to Székesfehérvár. It takes an hour to Velence from Budapest. In addition, there are good connections to Balaton – Siófok (seven), Balatonszentgyörgy (one), Fonyód (one) and Balatonfüred (one) – and trains to Nagykanizsa (two), Nyíregyháza (one), Tapolca and Püspökladány.

Buses to the Velence area are less frequent, except from nearby Székesfehérvár. Buses in Agárd leave and drop off from in front of the restaurant Nádas; there are four direct daily buses from Agárd to Budapest Népliget, over a dozen buses connecting Székesfehérvár and Gárdony, and even more connecting Székesfehérvár and Agárd.

INFORMATION AND OTHER PRACTICALITIES

🖪 **Hungarian National Angling Association (MOHOSZ)** Agárd, Tópart u., Pf 16; ❧ 22 370339. Can help with fishing permits & point you towards the top spots for hooking carp. Daily fishing permits are available all around the lake, often from private houses (look out for signs reading '*horgász jegy*').

Tourinform Gárdony, Szabadság út 16; ☎ 22 570078; e gardony@tourinform.hu. ⏱ Jun–Aug Mon–Sat 08.00–18.00, Sun 08.00–14.00; Sep–May Mon–Fri 09.00–17.00.

Velencetours Gárdony, Szabadság út 16; ☎ 22 355099; www.velencetours.hu. This office can recommend & book accommodation.

WHERE TO STAY AND EAT There are plenty of accommodation options around Lake Velence, mostly in the two-star hotel category, and some sections of the lakeside seem like one big camping ground. If you prefer smaller pensions, there are tiny, family-run places, as well as the ubiquitous private rooms (*'Zimmer frei/szoba kiadó'* signs). During the swimming season, cheap food ain't hard to come by at the lake side.

✘ **Gémeskút** Sukoró (northern shore), Fehérvári út 25/A; ☎ 22 476079; www.gemeskut.on.hu. A lovely restaurant overlooking the lake on a promontory with a large terrace. It is popular for weddings, so check availability at weekends. It also has a comfortable guest house, with 11 rooms. *Rooms 2,800Ft/pp; mains avg 2,000Ft;* ⏱ *May 1–Sep 19 Tue–Sun 12.00–22.00, Sep 20–Apr 30 Fri–Sun 12.00–21.00.*

🏠 **Hotel Juventus-Helios** (43 rooms) Velence (eastern tip of lake), Kis köz 6; ☎ 22 589330; www.hoteljuventus.hu. One of the most modern hotels in the area. Rooms are neat & clean, & the sheets crisp. There are also tennis courts, a sauna, a private beach, volleyball courts, a gym, water-sports equipment & bike rental. *Sgl 19,500Ft, dbl 25,900Ft.*

✘ **Szunyogszigeti Halászcsárda** (northern shore) ☎ 22 732003; www.halasz-csarda.fw.hu. This simple place off the beaten track (between Pákozd & Sukoró) is famous for its fish soups & other fish dishes. Follow the signs for the Doni Emlékhely (a memorial chapel to the Second Hungarian Army that was annihilated at

the Don River on the Russian front in the winter of 1942–43), pass the obelisk commemorating the Battle of Pákozd (the first victory of the new Hungarian army of 1848 over the Austrians) & – just as you're close to giving up all hope – you will reach the centuries-old reed-roofed building. Alternatively, you can take the boat from Agárd or Velence (*hourly during the summer;* 🚢 *750/460Ft*). No credit cards. *Mains avg 1,700;* ⏱ *Easter–Oct 23 10.00–22.00 daily.*

🏠 **Velencepart Hotel** (45 rooms) Gárdony (southeastern shore), Pisztráng ('trout', to maintain the fishy theme) u. 19; ☎ 06 20 460 2134; www.ohb.hu/velencepart. There are barbecue pits & tennis & volleyball courts in the grounds, & the use of bicycles, boats & surfboards is free for guests. *Sgl €38, dbl €52, trpl €61.*

🏠 **Youth Hostel** (Ifjúsági Fogadó; 64 rooms) Velence, Tópart u. 51; ☎ 22 355075. On a private beach (complete with a big waterslide) next to the lake. All rooms are clean & comfortable quads. *Rooms 6,100Ft.*

WHAT TO SEE AND DO Lake Velence is, unsurprisingly, all about the water; there are few other diversions. If the lake's not warm enough, head 1km to the **Agárdi Thermal Baths** (*Agárd, Határ út;* ☎ 22 579008; 🚢 *adult 1,000Ft/2 hrs, 1,500Ft/day;* ⏱ *Mon–Sat 08.00–22.00, Sun 08.00–19.00*), where the water is 35°C and is said to relieve locomotor diseases. There are two open-air thermal pools and a kids' pool, a sauna, a solarium, massages and a lengthy list of treatments; it also has a campsite.

One third of Lake Velence is a nature conservation area, covered with reeds and cut through with narrow passages and hidden inner bays. The area is encompassed by the Duna-Ipoly National Park, and you must be accompanied by a guide to visit. The 168ha **Velence Bird Reserve** (*call Péter Kiss to book a tour;* ☎ 06 30 663 4630) has been protected since 1958; 30,000 birds migrate here in spring to nest in the reeds and marshes, among them several species of heron. You'll also find a rare marsh orchid variety, *Liparis lueselii*. The **Dinnyés Fertő Nature Conservation Area** (*call László Fenyvesi to book a tour;* ☎ 06 30 663 4630) is much smaller, and was created to provide a nesting base for protected birds driven from other locations on the lake by tourism; standing next to a canal near Dinnyés village (southwestern shore), it attracts egrets, red herons, spoonbills (the largest population in Transdanubia), common herons and grey-leg geese. During October and early November, in excess of 20,000 geese pass through.

If you've developed a taste for Hungarian *pálinka* (fruit brandy), you can visit the **Agárd Distillery** (*Steiner Tanya;* ✆ *30 690 6570 or 22 579164; www.agardi.hu;* ⊕ *Mon–Fri 09.00–17.00, Sat 09.00–16.30*). There is a guided tour of the distillery, and a phenomenal range of brandies to taste (✚ *400Ft per 2cl or 500Ft per 2cl of specialities*). Take the turning to Zichyújfalú from Road 7 in Agárd, and follow the signs.

The **Lake Velence School of Watersports & Leisure Centre** (*Agárd, Tópart u. 17;* ✆ *22 370052; www.vvsi.hu*) is the best place to go for windsurfing lessons, or to rent boats, jet skis and other equipment. The centre also provides accommodation. There are opportunities for **horse-riding** at Lake Velence; contact the Csikós-Tanya Lovarda (*Agárd, Határ u.;* ✆ *06 30 246 7006*) or the Gárdonyi Equestrian Club (*Gárdony, Géza fejedelem u.;* ✆ *22 356860*).

EXCURSIONS Lying between Lake Velence and Budapest on Road 7 (and as much an excursion option from Budapest), **Martonvásár** holds the 18th-century Neo-Gothic country mansion (*Brunszvik u. 2*) of the Brunswicks, the aristocratic family that owned the area after the Turkish occupation. It now contains an agricultural institute, but is remembered for its connection with Beethoven who stayed here several times while visiting Count Brunswick and his daughters. It is possible that he was in love with the second of these, Josephine, and that she was the inspiration for the *Appassionata sonata* (which he composed at the house and dedicated to the count). Copies of some of the letters Beethoven penned to the family are held in the Beethoven Memorial Hall (✆ *22 569500;* ✚ *500/250Ft;* ⊕ *Mar 15–Oct 31 Tue–Fri 10.00–12.00 & 14.00–16.00, Sat–Sun 10.00–12.00 & 14.00–18.00, Nov 1–Mar 14 Tue–Sun 14.00–16.00*). The elder sister Teréz founded the first nursery school in central Europe in 1828; the Nursery School Museum (✆ *22 569518;* ✚ *340/170Ft;* ⊕ *Nov 1–Mar 15 Tue–Fri 10.00–14.00, Sun 11.00–15.00, Mar 16–Oct 31 Tue–Fri 10.00–14.00, Sat–Sun 11.00–17.00*), in a wooden chalet near the mansion, includes a memorial to her. All Beethoven concerts are held on Saturdays in July at the artificial lake set in the mansion's grounds. **Trains** stop regularly at Martonvásár on their way between Budapest and Székesfehérvár; the station is 1km or so northwest of the mansion (follow Brunszvik út).

The **Pannónia Golf and Country Club** (*Alcsútdoboz;* ✆ *22 594200; www.pannonia-golf.hu;* ✚ *green fee 16,500Ft weekdays, 22,000Ft w/ends;* ⊕ *Mar–Dec 1 from 09.00 daily*) in Máriavölgy is 20km north of Lake Velence and, like Martonvásár, as much an excursion option from Budapest or Székesfehérvár. The 18-hole British-built course is beautifully situated on the former estate of Archduke József, palatine of Hungary at the beginning of the 19th century. The clubhouse is based in the palace's former orangerie, where members and guests can enjoy a good meal or snack from the short menu.

A magnificient 200-year-old London Plane avenue leads to the village of Alcsútdoboz itself, where the ruins of Palatine József's palace (it was badly damaged during World War II and only the façade remains) form the backdrop of the most beautiful **arboretum** (✆ *20 4248995; www.alcsutiarboretum.hu;* ✚ *500/300Ft;* ⊕ *daily 10.00 to dusk, except Christmas & Jan 1*) in Hungary. The archduke started the herbaceous collection in the English garden/park complete with ruins, lake and small bridge, and the planting is ongoing. A magnificent spot.

Nearby Tabajd is not only home to the Hungarian Polo Club (*Magyar Polóklub;* ✆ *70 3806100; www.magyarpoloclub.hu*) but also to the **Bélápapuszta Equestrian Center and Hotel** (*6 rooms;* ✆ *22 594388; www.belapa.hu;* ✚ *riding 2,800Ft/hr; lunches 900–1,300Ft except Mon, other meals by prior arrangement;* ⊕ *Mar–Nov & Jun–Aug sgl/dbl 10,000/15,000Ft, rest of yr sgl/dbl 8,000/11,000Ft*). The latter is set in lightly wooded countryside, and accessed along a dirt road. Run by two sisters who speak excellent English; it caters both for experienced riders and beginners.

Don't allow your passage through the functional concrete of Székesfehérvár's outskirts to cloud your judgement; the cobbled streets and squares of the Belváros survived the last German offensive of 1945 that flattened all around them. Indeed, the industrial suburbs belie not only the architecture at the centre, but Székesfehérvár's status as 'Magyar' Hungary's earliest town – it is said that Árpád set up shop here after the land taking. Prince Géza constructed a castle, given defensive strength by the surrounding swamps, and a Byzantine-style church in which he was later buried. King István established the town as his capital (hence the meaning of its name 'Seat of the White Castle', white being the royal colour) and built a magnificent basilica. For 500 years this was the place of coronations, burials and national assemblies; 37 kings and 39 queens were crowned, 15 laid to rest, and 46 Diets convened within its walls.

The castle had succeeded in repelling even Mongol attack, but it fell to the Turks in 1543; the occupiers ransacked the royal graves and appropriated town buildings as mosques. The basilica, used as a gunpowder store, was destroyed after being hit by lightning during a storm. Székesfehérvár was put back together in the 18th century, filled with Baroque town houses and Franciscan and Carmelite churches, and developed apace after the marshes were drained in the 19th century. World War II hit hard, wiping out a third of its buildings and killing almost 10,000 of its citizens.

GETTING THERE AND AWAY The town's **bus station** is a five-minute walk south of the centre and looks after both local and regional travel. Buses depart for Budapest and Veszprém every half-hour and there is a regular service to Lake Velence. Other buses go to Tatabánya (nine), Siófok and Keszthely (seven), Pécs and Hévíz (five), Esztergom, Sümeg and Kecskemét (three), Baja and Sopron (two). In summer months there are two Sunday services to Stuttgart via Munich.

From the **railway station** (*Béke tér*) it's a ten-minute walk to the centre. Head northwest along Kégi György utca and left into Rákóczi út. There are two or three trains an hour to Budapest Déli every day, and Balaton is also well served with regular departures to Balatonfüred, Tapolca and Siófok. Other destinations include Veszprém (17), Szombathely (seven), Zalaegerszeg (five), Miskolc (two) and Szolnok (one). For Tatabánya, Győr, Pécs and Szeged you'll need to head to Budapest and pick up a connection.

INFORMATION AND OTHER PRACTICALITIES

🏬 **Alba Plaza** Palotai út. Large shopping mall with a 10-screen cinema. ⊕ Mon–Fri 09.00–21.00, Sun 10.00–19.00.

📧 **Ibusz** Táncsics Mihály u. 5; ✆ 22 312580; www.ibusz.hu. Offers regional & country-wide tour programmes, as well as currency exchange & private-accommodation bookings. ⊕ Mon–Fri 08.00–16.00.

📧 **Listings magazine** Fehérvári Est

📧 **Tourinform** (Hiemer Ház) Városház tér; ✆ 22 537261; www.szekesfehervar@tourinform.hu. Extremely helpful bureau where you can get maps & arrange sightseeing tips. ⊕ Sep 1–Jun 15 Mon–Fri 09.00–17.00, Jun 16–Aug 31 Mon–Fri 09.00–20.00, Sat–Sun 09.00–18.00.

WHERE TO STAY

🏠 **Hotel Magyar Király** (34 rooms) Fő u. 10; ✆ 22 311262; www.ohb.hu/magyarkiraly. Built in 1816 as a town house, it was later given its Neoclassical look by architect Mihály Pollack & operated as a hotel from 1870. The rooms are old-fashioned & unspecial, but the location is good. Sgl €45, dbl €60.

🏠 **Novotel** (96 rooms) Ady Endre u. 19–21; ✆ 22 534300; www.novotel-szekesfehervar.hu. Conference hotel with the usual 4-star trimmings (fitness room, sauna, etc). Dbl €120.

🏠 **Szent Gellért Tanulmányi Ház** (41 rooms) Mátyás király körút 1; ✆ 22 510810; e szentgellert@ axelero.hu; www.hotels.hu/szentgellert. The St Gellért

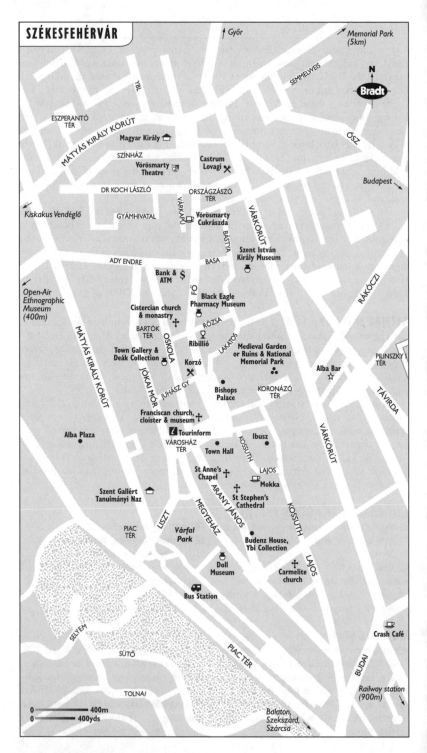

SZÉKESFEHÉRVÁR

Győr

Memorial Park (5km)

Bradt

N

SEMMELWEIS

ÓSZ

YBL

ESZPERANTÓ TÉR

MÁTYÁS KIRÁLY KÖRÚT

Magyar Király

SZÍNHÁZ

Vörösmarty Theatre

Castrum Lovagi

Budapest

DR KOCH LÁSZLÓ

ORSZÁGZÁSZLÓ TÉR

VÁRKÖRÚT

Kiskakus Vendéglő

GYÁMHIVATAL

VÁRKAPU

Vörösmarty Cukrászda

BÁSTYA

Szent István Király Museum

ADY ENDRE

BASA

Open-Air Ethnographic Museum (400m)

Bank & ATM

FŐ

Black Eagle Pharmacy Museum

RÁKÓCZI

Cistercian church & monastry

RÓZSA

BARTÓK TÉR

OSKOLA

Ribillió

Town Gallery & Deák Collection

LAKATÓS

Medieval Garden or Ruins & National Memorial Park

PILINSZKY TÉR

MÁTYÁS KIRÁLY KÖRÚT

JÓKAI MÓR

Korzó

Alba Bar

JUHÁSZ GY

Bishops Palace

KORONÁZÓ TÉR

TÁVIRDA

Franciscan church, cloister & museum

Tourinform

VÁROSHÁZ TÉR

Town Hall

Ibusz

KOSSUTH

VÁRKÖRÚT

Alba Plaza

St Anne's Chapel

LAJOS

Mokka

Szent Gallért Tanuimányi Naz

ARANY JÁNOS

St Stephen's Cathedral

KOSSUTH

PIAC TÉR

LISZT

Várfal Park

MEGYEHÁZ

Budenz House, Ybi Collection

Doll Museum

Carmelite church

LAJOS

Bus Station

SELYEM

Crash Café

BUDAI

SÜTŐ

PIAC TÉR

Railway station (900m)

TOLNAI

0 —————— 400m
0 —————— 400yds

Balaton, Szekszárd, Szárcsa

432

Study House is the best panzió, with modern rooms & a religious bent (it has its own chapel). There are rooms with or without bathrooms, & beds in dorm rooms. *Sgl 11,900Ft, dbl 14,700, dorms 3,900Ft/pp.*

☖ **Vadászkürt Panzió** (22 rooms) Berényi út 1; ☎ 22 507514; www.jagerhorn.hu. Slightly out from the centre – follow Szekfű György u. northeast into Berényi út – the Vadászkürt has uncluttered, whitewashed rooms with fridges. Buses 19, 26, 26A, 26G, 32 & 32G run here. *Dbl €38, apt (for 2) €50.*

✗ WHERE TO EAT AND DRINK

✗ **Castrum Lovagi Restaurant** Várkörút 3; ☎ 22 505720; www.castrumlovagietterem.hu. Medieval-cellar-style restaurant where meat feasts are served on wooden platters & you can eat with your fingers. Bring an appetite. Entrance on Országzászló tér. *Mains avg 2,500Ft;* ☉ *12.00–23.00 daily.*

✗ **Diófa Vendéglő** Kadocsa u. 32A; ☎ 22 300665; www.diofaetterem.hu. The Diófa has a mind-bogglingly extensive menu that includes Hungarian specialities & an eclectic mix of international dishes. It's a well-spaced & classy eatery with helpful staff, a pretty garden & good food at the upper end of the price range. Buses 24 & 25 from the centre stop 100m away. *Mains avg 2,300Ft;* ☉ *11.00–23.00 daily.*

✗ **Kiskakas Vendéglő** Kelemen Béla út 93; ☎ 22 340255. Twinned with the Diófa, the Kiskakas serves mainly Hungarian cuisine with a few international offerings. Casual but pleasant dining, with an atmospheric gallery eating area. *Mains avg 1,800Ft;* ☉ *11.00–22.00 daily.*

✗ **Korzó** Fő u. 1; ☎ 22 312674; www.korzosorozo.hu. A good pub & restaurant with a decked terrace overlooking Városház tér & the Bishop's Palace. Hungarian & German dishes. *Mains avg 2,200Ft;* ☉ *10.00–24.00 daily.*

🖵 **Mocca Kultúrkávézó** Kossuth u. 3; ☎ 22 500108; www.mokkakavezo,hu. Tucked behind the cathedral, this friendly café serves coffees, sandwiches, beers & *pálinka*. Jazz on Wed & Fri evenings. ☉ *Mon–Thu 08.30–21.00, Fri–Sat 10.00–22.00.*

✗ **Szárcsa Csárda** Szárcsa u. 1; ☎ 22 325700; www.szarcsa.hu. Although slightly out of the centre (on Road 63 to Sárbogárd), this restaurant is a local favourite. It is fairly formal in atmosphere; the imaginative menu features twists on Hungarian dishes. *Mains avg 2,200Ft;* ☉ *09.00–24.00 daily.*

🖵 **Vörösmarty Cukrászda** Fő u. 6. Popular café & cake shop. ☉ *Sun–Thu 09.00–21.00, Fri–Sat 09.00–24.00.*

ENTERTAINMENT AND NIGHTLIFE The Neoclassical **Vörösmarty Theatre** (*Fő u. 8; www.fehervar.hu/szinhaz*) sits just north of Országzászló tér, and hosts ballet and musicals as well as drama. It also has a smaller chamber theatre (*Kossuth u. 15*); for details and tickets to either, go to the **ticket office** (*Fő u. 3;* ☎ *22 327056;* e *jegyiroda@axelero.hu;* ☉ *Mon–Fri 08.00–17.30*). During summer, there is also a **kiosk** selling tickets to theatre and festival events on Kossuth Lajos utca, near the Carmelite church.

Alba Bár (*Rákóczi út 1;* ☎ *70 4554566; www.albabar.hu*) is a popular disco on the site of the former Hotel Alba Regia. **Ribillió** (*Rózsa u. 1;* ☉ *11.00–24.00 daily*) is a funky little joint over two levels, while **Crash Café** (☉ *Sun–Thu 10.00–24.00, Fri–Sat 10.00–02.00*) is generally full of young things catching up on the gossip and features DJs at weekends. The **West Side Music Club** (*Vörösmarty tér 1;* ☎ *06 30 936 6517*) is a small club south of the centre.

WHAT TO SEE AND DO

Városház tér and around The pretty main square holds the **town hall** (*Városház tér 1*) at its southern end, comprising two parts linked by a first-floor passage. That to the right is the older portion, built at the end of the 17th century, and with statues of Justice and Prudence at each corner of its balcony; its three-storey 18th-century counterpart was constructed as a palace for the Zichy family, whose coat of arms are visible above the gate on Kossuth utca. The square's naked equestrian statue is a monument to the 10th Hussar Regiment by Pál Pátzay, while the reddish stone orb supported by unconvincing lions is symbolic of the town's historic past and the franchise granted to it by King István. The memorial bell to the western side of the square fell from the Cistercian church during World War II.

Opposite the town hall is the **Franciscan church and cloister** (*Ferences templom & rendház; Városház tér 4*), built between 1720 and 1743, and believed to stand on the site of the medieval royal palace. Ferenc Megyessy's relief of a battle between Turks and Hungarians was added to one corner in 1938 on the 250th anniversary of liberation from Ottoman occupation. The former monastery contains the **Church Museum** (*Egyházmegye Múzeum;* ☎ 22 322247; 🎫 980/640Ft; ⊕ Apr–Oct Tue–Sat 10.00–18.00, Sun 14.00–18.00), with collections of religious art and a history of the diocese. Facing the monastery, the **Bishops' Palace** (*Püspöki Palota; Városház tér 10*) fills the wider part of the square and is a significant piece of Louis-XVI-style architecture. Built in 1801 from the ruins of the medieval basilica, its imposing central projection culminates in a tympanum bearing the episcopal coat of arms; the palace holds a significant library with early codices and incunabula.

The diminutive 15th-century **St Anna Chapel** (*Arany János u.;* ⊕ *Sun in summer*) – the town's only extant medieval building and a real gem by King Matyás's architects – is on Arany János utca, running south away from the town hall; its Gothic nave served as a prayer house during the Turkish period. Next to it stands the grand old lady that is **St István Cathedral** (*Géza Nagyfejedelem tér*). Remains of a quatrefoil chapel – thought to have been the burial place of Prince Géza (see page 431) – have been located in front of the entrance (the shape is marked with coloured paving). The cathedral was founded by King Béla IV in the 13th century, but it has undergone several reconstructions and bears no resemblance to its original Romanesque form. Parts of the royal coronation ceremonies were held inside. The statues above the entrance are of saints István, László and Imre, while the late-Baroque chancel and main altar were the work of Austrian court architect Franz Anton Hildebrandt in the 1770s.

The **Budenz House** (*Arany János u. 12*) was home to József Budenz, the founder of Hungarian comparative linguistics, who worked in the town as a teacher. Today it contains the **Ybl Collection** (☎ 22 317027; 🎫 400/200Ft; ⊕ Tue–Sun 10.00–16.00), a display of 20th-century art donated by art historian Ervin Ybl. There is also furniture belonging to the renowned Ybl family (including architect Miklós), who moved here from Austria in the early 1700s. A short distance to the east is the former **Carmelite church** (*Petőfi u.*), built in 1732 and restored after earthquake damage in 1800. It is a well-proportioned, elegant piece of Baroque architecture, complemented by Franz Anton Maulbertsch's interior frescoes – the painted crucifix in the oratory is particularly fine.

On the road running parallel to Arany János utca, the **Doll Museum** (*Megyeház u. 17;* ☎ 22 329504; 🎫 350/150Ft; ⊕ Tue–Sun 09.00–17.00) is tucked inside the old County Hall building, and holds dolls, toy furniture and miniature books (including a complete English bible) dating from the 18th, 19th and 20th centuries. The contemporary Hungarian art of the New Hungarian Gallery is also here. Head north up the same street for the **Town Gallery/Deák Collection** (*Oskola u. 10;* ☎ 22 329431; *www.deakgyujtemeny;* 🎫 500/350Ft; ⊕ Tue–Sun Apr–Oct 10.00–18.00, Nov–Mar 09.00–17.00) and a better collection of Magyar art by some major 19th- and 20th-century names.

Fő utca and around Fő utca runs north from Városház tér. Construction of the **Cistercian church and monastery** (*Ciszterci templom & rendház; Fő u. 6*) commenced in 1742; the former friary contains the **Szent István Király Museum** (☎ 22 315583; 🎫 350/150Ft; ⊕ Tue–Sun Apr 28–Oct 3 10.00–16.00, Mar 4–Apr 27 & Oct 4–Dec 21 10.00–14.00). The exhibition shows artefacts unearthed in Transdanubia from the Neolithic Age up to the period of Turkish occupation;

among them are linear pottery of 5000BC, finds relating to pre-Christian mystery religions, a significant collection of Roman stonework, fragments of the 11th-century royal castle and two pieces of what is believed to be the sarcophagus of King István (the main part of which is in the Garden of Ruins; see below). The museum has a second space at Országzászló tér 3, with temporary exhibitions.

The **Black Eagle Pharmacy Museum** (*Fekete SAS Patikamúzeum; Fő u. 5;* \ *22 315583;* ✆ *400/200Ft, free on Sun;* ⊕ *Tue–Sun 10.00–18.00*) contains Baroque furnishings carved by the Jesuits – who founded the church and monastery opposite before it was taken over by the Cistercians – in 1758. The pharmacy itself operated until 1971. Further north is a memorial to the Renaissance King Mátyás sculpted on the 500th anniversary of his death (he was buried in the basilica), and beyond that a statue of György Varkocs; Varkocs was a castellan who died defending Székesfehérvár from Sultan Suleiman II in 1543 after cowardly burghers closed the town gates on him.

Koronázó tér Behind the Bishops' Palace, to the east of Városház tér, are the **Medieval Garden of Ruins and National Memorial Park** (*Koronázó tér;* \ *22 315583;* ✆ *350/150Ft, free on Sun;* ⊕ *Apr 1–Oct 29 Tue–Sun 09.00–17.00*). This was the site of the original basilica established by King István – the national coronation church, home of the Holy Crown and royal insignia and one of the most significant buildings in medieval Hungary until it was destroyed during the Turkish period. You can see the excavated foundations (the majority of the stones were carted away for use in the Bishops' Palace), and a mausoleum decorated with paintings by Vilmos Aba Novák and containing what are thought to be the remains of King István's sarcophagus (although some argue it might actually be that of his son Imre) carved from an earlier Roman coffin. Part of the medieval city walls stands at the eastern side of the garden.

Beyond the centre On the northeastern outskirts of town, the extraordinary **Bory Castle** (*Bory Vár; Máriavölgyi u. 54;* \ *22 305570;* ✆ *500/250Ft;* ⊕ *Mar–Nov 09.00–17.00 daily*) was built up over decades by the sculptor and architect Jenő Bory (1879–1959). He blended architectural styles in creating this imaginative concrete edifice, taking inspiration from Gothic and Romanesque buildings and medieval Scottish hunting castles, and filled the whole with paintings (many of his wife, Ilona Komócsin) and statues. You can take buses 26A from the bus station or 32 from outside the railway station.

The western side of town – a district know today as Palotaváros – was settled by Serbs during and after the Turkish occupation. A Serb church of 1771 with a wonderful Rococo iconostasis survives, and an **Open-Air Ethnographic Museum** (*Rác u. 11;* \ *22 379078;* ✆ *350/150Ft;* ⊕ *Mar–Oct Wed–Sun 10.00–16.00*) has reconstructed rooms, examples of craft tools and other artefacts displayed in preserved peasant houses.

EXCURSION Around 10km south of Székesfehérvár, near the village of Tác, is the country's largest **Roman archaeological site** (*Gorsium Open-Air Museum;* ⊕ *daily Apr 28–Oct 31 08.00–18.00, Nov 1–Apr 27 10.00–16.00*). The settlement of Gorsium was mentioned in a late-3rd-century travel journal and spreads over 2km; originally a military camp defending the River Sárvíz, it developed into the religious centre and council seat of the Lower Pannonia province, and featured a sacred and administrative central quarter surrounded by residential areas. It was destroyed and rebuilt on several occasions, the last at the end of the 3rd century during the reign of Emperor Diocletian, when a grand palace and broad avenues were erected, and the town renamed Herculia. To the north of the ticket office is the sacred quarter of the 2nd and 3rd centuries, walls, towers and gates dating from AD300, and remains of the palace, Christian temples and an open-air theatre; to the south are houses and a 4th-century cemetery. Over a million items have been unearthed, and some of these are displayed in a former wine cellar built by the Zichy family (⊕ *Apr 28–Oct 31 Tue–Sun 10.00–18.00*). In spring (*Apr 28–May 3*), festival games are held to celebrate the ancient Floralia Feast, while there are theatre performances in summer (for details, see Tourinform in Székesfehérvár). You can catch **buses** from Székesfehérvár, which drop you in the village (the museum itself is a 15-minute walk from there).

VESZPRÉM

To the west of Székesfehérvár, the Bakony Hills blanket much of the Central Transdanubian region above Lake Balaton. Up until the mid 19th century, the forests in the hills were notoriously stuffed chock-full of outlaws, a breed that – according to the romantic canon – formed a parallel society governed by an alternative (and often preferable) creed; the similarities with Robin Hood and his men are obvious. The sympathetic contemporary portrayal of these people is perhaps in part due to the fact that many were servants who had fled cruelty under a feudal society (serfdom was not abolished until 1848). What is certainly true is that the Bakony landscape forms the backdrop for many of the country's ballads and legends.

Lying on five foothills 16km to the north of Balaton, Veszprém has a history to rival Székesfehérvár. During the rule of Prince Géza it was one of the country's earliest bishoprics; King István and his Bavarian Queen Gizella founded a cathedral and a castle here, and these subsequently became the places where queens were crowned and held court (leading to Veszprém's tag as the 'City of Queens'). It is said that the Hungarian coronation cloak (which is now on display in Budapest's National Museum; see page 165) was woven in a nearby nunnery, and that Gizella's own fair hand was involved – indeed it includes the only contemporary depiction of her in its design. Local literature frequently refers to the castle as though it remains a landmark, but in fact it was blown to smithereens by the Habsburgs. The town was also completely destroyed during the Turkish occupation and later independence struggles, and had to be rebuilt in the 18th century. The resulting Baroque historic district blends both with the broader avenues of the modern centre below it and the peaks and valleys of the surrounding Bakony countryside.

GETTING THERE AND AWAY It's a short walk westward along Csaplár János utca from the **bus station** (*Piac tér*) to Szabadság tér. There are up to four buses an hour to Balatonfüred and Herend, as well as twice-hourly connections to Budapest, Székesfehérvár and Tapolca. Other routes include Győr (11), Siófok (nine), Szekszárd and Nagykanizsa (four), Szombathely, Esztergom and Pécs (three). The **railway station** (*Jutasi út*) is 2½ km north of the castle area and has direct routes to Székesfehérvár (15), Sárvár and Szombathely (eight), Budapest Déli (seven) and Győr via Pannonhalma (five). Catch local buses 1, 2 or 4 to the centre.

INFORMATION AND OTHER PRACTICALITIES

🅱 **Ibusz** Rákóczi Ferenc u. 6; ☏ 88 565540. Currency exchange, travellers' cheques, car hire, tours & other programmes. They're also hot on village tourism. Situated just off Óváros tér. ⊕ *Mon–Fri 08.00–17.00, Sat 09.00–12.00.*

🅸 **Listings magazine** Veszprémi Est
🅸 **Tourinform** Vár u. 4; ☏ 88 404548; e tourinform@veszprem.hu. Helpful office that can arrange private rooms (*from 3,000Ft/pp*), & advise on rural tourism & accommodation in farm houses

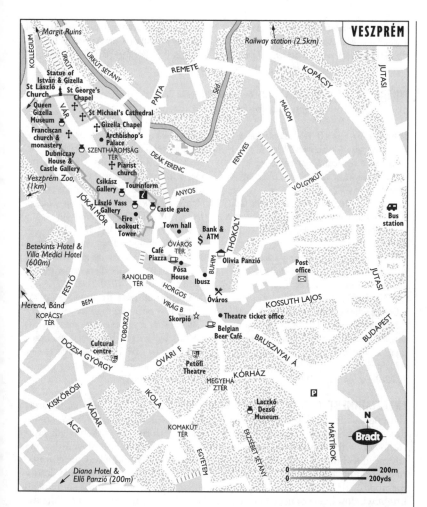

in surrounding villages. ⊕ May–Jun & Sep Mon–Fri
09.00–18.00, Sat–Sun 10.00–16.00, Jul–Aug

Mon–Fri 09.00–20.00, Sat–Sun 10.00–20.00; rest
of yr Mon–Fri 09.00–17.00, Sat 09.00–13.00.

WHERE TO STAY Veszprém has some excellent accommodation, but budget options
are thinner on the ground; contact Tourinform (see opposite) about private rooms
and for details of college rooms.

🏠 **Betekints Hotel** (38 rooms) Veszprémvölgyi u. 1;
📞 88 579280; www.betekints.hu. Stylish & upmarket
hotel with an adjacent wing of self-contained apts.
Outdoor swimming pool, sauna & fitness room. Located
in the Fejes Valley to the east of the centre, in the
shadow of the viaduct & a short distance from the
zoo. Sgl 21,700Ft, dbl 24,000Ft, apt (for 2) 29,300Ft.
🏠 **Diana Hotel** (10 rooms) József Attila u. 22; 📞 88
421061; www.panziodiana.hu. Run by a lovely family,
the Diana is more guesthouse than hotel; its rooms

are light & simply furnished. Lies to the south, on
the road towards Tapolca (take bus 4 from the
centre). Sgl 6,500Ft, dbl 8,500Ft, trpl 12,000Ft.
🏠 **Éllő Panzió** (18 rooms) József Attila u. 25; 📞 88
420097; www.ellopanzio.hu. Divided between two
houses, the Éllő offers large & clean rooms. Directly
opposite the Diana Hotel. Sgl 10,500Ft, dbl
12,000Ft, trpl 13,500Ft.
🏠 **Oliva Panzió** (11 rooms) Buhim u. 14–16; 📞 88
403875; www.oliva.hu. Delightful pension that

conjures a Mediterranean atmosphere & is superbly located. Sgl 17,860Ft, dbl 20,220Ft.

🏠 **Villa Medici** (26 rooms) Kittenberger Kálmán út 11; ✆ 88 590070; www.villamedici.hu. High-class

4-star hotel with sauna, solarium, English-style pub & indoor pool within a stone's throw of the Betekints Hotel (see page 437). Dbl 25,500Ft, apt 34,500Ft.

✗ **WHERE TO EAT AND DRINK** Classy places to rest your head are matched by classy places to fill your face; the top restaurants are attached to the hotels.

✗ **Betekints** See page 437. Polished restaurant & bar serving Hungarian & international dishes, & specialising in veal soup & pork medallions. Its reputation is good, & its prices high. Mains avg 2,400Ft; ⊕ 11.00–23.00.

🍴 **Café Piazza** Óváros tér 4; ✆ 88 406630. Coffee house at southwestern side of the square that offers light snacks, ice creams & cakes. ⊕ 08.30–22.00 daily.

♀ **Diana** See page 437. Good-value peasant-style restaurant serving Hungarian & international food, with game specialities. Mains avg 1,600Ft; ⊕ 07.00–23.00 daily.

♀ **Giselle Belgian Beer Café** Szabadság tér 1; ✆ 88 758058. One link in an international bar chain with an extensive selection of beers, a meat-heavy menu (steaks & grills), & a large courtyard. Mains avg 1,700Ft; ⊕ Mon–Fri 10.00–24.00, Sat 10.00–02.00, Sun 11.00–21.00.

✗ **Oliva** See page 437. You won't find a better place to eat in town. The seasonal menu features an eclectic choice of global flavours – & the olive-green walls & terraced garden make for an ambient setting. In summer, there's live jazz at the weekends. Mains avg 2,200Ft; ⊕ Mon–Wed 11.00–22.00, Thu–Sat 11.00–23.00, Sun 11.00–21.00.

✗ **Óváros** Szabadság tér 14; ✆ 88 326790. Traditional Hungarian food, with Transylvanian stuffed duck among the specialities. The three-tiered paved al-fresco eating area is the choice spot in summer. Mains avg 1,500Ft; ⊕ 10.00–22.00 daily.

✗ **Villa Medici** See above. The hotel has a pair of restaurants – one serving Hungarian (mains avg 2,400Ft) & the other international (mains avg 3,800Ft). Both are good but expensive, the latter – named after the hotel & voted one of the best 10 restaurants in Hungary – especially so. ⊕ 12.00–23.00 daily.

ENTERTAINMENT AND NIGHTLIFE Looking like a cross between a castle and a synagogue, the Art-Nouveau **Petőfi Theatre** (Óvári Ferenc u. 2; ✆ 88 424064) deserves a look at even if you're not taking in a performance. István Medgyaszay (follower of the renowned Viennese architect Otto Wagner) employed the most advanced technology available when designing it in 1908, and it was the country's first building constructed from reinforced concrete. Sándor Nagy, a leading member of the Gödöllő Pre-Raphaelite school, was responsible for some of the bright windows; one of his works depicts the Hungarian mythical story of the deer hunters Hunor and Magor. You can buy tickets or get information about what's on inside from the **ticket office** (Szabadság tér 7; ✆ 88 422440; e szervezes@ petofiszinhaz.hu; www.petofiszinhaz.hu ⊕ Mon–Fri 09.00–17.00). In July and August, many of the younger party-going locals head for the nearby Lake Balaton, and some of the clubs and bars close. As well as the **Belgian Beer Café** (see above), you could try the **Patrióta Bar** (⊕ from 18.00 daily) and, in the same building, **Skorpió Nightclub & Bar** (Virág Benedek u. 1; ⊕ Mon–Thu 10.00–02.00, Fri–Sat 10.00–04.00, Sun 10.00–01.00), an Irish theme bar with little Irish of note. It has ground- and basement-level areas, and hosts live jazz at weekends; there is an erotic club (⊕ Tue–Sat 22.00–05.00) at the top.

WHAT TO SEE AND DO
The Castle District The gateway to the historic centre on Castle Hill (Várhegy) is **Óváros tér**, a cobbled square with a landscaped feel to it and some handsome architecture. The Louis-XVI-style **Pósa House** (no 3) – with two chubby putti below the roof – is named after the printer Endre Pósa who once lived there; it was originally built in 1793 by the Cistercian order. The Neo-Romanesque

town hall (*no 9*), with shell motifs above its first-floor windows, was raised in 1857 as the church treasury, and has operated as municipal offices since 1990. To the right is the statue most favoured by locals; the bronze *Maid with Jar* by Lenke Kiss – pouring from a seemingly bottomless vase – is known affectionately as 'Zsuzsi' (Susy).

Behind the square's western side you'll see the **Fire Lookout Tower** (*Tűztorony; Vár u. 9; ✆ 300/200Ft; ☉ Mar–Oct 10.00–18.00 daily*), erected on the foundations of a watchtower that stood here during the reign of Béla IV. Every hour the clock plays the 'Csermák Verbunkos', a traditional recruiting song, and visitors can climb up to a gallery running around its outside. To get to it – it's reached via an arch at Vár utca 17 – you'll need to pass through **Castle (or Heroes') Gate** (Várkapu or Hősök kapuja). Once through the gate you join Vár utca, the spine of the Castle District. Several exhibitions of modern art fall beneath the umbrella of the **House of Arts** (*Művészetek Háza; Vár u. 17; ✆ 88 425204; www.arthouse.hu; ☉ Nov–Apr Tue–Sun 10.00–17.00, May–Oct 10.00–18.00 daily*). These include the Cellar Gallery (*Pince Galéria*), the Vass Collection (non-figurative Hungarian works of the last four decades collected by shoemaker László Vass), and the Csikász Gallery – all accessed through the arch at number 17 or the steps at numbers 3–7. The Castle Gallery (*Vár Galéria; Vár u. 29*) in the Dubniczay House, a Baroque palace further up the road, has a display of tiles and bricks dating from Roman times to the present in addition to a well-displayed collection of 20th-century Hungarian painting. Entrance to each costs 250–500Ft per adult; alternatively you can purchase a combined ticket that also covers the Fire Lookout Tower.

Today's courthouse was once the Louis-XVI-style **County Hall** (*Vár u. 19*); it stands opposite the Baroque former **Piarist school** (*Vár u. 10*) of 1778, whose pupils included the poet and monk Pál Ányos and the writer Viktor Cholnoky. The Neoclassical **Piarist church** (*Piarista templom; Vár u. 12–14; ☉ Tue–Sun 10.00–17.00*) was completed in 1833 and is currently an exhibition space, and its monastery (designed by Jakab Fellner, who was also responsible for the Bishop's Palace) is now a retirement home for priests. Across the road from the church (outside Vár utca 27) is a light-pink **altar stone**, a copy of an original (held in the county museum) that is the country's earliest piece of carved Renaissance stonework. It was made as a tribute to Albert Vetési in 1467, and is inscribed with the words 'Do good for God's sake'; Vetési was the Bishop of Veszprém, a diplomat for King Mátyás and a beneficent patron of the arts.

On the left, at the point where the street widens, is the **Dubniczay House** (*Vár u. 29*), built in 1751 and incorporating part of the castle wall; inside is the Castle Gallery (see above). When the imposing **Archbishop's Palace** (*Érseki Palota; Vár u. 16; ✆ 88 426088; ✆ 500/250Ft; ☉ Tue–Sun May–Aug 10.00–18.00, with free guide every hr, Sep 1–Oct 20 10.00–17.00, no guide available*) was under construction in the 1760s, the remains of a 13th-century Gothic chapel were uncovered. The so-called **Gizella Chapel** (*Vár u. 18; ✆ 88 426088; ✆ 200/100Ft; ☉ alternate weeks Tue–Sun 10.00–17.00,*) has a rib-vaulted ceiling and faded Byzantine frescoes of the apostles. The area in front of the palace is used for summer concerts. The **Trinity Monument** (*Szentháromság szobor*) was commissioned in 1750 by Bishop Márton Padányi Bíró, whose family crest it bears. The adjacent well reaches a depth of 40m.

The twin-towered, Neo-Romanesque **St Mihály Cathedral** (*Vár u. 18–20; ☉ Mon–Sat 10.00–17.00*) was founded in 1001 and decorated by Queen Gizella with vestments and chalices – her relics were moved here in 1996. The church underwent several reconstructions in subsequent centuries (most recently in the 20th), and only the crypt survives from the early days; Bishop Padányi Bíró's tomb is among those inside. Organ concerts are held in the cathedral. Opposite the entrance is the **Queen Gizella Museum** (*Vár u. 35;* ☏ *88 426088;* ✆ *400/200Ft;* ⊕ *daily May–Oct Mon–Sat 10.00–17.00,*) in the Tejfalussy House built in the 1770s. The religious pieces from the counties of Veszprém, Somogy and Zala include a replica of the coronation robe made in 1867 and a gold-threaded chasuble of 1480 that first belonged to Bishop Vetési. Just to the south of the museum, the **Franciscan church and monastery** (*Vár u. 33*) were built in the 18th century; Pál Ányos was buried in the church's crypt.

Next to the cathedral are the remains of **St György Chapel** (*Vár u. 20;* ✆ *100/70Ft;* ⊕ *Tue–Sun May–Aug 10.00–18.00, Sep 1–Oct 20 10.00–17.00*), probably built as a royal chapel even before the cathedral, and the earliest piece of architecture in the Castle District. It is believed to be the site where Imre, the son of King István, took a vow of chastity; later the relic of St George's head was kept in the chapel, which became a place of pilgrimage as a consequence. A set of steps behind the chapel leads down to the steep-sided finger of **Benedek Hill**, with a grassy strip along the top. If you don't fancy traipsing down to it, you can admire the views instead from the uppermost end of Vár utca, with its statues of István and Gizella (sculpted in 1938 on the 900th anniversary of the king's death) gazing from the ramparts. From here Benedek Hill extends away immediately in front, while to the left of its tip are the Margit Ruins – the walls of a convent built in 1240 where Margit (daughter of Béla IV) was educated for six years. In the distance around to the left is the unlovely St István Viaduct, its concrete arches spanning Fejes Valley. A little beyond that are the remains of the 10th-century Greek Orthodox nunnery where the coronation cloak was embroidered (see page 436).

Other sights Moving south from Óváros tér along Rákóczi utca, take a short detour to the right along Óváry Ferenc utca to see the Petőfi Theatre (see page 438) before continuing to Megyeház tér. On the eastern side is the Neo-Renaissance **County Hall**, designed in 1887 by István Kiss. Further down and set back from Erzsébet sétány among trees is the **Laczkó Dezső Museum** (*Erzsébet sétány 1;* ☏ *88 564310;* ✆ *1,400/800Ft;* ⊕ *Tue–Sun Mar 15–Oct 16 10.00–18.00, Oct 17–Mar 14 12.00–16.00*); it was voted the country's Museum of the Year in 2007. Among the permanent exhibits are items relating to Veszprém County, including Roman finds from Balácapuszta (see below). Next door is the **Bakony House** (*Bakonyi ház; Erzsébet sétány 3;* ☏ *88 561330;* ✆ *280/140Ft;* ⊕ *May 1–Oct 16 Tue–Sun 10.00–18.00*), a 20th-century reconstruction of a 19th-century peasant house in the village of Öcs, to the southwest of Veszprém. At the back is a flask-maker's workshop.

Veszprém Zoo (*Kittenberger út 17;* ☏ *88 421088; www.zoo.hu/veszprem;* ✆ *adult/student/child 1,320/1,170/900Ft;* ⊕ *May–Sep 09.00–18.00 daily, rest of yr 09.00–15.00*) is in Fejes Valley, a 15-minute walk west of the centre near the viaduct. The zoo also runs a riding school.

FESTIVALS AND EVENTS The main celebration is the Gizella Days Art Festival in May, when there are exhibitions of art, music and dance in Óvarós tér, Petőfi Theatre and elsewhere. The Summer Festival takes place in August.

EXCURSIONS Just under 10km to the southeast of Veszprém, at the edge of the village of Nemesvámos, is a place called **Balácapuszta** where Roman ruins (*Nemesvámos-Baláca;* ☏ *88 265050;* ⊕ *May–Sep Tue–Sun 10.00–18.00*) were unearthed at the turn of the 20th century. The settlement may have been called Caesariana, and fell at the junction of two main Roman roads. At the centre is a large 1st-century villa; finds from the site are exhibited in the cellars, and among them are two prize mosaics.

Turn your plate over in an upmarket restaurant, and there's a good chance that – as well as getting a lapful of soup – you'll see the mark of Herend. Since the early 19th century, this internationally renowned porcelain has emanated from the **Herend Porcelain Manufactory** (*Herend, Kossuth Lajos u. 140; www.herend.com*) in the village of Herend, 15km west of Veszprém on Road 8 towards Körmend. The company took off during the Great Exhibition of 1851 in London's Crystal Palace, when Queen Victoria was so impressed by the porcelain that she commissioned a dinner service. It was adorned with butterflies and oriental flowers; named after the monarch, it remains one of Herend's most popular designs. All the pieces are crafted by hand; figurines of the 1920s are considered the connoisseur's classics, but while the look of the porcelain has altered according to fashion the quality remains top-drawer. Today 250 potters and 630 painters work in the factory. The Porcelanium (☏ 88 523100; *www.porcelanium.com*; 🎫 1,500/500Ft, family 3,400Ft) is the visitor centre, and inside is a mini-manufactory (🕐 *daily 09.00–17.00*) where you can see some of the artists in action and a museum (🕐 *daily 09.00–16.00*) where you can take a trawl through the changing trends. There is also a café, a very high-class restaurant and a showroom where you can make purchases. The centre is a short walk northeast from the bus station; there are regular buses here from Veszprém.

Before you reach Herend on Road 8 you will pass the village of **Bánd**. Just visible from the road is the delightful old coaching inn, the Bándi Udvarház (*Bánd, Petőfi u. 2,* ☏ *88 272424; mains avg 2,000Ft;* 🕐 *Mar–Oct Tue–Sun 12.00–22.00*). This rustic thatched house is decorated with old kitchen and farming utensils, and serves honest Hungarian or Swabian (as ethnic Germans are called in the Danube valley) peasant dishes; the mutton *pörkölt* we ate was wholly authentic.

To Veszprém's north (20km along Road 82) is **Zirc**, whose Baroque Cistercian abbey and church (*Rákóczi tér*) of 1753 – with an altarpiece by F A Maulbertsch – stand on the site of a 12th-century predecessor destroyed by the Turks. The abbey's mid-19th-century Neoclassical library (*Reguly Antal Memorial Library;* ☏ *88 593800;* 🎫 *400/200Ft;* 🕐 *Tue–Sun 09.00–12.00, 13.00–17.00*) is furnished with wood from Bakony ash trees; named after a local linguist who was ahead of his time in arguing a link between Hungarian and Finnish, it was damaged in 1944 by pieces of a German war plane shot down overhead. The same building houses the Bakony Scientific Museum (☏ *88 414157;* 🎫 *400/200Ft;* 🕐 *10.00–17.00 daily*), devoted to the natural history of the Bakony, while next to the abbey is an arboretum (*Damjanich u. 19;* ☏ *88 414569;* 🕐 *Tue–Sun May–Aug 09.00–18.00, Sep 09.00–17.00, Oct–Nov & Mar 15–Apr 30 09.00–16.00*). The Tourinform (*Rákóczi tér 1;* ☏ *88 416816;* 🕐 *Jun 15–Aug 31 Mon–Fri 09.00–18.00, Sat–Sun 10.00–16.00, rest of yr Mon–Fri 09.00–17.00*) can provide details on walking routes in the surrounding hills.

About 6km outside Zirc at the end of a well signposted track is a beautifully restored and maintained hotel and riding centre called **Szépalma Hotel** (*26 rooms; H-8429 Porva-Szépalmapuszta;* ☏ *88 272424; www.szepalma.hu; sgl 16,800Ft, dbl 21,800Ft;* 🕐 *all yr except Christmas*). You can explore (on foot or horse) the castle ruins of Csesznek and the natural surroundings in Bakonybél. The hotel organises riding camps for 8–12-year-old children between June and August; its restaurant (*mains avg 2,200Ft*) has outdoor tables around an enclosed courtyard.

SÜMEG

Southwest of Veszprém, sandwiched in a valley between the Keszthely range and the western foothills of the Bakony, Sümeg was settled early – prehistoric man quarried flint near by, and Roman remains have also been discovered. The town's castle, of course, stands out like a sore thumb from its hilltop vantage point; a 13th-century version was reconstructed in the 16th century and successfully kept the Turks at bay, though not the Habsburgs (who set it ablaze in 1713). Picturesque as it is, however, the real thing of beauty in town is F A Maulbertsch's painting masterclass in the parish church, one of several significant commissions made during the 18th century while Sümeg was the seat of the bishops of Veszprém and it had to be resurrected after a devastating fire in 1700.

GETTING THERE AND AWAY The **bus station** (*Béke tér*) is just south of the centre; walk north through Béke tér and Flórián tér, and on to Kossuth Lajos utca. There are regular buses to Keszthely, Hévíz, Pápa, Veszprém and Tapolca, as well as services to Zalaegerszeg (ten), Győr (six), Sárvár (five), Szombathely and Sopron (four), Kaposvár and Kőszeg (two). Four buses a day make the four-hour journey to Budapest Népliget.

The modern **railway station** is 1km west of the centre. The most regular trains are to Celldömölk and Tapolca; there are also services to Keszthely (three), Szombathely (two), Sopron and Balatonfüred (one). Change at Celldömölk for Pápa, Tatabánya, Győr, Szombathely and Budapest.

INFORMATION AND OTHER PRACTICALITIES

🆔 **Balaton Tourist** Kossuth Lajos u. 15; ✆ 87 550259; e sumeg@balatontourist.hu. Arranges tours of the region. ☉ Mon 08.30–13.00, Tue–Fri 08.30–16.00, Sat 08.30–12.00.

✉ **Tourinform** Kossuth Lajos u. 15; ✆ 87 550276; e sumeg@tourinform.hu. Can organise private rooms (*from 2,000–5,000Ft/pp*). ☉ summer Mon–Fri 09.00–18.00, Sat–Sun 10.00–17.00, rest of yr Mon–Fri 08.00–16.00.

WHERE TO STAY

🏠 **Castle Stables** (*Váristálló*) Városldal u. 5; ✆ 87 550087; e varistallo@axelero.hu; www.sumeg.hu/capariplus. A rustic guesthouse at the Castle Stables, right at the foot of Castle Hill. *Rooms 3,500Ft/pp.*

🏠 **Hotel Kapitány** Tóth Tivadar u. 19; ✆ 87 352598; www.hotelkapitany.hu. On the road running past the northern side of Castle Hill, the Kapitány is a 4-star hotel with adequate (though not special) rooms that cashes in on the castle's proximity by hosting a range of themed programmes (horse shows, folk dances, wine-tastings, knights' tournaments, etc). There's an on-site cellar & a small outdoor pool. *Dbl 36,000Ft.*

🏠 **Hotel Vár** Vak Bottyán u. 2; ✆ 87 352352; www.hotelvar.hu. Despite its faux exterior – rigged to look like an austere castle – this hotel behind the Franciscan Church is modern & airy, with well-sized rooms. Good value. *Sgl 9,400Ft, dbl 11,800Ft, trpl 15,500Ft.*

🏠 **Krigler Panzió & Ramessetter Cellar** (8 rooms) Báróházi u. 1; ✆ 87 550320. When we visited, we found the owners occupied with gutting a pig for an evening feast; they are a hospitable bunch, who will prepare grills for their guests & serve wine from their 200-year-old cellar. The rooms are simple but comfortable; shared use of kitchen & TV. Recommended. *Sgl 5,000Ft, dbl 10,000Ft, trpl 15,000Ft.*

🏠 **Öreghegy Hotel** (20 rooms) Karolina u.; ✆ 87 350501; www.oreghegyhotel.hu; turn off Road 84 at the Shell filling station (well signposted). This new hotel definitely has the best views of the castle; the rooms are spacious & family-friendly, & there's a pool, sauna &WiFi. The road to it is unpaved. *Sgl 7,000Ft, dbl 14,000Ft, trpl 21,000Ft.*

✗ **WHERE TO EAT AND DRINK** There are a number of food stalls (as well as souvenir stands) on Vársétány (the road by the Carriage Museum that runs from Road 84 towards the castle).

✗ **Kisfaludy** Kossuth Lajos u. 13; ✆ 87 352128. The best restaurant in town. Its interior is hung with the skins & skulls of unfortunate boars &

deer. The Hungarian cuisine includes Balaton fish, steaks & – in the words of the great Bruce Forsyth – good game, good game. There is also an

ice-cream parlour. *Mains avg 1,700Ft;*
⊕ *09.00–23.00 daily.*

⌨ **Móri Fogadó** Kossuth Lajos u. 22; ☏ 87 352489.
Café-style eatery opposite the Tourinform office
serving cheap local nosh. *Mains avg 1,000Ft;*
⊕ *12.00–21.00 daily.*

✗ **Scotti** Szent István tér 1; ☏ 87 350997. Named
after the 19th-century owner of the house, Scotti is

primarily a pizza joint, with a limited selection of
other Hungarian dishes (their specialities the stuffed
cabbage & handmade strudel). The garden is
cluttered but inviting (with a fishpond, fountain &
creepers), the synthesiser music is dreadful, & the
ambience is good. The large pizzas could feed a
family for a week. Opposite the Town Museum.
Mains avg 2,000Ft; ⊕ *09.00–23.00 daily.*

WHAT TO SEE AND DO

Sümeg Castle Overlooking the whole shebang, the **castle** (☏ 87 352737;
www.sumegvar.hu; ☞ *1,500/500Ft inc programme;* ⊕ *daily Apr–Sep 09.00–19.00, rest of yr
10.00–18.00, depending on weather*) sits high on the 270m limestone Castle Hill and is
the dominant feature of the townscape. The journey up is rewarded not only with a
closer look at Transdanubia's biggest fort, but fabulous views. Razed by the Habsburgs
at the start of the 18th century, the castle wasn't restored until the 20th century. The
southern part of the courtyard contains the 13th-century Old Tower, inside which is
an exhibition detailing the castle's history and including pieces of weaponry.

In summer, there are **medieval programmes** hosted under the castle walls
(☞ *2,000/1,000Ft; Jun–Aug at 11.00, 14.30 & 17.00 daily*), and you can join an evening
banquet afterwards (☞ *5,000/4,000Ft*). A road leads around and up the hill, branching
from Vároldal utca near the Castle Stables (see opposite); you can get to Vároldal utca
either from the northeast by following Vársétány off Road 84 or from Szent István tér
to the southeast by following Vak Bottyán utca and Bem utca. If you don't want to
make the climb on foot, **jeep-like taxis** (☞ *400Ft/pp*) leave from the car park at the
northern end of Várodal utca; there need to be a minimum of two passengers.

Other sights and activities To the southwest of Szent István tér, at the end of Deák
Ferenc utca, the Roman Catholic parish **Church of the Ascension** (*Szent Imre tér;*
⊕ *Mon–Fri 09.00–17.00, Sat 10.00–12.00 & 17.00–19.00, Sun 10.00–12.00 &
14.00–17.00*) is a hulking Baroque temple constructed between 1756 and 1759 under
the stewardship of Bishop Márton Padányi Biró. What makes the church
extraordinary is what you'll find inside – namely some of the most beautiful Baroque
and Rococo paintings in the country. The bishop secured the services of Franz Anton
Maulbertsch, an Austrian painter in his early 30s, to decorate the interior; over a
period of 14 months, the young man surpassed any work he had or would produce,
conjuring what has been described as 'Hungary's Rococo Sistine Chapel'. Biró had
a say in the chosen biblical subjects, and it was then left to Maulbertsch to weave
magic in the colour, movement and play of light and shade. Pay particular attention
to the *Adoration of the Shepherds*, in which the artist has included a self portrait in the
figure offering a piece of ewe's cheese. He appears again on the back wall, dressed in
an orange tail coat in the company of his patron. The frescoes have been restored on
several occasions, most notably after a fire in 1799.

Across Kossuth Lajos utca, at the northern end of Kisfaludy tér, the **Town
Museum** (*Kisfaludy tér 2;* ☏ 87 550277; ☞ *400/200Ft;* ⊕ *May–Sep Tue–Sun
10.00–18.00; rest of yr Mon–Fri 08.00–16.00*) is housed in the birthplace of Sándor
Kisfaludy, who also lived here with his wife from 1800 and is buried in the town
cemetery. The influential poet was a fervent protector of his native language, a
leading member of the linguistic neology movement and one who wrote in
Hungarian at a time when the language of state was German. There is an
exhibition devoted to his life, as well as to other members of his family (his
younger brother was a writer of comedy and short stories). Also here are
collections of Bakony fossils, flints from the prehistoric mine found just outside

town, pieces of Sümeg pottery (including some Gothic and Renaissance examples excavated from the castle) and ecclesiastical art. Outside the gate is a pantheon to other famous local citizens such as József Németh and János Horváth.

Behind the trees just to the east is the 18th-century **Bishop's Palace** (*Szent István tér 8;* ☞ *400–200Ft;* ⊕ *May–Sep Wed–Sun 10.00–18.00, Oct–Apr Mon–Fri 08.00–16.00; please ring the bell*), built by Bishop Padányi Biró as a summer residence. Its crumbling plaster is being restored but the corner balconies and Neoclassical entrance give an idea of former splendour. The oval chapel with its frescoed ceiling and gilded episcopal coat of arms above the altar are particularly fine; the temporary exhibitions of local art can be uninspiring. Restoration is ongoing and more will be open to the public in due course. The central courtyard is used for summer concerts. One wing contains a **Wine Museum and Cellar** (*Bormúzeum & Borkóstolo Pince; www.palotapince.hu;* ☞ *entrance free;* ⊕ *10.00–21.00 daily*) where you can take a tasting (☞ *1,500Ft/5 wines*).

Across from the palace, the **Franciscan church and monastery** (*Szent István tér*) was built in Baroque style in 1657 and is (after the castle) the town's second-oldest structure. Frescoes of the Crucifixion and Ascension adorn the church's side chapels, there is an impressive altar of 1720 by Martin Witner, and a pulpit with gilded evangelists and a disembodied arm holding a crucifix. For the last 250 years, pilgrims have made the journey to see the church's statue of the Blessed Virgin in early September. This is an enjoyable, well-crafted church with much to admire in its details; it is unfortunate that it is destined always to suffer by comparison with the parish-church masterpiece to the west.

Follow Vak Bottyán utca up to Vároldal utca, and on the right are the **Castle Stables** (*Váristálló; Vároldal u. 5;* ☎ *87 550087; www.sumeg.hu/capari*); the Capári Riding School operates from here (☞ *riding from 3,500Ft/hr*) and offers tours, and there's an equestrian shop (⊕ *09.00–18.00 daily*). Behind the stables, on the other side of Vársétány, is the **Carriage Museum** (☞ *entry free, but donation appreciated of* ☞ *300/150Ft*), with horse-drawn carriages of the 19th and 20th centuries, and weaponry including a 16th-century crossbow.

PÁPA

Northwest of Veszprém and run through by Road 83, Pápa experienced its purple period in the 1750s when, under the ownership of the powerful Esterházys, its pretty Baroque core came to be; Károly Esterházy, the Bishop of Eger, was responsible for removing the medieval fortifications and modernising many of the streets and squares, flexing his wealthy muscles with an architectural flourish. During medieval times the settlement had been an important market town, but it subsequently became marked as a leading regional centre of Protestantism and learning. Its Calvinist college was founded in 1531, and it was here that Gál Huszár opened the faith to common Hungarians through his translation of the *Heidelberg Káté* in 1577. The college later boasted some of Hungary's cultural greats – including the author Mór Jókai and the poet Sándor Petőfi – among its 19th-century alumni. Despite its illustrious past, however, the town is now faded in look and could do with some tender loving care.

GETTING THERE AND AWAY The **bus station** is just west off the main strip on Szabadság utca, with regular buses running to Veszprém and Győr (up to 14 a day). Other destinations served include Tapolca (five), Sopron (four), Sárvár and Zalaegerszeg (three), Szombathely, Székesfehérvár and Tatabánya (two). Up to three buses a day make the four-hour trip to Budapest Népliget.

Trains run fairly regularly to Győr and Celldömölk from the **railway station** on Béke tér, north of the centre. There are also up to nine trains a day to Tatabánya, up to four to Budapest Keleti and two-daily to Szombathely and Sárvár. Change at Győr for access to Sopron, and Celldömölk for Tapolca and Veszprém.

INFORMATION AND OTHER PRACTICALITIES

🗹 **Listings magazine** Veszprémi Est

🗹 **Tourinform** Kossuth Lajos u. 18; ✆ 89 311535; e papa@tourinform.hu. ☉ Jun–Aug Mon–Fri 09.00–17.00, Sat 09.00–18.00, Sun 10.00–18.00, Sep–May Mon–Fri 09.00–17.00, Sat 09.00–12.00.

➦ WHERE TO STAY AND EAT

🏠 **Arany Griff Hotel** (24 rooms) Fő tér 15; ✆ 89 312000. Directly opposite the Great Church, the century-old Griff has bright & welcoming rooms with high ceilings, laminated floors & large windows. Its dance hall was once the scene for county balls. Its restaurant (*mains avg 1,800Ft;* ☉ 11.00–23.00 *daily*) – one of the town's rare places to eat – is plain but has a pleasant courtyard. We enjoyed a meal of turkey with sour cream, cheese & fried potato followed by banana pudding in hot-chocolate sauce; the arteries screamed 'no' but the tastebuds won the day. *Sgl 6,500–9,700Ft, dbl 9,700–12,600Ft, apt (for 2) 14,800Ft.*

🏠 **Főnix Panzió** (9 rooms) Jókai u. 4; ✆ 89 324361; www.fonpan.extra.hu. This small guesthouse above a dingy bar strays towards the shabby, but it is central & it's hard to quibble with the price. *Sgl 5,700Ft, dbl 7,400Ft.*

🏠 **Hotel Villa Classica** (20 rooms) Bástya u. 1; ✆ 89 512200; www.villaclassica.hu. Our favourite in Pápa, this delightful hotel to the southwest of Fő tér has chic & polished rooms. Its restaurant (*mains avg 2,000Ft;* ☉ 11.00–23.00 *daily*) dishes up fresh contemporary Hungarian & Mediterranean cuisine, & there's a bar & outdoor patio area. *Sgl 15,600Ft, dbl 18,000Ft.*

WHAT TO SEE AND DO The Baroque **Esterházy Palace** (*Esterházy-kastély; Fő tér 1;* ✆ *89 313584; closed for renovation*) at the northern side of Fő tér was designed by József Grossman for Count Ferenc Esterházy in the 1780s on the site of the town's medieval castle. It was badly damaged during World War II, and served as a Russian military barracks until 1990. There is a library (☉ *Mon 13.00–19.00, Tue, Thu, Fri 09.00–12.00 & 13.00–19.00*), music school and local-history museum inside, but ongoing renovation means the palace (with the exception of the library) is closed. However, its grounds – including a 100ha English garden at the back – make good strolling territory.

The late-18th-century **Great Church** (*Nagytemplom; Fő tér*), twin-towered and Neoclassical-Baroque, was the work of Jakab Fellner and József Grossman. It was commissioned by Károly Esterházy, the Bishop of Eger, as a family burial chamber. Each of the church's towers is broken by columns through which the bells are visible, and the nave is decorated with frescoes by Austrian master F A Maulbertsch.

Fő utca holds the town hall, built over a Benedictine monastery whose church of 1742 remains jammed next to it. On the same street is the smaller portion of the **Pápa Calvinist Collection**, which is divided in two. The late-Baroque church of 1784 (*Fő u. 6;* ✆ *89 324240;* ✆ *admission free;* ☉ *May–Oct Tue–Sun 09.00–16.00*) has exhibits relating to 500 years of Calvinism in Transdanubia. The main body of the collection is further south in the **Calvinist college** (*Március 15 tér 9;* ✆ *89 324240; www.papacollege.hu;* ✆ *500/300Ft;* ☉ *Nov–Apr Tue–Fri 08.00–16.00, May–Oct Tue–Fri 08.00–16.00, Sat–Sun 09.00–17.00*), and features ecclesiastical items, pieces of applied art and an Egyptian mummy donated by a former student.

The **Blue Dye Museum** (*Március 15 tér 12;* ✆ *89 324390;* ✆ *500/300Ft;* ☉ *Tue–Sat Nov–Mar 09.00–16.00, Tue–Sun Apr–Oct 09.00–17.00*) is in what was once one of the largest dye workshops in central Europe. During the 18th century, skilled textile workers migrated to Hungary from countries to the west in search of work. In 1786 Carl Friedrich Kluge, whose family had arrived from Saxony, established a business devoted to the process of dying cloth a fashionable indigo colour. The factory continued to operate through seven family generations until its closure in 1956, and the museum showcases the machinery and the final products, as well as some work by textile artist Irén Bódy.

The pedestrianised Kossuth Lajos utca runs parallel with Fő utca from the bottom of Fő tér; if you follow it down for 100m and turn right into Petőfi Sándor utca, you'll reach a derelict **synagogue** (*Petőfi Sándor u. 24*) of 1846; the construction was subsidised by the Esterházy family, who recognised the economic benefits Jewish settlers brought to Pápa and welcomed them accordingly. The adjacent Jewish cemetery is one of Hungary's earliest, with some headstones over three centuries old.

If you need a splash, the **Várkert Baths** (*Külső Várkert;* ✆ *89 311535; www.varkertfurdo.hu;* 🎟 *1,600/1,250Ft;* ☉ *thermal baths daily 09.00–21.00, indoor pools 06.00–22.00 daily, outdoor pools May 15–Sep 15 09.00–20.00 daily*) have indoor and outdoor pools, as well as other sports facilities and a bar and restaurant.

If you want a further fix of the Esterházy clan, you can visit the **family mausoleum** (*contact Mrs Otto Nagy in advance;* ✆ *06 30 304 3362*) in the village of Ganna (10km from Pápa); here over 50 Esterházys are buried, meeting their maker in palatial splendour.

FESTIVALS AND EVENTS August sees several of the town's main events, including the Historical Games and the International Hussar Camp (when there are costumed equestrian events) at the beginning of the month, and a three-day wine festival. The United Games Festival in June features concerts and exhibitions (*see www.papa.hu*).

TATA

Sitting between the Vértes and Gerecse hills above the industrial city of Tatabánya, Tata revolves around its Old Lake (Öreg-tó), a pretty pool that forms an appealing backdrop for walking and bird-watching and an enticing foreground for watersports. Predictably tagged with a 'Town of Waters' moniker, this is a place for 'doers' and avoids the sunbathing hordes. It was a favourite royal resort in the Middle Ages. King Zsigmond attached a palace to the 14th-century castle on the northern shore, and King Mátyás enjoyed hunting here. After the Turks had left, the landowning Eszterházys commissioned architect Jakab Fellner to rebuild the town during the 18th century, a period that also saw the Farkasházy-Fischer family establish their renowned delftware factory in 1758 (they later attracted further renown when founding the Herend factory; see page 441). Tata is famous too for having more watermills – 14 in total – than any other Hungarian town; the majority were constructed in the 18th century (although the Cifra Mill dates back 500 years) and today serve as hotels, residences and museums.

GETTING THERE, AWAY AND AROUND It's a five-minute walk to the centre of town from the **bus station** by following Váralija utca eastwards. Buses run every 30 minutes to Tatabánya, and there are services to Esztergom (eight), Székesfehérvár (four), Győr and Dunaújváros (three), and Szeged (once daily on Fri & Sun only).

The **railway station** is 2km north of the centre behind the castle and has very frequent services to Budapest (Déli and Keleti), Győr and Tatabánya. There are also regular trains to the Slovakian border crossing at Komárom. To cross into Austria you'll need to change at Győr.

A small **passenger ferry** (*Tópart sétány;* 🎟 *500/400Ft*) offers a 30-minute cruise around Öreg-tó whenever there are 12 or more passengers.

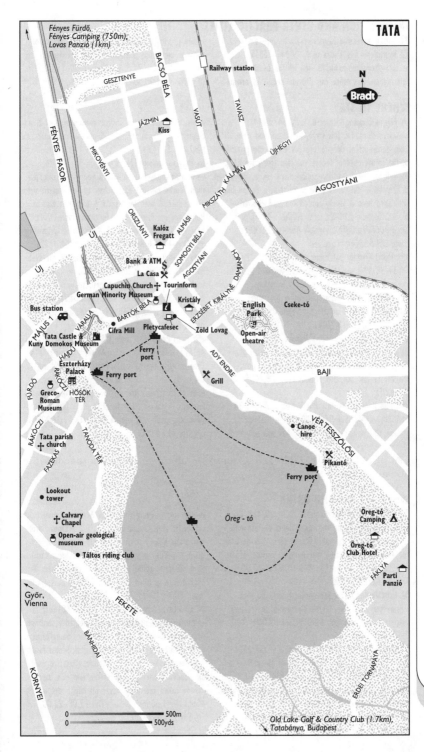

TATA

Fényes Fürdő,
Fényes Camping (750m),
Lovas Panzió (1km)

Railway station

N

Bradt

GESZTENYE

BACSÓ BÉLA

VASÚT

TAVASZ

ÚJHEGYI

JÁZMIN

Kiss

MIKOVÉNYI

FÉNYES   FASOR

ORSZLÁNYI

ÚJ

MIKSZÁTH KÁLMÁN

AGOSTYÁNI

ALMÁSI

Kalóz
Fregatt

SOMOGYI BÉLA

AGOSTYÁNI

Bank & ATM

La Casa

ÚJ

Capuchin Church

German Minority Museum

Tourinform

ERZSÉBET KIRÁLYNÉ DÁMJÁN

HOMANN

Kristály

English
Park

Cseke-tó

Bus station

BARTÓK BÉLA

Cifra Mill

Pletycafesec

Zöld Lovag

Open-air
theatre

Tata Castle &
Kuny Domokos Museum

VARALJA

HAJDÚ

Ferry
port

Eszterházy
Palace

Ferry port

ADY ENDRE

Grill

BAJI

FÜRDŐ

RÁKÓCZI

Greco-
Roman
Museum

HŐSÖK
TÉR

VÉRTESSZŐLŐSI

Canoe
hire

RÁKÓCZI

Tata parish
church

FAZEKAS

TÁNODA TÉR

Pikantó

Ferry port

Lookout
tower

Calvary
Chapel

Open-air geological
museum

Öreg - tó

Öreg-tó
Camping

Öreg-tó
Club Hotel

Táltos riding club

FAKLYA

Parti
Panzió

Győr,
Vienna

FEKETE

BÁNHIDAI

ERDEI TORNAPÁLYA

KÖRNYEI

0 _____ 500m
0 _____ 500yds

Old Lake Golf & Country Club (1.7km),
Tatabánya, Budapest

INFORMATION AND OTHER PRACTICALITIES

🖪 **Listings magazine** Komárom-Esztergomi Est
🖪 **Tourinform** Ady Endre u. 9; ✆ 34 586045;
e tata@tourinform.hu. As well as the usual information, this office can provide details of private rooms (from 2,500Ft/pp), although the quality of these is apparently variable. ⊕ Jun 15–Aug 31 Mon–Fri 08.00–17.00, Sat–Sun 10.00–19.00, rest of yr Mon–Fri 08.00–16.00.

🏠 WHERE TO STAY

🏕 **Fényes Camping** Környei u. 4; ✆ 34 588144; www.fenyesfurdo.hu. This large, well-manicured campsite 2km northwest of Öreg-tó site lies within the grounds of the town's outdoor leisure complex (see page 450). As well as tent & caravan space, there are bungalows & a motel – the latter little more than a Portakabin with hard beds & smelly shared toilets & shower blocks. Caravan 2,000Ft, tents 1,000–1,400Ft, plus 🛁 1,300Ft/1,000Ft; bungalow (for 4) 11,000Ft, motel dbl 6,500Ft; ⊕ all year.

🏠 **Hotel Kristály** (50 rooms) Ady Endre u. 22; ✆ 34 383577; www.hktata.hu. 230-year-old hotel in the centre. Renovation & extension is nearly complete; the rooms are spacious & pleasantly furnished, & there's an elegant vaulted restaurant. Sgl 13,800Ft, dbl 18,700Ft

🏠 **Kalóz Fregatt** (5 rooms) Alamási út 2; ✆ 34 382382; www.hotels.hu/kaloz. Pleasant rooms above the pirate-themed pub & restaurant (see opposite) in the centre. You can also hire bikes. Sgl 8,400Ft, dbl 14.000Ft.

🏠 **Kiss Hotel** (9 rooms) Bacsó Béla u. 54; ✆ 34 586888; www.ohb.hu/kiss. 200m from the railway station, this upmarket guesthouse has well-equipped rooms, a restaurant, an indoor swimming pool & a beauty salon (with solarium & massage options). Dbl €80, apt €104.

🏕 **Öreg-tó Camping** Fáklya u. 2; ✆ 34 383496; www.tatacamping.hu. More of a youngsters' campsite than Fényes, offering easy access to the eastern shore of the lake & with food stalls & bars just outside. Bungalows inc kitchenettes. Tent/caravan 1,000Ft, plus 1,000Ft/pp, bungalow 3,000Ft/pp; ⊕ May–Aug.

🏠 **Öreg-tó Club Hotel** Fáklya u. 4; ✆ 34 487960. Next to (but separate from) the campsite, the Club has a hotel (with en-suite rooms) as well as a hostel with 19 bungalows (shared shower & toilet facilities). On the shabby side, but prettily situated & cheap. Hotel sgl 3,900Ft, dbl 7,300Ft, trpl 9,200Ft, hostel 1,600Ft/pp.

🏠 **Parti Panzió** (12 rooms) Boróka u. 6–8; ✆ 34 481577; www.partipanzio.hu. At the eastern side of Öreg-tó, near the campsite, Parti is an excellent choice. As well as clean & cheerful standard rooms, each of its 4 apts are set in separate houses with kitchens & gardens. The hotel facilities include a swimming pool, whirlpool & sauna. Dbl 10,000Ft, apt (for 4) 18,000Ft.

See also Old Lake Golf and Country Club (page 450), for good-quality accommodation.

✕ WHERE TO EAT AND DRINK

✕ **Grill & Cocktail** Nagytó part; ✆ 34 383482. Classy restaurant overlooking the main sights of Tata on the other side of the lake. Glazed terrace & deck on the lake in the summer. International cuisine. Mains avg 2,200Ft; ⊕ Mon–Thu & Sun 12.00–22.00, Fri–Sat 12.00–01.00.

✕ **Kristály Restaurant** See above. Traditional local cuisine served in very agreeable turn-of-the-century surroundings. Mains avg 3,000Ft; ⊕ 07.00–10.00, 12.00–22.00 daily.

✕ **La Casa** Országgyűlés tér 3; ✆ 06 70 252 2884. One of the town's best, La Casa serves Mediterranean & local dishes – paella & Spanish frogs' legs sit alongside Hungarian stews – & has a quiet courtyard garden. Mains avg 1,800Ft; ⊕ 12.00–22.00 daily.

✕ **Pikantó** Tópart sétány; ✆ 34 489372. Wood-furnished restaurant with an upstairs gallery & a conservatory serving Hungarian & international cuisine. It also has an attached Mediterranean grill restaurant behind it that opens in summer only. Disco & parties every Fri–Sat. Located on a small road off Vértesszőlősi út that leads to the lake & boat pier, & is lined with food stalls & bars. Mains avg 1,800Ft; ⊕ 11.30–23.00 daily.

✕ **Zöld Lovag** Ady Endre u. 17; ✆ 34 481681; e z.lovag@freemail.hu. Medieval-themed restaurant with tacky heraldic shields dotting its dingy brick walls, & the obligatory costumed staff. Serves hearty portions (steaks the size of dinner plates) of food on wooden platters. Found at the end of a small parade called Esterházy udvar off Ady Endre u. Mains avg 1,600Ft; ⊕ Sun–Thu 12.00–22.00, Fri–Sat 12.00–24.00.

ENTERTAINMENT AND NIGHTLIFE The **Magyary Zoltán Cultural Centre** (*Váralja u. 4;* ✆ *34 380811;* e *muvhaz@tata.hu;* ⊕ *Mon–Fri 09.00–17.00*) can provide information on arts events, including those at an **open-air theatre** in the English Park (at the western side of Cseke-tó). The **Kalóz Fregatt** (see opposite; ⊕ *Sun–Thu 12.00–24.00, Sat–Sun 12.00–02.00*) is decked out like a frigate, and has the odd live band; off-key performers presumably risk a good keelhauling. The **Pletycafésec** (*Esterházy udvar;* ✆ *34 481402;* ⊕ *Mon–Thu 10.00–24.00, Fri 10.00–01.00, Sat 15.00–01.00, Sun 15.00–24.00*) – its name a play on the word '*pletykafészek*', meaning 'seat of gossip' – is an intimate little place in a shopping parade just off Ady Endre utca. It has a cellar bar and is a good spot for coffee or a drink; Friday is party night.

WHAT TO SEE AND DO **Öreg-tó**, spreading south from the centre, came into being during the 15th century when the Által Stream was dammed. It was once used to farm fish (although angling is no longer permitted), but is now a conservation area and a popular bird-watching haunt, particularly between the months of September and November when thousands of migrating wild geese rest their feathers and have a good honk (*for info,* ✆ *34 380851*). There are a couple of beaches, and you can hire kayaks and canoes (*just off Vértesszőlősi út;* ✆ *800–1,000Ft/hr;* ⊕ *Mon–Sun 09.00–12.00, 15.00–21.00*) 500m north of the Öreg-tó campsite on the eastern shore.

Tata Castle (*Váralja u.*), at the lake's northern tip, was constructed in the mid 14th century on a rocky outcrop ringed with water and marshland. At the end of the century, it became crown property and enjoyed a golden age as a beautiful Renaissance pile under kings Zsigmond and Mátyás. After the Turks had long gone, Lord Chief Justice József Eszterházy bought it in a far sorrier state – it had been burnt by the Habsburgs – and gave it a Romantic-style overhaul (which is what you see now). Precious little remains of the original castle beyond a single corner tower, ruined walls and some weathered stone sarcophagi in the grounds. The castle has recently been fully renovated; you can enter the castle chapel, while inside the main building is the **Kuny Domokos Museum** (✆ *34 381251;* ✆ *600/300Ft, free for families on Sun;* ⊕ *Tue–Sun 10.00–18.00*) containing Roman finds, a history of the castle, and displays of pieces produced in the 18th-century delftware factory. Fishy creatures were favoured subjects for the ceramicists, inspired by the water all about them.

A short distance anti-clockwise around the lake is the Louis-XVI-style **Eszterházy Palace** (*Hősök tere 6–8;* ✆ *34 708106;* ✆ *400/200Ft;* ⊕ *May–Sep Wed–Sun 10.00–18.00*), its bulging corner towers built to the design of Jakab Fellner in the 1760s. For much of the 20th century it served as a hospital, and was stripped of the majority of its fittings; as such, the museum inside is sterile, showing a few original bookshelves, a marble basin of 1887 and some old floorplans. There are vague murmurings of a renovation, but nothing firm. In the grounds are the remains of the palace's old theatre, and near by is one of the lake's small boat piers from where you can catch a ferry (✆ *400/300Ft*) across the water. Hősök tere also holds a **Greco-Roman Replica Statues Museum** (*Hősök tere 7;* ✆ *34 381251;* ✆ *200/100Ft;* ⊕ *Apr–Sep Tue–Sun 10.00–18.00, at other times of yr by prior notice*), housed in a former synagogue, and including the Venus de Milo among its 96 copies.

To the southwest (along Bercsényi utca or Rákóczi utca) is Kossuth tér, and next to it the late-Baroque **Tata parish church** (*Iskola tér*), built between 1751 and 1787 by Franz Anton Pilgram, Jakab Fellner and József Grossman. Fellner, whose hand was in so much of the town's architecture, actually died in 1780 before the church was completed. He was buried in the crypt, and there is a statue of him outside. Calvary Hill (Kálvária-domb) to the south has a chimney-like **lookout tower** (*Stavinovszki József-Fazekas u. 52/A;* ✆ *34 384306;* ✆ *160/120Ft;* ⊕ *May–Sep Tue–Sun 09.00–17.00*), standing just off Fazekas utca, as well as a sad-looking 18th-century **calvary** (Christ has neither head nor legs) and the odd-looking **Calvary Chapel**. The latter is so short in length that from the side it appears cut in half; this is because it was fashioned from the Gothic shrine of an earlier Medieval church on the site by Fellner in 1755. At the base of the hill's other side is an abandoned quarry whose rock layers preserve fossilised shells and a prehistoric fireplace. This nature conservation area is now an **Open-Air Geological Museum** (*Kálvária-domb, Fekete u. 2;* \ *34 381587;* &*200/100Ft;* ⊕ *Tue–Fri 10.00–16.00, Sat–Sun 10.00–17.00*).

Moving the other way around the top of the lake, the 16th-century **Cifra (Ornamental) Mill** is set back from the shore on Bartók Béla utca. Further on, another of the town's old watermills houses the **German Minority Museum** (*Német Nemzetiségi Múzeum; Alkotmány u. 1;* \ *34 487682;* & *200/100Ft;* ⊕ *every Thu 10.00–18.00*), which celebrates the German groups who settled in Transdanubia over the centuries; exhibits include pottery (some dating back to the 13th century), traditional dress and decorated furniture, 17th-century pistols and photos of pro-Hitler marches in the build up to World War II. Unfortunately there are no explanations in English.

A short distance to the north, Országyűlés tér (Parliament Square) commemorates the period in 1510 when the government convened in Tata after Buda was struck by plague. Its octagonal **clock tower** was made in 1763 completely from wood by local craftsman József Éder. Opposite is the **Capuchin church** (*Bartók Béla u.*), finished in 1746 with Fellner involved again. To the east (follow Ady Endre utca and turn left into Erzsébet királyné tér) is the smaller of the town's lakes – appropriately named Small Lake (Cseke-tó) – where fishermen angle for bream, catfish, common carp and pike (*licences available at Ady Endre u. 83;* \ *34 380160*). It is wrapped in an **English Park** (Angol Park), landscaped for the Eszterházys by Ferenc Bőhm, and featuring a family summer house, an artificial ruin constructed from the stones of a 12th-century abbey, and an outdoor theatre.

Other Two kilometres to the north of the centre, set to the west of Fényes fasor, is the **Fényes Fürdő** (*Fényes Fasor;* \ *34 588144; www.fenyesfurdo.hu;* & *850/550Ft, reduced admission after 15.00;* ⊕ *May–Sep daily 09.00–19.00*); the complex holds five pools (including one for young children), a waterslide, tennis courts, a fitness centre and sauna, as well as a campsite (see page 448). Bus 3 runs there.

There are several places to go horse-riding. The **Táltos Lovasklub** (*Fekete u. 2/A;* \ *06 20 242 2233;* & *riding 2,000Ft/hr;* ⊕ *Tue–Fri 09.00–12.00, 15.00–18.00*) is close to the Geological Museum (see above), and offers horse- or carriage-riding for all levels. The **Old Lake Golf and Country Club** (*Remeteségpuszta;* \ *34 587620;* e *old.lake.golf.club@axelero.hu; www.oldlakegolf.com*) is an extremely swish establishment 4km south of the centre (follow Fekete út to the end, around the western shore of the lake). Built on one of the Eszterházys' hunting estates, it has a golf course (& *weekdays 9,000Ft/round, weekends 14,500Ft/round*), indoor and outdoor swimming pools, a fitness centre, tennis courts, a restaurant, a hotel (*35 rooms; sgl 18,500Ft, dbl 24,500Ft*) and even its own fishing lake (Lake Derítő).

FESTIVALS AND EVENTS The Water, Music and Flower Festival takes place on the last weekend in June, and features a flower-arranging competition, medieval games and other events. There is a Theatre Festival at the open-air theatre in the third week of June.

EXCURSIONS For a little touch of godliness, travel 20km south from Tata (28 direct buses daily) to a lonely hill near the industrial town of Oroszlány. There you'll find the **Camaldolese Hermitage of Majkpuszta** (\ *34 361592; www.montecorona.hu;*

🍴 *880/580Ft;* ⊕ *Apr–Oct 10.00–18.00, free guided tour every half hour)*, a fabulous complex built in the 18th century for this silent order. It's a lovely, unexpected place. Each hermit lived in a small, separate house of four rooms built by a benefactor whose arms grace the dwelling's façade. Only the tower of the church remains, but beyond the hermitage is the old monastery building, which the Esterházys converted to a hunting lodge. The refectory is particularly beautiful; when we visited the corridors contained an atmospheric photo exhibition of a working Camadolese Hermitage near Krakow (Poland), which offered a glimpse into the austere life of the hermits. Five of the houses are available to rent (*whole house 10,000Ft/night, 6,000Ft for 1 room*), so you can get a taste of the hermit's life yourself; each sleeps four–six people, and has cooking facilities and a simple bathroom. The surrounding woods hold two 18th-century chapels where services were held for ordinary folk (men and women kept separate). Overlooking the monks' medieval fishpond is a simple restaurant called A Négy Remetéhez ('To the Four Hermits'; ☎ *34 364511; www.negyremete.hu; mains avg 2,000Ft;* ⊕ *11.00–21.00 daily*).

The road from Majk leads through the undulating Vértes forests to **Mór** (which is on Road 81 from Székesfehérvár to Győr). Originally a German village, Mór is famed for its white wine (Ezerjó of Mór). The top place to give it a try is a country inn called the Öreg Présház (*Arany János u. 4;* ☎ *22 407832; www.oregpres.hu; mains avg 2,500Ft;* ⊕ *Mon–Sat 11.00–22.00*), which has a large wooden wine press in front. It serves fine food and the best of the local vintage. If you want to stay in Mór, a row of village houses have been lovingly converted by their Hungarian/Austrian owners into a small hotel (*25 rooms; contact Öreg Presház; sgl 13,000Ft, dbl 19,000Ft*), each room decorated with country-style painting or carvings.

Western Transdanubia

A significant part of Western Transdanubia, the region to the west and northwest of Balaton, is in the shadow of the Alps foothills ranged along the Austrian border. This is among Hungary's most beautiful and interesting areas, one that formed part of Royal (Habsburg) Hungary during the Turkish occupation and which therefore preserves some medieval architecture that was destroyed in other parts. The towns of Kőszeg and Sopron are enchanting, while the villages of the Őrség retain traditional folk architecture. At the other end of the scale, Nagycenk and Fertőd hold two of the country's premier aristocratic mansions. For bird-watchers, Lake Fertő offers a significant swathe of wetland habitat. Ecclesiastical highlights can be found in Győr Cathedral, Pannonhalma Abbey, established by missionaries at the invitation of Prince Géza in the 10th century, and the 13th-century cathedral at Ják – possibly the best-preserved piece of Romanesque architecture.

GYŐR

Standing midships between Budapest and Vienna, and at the meeting point of the rivers Mosoni-Duna, Rábca and Rába, Győr's strategic position and natural transport links ensured that it developed into one of the country's throbbing industrial hubs. However, while its outer factories deter the timid, those who venture to the centre are well rewarded for their perseverance; at its Baroque heart are churches, palaces, museums and town houses with pretty corner balconies – all the trappings of a dense history. (In particular, Győr Cathedral's potent combination of stylish opulence and fascinating history is not to be missed.) Celts, Romans and Avars settled here on the Kisalföld (Small Plain), the latter constructing a round fort (*gyürü* in the Avar language) from which the city's name derives. King István made Győr an episcopal see during the 11th century. The

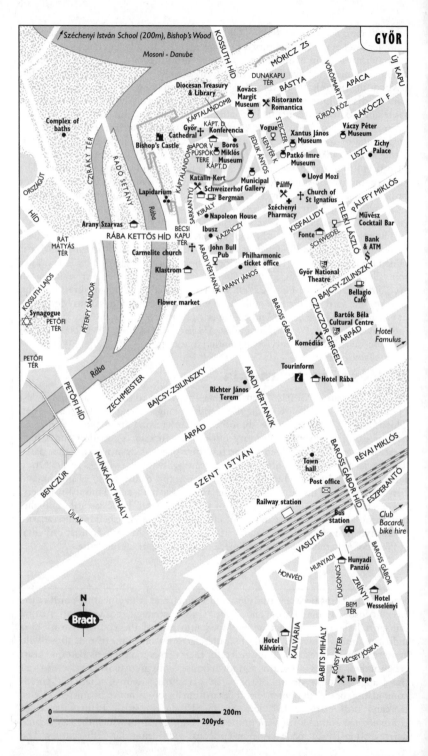

GYŐR

Széchenyi István School (200m), Bishop's Wood

Mosoni - Danube

KOSSUTH HÍD

MÓRICZ ZS

ÚJ KAPU

DUNAKAPU TÉR

BÁSTYA

VÖRÖSMARTY

APÁCA

Diocesan Treasury & Library

Kovács Margit Museum

Ristorante Romantica

FÜRDŐ KÖZ

RÁKÓCZI F

KAPTALANDOMB

KÁPT. D

Complex of baths

CZIRÁKY TÉR

Győr Cathedral

KÁPT. D Konferencia

Vogue

STEICZER

Xantus János Museum

Váczy Péter Museum

KENYÉR K

Zichy Palace

Bishop's Castle

SAPOR V PÜSPÖK TERE

Boros Miklós Museum

JEDLIK ÁNYOS

LISZT

RADÓ SÉTÁNY

KÁPT.D

Patkó Imre Museum

Katalin Kert

Municipal Gallery

Pálffy

Lloyd Mozi

PÁLFFY MIKLÓS

ORSZÁGÚT

Lapidarium

Rába

Schweizerhof Bergman

Church of St Ignatius

Széchenyi Pharmacy

KISFALUDY

TELEKI LÁSZLÓ

Művész Cocktail Bar

HÍD

KIRÁLY

Napoleon House

Fonte

SCHWEIDEL

Bank & ATM $

RÁT MÁTYÁS TÉR

Arany Szarvas

Ibusz

KAZINCZY

BÉCSI KAPU TÉR

RÁBA KETTŐS HÍD

Carmelite church

John Bull Pub

ARADI VÉRTANÚK

Philharmonic ticket office

Győr National Theatre

BAJCSY-ZSILINSZKY

Bellagio Café

Klastrom

ARANY JÁNOS

BAROSS GÁBOR

CZUCZOR GERGELY

Bartók Béla Cultural Centre

ÁRPÁD

Hotel Famulus

Flower market

KOSSUTH LAJOS

Synagogue

PETŐFI TÉR

PÉTERFY SÁNDOR

Komédiás

Tourinform

Hotel Rába

PETŐFI TÉR

Rába

ZECHMEISTER

BAJCSY-ZSILINSZKY

Richter János Terem

ARADI VÉRTANÚK

PETŐFI HÍD

ÁRPÁD

RÉVAI MIKLÓS

BAROSS GÁBOR HÍD

ESZPERANTÓ

SZENT ISTVÁN

Town hall

Post office

BENCZÚR

MUNKÁCSY MIHÁLY

Railway station

Bus station

Club Bacardi, bike hire

ÚJLAK

VASÚTAS

HUNYADI

DUGONICS

Hunyadi Panzió

ZRÍNYI

BAROSS GÁBOR

HONVÉD

BEM TÉR

Hotel Wesselényi

N

Bradt

KALVÁRIA

Hotel Kálvária

BABITS MIHÁLY

EÖRSY PÉTER

VÉCSEY JÓSIKA

Tio Pepe

0   200m
0   200yds

Turks were able to capture and hold it for just four years at the close of the 16th century, while Napoleon expended little energy in crushing a rebellion of nobles in 1809. It wasn't until World War II, when the factories and railway became targets for the Allies, that the city's architectural wings – the products of building by rich merchants and industrialists – were seriously singed.

GETTING THERE AND AWAY The main **railway station** is behind the town hall on Révai Miklós utca. From the station head northwards through the park (*Honvéd liget*) and along Aradi vértanút útja. Győr has excellent connections to Budapest's Déli, Keleti and Kelenföld stations, with up to 35 departures a day. Trains also run regularly to Pannonhalma (every 30 minutes), Csorna and Sopron. Other services are to Szombathely (eight), Szolnok (six), Veszprém (five) and Sárvár (two). Up to ten direct trains a day depart for Vienna, crossing the border at Hegyeshalom.

A subway links the railway station to the **bus station** (*Hunyadi u.*), with regular services to Budapest Népliget and Sopron, and very regular departures to Pannonhalma. Other buses run to Veszprém (12), Keszthely and Zalaegerszeg (five), Székesfehérvár (seven), Tapolca (four), Szombathely (five) and Pécs (two). There's also a bus that runs every morning to Vienna.

INFORMATION AND OTHER PRACTICALITIES

♿ **Álmos Vezér** Corvin u. 44; ☏ 96 335567. Bike hire for 1,000Ft/day (excl deposit). Tourinform can provide a cycling map. ⊕ Mon–Fri 12.00–17.00, Sat 10.00–13.00.

🔲 **Ibusz** Kazinczy u. 3; ☏ 96 314224; e gyor@ ibusz.hu. Private accommodation & local tours. ⊕ Mon–Fri 08.00–18.00, Sat 09.00–13.00.

🔲 **Listings magazine** *Győri Est*

🏛 **Virág Piac** Arany János u. (western end). Small outdoor vegetable & flower market that opens every morning.

🔲 **Tourinform** Árpád út 32; ☏ 96 311771; e gyor@tourinform.hu. Housed in a small glass pavilion outside the Hotel Rába; there is a currency-exchange service, as well as information on sights & events. ⊕ Jun 1–Sep 1 Mon–Fri 09.00–18.00, Sat–Sun 10.00–19.00, Mar–May Mon–Fri 09.00–17.00, Sat 09.00–13.00, Sep–Feb Mon–Fri 09.00–17.00, Sat 09.00–13.00.

🔲 **Vogue Music Caffe** See page 454. Offers free internet.

WHERE TO STAY

🏠 **Arany Szarvas** (16 rooms) Radó sétány 1; ☏ 96 517452. Attached to Captain Drakes Pub, the Arany Szarvas is scenically set on Radó Island, & has a fitness centre & sauna, & stands near the Thermal & Wellness Baths. *Sgl 12,900Ft, dbl 15,900Ft.*

🏠 **Famulus Kollégium** (50 apts) Budai út 4–6; ☏ 96 516732; www.kollegium.famulushotel.hu. Next to the Hotel Famulus, the accommodation is arranged in two-room apts for 4 people. *2,800Ft/pp.*

🏠 **Fonte Hotel** (29 rooms) Kisfaludy u. 38; ☏ 96 513810; www.hotelfonte.hu. The prices are on the high side, but this is a real treasure of a hotel with well-furnished, good-sized rooms, & an elegant restaurant (see page 454). Next to the National Theatre, & named after a fountain found when renovating the 18th-century townhouse. Free parking in the yard. *Sgl 13,900Ft, dbl 16,900Ft, apt (for 3) 23,900Ft.*

🏠 **Hotel Famulus** (60 rooms) Budai út 4–6; ☏ 96 547770; www.hotelfamulus.hu. This spanking new

business hotel is located at the crossroads of Győr, between the old city, the main shopping arcade & the old industrial area (to west of centre). Small but comfortable air-conditioned rooms, sauna, fitness, massage, bowling, squash, parking. *Sgl 19,000Ft, dbl 21,000Ft.*

🏠 **Hotel Kálvária** (19 rooms) Kálvária u. 22/d; ☏ 96 510800; www.hotel-kalvaria.hu. Newish 4-star hotel with tasteful standard rooms, plush suites & a tidy restaurant. Sauna, fitness room & solarium. A touch overpriced for its location. 15 mins south of the centre. *Sgl 20,500Ft, dbl dbl 21,700Ft.*

🏠 **Hotel Konferencia** (22 rooms) Apor Vilmos püspök tere 3; ☏ 96 511450; www.hotelkonferencia.hu. Although it is primarily a conference hotel (& feels almost like an office, because used by Audi staff for meetings), its location opposite the cathedral is superb. Well-equipped, modern rooms, swimming pool, sauna & parking. *Sgl 12,900Ft, dbl 16,000Ft.*

⌂ **Hotel Rába** (155 rooms) Árpád út 34; ✆ 96 889400; www.danubiushotels.com/raba. The first hotel in Győr – established in 1904 – the Rába is central & has a sauna, solarium, a small nightclub, as well as the Belgian Beer Café below. Guests get free admission to the casino opposite. The standard rooms are well-equipped & comfortable, & the business suites are excellent. *Standard/superior sgl €72/102, dbl €82/120.*

⌂ **Hotel Wesselényi** (30 rooms) Wesselényi u. 3; ✆ 96 510040. Pleasant hotel with a stylish bar, a 10-minute walk from the centre. Sauna & gym. *Sgl €57, dbl €62.*

⌂ **Hunyadi Panzió** (11 rooms) Hunyadi János út 10; ✆ 96 329162. A stone's throw from the bus station, this modern & welcoming guesthouse is good value compared with some of the other accommodation in town. *Sgl 9,900Ft, dbl 12,900Ft, trpl 15,000Ft.*

⌂ **Klastrom Hotel** (42 rooms) Zechmeister u. 1; ✆ 96 516910 www.hotels.hu/klastrom. Nestled for the past 50 years in the cloister at the back of the Carmelite church, the Klastrom has small, dated rooms in the former monks' cells. *Sgl €55, dbl €70, trpl €80.*

⌂ **Pihenő Camping & Motel** Kiskút liget; ✆ 96 318986. Tent & caravan pitches, bungalows & motel rooms at a fully equipped but average-feeling site. Tennis courts & a bufé. 3km east of the centre – follow Szent István út into Kiskúti & follow signs to the right, or jump on bus 8. *Camping 1,500Ft/pp, caravan 2,500Ft, motel room 2,500Ft/pp, bungalows (up to 4) 1,200Ft/pp.*

⌂ **Romantic Hotel Schweizerhof** (32 rooms) Sarkantyú köz 11–13; ✆ 96 512358; www.schweizerhof.hu. This Swiss-owned hotel in the historic town centre is conservatively furnished & well appointed. Sauna, fitness room, garage. *Sgl 16,000Ft, dbl 17,300Ft.*

✗ WHERE TO EAT AND DRINK

♀ **Belgian Beer Café** Árpád út 34; ✆ 96 507660. Bar & restaurant chain specialising – surprise, surprise – in Belgian beer (there are 15 different types on offer). Part of the Hotel Rába, it has an old-fashioned feel & a pavement terrace. The calorie-conscious can choose from the set 'wellness' menu. ⊕ *Mon–Fri 10.00–24.00, Sat 11.00–24.00, Sun 11.00–22.00.*

⊔ **Bergmann Cukrászda** Király u. 17, ✆ 96 322554. Well-established patisserie on the corner (behind some shrubs); it has an Art-Nouveau interior, as well as a few tables outside. Excellent cakes & their own ice-cream. ⊕ *Mon–Sat 10.00–18.00.*

✗ **Fonte Restaurant** Schweidel u. 17. Delightful, adventurous food in a classy setting at the Fonte Hotel. Specialities include salmon in lemon-crab sauce, chicken with apple purée & chateaubriand, & there's a good wine selection. *Mains avg 3,500Ft;* ⊕ *Mon–Sat 06.30–22.00.*

✗ **Katalin Kert** Sarkantyú köz 3, tel 96 542088. Tucked away under the city walls it has an enclosed garden & simply furnished dining room. *Mains avg 1,500Ft;* ⊕ *11.00–23.00.*

✗ **Klastrom Restaurant** See above. The Klastrom's claim to fame is that it prepared the food for a banquet served to Pope John Paul II in the Zichy Palace in 1996. Its international cuisine has a French twist; the cobbled courtyard is the spot to choose if the weather suits. *Mains avg 1,600Ft;* ⊕ *11.00–22.00 daily.*

✗ **Komédiás** Czuczor Gergely u. 30; ✆ 96 527217; e komedias@axelero.hu. Basic eatery serving good local dishes at reasonable prices. Large courtyard. *Mains avg 1,900Ft;* ⊕ *Mon–Sat 11.00–24.00.*

✗ **Pálffy Étterem** Jedlik Ányos u. 19; ✆ 96 524680; www.palffyetterem.hu. Hugely popular restaurant on the corner of beautiful Széchenyi tér; the menu is international, with a good selection of salads. *Mains avg 1,800Ft;* ⊕ *09.00–24.00 daily.*

✗ **Ristorante Romantica** Dunakapu tér 5; ✆ 96 314127. Brocade-heavy furnishings & tinkly Italian music does not romantic make. (The view of the unattractive square from the terrace does little to help the cause either.) Nevertheless, the Italian food is very good, if expensive. *Mains avg 2,200Ft;* ⊕ *Mon–Thu & Sun 11.30–23.00, Fri–Sat 11.30–24.00.*

✗ **Tio Pepe** Eörsi Péter u. 17; ✆ 96 439611; www.miwo.hu/tio. The owners have successfully created a Mediterranean atmosphere, & serve typical Spanish dishes. Sit at one of the booths outside, where there is a waterfall & ferns galore. A romantic, evenly priced treat. *Mains 650–1,090Ft, 2 courses for 700Ft;* ⊕ *12.00–24.00 daily.*

♀ **Vogue Music Caffe** Kenyér köz 4; ✆ 70 5502336; www.musiccaffe.hu. Busy bar with a varied music programme. *Mon–Thu 09.00–24, Fri–Sat 09.00–03.00, Sun 09.00–24.00.*

ENTERTAINMENT AND NIGHTLIFE The **Győr National Theatre** (*Győri Nemzeti Színház; Czuczor Gergely u. 7;* ✆ *96 314800;* e *szervezes@gyoriszinhaz.hu; www.gyoriszinhaz.hu; ticket office* ⊕ *Tue–Fri 10.00–13.00, 14.00–18.00*) is an angular, unattractive structure with a ramp-like roof that would look at home in a skateboard park. The side walls are decorated with ceramic Op-Art works by Victor Vasarely. The theatre plays host to the nationally acclaimed Győr Philharmonic and Győr Ballet companies, and has performances of folk dance, drama and musicals. The **Philharmonic Ticket Office** (*Kisfaludy u. 25;* ✆ *96 326323;* ⊕ *Mon–Thu 08.00–16.00, Fri 08.00–15.00*) sells tickets for orchestral performances at the Zichy Palace as well as the National Theatre. The **Bartók Béla Cultural Centre** (*Czuczor Gergely u. 17;* ✆ *96 326522;* ⊕ *Mon 13.00–21.00, Tue–Sat 10.00–21.00, Sun varies*) is one of several cultural centres in the city where you can obtain information on events, and has temporary exhibitions, concerts and lifestyle classes. **Bellagio Café** (*Teleki László u. 36;* ✆ *06 30 536 8545;* ⊕ *Mon–Fri 08.00–04.00, Sat–Sun 14.00–04.00*) is the bar to be seen in, with leather benches, a chrome bar and an elevated terrace from which to scowl at passers by. Also near the National Theatre is the small and busy **Művész Cocktail Bar** (*Schweidel u. 25;* ⊕ *Mon–Thu 07.00–23.00, Fri–Sat 07.00–02.00, Sun 11.00–23.00*).

John Bull Pub (*Aradi Vértanúk utja 3;* ✆ *96 618320;* ⊕ *10.00–24.00 daily*), just to the east of the Carmelite church, is an upmarket English-style boozer and a popular spot for a tipple. The **Hotel Wesselényi Bar** (see opposite; ⊕ *12.00–24.00 daily*) is a cool drinking hole with stylish furnishings. **Club Bacardi** (*Mészáros Lőrinc u. 11;* ⊕ *Fri–Sat 21.00–06.00*) is for the more serious clubbers, based on an industrial estate southeast of the centre (buses 23 and 27 stop 150m away), while the **Darius Music Club** (*Czuczor Gergely út 6;* ✆ *30 9944453;* ⊕ *Fri–Sat 22.00–04.00*) is a disco in the centre of town. **Rómer Ház – Underground Club** (*Teleki u. 21; www.mediawave.hu/romer*) has regular film screenings and cultural events for students.

WHAT TO SEE AND DO

Bécsi kapu tér Everthing of note in Győr is gathered in the area beside and around the confluence of the Rába and Mosoni-Duna rivers. Bécsi kapu tér, at the eastern head of the bridge that makes a skip and a jump on to Rába Island and the western bank, is the best place to begin your wanderings. It was originally closed by the Vienna Gate, but in 1809 Napoleon's troops destroyed the bastion while suppressing an uprising of Hungarian nobles, and opened it up to the river. The Baroque **Carmelite church** (*Karmelita templom*), with its elliptical nave and off-centre tower, was built by Márton Wittwer (a monk of the order) and consecrated in 1725. To the right of the entrance is an open chapel containing a statue of 'Foam Mary', which was moved from the island to this position of honour after supposedly protecting the city from 18th-century floods. The church interior contains high-altar paintings of István and his son Imre paying homage to the Virgin, carved walnut furnishings by Franz Richter and early-20th-century frescoes on the cupola. To the left of the nave is the Dark Chapel, which bears a sculpture of Mary made in Rome and touched with the holy statue in the Loretto Chapel before being shipped to Győr. Behind the church is the friary, built during the same period and currently home to the Klastrom Hotel (see opposite); the president of the National Assembly hid within after declaring independence from the Habsburgs in 1848.

Just off the eastern side of the square, **Napoleon House** (*Király u. 4;* ✆ *96 337742;* 🎫 *600/300Ft;* ⊕ *Mon–Fri 10.00–18.00, Sat 09.00–13.00*) is so-named because Napoleon spent the night of August 31 1809 there after his soldiers had captured the castle; there is now a small gallery on the first floor. At the northern end of the square

are some surviving walls of Győr's medieval castle. In the 16th century it was the biggest in Hungary, with three gates and seven bastions linked by 10m-high walls. The Turks occupied it for just four years before it was recaptured by the renowned generals Miklós Pálffy and Adolf Schwarzenberg; however, Napoleon inflicted considerable damage, and the bulk of the remains were demolished in 1820. A **lapidarium** (*Bécsi kapu tér 5;* ✆ *96 310588;* ✆ *600/300Ft;* ☉ *Apr–Oct Tue–Sun 10.00–18.00*) in the courtyard of what was the Sforza Bastion has pieces of the fortress, as well as Roman finds and a collection of bricks.

Káptalandomb To the north of Bécsi kapu tér is Káptalandomb (Chapter Hill), the nucleus of the medieval settlement and the site of the original cathedral established by King István in 1033. **Győr Cathedral** (*Székesegyház; Apor Vilmos püspök tere;* ☉ *closed for cleaning 12.00–14.00 daily*) weathered some considerable storms, attacked by the Mongols in the 13th century and used as both a stable and a gun emplacement by the Turks. Subsequent reconstructions resulted in a mish-mash of styles, and the building incorporates Romanesque, Gothic, Baroque and Neoclassical features. Its heavily gilded interior is adorned with 18th-century frescoes and an altarpiece depicting the Ascension of Mary by Franz Anton Maulbertsch.

The Héderváry (or Trinity) Chapel was added to the southern aisle in 1404 and contains the country's finest piece of medieval goldsmith's art – a bust of King László made in around 1400, and inlaid with Transylvanian enamelwork. The herm holds László's skull (a curator at the Episcopal Museum – one of the few people ever to have opened the reliquary – told us that beneath the crown is a plate, which is unscrewed to reveal a second silver crown with the skull inside); it is said that in 1763 the herm miraculously halted an earthquake, and every June it is paraded through the city in remembrance. At the other end of the chapel is the red-marble sarcophagus of Bishop Apor Vilmos, a vehement opponent of Nazism who was tragically killed at Easter in 1945 while protecting women from a drunk Russian soldier who'd taken part in the city's liberation. During the communist era it was prohibited even to mention his name; in 1997 he was beatified by the pope.

Outside the church are the sunken remains of a tiny 13th-century chapel discovered during late-20th-century excavations. Across the way, the **Borsos Miklós Museum** (*Apor Vilmos püspök tere 2;* ✆ *96 316329;* ✆ *600/300Ft;* ☉ *Tue–Sun*

THE WEEPING MADONNA

At the end of the cathedral's northern aisle is an altarpiece of particular interest. The silver-framed 'Weeping Madonna' painting was brought here by Walter Lynch, the Bishop of Clonfort in Ireland, who was fleeing persecution by Oliver Cromwell in 1655. On St Patrick's Day 1697, 34 years after his death – and at a time when further anti-Catholic laws were being passed in Britain – eyewitnesses (including General Siegbert Heister, the contemporary castle commander) recorded that the icon wept blood for three hours. The congregation mopped up the drops with a white cloth, still held in the sacristy. There followed a seven-year-long investigation that could find no rational explanation for the phenomenon, and in the years afterwards a strong cult developed around the painting. It has influenced many later artists – the depiction of Christ on a pillow, rather than in his mother's arms, was quite unusual – and pilgrims travel here annually on St Patrick's Day. In 1997 the Bishop of Clonfert travelled to Győr to take part in 300th-anniversary celebrations of the miracle. In 2004, a copy of the painting was taken to the church in Ireland from where it is believed Lynch brought the original, an act symbolic of the religious and historical parallels that many Hungarians see when they gaze across to Ireland.

Mar–Oct 10.00–18.00, Nov–Feb 10.00–17.00) displays the paintings, sculptures and bronze reliefs of Borsos, a 20th-century artist intrigued by tactile art and abstract portraiture, and responsible for the Zero Kilometre stone in Budapest (a sculpture near the funicular railway). He lived in this former bishop's courthouse between 1921 and 1945. Opposite the western entrance to the cathedral is the **Bishop's Castle** (*Püspökvár; Káptalandomb 1;* ☏ *20 3128735;* ⊕ *Tue–Sun 10.00–16.00*), which has a 15th-century Gothic chapel and a colourful tower (originally 14th-century but reconstructed in the 18th century). The Castle Garden was part of the 16th-century fortified complex, and is enclosed by some of the walls that still stand. Szent Mihály utca leaves the square's eastern side and leads to the **Diocesan Treasury and Library** (*Egyházmegyei Kincstár és Könyvtár; Káptalandomb 26;* ☏ *96 525090;* 🎟 *700/400Ft;* ⊕ *Mar–Oct Tue–Sun 10.00–16.00*), among the country's richest collection of sacred objects from Hungary and Transylvania. The hoard of manuscripts is the most valuable, including an 11th-century codex and a fabulous 15th-century illuminated manuscript from the library of Mátyás (one of a tiny number to survive the Turkish occupation in Buda; see page 166). In addition, there is an exhibition devoted to the 'Weeping Madonna' (see box opposite), a gold monstrance of 1500 from the Clarissa Convent in Buda's Castle District, and a piece of the bloodied shirt of Bishop Vilmos (see opposite).

Széchenyi tér and around The tarmacked Széchenyi tér is surrounded by historic buildings, many softening the square's points with the corner balconies for which the city is famous. Such window annexes provided the householder with unrestricted views, and allowed the wealthy to participate in street life – this used to be a market place – without having to hold their noses or dirty their shoes. In the square's southern section is the **Mária Column**, a Baroque monument consecrated in 1686 by Bishop Lipót Kollonich in thanks for the re-taking of Buda from the Turks. Behind it is the **Church of St Ignác**, built in 1641 by Jesuits and taken over later by the Benedictines (after József II had dissolved the Jesuit order). It is flanked by a Benedictine monastery and a Benedictine grammar school (the latter containing an exhibition to the acclaimed teachers Gergely Czuczor and Ányos Jedlik, whose statues are outside; *for admission,* ☏ *96 315988*). Beside the monastery is the still-working **Széchenyi Pharmacy** (*Széchenyi tér 9;* ☏ *96 320954; free admission;* ⊕ *Mon–Fri 07.30–16.00*), which was founded by the Jesuits in 1654 and has a ceiling fresco of Mary's Assumption surrounded by carved cherubs symbolic of the four seasons.

The **Patkó Imre Museum** (*Széchenyi tér 4;* ☏ *96 310588;* 🎟 *400/250Ft;* ⊕ *Apr–Sep Tue–Sun 10.00–18.00, rest of yr by appointment only*) is held in the Iron Stock House, so-named because of the stump outside into which wandering artisans hammered their nails. Entrance to the museum – which contains 20th-century European art and an ethnographic collection of objects from Africa and Oceania – is on Szelczer Lajos utca. The beautiful Baroque building next door – constructed in 1742 as lodgings for Pannonhalma abbots – hosts the **Xantus János Museum** (*Széchenyi tér 5;* ☏ *96 310588; www.gymsmuzeum.hu;* 🎟 *650/300Ft; combined ticket for Xantus, Patkó & Lapidarium 1,200/600Ft;* ⊕ *Tue–Sun May–Oct 10.00–18.00, Nov–Apr 10.00–14.00*). Named after a 19th-century globetrotter and naturalist, Győr's well-presented main museum features regional archaeological finds, items of local and medical history, and a massive collection of stamps. Highlights to look out for are a tiny pair of boots – after travelling for several years, craftsmen aspiring to membership of a guild had to submit a masterpiece of their art to the committee – and a 17th-century weathercock. The latter topped the Vienna Gate (see page 455) and is the symbol of the city. During their brief occupation, the confident Turks joked that a cock would crow beneath a full moon before Christians held Győr again; it is said that on the moonlit night the castle was re-taken, the weathercock creaked in the wind.

A short distance to the northeast of the square, an ex-hospice founded by Bishop György Széchenyi in 1666 now contains the **Váczy Péter Museum** (*Nefelejcs köz 3;* \ *96 318141;* & *600/300Ft;* ☉ *Tue–Sun Mar–Oct 10.00–18.00, Nov–Feb 10.00–17.00*), based on the private 20th-century collection of Renaissance and Baroque furniture and art gathered by an anti-communist professor. It is worth making a brief detour to see the nearby **Zichy Palace** (*Liszt Ferenc u. 20*) – built for Ferenc Zichy in 1720, and later providing accommodation for Ferenc Deák and Lajos Batthyány while they studied law – before crossing Széchenyi tér once more to the **Municipal Gallery** (*Király u. 17;* \ *96 322695;* & *800/300Ft, free for students on Sun;* ☉ *Tue–Sun 10.00–18.00*) in the former Esterházy Palace, with exhibitions of modern art.

Head north up Jedlik Ányos utca and you'll reach the Ark of the Covenant Statue (see box opposite) and the **Kovács Margit Museum** (*Apáca u. 1;* \ *96 326739;* & *600/300Ft;* ☉ *Tue–Sun Mar–Oct 10.00–18.00, Nov–Feb Tue–Sun 10.00–17.00*). The work of the 20th century's leading Hungarian ceramicist – who was born in Győr in 1902 – has always divided the opinion of experts. Influenced by religion, legend and folk art, her later work became increasingly abstract and informed by geometric shapes. The 100 pieces here include vases, animal-shaped vessels, religious paintings and Gothic figurines; for more, you'll need to visit the main museum in Szentendre (see pages 184–5).

Dunakapu tér, at the top of Jedlik Ányos utca, is named after the medieval gate that faced the river at this point. The fountain at the centre bears a copy of the weathercock now housed in the Xantus János Museum (see page 457). The square is filled with market stalls on Wednesdays and Saturdays.

Other If you arrive by bus or train and walk into the centre, you are likely to follow Baross Gábor út, the pedestrianised main shopping street. On the way there, you shouldn't miss the **town hall** (*Városház tér*), a magnificent Eclectic palace built in 1896 during the millennial celebrations to the design of Jenő Hübner. Every hour a piece of music by local composer Attila Reményi chimes from the building.

On the opposite side of the River Rába, roughly level with the southern end of the island, is an imposing **synagogue** (*Kossuth Lajos u. 5*). It was built between 1869 and 1870 with a quartet of octagonal corner turrets; it is now the venue for cultural performances and the Vasilescu Collection of 20th-century art. The former Jewish school next door now holds a music academy. The **Richter Hall** (*Aradi Vértanúk útja 16;* \ *96 312452; www.filharmonikusok.gyor.hu*) is home to the Győr Philharmonic Orchestra. János Richter was a famous conductor born in Győr, a champion of Wagner and Elgar, and first chief conductor of the London Symphonic Orchestra.

On the same bank, above the island's northern tip, is a big **complex of baths** (*Rába Quelle; Furdő tér 1;* \ *96 514900; www.gyortermal.hu;* & *1,950/1,350Ft;* ☉ *Sun–Thu 09.00–20.30, Fri–Sat & public holidays 09.00–21.00*); among the attractions are five swimming pools, two giant waterslides (of 64m and 38m), saunas and a thermal spa.

FESTIVALS AND EVENTS Győr prides itself on being a city of festivals, and there is no shortage of events every year. The Baroque Ball (*Feb*) features dancing and feasting in the Zichy Palace; the Spring Festival (*Mar–Apr*) involves music, theatre and dance; there is an international film competition and a programme of music, alternative drama and dance during Mediawave (*Apr–May*); Győr Summer (*Jun–Jul*) is a month of cultural events at several venues around the city; the Five Churches Festival (*Sep*) is a weekend of holy music in the city's churches; and Baroque Nostalgia (*Oct*) is another festival taking the Baroque for its watchword, with dance, music and art of the 17th and 18th centuries. For details see www.gyor.hu.

The masterful Ark of the Covenant Statue in Gutenberg János tér had an unusual conception. In 1729 a soldier accused of bigamy took refuge in the Benedictine monastery. When the friars refused to hand the man over, the soldiers that had come to arrest him posted themselves outside and waited. A stalemate ensued that the bishop of the day was determined to resolve. Easter was approaching, and it was decided to disguise the fugitive and smuggle him away as part of the Corpus Christi procession. As the group reached what is now Gutenberg János tér, however, the man was recognised; as the guards struggled to capture him, the Communion cup was dashed from the hands of the priest and broke on the stones. On hearing of this insult to the Church, Emperor Charles III commissioned the Ark of the Covenant Statue to be placed at the site. Ironically, the subject of the commotion was ultimately found innocent, while the soldiers who arrested him were thoroughly punished.

EXCURSIONS Thirty kilometres west of Győr along Road 85, **Csorna** is the centre of the Rábaköz (in the catchment of the River Rába), a region with a strong folk tradition of weaving and blue-dying. As well as embroidered bedclothes and table cloths, each village had its own individual patterned dress, often using the flowers of the local gardens as motifs. Csorna's 19th-century Baroque and Neoclassical buildings are capped by the Premonstratensian church, whose extravagant interior displays a replica of the Polish Czestochowa Madonna above the altar. The adjacent Premonstratensian palace was constructed on the site of the 13th-century monastery; the Csorna Museum (*Szent István tér 34;* \ *96 261527;* & *500/250Ft;* ⊕ *Tue–Fri 10.00–17.00, Sat–Sun 10.00–14.00*) inside has a collection of folk art covering the work of the town's blue-dyers and that of potters from nearby Dör. Csorna is linked by train to Győr, Sopron and Pápa; there are buses running from all three.

There's more folk art (as well as some regional archaeology and plaster and bronze works by 20th-century sculptor Pál Pátzay, who was born in the town) at **Kapuvár**, 17km further west. The Rábaköz Museum (*Fő tér 1;* \ *96 242557;* & *360/180Ft;* ⊕ *Wed–Sun May–Sep 10.00–18.00, rest of yr 10.00–14.00*) is housed in a Baroque mansion built in place of the 13th-century fortress that served as a gateway through the border defensive line (hence the town's name 'Gate Castle'); the castle was demolished by Rákóczi's *kuruc* soldiers to prevent it falling into the hands of imperial forces. Rising above is the main clocktower of St Anne's Church, built in 1884 and replacing a medieval wooden chapel that once stood outside the castle. If you look under the organ loft, you'll see some angels decked in the local Kapusvár costume. Kapuvár is on the same road and rail line as Csorna.

Fifteen kilometres northwest of Győr (take the left turn off the M1 or Road 1, or take on of around ten daily buses from Győr), **Lébény** has one of the country's leading pieces of Romanesque architecture. The Benedictine abbey was originally constructed in 1208 and, despite being seriously damaged by the Turks, was faithfully restored in the 19th century.

The **Szigetköz** running above Győr can lay claim to being Hungary's largest island, formed of alluvial deposit and surrounded by the Danube and Mosoni-Duna rivers. The area was badly hit by the diversion of water upriver for the Gabčikovo power station (see box, page 203) in the 1990s; although the water levels remain lower than they were, the wildlife has made a recovery, and this is rich territory for hiking or nature-spotting. There's forest of aspen, willow, ash and oak, and over 200 species of bird (including the purple heron, black stork,

Montagu's harrier and white-tailed eagle); rapid-flowing backwaters are ideal for canoeing and gravel-pit lakes for fishing. The Tourinforms in Győr (see page 453) or Mosonmagyaróvár (*Kápolna tér 16;* \ *96 206304;* e *mosonmagyarovar@ tourinform.hu;* ☺ *mid Jun–Aug 31 Mon–Fri 09.00–18.00, Sat–Sun 09.00–17.00, rest of yr Mon–Fri 08.00–16.00*) can provide information on accommodation, kayak and bike hire, horse-riding and fishing permits. The country-house hotel Hédervár (*18 rooms; Fő u. 47;* \ *96 213576; www.hedervar.hu; dbl from 20,000Ft*) in the middle of Szigetköz is quite exceptional: a graceful (but unstuffy) Renaissance palace surrounded by park containing original stone statues and pavilions. Meals (*mains avg 2,500Ft;* ☺ *11.00–21.00 daily*) are served in the elegant dining room or the wine cellar.

PANNONHALMA

Looming from one hill among a cluster of three at the edge of the Kisalföld, 20km southeast of Győr, Pannonhalma's Benedictine abbey – a UNESCO World Heritage Site since 1996 – wears that cloak of mystery and romance associated with monastic life very comfortably indeed. Its hilltop was the perfect site for Prince Géza to establish Hungary's first Christian community and take an early step towards Christianisation of the Magyar tribes. Firstly, it had special connotations for the Magyars – according to Anonymus, Árpád's 'heart was filled with joy' as he watered his horses up here and beheld the beauty of his newly acquired territory. Secondly, it had sacred connotations for some Benedictine monks arriving from Rome – they believed that St Martin, Bishop of Tours and patron saint of Western monasticism, had been born near by. And thirdly, its position was strategically strong – a vital ingredient in case of disgruntled grumblings among those to be converted. At Géza's invitation, the monks built a church on the 275m peak and consecrated it in 1002 in the presence of King István. This elevated symbol of kingly intent was invested with further significance in the shape of its first abbot, Astrik, who'd couriered the Holy Crown from Pope Sylvester II that legitimised István's rule. István was himself a regular visitor, praying with the monks for St Martin's assistance in his struggle against the rebellious pagans. The Turks later used the church as a mosque during their stay, but aside from that the complex was influential up until the dissolution of the order in 1786 by József II. The dictates of the Enlightenment meant that it was only allowed to re-open in 1802 if it were to be 'useful'; the resultant secondary boarding school remains an organic part of the monastery to this day, teaching 360 pupils. During the autumn of 1944, the abbey came under the protection of the Swiss Red Cross, and provided asylum for terrified Jews.

GETTING THERE AND AWAY There are **buses** to/from Győr every half-hour or so, arriving/departing from Pannonhalma village. From there you can board one of five daily buses running up to the abbey gates – failing that, you'll have to walk. The **railway station** is a little under 1km to the west of the village, at the end of Petőfi utca. There are up to eight trains a day to Győr and up to five to Veszprém.

INFORMATION AND OTHER PRACTICALITIES

🚩 **Tourinform** Petőfi u. 25; \ 96 471733; e pannonhalma@tourinform.hu. Small office at the western side of the village. ☺ Jun–Aug daily 09.00–18.00, rest of yr Mon–Fri 09.00–17.00, Sat–Sun 10.00–16.00.

🎫 **TriCollis** Vár 1; \ 96 570191; www.bences.hu. Positioned just outside the entrance, this is the ticket office for the Archabbey. As this is a working monastery & school, visiting is only possible on a guided tour (see page 462 for times).

🏠 **WHERE TO STAY, EAT AND DRINK** Unless you fancy a slurp of the local wine, there's little need to stay the night and most people visit on a day trip from Győr.

✕ **Borpince** Szabadság tér; ✆ 96 471240; www.borbirodalom.hu. This highly charming place caters for sales & tastings of local wine. Groups — for whom Hungarian food can also be cooked — should book ahead. *From 1,400Ft/pp;* ⊕ *11.00–19.00 daily (if not open, ring the bell).*

⌂ **Esthajnal Vendégház** (self-catering apt) Cseider völgy 6; ✆ 30 3655294; e nahalka1@freemail.hu. Freshly renovated peasant cottage in large garden with 2 double rooms. *3,500Ft/pp (if 4 people);* ⊕ *May 15–Sep 30.*

⌂ **Familia Panzió** Béke u. 61; ✆ 96 470192; e familiapanzio@enternet.hu. Welcoming family guesthouse northwest of the village centre (600m along a road running off Petőfi u.). Barbecue for balmy nights, & bike hire available. *Rooms €18/pp.*

⛺ **Panoráma Camping** Pannonhalma Pf 21; ✆ 96 471240. This basic campsite is quaint, well-cared-for & blessed with fab views. Short distance south of the centre. *Plot 1,000Ft, 900/550Ft/pp, bungalow rooms 7,000–8,000Ft.*

⌂ **Pannon Panzió** (16 rooms) Hunyadi u. 7; ✆ 96 470041. Comfortable guest rooms overlooking the Abbey. *Sgl 7,800Ft, dbl 9,700Ft, trpl 12,000Ft.*

✕ **Szent Márton Restaurant** Vár 1; ✆ 96 470798. Down wind of the abbey by just 100m, this timber restaurant has many windows for big views, a non-smoking room & primarily Hungarian fare (with the odd international dish). *Mains avg 1,400Ft;* ⊕ *Mon–Fri 09.00–17.00, Sat–Sun 09.00–18.00, closed on Mon Oct 1–Mar 15.*

PANNONHALMA ABBEY The seminal structure of 1002 – that at the very birth of the Christian State of Hungary – is invisible in today's **Pannonhalma Abbey** (*Vár u. 1;* ✆ *96 570100*), which is a medley of later styles. The original burnt down and was replaced in 1137 (only an arching wall of the western sanctuary remains, beneath floor level); the foundation of what you see now is a third, late-Romanesque version of 1224. The distinctive 55m **Neoclassical tower** buried at the heart of the complex, with its wedding cake columns and narrow dome, was added during the 19th century. The basilica's **main portal** (*Porta speciosa*) dates from the 13th century, and comprises a series of receding arches made of limestone and red marble, supported by sets of twin pillars. Above the doors is a fresco by Ferenc Storno, a 19th-century artist who carved and chipped at many of the region's churches in the name of aesthetic 'uniformity' and 'authentic' Gothic styling, and got thoroughly up the noses of present-day purists. The fresco shows St Martin of Tours – who started life as a Roman legionary before devoting himself to God – cutting his cloak and giving half to a beggar. While it might seem that he was being a touch miserly in his charity, a Roman soldier only paid for half his kit (the army bore the remaining cost) so he was giving all that was rightfully his. Storno's hand is in further features of the **basilica** interior, including the Romanesque and Gothic crypt – the oldest surviving section – which contains the red marble niche where the abbot sat during masses. Protocol dictated that the abbot gave up his spot to a royal visitor, and legend has it that this seat includes fragments of that on which István parked his backside.

Aside from some 18th-century Baroque buildings, much of the adjoining **monastery** dates to the 15th century, when it was rebuilt under the direction of King Mátyás. The cloister's covered walkway is adorned with diminutive stone faces representing human sins (as well as a bearded man thought to be the architect), and opens on to a quadrangle and garden; the latter contains a sundial inscribed with the deflating Latin truism 'One of you is my last hour'. The monastery's highly ornate refectory is among the finest Baroque halls in the country. To the south of the cloister are the **school buildings**, erected in the 1940s, while on the other side of the church is the stunning **Neoclassical library**. This was commissioned to serve the abbey's new educational role in the early 19th century, and was designed by József Ferenc Engel and then János Páckh (who also built the church tower). Its cherry-wood bookcases hold some of the library's 300,000 books. In the archives is the founding charter of the Abbey of Tihany (in Balaton) from 1055 – of special significance because among its Latin is a piece of the earliest-known sentence written in Hungarian. A **gallery** displays works including some European masterpieces of the 16th–18th centuries collected by one of the abbots, while the domed and vaulted basement has an **exhibition** of the abbey's history that opened during the order's millennial celebrations in 1996.

You can only visit the abbey on a **guided tour** (✆ *1,400/600Ft, foreign-lang tour, inc English, 2,400/1,800Ft; Eng-lang tours 11.20 & 13.20, additional one at 15.20 Jun–Sep*), which departs from the gate. Also look out for the annual celebratory **concerts** in the basilica; for information and bookings, contact Pax Tourist.

The other sights on the three hills are freely accessible. The middle peak holds the Neoclassical **Millennial Memorial**, built in 1896 as one of seven monuments (symbolic of the seven Magyar tribes) around the country to commemorate the conquest; Aba Novák Vilmos died before completing his frescoes inside. The **Chapel of the Blessed Virgin** on the hill to the southwest was completed in 1725, and has a pretty hexagonal belfry; its crypt remains a burial place for Benedictines. The crucifixion scene beside it was crafted in 1724 and moved here to make way for the Millennial Memorial. Behind it is a **lookout tower**.

SÁRVÁR

On the banks of the River Rába (and at the mouth of the Gyöngyös Brook) around 30km east of Szombathely, Sárvár has a long history. The Celts fortified the river crossing here and the Romans later established military camps on both sides of the water. Magyar earthworks defended against incursions by 10th-century Germanic tribes and the castle after which the town is named was first mentioned in documents of the 12th century. However, the Renaissance building of today dates to the 16th century when it came into possession of the Nádasdys, a significant dynasty that left a considerable mark. Tamás Nádasdy was a formidable politician – Governor of Croatia and later Palatine of Hungary – and he helped to make the town a religious and cultural centre of the Reformation. He surrounded himself with leading scientists, artists and humanist thinkers, and in 1537 established a printing house under the scholar János Sylvester; from this press rolled the first grammar book in 1539 and the first book in Hungarian (a translation of the New Testament) in 1541. Tamás's son Ferenc Nádasdy II (the so-called 'Black Captain') fought heroically (and winningly) against the Turks; much scandal surrounded his wife, however (see box opposite). The luck (and the family line) ran out with Ferenc Nádasdy III; the Lord Chief Justice was executed in 1671 for his part in the Zrínyi conspiracy (see page 18), a plot against Emperor Lipót hatched by a group of nobles angered by Habsburg concessions to the Turks. The 20th century saw the arrival of several factories, while in 1961 thermal water was discovered, which feeds the town's spa.

GETTING THERE AND AWAY The **bus station** (*Laktanya u.*) is west of town – follow Batthyány Lajos utca to reach the centre. There are up to 17 buses a day to Szombathely, as well as services to Veszprém (five) and Sopron (four), Budapest Népliget (three), Győr (two) and Zalaegerszeg (five). The **railway station** is northwest of the town on Selyemgyár utca; follow Hunyadi János utca southwards to the centre. Trains depart regularly to Szombathely, and there are up to eight daily to Budapest Deli and Keleti stations. Other destinations include Veszprém (eight), Székesfehérvár (seven), Pápa, Győr and Tatabánya (three), Tapolca (two), Sopron and Pécs (one).

INFORMATION AND OTHER PRACTICALITIES

Listings magazine *Szombathelyi Est*
Aqua Tours Batthyány út 19–21; ☎ 95 320578; www.aquatravel.hu. You can book private rooms or tours at this office. ☉ Mon–Sat 09.00–12.00 & 13.00–17.00.

Tourinform Várkerület 33; ☎ 95 520178; e sarvar@tourinform.hu. Near the castle entrance. ☉ Mon–Fri 08.00–17.00, Sat 08.00–12.00, May–Sep Sun 08.00–19.00.

WHERE TO STAY

Bassiana (19 rooms) Várkerület 2; ☎ 95 521300; www.hotelbassiana.hu. Pleasant, central hotel with a beautifully kept garden (inc children's play area) & its own entrance to the adjoining arboretum. Sauna, bike rental, child supervision, dental surgery (by prior appointment). *Dbl 19,000Ft, attic room 16,500Ft.*

BLOOD BATH-ORI

At the age of 54, Erzsébet Báthori was entombed in a room at her castle in Čachtice (now in Slovakia) to spend the last four years of her life in claustrophobic isolation. Such was her punishment for deeds so darkly devilish that they have been the stuff of horror ever since – inspiring, it is said, literary works as renowned as Bram Stoker's *Dracula*. She was accused of murdering over 600 women, of tearing lumps of flesh from their bodies, even of drinking and bathing in their blood in the belief it would rejuvenate her middle-aged complexion. She went down in history as one of the original vampires. The level of truth in these tales will probably never be known for sure.

What is beyond doubt is that those who made the accusations had a vested interest in making them. On the death of her husband Ferenc Nádasdy in 1604 she inherited a vast wealth, and Palatine of Hungary György Thurzó was concerned by the power the Báthoris would wield should she forge an alliance with her nephew Gábor (Prince of Transylvania). Others weren't happy either, among them the poet Miklós Zrínyi; he was Erzsébet's son-in-law, and was miffed that she wasn't channelling some of her fortune his way. In 1610, Thurzó took a body of guards to Čachtice and as he entered the door stumbled upon (literally) the corpse of a butchered servant. Or so he said.

'All rather convenient', we hear the defence lawyers cry. Yet there were factors that gave at least faint credence to the claim. There had been much inter-marriage in the Báthori clan, and Erzsébet would not have been the first among them to display signs of sadism or lunacy. Furthermore, Erzsébet had shown cruel tendencies in disciplining servants even prior to her husband's death, pouring freezing water over one until she died of the cold. And there were hundreds of statements gathered from those around her in support of the charges. Which case would have prevailed in court we'll never know, for while a maid accused of helping her was executed, the blue bloods were keen to hush up such crimes among their own (particularly after Gábor Báthori's death in 1613 removed the threat of an alliance). Erzsébet was incarcerated without trial, leaving behind a tale that has intrigued ghoulish story-tellers ever since; her body lies in the family vault at Nagyecsed.

⌂ **Platán Hotel** (18 rooms) Hunyadi u. 23; ☏ 95 320623; www.platanhotel.hu. Divided between new & old wings, this hotel is fine, but we feel the price is steep for rooms that are on the diminutive side. There is a swimming pool & sauna though, & you can rent bikes & fishing gear. Northwest of the castle — follow Ady Endre u. & look for the turning to the right. *Dbl 13,500Ft, trpl 17,500Ft.*

⌂ **Spirit Hotel** (273 rooms) Vadkert krt.5; ☏ 95 889500; www.spirithotel.hu. This 5-star hotel is Hungary's newest medical-wellness & spa hotel; it's surprising to find something so well equipped in such a quiet corner of the country. In addition to its own thermal-water supply for those seeking relief from ailments, the beauty & relaxation treatments are also comprehensive. Non-guests can use the facilities for 10,000Ft/pp. *Sgl €130, dbl €200.*

⚐ **Termál Camping** Vadkert u. 1; ☏ 95 320292, www.thermalcamping.com. Very popular campsite conveniently planted next to the thermal baths. It re-opened in 2006 after complete refurbishment. *Tent/caravan €6,90, plus ⊞ €7/5.*

⌂ **Thermal Hotel** (136 rooms) Rákóczi u. 1; ☏ 95 888400; www.danubiusgroup.com/sarvar. This semi-luxury hotel revolves solidly around its spa & wellness treatments. There is no gym to speak of (although there are a number of daily exercise classes), but otherwise every health & pampering need is met, from dentistry (popular with guests from Austria & Switzerland, where dental work is also expensive), hairdressing & beauty to massage, mud treatments & thermal/mineral water programmes (based around indoor & outdoor pools). There is even a pair of resident doctors. The comfortable & well-equipped (but not AC) rooms are ranged around two atriums. The hotel is largely empty in the hottest months, but very popular in spring & autumn. A variety of inclusive health packages are offered. *Sgl €110, dbl €145.*

⌂ **Vadkert Major** Vadkert u.; ☏ 95 320045. At the bottom of the road holding the thermal baths, this former hunting lodge is now a riding school, restaurant & inn. All rooms are en suite & most have TV; as well as the stables, there are also tennis courts & a sauna. *Sgl 6,700Ft, dbl 8,900Ft, trpl 12,300Ft.*

⌂ **Várkapu Panzió** (9 rooms) Várkerület 5; ☏ 95 326475; ℮ pentek@varkapu.hu; www.varkapu.hu. Just to the west of the castle, this family-run guesthouse has spic-and-span rooms, & is well priced. Its restaurant is the best. *Sgl 6,700Ft, dbl 8,900Ft, trpl 12,300Ft, room for 4 15,300Ft.*

✗ WHERE TO EAT AND DRINK

⊡ **Korona Fagylaltkert** Széchenyi István u. 2. A popular place to get your ice-cream licks & cake munches. Next to St László Church. ⊕ 09.00–22.00 daily.

✗ **Platán Restaurant** See above. Game predominates on the plate, & covers much of the walls too (in the form of hunting trophies not the spattered food of messy diners). Among the options are platters for 2 to share. Good food & healthy portions. *Mains avg 1,800Ft;* ⊕ 11.00–22.00 daily.

✗ **Várkapu Vendéglő** See above. Locally recommended as the best restaurant, Várkapu serves a varied menu of traditional Hungarian dishes, as well as pizzas & pastas. The imaginative chef changes the selection seasonally, & the food is excellent. *Mains avg 1,800Ft;* ⊕ Sun/Thu 08.30–22.00, Fri/Sat 08.30–23.00

✗ **Vadkert Major Fogadó** See above. Game is the speciality in this atmospheric & friendly basement restaurant attached to the riding school & inn (see opposite). *Mains avg 1,500Ft;* ⊕ daily 14.00–22.00 (closed Feb).

ENTERTAINMENT AND NIGHTLIFE You'll find the **Kossuth Lajos Cultural Centre** (*Várkerület 1;* ☏ *95 320063;* ⊕ *Mon–Fri 08.00–17.00*) in the castle courtyard; there are temporary exhibitions inside, and information on local events (including concerts at the castle itself). The **River Dance Club** (*Rákóczi Ferenc u. 91;* ⊕ *Sat & some Suns 22.00–07.00*) is set back from the main road to the south of the centre; the wooden, warehouse-like club is full of laser lights and sweaty bodies. There are theme nights, including foam parties and strip shows. **Club 63** (*Batthyány u. 63;* ☏ *95 326880; www.club63.hu;* ⊕ *Mon–Sat 9.00–23.00, Sun 9.00–22.00*) is a wood panelled 'English Pub' offering whiskies, beers, cocktails, teas, coffees, sandwiches and salads. Rather incongruously, it shares the building with a state-of-the-art fitness club.

WHAT TO SEE AND DO A wood-cobbled footbridge from Kossuth tér leads over the former moat and through a Gothic gatehouse to **Nádasdy Castle** (*Várkerület 1;*

\ *95 320158;* ⬛ *500/250Ft;* ☉ *Tue–Sun 09.00–17.00).* While there are earlier features, Tamás Nádasdy enlarged the castle in the 1560s and the bulk of the pentagonal structure dates from that time. On entering what is now the **Nádasdy Ferenc Museum**, you'll be met first by a state room decorated with ceiling frescoes by Hans Rudolf Miller; at the centre is the famous 'Battle of the Black Captain' led by Ferenc Nádasdy II at Sziszek, while around it are scenes of sieges against the Turks at other Transdanubian towns. The paintings of Old Testament stories that colour the walls were painted by István Dorfmeister in 1769. An adjoining room pays tribute to the weighty contribution the Nádasdy family made to the development of Hungarian printing, and an extensive exhibition devoted to the hussars (one regiment of which was named after the family) includes maces, carved powder horns and decorated rifles from the end of the 16th century (contemporary with the period when the Black Captain was routing the Ottomans). The Nádasdy Hussars, originally irregular soldiers who fought against the Turks, developed the strategy of using lightly armed and fast-moving cavalry that was later adopted internationally (hence the Queen's Own Hussars regiment in Britain).

The earliest piece in a valuable cartographic collection (donated by a Hungarian professor living in Oxford) is a map of Europe drawn in Strasbourg in 1520. The first map of Hungary produced in England appeared in an atlas of 1627. A helpful description on the back informs the user that Hungarian men 'are mostly strong, passionate and treat foreigners severely', and goes on to say that someone whose bravery is doubted can 'regain their honour by fighting with a Turk'. The rest of the castle is filled with tapestries, glassware, furniture and other fine art – the star piece a 17th-century wood cabinet with inlaid marble and a carving of Poseidon in the state room; they may reflect an aristocratic taste, but most of these objects did not actually belong to the Nádasdy family, whose castle was stripped by the Habsburgs after Ferenc III's execution. The castle's last owners were the Bavarian royal family, and they left most of the applied art collection hidden in the walls in 1945. The **Arcis Gallery** (⬛ *free;* ☉ *Mon–Fri 10.00–18.00, Sat 10.00–14.00*) can be found in the castle courtyard and has temporary exhibitions; the **Sylvester János Library** is in the same building.

Just to the northeast of the castle is a small **arboretum** (*Rákóczi u.;* ⬛ *250/150Ft;* ☉ *daily Apr 1–Oct 15 09.00–19.00, Oct 16–Mar 31 09.00–17.00*), rich and thick with foliage. Before heading there, take a look at **Szent László Church** (*Kossuth tér*), which was built by Ferenc Nádasdy III in 1645 after his conversion to Catholicism. It has been reconstructed several times since, once after it was damaged during the War of Independence. The statue of the Sorrowful Christ was sculpted in 1701.

ACTIVITIES The **Sárvár Thermal Baths** (*Vadkert u. 1;* \ *95 523600; www.badsarvar.hu;* ⬛ *1,950/1,100Ft, sliding rates after 17.00 & 20.00;* ☉ *08.00–22.00 daily*) make use of a hot spring discovered during oil surveying. A colourful new complex has rendered the older baths opposite redundant. There is a huge wellness centre, indoor and outdoor pools (including a kids area with a pirate ship and waterslides), a solarium, sauna, beauty emporium and state-of-the-art gym. All in all, this is a very swanky affair.

On the same road is the **Vadkert Major Riding School** (*Vadkert u.;* \ *95 320045; www.vadkertfogado.hu*), which has recently downsized from 70 to ten horses, but still offers horse-riding (⬛ *from 3,000Ft/hr*) and carriage driving (⬛ *from 6,000Ft/hr*). There's accommodation and a restaurant in the former hunting lodge (see opposite).

Southwest of the unexciting town of **Zalaegerszeg** (on the right bank of the River Zala, and recommended as a spring board or base rather than an end in itself), the rolling Göcsej is well worth exploring for its hilltop villages, vineyards, distinct folklore and unspoilt charm. The villages were once isolated by marshland (prior to the 19th century) and some of the old wood-carved houses – occupied until the 1950s – are preserved as museums (at Zalalövő, Felsőbagod and Kávás). This is not an affluent region: life for the villages is quiet and simple, almost self-sufficient. There is, however, private accommodation and small pensions are to be found in every village; it is an area that well rewards a couple of days spent touring by bicycle (or a day's digging around by car), and – with the airport at Balaton (albeit not receiving flights from Britain at present) – should become better-visited. This is a piece of the old world.

GETTING THERE AND AROUND There are hourly buses from Keszthely to Zalaegerszeg. It's a five-minute walk from the **bus station** (*Balatoni út*) to the centre of town. There are regular buses to Szombathely, Egervár and Nagykanizsa, and up to five trains a day to Budapest Déli (taking four hours). Other routes are to Sümeg (11), Balatonfüred (six), Pécs, Tapolca and Veszprém (five), Sárvár and Székesfehérvár (three).

Up to five **trains** leave daily for Budapest Déli, Veszprém, Székesfehérvár and Celldömölk, three to Szombathely and Nagykanizsa and one that crosses the Slovenia border at Hodoš to Ljubljana (taking 4½ hours). The **railway station** is 2km south of the centre on Bajcsy-Zsilinszky tér.

INFORMATION AND OTHER PRACTICALITIES (IN ZALAEGERSZEG)

Ibusz Eötvös u. 6–10; ✆ 92 311458. Currency exchange, regional tours & private rooms. ⊕ *Mon–Fri 08.30–16.30.*

Tourinform Széchenyi tér 4–6; ✆ 92 316160; e zalaegerszeg@tourinform.hu. Helpful office just south of Szabadság tér (through which the 74 & 76 roads run). ⊕ *Mon–Fri 09.00–18.00 all yr, Jun–Aug also Sat 09.00–12.00.*

Bicycles can be hired from Egerszegi Bringaklub (*Mártirok u. 3;* ✆ 92 313592; *www.bringaklub.extra.hu*) or Kerékvár (*Jákum u. 1;* ✆ 92 312433; *www.kerekvar.hu*).

 WHERE TO STAY, EAT AND DRINK Tourinform can provide a list of colleges offering cheap accommodation. The following places are in Zalaegerszeg unless otherwise stated in the contact information line.

AquaTherma Camping Gébárti-tó; ✆ 92 511268; e thermalpul@aquacity.hu; www.aquatherma.hu. Coiffured site next to Lake Gébárt & the thermal baths, & within easy access of Aqua City (an 8ha water park 2km north of the centre). On-site restaurant, pub & shop. *Tent/caravan 1,500Ft, plus 1,000/500Ft, 19,500Ft/night for 4-person chalet.*

Bella Pizzéria Kazinczy tér 11; ✆ 91 312687. One of several pizza joints in town. Right in the centre. ⊕ *12.00–24.00 daily.*

Erdőgyöngye (8 rooms) Alsóerdei út; ✆ 92 348067. A spacious, Austrian-inspired hotel in the woods just outside the town. Ask for a room at the back. The restaurant (*mains avg 2,000Ft;* ⊕ *11.00–22.00*) has an excellent reputation. *Sgl 9,000Ft, dbl 12,000Ft.*

Hotel Arany Bárány (50 rooms) Széchenyi tér 1; ✆ 92 550040; e info@aranybarany.hu; www.aranybarany.hu. The 3-star 'Golden Lamb' is the best in town, situated in an originally 18th-century building. Revamped in the 19th century, there was also a late-20th-century extension. *Dbl 18,800Ft.*

Kiskondás Panzió & Restaurant (10 rooms) Hock János u. 53; ✆ 92 321378; www.kiskondasetterem.hu. Friendly little guesthouse to the northwest of the centre (follow the road that starts as Rákóczi Ferenc u. out beyond the oil & village museums, or take bus 1). Its restaurant (*mains avg 1,900Ft;* ⊕ *Mon–Sat 10.00–22.00, Sun 10.00–16.00*) serves good Hungarian food & regional specialities, among them a mixed 'Kondás' platter of fish, pork & turkey for 2. *Dbl 7,000Ft, trpl 9,000Ft.*

🏠 **Sárkány Bio Panzió** Csöde, Erdész út 9; ☏ 92 371064; www.sarkanybiopanzio.hu. 30km west of Zalaegerszeg, this lovely guesthouse in a tiny village was constructed using traditional methods & materials. Fine Hungarian dishes made from local produce. Bike hire, riding, swimming pool. *Sgl 7,500Ft, dbl 9,600Ft, trpl 13,800Ft, half-board 2,100Ft/pp.*

🏠 **Zalai Lovarda** Zalaszentlászló, Szentmihálypuszta; ☏ 30 268 0832; www.zalailovarda.hu. Beautifully situated riding stables (with accommodation) between Keszthely & Zalaegerszeg in the valley of the River Zala. Riding 2,750Ft/hr, 7-day Balaton tour €750. *Sgl 3,000Ft, dbl 6,000Ft, half-board 2,600Ft/pp.*

WHAT TO SEE AND DO There is very little to hold your attention for long in Zalaegerszeg – its main merit is as a gateway to the villages beyond – but the **Göcsej Village Museum** (*Falumúzeum; Falumúzeum u.;* ☏ *92 703295; www.zmmi.hu;* 🎫 *500/250Ft;* 🕐 *Apr & Sep–Oct Tue–Sun 10.00–16.00, May–Aug 10.00–18.00*) next to the rail track (just off Ola utca, a continuation of Rákóczi utca, which runs west from Deák tér) illustrates the area's architectural heritage. Opened in 1968, this open-air museum was the first of its kind in the country and displays 19th- and 20th-century dwellings from 22 villages of Zala County.

Once you move beyond the main town, you have the chance to get a proper feel for a lifestyle that has long been lost in most areas of Europe. Each village has a few pretty houses and oozes an atmosphere of a bygone age which makes the walks between them a rare pleasure. Futhermore, the region has not been developed to the extent of the Őrség, and so there is just enough to enable you to visit comfortably without spoiling the ambience. There is a cycle road running between Zalaegerszeg and Zalalövő (where a Roman settlement was unearthed). The villages themselves have their own walking tours, running for two or three kilometres, but you should certainly pick up a map (such as Cartographia's *Az Őrség és a Göcsej*, 1:60,000) from the Tourinform in Zalaegerszeg before setting out.

THE ŐRSÉG

The Őrség, tucked into the country's most western place (where it moves out to meet Austria and Slovenia), has been the frontier limit since the Magyar conquest; one of the chieftains positioned his soldiers here to defend attack from Germanic peoples to the west, and this is reflected in the region's name (meaning 'guard').

UNDER SERF-ERRANCE

The Őrség villagers had for centuries enjoyed royal privileges granted in gratitude for their role as guardians of the western border. When the Turks invaded Europe, though, a Diet was convened in Sopron at which it was decided the favours should stop and the Őrség people should be subject to the same rules as peasants elsewhere in Hungary. However, the proud frontier citizens would not readily accept the mantle of serfs to the landowning Batthyány counts, and cocked a big fat snook to their noble betters. The Batthyánys were livid, and it is said that they hatched a cunning plan. They invited the bigwigs of the Őrség to a feast at their mansion in Körmend, asking them to bring with them the official documentation proving their right to special treatment so that the matter could finally be laid to rest. The naive leaders did so, and while they got stuck into the Batthyány victuals and drained the cellar dry their hosts swapped their contracts for crude forgeries. When they got down to business the next morning and the peasants produced their documents, the Batthyánys 'exposed' them as fakes – and the villagers had to endure the indignity of serfdom until its abolition in 1848. Undoubtedly a rural myth, but good fun nonetheless.

For centuries the residents swore to continue this role as stewards of the border, and were granted special privileges for doing so – the right to elect their own commanders, to be exempted from the usual royal taxes and to choose where to build their houses. The sentries cleared the woodland from the tops of local hills and constructed fenced settlements of between five and ten timber buildings (known as *szer* or *szeg* in ancient Hungarian) in which they lived with their families. Individually these were readily defended posts, while collectively they formed a system along which signals could be passed should enemies approach. Today the damp and lush landscape (which falls under the management of the recently established Őrség National Park) is popular with hikers and bikers, its wildlife supplemented by traditional folk architecture. Trails snake through the region and connect many of the villages; they are marked on Cartographia's *Az Őrség és a Göcsej* map (1:60,000). The Őrség is also famous for its pottery – look out for '*fazekas*' (potter) signs – but other crafts have also survived, and you'll find local produce such as honey, goat's cheese and pumpkinseed oil.

THE VILLAGES The 'capital' of the Őrség is **Őriszentpéter**, 21km south of Szentgotthárd. It is a model Őrség village, spread over several hills with clutches of thatched wooden dwellings – often erected without the use of metal nails – sitting well apart from each other. The 13th-century Romanesque St Peter's Church (*Templomszer 15*) that gives the village its name is on the northwestern edge, and with the exception of the 15th-century chancel retains much of its original character. Őriszentpéter is the village best-equipped for tourists in the region, and has several places to stay (in addition to the houses advertising private rooms); visit the information centre (2km from centre, but well signposted; *Siskaszer 26A;* ☏ *94 548034;* ⊕ *Jun 15–Aug 31 10.00–19.00, rest of yr Mon–Fri 10.00–16.00*) for details. You can hire bikes from József Gosztola (*Égésszer 53; tel 70 3785761*).

Close to the information centre, Fazekas Vendégház (*Kovács szer 72; 94 428 174*) has rustic rooms with wood-burning stoves in its main house (*2,500Ft/pp*), while the back garden holds basic bungalows with separate bathrooms and spaces for tents (*1,200Ft/pp*). Katalin Róka makes exquisite traditional pottery in the basement, and you can have a bash yourself too. Further down the road is Bodnár Étterem (*Kovács szer 96;* ☏ *94 428027; www.bognaretterem.hu; mains avg 1,500Ft;* ⊕ *10.00–21.00 daily*), a no-frills restaurant whose décor is somewhat 'socialist' in feel, but which offers decent, cheap food and excellent service. Near the centre of the village, Sziklakert (*6 rooms; Alszer 21/A;* ☏ *94/428828; 3,300Ft/pp;* ⊕ *Apr–Oct, depending on weather*) is a lovely choice of accommodation for a group of friends. The hostess is a keen cook, and you can enjoy lángos and apple cake baked in the bread oven in the pretty garden. Next door is the Dobokai Lovas Centre (*Alszer 26; tel 30 5070431; 2,500Ft/hr*), where you can arrange horse-riding.

Moving 10km north of Őriszentpéter, the village of **Kondorfa** has a restored traditional house where you can stay called Vadkörte Fogadó (*12 rooms; Kondorfa, Alvég 7;* ☏ *94 429031; www.vadkorte.hu; sgl 6,600Ft, dbl 11,200Ft*). Its cosy restaurant (*mains avg 2,000Ft;* ⊕ *10.00–22.00 daily*) serves a good choice of local dishes, including cep mushrooms picked in the surrounding forests. Bike hire is also available (*1,500Ft/day*).

Six kilometres to the northwest is **Szalafő**, whose eight *szer* have each expanded and grown together. The westernmost and highest of these is called Pityerszer; it was inhabited well into the 20th century, but is now the Open-Air Ethnographical Museum (*Pityerszer 12;* ☏ *06 30 467 7022;* ✆ *400/200Ft;* ⊕ *Jun–Aug daily 10.00–18.00, rest of yr Tue–Sun 10.00–18.00*). The houses consist of three rooms (a pantry, communal room and kitchen), are furnished with many of the original domestic objects, and have deep covered verandas that allowed the occupants to sit outside during the regular local showers. One of them has a defensive u-shaped

The Őrség National Park was founded in 2002 and covers 44,000ha of Hungary's westernmost corner, a place of babbling streams, shady valleys and forests, and verdant meadows. This is the rainiest part of the country and three rivers – the Rába, the Zala and the Ős ('Ancient') Mura – as well their many smaller tributaries, flow through it. One of the very few natural lakes is Fekete-tó (Black Lake), 5km northwest of Szalafő (near Orfalu); the lake is now filled with peat and moss. Around 60% of the park is forested; the most common type, because of the acidity of the soil, is Scots pine. You'll find junipers and downy birch among these forests, while dog's tooth violet and red cyclamen bloom in good quantities in the oak-hornbeam and beech woodland. The drier meadows hold various species of orchid, the green-winged orchid in greatest numbers; wet meadows along the numerous streams harbour round-leaf sundew, marsh cinquefoil and bogbean, all three typical inhabitants of peat bogs.

Thanks to the diversity of vegetation, Őrség National Park boasts the highest number of butterfly species in Hungary, and there are many unusual species of dragonfly too. One of Europe's rarest birds, the corncrake, nests in the wet meadows of the park, while the country's only population of Alpine newts is found in the waters. In addition to the wildlife attractions, the region has a strong folk tradition, and there are abundant examples of the typical u-shaped, wooden-walled Őrség dwellings. The national park was recently designated a European Destination of Excellence (*www.edenineurope.eu*), an award launched by the European Commission to recognise an 'emerging' tourist area's commitment to social, cultural and environmental sustainability. For further information, contact the Őrség National Park Directorate (*Őriszentpéter, Siskaszer 26/A;* ✆ *94 548033; www.onp.nemzetipark.gov.hu;* ⊕ *Mon–Fri 08.00–16.30*) at the turn-off to Szalafő.

layout, arranged around a courtyard. A walking trail leads from Őriszentpéter to Szalafő; alternatively you can catch one of a few daily buses (you'll need to walk the final kilometre to the museum). Both Szalafő and Őriszentpéter can be accessed by bus from Körmend, Zalaegerszeg, Kőszeg, Szentgotthárd and Sopron.

In the area south of Őriszentpéter, the heavy clay soil did not suit agriculture and so for centuries inhabitants supplemented incomes by making pottery. Today the main centre of pottery production is at **Magyarszombatfa**, where ten potting dynasties are still active. A potter's house built in 1780 serves as a museum (*Fazekasház;* ✆ *94 544003;* 🎟 *150/100Ft;* ⊕ *10.00–16.00 May–Sep daily, Oct Sat–Sun*). The shelves contain beautifully crafted containers and cooking vessels; these are unglazed because mineral glazes didn't emerge until the 1890s. The Ginti Panzió (*Fő u. 78;* ✆ *94 544028; 5,500Ft/pp, apt 16,000Ft*) is based around a few impeccably converted village houses, although there are modern comforts (swimming pool, darts, pool table, table tennis) alongside the traditional furnishings. The restaurant (*mains avg 1,400Ft;* ⊕ *daily 11.00–22.00*) serves local cuisine. There's excellent fried fish – sourced straight from the local fishponds – to be eaten in **Bajánsenye** (which you'll pass on your way to Magyarszombatfa) at the Berek Halászkert (*Rákóczi út 16;* ✆ *94 444143; www.berekhal.hu; mains avg 1,600Ft;* ⊕ *08.00–22.00 daily*).

Continuing south from Magyarszombatfa, the next two villages along the road are famed for their churches. The lone church in the forest in **Velemér** (✆ *94 429020;* 🎟 *300/150Ft;* ⊕ *Easter–Nov 1 09.00–16.00, rest of yr 11.00–13.00*) was built in 1270, and contains frescoes dating to 1377–78 by the Austrian painter Johannes Aquila (see box, page 470).

Central and Western Transdanubia THE ŐRSÉG

9

Johannes Aquila – responsible for the 14th-century frescoes in Velemér's church – was born in nearby Radkersburg in Austria, and worked as an architect and painter in the region. While the Gothic style still reigned supreme north of the Alps, Aquila's work betrays significant Italian Renaissance influence. Among the paintings in the Velemér church there is even a realistic self portrait of the artist, which was unusual during this period. Aquila's frescoes are arranged so that specific, relevant portions are illuminated by the sun's rays on different dates of the year – for instance, the scene showing the guiding star might be highlighted at Christmas or the crucifixion at Easter. This was not actually unique at the time because medieval architects knew their astronomy; they included tiny window slots in the walls, positioned to take account of changes in the angle of the sun's rays during the year, and the frescoes were then placed accordingly. However, few examples remain intact; as such, Austria, Slovenia and Hungary have developed a cross-border route that ekes out those churches painted by the master.

When you reach the next village of **Szentgyörgyvölgy**, turn at the Műemlék sign to visit its whitewashed Calvinist church (⊕ *May–end Oct 08.00–18.00 daily*). Church construction began after Joseph II's 'Edict of Tolerance' in 1787, the tower was added in 1792–3 and the astonishing interior was finally completed in 1830. While most other coffered church ceilings in Hungary have a different, polychrome painting in each square (of Renaissance-inspired subjects like flowers, heraldic animals and biblical motifs), the ceiling here is monochrome blue and adorned with swirls. The affect is stunning. It seems incredible now that a settlement of 470 people could sustain a Calvinist church, rectory and school in addition to an ornate Catholic church. However, until World War I this was a flourishing village. The Treaty of Trianon changed the borders in 1920 and significantly reduced the market for the villagers' produce, while during the darkest days of communism in the early 1950s the richer farmers (owning up to 60ha of land) were declared *kulaks* – their land and houses were confiscated and they were deported to endure forced labour (mainly in the Hortobágy region). The Calvinist congregation on a Sunday now numbers no more than 20.

KÖRMEND AND SZENTGOTTHÁRD

To the south of Szombathely, and perched on the northeastern brink of the Őrség – to which it is an upper gateway – **Körmend** is dominated by the Batthyány mansion (*Dr Batthyány-Strattmann u. 3*). This considerable pile was converted from a medieval castle into a Baroque palace after the town was acquired in 1604 by the Batthyány family – a powerful clan who within a few generations shifted from feudal enforcers (see box, page 467) to leading players in the revolutionary movement (Lajos Batthyány was prime minister during the 1848–49 War of Independence). The building now holds the Dr Batthyány-Strattmann László Museum (✆ *94 410425*; ✍ *500/2500Ft*; ⊕ *Tue–Sat Apr–Oct 09.00–12.00 & 13.00–17.00, rest of yr 10.00–12.00 & 14.00–16.00*), with displays of archaeology, natural history and products relating to local guilds. Rather appropriately, the museum specialises in exhibitions for sight-impared visitors – Dr Batthyány-Strattmann was an eye specialist who treated the poor free of charge in a wing of the mansion. An old building in the courtyard contains a Shoemakers' Museum, focusing on Hungarian cobblers. There are up to 13 trains a day to Szombathely, and eight to Zalaegerszeg. The railway station is 1km northwest of the centre on Vasútmellék utca. The bus station is on the same road and also serves Szombathely (11) and Zalaegerszeg (six), as well as Nagykanizsa (three).

Tight against the Austrian border 30km west along Road 8, **Szentgotthárd** takes its name from a 12th-century Cistercian abbey founded by Béla III, and in turn passes it on to a glorious struggle of 1664. The Battle of Szentgotthárd actually took place on the other side of the River Rába at what is now the Austrian town of Mögersdorf. There the Habsburg General Montecuccoli routed a Turkish army twice the size, with many of the vanquished drowning in the river. The victory is recorded in István Dorfmeister's fresco in a cupola of the mid-18th-century Baroque church (*Béke tér*). For all the strutting, however, the Treaty of Vasvár (see page 18) signed shortly afterwards by Emperor Lipót (Leopold I) was a crushing let down for the Hungarians – ceding as it did so much Magyar land to the Turks – and not only triggered the Zrínyi conspiracy (see page 18) but provoked a slow-burning sense of injustice that fuelled the independence cause long after the Ottomans had left.

Buses to Szentgotthárd are few and far between; the least-painful way of getting there is from Körmend (and even then there are only five on weekdays). A service also operates on weekdays only to Zalaegerszeg. Far more convenient is the train, with up to 18 services a day running to Szombathely via Körmend.

SZOMBATHELY

Szombathely translates as 'Saturday market' – a hangover from the medieval period when the weekend market was big business here. The shopping tag remains appropriate, however, for this is a great place for some retail therapy, and Austrian bargain-hunters are frequent faces. The town is the largest in Western Transdanubia. It came to prominence as early as the 1st century AD, when the Romans established a settlement called Savaria that by the dawn of the 2nd century was the capital of the Upper Pannonia province. The place thrived on trade, falling as it did (like Sopron) on the so-called Amber Road running between Italy and the Baltic Sea. Things declined after the Romans had left, and the town was plundered at several points over the centuries (most notably by the Mongols). The resurgence came in the 18th century when Maria Theresa made it an episcopal see, and come the 19th century it was a major junction of the railway network. The confusing street plan and architectural diversity is in part due to the different phases of expansion and partly due to heavy bombing during World War II, after which much had to be put back together again. As such, it's not attractive in the classical sense, but the main square is atmospheric and the old centre contains some interesting buildings. Szombathely – more precisely Fő tér 41 – is also the birthplace of the fictional anti-hero Leopold Bloom in James Joyce's novel *Ulysses*.

GETTING THERE AND AROUND The railway station is a 15-minute walk northeast of the centre at the culmination of Széll Kálmán út. Several lines branch out from it, and there are intercity trains to Budapest via Veszprém and Székesfehérvár, Győr, Nagykanizsa and Pécs, as well as services to closer towns like Kőszeg (16) and Sopron (12). There is a taxi rank here and the local bus station stops are outside. The **bus station** is northwest of Fő tér on Ady Endre tér (a short walk from the centre). You can get regular buses to Ják, Kőszeg and Körmend, and among other services are those to Budapest (four), Celldömölk (nine), Győr (seven), Sopron (nine), Zalaegerszeg (14) and Szeged (three). For **taxis**, try City (✆ 94 333666) or Centrum (✆ 94 311300).

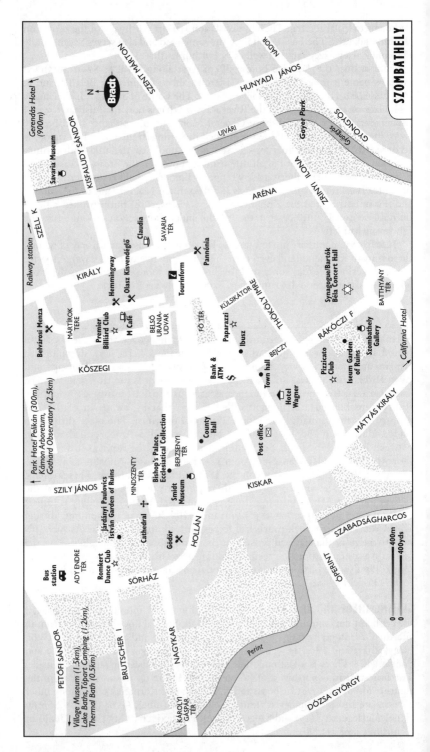

SZOMBATHELY

INFORMATION AND OTHER PRACTICALITIES

ℹ Listings magazine Szombathelyi Est

Ⓘ Ibusz Fő tér 44; ☎ 94 314141. Organises private rooms (from 5,000Ft/pp), currency exchange & local & regional tours. ⊕ Mon–Fri 08.00–17.00, Sat 08.00–12.00.

ⓔ Paparazzi Café and Club See page 474. Offers internet access for 200Ft/half-hour.

ℹ Tourinform Király u. 1A; ☎ 94 514451; e szombathely@tourinform.hu. Incredibly helpful office opposite McDonald's. ⊕ Jun 16–Sep 1 Mon–Fri 09.00–20.00, Sat–Sun 10.00–18.00, rest of yr Mon–Fri 09.00–17.00.

WHERE TO STAY

⌂ California Hotel (11 rooms) Rumi út 21; ☎ 94 509447; www.california-hotel.hu. More of a panzió than a hotel, with sweet little pine-furnished rooms. Around 500m south of Batthyány tér. Sgl 7,800Ft, dbl 8,500Ft.

⌂ Gerendás Hotel (19 rooms) 11-es Huszár u. 118; ☎ 94 509290; www.gerendashotel.hu. This 3-star is set back a little from the road, over 1km northeast of the centre. It's not central, but it is cheap & pleasant. It's also a favourite with athletes; Szombathely is renowned for its hammer-throwing coaches, & you'll often find some beefy chaps staying here while honing their skills. Gym, solarium, squash courts. Bus 3 runs here from the centre. Sgl 8,900Ft, dbl 11,900Ft, trpl 14,900Ft.

⌂ Hotel Wagner (12 rooms) Kossuth Lajos u. 15; ☎ 94 322208; www.hotelwagner.hu. Very nice, centrally located hotel with well-furnished rooms (the only possible complaint being they are on the small side). Sgl 11,000Ft, dbl 15,500Ft, apt (for 2/3) 21,500–23,500Ft.

⌂ Park Hotel Pelikán (42 rooms) Deák Ferenc u. 5; ☎ 94 513800; www.hotelpelikan.hu. This is a fabulous hotel that's well worth the extra cost – to our minds, one of the best in its bracket you'll find in Hungary. The town's only 4-star, it has standard & superior rooms, a lovely 25m pool (lit from underneath in the evening), a furiously bubbling jacuzzi, a sauna & small gym. The rooms are high-class, with soft lighting, plush red carpets & large bathrooms. Ask for one of the bigger rooms – they vary in size, even within their price brackets. The restaurant is appropriately excellent too (see below). To the north of centre. Standard/superior sgl 22,000/26,000Ft, dbl 25,500/33,200Ft.

Ⓐ Tópart Camping Kenderesi út 6; ☎ 94 509038; e savariatourist@axelero.hu. Next to the Lake Baths, to the northwest of the centre, this well-equipped site has 36 bungalows & a swimming pool. Bus 2A which stops outside. Camping 700Ft/pp; bungalow 8,000Ft (for 2); ⊕ May–Sep.

✗ WHERE TO EAT AND DRINK A good place to head is the Belső Uránia udvar, a narrow pedestrianised street accessed through an arched passage off Fő tér, which comes alive in the evening and is reminiscent of Budapest's Liszt Ferenc tér – with less of the 'look-at-me' pouting.

✗ Gödör Hollán Ernő u. 10–12; ☎ 94 510078; www.godorvendeglo.hu. Cellar eatery selling massive portions of hearty Hungarian grub. Come hungry. Mains 1,190–2,790Ft, avg 1,690Ft; ⊕ Mon–Thu 11.00–23.00, Fri–Sat 11.00–24.00, Sun 11.00–15.00.

♀ Hemmingway Club & Restaurant Belső Uránia udvar; ☎ 94 344978. Great place to chill out, eat & drink. Sells light snacks. Mains avg 1,300Ft; ⊕ Mon–Thu 11.00–23.00, Fri–Sat 11.00–02.00, Sun 16.00–23.00.

♀ M Café Belső Uránia udvar; ☎ 94 332300. Modern, open-fronted café-bar serving cocktails, coffees, cakes & ice cream. ⊕ Mon–Sun 09.00–22.00.

✗ Olasz Kisvendéglő Belső Uránia udvar; ☎ 94 342012. A substantial menu laden with Italian food – delicious & cheap. Recommended. Mains avg 1,500Ft; ⊕ Sun–Thu 11.00–23.00, Fri–Sat 11.00–24.00.

✗ Pannónia Restaurant Fő tér 29; ☎ 94 509588; e pannoniaetterem@freemail.hu. A cheerful place with a contemporary 'folksy' ambience. Hungarian & continental food. Next to McDonalds. Mains avg 1,750Ft; ⊕ 10.00–24.00 daily.

✗ Park Hotel Pelikán Restaurant See above. A beautiful, upmarket restaurant, surrounded with glass & with a classy upstairs bar. Perfect for a relaxed drink or a meal from the international menu. The staff are friendly & helpful. We can't find fault with this hotel & restaurant package. Mains avg 2,500Ft; ⊕ 07.00–22.00 daily.

✗ Wagner Restaurant See above. Along with the Pelikán, this is one of the top places to eat in town. It has a marble floor & a courtyard garden, & serves international fare peppered with Hungarian options & an extensive list of regional wines. *Mains avg 2,200Ft;* ⊕ *09.00–23.00 daily.*

ENTERTAINMENT AND NIGHTLIFE The **Bartók Béla Concert Hall** (*Ráckóczi Ferenc u. 3;* ↘ *94 313474; www.savaria_symphony.hu*) is housed in the Moorish former synagogue, built in 1881, and with a memorial to the Jews deported during World War II outside. It plays host to the town's symphony orchestra. The **cultural house** (*Fő tér 10;* ↘ *94 509641*) should be able to offer information on arts events. There are several bars on Belső Uránia udvar (see under *Where to eat and drink*). For a beer and a game of pool, head for the **Premier Billiárd Club** (*Belső Uránia udvar 4;* ↘ *94 330792;* ⊕ *Mon–Sun 09.00–04.00*), which has a younger crowd and turns into a nightclub come night. **Pizzicato Club** (*Thököly Imre u. 14;* ↘ *06 20 333 9700;* ⊕ *Tue–Sat 19.00–04.00, Sun 19.00–24.00*) is reached through an archway opposite the rear entrance of the Hotel Wagner. It holds Bacardi Breezer theme nights and booming parties, and offers live music sessions and DJs (usually at weekends). The **Romkert Dance Club** (*Ady Endre tér; www.olds-rom.hu*) is a pub-cum-disco next to the bus station with a definite youth-club feel (fruit machines, table football and thin walls). The **Paparazzi Café and Club** (*Fő tér 36;* ↘ *30 994036;* ⊕ *Mon–Wed 08.00–22.00, Thu 08.00–24.00, Fri–Sat 08.00–01.00, Sun 14.00–22.00*) is based in a dark cellar, although it also has a small terrace on the square in good weather.

WHAT TO SEE AND DO Fő tér is the heart of the modern town, wide and long without being classically quaint, and holding the shops and cafés. To its northwest is the **Savaria Museum** (*Kisfaludy Sándor u. 9;* ↘ *94 500720;* ⊕ *500/250Ft;* ⊕ *Tue–Sun 10.00–17.00*), which has archaeological, natural-history and ethnographic exhibitions, and is the place to head to get a flavour for the town's early history. The Roman flavour is particularly strong, with votive altars, burial stones (Christian and pagan), and a trio of carved deities that once stood in a temple here. The surviving milestone – erected to mark the distance (675 miles) from Savaria to Rome – is rare. Among the statues upstairs are the original apostles that adorned the 13th-century Benedictine church at Ják (see opposite), together with the moulds used to make the replicas that are now positioned above the portal.

There are more Roman remnants to be seen at the **Iseum Ruin Garden** next to the **Szombathely Gallery** (*Rákóczi Ferenc u. 12;* ↘ *94 508800;* ⊕ *600/300Ft;* ⊕ *Tue, Thu–Sun 10.00–17.00, Wed 10.00–18.00*). This 2nd-century Temple of Isis was discovered in the 1950s, and is one of only two or three in Europe (another is in Austria). Excavation and restoration is ongoing (including major reconstruction of the sanctuary). The gallery is primarily devoted to 20th-century Hungarian art, and has paintings by inter-war artists like Gyula Derkovits (a native of the town) as well as regular temporary exhibitions. The **former synagogue** (see above) is across the road.

Let's see yet more stones from Savaria – the last lot, we promise – in the **Járdányi Paulovics István Garden of Ruins** (*Romkert; Mindszenty József tér 1;* ↘ *94 313369;* ⊕ *400/200Ft;* ⊕ *Mar 15–Nov 30 Tue–Sat 09.00–17.00*), which is near the cathedral. This former bishop's garden contains what's left of buildings constructed throughout the Roman occupation. Among them are the public baths, a shrine to Mercury and the 4th-century imperial palace (which covered an area of 200m^2), with some of the best-preserved mosaics in Hungary. Also here is a portion of the basalt 'Amber Road', the route along which traders passed on their journey between the Baltic and the Adriatic; it was monitored by a customs house at the crossroads, and lined with craft shops.

The merging Mindszenty tér and Berzsenyi Dániel tér represent the town's historical core. When it was constructed for the first bishop, János Szily, in the late

18th century (when Maria Theresa made the town an episcopal see), the Neoclassical **Szombathely Cathedral** (*Mindszenty tér*) was graced with cupola frescoes and an altarpiece by the hand of F A Maulbertsch. Unfortunately an Allied bomb during World War II put paid to his hard work, and only a few of his decorative pieces remain. His work does survive in the reception hall of the late-Baroque **Bishop's Palace** (*Berzsenyi Daniel tér 3*) of 1783, but this is not open to the public. Instead you'll have to limit yourself to the Sala Terrena on the ground floor, where there's an **Ecclesiastical Collection** (*Egyházmegyei Múzeum;* ☏ 94 312056; ☞ 500/250Ft; ☉ Tue–Fri 09.30–15.30, Sat 09.30–11.30, Sun by appointment only) and walls frescoed by István Dorfmeister.

Behind the palace is the extraordinary **Smidt Museum** (*Hollán Ernő u. 2;* ☏ 94 311038; ☞ 450/250Ft; ☉ Tue–Sun 10.00–17.00, based upon the private collection of a respected local surgeon and containing a spread of items including those archaeological (including Roman – we lied when saying you'd seen the last of them!), medical, artistic and military.

Beyond the centre Around 3km to the northeast, the **Kámon Arborétum** (*Szent Imre herceg u. 102;* ☏ 94 311352; ☞ 400/300Ft; ☉ Apr 1–Oct 15 Mon–Fri 08.00–18.00, Sat–Sun 09.00–18.00, Oct 16–Mar 31 daily 08.00–16.00) is a 27ha botanical garden by the Gyöngyös Stream. There is a bus stop 200m away, served by numbers 1 or 1C. Near by is the **ELTE Gothard Astrophysical Observatory** (*Szent Imre herceg u. 112;* ☏ 94 522870; ☉ Mon–Fri 09.00–15.00), with various equipment from the turn of the 20th century and exhibits on modern astronomy.

To the northwest of the centre, just beyond Bartók Béla körút are a pair of lakes, the smaller **Fishing Lake** (*Horgásztó*) and the lower **Boating Lake** (*Csónakázótó*), a picturesque piece of water with an island on which you can hire rowing boats (*Mar 30–Sep 15 daily 13.00–19.00*). Facing the latter across the road are the **Lake Baths** (*Tófürdő; Kenderesi u.;* ☏ 94 505690; *www.varosgazd.hu;* ☞ 900/800Ft; ☉ May–Sep Sun–Thu 09.00–20.00, Fri 09.00–19.00), a huge open-air water park, with sunbathing areas and water chutes, while near that are the quieter **Thermal Baths** (*Bartók Béla körút;* ☏ 94 314336; ☞ 990/690Ft; ☉ Mon 14.00–21.30, Tue–Fri 06.00–21.30, Sat–Sun 09.00–18.00). Bus 2A stops 20m from the entrance.

At the western side of the Fishing Lake is the **Village Museum** (*Vasi Múzeumfalu; Árpád u. 30;* ☏ 94 311004; ☞ 500/250Ft; ☉ Apr 1–Nov 15 Tue–Sun 09.00–17.00), an outdoor collection of 18th- and 19th-century dwellings drawn from various pockets of Vas County. As well as the local styles, there are also examples of those built by Croatian, German and Slovene minorities. Bus 27 stops right outside.

EXCURSION Travel south of Szombathely by 12km and you'll arrive at one of the premium pieces of ecclesiastical art in Hungary – yes, we said *art*, for the nameless masters who created the **Benedictine abbey at Ják** (☞ 350/200Ft; ☉ Apr–Oct 08.00–18.00 daily, rest of yr by appointment), who chipped and carved at its west door, had artistic genius in every rough-skinned finger. While there are few good moments to die, Márton Nagy of the Ják clan had more reason than most to feel his time had come early; while work on the church he founded began in 1214, it wasn't completed until 1256 and by then he'd popped his clogs. He missed a treat.

Intact Romanesque architecture of the Árpád era is rare in Hungary, and this is undoubtedly the highlight of that left. It didn't survive the centuries wholly unscathed; it was severely ruffled during the Turkish siege of the village, and an adjacent monastery was dismantled in 1562. Subsequent Baroque additions were stripped away at the turn of the 20th century by the great Historicist Frigyes Schulek, and the restoration is considerably less divisive of opinion than his overhaul of the Mátyás Church in Buda. Some grumble about the choice of towers that he placed atop the original bases, but few dispute that Schulek's altars and vaulting complement an interior that oozes elegance and balance. The church's most-photographed feature is the western portal, a graceful beast of seven intricately carved receding arches surmounted by statues of Christ and his apostles. (There is a copy of this at the rear of Vajdahunyad Castle in Budapest's City Park.) The Chapel of St James to the west of the church was built in 1260 to serve non-monastic parishioners when the main church was in use. Up to 20 buses a day make the 20-minute journey between Ják and Szombathely. The bus stop is close to the abbey.

KŐSZEG

Jammed hard against the lower slopes of the Kőszeg Hills 20km north of Szombathely, Kőszeg is another of those towns that makes you wonder how you ever considered holidaying anywhere else. With Sopron just 50km away, this pocket of Western Transdanubia has a pair of the prettiest, most romantic and best-preserved urban centres in the country. Kőszeg's cobbled main square is dripping with Baroque, Neoclassical and Renaissance architecture, and buildings without plaques recording their historical significance are few and far between. Just take a pew at the square's heart and drink it all in.

A series of fires raged through the medieval mud-and-wood houses during the 17th and 18th centuries, and the core primarily consists of structures raised after that. (The repeated infernos were such a problem that citizens were fined if caught smoking in public – and even subjected to 50 lashes if 'a villain'.) The 13th-century castle is an exception, an important cog in the border fortifications during the Turkish occupation that saw considerable action in 1532. Then it was that a small force held out against Suleiman I's army of over 100,000, preventing the Turks from marching on to Vienna. All the while a nearby Habsburg army quietly looked on without raising a finger, happy to sacrifice heroic Magyar lives as long as the Turks were being stalled; this was a stance adopted at Szigetvár and other Hungarian battlefields – and one that helps explain the passion for independence from imperial rule displayed by townspeople here and elsewhere in the subsequent two centuries.

GETTING THERE, AWAY AND AROUND The **bus station** (*Liszt Ferenc u.*) is a few minutes' walk west of the centre; there is a frequent service to Szombathely and up to six daily buses to Sopron. The **railway station** is 1½km southwest of the town, at the end of Rákóczi Ferenc utca. Turn right from the station and follow this road into the centre. If you can't face the walk, local buses stop outside the station – there are up to 16 a day (ten at weekends). Kőszeg is at the end of a branch line from Szombathely, and there are up to 15 trains daily between the towns.

INFORMATION AND OTHER PRACTICALITIES

🖫 **Cultural centre** Rajnis u. 9; 🕾 94 360113; e jurisics@koszeg.hu; www.koszeg.hu. This arts centre at the castle can offer information on cultural events. ⊕ Mon–Fri 10.00–17.00.

🖪 **Savaria Tourist** Várkör 69; 🕾 94 563048; e tompasav@axelero.hu. The place to book local & regional tours. ⊕ Mon–Fri 08.00–12.00, 13.00–17.00, Sat 08.00–12.00.

🖪 **Tourinform** Jurisics tér 7; 🕾 94 563120. Helpful office by the Castle entrance. You can get information on the nature park here too (see page 479). ⊕ Jun 15–Aug 31 Mon–Fri 08.00–18.00, Sat–Sun 10.00–18.00, rest of yr Mon–Fri 08.00–16.00.

WHERE TO STAY

🏠 **Arany Strucc Szálloda** (15 rooms) Várkör 124; 🕾 94 360323; emails: strucc1@axelero.hu;

www.aranystrucc. Functioning as an inn from 1597, the 'Golden Ostrich' has a fair claim to being the country's oldest hotel. The original owner got into a fair tussle with the keeper of the White Horse Inn across the street (in what is now a bank), each accusing the other of stealing customers. In the end a magistrate had to intervene, threatening them with a heavy fine if the quarrel continued. Today the rooms have spacious bathrooms & are well-priced. *Sgl 6,400Ft, dbl 9,900/10,900Ft.*

🏠 **Gyöngyvirág Camping & Panzió** Bajcsy-Zsilinszky u. 6; ✆ 94 360454; www.gyongyviragpanzio.hu. This is a guesthouse with a camping site in its garden to the northeast of the centre (follow Dózsa György u. out from the curving Gyöngyös u.); there are rooms with or without ensuite facilities. *Sgl/dbl 6,500/7,500Ft (with bathroom); camping: tent/caravan/campervan 500/700/950Ft, plus adult/student/child 750/550/350Ft (all excl Tourist Tax).*

🏠 **Hotel Írottkő** (52 rooms) Fő tér 4; ✆ 94 360373; www.irottko.hu. The town's largest hotel; it's a little worn around the edges, despite its marble-floored lobby, but the location is excellent. *Sgl 12,300Ft, dbl 17,600Ft.*

🏠 **Jurisics Miklós Grammar School** Hunyadi János út 10; ✆ 94 361404. Dorm rooms available in summer. To the southwest of the castle. *Rooms 1,500–2,000Ft/pp.*

🏠 **Pont Vendégház** Táblaház u. 1; ✆ 94 563224; www.pontvendeghaz.hu. Opposite the castle, this welcoming burgher's house is individually furnished & room sizes vary. Ask for Room 1 for best view of the town. *Sgl 6,500Ft, dbl 9,000Ft.*

🏠 **Portré Hotel** (6 rooms) Fő tér 7; ✆ 94 363170; www.portre.com. This intimate, centrally placed & reasonably priced hotel has modern rooms above a coffee house. Sauna. *Sgl 7,000Ft, dbl 11,400Ft, trpl 17,000Ft.*

✖ WHERE TO EAT AND DRINK

🍵 **Arany Strucc Cukrászda** Várkör 126; ✆ 94 563345. The best place for ice cream & dreamy cakes; next to the hotel of the same name. ⏰ *09.00–19.00 daily.*

✖ **Bécsikapu Restaurant** Rajnics u. 5; ✆ 94 563122; www.becsikapu.hu. Playing on its proximity to the castle, this medieval-theme restaurant has a covered courtyard (adorned with maces & heraldic shields) & a cellar banqueting hall. Hungarian dishes include deer steak & stews of wild boar or tripe. *Mains avg 2,000Ft;* ⏰ *daily 11.00–22.00.*

✖ **Garabonciás Pizzéria** Jurisics tér 7. This pizzeria by St Jakab Church has an alfresco area overlooking the main square. It is known as the Sgraffito House because of the patterning on its façade, an Italian technique created by scratching through different layers of coloured plaster. The portions here are grand – don't order a large pizza unless you're famished or sharing. *Pizzas from 590Ft;* ⏰ *Mon–Thu 10.00–23.00, Fri–Sat 10.00–01.00, Sun 13.00–23.00.*

✖ **Taverna Flórián** Várkör 59; ✆ 94 563072; www.tavernaflorian.hu. It's on the expensive side, but this atmospheric brick-cellar restaurant in front of the Zwinger Tower is superb. The food is international/Mediterranean in influence – spaghetti, seared salmon, beef with cognac – & its beautiful garden has a rockery & trickling waterfall. You'll make no mistake in working out which are the male & female toilets – the door to the ladies is signalled by a pair of wooden breasts! *Mains avg 2,500Ft;* ⏰ *Wed–Sun 11.30–14.30, Tue–Sat 17.00–22.00.*

WHAT TO SEE AND DO Jurisics tér was the former market square, and the backdrop to the town's political and social life; here it was that the magistrates of the Middle Ages delivered sentence and naughty citizens were pinned in the stocks open to the abuse of all and sundry. You are ushered in through the **Heroes Gate** (*Hősök kapuja*) at the southern side, built in Eclectic style in 1932 on the site of a former 13th-century barbican that guarded the entrance to the town. The pseudo-medieval 20th-century gate was a monument to the 400th anniversary of the Turkish siege, but in fairness it represents something of a drab blot on the colourful surroundings. Next to it is the **General's House** (*Tábornok ház; Jurisics tér 6*), once the residence of the general of the town cavalry. Inside it the **Jurisics Miklós Town Museum** (🎟 *400/200Ft;* ⏰ *Tue–Sun 10.00–17.00*) has an exhibition about the local guilds and crafts, and the entrance ticket also gives access to a narrow gallery running around the outside of Heroes Gate, with views over the town's sloping terracotta roofs.

The cost of commissioning the **Blessed Virgin Mary statue** of 1739 – with chubby cherubic faces on its column – was met by fines imposed upon 'blasphemous' Lutherans. It is positioned on the site of the medieval pillory. The benches around it offer a good place to park yourself and have a proper glance around the square. What you'll immediately notice is that the buildings on the western side appear shorter than those opposite. In actual fact it's the road that's high rather than the buildings low, layers of rubble from the various fires having raised the street level here.

You're rather spoilt for choice architecturally, but the **town hall** (*Jurisics tér 8*) is the most striking of those around the outside. It has functioned continually as a civic centre since the 14th century; the façade is 18th-century and the portal 19th-century, but Gothic windows (visible from the gate at number 10) are reminders of its earlier heritage. The three coats of arms are those of Miklós Jurisics, historical Hungary and Kőszeg itself. The Ambrózy House (*Jurisics tér 14*) is named after the Lutheran merchant who lived inside until 1716; in 1708 it was the scene for the capture of a *kuruc* brigadier. The **Golden Unicorn Pharmacy Museum** (*Apotéka az Arany Egyszarvúhoz; Jurisics tér 11;* ↘ *94 360337;* 🎫 *400/200Ft;* ☉ *Tue–Sun 10.00–17.00*) showcases an 18th-century chemist's shop, and contains Baroque furniture stripped from the town's Jesuit cloister after the dissolution of the order in 1773 and secco painting added in 1777 by a Viennese master. Plants used for making the drugs were grown in the courtyard.

Of the square's two churches, **St Jakab Church** is the older, originally built in 1407 from the stones of a Minorite church brought down during a 13th-century siege. The 15th-century version was founded by Palatine Miklós Garai, but had to be reconstructed on several occasions after fires. Between 1554 and 1671, the church was used by the Lutherans, who whitewashed many of the frescoes and carted away extravagant altarpieces in their desire for simplicity in worship. Some of the original frescoes were uncovered during restoration, one of which shows Mary sheltering devotees under her cloak. The crypt contains the tomb of Miklós Jurisics and his children. **St Imre Church** came about as the result of a power struggle between Hungarian and German Protestants; they took over St Jakab Church after proving the victors, so another was constructed (completed in 1640) next to it for the native Lutherans. By comparison with its hulking exterior, the church feels surprisingly small on the inside; the carved ends to the Baroque pews are beautifully tactile, and the altar piece depicting *St Imre's Vow* is by István Dorfmeister (the younger).

Chernel utca runs away from the western side of the square, its Baroque residences reflecting the wealth of a quarter occupied by aristocratic members of the Zichy, Nádasdy and Festetics dynasties. You'll see parts of the southern section of the medieval city walls, demolished after a particularly destructive blaze in 1777, and the **Old Tower** at the end of the street. This stands in what was then a seven-metre-deep moat. During the Turkish siege the outer wall was breached, but pitch was poured upon the attackers from the walls of the castle proper and they were forced back.

Fő tér is younger than the medieval core, its tone set by the **Church of Jesus' Heart** (*Jézus Szíve templom*) that occupies its southwestern end. The 57m bell tower of this magnificent Neo-Gothic church peals at 11.00 every morning in memory of the end of Suleiman's siege. The church was built in 1894, and its interior is as resplendent as any you'll see, with the Austrian Otto Kott's painted columns and ceiling so vivid they look as though they've been wallpapered; it is especially worth seeing when the afternoon sun streams through its stained-glass windows (which show images of the Árpád saints, including István, Imre and Erzsébet). Carved stations of the cross line the sides of the nave, and the ornate pulpit canopy bears an image of the church itself. The **Holy Trinity Column** in front of the church was fashioned from stone quarried at Fertőrákos in 1713, and bears tribute to the 600 plague victims. Just off Fő tér is the town's second historic apothecary's shop, the **Black Saracen Pharmacy** (*Rákóczi u. 3;* ☉ *Tue–Fri*

13.00–17.00), which functioned for 300 years and only closed its doors to sneezing customers in 1983.

On the other side of the town's core, to the northeast of Jurisics tér, is a decrepit **synagogue** (*Várkör 38*) of 1859 that has lain empty since 1944 and the extermination programme of Eichmann. The nearby **Lutheran church** was consecrated in 1783; its separate Eclectic bell tower is not contemporaneous (it was built in 1930) because it was forbidden by József II for non-Catholic denominations to raise stone steeples or belfries.

Jurisics Castle Jurisics Castle (*Rajnis József u. 9*) is to the northwest of Jurisics tér. The chocolate-coloured inner buildings you see now are mainly the result of reconstruction after the fire of 1777, but there are Gothic and Renaissance features and remnants of the thick fortified outer wall running away from them. It was from the 14th-century castle that Miklós Jurisics and fewer than 500 garrison troops withstood a month-long Turkish assault in 1532. A statue of Jurisics stands in the yard, which is reached via a brick bridge spanning the former moat. The Knights' Hall is used for cultural events, while the southern and eastern wings are home to the **Miklós Jurisics Castle Museum** (94 360240; 1,000/700Ft; Feb–Dec Tue–Sun 10.00–17.00). The exhibitions contain items of local history, including those relating to the siege, and a vinicultural display (wine producing was strong in the area until the phylloxera epidemic hit).

Other A short distance to the west of the centre along Hunyadi utca is the **Chernel Botanical Garden** (*Arborétum u. 2;* 94 362676; Mon–Fri 09.00–15.00), which also contains a small museum (visits by prior notice only) dedicated to the wildlife of the Kőszeg Hills and the work of ornithologist István Chernel.

The **Kőszeg Hills** afford outdoor types good hiking terrain. The Írottkő Peak right on the border is the highest in Transdanubia (at 884m), and has a lookout tower (it falls on the Austria side, but the Schengen agreement means you don't need your passport to cross). There are hiking trails (of different lengths) to the Seven Springs (Hétforrás), a water source that once fed the castle and now flows through seven spouts representing the landtaking Magyar chieftains; to the Óház peak just to the south of it, which has a lookout tower; and to Calvary Hill, with its picturesque 18th-century chapel (whose 40,000 bricks were carried here by hand by the town citizens) and a bomb shelter where the Holy Crown was hidden in early 1945. The Írottkő Nature Park people have published leaflets outlining some favourite routes, including a cycle path starting at Kőszegfalva and passing through Kőszeg, Cák, Velem and Bozsok.

You should also buy a copy of Cartographia's *A Kőszegi-hegység és környékenek* (1:40,000). The literature and map are available from Tourinform.

FESTIVALS AND EVENTS Among the town's main events are medieval games and frolics held in the castle during summer months, and wine festivals in April and September. St Ursula's Day conveniently falls on October 21 (two days before the anniversary of the 1956 uprising, and a public holiday) and this is when honey and chestnuts are celebrated in and around the town. As in Italy and France, sweet chestnuts are much valued in Hungary, the purée a staple of cakes and other sweets. The country's best chestnuts are grown in the Kőszeg Hills. By October the honey harvest is also complete. You can sample honeys made from a range of flowers: the ubiquitous acacia (*Robinia pseudoacacia* was introduced from America, and its glorious scent is used to flavour firewood and honey), but also lime tree, clover and meadow flowers. Events include organised walks in the hills, tastings of the produce and general merrymaking. Be sure to book accommodation in advance.

9

About 30km east of Kőszeg lies the spa resort of Bükfürdő. Like Sárvár and Hajduszoboszló, the thermal water here was discovered during drilling activity in search of oil and gas, and the spa itself was established in the 1970s. The water is used to treat certain medical conditions; the pool complex is fabulous. In addition to the spa, Bük is popular among sporting tourists for the 18-hole golf course that opened in 1991 (Hungary's first championship course).

GETTING THERE Bük is connected to Sopron (16 daily) and Szombathely (15) by **train**, and to Szombathely(15) and Kőszeg (10) by **bus**. Both rail and bus stations are in the middle of the village, while the baths and the hotels are about 2km away.

INFORMATION AND OTHER PRACTICALITIES

Z Tourinform Eötvös u. 11; ⤨ 94 558419; e buk@tourinform.hu. Small, helpful office in the village centre; can help with private rooms. ① Mon–Fri 09.00–17.00.

⌂ WHERE TO STAY AND EAT Every other house has private accommodation in the village, and there are six large hotels around the baths.

⌂ Danubius Health Spa Resort Bük (200 rooms) Bükfürdő, Termál körút 27; ⤨ 94 889400; www.danubiushotels.com/buk. This fully equipped spa hotel has indoor & outdoor pools, saunas, wellness & the full range of therapeutic treatments. There's also a dental clinic & beauty saloon. The air-conditioned rooms are spacious, with balconies & tea/coffee making facilities. *Sgl 17,300Ft, dbl 26,000Ft.*

⌂ Hotel Öreg Malom (24 rooms) Csepreg; ⤨ 94 365505; wwworegmalom.hu. Standing in the neighbouring village (7km to the northwest of Bük), this 16th-century mill has been restored & converted to a hotel. The rooms are large & well furnished, those downstairs with their own terraces; the grounds could do with a little care & attention. Primarily, however, this is a place for an intimate meal (*mains avg 2,200Ft;* ① *10.00–14.00 &*

18.00–22.00 daily) away from the hustle of Bük. *Sgl 11,750Ft, dbl 18,800Ft.*

⌂ Radisson SAS Birdland Resort & Spa (202 rooms) Golf út 4; ⤨ 94 558700; www.buk.radissonsas.com. This new hotel overlooks the championship golf course. Aside from the golfing opportunities, however, the hotel also offers a 3,500m² wellness area devoted to health & beauty. Indoor & outdoor pools, thermal pools, extensive sauna facilities, tennis, bike hire. One of the restaurants is à la carte (*mains avg 3,000Ft*). Daily green fee €55–60. Dbl €129.

⌂ Rigótanya Étterem és Panzió (6 rooms) Kossuth Lajos u. 110; ⤨ 94 358160; www.rigotanya.hu. This restaurant (*mains avg 1,800Ft*) & pension is new to the scene, but it was built in traditional style with a reed roof & exposed beams. The rooms are large & air-conditioned, & there's WiFi access. Lovely enclosed terrace. Dbl 12,500Ft.

SOPRON

Heck, we love this place. We're sops to its architecture, its sense of past times in Fő tér, its museums and pubs and restaurants, its very proximity to the lungs of the Lővér Hills and Lake Fertő. We even love its title, 'Most Faithful City' (*Civitas Fidelissima*), a reference to a post-Trianon referendum of 1921 when its citizens elected to remain part of Hungary rather than be subsumed into Austria. Beautiful and constant: what more could one ask?

The country's westernmost city – pushing a bulge of border into Austria up to the foothills of the Alps – was settled first by the Celts and then the Romans, who called the place Scarbantia and thrived on the trade route known as the 'Amber Road' running between the Baltic Sea and the Adriatic. When the Magyars came they named it 'Suprun' after a contemporary county ruler, and merchants flourished throughout the medieval period. Unlike so much of the architecture further east, what was built here stayed built for the town remained untouched by Mongols and Turks. The slings and arrows of World War II left more considerable marks, but a committed programme of restoration put Sopron's houses in order – a programme that was deservedly rewarded with the Europa Award for preservation in 1975.

GETTING THERE AND AWAY The **Inner City bus station** (*Kristóf u.*) is a short walk from the centre along Lackner Kristóf utca and through Ógabona tér. Buses run hourly to Győr and very regularly to Fertőd, Fertőrákos and Nagycenk. There are also departures to Szombathely (seven), Budapest Népliget (four) and twice-daily services to Balatonfüred, Keszthely and Zalaegerszeg, and once-daily ones to Pécs, Tapolca, Esztergom and Vienna. A weekly (Sun evening) bus crosses the border to reach Stuttgart via Munich.

There are two **railway stations**, the main one (*Állomás u.*) 700m south of the Belváros. From here, walk in a southerly direction along Mátyás Király utca before turning left into Széchenyi tér. There are fairly regular trains to Győr and Szombathely (up to 14), and services to Budapest Keleti and Tatabánya (seven), Tapolca, Sárvár and Sümeg (one).

INFORMATION AND OTHER PRACTICALITIES

Escort Tourist Orsolya tér 4; ℡ 99 320670. Offers information & booklets on the region, as well as peddling souvenir tat. This is also the place to book tickets for concerts at the Esterházy Palace in Fertőd (see page 492). ⊕ Mon–Fri 09.00–17.00.
Listings magazine Soproni Est

Tourinform Liszt Ferenc u. 1; ℡ 99 517560; e sopron@tourinform.hu; www.tourinform.sopron.hu. Staff will trip over themselves to assist.A second Tourinform office (*Deák tér 45;* ℡ 99 505438) has free internet & offers bike hire (*1,500Ft/day*). ⊕ Jun 15–Aug 31 Mon–Fri 09.00–18.00, Sat–Sun 10.00–19.00; rest of yr Mon–Fri 09.00–17.00, Sat 09.00–12.00.

WHERE TO STAY Sopron is a popular place to be in summer, and you would do well to book your accommodation before you arrive.

Bio-Sport Hotel Lövér Várisi u. 4; ℡ 99 513840; www.danubiushotels.com/lover. 5km southwest of the centre, in the town's green belt at the edge of the Sopron Hills, there's clean air & lush woodland around this well-equipped 4-star. Facilities include swimming pool, sauna, fitness/wellness centre & a popular restaurant. Ideal for walks in the Lövér Hills. Local buses 1, 2 & 15 run here. Sgl 21,200Ft, dbl 24.000Ft.
Diána Panzió (9 rooms) Lövér körút 64; ℡ 99 329013; www.dianapanziosopron.hu. A cheaper alternative to the above, the Diána is a pleasant guesthouse also well-placed for hill walkers. It has a restaurant. Sgl 7,000, dbl 10,000Ft.
Hotel Sopron (100 rooms) Fövényverem u. 7; ℡ 99 512261;; www.hotelsopron.hu. Bland 4-star that lacks character but is within the city walls. Outdoor pool & solarium. Sgl/dbl 15,000/18,000Ft.
Hotel Wollner (18 rooms) Templom u. 20; ℡ 99 524400; www.wollner.hu. A touch of class in a 300-year-old Baroque building based around a narrow courtyard (with a restaurant – see page 483). Voted Best Hotel in Hungary 2008 (in its category). The

rooms are excellent, & there's a wine cellar for tastings. Highly recommended. Dbl 18,800Ft, trpl 22,900Ft.
Jégverem Inn (5 rooms) Jégverem u. 1; ℡ 99 510113; www.jegverem.hu. Built on the site of an 18th-century ice house, the rooms are whitewashed & simply furnished. 10-min walk northeast of the centre. Sgl 6,900Ft, dbl 8,900Ft.
Ózon Camping Erdei Malom köz 3; ℡ 99 523370; e ozoncamping@sopron.hu. Fabulously well-kept site with all the amenities – including restaurant, swimming pool & a few bungalows – to ensure campers are happy campers. 6km west of the centre – buses 3, 10 & 10B stop 200m away. Camping 1,500/850Ft; caravans/campervans/bungalows 2,500Ft, regular tent 800Ft; ⊕ Apr 15–Oct 15.
Pannonia Med Hotel (62 rooms) Várkerület 75; ℡ 99 312180; www.pannoniahotel.com. Possibly the city's most illustrious hotel, housed in a Neoclassical building of 1893. (A honeymooning Johann Strauss stayed in the previous hotel on this site in 1892.) The 4-star rooms are individually designed & the 14 suites

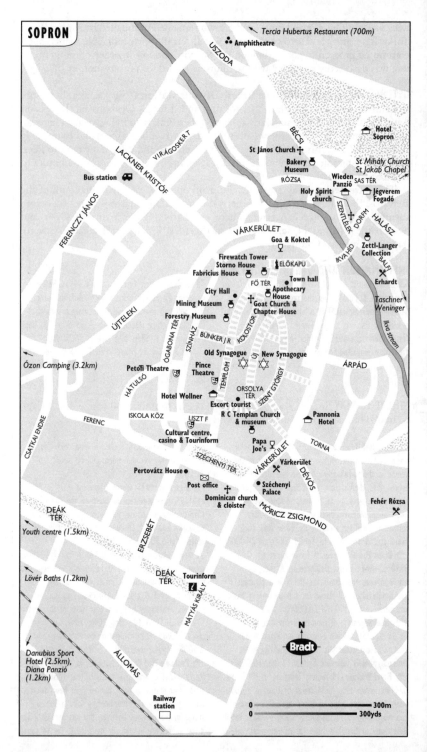

SOPRON

Tercia Hubertus Restaurant (700m)

Amphitheatre

USZODA

BÉCSI

Hotel Sopron

LACKNER KRISTÓF

VIRÁGOSKER T

St János Church

Bakery Museum

St Mihály Church
St Jakab Chapel

Bus station

FERENCZY JÁNOS

RÓZSA

Wieden Panzió

SAS TÉR

Holy Spirit church

SZENTLÉLEK

DORM

Jégverem Fogadó

HALÁSZ

VÁRKERÜLET

ÁKVA HID

BALF

Zettl-Langer Collection

Goa & Koktel

Firewatch Tower
Storno House
Fabricius House

ELŐKAPU

Town hall

Erhardt

FŐ TÉR

Apothecary House

Taschner
Weninger

City Hall

Mining Museum

Goat Church & Chapter House

Ikva stream

ÚJTELEKI

Forestry Museum

ÓGABONA TÉR

SZÍNHÁZ

BÜNKER J R

KOLOSTOR

Ózon Camping (3.2km)

Old Synagogue

New Synagogue

ÁRPÁD

Petőfi Theatre

HÁTULSÓ

Pince Theatre

TEMPLOM

ÚJ

SZENT GYÖRGY

Hotel Wollner

Escort tourist

ORSOLYA TÉR

CSATKAI ENDRE

FERENC

ISKOLA KÖZ

LISZT F

R C Templan Church & museum

Pannonia Hotel

TORNA

Cultural centre, casino & Tourinform

Papa Joe's

SZÉCHENYI TÉR

VÁRKERÜLET

Várkerület

DEVŐS

Pertovátz House

Post office

Dominican church & cloister

Széchenyi Palace

Fehér Rózsa

MÓRICZ ZSIGMOND

DEÁK TÉR

Youth centre (1.5km)

ERZSÉBET

Lövér Baths (1.2km)

DEÁK TÉR

Tourinform

MÁTYÁS KIRÁLY

N

Bradt

Danubius Sport Hotel (2.5km),
Diana Panzió (1.2km)

ÁLLOMÁS

Railway station

0 ——————— 300m
0 ——————— 300yds

482

furnished with tasteful antiques. Indoor pool, jacuzzi, gym & dental surgery. The hotel also owns 6 wooden apartments (for up to 10) 2km away & a gorgeous house on stilts on Lake Fertő. *Sgl €70, dbl €75.*

🛏 **Wieden Panzió** (9 rooms) Sas tér 13; ✎ 99 523222; e wieden@fullnet.hu; www.wieden.hu.

Comely place whose rooms could do with a touch of modernisation, but which includes a couple of very spacious apartments with kitchens. Stands to the northeast of the Belváros. Free bike rental. *Sgl 7,000Ft, dbl 9,900Ft, apt from 10,900Ft.*

✗ WHERE TO EAT AND DRINK

🍴 **Dömötöri Cukrászda & Coffee House** Széchenyi tér 13; ✎ 99 312781. Delicious ice creams, desserts & cakes. Take your treat on the outdoor terrace. ⊕ *Mon–Sat 07.00–24.00, Sun 08.00–24.00.*

✗ **Erhardt Restaurant & Wine Cellar** Balfi u. 10; ✎ 99 506711; www.borvendeglo.hu. Beautifully presented restaurant & wine cellar in an old burgher's house. Offers a large selection of Sopron wines (on the menu & in its shop). *Mains avg 2,000Ft;* ⊕ *Mon–Thu 11.30–23.00, Fri–Sat 11.30–24.00, Sun 11.30–22.00.*

✗ **Fehér Rózsa** Pócsi u. 21; ✎ 99 335270; www.feherrozsa.hu. This historic inn just outside the city walls is a prize-winning restaurant & the best in town. It specialises in traditional Hungarian dishes, & has a pleasant courtyard. *Mains avg 1,400Ft;* ⊕ *11.00–23.00.*

✗ **Fórum Pizzeria** Szent György u. 3. Good pizzas, as well as fish, grills & pasta dishes, & a beautiful setting. ⊕ *11.00–24.00 daily.*

✗ **Tercia Hubertus** Hubertusz út 1; ✎ 99 334290; www.terciarestaurant.hu. The Tercia Hubertus is large, lively & family-friendly (kids are given crayons to scribble with), & very convenient for travellers on Road 85 from Vienna. Traditional Hungarian fare, & live music at the weekend. Has some comfortable guestrooms (*dbl 8,500–9,500Ft*). *Mains avg 2,000Ft;* ⊕ *Sun–Thu 07.00–24.00, Fri–Sat 07.00–24.00.*

✗ **Várkerület Söröző** Várkerület 83; ✎ 99 319286; www.puskasrestaurant.hu. Friendly local place that stays busy till late. *Mains avg 1,900Ft;* ⊕ *11.00–24.00.*

✗ **Wollner Restaurant** See page 481. Super-stylish & ambient restaurant. A largely international à la carte menu is supplemented with tasty local specialities, & a set lunch menu (*available 12.30–15.00*) offers great value. *Mains avg 2,000Ft;* ⊕ *12.00–22.00 daily.*

ENTERTAINMENT AND NIGHTLIFE The Art-Nouveau **Sopron Petőfi Theatre** (*Petőfi tér 1;* ✎ *99 517542; www.prokultura.hu*) was erected in 1909; the main 400-seat arena hosts Hungarian and foreign drama, while a smaller theatre in the same building stages contemporary plays. There's no box office – get your tickets from the Liszt Ferenc Cultural Centre. To the south of Fő tér, the Neoclassical building housing the **Liszt Ferenc Conference and Cultural Centre** (*Liszt Ferenc u. 1;* ✎ *99 517517; ticket office* ⊕ *Mon–Fri 09.00–17.00, Sat 09.00–12.00*) once played host to the great Liszt (who performed here in 1874). Today you can get information on the city's arts events, and there is also a conference centre, concert room and theatre. Find out what's coming up in the *Soproni Program* (available from Tourinform). The **Civitas Cellar Theatre** (*Templom u. 16;* ✎ *99 332098; www.sopronnet.hu/civitas; ticket office* ⊕ *Tue–Sat 10.00–12.00, 17.00–20.00*) is a damp-smelling venue for theatre and cabaret accessed through an arch from Templom utca.

Goa C Bar (*Várkerület 24;* ⊕ *Sun–Thu 18.00–01.00, Fri–Sat 18.00–02.00*) is a chilled-out basement bar that plays acid-jazz and funky tunes, and has a huge selection of cocktails. **Papa Joe's Saloon** (*Várkerület 108;* ✎ *99 340933;* ⊕ *Sun–Thu & Sun 11.00–24.00, Fri–Sat 11.00–02.00*) has a Wild-West theme, but is less tacky than it sounds and has courtyard seating. For a bit of British, try **Perkovátz English Pub** (*Széchenyi tér;* ⊕ *daily 12.00–02.00*) – its un-English name refers to the Hungarian chap who worked in a Liverpool pub in 1908 and decided to open one himself on his return home. His grandson runs the place now. It's popular and well-frequented, and makes a decent stab at the traditional pub ambience; there's Guinness and a good selection of Scottish whiskies, but not a Yorkshire pud or fish and chip in sight on the Hungarian menu.

If you fancy something a bit more risky, try your hand at the **Casino Sopron** (*Liszt Ferenc u. 1;* \ *99 512350; www.casinosopron.hu;* ☉ *13.00–04.00 daily*) – where apparently 'luck knows no borders'. It's located on the ground floor of the cultural centre (entrance on Petőfi tér) and has slot machines and gaming tables. You'll need your passport to enter, and a few gambling chips are included in the entrance fee of €15 (the membership card also gives you a discount at some of the city's restaurants).

WHAT TO SEE AND DO
The Belváros
Fő tér The city's historic heartland is Fő tér, a gorgeous uneven square, and it is there you should begin any stroll about. Its northern gateway is the **Firewatch Tower** (*Tűztorony;* ✆ *700/350Ft;* ☉ *Apr & Sep 16–Oct 31 Tue–Sun 10.00–18.00, May–Sep 15 Tue–Sun 10.00–20.00*), which stands at the point of the medieval fortified gate (you can still see the remains of the original double drawbridge just outside). The tower – as you might have guessed – was used as an observation point to spot outbreaks of fire, although the watchmen were also on their guard for salesman trying to smuggle in non-Sopron wine. Maybe they'd been drinking it too, for while the lowest portion dates to the 13th century, the bulk of the Baroque form was built after a fire of 1676. A spiralling (and frequently congested) set of 200 steps takes you up to a viewing gallery. The archway leading through the tower's base is known as the **Gate of Fidelity**, a reference to the 1921 referendum at which the citizens voted to remain on Hungarian soil. The carved statues above represent the burghers praying to the allegorical figure of Hungaria, and were the work of Zsigmond Kisfaludy Strobl in 1928.

Much of the cobbled square dates from the aftermath of the 1676 fire, but the medieval layout is unchanged. In the centre is the Baroque **Trinity Column**, commissioned by two residents (shown kneeling at the base) to celebrate surviving the plague of 1695–1701. It's an extravagant affair and the first example of a corkscrew column – like a piece of twisted rope – in eastern Europe. Every Sunday it is kept company by stall-holders selling their wares at an **antiques market** (☉ *08.00–16.00*). Immediately to your left after passing through the arch is the Eclectic **town hall** (*Fő tér 1*), constructed as part of the millennial celebrations in 1896. Opposite that, the **Storno House** (*Fő tér 8*) had a Renaissance face before its 18th-century Baroque overhaul, and King Mátyás stayed inside in 1442–43 while he made an attack on nearby Vienna. It was also the venue for concerts by Ferenc Liszt in 1840 and 1881. In 1872 it became the residence of Ferenc Storno, who started life as a chimney sweep but whose extraordinary creative talent allowed him to become one of the period's leading art restorers. He re-styled many churches in Transdanubia (including Pannonhalma Abbey) in accordance with contemporary wishes for aesthetic unity, and he's therefore something of a pariah to architectural historians. He (and his offspring after him) went about hoarding paintings, furniture and weaponry, and these objects form the basis for the **Storno Collection** (\ *99 311327;* ✆ *1,000/500Ft;* ☉ *Tue–Sun Apr–Sep 10.00–18.00, Oct–Mar 14.00–18.00*). The intriguing exhibition includes a display of local history on the ground floor; foreign visitors can listen to a tape that explains the contents of each room.

The **Pharmacy Museum** (*Patikamúzeum; Fő tér 2;* \ *99 311327;* ✆ *300/150Ft;* ☉ *Tue–Sun Apr–Sep 10.00–18.00, Oct–Mar 14.00–18.00*) contains the original furnishings of a 19th-century chemist's shop. There is a valuable collection of medical books, as well as the superstitious trappings of a 17th-century apothecary's art – including an amulet to protect the bearer from the evil eye. The **Fabricius House** (*Fő tér 6;* \ *99 311327;* ✆ *700/350Ft;* ☉ *Tue–Sun Apr–Sep 10.00–18.00, Oct–Mar 14.00–18.00*) takes its name from the early 19th-century mayor and owner; he was friends with the poet Petőfi, who once changed his clothes inside after stealing away from his barracks to attend one of Liszt's concerts. Archaeologists uncovered a Roman bathhouse in the basement, and the Gothic cellar contains a display of other finds from Scarbantia – statues, sarcophagi and gravestones. At the rear of the building are even earlier finds from the time of the Illyrian and Celtic tribes, while at the front are pieces of 17th- and 18th-century furniture.

The **Kossow House** (*Fő tér 4*) has received some majestic guests in its time; Emperor Ferdinand II stayed in 1622 and 1625 when parliament met in Sopron, and Ferdinand III, Leopold I and Prince Charles of Lorraine all rested their heads inside during the 17th century, the latter while readying himself for the siege of Buda in 1684.

Templom utca, Orsolya tér and Új utca Templom utca leaves the southern side of Fő tér, passing to the right of the so-called **Goat Church** (*Kecske templom; Templom u. 1*). The Gothic church was built by the Franciscans in around 1280, supposedly from the proceeds of treasure unearthed by a foraging goat. Several sessions of the Hungarian Diet were convened in the church during the 16th and 17th centuries, and among the three coronations it witnessed was that of Ferdinand III in 1625. The southern wall bears the Kapisztrán pulpit from which the Franciscan monk – who fought alongside János Hunyadi in the famous victory at Nándorfehérvár in 1456 (see *Exploring Buda*, page 132) – is said to have called for Holy War against the Turks. The side altars were carved by Ferenc Storno (see opposite) in 1852. The tiny attached Gothic **Chapter House** (*Káptalanterem;* ☎ *99 523768;* ⊕ *Apr–Oct Mon–Fri at 10.00, 11.00, 14.00, 15.00, 16.00*) – just 5m² – served as the prayer house for the monastery, and subsequently as a burial chamber. It is adorned with fragments of medieval frescoes, as well as a ceiling painted by Dorfmeister in 1779.

A former Esterházy mansion now holds the collections of two adjacent museums. The **Central Mining Museum** (*Központi Bányászati Múzeum; Templom u. 2;* ☎ *99 312667;* 🎫 *500/300Ft;* ⊕ *Tue–Sun Apr–Oct 10.00–18.00, Nov–Mar 14.00–18.00*) focuses upon the history of digging in the Carpathian Basin. There's a reconstruction of part of a 20th-century mine shaft, and displays of earlier medieval and Stone-Age mining methods. Next door, the **Museum of Forestry** (*Erdészeti Múzeum; Templom u. 4;* ☎ *99 338870;* 🎫 *300/150Ft;* ⊕ *Thu–Tue May–Sep 13.00–18.00, Oct–Apr 10.00–13.00*) has the tools of 19th- and 20th-century woodsman; perhaps of more interest is the building's history, however, for it was here that the Allied representatives made their final judgement on the results of the 1921 referendum, and Sopron stayed Magyar. Also interesting is the 17th-century **Bezerédj House** (*Templom u. 6*), where Liszt – who spread himself thinly in Sopron – performed at a private gathering; afterwards there was a rather unbecoming spectacle as some of the ladies fought over one of his gloves.

Midway along Templom utca is the **Lutheran church**, built in 1782 after József II had issued his edict of religious tolerance and now frequently used for concerts. The tower wasn't added until the 1860s. The **National Lutheran Collection** (*Templom u. 12;* ☎ *99 523002;* 🎫 *80/40Ft; appointment necessary*) tells the history of the Lutherans and has documents dating back to the 16th century.

Towards the southern end of Templom utca is the **Körmendi-Csák Gallery** (*Templom u. 18–19;* ☎ *99 524012; www.kormendigaleria.hu;* 🎫 *entrance free; telephone in advance*), a collection of modern fine art from the mid 20th century onwards. Turning to the left brings you into **Orsolya tér**, with the Maria Fountain that once graced the courtyard of the Franciscan monastery before being moved here in the 1930s. The **Roman Catholic church** occupies the site of a wooden-steepled church where Maria Theresa attended mass during a visit in 1773. The current Gothic version dates to the 19th century, although it was reconstructed after being bombed in World War II. An Ursuline (Orsolya) convent was also built in the square in the 1860s, and its oratory (to the church's right) holds the **Roman Catholic Ecclesiastical Collection** (*Orsolya tér 2;* ✆ *99 312221;* ✆ *admission free;* ☉ *May–Oct Mon, Wed, Fri, Sat 10.00–16.00*).

Pop north up Új utca and on the left you'll see the **Old Synagogue** (*Ó Zsinagóga; Új u. 22–24;* ✆ *99 311327;* ✆ *600/300Ft;* ☉ *Tue–Sun May–Oct 10.00–18.00, Oct 10.00–14.00*). This street – formerly Zsidó (Jew) utca – was the Jewish quarter from as early as the 13th century (up until the Jews were banished in 1526 after being accused of plotting with the Turks). The Gothic synagogue was built around 1300; a corridor leads to the main hall, containing the base of the original pulpit and an alcove bearing traces of vine motifs. Opposite is the New Synagogue (*Új Zsinagóga; Új u. 11*), which was founded in 1350 as place of private prayer for a wealthy Viennese banker.

Széchenyi tér The southern end of Templom utca joins Széchenyi tér, at the far corner of which is a late-Baroque **Dominican church and cloister**, whose main body was completed in 1725 and the twin clock towers added 50 years later. The Neoclassical **Széchenyi Palace** (*Széchenyi tér 1–2*) ranged along the square's eastern side bears a plaque to István Széchenyi ('the greatest Hungarian') but it should perhaps bear testimony to his poor, overshadowed father; some of Ferenc's massive stash of books and maps were held here, later to become the core of the National Library that he founded (and which is now in Buda's Castle District).

Beyond the Belváros Moving away slightly from Sopron's medieval hub, there are plenty of other sights dotted around.

Draw a line diagonally to the northeast of the Belváros and you'll hit the **Zettl-Langer Collection** (*Balfi út 11;* ✆ *99 311136;* ✆ *adult 500Ft;* ☉ *Mar–Jan Tue–Sun 10.00–12.00*) on the other side of the Ikva Stream; like Ferenc Storno (see page 484), Gusztáv Zettl (1852–1917) was a young working-class man with artistic aspirations. While staying loyal to the family vinegar business, he also began collecting antiquities and fine art. Subsequent generations continued in the same vein, and the furniture, china, books and weapons are now on display in the family house.

A short distance away, across Dorfmeister utca, is the **Church of the Holy Spirit** (*Szent Lélek templom; Szent Lélek u.*), built in 1782 on the site of a 15th-century Gothic predecessor; it contains a flabbergastingly ornate altar and frescoes by Dorfmeister. Cut up Dorfmeister utca to Szent Mihály utca, rising up to Sopron's highest point. At the top is the Neo-Gothic **St Mihály Church**, originally 13th-century and reconstructed in the 15th century (when King Mátyás attended the consecration). At that time it is said to have been stuffed with up to 20 altar pieces, but much was destroyed in the 17th century. In the churchyard is the compact **St Jakab Chapel**, the earliest of the city's structures and showing elements of the transition between Romanesque and Gothic architectural styles.

Descend the hill again, and walk northwest a little further to Bécsi út. The **Bakery Museum** (*Pékház & Múzeum; Bécsi út 5;* ✆ *99 311327;* ✆ *400/200Ft;* ☉ *Apr–Sep Tue–Sun 14.00–18.00*) is located in a 16th-century baker's, and shows the grain store and preparation area, the shop where the bread was sold, and photos of the old bakers themselves. The living quarters are to the right of the entrance gate.

OTHER ACTIVITIES The **Vadon Equestrian Club** (*Sopron-Ágfalva, Magyar u. 25;* ✆ *99 505780; www.vadonlovasklub.hu*) is situated in the village of Ágfalva, 4km west of Sopron. It organises horse-riding tours and camps, as well as horse shows and other programmes. It also has a guesthouse with 14 rooms. There are regular buses here from Sopron, and the village has a small railway station. If you want a dip, the **Lővér Baths** (*Lővér körút 82; tel 99 510964;* 🎫 *800/470Ft;* ⊕ *Mon 14.00–21.00, Tue–Thu 05.30–21.00, Fri 05.30–20.00, Sat–Sun 09.00–20.00*) have indoor and outdoor pools (the latter open summer only); local buses 2 and 15 stop 100m from the entrance.

The Sopron region is known for its reds. The **Wollner Hotel** (see page 481) plans to open its wine cellar for tastings of exclusively Sopron wines; during the week, cold platters of cheese and charcuterie will be available, while simple warm food will be served at weekends. You can also take a tasting in the cellars of two nationally renowned winemakers. **Taschner** (*Balfi út 164;* ✎ *99 506605; www.taschnervin.hu;* ⊕ *Mon–Fri 08.00–16.00*) is a new cellar complex on the outskirts of Sopron. **Weninger** (*Fő u. 23;* ✎ *99 531082; www.weninger.hu; tasting 1,500Ft for 5 wines & 3,000Ft with cellar tour – appointment necessary;* ⊕ *Mon–Fri 08–16.00, Sat 12.00–16.00*) is actually in nearby Balf; the high-tech winery is slightly difficult to find (enter between two village houses on the main street).

The **Lővér Hills** to the south and southwest of Sopron feature forests and meadows, and offer good walking and hiking terrain. Head for the Bio-Sport Hotel (see page 481) from where you can pick up several trails, some of which go via the Károly Lookout Tower to the west. The hills fall under the auspices of the Sopron Landscape Preserve Area; the *Sopron környéke* (Kárpátia, 1:40,000) map shows all the hill paths, and should be available from Sopron's Tourinform.

FESTIVALS AND EVENTS Liszt was born in Sopron County and played on several occasions in the city, and it is inevitable that there are important festivals devoted to culture and the arts. Sopron was the first place to join Budapest in holding a Spring Festival (*Mar*), when there are performances of theatre, music and dance. The main events of Sopron Festive Weeks (*Jun–Jul*) take place in the Quarry Theatre at Fertőrákos (see below), but there are also concerts and folkloric exhibitions in the city squares. At the beginning of July the VOLT Festival of popular music fills the city to the brim. September sees the Festival of Kékfrankos, the fiery local red wine produced in the hills above Lake Fertő. For details see www.prokultura.hu.

EXCURSIONS FROM SOPRON

Fertőrákos Travel 12km northeast of Sopron and you'll reach Fertőrákos. A break in the rushes offers access to the only recreational area on Lake Fertő, and the **strand** (🎫 *525/360Ft;* ⊕ *daily May & Aug 24–Sep 15 09.00–20.00, Jun 1–Aug 23 09.00–21.00*) has a grassy sunbathing area, a number of *bufés* and water craft for hire. It is also possible to catch a Drescher Line **ferry** (✎ *99 355361; adult/child €8/5 rtn; Jul 1–Oct 15 daily 10.00, 12.00, 14.00 & 16.00*) from here across to Morbisch in Austria. However, the village is known widely for its rock rather than its water. The legacy of a Pannonian Sea that covered the area 15 million years ago is a rich seam of limestone, formed of dead fishy matter that settled on the seabed. Travel back 2,000 years, and the Romans were mining the stone (which is of a good colour and readily carved) and using it to build Scarbantia (Sopron); in later centuries it formed building blocks for cities including Vienna. The **quarry** (*Fertőrákos kőfejtő; Fő u. 1;* ✎ *99 355026;* 🎫 *300/200Ft;* ⊕ *daily Feb, Nov & Dec 08.00–16.00, Mar–Apr & Oct 08.00–17.00, May–Sep 08.00–19.00*), at the northern end of the village, operated until World War II, after which artificial materials like concrete became the vogue. In the 1970s it was decided to make use of the space by establishing a cave theatre, and this now provides a quite unique setting for concerts, theatre and opera, particularly during the Sopron Festival Weeks in summer. The steep quarry sides also form a popular nesting side for birds, and a study path runs around the top.

Moving down from the quarry along Fő utca (which stretches the length of the village), other sights to look out for are the **Crystal Museum** (*Fő u. 99;* ᴁ *200/100Ft;* ☉ *May 1–Nov 1 daily 09.00–19.00*), with its collection of Hungarian minerals, the 18th-century Rococo **Bishop's Palace** (*Fő u. 153*), a 16th-century public pillory (the only one of its kind in Hungary) and the **Mithras Chapel** (a Roman cave temple near the border – follow Meggyesi utca to the right from the top of the village for 2km). If you need **accommodation**, there are regular signs advertising free rooms (*szoba kiadó*). Alternatively, Huber Panzió (*Fertő u. 1;* ❑ *99 355149; www.huberpanzio.hu*) is a good-looking guesthouse with lovely gardens. You can **eat** Hungarian specialities and grills at Puskás Sörkert (*Fő u. 175;* ❑ *99 355506; mains avg 1,500Ft;* ☉ *daily 10.00–23.00*), which has a large garden and is the main place for food and beer. There is live music at the weekends. The rustic Ráspi (*Fő u. 72;* ❑ *99 355146; www.raspi.hu; degustation: 3 courses 3,500Ft, 5 courses 5,500Ft*) is well known for its adventurous cooking; it's worth ditching the car so you can enjoy a meal accompanied by their own wines. It's also a popular watering hole for the cyclists rounding Lake Fertő.

Buses from Sopron (up to nine daily) stop at the strand car park, and continue down Fő utca. En route you'll pass the **memorial site of the Pan-European Picnic** (see box, page 22), a momentous event in the history of the Iron Curtain. At the instigation of Otto von Habsburg, then President of the European Parliament, the border between Hungary and Austria was opened for a few hours in August 1989. A fleet of Trabants from East Germany poured through the breach, visibly demonstrating how untenable the Iron Curtain had become. A few months later, the Berlin wall fell.

FERTŐ-HANSÁG NATIONAL PARK

Jutting between Sopron and Fertőd, the 23,600ha national park was founded in 1991 to protect the Hungarian section of Lake Fertő (which straddles the Austrian border, and is known on the other side as Neusiedler See), the remaining marshes and bogs of the Hanság (which lies around the south of the lake), and the most valuable natural parts of the Répce valley (as it runs above Csorna and Kapuvár).

The shallow **Lake Fertő** is the second-largest wetland in Hungary (the fifth-largest in Europe), and the westernmost alkaline steppe lake. It has receded on several occasions, and this indirectly led to the Austrian name for it; people built houses on the dry bed in 1868 but they were forced to up sticks to a new settlement ('neue Siedlung') when the water returned four years later. An important stopover site for migratory birds, the lake regularly hosts over 20,000 water-loving flappers – mainly geese, ducks and shorebirds – both during migration periods and in winter. (Some good towers – such as that by the road from Fertőújlak (at the lake's southeastern tip) to Mekszikópuszta, and at the Rábca Stream near Bősárkány – offer birders excellent views of the area, and passages have been cut through the reeds for those with guides in rowing boats.) The plains around the shores are filled with alkaline grasslands, rich in species of salt-tolerant plant. Among these are the Pannonic lepidium, *Puccinellia limosa*, and the Pannonic salt-land cyperus, while the surrounding hillsides are home to rare Pannonian steppe vegetation.

One of the missions of those cultivating the national park is to preserve the remains of what was once a massive area of peat landscape (depleted by human hand in the past through peat cutting and drainage). You will find peat forests, peat meadows and peat lakes, all subject to restoration projects (notably in Bősárkány, on the shores of the Rábca Stream near Csorna). As a consequence of such a conservation drive, species associated with peat are re-colonising the area. The smallest piece of the park's jigsaw is the **River Répce**; a section of its course harbours swamp meadows and one of the largest swamp forests in Hungary.

Nagycenk To the southeast of Sopron at the juncture of roads 84 and 85 is Nagycenk, site of the plain Baroque mansion of the Széchenyi family. The achievements of Ferenc Széchenyi – founder of Budapest's National Library – were far from inconsiderable, but it was his son István (1791–1860) who became the leading light of the reform era and earned the flattering tag of 'the greatest Hungarian'. Among the visible monuments to his progressive vision are Budapest's Chain Bridge (the city's first permanent river crossing) and the Hungarian Academy of Sciences (towards which he donated a year's income; see page 147), but perhaps of even more significance were his investment in the railway network and his river-regulation schemes that reclaimed vast areas of swampland in the Great Plain for agriculture. While his practical reformatory zeal – influenced greatly by what he saw during visits to Britain – was unsurpassed, in political terms he urged gradual, evolutionary change and attempted unsuccessfully to put the breaks on the revolutionary stance of Batthyány's government of 1848. He watched the increasingly radical turn of events with the horror of a helpless witness to a train crash, and the pressure triggered a total nervous breakdown. After several years spent in a Viennese asylum, he returned to his political writings; however, he never fully emerged from his black hole and shot his considerable brains out in 1860. His **mauselum** (*$200/100Ft;* ⊕ *May–Oct Tue–Sun 10.00–18.00*) stands in the village cemetery of the Neo-Romanesque, Ybl-designed **St István Church** (*Széchenyi tér*) – whose organ was played once by Liszt. Its Neoclassical form bears a gilded allegory of Hope – which guided Széchenyi for much of his life but appeared a treacherous mistress by the end. The supreme

Herds of ancient indigenous breeds (grey cattle, racka sheep and water buffalo) are also kept in the park, as well as ethnographic displays recording the lives of the people who once lived here – including marsh dwellers and fishermen, who wove traps from the lakeside rushes. While South Hanság can be visited freely along marked walking routes, access to the reed beds and the immediate area of the lake is generally only permitted with a guide; between May and September, however, a 6km canoe trail is opened for adults. A month-long bird-ringing camp is also held annually in the Madárvárta (Birdwatcher's House) to the south of the lake.

The place to start is the **Fertő-Hanság National Park visitor centre** (*Sarród, Rév-Kócsagvár;* ☏ *99 537620; www.ferto-hansag.hu*) – known as Egret Castle (Kócsagvár) – located just northwest of Fertőd at the park boundary. The centre organises three-hour tours (*Wed & Sat departing 09.00 in summer; * *adult 2,500Ft*) of the park's restricted areas. The tours either take in the sodic waters, grasslands and puszta of the eastern shore, the reedbeds of the western shore (by canoe) or the wetland forest and marsh of the Hanság. (Note that sometimes these leave from Öntésmajor, where you'll also find an exhibition on the region's flora and fauna.) There are study trails that you can join from here. You can reach Lake Fertő by **bus** from Sopron, and Sarród has a **railway station** on a branch line from Fertőszentmiklós (which is itself on the Sopron line). A more pleasant way to get there, however, is by joining the **cycle route** that runs all the way around the lake. On the Hungarian side you can take in Fertőrákos and Fertőd on your journey along the southern shore; if you wish to pass over the border to cycle the Austrian portion too, you can do so between April and November only (and will need your passport for the checkpoint at Mörbisch, just north of Fertőrákos). Both bicycles and canoes are available for hire at the visitor centre, and there is **accommodation** (*dbl 5,500Ft*) too. Pick up a copy of the *Fertő-Hanság Nemzeti Park* (Paulus, 1:60,000) map to get a clearer picture of the nature trails and birdwatching towers.

Despite the excellent pay and regular work, Haydn and the musicians and other artists of Esterháza weren't wholly content. They were required to stage as many as three opera performances and two concerts a week for the ducal court and this meant they were kept from their families for long periods. In 1772, Prince Miklós unexpectedly announced he was to extend his stay in Esterháza for a few weeks (thus postponing the date when the musicians could leave). This inspired Haydn to write a piece in which the instruments gradually fall silent, one by one – his *Farewell Symphony*. The symphony was performed in front of the count, and as each player finished he blew out his candle and left the room. Miklós wasn't stupid, recognising the unhappiness and homesickness of the orchestra, and ordered them home the following day.

Haydn died in 1809 and was laid to rest at a simple funeral attended by Viennese aristocrats and French generals. In 1820, however, the coffin was opened while being moved for re-burial in Kismarton and while Haydn's wig was inside the skull on which it should have perched was not. They hunted high and low, and eventually the culprit was uncovered – a Karl Rosenbaum, who had stolen the head for scientific research. It wasn't until 1954 that the skull was finally reunited with its body in the mausoleum at the hill church in Kismarton (now Eisenstadt).

irony, of course, is that hope returned with the Compromise just seven short years after the count's death.

The **Széchenyi Mansion** itself stands just under 1km to the northeast, beside Road 85. While the horseshoe-shaped building is hardly sober, it lacks the feudal extravagance of palaces at Gödöllő or Fertőd and is wholly in tune with one so immersed in the middle-class, anti-aristocratic ethic. Two decades before serfdom was abolished, István actually gave over a considerable area of his estate to serfs, who had no land for themselves. However, that didn't mean he did away with the trappings of comfort, and the mansion was furnished with cutting-edge technology – including flushing toilets. (The villagers also benefited from the count's passion for English innovation, and Nagycenk was the first settlement with gas lamps from 1815.) Built at the end of the 18th century for Antal Széchenyi, and enlarged upon by Mihály Pollack in 1838, the mansion burned down during World War II but was faithfully restored and is beautifully maintained. The **Széchenyi Memorial Museum** (*Kiscenki út 3;* ✆ *99 360023;* 🎟 *600/300Ft;* 🕐 *Tue–Sun Apr–Oct 10.00–18.00, Jan–Mar 10.00–14.00, Nov–Dec 10.00–17.00*) holds furniture, documents, personal belongings and portraits of the Széchenyi family, as well as an exhibition devoted to István's practical achievements. The history of Hungary's industrial development is also laid bare, and there's a collection of coins. The eastern wing contains a stud, the western 'Red Mansion' the Széchenyi Castle Hotel (✆ *99 360061; www.szechenyikastelyszallo.hu; 19 rooms; sgl 12,600Ft, dbl 16,800Ft; guests can visit museum free*) and restaurant, and a 3km-long avenue of lime trees leads away from the whole shebang.

Cross Kiscenki utca and head up Hársfa sor for the **Kastély narrow-gauge station**, which runs summer weekend journeys northward to Fertőboz (*Apr 5–Sep 28 Sat–Sun & hols 10.10, 11.28, 14.00, 15.25 & 17.45;* 🎟 *adult sgl/rtn 150/300Ft, child 75/150Ft*), whose Gloriette Tower of 1802 provides views of Lake Fertő. (There are also trains to the nearer Barátság, for which tickets cost the same.) Special trains are available on weekdays (✆ *99 517384 a week in advance*), and you can actually have a go at driving the locomotive. Behind the station is an open-air **Train Museum** (*free to visit*).

There are very regular **buses** to Nagycenk from Sopron, and services too from Győr (passing through Csorna and Kapuvár on the way); the bus stop is near the mansion. Nagycenk's main **railway station** (near the church and mausoleum) is on the line between Sopron and Szombathely.

FERTŐD

The village of Fertőd, 30km southeast of Sopron, is on the map because of the Esterházy Palace. The Esterházy family came to prominence during the 17th century, and in 1711 a hereditary dukedom was bestowed upon Pál Esterházy – palatine since 1681 – as reward for his loyalty to the Habsburgs. His grandson, Miklós 'the Magnificent' Esterházy, built the mansion in 1766 as a conscious effort to match the opulent lifestyle of the Habsburg emperor; his yearly income was enormous, and he is famously said to have boasted 'What the emperor can afford, I can afford'. It is undoubtedly the country's leading piece of Rococo architecture, and guests including Goethe were blown away by its high-blown elegance – as well as the lustrous parties hosted by Miklós, characterised by fairy lights, pomp, ceremony and the duke in his diamond-studded robe. What you see now is actually but a part of the complex as it appeared in its prime. Taking the palace at Versailles for its inspiration, 'Esterháza' (as it was then known) was set in 3,000ha of grounds filled with statues, fountains and temples, an oriental pagoda hung with wind chimes, a puppet theatre and an opera house where Maria Theresa enjoyed a performance in 1773. The opera house was particularly significant because Haydn lived on the estate for 30 years and the majority of his pieces were first played within its walls. After the death of Miklós in 1790, the palace rapidly fell away (just a few years later parts of it were being used as stables for livestock) and it served as a hospital under the Russians. The restoration job began in the 1950s, and is still ongoing.

GETTING THERE AND AWAY There are **bus stops** directly outside the entrance to the palace (on Bartók Béla utca), with regular services to Sopron, Balf and Kapuvár. The nearest **railway station** is at the end of Fő utca in Fertőszéplak (a couple of kilometres to the west), which sits on a branch running from Fertőszentmiklós (on the Sopron–Győr main line). Fertőszentmiklós is itself around 4km south of Fertőd.

INFORMATION
Tourinform Joseph Haydn u. 3; ℡ 99 537140; e fertod@tourinform.hu. By the ticket office to the palace. ☉ Jun 15–Sep 15 Mon–Fri 09.00–18.00, Sat–Sun 09.00–17.00, rest of yr 09.00–17.00.

WHERE TO STAY AND EAT
Dori Hotel & Camping Pomogyi út 1; ℡ 99 370838; www.dorihotel.hu. Behind the Kastélykert, the Dori certainly stands out with its asymmetrical timber chalet of a hotel. The rooms inside are of a good standard. The campsite is lovely, & includes wooden bungalows; the site has its own restaurant (☉ 07.00–22.00 daily). Hotel: sgl 6,500Ft, dbl 4,900Ft, trpl 4,300Ft; ☉ all yr. Bungalows from 3,100Ft/pp; ☉ Apr 15–Oct 15.

Gránátos Joseph Haydn u. 1; ℡ 99 370944; www.rabensteiner.hu. Opposite the palace entrance, the Gránátos (together with the Kastélykert) was once the lodgings for the grenadiers who rode the 100 horses of the Esterházy stables. The restaurant serves Hungarian food (inc b/fast); in terms of cuisine & price, there's little difference between it & the Kastélykert, but the latter shades things with marginally more elegant surroundings. Mains avg 1,500Ft; ☉ 09.00–22.00 daily.

Kastélykert Joseph Haydn u. 3; ℡ 99 349418; www.kastelykert.hu. Next to the Gránátos, this restaurant & café serves some international dishes but its menu is primarily Hungarian in flavour. Mains avg 1,500Ft; ☉ 09.00–22.00 daily.

🏠 **Szidónia Kastélyszálló** (52 rooms) Röjtökmuzsaj, Röjtöki u. 37; ☎ 99 544810; www.szidonia.hu. This beautifully furnished country house hotel is about 9km away from Fertőd, to the south on the road to Kőszeg. Some of the Louis-XVI-style rooms have palatial bathrooms; the 7ha grounds contain a hunting lodge, while the converted stables & granary have rooms more in the contemporary style. Pool table, tennis court, bike hire, comprehensive wellness (indoor & outdoor pools, saunas, beauty treatments, massage, Kneipp baths). Restaurant (*mains avg 4,000Ft*; ⏱ *12.00–15.00 & 18.00–22.00; coffee shop 07.00–22.00*) in an orangerie-style extension with a lovely terrace. Dbl *19,900Ft (main house)*, *15,900Ft (granary)*, *14,900Ft (stables)*.

THE ESTERHÁZY PALACE The horseshoe-shaped Esterházy Palace (*Esterházy-kastély; Joseph Haydn u. 2;* ☎ *99 537640; www.mag.hu*) is one of the top-three Baroque-Rococo edifices in the country. So important was it as a centre for European nobility that the post-coach to Vienna had its terminus here. When Maria Theresa visited in 1773, the French-style park was adorned with 24,000 Chinese lanterns, and the festivities culminated in a firework display whose touch paper was lit by the empress herself. Count Miklós presented her with a sleigh encrusted with precious stones (now on display at the Imperial Palace in Vienna) and salt was laid on the road so that she could ride it away.

The family occupied the ground-floor wings and above them were rooms to accommodate the servants and the regular flow of guests. At the end of World War II, many of the furnishings were removed, but some period furniture and restored wood panels are on display in the **Esterházy Palace Museum** (☞ *1,500/750Ft*; ⏱ *Mar 15–Oct 31 Tue–Sun 10.00–18.00, rest of yr Fri–Sun 10.00–16.00; park 06.00–dusk*) in the palace's central portion (much of which was originally given over to ceremonial occasions). Around 30kg of gold was used for the gilding on the walls of the 26 rooms open to the public. The ground level includes the apartments of the count and countess, featuring Chinese-style paintings and furniture, together with the reception room (**Sala Terrena**) whose floor of Italian marble was heated from beneath. Haydn worked for several decades in the **Concert Hall** on the first floor – it was here that the *Farewell Symphony* was first performed in 1772 – and there is a display of documents relating to his life and work. The **Gala Room** has red marble fireplaces, Flemish tapestries and the best of the mansion's frescoes – a ceiling painting by the Austrian J I Milldorfer of the *Glory of Apollo*; wherever you stand, you appear to be in the path of the chariot's charging horses. The corner room of the apartments where Maria Theresa stayed includes a portrait of her by the court painter Glunck.

Moving outside, it is noticeable that the mustard-coloured façade is considerably less vibrant than it appears in the multitude of images that adorn the country's tourist literature. The **Music House**, 300m to the west of the palace, is where Haydn lived; there is a commemorative tablet by the sculptor Jenő Bory. Behind the palace French gardens stretch away as far as the village of Fertőszentmiklós. Regular **concerts** are staged in the palace's Concert Hall between June and September. Look out in particular for the Haydn Festival of Strings (*Jul*) and the Haydn Esterháza Festival (*Aug/Sep*); they book up quickly – for tickets, call 99 537640 or contact Escort Tourist (*Sopron, Orsolya tér 4;* ☎ *99 320670; www.escorttourist.hu*).

The almost adjoining village of **Fertőszéplak** was the ancestral home of the Széchenyi family, and Ferenc was born there. In the middle of the village, opposite the church, is his somewhat dilapidated birthplace and the fabulously ornate gate to the small cemetery. Further down the main road towards Fertőd are five virtually identical houses from the early 19th century; these contain a rich collection (☞ *500/250Ft*; ⏱ *Tue–Sun 10.00–18.00*) of local vernacular craftwork (embroidered bedspreads, carved spoons, etc).

10

Lake Balaton

The 'Hungarian sea' in the middle of Transdanubia is where Hungarians come to play. They're not the only ones. During the communist period, the lake represented a convenient meeting place for those divided by the Berlin Wall, and Germans continue to provide a decent chunk of the tourist revenue. With a length of 77km and a total area of 600km², Balaton is the largest lake in central Europe, and its shallow depth (particularly on the southern side) – on average, just two–three metres – means both that it is relatively family-friendly and that it warms up quickly in the sun. The water harbours ample stocks of fish such as carp, bream and the native *fogas* (pike-perch), and is a popular place for windsurfing and rowing. Motorboats are prohibited, so you will not find yourself swamped in a waterskiier's wash; instead wakeboarding – where the skiier is pulled around a circuit by a mechanised pulley – is very much *de rigeur*.

There's a distinct north-south divide where the lake's concerned. The southern shore is the favourite with the water-baby masses intent on sun-worshipping, soaking and wakeboarding, and where the real concentration of hotels, bars and clubs is to be found. The southern resorts attract those with young children and the party crowd, and Siófok – stretching for a full 15km – is the brash leader of the pack. On the other side of the lake, the reeds, volcanic hills and cooler water make for an atmosphere less fevered: Keszthely is a university town that has a life beyond the tourist season; Balatonfüred has always taken its water with a graceful air; Tihany and Badacsony have stunning scenery and wonderful walking terrain. The northern side also boasts the best of the wines.

It used to be the case that the main season at Balaton lasted over three months, and the water is certainly a pleasant enough temperature in late spring and early autumn. However, the hotels and restaurants have been flogging the cash cow with increasing severity, and it is noticeable that the season appears to have narrowed as many potential visitors look for cheaper beach holidays elsewhere. Despite that, the most popular resorts heave with bodies in July and August, and you'd be wise to come outside those months if you can possibly help it.

Balaton is easily reached by train from Budapest Déli, and by bus or train from other towns in Transdanubia. Buses and trains are convenient links between resorts on the same shore, but the ferry is the way to go if you want to get to the other side – indeed even if you don't, it's a pleasant way of viewing the lake from a different angle. From April until October, ferries for foot passengers travel a route between Siófok, Balatonfüred, Tihany and Balatonföldvár, and between Fonyód and Badacsony; during the high-season months these run more often, and there are additional services to other resorts around the lake. There is only one crossing available for cars, that between Tihany and Szántód. See page 43 for details of the airport near Keszthely.

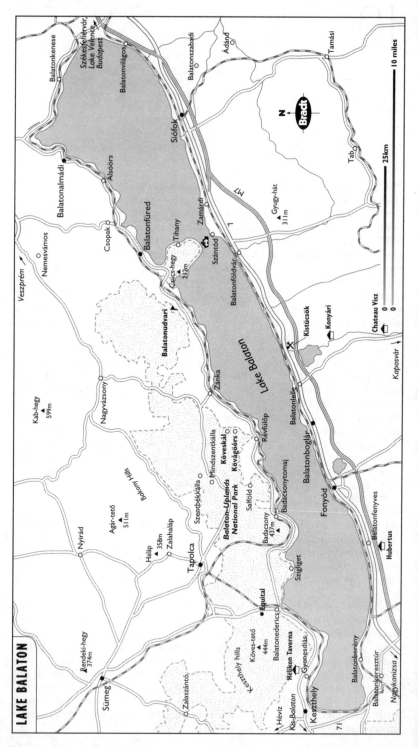

LAKE BALATON

Siófok is the biggest of Balaton's resorts; it's traditionally been seen as the party place – a spot for eating, drinking and basking bodies in the height of summer – but recently it has positioned itself as something of an 'urban resort' (to balance the historic and cultural attractions of Keszthely and Balatonfüred), and has done so with some success. The explosion in Siófok's popularity came after the railway line from Budapest Déli reached here in the late 20th century, and allowed those from the capital to come along and let off steam. There's little that will stimulate you culturally here; instead this is the place to try your hand at some watersports and enjoy a flourishing night scene. Despite the many bleary eyes you'll encounter of a morning, the town is also growing as a centre of health tourism, and there are several new wellness hotels.

GETTING THERE, AWAY AND AROUND Both the **bus station** and main **railway station** (there are several to the east and west of the centre on the same line) are just to the northeast of the Tourinform, on Milleneum tér. Trains run westward through Siófok to the other shore resorts and on to Nagykanizsa (15 daily), and eastward to Székesfehérvár (four) and Budapest (mainly Déli; up to 21 in summer). Buses are less regular, apart from those to Kaposvár; among the services are those to Budapest (three direct daily, three via Székesfehérvár), Hévíz (four), Pécs (seven), Szeged (three), Szekszárd (seven), Tatabánya (three) and Veszprém (ten).

Balaton Shipping Co **ferries** leave from the pier at the point where the lake and the Sió Canal meet, and the ticket office is near by on Krúdy sétány; between late March and late October, there are up to seven services to Balatonfüred and Tihany.

If you want a **taxi**, try Bokros ($\searrow$ 84 317713). The Gold Coast is served by local bus 2 and by Szabadifürdő railway station, the Silver Coast by buses 1, 7 and 5 and by trains to Balatonszéplak felső.

INFORMATION AND OTHER PRACTICALITIES

🚴 **Bike hire** Vitorlás u. 4; $\searrow$ 20 9451279. Bikes for 1,700Ft/day, 8,000Ft/week. You can also hire mopeds on the way to the jetty. ⏲ daily 09.00–21.00.

📧 **Ibusz** Fő u. 176; $\searrow$ 84 510720. Programmes, tours & private rooms from 7,000Ft. On 1st floor of shopping arcade. ⏲ Jun–Aug Mon–Fri 08.00–18.00, Sat 08.00–13.00, rest of yr Mon–Fri 08.00–16.00.

📧 **Internet** There are terminals at the Big Shots Pub (see page 497) & Planet Café (Kele u. 5; $\searrow$ 84 311416; ⏲ Mon–Fri 10.00–20.00, Sat 10.00–16.00).

📧 **Julius Ferien Reisebüro** Petőfi sétány 26; www.juliusferien.de. Main office of a company that arranges apts & private rooms, from basic to luxury. Prices start at 18,000Ft (apt for 4).

🗞 **Listings magazine** Kapos Est

🏢 **Tourinform** Víztorony, Szabadság tér; $\searrow$ 84 310117; e tourinform@siofokportal.com. Housed at the bottom of the ivy-clad water tower. ⏲ Jul–Aug of yr Mon–Fri 08.00–16.00, Sat 10.00–12.00.

🛏 **WHERE TO STAY** There are many hotels and campsites in Siófok, but the resort gets very crowded in high season and bookings are recommended.

⛺ **Aranypart Camping** Szent László u. 183–185; $\searrow$ 84 353399; e siotour.aranypart@balatontourist.hu. Huge site with camping pitches & 76 bungalows (most complete with kitchenettes, bathrooms, etc); you can hire a host of contraptions for getting about – among them electric scooters & mopeds. One of several campsites by the Gold Coast. Alight at the Szabadifürdő railway station if you are coming from Budapest, or take bus 2 from the centre. Bungalows: class I (for 4) 9,000–24,000Ft, class II (for 7) 12,000–35,000Ft; ⏲ Apr 25–Sep 14

🏨 **Hotel Panoráma** (328 rooms) Beszédes József sétány 80; $\searrow$ 84 311638; www.panoramahotel-siofok.hu. 4-star hotel with cheerful, if small, rooms (most of

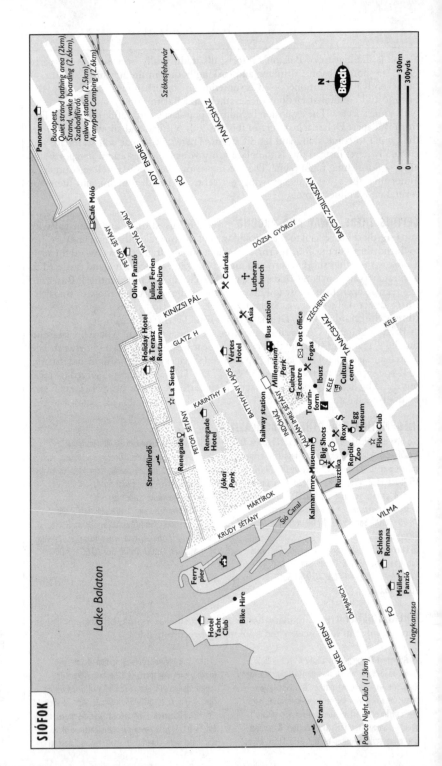

which have balconies). Swimming pool, sauna, jacuzzi, tennis court, bike rental. At the Gold Coast. *Sgl 18,300Ft, dbl 22,800Ft;* ⊕ *all yr.*

⌂ **Hotel Vértes** (58 rooms) Batthyány u. 24; ☎ 84 312422; e sales@hotelvertes.hu; www.hotelvertes.hu. One of 3 newish wellness hotels in Siófok – the others are the Hotel Residence (*www.hotel-residence.hu*) & Hotel Azúr (*www.azurhotel.hu*). Among the facilities are a thermal pool, jacuzzi, fitness centre & sauna, & there are various massages & therapies on offer. *Sgl 14,500Ft, dbl 20,500Ft.*

⌂ **Hotel Yacht Club** (29 rooms) Vitorlás u. 14; ☎ 84 311161; www.hotel-yachtclub.hu. Near the ferry pier, this quiet hotel has lake views from half of its rooms. There's a 25m pool overlooking the yacht harbour, & a range of sauna, jacuzzi &

massage options. The private strand has a fabulous view of the Tihany peninsula & the north shore. A shaded grill terrace operates from 17.00. *Sgl 11,900Ft, dbl 19,000Ft;* ⊕ *all yr.*

⌂ **Olivia Panzió** (11 rooms) Petőfi sétány 38; ☎ 84 311105. The Olivia is run by Julius Ferien Reisebüro (see page 495). The pension rooms are old-fashioned & plain. *Dbl 13,000Ft, trpl 18,000Ft, apt (for 4) 26,000Ft.*

⌂ **Renegade Sport Hotel** (70 rooms) Petőfi sétány 3; ☎ 84 311506; e renegadesporthotel@renegadehotel.hu; www.renegadehotel.hu. Don't be put off by its link with the lively pub across the road, for the Renegade's rooms are good & characterful, furnished with terracotta colours & stone-effect tiles. *Dbl 20,000Ft.*

✕ WHERE TO EAT AND DRINK

✕ **Asia Restaurant** Fő u. 93–95; ☎ 84 312546. An elegant restaurant serving Thai & Chinese specialities. If you've a goodly appetite, you might find some of the portions slightly undersized. *Mains avg 2,200Ft;* ⊕ 11.30–22.00 daily.

✕ **Borharapó** Fő u. 43; ☎ 30 5685963; www.piknik.hu. This newly refurbished 18th-century inn has a pleasant courtyard on the banks of the Sió & beautiful vaulted rooms for colder days. There's a huge Hungarian wine list, & the inn also offers wine tastings featuring those from regions all over the country. Fedák Sári's pancake – named after a famous actress – is a delicious, melting combination of oranges & chocolate sauce. *Mains 1,500–3,000Ft;* ⊕ 12.00–22.00 daily

⌷ **Café Móló** Szent István sétány 1; ☎ 84 317617; www.cafemolo.hu. Funky beach-house café serving

good Mediterranean food & excellent iced coffee. *Mains avg 1,450Ft;* ⊕ May 15–Sep 15 Sun–Thu 12.00–02.00, Fri 12.00–04.00, Sat 12.00–05.00.

✕ **Csárdás** Fő u. 105; ☎ 84 310642. Good, traditional Hungarian restaurant. *Mains avg 1,500Ft;* ⊕ 12.00–23.00 daily.

✕ **Fogas** Fő u. 184; ☎ 84 311405. Specialises in fish, including freshwater specimens from Balaton (pike-perch, or fogas, in particular) & seafish including shark & calamari. Live music from 18.00. Opposite the railway station. *Mains avg 1,700Ft;* ⊕ Mar–Nov 12.00–22.00 daily.

✕ **Roxy** Szabadság tér; ☎ 84 306373. Bundles of character in this brick-walled restaurant & bar near the water tower. There are pizzas, pastas & Hungarian & German dishes in good portions. Also does b/fast. *Mains avg 1,700Ft;* ⊕ 08.00–02.00 daily.

ENTERTAINMENT AND NIGHTLIFE Behind the water tower, the **Imre Kálmán Cultural Centre** (*Fő tér 2;* ☎ 84 311855; ⊕ *Mon–Fri 08.00–20.00, Sat 08.00–18.00, Sun 10.00–18.00*) has temporary exhibitions and performances of folk dancing and operetta. Imre Kálmán – who composed the operetta *Countess Maritza* – is the most famous son of the city. The **Palace Disco** (*Deák Ferenc sétány 2;* ☎ 84 351295; *www.palace.hu;* ⊕ *May 15–Sep 15 21.00–04.00 daily*) is situated 2km west of the centre, and features big-name guest DJs and themed party nights. A free bus runs there leaving from the water tower every hour between 21.00 and 24.00 (although you can also flag it down if it passes you elsewhere). **Flört Club** (*Sió u. 4;* ☎ 06 20 333 3303; *www.flort.hu;* ☞ *admission 2,000–4,500Ft;* ⊕ *May 15–Sep 15 daily*) is another of the town's main clubs; Tuesday is singles' night.. You can get a free ride there aboard a yellow 'Flört Free Taxi' (as long as you are paying the full, undiscounted cost of entry to the club), which you'll see outside the railway station and at other points around town. **Big Shots Pub** (*Fő u. 43;* ☎ 84 310818; ⊕ *11.00–04.00 daily*) is a large open-fronted bar just off the main road that serves snack food and hosts live music and theme nights. **Renegade Pub** (*Petőfi sétány 3;* ⊕ *May 30–Sep 15 daily 20.00–04.00*) is a popular spot with its own hotel opposite.

WHAT TO SEE AND DO Most come to Siófok for watersports, sunbathing and nightlife. The centre is to the east of the **Sió Canal**, whose sluice regulates the level of the lake. **Fő utca** is where you'll find the Tourinform (in a former water tower built in 1912), shops and several bars. The **Hüllő Zoo** (*Fő u. 156–160; www.hullozoo.hu;* ✆ *500/350Ft;* ☉ *Tue–Sun 10.00–24.00*) is a reptile house close to the bridge over the canal, while the striking **Lutheran church** in Oulu Park – with its eyes and wings above the entrance – was designed by organic architect Imre Makovecz in 1985 and constructed from Finnish wood.

On the parallel road to the north is the **Kálmán Imre Museum** (*Kálmán Imre sétány 5;* ✆ *84 311287;* ✆ *adult 300Ft;* ☉ *Tue–Sun Apr–Oct 09.00–17.00, rest of yr 11.00–15.00*), which holds an exhibition devoted to 19th-century Siófok. It bore a very different face then, and attracted writers, artists and musicians; among them was Kálmán himself, who was born in this house in 1882, and the collection includes items belonging to the composer including his ashtray, pencil sharpener and wallet. In addition to myriad stalls selling tourist tat, the same road contains the **Mineral Museum** (*Ásványmúzeum; Kálmán Imre sétány 10;* ✆ *84 350038;* ✆ *250/125Ft;* ☉ *09.00–21.00 daily*), with rocks from the Carpathian Basin in glass cases. The **Egg Museum** (*Tojás Muzeum; Szűcs u. 4;* ✆ *84 310276; www.tojasmuzeum.hu;* ✆ *400/200Ft;* ☉ *20.00–18.00 daily*) has 2,000 decorated eggs from around the world.

Closer to the shore is **Petőfi sétány**, a 200m segment of which is packed with bars, clubs, arcades and pizza joints. The **main strand** (*Petőfi sétány 3;* ✆ *1,000Ft, free entry after 18.00;* ☉ *08.00–03.00 daily in summer*) lies in front, and has a grassed area and places to hire water craft and even go bungee jumping. Between July 1 and August 20, the main beach hosts the '**Coke Club**' – a free party starting at 18.00 daily. The other main resort and strand sections are known as the **Gold Coast** (Aranypart), which stretches along the shore to the east of the centre, and the **Silver Coast** (Ezüstpart) to the west. Aranypart is the livelier of the two, with hotels, bars and stalls; among its attractions is a **wakeboarding circuit** (✆ *850Ft/2 rounds, 4,200Ft/12, 7,500Ft/24;* ☉ *May 15–Sep 15 08.00–20.00 daily*). You'll pay to enter the main strands of these resorts, but 1km further along in each case are areas that are both quieter and freely accessible.

Jókai Park is just beyond the bars of Petőfi sétány. It nudges up against the canal – which the Romans started building in the 3rd century – and its edge is a popular fishing spot. The weather observatory which issues warnings of impending storms, stands at the canal mouth (just across from the ferry pier).

Other A summer **sightseeing train** (✆ *600/300Ft*) leaves 13 times a dayfrom opposite the Hotel Holiday on Petőfi sétány. For **sightseeing by water**, the

SAILING ON BALATON

There are 22 yacht harbours around the lake (main centres are Balatonfüred, Balatonkenese and Siófok). Most boats are fairly large (so that they can cope with sudden storms); similarly, sailing boats are permitted to have motors (motorboats are otherwise prohibited on the lake).

While you can mess about in a dinghy (from 8,000Ft per day), if you wish to sail a yacht you will need an International Certificate of Competence (Inland Waterways) or hire a boat with a captain. Reliable charter companies are www.balatoncharter.hu (based in Siófok) and www.vegayacht.hu (in Balatonfüred); prices are around 28,000Ft/day and 180,000Ft/week. Alternatively, take an afternoon trip on a large sailing boat from Siófok or Keszthely, or book a three day trip on the Pelso, an older boat beautifully restored and fully staffed (see *www.pelsoline.hu*).

Excellence Yacht operates a one-hour trip (☞ *1,000/500Ft; departs on the hour 16.00–22.00 in summer*) leaving from the pier. A selection of other programmes runs in high season (*Jun 28–Aug 24*); for example, *Saturnus* is an old wooden sailing boat that plies the waters to Tihany. Check www.balatonihajozas.hu or call ☎ 84 310050.

Just to the west of Siófok, the 300ha nature conservation area and ten fish ponds at **Töreki** offer the chance for some peaceful walks, picnics and fishing. A 9km-long trail through the area begins outside the village. The landscape is varied, featuring lakes, marsh, meadow, grassland and forest; the fish ponds provide resting places for migrating bird species, and there are colonies of swallows in the banks. You can get there on Road 7, and bus 7 runs from Siófok bus station.

ELSEWHERE ON THE SOUTHERN SHORE

Going west from Siófok, your first stop should be the Kistücsök Restaurant in **Balatonszemes** (*Bajcsy-Zsilinszky u. 25;* ☎ *84 360133; www.kistucsok.hu; mains avg 1,600Ft;* ✆ *daily 11.00–23.00*). A popular spot on the old Road 70, the exterior is unprepossessing but it has imaginative menu choices excellently executed. The chef uses local and seasonal ingredients; the Serbian carp we ate was outstanding.

Up the road in **Balatonlelle**, look for the signpost to Kishegy (by the St John statue), which directs you out of town to the local vineyards. Follow the signs to Majthényi Présház (*Kishegy;* ☎ *20 9682397*), which occupies a wonderful spot next to a whitewashed 1784 chapel. The restaurant in the press-house (*mains avg 1,900Ft;* ✆ *May–Sep 12.00–22.00 daily*) offers spectacular views of Balaton from its atmospheric loggia. A little down the hill is the Konyári Winery (*Kishegy;* ☎ *85 700037; ☞ 1,500Ft/pp for tasting of 5 wines;* ✆ *May 15–Aug 20 Mon–Sat 10.00–18.00*), where you can sample the wines of one of Hungary's premier vintners and also have a look around the winery's state-of-the-art equipment. Konyári also has some charming accommodation in their guest house (*3 rooms; min 2-night stay; dbl 10,000Ft*); the really lucky guests get to stay in one of the peasant cottages in the *tanya* (ranch), all of which are furnished in 1920s style.

Ten kilometres south of Balatonlelle, on Road 67 to Kaposvár, Chateau Visz (*Visz, Berencsepuszta;* ☎ *85 710003; www.chateau-visz.com; 13 rooms; dbl from 51,000Ft*) sits in dense forest just past the village of **Visz**. This immaculately restored former hunting lodge has elegant rooms decorated with 20th-century art and furniture handmade in Transylvania, as well as a wine cellar and well-equipped wellness facilities. Its main draw is its gourmet restaurant (*3-course meal 12,300Ft*), which aspires to blend the flavours of the classic Hungarian kitchen with the subtle class of French cuisine. Non-residents wishing to eat here will need to book in advance.

In **Balatonfenyves**, Hubertus-Hof (*Nimród u. 1;* ☎ *85 560930; www.hubertus.hu; dbl 15,000Ft*) is a spacious hunting lodge with comfortable rooms in separate buildings. The restaurant (*mains avg 2,000Ft;* ✆ *12.00–22.00 daily all yr*) has an informal atmosphere and serves game from their own estate, while the terrace is surrounded by mature trees and there's a relaxing reading room. This is a perfect base for a holiday of riding, cycling and swimming (and even shooting, for those who wish to do so).

KESZTHELY

If it weren't for the lake, you could be forgiven for forgetting you were at Lake Balaton. It is true that Keszthely sees the inevitable crowds in high season, but there's life beyond the tourist dollar here and a whiff of culture that comes as a surprise after the more hedonistic pleasures of Siófok. There's nobility in its architecture, a legacy of the Festetics family, aristocrats whose star rose

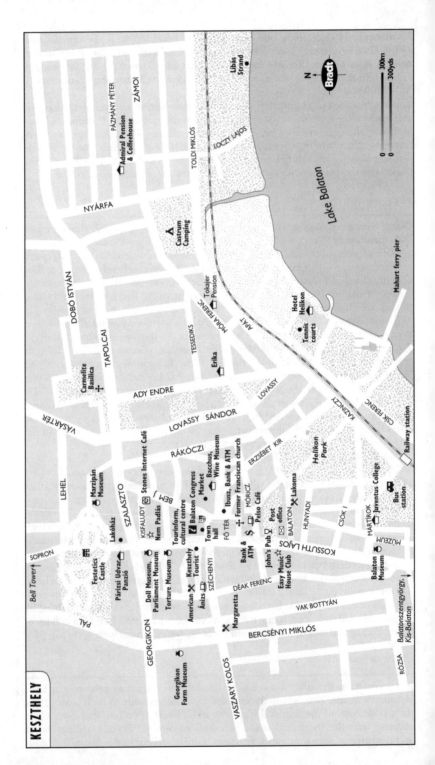

KESZTHELY

Bell Tower

SOPRON

PÁL

GEORGIKON

Festetics Castle

Párizsi Udvar Panzió

Lakóház

Marzipán Museum

VÁSÁRTÉR

LEHEL

SZALASZTO

Stones Internet Café

KISFALUDY

Nem Padlás

BEM J

Carmelite Basilica

TAPOLCAI

DOBÓ ISTVÁN

NYÁRFA

PÁZMÁNY PÉTER

ZÁMOI

Admiral Pension & Coffeehouse

Castrum Camping

Tokajer Pension

TOLDI MIKLÓS

LÓCZY LAJOS

ADY ENDRE

TESSEDIKS

MÓRA FERENC

Erika

APÁT

LOVASSY SÁNDOR

RÁKÓCZI

LOVASSY

Lake Balaton

Mahart ferry pier

Hotel Helikon

Tennis courts

Doll Museum, Parliament Museum

Torture Museum

Georgikon Farm Museum

American

Ánizs

Keszthely Tourist

SZÉCHENYI

Margaretta

DEÁK FERENC

VASZARY KOLOS

Balaton Congress

Market

Tourinform, cultural centre

Town hall

FŐ TÉR

Bank & ATM

Bacchus, Wine Museum

Ibusz, Bank & ATM

Former Franciscan church

MÓRICZ

Pelso Café

BALATON

Post office

John's Pub

KOSSUTH LAJOS

Easy Music House Club

BERCSÉNYI MIKLÓS

VAK BOTTYÁN

ERZSÉBET KIR

Lakoma

HUNYADI

CSOK I

MÁRTÍROK

MÚZEUM

Balaton Museum

Juventus College

Bus station

Helikon Park

KAZINCZY

CSÍK FERENC

Railway station

ROZSA

Balatonszentgyörgy, Kis-Balaton

N

Bradt

0   300m
0   300yds

500

considerably as a consequence of their loyalty to the Habsburgs, and who acquired the Keszthely estate in 1739. This was not a dynasty of mere shoe-licking self-servers, however; at the beginning of the 19th century they were enthusiastic supporters of the reform drive and György Festetics was actually involved in the Jacobin plot led by Martinovics (see box, page 132) in 1792. Fortunate to avoid the fate of some of his fellow conspirators on Castle Hill's 'Field of Blood', he subsequently got stuck into progressive projects, founding Europe's first agricultural college and working to improve the breeding stock of Hungarian horses – passions shared by István Széchenyi, which is unsurprising when the 'greatest Hungarian' was György's nephew.

GETTING THERE, AWAY AND AROUND The **bus** and **railway stations** are 600m to the southeast of the centre, at the end of Mártírok útja. Keszthely is on the line between Tapolca and Balatonszentgyörgy, and you can change at one of these for journeys around the lake and beyond if the direct services don't suit your schedule. There are up to 15 daily trains to Tapolca and 20 to Balatonszentgyörgy; direct trains elsewhere include those to Budapest (Déli or Keleti; seven), Balatonfüred (one), Siófok (six), Sümeg (three), Pécs (two), Celldömölk (two), Székesfehérvár (one) and Szomabathely (two). In addition, There are regular buses to Tapolca, Sümeg, Balatongyörök, Veszprém, Zalaegerszeg and Hévíz, as well as services to Badacsony (12), Balatonfüred (13), Balatonszentgyörgy (14), Budapest Népliget (six), Győr (six), Kaposvár (ten), Nagykanizsa (15), Pápa (ten), Pécs (six), Siofók (six) and Sopron (three).

Ferries dock at the pier near the main strand. In summer, there are four daily services to Badacsony (via Balatonmária, Balatongyörök and Szigliget) at 09.30, 10.30, 13.50 (going on as far as Balatonszemes) and 18.30; the last boat back to Keszthely from Badacsony is at 18.00. Two **sailing boats** also operate from the pier; the 100-year-old *Juditta* (*www.pelsoline.hu*) takes regular one-hour tours, and once a week offers an excursion to Szigliget with wine tasting. If you need a **taxi**, try Georgikon (\ *83 333666*).

INFORMATION AND OTHER PRACTICALITIES

Ibusz Fő tér 7–8. Exchanges travellers' cheques & arrange private accommodation. ⊕ *Mon–Thu 08.30–16.30, Fri 08.30–15.30.*

Internet Stones Cyber & Dance Café (*Kisfaludy u. 17;* \ *83 510109;* ⊕ *Sun–Thu 11.00–23.00, Fri 13.00–02.00, Sat 18.00–04.00*), on the corner Bem József utca, has a couple of internet terminals.

Keszthely Tourist Kossuth Lajos u. 25; \ *83 314031;* e info@keszthelytourist.hu; www.keszthelytourist.hu. Arranges tours & private rooms, but we found the staff rather unhelpful. Hope you receive better service. ⊕ *Mon–Sat 08.00–19.00, Sun 09.00–17.00 (in summer).*

Tourinform Kossuth Lajos u. 28; \ *83 314144;* e keszthely@tourinform.hu; www.west-balaton.hu. Housed in the 19th-century former town hall building. ⊕ *May 15–Sep 15 Mon–Fri 09.00–20.00, Sat–Sun 09.00–18.00, rest of yr Mon–Fri 09.00–17.00, Sat–Sun 09.00–13.00.*

WHERE TO STAY
Keszthely's pensions appear eager to out-do each other with 'luxury' facilities – small swimming pools are far from unusual.

Admiral Pension Pázmány Péter u. 1; \ *83 314368;www.admiralpanzio.hu.* Large guesthouse with inviting rooms. Facilities inc solarium, sauna & postage-stamp-sized pool, & you can rent bikes. *Sgl 13,000Ft, dbl 15,200Ft, trpl 18,500Ft.*

Camping Castrum Móra Ferenc u. 48; \ *83 312120; www.castrum-group.hu.* Large site with 330 tent pitches & lots of amenities. There's a decent-sized pool & 4 clay tennis courts (lessons & equipment available). *700Ft for smallest plot, plus 750Ft/pp;* ⊕ *Apr–Oct.*

Erika Panzió (10 rooms/apts) Ady Endre u. 14–16; \ *83 314591; www.erika-pension.hu.* Set in 2 detached houses, this good-looking guesthouse is well equipped & only 200m from the lake. *Sgl 7,500Ft, dbl 9,000Ft;* ⊕ *all yr.*

⌂ **Hotel Helikon** (240 rooms) Balatonpart 5; ☎ 83 889600; www.danubiushotels.com. 3-star hotel in the pleasant park to the northeast of the ferry pier with 10 indoor & outdoor tennis courts, a large swimming pool & fitness centre. You can also use the hotel's windsurfs, kayaks & sailing boats free of charge. The exterior is ugly, but the bar is located in a glass atrium & the lakeside rooms have lovely views. They keep the kids well entertained here. *Sgl standard/superior €77/92, dbl €104/128.*

⌂ **Hotel Bacchus** (26 rooms) Erzsébet királyné u. 18; ☎ 83 314096; www.bacchushotel.hu. Centrally located 3-star with its own 'wine museum' in the cellar & wine-tasting programmes (*from €10 for 10 wines*). Rooms are plainly furnished but comfortable; those downstairs have terraces, those upstairs have balconies. *Sgl €33, dbl €44, apt €66.*

⌂ **Lehner Major B&B** H-8714 Keleviz, Lehner Major; ☎ 85 708142; e info@hunyady.hu. This guesthouse is actually around 30 mins from Keszthely, but is worth mentioning for its noble splendour & friendly owner, who organises riding tours around Balaton (see Somogy Nature Association under *Tour operators*, page 40). The owner is a keen vintner & arranges wine tastings of his wines in a cellar overlooking Balaton. Great value. *Rooms €40/pp.*

⌂ **Tokajer Pension** Apát u. 21; ☎ 83 319875; e pensiontokajer@hotmail.com; www.pensiontokajer.hu. When grandma chucked the chintz out it ended up here; the rooms are extremely flowery, but clean & homely with it. This welcoming pension also boasts amenities including a pool, summer terrace, sauna, whirlpool & solarium; they lay on a feast of a b/fast too. Bicycle hire. Located 600m from the pier. Recommended. *Sgl 7,700Ft. dbl 20,400Ft, apts 14,200Ft.*

✖ WHERE TO EAT AND DRINK

✖ **Amerikai Pizzéria** Városház u. 5/A; ☎ 70 9434359. This is a small place that opens into the early hours & offers a large choice of pizzas. ⊕ *Mon–Sat 19.00–04.00*

🍺 **Ánizs Art Café** Városház u. 6; ☎ 30 2379909. A brick-vaulted & stylish café tucked away in a side street. You can enjoy Illy coffee with your breakfast, & well-priced, simple dishes are available all day. Internet. *Mains 490–990Ft,* ⊕ *Mon–Thu 16.00–24.00, Fri/Sat 16.00–02.00.*

✖ **Bacchus** See above. Atmospheric, rustic hotel restaurant. Good food to go with an excellent wine list. *Mains avg 2,200Ft;* ⊕ *12.00–23.00 daily.*

✖ **Lakoma** Balaton u. 9; ☎ 83 313129. Offers specialities of Zala county in addition to the usual Hungarian fare. The décor is nothing to write home about. *Mains avg 1,600Ft;* ⊕ *daily 12.00–23.00.*

✖ **Margaretta** Bercsényi Miklós u. 60; ☎ 83 314882. Hungarian food, including a wide selection of goose liver, fish, pork & poultry. The outdoor eating area looks faintly cheap, but this is one of the town's top eateries & the well-priced & hearty portions are accompanied by good service. Appearance, in this instance, is deceptive. *Mains avg 1,300Ft;* ⊕ *11.30–22.00 daily.*

✖ **Park Vendeglő** Vörösmarty u. 1/A; ☎ 83 311654. This restaurant is popular with locals & foreigners alike, & is unusual in offering half portions (at half the price) for those with smaller appetites. *Mains avg 1,500Ft;* ⊕ *daily 11.00–23.00.*

🍺 **Pelso Café** Kossuth Lajos u. 38; ☎ 83 315415. Two-tiered beach hut with wicker furnishings in the garden of the Fő tér church. We still haven't forgotten their After Eight ice cream with peppermint liqueur – delicious! 'Pelso' was the Roman name for Lake Balaton. ⊕ *Mon–Thu 09.00–21.00, Fri–Sat 09.00–22.00, Sun 09.00–20.00.*

✖ **Piccola Post Pizzeria** József Attila u. 6; ☎ 83 312689. Family-run establishment offering the very best pizzas in town. ⊕ *Mon–Sat 12.00–22.00.*

ENTERTAINMENT AND NIGHTLIFE The **Balaton Congress Centre and Theatre** (*Fő tér 3;* ☎ *83 515230*) offers drama, dance and classical music (with appearances by the Budapest Philharmonic), and also puts on temporary exhibitions. The ticket office (⊕ *Tue–Thu 08.30–12.00 & 12.30–17.00*) is next door. The **Goldmark Károly Cultural Centre** (*Kossuth Lajos u. 28;* ☎ *83 515257*) is accessed through an archway at the Tourinform; it has folk-dancing performances in summer.

Keszthely is a university town, and the students are clearly fond of their strip joints.

John's Pub & Restaurant (*Kossuth Lajos u. 46;* ☎ *30 9931140;* ⊕ *Mon–Fri 12.00–24.00, Sat 18.00–04.00, in summer Sun 18.00–24.00*) is a popular place with internet, WiFi, garden, and a choice between steaks and Italian food. There's a DJ at weekends. **Nem Padlás** (*Kisfaludy u. 3;* ☏ *70 3332916;* ☉ *Mon–Sat 18.00–03.00*) is a cellar bar that offers blues and classic rock. From June to September the Town Strand hosts the **Viviere Stones Beach**, with concerts and a disco on Fridays and Saturdays. The **Easy Music House** (*Kossuth Lajos u.;* ☉ *Wed, Fri & Sat 22.00–late*) is the most popular of several bars and clubs along Kossuth Lajos utca to the south of Fő tér. Women are admitted free before midnight.

WHAT TO SEE AND DO The **Festetics Palace** (*Festetics kastély; Kastély u. 1;* ☏ *83 312194; www.helikonkastely.hu;* ☞ *1,800/1000Ft;* ☉ *Tue–Sun Sep–May Tue–Sun10.00–17.00, Jun–Aug 09.00–18.00 daily,*) ranks among the most impressive aristocratic mansions in the country. It was originally built in the mid 18th century – the Baroque south wing dates to this period – before 19th-century extensions resulted in its pleasingly asymmetrical façade. Many of the family's Rococo and Biedermeier furnishings remain inside the rooms that are open to the public. The Helikon Library, with its coffered ceiling and 86,000 books, was one of the great personal collections and is indicative of the Festetics' interest in the arts; during the early 19th century, members of the literary élite were regular visitors. There are exhibitions of the trappings of aristocratic life during the 18th and 19th centuries, as well as a display of weaponry. The significant cloud that hangs over the palace is the extortionate admission price. Thankfully the beautiful grounds can be strolled without denting the personal finances, and are particularly worth visiting at around 21.30 when the fountain at the entrance is illuminated with changing colours; in summer the gardens become the backdrop for a series of theatre performances (see Tourinform for details).

The 16th-century cellar of the Palace is home to the House of Balaton Wines (☉ *10.00–18.00 daily*), where 50 varieties of Hungarian wine can be tasted.

To the southwest of the palace is the **Georgikon Major Museum** (*Bercsényi Miklós 65–67;* ☏ *83 311563;* ☞ *200/100Ft;* ☉ *May–Oct Tue–Sat 10.00–17.00, Sun 10.00–18.00*), housed in courtyard buildings that accommodated students of the agricultural college founded by György (hence its name) Festetics in 1797. The museum contains a history of the college, together with exhibitions on 19th-century viniculture, farming in Transdanubia and a blacksmith's workshop. The **Marzipan Museum** (*Katona József u. 19;* ☏ *83 319322;* ☞ *160/100Ft;* ☉ *Mar 1–Jan 6 Tue–Sun 10.00–18.00*) is to the east of the palace, featuring 100 pieces of shaped marzipan – including an intricate model of the palace itself – and selling cakes to take away.

Walking south from the palace down Kossuth Lajos utca, a turn into Bakacs utca will bring you to the **Doll Museum** (*Bakacs u. 2;* ☏ *83 318855;* ☞ *390/330Ft;* ☉ *daily May–Oct 09.00–19.00, rest of yr 09.00–17.00*); in addition to its dolls in folk costume from all regions of Hungary and models of traditional dwellings, there are also life-sized mannequins in historical dress and a model of parliament made from the shells of sea snails. You pay separately to access each display in the complex. Sharing the same building as the Casablanca strip club, the **Torture Museum** (*Bakacs u. 2;* ☏ *83 318855;* ☞ *300/200Ft;* ☉ *daily 10.00–18.00*) has puppets in various states of dismemberment and uses more fake blood than a Christopher Lee film.

Continuing down Kossuth Lajos utca brings you to Fő tér, whose Louis-XVI-style **town hall** (*no 1*) was built in 1790. Outside it is a weather-worn Trinity Column of 1770 – a stone island in a sea of flowers – while set back at the southeastern side is the former **Franciscan church** (*no 10*). The church was constructed in the 14th century, during the reign of Palatine István Lackfi II, and in 1560 was converted into a fortress to defend the town against Turkish assaults. There was much reconstruction over the centuries (the Neo-Gothic tower, for instance, was added in 1896) but the rose window dates to the 14th century, and 15th-century frescoes were uncovered during restoration. The tomb of György Festetics is in the crypt.

Lake Balaton KESZTHELY

10

The entrance to the vast **Balaton Museum** (*Múzeum u. 2;* \ *83 312351;*
🎟 *500/250Ft;* ☉ *May–Oct Tue–Sat 10.00–18.00, Nov–Apr Tue–Sat 09.00–17.00*) is at
Kossuth Lajos utca 74. Among its holdings are regional Roman finds and an
exhibition focusing on life around Balaton, from the wildlife to the 19th-century
steamships used to transport goods and passengers from one shore to the other.
Around 100m further south along Kossuth Lajos utca is the **St Miklós Cemetery**
(☉ *daily Mar 15–Aug 31 07.00–20.00, Sep 1–Oct 25 07.00–19.00, Oct 26–Nov 5
07.00–20.00, Nov 6–Mar 14 07.00–18.00*). The resplendently yellow cemetery
chapel was built on medieval foundations in 1713, while the Neoclassical
Festetics Mausoleum stands towards the back of the plot.

Other activities There are three stretches to **take a dip** along the shoreline at
Keszthely – the Városi and Helikon strands near the ferry pier and the Libás strand
further to the northeast. You will pay to enter the first two (🎟 *600/ 550Ft, reductions
after 16.00;* ☉ *May 15–Sep 15 08.30–19.00 daily*); a Keszthely Card, which you can
pick up from Tourinform or hotels if you have proof you are staying in town for
six nights or more, gives a 50% discount. There are waterslides, and water craft for
hire, and the Városi has a reconstructed 19th-century pier (known as the
Szigetfürdő) that juts out into the lake and has decked areas branching from it.
Libás Strand (accessed via a narrow track at the end of Lóczy Lajos utca) is hidden
behind reeds and is both quieter and free to use. You can also fish here.

Sightseeing boats leave from the pier (\ *84 310050*); a one-hour tour goes up to
five times daily in summer, and there are various other boating programmes too.
Check the information boards. A motorised **tourist train** (\ *06 20 957 1436; runs
09.00–21.00 daily in summer*) runs between the Helikon Hotel and the palace.

If **birdwatching** is your passion, a visit to Kis-Balaton is a must: the River Zala
floods this large area where the water is cleansed before flowing into Lake Balaton.
You get much more than the usual ducks and geese – we saw white-tailed eagles
and a colony of European bee-eaters. For guided tours, call Anna Knauer (\ *87
555290*); see also pages 39–41. Keszthely is also the best starting point for exploring
the ethnographically distinct **Göcsej region** southwest of Zalaegerszeg (around
50km from Keszthely). For details of a tour of some of the villages, walking trails
and other sights, see pages 466–7.

VILLAGES NEAR KESZTHELY

The villages near by offer something different from the cultured Keszthely – the
opportunity for relaxing 'family' holidays that take proper advantage of the lake on
the one side and the Keszthely Hills on the other. Gyenesdiás, Vonyarcvashegy and
Balatongyörök are three villages running eastward of Keszthely along the shore
(Road 71) – there is then a gap before you reach Szigliget (see page 509) – and each
offers excellent private accommodation at very cheap prices. You can obtain
information from the Gyenesdiás Tourinform office (*Kossuth Lajos u. 97;* \ *83
314144;* e *gyenesdias@tourinform.hu*).

🏠 **WHERE TO STAY AND EAT** Basic but well-equipped **private houses** and
apartments can be rented in each of the villages from €10 per person per night
– check out the relevant village websites (*www.gyenesdias.hu, www.vonyarcvashegy.hu
& www.bala tongyorok.hu*) for further information. In addition, the recently opened
Hotel Katalin (*Gyenesdiás; Szent István út 5;* \ *83 311324; www.hotelkatalin.hu; dbl
18,900–22,000Ft, inc half board & wellness facilities*) is worth particular mention; this
four-star wellness hotel close to the main strand at Diás has impressive facilities
caters for families and is beautifully kept, with a blaze of flowers.

There are many restaurants in the villages. **Piroska** (*Gyenesdiás; Csokonai Vitéz Mihály utca;* \ *83 316301; mains avg 1,800Ft;* ⊕ *daily 11.00–23.00 all yr*) is said to have the best kitchen in the area (it was recommended to us by a chef) and is decorated in Transylvanian style with painted pottery and a carved gateway. It is signposted from the road. **Helikon Taverna** (*Vonyarcvashegy; Helikon u. 22;* \ *83 348004;* ⊕ *15.00–23.00 daily; mains avg 2,000Ft*) is the spot for a meal if you fancy a view over the lake. This 19th-century wine cellar of the Festetics family has recently been fully refurbished and offers a large selection of Hungarian specialities and wines. There are also 13 simply furnished en-suite rooms with air-conditioning (*from 7,900Ft*).

ACTIVITIES The Keszthely Hills north of the town offer excellent **walking** and **cycling**. Pick up a free walking and cycling map from the Tourinform office (see page 501). Bicycle rental is available from the shopping arcade in Keszthely (*Rákóczi u. 15;* \ *83 315463;* ⊕ *Mon–Fri 09.00–18.00, Sat 09.00–13.00;* ☞ *2,000Ft/day, 12,000Ft/week*).

Gyenesdiás is the starting point for a 16.8km-long **walking tour** (called the Darnay-Dornyai Emléktúra) leading to seven lookout points over the lake. The marked tour starts at Nagymező (approach from Faludi utca by the roundabout on Road 71) and finishes at Balatongyörök. Regular buses connect Balatongyörök and Keszthely.

Those wishing to play a round of **golf** can head for the Balatongyörök golf course (currently under construction, but due to open in summer 2010.

Equital Lovasudvar (\ *30 659 3904; www.equital.hu*), in the lovely village of Nemesvita on the eastern side of the Keszthely Hills (on Road 84), is a new and well-equipped **riding** establishment off the beaten track. One-hour's riding costs €10 per person, and there are cross-country riding trips, pony trekking and riding lessons. A seven-day tour (featuring five days' riding) with full board costs €469 per person. It also offers accommodation (*dbl €30–34*) for riders and non-riders alike.

You can have **watersports lessons** at the strand at Vonyarcvashegy (\ *70 335 4681*); sailing boats (☞ *4,000Ft/hr, 16,000Ft/5hrs*), windsurfers (☞ *1,250Ft/hr, 5,000Ft/5hrs*) and kayaks are all available to hire. In addition, there is a wakeboarding circuit.

HÉVÍZ

We find Hévíz, 8km northwest of Keszthely, a rather over-bearing resort; its every cranny is packed with expensive hotels, guesthouses, souvenir shops and cafés coining it in on the back of the town's thermal lake. **Tó-fürdő** (*Parkerdő;* ☞ *3-hr ticket 1,900Ft, 5-hr ticket 2,500Ft, daily ticket 2,900Ft;* ⊕ *daily 08.00–20.00 in Jun–Aug, 08.30–18.00 rest of yr*) is formed of a crater 39m deep that's kept filled by hot springs gushing 60 million litres of water a day; it is the largest of its type in Europe, and the second-largest (to New Zealand's Lake Tarawera, which you can't bathe in) on the planet. During summer the water temperature is 32–35°, falling slightly to around 26°C in winter, and it's a pretty (if sulphurously smelly) thing, with a central pavilion and piers, lilies on the surface and steam rising from it in colder months. The year-round warmth means that wallowers come in all seasons, but late spring and early autumn are particularly popular. The water is mildly radioactive – prolonged immersion isn't recommended – and relieves rheumatic disorders. The mud dredged from the lake bed is also used in face packs and the like. The Szent András Kórház (*Dr Schulhof Vilmos u. 1;* \ *83 340587; www.spaheviz.hu*) is a hospital by the lake that tailors individual programmes (on average lasting two–three weeks) using the water, mud and other medical treatments. There are entrances to the lake complex in Deák tér (on the northern side, near the bus station) and on Ady Endre utca (to the southeast, by Castrum Camping). Ticket reservation is recommended to avoid queues.

After a swim in the lake, you might take a stroll to the charming late-20th-century **Blue Church** (*Szent Lélek templom; Zrínyi u.*), with five narrow towers and a rounded nave, half way up the sloping Széchenyi utca. From here, follow signs to the little **Romanesque church at Egregy** on the eastern outskirts of town. Beyond the church are some lovely vineyards with simple restaurants offering terraces overlooking the valley. The last of these is the **Vadász Borozó** (*Dombföldi út 17;* ✆ *30 3480970; mains avg 2,000Ft;* ⊕ *Easter–Nov 17.00–22.00*). If you turn left up the hill by the green church you will find a small **pottery sales room** with a large selection of Hungarian gift items by potter István Barakonyi (*Dr Babócsay u. 98;* ✆ *20 9711728; ring the bell*). The motorised tourist train starting from the lake will take you there.

GETTING THERE AND AWAY The **bus station** (*Deák Ferenc tér*) is at the northern entrance to Parkerdő and the lake. There are very regular buses to Keszthely, and regular services to Sümeg and Zalaegerszeg; other destinations include Badacsony (nine), Balatonfüred (12), Budapest (six), Tapolca (nine), Veszprém (12) and Nagykanizsa (12). There is no railway station.

🏠 **WHERE TO STAY AND EAT** Unless you're on an intensive programme of therapy, there really is little reason to stay in Hévíz when Keszthely is so close. The restaurants are generally touristy.

⛺ **Castrum Camping** Tó-part; ✆ 83 343198; info@castrum-group.hu; www.castrum-group.hu. This is the most convenient campsite, near the southeastern entrance to the lake.

🏠 **Danubius Thermal Hotel Hévíz** (210 rooms) Kossuth Lajos u. 9–11; ✆ 83 8895400; e heviz@danubiushotels.hu; www.danubiushotels.hu/heviz. This wellness hotel has an indoor thermal spa & fun bath, as well as an outdoor pool, & offers beauty & health treatments, 16 different massages. All rooms above the 1st floor have small balconies, & it's 500m to the lake. Sauna, solarium, fitness room. *Sgl €83, dbl €138.*

🏠 **Europa Fit** (230 rooms) Jókai u. 3; ✆ 83 501100; www.europafit.hu. This is the top hotel in Hévíz; with beautiful pools & wellness facilities, it is more of a spa hotel in the Western sense than a 'treatment' centre. Its beauty salon was voted the best in Hungary in 2006, & all the staff speak some English. The hotel is particularly suited to families in summer months. *Sgl €75, dbl €118.*

🏠 **Guszti Villa** (12 rooms) Széchenyi u. 18; ✆ 83 341266; www.gusztivilla.hu. This centrally located guesthouse has spacious, simple double rooms with showers. The guests share the kitchen facilities. *Dbl 7,100Ft.*

✖ **Gyönyösi Betyárcsárda** ✆ 83 373006. Built in 1728, this inn was once the favourite haunt of outlaws; inside are their weapons & near by are the graves of two of their number executed in 1862.

The cuisine is traditional, & there are evening horse & folk shows in summer (*May 15–Jun 30 Wed 20.00, Jul–Aug Mon, Wed & Fri 20.00*). 6km north of Hévíz on the road leading north to Sümeg, just before the branch left towards Karmacs. *Mains 1,500–3,000Ft;* ⊕ *12.00–23.00 daily, closed in Feb.*

✖ **Magyar Csárda** Tavirózsa u. 2; ✆ 83 343271; www.magyarcsarda.hu. The best of a bunch of restaurants lining this street, with a pretty patio area & typical Hungarian fare. There's gypsy music 17.00–23.00. To the west of the lake – take Helikon u. off Kossuth Lajos utca, & Tavirózsa u. runs off it. *Mains 1,20–4,400Ft;* ⊕ *11.00–23.00 daily.*

🏠 **Naturmed Hotel Carbona** (261 rooms) Attila u. 1; ✆ 83 501500; www.carbona.hu. This large hotel has a host of spa facilities, including spring-fed thermal baths, a Kneipp cold-water treading pool, open-air activity pools (with massage jets & water chutes), an indoor swimming pool, sauna, steam bath & more. The medical team can tailor a health or relaxation programme of treatments. *Sgl €110, dbl €157, suite €266, excl Tourist Tax.*

🏠 **Wellness Hotel Hévíz** (19 rooms) Hévíz-Cserszegtomaj, Sümeg u. 35; ✆ 83 330200; www.wellnesshotelheviz.hu. Handsome & smallish wellness hotel, with swimming pool, sauna, fitness room & a selection of beauty/health packages. Situated just off the road running north towards Sümeg, in between Hévíz & Cserszegtomaj. *Dbl €60.*

Settled in the Tapolca basin, the Badacsony region comprises a pocket of volcanic cones and hills clustered behind the flat-topped, 400m-high Badacsony Hill. There are four villages in the area (all with the Badacsony- prefix), but it is the resort to the southwest of Badacsonytomaj – in the bump of shoreline that presses out slightly into the lake – that is usually meant when people refer to Badacsony. Like Tihany, Badacsony is beautiful and offers some good walking trails to supplement the splashing at the strands. The slopes of Badacsony are littered with cellars whose vineyards thrive on the fertile volcanic soil (Kéknyelű, or Blue Stem, is the name most associated with its wines). The oft-trod path is Kisfaludy utca, which leads uphill from Római út and promises wine shacks and pinces along the route; despite the crowds moving up and down, it is an enjoyable excursion laced with a frisson of wine-induced camaraderie.

GETTING THERE, AWAY AND AROUND The **railway station** (*Park u. 1*) – built from the dark basalt typical of the region – is in the centre of town, right in front of the ferry pier. It is on the line connecting the settlements of the northern shore, and there are direct services to Tapolca, Balatonfüred (15), Székesfehérvár (12) and Budapest Déli (eight). (It's worth casting a glance at the walking map outside the station, which shows the route to the Kisfaludy-ház, from where trails into Badacsony start in earnest.) **Buses** arrive and depart from the stop on Balatoni út just outside the railway station; among the services are buses to Balatonfüred (three daily), Székesfehérvár (four), Tapolca (two), Budapest (two) and Hévíz (up to four in summer only).

Passenger **ferries** run to Fonyód up to ten times a day in peak season (*Jul–Aug; first at 10.00, last at 17.30*), with less frequent services in other months between April and October. In summer, there are also ferries to Balatonföldvár, Balatonmáriafürdő and Keszthely (four), Balatonlelle and Szigliget. Open-top **jeep taxis** (\ *06 30 939 5346*) wait near the post office on Park utca and are an easy way to reach the wine cellars. Alternatively you could take a horsedrawn carriage from near the Neptun Hotel on Római út.

INFORMATION AND OTHER PRACTICALITIES

🎭 **Egry József Cultural Centre** Badacsonytomaj, Romai út 69; \ 87 571115. Cultural centre & cinema opposite the Borbarátok Panzió.

📧 **Midi Tourist** Park u. 53; \ 87 431028; www.miditourist.hu. Can help with private accommodation, & also offers internet access. This branch is in the centre, & there is a 2nd (main) office a few hundred metres northeast (*Park u. 53*). ⊕ *08.00–19.00 daily.*

ℹ️ **Tourinform** Park u. 6; \ 87 431046; e badacsonytomaj@tourinform.hu; www.badacsonytomaj.hu. Just to the north of the railway station. ⊕ *Oct–Apr Mon–Fri 09.00–15.00, May–Jun 09.00–17.00 daily, Jul–Aug 09.00–19.00 daily, Sep Mon–Fri 09.00–17.00, Sat–Sun 09.00–16.00.*

WHERE TO STAY In addition to the accommodation listed below, there are several private rooms and apartments on offer along Romai út.

🏠 **Andreas Wellness Panzió** (8 rooms) Badacsonytördemic, Debreczenyi u. 4; \ 87 433108. A quiet village house somewhat off the tourist route (turn off Road 71 towards Badacsonytördemic, & the guesthouse is on the left). The rooms are neat and the unpretentious restaurant offers food cooked by the owner. Dbl 9,600Ft; ⊕ *all yr.*

🏠 **Borbarátok Panzió** (6 rooms) Badacsonytomaj, Római út 88; \ 87 471000; www.borbaratok.hu. This comfortable guesthouse is nearly always full, so bookings are advised in peak periods. The rooms are on the 'cosy' side, but are lovely nevertheless; the restaurant (see page 508) is out of the top drawer. It's located 1km or so northeast of Badacsony on

the road to Badacsonytomaj. *Dbl 12,600Ft;*
⊕ *Mar–Dec.*

⌂ **Hotel Neptun** (16 rooms) Római út 170; ☎ 87
431293. Renovated, turn-of-the-century house offering
en-suite rooms. Centrally located 200m from the
beach. Reliable, cheap choice. *Dbl 12,600Ft.*

✗ WHERE TO EAT AND DRINK

✗ **Bacchus** Kossuth Lajos u. 1; ☎ 87 531031;
www.bacchusinfo.hu. the food menu at this wine
restaurant – located among the grapes & with
lovely views – is short & sweet, but there's a
huge selection of wines from all regions of
Hungary. definitely a place for wine buffs. *Mains
avg 2,000Ft;* ⊕ *May–start of Oct daily
12.00–22.00.*

✗ **Borbarátok** See page 507. Bubbly, busy &
atmospheric, this restaurant combines traditional &
modern touches, & serves a mean kettle goulash.
They serve their own wines, the sweet Ürmös being
the best. Highly recommended. Some evenings
Gypsy music, on others hungarian classic songs.
Mains avg 1,800Ft; ⊕ *daily 12.00–22.00 Mar
11–Dec 31.*

✗ **Imre Borozó** Kisfaludy u. 11; ☎ 06 20 347 2274.
Further up the hill from the Szent Orbán (see
opposite), this wine bar is run by a fourth generation
of family winegrowers. They sell & bottle Riesling,
Pinot Gris & Muscat. You can visit their cellar for
wine tastings. ⊕ *May 1–Sep 15 12.00–19.00 daily,
Sep 16–Apr 30 by appointment only.*

✗ **Istvándy Pince** Káptalantóti, Rózsadomb 121;
☎ 70 2304713; www.istvandy-pinceszet.hu. It is a
challenge to find this gem: take the road from
Badacsonytomaj to Káptalantóti – & be sure to
persevere. When you arrive at the estate the
panoramic views of the hills & the lake are quite
overwhelming. Taste their wines (17 varieties) & cold
platters of produce from their own farm.
⊕ *May–Sep Tue–Sun 13.00–20.00.*

✗ **Kisfaludy-ház** Kisfaludy u.; ☎ 87 431016. The
food here in the Kisfaludy family's 18th-century
press house (see below) is excellent, & there are
breathtaking views & gypsy music . *Mains avg
2,400Ft;* ⊕ *Apr 15–start Oct daily 11.00–23.00.*

✗ **Szent Orbán** Kisfaludy u. 5; ☎ 87 431382;
www.szeremley.com. Nestled on the lower slope of
Badacsony-hegy (on the walking route up to the
Kisfaludy-ház), this is a beautiful place to dine & a
restful spot. On the menu is organic produce from
their own farm. The restaurant can arrange wine
tasting in its nearby cellar. *Mains avg 1,900Ft;*
⊕ *daily 12.00–22.00 Easter–end Oct, w/ends only
in winter.*

WHAT TO SEE AND DO The **Egry József Memorial Museum** (*Egry sétány 12;* ☎ *87
431044;* ☞ *500/250Ft;* ⊕ *Tue–Sun May–Sep,* on the road linking Balatoni út and
Park utca (100m from the bus station), showcases photos, documents and early
works by József Egry (1883–1951). Egry – an artist compared in style with William
Turner – lived in this house for 30 years, and was hugely productive here. His
paintings are wonderful representations of the changing light and moods of the
lake, which he was inspired by (and obsessed with).

From the museum, continue away from the lake until you hit Római út, from
which Szegedi Róza utca makes the relatively steep and sapping climb up
Badacsony-hegy. You are flanked by vineyards all the way up, and there are small
wine shacks and bigger wine houses to stop off at on the way. (Alternatively you
can catch a jeep taxi; see under *Getting there, away and around*). After 1km or so you'll
reach the **Szegedi Róza Literary Museum** (*Kisfaludy u. 17;* ☎ *87 431906;*
☞ *360/180Ft;* ⊕ *May–Sep Tue–Sun 10.00–18.00*), and if you're still sober you can
take a look around the house of actress Róza Szegedi, who married the poet Sándor
Kisfaludy in 1800. The pair spent much time here, and dabbled in viniculture
themselves (in the wine press that now holds the Kisfaludy-ház restaurant);
apparently Róza's vermouth in particular was highly regarded.

The **Kisfaludy-ház** is 100m further on, and stands at the starting post for a
series of **marked trails** running across the top of Badacsony-hegy. A map at the
car park displays the routes, and a nature trail is accompanied by explanatory
boards. The plateau is covered with forest, which grows in the rich soil that is so
frequently washed from the steeper peaks elsewhere, and is home to the great

spotted woodpecker, the great black woodpecker, the nuthatch and the tree-creeper. The landscape also harbours 11 protected plant species. A short distance along a footpath brings you to some basalt stone blocks, one of which has a carved surface and is known as the **Rose Stone** (*Rózsa-kő*); it is said that if a couple sit on it with their backs to the lake, and think sweet thoughts of each other, they will be married within the year. Some people linger hopefully at the rock, while others suddenly find something terribly interesting in the opposite direction.

Other highlights on the trail are the **Páholy** and **Kisfaludy lookout towers**, and unusual rock formations like the **Stone Gate** (with its horizontal layers in the cliff sides) and the **Exiles' Stairs** (the latter leading to the Tördemic lookout point). If you choose to hike to the hills beyond the plateau, pick up a map from Tourinform.

EXCURSION To the west of Badacsony is the **Szigliget peninsula**, which has a castle first constructed by Benedictine monks from Pannonhalma in 1260 as protection from any further Mongol invasions. It was extended several times over subsequent centuries, the last renovation in 1540 when the round bastion was added. The fortress saw action in 1664 when the Turks tried and failed to capture it on three separate occasions, but lightning hit the powder store in 1697 and Lipót I ensured there was no chance of a resurrection during his demolition programme of 1702. The ruins are a steep 20-minute walk up the hill from the village below; the effort is rewarded with beautiful views over the lake, the valleys and the vineyards, and is particularly atmospheric at sunset. Road 71 leads into Köz út and Fő tér, from where several flights of steps take you over Petőfi utca and on to Kisfaludy utca from where the climb begins in earnest.

Szent Antal Pince (*Szigliget-Antalhegy*; ✆ 87 708082; *www.szentantalpince.hu*; ☉ *daily 14.00–dusk, 14.00–17.00 in winter*) is another beautiful winery with fabulous views. Kikötő (✆ 70 3106450; ☉ *Apr–Nov 08.00–22.00 daily; mains 1,000–2,000Ft*) is a very friendly, simple restaurant in the yacht harbour by the pier; there's a short menu of daily specials and the staff provide excellent service. It also has two apartments available at 10,000Ft. A walk up the hill from the harbour will take you to the charming Chapel of the Holy Trinity; in front of it are the graves of five US servicemen shot down in one of the last great battles of World War II in the spring of 1945.

There is a bus stop in Fő tér, served by buses from Tapolca and Badacsony. The ferry pier (*Réhelyi út*) is 2km south of the castle, and has up to five daily services to towns around Balaton (including Keszthely and Badacsony); evening sightseeing boats also depart from here (🚢 *1,250/625Ft; Jul 5–Aug 24 Tue & Sat 18.30*). Buses run between the pier and Fő tér.

TAPOLCA

Set 10km back from the northern shore of Balaton, Tapolca has prospered in modern times on the back of mining for the clay-like mineral bauxite. It is an attractive little town with a watermill and pond, and a water-filled cave.

GETTING THERE, AWAY AND AROUND The **bus station** is at the northwestern side of Hősök tere, from where Deák Ferenc utca runs east towards the Mill Pond and the Cave Lake. There are very regular services to Keszthely, Veszprém and Sümeg, as well as buses to Budapest (five daily), Badacsony (12), Hévíz (11), Szigliget (14), Székesfehérvár, Szombathely (three) and other destinations in Transdanubia. The **railway station** at the end of Dózsa György út is around 2km southwest of the centre, and represents the connecting point between towns around Lake Balaton and those in Western Transdanubia. There are good links with Balatonfüred (13 daily) and Keszthely (eight), as well as Celldömölk (seven) and Szombathely (four). Going further eastward, there are trains to Székesfehérvár and Budapest (ten). From the station you can catch buses 1 and 2 to Fő tér (every 15–30 mins).

INFORMATION AND OTHER PRACTICALITIES

E Balaton Tourist Arany János u. 2; \ 87 510131; www.balatontouristutazas.hu. Can arrange private accommodation, with rooms (for 2) starting at 3,500Ft & apts (for 4) at 10,000Ft. ⊕ Mon–Fri 08.00–16.00, Sat 09.00–11.30.

Z Tourinform Fő tér 17; \ 87 510777; e tapolca@ tourinform.hu. Directly above the Mill Lake. ⊕ Jun 15–Sep 15 Mon–Fri 09.00–19.00, Sat–Sun 10.00–20.00, rest of yr Mon–Fri 09.00–16.00, Sat 09.00–14.00.

 WHERE TO STAY AND EAT

✗ **Peppino Pizzeria** Kisfaludy u. 7; \ 87 414133. The place to grab a pizza, with a selection of nearly 40 to choose from, as well as salads, pastas & grills. Also sells ice cream. Opposite the cultural centre. Pizzas 650–1,200Ft, avg 1,000Ft; ⊕ 11.00–23.00 daily.

🏠 **Tavasbarlang Szálló** Hősök tere 5; \ 87 514100. Grim building next to the bus station – but you get what you pay for in this old workers' hostel. Beds 2,500Ft/pp, private sgl 4,000Ft.

🏠 **Szent György Panzió & Restaurant** (8 rooms) Kisfaludy Sándor u. 1; \ 87 413593. Sitting right next to the entrance to the Cave Lake, the elegant Hungarian restaurant (mains avg 1,800Ft; ⊕ 07.00–22.00 daily) has high-ceilinged rooms, an outdoor café terrace & helpful staff. The pension is similarly well-turned-out, with tidy rooms. A good choice in a good location. Dbl 19,200Ft..

🏠 **Hotel Pelion** (228 rooms) Köztársaság tér 10; \ 87 513101; e reserve@ hotelpelion.hunguesthotels.hu. This is an excellent

hotel, and very reasonably priced. Among the facilities are thermal & fun baths, various saunas & steam cabins, a jacuzzi & squash courts. The rooms are of a good size, & the deluxe apartments even have their own jacuzzis. From here, you can access a large underground cave whose pollen-free air is used to treat asthma sufferers. To the north of the Cave Lake. Dbl 41,400Ft.

🍴 **Dolce Cukrászda** Csobánc u. 55; \ 87 412015. The best of the places to get a cake. East of Templom domb. ⊕ Tue–Sun 10.00–19.00.

🏠 **Hotel Gabriella** (16 rooms) Batsányi tér 7; \ 87 511070; www.hotelgabriella.hu. The Gabriella is housed in a quiet location inside the original watermill, & has small & large dbl rooms, as well as apartments. Its restaurant (mains avg 1,800Ft; ⊕ 07.00–22.00 daily) has a terrace overlooking the lake; the menu includes Hungarian & international food, with goose-dish specialities. Dbl 14,800; ⊕ all yr.

ENTERTAINMENT AND NIGHTLIFE Dreamteam Café, Bar and Restaurant (*Kossuth u. 4 & 8;* \ *87 321637; www.dreamteamcafe.hu; mains 1,100–2,500Ft;* ⊕ *11.00–23.00 daily*) is the most popular place – actually two places – to while away time right in the centre of town. On Saturday night there is a varied programme of live entertainment. **Teke Club** (*Kossuth Lajos u. 12;* ⊕ *18.00–late*) is Tapolca's primary nightspot. The bowling alley is a popular attraction.

WHAT TO SEE AND DO Fő tér, which leads east into Kossuth Lajos utca and west into Deák Ferenc utca, is the main drag (and lined with banks and shops). To the south of it lies the **Mill Pond** (Malom-tó), divided between an upper lake surrounded by a low stone wall and a lower lake into which water flows to drive the wheel of the mill sitting at the juncture between the two. The mill how holds the Hotel Gabriella, and near by is a bust of the Austrian poet Baumberg Gabriella (1766–1839); she was married to the revolutionary 18th-century poet János Batsányi. This is a popular spot for lingering walks, idly watching the goldfish dart about in the smaller lake and enjoying the water lilies in the longer section.

The mild incline to the east of the lower lake is Templom domb, at the top of which is a **Roman Catholic church**. This was enlarged in the 18th century, but it retains earlier parts from the 13th and 15th centuries and has an 11th-century Gothic sanctuary. In front are some wall remains; while the majority of these belonged to the town's **15th-century castle** (which was brought down by the Turks), there are also portions dating forward to the 17th century and back as far as the Roman period. The **Town and School Museum** (*Templom domb 15;* ❜ *87 412246;* ℰ *500/200Ft;* ⊕ *Tue–Sun 09.00–16.00*) at one side of the primary school building has been reconstructed to mimic a turn-of-the-20th-century classroom. The teacher's hat and walking stick hang from pegs, while an adjacent room holds his bed.

The town's major highlight is of course its **Cave Lake** (*Tavasbarlang; Kisfaludy u. 3;* ❜ *87 412579;* ℰ *1,000/500Ft, boat tour 400Ft;* ⊕ *Tue–Sun 10.00–17.00*). There are crowds in high season, but it's well worth the wait to propel yourself in a tin boat through craggy white channels. The ride takes around 15 minutes and is great fun, the water beautiful, clear and cool. A few kilometres to the east in the village of Tapolca-Diszel is the **Reiterhof Villám Lovaspanzió** (*Templom tér 4;* ❜ *87 413943;* e *villam48@axelero.hu*), a family-run riding school with 7 *kisbér* (Hungarian half-bred) horses and an assortment of dogs. The accommodation (*5 rooms; dbl 20,000Ft*) is 'puritan' in its lack of frills, but spacious nevertheless. As well as lessons (*2,500Ft/hr*), the school offers tailor-made tours. There are buses to the village from Tapolca, or the company can collect you from Budapest airport.

KÁLI BASIN

East of Tapolca and north of Lake Balaton is the geological wonder of the Káli Basin: formed by the violence of volcanic activity it is now a gentle area of meadows, forests and vineyards, and small villages with steepled churches. This is rambling and cycling country, and the Balaton Uplands National Park maintains a network of study trails that explain the geological and botanical importance of the locations. It is worth buying the 1:90,000 ordinance map of the *Balaton-Felvidéki Nemzeti Park* (ℰ *1,800Ft*) from Tourinform.

WHERE TO STAY AND EAT A great variety of accommodation is available that caters to those after a peaceful break. In **Köveskál**, the manicured lawns of the superb Káli Art Inn (*12 rooms; Köveskál, Fő u. 8;* ❜ *87 706090; www.kaliartinn.com; dbl 28,500Ft;* ⊕ *Easter–mid Nov*) are popular with the Brits; the inn now employs an inventive young chef who prepares meals with local ingredients (*three courses 5,500Ft;* ⊕ *daily 08.00–22.00*). The inn has received good coverage in the UK travel press, and offers an intimate, rustic alternative to some of the high-rise hotels on the Balaton shoreline. Opposite is the Kővirág (*6 apts; Fő u. 9/A;* ❜ *20 5684724; www.kali.hu/szallas/kovirag; dbl 11,000Ft;* ⊕ *Easter–end Oct*), a stylish country house run by an enthusiastic couple; this is an easygoing place serving hearty fare (*mains 1,300–3,000Ft;* ⊕ *Mon–Thu 17.00–22.00, Fri–Sun 12.00–22.00*).

In nearby **Kővágóörs**, the Pálos Kuria (*Vörösmarty u. 11;* ❜ *87 707997; www.kali.hu/szallas/palos; dbl 15,000Ft;* ⊕ *May–Sep*) is a well-hidden gem (turn off the main road in the village by the school and take the left fork). A thatched house of a well-to-do 19th-century villager, it has been carefully restored and furnished with family heirlooms. Breakfast is served in the open barn. Three kilometres away in **Révfülöp**, try the Mákvirág Borház (*Petőfi u. 4;* ❜ *87 464754; mains 1,000–3,000Ft; wine tasting 1,500Ft*) for grilled food with a variety of sauces or for winetasting. Pajta Galléria in **Salföld** (*Petőfi u. 9;* ❜ *30 2890715; www.salfold.hu; 4 rooms; dbl 8,000Ft;* ⊕ *May–Sep*) is a popular eating place at the edge of the village where the Balaton Uplands National Park operates a traditional model farm. The owner is a professional photographer who runs courses from here. The short Hungarian menu changes weekly, and there is accommodation in two small houses.

The Sárvári Vendégház (*Zrínyi u. 41;* ↘ *06 30 205 2139; www.savarivendeghaz.hu; dbl 9,500Ft*) is a well-kept, rustic guesthouse with a lot of character on a decent plot of land in **Szentbékkálla**.

ACTIVITIES For horse lovers, Szentbékkálla is home to the **Káli Polo Ground** (one of two polo grounds in Hungary; www.magyarpoloclub.hu), and nearby **Tusculanum** in Mindszentkálla (*Szent Imre Major 66;* ↘ *87 478062; dbl 14,400Ft;* ⊕ *all yr*) is a large and somewhat derelict farm home to 14 horses and seven dogs. However, the rooms are spacious and meals are served in the family house, which is furnished in the bourgeois style of pre-war Hungary. Your hostess will prepare dinner for you – it is a rare treat to sample home-cooked, middle-class food. **Gyulakeszi Lovasudvar** (*Gyulakeszi;* ↘ *20 931 7446; www.gyulavezer.hu; dbl 9,000Ft*) is one of the larger riding establishments, with 24 horses. They arrange hunting in the autumn and a seven-day castle tour connecting historical points of the uplands. Accommodation is above the stables; the basic rooms all have balconies.

If you take the road from Szigliget to Tapolca off Road 71, you will come to **Szent György hegy**, another volcanic hill producing excellent wines. The Lengyel Chapel on this hillside is surrounded by vineyards and wine cellars, of which **Szent György Pince** (*Hegymagas;* ↘ *87 709469; www.nyaripince.hu;* ⊕ *May–Sep 14.00–16.00 daily*) is one of the best.

NAGYVÁZSONY

To the northeast of Tapolca, on the way to Veszprém, Nagyvázsony holds the **Kinizsi Castle** (*Vár utca;* ↘ *88 264786;* ☜ *500/300Ft;* ⊕ *Mar 15–Oct 31 Tue–Sun 0.9.00–17.00*), an originally 14th-century fort that was enlarged and reinforced by King Mátyás's military commander Pál Kinizsi in the 15th century. Kinizsi's strength was the stuff of legend; he is said once to have performed a victory dance while bearing a slain Turk in each hand. Pieces of his red-marble sarcophagus can be seen in the castle chapel. Much of the castle's structure remains – including a 30m-high keep and a six-storey tower – because it was owned by the Zichys in the 18th century, a family loyal to the Habsburgs, and therefore wasn't levelled after the Independence Wars. At the bottom of the barbican is the former dungeon, complete with waxworks of torturers at their grisly task, while the upper rooms have an exhibition of the castle's history. From the top of the barbican you can enjoy wonderful views over the turrets and through the gun-holes. The journey back down can be slightly hair raising, particularly at points where the steps are thrown into darkness, so please be careful. Displays of **medieval jousting** (☜ *1,000/600Ft; Jul 1–Aug 20 daily 11.00 & 15.00*) are held in a stretch just inside the outer castle walls. **Concerts** take place in the castle in summer; tickets for these and others in St István Church can be purchased from the ticket office (*Sörház u. 2;* ↘ *88 509516*), just off Vár utca to the southeast.

Opposite the castle is a rotund **Calvinist church** of 1796 with a wood-framed bell tower. The **Postal Museum** (*Temető u. 3;* ↘ *88 264300;* ☜ *500/250Ft;* ⊕ *Apr–Oct Tue–Sun 10.00–18.00*) is housed in a renovated peasant cottage, while behind that is an **Open-Air Folk Museum** (*Szabadtéri Néprajzi Múzeum; Bercsényi u. 21;* ☜ *300/150Ft;* ⊕ *May–Sep Tue–Sun 10.00–17.00*) with a pair of early-19th-century thatched cottages (including a coppersmith's house).

Just over 1km southwest of the centre (and signposted on Kinizsi utca), the **Nagyvázsony Leányfalui Horse Club** (*Leányfalui út 10;* ↘ *06 30 318771; www.vazsony.hu*) offers horse-riding (☜ *2,500Ft/hr*) and lessons, as well as carriage-driving lessons. Guests can stay in the three-room pension (*dbl 8,000Ft*); buses don't come here, but the owners can pick you up from the centre.

The area's main annual event is the Valley of Arts Festival (*www.kapolcs.hu*) at the end of July. Seven villages celebrate 19th-century rural life with folk, jazz, theatre productions, markets and general jolliness. Nagyvázsony's contribution is medieval in thrust – demonstrations of jousting and archery, in addition to a market.

GETTING THERE AND AWAY Buses run to Kinizsi Pál utca, the town's main street, and serve Veszprém regularly; there are also buses to Budapest (one on weekdays), Balatonfüred (three) and Tapolca (eight).

WHERE TO STAY AND EAT

🏠 **Várcsárda** Temetö u. 7; 🔌 88 264 344. Overlooking the castle, the peasant-style restaurant has individual thatched gazebos. The Hungarian food is well executed & the helpings are large; the carp with *lecso* (a dish similar to ratatouille, but of Ottoman origin) was very tasty. *Mains 1,200–2,300Ft, avg 1,500Ft;* ⊕ *Jul–Aug 12.00–23.00 daily, Apr–Jun & Sep closed on Mon.*

🏠 **Vázsonyvölgy Panzió & Restaurant** (10 rooms) Sörház u. 2; 🔌 88 264289; www.vazsonyvolgy.fw.hu Simple, friendly guesthouse 200m from the castle, with an elevated restaurant (*mains 900–3,000Ft, avg 1,500Ft;* ⊕ *10.00–22.00 daily*) preparing Hungarian food. Tennis, riding & bike hire available. *Sgl 5,500Ft, dbl 7,500Ft;* ⊕ *all yr.*

TIHANY

To the west of Balatonfüred – but nothing like it – the volcanic peninsula of Tihany feels like a heady mix of Cotswold town, Mediterranean cliff and national park. Its surface was formed by debris spewed from ancient volcanoes, and at its heart – alongside the hills, marshes and old geyser cones – are two crater lakes. This adds up to top-rate hiking territory, served by several marked trails, and it was declared the country's first nature reserve in 1952. Belső-tó (Inner Lake) is popular with anglers and Külső-tó with birdwatchers, while romantics head for the village at the eastern side, with its peasant houses and abbey. The first written reference to Tihany came in deeds recording the foundation of the Benedictine abbey by András I in 1055; this document – now held at Pannonhalma – is a particular treasure because it contains some Hungarian words among its Latin (the earliest surviving example of the native language in writing). In the 13th century the monastery was fortified and later resisted Turkish attempts to take it; however, the castle walls were reduced to ruins by the Habsburgs as part of the demolition programme of 1702, and the symbol of Tihany today is 18th-century and Baroque.

GETTING THERE AND AROUND There is no railway station, but **buses** go to seven or eight stops along the main stretch of Kossuth Lajos utca, which runs through the village centre. They also stop at the two ferry stations. There are regular services to Balatonfüred and up to six a day to Veszprém. **Passenger ferries** for Balatonfüred and Siófok (*Apr–Oct*) and Balatonföldvar (*Jun–Aug*) arrive/depart from Belső Kikötő (Inner Harbour), lying below the village. **Car ferries** crossing to Szántód (*Mar–Nov*) use the pier (Tihanyi-rév) at the peninsula's southern tip, leaving every 30 minutes or so in peak season. In summer, a motorised **sightseeing train** departs from Posta köz (opposite Paprika-ház) every 20 minutes (🚃 *700/500Ft; 09.00–20.00*), circles the town and continues down to Tihany-rév.

INFORMATION AND OTHER PRACTICALITIES

🚲 **Rent a bike** Kossuth Lajos u. 32; 🔌 30 393 8560. Bike hire by the hour, day or week. *1,100Ft/hr, 3,000Ft/day, 13,000Ft/week;* ⊕ *May–Sep daily 10.00–19.00.*

🛈 **Tihany Tourist** Kossuth Lajos u. 11; 🔌 87 448481; www.tihanytourist.hu. This office can arrange private accommodation (*from 3,000Ft/pp*), including peasant-style houses for 4 (*from 12,000Ft/night*), &

bus & boat tours. ☺ 09.00–16.00 daily
(09.00–19.00 in Jul & Aug).
🖬 Tourinform Kossuth Lajos u. 20; ☎ 87 438016;
🄴 tihany@tourinform.hu. In the centre of the
village, at the top of some steps (above a wine

shop). ☺ Jun–Aug Mon–Fri 09.00–19.00, Sat–Sun
10.00–20.00; Sep–Nov & Mar–May Mon–Fri
10.00–17.00, Sat–Sun 10.00–16.00; Dec–Feb daily
10.00–16.00.

 WHERE TO STAY You can rent peasant houses through Tihany Tourist (see page
513).

🏠 **Adler Fogadó** (11 rooms) Felsőkopaszhegyi u.
1/a; tel 87 538000; www.adler-tihany.hu. We were
beckoned over by an English couple sitting on the
terrace & they could not praise the hotel in more
superlative terms. Pleasant rooms with small terraces
or balconies, air-con, swimming pool, sauna,
restaurant. Dbl from €45; ☺ mid-Mar–Oct.
🏠 **Club Tihany** (330 rooms) Rév u. 3; ☎ 87
538564; www.clubtihany.hu. At the southernmost
point of the peninsula (next to the car-ferry pier),
this massive resort has a plethora of sporting
facilities – swimming pool, gym, beauty centre,

tennis courts & surfing/sailing school – &
bungalows. It's pricey, but the rooms are modern;
take a lake-facing one if you don't mind paying
extra. Rooms from sgl 15,750Ft, dbl 26,500Ft.
🏠 **Echo Residence** (18 apts) Felsőkopaszhegyi út
35; ☎ 87 448043; www.echoresidence.hu. The first
5-star development on the lake, with unusual &
contemporary décor, & an extensive wellness
complex. The larger apartments have their own
sauna. Its private strand is 5 mins' walk away; the
Balaton Golf Club (see page 517) is 20 mins by car.
Deluxe apts from 55,000Ft (for 2).

BALATON UPLANDS NATIONAL PARK

The Balaton National Park was founded in 1997 and extends over 57,000ha, starting at
the lake's western corner and covering the bulk of the northern shore up to the Tihany
peninsula. It is probably the most-visited of the country's national parks, and can be
divided into five main sections.

Kis (or 'Small') Balaton is a vast reedbed that came into being as a consequence
of hydrological works aimed at restoring the water quality in Lake Balaton – the River
Zala feeds into it and is slowed (depositing its sediment) before continuing into Balaton.
Pollution resulting from chemicals dumped in the Zala remains a problem, but that has
not deterred the birdlife – it is home to all species of European heron, to the great
white egret and to large numbers of nesting greylag geese. Up to 20,000 bean goose
stop here during migration. With the exception of Kányavári Island, the lake can only
be visited with a guide (arranged through the national-park directorate), and it is closed
during the breeding season. Fishermen angle from the Zalavár road crossing the
northern tip or from Kányavári Island (reached over a wooden bridge from
Balatonmagyaród), which also has a 3km nature trail. From Balatonmagyaród (which
can be reached by bus direct from Keszthely or with a change at Sármellék), you can
walk to the Kápolnapuszta Buffalo Reserve (🄳 400/150Ft; ☺ 08.00–dusk daily). The
traditional Hungarian buffalo was brought over by Asiatic tribes, and used in agriculture
up until the 1950s; while there were 200,000 in the early 1900s, there are now only
350 left and the reserve – which holds a third of the country's – plays a vital role in
their survival.

The **Keszthely range** is dominated by forest. The steeper dolomite slopes hold
steppeland and dry scrub forest of Hungarian oak, sumach and butcher's broom. The
rarest plant species here is the leopard's bane. The hills have several lookout points –
Batsányi on Pap-hegy, Szép on Kápolna-hegy, Bél Mátyás on Galga-hegy and Berzsenyi
on Pető-hegy. A study trail running up Kovácsi-hegy begins from the edge of Zalaszántó
village, which sits between Hévíz and Sümeg. The hill is notable for its 1km-long lava
formation known as the 'basalt road'.

⌂ Hotel Tihany Atrium (24 rooms) Kenderföld u. 9; ☎ 87 538100; www.hoteltihany.com. This 4-star hotel is just over 1km to the south of the village, next to a strand & private yacht club. The rooms are large & very comfortable. *Sgl 13,300Ft, dbl 17,700Ft (excl Tourist Tax).*

⌂ Kántás Panzió (6 rooms) Csokonai u. 49; ☎ 87 448072; e kantaspension@canet.hu; www.hotels.hu/kantas. Delightfully quaint guesthouse in the heart of the village (take József Attila u. off Kossuth Lajos utca, & Csokonai u. is on the left). *Rooms €20/pp.*

✖ WHERE TO EAT AND DRINK Restaurants without a fabulous view aren't worth a second glance in Tihany.

✖ Balatoni Ház Halászköz 8–9; ☎ 87 448608. The spot for an al-fresco meal with a view. It is difficult to miss, sitting on the promenade behind the abbey, & is a busy place with quick service. Large helpings of Hungarian fare. *Mains avg 2,000Ft;* ⊕ *Apr–Oct 11.00–21.30 daily.*

✖ Ferenc Pince Cserhegy u. 9; ☎ 87 448575. Surrounded by a picket fence & lime trees, this popular restaurant enjoys fabulous views of the lake. Good Hungarian food & an extensive list of local wines. It is located 1½km south of the village, up a

track leading off the road to Tihany-rév; if you take the bus, alight at the point where Kossuth Lajos u. meets Cserhegyi utca & walk the remaining 200m. *Mains avg 1,650Ft;* ⊕ *Apr–Oct Wed–Mon 12.00–23.00.*

✖ Oázis Major u. 47; ☎ 87 438008; www.oazis.net. Thatched restaurant with an open-fronted bar overlooking Belső-tó. The Hungarian food is good; we recommend the fish platters for 2. It's a 10-min walk southeast from the abbey. *Mains avg 1,700Ft;* ⊕ *May–Sep 11.00–23.00 daily.*

The **Tapolca basin** features arguably the country's most beautiful landscape, with the volcanic hills of Badacsony, Csobánc and Szent György that formed four–five million years ago. The lip fern (*Ceilanthus marantae*) is found only in this part of Hungary and grows on the exposed basalt slopes. Orchids and the marsh gladiolus prospers on the remains of ancient marshes in the foothills.

The **Káli basin** – named after the Magyar Kál tribe that settled in the area – is known primarily for its geological features. The highlight is Hegyestű, to the east of Köveskál village, a two-layered series of rock pillars formed by several volcanic eruptions. Other rocky rarities include the 'seas of stones', the best of which can be found near Salföld and to the northwest of Szentbékkálla. These were formed when pockets of sand became petrified at the bottom of the Pannonian Sea during the Miocene period. The area is also rich in bogs. Among these is the Sásd Meadow in Köveskál, home to a significant population of a rare sub-alpine primrose. In two bogs at Kövágóőrs you'll find floating sphagnum, a survivor from the ice age. The Salföld Nature Conservation Site (*Salföld Major;* ☎ *06 30 939 0770; www.kali.hu/salfoldmajor;* ✆ *250/100Ft;* ⊕ *09.00–18.00 daily*), to the northeast of Badacsony, showcases ancient Hungarian animal breeds. There are also opportunities for horse- riding here. Horse shows are held at the adjacent '*puszta*' (✆ *2,500/1,700Ft; shows May–Jun & Sep Sat 15.00, Jul–Aug Tue–Sat 18.00*). Buses run to Salföld from Badascony and Badascony-Tomaj, and the conservation site is a short distance to the east.

The **Pécsely basin and Tihany peninsula** is also volcanic in origin and it boasts Hungary's mildest micro-climate. Here are significant populations of sub-Mediterranean plant species such as burning bush, pheasant's eye, pyramidal orchid and the *Sternbergia colchiciflora*. In addition, the scops owl, a typically Mediterranean bird, nests in the area.

For further information on any of the above or to arrange guides, contact the **Balaton Uplands National Park Directorate** (*Veszprém, Vár u. 31;* ☎ *88 577730; www.bfnpi.hu*). The office should also be able to sell you a copy of the *Balaton-Felvidéki Nemzeti Park* (Paulus, 1:90,000) map on which are marked all the walking trails and viewing points.

✘ **Rege Kávézó** Kossuth Lajos u. 22; ☎ 87 448280. Occupying a side wing of the former convent, this café has good cakes & a rear terrace. To the left as you leave the gallery. ⊕ *Easter–Oct 10.00–20.00 daily.*
✘ **Regi idők udvara** Batthyany út 3; tel 70 284 6705. This is a quirky place in a courtyard decorated with everything old – from kitchen tools to farm implements. The home-brewed beer is excellent, as is the elderflower cordial. We ate fish which was simple but good. *Mains avg 2,000Ft;* ⊕ *May–Oct 11.00–19.00, later at w/end.*

WHAT TO SEE AND DO The cream-coloured, two-towered **Tihany Abbey** (*Apátsági templom; I András tér;* ☎ 87 538200; ☞ 700/300Ft, foreign-lang guide 8,000Ft; ⊕ daily Mar 27–Apr 30 10.00–17.00, May–Sep 09.00–18.00) stands at the southeastern side of I András tér. It was built between 1719 and 1754 on the site of András I's 11th-century abbey; the Romanesque crypt survives, and contains the marble tomb of the king (the only Árpád royal grave still in its original resting place) and that of his son. The church was constructed by local, unschooled craftsmen, but the extravagance and intricacy of some of the interior furnishings – the elaborate pulpit (with putti on its canopy) and heavily gilded altars – belies a hand more skilled. The whys and wherefores of Austrian wood-carver Sebestyén Stulhoff's arrival at Tihany are unclear; what is certain is that he pitched up in 1754 and stayed 25 years until his death. He did not take monastic orders, yet he received no payment and the interior of this church is the only known example of his work. A popular belief is that he came here as a broken-hearted young man after the death of his bride-to-be. It would be lovely to believe the story that the angel kneeling before Mary in the first altar bears the likeness of his departed fiancée. The frescoes on the arching ceiling were added in the 19th century by artists including Károly Lotz and Bertalan Székely. There are organ recitals in summer (see Tourinform for details).

From the main altar, you move through into the **Benedictine Abbey Museum**, housed in the former monastery adjoining the church. Inside is a lapidarium of stones dating back as far as the Roman period, and including pieces of the 11th-century abbey, together with temporary art exhibitions usually focused on the Balaton region. The ticket to the church also gives access to the museum. In front of the church is a surreal statue of András I entitled *The Founder* (*Az Alapító;* 1972); the intriguing use of metal and stone betrays the artist as Imre Varga. Also here is the **Spring Cave** (*Forrás Barlang*), one of the peninsula's many cones formed by post-volcanic thermal activity.

A hillside promenade (Pisky sétány) leads away from the northern side of the church, along which is a pair of 19th-century thatched peasant houses belonging to the **Open-Air Museum** (*Néprajzi Múzeum; Pisky sétány 12;* ☎ 87 438960; ☞ 350/250Ft; ⊕ May–Sep 10.00–18.00 daily). One of these was the meeting place of the fishermen's guild and contains a smoke kitchen and equipment used for ice fishing. The other was a farmer's abode, filled with the modest possessions of a family that would never make it rich on the unfertile ground of Tihany. From here, turn left and then right on to Visszhang utca, where you'll find the **Doll Museum** (*Visszhang u. 4;* ☎ 87 448431; ☞ 400/300Ft; ⊕ daily Mar 15–May 31 10.00–15.00, Jun–Aug 10.00–19.00, Sep–Oct 10.00–15.00). The collection features 600 porcelain dolls gathered over four decades and dating back as far as 1840. The accessories and clothing offer an interesting insight into 19th-century aristocratic and upper-middle-class tastes.

Opposite the museum stands a 19th-century **peasant house**, one of many to be found in Tihany. They were traditionally built from basalt tuff, with whitewashed walls and broad thatched roofs that provided a second-storey living space. Continue along Visszhang utca (back towards Pisky sétány) and you'll reach **Echo Hill** (Visszhang domb), so-named because of the echoes that bounced back when people shouted from here towards the abbey. The increased number of buildings means that the clarity is no longer what it was, but you can holler away if you don't mind irritating everybody around you. From here you can join a path leading around the Óvár to a series of **cells** hewn (for private contemplation) by the Russian Orthodox monks brought to the abbey by Ándrás I.

If you fancy picking up some traditional produce or crafts, there's a vivid-red **Paprika House** (*Kossuth Lajos u. 16;* ⟍ *06 70 257 8642;* ⊕ *Mar–Nov 09.00–21.00 daily*) selling things pepper-related, and a **Pottery House** (*Fazekasház; Batthyány u. 26;* ⟍ *87 448159;* ⊕ *08.00–20.00 daily*) with a cluttered display of hand-made earthenware items. Stalls offering lacework, handbags and other goods line Batthyány utca in summer.

Other While Tihany isn't a writhing sunbathing haven in the mould of other Balaton resorts, there are **strands** on all sides of the peninsula. Those to the southeast, around the Tihany-rév ferry port, are the busiest; if you want something simpler, quieter and free to use, try the strand (⊕ *Jun–Sep 08.00–19.00*) 500m south of the village, or those to the north in between the settlements of Diós and Gödrös. To really get away from the crowds, head inland to the nature reserve. The **Lóczy Geyser Trail** runs a total length of 18km, with information boards in English; among the geological highlights are the Golden House (Aranyház) geyser cones to the south. Pick up a map from Tourinform showing the various marked routes.

The **Royal Balaton Golf & Yacht Club** (*Balatonudvari, Vászolyi utca;* ⟍ *87 549200; www.balatongolf.hu*) is the first golf course on the lake, about 20 minutes by car from Tihany on Road 71 towards Keszthely. Beautifully situated in an elevated position surrounded by indigenous forest and vineyards, it is a quiet spot away from the crowds. More development is in the pipeline, including a yacht harbour and a golf and wellness hotel.

Just north of Tihany, inside the national park, is the **Csikós Lovasudvar** (*Pécsely, Klára-puszta;* ⟍ *87 445308; www.csikos-lovasudvar.hu; dbl from €50; cross-country rides €9.50/hr;* ⊕ *Mar–Nov*). This impeccably kept riding establishment has 21 traditionally furnished rooms in a building reconstructed from ruins; in addition, there's a swimming pool, tennis courts and, of course, stables. Star tours are possible into the rolling countryside and forests of the national park. The à-la-carte restaurant and terrace serves Hungarian dishes and local wines, accompanied by gypsy music. A quiet place in the country, and enjoyable as such even if you are not passionate about riding.

BALATONFÜRED

The first written allusion to Balatonfüred came in Tihany Abbey's land register of 1211. However, it properly rose to prominence in the early 1700s when a spa was established harnessing the health-giving properties of its sulphurous springs. Come the 19th century, it was a favourite with progressive aristocrats at the head of the reform drive and in summer skimmed the cream from the worlds of art and politics. The names of literary men like Mór Jókai and Sándor Kisfaludy are linked with Balatonfüred' development, and their legacy is a noble, even cerebral resort that looks with lofty disdain across the water to vulgar bruisers like Siófok.

GETTING THERE, AWAY AND AROUND Balatonfüred lies on Road 71, which leads along the northern shore. The **bus** and **railway stations** are adjacent to each other on Castricum tér, roughly equidistant between the shore resort and the old town centre. Buses 1, 1A and 2 run to the shore from the stations, numbers 10 and 11 continuing west down Széchenyi utca. The railway lies on the Budapest–Tapolca line, and there are frequent services to Budapest's Déli and Kelenföld (through

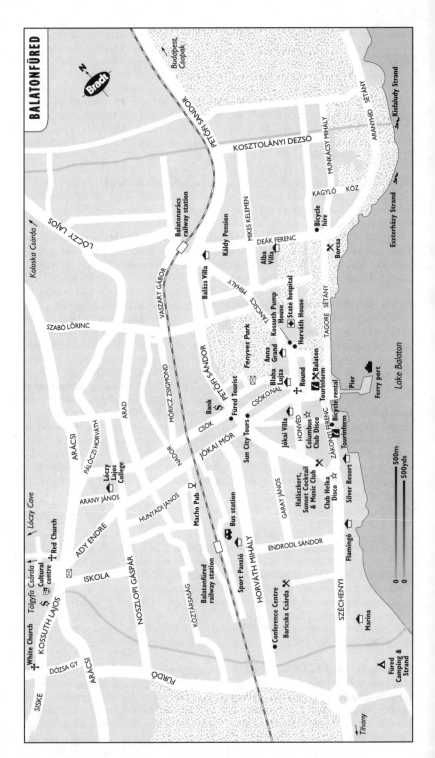

BALATONFÜRED

SISKE
DÓZSA GY
ARÁCSI
FÜRDŐ
NOSZLOPI GÁSPÁR
KÖZTÁRSASÁG
ISKOLA
ADY ENDRE
ARANY JÁNOS
HUNYADI JÁNOS
PÁLÓCZI HORVÁTH
ARÁCSI
ARAD
SZABÓ LŐRINC
LÓCZY LAJOS
Koloska Csárda
KOSSUTH LAJOS

† White Church
$ Cultural centre
⌖ Red Church
Tölgyfa Csárda
Lóczy Cave
Lóczy Lajos College
Macho Pub
Bus station
Balatonfüred railway station
Sport Panzió
HORVÁTH MIHÁLY
ENDRŐDL SÁNDOR
GARAY JÁNOS
Conference Centre
Baricska Csárda ✗
SZÉCHENYI
Flamingó
Silver Resort
Club Helka Disco ☆
Halászkert, Sunset Cocktail & Music Club
ZÁKONYI FERENC
Tourinform
Marina
Füred Camping & Strand
Tihany

NÁDOR
MÓRICZ ZSIGMOND
CSOK
Bank $
Füred Tourist
Sun City Tours
JÓKAI MÓR
CSOKONAL
Jókai Villa
HONVÉD
Columbus ☆ Club Disco
Bicycle rental
Tourinform

VASZARY GÁBOR
PETŐFI SÁNDOR
Fenyves Park
Blaha Lujza
Anna Grand
† Round
Balaton ✗
Tourinform
Pier
Ferry port

Balatonarács railway station
Balázs Villa
MIHÁLY
TÁNCSICS
Káldy Pension
MIKES KELEMEN
DEÁK FERENC
Alba Villa
Kossuth Pump House
✚ State hospital
Horváth House
TAGORE SÉTÁNY

KOSZTOLÁNYI DEZSŐ
Budapest, Csopak
PETŐFI SÁNDOR
KAGYLÓ KÖZ
MUNKÁCSY MIHÁLY
ARANYHÍD SÉTÁNY
Bicycle hire
Borcsa
Eszterházy Strand
Kisfaludy Strand

Lake Balaton

N Bradt

0 500m
0 500yds

Székesfehérvár) and to Tapolca (through Badacsony). There are regular buses to Tihany, Hévíz and Veszprém, as well as services to Budapest (five), Tapolca (four), Győr (eight), Zalaegerszeg (seven) and other towns in Transdanubia.

The **Balaton Ferry** (*Balatoni Hajózás;* 87 342230; *www.balatonihajozas.hu;* 1,430/715Ft) leaves from the pier at the end of Tagore sétány, travelling to Siófok and Tihany. It operates April–September, and there are up to eight daily departures in high season (*Jul 5–Aug 24*); these are for foot passengers only. If you need a taxi, try **Taxi Balatonfüred** (87 444444).

INFORMATION AND OTHER PRACTICALITIES

Füred Tourist Petőfi Sándor u. 2; 87 481605; e info@furedtourist.hu. Broad selection of excursions. Doesn't organise private rooms. May–Oct 08.00–20.00 daily.

Sun City Tours Csokonai u. 1; 87 481798; www.suncity.hu. Apts & private rooms arranged from 8,000Ft (for 2). all yr 09.00–17.00 daily.

Tempo 21 Rent A Bike Ady Endre u. 52; 87 480671; www.kerekparkolcsonzes.hu. The main office

is opposite the entrance to the Eszterházy Strand. Costs hour/day/week 450/2,600/12,500Ft; 09.00–19.00 daily.

Tourinform Kisfaludy u. 1; 87 580480; e balatonfured@tourinform.hu; Jun 15–Aug 31 Mon–Sat 09.00–19.00, Sun 10.00–20.00, Sep Mon–Fri 09.00–17.00, Sat 09.00–13.00, Oct 1–Jun 15 Mon–Fri 09.00–16.00.

WHERE TO STAY

Alba Villa (13 apts) Deák Ferenc u. 23; 87 580124; www.albavilla.hu. The modern apartments have 2 bedrooms, well-equipped kitchen, air-con, TV with cable channels & balcony. Swimming pool, sauna, jacuzzi, steam bath, children's pool. In the adjoining Alba Villa a reasonably priced à-la-carte restaurant operates. *From 19,800Ft (min 5 nights in main season).*

Anna Grand Hotel (101 rooms) Gyógy tér 1; 87 581200; www.annagrandhotel.eu. Right in the newly restored historic centre of town, this venerable hotel is being reborn. Some of the elegant rooms are traditionally furnished, others have a contemporary feel. Sixty per cent of all cultural events in Balatonfüred take place in the beautiful upstairs theatre hall, but the main event of the year is the famous Anna Ball in July. The large, high-ceilinged restaurant exudes grandeur. Large wellness/fitness centre, squash, bowling. *Sgl €65, dbl €130 half board.*

Balázs Villa (5 rooms) Deák Ferenc u. 1; 87 580060; www.balazsvilla.hu. Next door to the Káldy (see page 520), but a better option with spacious & inviting rooms. Swimming pool, solarium, sauna. *Sgl/dbl 7,000/8,500Ft;* all yr.

Blaha Lujza Hotel (22 rooms) Blaha Lujza u. 4; 87 581210; www.hotelblaha.hu. This Neoclassical villa was once the summer house of the famous Hungarian singer Blaha Lujza (1893–1916). It now holds the hotel restaurant, while the rear of the building has been extended over 2 storeys, & offers neat rooms. Sauna, fitness room, solarium. *Sgl 10,000, dbl 16,000Ft.*

Camping Füred & Strand Széchenyi u. 24; 87 580241; e fured@balatontourist.hu. A mammoth site on the shore. There's so much to do you need never leave — watersports, fishing, football, tennis, minigolf... As well as tent pitches, there are also bungalows & motel rooms. *Tent/caravan from 3,150Ft, plus adults/concessions 1,500/1,100Ft;* Apr–mid Oct.

Flamingo Hotel (181 rooms) Széchenyi u. 16; 87 581060; www.flamingohotel.hu. One of the area's best, this hotel has large & tasteful rooms (some modern, some with 'antique' furnishings), an indoor pool, whirlpool, jacuzzi & private beach. 42 rooms offer Balaton views. Non-residents can use the leisure pool & wellness facilities for 4,500Ft/day. *Dbl with/without balcony 33,000/25,800Ft (excl Tourist Tax).*

Hotel Marina (349 rooms) Széchenyi u. 26; 87 889500; www.danubiushotels.com/marina. This family-oriented hotel is housed in an ugly block, but has its own private beach, indoor pool & plenty to keep the kids occupied. Stays are all-inclusive (facilities & meals). The standard rooms have small balconies — request a lake view. *Dbl 34,600Ft;* Apr 30–Sep 28.

Hotel Silver Resort (71 rooms, 23 with lake views) Zákonyi Ferenc u. 4; 87 583000; www.silverresort.hu. This brand-new hotel is fully equipped with indoor & outdoor pools, children's pool, selection of saunas, jacuzzi & beauty treatments. It has its own harbour & yacht hire is possible. Bike hire. The restaurant (*mains 1,500–6,000Ft*) overlooks the lake & the harbour. *Dbl 27,800Ft (inc wellness facilities).*

🏠 **Káldy Panzió** (8 rooms) Deák Ferenc u. 5; 📞 87 340760; e varga37@t-online.hu. One of the cheaper options in town, but basic with it. *Dbl 9,500Ft, trpl 10,500Ft, apt (for 4) 17,000Ft.*

🏠 **Sport Panzió** (7 rooms) Horváth Mihály u. 35; 📞 87 340720; e pulsport@t-online.hu. Modern guesthouse with a chalet-style feel to it. Small & reasonably priced, & a good choice. 2 squash courts & sauna. *Rooms 9,000Ft/pp.*

✕ WHERE TO EAT AND DRINK

✕ **Balaton Restaurant** Kisfaludy út 5; 📞 87 481319. Set in the park running above Tagore sétány, this restaurant has a cultivated wooded-glade feel to it & an extensive menu featuring much fish. *Mains avg 1,900Ft;* ⏰ *11.00–23.00 daily.*

✕ **Baricska Csárda** Széchenyi u.; 📞 87 580247; www.baricskacsarda.hu. Kitsch but pleasing peasant-style inn set back 200m from the road, & serving Hungarian cuisine (crispy piglet, stuffed cabbage, pike perch in beer dough & speciality plates for 2–3). Gypsy music. *Mains avg 2,700Ft;* ⏰ *Mar–Oct 11.00–23.00 daily.*

✕ **Borcsa Restaurant** Tagore sétány; 📞 87 580070; www.borcsaetterem.hu. Hungarian & international cuisine, including haunch of deer in red wine with cranberries, stuffed pear & potato croquettes, rumpsteaks, pizzas & a few pasta dishes. Modern interior with open front in good weather & a terrace. There are cocktails & ice cream on the upper level, decked out like a cruise liner in the main season. Accessible from both Tagore sétány & from within Eszterházy Strand. *Mains avg 1,600Ft;* ⏰ *11.00–22.00 daily.*

✕ **Blaha Étterem** Blaha Lujza u. 4; 📞 87 581210. This elegant restaurant in the centre of town has a quiet terrace. The food choices are Hungarian, & the pancakes are especially wonderful. *Mains avg 2,200Ft;* ⏰ *08.00–23.00 in summer, 08.00–22.00 in winter.*

✕ **Halászkert Restaurant** Zákonyi Ferenc u. 3; 📞 87 581050; www.halaszkert.hu. Delish fish, including those from the sea as well as the lake. *Mains avg 1,800Ft;* ⏰ *12.00–23.00 in summer (nightclub till 04.00); 12.00–22.00 in winter daily.*

✕ **Koloska Csárda** Koloska Völgy; 📞 87 703037; www.koloskacsarda.hu. This popular excursion spot is about 4km from the centre; follow the signs from Balatonarács. The walks are lovely in the surrounding forests & meadows & your reward is a Hungarian meal in rustic surroundings. Gypsy music in the summer months. *Mains avg 1,800Ft;* ⏰ *Apr–Oct 11.00–23.00 daily.*

✕ **Tölgyfa Csárda** Meleghegyi Dűlő; 📞 87 343036; www.tolgyfacsarda.hu. Among the vineyards, this folksy restaurant offers superb views of the lake. The food is traditional Hungarian with fish & game specialities. Well-signposted access from the town centre; turn right at the Red Church. *Mains avg 2,000Ft;* ⏰ *Apr–Oct 11.00–23.00 daily.*

ENTERTAINMENT AND NIGHTLIFE The **cultural centre** (*Kossuth Lajos u. 3;* 📞 *87 480872;* ⏰ *Mon–Fri 07.00–17.00*) is opposite the Red Church, and can offer advice on arts events in town. Local buses 1, 1A, 1B, 5, 5A and 5B run here from the lake-shore promenade (as well as the motorised train). The Round and White churches are sometimes used for concerts. The **Columbus Club Disco** (*Honvéd u. 3; www.columbusclub.hu;* ⏰ *in summer 22.00–05.00 daily*), just back from Tagore sétány, is the current club of choice (although things move fast at Balaton); guest DJs play chart and dance music. **Club Helka Disco** (*Zákonyi Ferenc utca;* 📞 *87 788013; www.clubhelka.hu;* ⏰ *22.00–04.00 daily in summer*) is a prominent club on the main drag, with regular DJs from Budapest and abroad. **Macho Pub** (*Vasút u. 4;* 📞 *87 3421769;* ⏰ *Sun–Thu 18.00–02.00, Fri–Sat 18.00–05.00*) is a Mexican-style theme pub. **Sunset Cocktail & Music Club** (*Zákonyi Ferenc u. 3;* 📞 *70 3146677;* ⏰ *daily 20.00–04.00 in summer, Fri–Sat 20.00–04.00 in winter*) is difficult to miss, with spotlights arcing into the night sky; great place for cocktails and toe-tapping, and very busy.

WHAT TO SEE AND DO One of Balatonfüred's greatest features is a simple thing – a straight promenade leading along the lake edge away from the pier. It is lined with acacias, and affords peaceful views of the southern shore as well as rocky crops dotted with anglers. **Tagore sétány** is named after the Hindu poet Rabindranath Tagore, who took the water here to relieve his heart disease in 1926. In thanks for his recovery he planted a lime tree in the park next to the promenade; in front of it is his bust, bearing his words 'When I am no longer on this earth, my tree, let the ever-renewed leaves of thy spring murmur to the wayfarer; the poet did love thee while he lived'. Other prominent figures have followed his lead, and the park contains the trees of President Indira Gandhi, Fidesz leader Viktor Orbán, and various Nobel-prize-winning poets and scientists. There are several statues and monuments along the route; look out for the haunting sculpture of a hand being sucked into its stone block, a memorial to those who drowned when the *Pajtás* sank on the lake in 1954.

Moving back from the shore, the Neoclassical **Round Church** (*Kerektemplom; Blaha Lujza u. 1*) stands at the western end of Blaha Lujza and was modelled on the Pantheon in Rome. Consecrated in 1846, it bears a late-19th-century painting of *The Crucifixion* by János Vaszary above a side altar. Continuing along the same road, you'll pass the summer villa of the famed singer Blaha Lujza (now housing the hotel of the same name) on your way to the gravelled Gyógy tér. At the square's centre is the **Kossuth Spring** (*Forrás*) of 1802, a pumphouse from which four spouts dispense the town's therapeutic water; lick a two-pence piece and you'll get an idea of the notoriously 'sour' taste.

The **State Hospital for Heart Disease** at the eastern side bases its treatments on this water. Behind the pump house is a parade with plaques recording famous figures who have received the cure – among them Mór Jókai, Sándor Kisfaludy, Mihály Vörösmarty and Endre Ady. The pantheon's building was originally a **sanatorium**. The elegant building opposite (and incorporating the pantheon) is the newly opened Anna Grand Hotel (see page 519). The major event in the town's social calendar – the Anna Ball (see page 522) – is again taking place in its hall. A rose garden in front contains a gentle sculpture of a bathing woman by Zsigmond Kisfaludy Stróbl; the first Hungarian-language theatre in Transdanubia (built 1831) once stood on the site. The inaugural Anna Ball was held in the Louis-VI-style **Horváth House** (*Gyógy tér 3*) in 1825 (although it later moved to what is now the Anna Grand Hotel); this former inn, which hosted many of the big cheeses of the 19th century, has been transformed into private apartments.

Retrace your steps past the Round Church and cross the road to the **Jókai Memorial Museum** (*Honvéd u. 1;* ✆ *87 343426;* ✆ *570/280Ft;* ☉ *Tue–Sun Jul–Aug 10.00–20.00*), which was closed for refurbishment as we went to press. Jókai (1825–1904) is rated as one of the country's greatest Romantic prose writers. Many of his 200 published works were written from this villa – including *The Golden Man* – which he used as a summer residence for 20 years after finding the town's air and water relieved his chronic bronchitis. He is probably best known to the outside world as the source of the libretto of The Gypsy Baron by Johann Strauss. The museum displays some of his furnishings, photos, letters and early editions of his works.

A kilometre further northwest is Balatonfüred's older centre, containing administrative and cultural offices. The Neo-Romanesque **Red Church** (*Vöröstemplom; Szent István tér*) is made of the red stone local to the area. Further west along Kossuth Lajos utca is the Calvinist **White Church** (*Fehér templom; Óvoda u. 1*) of 1829.

Other The town has three public beaches, all busy in summer. **Eszterházy Strand** (*Tagore sétány;* ✆ *87 343817; daily pass* ✆ *600/400Ft;* ☉ *Jun 25–Sep 15 09.00–18.00 daily*) has a section of sandy beach, together with pedalos and windsurfers for hire, a pizzeria and bar, and activities like mini golf and trampolining. **Kisfaludy Strand** (*Aranyhíd sétány;* ✆ *87 342916; daily pass* ✆ *400/300Ft;* ☉ *Jun 15–Sep 15 09.00–22.00*) has similar offerings, while **Brázay Strand** is the smallest, sandwiched between the other two.

If you fancy some **sailing**, you can hire boats from Opti Yacht (*Köztársaság u. 1/A;* \ *87 341188;* ✆ *4–5-man yachts 10,000Ft/hr*). You'll need an international licence to sail unaccompanied, but if you don't have one both companies can provide a 'captain'. Book in advance. **Sightseeing boats** depart daily from the pier in high season (*Jun–Aug*); there are trips lasting one hour (✆ *1,000/500Ft; 12.30, 14.00, 16.00, 18.00 & 20.00*) and two hours (✆ *1,600/800Ft; 10.00*), and a disco boat (✆ *1,300/1,000Ft; 21.00*) in the evening. A motorised **mini train** (✆ *600/300Ft; every 30 mins 09.00–24.00 daily in summer*) offers sightseeing on land, and starts from the pier. Permits are required to go **fishing**; you can buy these at Tourinform (among other places), and there are several shops selling tackle.

The wooded hills and valleys above Balatonfüred offer ample opportunity for **hiking**. A blue trail leads up Tamás-hegy to the **Jókai Lookout Tower**, which sadly burnt down recently but will be rebuilt soon, while on the hill's western side is the **Lóczy Cave** (*Öreghegyi utca;* ✆ *400/300Ft;* ☉ *May 1–Sep 15 Tue–Sun 10.00–17.00*). This cave is the largest in the Balaton Uplands and consists of a series of linked chambers; the wonder here is in the walls' limestone layers – like stacks of toast – that were formed by the pressures that forced the hill upwards. You can reach the cave by following Öreghegyi utca for 1km from near Szent István tér.

FESTIVALS AND EVENTS The annual highlight is the Anna Ball of July 26 (or the weekend closest to it), which features dancing and the election of a queen and courtiers (who are driven through the streets in a carriage). Tickets are expensive and hotly sought after. The Balatonfüred Wine Weeks take place in August, with wine growers showcasing their products along Tagore sétány, and there is more wine at the Vintage Procession in September. The last weekend in September is devoted to the Romantic Reform Age, when the early-19th-century core of the town becomes the scene for celebrations to commemorate the town founders. There are costumes and dishes influenced by the 1830s; for more details on the programmes, see www.balatonfured.info.hu.

Appendix I

LANGUAGE

The Nobel-Prize-winning physicist Enrico Fermi was fascinated by the possible existence of extra terrestrials. 'Where are they?' he once blurted out. The Hungarian-born scientist Leó Szilárd paused from his lunch, looked up at his colleague, and replied, 'They are among us, but they call themselves Hungarians'. Alien speech betrayed these Martians in central Europe. Hungarian bears no relation to the Indo-European languages of neighbouring countries. While there's a distant link with Finnish and Estonian (of the Finno-Ugric linguistic group), we find the ET theory as credible as any other.

Staff in Budapest's restaurants and bars will usually speak some English, but you'll endear yourself by trying a word or two magyarul (Hungarian-ly). Small tourist dictionaries (*Magyar-Angol/Angol-Magyar útiszótár*) are available from bookshops, and should provide most of what you'll need. Don't worry about the grammar – life (and your stay) is too short. Good luck! – *Sok szerencsét!*

PRONUNCIATION Perfect pronunciation is a rare thing from beginners. No matter; be determined – and free with the odd descriptive hand signal – and you'll make yourself understood. The golden rules are that the stress should always fall on the word's first syllable, that there are no silent vowels, and that letters (or combinations of letters) are consistent in their sound values. Below is a list of letters with phonetic transcriptions; those not included are pronounced as in English, with the exception of *q, w, x* and *y*, which don't appear in Hungarian (except in foreign derivatives and some names). And did you know that every single word under *ty* in the Hungarian dictionary is related to, or begins with, the word for 'chicken' (*tyúk*)?

a	as in d**o**t		**ó**	as for o, but held for longer
á	as in r**a**ther		**ö**	as the u in **u**rn
c	as the ts in ac**ts**		**ő**	as above, but held for longer
cs	as the ch in bir**ch**		**r**	rolled, as in the Scottish accent
é	as the a in d**a**y		**s**	as the sh in **sh**opping
g	always hard as in **g**ood, never soft as in germ		**sz**	as the s in **s**ell
gy	as the dy sound in **du**ring		**t**	with the **t**ongue
i	as in sp**i**t		**ty**	as the tu in **tu**lip
í	as the ie in n**ie**ce		**u**	as in p**u**ll
j	as the y in **y**esterday		**ú**	as the oo in m**oo**dy
ly	as the y in **y**esterday (as above)		**ü**	as in c**u**te
ny	as the ny sound in **ne**w		**ű**	as above, but held for longer
o	as the or sound in s**o**re		**w**	as the v in **v**an
			zs	as the zs sound in trea**su**re

WORDS & PHRASES
Numbers

0	*nulla*	(nool-loh)		3	*három*	(haa-rom)
1	*egy*	(edj)		4	*négy*	(naidj)
2	*kettő*	(ket-töh)		5	*öt*	(öt)

6	*hat*	(hot)		10	*tíz*	(teez)
7	*hét*	(hait)		100	*száz*	(saaz)
8	*nyolc*	(nyolts)		1,000	*ezer*	(eh-zer)
9	*kilenc*	(kee-lents)				

Days

Monday	*hétfő*	(hait-foh)	Friday	*péntek*	(pain-tek)
Tuesday	*kedd*	(kedd)	Saturday	*szombat*	(som-bot)
Wednesday	*szerda*	(ser-doh)	Sunday	*vasárnap*	(vosh-aar-nop)
Thursday	*csütörtök*	(choot-ör-tök)			

Months

January	*január*	(yon-ooh-aar)	July	*július*	(yool-yoosh)
February	*február*	(feb-rooh-aar)	August	*augusztus*	(ah-ooh-goos-toosh)
March	*március*	(maar-tsee-oosh)	September	*szeptember*	(sep-tem-ber)
April	*április*	(aap-ree-lish)	October	*október*	(ok-tow-ber)
May	*május*	(maay-oosh)	November	*november*	(noh-vem-ber)
June	*június*	(yoon-eeh-oosh)	December	*december*	(deh-tsem-ber)

Basics

hello (familiar)	*szervusz/szervusztok* (to one/more)	(ser-voos/ser-voos-tok)
	szia/sziasztok (to one/more)	(see-yah/see-yah-stok)
hello/goodbye (on telephone)	*halló*	(hol-low)
hello/goodbye (not on telephone)	*heló*	(hay-low)
goodbye (polite)	*viszontlátásra*	(vee-sont-laa-taash-roh)
	(*visz'lát* a shortened version)	
Pardon?/At your service	*Tessék?*	(tesh-ayk)
good day (polite)	*jó napot*	(yo nop-pot)
good morning	*jó reggelt*	(yo reg-gelt)
please	*kérem*	(kay-rem)
goodnight	*jó éjszakát*	(yo ey-so-kaat)
sorry	*bocsánat*	(bo-chaanot)
no	*nem*	(nem)
yes	*igen*	(ee-gen)
thank you	*köszönöm*	(kö-sö-nöm)
you're welcome	*szívesen*	(see-ve-shen)

Meeting people

Do you speak English?	*Beszél angolul?*	(beh-sail on-gow-lool)
How are you?	*Hogy van?*	(hodj von)
I am fine.	*Jól vagyok.*	(yol vod-yok)
My name is...	*Az én nevem...*	(oz ain neh-vem)
Pleased to meet you	*Örülök, hogy megismerkedhettem önnel*	(ö-roo-lök, hodj meg-eesh-mer-ked-het-tem ön-nel)
What's your name?	*Mi az Ön neve?*	(mee oz ön neh-veh)
Where is...?	*Hol van...*	(hol von)

Transport

bicycle	*kerékpár*	(keh-rayk-par)
bus	*busz*	(boos)
bus station	*autóbusz-állomás*	(ow-toh-boos aal-lomaash)
bus stop	*autóbusz-megálló*	(ow-toh-boos meg-aal-low)
car park	*parkoló*	(park-ow-low)

railway station	*pályaudvar*	(paayoh-oodvor)
ticket	*jegy*	(yedj)
ticket office	*jegypénztár*	(yedj-painz-tar)
timetable	*menetrend*	(menet-rend)
train	*vonat*	(vonot)
tram	*villamos*	(veel-law-mosh)
underground/metro	*metró*	(metro)

Eating & drinking

A glass of...	*Egy pohár...*	(edj poh-haar)
A table for two please.	*Egy asztal kettő személyre*	(edj ostol ket-töh se-may-reh)
Is service included?	*A felszolgálás benne van?*	(aw fell-sol-gaah-laash ben-neh von)
One beer, please.	*Egy sört kérek.*	(edj sört kay-rek)
The bill, please.	*Kérem a számlát*	(kay-rem aw saam-lat)
The menu, please.	*Kérem az étlapot*	(key-rem oz ayt-la-pot)
Bon appétit!	*Jó étvágyat!*	(yo ayt-vah-djot)
Cheers	*Egészégére*	(egaish-shaigai-re)
I'd like to pay	*Fizetni szeretnék*	(fee-zet-nee sehr-ret-nehk)
beer	*sör*	(shör)
bread	*kenyér*	(kenj-air)
breakfast	*reggeli*	
cake shop	*cukrászda*	(tsook-raas-dow)
chicken	*csirke*	(chirke)
coffee bar	*eszpresszó*	(es-pres-sow)
coffee	*kávé*	(kaah-vay)
coffee house	*kávéház*	(kaah-vah-haaz)
dinner/supper	*vacsora*	(vochoro)
duck	*kacsa*	(kocho)
dumplings	*galuska*	(gah-loosh-kah)
fish	*hal*	(hol)
goulash	*gulyás*	(ghoo-yaash)
ham	*sonka*	(shonko)
ice-cream	*fagylalt*	(fodj-lolt)
lunch	*ebéd*	(ebaid)
mineral water	*ásványvíz*	(aash-vaanj-veez)
pancake	*palacsinta*	(pah-lah-chin-tah)
pork	*sertés*	(shair-taish)
pub	*söröző*	(shöh-röh-zöh)
red wine	*vörös bor*	(vöh-rösh bowr)
restaurant	*étterem, vendéglő*	(ait-terem, ven-day-gloh)
salad	*saláta*	(sholaato)
soup	*leves*	(levesh)
tea	*tea*	(teya)
turkey	*pulyka*	(pooyko)
vegetarian	*vegetáriánus*	(veghetaariyaanoosh)
waiter	*pincer*	(pintsair)
water	*víz*	(veez)
white wine	*fehér bor*	(fahair bowr)
winebar	*borozó*	(boh-row-zow)

Accommodation

bed and breakfast	*szoba reggelivel*	(sow-boh reg-ghelee-vel)
breakfast	*reggeli*	(reg-ghelee)
camping	*kemping*	
caravan	*lakókocsi*	(lokaw-kochi)
double room	*kétágyas szoba*	(kait-aadjosh sobo)
for one night	*egy éjszakára*	(edj aysaw-kaw-roh)
for two people	*két személyre*	(kait semay-reh)
guesthouse	*panzió*	(pahn-zee-ow)
hotel	*szálloda*	(saal-low-doh)
room reservation	*szobafoglalás*	(sobo-fog-lolaash)
single room	*egyágyas szoba*	(edjaadjosh sobo)
tent	*sátor*	(shaator)

Miscellaneous

adult	*felnőtt*	(fel-nöt)
and	*és*	(aish)
big	*nagy*	(nahdj)
boulevard	*körút*	(köh-root)
bridge	*híd*	(heed)
cash desk	*pénztár*	(pains-taah)
chapel	*kápolna*	
chemist	*gyógyszertár/patika*	(djowdj-sehr-taah/pah-tee-kah)
church	*templom*	
child	*gyerek*	(djeh-rek)
cinema	*mozi*	(mow-zee)
city	*város*	(vaah-rosh)
closed	*zárva*	(zaahr-vah)
English (adverb)	*angolul*	(on-gow-lool)
Franciscan	*Ferences*	(Ferentsesh)
entry	*bejárat*	(beh-yaah-raat)
exit	*kijárat*	(kee-yaah-raat)
exhibition	*kiállitás*	(ki-aaleetaash)
garden	*kert*	
gate	*kapu*	
gentlemen	*férfi*	(fehr-fee)
hill	*hegy*	(hedj)
hospital	*kórház*	(kowr-haaz)
island	*sziget*	(see-get)
ladies	*nők*	(nöhk)
lake	*tó*	(taw)
Lutheran	*Evangélikus*	
market	*piac*	(piyots)
no smoking	*tilos a dohányzás*	(tee-losh ah dow-haanj-zaash)
open	*nyitva*	(njeet-vah)
opening hours	*nyitvatartás*	(njeet-vah-taah-tash)
park	*liget*	(leeget)
police	*rendőrség*	(ren-dör-shaig)
road	*út*	(oot)
small	*kis/kicsi*	(keesh/kee-chee)
square	*tér*	(tehr)
street	*utca*	(ootsah)
swimming pool	*uszoda*	(oo-sow-dah)

synagogue	*zsinagóga*	(zsinogawgo)
theatre	*színház*	(seen-haaz)
toilet	*vécé/toalett/mosdó*	(vay-tsay/to-wa-let/mosh-doh)
town hall	*városháza*	(vaarosh-haazo)
zoo	*állatkert*	(al-lot-kert)

SOME PROVERBS Like sayings around the world, Hungarian proverbs tend to be cautionary in nature. However, the tailored proverbs of a nation say much about its outlook. Those below are indicative of a character that is sceptical, but one that recognises everyday pitfalls for the minor inconsequences that they are. They also show a sharp, if dark, sense of humour.

Aki korpa közé keveredik azt megeszik a disznók	'Those who get mixed up with bran will be eaten by pigs'	If you take risks be prepared for the consequences
A kutyából nem lesz szalonna	'You can't get bacon from dog'	You can't change a person
A kerítés is kolbászból van	'Even the fence is made of sausage'	They are doing really well
Több is veszett Mohácsnál	'More was lost at Mohács' (defeat in 1526 that let the Turks into Hungary)	It is not a serious problem
Nem hajt a tatár	'The Tatars are not chasing us'	We have time, no hurry
Sok beszédnek sok az alja	'A lot of talk has a lot of dregs'	Too much talk and no action
Megfota az isten lábát	'He/she grabbed the leg of God'	He/she was very lucky

AND SOME SLANG...

szellemi rövidnadrágos	'mentally short-trousered' (stupid)
baromarcú	'cattle-faced' (annoying)
kerítésszaggató	'fence ripper' (strong booze)
lónyál	'horse's saliva' (soft drink)
a béka segge alatt	'under a frog's arse' (in a poor financial state)

Appendix 2

FURTHER INFORMATION
BOOKS
History and culture
Ardó, Zsuzsanna. *Culture Shock: A Guide to Customs & Etiquette in Hungary.* Times Media, 2003
Ash, Timothy Garton. *The Magic Lantern: The Revolution of '89.* Vintage, 1993
Balázs, Géza. *The Story of Hungarian: A Guide to the Language.* Corvina, 1997.
Dent, Bob. *Budapest 1956: Locations of Drama.* Europa Könyvkiadó, 2006. An interesting survey of the key spots in Budapest during the revolution.
Fonseca, Isabel. *Bury Me Standing.* Vintage, 1996. The Roma (gypsies) in central Europe.
Kontler László. *Millennium in Central Europe: A History of Hungary.* Atlantisz, 1999
Lang, George. *The Cuisine of Hungary.* Penguin, 1985. Recipes and anecdotes.
Lang, George. *Nobody Knows the Truffles I've Seen.* Alfred A Knoff, 1998. Autobiography by Gundel.
Lázár István. *Hungary: A Brief History.* Corvina, 1989
Liddell, Alex. *The Wines of Hungary.* Mitchell Beazley, 2003.
Lukacs, John. *Budapest 1900: A Historical Portrait of the City & its Culture.* Grove, 1990
Molnár, Miklós. *A Concise History of Hungary.* CUP, 2001
Móra, Imre. *Budapest Then & Now.* New World, 2001. Articles about Budapest.

Literature
Bíró, Val. *Hungarian Folk-Tales.* OUP, 1992
Eszterházy, Péter. *The Glance of Countess Hahn-Hahn.* Northwestern, 2000. A meditation on travel, the Danube and its history.
Eszterházy, Péter. *Celestial Harmonies.* Flamingo, 2004. Dynastic saga of the Eszterházys.
Fischer, Tibor. *Under the Frog.* Henry Holt, 1997. Ironic and humorous tale against the backdrop of the 1956 revolution.
Kertész, Imre. *Fateless, 1992.* Nobel-Prize-winning novel.
Konrad, George. *A Feast in the Garden.* Harvest, 1993. Boy escapes the Nazi horrors.
Kosztolányi, Dezső. *Anna Édes.* New Directions, 1993. Classic 1920s novel depicting bourgeois pretences in Budapest.
Márai, Sándor. *Embers.*
Márai, Sándor. *Memoir of Hungary.* Life under the Arrow Cross and the Communists (1944–45).
Petőfi, Sándor. *John the Valiant.* Hesperus, 2004. Epic Hungarian poem.
Various. *The Lost Rider: A Bilingual Anthology.* Corvina, 1997. Selection of works by Hungarian poets.

GUIDEBOOKS & MAPS
Bánfalvi, Carolyn. *Food & Wine Lover's Guide to Hungary.* Park kiadó, 2008.
Budapest 'Classic' map (1:30,000) Cartographia, 2008
Garami, László. *Treasure Trekking.* Athenaeum, 2000. Very useful guide to Hungary's national parks and protected areas.
Gorman, Gerard. *Birding in Eastern Europe.* Wildsounds, 1996.
Gorman, Gerard. *Birds of Hungary.* Christopher Helm, 1996.

Gorman, Gerard. *Central & Eastern European Wildlife*. Bradt, 2008. A full-colour Bradt wildlife guide, covering the region's most interesting flora and fauna.

Hilbers, Dirk. *Nature Guide to the Hortobágy and Tisza Flood Plain*. Crossbill Guides, 2008. Hungary's national parks and protected areas.

Hungary map (1:450,000). Cartographia.

Hungary map. International Travel Maps (ITMB Publishing).

Lőrinczi, Zsuzsa & Vargha, Mihály. *Architectural Guide, 20th Century*. Budapest, 1997

Németh, Gyula. *Hungary, A Complete Guide*. Corvina Books, 1992

Parsons, Nicholas T. *Hungary: A Traveller's Guide*. Christopher Helm, 1990. Good historical guide.

Phillips, Adrian and Scotchmer, Jo. *Budapest: The Bradt City Guide*. Bradt, 2nd edition, 2009. If you require detail beyond that offered in the Budapest chapter here, this is the book for you!

Pintér, Tamás K & Kaiser, Anna. *Churches of Budapest*. Corvina, 1993

Svensson, Lars. *Birds of Europe*. Princeton, 2010.

Svensson, Lars. *Collins Bird Guide*. Collins, 2010.

Szatmári Gizella. *Walks in the Castle District*. Budapest Municipality, 2001

Török, András *Budapest: A Critical Guide*. Pallas Athene, 2000. Eccentric look at Budapest.

Various. *Out and About in Hungary*. Well-PRess, 2001. Comprehensive tome.

WEBSITES

http://english.mti.hu Comprehensive and up-to-date news-agency site. In English.
www.balatonihajozas.hu Boating information on Lake Balaton.
www.bbj.hu Online edition of the Budapest Business Journal..
www.bkv.hu Useful details on Budapest transport. English section.
www.bortarsasag.hu Website of the wine society and shops.
www.budacast.hu Podcasts on all things Budapest (including a few recordings by Adrian Phillips).
www.budapestinfo.hu Budapest's official tourist website.
www.budapestpanorama.com For events information.
www.budapestsun.com Online version of the English-language newspaper.
www.budapesttimes.hu As above, for its rival.
www.caboodle.hu Information on clubs, restaurants and much more. Useful.
www.chew.hu Reviews of restaurants.
www.elvira.hu Useful timetable of the MÁV Hungarian Railway. In English.
www.findagrave.com Fascinating site holding 6 million grave records.
www.funzine.hu Website of the Budapest events magazine.
www.gay.hu Latest information on the gay scene.
www.gotohungary.co.uk UK website of the HNTO.
www.gotohungary.com US website of the HNTO.
www.hotelshungary.com Competitively priced accommodation.
www.hungarytourism.hu Tourist office website.
www.insidehungary.com From current affairs to entertainment.
www.longitudebooks.com A good further-reading resource.
www.mav-start.hu Train ticket and timetabling information.
www.menetrendek.hu Timetable for domestic buses.
www.museum.hu Website listing details of all Hungarian museums.
www.pestiside.hu An amusing Budapest news portal.
www.pepmagazin.hu English–German magazine portal.
www.spasbudapest.com Budapest's spas.
www.talkingcities.co.uk/budapest Tourist sights and more.
www.tokaji.hu Website of the association of top Tokaji estates.
www.tourist-offices.org.uk/hungary UK-specific information.
www.winesofhungary.com Maps of Hungarian towns and villages. In Hungarian.
www.volan.hu Information on the Hungarian bus network. In Hungarian.
www.wherebudapest.com Online version of *Where Budapest* (page 59).

Bradt Travel Guides

www.bradtguides.com

Africa

Access Africa: Safaris for People with Limited Mobility	£16.99
Africa Overland	£16.99
Algeria	£15.99
Botswana: Okavango, Chobe, Northern Kalahari	£15.99
Burkina Faso	£14.99
Cameroon	£15.99
Cape Verde Islands	£14.99
Congo	£15.99
Eritrea	£15.99
Ethiopia	£16.99
Gambia, The	£13.99
Ghana	£15.99
Johannesburg	£6.99
Madagascar	£15.99
Malawi	£13.99
Mali	£14.99
Mauritius, Rodrigues & Réunion	£15.99
Mozambique	£13.99
Namibia	£15.99
Niger	£14.99
Nigeria	£17.99
North Africa: Roman Coast	£15.99
Rwanda	£14.99
São Tomé & Principe	£14.99
Seychelles	£14.99
Sierra Leone	£16.99
Sudan	£15.99
Tanzania, Northern	£14.99
Tanzania	£17.99
Uganda	£15.99
Zambia	£17.99
Zanzibar	£14.99

Britain and Europe

Albania	£15.99
Armenia, Nagorno Karabagh	£14.99
Azores	£13.99
Baltic Cities	£14.99
Belarus	£14.99
Bosnia & Herzegovina	£13.99
Bratislava	£9.99
Britain from the Rails	£17.99
Budapest	£9.99
Bulgaria	£13.99
Cork	£6.99
Croatia	£13.99
Cyprus see North Cyprus	

Czech Republic	£13.99
Dresden	£7.99
Dubrovnik	£6.99
Estonia	£13.99
Faroe Islands	£15.99
Georgia	£14.99
Hungary	£14.99
Iceland	£14.99
Kosovo	£14.99
Lapland	£13.99
Latvia	£13.99
Lille	£9.99
Lithuania	£14.99
Ljubljana	£7.99
Luxembourg	£13.99
Macedonia	£14.99
Montenegro	£14.99
North Cyprus	£12.99
Riga	£6.99
Serbia	£14.99
Slovakia	£14.99
Slovenia	£13.99
Spitsbergen	£16.99
Switzerland Without a Car	£14.99
Tallinn	£6.99
Transylvania	£14.99
Ukraine	£14.99
Vilnius	£6.99
Zagreb	£6.99

Middle East, Asia and Australasia

Bangladesh	£15.99
Borneo	£17.99
China: Yunnan Province	£13.99
Great Wall of China	£13.99
Iran	£15.99
Iraq: Then & Now	£15.99
Israel	£15.99
Kazakhstan	£15.99
Kyrgyzstan	£15.99
Maldives	£15.99
Mongolia	£16.99
North Korea	£14.99
Oman	£13.99
Shangri-La: A Travel Guide to the Himalayan Dream	£14.99
Sri Lanka	£15.99
Syria	£14.99
Tibet	£13.99
Turkmenistan	£14.99
Yemen	£14.99

The Americas and the Caribbean

Amazon, The	£14.99
Argentina	£15.99
Bolivia	£14.99
Cayman Islands	£14.99
Chile	£16.95
Colombia	£16.99
Costa Rica	£13.99
Dominica	£14.99
Grenada, Carriacou & Petite Martinique	£14.99
Guyana	£14.99
Panama	£14.99
St Helena	£14.99
Turks & Caicos Islands	£14.99
USA by Rail	£14.99

Wildlife

100 Animals to See Before They Die	£16.99
Antarctica: Guide to the Wildlife	£15.99
Arctic: Guide to the Wildlife	£15.99
Central & Eastern European Wildlife	£15.99
Chinese Wildlife	£16.99
East African Wildlife	£19.99
Galápagos Wildlife	£15.99
Madagascar Wildlife	£16.99
New Zealand Wildlife	£14.99
North Atlantic Wildlife	£16.99
Peruvian Wildlife	£15.99
Southern African Wildlife	£18.95
Sri Lankan Wildlife	£15.99
Wildlife and Conservation Volunteering: The Complete Guide	£13.99

Eccentric Guides

Eccentric Australia	£12.99
Eccentric Britain	£13.99
Eccentric California	£13.99
Eccentric Cambridge	£6.99
Eccentric Edinburgh	£5.95
Eccentric France	£12.95
Eccentric London	£13.99

Others

Something Different for the Weekend	£9.99
Weird World	£14.99
Your Child Abroad: A Travel Health Guide	£10.95

Index